CORPORATE FINANCE

This book is unique – one of the ultimate study and reference guides for European financiers from students to CFOs. The French-language versions of the *Vernimmen* have been for me some of the most helpful and trusted companions throughout my professional career.

Dan Arendt, Corporate Finance partner at Deloitte in Luxembourg

This book is particularly useful for those people who look for the bridge between strategic, operational and investment decisions on one hand, and financial accounts on the other. The authors' approach, which consists of guiding the reader from financial accounting to most complex deals that have strategic implications for firms, is new and very useful. I would recommend this book to those who want to succeed in both the in-house and the external consulting world, as well as in the area of Corporate Finance.

Stephan Dertnig, Vice President, Moscow Office, The Boston Consulting Group

I'm glad to hear that Vernimmen's unique book on finance is now available for English-speaking readers. I have known this excellent book for many years, which all professionals can easily use when they need to go back to the basics of modern Corporate Finance. Smartly written, thorough, lively, and regularly updated. I strongly recommend it to everyone – from the debutant in finance to high-level experts. Learning with *Vernimmen* is a real pleasure.

Antoine Giscard d'Estaing, CFO of Danone

Vernimmen's *Corporate Finance*, long overdue in English, is an outstandingly clear and complete manual, a wonderful merger of practice and theory. Its coverage of the market aspects of Corporate Finance and of European practices distinguishes its content, but its treatment of all the material makes it essential reading for the student, financier or industrialist.

Howard Jones, Fellow in Finance at the Saïd Business School, Oxford University, UK

This book was the first finance book I read as a student in my twenties. I read it again in my thirties to review some of the key finance challenges I was facing in my professional life. Now, in my forties, I am reviewing it once more to compare the reality I have to face now in Asia, with the most advanced financial concepts. I have never been disappointed and have always been able to find the appropriate answer to my questions, as well as food for thought. I am sure my children will read it when I am in my fifties, as *Vernimmen* is not just another book on finance: this is finance as a life experiment.

I strongly recommend this book to all the corporate managers facing new questions or challenges in their professional lives, especially in an international multi-currency context. You do not need to be a finance expert to enjoy reading it, as it's really easy to understand, with enough explanations, concrete examples . . . and humour, to help you jump successfully into the most sophisticated theories. But, if you are an expert, you will also find food for thought, as its methodological bases are strong enough to satisfy the most demanding CFO.

Jean-Michel Moutin, CFO, Louis Vuitton Asia Pacific-Japan

Understanding Corporate Finance is key to successful company management. From a banker's point of view, a good understanding of Corporate Finance is crucial to assist a company. The *Vernimmen*, written for Europeans by Europeans is a most useful reference for the student as well as the practitioner. The style of the book is concise, yet every conceivable aspect of Corporate Finance is covered. Complemented by an exhaustive website containing summaries of key concepts, of formulae, and of financial statements from a wide range of companies, the *Vernimmen* is a must.

Michael Rockinger, Professor of Finance, Director of the Institute of Banking and Finance, HEC & FAME, University of Lausanne, Switzerland

This book efficiently bridges financial theory and practice, and encapsulates everything a Corporate Finance banker will ever need to know and understand. It is obvious that the authors are passionate about finance, and their enthusiasm is contagious. Written in an easy and accessible style, this book deserves to become a reference work.

Jan Zarzycki, Director, Equity Capital Markets, Deutsche Bank

Pierre Vernimmen

CORPORATE FINANCE

THEORY AND PRACTICE

Pascal Quiry
Maurizio Dallocchio
Yann Le Fur
Antonio Salvi

John Wiley & Sons, Ltd

Adapted and updated from the original French, first published by Éditions Dalloz, Paris, 1994
(sixth edition 2005).

Other Wiley Editorial Offices

John Wiley & Sons Inc., 111 River Street, Hoboken, NJ 07030, USA

Jossey-Bass, 989 Market Street, San Francisco, CA 94103-1741, USA

Wiley-VCH Verlag GmbH, Boschstr. 12, D-69469 Weinheim, Germany

John Wiley & Sons Australia Ltd, 42 McDougall Street, Milton, Queensland 4064, Australia

John Wiley & Sons (Asia) Pte Ltd, 2 Clementi Loop #02-01, Jin Xing Distripark, Singapore 129809

John Wiley & Sons Canada Ltd, 22 Worcester Road, Etobicoke, Ontario, Canada M9W 1L1

Wiley also publishes its books in a variety of electronic formats. Some content that appears in
print may not be available in electronic books.

British Library Cataloguing in Publication Data

A catalogue record for this book is available from the British Library

ISBN-13 978-0-470-09225-5 (PB)
ISBN-10 0-470-09225-4 (PB)

Project management by Originator, Gt Yarmouth, Norfolk (typeset in 10/12pt Times and Meta)
Printed and bound in Great Britain by Scotprint, Haddington, Scotland

This book is printed on acid-free paper responsibly manufactured from sustainable forestry
in which at least two trees are planted for each one used for paper production.

About the authors

Pascal Quiry is an adjunct finance teacher in the leading French business school HEC Paris, and a managing director at BNP Paribas Corporate Finance, specialising in M&A transactions for listed companies.

Maurizio Dallocchio is the current Dean of the leading Italian business school Bocconi (Milan) and Lehman Brothers Chair of Corporate Finance. He is also a board member of several listed and unlisted companies and is one of the most distinguished Italian authorities on finance.

Yann Le Fur is a corporate finance teacher at HEC Paris business school and an investment banker with Mediobanca in Paris (after several years with Schroders and Citigroup).

Antonio Salvi is an Assistant Professor of Finance at Bocconi and the University of Venice where he teaches Corporate Finance. His areas of research cover cost of capital, structure of debt finance and corporate governance.

Pierre Vernimmen, who died in 1996, was both an M&A dealmaker (he advised Louis Vuitton on its merger with Moët Henessy to create LVMH, the world luxury goods leader) and a finance teacher at HEC Paris. His book, *Finance d'Entreprise*, was and still is the top-selling financial textbook in French-speaking countries and is the forebear of *Corporate Finance: Theory and Practice*.

The authors of this book wish to express their profound thanks to the HEC Paris Business School and Foundation, ABN Amro, Barclays, BNP Paribas, DGPA, HSBC, Lazard, and Nomura for their generous financial support; also Matthew Cush, Robert Killingsworth, John Olds, Gita Roux, Steven Sklar and Patrice Carlean-Jones who helped us tremendously in writing this book.

Summary

Section III
CORPORATE FINANCIAL POLICIES   473

Part One
FINANCIAL SECURITIES   475

Part Two
CAPITAL STRUCTURE POLICIES   635

Part Three
EQUITY CAPITAL AND DIVIDEND POLICIES   753

Section IV
FINANCIAL MANAGEMENT   809

Part One
VALUATION AND FINANCIAL ENGINEERING   811

Part Two
MANAGING NET DEBT AND FINANCIAL RISKS   937

Contents

Part Two   Capital structure policies

Part Two   Managing net debt and financial risks

Foreword by Richard Roll

Thirty years ago, when I lived and worked in Europe, only a handful of financial scholars resided on that continent and no finance texts had a European focus. How things have changed! This book is a wonderful example of the progress that has been made. Pierre Vernimmen became an important catalyst for change when he published (in French) one of the first European-oriented corporate finance texts in the 1970s. It is now available in English, updated, expanded and rendered invaluable not only to students but also to practising financial managers.

The book itself covers all the important techniques that a financial manager must have in his repertoire of tools. Its scope is breathtaking: from the basics of financial analysis through accounting, capital markets, risk, arbitrage, portfolio analysis, options, agency and signalling concepts, to the ultimate goal of corporate finance, decision making about equity issuance, leverage, mergers, bankruptcy and other important financial events. The exposition is clear and concise and, most importantly, relies on commonsense reasoning throughout. This is not a book with obscure formulae, yet is still rigorous and at the same time a model of clarity.

Two noteworthy attributes of the book are, first, its association with an excellent website and, second, the commitment of the authors to issue a monthly newsletter with updated research information about topical issues. In the December 2004 newsletter, for example, we find a tabulation of corporate income tax rates compared across countries and traced over time. There are also fascinating articles about forming a European-wide company, on how joining or leaving an index affects an individual firm's stock price and on whether it makes sense for European firms to list their stock on an American exchange (in general, it doesn't).

The website is even better. It provides lots of data to those who feel a burning need to perform a few statistical calculations. It has an extensive glossary and a comprehensive research bibliography about every important topic in finance. It even has quizzes to test your financial acumen, cross-referenced against chapters in *Corporate Finance* where the answers, given briefly on the Web, are explained in detail. I enjoyed going through these quizzes even though getting a few wrong answers was humbling.

It seems to me that the European focus of this book is entirely appropriate for European financial managers and for students who wish to pursue careers in finance. There are enough international differences in legal systems, accounting methods and management practices to make a focused text invaluable. Of course, the basic principals of finance are universal, but examples, case studies, problem sets and quizzes are much more transparent when they involve a familiar and realistic setting. In summary, if I were teaching corporate finance in Europe or consulting with a financial team at a European company, I would strongly urge everyone, from students up through the CFO, to possess this book. It contains the answers to most questions that financial managers ask every day and, most importantly, the answers are easy to find.

Richard Roll
Japan Alumni Chair in International Finance at the UCLA Anderson School

Preface

This book aims to cover the full scope of corporate finance as it is practised today in Europe.

A way of thinking about finance

There are four key features that distinguish this book from the many other corporate finance textbooks available on the market today:

- Our strong belief that financial analysis is part of corporate finance. Pierre Vernimmen, who was the mentor and partner in the practice of corporate finance of some of us, understood very early on that a good financial manager must first be able to analyse a company's economic, financial and strategic situation, and then value it, while at the same time mastering the conceptual underpinnings of all financial decisions.
- *Corporate Finance* is neither a theoretical textbook nor a practical workbook. It is a book in which theory and practice are constantly set off against each other, in the same way as we do in our daily practice of corporate finance, as investment bankers at BNP Paribas, DGPA, Mediobanca, as board members of several listed and unlisted companies, and as teachers at the Bocconi and HEC business schools.
- Emphasis is placed on concepts intended to give you an understanding of situations, rather than on techniques, which tend to shift and change over time. We confess to believing that the former will still be valid in 20 years time, whereas the latter will for the most part be long forgotten!
- Financial concepts are international, but they are much easier to grasp when they are set in a familiar context. Written by Europeans for Europeans, *Corporate Finance* explains how finance works on European markets, such as London, Frankfurt and Madrid.

The four sections

This book starts with an introductory chapter reiterating the idea that corporate financiers are the bridge between the economy and the realm of finance. Increasingly, they must play the role of marketing manager and negotiator. Their products are financial securities that represent rights to the firm's cash flows. Their customers are bankers and investors. A good financial manager listens to customers and sells them good products at high prices. A good financial manager always thinks in terms of value rather than costs or earnings.

Section I goes over the basics of financial analysis – i.e., understanding the company based on a detailed analysis of its accounts. We are amazed at the extent to which large numbers of investors neglected this approach during the latest stockmarket euphoria. When share prices everywhere are rising, why stick to a rigorous approach? For one thing, to avoid being caught in the crash that inevitably follows. How many investors took the trouble to read Enron's annual report? Those who did found that it spoke volumes!

We are convinced that a return to reason will also return financial analysis to its rightful place as a cornerstone of economic decision making. To perform financial analysis, you must first understand the firm's basic financial mechanics (Chapters 2–5), master the basic techniques of accounting, including accounting principles, consolidation techniques, and certain complexities (Chapters 6–7), based on international (IAS) standards, now mandatory for listed European companies. In order to make things easier for the newcomer to finance, we have structured the presentation of financial analysis itself around its guiding principle: in the long run, a company can survive only if it is solvent and creates value for its shareholders. To do so, it must create value (Chapters 9 and 10), invest (Chapter 11), finance its investments (Chapter 12) and generate a sufficient return (Chapter 13). The illustrative financial analysis of Ericsson will guide you throughout this section of the book.

Section II reviews the basic theoretical knowledge you will need to make an assessment of the value of the firm. Here again, the emphasis is on reasoning, which in many cases will become automatic (Chapters 15–24): efficient capital markets, the time value of money, the price of risk, volatility, arbitrage, return, portfolio theory, present value and future value, market risk, beta, etc.

In **Section III**, "Corporate financial policies", we review the major types of financial securities: equity, debt and options, for the purposes of valuation, along with the techniques for issuing and placing them (Chapters 25–31). Then, we analyse each financial decision in terms of:

- value in the context of the theory of efficient capital markets;
- balance of power between owners and managers, shareholders and debtholders (agency theory);
- communication (signal theory).

Such decisions include choosing a capital structure, investment decisions, cost of capital, dividend policy, share repurchases, capital increases, hybrid security issues, etc.

In the course of this section, we call your attention to today's obsession with earnings per share, return on equity and other measures whose underlying basis we have a tendency to forget and which may, in some cases, be only distantly related to value creation. We have devoted considerable space to the use of options (as a technique or a type of reasoning) in each financial decision (Chapters 32–39).

When you start reading **Section IV**, "Financial management", you will be ready to examine and take the remaining decisions: how to organise a company's equity capital, buying and selling companies, mergers, demergers, LBOs, bankruptcy and restructuring (Chapters 40–45). Lastly, this section presents cash flow management, asset-based financing and management of the firm's financial risks (Chapters 46–48).

Instructions to the reader

To make sure that you get the most out of your book, each chapter ends with a summary, a series of problems and questions (a total of 746) (solutions provided). The appendix contains a 75-entry glossary, with a further 1,300 terms defined on the site *www.vernimmen.com*. We've used the last page of the book to provide a cribsheet (nearly 1,000 pages of this book summarised on one page!). For those interested in exploring the topics discussed in greater depth, there is an end-of-chapter bibliography giving suggestions for further reading, covering fundamental research papers, articles in the press and published books. A large number of graphs and tables (over 100!) have been included in the body of the text which can be used for comparative analyses. Finally, the index is fully comprehensive.

An Internet site with huge and diversified content

www.vernimmen.com provides free access to tools (formulas, tables, statistics, lexicons, glossaries), resources that supplement the book (articles, prospectuses of financial transactions, financial figures for more than 10,000 European and North American listed companies, thesis topics, thematic links, a list of must-have books for your bookshelf, an Excel file providing detailed solutions to all of the problems set in the book), problems, case studies, quizzes for testing and improving your knowledge. There is a letterbox for your questions to the authors (we aim to reply within 72 hours, unless of course you manage to stump us!). There are questions and answers and much more. New services are put onto the site, which has its own internal search engine, on a regular basis.

A free monthly newsletter on corporate finance

Since (unfortunately) we can't bring out a new edition of the *Vernimmen* every month, we have set up the *Vernimmen.com Newsletter*, which is sent out free of charge to subscribers by means of the Internet. It contains:

- A conceptual look at a topical corporate finance problem (*e.g., the European company: a new tool to facilitate cross-border mergers, EU anti-concentration regulations, the value of synergies*).
- Statistics or tables that you are likely to find useful in the day-to-day practice of corporate finance (*e.g., worldwide corporate income tax rates, yield curves, IPOs since 1987*).
- A critical review of a financial research paper with a concrete dimension (*e.g., conglomerates and diversification, new ideas on financial structure, leasing vs. bank loans*).

- A question left on the vernimmen.com site by a visitor plus a response (*e.g., What are the advantages and drawbacks of spinning off a division? Does writedown of goodwill impact on values? What is dilution?*)

Subscribe on *www.vernimmen.com* and become one of the many readers of the *Vernimmen.com Newsletter*.

Many thanks

- To Eric Briys, Didier Kunstlinger and Renaud Lefebvre for their seminal, friendly and efficient support.
- To Richard Roll for the many kind words included in the foreword.
- To Sebastian Cardarelli, Benoît de Courcelles, Evgueni Madorski, Ryan McGovern, and the other students of HEC and Bocconi MBA programmes for their help in improving the manuscript.
- To Vincent Jacques, the *vernimmen.com* webmaster.
- To Isabelle Marié-Sall for her help in transforming our scribblings into a proper manuscript.
- And last but not least to our relatives and our many friends who have had to endure our endless absences over the last two and a half years, and of course Catherine Vernimmen and her children for their everlasting and kind support.

We hope that you will gain as much enjoyment from your *Vernimmen*, whether you are a new student of corporate finance or whether you are using it to revise and hone your financial skills, as we have had in editing this edition and in expanding the services and products that go with the book.

We wish you well in your studies!

Milan and Paris, May 2005

Pascal Quiry   *Maurizio Dallocchio*

Yann Le Fur   *Antonio Salvi*

Frequently used symbols

A_k^N	Annuity factor for N years and an interest rate of k
ABCP	Asset Backed Commercial Paper
ACES	Advanced Computerised Execution System
ADR	American Depositary Receipt
APT	Arbitrage Pricing Theory
APV	Adjusted Present Value
ARR	Accounting Rate of Return
BIMBO	Buy In Management Buy Out
BV	Book Value
Capex	Capital Expenditures
CAPM	Capital Asset Pricing Model
CAR	Cumulative Abnormal Return
CB	Convertible Bond
CD	Certificate of Deposit
CDO	Collateralised Debt Obligation
CE	Capital Employed
CFROI	Cash Flow Return On Investment
COV	Covariance
CVR	Contingent Value Right
D	Debt, net financial and banking debt
d	Payout ratio
DCF	Discounted Cash Flows
DDM	Dividend Discount Model
DECS	Debt Exchangeable for Common Stock; Dividend Enhanced Convertible Securities
DFL	Degree of Financial Leverage
Div	Dividend
DJ	Dow Jones
DOL	Degree of Operating Leverage
DPS	Dividend Per Share
DR	Depositary Receipt
EAT	Earnings After Tax
EBIT	Earnings Before Interest and Taxes
EBITDA	Earnings Before Interest, Taxes, Depreciation and Amortisation
EBRD	European Bank for Reconstruction and Development
ECAI	External Credit Assessment Institution
ECP	European Commercial Paper
EGM	Extraordinary General Meeting
EMTN	European Medium Term Note
ENPV	Expanded Net Present Value
EONIA	European Over Night Index Average
EPS	Earnings Per Share
$E(r)$	Expected return
ESOP	Employee Stock Ownership Programme
EURIBOR	EURopean Inter Bank Offer Rate
EV	Enterprise Value

EVA	Economic Value Added
EVCA	European Private Equity and Venture Capital Association
f	Forward rate
F	Cash flow
FA	Fixed Assets
FASB	Financial Accounting Standards Board
FC	Fixed Costs
FCF	Free Cash Flow
FCFF	Free Cash Flow to Firm
FCFE	Free Cash Flow to Equity
FE	Financial Expenses
FIFO	First In, First Out
FRA	Forward Rate Agreement
g	Growth rate
GAAP	Generally Accepted Accounting Principles
GCE	Gross Capital Employed
GCF	Gross Cash Flow
GDP	Global Depositary Receipt
i	After-tax cost of debt
IASB	International Accounting Standards Board
IFRS	International Financial Reporting Standard
IPO	Initial Public Offering
IRR	Internal Rate of Return
IRS	Interest Rate Swap
IT	Income Taxes
k	Cost of capital, discount rate
k_D	Cost of debt
k_E	Cost of equity
K	Option strike price
KPI	Key Performance Indicator
LBO	Leveraged Buy Out
LBU	Leveraged Build Up
L/C	Letter of Credit
LIBOR	London Inter Bank Offer Rate
LIFO	Last In, First Out
LMBO	Leveraged Management Buy Out
ln	Naperian logarithm
LOI	Letter Of Intent
LSP	Liquid Share Partnership
LYON	Liquid Yield Option Note
m	Contribution margin
MM	Modigliani–Miller
MOU	Memorandum Of Understanding
MTN	Medium Term Notes
MVA	Market Value Added
n	Years, periods
N	Number of years
$N(d)$	Cumulative standard normal distribution
NASDAQ	National Association of Securities Dealers Automatic Quotation system
NAV	Net Asset Value
NM	Not Meaningful
NMS	National Market System
NOPAT	Net Operating Profit After Tax
NPV	Net Present Value
NYSE	New York Stock Exchange
OGM	Ordinary General Meeting
OTC	Over The Counter

P	price
PBO	Projected Benefit Obligation
PBR	Price to Book Ratio
PBT	Profit Before Tax
P/E ratio	Price Earnings ratio
PERCS	Preferred Equity Redemption Cumulative Stock
PEPs	Personal Equity Plans
POW	Path Of Wealth
PRIDES	Preferred Redeemable Increased Dividend Equity Security
PSR	Price to Sales Ratio
P to P	Public to Private
PV	Present Value
PVI	Present Value Index
QIB	Qualified Institutional Buyer
r	Rate of return, interest rate
r_f	Risk-free rate
r_m	Expected return of the market
RNAV	Restated Net Asset Value
ROA	Return On Assets
ROCE	Return On Capital Employed
ROE	Return On Equity
ROI	Return On Investment
RWA	Risk Weighted Assessment
S	Sales
SA	Standardised Approach
SEC	Securities Exchange Commission
SEO	Seasoned Equity Offering
SPV	Special Purpose Vehicle
STEP	Short Term European Paper
SV	Salvage Value
t	Interest rate, discount rate
T	Time remaining until maturity
T_c	Corporate tax rate
TCN	Titres de Créances Negociables
TMT	Technology, Media, Telecommunications
TSR	Total Shareholders Return
V	Value
VAT	Value Added Tax
VC	Variable Cost
V_D	Value of Debt
V_E	Value of Equity
$V(r)$	Variance of return
WACC	Weighted Average Cost of Capital
WC	Working Capital
y	Yield to maturity
YTM	Yield to Maturity
Z	Scoring function
ZBA	Zero Balance Account
β or β_E	Beta coefficient for a share or an equity instrument
β_A	Beta coefficient for an asset or unlevered beta
β_D	Beta coefficient of a debt instrument
$\sigma(r)$	Standard deviation of return
$\rho_{A,B}$	Correlation coefficient of return between shares A and B

Chapter 1
WHAT IS CORPORATE FINANCE?

To whet your appetite . . .

The primary role of the financial manager is to ensure that his company has a sufficient supply of capital.

The financial manager is at the crossroads of the real **economy**, with its industries and services, and the world of **finance**, with its various financial markets and structures.

There are two ways of looking at the financial manager's role:

- a buyer of capital who seeks to minimise its cost, i.e., the traditional view;
- a seller of financial securities who tries to maximise their value. This is the view we will develop throughout this book. It corresponds, to a greater or lesser extent, to the situation that exists in a capital market economy, as opposed to a credit-based economy.

At the risk of oversimplifying, we will use the following terminology in this book:

- The **financial manager** or **Chief Financial Officer** (CFO) is responsible for financing the enterprise and acts as an intermediary between the financial system's institutions and markets, on the one hand, and the enterprise, on the other.
- The **business manager** invests in plant and equipment, undertakes research, hires staff and sells the firm's products, whether the firm is a manufacturer, a retailer or a service company.
- The **financial investor** invests in financial securities. More generally, the financial investor provides the enterprise with financial resources, and may be either an equity investor or a lender.

Section 1.1
THE FINANCIAL MANAGER IS FIRST AND FOREMOST A SALESMAN . . .

1/THE FINANCIAL MANAGER'S JOB IS NOT ONLY TO "BUY" FINANCIAL RESOURCES . . .

The financial manager is traditionally perceived as a buyer of capital. He negotiates with a variety of investors – bankers, shareholders, long-term lenders – to obtain funds at the lowest possible cost.

Transactions that take place on the **capital markets** are made up of the following elements:

- a commodity: money;
- a price: the interest rate in the case of debt, dividends and/or capital gains in the case of equities.

In the traditional view the financial manager is responsible for the company's financial procurement. His job is to minimise the price of the **commodity** to be purchased, i.e., the **cost of the funds** he raises.

We have no intention of contesting this view of the world. It is obvious and is confirmed everyday, in particular in the following types of negotiations:

- between corporate treasurers and bankers, regarding interest rates and value dates applied to bank balances (see Chapter 46);
- between chief financial officers and financial market intermediaries, where negotiation focuses on the commissions paid to arrangers of financial transactions (see Chapter 31).

2/... BUT ALSO TO SELL FINANCIAL SECURITIES

This said, let's now take a look at the financial manager's job from a different angle:

- he is not a buyer but a **seller**;
- his aim is not to reduce the cost of the raw material he buys but to **maximise a selling price**;
- he practises his art not on the capital markets, but on the market for financial instruments, be they loans, bonds, shares, etc.

We are not changing the world here; we are merely looking at the same market from another point of view:

- the **supply** of financial securities corresponds to the demand for capital;
- the **demand** for financial securities corresponds to the supply of capital;
- the price, the point at which the supply and demand for financial securities are in equilibrium, is therefore the **value of security**. In contrast, the equilibrium price in the traditional view is considered to be the interest rate, or the cost of capital.

We can summarise these two ways of looking at the same capital market in the following table:

Analysis/Approach	Financial	Traditional
Market	Securities	Capital
Supply	Issuer	Investor
Demand	Investor	Issuer
Price	Value of security	Interest rate

Depending on your point of view – i.e., traditional or financial – supply and demand are reversed, as follows:

- when the **cost of money** – the interest rate, for example – **rises**, demand for funds is greater than supply. In other words, the supply of financial securities is greater than the demand for financial securities, and **the value of the securities falls**;
- conversely, when **the cost of money falls**, the supply of funds is greater than demand. In other words, the demand for financial instruments is greater than their supply and **the value of the securities rises**.

The cost of capital and the value of the securities vary in opposite directions. We can summarise with the following theorem, fundamental to this entire book:

Minimising financing cost is synonymous with maximising the value of the underlying securities.

For two practical reasons, one minor and one major, we prefer to present the financial manager as a seller of financial securities.

The minor reason is that viewing the financial manager as a salesman trying to sell his products at the highest price casts his role in a different light. As the merchant does not want to sell low-quality products but products that respond to the needs of his customers, so the financial manager must understand his capital suppliers and satisfy their needs without putting the company or its other capital suppliers at a disadvantage. **He must sell high-quality products at high prices.** We cannot emphasise this enough.

The more important reason is that when a financial manager applies the traditional approach of minimising the cost of the company's financing too strictly, erroneous decisions may easily follow. The traditional approach can make the financial manager **short-sighted**, tempting him to take decisions that emphasise the short term to the detriment of the long term.

For instance, choosing between a capital increase, a bank loan and a bond issue with lowest cost as the only criterion reflects flawed reasoning. Why? Because suppliers of capital (i.e., the buyers of the corresponding instruments) do not all face the same level of risk.

The investor's risk must be taken into account in evaluating the cost of a source of financing.

The cost of two sources of financing can be compared only when the suppliers of the funds incur the same level of risk.

All too often we have seen corporate leaders or treasurers assume excessive risk when choosing a source of financing because they have based their decision on a single criterion: the respective cost of the different sources of funds.

For example:

- increasing short-term debt on the pretext that short-term interest rates are lower than long-term rates can be a serious mistake;

- granting a mortgage in return for a slight decrease in the interest rate on a loan can be very harmful for the future;
- increasing debt systematically on the sole pretext that debt costs less than equity capital jeopardises the company's prospects for long-term survival.

We will develop this theme further throughout in Section III of this book, but we would like to warn you now of the pitfalls of faulty financial reasoning. **The most dangerous thing a financial manager can say is, "It doesn't cost anything." This sentence should be banished and replaced with the following question: "What is the impact of this action on value?"**

Section 1.2
... OF FINANCIAL SECURITIES ...

Let's now take a look at the overall concept of a financial security, the product created by the financial manager.

1/ISSUANCE OR CREATION OF SECURITIES

There is a great variety of financial instruments, each of which has the following characteristics:

- it is a contract;
- the contract is executed over time;
- its value derives solely from the series of cash flows it represents.

Indeed, from a mathematical and more theoretical viewpoint, a financial instrument is defined as a **schedule of future cash flows**.

Holding a financial security is the same as holding the right to receive the cash flows, as defined in the terms and conditions of the issue that gave rise to the financial instrument. Conversely, for the issuer, creating a financial instrument is the same as committing to paying out a series of cash flows. In return for this right to receive cash flows or for taking on this commitment, the company will issue a security at a certain price, enabling it to raise the funds needed to run its business.

A financial security is a contract . . .

You've undoubtedly heard people say that the financial manager's stock-in-trade is "paper". Computerisation has now turned financial instruments from paper documents into intangible book entries, reducing them to the information they contain; i.e., the contract. The essence of finance is and will always be **negotiation** between an issuer seeking new funds and the investors interested in buying the instruments that represent the underlying obligations. And negotiation means markets, be they credit markets, bond markets, stock markets, etc.

. . . executed over time . . .

Time, or the term of the financial security, introduces the notion of **risk**. A debt instrument that promises cash flows over time, for example, entails risk, even if the borrower is very creditworthy. This seems strange to many people who consider that "a deal is a deal" or "a man's word is his bond". Yet, experience has shown that a wide variety of risks can affect the payment of those cash flows, including political risk, strikes, natural disasters and other events.

. . . and materialised by cash flows.

Further on in this book you will see that financial logic is used to analyse and choose among an enterprise's investment options. The financial manager transforms flows of goods and services, deriving from the company's industrial and other business assets, into cash flows. You will soon understand that the world of finance is one of **managing rights, on the one hand, and commitments, on the other, both expressed in terms of cash flows**.

In a market for financial instruments, it is not the actual flows that are sold, but the rights associated with them. The investor – i.e., the buyer of the security – acquires the rights granted by the instrument. The issuing company assumes contractual obligations deriving from the instrument, regardless of who the owner of the instrument is.

For example, commodity futures markets make it possible to perform purely financial transactions. You can buy sugar "forward", via financial instruments called futures contracts, knowing full well that you will never take delivery of the sugar into your warehouse. Instead, you will close out the position prior to maturity. The financial manager thus trades on a market for real goods (sugar), using contracts that can be unwound prior to or at maturity.

A property investor acts similarly. After acquiring real property, whose value fluctuates, he can lease it or resell it. Viewed this way, real property is as fungible as any other property and is akin to a financial asset.

Clearly, these assets exhibit different degrees of "financiality". To take the argument one step further, you turn a painting into a financial instrument when you put it in your safe in the hope of realising a gain when you sell it.

The distinction between a real asset and a financial asset is therefore subtle but fundamental. It lies either in the nature of the contract or in the investor's motivation, as in the example of the painting.

Lastly, the purchase of a financial security, with certain exceptions such as life estates, differs from the purchase of a durable good in that the financial security is undifferentiated. A large number of investors can buy the same financial security. In contrast, acquiring a specific office building or building an industrial plant is a very specific, unique investment.

In conclusion, every financial instrument represents a series of cash flows to be received according to a set timetable. Mathematically, it can be expressed as a series of future cash flows $F_1, F_2, F_3, F_4, \ldots, F_n$ over n periods.

2/TYPES OF FINANCIAL SECURITIES

(a) Debt instruments (Chapters 26 and 27)

The simplest financial instrument is undoubtedly the contract that ties a lender (investor) to a borrower (the company). It represents a very strong commitment, not only to repay, but to repay with interest. Loans become financial securities when they are made negotiable on a secondary market (see p. 7) and "listed". Bonds and commercial paper fall into this category.

A bond is negotiable debt security representing a fraction of a borrowing contracted by an industrial company, a financial institution or a sovereign state (Gilts in the UK, Bunds in Germany, etc.).

Commercial paper is a negotiable debt security representing a fraction of a short-term borrowing (generally between 1 day and 2 years) contracted by a company. If the company is a bank, the security will be called a **certificate of deposit**. Short-term sovereign debt instruments go by different names depending on the country; in Spain, for example, they are called *Bonos del Estado*.

Strictly speaking, these investors do not assume any industrial risk. **Their return is set contractually** and may be fixed or variable. If it is variable, it will be indexed on an interest rate and not on the results of the company.

We will see in Chapter 14 that the lender nevertheless assumes certain risks, namely the failure of the borrower to honour the debt contract.

(b) Equity securities (Chapter 28)

Equity represents the capital injected into a company by an investor who bears the full risk of the company's industrial undertakings in return for a share of the profits.

If the company is organised under a limited liability structure, the equity is divided into **shares**. The risk borne by the shareholders is limited to the amount they contribute to the enterprise. Unless otherwise noted, we will be dealing in this book with finance as it relates to the various forms of "limited companies".

Shareholders' equity is a source of financing for the enterprise, but the related financial security, the share, guarantees the investor neither a fixed level of income nor repayment. The shareholder can "cash in" his investment only by selling it to someone else. The investor obtains certain corporate rights, however: a claim on the company's earnings and – via his voting rights – management oversight.

(c) Other securities (Chapters 29 and 30)

As you will discover in Chapter 30, financial engineering specialists have invented hybrid securities that combine the characteristics of the two categories discussed above. Some securities have the look and feel of equity from the point of view of the company, but the corresponding cash flows are fixed, at least partially. Other instruments have yields that are dependent on the performance of the company, but are considered loans, not equity capital. Financial imagination knows no bounds. Keep in mind that these instruments are peripheral to our primary focus in this book. As such, we won't burden you with them until Chapter 30!

There is a specific type of financial instrument, however, **the option**, whose associated cash flows are actually less "important" to the investor than the rights the options conveys. This instrument grants the right, but not the obligation, to do something. Options either grant this right at any time ("American" options) or at maturity ("European" options).

In sum, financial instruments carry a wide spectrum of characteristics, which, from the investor's point of view, range from rights to obligations.

Section 1.3
. . . VALUED CONTINUOUSLY IN THE FINANCIAL MARKETS

Our view of finance can take shape only in the context of well-developed financial markets. But before examining the technical characteristics of markets (Section II of this book), let's spend a moment on definitions.

1/FROM THE PRIMARY MARKET TO THE SECONDARY MARKET

Once launched by its issuer, a financial security lives a life of its own. It is sold from one investor to another, and it serves as support for other transactions. The instrument itself evolves, but the terms of the contract under which it was issued do not.

The life of a financial security is intimately connected with the fact that it can be bought or sold at any moment. For example, shares issued or created when a company is founded can later be floated on a stock exchange, just as long-term bonds may be used by speculators for short-term strategies.

The new issues market (i.e., creation of securities) is called the primary market. Subsequent transactions involving these securities take place on the **secondary market**. Both markets, like any market, are defined by two basic elements: the product (the security) and the price (its value).

From the point of view of the company, the distinction between the primary and secondary markets is fundamental. **The primary market is the market for "new" financial products**, from equity issues to bond issues and everything in-between. It is the market for newly minted financial securities.

Conversely, the secondary market is the market for "used" financial products. Securities bought and sold on this market have already been created and are now simply changing hands, without any new securities being created.

The primary market enables companies, financial institutions, governments and local authorities to obtain financial resources by issuing securities. These securities are then listed and traded on secondary markets. The job of the secondary market is to ensure that securities are properly priced and traded. This is the essence of **liquidity**: facilitating the purchase or sale of a security.

The distinction between primary and secondary markets is conceptual only. The two markets are not separated from each other. A given financial investor can buy either existing shares or new shares issued during a capital increase, for example.

If there is often more emphasis placed on the primary market, it is because the function of the financial markets is first and foremost to ensure equilibrium between financing needs and the sources of finance. Secondary markets, where securities can change hands, constitute a kind of financial "innovation".

2/THE FUNCTION OF THE SECONDARY MARKET

Financial investors do not intend to remain invested in a particular asset indefinitely. From the moment they buy a security, they begin thinking about how they will **exit**. As a result, they are constantly evaluating whether they should buy or sell such and such asset.

Exiting is relatively easy when the security is a short-term one. All the investor has to do is wait until maturity.[1] The need for an exit strategy grows with the maturity of the investment and is greatest for equity investments whose maturity is unlimited. The only way a shareholder can exit his investment is to sell his shares to someone else.

Similarly, the successful businessman who floats his company on the stock exchange, thereby bringing in new shareholders, diversifies his own portfolio, which before flotation was essentially concentrated in one investment.

The secondary market makes the investor's investments liquid.

Liquidity refers to the ability to convert an instrument into cash quickly and without loss of value. It affords the opportunity to trade a financial instrument at a "listed" price and in large quantities without disrupting the market. An investment is liquid when an investor can buy or sell it in large quantities without causing a change in its market price.

The secondary market is therefore a **zero-sum game** between investors, because what one investor buys another investor sells. In principle, the secondary market operates completely independently from the issuer of the securities.

A company that issues a bond today knows that a certain amount of funds will remain available in each future year. This knowledge is based on the bond's amortisation schedule. During that time, however, the investors holding the bonds will have changed.

Secondary market transactions do not show up in macroeconomic statistics on capital formation, earning them the scorn of some observers, who claim that the secondary market does nothing to further economic development, but only bails out the initial investors.

We believe this thinking is misguided and reflects great ignorance about the function of secondary markets in the economy. Remember that a financial investor is constantly comparing the primary and secondary markets. He cares little whether he is buying a "new" or a "used" security, so long as they have the same characteristics.

1 *However, in periods of market crisis, even 24 hours can seem like an eternity.*

The secondary market plays the fundamental role of valuing securities.

In fact, the quality of a primary market for a security depends greatly on the quality of its secondary market. Think about it: who would want to buy a financial security on the primary market, knowing that it will be difficult to sell it on the secondary market?

Consequently, it makes no economic sense to grant tax advantages, for example, to investments in the primary market without offering the same advantages to investments in the secondary market. Otherwise, investors quickly realise that the advantage is fictitious, because they will lose out when they try to sell the investment in the secondary market.

The secondary market determines the price at which the company can issue its securities on the primary market, because investors are constantly deciding between existing investments and proposed new investments.

We have seen that it would be a mistake to think that a financial manager takes no interest in the secondary market for the securities issued by his company. Much to the contrary, it is on the secondary market that his company's financial "raw material" is priced every day. When the raw material is equities, there is another reason the company cannot afford to turn its back on the secondary market: this is where investors trade the right to vote in the company's affairs and, by extension, to control the company.

3/ DERIVATIVE MARKETS: FUTURES AND OPTIONS

Over the last 30 years, fluctuations in interest rates, currencies and the prices of raw materials have become so great that financial risks have become as important as industrial risks. Consider a Swiss company that buys copper in the world market, then processes it and sells it in Switzerland and abroad.

Its performance depends not only on the price of copper but also on the exchange rate of the US dollar vs. the Swiss franc, because it uses the dollar to make purchases abroad and receives payment in dollars for international sales. Lastly, interest-rate fluctuations have an impact on the company's financial flows. A multi-headed dragon!

The company must manage its specific interest-rate and exchange-rate risks, because doing nothing can also have serious consequences. As the bumper sticker says, "if you think education is expensive, try ignorance!"

Take an example of an economy with no derivative markets. A corporate treasurer anticipating a decline in long-term interest rates and whose company has long-term debt has no choice but to borrow short-term, invest the proceeds long-term, wait for interest rates to decline, pay off the short-term loans and borrow again. You will have no trouble understanding that this strategy has its limits. The balance sheet becomes inflated, intermediation costs rise and so on. Derivative markets enable him to manage this long-term interest-rate risk without touching his company's balance sheet.

Derivatives are instruments for taking positions on other instruments, or "contracts" on "contracts". They let you take significant short or long positions on other assets with a limited outlay of funds.

Derivative instruments are tailored especially to the management of these types of financial risk. By using derivatives, the financial manager chooses a price – expressed as an interest rate, an exchange rate or the price of a raw material – that is independent of the company's financing or investment term. Derivatives are also highly liquid. The financial manager can change his mind at any time at a minimal cost.

Similarly, options enable the investor to take advantage of leverage with a limited outlay of funds, but entail higher risks.

Section 1.4
MOST IMPORTANTLY, HE IS A NEGOTIATOR ...

Let's return to our financial manager who has just created a financial security. Because the security is traded on a secondary market, he doesn't know who holds the securities. Nor does he know who has sold it, especially as, via the futures market, investors can sell the security without ever having bought it.

But what exactly is our financial manager selling? Or put another way: how can the value of the financial security be determined?

From a practical standpoint, the financial manager "sells" management's reputation for integrity, its expertise, the quality of the company's assets, its overall financial health, its ability to generate a certain level of profitability over a given period and its commitment to more or less restrictive legal terms. Note that the quality of assets will be particularly important in the case of a loan tied to and often secured by specific assets, while the overall financial health will dominate when financing is not tied to specific assets.

Theoretically, the financial manager sells expected future cash flows that can derive only from the company's business operations.

A company cannot distribute more cash flow to its providers of capital than its business generates. A money-losing company pays its creditors only at the expense of its shareholders. When a company with sub-par profitability pays a dividend, it jeopardises its financial health.

The financial manager's role is to transform the company's commercial and industrial business assets and commitments into financial assets and commitments.

In so doing, he spreads the expected cash flows among many different investor groups: banks, financial investors, family shareholders, individual investors, etc.

Far from building castles in the sky, the corporate financial manager transforms the company's economic activity into cash flows that he offers to financial investors.

Financial investors then turn these flows into negotiable instruments traded on an open market, which value the instruments in relation to other opportunities available on the market.

Underlying the securities is the market's evaluation of the company. A company considered to be poorly managed will see investors vote with their feet. Yields on the company's securities will rise to prohibitive levels and prices on them will fall. Financial difficulties, if not already present, will soon follow. The financial manager must therefore keep the market convinced at all times of the quality of his company, because that is what is backing up the securities it issues!

Diverse financial partners hold a portion of the value of the company. This diversity gives rise to yet another job for the financial manager: **he must adroitly steer the company through the distribution of the overall value of the company**.

Like any dealmaker, he has something to sell, but he must also:

- assess his company's overall financial situation;
- understand the motivations of the various participants; and
- analyse the relative powers of the parties involved.

Section 1.5

. . . AND HE REMEMBERS TO DO AN OCCASIONAL REALITY CHECK!

The financial investors who buy the company's securities do so not out of altruism, but because they hope to realise a certain rate of return on their investment, in the form of interest, dividends or capital gains. In other words, in return for entrusting the company with their money via their purchase of the company's securities, they require a minimum return on their investment.

Consequently, the financial manager must make sure that, over the medium term, the company makes investments whose returns are by and large at least equal to the rate of return expected by the company's providers of capital. If so, all is well. If not and if the company is consistently falling short of this goal, it will destroy value, turning what was worth 100 into 90, or 80. This is corporate purgatory. On the other hand, if the profitability of its investments consistently exceeds investor demands, transforming 100 into 120 or more, the company deserves the kudos it will get. But it should also remain humble. With technological progress and deregulation advancing apace, repeat performances are becoming more and more challenging.

The financial manager must therefore analyse proposed investment projects and explain to his colleagues that some should not be undertaken because they are not profitable enough. In short, he sometimes has to be a "party-pooper". He is indirectly the spokesman of the financial investment community.

The financial manager must ensure that the company creates value, that the assets it has assembled will generate a rate of return into the medium term that is at least equal to the rate required by the investors whose capital has enabled the company to build those assets.

How's that appetite?

We're going to leave you with these appetizers in the hope that you are now hungry for more. But beware of taking the principles briefly presented here and skipping directly to Section III of the book. If you are looking for high-finance and get-rich-quick schemes, this book might not be for you. The menu we propose is as follows:

- First, an understanding of the firm, i.e., the source of all the cash flows that are the subject of our analysis (**Section I: A financial assessment of the firm**).
- Then an appreciation of markets, because it is they who are constantly valuing the firm (**Section II: Investors and financial markets**).
- To be followed by the major financial decisions of the firm, viewed in the light of both market theory and organisational theory (**Section III: Value and financial strategy**).

Finally, if you persevere through the foregoing, you will get to taste the dessert, as **Section IV** presents several practical, current topics in financial management.

SUMMARY

download

The financial manager has two roles:

- Ensure the company has enough funds to finance its expansion and meet its obligations.
  To do this, the company issues securities (equity and debt) and the financial manager tries to sell them to financial investors at the highest possible price. In today's capital market economy, the role of the financial manager is less a buyer of capital, with an objective to minimise cost, but more a seller of financial securities. By emphasising the financial security, we focus on its value, which combines the notions of return and risk. We thereby de-emphasise the importance of minimising the cost of financial resources, because this approach ignores the risk factor. Casting the financial manager in the role of salesman also underlines the marketing aspect of his job, which is far from theoretical. He has customers (investors) that he must persuade to buy the securities his company issues. The better he understands their needs, the more successful he will be.

- Ensure that over the long run the company uses the resources investors put at its disposal to generate a rate of return at least equal to the rate of return the investors require. If it does, the company creates value. If it does not, it destroys value. If it continues to destroy value, investors will turn their backs on the company and the value of its securities will decline. Ultimately, the company will have to change its senior managers, or face bankruptcy.

In his first role, the financial manager transforms the company's real assets into financial assets. He must maximise the value of these financial assets, while selling them to the various categories of investors.

His second role is a thankless one. He must be a "party-pooper", a "Mr No" who examines every proposed investment project under the microscope of expected returns and advises on whether to reject those that fall below the cost of funds available to the company.

QUESTIONS

quiz

1/ Should the unexpected announcement of a rise in interest rates automatically result in a drop in the stock market index?

2/ Would your answer be the same if the announcement had been anticipated by the market? So what is the most important factor when valuing securities?

3/ Other than the word "market", what in your view is the key word in corporate finance?

4/ How is it possible to sell something without actually having bought anything?

5/ You are offered a loan at 7.5% over 10 years without guarantee, and a loan at 7% over 10 years with guarantee. You need the loan. How should you go about deciding which loan to take out?

6/ Can you define a financial security?

7/ Is a financial security a financial asset or a financial liability? Why?

8/ Provide an example of something that was assumed to be a financial asset, but which proved on analysis to be a financial liability.

9/ How important is it to think in terms of an offer of and a demand for securities, and not in terms of an offer of and a demand for capital, for:

- shares;
- bonds;
- medium-term international loan;
- domestic bank loans.

Why?

10/ What other financial term should immediately spring to mind when you hear the word "returns"?

11/ In your view, are more securities issued on the primary market than exchanged on the secondary market?

12/ What other financial term should immediately spring to mind when you hear the word "risk"?

13/ Which instrument carries the greater risk – shares or bonds? Why?

14/ Explain how the poor performance of the secondary market can impact the primary market.

15/ What are the two biggest flaws of a bad financial manager?

ANSWERS

1/ *As an automatic reaction, yes.*

2/ *No, the answer in this case would be no. The most important factor in valuing securities is anticipation.*

3/ *Value.*

4/ *On the futures market.*

5/ *Is it worth providing a guarantee for a gain of 0.5%?*

6/ *A financial instrument represents a series of cash flows to be received according to a set timetable.*

7/ *A financial asset if the present value of future flows is positive (which it is for the investor), and a liability if not (which is the case for the issuer).*

8/ *The inheritance of an estate, the debts of which exceed the value of the assets.*

9/ *In order – 1 = very important; 2 = of moderate importance; 3 = unimportant: 1–2–2–3, because they are more easily traded.*

10/ *Risk.*

11/ *No, far fewer securities are issued on the primary market than exchanged on the secondary market. In 2004, on the London Stock Exchange, listed companies issued €22bn worth of new shares, whereas the value of shares exchanged was €6,700bn.*

12/ *Returns, the two are inextricably linked.*

13/ *Shares, as returns are not guaranteed for the investor, and creditors are paid out before shareholders.*

14/ *If the value of shares continues to decline long-term, market pessimism descends, and investors become reluctant to subscribe shares on the primary market, as they are convinced that the value of such shares will fall once issued.*

15/ *Short-sightedness and poor marketing skills.*

Section I

FINANCIAL ANALYSIS

PART ONE
FUNDAMENTAL CONCEPTS IN FINANCIAL ANALYSIS

The following six chapters provide a gradual introduction to the foundations of financial analysis. They examine the concepts of cash flow, earnings, capital employed and invested capital, and look at the ways in which these concepts are linked.

Chapter 2
CASH FLOWS

Let's work from A to Z (unless it turns out to be Z to A!)

In the introduction, we emphasised the importance of cash flows as the basic building block of securities. Likewise, we need to start our study of corporate finance by analysing company cash flows.

CLASSIFYING COMPANY CASH FLOWS

Let's consider, for example, the monthly account statement that individual customers receive from their bank. It is presented as a series of lines showing the various inflows and outflows of money on precise dates and in some cases the type of transaction (deposit of cheques, for instance).

Our first step is to trace the rationale for each of the entries on the statement, which could be everyday purchases, payment of a salary, automatic transfers, loan repayments or the receipt of bond coupons, to cite but a few examples.

The corresponding task for a financial manager is to reclassify company cash flows by category to draw up a cash flow document that can be used to:

- analyse past trends in cash flow (generally known as a **cash flow statement**[1]); or
- project future trends in cash flow, over a shorter or longer period (known as a cash flow budget or plan).

1 Or sometimes as statement of changes in financial position

With this goal in mind, we will now demonstrate that cash flows can be classified as one of the following processes:

- Activities that form part of the industrial and commercial life of a company:

  - operating cycle;
  - investment cycle.

- Financing activities to fund these cycles:

  - the debt cycle;
  - the equity cycle.

Section 2.1
OPERATING AND INVESTMENT CYCLES

1/THE IMPORTANCE OF THE OPERATING CYCLE

Let's take the example of a greengrocer, who is "cashing up" one evening. What does he find? First, he sees how much he spent in cash at the wholesale market in the morning and then the cash proceeds from fruit and vegetable sales during the day. If we assume that the greengrocer sold all the produce he bought in the morning at a mark-up, the balance of receipts and payments for the day will deliver a cash surplus.

Unfortunately, things are usually more complicated in practice. Rarely is all the produce bought in the morning sold by the evening, especially in the case of a manufacturing business.

A company processes raw materials as part of an operating cycle, the length of which varies tremendously, from a day in the newspaper sector to 7 years in the cognac sector. There is thus a time lag between purchases of raw materials and the sale of the corresponding finished goods.

And this time lag is not the only complicating factor. It is unusual for companies to buy and sell in cash. Usually, their suppliers grant them extended payment periods, and they in turn grant their customers extended payment periods. The money received during the day does not necessarily come from sales made on the same day.

As a result of customer credit,[2] supplier credit[3] and the time it takes to manufacture and sell products or services, the operating cycle of each and every company spans a certain period, **leading to timing differences between operating outflows and the corresponding operating inflows**.

Each business has its own operating cycle of a certain length that, from a cash flow standpoint, may lead to positive or negative cash flows at different times. Operating outflows and inflows from different cycles are analysed by period, e.g., by month or by year. The balance of these flows is called **operating cash flow**. Operating cash flow reflects the cash flows generated by operations during a given period.

In concrete terms, operating cash flow represents the cash flow generated by the company's day-to-day operations. Returning to our initial example of an individual looking at his bank statement, it represents the difference between the receipts and normal outgoings, such as on food, electricity and car maintenance costs.

Naturally, unless there is a major timing difference caused by some unusual circumstances (start-up period of a business, very strong growth, very strong seasonal fluctuations), the balance of operating receipts and payments should be positive.

Readers with accounting knowledge will note that operating cash flow is independent of any accounting policies, which makes sense since it relates only to cash flows. More specifically:

- neither the company's depreciation and provisioning policy;

2 *That is, credit granted by the company to its customers, allowing them to pay the bill several days, weeks or, in some countries, even several months after receiving the invoice.*

3 *That is, credit granted by suppliers to the company.*

- nor its inventory valuation method;
- nor the techniques used to defer costs over several periods

have any impact on the figure.

However, the concept is affected by decisions about how to classify payments between investment and operating outlays, as we will now examine more closely.

2/ INVESTMENT AND OPERATING OUTFLOWS

Let's return to the example of our greengrocer, who now decides to add frozen food to his business.

The operating cycle will no longer be the same. The greengrocer may, for instance, begin receiving deliveries once a week only and will therefore have to run much larger inventories. Admittedly, the impact of the longer operating cycle due to much larger inventories may be offset by larger credit from his suppliers. The key point here is to recognise that the operating cycle will change.

The operating cycle is different for each business and, generally speaking, the more sophisticated the end product, the longer the operating cycle.

But, most importantly, before he can start up this new activity, our greengrocer needs to invest in a freezer chest.

What difference is there from solely a cash flow standpoint between this investment and operating outlays?

The outlay on the freezer chest seems to be a prerequisite. It forms the basis for a new activity, the success of which is unknown. It appears to carry higher risks and will be beneficial only if overall operating cash flow generated by the greengrocer increases. Lastly, **investments are carried out from a long-term perspective and have a longer life than that of the operating cycle**. Indeed, they last for several operating cycles, even if they do not last for ever given the fast pace of technological progress.

This justifies the distinction, from a cash flow perspective, between operating and investment outflows.

Normal outflows, from an individual's perspective, differ from an investment outflow in that they afford enjoyment, whereas investment represents abstinence. As we will see, this type of decision represents one of the vital underpinnings of finance. Only the very puritan-minded would take more pleasure from buying a microwave oven than from spending the same amount of money at a restaurant! One of these choices can only be an investment and the other an ordinary outflow. So what purpose do investments serve? Investment is worthwhile only if the decision to forgo normal spending, which gives instant pleasure, will subsequently lead to greater gratification.

From a cash flow standpoint, an investment is an outlay that is subsequently expected to increase operating cash flow such that overall the individual will be happy to have forsaken instant gratification.

This is the definition of the **return on investment** (be it industrial or financial) from a cash flow standpoint. We will use this definition throughout this book.

Like the operating cycle, the investment cycle is characterised by a series of inflows and outflows. But the length of the investment cycle is far larger than the length of the operating cycle.

The purpose of investment outlays (also frequently called capital expenditures) is to alter the operating cycle; e.g., to boost or enhance the cash flows that it generates.

The impact of investment outlays is spread over several operating cycles. Financially, capital expenditures are worthwhile only if inflows generated thanks to these expenditures exceed the required outflows by an amount yielding at least the return on investment expected by the investor.

Note also that a company may sell some assets in which it has invested in the past. For instance, our greengrocer may decide after several years to trade in his freezer for a larger model. The proceeds would also be part of the investment cycle.

3/FREE CASH FLOW

Before-tax free cash flow is defined as the difference between operating cash flow and capital expenditure net of fixed assets disposals.

As we will see in Sections II and III of this book, free cash flow can be calculated before or after tax. It also forms the basis for the most important valuation technique. Operating cash flow is a concept that depends on how expenditure is classified between operating and investment outlays. Since this distinction is not always clearcut, operating cash flow is not widely used in practice, with free cash flow being far more popular. If free cash flow turns negative, additional financial resources will have to be raised to cover the company's cash flow requirements.

Section 2.2
FINANCIAL RESOURCES

The operating and investment cycles give rise to a timing difference in cash flows. Employees and suppliers have to be paid before customers settle up. Likewise, investments have to be completed before they generate any receipts. Naturally, this cash flow deficit needs to be filled. This is the role of **financial resources**.

The purpose of financial resources is simple: they must cover the shortfalls resulting from these timing differences by providing the company with sufficient funds to balance its cash flow.

These financial resources are provided by investors: shareholders, debtholders, lenders, etc. These financial resources are not provided "no strings attached". In return for providing the funds, investors expect to be subsequently "rewarded" by receiving dividends or interest payments, registering capital gains, etc. This can happen only if the operating and investment cycles generate positive cash flows.

To the extent that the financial investors have made the investment and operating activities possible, they expect to receive, in various different forms, their fair share of the surplus cash flows generated by these cycles.

The financing cycle is therefore the "flip side" of the investment and operating cycles.

At its most basic, the principle would be to finance these shortfalls solely using capital that incurs the risk of the business. Such capital is known as **shareholders' equity**. This type of financial resource forms the cornerstone of the entire financial system. Its importance is such that shareholders providing it are granted decision-making powers and control over the business in various different ways. From a cash flow standpoint, the equity cycle comprises inflows from capital increases and outflows in the form of dividend payments to the shareholders.

Without casting any doubt on their managerial capabilities, all our readers have probably had to cope with cash flow shortfalls, if only as part of their personal financial affairs. The usual approach in such circumstances is to talk to a banker. Your banker will only give you a loan if he believes that you will be able to repay the loan with interest. Bank loans may be short-term (overdraft facilities) or long-term (e.g., a loan to buy an apartment).

Like individuals, a business may decide to ask lenders rather than shareholders to help it cover a cash flow shortage. Bankers will lend funds only after they have carefully analysed the company's financial health. They want to be nearly certain of being repaid and do not want exposure to the company's business risk. These cash flow shortages may be short-term, long-term or even permanent, but lenders do not want to take on business risk. The capital they provide represents the company's **debt capital**.

The debt cycle is the following: the business arranges borrowings in return for a commitment to repay the capital and make interest payments regardless of trends in its operating and investment cycles. These undertakings represent firm commitments ensuring that the lender is certain of recovering its funds provided that the commitments are met. This definition applies to both:

- financing for the investment cycle, with the increase in future net receipts set to cover capital repayments and interest payments on borrowings; and
- financing for the operating cycle, with credit making it possible to bring forward certain inflows or to defer certain outflows.

From a cash flow standpoint, the life of a business comprises an operating and an investment cycle, leading to a positive or negative free cash flow. If free cash flow is negative, the financing cycle covers the funding shortfall.

As the future is unknown, a distinction has to be drawn between:

- equity, where the only commitment is to enable the shareholders to benefit fully from the success of the venture;
- debt capital, where the only commitment is to meet the capital repayments and interest payments regardless of the success or failure of the venture.

The risk incurred by the lender is that this commitment will not be met. Theoretically speaking, debt may be regarded as an advance on future cash flows generated by the investments made and guaranteed by the company's shareholders' equity.

Although a business needs to raise funds to finance investments, it may also find at a given point in time that it has a cash surplus, i.e., the funds available exceed cash requirements.

These surplus funds are then invested in short-term investments and marketable securities that generate revenue, called financial income.

Although at first sight short-term financial investments (marketable securities) may be regarded as investments since they generate a rate of return, we advise readers to consider them instead as the opposite of debt. As we will see, company treasurers often have to raise additional debt just to reinvest those funds in short-term investments without speculating in any way.

These investments are generally realised with a view to ensuring the possibility of a very quick exit without any risk of losses.

Debt and short-term financial investments or marketable securities should not be considered independently of each other, but as inextricably linked. We suggest that readers **reason in terms of debt net of short-term financial investments** and **financial expense net of financial income**.

Putting all the individual pieces together, we arrive at the following simplified cash flow statement, with the balance reflecting the net decrease in the company's debt during a given period:

SIMPLIFIED CASH FLOW STATEMENT

		2005	2006	2007
	Operating receipts			
−	Operating payments			
=	**Operating cash flow**			
−	Capital expenditure			
+	Fixed asset disposals			
=	**Free cash flow before tax**			
−	Financial expense net of financial income			
−	Corporate income tax			
+	Proceeds from share issue			
−	Dividends paid			
=	**Net decrease in debt**			
	With:			
	Repayments of borrowings			
−	New bank and other borrowings			
+	Change in marketable securities			
+	Change in cash and cash equivalents			
=	**Net decrease in debt**			

The cash flows of a company can be divided into four categories, i.e., operating and investment flows, which are generated as part of its business activities, and debt and equity flows, which finance these activities.

The operating cycle is characterised by a time lag between the positive and negative cash flows deriving from the length of the production process (which varies from business to business) and the commercial policy (customer and supplier credit).

Operating cash flow, the balance of funds generated by the various operating cycles in progress, comprises the cash flows generated by a company's operations during a given period. It represents the (usually positive) difference between operating receipts and payments.

From a cash flow standpoint, capital expenditures must alter the operating cycle in such a way as to generate higher operating inflows going forward than would otherwise have been the case. Capital expenditures are intended to enhance the operating cycle by enabling it to achieve a higher level of profitability in the long term. This profitability can be measured only over several operating cycles, unlike operating payments, which belong to a single cycle. As a result, investors forgo immediate use of their funds in return for higher cash flows over several operating cycles.

Free cash flow (before tax) can be defined as operating cash flow less capital expenditure (investment outlays).

When a company's free cash flow is negative, it covers its funding shortfall through its financing cycle by raising equity and debt capital.

Since shareholders' equity is exposed to business risk, the returns paid on it are unpredictable and depend on the success of the venture. Where a business rounds out its financing with debt capital, it undertakes to make capital repayments and interest payments (financial expense) to its lenders regardless of the success of the venture. Accordingly, debt represents an advance on the operating receipts generated by the investment that is guaranteed by the company's shareholders' equity.

Short-term financial investment, the rationale for which differs from investment, and cash should be considered in conjunction with debt. We will always reason in terms of net debt (i.e., net of cash and of marketable securities, which are short-term financial investments) and net financial expense (i.e., net of financial income).

SUMMARY

download

1/ What are the four basic cycles of a company?

2/ Why do we say that financial flows are the flip side of investment and operating flows?

3/ Define operating cash flow. Should the company be able to spend this surplus as it likes?

4/ Is operating cash flow an accounting profit?

5/ Why do we say that, as a general rule, operating cash flow should be positive? Provide a simple example that demonstrates that operating cash flow can be negative during periods of strong growth, start-up periods and in the event of strong seasonal fluctuations.

QUESTIONS

quiz

6/ When a cash flow budget is drawn up for the purposes of assessing an investment, can free cash flows be negative? If so, is it more likely that this will be the case at the beginning or at the end of the business plan period? Why?

7/ Among the following different flows, which will be appropriated by both shareholders and lenders: operating receipts, operating cash flow, free cash flows? Who has priority, shareholders or lenders? Why?

8/ A feature of a supermarket chain such as Tesco or Ahold is the very fast rotation of food stocks (6 days), cash payments by customers, long supplier credit periods (60 days) and very low administrative costs. Will the operating cycle generate cash requirements or a cash surplus?

9/ From a cash flow standpoint, should the costs of launching a new perfume be considered as an operating outlay or an investment outlay?

10/ How is an investment decision analysed from a cash standpoint?

11/ After reading this chapter, are you able to define bankruptcy?

12/ Is debt capital risk-free for the lender? Can you analyse what the risk is? Why do some borrowers default on loans?

EXERCISES

1/ Boomwichers NV, a Dutch company financed by shareholders' equity only, decides during the course of 2005 to finance an investment project worth €200m using shareholders' equity (50%) and debt (50%). The loan it takes out (€100m) will be paid off in full in $n + 5$ years, and the company will pay 5% interest per year over the period. At the end of the period, you are asked to complete the following simplified table (no further investments were made):

Period	2005	2006	2007	2008	2009	2010
Operating inflows	165	200	240	280	320	360
Operating outflows	165	175	180	185	180	190
Operating cash flows						
Investments	−200					
Free cash flows						
Flows . . .						
. . . *to creditors*						
. . . *to shareholders*						

What do you conclude from the above?

2/ Ellingham plc opens a Spanish subsidiary, which starts operating on 2 January 2005. On 2 January 2005 it has to buy a machine costing €30m, partly financed by a €20m bank loan repayable in instalments of €2m every 15 July and 15 January over 5 years. Financial expenses, payable on a half-yearly basis, are as follows:

2005		2006		2007		2008		2009	
Jun	Dec	Jun	Dec	Jun	Dec	Jun	Dec	Jun	Dec
1	0.9	0.8	0.7	0.6	0.5	0.4	0.3	0.2	0.1

Profits are tax-free. Sales will be €12m per month. A month's inventory of finished products will have to be built up. Customers pay at 90 days.

The company is keen to have a month's worth of advance purchases and, accordingly, plans to buy 2 months' worth of supplies in January 2005. Requirements in a normal month amount to €4m.

The supplier grants the company a 90-day payment period. Other costs are:

○ personnel costs of €4m per month;
○ shipping, packaging and other costs, amounting to €2m per month and paid at 30 days. These costs are incurred from 1 January 2005.

Draw up a monthly and an annual cash flow plan.

How much cash will the subsidiary need at the end of each month over the first year? And if operations are identical, how much will it need each month over 2006? What is the change in the cash position over 2006 (no additional investments are planned)?

Questions

ANSWERS

1/ *Operating, investment, debt and equity cycles.*
2/ *Because negative free cash flows generated by operating and investment cycles must be compensated by resources from the financial cycle. When free cash flows are positive, they are entirely absorbed by the financial cycle (debts are repaid, dividends are paid, etc.).*
3/ *It is the balance of the operating cycle. No, as it has to repay banking debts when they are due, for example.*
4/ *No, it is a cash flow, not an accounting profit.*
5/ *It measures flows generated by the company's operations (i.e., its business or "raison d'être". If it is not positive in the long term, the company will be in trouble. Major shortfall due to operating cycle, large inventories, operating losses on start-up, heavy swings in operating cycle.*
6/ *Yes. At the beginning, an investment may need time to run at full speed.*
7/ *Free cash flows, since all operating or investment outlays have been paid. The lenders because of contractual agreement.*
8/ *A cash surplus, as customer receipts come in before suppliers are paid.*
9/ *Investment outlays, from which the company will benefit over several financial years as the product is being put onto the market.*
10/ *Expenditure should generate inflows over several financial periods.*
11/ *The inability to find additional resources to meet the company's financial obligations.*
12/ *No. The risk is the borrower's failure to honour contracts either because of inability to repay due to poor business conditions or because of bad faith.*

Exercises

1/ *Boomwichers NV*

Period	2005	2006	2007	2008	2009	2010
Operating inflows	165	200	240	280	320	360
Operating outflows	165	175	180	185	180	190
Operating cash flows	**0**	**25**	**60**	**95**	**140**	**170**
Investments	−200	0	0	0	0	0
Free cash flows	**−200**	**25**	**60**	**95**	**140**	**170**
Flows ...						
... to creditors	−100	5	5	5	5	105
... to shareholders	−100	20	55	90	135	65

The investment makes it possible to repay creditors and leave cash for shareholders.

2/ *Ellingham plc exercise, see p. 69.*

BIBLIOGRAPHY

To learn more about the notion of flows:

K. Checkley, *Strategic Cash Flow Management*, Capstone Express, 2002.
E. Helfert, *Techniques of Financial Analysis*, Irwin, 11th edn, 2002.

Chapter 3
EARNINGS

Time to put our accounting hat on!

Following our analysis of company cash flows, it is time to consider the issue of how a company creates wealth. In this chapter, we are going to study the income statement to show how the various cycles of a company create wealth.

Section 3.1
ADDITIONS TO WEALTH AND DEDUCTIONS TO WEALTH

What would your spontaneous answer be to the following questions?

- Does purchasing an apartment make you richer or poorer?
- Would your answer change if you were to buy the apartment on credit?

There can be no doubt as to the correct answer. Provided that you pay the going rate for the apartment, your wealth is not affected whether or not you buy it on credit. Our experience as university lecturers has shown us that students often confuse cash and wealth.

Cash and wealth are two of the fundamental concepts of corporate finance. It is vital to be able to juggle them around and thus to be able to differentiate between them confidently.

Consequently, we advise readers to train their minds by analysing the impact of all transactions in terms of cash flows and wealth impacts.

For instance, when you buy an apartment, you become neither richer, nor poorer, but your cash decreases. Arranging a loan makes you no richer or poorer than you were before (you owe the money), but your cash has increased. In this respect, the proverb "He who pays his debts gets richer" is nonsense from a financial viewpoint. If a fire destroys your house and it was not insured, you are worse off, but your cash position has not changed, since you have not spent any money.

Raising debt is tantamount to increasing your financial resources and commitments at the same time. As a result, it has no impact on your net worth. Buying an apartment for cash results in a change in your assets (reduction in cash, increase in property assets) without any change in net worth. The possible examples are endless. **Spending money does not necessarily make you poorer. Likewise, receiving money does not necessarily make you richer**.

1 *Also called Profit and Loss statement, P&L account.*

The job of listing all the cash flows that positively or negatively affect a company's wealth is performed by the **income statement**,[1] which shows all the additions to wealth (**revenues**) and all the deductions to wealth (**charges or expenses or costs**). The fundamental aim of all businesses is to increase wealth. Additions to wealth cannot be achieved without some deductions to wealth. In sum, earnings represent the difference between additions and deductions to wealth:

	Revenues	Gross additions to wealth
−	Charges	− Gross deductions from wealth
=	Earnings	= Net additions to wealth (deduction from)

Earnings represent the difference between revenues and charges, leading to a change in net worth during a given period. Earnings are positive when wealth is created or negative when wealth is destroyed.

Since the rationale behind the income statement is not the same as for a cash flow statement, some cash flows do not appear on the income statement (those that neither generate nor destroy wealth). Likewise, some revenues and charges are not shown on the cash flow statement (because they have no impact on the company's cash position).

1/THE DISTINCTION BETWEEN OPERATING CHARGES AND FIXED ASSETS

Although we were easily able to define investment from a cash flow perspective, we recognise that our approach went against the grain of the traditional presentation, especially as far as those familiar with accounting are concerned:

- whatever is consumed as part of the operating cycle to create something new belongs to the operating cycle. Without wishing to philosophise, we note that the act of creation always entails some form of destruction;
- whatever is used without being destroyed directly and thus retaining its value belongs to the investment cycle. This represents an immutable asset or, in accounting terms, a fixed asset.

For instance, to make bread, a baker uses flour, salt and water, all of which form part of the end product. The process also entails labour, which has a value only in so far as it transforms the raw material into the end product. At the same time, the baker also needs a bread oven, which is absolutely essential for the production process, but is not destroyed by it. Though this oven may experience wear and tear it will be used many times over.

This is the major distinction that can be drawn between operating charges and fixed assets. It may look deceptively straightforward, but in practice is no clearer than the distinction between investment and operating outlays. For instance, does an advertising campaign represent a charge linked solely to one period with no impact on any other? Or does it represent the creation of an asset (e.g., a brand)?

2/EARNINGS AND THE OPERATING CYCLE

The operating cycle forms the basis of the company's wealth. It consists in both:

- additions to wealth (products and services sold, i.e. products and services whose worth is recognised in the market);
- deductions from wealth (consumption of raw materials or goods for resale, use of labour, use of external services, such as transportation, taxes and other duties).

The very essence of a business is to increase wealth by means of its operating cycle:

Additions to wealth		Operating revenues
Deductions from wealth	−	Cash operating charges
	=	EBITDA[2]

2 Earnings Before Interest, Taxes, Depreciation and Amortisation.

Put another way, the result of the operating cycle is the balance of operating revenues and cash operating charges incurred to obtain these revenues. We will refer to it as gross operating profit or EBITDA.

It may be described as gross insofar as it covers just the operating cycle and is calculated before noncash expenses such as depreciation and amortisation, and before interest and taxes.

3/EARNINGS AND THE INVESTING CYCLE

(a) Principles

Investing activities do not appear directly on the income statement. In a wealth-oriented approach, an investment represents a use of funds that retains some value.

To invest is to forgo liquid funds: an asset is purchased but no wealth is destroyed. As a result, investments never appear directly on the income statement.

This said, the value of investments may change during a financial year:

- it may decrease if they suffer wear and tear or become obsolete;
- it may increase if the market value of certain assets rises.

Even so, by virtue of the principle of prudence, increases in value are recorded only if realised through the disposal of the asset.

(b) Accounting for loss in the value of fixed assets

The loss in value of a fixed asset due to its use by the company is accounted for by means of **depreciation** and **amortisation**.[3]

    Impairment losses or write-downs on fixed assets recognise the loss in value of an asset not related to its day-to-day use; i.e., the unforeseen diminution in the value of:

3 Amortisation is sometimes used instead of depreciation, particularly in the context of intangible assets.

- an intangible asset (goodwill, patents, etc.);
- a tangible asset (property, plant, and equipment);
- an investment in a subsidiary.

Depreciation and amortisation on fixed assets are so-called "noncash" charges in so far as they merely reflect arbitrary accounting assessments of the loss in value.

As we will see, there are other types of noncash charges, such as impairment losses on fixed assets, write-downs on current assets (which are included in operating charges) and provisions for liabilities and charges.

4/THE COMPANY'S OPERATING PROFIT

From EBITDA, which is linked to the operating cycle, we deduct noncash charges, which comprises depreciation and amortisation and impairment losses or write-downs on fixed assets.

This gives us operating income or operating profit or EBIT (Earnings Before Interest and Taxes), which reflects the increase in wealth generated by the company's industrial and commercial activities.

Operating profit or EBIT represents the earnings generated by investment and operating cycles for a given period.

The term "operating" contrasts with the term "financial", reflecting the distinction between the real world and the realms of finance. Indeed, operating income is the product of the company's industrial and commercial activities before its financing operations are taken into account. Operating profit or EBIT may also be called operating income, trading profit, or operating result.

5/EARNINGS AND THE FINANCING CYCLE

(a) Debt capital

Repayments of borrowings do not constitute costs, but as their name suggests, merely repayments.

Just as common sense tells us that securing a loan does not increase wealth, neither does repaying a borrowing represent a charge.

The income statement shows only charges related to borrowings. It never shows the repayments of borrowings, which are deducted from the debt recorded on the balance sheet.

We emphasise this point because our experience tells us that many mistakes are made in this area.

Conversely, we should note that the interest payments made on borrowings lead to a decrease in the wealth of the company and thus represent an expense for the company. As a result, they are shown on the income statement.

The difference between financial income and financial expense is called **net financial expense/(income)**.

The difference between operating profit and financial expense net of financial income is called **profit before tax** and **nonrecurring items**.[4]

4 *Or nonrecurrent items.*

(b) Shareholders' equity

From a cash flow standpoint, shareholders' equity is formed through issuance of shares less outflows in the form of dividends or share buybacks. These cash inflows give rise to ownership rights over the company. Dividends are a way of apportioning earnings voted on at the general meeting of the shareholders once the company's accounts have been approved. For technical, tax and legal reasons, most of the time they are not shown on the income statement, except in the United Kingdom.

"Retained earnings" is the term frequently used to designate the portion of earnings not distributed as a dividend. This said, if we take a step back, we see that dividends and financial interest are based on the same principle of distributing the wealth created by the company.[5] Likewise, income tax represents earnings paid to the State in spite of the fact that it does not contribute any funds to the company.

5 *This is why dividends appear on the income statement in UK accounting, the last line of which shows retained earnings.*

6/ RECURRENT AND NONRECURRENT ITEMS: EXTRAORDINARY AND EXCEPTIONAL ITEMS, DISCONTINUING OPERATIONS

We have now considered all the operations of a business that may be allocated to the operating, investing and financing cycles of a company. This said, it is not hard to imagine the difficulties involved in classifying the financial consequences of certain **extraordinary** events, such as losses incurred as a result of earthquakes, other natural disasters or the expropriation of assets by a government.

They are not expected to recur frequently or regularly and are beyond the control of a company's management. Hence the idea of creating a separate catch-all category for precisely such extraordinary items.

Among the many different types of **exceptional** events, we will briefly focus on asset disposals. Investing forms an integral part of the industrial and commercial activities of businesses. But it would be foolhardy to believe that investment is a one-way process. The best-laid plans may fail, while others may lead down a strategic impasse.

Put another way, disinvesting is also a key part of an entrepreneur's activities. It generates exceptional "asset disposal" inflows on the cash flow statement and capital gains and losses on the income statement, which usually appear under exceptional items.

Lastly, when a company disposes of some segments of its activity or entire sections of a business, the corresponding gains or losses are recorded under **discontinuing operations**.

One of the main puzzles for the financial analyst is to identify whether an extraordinary or exceptional item can be described as recurrent or nonrecurrent. If it is recurrent, it will occur again and again in the future. If it is not recurrent, it is simply a one-off item.

Without any doubt extraordinary items and results for discontinuing operations are nonrecurrent items.

Exceptional items are much more tricky to analyse. For large groups, closure of plants, provisions for restructuring, etc. tend to happen every year in different divisions or countries. In some sectors, exceptional items are an intrinsic part of the business. A car rental company renews its fleet of cars every 9 months and regularly registers capital gains. Exceptional items should then be analysed as recurrent items and as such be included in the operating profit. For smaller companies, exceptional items tend to be one-off items and as such should be seen as nonrecurrent items.

The International Accounting Standards Board (IASB) has decided to include extraordinary and exceptional items within operating charges without identifying them as such. We think it is unwise and hope that, one day or another, accountants will switch to the more relevant recurrent vs. nonrecurrent items classification.

By definition, it is easier to analyse and forecast profit before tax and non-recurrent items than **net income or net profit**, which is calculated after the impact of nonrecurrent items and tax.

Section 3.2
DIFFERENT INCOME STATEMENT FORMATS

Two main formats of income statement are frequently used, which differ in the way they present revenues and expenses related to the operating and investment cycles. They may be presented either:

6 *Also called by-destination income statement.*

7 *Also called by-category income statement.*

- **by function**;[6] i.e., according to the way revenues and charges are used in the operating and investing cycle. This shows the cost of goods sold, selling and marketing costs, research and development costs and general and administrative costs; or
- **by nature**;[7] i.e., by type of expenditure or revenue which shows the change in inventories of finished goods and in work in progress (closing less opening inventory), purchases of and changes in inventories (closing less opening inventory) of goods for resale and raw materials, other external charges, personnel expense, taxes and other duties, depreciation and amortisation.

Thankfully, operating profit works out to be the same, irrespective of the format used!

The two different income statement formats can be summarised as shown in the diagram at the top of the next page.

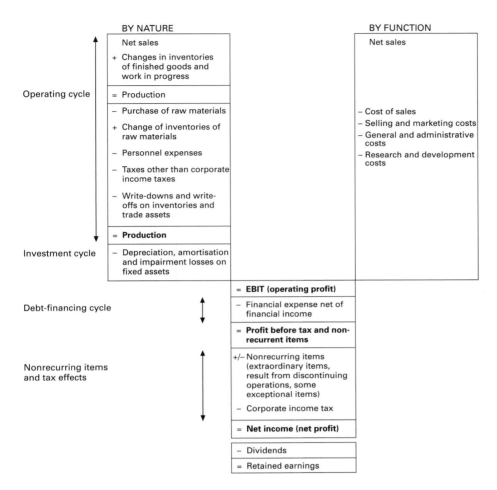

The by-nature presentation predominates to a great extent in Italy, Spain and Belgium. In the US, the by-function presentation is used almost to the exclusion of any other format.[8]

8 The US airline companies are an exception as most of them use the by-nature income statement.

	France	Germany	Italy	Japan	Netherlands	Poland	Russia	Spain	Scandinavia	Switzerland	UK	US
By nature	28%	7%	87%	7%	51%	10%	25%	97%	24%	34%	29%	3%
By function	56%	86%	13%	80%	49%	90%	55%	0%	73%	66%	68%	84%
Other	16%	7%	0%	13%	0%	0%	20%	3%	3%	0%	3%	13%

Source: 2003 annual reports from the top 30 listed nonfinancial groups in each country.

Whereas in the past France, Germany, the Netherlands, Switzerland and the UK tended to use systematically the by-nature or by-function format, the current situation is less clear-cut. Moreover, a new presentation is making some headway, it is mainly a by-function format but depreciation and amortisation are not included in the cost of goods sold, or in selling and marketing costs, or in research development costs, but are isolated on a separate line.[9]

9 See, for example the income statement of Adidas on www.adidas-salomon.com

1/THE BY-FUNCTION INCOME STATEMENT FORMAT

This presentation is based on a management accounting approach, in which costs are allocated to the main corporate functions:

Function	Corresponding cost
Production	Cost of sales
Commercial	Selling and marketing costs
Research and development	Research and development costs
Administration	General and administrative costs

As a result, personnel expense is allocated to each of these four categories (or three where selling, general and administrative costs are pooled into a single category) depending on whether an individual employee works in production, sales, research or administration. Likewise, depreciation expense for a tangible fixed asset is allocated to production if it relates to production machinery, to selling and market-ing costs if it concerns a car used by the sales team, to research and development costs if it relates to laboratory equipment, or to general and administrative costs in the case of the accounting department's computers, for example.

The underlying principle is very simple indeed. This format shows very clearly that operating profit is the difference between sales and the cost of sales irrespective of their nature (i.e., production, sales, research and development, administration).

On the other hand, it does not differentiate between the operating and investment processes since depreciation and amortisation is not shown directly on the income statement (it is split up between the four main corporate functions), obliging analysts to track down the information in the cash flow statement or in the notes to the accounts.

2/THE BY-NATURE INCOME STATEMENT FORMAT

This is the traditional presentation of income statements in many Continental European countries, even if some groups are dropping it in favour of the by-function format in their consolidated accounts.

The by-nature format is simple to apply, even for small companies, because no allocation of expenses is required. It offers a more detailed breakdown of costs.

Naturally, operating profit is still, as in the previous approach, the difference between sales and the cost of sales.

In this format, charges are recognised as they are incurred rather than when the corresponding items are used. Showing on the income statement all purchases made and all invoices sent to customers during the same period would not be comparing like with like.

A business may transfer to the inventory some of the purchases made during a given year. The transfer of these purchases to the inventory does not destroy any wealth. Instead, it represents the formation of an asset, albeit probably a temporary one, but one that has real value at a given point in time. Secondly, some of the end products produced by the company may not be sold during the year and yet the corresponding charges appear on the income statement.

To compare like with like, it is necessary to:

- eliminate changes in inventories of raw materials and goods for resale from purchases to get raw materials and goods for resale used rather than simply purchased;
- add changes in the inventory of finished products and work in progress back to sales. As a result, the income statement shows **production** rather than just sales.

The by-nature format shows the amount spent on production for the period and not the total expenses under the accruals convention. It has the logical disadvantage that it seems to imply that changes in inventory are a revenue or an expense in their own right, which they are not. They are only an adjustment to purchases to obtain relevant costs.

Exercise 1 will help readers get to grips with the concept of changes in inventories of finished goods and work in progress.

To sum up, there are two different income statement formats:

- the **by-nature format** which is focused on production in which all the charges incurred during a given period are recorded. This amount then needs to be adjusted (for changes in inventories) so that it may be compared with products sold during the period;
- the **by-function format** which reasons directly in terms of the cost price of goods or services sold.

Either way, it is worth noting that EBITDA depends heavily on the inventory valuation methods used by the business. This emphasises the appeal of the by-nature format, which shows inventory changes on a separate line of the income statement and thus clearly indicates their order of magnitude.

Like operating cash flow, EBITDA is not influenced by the valuation methods applied to tangible and intangible fixed assets or the taxation system.

SUMMARY

download

A distinction needs to be made between cash and wealth. Spending money does not necessarily make you poorer and neither does receiving money necessarily make you any richer. Additions to wealth or deductions to wealth by a company is measured on the income statement. It is the difference between revenues and charges that increases a company's net worth during a given period.

From an accounting standpoint, operating charges reflect what is used up immediately in the operating cycle and somehow forms part of the end product. On the contrary, fixed assets are not destroyed directly during the production process and retain some of their value.

EBITDA shows the profit generated by the operating cycle (operating revenues − operating charges).

As part of the operating cycle, a business naturally builds up inventories, which are assets. These represent deferred charges, the impact of which needs to be eliminated in the calculation of EBITDA. In the by-nature format, this adjustment is made to operating revenues (by adding back changes in finished goods inventories) and to operating charges (by subtracting changes in inventories of raw materials and goods for resale from purchases). The by-function income statement merely shows sales and the cost of goods sold requiring no adjustment.

Capital expenditures never appear directly on the income statement, but they lead to an increase in the amount of fixed assets held. This said, an accounting assessment of impairment in the value of these investments leads to noncash expenses, which are shown on the income statement (depreciation, amortisation and impairment losses on fixed assets).

EBIT shows the profit generated by the operating and investment cycles. In concrete terms, it represents the profit generated by the industrial and commercial activities of a business. It is allocated to:

● financial expense: only charges related to borrowings appear on the income statement, since capital repayments do not represent a destruction of wealth;

● corporate income tax;

● net income that is distributed to shareholders as dividends or transferred to the reserves (as retained earnings).

QUESTIONS

quiz

1/ A company raises €500m in shareholders' equity for an R&D project. Has it become richer or poorer? By how much? What is your answer if the company spends half of the funds in the first 2 years, and the project does not produce results? In the 3rd year, the company uses the remaining funds to acquire a competitor that is overvalued by 25%. But, thanks to synergies with this new subsidiary, it is able to improve its earnings by €75m. Has it become richer or poorer? By how much?

2/ What are the accounting items corresponding to additions to wealth for shareholders, lenders and the State?

3/ In concrete terms, based on the diagram on p. 35, by how much does a company create wealth over a given financial period? Why?

4/ Comment on the following two statements: "This year, we're going to have to go into debt to cover our losses" and "We'll be able to buy out our main competitor, thanks to the profits we made this year".

5/ In 2005, a company's free cash flow turns negative. Has the company created or destroyed wealth?

6/ Does EBITDA always flow directly into a company's bank account?

7/ Is it correct to say that a company's wealth is increased each year by the amount of EBITDA?

8/ According to the terminology used in Chapter 2, is depreciation a cash expense or a noncash charge? What is the difference between these two concepts?

9/ Analyse the similarities of and the differences between cash and wealth, looking at, for example, investment in real estate and investment in research.

10/ Will repayment of a loan always be recorded on the income statement? Will it always be recorded under a cash item?

11/ Does the inflation-related increase in the nominal value of an asset appear on the income statement?

12/ Why is the increase in inventories of raw materials deducted from purchases in the by-nature income statement format?

13/ Why is change in finished goods' inventories recorded under income in the by-nature income statement format?

14/ Should the sale of a fixed asset be classified as part of the "ordinary course of business" of a company? How is it recorded on the income statement? Why under this heading?

15/ Provide several examples illustrating the difference between cash receipts and revenues, cash expenses and charges.

16/ Is there a substantial difference between the income statement and the cash flow statement?

17/ What is a noncash expense? What is a deferred charge? Describe their similarities and the differences between them.

EXERCISES

1/ **Starjö AB**

You are asked by a Swedish company that assembles computers to draw up a by-nature and by-function income statement for year n. You are provided with the following information: Retail price of a PC: €1,500.

Cost of various components:

Parts	Price	Opening inventory	Closing inventory
Case	50	5	13
Mother board	200	8	2
Processor	300	4	11
Memory	100	6	4
Graphics card	50	1	13
Hard disk	150	5	10
Screen	200	3	3
CD-ROM reader	50	7	19

Over the financial period, the company paid out €60,000 in salaries and social security contributions of 50% of that amount. The company produced 240 PCs. Closing stock of finished products was 27 units and opening stock 14 units.

At the end of the financial period, the manager of the company sells the premises that he had bought for €200,000 3 years ago (which was depreciated over 40 years) for €230,000, rents other premises for €1,000 per month, and pays off a €12,000 loan on which the company was paying interest at 5%. What impact do these transactions have on EBITDA, operating profits and net incomes? Tax is levied at a rate of 35%.

Over the course of the financial period, by how much did the company/the lenders/the company manager (who owns 50% of the shares) get richer/poorer?

2/ **Ellingham plc**

Draw up the income statement for 2005 in both the by-nature and by-function formats. Depreciation and amortisation come to €6m.

3/ **Carvalho SA**

Consider a Portuguese business that sells oak barrels to vineyards. At the start of the year, its inventory of finished products was zero. It sold 800 of the 900 barrels it had produced, leaving the closing inventory at 100 barrels. Each barrel sells for €100. To produce one barrel, the company spends €50 on oak purchases and incurs €20 in labour costs. In addition, the sales force generates costs of €4,500 per year and the fully outsourced administrative department incurs costs of €4,000 p.a. Annual depreciation expense related to the production facilities comes to €3,000. The opening inventory of raw materials was €4,000 and the closing inventory €5,000. In sum, the business spent €46,000 on raw materials.

Produce the by-nature income statement.

Assuming that depreciation breaks down into €2,000 for the production machinery, €700 for the sales facilities and €300 for the administrative facilities, produce the by-function income statement. Are you surprised that both formats give the same EBIT? Why? What do you think about Carvalho's EBIT margin?

ANSWERS

Questions

1/ *Neither. Zero, poorer by €250m. Richer by €25m: $75 - 250 \times [25\%/(1 + 25\%)]$.*
2/ *Net income, financial expenses, corporate income tax.*
3/ *EBIT (Operating profit) + Non-recurring items − Corporate income tax. The wealth created is the wealth to be divided up between lenders (financial expenses), the State (corporate income tax) and shareholders (the balance).*
4/ *Confusion between additions to and deductions from wealth (which is an accounting issue) and cash: in the former, new borrowings do not add wealth to cover the losses; in the latter, profit is not the means used to finance an investment as it does not translate 100% in cash.*
5/ *There is nothing that tells us whether wealth has been destroyed or created as we do not know what net income for 2005 is.*
6/ *No, because income and charges may not necessarily correspond to immediate cash receipts or expenses.*
7/ *No, because a company takes on costs that are deductible from EBITDA to form net income depreciation, financial costs, etc.*
8/ *It is a noncash charge, not a cash expense, i.e., a cost that is recorded, but which does not have to be cashed out.*
9/ *From a cash standpoint, an investment in real estate is a cash expense which will only generate income on the day it is sold. From a wealth standpoint, real estate is an attractive asset. For investments in R&D, returns must be quicker from a cash standpoint. In terms of wealth, however, the disposal value of R&D is nil.*
10/ *No, only financial interest is recorded in the income statement. Yes, because debts are repaid in cash.*
11/ *No, because of the prudence principle.*

12/ *In order to obtain a figure for purchases consumed in the business in the current year.*

13/ *In order to counterbalance charges recorded in the income statement which should not affect this year net income as they are related to unsold products.*

14/ *No, except if the company is in the business of regularly selling fixed assets, like a car rental company, for example. Capital gains or losses on the sale of a fixed asset will be recorded as exceptional gains/losses.*

15/ *Sales (revenues) and customer payments (cash receipts). Depreciation and amortisation (charges without cash expenses). Purchase of a machine (cash expense but not a charge).*

16/ *Yes. See flow chart in Chapter 5 (p. 59).*

17/ *A noncash expense is a charge which does not reflect a specific expense, but an accounting valuation of how much wealth has been destroyed. A deferred charge is one that is carried over to the next financial period. Common point: both are based on an accounting decision, resulting in a dilemma for the financial manager: Have they been properly measured?*

Exercises

1/ **Starjö AB**

Production sold	340,500	Sales	340,500
Change in finished goods and in-progress inventory	19,175		
Purchases of raw materials and goods for resale	267,050		
Change in raw materials and goods for resale	3,050		
Personnel costs, including payroll taxes	90,000		
Other purchases and external charges, including lease payments	0		
EBITDA	5,675		
Depreciation and amortisation	5,000	Cost of goods sold	339,825
Operating income		675	
Net interest and other financial charges		600	
Exceptional gains		45,000	
Tax		15,776	
Net earnings		29,299	

Sale of premises: capital gain of €45,000 booked as an exceptional gain. Rental of premises: extra €12,000 in operating charges (recorded under "Other purchases and external charges", and disappearance of depreciation and amortisation the following year. Repayment of the loan: disappearance of €600 in interest expenses the following financial year. Over the course of the financial year, and after booking these transactions, the company became richer by €29,299 (after tax), the creditors by €600 and the company manager by €14,649.

2/ **Ellingham plc:** *see Chapter 5 (p. 69).*

3/ **Carvalho SA**

By-nature income statement:

	Net sales	$800 \times €100 = 80,000$	
+	Closing inventory of finished products	$100 \times (50 + 70) = +7,000$	+ Changes in
−	Opening inventory and work in progress	−0	inventories of finished goods and work in progress
=	Production for the year	87,000	
−	Purchases of raw materials and goods for resale	−46,000	
−	Opening inventory of raw materials and goods for resale	−4,000 +5,000	= Raw materials and goods for resale consumed
+	Closing inventory of raw materials and goods for resale		
=	Gross profit on raw materials and goods for resale used	42,000	
−	Personnel expenses	$900 \times €20 + €4,500 = -22,500$	
−	Services (other operating expenses)	−4,000	
−	Depreciation and amortisation	−3,000	
=	EBIT (operating profit)	12,500	

By-function income statement:

Sales (products)	800 units × 100 = €80,000
Cost of sales	2,000 + 800 units × 70 = €58,000
Selling and marketing costs	700 + 4,500 = €5,200
General and administrative costs	300 + 4,000 = €4,300

EBIT (operating profit)	€12,500

This corresponds exactly to the gross margin per unit of €30 multiplied by the 800 units sold less fixed costs of €4,500 (sales force), €4,000 (administration) and €3,000 (depreciation).

As by-nature and by-function formats differ only by presentation and not substance it is quite logical that the different formats do not lead to a difference in reported EBIT!

Achieving an EBIT of €12,500 out of a turnover of €80,000 is a very nice margin (15.6%). Most industrial groups do not achieve this kind of margin. This may be due to the fact that in most small companies, owners prefer to be paid a low wage and receive higher dividends which are generally taxed at a lower rate than ordinary salaries.

For the basics of income statements:

F. Plewa, G. Friedlob, *Understanding Income Statements*, John Wiley & Sons, 1995.

For a thorough explanation of the structure of the income statement:

C.R. Baker, Y. Ding, H. Stolowy, The statement of intermediate balance: A tool for international financial statement analysis based on income statement 'by nature', an application to the airline industry, *Advances in International Accounting*, **18**, 2005.
H. Stolowy, M. Lebas, *Corporate Financial Reporting: A Global Perspective*, Thomson, 2002.

BIBLIOGRAPHY

Chapter 4
CAPITAL EMPLOYED AND INVESTED CAPITAL

The end-of-period snapshot

So far in our analysis we have looked at inflows and outflows, or revenues and costs during a given period. We will now temporarily set aside this dynamic approach and place ourselves at the end of the period (rather than considering changes over a given period) and analyse the balances outstanding.

For instance, in addition to changes in net debt over a period we also need to analyse net debt at a given point in time. Likewise, we will study here the wealth that has been accumulated up to a given point in time, rather than that generated over a period.

The balance represents a snapshot of the cumulative inflows and outflows previously generated by the business

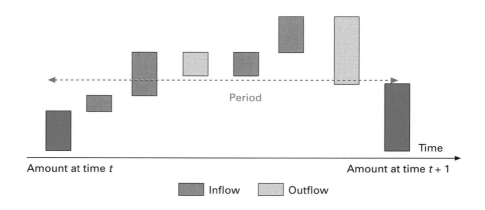

To summarise, we can make the following connections:

- an inflow or outflow represents a change in "stock"; i.e., in the balance outstanding;
- a "stock" is the arithmetic sum of inflows and outflows since a given date (when the business started up) through to a given point in time. For instance, at any moment shareholders' equity is equal to the sum of capital increases by shareholders and annual net income for past years not distributed in the form of dividends plus the original share capital.

THE BALANCE SHEET: DEFINITIONS AND CONCEPTS

The purpose of a balance sheet is to list all the assets of a business and all of its financial resources at a given point in time.

1/MAIN ITEMS ON A BALANCE SHEET

Assets on the balance sheet comprise:

- **fixed assets**; i.e., everything required for the operating cycle that is not destroyed as part of it. These items retain some value (any loss in their value is accounted for through depreciation, amortisation and impairment losses). A distinction is drawn between **tangible fixed assets** (land, buildings, machinery, etc.[1]), **intangible fixed assets** (brands, patents, goodwill, etc.) and **investments**. When a business holds shares in another company (in the long term), they are accounted for under investments;

- inventories and trade receivables; i.e., temporary assets created as part of the operating cycle;

- lastly, marketable securities and cash that belong to the company and are thus assets.

1 Known as property, plant and equipment in the US.

Inventories, receivables,[2] marketable securities and cash represent the **current assets**, a term reflecting the fact that these assets tend to "turn over" during the operating cycle.

Resources on the balance sheet comprise:

2 Known as debtors in the UK.

- capital provided by shareholders, plus retained earnings, known as **shareholders' equity**;

- borrowings of any kind that the business may have arranged – e.g., bank loans, supplier credits, etc. – known as **liabilities**.

By definition, a company's assets and resources must be exactly equal. This is the fundamental principle of double-entry accounting. When an item is purchased, it is either capitalised or expensed. If it is capitalised, it will appear on the asset side of the balance sheet, and, if expensed, it will lead to a reduction in earnings and thus shareholders' equity. The double-entry for this purchase is either a reduction in cash (i.e., a decrease in an asset) or a commitment (i.e., a liability) to the vendor (i.e., an increase in a liability). According to the algebra of accounting, assets and resources (equity and liabilities) always carry the opposite sign, so the equilibrium of the balance sheet is always maintained.

It is European practice to classify assets starting with fixed assets and to end with cash,[3] whereas it is North American and Japanese practice to start with cash. The same is true for the equity and liabilities side of the balance sheet: Europeans start with equity, whereas North Americans and the Japanese end with it.

3 Which is required by the European Fourth Directive.

A "horizontal" format is common in Continental Europe with assets on the left and resources on the right. In the United Kingdom, the more common format is a "vertical" one, starting from fixed assets plus current assets and deducting liabilities to end up with equity.

THE BALANCE SHEET

FIXED ASSETS	SHAREHOLDERS' EQUITY
CURRENT ASSETS	LIABILITIES

2/TWO WAYS OF ANALYSING THE BALANCE SHEET

A balance sheet can be analysed either from a capital-employed perspective or from a solvency-and-liquidity perspective.

In the capital-employed analysis, the balance sheet shows all the uses of funds for the company's operating cycle and analyses the origin of its sources of funds.

A capital-employed analysis of the balance sheet serves three main purposes:

- to understand how a company finances its operating assets (see Chapter 12);
- to compute the rate of return either on capital employed or on equity (see Chapter 13); and
- as a first step to valuing the equity of a company as a going concern (see Chapter 40).

In a solvency-and-liquidity analysis, a business is regarded as a set of assets and liabilities, the difference between them representing the book value of the equity provided by shareholders. From this perspective, the balance sheet lists everything that a company owns and everything that it owes.

A solvency-and-liquidity analysis of the balance sheet serves three purposes:

- to measure the solvency of a company (see Chapter 14);
- to measure the liquidity of a company (see Chapter 12); and
- as a first step to valuing its equity in a bankruptcy scenario.

CAPITAL-EMPLOYED ANALYSIS OF THE BALANCE SHEET	
All USES OF FUNDS	Origin of SOURCES OF FUNDS

SOLVENCY-AND-LIQUIDITY ANALYSIS OF THE BALANCE SHEET	
List of all ASSETS	SHAREHOLDERS' EQUITY
	List of all LIABILITIES

Section 4.2
THE CAPITAL-EMPLOYED ANALYSIS OF THE BALANCE SHEET

To gain a firm understanding of the capital-employed analysis of the balance sheet, we believe it is best approached in the same way as the analysis in the previous chapter, except that here we will be considering "stocks" rather than inflows and outflows.

The purpose of a capital-employed analysis of the balance sheet is to analyse the capital employed in the operating cycle and how this capital is financed.

More specifically, in a capital-employed analysis a balance sheet is divided into the following main headings:

1/FIXED ASSETS

These represent all the investments carried out by the business, based on our financial and accounting definition.

It is helpful to distinguish wherever possible between operating and non-operating assets that have nothing to do with the company's business activities; e.g., land, buildings and subsidiaries active in significantly different or noncore businesses. Nonoperating assets can thus be excluded from the company's capital employed. By isolating nonoperating assets, we can assess the resources the company may be able to call upon in hard times (i.e., through the disposal of nonoperating assets).

The difference between operating and nonoperating assets can be subtle in certain circumstances. For instance, how should a company's head office on Bond Street or on the Champs-Elysées be classified? Probably under operating assets for a fashion house or a car manufacturer, but under nonoperating assets for an engineering or construction group which has no business reason to be on Bond Street, unlike Burberry or Jaguar.

2/ WORKING CAPITAL

Uses of funds comprise all the operating costs incurred but not yet used or sold (i.e., inventories) and all sales that have not yet been paid for (trade receivables).

Sources of funds comprise all charges incurred but not yet paid for (trade payables, social security and tax payables), as well as operating revenues from products that have not yet been delivered (advance payments on orders).

The net balance of operating uses and sources of funds is called the **working capital**.

If uses of funds exceed sources of funds, the balance is positive and working capital needs to be financed. This is the most frequent case. If negative, it represents a source of funds generated by the operating cycle. This is a nice but rare situation!

It is described as "working capital" because the figure reflects the cash required to cover financing shortfalls arising from day-to-day operations.

Sometimes working capital is defined as current assets less current liabilities. This definition corresponds to our working capital definition + marketable securities and net cash − short-term borrowings. We think that this is an improper definition of working capital as it mixes items from the operating cycle (inventories, receivables, payables) and items from the financing cycle (marketable securities, net cash and short-term bank and financial borrowings). You may also find in some documents expressions such as "working capital needs" or "requirements in working capital". They are synonyms for working capital.

Working capital can be divided between operating working capital and nonoperating working capital.

3/ OPERATING WORKING CAPITAL

Operating working capital comprises the following accounting entries:

	Inventories	Raw materials, goods for resale, products and work in progress, finished products
+	**Trade receivables**	Amounts owed by customers, prepayments to suppliers and other trade receivables
−	**Trade payables**	Amounts owed to trade suppliers, social security and tax payables, prepayments by customers and other trade payables
=	**Operating working capital**	

Only the normal amount of operating sources of funds is included in calculations of operating working capital. Unusually long payment periods granted by suppliers should not be included as a component of normal operating working capital.

Where it is permanent, the abnormal portion should be treated as a source of cash, with the suppliers thus being considered as playing the role of the company's banker.

Inventories of raw materials and goods for resale should be included only at their normal amount. Under no circumstances should an unusually large figure for inventories of raw materials and goods for resale be included in the calculation of operating working capital.

Where appropriate, the excess portion of inventories or the amount considered as inventory held for speculative purposes can be treated as a high-risk short-term investment.

Working capital is totally independent of the methods used to value fixed assets, depreciation, amortisation and impairment losses on fixed assets. However, it is influenced by:

- inventory valuation methods;
- deferred income and cost (over one or more years);
- the company's provisioning policy for current assets and operating liabilities and costs.

As we will see in Chapter 5, working capital represents a key principle of financial analysis.

The amount of working capital depends on the accounting methods used to determine earnings, as well as the operating cycle.

Theoretically, working capital is independent of the accounting methods used by a company since working capital is nothing but the difference at a given moment between operating inflows and outflows. Nevertheless, working capital is dependent on the accounting methods used to value inventories and trade receivables when it is calculated from these balance sheet items.

4/NONOPERATING WORKING CAPITAL

Although we have considered in sufficient detail the timing differences between inflows and outflows that arise during the operating cycle, we have until now always assumed that capital expenditures were paid for when purchased and that nonrecurring costs are paid for when they are recognised in the income statement. Naturally, there may be timing differences here, too, giving rise to what is known as **nonoperating working capital**.

Nonoperating working capital, which is not a very robust concept from a theoretical perspective, is hard to predict and to analyse, because it depends on individual transactions, unlike operating working capital which is recurring.

In practice, nonoperating working capital is a catch-all category for items that cannot be classified anywhere else. It includes amounts due on fixed assets, dividends to be paid, extraordinary items, etc.

5/CAPITAL EMPLOYED

Capital employed is the sum of a company's fixed assets and its working capital (i.e., operating and nonoperating working capital). It is, therefore, equal to the sum of the net amounts devoted by a business to both the operating and investing cycles. It is also known as **operating assets**.

Capital employed is financed by two main types of funds, shareholders' equity and net debt, sometimes grouped together under the heading of **invested capital**.

6/SHAREHOLDERS' EQUITY

Shareholders' equity comprises capital provided by shareholders when the company is initially formed and at subsequent capital increases, as well as capital left at the company's disposal in the form of earnings transferred to the reserves.

7/NET DEBT

The company's gross debt comprises **debt financing**, irrespective of its maturity; i.e., medium- and long-term (various borrowings due in more than 1 year that have not yet been repaid) and short-term bank or financial borrowings (portion of long-term borrowings due in less than 1 year, discounted notes, bank overdrafts, etc.). A company's **net debt** goes further by taking into account cash and equivalents (e.g., petty cash and bank accounts) and marketable securities.

All things considered, the equation is as follows:

	Medium- and long-term bank and other borrowings (bond issues, commitment under finance lease, etc.)
+	Short-term bank or financial borrowings (discounted notes, bank overdrafts, etc.)
−	Marketable securities (marketable securities)
−	Cash and equivalents (petty cash and bank accounts)
=	Net debt

A company's net debt can either be positive or negative. If it is negative, the company is said to have net cash.

The balance of provisions for liabilities and charges not treated as equity or net debt (see p. 111) is included in the calculation of the working capital.

From a capital-employed standpoint, a company balance sheet can be analysed as follows:

		2005	2006	2007
	Fixed assets (**A**)			
	Inventories			
+	Accounts receivables			
−	Accounts payables			
=	Operating working capital			
+	Nonoperating working capital			
=	Working capital (**B**)			
Capital employed (A + B)				
	Shareholders' equity (**C**)			
	Short-, medium- and long-term bank and other borrowings			
−	Marketable securities			
−	Cash and equivalents			
=	Net debt (**D**)			
Invested capital (C + D) = Capital employed (A + B)				

A SOLVENCY-AND-LIQUIDITY ANALYSIS OF THE BALANCE SHEET

The solvency-and-liquidity analysis of the balance sheet, which presents a statement of what is owned and what is owed by the company at the end of the year, can be used:

- by shareholders to list everything that the company owns and owes, bearing in mind that these amounts may need to be revalued;
- by creditors looking to assess the risk associated with loans granted to the company. In a capitalist system, shareholders' equity is the ultimate guarantee in the event of liquidation since the claims of creditors are met before those of shareholders.

Hence the importance attached to a solvency-and-liquidity analysis of the balance sheet in traditional financial analysis. As we will see in detail in Chapters 12 and 14, it may be analysed from either a liquidity or solvency perspective.

1/BALANCE SHEET LIQUIDITY

A classification of the balance sheet items needs to be carried out prior to the liquidity analysis. Liabilities are classified in the order in which they fall due for repayment. Since balance sheets are published annually, a distinction between the short term and long term turns on whether a liability is due in less than or more than 1 year. Accordingly, liabilities are classified into those due in the short term (less than 1 year), in the medium and long term (i.e., in more than 1 year) and those that are not due for repayment.

Likewise, what the company owns can also be classified by duration as follows:

- assets that will have disappeared from the balance sheet by the following year, which comprise current assets in the vast majority of cases;
- assets that will still appear on the balance sheet the following year, which comprise fixed assets in the vast majority of cases.

Consequently, from a liquidity perspective we classify liabilities by their due date, investments by their maturity date and assets as follows:

Assets are regarded as liquid where, as part of the normal operating cycle, they will be monetised in the same year.

Thus, they comprise (unless the operating cycle is unusually long) inventories and trade receivables.

Assets that, regardless of their nature (head office, plant, etc.), are not intended for sale during the normal course of business are regarded as fixed and not liquid.

Balance sheet liquidity, therefore, derives from the fact that the turnover of assets (i.e., the speed at which they are monetised within the operating cycle) is faster than the turnover of liabilities (i.e., when they fall due). The maturity schedule of liabilities is known in advance because it is defined contractually. However, the liquidity of current assets is unpredictable (risk of sales flops or inventory write-downs, etc.). **Consequently, the clearly defined maturity structure of company's liabilities contrasts with the unpredictable liquidity of its assets.**

Therefore, short-term creditors will take into account differences between a company's asset liquidity and its liability structure. They will require the company to maintain current assets at a level exceeding that of short-term liabilities to provide a margin of safety. Hence the sacrosanct rule in finance that each and every company must have assets due to be monetised in less than 1 year at least equal to its liabilities falling due within 1 year.

2/SOLVENCY

Solvency reflects the ability of a company to honour its commitments in the event of liquidation; i.e., if its operations are wound up and are put up for sale.

A company may be regarded as insolvent once its shareholders' equity turns negative. This means that it owes more than it owns.

3/NET ASSET VALUE OR THE BOOK VALUE OF SHAREHOLDERS' EQUITY

This is a solvency-oriented concept that attempts to compute the funds invested by shareholders by valuing the company's various assets under deduction of liabilities. Net asset value is an accounting and, in some instances, tax-related term, rather than a financial one.

The book value of shareholders' equity is equal to everything a company owns less everything it already owes or may owe. Financiers often talk about net asset value, which leads to confusion among nonspecialists, who can understand them as total assets net of depreciation, amortisation and impairment losses.

Book value of equity is thus equal to the sum of:

> **Fixed assets**
> + **Current assets**
> − **All borrowings of any kind.**

When a company is sold, the buyer will be keen to adopt an even stricter approach:

- by factoring in contingent liabilities (which do not appear on the balance sheet);
- by excluding worthless assets; i.e., of zero value. This very often applies to most intangible assets owing to the complexity of the way in which they are accounted for (see Chapter 7).

Section 4.4
A detailed example of a capital-employed balance sheet

On the following page, our reader will find the capital-employed balance sheet of the Swedish group Ericsson. This balance sheet will be used in future chapters.

Items specific to consolidated accounts are highlighted in blue and will be described in detail in Chapter 6.

download

Summary

download

The balance sheet shows a snapshot of cumulative inflows and outflows from the company classified into assets and resources (liabilities and shareholders' equity).

Assets comprise fixed assets (intangible and tangible fixed assets and long-term investments) and current assets (inventories, accounts receivable, marketable securities and cash and equivalents). Resources comprise shareholders' equity and bank and financial borrowings, plus trade payables.

A capital-employed analysis of the balance sheet shows all the uses of funds by a company as part of the operating cycle and analyses the origin of the sources of a company's funds at a given point in time.

On the asset side, the capital-employed balance sheet has the following main headings:

- fixed assets; i.e., investments made by the company;

- operating working capital (inventories and trade receivables under deduction of trade payables). The size of the operating working capital depends on the operating cycle and the accounting methods used to determine earnings;

- nonoperating working capital, a catch-all category for the rest.

The sum of fixed assets and working capital is called capital employed.

Capital employed is financed by capital invested; i.e., shareholders' equity and net debt.

Net debt is defined as bank and financial borrowings, be they short, medium or long term, less marketable securities (short-term investments) and cash and equivalents.

A solvency-and-liquidity analysis lists everything the company owns and everything that it owes, the balance being the book value of shareholders' equity or net asset value. It can be analysed from either a solvency or liquidity perspective.

Solvency measures the company's ability to honour its commitments in the event of liquidation, whereas liquidity measures its ability to meet its commitments up to a certain date by monetising assets in the ordinary course of business.

BALANCE SHEET FOR ERICSSON (€m)

	Date	1999	2000	2001	2002	2003
	Goodwill	1,039	1,297	1,319	939	627
+	Other intangible fixed assets	112	104	108	437	597
+	Tangible fixed assets	2,666	2,404	1,688	1,088	580
+	Fixed assets held under finance lease	32	39	129	0	130
+	Equity in associated companies	296	305	342	200	324
+	Long-term investments	191	271	339	245	47
=	**FIXED ASSETS (FA)**	**4,336**	**4,420**	**3,924**	**2,909**	**2,305**
	Inventories of goods for resale					
+	Inventories of raw materials and other suppliers	1,455	2,173	1,003	475	473
+	Work in progress	1,662	2,347	1,624	1,156	1,039
+	Finished goods inventories	215	491	625	326	30
+	Trade receivables	5,713	7,223	5,191	3,205	2,776
+	Other operating receivables	3,036	4,093	3,040	2,544	1,388
−	Trade payables	2,360	3,292	2,130	1,361	971
−	Tax and social security liabilities	262	555	203	68	212
−	Other operating payables	4,509	5,279	4,978	3,661	3,287
=	**OPERATING WORKING CAPITAL (1)**	**4,950**	**7,201**	**4,172**	**2,616**	**1,236**
	Nonoperating receivables	1,460	1,232	2,374	1,757	584
−	Nonoperating payables	1,412	1,665	2,273	2,167	3,013
=	**NONOPERATING WORKING CAPITAL (2)**	**48**	**−433**	**101**	**−409**	**−2,429**
=	**WORKING CAPITAL (1 + 2)**	**4,999**	**6,768**	**4,273**	**2,207**	**1,193**
	CAPITAL EMPLOYED = FIXED ASSET + WORKING CAPITAL	**9,336**	**11,188**	**8,197**	**5,116**	**1,113**
	Share capital	534	864	881	1,744	1,761
+	Retained earnings	2,133	3,292	5,698	4,006	1,626
+	Net income for the year	1,281	2,184	−3,815	−2,949	−1,526
+	Revaluation and consolidation reserves					
+	Others	3,365	3,292	2,660	2,556	1,831
+	Investment grants					
+	Other equity (shareholders' advances, mandatory convertible bonds, etc.)					
=	**SHAREHOLDERS' EQUITY, GROUP SHARE**	**7,313**	**9,632**	**5,423**	**5,357**	**3,691**
+	Minority interests in consolidated subsidiaries	238	302	399	270	251
=	**TOTAL GROUP EQUITY**	**7,551**	**9,934**	**5,822**	**5,627**	**3,942**
	Medium- and long-term borrowings and liabilities	3,641	3,451	7,095	5,247	4,124
+	Commitments under finance leases					
+	Bank overdrafts and short-term borrowings	1,311	1,690	2,805	1,471	1,038
−	Marketable securities (short-term investments)	1,465	2,050	3,935	5,268	6,181
−	Cash and equivalents	1,702	1,837	3,589	1,961	1,811
=	**NET DEBT**	**1,785**	**1,254**	**2,375**	**−510**	**−2,830**
=	**INVESTED CAPITAL = (GROUP EQUITY + NET DEBT) CAPITAL EMPLOYED**	**9,336**	**11,188**	**8,197**	**5,116**	**1,113**

1/ When do we use a capital-employed analysis of the balance sheet? And when do we use a solvency-and-liquidity analysis of the balance sheet?

2/ Which approach to the balance sheet should you adopt:

  ○   when warranting a company's balance sheet when it is being sold?
  ○   when forecasting a company's working capital?

3/ Do liabilities that arise during the operating cycle always have a maturity of less than 1 year?

4/ Classify the following as "stocks", in/outflows or change in in/outflows: sales, trade receivables, change in trade receivables, increase in dividends, financial expense, increase in sales, EBITDA.

5/ A company's sales clearly represent a source of funds. However, they do not appear on the balance sheet. Why?

6/ Classify the following balance sheet items under fixed assets, working capital, shareholders' equity or net debt: overdraft, retained earnings, brands, taxes payable, finished goods inventories, bonds.

7/ Is a company that is currently unable to pay its debts always insolvent?

8/ Assess the liquidity of the following assets: plant, unlisted securities, listed securities, head office building located in the centre of a large city, ships and aircraft, commercial papers, raw materials inventories, work-in-progress inventories.

9/ Provide examples of items classified under nonoperating working capital.

10/ Give a synonym for net assets.

11/ What is another way of describing a difference in "stocks"?

12/ What is the difference between liabilities and sources of funds?

13/ What is another way of describing a cumulative inflow or outflow?

14/ The main manufacturers of telephony equipment (Ericsson, Nokia, etc.) provided telecom operators (Deutsche Telekom, Swisscom, etc.) with substantial supplier credit lines, in order to assist them in financing the construction of their UMTS networks. State your views.

Ellingham plc exercise

Draw up the balance sheet showing capital-employed and invested capital (1 January 2005, end 2005, 2006) assuming that the company has equity of €40m.

QUESTIONS

quiz

ANSWERS

Questions

1/ *Capital-employed analysis of the balance sheet: for understanding the company's use of funds and how they were financed. Solvency-and-liability analysis of the balance sheet: for listing all assets and liabilities.*

2/ *The solvency-and-liquidity analysis, the capital-employed analysis.*

3/ *No, in some industries, there is a long period between the invoice date and customer payment (e.g., movie rights).*

4/ *Inflow, ''stocks'', inflow, change in outflow, outflow, change in inflow, inflow.*

5/ *The balance resulting from the activity is what appears on the balance sheet – i.e., the profit or loss – not the activity itself measured by sales.*

6/ *In order of listing: net debt, shareholders' equity, fixed assets, working capital, working capital, net debt.*

7/ *In theory no, as the company may be facing a temporary credit crunch, but most of the time yes because it will have to dispose of assets quickly or stop its activities which will result in a big reduction in equity, and then in its solvency.*

8/ *In order of decreasing liquidity: listed securities, commercial paper, raw materials inventories, head office, unlisted securities, ships and aircraft, work-in-progress inventories, plant.*

9/ *Credit from machine supplier, insurance payout not yet received for burnt-out factory, payment from purchaser of a subsidiary.*

10/ *Shareholders' equity.*

11/ *An inflow or outflow.*

12/ *Sources of funds include shareholders' equity (which does not have to be repaid and is consequently not a liability) and liabilities (which sooner or later have to be repaid).*

13/ *A ''stock''.*

14/ *These are in fact merely financial loans, and not operating loans, granted to enable the telecoms operator to buy the equipment made by the manufacturer. Those loans should be treated as fixed assets on the manufacturer's balance sheet and as financial debts on the telecom operator's balance sheet.*

Ellingham plc case – see Chapter 5

BIBLIOGRAPHY

For a thorough explanation of the balance sheet:

G. Friedlob, F. Plewa, *Understanding Balance Sheets*, John Wiley and Sons, 1996.

For more advanced topics on balance sheets:

H. Stolowy, M. Lebas, *Corporate Financial Reporting: A Global Perspective*, Thomson, 2002.

Chapter 5
WALKING THROUGH FROM EARNINGS TO CASH FLOW

Or how to move mountains together!

Chapter 2 showed the structure of the cash flow statement, which brings together all the receipts and payments recorded during a given period and determines the change in net debt position.

Chapter 3 covered the structure of the income statement, which summarises all the revenues and charges during a period.

It may appear that these two radically different approaches have nothing in common. But common sense tells us that a rich woman will sooner or later have cash in her pocket, while a poor woman is likely to be strapped for cash – unless she should make her fortune along the way.

Although the complex workings of a business lead to differences between profits and cash, they converge at some point or another.

The aim of this chapter is to reconcile the cash flow and earnings approaches.

First of all, we will examine revenues and charges from a cash flow standpoint. Based on this analysis, we will establish a link between changes in wealth and the change in net debt that bridges the two approaches.

We recommend that readers get to grips with this chapter because understanding the transition from earnings to the change in net debt represents a key step in comprehending the financial workings of a business.

Section 5.1
ANALYSIS OF EARNINGS FROM A CASH FLOW PERSPECTIVE

This section is included merely for explanatory and conceptual purposes. Even so, it is vital for an understanding of the basic financial workings of a company.

1/OPERATING REVENUES

Operating receipts should correspond to sales for the same period, but they differ because customers may be granted a payment period or payments of invoices from the previous period may be received during the current period. As a result, operating receipts are equal to sales only if sales are immediately paid in cash. Otherwise, they generate a change in trade receivables.

$$
\text{Sales for the period} \quad
\begin{array}{c}
- \quad \text{Increase in trade receivables} \\
\text{or} \\
+ \quad \text{Reduction in trade receivables}
\end{array}
\quad = \quad \text{Operating receipts}
$$

2/CHANGES IN INVENTORIES OF FINISHED GOODS AND WORK IN PROGRESS

As we have already seen in by-nature income statements, the difference between production and sales is adjusted for through changes in inventories of finished goods and work in progress.[1] But this is merely an accounting entry to deduct from operating costs costs that do not correspond to products sold. It has no impact from a cash standpoint.[2] As a result, changes in inventories need to be reversed in a cash flow analysis.

3/OPERATING COSTS

Operating costs differ from operating payments in the same way that operating revenues differ from operating receipts. Operating payments are the same as operating costs for a given period only when adjusted for:

- timing differences arising from the company's payment terms (credit granted by its suppliers, etc.);
- the fact that some purchases are not used during the same period. The difference between purchases made and purchases used is adjusted for through change in inventories of raw materials.

These timing differences give rise to:

- changes in trade payables in the first case;
- discrepancy between raw materials used and purchases made, which is equal to change in inventories of raw materials and goods for resale.

1 This adjustment is not necessary in by-function income statements as explained in Chapter 3.

2 In accounting parlance, this is known as a "closing entry".

$$
\begin{array}{l}
\text{Operating payments} \\
= \\
\text{operating costs except} \\
\text{depreciation, amortisation} \\
\text{and impairment losses}
\end{array}
\left\{
\begin{array}{l}
+ \text{ reduction in supplier credit} \\
\quad\quad\quad\quad \text{or} \\
- \text{ increase in supplier credit} \\
\\
\\
+ \text{ increase in inventories of raw materials and good for resale} \\
\quad\quad\quad\quad \text{or} \\
- \text{ Reduction in inventories of raw materials and good for resale}
\end{array}
\right.
$$

The only differences between operating revenues and receipts and between operating charges and payments are timing differences deriving from deferred payments (payment terms) and deferred charges (changes in inventories).

The total amount of the timing differences between operating revenues and charges and between operating receipts and payments can thus be summarised as follows for by-nature and by-function income statements:

BY-NATURE INCOME STATEMENT	DIFFERENCE	CASH FLOW STATEMENT
Net sales	− Change in trade receivables (deferred payment)	= **Operating receipts**
+ **Changes in inventories of finished goods and work in progress**	− Changes in inventories of finished goods and work in progress (deferred charges)	
− **Operating costs except depreciation, amortisation and impairment losses**	+ Change in trade payables (deferred payments) − Change in inventories of raw materials and goods for resale (deferred charges)	= − **Operating payments**
= **EBITDA**	− Change in operating working capital	= **Operating cash flows**

BY-FUNCTION INCOME STATEMENT	DIFFERENCE	CASH FLOW STATEMENT
Net sales	− Change in trade receivables (deferred payment)	= **Operating receipts**
− **Operating costs except depreciation, amortisation and impairment losses**	+ Change in trade payables (deferred payments) − Change in inventories of finished goods, work in progress, raw materials and goods for resale (deferred changes)	= − **Operating payments**
= **EBITDA**	− Change in operating working capital	= **Operating cash flows**

Astute readers will have noticed that the items in the central column of the above table are the components of the change in operating working capital between two periods, as defined in Chapter 4.

Over a given period, the change in operating working capital represents a need for or a source of financing that must be added to or subtracted from the other financing requirements or resources.

The change in operating working capital accounts for the difference between EBITDA and operating cash flow.

If positive, it represents a financing requirement, and we refer to an increase in operating working capital. If negative, it represents a source of funds, and we refer to a reduction in operating working capital.

The change in working capital merely represents a straightforward timing difference between the balance of operating cash flows (operating cash flow) and the wealth created by the operating cycle (EBITDA). As we will see, it is important to remember that timing differences may not necessarily be small, of limited importance, short or negligible in any way.

An analysis of changes in working capital is one of the key pillars of financial analysis.

4 / CAPITAL EXPENDITURE

3 *Or investments in fixed assets.*

Capital expenditures[3] lead to a change in what the company owns without any immediate increase or decrease in its wealth. Consequently, they are not shown directly on the income statement. Conversely, capital expenditures have a direct impact on the cash flow statement.

From a capital expenditure perspective, there is a fundamental gulf separating the income statement and the cash flow statement. The income statement spreads the capital expenditure charge over the entire life of the asset (through depreciation), while the cash flow statement records it only in the period in which it is purchased.

A company's capital expenditure process leads to both cash outflows that do not diminish its wealth at all and the accounting recognition of impairment in the purchased assets through depreciation and amortisation that do not reflect any cash outflows.

Accordingly, there is no direct link between cash flow and net income for the capital expenditure process, as we knew already.

5 / FINANCING

4 *Except in the UK where companies deduct dividends from net income and end the income statement with "retained profit".*

Financing is by its very nature a cycle that is specific to inflows and outflows. Sources of financing (new borrowings, capital increases, etc.) do not appear on the income statement, which shows only the remuneration paid on some of these resources; i.e., interest on borrowings but not dividend on equity.[4]

Outflows representing a return on sources of financing may be analysed as either charges (i.e., interest) or a distribution of wealth created by the company among its equity capital providers (i.e., dividends).

The distinction between capital and interest payments is not of paramount importance in the cash flow statement, but is essential in the income statement.

Assuming, to keep things simple, that there are no timing differences between the recognition of a cost and the corresponding cash outflow, a distinction needs to be drawn between:

- interest payments on debt financing (financial expense) and income tax, which affect the company's cash position and its earnings;
- the remuneration paid to equity capital providers (dividends), which affects the company's cash position and earnings transferred to reserves;
- new borrowings and repayment of borrowings, capital increases and share buybacks,[5] which affect its cash position, but have no impact on earnings.

Lastly, corporate income tax represents a charge that appears on the income statement and a cash payment to the State, which, though it may not provide any financing to the company, provides it with a range of free services and entitlements – e.g., police, education, roads, etc.

We can now finish off our table and walk through from earnings to decrease in net debt:

5 *When a company buys back some of its shares from some of its shareholders. For more see Chapter 38.*

@
download

FROM THE INCOME STATEMENT ... TO THE CASH FLOW STATEMENT

INCOME STATEMENT	DIFFERENCE	CASH FLOW STATEMENT
EBITDA	− Change in operating working capital =	**Operating cash flow**
− Depreciation, amortisation and impairment losses on fixed assets	− Capital expenditure = + Disposals = + Depreciation, amortisation and impairment losses on fixed assets (noncash charges) =	− Capital expenditure + Disposals
= **EBIT (operating profit)** − Financial expense net of financial income − Corporate income tax		= **Free cash flow before tax** = − Financial expense net of financial income = − Corporate income tax
	+ Proceeds from share issues = − Share buybacks − Dividends paid =	= − Proceeds from share issues − Share buybacks − Dividends paid
= **Net income (net earnings)**	+ Column total	= **Decrease in net debt**

Section 5.2

CASH FLOW STATEMENT

The same table enables us to move in the opposite direction and, thus, account for the decrease in net debt based on the income statement. To do so, we simply need to add back all the movements shown in the central column to net profit.

> **Net income**
> + Depreciation, amortisation and impairment losses on fixed assets
> − Change in operating working capital
> − Capital expenditure net of asset disposals
> + Disposals
> + Proceeds from share issue
> − Share buybacks
> − Dividends paid
> = Decrease in net debt

The following reasoning may help our attempt to classify the various line items that enable us to make the transition from net income to decrease in net debt.

Net income should normally turn up in "cash at hand". This said, we also need to add back certain noncash charges (depreciation, amortisation and impairment losses on fixed assets), which were deducted on the way down the income statement but have no cash impact, to arrive at what is known as **cash flow**.

Cash flow will appear in "cash at hand" only once the timing differences related to the operating cycle as measured by change in operating working capital have been taken into account.

Lastly, the investing and financing cycles give rise to uses and sources of funds that have no immediate impact on net income.

1/FROM NET INCOME TO CASH FLOW

As we have just seen, depreciation, amortisation, impairment losses on fixed assets and provisions for liabilities and charges are noncash charges that have no impact on a company's cash position. From a cash flow standpoint, they are no different to net income.

Consequently, they are added back to net income to show the total financing generated internally by the company.

These two items form the company's cash flow, which accountants allocate between net income, on the one hand, and depreciation, amortisation and impairment losses, on the other hand, according to the relevant accounting and tax legislation.

Cash flow can therefore be calculated by adding certain noncash charges net of writebacks to net income.

The simplicity of the cash flow statement shown in Chapter 2 was probably evident to our readers, but it would not fail to shock traditional accountants, who would find it hard to accept that financial expense should be placed on a par with repayments of borrowings. Raising debt to pay financial expense is not the same as replacing one debt with another. The former makes the company poorer, whereas the latter constitutes liability management.

As a result, traditionalists have managed to establish the concept of cash flow. We need to point out that we would advise computing cash flow before any capital gains (or losses) on asset disposals and before extraordinary items, which do not affect it.

Cash flow is not as pure a concept as EBITDA. This said, a direct link may be established between these two concepts by deriving cash flow from the income statement using the top-down method:

> EBITDA
> — Financial expense net of financial income
> — Corporate income tax
> = Cash flow

or the bottom-up method:

> Net income
> + Depreciation, amortisation and impairment losses
> +/− Capital losses/gains on asset disposal
> +/− Extraordinary losses/gains
> = Cash flow

Cash flow is influenced by the same accounting policies as EBITDA. Likewise, it is not affected by the accounting policies applied to tangible and intangible fixed assets.

Note that the calculation method differs slightly for consolidated accounts[6] since the contribution to consolidated net profit made by equity-accounted income is replaced by the dividend payment received. This is attributable to the fact that the parent company does not actually receive the earnings of an associate company,[5] since it does not control it but merely receives a dividend.

6 *For details on consolidated accounts see Chapter 6.*

Furthermore, cash flow is calculated at group level without taking into account minority interests. This seems logical since the parent company has control of and allocates the cash flows of its fully consolidated subsidiaries.[6] In the cash flow statement, minority interests[6] in the controlled subsidiaries are reflected only through the dividend payments that they receive.

Lastly, readers should beware of cash flow as there are nearly as many definitions of cash flow as there are companies in the world!

The upper definition is widely used but, frequently, free cash flows, cash flow from operating activities, operating cash flow are simply called "cash flow" by some professionals. So it is safest to check which cash flow they are talking about.

2/FROM CASH FLOW TO CASH FLOW FROM OPERATING ACTIVITIES

We introduced in Chapter 2 the concept of cash flow from operating activities, which is not the same as cash flow.

To go from cash flow to cash flow from operating activities, we need to adjust for the timing differences in cash flows linked to the operating cycle.

This gives us the following equation:

Cash flow from operating activities = Cash flow − Change in operating working capital.

Note that the term "operating activities" is used here in a fairly broad sense, since it includes financial expense and corporate income tax.

3/OTHER MOVEMENTS IN CASH

We have now isolated the movements in cash deriving from the operating cycle, so we can proceed to allocate the other movements to the investment and financing cycles.

The investment cycle includes:

- capital expenditures (acquisitions of tangible and intangible assets);
- disposals of fixed assets; i.e., the price at which fixed assets are sold and not any capital gains or losses (which do not represent cash flows);
- changes in long-term investments (i.e., financial assets).

Where appropriate, we may also factor in the impact of timing differences in cash flows generated by this cycle, notably nonoperating working capital.

The financing cycle includes:

- capital increases in cash, the payment of dividends (i.e., payment out of the previous year's net profit) and share buybacks;
- change in net debt resulting from the repayment of (short-, medium- and long-term) borrowings, new borrowings, changes in marketable securities (short-term investments) and changes in cash and equivalents.

This brings us back to the cash flow statement in Chapter 2, but using the indirect method, which starts with net income and classifies cash flows by cycle (i.e., operating, investing or financing activities; see p. 65).

Items specific to consolidated accounts are highlighted in blue and will be described in detail in Chapter 6.

This format calls for the following comments:

(a) Even though the order used in cash flow statements indicates the pre-eminence of operating activities, it is important to recognise that operating activities are to some extent a catch-all category containing all the items not allocated to investing or financing activities. Indeed, the scope of operating activities is in most cases different to the operating cycle in the strict sense of the term, as described in Chapter 2. Aside from the items falling within a narrower definition of the operating cycle, operating activities include financial expense and income tax which, logic dictates, should appear under financing activities or be split among the three cycles.

Readers may legitimately ask whether the best indicator of the company's operating performance is:

- operating cash flow less theoretical tax on operating profit; or
- cash flow less the change in working capital, which is cash flow from operating activities.

First of all, we note that the difference between these two indicators is attributable primarily to financial expense after tax, which is generally modest in a low-interest-rate environment.

In our view, operating cash flow less theoretical tax on operating profit is the more useful because it is a key factor influencing both investment decisions (Chapter 18) and valuations (Chapter 40). However, most if not all cash flow

CASH FLOW STATEMENT FOR ERICSSON (€m)

		1999	2000	2001	2002	2003
	OPERATING ACTIVITES					
	Net income	1,281	2,184	−3,815	−2,949	1,526
+	Minority interest in net income	44	68	101	37	22
+	Depreciation, amortisation and impairment losses on fixed assets	806	1,203	855	714	916
−	Capital gains + capital losses on asset disposals	−153	−2,760	−669	79	−101
+	Other noncash items	−6	171	−296	−566	192
=	**Cash flow**	**1,972**	**867**	**−3,825**	**−2,685**	**−679**
−	Change in working capital	556	1,769	−2,495	−2,067	3,400
=	**CASH FLOW FROM OPERATING ACTIVITIES (A)**	**1,416**	**−902**	**−1,330**	**−618**	**2,720**
	INVESTING ACTIVITES					
	Capital expenditure	992	1,380	953	299	455
−	Disposal of fixed assets	68	700	1,109	325	165
+/−	Change in investments	803	−2,392	−521	−389	89
=	**CASH FLOW FROM INVESTING ACTIVITIES (B)**	**1,726**	**−1,712**	**−677**	**−415**	**379**
=	**FREE CASH FLOW AFTER FINANCIAL EXPENSE (A − B)**	**−310**	**810**	**−653**	**−204**	**2,341**
	FINANCING ACTIVITIES					
	Proceeds from share issues (C)	0	178	0	3,160	1
	Dividends paid (D)	438	456	469	70	22
	A − B + C − D = DECREASE/(INCREASE) IN NET DEBT	**−748**	**532**	**−1,122**	**2,886**	**2,319**

Decrease in net debt can be broken down as follows :

		1999	2000	2001	2002	2003
	Repayment of short-, medium- and long-term borrowings	−703	1,032	756	3,240	1,559
−	New short-, medium- and long-term borrowings	1,221	1,221	5,514	59	3
+	Change in marketable securities (short-term investments)	771	586	1,885	1,333	914
+	Change in cash and equivalents	406	135	1,752	−1,628	−150
=	**DECREASE IN NET DEBT**	**−748**	**532**	**−1,122**	**2,886**	**2,319**

statements define cash flow from operating activities as cash flow less the change in working capital.

Cash flow is a fairly mongrel concept because it is calculated before the return (dividends) paid on certain funds (i.e., shareholders' equity) but after that (financial expense) paid on other funds (i.e., debt).

(b) Investing activities are shown as a financing requirement (or a surplus in rare cases), which is calculated as the difference between capital expenditure and disposals.

(c) In practice, most companies publish a cash flow statement that starts with net income and moves down to changes in "cash and equivalents" or change in "cash", a poorly defined concept since certain companies include marketable securities while others deduct bank overdrafts and short-term borrowings.

Furthermore, net debt reflects the level of indebtedness of a company much better than cash and cash equivalents or than cash and cash equivalents less short-term borrowings, since the latter two are only a portion of the debt position of a company. On one hand, one can infer relevant comments from changes in the net debt position of a company. On the other hand, changes in cash and cash equivalents are rarely relevant as it is so easy to increase cash in the balance sheet at the closing date: simply get into long-term debt and put the proceeds in a bank account! Cash on the balance sheet has increased but net debt is still the same.

As we will see in Chapter 27 net debt is managed globally, and looking at only one side (cash and cash equivalents and marketable securities) is, therefore, of little interest.

SUMMARY

download

The first step in the process of moving from the income statement to a cash flow perspective is to recreate operating cash flows. The only differences between operating receipts and operating revenues and between operating costs and operating payments are timing differences related to payment terms (deferred payments) and changes in inventories (deferred charges).

The change in operating working capital accounts for the difference between operating cash flow and the generation of wealth within the operating cycle (EBITDA).

For capital expenditures, there is no direct link between cash flow and net income, since the former records capital expenditures as they are paid and the latter spreads the cost of capital expenditures over their whole useful life.

From a financing standpoint, the cash flow statement does not distinguish between capital and remuneration related to sources of financing, while the income statement shows only returns on debt financing (interest expenses) and corporate income tax.

Net income should normally appear in "cash at hand", along with certain noncash charges that together form cash flow. Cash flow may be translated into an inflow or outflow of cash only once adjusted for the change in operating working capital to arrive at cash flow from operating activities in a broad sense of the term.

Lastly, factoring in the investment cycle, which gives rise to outflows sometimes offset by fixed asset disposals, and the equity financing cycle, we arrive at the decrease in net debt.

1/ Do inventories valuation methods influence:

- ○ The company's net income?
- ○ The company's cash position?

2/ Same question for the following:

(a) depreciation and amortisation;
(b) corporate income tax;
(c) capital increase through cash contribution;
(d) cash purchase of fixed assets;
(e) recognition and payment of salaries;
(f) disposal for cash of an asset at its book value;
(g) sale of goods on credit;
(h) payment for these goods;
(i) repayment of medium-term loan;
(j) financial expenses.

3/ What differences are there between cash flow from operating activities and operating cash flow?

4/ What noncash charges must be factored back into calculations of cash flow?

5/ Is cash flow a measure of an increase in wealth? Or an increase in cash?

6/ Why is the difference between EBITDA and operating cash flows equal to a change in working capital?

7/ What difference is there between sales in a financial year and operating receipts over the same period?

8/ What is the difference between cash flow and cash flow from operating activities?

9/ Why is decrease in net debt more relevant than change in cash position or marketable securities?

10/ Make use of the cash flow statement to show how impairment losses on current assets have no impact on cash.

11/ Will a capital increase by way of incorporation of reserves appear on the cash flow statement?

12/ Pearson plc is in the process of revaluing all of its tangible assets. How will this impact on the cash flow statement?

Ellingham plc exercise

Draw up a cash flow statement for Ellingham for 2005 and 2006. If you so wish, create a cash–earnings link at each level. What is your interpretation of these figures?

QUESTIONS

quiz

Answers

Questions

1/ *Yes, the lower inventories are valued, the lower net income for the current year. No, except for corporate income tax.*

2/ *(a) Yes, as depreciation and amortisation are expenses; no, as depreciation and amortisation are noncash expenses. (b) Yes, yes, as corporate income tax is a cash expense. (c) No, yes, as a source of financing is neither a revenue nor an expense. (d) No, yes, as the cash purchase of a fixed asset is not an expense but a cash payment. (e) Yes, yes, as salaries paid are a cash expense. (f) No, yes, as no capital gain is registered. (g) Yes, no, as a revenue is registered but the cash receipt has still to be received (goods sold on credit). (h) No, yes, as the cash receipt is now received but the revenue has already been registered. (i) No, yes, as repayment of a loan does not modify the wealth of the company but its cash position. (j) Yes, yes, as financial expenses reduce the wealth of the company and its cash position.*

3/ *Unlike operating cash flow, cash flow from operating activities encompasses not only operations but also financial expense, tax and some exceptional items.*

4/ *Depreciation, amortisation and impairment losses on fixed assets and provisions for liabilities and charges.*

5/ *No, cash flow is not a measure of increase in wealth because it does not take into account depreciation, which reflects the wear and tear of fixed assets and, thus, a source of wealth destruction. No, because customers do not pay cash and suppliers are not paid in cash.*

6/ *The difference between EBITDA and operating cash flow is nothing but new invoices received or sent but not yet paid either by the company or its customers, or variation in inventories; i.e., increase in working capital.*

7/ *Change in trade receivables.*

8/ *Changes in working capital.*

9/ *Because it is easier to modify the cash position of a company at year end than the net debt position which reflects its true level of indebtedness.*

10/ *Impairment losses reduce earnings, but also bring down working capital: they cancel each other out at the level of the cash flow from operating activities.*

11/ *No, it will not impact on the company's cash flow as it is a pure accounting entry.*

12/ *It will have no impact as it is a noncash operation.*

Ellingham plc exercise

Cash forecast	Jan 2005	Feb 2005	Mar 2005	Apr 2005	May 2005	Jun 2005	Jul 2005	Aug 2005	Sep 2005	Oct 2005	Nov 2005	Dec 2005	2005	2006	2007
Operating inflows															
Sales					12	12	12	12	12	12	12	12	96	144	144
Operating outflows															
− Purchases				8	4	4	4	4	4	4	4	4	40	48	48
− Personnel costs	4	4	4	4	4	4	4	4	4	4	4	4	48	48	48
− Shipping		2	2	2	2	2	2	2	2	2	2	2	22	24	24
− Interest expense						1						0.9	1.9	1.5	1.1
− Capital expenditure	30												30		
+ New borrowings	20												20		
− Repayment of borrowings	2						2						4	4	4
Change in cash	−16	−6	−6	−14	2	1	0	2	2	2	2	1.1	−29.9	18.5	18.9
Cumulated balance	−16	−22	−28	−42	−40	−39	−39	−37	−35	−33	−31	−29.9			

(N.B.: No sales in January 2005 in order to build up initial stock of finished goods.)

Income statement (by nature)	2005	2006	2007
Sales	132	144	144
+ Change in finished goods and in—progress inventory[1]	10	0	0
= **Production for period**	**142**	**144**	**144**
− Raw materials used in the business[2]	48	48	48
− Payroll costs	48	48	48
− Shipping	24	24	24
= **EBITDA**	**22**	**24**	**24**
− Depreciation and amortisation	6	6	6
= **Operating income**	**16**	**18**	**18**
− Interest expense	1.9	1.5	1.1
= **Net earnings**	**14.1**	**16.5**	**16.9**

[1] Change in finished goods and in—progress inventory: €4m in raw materials + €4m in payroll costs + €2m in shipping costs = €10m.
[2] Breakdown of raw materials used in the business in year 1: €52m (purchases) −€4m (increase in raw materials inventories) = €48m.

Income statement (by function)	2005	2006	2007
Sales	**132**	**144**	**144**
− Cost of sales	116	126	126
= **Operating income**	**16**	**18**	**18**
− Interest expense	1.9	1.5	1.1
= **Net income**	**14.1**	**16.5**	**16.9**

Cash flow statement – Format 1	2005	2006	2007
EBITDA	22	24	24
− Change in working capital	36	0	0
= **Operating cash flows**	**−14**	**24**	**24**
− Capital expenditure	30	0	0
− Interest expense	1.9	1.5	1.1
= **Net decrease in debt**	**−45.9**	**22.5**	**22.9**
New borrowings	20	0	0
− Debt repayments	4	4	4
− Change in cash and equivalents	−29.9	18.5	18.9

Cash flow statement – Format 2	2005	2006	2007
Net income	14.1	16.5	16.9
+ Depreciation and amortisation	6	6	6
= **Cash flow**	**20.1**	**22.5**	**22.9**
− Change in working capital	36	0	0
= **Cash flow from operating activities**	**−15.9**	**22.5**	**22.9**
− Capital expenditure	30	0	0
= **Net decrease in debt**	**−45.9**	**22.5**	**22.9**
New borrowings	20	0	0
− Debt repayments	4	4	4
− Change in cash and equivalents	−29.9	18.5	18.9

Balance sheet	Date 0	End 2005	End 2006
Fixed assets, net (A)	0	24	18
Inventories	0	14	14
+ Trade receivables	0	36	36
− Trade payables and other debts	0	14	14
= **Working capital (B)**	0	36	36
= *Capital employed (A+B)*	0	60	54
Shareholders' equity (C)	40	54.1	70.6
Bank and financial debts	0	16	12
− Marketable securities	0	0	0
− Cash and equivalents	40	10.1	28.6
= **Net debt (D)**	−40	5.9	−16.6
= *Invested capital (C+D)*	0	60	54

The creation of their Spanish subsidiary is a clever move. This outfit is profitable the first year, capital expenditure and increase in working capital (30 + 36) are nearly entirely paid back at end-2007 after only 3 years of activity. It is almost too good to be true!

BIBLIOGRAPHY

For more on the topics covered in this chapter:

K. Checkley, *Strategic Cash Flow management*, Capstone Express, 2002.
J. Kinnunen, M. Koskela, Do cash flows reported by firms articulate with their income statements and balance sheets? Descriptive evidence from Finland, *European Accounting Review*, **8**, 631–654, 1999.
O. Whitfield Broome, Statement of cash flows: Time for change!, *Financial Analysts Journal*, 16–22, March–April 2004.

Chapter 6
GETTING TO GRIPS WITH CONSOLIDATED ACCOUNTS

A group-building exercise

The purpose of consolidated accounts is to present the financial situation of a group of companies as if they formed one single entity. This chapter deals with the basic aspects of consolidation that anyone interested in corporate finance should fully master.

An analysis of the accounting documents of each individual company belonging to a group does not serve as a very accurate or useful guide to the economic health of the whole group. The accounts of a company reflect the other companies that it controls only through the cost of its shareholdings (revalued or written down, where appropriate) and the size of the dividends that it receives.

Consolidation is intended to remedy these deficiencies.

The purpose of consolidated accounts is to present the financial situation of a group of companies as if they formed one single entity.

The goal of this chapter is to familiarise readers with the problems arising from consolidation. Consequently, we present an example-based guide to the main aspects of consolidation to facilitate analysis of consolidated accounts.

In some cases, consolidated accounts take some time to come out or do not even exist.[1] That said, for various reasons financial analysts may need to know, albeit only approximately, some of the key consolidated figures, such as earnings and shareholders' equity.

The aggregation of accounts may give analysts this overview provided that they roughly apply the various preconsolidation adjustments explained in this chapter.

Section 6.1
CONSOLIDATION METHODS

Any firm that controls other companies exclusively or that exercises significant influence over them should prepare consolidated accounts and a management report for the group.[2]

1 For example, it took 9 months for Dutch supermarket group Ahold to produce its 2002 consolidated accounts after it had discovered accounting frauds in its US subsidiary.

2 Unless the parent is itself a wholly owned subsidiary or is virtually wholly owned.

Consolidated accounts must be certified by the statutory auditors and made available, together with the group's management report, to shareholders, debt-holders and all interested parties.

3 *IAS/IFR rules are produced by the International Accounting Standards Board (IASB), a private organisation made up of most accountancy bodies in the world.*

Listed European companies will be required to use IAS/IFR[3] rules for their consolidated financial statements from 2005.[4] Accounts for 2005 will be published with 2004 accounts restated to fully comply with IAS/IFRS[5] rules to allow for meaningful comparisons.

The companies to be included in the preparation of consolidated accounts form what is known as the **scope of consolidation**. Scope of consolidation comprises:

4 *Except for groups already publishing their accounts following internationally recognised rules (applies to Austrian, Dutch and German groups using US rules). They will need to switch to IFRS rules from 2007 onwards.*

- the parent company;
- the companies in which the parent company holds directly or indirectly at least 20% of the voting rights.

However, a subsidiary should be excluded from consolidation when its parent loses the power to govern its financial and operating policies – for example, when the subsidiary becomes subject to the control of a government, a court or an administrator. Such subsidiaries should be accounted for at fair market value.

5 *IAS: International Accounting Standards; IFRS: International Financial Reporting Standards.*

The basic principle behind consolidation consists in replacing the historical cost of the parent's investment in the company being consolidated with its assets, liabilities and equity.

For instance, let us consider a company with a subsidiary that appears on its balance sheet with an amount of 20. Consolidation entails replacing the historical cost of 20 with all or some of the assets, liabilities and equity of the company being consolidated.

There are three methods of consolidation that are used, depending on the strength of the parent company's control or influence over its subsidiary:

6 *Or simply consolidation.*

Type of relationship	Type of company	Consolidation method
Control	Subsidiary	Full consolidation[6]
Joint control	Joint venture	Proportionate consolidation
Significant influence	Associate	Equity method

We will now examine each of these three methods in terms of its impact on sales, net profit and shareholders' equity.

1/FULL CONSOLIDATION

The accounts of a subsidiary are fully consolidated if it is controlled by its parent. Control is presumed to exist when the parent company:

- holds, directly or indirectly, over 50% of the voting rights in its subsidiary;
- holds, directly or indirectly, less than 50% of the voting rights but has power

over more than 50% of the voting rights by virtue of an agreement with other investors;

- has power to govern the financial and operating policies of the subsidiary under a statute or an agreement;
- has power to cast the majority of votes at meetings of the board of directors; or
- has power to appoint or remove the majority of the members of the board.

The criterion of exclusive control is the key factor under IAS. Under US GAAP, the determining factor is whether or not the parent company holds the majority of voting rights. This requirement is currently being revised by the FASB[7] and the IASB. They want to introduce a broader definition of control, such as the power to make decisions regarding the company's strategy and management with a view to increase its own profits or limiting its losses.

As its name suggests, full consolidation consists in transferring all the subsidiary's assets, liabilities and equity to the parent company's balance sheet and all the revenues and costs to the parent company's income statement.

The assets, liabilities and equity thus replace the investments held by the parent company, which therefore disappear from its balance sheet.

That said, when the subsidiary is not controlled exclusively by the parent company, the claims of the other "minority" shareholders on the subsidiary's equity and net income also need to be shown on the consolidated balance sheet and income statement of the group.

Assuming there is no difference between the book value of the parent's investment in the subsidiary and the book value of the subsidiary's equity,[8] full consolidation works as follows:

- On the balance sheet:

  o the subsidiary's assets and liabilities are **added item by item** to the parent company's balance sheet;

  o the historical cost amount of the shares in the consolidated subsidiary held by the parent is eliminated from the parent company's balance sheet and the same amount is deducted from the parent company's reserves;

  o the subsidiary's equity (including net income) is added to the parent company's equity and then allocated between the interests of the parent company (added to its reserves) and those of minority investors, which is added to a special **minority interests** line below the line item showing the parent company's shareholders' equity.

- On the income statement, all the subsidiary's revenues and charges are added item by item to the parent company's income statement. The parent company's net income is then broken down into:

  o the portion attributable to the parent company, which is added to the parent company's net income on both the income statement and the balance sheet;

  o the portion attributable to third-party investors, which is shown on a separate line of the income statement under the heading "minority interests".

Minority interests represent the share attributable to minority shareholders in the shareholders' equity and net income of fully consolidated subsidiaries.

7 *Financial Accounting Standards Board: the US accounting standard setter.*

8 *Which means "no goodwill", a topic to which we will return.*

From a solvency standpoint, minority interests certainly represent shareholders' equity. But from a valuation standpoint, they add no value to the group since minority interests represent shareholders' equity and net profit attributable to third parties and not to shareholders of the parent company.

Right up until the penultimate line of the income statement, financial analysis assumes that the parent company owns 100% of the subsidiary's assets and liabilities and, implicitly, that all the liabilities finance all the assets. This is true from an economic, but not from a legal perspective.

To illustrate the full consolidation method, consider the following example assuming that the parent company owns 75% of the subsidiary company.

The original balance sheets are as follows:

9 *Valued at historical cost less depreciation if any.*

Parent company's balance sheet				Subsidiary's balance sheet			
Investment in the subsidiary[9]	15	Shareholders' equity	70	Assets	28	Shareholders' equity	20
Other assets	57	Liabilities	2			Liabilities	8

In this scenario, the consolidated balance sheet would be as follows:

Consolidated balance sheet			
Investment in the subsidiary $(15-15)$	0	Shareholder' equity $(70+20-15)$	75
Assets $(57+28)$	85	Liabilities $(2+8)$	10

Or in a more detailed form:

Consolidated balance sheet		
Assets	85	Shareholder' equity group share $(75-5)$	70
		Minority interests $(20 \times 25\%)$	5
		Liabilities	10

The original income statements are as follows:

Parent company's income statement				Subsidiary's income statement			
Charges	80	Net sales	100	Charges	30	Net sales	38
Net income	20			Net income	8		

In this scenario, the consolidated income statement would be as follows:

Consolidated income statement			
Charges $(80+30)$	110	Net sales $(100+38)$	138
Net income $(20+8)$	28		

Or in a more detailed form:

Consolidated income statement

Charges	110	Net sales	138
Net income:			
Group share	26		
Minority interest (8 × 25%)	2		

2/PROPORTIONATE CONSOLIDATION

When the parent company exercises joint control with a limited number of partners over another company, this company is accounted for using the **proportionate consolidation** method. The key factors determining joint control are: (i) a limited number of partners sharing control (without any partner able to claim exclusive control), and (ii) a contractual arrangement outlining and defining how this joint control is to be exercised.

Proportionate consolidation is used to consolidate the accounts of companies controlled jointly with a limited number of partners. Such companies are known as **joint ventures**. Similar to full consolidation, proportionate consolidation leads to the replacement of the investment held in the joint venture with the assets, liabilities and equity of the joint venture. As its name suggests, the key difference with respect to full consolidation is that assets and liabilities are transferred to the parent company's balance sheet **only in proportion to the parent company's interest in the joint venture**. Likewise, the joint venture's revenues and charges are added to those of the parent company on the consolidated income statement only in proportion to its participation in the joint venture.

From a technical standpoint, proportionate consolidation is carried out as follows:

- the joint venture's assets and liabilities are added to the parent company's assets and liabilities in proportion to the latter's interest in the joint venture;
- the carrying amount of the shares in the joint venture held by the parent company is subtracted from long-term investments and from reserves in the balance sheet;
- the parent company's share in the shareholders' equity of the joint venture excluding the latter's net income is added to the parent company's reserves;
- all the joint venture's revenues and charges are added in proportion to the level of the parent company's shareholding to the corresponding line items of the parent company's income statement;
- the portion of the joint venture's net income attributable to the parent company is added to its net income on the balance sheet and income statement.

To illustrate the proportionate consolidation method, let us analyse the following example assuming that the parent company owns 33% of the joint venture:

The original balance sheets are as follows:

Parent company's balance sheet				Joint venture's balance sheet			
Investment in the joint venture	6	Shareholders' equity	62	Assets	30	Shareholders' equity	18
Other assets	58	Liabilities	2			Liabilities	12

In this scenario, the consolidated balance sheet would be as follows:

Consolidated balance sheet

Investment in the joint venture $(6 - 6)$	0	Shareholder' equity $(62 - 6 + 18 \times 33\%)$	62
Assets $(58 + 30 \times 33\%)$	68	Liabilities $(2 + 12 \times 33\%)$	6

The original income statements are as follows:

Parent company's income statement				Joint venture's income statement			
Charges	80	Net sales	100	Charges	30	Net sales	36
Net income	20			Net income	6		

In this scenario, the consolidated income statement would be as follows:

Consolidated income statement

Charges $(80 + 30 \times 33\%)$	90	Net sales $(100 + 36 \times 33\%)$	112
Net income $(20 + 6 \times 33\%)$	22		

Proportionate consolidation does not give rise to any minority interests.

One shortcoming of proportionate consolidation is that it appears to exaggerate the group's power since a portion of the turnover, cash flow, equity, fixed assets, etc. of joint ventures is included in the parent company's financial statements even if the group does not have exclusive control over those joint ventures.

3/EQUITY METHOD OF ACCOUNTING

Finally, when the parent company exercises significant influence over the operating and financial policy of its associate, the latter is accounted for under the equity method. Significant influence over the operating and financial policy of a company is assumed when the parent holds, directly or indirectly, at least 20% of the voting rights. Significant influence may be reflected by participation on the executive and supervisory bodies, participation in strategic decisions, the existence of major intercompany links, exchanges of management personnel and a relationship of dependence from a technical standpoint.

Equity accounting consists in replacing the carrying amount of the shares held in an associate (also known as an **equity affiliate** or **associated undertaking**) with the corresponding portion of the associate's shareholders' equity (including net income).

This method is purely financial. Both the group's investments and aggregate profit are thus reassessed on an annual basis. Accordingly, the IASB regards equity accounting as being more of a valuation method than a method of consolidation.

From a technical standpoint, equity accounting takes place as follows:

- the historical cost amount of shares held in the associate is subtracted from the parent company's investments and replaced by the share attributable to the parent company in the associate's shareholders' equity **including net income** for the year;
- the carrying value of the associate's shares is subtracted from the parent company's reserves, to which is added the share in the associate's shareholders' equity, **excluding the associate's income** attributable to the parent company;
- the portion of the associate's net income attributable to the parent company is added to its net income on the balance sheet and the income statement.

Investments in associates represent the share attributable to the parent company in associates shareholders' equity attributable to the parent company.

The equity method of accounting therefore leads to an increase each year in the carrying amount of the shareholding on the consolidated balance sheet, by an amount equal to the net income transferred to reserves by the associate.

However, from a solvency standpoint, this method does not provide any clues to the group's risk exposure and liabilities *vis-à-vis* its associate. The implication is that the group's risk exposure is restricted to the value of its shareholding.

The equity method of accounting is more a method used to revalue certain participating interests than a genuine form of consolidation.

To illustrate the equity method of accounting, let us consider the following example based on the assumption that the parent company owns 20% of its associate.

The original balance sheets are as follows:

Parent company's balance sheet				Associate's balance sheet			
Investment in the associate	5	Shareholders' equity	60	Assets	35	Shareholders' equity	25
Other assets	57	Liabilities	2			Liabilities	10

In this scenario, the consolidated balance sheet would be as follows:

Consolidated balance sheet			
Investment in the associate (20% × 25)	5	Shareholder' equity (60 + 5 − 5)	60
Other assets	57	Liabilities	2

The original income statements are as follows:

Parent company's income statement				Associate's income statement			
Charges	80	Net sales	100	Charges	30	Net sales	35
Net income	20			Net income	5		

In this scenario, the consolidated income statement would be as follows:

Consolidated income statement

Charges	80	Net sales	100
Net income (20 + 5 × 20%)	21	Income from associates (5 × 20%)	1

Section 6.2
CONSOLIDATION-RELATED ISSUES

1/SCOPE OF CONSOLIDATION

The scope of consolidation – i.e., the companies to be consolidated – is determined using the rules we presented in Section 6.1. To determine the scope of consolidation, one needs to establish the level of control exercised by the parent company over each of the companies in which it owns shares.

(a) Level of control and ownership level

The **level of control**[10] measures the strength of direct or indirect dependence that exists between the parent company and its subsidiaries, joint venture or associates. This level reflects the percentage of voting rights held by the parent company in these companies.

To calculate the level of control, the percentage of voting rights held by all group companies in the subsidiary, the joint venture or the associates are added together, provided that the group companies are controlled directly or indirectly by the parent company. Control is assumed when the percentage of voting rights held is 50% or higher or when a situation of de facto control exists at each link in the chain.

It is important not to confuse the level of control with the level of ownership. Generally speaking, these two concepts are different. The **ownership level**[11] is used to calculate the parent company's claims on its subsidiaries, joint ventures or associates. It reflects the proportion of their capital held directly or indirectly by the parent company. It is a financial concept, unlike the level of control, which is a power-related concept.

The ownership level is the sum of the product of the direct and indirect percentage stakes held by the parent company in a given company. The ownership level differs from the level of control which is calculated by adding together the investments made by all group companies in another company, provided that these group companies are controlled directly or indirectly by the parent company.

Consider the following example:

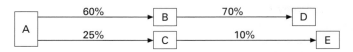

A controls 60% of B, B controls 70% of D, so A controls 70% of D. D and B are

---

10 *Or percentage control.*

11 *Or percentage interest.*

therefore fully consolidated by A. But A owns not 70%, but 42% of D (i.e., 60% × 70%). The ownership level of A over D is then 42%: only 42% of D's net income is attributable to A.

Since C owns just 10% of E, C will not consolidate E. But since A controls 25% of C, A will account for C under the equity method and will show 25% of C's net income in its income statement.

How the ownership level is used varies from one consolidation method to another:

- with full consolidation, the **ownership level** is used only to allocate the subsidiary's reserves and net income between the parent company and minority interests in the subsidiary;
- with proportionate consolidation, all the joint venture's balance sheet and income statement items are added in proportion to the **ownership level** to the balance sheet and income statement items of the parent company;
- with the equity method of accounting, the **ownership level** is used to determine the portion of the subsidiary's shareholders' equity and net income attributable to the parent company.

(b) Changes in the scope of consolidation

It is important to analyse the scope of consolidation, especially with regard to what has changed and what is excluded. A decision not to consolidate a company means:

- neither its losses nor its shareholders' equity will appear on the balance sheet[12] of the group;
- its liabilities will not appear on the balance sheet of the group.

The equity method of accounting also means that not all the group's liabilities are shown on the balance sheet as readers will see with the example of Coca-Cola in Chapter 13.

Changes in the scope of consolidation require the preparation of **pro forma** financial statements. Pro forma statements enable analysts to compare the company's performances on a consistent basis. In these pro forma statements, the company may either:

- restate past accounts to make them comparable with the current scope of consolidation; or
- remove from the current scope of consolidation any items that were not present in the previous period to maintain its previous configuration. The latter option is, however, less interesting for financial analysts.

Finally, as we will see in Chapter 47, certain techniques can be used to remove subsidiaries still controlled by the parent company from the scope of consolidation. These techniques have been developed to make certain consolidated accounts look more attractive and they frequently involve a Special Purpose Vehicle (SPV). The SPV is a separate legal entity created specially to handle a venture on behalf of a company. In many cases the SPV belongs from a legal standpoint to banks or to investors rather than to the company. This said, the IASB has stipulated that the company should consolidate the SPV if:

12 *Unless the losses are such that the portion of the subsidiary's shareholders' equity attributable to the parent company is lower than the net book value of the shares in the subsidiary held by the parent. In which case, an impairment loss is recognised on the shareholding.*

- it enjoys the majority of the benefits; or
- if it incurs the residual risks arising from the SPV even if it does not own a single share of the SPV.

2/GOODWILL

It is very unusual for one company to acquire another for exactly its book value.

Generally speaking, there is a difference between the acquisition price, which may be paid in cash or in shares, and the portion of the target company's shareholders' equity attributable to the parent company. In most cases, this difference is positive as the price paid exceeds the target's book value.

(a) What does this difference represent?

In other words, why should a company agree to pay out more for another company than its book value? There are several possible explanations:

- the assets recorded on the acquired company's balance sheet are worth more than their historical cost. This situation may result from the prudence principle, which means that unrealised capital losses have to be taken into account, but not unrealised capital gains;
- it is perfectly conceivable that assets, such as patents, licences and market share, that the company has accumulated over the years without wishing to or even being able to account for them, may not appear on the balance sheet. This situation is especially true if the company is highly profitable;
- the merger between the two companies may create synergies, either in the form of cost reductions and/or revenue enhancement. The buyer is likely to partly reflect them in the price offered to the seller;
- the buyer may be ready to pay a high price for a target just to prevent a new player from buying it, entering the market and putting the current level of the buyer's profitability under pressure;
- finally, the buyer may quite simply have overpaid for the deal.

(b) How is goodwill accounted for?

Goodwill is shown under intangible fixed assets of the new group's balance sheet at an amount equal to the difference between the acquisition price and the share of the new subsidiary's equity adjusted for unrealised capital gains net of unrealised capital losses on assets and liabilities. Assets, liabilities and equity of the new subsidiary are transferred to the group's balance sheet at their estimated value rather than their book value. In this case, the intangible assets acquired are recorded on the group's balance sheet even if they did not originally appear on the acquired company's balance sheet; i.e., brands, patents, licences, landing slots, data bases, etc.

The difference between the purchase cost and the fair market value of the assets and liabilities acquired with a company is called goodwill.

Goodwill is assessed each year to verify whether its value is at least equal to its net book value as shown on the group's balance sheet. This assessment is done by means of **impairment** tests. If the market value of goodwill is below its book value, goodwill is written down to its fair market value and a corresponding impairment loss is recorded in the income statement.

This method is known as the **purchase method**. This is the method prescribed by US GAAP since December 2001 and IAS from 1 January 2006.[13] The **pooling of interest method** was abolished by the US authorities in December 2001 and will be abolished by the IASB from 2006. It allowed the assets and liabilities of the newly acquired company to be included in the group's accounts at their book value without any goodwill being recorded.[14]

To illustrate the purchase method, let's analyse now how Pfizer, the US pharmaceutical group, accounted for the acquisition of its rival, Pharmacia.

Prior to the acquisition, the Pfizer balance sheet (in $bn) can be summarised as follows:

Goodwill	1.2	Shareholders' equity	20.0
Other fixed assets	21.6		
Working capital	−1.7	Net debt	1.1

While Pharmacia's balance sheet was as follows:

Goodwill	1.5	Shareholders' equity	8.0
Other fixed assets	6.0		
Working capital	1.4	Net debt	0.9

During 2003, Pfizer acquired 100% of Pharmacia for $56bn paid in Pfizer shares. Since Pharmacia's equity stood at $8bn, this transaction gave rise to $48bn in goodwill.

Pharmacia's assets and liabilities were revalued by $27.6bn:

* intangible assets (technology rights, brands): +$37.2bn;
* current research and development: +$5.1bn, which was nonetheless fully charged off against income for 2003, in accordance with US accounting standards;
* inventories: +$1.6bn;
* deferred tax: +$13.5bn (increase in liabilities); and
* sundry other items: €2.8bn (increase in liabilities).

Consequently, the amount of goodwill created was reduced to $20.4bn The simplified balance sheet of the combined entity was therefore as follows:

Goodwill	23.1[15]	Shareholders' equity	76.0[16]
Other fixed assets	69.9[17]	Deferred taxes and other	16.3
Working capital	1.3	Net debt	2.0

13 *But early application is encouraged.*

14 *As the difference between the price paid for the shares and their book value was deducted from the acquiror's equity.*

15 *23.1 = 1.2 + 1.5 + 20.4*

16 *76.0 = 20 + 56*

17 *69.9 = 21.6 + 6.0 + 37.2 + 5.1*

It is worth noting that the combined entity's capital employed would have been $28.5bn[18] under the pooling of interests method compared with $94.3bn under the purchase method – i.e., a difference of 230% for the same operating assets! Likewise, return on equity would be calculated on shareholders' equity of $28bn[19] under the pooling of interests method and $76bn under the purchase method. It is therefore easy to see why the abandonment of the pooling of interests method has made accounts more rigorous.

Finally, transactions may give rise to negative goodwill under certain circumstances. Under IAS, negative goodwill is immediately recognised as a profit in the income statement of the new groups.

All in all, the difference between the purchase price and the share in equity is broken down into two portions. One reflects unrealised capital gains on the assets of the target company and is factored into the valuation of the consolidated assets. The other one, the residual portion, is called goodwill, and is not accounted for by unrealised capital gains.

The consolidated company's assets and liabilities are therefore revalued upon its first-time consolidation. Its accounts are adjusted to bring them into line with the accounting policies applied by its new parent company.

(c) How financial analysts should treat goodwill?

From a financial standpoint, it is sensible to regard goodwill as an asset like any other that may suffer sudden falls in value that need to be recognised by means of an impairment charge.

Can it be argued that goodwill impairment losses do not reflect any decrease in the company's wealth because there is no outflow of cash? We do not think so.

Granted, goodwill impairment losses are a noncash item, but it would be wrong to say that only decisions giving rise to cash flows affect a company's value. For instance, setting a maximum limit on voting rights or attributing ten voting rights to certain categories of share does not have any cash impact, but definitely reduces the value of shareholders' equity.

Recognising the impairment of goodwill related to a past acquisition is tantamount to admitting that the price paid was too high. But what if the acquisition was paid for in shares? This makes no difference whatsoever, irrespective of whether the buyer's shares were overvalued at the same time.

Had the company carried out a share issue rather than overpaying for an acquisition, it would have been able to capitalise on its lofty share price to the great benefit of existing shareholders. The cash raised through the share issue would have been used to make acquisitions at much more reasonable prices once the wave of euphoria had subsided. This is precisely the strategy adopted by Bouygues. It raised €1.5bn of new equity in March 2000 at a very high share price, refused to participate in the UMTS auctions and used its cash pile only in 2002 to buy out minority interests in its telecom subsidiary at a far lower level than the rumoured price in 2000.

It is essential to remember that shareholders in a company that pays for a deal in shares suffer dilution in their interest. They accept this dilution because they take the view that the size of the cake will grow at a faster rate (e.g., by 30%) than the

[18] $28.5 = 1.2 + 21.6 - 1.7 + 6 + 1.4$

[19] $28 = 20 + 8$

number of guests invited to the party (e.g., by over 25%). Should it transpire that the cake grows at merely 10% rather than the expected 30% because the purchased assets prove to be worth less than anticipated, the number of guests at the party will unfortunately stay the same. Accordingly, the size of each guest's slice of the cake falls by 12% (110/125 − 1), so shareholders' wealth has certainly diminished.

Finally, testing each year whether the capital employed of each company segment is greater than its book value so as to determine whether the purchased goodwill needs to be written down is implicitly tantamount to recording internally generated goodwill that gradually replaces the purchased goodwill. As we know, goodwill has a limited lifespan in view of the competition prevailing in the business world.

(d) How financial analysts should treat "adjusted income"

Following the acquisition of Phamarcia, Pfizer was the first group to publish an "adjusted income" to neutralise the P&L impact of the revaluation of assets and liabilities of its newly acquired subsidiary.

Note that, by virtue of the revaluation of Pharmacia's inventories to their market value, the normal process of selling the inventories will generate no profit. So how relevant will the P&L be in the first year after the merger? Say somebody took over Rémy Cointreau. Since cognac inventories would have an average lifespan of 7 years, that would mean several lacklustre years for the P&L!

As a result, Pfizer decided to report on the basis of "adjusted income", which fully neutralised the P&L impact of purchase accounting. It was as if the entire difference between the acquisition price and book value was booked under goodwill. Naturally, a P&L account is drawn up under normal standards, but it carries an audited table showing the impact of the switch to adjusted income.

For 2003, Pfizer reported net attributable profit of $3.9bn, down 57% from the $9.1bn figure of 1 year earlier. On an adjusted basis, net profit rose 42% to $10.5bn. Not exactly in the same ballpark, is it? The adjustments reflect the reversal of the 100% depreciation of the cost of acquired R&D, the reversal of Pharmacia's depreciations, which were revalued at the acquisition, and the reversal of the reappraisal of Pharmacia's inventories, net of tax impact.

To the extent that Pfizer is one of the biggest US market caps ($190bn in March 2005), its practice is likely to be copied. Already, all analysts who cover Pfizer go on the adjusted figures, not the accounting data. We believe they are right to do so.

Section 6.3
TECHNICAL ASPECTS OF CONSOLIDATION

1/HARMONISING ACCOUNTING DATA

Since consolidation consists of aggregating accounts, give or take some adjustments, it is important to ensure that the accounting data used are consistent; i.e., based on the same principles.

Usually, the valuation methods used in individual company accounts are determined by accounting or tax issues specific to each subsidiary, especially when some of them are located outside the group's home country. This is particularly true for provisions, depreciation and amortisation, fixed assets, inventories and work in progress, deferred charges and shareholders' equity.

These differences need to be eliminated upon consolidation. This process is facilitated by the fact that most of the time consolidated accounts are not prepared to calculate taxable income, so groups may disregard the prevailing tax regulations.

2/ ELIMINATING INTRA-GROUP TRANSACTIONS

Consolidation entails more than the mere aggregation of accounts. Before the consolidation process as such can begin, intra-group transactions and their impact on net income have to be eliminated from the accounts of both the parent company and of its consolidated companies.

Assume, for instance, that the parent company has sold to subsidiaries products at cost plus a margin. An entirely fictitious gain would show up in the group's accounts if the relevant products were merely held in stock by the subsidiaries rather than being sold on to third parties. Naturally, this fictitious gain, which would be a distortion of reality, needs to be eliminated.

Intra-group transactions to be eliminated upon consolidation can be broken down into two categories:

- Those that are very significant because they affect consolidated net income. It is therefore vital for such transactions to be reversed. The goal is to avoid showing two profits or showing the same profit twice. The reversal of these transactions upon consolidation leads primarily to the elimination of:
  - intra-group profits included in inventories;
  - capital gains arising on the transfer or contribution of investments;
  - dividends received from consolidated companies;
  - impairment losses on intra-group loans or investments; and
  - tax on intra-group profits.
- Those that are not fundamental because they have no impact on consolidated net income or those affecting the assets or liabilities of the consolidated entities. These transactions are eliminated through netting, so as to show the real level of the group's debt. They include:
  - parent-to-subsidiary loans (advances to the subsidiary) and vice versa;
  - interest paid by the parent company to the consolidated companies (financial income of the latter) and vice versa.

3/ TRANSLATING THE ACCOUNTS OF FOREIGN SUBSIDIARIES

(a) The problem

The translation of the accounts of foreign companies is a thorny issue because of exchange rate fluctuations and the difference between inflation rates, which may distort the picture provided by company accounts.

For instance, a parent company located in the euro zone may own a subsidiary in a country with a soft currency.[20]

Using year-end exchange rates to convert the assets of its subsidiary into the parent company's currency understates their value. From an economic standpoint, all the assets do not suffer depreciation proportional to that of the subsidiary's home currency.

On one hand, fixed assets are protected to some extent. Inflation means that it would cost more in the subsidiary's local currency to replace them after the devaluation in the currency than before. All in all, the inflation and devaluation phenomena may actually offset each other, so the value of the subsidiary's fixed assets in the parent company's currency is roughly stable. On the other hand, inventories, receivables and liabilities (irrespective of their maturity) denominated in the devalued currency all depreciate in tandem with the currency.

If the subsidiary is located in a country with a hard currency (i.e., a stronger one than that of the parent company), the situation is similar, but the implications are reversed.

To present an accurate image of developments in the foreign subsidiary's situation, it is necessary to take into account:

- the impact on the consolidated accounts of the translation of the subsidiary's currency into the parent company's currency;
- the adjustment that would stem from translation of the foreign subsidiary's fixed assets into the local currency.

(b) Methods

Several methods may be used at the same time to translate different items in the balance sheet and income statement of foreign subsidiaries giving rise to currency translation differences:

- if the subsidiary is economically and financially independent of its parent company, which is the most common situation, the **closing rate method** is used;
- if the subsidiary is not independent of its parent company, because its operations are an integral part of another company, the **temporal method**[21] is used;
- finally, if the subsidiary is based in a country with high inflation, a special method is used.

Under the **closing rate method**, all assets and liabilities are translated at the closing rate which is the rate of exchange at the balance sheet date.[22] IAS recommends using the exchange rate prevailing on the transaction date to translate revenues and charges on the income statement or, failing this, the average exchange rate for the period, which is what most companies do. Currency translation differences are recorded under shareholders' equity, with a distinction being made between the group's share and that attributable to minority investors. This translation method is relatively comparable with the US standard.

The **temporal method** consists of translating:

- monetary items (i.e., cash and sums receivable or payable denominated in the foreign company's currency and determined in advance) at the closing rate;
- nonmonetary items (fixed assets and the corresponding depreciation and

20 *A soft or weak currency is a currency that tends to fall in value because of political or economic uncertainty (high inflation rate). The Nepal rupee is a good example.*

21 *Based on the historical exchange rate method.*

22 *This method is also called the* **current rate method**.

amortisation,[23] goodwill, inventories, prepayments, shareholders' equity, investments, etc.) at the exchange rate at the date to which the historical cost or valuation pertains;

- revenues and charges on the income statement theoretically at the exchange rate prevailing on the transaction date. In practice, however, they are usually translated at an average exchange rate for the period.

Under the temporal method, the difference between the net income on the balance sheet and that on the income statement is recorded on the income statement under foreign exchange gains and losses.

(c) Translating the accounts of subsidiaries located in hyperinflationary countries

A hyperinflationary country is one where inflation is both chronic and out of control. In such circumstances, the previous methods are not suitable for translating the effects of inflation into the accounts.

Hence the use of a specific method based on restatements made by applying a general price index. Items such as monetary items that are already stated at the measuring unit at the balance sheet date are not restated. Other items are restated based on the change in the general price index between the date those items were acquired or incurred and the balance sheet consolidation. A gain or loss on the net monetary position is included in net income.

The temporal method is prescribed in the US.

SUMMARY

download

Consolidation aims to present the financial position of a group of companies as if they formed one single entity. It is an obligation for companies that exclusively control other companies or exercise significant influence over them. The scope of consolidation encompasses the parent company and the companies in which the parent company holds at least 20% of the voting rights. The basic principle of consolidation is to replace the book value of investments on the parent company's balance sheet with the assets, liabilities and equity of the consolidated subsidiaries.

Full consolidation, which is generally applied when the parent company holds more than 50% of voting rights in its subsidiary, consists of replacing the investments on the parent company's balance sheet with all the subsidiary's assets, liabilities and equity, as well as adding all the revenues and charges from its income statement. This method gives rise to minority interests in the subsidiary's net income and shareholders' equity.

Proportionate consolidation is used where the parent company shares control over a joint venture with a limited number of partners. The approach is the same as for full consolidation, but assets, liabilities, equity, revenues and charges are transferred only in proportion to the stake of the parent company in the joint venture.

Where the parent company exercises significant influence (usually by holding over 20% of the voting rights) over another company called an associate, the equity method of accounting is used. The book value of investments is replaced by the parent company's share in the associate's equity (including net income). This method is actually equivalent to an annual revaluation of these investments.

From a financial standpoint, the ownership level, which represents the percentage of the capital held directly or indirectly by the parent company, is not equal to the level of control, which reflects the proportion of voting rights held. The level of control is used to determine which consolidation method is applied. The ownership level is used to separate groups' interests from minorities' interests in equity and net income.

A group often acquires a company by paying more than the book value of the company's equity. The difference is recorded as goodwill under intangible assets, less any unrealised capital gains or losses on the acquired company's assets and liabilities. This goodwill arising on consolidation is compared each year with its estimated value and written down to fair market value, where appropriate.

When analysing a group, it is essential to ensure that the basic accounting data are consistent from one company to another. Likewise, intra-group transactions, especially those affecting consolidated net income (intra-group profits, dividends received from subsidiaries, etc.), must be eliminated upon consolidation.

Two methods are used to translate the accounts of foreign subsidiaries: the closing rate and the temporal method for currency exchange rate translations. In addition, specific currency translation methods are used for companies in hyperinflationary countries.

QUESTIONS

quiz

1/ Describe the three methods used for consolidating accounts.

2/ What criticism can be made of the equity method of accounting?

3/ What criticism can be made of proportionate consolidation?

4/ What is the difference between the proportion of voting rights held and the ownership level?

5/ On the consolidated income statement, what is the "share of earnings in companies accounted for under the equity method" similar to?

6/ In what circumstances should the group's share be separated from that attributable to minority investors?

7/ Will opening up the capital of a subsidiary to shareholders outside the group have an impact on the group's earnings? Is this a paradox? Explain.

8/ Why do dividends paid by subsidiaries have to be restated when consolidated accounts are drawn up?

9/ What is goodwill and how is it stated?

10/ What is the most frequently used method of consolidation? Why?

11/ In France, the UK or Italy, does the rate at which goodwill is written down have an impact on the amount of tax paid by the group?

12/ What is the pooling of interests method?

13/ Is an impairment loss in the amount of goodwill a recurrent or a nonrecurrent item? Explain why, nevertheless, it has a negative impact on the share price.

14/ Why has the phasing out of the pooling of interests method made accounts more rigorous?

15/ What is the logic behind the temporal method of translating fixed assets at the historical exchange rate?

EXERCISES

The financial statements of company M and its subsidiary S are shown here (in €m).

Balance sheet

Assets	M	S	Equity and liabilities	M	S
Tangible and intangible fixed assets	100	30	Equity and share capital	40	10
Investment in subsidiary S	16	—	Reserves	80	10
Other investments	5	—	Net earnings	10	5
Current assets	200	70	Debt	191	75
Total	**321**	**100**	**Total**	**321**	**100**

Income statement

	M	S
Sales	200	90
− Purchases of raw materials	100	50
− Change in inventories	—	2
− Other external services	25	20
− Personnel costs	40	8
− Interest and other financial charges	10	1
+ Interest, dividends and other financial income	3	—
− Exceptional costs	9	—
+ Exceptional income	2	—
− Corporate income tax	11	4
= **Net income**	**10**	**5**

Draw up the consolidated accounts for the group M + S in the following circumstances:

(a) M has an 80% stake in S (full consolidation).

(b) M has a 50% stake in S (proportional consolidation).

(c) M has a 20% stake in S (equity method consolidation).

(N.B.: It is assumed that there are no flows between M and S.)

ANSWERS

Questions

1/ *See chapter.*

2/ *It is not a consolidation method but a method for revaluing assets.*

3/ *It is misleading in the sense that, if you own a third of the joint venture, you do not own a third of the assets and are not liable for a third of liabilities.*

4/ *See chapter.*

5/ *Financial income on long-term investments.*

6/ *When valuing shares of the group because shareholders of the group have no claim whatsoever on stakes owned by minority interests in subsidiaries.*

7/ *Yes, it results in minority interests. This is a paradox since the group registers a profit or a loss without receiving cash. This is because of the increase or reduction in the group's share in shareholders' equity.*

8/ *Because they are internal flows.*

9/ *Goodwill is the difference between the price paid for the subsidiary minus the estimated value of its assets and liabilities. Goodwill is an intangible asset whose value will be tested every year and impaired if need be.*

10/ *Full consolidation. because groups tend to prefer exclusive control over joint control or significant influence.*

11/ *No, it is a consolidated accounting entry; and corporate income taxes are not computed on consolidated accounts but in individual accounts in France, the UK and Italy.*

12/ *See chapter.*

13/ *It should normally be a nonrecurrent item, if not the future of the company is doomed! Because it is a clear indication that the future profitability of the company will be lower than initially anticipated.*

14/ *Because it is no longer possible to reduce capital employed and capital invested by writing off goodwill against equity, artificially boosting return on equity or return on capital employed.*

15/ *The temporal method is only used for subsidiaries that are dependent on the parent company. It is considered that their fixed assets are accordingly the property of the parent company but that they just happen to be abroad. Consequently, their value appears on the balance sheet of the groups as if those fixed assets had been bought by the parent company at a price translated on the purchase date at the then exchange rate.*

Exercise

M + S balance sheet (€m)	80%	50%	20%
Assets			
Tangible and intangible fixed assets	130	115	100
Equity in associated companies			5
Investments	5	5	5
Current assets	270	235	200
Total	405	355	310
Equity and liabilities			
Share capital	40	40	40
Reserves	80*	74	68
Minority interests in equity	4		
Net earnings (group share)	14	12.5	11
Minority interests in net earnings	1		
Debt	266	228.5	191
Total	405	355	310

* Group share

M + S income statement (€m)	80%	50%	20%
Sales	290	245	200
− Purchases of raw materials	150	125	100
− Change in inventories	2	1	
− Other external services	45	35	25
− Personnel costs	48	44	40
− Interest and other finance charges	11	10.5	10
+ Interest, dividends and other financial income	3	3	3
− Exceptional costs	9	9	9
+ Exceptional income	2	2	2
− Corporate income tax	15	13	11
+ Income from associates			1
= Net earnings	15	12.5	11
− Minority interests	1		
= Net earnings, group share	14		

For more about consolidation techniques:

D. Alexander, C. Nobes, *Financial Accounting*, Prentice Hall, 2001.
H. Stolowy, M. Lebas, *Corporate Financial Reporting: A Global Perspective*, Thomson, 2002.

To get the latest version of US and International GAAPs:

B. Epstein, A.A. Mirza, *Interpretation and Application of International Accounting Standards*, John Wiley & Sons, published every year.
www.fasb.org, the website of the US Accounting Standards Board.
www.iasb.org.uk, the website of the International Accounting Standards Board.
www.iasplus.com, the website of Deloitte about IAS rules.
www.pwcglobal.com/Extweb/service.nsf/docid/981951434174C5ED80256C7E004BBC97, clearly the best website to help you solve complex accounting issues, but an incredibly complex name to remember!

To understand how financial markets react to impairment losses in goodwill:

M. Hirschey, V. Richardson, Investor underreaction to goodwill write-offs, *Financial Analysts Journal*, 75–84, November/December 2003.

BIBLIOGRAPHY

Chapter 7

HOW TO COPE WITH THE MOST COMPLEX POINTS IN FINANCIAL ACCOUNTS

Everything you always wanted to know but never dared to ask!

This chapter is rather different from the others. It is not intended to be read from start to finish, but consulted from time to time, whenever readers experience problems interpreting, analysing or processing a particular accounting item.

Each of these complex points will be analysed from these angles:

- **from an economic standpoint** so that readers gain a thorough understanding of its real substance;
- **from an accounting standpoint** to help readers understand the accounting treatment applied and how this treatment affects the published accounts;
- **from a financial standpoint** to draw a conclusion as to how it is best to deal with this problem.

Our experience tells us that this is the best way of getting to grips with and solving problems. The key point to note in this chapter is the method we use to deal with complex issues, since we cannot look at every single point here. When faced with a different problem, readers will have to come up with their own solutions using our methodology – unless they contact us through the *vernimmen.com* website.

The following bullet list shows, in alphabetical order, the main line items and principal problems that readers are likely to experience:

- accruals in the income statement;
- construction contracts;
- convertible bonds or loans;
- currency translation adjustments;
- deferred tax assets and liabilities;
- dilution profits or losses;
- exchangeable bonds;
- goodwill;
- intangible fixed assets;
- inventories;
- leases;
- mandatory convertible bonds;
- off-balance-sheet commitments;
- preference shares;
- perpetual subordinated loans or notes;
- provisions;
- stock options;
- tangible fixed assets;
- treasury shares.

Section 7.1
ACCRUALS

1/WHAT ARE ACCRUALS?

Accruals are used to recognise revenues and costs booked in one period but relating to another period.

2/HOW ARE THEY ACCOUNTED FOR?

The main categories of accruals are:

- **prepaid costs**; i.e., charges relating to goods or services to be supplied later. For instance, three-quarters of a rental charge payable in advance for a 12-month period on 1 October each year will be recorded under prepaid costs on the asset side of the balance sheet at 31 December;[1]
- **prepaid income**; i.e., income accounted for before the corresponding goods or services have been delivered or carried out. For instance, a cable company records three-quarters of the annual subscription payments it receives on 1 October under prepaid income on the liabilities side of its balance sheet at 31 December.[1]

1 If the company's financial year starts as of January 1st.

We should also cite accrued income and cost, which work in the same way as prepaid income and cost, only in reverse.

3/HOW SHOULD FINANCIAL ANALYSTS TREAT THEM?

Prepaid income and cost form part of operating working capital.

Section 7.2
CONSTRUCTION CONTRACTS

1/WHAT ARE CONSTRUCTION CONTRACTS?

In some cases, it may take more than a year for a company to complete a project. For instance, a group that builds dams or ships may work for several years on a single project.

2/HOW ARE THEY ACCOUNTED FOR?

Construction contracts are accounted for using the percentage of completion method, which consists in recognising at the end of each financial year the sales and profit/loss anticipated on the project in proportion to the percentage of the work completed at that time. US accounting rules recognise both the percentage of completion method and the completed contract method where revenue recognition is deferred until completion of the contract.[2]

3/How should financial analysts treat them?

In order to assess the earnings quality of a company, analysts need to check whether or not a change in method has occurred recently.

Construction projects in progress are part of the operating working capital. The percentage of completion method results in less volatile profits, as they are spread over several fiscal years, even if the completed contract method may seem more prudent. Analysts should beware of changes in accounting methods for construction contracts (which are not possible under IAS) as such change may indicate an attempt to improve artificially the published net income for a given year.

Section 7.3
Convertible bonds and loans

1/What are convertible bonds and loans?

Convertible bonds are bonds that may be converted at the request of their holders into shares in the issuing company. Conversion is thus initiated by the investor.

2/How are they accounted for?

When they are issued, convertible bonds and loans are allocated between debt and equity accounts since they are analysed under International Accounting Standards (IAS) as compound financial instruments made up of a straight bond and a call option (see Chapter 30).

3/How should financial analysts treat them?

Some analysts take the view that convertible bonds lie halfway between equity and debt, so treat them as 50% shareholders' equity and 50% debt. We believe this to be a totally arbitrary and unjustified approach. The approach we recommend is to examine the conditions governing conversion of the bonds and to make the equity/debt classification based on the results of this analysis. For instance, if the share price already lies well above the conversion price, the bonds are very likely indeed to be converted, so the issue should be treated as equity. For valuation purposes, the related interest expense net of tax should be reversed out of the income statement, leading to an increase in net income. The number of shares should also be increased by those to be issued through the conversion of the convertible bonds.

---

2 *The completed contract method consists of recognising the sales and earnings on a project only when the project has been completed or the last batch delivered. Nonetheless, by virtue of the conservatism principle, any losses anticipated are fully provisioned. This method is thus equivalent to recognising only unrealised losses while the project is underway. It may be used in the US where the recommended method is the percentage of completion method.*

On the other hand, if the share price is below the conversion price, convertible bonds should be treated as conventional bonds and stay classified as borrowings.

Section 7.4
CURRENCY TRANSLATION ADJUSTMENTS

See Chapter 6.

Section 7.5
DEFERRED TAX ASSETS AND LIABILITIES

1/WHAT ARE DEFERRED TAX ASSETS AND LIABILITIES?

Deferred taxation giving rise to deferred tax assets or liabilities. It stems:

- either from differences in periods in which the income or cost is recognised for tax and accounting purposes;
- or from differences between the taxable and book values of assets and liabilities.

On the income statement, certain revenues and charges are recognised in different periods for the purpose of calculating pre-tax accounting profit and taxable profit.

In some cases, the difference may be temporary due to the method used to derive taxable profit from pre-tax accounting profit. For instance, a charge has been recognised in the accounts, but is not yet deductible for tax purposes (e.g., employee profit-sharing in some countries); or vice versa. The same may apply to certain types of revenue. Such differences are known as **timing differences**.

In other circumstances, the differences may be definitive or permanent; i.e., for revenue or charges that will never be taken into account in the computation of taxable profit (e.g., tax penalties or fines that are not deductible for tax purposes). Consequently, there is no deferred tax recognition.

On the balance sheet, the historical cost of an asset or liability may not be the same as its tax base, which creates a **temporary difference**. Depending on the situation, temporary differences may give rise to a future tax charge and thus deferred tax liabilities, while others may lead to future tax deductions and thus deferred tax assets. For instance, deferred tax liabilities may arise from:

- assets that give rise to tax deductions that are lower than their book value when sold or used. The most common example of this derives from the revaluation of assets upon the first-time consolidation of a subsidiary. Their value on the consolidated balance sheet is higher than the tax base used to calculate depreciation and amortisation or capital gains and losses;
- capitalised financial costs that are deductible immediately for tax purposes, but that are accounted for on the income statement over several years or deferred;

- revenues, the taxation of which is deferred, such as accrued financial income that becomes taxable only once it has been actually received.

Deferred tax assets may arise in various situations including charges that are expensed in the accounts but are deductible for tax purposes in later years only, such as:

- provisions that are deductible only when the stated risk or liability materialises (for retirement indemnities in certain countries);
- certain tax losses that may be offset against tax expense in the future (i.e., tax loss carryforwards, long-term capital losses).

Finally, if the company were to take certain decisions, it would have to pay additional tax. These taxes represent **contingent tax liabilities**; e.g., stemming from the distribution of reserves on which tax has not been paid at the standard rate.

2/HOW ARE THEY ACCOUNTED FOR?

It is mandatory for companies to recognise all their deferred tax liabilities in consolidated accounts. Deferred tax assets arising from tax losses should be recognised when it is probable that the deferred tax asset can be used to reduce tax to be paid.

Deferred tax liabilities are not recognised on goodwill where goodwill depreciation is not deductible for tax purposes, as is the case in the UK, Italy or France. Likewise, they are not recorded in respect of tax payable by the consolidating company on distributions (e.g., dividend-withholding tax) since they are taken directly to shareholders' equity.

In some more unusual circumstances, the temporary difference relates to a transaction that directly affects shareholders' equity (e.g., a change in accounting method), in which case the temporary difference will also be set off against the company's shareholders' equity.

IAS do not permit the discounting of deferred tax assets and liabilities to net present value.

Deferred tax is not the same as **contingent taxation**, which reflects the tax payable by the company if it takes certain decisions. For instance, tax charges payable if certain reserves are distributed (i.e., dividend-withholding tax), or if assets are sold and a capital gain is registered, revenues qualifying for a lower rate of tax provided they are not distributed to shareholders (long-term capital gains in some countries, etc.). The principle governing contingent taxation is straightforward: it is not recorded on the balance sheet and no charge appears on the income statement.

3/HOW SHOULD FINANCIAL ANALYSTS TREAT THEM?

It is important to recognise that deferred taxation does not represent an amount of tax currently due to or from the tax authorities, but consists of accounting entries with, most of the time, no economic underpinnings and with no corresponding cash flows.

Deferred taxation is the product of accounting entries triggered by differences between accounting values and tax bases (on the balance sheet) or between accounting and tax treatments (on the income statement). The corresponding double entry is made either on the income statement or to shareholders' equity.

For instance, a company that posts a loss for a given period owing to exceptional circumstances will recognise a deferred tax asset in its consolidated accounts, the double entry to which will be a tax benefit that reduces the amount of the after-tax reported loss. Please note that the deferred tax asset does not represent an amount due from the State, but only a future tax saving assuming positive net income in the near future.

Accordingly, we would advise treating deferred tax assets due to past losses as an intangible asset or to deduct it from shareholders' equity to arrive back at the original amount of the nonrecurrent loss for the year.

For deferred tax assets linked to provisions that are not tax-deductible, we would advise deducting the related deferred tax asset from the provision (which will appear after tax on the balance sheet) or deducting it from shareholders' equity.

We recommend adding the deferred tax assets linked to assets with a different tax and accounting base (a frequent case after an acquisition booked under purchase accounting[3]) to goodwill (as goodwill was initially reduced by accounting for their deferred tax assets which has no real value). We advise adding deferred tax liabilities created by differences between tax and accounting base to shareholders' equity.

3 *See Chapter 6.*

Lastly, contingent tax liabilities, which do not appear in company accounts, are of interest only for the computation of the net asset value of the company (see Chapter 40).

Section 7.6
DILUTION PROFIT AND LOSSES

1/WHAT ARE DILUTION PROFIT AND LOSSES?

Where a parent company does not subscribe either at all or only partially to a capital increase by one of its subsidiaries, which takes place above the subsidiary's book value, the parent company records a **dilution profit**.

Likewise, if the valuation of the subsidiary for the purpose of the capital increase is less than its book value, the parent company records a **dilution loss**.

2/HOW ARE THEY ACCOUNTED FOR?

For instance, let us consider the case of a parent company that has paid 200 for a 50% shareholding in a subsidiary with shareholders' equity of 100. A capital increase of 80 then takes place valuing the subsidiary at a total of 400. Since the parent company does not take up its allocation, its shareholding is diluted from 50% to 41.67%.

The parent company's share of the subsidiary's equity decreases from $50\% \times 100 = 50$ to $41.67\% \times (100 + 80) = 75$, which generates a nonrecurrent gain of $75 - 50 = 25$. This profit of 25 corresponds exactly to the profit that the parent company would have made by selling an interest of $50\% - 41.67\% = 8.33\%$ based on a valuation of 400 and a cost price of 100 for 100%, since $25 = 8.33\% \times (400 - 100)$.

3/How should financial analysts treat them?

Dilution gains and losses generate an accounting profit, whereas the parent company has not received any cash payments. They are by their very nature nonrecurring. Otherwise, the group would soon have no subsidiaries left. Naturally, they do not form part of a company's normal earnings power and so they should be totally disregarded.

Section 7.7
Exchangeable bonds

1/What are exchangeable bonds?

Exchangeable bonds are bonds issued by a company that may be redeemed at the request of their holders into shares of a company other than the issuer of the bonds or in cash.

2/How are they accounted for?

Exchangeable bonds are accounted for as financial debt.

3/How should financial analysts treat them?

Financial analysts must treat exchangeable bonds as financial debt as they will be redeemed either in cash or in shares of a company other than the issuer, and never in shares of the issuer. They have no equity component at all.

Section 7.8
Goodwill

See Chapter 6.

Section 7.9
Intangible fixed assets

These primarily encompass startup costs, capitalised development costs, patents, licences, concessions and similar rights, leasehold rights, brands, market share, software and goodwill arising on acquisitions (see Chapter 6).

Under IAS, a company is required to recognise an intangible asset (at cost) if and only if:

- it is probable that the future economic benefits that are attributable to the asset will flow to the company; and if
- the cost of the asset can be reliably measured.

Internally generated goodwill, brands, mastheads, publishing titles, customer lists should not be recognized as intangible assets. Internally generated goodwill is expensed as incurred. Costs on starting up a business, on training, on advertising, on relocating or reorganizing a company receive the same treatment.

This line item requires special attention since companies have some degree of latitude in treating these items that now represent a significant portion of companies' balance sheets.

1/Startup costs

(a) What are startup costs?

Startup costs are costs incurred in relation to the creation and the development of a company, such as incorporation, customer canvassing and advertising costs incurred when the business first starts operating, together with capital increase, merger and conversion fees.

(b) How are they accounted for?

Startup costs are to be expensed as incurred under IAS. In the US, pre-operating costs may be included in "Other noncurrent assets" and are generally amortised over 3–5 years.

(c) How should financial analysts treat them?

It is easy to analyse such costs from a financial perspective. They have no value and should thus be deducted from the company's shareholders' equity.

2/Research and development costs

(a) What are research and development costs?

These costs are those incurred by a company on research and development for its own benefit.

(b) How are they accounted for?

Under IAS, research costs are expensed as incurred in line with the conservatism principle governing the unpredictable nature of such activities.

Development costs should be capitalised on the balance sheet if the following conditions are met:

- the project or product is clearly identifiable and its costs measurable;
- the product's feasibility can be demonstrated;
- the company intends to produce, market or use the product or project;
- the existence of a market for the project or product can be demonstrated;
- the utility of the product for the company, where it is intended for internal use, can be demonstrated;
- the company has or will have the resources to see the project through to completion and use or market the end product.

The recommended amortisation period is not longer than 20 years and shorter if the useful economic life is known.

Under US GAAP, research and development costs cannot be capitalised.

(c) Financial analysis

We recommend leaving development costs in intangible fixed assets, while monitoring closely any increases in this category, since those could represent an attempt to hide losses.

3/ BRANDS AND MARKET SHARE

(a) What are brands and market share?

These are brands or market share purchased from third parties and valued upon their first-time consolidation by their new parent company.

(b) How are they accounted for?

Brands are not valued in the accounts unless they have been acquired. This gives rise to an accounting deficiency, which is especially critical in the mass consumer (e.g., food, textiles, automotive sectors) and luxury goods industries, particularly from a valuation standpoint. Brands have considerable value, so it makes no sense whatsoever not to take them into account in a company valuation. As we saw in Chapter 6, the allocation of goodwill on first-time consolidation to brands and market share leads to an accumulation of such assets on groups' balance sheets. For instance, LVMH carries brands for €4bn on its balance sheet, which thus account for one-quarter of its capital employed. Since the amortisation of brands is not tax-deductible in most countries, it has become common practice not to amortise such assets, all the more so as they have an indefinite life. Brands are at most written down, where appropriate.

Under IAS, market share cannot be carried on the balance sheet unless the company has protection enabling it to protect or control its customer relationships (which is difficult to get and demonstrate).

(c) How financial analysts should treat them?

Some analysts, especially those working for banks, regard brands as having nil value from a financial standpoint. Such a view leads to deducting these items peremptorily from shareholders' equity. We beg to differ.

These items usually add considerably to a company's valuation, even though they may be intangible. For instance, what value would a top fashion house or a consumer goods company have without its brands?

4/Conclusion

To sum up, our approach to intangible fixed items is as follows: the higher the book value of intangibles, the lower their market value is likely to be; and the lower their book value, the more valuable they are likely to be. This situation is attributable to the accounting and financial policy of a profitable company that seeks to minimise as much as possible its tax expense by expensing every possible cost. Conversely, an ailing company or one that has made a very large acquisition may seek to maximise its intangible assets in order to keep its net profit and shareholders' equity in positive territory.

From a financial standpoint, intangible fixed assets form a key part of a company's value. This said, we believe that their book value is purely formal and has little to do with financial reality.

Readers familiar with traditional accounting must understand that no difference is now made between:

- intangible fixed assets that are by nature immune to wear and tear and, thus, not subject to amortisation, aside from writedowns in the event of a crisis; and
- tangible fixed assets that are depreciated.

Intangible assets with finite lives are amortised over their useful life. The International Accounting Standards Board (IASB) also requires that the relevant intangible assets undergo an impairment test each year to verify that their net book value is consistent with the recoverable value of the corresponding assets. The recoverable value is defined as the highest of:

- the value in use – i.e., the present value of the cash flows expected to be realised from the asset;
- the net selling price – i.e., the amount obtainable from the sale of an asset in an arm's length transaction, less the costs of disposal.

From this standpoint, it would be sufficient for one of these two amounts to be higher than an asset's book value for the asset not to be written down. But if the result of the impairment review is negative, the intangible asset has to be written down by recognising an impairment loss.

Intangible assets with indefinite lives are not amortised but they are assessed for impairment at least every year.

US rules are very similar to the IASB's.

Depreciation and amortisation indicate a desire to reflect the turnover in fixed assets, be they tangible or intangible, and thus recognise the ephemeral nature of all assets.

Section 7.10
INVENTORIES

1/WHAT ARE INVENTORIES?

Inventories include items used as part of the company's operating cycle. More specifically, they are:

- used up in the production process (inventories of raw materials and goods for resale);
- sold as they are (inventories of finished goods) or sold at the end of a transformation process that is either underway or will take place in the future (work in progress).

2/HOW ARE THEY ACCOUNTED FOR?

(a) Costs that should be included in inventories

The way inventories are valued varies according to their nature: supplies of raw materials and goods for resale or finished products and work in progress. Supplies are valued at acquisition cost, including the purchase price before taxes, customs duties and related purchase costs. Finished products and work in progress are valued at production cost, which includes the acquisition cost of raw materials used, plus direct and indirect production costs insofar as the latter may reasonably be allocated to the production of an item.

Costs must be calculated based on normal levels of activity, since allocating the costs of below-par business levels would be equivalent to deferring losses to future periods and artificially inflating profit for the current year. In practice, this calculation is not always properly performed, so we would advise readers to closely follow the cost allocation.

Financial charges, research and development costs and general and administrative costs are not usually included in the valuation of inventories unless specific operating conditions justify such a decision. Interim interest payments[4] may be included in the cost of inventories where the production cycle is very long.

4 *Interest on capital borrowed to finance production.*

In all sectors of activity where inventories account for a significant proportion of the assets, we would strongly urge readers to study closely the impact of inventory valuation methods on the company's net income.

(b) Valuation methods

Under IAS, there are three main methods for valuing inventories:

- the weighted average cost method;
- the FIFO (First In, First Out) method;
- the identified purchase cost method.

Weighted average cost consists in valuing items withdrawn from the inventory at their weighted average cost, which is equal to the total purchase cost divided by quantities purchased.

The **FIFO** method values inventory withdrawals at the cost of the item that has been held in inventory for the longest.

The **identified purchase** cost is used for noninterchangeable items and goods or services produced and assigned to specific projects.

For items that are interchangeable, the IASB allows the weighted average cost and FIFO methods but no longer accepts the LIFO method (Last In, First Out) that values inventory withdrawals at the cost of the most recent addition to the inventory. US GAAPs permit all methods (including LIFO) but the identified cost method.

During periods of inflation, the FIFO method enables a company to post a higher profit than under the LIFO method. The FIFO method values items withdrawn from the inventory at the purchase cost of the items that were held for longest and thus at the lowest cost, hence a high net income. The LIFO method produces a smaller net income as it values items withdrawn from the inventory at the most recent and, thus, the highest purchase cost. The net income figure generated by the weighted average cost method lies midway between these two figures.

Analysts need to be particularly careful when a company changes its inventory valuation method. These changes, which must be disclosed and justified in the notes to the accounts, make it harder to carry out comparisons between periods and may artificially inflate net profit or help to curb a loss.

Finally, where the market value of an inventory item is less than its calculated carrying amount, the company is obliged to recognise an impairment loss for the difference (i.e., an impairment loss on current assets).

3/How should financial analysts treat them?

First, let us reiterate the importance of inventories from a financial standpoint. Inventories are assets booked by recognising deferred costs. Assuming quantities remain unchanged, the higher the carrying amount of inventories, the lower future profits will be. Put more precisely, assuming inventory volumes remain constant in real terms, **valuation methods do not affect net profit for a given period**. But, depending on the method used, inventory receives a higher or lower valuation, making shareholders' equity higher or lower accordingly.

When inventories are being built up, the higher the carrying amount of inventories, the faster profits will appear. The reverse is true when inventories are decreasing. Overvalued inventories that are being run down generate a fall in net income.

Hence the reticence of certain managers to scale down their production even when demand contracts. Finally, we note that, tax-related effects apart, inventory valuation methods have no impact on a company's cash position.

From a financial standpoint, it is true to say that the higher the level of inventories, the greater the vulnerability and uncertainty affecting net income for the given period. We recommend adopting a cash-oriented approach if, in addition, there is no market serving as a point of reference for valuing inventories, such as in the building and public infrastructure sectors. In such circumstances, cash generated by operating activities is a much more reliable indicator than net income, which is much too heavily influenced by the application of inventory valuation methods.

Inventories are merely accruals (deferred costs), which are always slightly speculative and arbitrary in nature, even when accounting rules are applied bona fide.

Consequently, **during inflationary periods**, inventories carry unrealised capital gains that are larger when inventories are moving slower. In the accounts, these gains will appear only as these inventories are being sold, even though these gains are there already. When prices are falling, inventories carry real losses that will appear only gradually in the accounts, unless the company writes down inventories.

The only financial approach that makes sense would be to work on a replacement cost basis and, thus, to recognise gains and losses incurred on inventories each year. In some sectors of activity where inventories move very slowly, this approach seems particularly important. In 1993, champagne houses carried inventories at prices that were well above their replacement cost. We firmly believe that had inventories been written down to their replacement cost, the ensuing crisis in the sector would have been less severe. The companies would have recognised losses in one year and then posted decent profits the next instead of resorting to all kinds of creative solutions to defer losses. The same can be argued regarding the loan portfolios carried by the Japanese banks in the early 2000s.

Section 7.11
LEASES

1/WHAT ARE LEASES?

Leases allow a company to use some of its operating fixed assets (i.e., buildings, plant and other fixed assets) under a rental system. In certain cases, the company may purchase the asset at the end of the contract for a predetermined and usually very low amount (see p. 959).

Leases pose two relatively complicated problems for external financial analysts:

- First, leases are used by companies to finance the assets. Even if those items are not shown on the balance sheet, they may represent a considerable part of a company's assets.
- Second, they represent a commitment whose extent varies depending on the type of contract:
  - equipment leasing may be treated as similar to debt, depending on the length of the period during which the agreement may not be terminated;
  - real estate leasing for buildings may not be treated as actual debt in view of the termination clause contained in the contract. Nonetheless, the utility of the leased property usually leads the company to see out the initially determined length of the lease, and the termination of a lease may then be treated as the early repayment of a borrowing (financed by the sale of the relevant asset).

2/HOW ARE THEY ACCOUNTED FOR?

A lease is either a **finance lease** or an **operating lease**.

A finance lease[5] according to the IASB is "a lease that transfers substantially all the risk and rewards incident to ownership of an asset. Title may or may not eventually be transferred."[6]

An operating lease is a lease that is not a finance lease.

Under IAS, finance leases are capitalised, which means they are recorded under fixed assets and a corresponding amount is booked under financial debt.

The lease payments to the lessor are treated partly as a reduction in financial debt and partly as financial expense. The capitalised asset under a finance lease is depreciated over its life. Accordingly, no rental costs are recorded on the income statement, merely financial and depreciation costs.

Operating leases are not capitalised and are treated as rentals.

Sale and leaseback transactions, where an asset is sold only to be taken back immediately under a lease (see Chapter 47), are restated as follows: any capital gain on the disposal is deferred and recognised in income over the duration of the lease for finance leases or immediately for operating leases.

5 *Capital lease in the United States.*

6 *IAS 17.*

3/HOW SHOULD FINANCIAL ANALYSTS TREAT THEM?

As the reader can see, the distinction between a finance lease and an operating lease is fairly vague; it remains nonetheless a vital one for analysing the real level of a group's indebtedness.

US GAAP contain precise criteria (see p. 959) used in Europe. But they may be too precise, as companies wanting to avoid capitalising leases in their balance sheet may artificially structure leases in a way to avoid being qualified as a finance lease, so as not to show additional liabilities.

Eventually, accountants may decide that all leases are financial leases. Such a decision is not as dramatic as it seems at first sight since, when a lessee signs a contract with a lessor and pays it a rent, this commitment gives rise to a liability, at least from a financial point of view.

So the reader should beware of a company with large operating leases. They add fixed costs to its income statement and raise its breakeven point.

Section 7.12
MANDATORY CONVERTIBLE BONDS

1/WHAT ARE MANDATORY CONVERTIBLE BONDS?

Mandatory convertible bonds are bonds that initially pay a rate of interest not linked to the company's earnings performance and are redeemed in shares of the issuing company. For further details, please refer to Chapter 30 on hybrid securities.

2/HOW ARE THEY ACCOUNTED FOR?

Proceeds from the issue of mandatory convertible bonds are allocated between debt (present value of coupons) and equity (present value of shares to be issued to redeem the bonds). Such treatment is due to IASB seeing mandatory convertible bonds as compound financial instruments made up of a straight bond and a deferred issue of shares.

3/HOW SHOULD FINANCIAL ANALYSTS TREAT THEM?

We treat mandatory convertible bonds as equity, since this is what they are certain to become. For valuation purposes, interest payments net of tax should be reversed. This boosts net profit and increases the number of shares outstanding to reflect those to be issued upon redemption of the bonds.

Section 7.13
OFF-BALANCE-SHEET COMMITMENTS

1/WHAT ARE OFF-BALANCE-SHEET COMMITMENTS?

The balance sheet shows all the items resulting from transactions that were realised. But it is hard to show in company accounts transactions that have not yet been realised (e.g., the remaining payments due under an operating lease, orders placed but not yet recorded or paid for because the goods have not yet been delivered).

And yet such items may have a significant impact on a company's financial position.

2/How are they accounted for?

These commitments may have:

- either a positive impact – they are not recorded on the balance sheet, but are stated in the notes to the accounts, hence the term "off-balance-sheet". These are known as **contingent assets**;
- or a negative impact that causes a provision to be set aside if likely to be realised, or gives rise to a note to the accounts if it remains a possibility only. These are called **contingent liabilities**.

3/How financial analysts should treat them?

Analysts should always be concerned that a company may show some items as off-balance entries while they should actually appear on the balance sheet. It is therefore very important to analyse off-balance-sheet items because they reflect:

- the degree of accounting ingenuity used by the company, this judgement provides the basis for an opinion about the quality of the published accounts;
- the subsequent arrival on the balance sheet of the effects of the commitments (purchase of fixed assets or purchase commitment that will have to be financed with debt, guarantees given to a failed third party that will lead to losses and payments with nothing received in return).

The key points to watch for are as follows:

	Item	Comments
Financial commitments	Sureties and guarantees granted (including representations and warranties, product warranties).	Analyse the situation of the relevant entity to estimate the size of the commitment.
	Commitments given as partners, whether unlimited or not, put options written on assets.	
	Claw-back commitments.	Same as above.
Liabilities	Debts backed by tangible collateral.	Reflects bankers' confidence in the company.
Other	Orders to suppliers of fixed assets and other purchase commitments.	These will alter the balance sheet in the short term.
	Transactions involving interest rate, currency or commodities futures and options (forwards, swaps, options).	To be assessed with regard to the company's financial strength.

7 *That is, Future Rate Agreements (FRAs), swaps, options, see Chapter 48 for further details.*

Under IAS, companies must disclose information about instruments used to manage interest rate and currency risks,[7] whether or not they are shown in the accounts. Consequently, future cash flows and their probability of occurrence may be assessed.

For each type of financial instrument, a company must specify its nature and how it is accounted for. There has been a very lively debate between the standard-setting bodies over how the financial instruments market value should be computed (i.e., marked to market) or even included on the balance sheet.

When companies are sold, the seller usually gives the buyer representations and warranties (see Chapter 42), which are included in off-balance-sheet items.

8 *Also called "preferred shares".*

Section 7.14
PREFERENCE SHARES[8]

1/WHAT ARE PREFERENCE SHARES?

Preference shares combine characteristics of shares and bonds. They may have a fixed dividend (bonds pay interest), a redemption price (bonds), a redemption date (bonds). If the company were to be liquidated, the preference shareholders would be paid a given amount before the common shareholders would have a right to receive any of the proceeds. Sometimes the holders of preference shares may participate in earnings beyond the ordinary dividend rate; have a cumulative feature allowing their dividends in arrears, if any, to be paid in full before shareholders can get a dividend, etc.

9 *For more details about preference shares see Chapter 30.*

Most of the time, in exchange for these financial advantages, the preference shares have no voting rights. They are known as *actions à dividende prioritaire* (ADP) in France, *Vorzugsaktien* in Germany, *azioni risparmio* in Italy, preferred stock in the US, etc.[9]

2/HOW ARE THEY ACCOUNTED FOR?

Under IAS, preference shares are accounted either as equity or financial debt, depending on the results of a "substance over form" analysis. If the preference share:

10 *Or determinable.*

- provides for mandatory redemption by the issuer at a fixed[10] date in the future, or
- if the holder has the right to put the preference share to the issuer in the future, or
- if the preference share pays a fixed dividend regardless of the net income of the company,

it is a financial debt.

Under US GAAP, preference shares are treated as equity.

3/ How should financial analysts treat them?

Let's call a spade a spade: if the preference share meets all our criteria for consideration as equity:

- returns linked solely to the company's earnings,
- no repayment commitment,
- claims on the company ranking last in the event of liquidation,

then it is equity. If not, it is a financial debt.

Section 7.15
PERPETUAL SUBORDINATED LOANS AND NOTES

1/ What are perpetual subordinated loans and notes?

As their name suggests, these instruments are never redeemable and thus continue to pay interest as long as the borrower remains solvent.

They have no duration because there is no contractual undertaking for repayment, which may take place when the issuer so wishes. **If the issuer is liquidated, note holders rank for repayment after other creditors** (as they are subordinated loans) but before shareholders.

2/ How are they accounted for?

Perpetuals are booked under financial debt.

3/ How should financial analysts treat them?

We regard perpetual subordinated notes as financial debt. They do not meet one of the three criteria needed to be ranked as equity: their returns are not linked to the company's earnings.

Section 7.16
PROVISIONS

1/ General principles

The term "provision" covers a wide range of different items:

- **impairment losses**[11] that recognise a diminution in a company's wealth owing to impairment in the value of an asset or the likely loss on an asset due, for example, to the risk of uncollectibility;

11 *Not generally referred to as "provisions" in this book.*

- **provisions** that reflect an increase in the company's liabilities in the shorter or longer term relating to a charge that has not yet been incurred by the financial year-end, but is likely to arise and is connected with operations carried out during the year. Provisions may cover restructuring, warranty, environmental, litigation, pension costs, etc., which can be reliably estimated;
- **tax-regulated provisions** that stem from tax concessions and have nothing to do with future losses or liabilities (strictly speaking they are not provisions).

Aside from tax-regulated provisions, provisions are set aside in anticipation of a charge. Additions to provisions reduce net income in the year they are set aside and not in the year the corresponding charge will actually be incurred. Provisions will actually be written back the year the corresponding charge will be incurred, thereby neutralising the impact of recognising the charges in the income statement. Additions to provisions are therefore equivalent to an anticipation of costs.

2/Impairment losses

(a) What are impairment losses?

Impairment losses are set aside to cover capital losses or those that may be reasonably anticipated on assets. They cover mainly depreciation for doubtful receivables, inventories or goodwill and other intangible assets.

(b) How are they accounted for?

These provisions are netted off against the value of the corresponding assets. Impairment must relate to a specific and individual asset, be permanent in nature and be borne during the period in which it is recognised. Groups tend to be discreet about impairment in their consolidated tangible fixed assets, and analysts will be very lucky to find any detailed explanations in the notes to the accounts.

(c) How should financial analysts treat them?

Impairment losses are netted off directly against assets and, provided that these losses are justified, there is no need for any restatements. We consider impairment losses on current assets as lost profit, which should thus come to reduce EBITDA.[12] Conversely, we regard impairment losses on tangible fixed assets as nonrecurrent items.

As discussed on p. 167, we consider impairment losses on intangible fixed assets (including goodwill) as nonoperating items to be excluded from EBITDA and EBIT.[13]

3/Restructuring provisions

(a) What are restructuring provisions?

Restructuring charges consist in taking a heavy upfront charge against earnings in a given year to cover a restructuring programme (site closures, redundancies, etc.).

12 *Earnings Before Interest, Taxes, Depreciation and Amortisation.*

13 *Earnings Before Interest and Taxes.*

The future costs of this restructuring programme are eliminated through the gradual writeback of the provision, thereby smoothing future earnings performance.

(b) How are they accounted for?

Restructuring costs represent a liability if they derive from an obligation for a company *vis-à-vis* third parties or members of its workforce. This liability must arise from a decision by the relevant authority and be confirmed prior to the end of the accounting period by the announcement of this decision to third parties and the affected members of the workforce. The company must not anticipate anything more from those third parties or members of its workforce. Conversely, a relocation leading to profits further ahead in the future should not give rise to such a provision.

(c) How should financial analysts treat them?

The whole crux of the matter boils down to whether restructuring provisions should be recorded under operating or nonoperating items: the former are recurrent in nature, unlike the latter. Some groups consider productivity-enhancing restructuring charges as operating items and business shutdowns as nonrecurrent items. This may be acceptable when the external analyst is able to verify the breakdown between these two categories. Other companies tend to treat the entire restructuring charge as nonrecurrent items.

Our view is that in today's world of rapid technological change and endless restructuring in one division or another, restructuring charges are usually structural in nature, which means they should be charged against operating profit. The situation may be different for SMEs,[14] where those charges are more likely to be of a nonoperating nature.

14 *Small- and Medium-sized Enterprises.*

On the liability side of the balance sheet, we treat these restructuring provisions as comparable to financial debt.

4/Provisions for employee benefits and pensions

(a) What are provisions for employee benefits and pensions?

Pension and related commitments include severance payments, early retirement and related payments, special retirement plans, top-up plans providing guaranteed resources and healthcare benefits, life insurance and similar entitlements that, in some cases, are granted under employment contracts and collective labour agreements.

A distinction is made between:

- **defined benefit plans**, where the employer commits to the amount or guarantees the level of benefits defined by the agreement. This is a commitment to a certain level of performance, usually according to the final salary and length of service of the retiring employee. These plans may be managed internally or externally;
- **defined contribution plans**, where the employer commits to making regular payments to an external organisation. Those payments are paid back to

employees when they retire in the form of pensions together with the corresponding investment revenue. The size of the pension payments depends on the investment performance of the external organisation managing the plan. The employer does not guarantee the level of the pension paid (a resource-related obligation). This applies to most national social security systems.

(b) How are they accounted for?

Only defined benefit plans require specific information disclosures in accounts. Contributions to defined contribution plans are expensed each year as incurred. A defined benefit plan gives rise to a liability corresponding to the **actuarial present value of all the pension payments due at the balance sheet closing date** (Projected Benefit Obligation – PBO).

In countries where independent pension funds handle the company's commitments to its workforce, the market value of the pension fund's assets are set off against the actuarial value of the liability. The method used to assess the actuarial value is the projected unit credit method that models the benefits vested with the entire workforce of the company at the assessment date. It is based on certain demographic and staff turnover assumptions (resignations, redundancies, mortality rates, etc.).

Each year, changes in actuarial assumptions (especially the discount rate) and changes to retirement benefit plans give rise to adjustments in the calculation of pension liabilities. These adjustments may be recognised immediately in the income statement. They may be amortised on a straight-line basis over the service life of employees for amounts exceeding 10% of the provision for retirement benefit plans.

In a move that has broadened the debate, the IASB has stipulated that all benefits payable to employees – i.e., retirement savings, pensions, insurance and healthcare cover and severance payments – should be accounted for. These standards state in detail how the employee liabilities deriving from these benefits should be calculated. US accounting standards also provide for the inclusion of retirement benefits and commitments other than just pension obligations; i.e., mainly the reimbursement of medical costs by companies during the active service life of employees.

Consequently, the net pension costs in the income statement for a given year are mainly composed of:

- a service cost, which represents the present value of benefits earned by employees during the year;
- an interest cost, which represents increase in the present value of the pensions payments due at the balance sheet closing date since last year due to the passage of time;
- an expected return on assets, which represents what management expects to earn on the pension plan assets;
- an amortisation of unrecognised profit or loss on the pension plan assets if they exceed 10% of the projected benefit obligation or the fair value of plan assets, whichever is greater.

(c) How should financial analysts treat them?

How then should we treat provisions for employees' benefits and pensions that may in some cases reach very high levels, as is often the case with German companies?

Our view is that provisions for retirement benefit plans are very similar to a financial liability *vis-à-vis* employees. This liability is adjusted each year to reflect the actuarial (and automatic) increase in employees' accrued benefits, just like a zero-coupon bond,[15] where the company recognises an annual financial charge that is not paid until the bond is redeemed. Consequently, we suggest treating such provisions minus the market value of the pension fund's assets as a financial debt.

15 *See p. 966.*

In the income statement, we regard only pension service costs as operating costs and the balance of net pension costs (interest costs, notional return on pension assets, amortisation of various types, etc.) as financial charges. Consequently the balance of net pension costs must be deducted from EBITDA and EBIT and added to financial charges unless the company has already applied this rule in its accounts, as it happens sometimes.

Where defined benefit plans are contracted out to a third-party company, the charge is booked under insurance premiums and no provisions appear on the liabilities side of the balance sheet. Hence, there is no need for restatements. This said, the involvement of the third party does not free the company from all future liabilities, because this third party is obliged to do its best rather than to guarantee the results.

5/ PROVISIONS FOR DEFERRED TAXATION

See deferred taxation.

Section 7.17
STOCK OPTIONS

1/ WHAT ARE STOCK OPTIONS?

Stock options are options to buy existing or to subscribe to new shares at a fixed price. Their maturity is generally between 3 and 10 years after their issuance. They are granted free of charge to company employees, usually senior executives. Their purpose is to motivate executives to manage the company as efficiently as possible, thereby increasing its value and delivering them a financial gain when they exercise the stock options. As we will see in Chapter 32, they represent one of the ways of aligning the interests of managers with those of shareholders.

2/ HOW ARE THEY ACCOUNTED FOR?

Under IAS, the issuance of fully vested stock options is presumed to relate to past service, requiring the full amount of the grant date fair value to be expensed immediately. The issuance of stock options to employees with, say, a 4-year vesting

16 *Which means that stock options cannot be exercised before at least 4 years.*

17 *For more see Chapter 29.*

period[16] is considered to relate to services over the vesting period. Therefore, the fair value of the share-based payment, determined at the grant date, should be expensed on the income statement over the vesting period. The corresponding entry is an increase in equity for the same amount.

Stock options are usually valued using standard option-pricing models[17] with some alterations or discounts to take into account cancellations of stock options during the vesting period (some holders may resign), conditions which may be attached to their exercise such as the share price reaching a minimum threshold or outperforming an index.

3/HOW FINANCIAL ANALYSTS SHOULD TREAT THEM

We are not in favour of expensing stock options as:

- the issuance of stock options means that existing shareholders potentially transfer some of their ownership interests to employees without any impoverishment for the company;
- there is no cost for the company itself, because stock option flows do not require the company to sacrifice any cash or other assets at any point in time;
- cost recognition is inconsistent with the definition of a cost. If services are received in a stock option payment, there is no transaction or event that meets the definition of a cost: there is no outflow of assets and no liability is incurred.

18 *For a valuation exercise see p. 568.*

If the company has expensed stock options and if the amounts are material, we recommend reversing the relevant entries.[18]

Section 7.18
TANGIBLE FIXED ASSETS

1/WHAT ARE TANGIBLE FIXED ASSETS?

19 *Known as PPE.*

Tangible fixed assets (property, plant and equipment[19] in US accounting) comprise **land, buildings, technical assets, industrial equipment and tools, other tangible fixed assets and tangible fixed assets in process.**

Together with intangible assets, tangible fixed assets form the backbone of a company, namely its **industrial and commercial base**.

2/HOW ARE THEY ACCOUNTED FOR?

Tangible assets are booked at acquisition costs and depreciated over time (except for land). IAS allow them to be revalued at fair value, but this option is not widely used by companies except following an acquisition where it is requisite for the

20 *See p. 82.*

tangible assets of the purchased company.[20]

Some tangible fixed assets may be very substantial; they may have increased in value (e.g., a head office, a store, a plant located in an urban centre) and thus become much more valuable than their historical costs suggests. Conversely, some tangible assets have virtually no value outside the company's operations. Though it may be an exaggeration, we can say that they have no more value than certain startup costs.

It is clear that showing assets at historical cost, in line with the historical cost principle, does not have any benefits for the analyst from a financial standpoint.

Note that certain companies also include interim financial expense into internally produced fixed assets (provided that this cost is clearly identified). IAS provide for the possibility of including borrowing costs related to the acquisition cost or the production of fixed assets when it is likely that they will give rise to future economic benefits for the company and that their cost be may reliably assessed. Under US GAAP, these financial costs must be included in the cost of fixed assets.

3/How should financial analysts treat them?

The accounting policies applied with respect to fixed assets may have a significant impact on various parameters, including the company's or group's net income and apparent solvency level.

For instance, a decision to capitalise a charge by recording it as an asset **increases net income in the corresponding year, but depresses earnings performance in subsequent periods because it leads to higher depreciation charges**.

The way tangible fixed assets are accounted for:

- is formal in a capital-employed analysis of the balance sheet;
- is partial in an analysis seeking to establish the company's value or its solvency.

Accordingly, financial analysts need to take a much closer look at changes in fixed assets rather than fixed assets at a given point in time. The advantage of movements is that they are shown at their current value.

Section 7.19
TREASURY SHARES

1/What are treasury shares?

Treasury shares are shares that a company or its subsidiaries own in the company after buying them either for the purpose:

- of stabilising the share price (i.e., for listed companies); or
- of being granted to employees – i.e., as part of a stock option plan; or
- of being remitted to holders of convertible bonds if they request conversion of their bonds into shares; or
- simply because they were considered at a given moment to be a good investment.

We will examine in more detail how such situations arise in Chapter 38.

2/HOW ARE THEY ACCOUNTED FOR?

Under IAS, treasury shares are systematically deducted from shareholders' equity.

3/HOW SHOULD FINANCIAL ANALYSTS TREAT THEM?

Whatever their original purpose, we recommend deducting treasury shares from assets and from shareholders' equity if this has not yet been done by accountants. From a financial standpoint, we believe that share repurchases are equivalent to a capital reduction, regardless of the legal treatment. Likewise, if the company sells the shares, we recommend that these sales be analysed as a capital increase.

Treasury shares must thus be subtracted from the number of shares outstanding when calculating earnings per share or valuing the equity.

BIBLIOGRAPHY

B. Lev, Intangibles at a crossroads: What's next? *Financial Executive*, 34–39, March/April 2002.

To better understand accounting rules:

International Financial Reporting Standards, a yearly publication from the IASB.
B. Epstein, A. Mirza, *Interpretation and Application of International Accounting Standards*, published every year by John Wiley & Sons.
www.fasb.org, the US accounting setter website.
www.iasb.org.uk, the IASB website.
www.iasplus.com, the Deloitte website dedicated to IFRS.

APPENDIX: MAIN DIFFERENCES BETWEEN INTERNATIONAL AND US ACCOUNTING STANDARDS

	IAS	US GAAP
Capitalisation of R&D costs	Research costs must be expensed. Development costs may be treated as intangible fixed assets provided that a whole series of conditions are met related to: • the technical feasibility of the project such that the final asset may be used or sold; • the intention of completing the project; • the ability to sell or use the asset; • the way in which the asset will generate future profits; • the ability to measure cost related to the project's development.	All R&D costs without exception must be expensed as incurred.
Consolidation policy for subsidiaries	Control (look to governance and risk and rewards).	Majority voting rights.
Construction contracts	The percentage of completion method is the only method accepted.	The percentage of completion method is the recommended method. The completed contract method may also be used.
Convertible debt	Split the convertible debt into its debt and equity components at issuance.	Classified as a debt.
Extraordinary items	Prohibited.	Permitted but restricted to infrequent, unusual and rare items that affect profit and loss.
Foreign currency hedging	Currency futures belong to the group of instruments subject to IAS 39 and must thus be marked to market (with capital gains and losses included in the income statement). This rule may be overridden in certain cases when the instrument is clearly identified as a hedge. There are three clearly identified categories of hedge: • fair value hedges for an instrument denominated in a foreign currency; • cash flow hedges; • investment hedges.	Identical to IAS rules except for the fact that fair value hedges include firm commitments (e.g., a signed order).
Impairment loss subsequent reversal	Required if certain criteria are met, except for goodwill.	Prohibited.
Intangible assets reevaluation	Permitted if the intangible assets trades in an active market.	Prohibited.

	IAS	US GAAP
Interim financial expenses on internally produced fixed assets	Could be included in the cost of fixed assets.	Must be included in the cost of fixed assets.
Investment accounting in parent company financial statements	Either at cost or fair value but not equity method.	At cost or equity value.
Inventory cost	LIFO is prohibited.	LIFO is permitted.
Joint ventures	Consolidated with the equity method or the proportionate consolidation.	Generally the equity method is used.
Negative goodwill	Recognised immediately as a gain.	Allocated on a pro-rata basis against the carrying amounts of certain acquired nonfinancial assets with any excess recognised as extraordinary gain.
Preference shares	A "substance-over-form" analysis is carried out before deciding whether to include them in equity or financial debt.	Rank as equity.
Provisions	Best estimate to settle the obligation.	Low end of the range of possible amounts.
Special purpose entity (SPE)	Consolidated if controlled.	Consolidated if certain criteria for qualifying SPE are not met, depends on whether the SPE has sufficient level of equity at risk.
Startup costs	The costs arising in the period following an acquisition/receipt of an asset (e.g., a plant), until the asset enters service may be capitalised.	All startup costs are expensed as incurred.
Stock options	Expensed in the P&L based on fair value.	Likely the move towards IAS.
Tangible assets	Valued at historical costs or fair value.	Valued at historical costs.

Adapted from "Key differences between IFS and US GAAP", June 2004, Deloitte.

In this part, we will gradually introduce more aspects of financial analysis, including how to analyse wealth creation, investments either in working capital or capital expenditure and their profitability. But we first need to look at how to carry out an economic and strategic analysis of a company.

Chapter 8
HOW TO PERFORM A FINANCIAL ANALYSIS

Opening up the toolbox

Before embarking on an examination of a company's accounts, readers should take the time to:

- carry out a strategic and economic assessment, with particular attention paid to the characteristics of the sector in which the company operates, the quality of its positions and how well its production model, distribution network and ownership structure fit with its business strategy;
- carefully read and critically analyse the auditors' report and the accounting rules and principles adopted by the company to prepare its accounts. These documents describe how the company's economic and financial situation is translated by means of a code (i.e., accounting) into tables of figures (accounts).

Since the aim of financial analysis is to portray a company's economic reality by going beyond just the figures, it is vital to think about what this reality is and how well it is reflected by the figures before embarking on an analysis of the accounts. Otherwise, the resulting analysis may be sterile, highly descriptive and contain very little insight. It would not identify problems until they have shown up in the numbers – i.e., after they have occurred and when it is too late for investors to sell their shares or reduce their credit exposure.

Once this preliminary task has been completed, readers can embark on the standard type of financial analysis that we suggest and use more sophisticated tools, such as credit scoring and ratings.

But, first and foremost, we need to deal with the issue of what financial analysis actually is.

Section 8.1
WHAT IS FINANCIAL ANALYSIS?

1/ WHAT IS FINANCIAL ANALYSIS FOR?

Financial analysis is a tool used by existing and potential shareholders of a company, as well as lenders or rating agencies. For shareholders, financial analysis assesses whether the company is able to create value. It usually involves an analysis of the value of the share and ends with the formulation of a buy or a sell recommendation on the share. For lenders, financial analysis assesses the solvency and liquidity of a company – i.e., its ability to honour its commitments and to repay its debts on time.

We should emphasise, however, that there are not two different sets of processes depending on whether an assessment is being carried out for shareholders or lenders. Even though the purposes are different, the techniques used are the same, for the very simple reason that a value-creating company will be solvent and a value-destroying company will sooner or later face solvency problems. Nowadays, both lenders and shareholders look very carefully at a company's cash flow statement because it shows the company's ability to repay debts to lenders and to generate free cash flows, the key value driver for shareholders.

2/FINANCIAL ANALYSIS IS MORE OF A PRACTICE THAN A THEORY

The purpose of financial analysis, which primarily involves dealing with economic and accounting data, is to provide insight into the reality of a company's situation on the basis of figures. Naturally, knowledge of an economic sector and a company and, more simply, some common sense may easily replace some of the techniques of financial analysis. Very precise conclusions may be made without sophisticated analytical techniques.

Financial analysis should be regarded as **a rigorous approach to the issues facing a business that helps rationalise the study of economic and accounting data**.

3/IT REPRESENTS A RESOLUTELY GLOBAL VISION OF THE COMPANY

It is worth noting that, although financial analysis carried out internally within a company and externally by an outside observer is based on different information, the logic behind it is the same in both cases. Financial analysis is intended to provide a global assessment of the company's current and future position.

Whether carrying out an internal or external analysis, an analyst should endeavour to study the company primarily from the standpoint of an outsider looking **to achieve a comprehensive assessment of abstract data, such as the company's policies and earnings**. Fundamentally speaking, financial analysis is thus a method that helps to describe the company in broad terms on the basis of a few key points.

From a practical standpoint, the analyst has to piece together the policies adopted by the company and its real situation. Therefore, analysts' effectiveness are not measured by their use of sophisticated techniques, but by their ability to uncover evidence of the inaccurateness of the accounting data or of serious problems being concealed. As an example, a company's earnings power may be maintained artificially through a revaluation or through asset disposals, while the company is experiencing serious cash flow problems. In such circumstances, competent analysts will cast doubt on the company's earnings power and track down the root cause of the deterioration in profitability.

We frequently see that external analysts are able to piece together the global economic model of a company and place it in the context of its main competitors. By analysing a company's economic model over the medium term, analysts are able to detect chronic weaknesses and to separate them from temporary glitches. For instance, an isolated incident may be attributable to a precise and nonrecurring factor, whereas a string of several incidents caused by different factors will prompt an external analyst to look for more fundamental problems likely to affect the company as a whole.

Naturally, it is impossible to appreciate the finer points of financial analysis without grasping the fact that a set of accounts represents a compromise between different concerns. Let's consider, for instance, a company that is highly profitable because it has a very efficient operating structure, but also posts a nonrecurrent profit that was "unavoidable". As a result, we see a slight deterioration in its operating ratios. In our view, it is important not to rush into making what may be overhasty judgements. The company probably attempted to adjust the size of the exceptional gain by being very strict in the way that it accounts for operating revenues and charges.

Section 8.2
ECONOMIC ANALYSIS OF COMPANIES

An economic analysis of a company does not require cutting edge expertise in industrial economics or encyclopaedic knowledge of economic sectors. Instead, it entails straightforward reasoning and a good deal of common sense, with an emphasis on:

- analysing the company's market;
- understanding the company's position within its market;
- studying its production model;
- analysing its distribution networks; and
- lastly, identifying what motivates the company's key people.

1/ANALYSIS OF THE COMPANY'S MARKET

Understanding the company's market also generally leads analysts to arrive at conclusions that are important for the analysis of the company as a whole.

(a) What is a market?

First of all, a market is not an economic sector, as statistical institutes, central banks or professional associations would define it. Markets and economic sectors are two completely separate concepts.

What is the market for pay TV operators such as BSkyB, Premiere, Telepiù or Canal+? It is the entertainment market and not just the TV market. Competition comes from cinema multiplexes, DVDs, live sporting events rather than from ITV,

RTL TV, Rai Uno or TF1 that mainly sell advertising slots to advertisers seeking to target the legendary housewife below 50 years of age.

So, what is a market? A market is defined by consistent behaviour – e.g., a product satisfying similar needs, purchased through a similar distribution network by the same customers.

A market is therefore not the same as an economic sector. Rather, it is a niche or space in which a business has some industrial, commercial or service-oriented expertise. It is the arena in which it competes.

Once a market has been defined, it can then be segmented using geographical (i.e., local, regional, national, European, worldwide market) and sociological (luxury, mid-range, entry level products) variables. This is also an obvious tactic by companies seeking to gain protection from their rivals. If such a tactic succeeds, a company will create its own market in which it reigns supreme, as does Club Méditerranée, which is neither a tour operator nor a hotel group, nor a travel agency, but sells a unique product. But, before readers get carried away and rush off to create their very own markets arenas, it is well to remember that a market always comes under threat, sooner or later.

Segmenting markets is never a problem for analysts, but it is vital to get the segmentation right! To say that a manufacturer of tennis rackets has a 30% share of the German racket market may be correct from a statistical standpoint, but is totally irrelevant from an economic standpoint because this is a worldwide market with global brands backed by marketing campaigns featuring international champions. Conversely, a 40% share of the northern Italian cement market is a meaningful number, because cement is a heavy product with a low unit value that cannot be stored for long and is not usually transported more than 150–200 km from the cement plants.

(b) Market growth

Once a financial analyst has studied and defined a market, his or her natural reflex is then to attempt to assess the growth opportunities and identify the risk factors. The simplest form of growth is organic volume growth – i.e., selling more and more products.

This said, it is worth noting that volume growth is not always as easy as it may sound in developed countries, given the weak demographic growth (0.2% p.a. in Europe). Booming markets do exist (such as DVDs), but others are rapidly contracting (nuclear power stations, daily newspapers, etc.) or are cyclical (transportation, paper production, etc.).

At the end of the day, the most important type of growth is value growth. Let's imagine that we sell a staple product satisfying a basic need, such as bread. Demand does not grow much and, if anything, appears to be on the wane. So we attempt to move upmarket by means of either marketing or packaging, or by innovating. As a result, we decide to switch from selling bread to a whole range of speciality products, such as baguettes, rye bread and farmhouse loaves, and we start charging €0.90, €1.10 or even €1.30, rather than €0.70 per item. The risk of pursuing this strategy is that our rivals may react by focusing on a narrow range of straightforward, unembellished products that sell for less than ours; e.g., a small shop that bakes pre-prepared dough in its ovens or the in-store bakeries at food superstores.

Once we have analysed the type of growth, we need to attempt to predict its duration, and this is no easy task. The famous 17th century letter writer Mme de Sévigné once forecast that coffee was just a fad and would not last for more than a week ... At the other end of the spectrum, it is not uncommon to hear entrepreneurs claiming that their products will revolutionise consumers' lifestyles and even outlast the wheel!

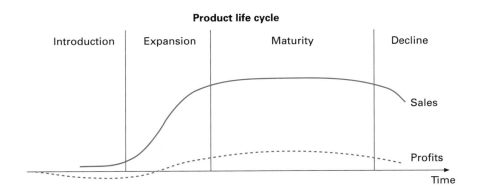

Product life cycle

Introduction   Expansion   Maturity   Decline

Sales

Profits

Time

To tackle the question of market growth, we need to look at the product life cycle.

download

Growth drivers in a developed economy are often highly complex. They may include:

- technological advances, new products (e.g., high-speed Internet connection, etc.);
- changes in the economic situation (e.g., expansion of air travel with the rise in living standards);
- changes in consumer lifestyles (e.g., eating out, etc.);
- changing fashions (e.g., blogs);
- demographic trends (e.g., the popularity of cruises owing to the ageing of the population);
- delayed uptake of a product (e.g., Internet access in France owing to the success of the previous generation Minitel videotext information system).

In its early days, the market is in a constant state of flux, as products are still poorly geared to consumers' needs. During the growth phase, the technological risk has disappeared, the market has become established and expands rapidly, being fairly insensitive to fluctuations in the economy at large. As the market reaches maturity, sales become sensitive to ups and downs in general economic conditions. And, as the market ages and goes into decline, price competition increases and certain market participants fall by the wayside. Those that remain may be able to post very attractive margins, and no more investment is required.

Lastly, readers should note that an expanding sector is not necessarily an attractive sector from a financial standpoint. Where future growth has been over-estimated, supply exceeds demand, even when growth is strong, and all market participants lose money. For instance, after a false start in the 1980s (when the leading player Atari went bankrupt), the video games sector have experienced growth rates of well over 20%, but returns on capital employed of most companies are at best poor. Conversely, tobacco, which is one of the most mature markets in existence, generates a very high level of return on capital employed for the last few remaining companies operating in the sector.

(c) Market risk

Market risk varies according to whether the product in question is original equipment or a replacement item. A product sold as original equipment will also seem more compelling in the eyes of consumers who do not already possess it. And it is the role of advertising to make sure this is how they feel. Conversely, should consumers already own a product, they will always be tempted to delay replacing it until their conditions improve and, thus, to spend their limited funds on another new product. Needs come first! Put another way, replacement products are much more sensitive to general economic conditions than original equipment. For instance, sales in the European motor industry beat all existing records in 2000, when the economy was in excellent shape, but sales slumped to new lows in 2004 when the economic conditions were poorer.

As a result, it is vital for an analyst to establish whether a company's products are acquired as original equipment or as part of a replacement cycle because this directly affects its sensitivity to general economic conditions.

All too often we have heard analysts claim that a particular sector, such as the food industry, does not carry any risk (because we will always need to eat!). These analysts either cannot see the risks or disregard them. Granted, we will always need to eat and drink, but not necessarily in the same way. For instance, eating out is on the increase, while wine consumption is declining, and fresh fruit juice is growing fast, while the average length of mealtimes is on the decline.

Risk also depends on the nature of barriers to entry to the company's market and whether or not alternative products exist. Nowadays, barriers to entry tend to weaken constantly owing to:

- a powerful worldwide trend towards deregulation (there are fewer and fewer legally enshrined monopolies – e.g., in railways or postal services);
- technological advances (e.g., the Internet);
- a strong trend towards internationalisation.

All these factors have increased the number of potential competitors and made the barriers to entry erected by existing players far less sturdy.

For instance, the five record industry majors, Sony, Bertelsmann, Universal, Warner and EMI, had achieved worldwide domination of their market, with a combined market share of 85%. They have nevertheless seen their grip loosened by the development of the Internet and artists' ability to sell their products directly to consumers through music downloads, without even mentioning the impact of piracy!

(d) Market share

The position held by a company in its market is reflected by its market share, which indicates the share of business in the market (in volume or value terms) achieved by the company.

A company with substantial market share has the advantage of:

- some degree of loyalty among its customers, who regularly make purchases from the company. As a result, the company reduces the volatility of its business;
- a position of strength *vis-à-vis* its customers and suppliers. Mass retailers are a perfect example of this;
- an attractive position, which means that any small producer wishing to put itself up for sale, any inventor of a new product or new technique or any talented new graduate will usually come to see this market leader first, because a company with large market share is a force to be reckoned with in its market.

This said, just because market share is quantifiable does not mean that the numbers are always relevant. For instance, market share is meaningless in the construction and public works market (and indeed is never calculated). Customers in this sector do not renew their purchases on a regular basis (e.g., town halls, swimming pools and roads have a long useful life). Even if they do, contracts are awarded through a bidding process, meaning that there is no special link between customers and suppliers. Likewise, building up market share by slashing prices without being able to hold onto the market share accumulated after prices are raised again is pointless. This inability demonstrates the second limit on the importance of market share: the acquisition of market share must create value, otherwise it serves no purpose.

Lastly, market share is not the same as size. For instance, a large share of a small market is far more valuable than middling sales in a vast market.

(e) The competition

If the market is expanding, it is better to have smaller rivals than several large ones with the financial and marketing clout to cream off all the market's expansion. Where possible, it is best not to try to compete against the likes of Microsoft. Conversely, if the market has reached maturity, it is better for the few remaining companies that have specialised in particular niches to have large rivals that will not take the risk of attacking them because the potential gains would be too small. Conversely, a stable market with a large number of small rivals frequently degenerates into a price war that drives some players out of business.

But since a company cannot choose its rivals, it is important to understand what drives them. Some rivals may be pursuing power or scale-related targets (e.g., biggest turnover in the industry) that are frequently far removed from profitability targets. Consequently, it is very hard for groups pursuing profitability targets to grow in such conditions. So, how can a company achieve profitability when its main rivals – e.g., farming cooperatives in the canned vegetables sector – are not profit-driven? It is very hard indeed because it will struggle to develop since it will generate weak profits and thus have few resources at its disposal.

(f) How does competition work?

Roughly speaking, competition is driven either by prices or by products:

- where competition is price-driven, pricing is the main, if not the only factor, that clinches a purchase. Consequently, costs need to be kept under tight control so that products are manufactured as cheaply as possible, product lines need to be pared down to maximise economies of scale and the production process needs to be automated as far as possible, etc. As a result, market share is a key success factor since higher sales volumes help keep down unit costs (see BCG's famous experience curve which showed that unit costs fall by 20% when total production volumes double in size). This is where engineers and financial controllers are most at home! It applies to markets, such as petrol, milk, phone calls, etc.;
- where competition is product-driven, customers make purchases based on after-sales service, quality, image, etc., that are not necessarily pricing-related. Therefore, companies attempt to set themselves apart from their rivals and pay close attention to their sales and customer loyalty techniques. This is where the marketing specialists are in demand! Think about Bang and Olufsen's image, Harrod's atmosphere or the after-sales service of Volvo.

The real world is never quite as simple, and competition is rarely only price- or product-driven, but is usually dominated by one or the other or may even be a combination of both – e.g., lead-free petrol, vitamin-enhanced milk, caller display services for phone calls, etc.

2/PRODUCTION

(a) Value chain

A value chain comprises all the companies involved in the manufacturing process, from the raw materials to the end product. Depending on the exact circumstances, a value chain may encompass the processing of raw materials, R&D, secondary processing, trading activities, a third or fourth processing process, further trading and, lastly, the end distributor. Increasingly in our service-oriented society, grey matter is the raw material, and processing is replaced by a series of services involving some degree of added value, with distribution retaining its role.

The point of analysing a value chain is to understand the role played by the market participants, as well as their respective strengths and weaknesses. Naturally, in times of crisis, all participants in the value chain come under pressure. But some of them will fare worse than others, and some may even disappear altogether because they are structurally in a weak position within the value chain. Analysts need to determine where the structural weaknesses lie. They must be able to look beyond good performance when times are good because it may conceal such weaknesses. Analysts' ultimate goals are to identify where not to invest or not to lend within the value chain.

Let's consider the example of the film industry. The main players are:

- the production company, which plays both an artistic and a financial role. The producer writes or adapts the screenplay and brings together a director and actors. In addition, the production company finances the film using its own funds and by arranging contributions from third parties, such as co-producers and television companies, which secure the right to broadcast the film, as well as by earning advances from film distribution companies (guaranteed minimum payment);

- the distributor, which also has a dual role assuming responsibility for logistics and financial aspects. It distributes the film reels to dozens, if not hundreds, of cinemas and promotes the film. In addition, it helps finance the film by guaranteeing the producer minimum income from cinema operators, regardless of the actual level of box office receipts generated by the film;
- lastly, the cinema operator that owns or leases its cinemas, organises the screenings and collects the box office receipts.

Going beyond a review of a particular value chain, additional insight can be gained into the balance of power by modelling the effects of a crisis and assessing the impact on the different players. During the 1980s, the number of box office admissions fell right across Europe owing to the advent of new TV channels and video cassettes.

Which category of player was worst affected and has now generally lost its independence?

Cinema operators? Granted, the fall in box office admissions led to a contraction in their sales. Some had to shut down cinemas, but since their properties were located in town and city centres, cinema operators that owned the premises had no trouble in finding buyers, such as banks and shops, that were prepared to pay a decent price for these properties. The others modernised their theatres, built up their sales of confectionery that carry very high margins and have capitalised on the renewed growth in cinema audiences across Europe over the past 10 years.

What about the production companies? Obviously, lower audiences meant lower box office receipts but, at the same time, other media outlets developed for films (television channels, video cassettes), generating new sources of revenue for film producers.

All things considered, film distribution companies were the worst hit. Some went bankrupt, while others were snapped up by film producers or cinema operators. Film distribution companies had only one source of revenue: box office receipts. Unlike cinema operators, they had no bricks-and-mortar assets which could be redeveloped. Unlike film production companies, they had no access to the alternative sources of income (royalties from pay TV or video cassettes) which caused the slump in the number of tickets sold. They had agreed to pay a guaranteed minimum to film production companies based on estimated box office receipts but, given the steady decline in admissions, these estimates systematically proved overoptimistic. As a result, distributors failed to cover the guaranteed minimum and were doomed to failure.

When studying a value chain, analysts need to identify weaknesses where a particular category of player has no or very little room for manoeuvre (scope for developing new activities, for selling operating assets with value independent of their current use, etc.).

(b) Production models

In a service-dominated economy, the production models used by an industrial company are rarely analysed, even though we believe this is a very worthwhile exercise.

The first step is to establish whether the company assumes responsibility for or subcontracts the production function, whether production takes place in Europe or whether it has been transferred to low-labour-cost countries and whether the labour force is made up of permanent or temporary staff, etc. This step allows the analyst to measure the flexibility of the income statement in the event of a recession or strong growth in the market.

In doing so, the analyst can detect any inconsistencies between the product and the industrial organisation adopted to produce it. As indicated in the following diagram, there are four different types of industrial organisation:

Products: Processes:	Unique, custom-made, designed for the user	Multiple, differentiated, not stand-ardised, produced on demand	Diversified, but made up of standardised components, high volumes	Unique, complex, very high volumes
Project: Specific and temporary organisation comprising experts	Pyramids in Egypt Cathedrals Hubble telescope			
Workshop: Flexibility through overcapacity, not very specialised equipment, multi-skilled workforce		Aerospace Catering Machine tools		
Mass production: Flexibility through semi-finished inventories, not very qualified or multi-skilled workforce			Customer appliances Shoes Textiles	
Process-specific: Total lack of flexibility, but no semi-finished inventories, advanced automatisation, small and highly technical workforce				Automotive Energy Sugar production Chemicals

Source: adapted from J.C. Tarondeau.

The **project**-type organisation falls outside the scope of financial analysts. Although it exists, its economic impact is very modest indeed.

The **workshop** model may be adopted by craftsmen, in the luxury goods sector or for research purposes, but, as soon as a product starts to develop, the workshop should be discarded as soon as possible.

Mass production is suitable for products with a low unit cost, but gives rise to very high working capital owing to the inventories of semi-finished goods that provide its flexibility. With this type of organisation, barriers to entry are low because, as soon as a process designer develops an innovative method, it can be sold to all the market players. This type of production is frequently relocated to emerging markets.

Process-oriented production is a type of industrial organisation that took shape in the late 1970s and revolutionised production methods. It has led to a major decline in working capital because inventories of semi-finished goods have almost disappeared. It is a continuous production process from the raw material to the end product, which requires the suppliers, subcontractors and producers to be located close to each other and to work on a just-in-time basis. This type of production is hard to relocate to countries with low labour costs owing to its complexity (fine-tuning) and it does not provide any flexibility given the elimination of the inventories of semi-finished goods. A strike affecting a supplier or subcontractor may bring the entire group to a standstill.

EVOLUTION IN THE MOTOR INDUSTRY'S PRODUCTION MODEL

But readers should not allow themselves to get carried away with the details of these industrial processes. Instead, readers should examine the pros and cons of each process and consider how well the company's business strategy fits with its selected production model. Workshops will never be able to deliver the same volumes as mass production!

> The natural tendency for all industries is to evolve gradually, mirroring trends in the motor industry during the 20th century.

download

(c) Capital expenditure

A company should not invest too early in the production process. When a new product is launched on the market, there is an initial phase during which the product must show that it is well suited to consumers' needs. Then, the product will evolve, more minor new features will be built in and its sales will increase.

From then on, the priority is to lower costs; all attention and attempts at innovation will then gradually shift from the product to the production model.

INNOVATION IN PRODUCTS AND PRODUCTION SYSTEMS

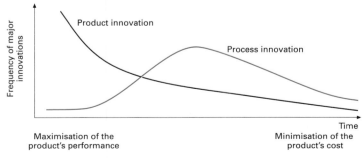

Source: Utterback and Abernathy (1975).

Investing too early in the production process is a mistake for two reasons. First, money should not be invested in production facilities that are not yet stable and might even have to be abandoned. Second, it is preferable to use the same funds to anchor the product more firmly in its market through technical innovation and marketing campaigns. Consequently, it may be wiser to outsource the production process and not incur production-related risks on top of the product risk. Conversely, once the production process has stabilised, it is in the company's best interests to invest in securing a tighter grip over the production process and unlocking productivity gains that will lead it to lower costs.

More and more, companies are looking to outsource their manufacturing or service operations, thereby reducing their core expertise to project design and management. Roughly speaking, companies in the past were geared mainly to production and had a vertical organisation structure because value was concentrated in the production function. Nowadays, in a large number of sectors (telecoms equipment, computer production, etc.), value lies primarily in the research, innovation and marketing functions.

Companies therefore have to be able to organise and coordinate production carried out externally. This outsourcing trend has given rise to companies such as Solectron, Flextronics and Celestica, whose sole expertise is industrial manufacturing and which are able to secure low costs and prices by leveraging economies of scale because they produce items on behalf of several competing groups.

3/ DISTRIBUTION SYSTEMS

A distribution system usually plays three roles:

- **logistics**: displaying, delivering and storing products;
- **advice and services**: providing details about and promoting the product, providing after-sales service and circulating information between the producer and consumers, and vice versa;
- **financing**: making firm purchases of the product – i.e., assuming the risk of poor sales.

These three roles are vital and, where the distribution system does not fulfil them or does so only partially, the producer will find itself in a very difficult position and will struggle to expand.

Let's consider the example of the furniture retail sector. It does not perform the financing role because it does not carry any inventories aside from a few demonstration items. The logistics side merely entails displaying items, and advice is limited to say the least. As a result, the role of furniture producers is merely that of piece workers that are unable to build their own brand (a proof of their weakness), the only well-known brands being private-label brands, such as Ikea and Habitat.

It is easy to say that producers and distributors have diverging interests, but this is not true. Their overriding goal is the same: i.e., that consumers buy the product. Inevitably, producers and distributors squabble over their respective share of the selling price, but that is a secondary issue. A producer will never be efficient if the distribution network is inefficient.

The risk of a distribution network is that it does not perform its role properly and that it restricts the flow of information between the producer and consumers, and vice versa.

So, what type of distribution system should a company choose? This is naturally a key decision for companies. The closer they can get to their end-customers, possibly even handling the distribution role themselves, the faster and more accurately they will find out what their customers want (i.e., pricing, product ranges, innovation, etc.). And the earlier they become aware of fluctuations in trading conditions, the sooner they will be able to adjust their output. But such choice requires special human skills, as well as investment in logistics and sales facilities, and substantial working capital.

This approach makes more sense where the key factor motivating customer purchases is not pricing but the product's image, after-sales service and quality, which must be tightly controlled by the company itself rather than an external player. For instance, following the Gucci Group's decision to take control of Yves Saint-Laurent, its first decision was to call a halt to the distribution of its products through department stores and to concentrate it in Yves Saint-Laurent stores.[1]

Being far from end-customers brings the opposite pros and cons. The requisite investment is minimal, but the company is less aware of its customers' preferences and the risks associated with cyclical ups and downs are amplified. If end-customers slow down their purchases, it may take some time before the end-retailer becomes aware of the trend and reduces its purchases from the wholesaler. The wholesaler will in turn suffer from an inertia effect before scaling down its purchases from the producer, which will not therefore have been made aware of the slowdown until several weeks or even months after it started. And, when conditions pick up again, it is not unusual for distributors to run out of stock even though the producer still has vast inventories.

Where price competition predominates, it is better for the producer to focus its investment on production facilities to lower its costs, rather than to spread it thinly across a distribution network that requires different expertise from the production side.

1 *Which, sometimes, are inside department stores, but are run by Yves Saint-Laurent.*

4/THE COMPANY AND ITS PEOPLE

All too often, we have heard it said that a company's human resources are what really count. In certain cases, this is used to justify all kinds of strange decisions. There may be some truth to it in smaller companies, which do not have strategic positions and survive thanks to the personal qualities and charisma of their top managers. Such a situation represents a major source of uncertainty for lenders and shareholders. To say that the men and women employed by a company are important may well be true, but management will still have to establish strategic positions and build up economic rents that give some value to the company aside from its founder or manager.

(a) Shareholders

From a purely financial standpoint, the most important men and women of a company are its shareholders. They appoint its executives and determine its strategy. It is important to know who they are and what their aims are, as we will see in Chapter 41. There are two types of shareholder: inside and outside shareholders.

Inside shareholders are shareholders who also perform a role within the company, usually with management responsibilities. This fosters strong attachment to the company and sometimes leads to the pursuit of scale-, power- and prestige-related objectives that may have very little to do with financial targets. **Outside shareholders** do not work within the company and behave in a purely financial manner.

What sets inside shareholders apart is that they assume substantial personal risks because both their assets and income are dependent on the same source: i.e., the company. Consequently, inside shareholders usually pay closer attention than a manager who is not a shareholder and whose wealth is only partly tied up in the company. Nonetheless, the danger is that inside shareholders may not take the right decisions – e.g., to shut down a unit, dispose of a business or discontinue an unsuccessful diversification venture – owing to emotional ties or out of obstinacy. The Kirch Group would probably have fared better during the early 2000s had the Group's founder not clung on to his position as CEO well into retirement age and had he groomed a successor.

Outside shareholders have a natural advantage. Because their behaviour is guided purely by financial criteria, they will serve as a very useful pointer for the group's strategy and financial policy. This said, if the company runs into problems, they may act very passively and show a lack of resolve that will not help managers very much.

Lastly, analysts should watch out for conflicts among shareholders that may paralyse the normal life of the company. As an example, disputes among the founding family members almost ruined Gucci.

(b) Managers

It is important to understand managers' objectives and attitudes *vis-à-vis* shareholders. The reader needs to bear in mind that the widespread development of share-option-based incentive systems in particular has aligned the managers' financial interests with those of shareholders. We will examine this topic in greater depth in Chapter 32.

We would advise readers to be very wary where incentive systems have been extended to include the majority of a company's employees. First, stock options cannot yet be used to buy staple products and, so, salaries must remain the main source of income for unskilled employees. Second, should a company's position start to deteriorate, its top talent will be fairly quick to jump ship after having exercised their stock options before they become worthless. Those that remain on board may fail to grasp what is happening until it is too late, thereby losing precious time. This is what happened to so-called new economy companies, which distributed stock options as a standard form of remuneration. It is an ideal system when everything is going well, but highly dangerous in the event of a crisis because it exacerbates the company's difficulties.

(c) Corporate culture

Corporate culture is probably very difficult for an outside observer to assess. Nonetheless, it represents a key factor, particularly when a company embarks on acquisitions or diversification ventures. A monolithic and highly centralised company with specific expertise in a limited number of products will struggle to diversify its businesses because it will probably seek to apply the same methods to its target, thereby disrupting the latter's impetus.

For instance, Matsushita of Japan acquired US film producer Universal, but the deal never really worked because Matsushita's engineering culture was far removed from the artistic culture prevailing in Hollywood studios.

Conversely, Danone has turned itself from a European glass producer into a worldwide food giant because its chairman fully grasped that he needed marketing specialists rather than engineers to manage this diversification, which has now become the group's sole business. So, he hired staff from Procter & Gamble, Unilever, etc.

Section 8.3
AN ASSESSMENT OF A COMPANY'S ACCOUNTING POLICY

We cannot overemphasise the importance of analysing the auditors' report and considering the accounting principles adopted, before embarking on a financial analysis of a group's accounts based on the guide that we will present in Section 8.4.

If a company's accounting principles are in line with practices, readers will be able to study the accounts with a fairly high level of assurance about their relevance – i.e., their ability to provide a decent reflection of the company's economic reality.

Conversely, if readers detect anomalies or accounting practices that depart from the norm, there is no need to examine the accounts, because they provide a distorted picture of the company's economic reality. In such circumstances, we can only advise the lender not to lend or to dispose of its loans as soon as possible and the shareholder not to buy shares or to sell any held already as soon as possible. A company that adopts accounting principles that deviate from the usual standards does not do so by chance. In all likelihood the company will be seeking to window-dress a fairly grim reality. We refer readers to Chapter 7, which deals with this issue.

To facilitate this task, the appendix to this chapter includes tables showing the main creative accounting techniques used to distort earnings, the shape of the income statement or the balance sheet.

Section 8.4
STANDARD FINANCIAL ANALYSIS PLAN

Experience has taught us that novices are often disconcerted when faced with the task of carrying out their first financial analysis because they do not know where to start and what to aim for. They risk producing a collection of mainly descriptive comments, without connecting them or verifying their internal consistency; i.e., without establishing any causal links.

A financial analysis is an investigation that must be carried out in a logical order. It comprises parts that are interlinked and should not therefore be carried out in isolation. Financial analysts are detectives, constantly on the lookout for clues, seeking to establish a logical sequence, as well as any disruptive factors that may be a prelude to problems in the future. The questions they most often need to ask are: "Is this logical? Is this consistent with what I have already found? If so, why? If not, why not?"

We suggest that readers remember the following sentence, which can be used as the basis for all types of financial analysis:

Wealth creation requires investments that must be financed and provide sufficient return.

Let us analyse this sentence in more depth. A company will be able to remain viable and ultimately survive only if it manages to find customers ready to buy its goods or services in the long term at a price that enables it to post a sufficient operating profit. This forms the base for everything else. Consequently, it is important to look first at the structure of the company's earnings. But the company needs to make capital expenditures to start operations: acquire equipment, buildings, patents, subsidiaries, etc. (which are fixed assets) and set aside amounts to cover working capital. Fixed assets and working capital jointly form its capital employed. Naturally, these outlays will have to be financed either through equity or bank loans and other borrowings.

Once these three factors (margins, capital employed and financing) have been examined, the company's profitability – i.e., its efficiency – can be calculated, in terms of either its Return On Capital Employed (ROCE) or its Return On Equity (ROE). This marks the end of the analyst's task and provides the answers to the original questions: Is the company able to honour the commitments it has made to its creditors? Is it able to create value for its shareholders?

Consequently, we have to study the company's:

➢ **wealth creation**, by focusing on:

  ○ trends in the company's sales, including an analysis of both prices and volumes. This is a key variable that sets the backdrop for a financial analysis. An expanding company does not face the same problems as a company in decline, in a recession, pursuing a recovery plan or experiencing exponential growth;

- o the impact of business trends, the strength of the cycle and its implications in terms of volumes and prices (gap vs. those seen at the top or bottom of the cycle);
- o trends in margins and particularly the EBITDA[2] margin;
- o an examination of the scissors effect (see Chapter 9) and the operating leverage (see Chapter 10), without which the analysis is not very robust from a conceptual standpoint.

➤ **capital-employed policy**; i.e., capital expenditure and working capital (see Chapter 11);

➤ **financing policy**. This involves examining how the company has financed capital expenditure and working capital either by means of debt, equity or internally generated cash flow. The best way of doing so is to look at the cash flow statement for a dynamic analysis and the balance sheet for a snapshot of the situation at the company's year-end (see Chapter 12).

➤ **profitability** by:

- o analysing its ROCE and ROE, leverage effect and associated risk (see Chapter 13;
- o comparing actual profitability with the required rate of return (on capital employed or shareholders' equity) to determine whether the company is creating value and whether the company is solvent (see Chapter 14).

In the following chapters we use the case of the Ericsson Group as an example of how to carry out a financial analysis.

Ericsson is one of the world's largest telecom equipment suppliers. It offers wireless and wireline networking equipment, wireless handsets and related platform technologies as well as some defence-related solutions.

Net sales in 2003 were €12.9bn in three main lines of products: systems, phones and other (mainly defence-related) operations. It generates 48% of its sales in Europe, the Middle East and Africa, 26% in Asia and the Pacific, 18% in North America and 8% in Latin America.

Annual reports of Ericsson from 1999 through 2003 are now available at *www.vernimmen.com*

Let's now see the various techniques that can be used in financial analysis.

2 Earnings Before Interest, Taxes, Depreciation and Amortisation.

Section 8.5
THE VARIOUS TECHNIQUES OF FINANCIAL ANALYSIS

1/TREND ANALYSIS OR THE STUDY OF THE SAME COMPANY OVER SEVERAL PERIODS

Financial analysis always takes into account trends over several years because its role is to **look at the past to assess the present situation and to forecast the future**. It may also be applied to projected financial statements prepared by the company. The only way of teasing out trends is to look at performance over several years (usually three where the information is available).

OVERVIEW OF A STANDARD PLAN FOR A FINANCIAL ANALYSIS

Two preliminary tasks

GET TO KNOW THE BUSINESS WELL ...
• *The market(s)* • *The product(s)* • *Production model(s)* • *Distribution network* • *Human resources*

... AS WELL AS THE COMPANY'S ACCOUNTING POLICIES
Auditors' reports • *Accounting principles* • *Consolidation techniques and scope* • *Goodwill, brands and other intangibles* • *Provisions* • *Inventories* • *Unconsolidated subsidiaries etc.*

download

Four-stage plan

WEALTH CREATION ...

• *Margin analysis:*
  – structure
  – scissors effect
  – operating leaverage (breakeven point)

... REQUIRES CAPITAL EMPLOYED ...
• *Working capital* • *Capital expenditures*

... THAT MUST BE FINANCED
• *Cash flows* • *Equity/Debt* • *Liquidity, interest rate and currency risk*

... AND PROVIDE A SUFFICIENT RETURN

• *Analysis of return on capital employed and return on equity: leverage effect*
• *Comparison between ROCE/rate of return required by shareholders and lenders*
    → *Value*
    → *Solvency risk*

Analysts need to bring to light any possible deterioration so that they can seize on any warning signals pointing to major problems facing the company. All too often we have seen lazy analysts look at the key profit indicators without bothering to take a step back and analyse trends. Nonetheless, this approach has two important drawbacks:

- trend analysis only makes sense where the data are roughly comparable from one year to the next. This is not the case if the company's business activities, business model (e.g., massive use of outsourcing), or scope of consolidation change partially or entirely, not to mention any changes in the accounting rules used to translate its economic reality;
- accounting information is always published with a delay. Broadly speaking, the accounts for a financial year are published between 2 and 5 months after the year-end, and they may no longer bear any relation to the company's present situation. In this respect, external analysts stand at a disadvantage to their internal counterparts who are able to obtain data much more rapidly if the company has an efficient information system.

2/COMPARATIVE ANALYSIS OR COMPARING SIMILAR COMPANIES

Comparative analysis consists of evaluating a company's key profit indicators and ratios so that they can be compared with the typical indicators and ratios of companies operating in the same sector of activity. The basic idea is that one should not get up to any more nonsense than one's neighbours, particularly when it comes to a company's balance sheet. Why is that? Simply because during a recession most of the lame ducks will be eliminated and only healthy companies will be left standing. **A company is not viable or unviable in absolute terms. It is merely more or less viable than others.**

The comparative method is often used by financial analysts to compare the financial performance of companies operating in the same sector, by certain companies to set customer payment periods, by banks to assess the abnormal nature of certain payment periods and of certain inventory turnover rates and by those examining a company's financial structure. It may be used systematically by drawing on the research published by organisations (such as central banks, Datastream, Standard & Poor's, Moody's) that compile the financial information supplied by a large number of companies. They publish the main financial characteristics in a standardised format of companies operating in different sectors of activity, as well as the norm (average) for each indicator or ratio in each sector. This is the realm of **benchmarking**.

This approach has two drawbacks:

- The concept of sector is a vague one and depends on the level of detail applied. For this approach, which analyses a company based on rival firms, to be of any value, the information compiled from the various companies in the sector must be consistent and the sample must be sufficiently representative.
- There may be cases of mass delusions, leading all the stocks in a particular sector to be temporarily overvalued. Financial investors should then withdraw from the sector.

3/ NORMATIVE ANALYSIS AND FINANCIAL RULES OF THUMB

Normative analysis represents an extension of comparative analysis. It is based on a comparison of certain company ratios or indicators with rules or standards derived from a vast sample of companies.

For instance, there are norms specific to certain industries:

- in the hotel sector, the bed–night cost must be at least 1/1,000 of the cost of building the room, or the sales generated after 3 years should be at least one-third of the investment cost;
- the level of work in progress relative to the company's shareholders' equity in the construction sector;
- the level of sales generated per m^2 in supermarkets, etc.

There are also some financial rules of thumb applicable to all companies regardless of the sector in which they operate and relating to their balance sheet structure:

- fixed assets should be financed by stable sources of funds;
- net debt should be no greater than around four times EBITDA;
- etc.

Readers should be careful not to set too much store by these norms that are often not very robust from a conceptual standpoint because they are determined from statistical studies. These ratios are hard to interpret, except perhaps where capital structure is concerned. After all, profitable companies can afford to do what they want, and some may indeed appear to be acting rather whimsically, but profitability is what really matters. Likewise, we will illustrate in Section III of this book that there is no such thing as an ideal capital structure.

Section 8.6
RATINGS

Credit ratings are the result of a continuous assessment of a borrower's solvency by a specialised agency (Standard & Poor's, Moody's, Fitch, etc.), by banks for internal purposes to ensure that they meet prudential ratios and by credit insurers (e.g., Coface, Hermes, etc.). As we will see in Chapter 26, this assessment leads to the award of a rating reflecting an opinion about the risk of a borrowing. The financial risk derives both from:

- the borrower's ability to honour the stipulated payments; and
- the specific characteristics of the borrowing, notably its guarantees and legal characteristics.

The rating is awarded at the end of a fairly lengthy process. Rating agencies assess the company's strategic risks by analysing its market position within the sector (market share, industrial efficiency, size, quality of management, etc.) and by conducting a financial analysis.

The main aspects considered include trends in the operating margin, trends and sustainability of return on capital employed, analysis of capital structure (and notably coverage of financial expense by operating profit and coverage of net debt by cash generated by operations or cash flow). We will deal with these ratios in more depth in Chapters 9–14.

Let us now deal with what may be described as "automated" financial analysis techniques, to which we will not return.

Section 8.7
SCORING TECHNIQUES

1/THE PRINCIPLES OF CREDIT SCORING

Credit scoring is an analytical technique intended to carry out a pre-emptive checkup of a company.

The basic idea is to prepare ratios from companies' accounts that are leading indicators (i.e., 2 or 3 years ahead) of potential difficulties. Once the ratios have been established, they merely have to be calculated for a given company and cross-checked against the values obtained for companies that are known to have run into problems or have failed. Comparisons are not made ratio by ratio, but globally. The ratios are combined in a function known as the Z-score that yields a score for each company. The equation for calculating Z-scores is as follows:

$$Z = a + \sum_{i=1}^{n} \beta_i \times R_i$$

where a is a constant, R_i the ratios, β_i the relative weighting applied to ratio R_i and n the number of ratios used.

Depending on whether a given company's Z-score is close to or a long way off from normative values based on a set of companies that ran into trouble, the company in question is said to have a certain probability of experiencing trouble or remaining healthy over the following 2- or 3-year period. Originally developed in the US during the late 1960s by Edward Altman, the family of Z-scores has been highly popular, the latest version of the Z'' equation being:

$$Z'' = 6.56X_1 + 3.26X_2 + 6.72X_3 + 1.05X_4$$

where X_1 is working capital/total assets, X_2 is retained earnings/total assets, X_3 is operating profit/total assets and X_4 is shareholders' equity/net debt.

If Z'' is less than 1.1, the probability of corporate failure is high, and if Z'' is higher than 2.6, the probability of corporate failure is low, the grey area being values of between 1.1 and 2.6. The Z''-score has not yet been replaced by the Zeta Score, which introduces into the equation the criteria of earnings stability, debt servicing and balance sheet liquidity.

2/BENEFITS AND DRAWBACKS OF SCORING TECHNIQUES

Scoring techniques represent an enhancement of traditional ratio analysis, which is based on the isolated use of certain ratios. With scoring techniques, the problem of the relative importance to be attached to each ratio has been solved because each is weighted according to its ability to pick out the "bad" companies from the "good" ones.

This said, scoring techniques still have a number of drawbacks.

Some weaknesses derive from the statistical underpinnings of the scoring equation. The sample needs to be sufficiently large, the database accurate and consistent and the period considered sufficiently long to reveal trends in the behaviour of companies and to measure its impact.

The scoring equation has to be based on historical data from the fairly recent past and, thus, needs to be updated over time. Can the same equation be used several years later when the economic and financial environment in which companies operate may have changed considerably? It is thus vital for scoring equations **to be kept up to date**.

The design of scoring equations is heavily influenced by their designers' top priority; i.e., to measure the risk of failure for small- and medium-sized enterprises. They are not well suited for any other purpose (e.g., predicting in advance which companies will be highly profitable) or for measuring the risk of failure for large groups. Scoring equations should thus be used only for companies whose business activities and size is on a par with those in the original sample.

Scoring techniques, which are a straightforward and rapid way of synthesising figures, have considerable appeal. Their development may even have perverse self-fulfilling effects. Prior awareness of the risk of failure (which scoring techniques aim to provide) may lead some of the companies' business partners to adopt behaviour that hastens their demise. Suppliers may refuse to provide credit, banks may call in their loans, customers may be harder to come by because they are worried about not receiving delivery of the goods they buy or not being able to rely on after-sales service, etc.

Section 8.8
EXPERT SYSTEMS

Expert systems comprise software developed to carry out financial analysis using a knowledge base consisting of rules of financial analysis, enriched with the result of each analysis performed. The goal of expert systems is to develop lines of reasoning akin to those used by human analysts. This is the realm of artificial intelligence.

To begin with, the company's latest financial statements and certain market and social indicators are entered and serve as the basis for the expert system's analysis. It then poses certain questions about the company, its environment and its business activities to enrich the database. It proceeds on a step-by-step basis by activating the rules contained in its database.

Third, the expert system produces a financial report that may comprise an assessment of the company, plus recommendations about certain measures that need to be considered.

The goal is to develop a tool providing early warnings of corporate failures, which can, for instance, be used by financial institutions.

APPENDIX 8A: ACCOUNTING PROCEDURES WITH AN IMPACT ON EARNINGS

Main items affected	Mechanism used	Impact on the accounts	Drawbacks
Fixed assets and financial expense	Financial expense included in the cost of fixed assets produced internally by the company	• Increase in earnings in the year when the charges are transferred • Decrease in earnings in the year of the transfer and following years through depreciation of the fixed asset produced	Procedure often regarded as exceptional in practice
Development costs	Development costs capitalised on the balance sheet	• Increase in earnings in the year the development costs are capitalised • Decrease in earnings in the year of the transfer and following years through amortisation of the fixed asset produced • Impact of the date chosen to start amortisation	• Conditions relating to individualised projects, technical feasibility and commercial profitability must be satisfied • Risk of a boomerang effect whereby development research costs may have to be capitalised artificially to offset the impact of amortising past expenditure
Fixed assets	Sale and leaseback; i.e., the sale of a fixed asset, which is then leased back by the company	• A leaseback gain may be recorded on the sale • Leasing costs are recorded for the duration of the lease	• Artificial increase in earnings because the company undertakes to pay leasing costs for a certain period • Hence it is recommended that the capital gain should be spread over the relevant period
Depreciation and amortisation	When a depreciation schedule is drawn up, a company has numerous options: • Determine the likely useful life • Fix a residual value • Take into account the rate of use • Use physical working units, etc.	Depending on the option selected, the size of depreciation and amortisation allowances may change, leading to a change in the profile of depreciation and amortisation over time	• Need for a depreciation schedule • Methods to be applied consistently
Depreciation and fixed assets	Revise the depreciation schedule, e.g. by increasing (or decreasing) the residual depreciation period	Decrease (or increase) in future allowances over a longer (shorter) period	Change in accounting method: disclosures required in the notes to the accounts
Depreciation and intangible assets or investment	Understatement (overstatement) of impairment losses on investment or intangible assets (goodwill), notably made possible by the existence of various different valuation methods	• Increase (or decrease) in earnings when the impairment losses are recognised; • Opposite effect when the impairment losses are reversed	• Prudence principle; • Boomerang effect when the impairment losses are reversed
Inventories	Financial expense included in the production cost of inventories	• Increase in earnings in the year when the charges are transferred; • Decrease in earnings when the inventory is eliminated	Justification and amount of the relevant expenses must be disclosed in the notes to the accounts

APPENDIX 8A: ACCOUNTING PROCEDURES WITH AN IMPACT ON EARNINGS (cont.)

Main items affected	Mechanism used	Impact on the accounts	Drawbacks
Inventories	Change in inventory valuation method	Earnings modified as a result of the change	Change in accounting method: disclosures must be disclosed in the notes to the accounts
Inventories	Incorporation of costs related to below-normal activity in the valuation of items held in inventory	• Transfer of the loss arising from below-normal activity to the following year • Increase in earnings for the current year • Decrease in earnings for the following year	• IASB states that the cost of below-normal activity should not be taken into account in inventory valuations • It is hard to determine the normal level of production
Impairment losses and current assets	• Understatement/ (overstatement) of impairment losses on doubtful receivables • Understatement/ (overstatement) of impairment losses on inventories	• Increase (or decrease) in earnings when the impairment losses are recognised • Opposite effect when the impairment losses are reversed	• Conservatism principle • Boomerang effect when the impairment losses are reversed
Deferred costs and start-up costs (especially pre-opening and research costs)	Change in accounting method: • Deferral of charges through amortisation whereas the charges were previously recorded in an earlier year • or vice versa	• Deferral of charges • Or, on the contrary, recognition of changes in a single period	• Consistency principle undermined • Disclosures required in the notes to the accounts
Costs related to the acquisition of fixed assets	Acquisition-related costs (which cannot be included in acquisition costs) – e.g., professional fees, commission payments, registration fees left under costs or deferred costs	• Immediate decrease in earnings if left under costs • Deferral of costs if transferred to assets	Consistency principle (type of costs, amortisation period)
Grants and subsidies	• Investment subsidy added to shareholders' equity • Several possibilities for its inclusion on the income statement	• Affects return on invested capital calculations	Consistency principle
Provisions for liabilities and charges	Provisions for restructuring. Several problems exist: • What is the decision date? • Degree of precision and impact on the valuation; • Recognition of potential capital gains in the assessment of the provision	• Impact on earnings depends on the size of the provision • Opposite effect when reversed	• Consistency principle • Checked by auditors
Financial income	Artificial sale of securities – i.e., sale followed by repurchase	Unrealised capital gain turned into a real capital gain	• Transaction expenses • Neutral impact on cash
Financial income	Securities sold with a repurchase option at a fixed price (i.e., less accrued interest) for a certain period	• Unrealised capital gain turned into a real capital gain • Shape of balance sheet improves: financing guaranteed by securities with no increase in debt • Payment of accrued interest and decrease in earnings in the year the option is exercised	• Where the parties intend to return the securities sold within the given period, the capital gain arising on the sale is eliminated and a provision set aside for the accrued interest

APPENDIX 8A: ACCOUNTING PROCEDURES WITH AN IMPACT ON EARNINGS (cont.)

Main items affected	Mechanism used	Impact on the accounts	Drawbacks
Goodwill	Goodwill allocated to nondepreciable items (i.e., brands, etc.) with no revaluation of depreciable items (i.e., fixed assets)	No reduction in consolidated earnings in future years	• Hard to establish the value of brands • Closely watched by auditors • Requires an annual impairment review and possibly recognition of impairment losses
Scope of consolidation	Change in scope of consolidation to include profitable subsidiaries. Use of the following options: • Concept of nonmaterial subsidiaries • Fully consolidated when less than 50%-owned	Change in earnings dependent on the change in the scope of consolidation	• Consistency principle • Disclosure of details adjusted for the change in scope of consolidation
Deferred taxation	Recognition of deferred tax assets	Increase in consolidated earnings	• Conservatism principle • Restrictive conditions to be checked (in particular, it must be probable that the company will return to profit). Hence the need for verifiable budgeted statements based on conservative and coherent assumptions
Accounting year-end	Change in the year-end date	The company may hope to increase its earnings during the additional months	Numerous drawbacks: organisation of accounting, consolidation and tax arrangements
Earnings generated by subsidiaries	Accelerate the transfer of subsidiaries' earnings Profitable subsidiaries: • Interim dividends • Difference in year-end dates • Partnership status Loss-making subsidiaries: • Subsidies or debt waivers • Impairment losses proportional to the change in shareholders' equity • Partnership status	Positive or negative impact on earnings depending on the entry	Works for unconsolidated accounts

Excerpt adapted from H. Stolowy, *Comptabilité Creative, Encyclopédie de Comptabilité, Contrôle de Gestion et Audit*, pp. 157–178, Economica 2000.

APPENDIX 8B: ACCOUNTING PROCEDURES WITH AN IMPACT ON THE SHAPE OF THE BALANCE SHEET

Main items affected	Mechanism used	Impact on the accounts	Drawbacks
Fixed assets	Sale and leaseback;[1] i.e., the sale of a fixed asset, which is then leased back by the company	Reduction in debt	• Artificial improvement in financial situation • Restatement of the lease shows the real level of debt
Fixed assets and shareholders' equity	Revaluation of tangible fixed assets	• Increase in assets • Increase in shareholders' equity (an attractive way of building capital back up for thinly capitalised companies)	Revaluation gains may be liable to tax
Trade receivables	Discounting of a bill of exchange or promissory note	Accounting view: • Reduction in working capital • Reduction in debt	After restatement: • No reduction in working capital • No reduction in debt
Trade receivables	Securitisation: sale of receivables to a mutual fund in return for cash	Reduction in working capital and debt	Need to be restated in financial analysis
Shareholders' equity	Issue of hybrid securities that are hard to classify between debt and equity	Change in gearing and return on equity	
Minority interests	Inclusion in shareholders' equity, with debt apportioned separately, or other solutions	Change in gearing and return on equity	
Borrowings	Use of sale and operating leaseback	Operating lease-related debt does not appear on the balance sheet	More likely than not to be restated in a financial analysis
Minority interests	Inclusion in shareholders' equity, with debt apportioned separately, or other solutions	Change in gearing and return on equity	

[1] This mechanism also serves to alter the level of earnings (see Appendix 8A).

The aim of financial analysis is to explain how a company can create value in the medium term (shareholders' viewpoint) or to determine whether it is solvent (lenders' standpoint). Either way, the techniques applied in financial analysis are the same.

First of all, financial analysis involves a detailed examination of the company's economics; i.e., the market in which it operates, its position within this market and the suitability of its production, distribution and human ressources management systems to its strategy. Next, it entails a detailed analysis of the company's accounting principles to ensure that they reflect and not distort the company's economic reality. Otherwise, there is no need to study the accounts, since they are not worth bothering with, and the company should be avoided like the plague, as far as shareholders, lenders and employees are concerned.

A standard financial analysis can be broken down into four stages:

- Wealth creation (sales trends, margin analysis) . . .

- . . . requires capital employed (fixed assets, working capital) . . .

- . . . that must be financed (by internal financing, shareholders' equity or bank loans and borrowings) . . .

- . . . and be sufficiently profitable (return on capital employed, return on equity, leverage effect).

Only then can the analyst come to a conclusion about the solvency of the company and its ability to create value.

Analysts may use trend analysis, which uses past trends to assess the present and predict the future; comparative analysis, which uses comparisons with similar companies operating in the same sector as a point of reference; and normative analysis, which is based on financial rules of thumb.

Ratings represent an evaluation of a borrower's ability to repay its borrowings. Ratings are produced through a comprehensive financial analysis of groups, part of whose debt is traded on a market. The process is greatly facilitated by the use of scoring techniques by credit insurers and banks for their internal purposes.

Scoring techniques are underpinned by a statistical analysis of the accounts of companies, which are compared with accounts of companies that have experienced problems, including bankruptcy in some cases. This automated process yields a probability of corporate failure. Scoring is primarily used for small- and medium-sized companies.

SUMMARY

download

QUESTIONS

quiz

1/ Do shareholders and lenders carry out financial analysis in the same way?

2/ What are the two prerequisites for financial analysis?

3/ Is a market an economic sector? Why?

4/ Why is there less risk on an original equipment market than on a replacement product market?

5/ When a new product is launched, should the company invest in the production process or in the product itself? Why?

6/ What is a standard financial analysis plan?

7/ What standard ratios are applicable to all companies?

8/ When is it possible to compare the EBIT of two companies?

9/ What criticism can be directed at scoring techniques?

10/ Why does the financial expense/EBITDA ratio play such a fundamental role in scoring techniques?

11/ What are the strengths of a trends analysis?

12/ Why start a financial analysis with a study of wealth creation?

13/ Is financial analysis always doomed to be too late to be useful?

14/ What is your view of the Italian proverb *traduttore, traditore* (to translate is to betray)?

15/ Why will vertical integration be dismissed as being of little value after an analysis of the value chain?

16/ What assumptions are made in a comparative financial analysis, especially on an international scale?

EXERCISES

1/ Carry out an analysis of the frozen chicken value chain and decide which participants in the value chain are in a structurally weak position. The main participants in the chicken value chain are:

- research: genetic selection of the best laying hens;
- breeding of laying hens: a laying hen lays eggs for 18 months nonstop, after which it is sold to the pet food industry;
- hatcheries: the eggs are placed in incubators stacked in batteries for an 18-day incubation period followed by a 3-day hatching period, and kept at the appropriate temperature and level of humidity;
- rearing: chickens are reared for around 40 days, until they reach a weight of 1.8 kg. This function provides additional income for a couple who, thanks to computerised equipment, only need to spend 2–3 hours/day attending to the chickens;
- feed: produced by animal feed groups, which develop subtle blends of wheat, maize and soya or rape seed proteins;
- slaughterhouses: 20,000 chickens are anaesthetised, decapitated, processed, and frozen per hour, then exported mainly to the Middle East.

2/ Guizzardi is one of the main Italian producers of synthetic raincoats. It sells two product ranges – the fashion and the classic raincoat – through supermarkets. Most of the Guizzardi workforce is paid the minimum wage.

Key figures (€m):

	2001	2002	2003
Sales	256	326	422
Raw materials used	78	104	143
Personnel cost	102	139	190
Operating income	41	52	59
Net income	23	27	30
Shareholders' equity	119	129	152
Net bank borrowings	42	125	150

(a) What is your view on the financial health of Guizzardi?

(b) Would you be of the same opinion if you had carried out an analysis beforehand of the company's value chain and simulated the impact of a crisis in 2004 (11% increase in labour costs due to introduction of a shorter working week with no reduction in wages, 40% rise in cost of raw materials due to the drop in the value of the euro against the dollar and the 2004 hike in the price of oil), with a 17% drop in the price of cotton in 2003?

3/ The table below appears on p. 2 of the annual report of the Norne group:

Key financials (unaudited, in millions of $, excluding earnings per share and dividends):

	1996	1997	1998	1999	2000
Sales	13,289	20,273	31,260	40,112	100,789
Net income:					
EBIT	493	515	698	957	1,266
Items impacting comparability	91	−410	5	−64	−287
Total	**584**	**105**	**703**	**893**	**979**
Diluted earnings per share:					
EBIT	0.91	0.87	1.00	1.18	1.47
Items impacting comparability	0.17	−0.71	0.01	−0.08	−0.35
Total	**1.08**	**0.16**	**1.01**	**1.10**	**1.12**
Dividend per share	0.43	0.46	0.48	0.50	0.50
Total assets	16,137	22,552	29,350	33,381	65,503
Cash from operating activities (excluding change in working capital)	742	276	1,873	2,228	3,010
Capital expenditures	1,483	2,092	3,564	3,085	3,314
Share price at 31 Dec	22	21	29	44	83

State your views.

ANSWERS

Questions

1/ *Yes, because a company that creates value (for shareholders) will be solvent (for lenders).*

2/ *An understanding of the company's "economics" (market, competitive position, production and distribution system, staff) and the accounting principles used.*

3/ *No, a market is defined by consistent behaviour of customers who buy products in order to meet similar needs.*

4/ *The replacement products market is far more sensitive to general economic conditions because, when consumers already own a product, they can postpone replacing it until the economy picks up.*

5/ *When a product is launched, it is better to invest in the product and the marketing thereof than in the production facilities or process that could change in the future.*

6/ *Wealth creation requires investments that must be financed and be sufficiently profitable.*

7/ *None.*

8/ *When the companies operate in the same sector.*

9/ To be effective, a sample must be sufficiently large and scores need to be updated regularly. Priority is to measure the risk of failure, which may have perverse self-fulfilling effects.

10/ Because it reveals both high levels of debt (substantial financial expense) and low returns (low EBITDA).

11/ It helps in understanding the company's strategy.

12/ Because this is the very reason the company exists.

13/ In theory, yes, if the analyst merely studies the company's financial statements. In practice, no, if the analyst has factored in the "economics" of the company.

14/ This saying demonstrates why it is important to take a close look at the accounting principles used by the company.

15/ Because, in a value chain, there are positions of structural weakness, where it is better to let others invest, even if it means handling them through supply contracts.

16/ Comparable accounting principles.

Exercises

1/ Position of structural weakness: (a) breeding of laying hens – in times of crisis, all of the hens (which are unable to stop laying) have to be slaughtered and sold at a knockdown price to pet food manufacturers (the couple thus lose their asset and their source of income); (b) the hatchery and chicken rearing – no special skills or technology required. Position of strength: (a) research and animal feed – many opportunities outside the chicken segment; (b) the slaughterhouse – control over the whole of the chain upstream, through supply contracts and sales to the finished product.

2/ (a) Very good financial health, with a 20% return on equity in 2003 and 12% ROCE with sales growing briskly. (b) Guizzardi is in a position of structural weakness which is hidden by the good performance of the very volatile fashion range. It has no control over 92% of its costs (labour, oil, dollar). Its customers – supermarkets – would be reluctant to increase sales prices given that the competition (manufacturers of cotton raincoats) is not facing the same problems (drop in the price of cotton, rise in the price of oil). It is too small a business to expect any help from its suppliers (the big petrochemical groups).

3/ Why have these figures not been audited? Are the negative items impacting comparability really nonrecurring (3 out of 5 years)? Should the presentation of the results not be improved? Why talk about cash flow from operating activities excluding changes in working capital – change in working capital is a natural constituent of cash flow from operating activities. The share is very highly valued (adjusted P/E of 56 (74 nonadjusted). All of the above should set alarm bells ringing. These are in fact the financial statements for Enron, which went bankrupt with a big bang in 2001.

BIBLIOGRAPHY

For more about the economic analysis of companies:

S. Chopra, P. Meindl, *Supply Chain Management*, 2nd edn, Prentice Hall, 2003.
Ph. Kotler, *Marketing Management*, 11th edn, Prentice Hall, 2003.
B. Moingeon and G. Soenen, *Corporate and Organisational Identities*, Routledge, 2003.
M. Porter, *Competitive Strategy: Techniques for Analyzing Industries and Competitors*, Free Press, 1998.
W. Stevenson, *Operations Management*, McGraw-Hill/Irwin, 2004.
J.C. Utterback, W.J. Abernathy, A dynamic model of process and product innovations, *Omega*, 3(6), 1975.
J.C. Tarondeau, *Stratégie Industrielle*, 2nd edn, Vuibert, 1998 [in French].
J. Woodward, *Industrial Organization: Theory and Practice*, 2nd edn, Oxford University Press, 1980.

For more about company accounting practices:

AIMR, *Finding Reality in Reported Earnings*, Association for Investment Management and Research, 1997.
AIMR, *Closing the Gap between Financial Reporting and Reality*, Association for Investment Management and Research,, 2003.
AIMR, *Financial Reporting in the 1990s and Beyond*, Association for Investment Management and Research,, 1993.
C. Mulford, E. Comiskey, *The Financial Number Game: Detecting Creative Accounting Practices*, John Wiley & Sons, 2002.
T. O'glove, *Quality of Earnings*, Free Press, 1998.
H. Schilit, *Financial Shenanigans: How to Detect Accounting Gimmicks and Fraud in Financial Reports*, 2nd edn, McGraw-Hill Trade, 2002.

For more on automated financial analysis:

E. Altman, *Bankruptcy, Credit Risk and High Yield Junk Bonds*, Blackwell, 2002.
Standard & Poor, *Corporate Ratings Criteria*, 2004 (*www.standardpoors.com/ratings*).

Chapter 9
MARGIN ANALYSIS: STRUCTURE

If financial analysis were a puppet, company strategy would be pulling its strings

An analysis of a company's margins is the first step in any financial analysis. It is a key stage because a company that does not manage to sell its products or services for more than the corresponding production costs is clearly doomed to fail. But, as we will see, positive margins are not sufficient on their own to create value or to escape bankruptcy.

Net income is what is left after all the revenues and charges shown on the income statement have been taken into account. Readers will not therefore be very surprised to learn that we will not spend too much time on analysing net income as such. A company's performance depends primarily on its operating performance, which explains why operating profit is the focus of analysts' attention. Financial and nonrecurrent items are regarded as being almost "inevitable" or "automatic" and are thus less interesting, particularly when it comes to forecasting a company's future prospects.

For the purposes of this chapter, we will assume that the analyst has drawn up an income statement as shown on pp. 173 and 174, which will serve as a point of reference. What's more, we will assume that additional information, such as average headcount, sales and production volumes, as well as industry data, such as prices in the sector and rivals' market share, is also available.

The first step in margin analysis is to examine the accounting practices used by the company to draw up its income statement. We dealt with this subject in Chapter 8 and will not restate it here, except to stress how important it is. Given the emphasis placed by analysts on studying operating profit (or EBIT[1]), there is a big temptation for companies to boost their operating profit by transferring operating charges to financial or nonrecurrent items.

The next stage involves a trend analysis based on an examination of the revenues and charges that determined the company's operating performance. This is useful only insofar as it sheds light on the past to help predict the future. Therefore, it is based on historical data and should cover several financial years. Naturally, this exercise is based on the assumption that the company's business activities have not altered significantly during the period under consideration.

1 *Earnings Before Interest and Taxes.*

The main aim here is to calculate the rate of change in the main sources of revenue and the main costs, to examine their respective trends and, thus, to account for the relative change in the margins posted by the company over the period.

The main potential pitfall in this exercise is to adopt a purely descriptive approach, without much or any analytical input; e.g., statements such as "personnel cost increased by 10%, rising from 100 to 110 …".

Margin trends are a reflection of a company's:

- strategic position, which may be stronger or weaker depending on the scissors effect; and
- risk profile, which may be stronger or weaker depending on the breakeven effect that we will examine in Chapter 10.

All too often the strategic aspects are neglected, with the lion's share of the study being devoted to figures and no assessment being made of what these figures tell us about a company's strategic position.

As we saw in Chapter 8, analysing a company's operating profit involves assessing what these figures tell us about its strategic position, which directly influences the size of its margins and its profitability:

- a company lacking any strategic power will sooner or later post a poor, if not a negative operating performance;
- a company with strategic power will be more profitable than the other companies in its business sector.

In our income statement analysis, our approach therefore needs to be far more qualitative than quantitative.

Section 9.1
HOW OPERATING PROFIT IS FORMED

By-nature format income statements (raw material purchases, personnel cost, etc.), which predominate in continental Europe, provide a more in-depth analysis than the by-function format that developed in the Anglo-Saxon tradition of accounting (cost of sales, selling and marketing costs, research and development costs, etc.). Granted, analysts only have to page through the notes to the accounts for the more detailed information that they need to get to grips with the following questions. In most cases, they will at best be able to work back towards EBITDA[2] by using the depreciation and amortisation data that must be included in the notes or in the cash flow statement.

2 *Earnings Before Interest, Taxes, Depreciation and Amortisation.*

1/Sales

Sales trends are an essential factor in all financial analysis and company assessments. A company whose business activities are expanding rapidly, stagnating, growing slowly, turning lower or depressed will encounter different problems. An examination of sales trends sets the scene for an entire financial analysis.
Sales growth forms the cornerstone for all financial analysis. Sales growth needs to be analysed in terms of volume (quantities sold) and price trends, organic and acquisition-led growth.

Before sales volumes can be analysed, acquisition-led growth needs to be separated from the company's organic growth, so that like can be compared with like. This means analysing the company's performance (in terms of its volumes and prices) on a comparable structure basis and then assessing additions to and withdrawals from the scope of consolidation. In practice, most groups publish **pro forma accounts** in the notes to their accounts showing the income statements for the relevant and previous periods based on the same scope of consolidation and using the same consolidation methods.

If a company is experiencing very brisk growth, analysts will need to look closely at the growth in operating costs and the financial requirements generated by this growth.

A company experiencing a period of stagnation will have to scale down its operating costs and financial requirements. As we will see later in this chapter, production factors do not have the same flexibility profile when sales are growing as when sales are declining.

Where a company sells a single product, volume growth can easily be calculated as the difference between the overall increase in sales and that in the selling price of its product. Where it sells a variety of different products or services, analysts face a trickier task. In such circumstances, they have the option of either working along the same lines by studying the company's main products or calculating an average price increase, based on which the average growth in volumes can be estimated.

An analysis of price increases provides valuable insight into the extent to which overall growth in sales is attributable to inflation. This can be carried out by comparing trends in the company's prices with those in the general price index for its sector of activity. Account also needs to be taken of currency fluctuations and changes in the product mix, which may sometimes significantly affect sales, especially in consolidated accounts.

In turn, this process helps to shed light on the company's strategy; that is:

- whether its prices have increased through efforts to sell higher value-added products;
- whether they have been hiked owing to a lack of control on administrative overheads, which will gradually erode its sales performance;
- whether the company has lowered its prices in a bid to pass on efficiency gains to customers and thus to strengthen its market position;
- etc.

In the retail sector, the sales density ratio (i.e., sales per m^2 calculated as sales/sales space) measures the company's performance and is a key strategic indicator. Consequently, the sale density ratio obviously needs to be calculated, measured and its annual fluctuations need to be accounted for.

Key points and indicators:
- The rate of growth in sales is the key indicator that needs to be analysed.
- It should be broken down into volume and price trends, as well as into product and regional trends.
- These different rates of growth should then be compared with those for the market at large and (general and sectoral) price indices. Currency effects should be taken into account.
- The impact of changes in the scope of consolidation on sales needs to be studied.

2/PRODUCTION

Sales represent what the company has been able to sell to its customers. Production represents what the company has produced during the year and is computed as follows:

	Production sold; i.e., sales
+	Changes in inventories of finished goods and work in progress at cost price;
+	Production for own use, reflecting the work performed by the company for itself and carried at cost
=	**Production**

First and foremost, production provides a way of establishing a relationship between the materials used during a given period and the corresponding sales generated. As a result, it is particularly important where the company carries high levels of inventories or work in progress. Unfortunately, production is not entirely consistent insofar as it lumps together:

- production sold (sales), shown at the selling price;
- changes in inventories of finished goods and work in progress and production for own use, stated at cost price.

Consequently, production is primarily an accounting concept that depends on the methods used to value the company's inventories of finished goods and work in progress.

A faster rate of growth in production than in sales may be the result of serious problems:

- **overproduction**, which the company will have to absorb in the following year by curbing its activities, bringing additional costs;
- **overstatement of inventories' value**, which will gradually reduce the margins posted by the company in future periods.

Production for own use does not constitute a problem unless its size seems relatively large. From a tax standpoint, it is good practice to maximise the amount of capital expenditure that can be expensed, in which case production for own use is kept to a minimum. An unusually high amount may conceal problems and an effort by management to boost book profit superficially.

Key points and indicators:
- The growth rate in production and the production/sales ratio are the two key indicators.
- They naturally require an analysis of production volumes and inventory valuation methods.

3/ Gross trading profit

Gross trading profit is the difference between the selling price of goods for resale and their purchase cost. It is useful only in the retail and wholesale sectors, where it is a crucial indicator, and it helps to shed light on a company's strategy. It is usually more stable than its components (i.e., sales and the cost of goods for resale sold).

4/ Raw materials used and other operating costs

This is another arena in which price and volume effects are at work, but it is almost impossible to separate them out because of the variety of items involved. At this general level, it is very hard to calculate productivity ratios for raw materials. Consequently, analysts may have to make do with a comparison between the rate of growth in cost of sales and that in net sales (for by-function income statements) or the rate of growth of raw material and other operating costs and that in production (by-nature income statements). A sustained difference between these figures may be attributable to changes in the products manufactured by the company or improvements (deterioration) in the production process.

Conversely, internal analysts may be able to calculate productivity ratios based on actual raw material costs used in the operating cycle since they have access to the company's management accounts.

Key points and indicators:
- What are the main components of this item (raw materials, transportation costs, energy, advertising, etc.), and to what extent have they changed and are they forecast to change?
- Have there been any major changes in the price of each of these components?

5/ Value added

This represents the value added by the company to goods and services purchased from third parties through its activities. It is equivalent to the sum of gross trading profit and profit on raw materials used, less other goods and services purchased from third parties.

It may thus be calculated as follows for by-nature income statements:

> Gross trading profit
> + Profit on raw materials used
> − Other operating costs
> = **Value added**

Other operating costs comprise outsourcing costs, property or equipment rental charges, the cost of raw materials and supplies that cannot be held in inventory (i.e., water, energy, small items of equipment, maintenance-related items, administrative supplies, etc.), maintenance and repair work, insurance premiums, studies and research costs, external personnel charges, fees payable to intermediaries and professional costs, advertising costs, transportation charges, travel costs, the cost of meetings and receptions, postal charges and bank charges (i.e., not interest on bank loans, which is booked under interest expense).

For by-function income statements, value added may be calculated as follows:

> Operating profit (EBIT)
> + Depreciation, amortisation and impairment losses on fixed assets
> + Personnel costs
> + Tax other than corporate income tax
> = **Value added**

At company level, value added is of interest only insofar as it provides valuable insight regarding the degree of a company's integration within its sector. It is not uncommon for an analyst to say that average value added in sector X stands at A, as opposed to B in sector Y. But such comparisons may be seriously flawed, especially if a company relies heavily on outsourcing.

Besides that, we do not regard the concept of value added as being very useful. In our view, it is not very helpful to make a distinction between what a company adds to a product or service internally and what it buys in from the outside. This is because all a company's decisions are tailored to the various markets in which it operates; i.e., the markets for labour, raw materials, capital and capital goods, to cite but a few. Against this backdrop, a company formulates a specific value creation strategy; i.e., a way of differentiating its offering from that of its rivals in order to generate a revenue stream.

This is what really matters – not the internal/external distinction.

In addition, value added is only useful where a market-based relationship exists between the company and its suppliers in the broad sense of the term – e.g., suppliers of raw materials, capital providers, and suppliers of labour. In the food sector, food processing companies usually establish special relationships with the farming industry. As a result, a company with a workforce of 1,000 may actually keep 10,000 farmers in work. This raises the issue of what such a company's real value added is.

Where a company has established special contractual ties with its supplier base, the concept of value added loses its meaning.

Value added is a useful concept only where a market-based relationship exists between a company and its suppliers.

6/PERSONNEL COST

This is a very important item, because it is often high in relative terms and because it is usually very inert. Although personnel cost is theoretically a variable cost par excellence, it actually represents a genuinely fixed cost item from a short-term perspective.

A financial analysis should focus both on volume and price effects (measured by the $\frac{\text{Personnel expense}}{\text{Average headcount}}$ratio) as well as the employee productivity ratio, which is measured by the following ratios:[3]

$$\frac{\text{Sales}}{\text{Average headcount}}, \quad \frac{\text{Production}}{\text{Average headcount}} \quad or \quad \frac{\text{Value added}}{\text{Average headcount}}$$

Since external analysts are unable to make more accurate calculations, they have to make a rough approximation of the actual situation. In general, productivity gains are limited and are thinly spread across most income statement items, making them hard to isolate.

Analysts should not neglect the inertia of personnel cost, either as regards increases or decreases in the headcount. If 100 additional staff are hired throughout the year, this means that only 50% of their salary costs will appear in the first year, with the full amount showing up in the following period. The same applies if employees are laid off.

Key points and indicators:
Personnel cost should be analysed in terms of:
* productivity – sales/average headcount, value added/average headcount and production/average headcount;
* cost control – personnel cost/average headcount;
* growth.

7/AN ANALYSIS OF THE EBITDA MARGIN FORMS A NATURAL CONCLUSION TO THE POINTS CONSIDERED SO FAR

As we saw in Chapter 3, EBITDA is a key concept in the analysis of income statements. The concepts we have just examined – i.e., value added and production – have more to do with macroeconomics, whereas EBITDA belongs firmly to the field of microeconomics.

3 *For year 2005, the first ratio is*

$$\frac{\text{2005 sales}}{\text{Average 2005 headcount}},$$

Average 2005 headcount being equal to Average of 2004 year-end and 2005 year-end headcounts.

We cannot stress more heavily the importance of EBITDA in income statement analysis.

EBITDA represents the difference between operating revenues and cash operating charges. Consequently, it is computed as follows:

	Operating profit (EBIT)
+	Depreciation, amortisation and impairment losses on fixed assets
=	**EBITDA**

Alternatively, for by-nature income statements, EBITDA can be computed as follows:

	Value added
−	Taxes other than on income
−	Personnel cost and payroll charges
−	Impairment losses on current assets and additions to provisions for operating liabilities and charges
+	Other operating revenues
−	Other operating cost
=	**EBITDA**

Other operating cost comprises charges that are not used up as part of the production process and include items such as redundancy payments, recurring restructuring charges payments relating to patents, licences, concessions, representation agreements and directors' fees. Other operating revenues include payments received in respect of patents, licences, concessions, representation agreements, directors' fees, operating subsidies received, etc.

Impairment losses on current assets include impairment losses related to receivables (doubtful receivables), inventories, work in progress and various other receivables related to the current or previous periods. Additions to provisions for operating liabilities and charges primarily include provisions for retirement benefit costs, litigation, major repairs and deferred costs, statutory leave, redundancy or pre-redundancy payments, early retirement, future underactivity, relocation, etc., provided that they relate to the company's normal business activities. In fact, these provisions represent losses for the company and should be deducted from its EBITDA.

Personnel expense and payroll charges also include employee incentive payments, stock options and profit-sharing.

Since it is unaffected by noncash charges – i.e., depreciation, amortisation, impairment charges and provisions, which may leave analysts rather blind-sighted – trends in the EBITDA/sales ratio, commonly known as the **EBITDA margin**, form a central part of a financial analysis. All the points we have dealt with so far in this section should enable a financial analyst to explain why a group's EBITDA margin expanded or contracted by X points between one period and the next. The EBITDA margin change can be attributable to an overrun on production costs, to personnel cost, to the price effect on sales or to a combination of all these factors.

Our experience tells us that competitive pressures are making it increasingly hard for companies to keep their EBITDA margin moving in the right direction!

The following table shows trends in the EBITDA margins posted by various different sectors in Europe over the 1995–2005 period.

download

EBITDA MARGIN IN % OF SALES FOR LEADING LISTED EUROPEAN COMPANIES

Sector	1996	1997	1998	1999	2000	2001	2002	2003	2004	2005e	2006e
Aerospace and defence	7.8	9.1	5.6	10.1	10.0	10.8	9.7	9.8	11.2	11.0	11.0
Automotive	8.1	9.1	9.6	9.3	8.8	8.0	8.3	8.1	8.8	9.0	9.6
Beverages	15.6	18.4	19.1	20.1	20.5	20.5	21.3	21.4	21.2	21.6	22.1
Building materials	13.1	13.2	14.3	16.8	15.5	15.7	15.7	15.4	15.6	16.0	16.2
Capital goods	9.3	8.9	9.6	8.3	8.7	6.8	7.8	7.7	9.7	10.8	11.1
Chemicals	17.1	17.2	17.9	16.9	17.3	16.3	16.8	16.2	17.9	18.1	17.9
Consumer goods	9.5	9.7	9.8	10.6	10.9	10.0	10.8	10.7	10.4	10.5	10.9
Food and home care	12.8	12.9	13.7	14.5	15.2	14.5	14.9	16.3	16.0	16.5	16.8
Food retail	5.8	6.1	6.1	6.0	6.1	6.1	6.4	6.2	6.2	6.5	6.6
General retail	5.8	7.2	9.8	10.1	10.4	10.8	11.4	11.5	12.1	13.3	13.4
IT hardware	10.2	12.7	10.8	12.6	13.6	6.1	9.3	12.9	16.3	16.1	15.4
IT services	10.6	11.5	12.9	12.8	12.7	10.8	7.7	7.7	7.4	8.6	9.5
Leisure and hotels	8.9	10.5	10.0	11.7	11.5	11.8	10.2	9.7	11.0	11.5	10.6
Luxury goods	24.0	22.6	20.4	21.7	21.1	17.3	19.1	21.9	22.4	23.6	24.5
Media	12.6	13.6	16.2	16.1	17.0	16.4	16.9	20.1	21.9	23.0	23.6
Metals and mining	14.6	9.3	11.8	13.8	15.7	13.2	12.9	13.3	18.0	20.0	19.1
Oil and gas	16.7	16.8	18.1	16.7	19.2	18.2	14.8	15.6	16.9	15.7	15.6
Personal care	14.4	14.6	14.8	14.8	15.6	15.1	15.8	16.4	17.7	18.0	18.6
Pharmaceuticals	25.2	23.6	26.6	26.5	27.5	29.0	30.6	30.3	29.3	32.0	32.5
Software	27.6	28.7	24.5	19.7	17.5	20.9	23.7	26.1	27.6	27.4	28.0
Support services	9.5	9.0	8.6	10.0	9.4	8.2	7.6	7.6	7.4	7.6	7.7
Telecom operators and ISPs	39.2	34.3	40.4	37.9	31.1	30.7	32.0	34.9	35.1	35.4	35.7
Transport	18.2	12.9	13.1	14.6	16.6	13.5	17.7	16.4	15.9	16.8	16.8
Utilities	16.1	18.8	18.5	16.4	14.9	15.0	19.0	19.3	19.9	19.5	20.4

Source: Exane BNP Paribas.

It clearly shows, among other things, the tiny but stable EBITDA margin of food retailers, the ever-increasing and very high EBITDA margin of pharmaceutical groups and the large impact of the Internet bubble blowout for telecom operators in 2000–2002.

8/DEPRECIATION, AMORTISATION

In a given period, this income statement item is relatively independent of the operating cycle. Aside from accounting policies, it depends on the company's investment policy, which we examine in greater detail in Chapter 11.

Now we arrive at operating profit (EBIT), an indicator whose stock has risen substantially of late. Analysts usually refer to the operating profit/sales ratio as the **operating margin**, trends in which must also be explained.

9/OPERATING PROFIT OR EBIT

Operating profit is EBITDA less noncash operating costs. It may thus be calculated as follows:

	EBITDA
−	Depreciation and amortisation
+	Writebacks of depreciation and amortisation
=	**Operating profit or EBIT**

Impairment losses on fixed assets relate to operating assets (i.e., brands, purchased goodwill, etc.) are normally included with depreciation and amortisation by accountants. We beg to differ, as impairment losses are normally nonrecurring items and as such should be excluded by the analyst from the operating profit and relegated to the bottom of the income statement.

As we saw in Chapter 3, the by-function format directly reaches operating profit without passing through EBITDA:

	Sales
−	Cost of sales
−	Selling, general and administrative costs
−	Research and development costs
+/−	Other operating income and cost
=	**Operating profit (or EBIT)**

The emphasis placed by analysts on operating performance over the past decade or so has led many companies to attempt to boost their operating profit artificially by excluding charges that should logically be included. These charges are usually to be found on the separate Other income and cost line, below operating profit, and are, of course, normally negative ... as companies want to boost their EBIT.

Other companies publish an operating profit figure and a separate EBIT figure, presented as being more significant than operating profit. Naturally, it is always higher, too ...

For instance, we have seen foreign currency losses of a debt-free company,[4] recurring provisions for length-of-service awards or environmental liabilities, costs related to underactivity and anticipated losses on contracts excluded from

4 Which are necessarily related to the operating process and not the financing process as the

operating profit. In other cases, capital gains on asset disposals have been included in EBIT.

company is debt-free.

We believe it is vital for readers to avoid preconceptions and to analyse precisely what is included and what is not included in operating profit. In our opinion, the broader the operating profit definition, the better!

The following table shows trends in the operating margin posted by various different sectors over the 1995–2005 period.

download

OPERATING PROFIT IN % OF SALES FOR LEADING LISTED EUROPEAN COMPANIES

Sector	1996	1997	1998	1999	2000	2001	2002	2003	2004	2005e	2006e
Aerospace and defence	4.8	6.2	6.6	7.1	5.6	7.3	6.3	6.3	7.8	7.7	7.8
Automotive	3.0	3.9	4.8	4.7	4.0	2.9	3.7	3.3	4.0	4.2	4.9
Beverages	11.3	14.4	14.6	15.6	15.7	16.1	16.9	16.9	16.4	16.9	17.4
Building materials	8.0	8.7	9.5	11.3	10.4	10.4	10.4	10.2	10.8	11.1	11.5
Capital goods	5.3	4.9	4.9	4.2	5.1	1.6	3.7	3.9	5.8	7.1	7.5
Chemicals	9.9	10.9	10.6	9.6	10.4	8.7	9.5	9.0	11.0	11.3	11.2
Consumer goods	5.4	5.8	6.1	7.0	7.5	6.6	7.5	7.5	7.2	7.2	7.7
Food and home care	9.3	9.5	10.4	11.0	12.0	11.6	11.8	13.3	13.0	13.3	13.5
Food retail	3.7	3.9	3.9	3.8	3.8	3.9	4.0	4.0	3.9	4.2	4.3
General retail	4.2	5.6	7.4	7.6	7.8	8.3	8.9	8.9	9.4	10.5	10.7
IT hardware	5.4	7.5	5.4	7.8	8.8	0.0	2.3	5.9	10.2	10.1	9.8
IT services	7.7	8.8	10.4	10.8	10.3	8.0	5.3	5.2	5.3	6.5	7.4
Leisure and hotels	3.2	4.9	5.8	7.1	7.1	7.4	5.6	4.8	6.3	6.9	6.5
Luxury goods	20.4	18.3	16.6	17.7	17.3	13.4	15.1	17.1	18.3	19.2	20.2
Media	7.2	8.2	10.7	10.5	11.1	10.6	10.6	14.3	16.3	17.4	18.1
Metals and mining	7.1	2.0	4.1	7.2	9.7	6.8	6.8	7.6	13.1	15.4	14.3
Oil and gas	10.4	10.8	9.4	10.1	13.8	12.8	9.0	10.0	12.1	11.7	11.0
Personal care	11.1	11.4	11,7	11.6	12.1	11.7	12.2	12.9	14.1	14.4	14.9
Pharmaceuticals	20.0	19.1	21.2	21.3	22.5	23.9	25.0	24.6	25.6	26.5	27.2
Software	22.5	25.6	21.5	17.0	14.8	18.4	21.2	23.4	25.0	25.0	25.7
Support services	7.0	6.8	6.6	8.0	7.4	6.4	5.6	5.6	5.4	5.6	5.8
Telecom operators and ISPs	19.2	13.8	19.9	19.3	14.8	13.6	15.1	19.3	20.0	20.7	21.5
Transport	11.2	6.5	6.5	6.0	8.0	4.3	7.9	6.7	6.8	7.9	8.5
Utilities	9.9	10.7	10.9	9.3	8.2	8.7	11.2	11.8	12.6	12.7	13.1

Source: Exane BNP Paribas.

The reader may notice, for example, how cyclical are the automotive and capital goods sectors in stark contrast to the beverage or food and home care businesses.

Section 9.2
HOW OPERATING PROFIT IS ALLOCATED

1/NET FINANCIAL EXPENSE/INCOME

It may seem strange to talk about net financial income for an industrial or service company whose activities are not primarily geared towards generating financial income. Since finance is merely supposed to be a form of financing a company's operating assets, financial items should normally show a negative balance, and this is generally the case. That said, some companies, particularly large groups generating substantial negative working capital (like big retailers, for instance), have financial aspirations and generate net financial income, to which their financial income makes a significant contribution.

Net financial expense thus equates to financial expense less financial income. Where financial income is greater than financial expense, we naturally refer to it as net financial income.

Financial income includes:

- income from other securities and from loans recorded as fixed assets. This covers all income received from investments other than participating interests – i.e., dividends and interest on loans;
- other interest and related income – i.e., income from commercial and other loans, income from marketable securities, discounts obtained from suppliers, other financial income;
- writebacks of certain provisions and charges transferred – i.e., writebacks of provisions for financial liabilities and charges, of impairment losses on financial items and, lastly, writebacks of financial charges transferred;
- foreign exchange gains on debt;
- net income on the disposal of marketable securities – i.e., capital gains on the disposal of marketable securities.

Financial expense includes:

- interest and related charges;
- foreign exchange losses on debt;
- net expense on the disposal of marketable securities – i.e., capital losses on the disposal of marketable securities;
- amortisation of bond redemption premiums;
- additions to provisions for financial liabilities and charges and impairment losses on investments.

Where a company uses sophisticated financial liabilities and treasury management techniques, we advise readers to analyse its net financial income/(expense) carefully.

Net financial expense is not directly related to the operating cycle but, instead, reflects the size of the company's debt burden and the level of interest rates. There is no volume or price effect to be seen at this level. Chapter 12, which is devoted to the issue of how companies are financed, covers the analysis of net financial expense in much greater detail.

Profit before tax and nonrecurring items or profit on ordinary activities is the difference between operating profit and financial expense net of financial income.

2/INCOME FROM ASSOCIATES, MINORITY INTERESTS, INCOME TAX

Depending on its size, the share of net profits (losses) of associates[5] deserves special attention. Where these profits or losses account for a significant part of net income, either they should be separated out into operating, financial and nonrecurring items to provide greater insight into the contribution made by the equity-accounted associates, or a separate financial analysis should be carried out of the relevant associate.

Minority interests[6] are always an interesting subject and beg the following questions: Where do they come from? Which subsidiaries do they relate to? Do the minority investors finance losses or do they grab a large share of the profits? An analysis of minority interests often proves to be a useful way of working out which subsidiary(ies) generate(s) the group's profits.

Last comes the corporate income tax line, which can be difficult to analyse owing to the effects of deferred taxation, the impact of foreign subsidiaries and tax loss carryforwards. Analysts usually calculate the group's effective tax rate (i.e., corporate income tax divided by profit before tax), which they monitor over time to assess how well the company has managed its tax affairs.

5 *For more on associates see p. 79.*

6 *For more on minority interests see p. 75.*

3/NONRECURRING ITEMS

Nonrecurring items are not an accounting entry but a category of items defined on a case-by-case basis by the analyst and include some exceptional items, extraordinary items, impairment losses on fixed assets and results from discontinuing operations. It makes no sense to assess the current level of nonrecurring items from the perspective of the company's profitability or to predict their future trends. Analysts should limit themselves to understanding their origin and why, for example, the company needed to write down the goodwill.

Section 9.3
FINANCIAL ASSESSMENT

1/THE SCISSORS EFFECT

The scissors effect is first and foremost the product of a simple phenomenon.

The scissors effect is what takes place when revenues and costs move in different or diverging directions. It accounts for trends in profits.

If revenues are growing by 5% p.a. and certain costs are growing at a faster rate, earnings naturally decrease. If this trend continues, earnings will decline further each year and, ultimately, the company will sink into the red. This is what is known as the scissors effect.

DIFFERENT EXAMPLES OF THE SCISSORS EFFECT

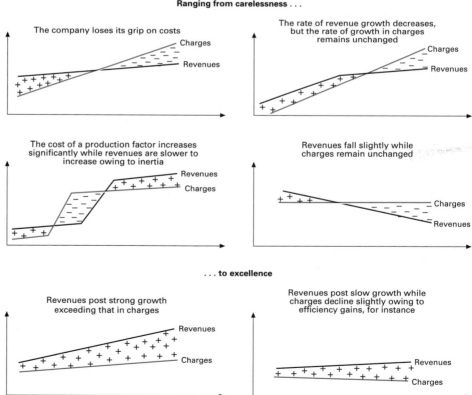

Whether or not a scissors effect is identified matters little. What really counts is establishing the causes of the phenomenon. A scissors effect may occur for all kinds of reasons (regulatory developments, intense competition, mismanagement in a sector, etc.) **that reflect the higher or lower quality of the company's strategic position in its market**. If it has a strong position, it will be able to pass on any increase in its costs to its customers by raising its selling prices and thus gradually widening its margins.

A scissors effect may arise in different situations, some examples of which are given on the previous page.

Where it reduces profits, the scissors effect may be attributable to:

- a statutory freeze on selling prices, making it impossible to pass on the rising cost of production factors;
- psychological reluctance to put up prices. During the 1970s, the impact of higher interest rates was very slow to be reflected in selling prices in certain debt-laden sectors;
- poor cost control – e.g., where a company does not have a tight grip on its cost base and may not be able to pass rising costs on in full to its selling prices. As a result, the company no longer grows, but its cost base continues to expand.

The impact of trends in the cost of production factors is especially important because these factors represent a key component of the cost price of products.

In such cases, analysts have to try to estimate the likely impact of a delayed adjustment in prices. This depends primarily on how the company and its rivals behave and on their relative strength within the marketplace.

But the scissors effect may also work to the company's benefit, as shown by the last two charts.

A company's accounts are littered with potential pitfalls, which must be sidestepped to avoid errors of interpretation during an analysis. The main types of potential traps are as follows.

2/THE STABILITY PRINCIPLE (WHICH PREVENTS ANY SIMPLISTIC REASONING)

This principle holds that a company's earnings are much more stable than we would expect. Net income is frequently a modest amount that remains when **charges are offset against revenues**. Net income represents an equilibrium that is not necessarily upset by external factors. Let's consider, for instance, a supermarket chain, whose net income is roughly equal to its net financial income. It would be a mistake to say that if interest rates decline the company's earnings will be wiped out. The key issue here is whether the company will be able to slightly raise its prices to offset the impact of lower interest rates, without eroding its competitiveness. It probably will be able to do so if all its rivals are in the same boat. But the company may be doomed to fail if more efficient distribution channels exist.

The situation is very similar for champagne houses. A poor harvest drives up the cost of grapes and pushes up the selling price of champagne bottles. Here the key issue is when prices should be increased in view of the competition from sparkling wines, the likely emergence of an alternative product at some point in the future and consumers' ability to make do without champagne, if it is too expensive.

It is important not to repeat the common mistake of establishing a direct link between two parameters and explaining one by trends in the other.

A company's margins also depend to a great extent on those of its rivals. The purpose of financial analysis is to understand why they are above or below those of its rivals.

This said, there are limits to the stability principle.

3/ Regulatory changes

These are controls imposed on a company by an authority (usually the government) that generally restricts the "natural" direction in which the company is moving. For instance, an aggressive devaluation, the introduction of a shorter working week or measures to reduce the opening hours of shops.

4/ External factors

Like regulatory changes, these are imposed on the company. This said, they are more common and are specific to the company's sector of activity; e.g., pressures in a market, arrival (or sudden reawakening) of a very powerful competitor or changes to a collective bargaining agreement.

5/ Pre-emptive action

Pre-emptive action is where a company immediately reflects expectations of an increase in the cost of a production factor by charging higher selling prices. This occurs in the champagne sector where the buildup of pressure in the raw materials market following a poor grape harvest very soon leads to an increase in prices per bottle. Such action is taken even though it will be another 2 or 3 years before the champagne comes onto the marketplace.

Pre-emptive action is particularly rapid where no alternative products exist in the short to medium term and competition in the sector is not very intense. It leads to gains or losses on inventories that can be established by valuing them only at their replacement cost.

6/ Inertia effects

Inertia effects are much more common than those we have just described, and they work in the opposite direction. Owing to inertia, a company may struggle to pass on fluctuations in the cost of its production factors immediately by upping its selling prices. For instance, in a sector that is as competitive and has such low barriers to entry as the road haulage business, there is usually a delay before an increase in diesel fuel prices is passed on to customers in the form of higher shipping charges.

7/INFLATION EFFECTS

Particularly when it is high (e.g., during the 1970s and the early 1980s), inflation distorts company earnings because it acts as an incentive for them to overinvest and overproduce. Should a company planning to expand the capacity of a plant around 4 years in the future decide to build it immediately, it would save 30–40% of its cost in nominal terms, giving it a competitive advantage in terms of accounting costs. Building up excess inventories is another temptation in high-inflation environments because time increases the value of inventories, thereby offsetting the financial expense involved in carrying them and giving rise to inflation gains in the accounts.

Inflation gives rise to a whole series of similar temptations of artificial gains, and any players opting for a more cautious approach during such periods of madness may find themselves steamrollered out of existence. By refusing to build up their inventories to an excessively high level and missing out on inflation gains, they are unable to pass on a portion of them to consumers, as their competitors do. Consequently, during periods of inflation:

- depreciation and amortisation are in most cases insufficient to cover the replacement cost of an investment, the price of which has risen;
- inventories yield especially large nominal inflation gains where they are slow-moving.

Deflation leads to the opposite results.

8/CAPITAL EXPENDITURE AND RESTRUCTURING

It is fairly common for major investments (e.g., the construction of a new plant) to depress operating performance and even lead to operating losses during the first few years after they enter service.

For instance, the construction of a new plant generally leads to:

- additional general and administrative costs, such as R&D and launch costs, professional fees, etc;
- financial charges that are not matched by any corresponding operating revenues until the investment comes on stream (this is a common phenomenon in the hotel sector given the length of the payback periods on investments). In certain cases, they may be capitalised and added to the cost of fixed assets, but this is even more dangerous;
- additional personnel cost deriving from the early recruitment of line staff and managers, who have to be in place by the time the new plant enters service;
- lower productivity owing both to the time it takes to get the new plant and equipment running and the inexperience of staff at the new production facilities.

As a result of these factors, some of the investment spending finds its way onto the income statement, which is thus weighed down considerably by the implications of the investment programme.

Conversely, a company may deliberately decide to pursue a policy of under-investment to enhance its bottom line (so as to be sold at an inflated price) and to maximise the profitability of investments it carried out some time ago. But this type of strategy of maximising margins jeopardises its scope for value creation in the future (it will not create any new products, it will not train sufficient staff to prepare for changes in its business, etc.).

Section 9.4
PRO FORMA INCOME STATEMENTS (INDIVIDUAL AND CONSOLIDATED ACCOUNTS)

The tables on the next two pages show two model income statements, the first of which has been adapted to the needs of individual company accounts and is based on the by-nature format. The second model income statement is based on the by-function format as used in Ericsson Group's consolidated accounts.

The line items shown in blue are specific to consolidated accounts.

Section 9.5
CASE STUDY: ERICSSON

In just two years (from 1998 to 2000) Ericsson's net sales increased by 49% on the back of ever-increasing orders from incumbent phone operators and from new players which secured cheap financing thanks to the Internet bubble. When the bubble burst, some of Ericsson's customers went bankrupt or nearly bankrupt (WorldCom, Mobilcom, KPN) and others dramatically reduced their capital expenditure. Consequently, Ericsson's net sales collapsed by 50% in just 3 years (from 2001 to 2003) and went back to where they were in 1995.

Operating margins plummeted from 8.1% to −13.6% before creeping back to −9.3% as Ericsson fell victim to a scissors effect and an unfavourable mix of fixed and variable costs (as we will see in Chapter 10). During this period many of Ericsson's customers merged (MCI–Worldcom, Vodafone–Manesmann, France Télécom–Orange, etc.), reducing the number of potential customers. No large telecom equipment suppliers made the same strategic move.[7] This naturally weakened their bargaining power *vis-à-vis* their customers.

As a result, Ericsson was not able to reduce its cost of sales as fast as sales collapsed. Costs worryingly increased from 58.4% to 71.4% of sales before falling to a slightly healthier 62.9%. On a more positive note, Ericsson does not seem to have been obliged to cut its R&D spending too far. This is an important point because maintaining R&D is vital for future sales in a sector marked by constant advances in technology.

7 *Lucent and Alcatel tried to merge but failed to agree on who would run the merged entity.*

BY-NATURE INCOME STATEMENT – INDIVIDUAL COMPANY ACCOUNTS

Periods	2005	2006	2007
NET SALES			
+ Changes in inventories of finished goods and work in progress			
+ Production for own use			
= **PRODUCTION**			
− Raw materials used			
− Cost of goods for resale sold			
= Profit on raw materials used/goods for resale sold			
− Other purchases and external charges			
= **VALUE ADDED**			
− Personnel cost (incl. employee profit-sharing and incentives)			
− Taxes other than on income			
+ Operating subsidies			
− Change in operating provisions[8]			
+ Other operating income and cost			
= **EBITDA**			
− Depreciation and amortisation			
= **EBIT (OPERATING PROFIT) (A)**			
Financial expense			
− Financial income			
− Net capital gains/(losses) on the disposal of marketable securities			
+ Change in financial provisions			
= **NET FINANCIAL EXPENSE (B)**			
(A) − (B) = PROFIT BEFORE TAX AND NON RECURRING ITEMS			
+/− Nonrecurring items including impairment losses on fixed assets			
− Corporate income tax			
= **NET INCOME (net profit)**			

8 *Impairment losses on current assets and provisions for operating liabilities and charges.*

BY-FUNCTION INCOME STATEMENT – CONSOLIDATED ACCOUNTS

	1999		2000		2001		2002		2003	
	€m	%	€m	%	€m	%	€m	%	€m	%
NET SALES	23,516	100	24,191	100	25,310	100	15,914	100	12,853	100
− Cost of sales	13,742	58.4	13,168	54.4	18,074	71.4	10,768	67.7	8,091	62.9
= GROSS MARGIN	9,773	41.6	11,023	45.6	7,236	28.6	5,146	32.3	4,763	37.1
− Selling and marketing costs	3,276	13.9	2,900	12.0	3,367	13.3	2,229	14.0	1,306	10.2
− General and administrative costs	1,231	5.2	1,310	5.4	1,355	5.4	1,015	6.4	687	5.3
− Research and development costs	3,616	15.4	3,815	15.8	4,705	18.6	2,881	18.1	2,377	18.5
+/− Other operating income and expense	243	1.0	247	1.0	917	3.6	118	0.7	206	1.6
− Restructuring costs	—	0.0	873	3.6	1,638	6.5	1,306	8.2	1,797	14.0
= OPERATING PROFIT	1,893	8.1	2,371	9.8	−2,911	11.5	−2,167	−13.6	−1,199	−9.3
− Financial expense	324	1.4	534	2.2	719	2.8	632	4.0	530	4.1
+ Financial income	248	1.1	404	1.7	526	2.1	464	2.9	436	3.4
= PROFIT BEFORE TAX AND NONRECURRING ITEMS	1,817	7.7	2,241	9.3	−3,105	12.3	−2,335	−14.7	−1,294	−10.1
+ Income from associates	27	0.1	−1,756	−7.3	−78	0.3	−158	−1.0	−28	−0.2
− Corporate income tax	519	2.2	983	4.1	531	2.1	418	2.6	183	1.4
− Minority interests	44	0.2	68	0.3	101	0.4	37	0.2	22	0.2
NET PROFIT BEFORE IMPAIRMENT LOSSES ON FIXED ASSETS AND NONRECURRING ITEMS	1,281	5.4	−567	2.3	−3,815	−15.1	−2,949	−18.5	−1,526	−11.9
− Impairment losses on fixed assets	—	0.0	—	0.0	—	0.0	—	0.0	—	0.0
+ Nonrecurrent items net of tax	—	0.0	2,751	11.4	—	0.0	—	0.0	—	0.0
= PUBLISHED NET PROFIT	1,281	5.4	2,184	9.0	−3,815	−15.1	−2,949	−18.5	−1,526	−11.9

The first step in any financial analysis is to analyse a company's margins. This is absolutely vital because a company that fails to sell its products or services to its customers at above their cost is doomed.

An analysis of margins and of their level relative to those of a company's competitors reveals a good deal about the strength of company's strategic position in its sector.

Operating profit, which reflects the profits generated by the operating cycle, is a central figure in income statement analysis. First of all, we look at how the figure is formed based on the following factors:

- sales, which are broken down to show the rate of growth in volumes and prices, with trends being compared with growth rates in the market or the sector;

- production, which leads to an examination of the level of unsold products and the accounting method used to value inventories, with overproduction possibly heralding a serious crisis;

- raw materials used and other external charges, which need to be broken down into their main components (i.e., raw materials, transportation, distribution costs, advertising, etc.) and analysed in terms of their quantities and costs;

- personnel cost, which can be used to assess the workforce's productivity (sales/average headcount, value added/average headcount) and the company's grip on costs (personnel cost/average headcount);

- depreciation and amortisation, which reflect the company's investment policy.

Further down the income statement, operating profit is allocated as follows:

- net financial expense, which reflects the company's financial policy. Heavy financial expense is not sufficient to account for a company's problems, it merely indicates that its profitability is not sufficient to cover the risks it has taken;

- nonrecurring items (extraordinary items, some exceptional items and results from discontinuing operations) and the items specific to consolidated accounts (income or losses from associates, minority interests and impairment losses on fixed assets);

- corporate income tax.

Diverging trends in revenues and charges produce a scissors effect, which may be attributable to failures in the market in which the company operates; e.g., economic rents, monopolies, regulatory changes, pre-emptive action, inertia. Identifying the cause of a scissors effect provides valuable insight into the economic forces at work and the strength of the company's strategic position in its sector. We are able to understand why the company generates a profit, and get clues about its future prospects.

SUMMARY

download

1/ Why can a direct link not be drawn between an increase in production costs and the corresponding drop in profits?

2/ What steps can be taken to help offset the impact of a negative scissors effect?

3/ Using the pro forma income statement, carry out a study on the impact that a high rate of inflation will have on earnings. Assume that the quantities sold by the company do not increase, but that sales prices and cash operating charges rise at

QUESTIONS

quiz

the rate of inflation. Perform a careful study of financial expense and depreciation and amortisation, which will lead you to a thorough analysis of EBITDA, EBIT, profit before tax and nonrecurring items and net income.

4/ Of the following companies, which would you define as making "a margin between the end market and an upstream market":
  ○   temporary employment agency;
  ○   storage company (warehouse);
  ○   slaughterhouse;
  ○   furniture manufacturer;
  ○   supermarket.

5/ What does the stability of a company's net profits depend on?
6/ Van Breda NV has positive EBITDA and growth, but negative operating profit. State your views.
7/ What is your view of a company which has seen a huge increase in sales due to a significant drop in prices and a strong volume effect?
8/ Why analyse minority interests on the consolidated income statement?
9/ Why break down contributions made by associate companies into operating, financial and nonrecurring items?

EXERCISES

1/ Identify the sector to which each of the following types of company belongs: electricity producer, supermarket, temporary employment agency, specialised retailer, building and public infrastructure.

Company	1	2	3	4	5
Sales	100	100	100	100	100
Production	100	100	104	99	0
Trading profit	23.0	24.8	0	0	0
Raw materials used	0	0	}46.6	23.6	0
Other external charges	7.8	7.0		46.9	14.1
Personnel cost	9.3	11.7	21.5	24.1	88.2
EBITDA	6.8	6.7	28.1	3.7	4.6
Depreciation and amortisation	2.6	0.9	14.4	1.2	0.7
Operating income	4.2	5.8	7.1	2.9	3.1

2/ Identify the sector to which each of the following types of company belongs: cement, luxury products, travel agency, stationery, telecom equipment.

Company	1	2	3	4	5
Sales	100	100	100	100	100
Cost of sales	35.9	84.0	67.7	44.3	52.2
Marketing and selling costs	37.0	4.4	14.0	23.1	21.8
Administrative costs	11.1	10.0	6.6	10.7	9.3
R&D costs	0	0	20.1	6.6	2.1
Operating income	16.0	1.6	−8.3	15.3	14.6

Questions

1/ *Because of the very complex issues at work which will require further study.*

2/ *Be flexible: outsource, bring in temporary staff.*

3/ *EBITDA keeps pace with inflation, operating income rises faster due to undervaluation of depreciation and amortisation, net income, possibly fictitious (because of understatement of depreciation and amortisation), look acceptable as a result of low financial expense.*

4/ *Temporary employment agency: margin between the direct employment market and the temporary employment market. Warehouse: fixed costs although margins are linked to volumes of business. Slaughterhouse: margin between downstream and upstream. Manufacturer of furniture: margin between raw material, the wood and the sales price. Supermarket: fixed costs, although margins are linked to volumes of business.*

5/ *On the cyclical nature of sales, the flexibility of the company (fixed/variable cost split) and the margin in absolute value.*

6/ *Analyse the investments and amortisation policy, along with impairment losses on fixed assets.*

7/ *What is the impact on EBITDA?*

8/ *In order to find out which of the group's entities is making profits.*

9/ *To obtain a clearer view of the entirety of the income statement, especially operating income.*

Exercises

1/ *Electricity production: 3 (large amount booked under depreciation and amortisation); supermarkets: 1 (lowest trading profits, it is a low-margins business); temporary employment agency: 5 (high personnel cost); specialised retail: 2 (highest trading profits); building and public infrastructure: 4 (high outsourcing costs).*

2/ *Luxury products group: 1 (high operating income margin and high marketing costs. Travel agency: 2 (very low operating income, very high cost of sales, no R&D). Telecom equipment supplier: 3 (high R&D costs). Stationery products group: 4 (high marketing costs but lower than for the luxury products group). Cement group: 5 (the last one! Some R&D).*

Chapter 10
MARGIN ANALYSIS: RISKS

Costs are not like problems, people do not like them to be fixed.

In Chapter 9 we compared the respective growth rates of revenues and costs. In this chapter, we will compare all company revenues, charges, key profit indicators as a percentage of its business – i.e., sales in most cases – and production for companies that experience major swings in their inventories of finished goods and work in progress.

The purpose of this analysis is to avoid extrapolating into the future the rate of earnings growth recorded in the past. Just because profits grew by 30% p.a. for two years as a result of a number of factors, they will not necessarily keep growing at the same pace going forward.

Earnings and sales may not grow at the same pace owing to the following factors:

- structural changes in production;
- the scissors effect (see Chapter 9); or
- **simply a cyclical effect accentuated by the company's cost structure. This is what we will be examining in more detail in this chapter.**

Section 10.1
HOW OPERATING LEVERAGE WORKS

Operating leverage links variation in activity (measured by sales) with variations in result (either operating profit or net income). Operating leverage depends on the level and nature of the breakeven point.

1/DEFINITION

Breakeven is the point at which total revenues cover total charges. With business running at this level, earnings are thus zero.

Put another way:

- if the company does not reach breakeven (i.e., insufficient sales), the company posts losses;

- if sales are exactly equal to the breakeven point, profits are zero;
- if the company exceeds its breakeven point, it generates a profit.

A company's breakeven point depends on its cost structure.

2/CALCULATING BREAKEVEN POINT

Before breakeven point can be calculated, it is vital for costs to be divided up into fixed and variable. This classification depends on the period under consideration. For instance, it is legitimate to say that:

- in the long term, all costs are variable, irrespective of their nature. If a company is unable to adjust its cost base, it is not a viable company;
- in the very short term (less than 3 months), almost all costs are fixed, with the exception of certain direct costs (i.e., some raw materials);
- from a medium-term perspective, certain costs can be considered variable (e.g., indirect personnel cost, etc.).

Breakeven point cannot be defined in absolute terms. It depends first and foremost on the length of the period under consideration. It usually decreases as the period in question increases.

Before starting to calculate a company's breakeven point, it is wise to define which type of breakeven point is needed. This obvious step is all too commonly forgotten. For instance, we may want to assess:

- the projected change in the company's earnings in the event of a partial recession with or without a reduction in the company's output;
- the sensitivity of earnings to particularly strong business levels at the end of the year;
- the breakeven point implied by a strategic plan, particularly that resulting from the launch of a new business venture.

Breakeven point can also be presented graphically:

This chart is fairly basic since fixed costs cannot be considered as such whatever the level of sales, but should be regarded as being fixed only for a certain activity range and increasing or decreasing in steps above or below this range.

Breakeven point is the level of sales at which fixed costs are equal to the contribution margin, which is defined as the difference between sales and variable costs. At the breakeven point, the following equation therefore holds true:

$$\text{Contribution margin} = \text{Fixed costs}$$

$$\text{or} \quad m \times \text{Sales}_0 = \text{Fixed costs}$$

$$\text{i.e.,} \quad \text{Sales}_0 = \frac{\text{Fixed costs}}{m}$$

$$\text{with} \quad m = \frac{\text{Sales} - \text{Variable costs}}{\text{Sales}}$$

where Sales_0 is the level of sales at the breakeven point and m is the contribution margin expressed as a percentage of sales.

Example   A company has sales of €150m, fixed costs of €90m and variable costs of €50m.

Its contribution margin is thus $150 - 50 = 100$; i.e., $100/150 = 66.67\%$ when expressed as a percentage of sales.

Breakeven point thus lies at: $90/0.6667 = €135m$. In this example, the company is 11.1% above its breakeven point.

1 *In: The power of pricing*, *McKinsey Quarterly*, **1**, 29, 2003.

At the beginning of 2003, McKinsey[1] estimated that the typical economics of an S & P 1500 company with a revenue of $100 was $19.2 fixed costs, $68.3 variable costs and an operating profit of $12.5. Accordingly, a decrease of 1% in turnover results in a decrease of 2.5% in operating profit.

3/THREE DIFFERENT BREAKEVEN POINTS

Breakeven point may be calculated before or after payments to the company's providers of funds. As a result, three different breakeven points may be calculated:

- **operating breakeven**, which is a function of the company's fixed and variable production costs that determine the stability of operating profit;
- **financial breakeven**, which takes into account the interest costs incurred by the company that determine the stability of profit before tax and nonrecurring items;
- **total breakeven**, which takes into account all the returns required by the company's lenders **and** shareholders.

Operating breakeven is a dangerous concept because it disregards any returns on capital invested in the company, while financial breakeven understates the actual breakeven point because it does not reflect any return on equity, which is the basis of all value creation.

Consequently, we recommend that readers calculate the breakeven point at which the company is able to generate not a zero net income but a positive net income high enough to provide shareholders with the return they required. To this end, we need to adjust the company's cost base by the profit before tax expected by shareholders. Below this breakeven point, the company may generate a profit, but will not (totally) satisfy the profitability requirements of its shareholders.

Interest charges represent a fixed cost at a given level of sales (and thus capital requirement). A company that experiences significant volatility in its operating profit may thus compensate partially for this instability through modest financial expense; i.e., by pursuing a strategy of limited debt. In any event, earnings instability is greater for a highly indebted company owing to its financial expense, which represents a fixed cost.

To illustrate these concepts in concrete terms, we have prepared the following table calculating the various breakeven points for Ericsson:[2]

2 We analyse the table for Ericsson in Section 10.4 (see p. 188). We have assumed that costs of sales and selling and marketing costs are all variable costs and that other operating costs are fixed. This is evidently a rough cut, but nevertheless gives a reasonable estimate.

BREAKEVEN POINTS (e.g., Ericsson)

€m		1999	2000	2001	2002	2003
Sales		23,516	24,191	25,310	15,914	12,853
Operating fixed costs	FC	4,604	5,751	6,781	5,084	4,655
Financial fixed costs	FiC	76	130	193	168	94
Variable costs	VC	17,018	16,068	21,441	12,937	9,397
Contribution margin as a % of sales	$m = \dfrac{Sales - VC}{Sales}$	27.6%	33.6%	15.3%	18.3%	26.9%
Operating breakeven	$Sales_{op} = \dfrac{FC}{m}$	16,681	17,116	44,310	27,781	17,305
Position of the company relative to operating breakeven as a %	$\dfrac{Sales}{Sales_{op}} - 1$	+41%	+41%	−43%	−43%	−26%
Financial breakeven	$Sales_f = \dfrac{(FC + FiC)}{m}$	16,957	17,503	45,588	28,699	17,654
Position of the company relative to financial breakeven	$\dfrac{Sales}{Sales_f} - 1$	+39%	+38%	−44%	−44%	−27%
Total breakeven [(1)]	$Sales_t = \dfrac{FC + FiC + PBT}{m}$	19,703	20,622	54,248	37,890	23,156
Position of the company relative to total breakeven	$\dfrac{Sales}{Sales_t} - 1$	+19%	+17%	−53%	−58%	−45%

(1): *PBT*: profit before tax expected by shareholders, assumed to be €1,577 m in this analysis for 2003.

Based on these considerations, we see that operating leverage depends on four key parameters:

download

- the three factors determining the stability of operating profit – i.e., the stability of sales, the structure of production costs and the company's position relative to its breakeven point;
- the level of interest expense, which is itself a function of the debt policy pursued by the company.

We saw from our experience up to the late 1990s that, in practice, a company is in an unstable position when its sales are less than 10% above its financial breakeven point. Sales 20% above financial breakeven point reflected a relatively stable situation and sales over 20% above financial breakeven point for a given business structure indicated an exceptional and comfortable situation.

In the highly competitive and unstable conditions that we are currently experiencing, these figures may not be high enough as Ericsson illustrates.

Section 10.2

A MORE REFINED ANALYSIS PROVIDES GREATER INSIGHT

1/ANALYSIS OF PAST SITUATIONS

Breakeven analysis (also known as cost–volume–profit analysis) may be used for three different purposes:

- to analyse earnings stability taking into account the characteristics of the market and the structure of production costs;
- to assess a company's real earnings power;
- to analyse the difference between forecasts and actual performance.

(a) Analysis of earnings stability

Here the level of the breakeven point in absolute terms matters much less than the company's position relative to its breakeven point.

The closer a company is to its breakeven point, the higher its earnings instability.

When a company is close to its breakeven point, a small change in sales triggers a steep change in its net income, so a strong rate of earnings growth may simply reflect a company's proximity to its breakeven point. This is the real problem affecting Japanese industry, the profitability of which is weak compared with that of industrial sectors in other countries.

Consider a company with the following manufacturing and sales characteristics:

Total fixed costs	=	€200,000
Variable costs per unit	=	€50
Unit selling price	=	€100

Its breakeven point stands at 4,000 units. To make a profit, the company therefore has to sell at least 4,000 units.

The following table shows a comparison of the relative increases (or reductions) in sales and earnings at five different sales volumes:

	Sales volumes		Net income		Sensitivity
Number of units sold	% increase compared with previous level (A)	Amount	% increase compared with previous level (B)		(A)/(B)
4,000		0			
5,000	25%	50,000	Infinite		Infinite
6,000	20%	100,000	100%		5
7,200	20%	160,000	60%		3
8,640	20%	232,000	45%		2.25

This table clearly shows that the closer the breakeven point, the higher the sensitivity of a company's earnings to changes in sales volumes. This phenomenon holds true both above and below the breakeven point.

We should be wary when profits are increasing much faster than sales for a company with low margins since this phenomenon may be attributable to the operating leverage.

Consequently, breakeven analysis helps put into perspective a very strong rate of earnings growth during a good year. Rather than getting carried away with one good performance, analysts should attempt to assess the risks of subsequent downturns in reported profits.

For instance, BMW and Volkswagen posted similar sales trends, but completely different earnings trends during 2003 because their proximity to breakeven point was very different. BMW was clearly farther from its breakeven point than Volkswagen as can be seen by comparing operating margins: 8.1% vs. 2.9%.

	Sales	Operating income
BMW	€41,525m (−2%)	€3,353m (−4%)
Volkswagen	€87,153m (−2%)	€2,491m (−48%)

Likewise, the sensitivity of a company's earnings to changes in sales depends to a great extent on its cost structure. The higher a company's fixed costs, the greater the volatility of its earnings as illustrated by the following example.

	Sales	Net income
Tesco	€20,646m (+18%)	€808m (+22%)
Roche	€21,000m (+11%)	€2,691m (+24%)
Heidelberg Cement	€6,908m (+9%)	€334m (+215%)

Tesco, the UK food retailer, has the lowest fixed costs of the three and Heidelberg Cement the highest. An increase in the turnover of 9% of the cement producer pushes up its earnings by 215%, whereas an increase in sales double that percentage (18%) only increased Tesco's net income by 22%. Roche, the Swiss pharmaceutical group whose fixed costs are in between those of Tesco and Heidelberg Cement, registers about the same increase in net income as Tesco (+24%) prompted by an increase in sales of 11%, similar to that of Heidelberg Cement.

(b) Assessment of normal earnings power

Operating leverage, which accelerates the pace of growth or contraction in a company's earnings triggered by changes in its sales performance, means that the significance of income-statement-based margin analysis should be kept in perspective.

The reason for this is that an exceptionally high level of profits may be attributable to exceptionally good conditions that will not last. In such conditions good performance does not necessarily indicate a high level of structural profitability. This held true for a large number of companies during 2000.

Consequently, an assessment of a company's earnings power deriving from its structural profitability drivers needs to take account of the operating leverage and cyclical trends; i.e.: Are we currently in an expansion phase of the cycle?

We have been struck by the fact that certain analysts have described as growth companies groups (such as commercial TV groups) whose earnings have posted very strong increases owing to exceptionally supportive conditions to a much greater extent than structural growth.

(c) Variance analysis

Breakeven analysis helps analysts account for differences between the budgeted and actual performance of a company over a given period.

The following table helps illustrate this phenomenon:

	Value in absolute terms				Structure	
	Budget	Actual (A)	Change	% difference	Actual sales (B)/ Budgeted margin	% difference (A) − (B)
Sales	240	180	−60	−25%	180	—
Variable costs	200	155	−45	−22.5%	150	+5%
Contribution margin	40	25	−15	−37.5%	30	−5%
Margin	16.66%	13.9%			16.66%	
Fixed costs	20	25	+5	+25%	20	+5%
Earnings	20	0	−20	−100%	10	−10%

This table shows the collapse in the company's earnings of 20 is attributable to both:

- the fall in sales (−25%);
- the surge in fixed costs (+25%);
- the surge in variable costs as a proportion of sales from 83.33% to 86.1%.

The cost structure effect accounts for 50% of the earnings decline (5 in higher fixed costs and 5 in higher variable costs), **with the impact of the sales contraction** accounting for the remaining 50% of the decline (10 lost in contribution margin).

2/ STRATEGIC ANALYSIS

(a) Industrial strategy

A company's breakeven point is influenced by its industrial strategy.

A large number of companies operating in cyclical sectors made a mistake by raising their breakeven point through heavy investment. In fact, they should have been seeking to achieve the lowest possible breakeven point and, above all, the most flexible possible cost structure to curb the effects of major swings in business levels on their profitability.

For instance, integration has often turned out to be a costly mistake in the construction sector. Only companies that have maintained a lean cost structure through a strategy of outsourcing have been able to survive the successive cycles of boom and bust in the sector.

In highly capital-intensive sectors and those with high fixed costs (pulp, metal tubing, cement, etc.), it is in companies' interests to use equity financing. Such financing does not accentuate the impact of ups and downs in their sales on their bottom line through the leverage effect of debt, but in fact attenuates their impact on earnings.

A breakeven analysis provides a link between financial and industrial strategy.

When a company finds itself in a tight spot, its best financial strategy is to reduce its financial breakeven point by raising fresh equity rather than debt capital, since the latter actually increases its breakeven point, as we have seen.

If the outlook for its market points to strong sales growth in the long term, a company may decide to pick up the gauntlet and invest. In doing so, it raises its breakeven point, while retaining substantial room for manoeuvre. It may thus decide to take on additional debt.

As we will see in Chapter 36, the only real difference in terms of cost between debt and equity financing can be analysed in terms of a company's breakeven point.

(b) Restructuring

When a company falls below its breakeven point, it sinks into the red. It can return to the black only by increasing its sales, lowering its breakeven point or boosting its margins.

Increasing its sales is only a possibility if the company has real strategic clout in its marketplace. Otherwise, it is merely delaying the inevitable: sales will grow at the expense of the company's profitability, thereby creating an illusion of improvement for a while, but inevitably precipitating cash problems.

Lowering the breakeven point entails restructuring industrial and commercial operations; e.g., modernisation, reductions in production capacity, cuts in overheads. The danger with this approach is that management may fall into the trap of believing that it is reducing only the company's breakeven point when it is actually shrinking its business. In many cases, **a vicious circle sets in, as the measures taken to lower breakeven trigger a major business contraction, obliging the company to lower its breakeven point further, thereby sparking another business contraction, etc.**

Boosting margins means improving management, enhancing the competitiveness of products, eliminating low- or zero-margin products, and consolidating operations around their existing strengths.

(c) Analysis of cyclical risks

As we stated earlier, there is no such thing as an absolute breakeven point, but there are as many breakeven points as there are periods of analysis. But, first and foremost, the breakeven point is a dynamic rather than static concept. If sales fall by 5%, the mathematical formulae will suggest that earnings may decline by 20%, 30% or more, depending on the exact circumstances. In fact, experience shows that earnings usually fall much further than breakeven analysis predicts.

A contraction in market volumes is often accompanied by a price war, leading to a decline in the contribution margin. In this situation, fixed costs may increase, as customers are slower to pay; inventories build up leading to higher interest costs and higher operating provisions. All these factors may trigger a larger reduction in earnings than that implied by the mathematical formulae of breakeven analysis.

During cyclical downturns, contribution margins tend to decline, while fixed costs are often higher than expected.

Consequently, breakeven point increases while sales decline as many recent examples show. Any serious forecasting thus requires modelling based on a thorough analysis of the situation.

During the German property slump mid-1990 (after the reunification boom), a mere slowdown in growth halted the speculators in their tracks. Crippled by their interest expense, they were obliged to lower prices, which led to speculation of a fall in the market (purchases were delayed in expectation of an additional fall in prices).

Businesses such as telecoms and paper production, which require substantial production capacity that takes time to set up, periodically experience production gluts or shortages. As readers are aware, if supply is inflexible, a volume glut (or shortage) of just 5% may be sufficient to trigger far larger price reductions (or hikes) (i.e., 30%, 50% and sometimes even more).

Here, again, an analysis of competition (its strength, patterns and financial structure) is a key factor when assessing the scale of a crisis.

Section 10.3
FROM ANALYSIS TO FORECASTING: THE CONCEPT OF NORMATIVE MARGIN

Nowadays, a great deal of the analysis of financial statements for past periods is carried out for the purpose of preparing financial projections. These forecasts are based on the company's past and the decisions taken by management. This section contains some advice about how best to go about this type of exercise.

All too often, it is not sufficient merely to set up a spreadsheet, click on the main income statement items determining EBITDA[3] (or operating profit if depreciation and amortisation are also to be forecast) and then apply to all of these items a fixed rate of growth, which may be reasonable in itself, but implies unreasonable assumptions when applied systematically. Growth is not a process that can continue endlessly!

Instead, readers should:

- gain a full understanding of the company and especially its key drivers and margins;
- build growth scenarios, as well as possible reactions by the competition, the environment, international economic conditions, etc.;
- draw up projections and analyse the coherence of the company's economic (is its investment sufficient? etc.) and strategic policy.

To this end, financial analysts have developed the concept of normalised earnings; i.e., a given company in a given sector should achieve an operating margin of x% (i.e., operating profit/sales).

This type of approach is entirely consistent with financial theory, which states that in each sector profitability should be commensurate with the sector's risks and that, sooner or later, these margins will be achieved, even though adjustments may take some considerable time (i.e., 5 years or even more); in any case, much longer than they do in the financial markets.

What factors influence the size of these margins? This question can be answered only in qualitative terms and by performing an analysis of the strategic strengths and weaknesses of a company, which are all related to the concept of barriers to entry:

- the degree of maturity of the business;
- the strength of competition and quality of other market players;
- the importance of commercial factors, such as market share, brands, distribution networks, etc.;
- the type of industrial process and incremental productivity gains, etc.

This approach is helpful because it takes into consideration the economic underpinnings of margins. Its drawback lies in the fact that analysts may be tempted to overlook the company's actual margin and concentrate more on its future, theoretical margins.

We cannot overemphasise the importance of explicitly stating and verifying the significance of all forecasts.

3 *Earnings Before Interest, Taxes, Depreciation and Amortisation.*

4 *The breakeven table for Ericsson is on p. 181.*

Section 10.4
Case study[4]: Ericsson

Most of the time the information provided by listed companies is not enough for an external analyst to be able to compute precisely the breakeven point.

Nonetheless, a rough estimate may be made using linear regression of each cost against net sales to approximate the breakdown between fixed and variable costs. This is what we have done for Ericsson to fill in the table on p. 181.

As expected, Ericsson went from a comfortable position (41% above the operating breakeven point in 1999) to an uneasy one in 2001 (43% below breakeven). As the group had hardly any net financial costs, its financial breakeven point was not substantially different from its operating one.

To escape bankruptcy, Ericsson drastically reduced its fixed costs (−25% in 2002, and −8% again in 2003) and pushed its 2003 contribution margin back to its 1999's level: around 27% of sales. To achieve that result, Ericsson has had to spend €5.6bn in restructuring costs since 2001 and lay off 54% of its employees ... In 2003, fixed costs were back at 1999 levels, but sales were still down 45% on that year, which explains why the group was still posting heavy losses.

To be able to move back into profit, Ericsson would need either to increase its sales by 35% with no further fixed costs or to reduce its fixed costs by 26% while keeping the same level of net sales.

A daunting challenge!

SUMMARY

download

Breakeven point is the level of business activity, measured in terms of production, sales or the quantity of goods sold, at which total revenues cover total charges. At this level of sales, a company makes zero profit.

Breakeven point is not an absolute level – it depends on the length of period being considered because the distinction between fixed and variable costs can be justified only by a set of assumptions and, sooner or later, any fixed cost can be made variable.

Three different breakeven points may be calculated:

- operating breakeven, which is a function of the company's fixed and variable production costs. It determines the stability of operating activities, but may lead to financing costs being overlooked;

- financial breakeven, which takes into account the interest expense incurred by the company, but not its cost of equity;

- total breakeven, which takes into account both interest expense and the net profit required by shareholders. As a result, it takes into account all the returns required by all the company's providers of funds.

Operating breakeven is calculated by dividing a company's fixed costs by its contribution margin ((Sales − Variable costs)/Sales). Financial breakeven is calculated by adding interest expense to the fixed costs in the previous formula. Total breakeven is computed by adding the net income required to cover the cost of equity to fixed operating costs and interest costs.

The calculation and a static analysis of a company's breakeven point can be used to assess the stability of its earnings, its normal earnings power and the actual importance of the differences between budgeted and actual performance. The further away a company lies from its breakeven point, the more stable its earnings and the more significant its earnings trends are. The higher its fixed costs as a share of total costs are, the higher the breakeven point and the greater the operating leverage and the volatility of its earnings are.

An analysis of trends in the operating leverage over time reveals a good deal about the company's industrial strategy. An attempt to harness economies of scale will raise the breakeven point and thus make a company more sensitive to economic trends. Efforts to make its industrial base more flexible will lower its breakeven point, but may also reduce its potential earnings power.

QUESTIONS

@
quiz

1/ A company's net income, which was 0.2% of sales in year 1, leaps by 40% in year 2. State your views.

2/ Would it be better for an oil refinery to finance its needs using equity or debt?

3/ Would it be better for an Internet startup company to finance its needs using equity or debt?

4/ You are appointed financial director of a cement group which has no debt. What should you be concerned about?

5/ You are appointed financial director of a cement group which has a fairly substantial amount of debts. What should you be concerned about?

6/ Is personnel cost a variable or a fixed cost?

7/ A major investment bank announces the best half-year results it has ever achieved. State your views.

EXERCISES

1/ Below are the income statements of four companies with the same level of sales, but with different production costs and financial structures.

	A	B	C	D
Sales	100	100	100	100
Variable costs	65	55	36	30
Fixed costs	25	29	50	55
EBITDA	10	16	14	15
Depreciation and amortisation	2	8	4	6
EBIT[5]	8	8	10	9
Financial expense	2	6	1.5	6
Profit before tax and nonrecurring items	6	2	8.5	3

5 _Earnings Before Interest and Taxes._

For each company, calculate the breakeven point, before and after financial costs, and the company's position relative to its breakeven point.

2/ Below are the income statements for the Spanish Hoyos Group. The company asks you to analyse these statements and answer the following questions:

(a) What is your opinion of the company?
(b) Is the company moving closer towards or further away from breakeven point?
(c) In your view, is the company in a period of heavy capital expenditures?
(d) What choices are made with regard to cost control?
(e) Explain the rise in financial expense.

Grupo Hoyos	1	2	3
Sales	82,000	92,000	97,000
Change in finished goods and in-progress inventory	500	1,400	2,800
Operating revenues	82,500	93,400	99,800
Purchases of raw materials and goods for resale	24,800	27,400	29,900
Change in inventories	−1,700	−500	−1,600
Other external charges	20,200	23,000	23,500
Taxes	1,200	1,400	1,500
Personnel cost	29,000	33,000	37,000
Depreciation and amortisation	5,200	4,900	4,800
Provisions	100	200	—
Operating charges	78,800	89,400	95,100
Operating income	3,700	4,000	4,700
Interest, dividends and other financial income	300	400	300
Interest and other finance charges	2,300	2,900	3,900
Financial income	−2,000	−2,500	−3,600
Nonrecurring income	−100	−100	+100
Tax	800	700	600
Net income	800	700	600

3/ In January of year 0, the Swiss group Schmidheiny published the following projected figures:

Projected	0	1	2	3
Production	70.2	106	132	161
Raw materials used	29.4	35.4	44.3	53.8
Personnel cost	22.2	29.4	36.7	41.1
Taxes	0.5	0.7	0.7	0.8
Other external services	13.7	19.8	24.6	30.5
Outsourcing	2.5	8.9	11.2	11.3
Depreciation and amortisation	1.4	2.7	3.6	5

(a) Calculate the breakeven point for each year. The cost structure is as follows:
  ○ variable costs: raw materials used, outsourcing, 50% of other external services;
  ○ fixed costs: all other costs.

(b) Schmidheiny is planning a capital expenditure programme which should increase its production capacity threefold. This programme, which is spread over years 0 to 1, includes the construction of four factories and the launch of new products. The income statements for years 1, 2 and 3 factor in these investments. State your views.

(c) The company will need to raise around €30m to finance this capital expenditure programme. Financial expense before this capital expenditure programme amounts to €1.6m, and Schmidheiny is planning to finance its new requirements using debt exclusively (average cost of debt: 10% before tax).

What is your view of the debt policy the company intends to pursue?

ANSWERS

Questions

1/ *Low profit levels mean that any improvement in the economic situation will very quickly lead to higher profits (company close to breakeven point).*
2/ *A company with a very cyclical activity: financing with equity.*
3/ *Shareholders' equity.*
4/ *Turn a maximum of costs into variable costs, and bring down fixed costs.*
5/ *The same concerns as question 4, and get rid of your debts!*
6/ *It depends on whether the staff are permanent or temporary and on the breakdown of salaries between fixed salary and commissions/bonuses and on whether local rules allow you to fire people rapidly (as in UK) or not (as in Germany or France).*
7/ *How much of this improvement can be attributed to an improvement in the economy, and how much to structural improvements?*

Exercises

1/

	A	B	C	D
Sales	100	100	100	100
Contribution	35	45	64	70
Contribution in % of sales	35%	45%	64%	7%
Breakeven point before financial expense[6]	77	82	84	87
Sales/breakeven	129.6%	121.6%	118.5%	114.8%
Breakeven point after financial expense	83	96	87	96
Sales/breakeven	120.7%	104.7%	115.3%	104.5%

6 *Total fixed costs = Fixed operating costs + Depreciation and amortisation.*

2/ (a) *Personnel cost will increasingly eat into EBITDA. Given the steep rise in financial expense, profit before tax and nonrecurring items decreases in both absolute and relative value. The company is becoming less and less profitable, and accumulating more and more debts. One-quarter of increased production is artificial, as it is tied up in inventories and finished products. The company is producing more but cannot shift its products.*

(b) With stable margins on purchases and an increase in other costs, the company is clearly approaching its breakeven point.

(c) With depreciation and amortisation down in absolute value, we can conclude that the company is not overinvesting in fixed assets.

(d) The management of Grupo Hoyos keeps tight control over raw materials, probably a reflection of a sound procurement policy. External charges are also well-managed. Personnel cost is, however, out of control.

(e) The company is not investing, and the explanation for the increase in financial expense probably lies in the rise in working capital (increase in inventories).

3/ (a) Economic breakeven point

Schmidheiny	0	1	2	3
Production	70.2	106	132	161
Variable costs	38.75	54.2	67.8	80.35
Contribution	31.45	51.8	64.2	80.65
Contribution as a % of sales	44.80	48.87	48.64	50.09
Fixed costs	30.95	42.7	53.3	62.15
Breakeven	69.08	87.38	109.59	124.07

(b) A good investment: improvement in earnings with fixed costs rising at a slower rate than production. The company is moving further away from its breakeven point. Trebling production capacity only results in a doubling of fixed costs. Improvement in production or overoptimistic projections?

(c) Breakeven point after financial expense with the envisaged level of debt.

	1	2	3
Breakeven point after financial expense	96.8	119.0	133.3

Debt capital significantly increases breakeven point and accordingly, the risk.

BIBLIOGRAPHY

G. Buccino, K. McKinley, The importance of operating leverage in a turnaround, *Secured Lender*, 64–68, Sept./Oct. 1997.

M. Marn, E. Roegner, C. Zawada, The power of pricing, *McKinsey Quarterly*, **1**, 27–36, 2003.

Chapter 11
WORKING CAPITAL AND
CAPITAL EXPENDITURES

The company's lifeblood ...

As we saw in the standard financial analysis, all value creation requires investment. In finance, investment means creating either new fixed assets or working capital. The latter, often high in continental Europe, merits some explanation.

Section 11.1
THE NATURE OF WORKING CAPITAL

Every analyst intuitively tries to establish a percentage relationship between the working capital of a company and one or more of the measures of the volume of its business activities. In most cases, the chosen measure is annual turnover or sales (excl. VAT).

The ratio

$$\frac{\text{Operating working capital}}{\text{Annual sales (excl. VAT)}}$$

reflects the fact that the operating cycle generates an operating working capital that includes:

- capital "frozen" in the form of inventories, representing procurement and production costs that have not yet resulted in the sale of the company's products;
- funds "frozen" in customer receivables, representing sales that customers have not yet paid for;
- accounts payable that the company owes to suppliers.

The balance of these three items represents the net amount of money tied up in the operating cycle of the company. In other words, if the working capital turnover ratio is 25% (which is high), this means that 25% of the company's annual sales volume is "frozen" in inventories and customer receivables not financed by supplier credit. This also means that, at any moment, the company needs to have on hand funds equal to a quarter of its annual sales to pay suppliers and employee salaries for materials and work performed on products or services that have not yet been manufactured, sold or paid for by customers.

The following table shows trends in the working capital turnover ratio by various sectors over the 1995–2005 period.

WORKING CAPITAL IN % OF SALES FOR LEADING LISTED EUROPEAN COMPANIES

Sector	1996	1997	1998	1999	2000	2001	2002	2003	2004	2005e	2006e
Aerospace and defence	3	3	−1	1	−5	−1	−6	−2	−6	−3	−3
Automotive	3	12	11	13	16	16	17	17	15	15	14
Beverages	8	7	10	9	11	13	10	8	7	9	9
Building materials	10	10	9	8	7	6	6	6	6	6	6
Capital goods	17	17	18	8	9	4	4	5	4	5	5
Chemicals	16	16	17	18	19	18	18	18	16	17	17
Consumer goods	20	20	20	18	19	16	12	12	12	12	12
Food and home care	9	6	6	6	5	4	1	2	1	1	1
Food retail	−6	−6	−4	−5	−5	−5	−5	−6	−6	−6	−6
General retail	3	4	12	10	8	6	5	4	4	4	3
IT hardware	18	17	20	17	18	16	11	10	10	11	12
IT services	10	4	2	4	9	8	6	6	5	4	5
Leisure and hotels	3	7	3	−9	−1	−2	−1	−4	−6	−6	−2
Luxury goods	34	26	32	39	35	36	29	31	30	30	29
Media	−1	−3	−5	−2	−12	−9	−8	−10	−11	−11	−10
Metals and mining	17	14	14	21	19	19	18	16	14	14	15
Oil and gas	4	1	0	3	0	1	1	1	1	1	1
Personal care	14	14	13	13	16	15	13	12	12	12	12
Pharmaceuticals	19	19	22	21	15	14	17	18	17	17	18
Software	−4	25	3	−1	5	5	2	1	−2	−2	−2
Support services	0	1	0	1	0	−2	−3	−2	−2	−2	−2
Telecom operators and ISPs	−7	−11	−6	−4	−8	−7	−9	−11	−10	−10	−9
Transport	−17	−7	−7	−11	−11	−12	−13	−14	−10	−10	−9
Utilities	3	9	10	3	4	2	2	−1	−3	−3	−3

Source: Exane BNP Paribas.

In the economy, working capital is clearly down over the last 10 years from 9% in average of sales to 5% in 2005. Some sectors benefit from negative working capital: transport (you buy your airline ticket in advance), media (subscription to pay TV or magazine), food retail. Others are less fortunate: chemicals, luxury goods, metals and mining with high working capital due to the weight of inventories.

As we will see in Section 11.2, working capital is often expressed as a number of days of sales. This figure is arrived at by multiplying a percentage ratio by 365. In our example, a ratio of 25% indicates that working capital totals around 90 days of the company's sales.

1/STEADY BUSINESS, PERMANENT WORKING CAPITAL

Calculated from the balance sheet, a company's working capital is the balance of the accounts directly related to the operating cycle. According to traditional financial theory, these amounts are very liquid; that is, they will either be collected or paid within a very short period of time. **But, in fact, although it is liquid, working capital also reflects a permanent requirement.**

No matter when the books are closed, the balance sheet always shows working capital, although the amount changes depending on the statement date. The only exceptions are the rare companies whose operating cycle actually generates cash rather than absorbs it.

There is an apparent contradiction between the essentially liquid nature of working capital on the one hand and its permanence on the other hand.

Working capital is liquid in the sense that every element of it disappears in the ordinary course of business. Raw materials and inventories are consumed in the manufacturing process. Work in progress is gradually transformed into finished products. Finished products are (usually) sold. Receivables are (ordinarily) collected and become cash, bank balances, etc. Similarly, debts to suppliers become outflows of cash when they are paid.

As a result, if the production cycle is less than a year (which is usually the case) all of the components of working capital at the statement date will disappear in the course of the following year. But, at the next statement date, other operating assets will have taken their place. **This is why we view working capital as a permanent requirement.**

Even if each component of working capital has a relatively short lifetime, the operating cycles are such that the contents of each are replaced by new contents. As a result, if the level of business activity is held constant, the various working capital accounts remain at a constant level.

In sum, at any given point in time, a company's working capital is indeed liquid. It represents the difference between some current assets and some current liabilities. But thinking in terms of a "permanent working capital" introduces a radically different concept. It suggests that if business is stable, current (liquid) operating assets and current operating liabilities will be renewed and new funds will be tied up, constituting a permanent capital requirement as surely as fixed assets are a permanent capital requirement.

Working capital is two-sided. From the point of view of balance sheet value, it is liquid. From a going concern point of view, it is permanent.

2/SEASONAL BUSINESS ACTIVITY, PARTLY SEASONAL REQUIREMENT

When a business is seasonal, purchases, production and sales do not take place evenly throughout the year. As a result, working capital also varies during the course of the year, expanding, then contracting.

The following graphs show that the working capital of a seasonal business never falls to zero. Whether the company sells canned vegetables or raincoats, a minimum level of inventories is always needed to carry the company over to the next production cycle.

download

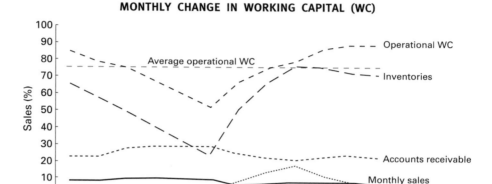

Question 10 at the end of this chapter will ask you to take a closer look at these graphs.

In our experience, companies in seasonal businesses often pay too much attention to the seasonal aspect of their working capital and ignore that a significant part of it is permanent. As some costs are fixed, so are some parts of the working capital.

We have observed, for example, that in some very seasonal businesses, such as toys, the peak working capital is only twice the minimum. This means that half of the working capital is permanent, the other half seasonal.

3/CONCLUSION: PERMANENT WORKING CAPITAL AND THE COMPANY'S ONGOING NEEDS

An external analyst risks confusing the working capital on the balance sheet with the permanent working capital.

About 30% of all companies close their books at a date other than 31 December. Bordeaux vineyards close on 30 September, Caribbean car rental companies on 30 April. They choose these dates because that is when the working capital requirement shown on their balance sheets is lowest. This is pure window-dressing.

A company in trouble uses trade credit to the maximum possible extent. In this case, you must restate working capital by eliminating trade credit that is in excess of normal levels. Similarly, if inventory is unusually high at the end of the year because the company speculated that raw material prices would rise, then the excess over normal levels should be eliminated in the calculation of permanent working capital. Lastly, to avoid giving the impression that the company is too cash-rich, some companies make an extra effort to pay their suppliers before the end of the year. This is more akin to investing cash balances than to managing working capital.

It may be rash to say that the working capital at fiscal year-end is the company's permanent working capital.

Although the working capital on the balance sheet at year-end cannot be used as an indicator of the company's permanent requirement, its year-to-year change can still be informative. Calculated at the same date every year, there should be no seasonal impact. Analysing how the requirement has changed from year-end to year-end can shed light on whether the company's operations are improving or deteriorating.

The year-end working capital is informative only if compared with the working capital at other year-end dates.

You are therefore faced with a choice:

- if the company publishes quarterly financial statements, you can take the permanent working capital to be the lowest of the quarterly balances;
- if the company publishes only year-end statements, you must reason in terms of year-to-year trends and comparisons with competitors.[1]

1 *Provided competitors have the same balance sheet closing date.*

Section 11.2

WORKING CAPITAL TURNOVER RATIOS

As financial analysis consists of uncovering hidden realities, let's simulate reality to help us understand the analytical tools.

Working capital accounts are composed of uncollected sales, unsold production and unpaid-for purchases. In other words, the business activities that took place during the days preceding the statement date. Specifically:

- if customers pay in 15 days, receivables represent the last 15 days of sales;
- if the company pays suppliers in 30 days, accounts payable represent the last 30 days of purchases;
- if the company stores raw materials for 3 weeks before consuming them in production, the inventory of raw materials represents the last 3 weeks of purchases.

These are the principles. Naturally, the reality is more complex, because:

- payment periods can change;
- business is often seasonal, so the year-end balance sheet may not be a real picture of the company;
- payment terms are not the same for all suppliers or all customers;
- manufacturing process is not the same for all products.

Nevertheless, working capital turnover ratios calculated on the basis of accounting balances represent an attempt to see the reality behind the figures.

1/THE MENU OF RATIOS

(a) Days/receivables

The days/receivables ratio measures the average payment terms the company grants to its customers (or the average actual payment period). It is calculated by dividing the receivables balance by the company's average daily sales, as follows:

$$\frac{\text{Receivables}}{\text{Annual sales (incl. VAT)}} \times 365 = \text{Days sales outstanding}$$

As the receivables on the balance sheet are shown inclusive of VAT, for consistency, sales must be shown on the same basis. But the sales shown on the profit and loss statement are exclusive of VAT. You must therefore increase it by the applicable VAT rate for the products the company sells or by an average rate if it sells products taxed at different rates.

VAT RATES ACROSS EUROPE, JAPAN AND THE USA

	Reduced rate	Normal rate
France	2.1 or 5.5%	19.6%
Germany	7%	16%
Italy	4–10%	20%
Japan	—	5%
Netherlands	6%	19%
Poland	0–7%	22%
Russia	10%	18%
Spain	4–7%	16%
Sweden	6–12%	25%
Switzerland	2.4–3.6%	7.6%
United Kingdom	0–5%	17.5%
United States of America*	—	—

*VAT does not exist in the USA. A sale tax is paid. Its rate varies across states.

Receivables are calculated as follows:

	Customer receivables and related accounts
+	Outstanding bills discounted
−	Advances and deposits on orders being processed
=	Total receivables

(b) Days/payables

The days/payables ratio measures the average payment terms granted to the company by its suppliers (or the average actual payment period). It is calculated by dividing accounts payable by average daily purchases, as follows:

$$\frac{\text{Accounts payable}}{\text{Annual purchases (incl. VAT)}} \times 365 = \text{Number of days of payables}$$

Accounts payable are calculated as follows:

	Accounts payable and related accounts
−	Advances and deposits paid on orders
=	Total accounts payable

To ensure consistency, purchases are valued inclusive of VAT. They are calculated as follows:

	Purchase of goods held for resale (incl. VAT)
+	Purchase of raw materials (incl. VAT)
+	Other external costs (incl. VAT)

The amounts shown on the profit and loss statement must be increased by the appropriate VAT rate.

When the figure for annual purchases is not available (mainly when the income statement is published in the by-function format), the days/payables ratio is approximated as:

$$\frac{\text{Accounts payable}}{\text{Sales (incl. VAT)}} \times 365 = \text{Payables in number of days of sales}$$

(c) Days' inventory

The significance of the inventory turnover ratios depends on the quality of the available accounting information. If it is detailed enough, you can calculate true turnover ratios. If not, you will have to settle for approximations that compare dissimilar data.

You can start by calculating an overall turnover ratio, not meaningful in an absolute sense, but useful in analysing trends:

$$\frac{\text{Inventories and work in progress}}{\text{Annual sales (excl. VAT)}} \times 365$$

$$= \text{Approximate in number of days of inventory}$$

Depending on the available accounting information, you can also calculate the turnover of each component of inventory – in particular, raw material and goods held for resale – and distil the following turnover ratios:

➤ **Days of raw material**, reflecting the number of days of purchases the inventory represents or, viewed the other way round, the number of days necessary for raw material on the balance sheet to be consumed:

$$\frac{\text{Inventory of raw material}}{\text{Annual purchases of raw material (excl. VAT)}} \times 365$$

$$= \text{Number of days of purchase}$$

➤ **Days of goods held for resale**, reflecting the period between the time the company purchases goods and the time it resells them:

$$\frac{\text{Inventory of goods held for resale}}{\text{Annual purchases of goods held for resale (excl. VAT)}} \times 365$$

$$= \text{Number of days of goods held for resale}$$

➤ **Days of finished goods inventory**, reflecting the time it takes the company to sell the products it manufactures, and calculated with respect to cost of goods sold:

$$\frac{\text{Inventory of finished goods}}{\text{Annual cost of goods sold}} \times 365$$

$$= \text{Number of days of finished goods inventory}$$

If cost of goods sold is unavailable, it is calculated with respect to the sales price:

$$\frac{\text{Finished goods inventory}}{\text{Annual sales (excl. VAT)}} \times 365$$

➤ **Days of work in progress**, reflecting the time required for work in progress and semi-finished goods to be completed – in other words, the length of the production cycle:

$$\frac{\text{(Work in progress)} + \text{(Semi-finished products)}}{\text{Annual cost of goods sold}} \times 365$$

$$= \text{Length of production cycle}$$

For companies that present their profit and loss statement by-nature, this last ratio can be calculated only from internal sources as cost of goods sold does not appear as such on the P&L. The calculation is therefore easier for companies that use the by-function presentation for their profit and loss statement.

2/THE LIMITS OF RATIO ANALYSIS

Remember that, in calculating the foregoing ratios, you must follow two rules:

• make sure the base of comparison is the same: sales price or production cost, inclusive or exclusive of VAT;

• compare outstandings in the balance sheet with their corresponding cash flows.

Turnover ratios have their limitations:

*   they can be completely misleading if the business of the company is seasonal. In this case, the calculated figures will be irrelevant. To take an extreme example, imagine a company that realises all of its sales in a single month. If it grants payment terms of 1 month, its number of days/receivables at the end of that month will be 365;
*   they provide no breakdown – unless more detailed information is available – of the turnover of the components of each asset (or liability) item related to the operating cycle. For example, receivables might include receivables from private sector customers, receivables from international customers and receivables from government agencies. These three categories can have very different collection periods (governments agencies, for instance, are known to pay late).

You must ask yourself what degree of precision you want to achieve in your analysis of the company. If a general idea is enough, you might be satisfied with average ratios, as calculated above after verifying that:

*   the business is not too seasonal;
*   if it is seasonal, that the available data refer to the same point in time during the year. If this is your case, we advise you to express the ratios in terms of a percentage (receivables/sales), which do not imply a direct link with actual conditions.

If you need a more detailed analysis, you will have to look at the actual business volumes in the period just prior to the statement date. In this case, the daily sales figure will not be the annual sales divided by 365, but the last quarter's sales divided by 90, the last 2 months divided by 60, etc.

If you must perform an in-depth audit of outstandings in the balance sheet, averages are not enough. You must compare outstandings with the transactions that gave rise to them.

Section 11.3
READING BETWEEN THE LINES OF WORKING CAPITAL

Evaluating working capital is an important part of an analyst's job in continental Europe, because intercompany financing plays a prominent role in the economy. In Anglo-Saxon countries this analysis is less important, because commercial practice is stricter.

1/GROWTH OF THE COMPANY

In principle, the ratio of working capital to annual sales should remain stable.

If the permanent requirement equals 25% of annual sales and sales grow from €100m to €140m, working capital requirement should grow by €10m (€40m × 25%).

Growth in business volume causes an increase in working capital. This increase appears, either implicitly or explicitly, in the cash flow statement.

Growth in the company's business tends to increase the amount of working capital. This increase represents an additional need that a business plan must take into account.

We might be tempted to think that working capital does not grow as fast as sales, because certain items, such as minimum inventory levels, are not necessarily proportional to the level of business volume. Experience shows, however, that growth very often causes a sharp, sometimes poorly controlled, increase in working capital at least equal to the growth in the company's sales volume.

In fact, a growing company is often confronted with **working capital that grows faster than sales**, for various reasons:

- management sometimes neglects to manage working capital rigorously, concentrating instead on strategy and on increasing sales;
- management often tends to integrate vertically, both upstream and downstream. Consequently, structural changes to working capital are introduced as it starts growing much more rapidly than sales.

When a company is growing, the increase in working capital constitutes a real use of funds, just as surely as capital expenditures do. For this reason, increases in working capital must be analysed and projected with equal care.

Efficient companies are characterised by controlled growth in working capital. Indeed, successful expansion often depends on the following two conditions:

- ensuring that the growth in working capital tracks the growth in sales rather than zooms ahead of it;
- creating a corporate culture that strives to contain working capital. If working capital grows unchecked, sooner or later it will lead to serious financial difficulties and compromise the company's independence.

Today, companies faced with slower growth in business manage working capital strictly through just-in-time inventory management, greater use of outsourcing, etc.

Note that, **in inflationary periods, working capital increases** even if the quantities the company produces do not. This increase is primarily due to the rise in prices, which, at constant payment terms, increases production costs and receivables.

The foregoing analysis sheds light on two models of growth. A company can:

- Grow without changing its production cycle and its relative working capital.
- Grow on the basis of:
  - a change in its manufacturing processes related, for example, to diversification into new products;
  - a change in the composition of the customer base, leading to a change in overall payment terms granted to customers. For example, if a growing part of sales is realised with international companies, receivables will take longer to collect.

In the first case, growth in sales will lead to proportional growth in working capital.

For example, imagine the company's sales rise from €100m to €140m and working capital is 72 days of sales. In absolute terms, working capital rises from €20m to €28m, or by 40%, the same as the percentage rise in sales. The company will have to finance an increase in working capital of €8m as a result of increasing its sales by €40m.

In the second case, growth in sales can lead to a more-than-proportional increase in permanent working capital.

Using the figures from the same example, we suppose receivables used to represent 62 days of sales on average. Now suppose the 40% increase in sales results primarily from an increase in exports, to customers who are granted more generous payment terms. Receivables rise by 18 days to 80 days of sales on average. Because sales have increased, permanent working capital rises to 90 days $(72 + 18)$ of sales, or $140 \times 90/365 = €35m$, representing an increase of 75% from its initial volume of €20m.

Consequently, the company will have to finance an additional working capital of €15m and will be confronted with a much bigger financing problem than the company in the first example.

2/ RECESSION

By analysing the working capital of a company facing a sudden drop in its sales, we can see that working capital reacts in stages.

Initially, the company does not adjust its production levels. Instead, it tries other ways to shore up sales. The recession also leads to difficulty in controlling accounts receivable, because customers start having financial difficulties and stretch out their payments over time. The company's cash situation deteriorates, and it has trouble honouring its commercial obligations, so it obtains more favourable payment terms from its suppliers. At the end of this first phase, working capital, the balance between the various items affected by divergent forces, stabilises at a higher level.

In the second phase, the company begins to adopt measures to adjust its operating cycle to its new level of sales. It cuts back on production, trims raw material inventories and ratchets customer payment terms down to normal levels. By limiting purchases, accounts payable also decline. These measures, salutary in the short term, have the paradoxical effect of inflating working capital because certain items remain stubbornly high while accounts payable decline.

As a result, the company produces (and sells) below capacity, causing unit costs to rise and the bottom line to deteriorate.

Finally, in the third phase, the company returns to a sound footing:

- sales surpass production;
- the cap on purchases has stabilised raw material inventories. When purchases return to their normal level, the company again benefits from a "normal" level of supplier credit.

Against this background, working capital stabilises at a low level that is once again proportional to sales, but only after a crisis that might last as long as a year.

It is important to recognise that any contraction strategy, regardless of the method chosen, requires a certain period of psychological adjustment. Management must be convinced that the company is moving from a period of expansion to a period of recession. This psychological change may take several weeks but, once it is accomplished, the company can:

- decrease purchases;
- adjust production to actual sales;
- reduce supplier credit which the company had tried to maximise. Of course, this slows down reduction in working capital.

We have rarely seen a company take less than 9 months to significantly reduce its working capital and improve the bottom line (unless it liquidates inventories at fire sale prices).

During a recession, working capital has a paradoxical tendency to grow; then, despite restructuring measures, it still doesn't budge. It is only towards the end of the recession that working capital subsides and the company gains breathing space.

3/COMPANY STRATEGY AND ITS IMPACT ON WORKING CAPITAL

Companies that expand vertically by acquiring suppliers or distributors lengthen their production cycle. In so doing, they increase their value added. But this very process also increases their working capital because the increased value added is incorporated in the various line items that make up working capital, notably receivables and finished goods inventories. Conversely, accounts payable reflect purchases made further upstream and therefore contain less value added. So they become proportionately lower.

4/NEGATIVE WORKING CAPITAL

The operating cycles of companies with negative working capital are such that, thanks to a favourable timing mismatch, they collect funds prior to disbursing certain payments. There are two basic scenarios:

- supplier credit is much greater than inventory turnover while, at the same time, customers pay quickly, in some cases in cash;
- customers pay in advance. This is the case for companies that work on military contracts, collective catering companies, companies that sell subscriptions, etc. Nevertheless, these companies are sometimes required to lock up their excess cash so long as the customer has not yet "consumed" the corresponding service. In this case, negative working capital offers a way of earning significant investment income rather than presenting a source of funding that can be freely used by the firm to finance its operations.

The companies in the examples below receive the proceeds of their sales before paying for all of their production costs; in particular, their suppliers of raw materials or merchandise intended for resale. They are few in number and are concentrated in the following sectors:

- supermarkets;
- retailing of goods under special terms, such as consignment sales stores, which enjoy high supplier credit;
- companies that receive advance payments on work in progress, such as aerospace and telecoms contractors working for public entities, and certain companies operating in the public works sector;
- collective catering companies;
- mail order companies or online retailers, when the customer pays upon ordering;
- certain newspaper and magazine publishers or pay TV channels, since a large part of their sales volume derives from subscriptions;
- companies whose suppliers are in a position of such weakness – printers or hauliers that face stiff competition, for example – that they are forced to offer inordinately long payment terms to their customers.

A low or negative working capital is a boon to a company looking to expand without recourse to external capital. Efficient companies – in particular, in mass-market retailing – all benefit from low or negative working capital. Put another way, certain companies are adept at using intercompany credit to their best advantage.

The presence of negative working capital can however lead to management errors. We once saw an industrial group that was loath to sell a loss-making division because it had a negative working capital. Selling the division would have shored up the group's profitability but would also have created a serious cash management problem, because the negative working capital of the unprofitable division was financing the working capital of the profitable divisions. Short-sightedness blinded the company to everything but the cash management problem it would have had immediately after the disposal.

5/Working capital as an expression of balance of power

Economists have tried to understand the theoretical justification for intercompany credit, as represented by working capital. To begin with, they have found that there are certain minimum technical turnaround times. For example, a customer must verify that the delivery corresponds to his order and that the invoice is correct. Some time is also necessary to actually effect the payment.

But this explains only a small portion of intercompany credit, which varies greatly from one country to another:

PROPORTION OF ACCOUNTS RECEIVABLE IN TOTAL ASSETS OF INDUSTRIAL COMPANIES

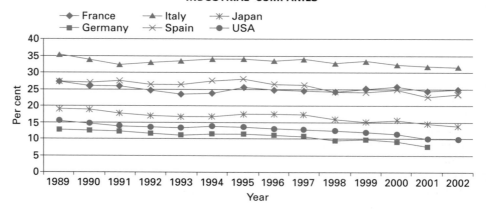

Source: Bulletin de la Banque de France, **132**, December 2004.

PROPORTION OF ACCOUNTS PAYABLE IN TOTAL ASSETS OF INDUSTRIAL COMPANIES

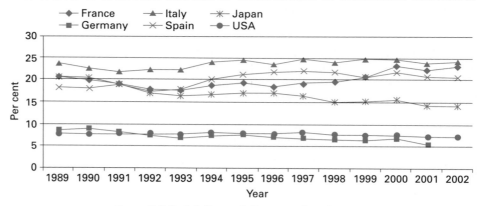

Source: Bulletin de la Banque de France, **132**, December 2004.

Several factors can explain the disparity:

* cultural differences. In Germanic countries, the law stipulates that title does not pass to the buyer until the seller is paid. This makes generous payment terms much less attractive for the buyer, because as long as his supplier is not paid, he cannot process the raw material;
* historical factors in France, Italy and Spain, where for a long time bank credit was restricted. Companies whose businesses were not subject to credit restrictions (building, exports, energy, etc.) used their bank-borrowing capacity to support companies subject to the restrictions by granting them generous payment terms. Tweaking payment terms was also a way of circumventing price controls in Mediterranean countries;
* technical factors in the USA where suppliers often offer two-part trade credit, in which a substantial discount is offered for relatively early payment, such as a 2% discount for payment made within 10 days. Most buyers take this discount.

This discount explains the low level of accounts payable in US groups' balance sheets. As a byproduct, failure of a buyer to take this discount could serve as a very strong and early signal of financial distress.

There are numerous theories that provide explanations for the provision of trade credit by suppliers.

Mian and Smith suggested that credit provisions will be more likely in circumstances where it is easy to resell the product being sold, since this will allow the seller to seize and resell the product if the buyer defaults.

Cunat argued that the provision of trade credit ties customers to particular suppliers, thereby increasing the scope for punishment of nonpayment.

Some industries may require trade credit as a guarantee for product quality.[2] Certainly some products – for example, high-tech or newly developed products – need more quality assurance for their inputs than others, such as commodities.

2 *As in Long, Malitz and Ravid.*

Furthermore, Dietsch has shown that supplier credit acts as a financial shock absorber for companies in difficulty. For commercial reasons, suppliers feel obligated to support companies whose collateral or standing is insufficient (or has become insufficient) to borrow from banks. Suppliers know that they will not have complete control over payment terms. They have unwittingly become bankers, and, like bankers, they attempt to limit payment terms on the basis of the backup represented by the customer's assets and capital.

This said, it is unhealthy for companies to offer overly generous payment terms to their customers. In so doing, they run a credit risk. Even though the corporate credit manager function is more and more prevalent, even in small companies, credit managers are not in the best position to appreciate and manage this risk. Moreover, intercompany credit is one of the causes of the domino effect in corporate bankruptcies.

In conclusion, we reiterate that intercompany credit is one of the most visible manifestations of the balance of power between customers and suppliers. The size of the intercompany credit serves as an indication of the strength of the company's strategic position *vis-à-vis* its customers and suppliers. How else can we explain why the industrial gases group Air Liquide enjoys working capital that is at worst zero and the rest of the time negative?

Section 11.4
ANALYSING CAPITAL EXPENDITURES

The following three questions should guide your analysis of the company's investments:

- What is the state of the company's plant and equipment?
- What is the company's capital expenditure policy?
- What are the cash flows generated by these investments?

1/ANALYSING THE COMPANY'S CURRENT PRODUCTION CAPACITY

3 Net fixed assets are gross fixed assets minus cumulative depreciation.

The current state of the company's fixed assets is measured by the ratio:

$$\frac{\text{Net fixed assets}}{\text{Gross fixed assets}} \cdot {}_3$$

A very low ratio (less than 25%) indicates that the company's plant and equipment are probably worn out. In the near term, the company will be able to generate robust margins because depreciation charges will be minimal. But don't be fooled, this situation cannot last for ever. In all likelihood, the company will soon have trouble because its manufacturing costs will be higher than those of its competitors, who have modernised their production facilities or innovated. Such a company will soon lose market share and its profitability will decline.

If the ratio is close to 100%, the company's fixed assets are recent, and it will probably be able to reduce its capital expenditure in the next few years.

2/ANALYSING THE COMPANY'S INVESTMENT POLICY

Through the production process, fixed assets are used up. The annual depreciation charge is supposed to reflect this wearing out. By comparing capital expenditure with depreciation charges, you can determine whether the company is:

- expanding its industrial base by increasing production capacity. In this case, capital expenditure is higher than depreciation as the company invests more than to simply compensate for the annual wearing out of fixed assets;
- maintaining its industrial base, replacing production capacity as necessary. In this case, capital expenditure approximately equals depreciation as the company invests just to compensate for the annual wearing out of fixed assets;
- underinvesting or divesting (capital expenditure below depreciation). This situation can only be temporary or the company's future will be in danger, unless the objective is to liquidate the company.

Comparing capital expenditure with net fixed assets at the beginning of the period gives you an idea of the size of the investment programme with respect to the company's existing production facilities. A company that invests an amount equal to 50% of its existing net fixed assets is building new facilities worth half what it has at the beginning of the year. This strategy carries certain risks:

- risk that economic conditions will take a turn for the worse;
- risk that production costs will be difficult to control (productivity deteriorates);
- technology risks, etc.

3/ANALYSING THE CASH FLOWS GENERATED BY INVESTMENTS

The theoretical relationship between capital expenditures, on the one hand, and the cash flow from operating activities, on the other hand, is not simple. New fixed assets are combined with those already on the balance sheet and, together, they generate the cash flow of the period. Consequently, there is no direct link between operating cash flow and the capital expenditure of the period.

Comparing cash flow from operating activities with capital expenditure makes sense only in the context of overall profitability and the dynamic equilibrium between sources and uses of funds.

The only reason to invest in fixed assets is to generate profits; i.e., positive cash flows. Any other objective turns finance on its head. You must therefore be very careful when comparing the trends in capital expenditure, cash flow and cash flow from operating activities. This analysis can be done by examining the cash flow statement.

Any investment strategy must sooner or later result in an increase in cash flow from operating activities. If it doesn't, then the investments are not profitable enough. The company is heading for trouble or, more likely, is already in trouble.

Be on the lookout for companies that, for reasons of hubris, grossly overinvest, whereas their cash flow from operating activities is not growing at the same rate as their investments. Management has lost sight of the all-important criterion that is profitability.

All the above said does not mean that capital expenditure should be financed by internal sources only. Our point is simply that a good investment policy grows cash flow at the same rate as capital expenditure and leads to a virtuous circle of growth, a necessary condition for the company's financial equilibrium, as shown in graph A below.

EXAMPLE OF INVESTMENT POLICY ANALYSIS

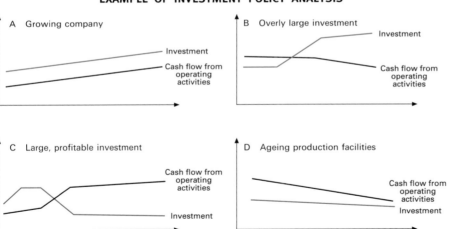

Graphs B, C and D illustrate other corporate situations. In D, investment is far below the company's cash flow from operations. You must compare investment with depreciation charges so as to answer the following questions:

- Is the company living off the assets it has already acquired (profit generated by existing fixed assets)?
- Is the company's production equipment ageing?
- Are the company's current capital expenditures appropriate, given the rate of technological innovation in the sector?

Naturally, the risk in this situation is that the company is "resting on its laurels", and that its technology is falling behind that of its competitors. This will eat into the company's profitability and, as a result, into its cash flow from operating activities at the very moment it will need cash the most in order to make the investments necessary to close the gap *vis-à-vis* its rivals.

The most important piece of information to be gleaned from a cash flow statement is the relationship between capital expenditure and cash flow from operating activities and their respective growth rates.

Generally speaking, you must understand that there are certain logical inferences that can be made by looking at the company's investment policy. If its capital expenditure is very high, the company is embarking on a project to create significant new value rather than simply growing. Accordingly, future cash flow from operating activities will depend on the profitability of these new investments and is thus highly uncertain.

Lastly, ask yourself the following questions about the company's divestments. Do they represent recurrent transactions, such as the gradual replacement of a rental car company's fleet of vehicles? Or, are they one-off disposals? In the latter case, is the company's insufficient cash flow forcing the company to divest? Or, is the company selling old, outdated assets in order to turn itself into a dynamic, strategically rejuvenated company?

Section 11.5
CASE STUDY[4]: ERICSSON

4 Financial statements for Ericsson are shown on pp. 54 and 174.

1/WORKING CAPITAL ANALYSIS

As the average VAT rate of Ericsson is not made public, and as it is difficult to estimate it since the group's activities span over several continents, working capital ratios has been computed without taking VAT into account:

In days of net sales	1999	2000	2001	2002	2003
$\dfrac{\text{Operating working capital}}{\text{Net sales}} \times 365$	77	109	60	60	35
$\dfrac{\text{Inventories and work in progress}}{\text{Net sales}} \times 365$	52	76	47	45	44
$\dfrac{\text{Receivables}}{\text{Net sales}} \times 365$	136	171	119	132	118
$\dfrac{\text{Payables}}{\text{Net sales}} \times 365$	111	138	105	117	127

By the end of year 2000, the operating working capital of Ericsson was no longer under control (42% increase in days of net sales!). Clearly, after the Internet bubble burst in mid-2000, some customers had financial difficulties and were given extended payment terms by Ericsson. The Swedish group itself adapted slowly to the collapse in its orders as illustrated by the huge increase in inventories and work in progress (from 52 days in 1999 to 76 days in 2000!).

One year later, the situation was back under control with Ericsson striving successfully to further reduce its operating working capital: 2003 inventories and receivables were well below their relative level of 1999, while payables were above. In 3 years, Ericsson has been able to reduce its relative operating working capital by half and by four in absolute terms.

As usual, nonoperating working capital is difficult to explain. It was mainly made up of loans provided on favourable terms to customers on condition they buy equipment from Ericsson, which does not suggest that the Swedish group was in a strong bargaining position! Nonoperating working capital also includes warranty commitments and restructuring costs.

2/CAPITAL EXPENDITURE ANALYSIS

From 1999 to 2001, Ericsson invested moderately in new fixed assets (capital expenditure for those years are 6% higher than the corresponding depreciation), but seems to have divested a lot of old ones for €1.9bn in value. With the collapse in its market, Ericsson rightly decided practically to stop spending money on capital expenditure: in 2002 and in 2003, €754m was spent in capex,[5] only 46% of the depreciation cost for these years, and Ericsson divested tangible assets worth €490m.

5 *Capital expenditure.*

It goes without saying that this is a nice move from a cash flow point of view but it cannot last for long as it jeopardises Ericsson's medium-term ability to produce at competitive costs: net tangible assets represented 47% of gross tangible assets at the beginning of 2000 and only 26% at the end of 2003.

SUMMARY

download

A company's working capital is the balance of the accounts directly related to its operating cycle (essentially customer receivables, accounts payable and inventories). Calculated at the year-end closing date, it is not necessarily representative of the company's permanent requirement. Therefore, you must look at how it has evolved over time.

All of the components of working capital at a given point in time disappear shortly thereafter. Inventories are consumed, suppliers are paid and receivables are collected. But, even if these components are being consumed, paid and collected, they are being replaced by others. Working capital is therefore both liquid and permanent.

Working capital turnover ratios measure the average proportion of funds tied up in the operating cycle. The principal ratios are:

- days/receivables: Accounts receivable/Sales (incl. VAT) × 365;

- days/payables: Accounts payable/Purchases (incl. VAT) × 365;

- days' inventory: Inventories and work in progress/Sales (excl. VAT) × 365;

- working capital turnover: Working capital/Sales (excl. VAT) × 365.

When a company grows, its working capital has a tendency to grow, because inventories and accounts receivable (via payment terms) increase faster than sales. Paradoxically, during periods of recession, working capital continues to grow because restrictive measures do not immediately deliver their desired effect. It is only at the end of the recession that working capital subsides and cash flow problems ease.

A low or negative working capital is a boon to a company looking to expand.

The level of working capital is an indication of the strength of the company's strategic position, because it reflects the balance of power between the company and its customers and suppliers.

We evaluate a company's investment policy by looking at the following three criteria:

- the extent to which production facilities are worn out, as measured by the net fixed assets/gross fixed assets ratio;

- the purpose of capital expenditure – build up fixed assets, maintain them or let them run down – determined by whether capital expenditure is greater than, equal to or less than depreciation;

- analysis of the cash flow generated by investments.

QUESTIONS

quiz

1/ Can it be said that the working capital calculated on the balance sheet is representative of the company's permanent needs?

2/ If income is recorded on a company's books on the day it is received (and not on the invoice date) and costs on the date of payment, would this generate working capital? If so, how would this working capital differ from the working capital as calculated today?

3/ Is the permanent part of working capital liquid?

4/ Explain why, during a recession, working capital will decline at a slower pace than sales.

5/ How does working capital behave in an inflationary period?

6/ The financial director of a company makes the following comments: "The company performed remarkably well this year. You be the judge – our depreciation policy enabled us to generate 50% more EBITDA[6] than last year. Our working capital has increased sharply, due to a more generous customer credit policy (3 months instead of 2) and to a significant increase in our inventories." What is your response? What advice would you give?

7/ The perfume division of Unilever has decided to launch a new perfume. During the first weeks following the launch, sales to retailers are high. Can the new perfume be considered to be a success?

8/ An aeronautics group has substantial inventories of unfinished goods. What consequences will this have? What measures would you suggest to improve this situation?

9/ Is calculating the ratio of nonoperating working capital/sales a worthwhile exercise?

10/ Explain the two graphs on p. 196.

6 *Earnings Before Interest, Taxes, Depreciation and Amortisation.*

1/ The Belgian Van de Putte Group has the following operating structure: sales = 100, raw materials used in the business = 30, direct production costs = 40, administrative costs = 20. Operating cycle – raw materials inventories: 15 days, length of production cycle: 1 month, inventories of finished products: 15 days. Payment terms – suppliers 2 months, customers 1 month, other costs paid in cash.

Assuming zero VAT, calculate working capital in days of sales. The production cycle lasts 1 month, which means that in-progress inventories represent 1 month of raw materials and 15 days of production costs.

2/ The operating details for Spalton plc are as follows:

- permanent working capital equal to 25% of sales;
- sales rise from 100 million to 120 million in year 2;
- EBITDA rises to 15% of sales in year 2.

Calculate operating cash flow (before financial expense and tax) in year 2.

3/ Calculation of turnover ratios.

Working capital for Moretti Spa over the last 5 years (at 31 December) was as follows:

(in €m)	2001	2002	2003	2004	2005
Inventories of finished goods	6.1	7.4	9.1	13	15.4
Trade and notes receivable	6.4	8.9	10.5	11.1	11.6
Trade and notes payable	2.1	3.5	3.5	3.8	3.4

The income statement includes the following data:

(in €m)	2001	2002	2003	2004	2005
Sales (excl. VAT)	32.8	44.7	49.4	48.9	50
Sales (incl. VAT)	38.9	52.6	58.1	57.4	57.2
Purchases (incl. VAT)	12.5	19.2	19.6	20.9	20.4

Calculate the different turnover ratios for working capital.

4/ Below are the operating terms and conditions of a trading company:

- goods held for resale rotate four times a year;
- cost of goods sold is equal to 60% of sales (excl. tax);
- customers pay at 45 days month-end;
- suppliers are paid at 30 days;
- salaries, which amount to 10% of pre-tax sales, are paid at the end of every month;
- payroll taxes, which amount to 50% of salaries, are paid on the 15th of the following month;
- operating charges other than purchases of goods for resale and staff costs are paid in cash;
- VAT is payable at 19.6% on sales and purchases. VAT payable for month n, equal to the difference between VAT collected on sales in month n and VAT recoverable on sales in month n, is paid at the latest on the 25th of the month $(n + 1)$.

Using the above data, calculate the working capital of the company in days of sales (excl. VAT).

5/ Below are details of a distribution company's operating terms and conditions: days of goods held for resale: 24 days; supplier credit: 90 days; customer credit: 10 days; purchases: 75% of sales; no VAT. Calculate normal working capital as a percentage of sales.

6/ Give your views of Air Liquide's investment policy since 1990, as represented in the following graph (data in €m):

Source: Annual report.

ANSWERS

Questions

1/ *No, because of the seasonality of most business.*

2/ *Yes, it would, as working capital depends primarily on the time difference between payment to suppliers and payment from customers which would not be substantially modified by a change in accounting rules; with an adjustment of working capital and shareholders' equity.*

3/ *Yes, because each item of working capital is sold, paid by the company or its suppliers.*

4/ *As a result of inertia.*

5/ *It tends to increase even if the number of products sold stays constant.*

6/ *This is not borne out by an analysis of the information. A depreciation charge does not affect EBITDA (as EBITDA is computed before depreciation charge). Working capital has increased considerably. Note the change in net debt.*

7/ *No, the retailers are getting in stock, but not necessarily selling any!*

8/ *Very high working capital. Downpayments by customers, prefinancing of series by state authorities, pass on to subcontractors, etc.*

9/ *Not really, given that nonoperating working capital is such a catch-all category.*

10/ *Sales in the raincoat business are linked to two weather-related peaks – in early autumn and early spring, but with delivery periods to supermarkets, the peaks in sales figures will occur 3 months later (July, October). The rate of production would appear to be constant throughout the year. Most of the vegetable canning factory's production is completed during the summer (3 months) and then sold over the rest of the year, especially in winter.*

Exercises

1/

Working capital component	% of sales	Time taken to shift goods or payment period	Value in days of sales
Raw materials inventories	30%	15 days	4.5 days
+ Work in progress		30% × 30 days + 40% × 15 days	15.0 days
+ Inventories of finished products	90%	15 days	13.5 days
+ Trade receivables	100%	30 days	30.0 days
− Trade payables	30%	60 days	18.0 days
= Total			45.0 days

2/ *Operating cash flow (before taxes and financial expense) = EBITDA $-\Delta WC = 15\%$ × 120 − 25% × (120 − 100) = €13m.*

3/

	1	2	3	4	5
Working capital (WC)	10,400	12,800	16,100	20,300	23,600
WC in days of sales (excl. VAT)	116	105	119	152	172
Outstanding receivables in days of sales (including VAT)	60	62	66	71	74
Days of inventories	68	60	67	97	112
Days of payables in days of purchase (including tax)	61	67	65	66	61

The economy is in recession and the company has not yet adjusted production and is keeping sales up by offering customers better payment terms.

4/

Working capital component	% of sales	Time taken to shift goods or payment period	Value in days of sales
Inventories of goods for resale	60%	90 days	54.0 days
+ Trade receivables	119.60%	30/2 + 45 = 60 days	71.8 days
− Accounts payable	−71.76%	30 days	21.5 days
− Personnel cost	10%	15 days	1.5 days
− Social security contributions payable	5%	30/2 + 15 = 30 days	1.5 days
− VAT payable	(19.6 − 19.6 ×60% = 7.84%)	30/2 +25 = 40 days	3.1 days
= Total			98.1 days

5/

Working capital component	% of sales	Time taken to shift goods or payment period	Value in days of sales
Inventories of goods for resale	75%	24.3 days	18.2 days
+ Trade receivables	100%	10 days	10.0 days
− Accounts payable	75%	90 days	67.5 days
= Total			−39.2 days

6/ *Until 1995, Air Liquide reaps the benefits of capital expenditure prior to 1990 and generates cash flow which is stagnant but much higher than its capital expenditure. Between 1996 and 2000, seeking to achieve the growth it had previously recorded, Air Liquide lays out large amounts on capital expenditure, resulting in an increase in cash flow. After making these capital expenditures, Air Liquide can reduce the amount of its capital expenditure for a few years (1999–2003) and reap large amounts of cash from operating activities. When cash from operating activities starts to stagnate (2002–2004), Air Liquide increases again its capital expenditure (2004). It is a never-ending story of low capex and high cash flows or high capex and low cash flows, capex being increased when cash flows are decreasing, and capex being reduced when past capex results in higher cash flows.*

BIBLIOGRAPHY

To get deeper into the analysis of working capital:

B. Bardes, Délais de paiement et solde du crédit inter-entreprises de 1989 à 2002, *Bulletin de la Banque de France*, **132**, 69–82, December 2004 [in French].

B. Biais, Ch. Grolier, Trade credit and credit rationing, *Review of Financial Studies*, **10**, 903–937, 1997.

V. Cunat, *Inter-firm Credit and Industrial Links*, Mimeo, London School of Economics, 2000.

A.-F. Delaunay, M. Dietsch, Le crédit interentreprises joue un rôle d'amortisseur des tensions conjoncturelles, *Revue d'Economie Financière*, **54**, 121–136, October 1999 [in French].

M. Long, I. Malitz, A. Ravid, Trade credit, quality guarantees, and product marketability, *Financial Management*, **22**, 117–127, 1993.

C. Maxwell, L. Gitman, S. Smith, Working capital management and financial-service consumption preferences of US and foreign firms: A comparison of 1979 and 1996 preferences, *Financial Practice and Education*, 46–52, Autumn/Winter 1998.

S. Mian, C. Smith, Accounts receivable management policy: Theory and evidence, *Journal of Finance*, **47**, 169–200, 1992.

C. Ng, J. Smith, R. Smith, Evidence on the determinants of credit terms used in interfirm trade, *Journal of Finance*, **54**, 1109–1129, June 1999.

H-H. Shin, L. Soenen, Efficiency of working capital management and corporate profitability, *Financial Practice and Education*, 37–45, Autumn/Winter 1998.

Y. Kim, *Advances in Working Capital Management*, Elsevier Sciences, 1996.

Chapter 12
FINANCING

Tell me how you're financed and I'll tell you who you are

When you evaluate how a company is financed, you must perform both dynamic and static analyses.

● When it is founded, a company makes two types of investments. First, it invests to acquire land, buildings, equipment, etc. Second, it makes operating investments; specifically, startup costs and building up working capital.

To finance these investments, the company must raise either equity or debt financing. The investments, which initially generate negative cash flows, must generate positive cash flows over time. After subtracting returns to the providers of the company's financing (interest and dividends), as well as taxes, these cash flows must enable the company to repay its borrowings.

If the circle is a virtuous one – i.e., if the cash flows generated are enough to meet interest and dividend payments and repay debt – the company will gradually be able to grow and, as it repays its debt, it will be able to borrow more (the origin of the illusion that companies never repay their loans).

Conversely, the circle becomes a vicious one if the company's resources are constantly tied up in new investments or if cash flow from operating activities is chronically low. The company systematically needs to borrow to finance capital expenditure, and it may never be able to pay off its debt, not to mention pay dividends.

This is the dynamic approach.

➤ In parallel with the dynamic approach, you must look at the current state of the company's finances with two questions in mind:

○ Given the proportion of the company's assets financed by bank and other financial debt and the free cash flow generated by the company, can the company repay its debt?
○ Given the term structure of the company's debt, is the company running a high risk of illiquidity?

This is the static approach.

A DYNAMIC ANALYSIS OF THE COMPANY'S FINANCING

To perform this analysis you will rely on the cash flow statement.

1/THE FUNDAMENTAL CONCEPT OF CASH FLOW FROM OPERATING ACTIVITIES

The cash flow statement (see Chapter 5) is designed to separate operating activities from investing and financing activities. Accordingly, it shows cash flows from operating and investing activities and investments on the one hand and from financing activities on the other hand. This breakdown will also be very useful to you in valuing the company and in examining investment decisions.

The concept of cash flow from operating activities, as shown by the cash flow statement, is of utmost importance. It depends on three fundamental parameters:

- the rate of growth in the company's business;
- the amount and nature of operating margins;
- the amount and nature of working capital.

An analysis of the cash flow statement is therefore the logical extension of the analysis of the company's margins and the changes in working capital.

Several problems can be dealt with using the concept of cash flow.

By dissociating industrial and financial policy, the cash flow statement emphasises the cash flow from operating activities. Cash flow from operating activities constitutes a fundamental aspect of the company's profitability, especially in an economy where the value of assets on the balance sheet is low. There is no way round the following basic truth: to be profitable, a company must sooner or later generate cash in excess of what it spends. In other words, it must generate a net positive cash flow from operating activities.

Analysing the cash flow statement means analysing the profitability of the company from the point of view of its operating dynamics, rather than the value of its assets.

We once analysed a fast-growing company with a high working capital. Its cash flow from operating activities was insufficient, but its inventories increased in value every year. We found that the company was turning a handsome net income, but its return on capital employed was poor, as most of its profit was made on capital gains on the value of its inventories. Because of this, the company was very vulnerable to any recession in its sector.

In this case, we analysed the cash flow statement and were able to show that the company's trade activity was not profitable and that the capital gains just barely covered its operating losses. It also became apparent that the company's growth process led to huge borrowings, making the company even more vulnerable in the event of a recession.

2/HOW IS THE COMPANY FINANCED?

As an analyst, you must understand how the company finances its growth over the period in question. New equity capital? New debt? Reinvesting cash flow from operating activities? Asset disposals can contribute additional financial resources. The cash flow statement will enable you to understand the origin of the company's financial resources over the period.

Did the company issue new equity capital during the period, and, if so, for what purpose? To pay down debt or to finance a large investment programme?

As we will see in Chapter 38, the company's dividend policy is also an important aspect of its financial policy. It is a valuable piece of information when evaluating the company's strategy during periods of growth or recession:

- Is the company's dividend policy out of step with its growth strategy?
- Is the company's cash flow reinvestment policy in line with its capital expenditure programme?

You must compare the amount of dividends with the investments and cash flows from operating activities of the period. For a family-owned company, we would also advise increasing dividends by repayment of shareholders loans, and any other unusual operating costs or payments that could be substitutes for dividend payments. You could also look at the company's payout ratio (see p. 541).

Analysing the net increase or decrease in the company's debt burden is a question of financial structure:

- If the company is paying down debt, is it doing so in order to improve its financial structure? Has it run out of growth opportunities? Is it to pay back loans that were contracted when interest rates were high?
- If the company is increasing its debt burden, is it taking advantage of unutilised debt capacity? Or, is it financing a huge investment project or reducing its shareholders' equity and upsetting its financial equilibrium in the process?

In conclusion, it is imperative that you analyse the cash flow statement to understand the dynamics of the company's cash flows.

In Section III, we will examine the more complex reasoning processes that go into determining investment and financing strategies. For the moment, keep in mind that analysis of the financial statements alone can only result in elementary, common sense rules.

As you will see later, we stand firmly **against** the following "principles":

- the amount of capital expenditure must be limited to the cash flow from operating activities. **No!** After reading Section III you will understand that the company should continue to invest in new projects until their marginal profitability is equal to the required rate of return. If it invests less, it is under-investing; if it invests more, it is overinvesting, even if it has the cash to do so;
- the company can achieve equilibrium by having the "cash cow" divisions finance the "glamour" divisions. **No!** With the development of financial markets, every division whose profitability is commensurate with its risk must be able to finance itself. A "cash cow" division should pay the cash flow it generates over to its providers of capital.

Studying the equilibrium between the company's various cash flows in order to set rules is tantamount to considering the company as a world unto itself. This approach is diametrically opposed to financial theory. It goes without saying, however, that you must determine the investment cycle that the company's financing cycle can support. In particular, debt repayment ability remains paramount. We warned you about that already in Chapter 2!

Section 12.2
A STATIC ANALYSIS OF THE COMPANY'S FINANCING

Focusing on a multi-year period, we have examined how the company's margins, working capital and capital expenditure programmes determine its various cash flows. We can now turn our attention to the company's absolute level of debt at a given point in time and to its capacity to meet its commitments while avoiding liquidity crises.

1/CAN THE COMPANY REPAY ITS DEBTS?

The best way to answer this simple, fundamental question is to take the company's business plan and project future cash flow statements. These statements will show you whether the company generates enough cash flow from operating activities such that, after financing its capital expenditure, it has enough left over to meet its debt repayment obligations without asking shareholders to reach into their pockets. If the company must indeed solicit additional equity capital, you must evaluate the market's appetite for such a capital increase. This will depend on who the current shareholders are. A company with a core shareholder will have an easier time than one whose shares are widely held. It will also depend on the value of equity capital (if it is near zero, maybe only a **vulture fund**[1] will be interested).

Naturally, this assumes that you have access to the company's business plan, or that you can construct your own from scenarios of business growth, margins, changes in working capital and likely levels of capital expenditure. We will take a closer look at this approach in Chapter 40.

Analysts have in the meantime adopted a "quick-and-dirty" way to appreciate the company's ability to repay its debt: the ratio of net debt to EBITDA.[2]

This highly empirical measure is nonetheless considered useful, because EBITDA is very close to cash flow from operating activities, give or take changes in working capital corporate and income tax. A value of 4 is considered a critical level, below which the company should generally be able to meet its repayment obligations.

If we were to oversimplify, we would say that a value of 3 signifies that the debt could be repaid in 3 years provided the company halted all capital expenditure and didn't pay corporate income tax during that period. Of course, no one would ask the company to pay off all its debt in the span of 3 years, but the idea is that if it had to, it could.

Conversely, bank and other financial borrowings equal to more than 4 times EBITDA is considered a heavy debt load, and gives rise to serious doubts about the

1 *An investment fund that buys the debt of companies in difficulty or subscribes to equity issues with the aim of taking control of the company at a very low price.*

2 *Earnings Before Interest, Taxes, Depreciation and Amortisation.*

company's ability to meet its repayment commitments as scheduled. As we will see in Chapter 44, LBOs display this type of ratio. When the value of the ratio exceeds 5 or 6, the debt becomes "high-yield", the politically correct euphemism for "junk bonds".

Bankers are more willing to lend money to sectors with stable and highly predictable cash flows (food retail, utilities, reference books, etc.), even on the basis of high net debt to EBITDA ratio, than to others where cash flows are more volatile (media, capital goods, etc.).

The following table shows trends in the net debt/EBITDA ratio posted by various sectors in Europe over 1995–2005.

download

NET DEBT/EBITDA RATIO FOR LEADING LISTED EUROPEAN COMPANIES (%)

Sector	1996	1997	1998	1999	2000	2001	2002	2003	2004	2005e	2006e
Aerospace and defence	NM*	NM	NM	37	87	104	83	83	44	54	54
Automotive	7	NM	NM	NM	38	62	37	24	9	NM	NM
Beverages	119	124	171	178	187	202	231	185	165	143	114
Building materials	165	174	174	246	262	305	279	251	213	190	159
Capital goods	NM	48	26	121	130	235	140	117	55	20	NM
Chemicals	65	87	97	130	186	154	129	136	93	73	51
Consumer goods	140	139	140	102	115	83	36	27	42	28	2
Food and home care	92	15	67	43	189	230	167	154	121	98	76
Food retail	67	104	151	195	246	217	208	186	173	159	146
General retail	171	109	144	116	144	149	150	117	104	77	47
IT hardware	77	31	NM	5	21	84	NM	NM	NM	NM	NM
IT services	123	32	NM	NM	NM	NM	51	50	22	4	NM
Leisure and hotels	896	795	588	509	602	565	636	631	527	453	151
Luxury goods	119	162	242	317	243	325	224	165	121	82	39
Media	170	115	161	261	236	277	244	170	107	69	39
Metals and mining	161	328	258	189	172	217	197	152	77	44	27
Oil and gas	48	64	86	110	40	52	85	70	44	35	30
Personal care	49	40	27	52	88	65	39	10	44	9	NM
Support services	151	140	156	218	271	258	273	243	215	183	151
Telecom operators and ISPs	116	165	157	178	301	260	237	165	145	131	105
Transport	335	272	270	327	304	399	251	252	282	259	248
Utilities	146	101	126	221	261	244	304	239	229	221	262

Source: Exane BNP Paribas. Figures for the pharmaceutical and software sectors are missing as they are not meaningful (negative net debt).
*NM = Not meaningful (i.e., negative net debt).

Leisure/hotels and transport sectors are the most highly leveraged sectors. One explanation is naturally their capital intensity, which is strong. Another one is the willingness of lenders to lend money to these sectors as they own real estate assets with a value independent from the business (a film theatre can be redeveloped into a commercial area) or with a strong secondary market (like for planes). Similarly, analysts look at the debt service ratio (or debt service coverage) – i.e., the ratio of EBIT[3] to net interest expense. A ratio of 3 : 1 is considered the critical level. Below this level, there are serious doubts as to the company's ability to meet its obligations as scheduled, as for the transport sector post-9/11. Above it, the company's lenders can sleep more easily at night!

The following table shows trends in the net debt service coverage ratio posted by various different sectors in Europe over 1995–2005.

3 *Earnings Before Interest and Taxes.*

@
download

DEBT SERVICE COVERAGE RATIO FOR LEADING LISTED EUROPEAN COMPANIES

Sector	1996	1997	1998	1999	2000	2001	2002	2003	2004	2005e	2006e
Aerospace and defence	−14.1	−19.0	−3.2	2.2	2.1	5.2	6.3	5.7	7.2	8.5	−9.5
Automotive	−12.6	−13.9	−19.1	−191	18.7	4.4	5.2	3.0	5.1	7.6	−9.2
Beverages	5.7	6.2	6.3	6.5	5.8	7.1	6.2	6.4	8.1	9.0	−10.1
Building materials	5.3	5.9	6.0	5.0	3.9	3.5	4.0	4.2	5.1	5.6	−6.5
Capital goods	1563	9.9	9.8	−6.4	−4.6	2.7	9.4	5.9	13.2	29.9	−104
Chemicals	15.9	13.8	11.5	8.0	6.2	4.7	6.9	6.9	9.1	10.7	−15.4
Consumer goods	5.0	5.1	7.0	8.2	7.8	7.4	20.8	22.0	17.1	18.7	−28.1
Food and home care	7.7	10.5	12.8	13.9	10.6	6.7	8.2	9.6	10.4	13.4	−16.3
Food retail	22.8	18.5	7.7	6.2	4.2	4.3	4.2	4.4	4.7	5.2	−5.7
General retail	18.1	85.5	18.0	23.4	12.0	10.4	10.5	13.5	12.4	15.9	−19.5
IT hardware	6.6	12.9	9.1	25.6	22.1	−0.0	1.0	15.2	−43.5	367	509
IT services	8.6	16.3	101	−138	−305	408	12.2	9.7	8.6	15.0	−23.9
Leisure and hotels	0.6	0.9	2.0	2.5	2.6	2.5	1.9	1.9	2.3	2.8	−6.8
Luxury goods	26.1	19.3	8.7	15.3	7.0	4.6	7.7	12.1	15.6	18.6	−26.1
Media	6.7	8.7	18.8	8.8	5.7	3.8	2.2	5.6	8.8	12.3	−36.0
Metals and mining	8.4	2.1	3.2	4.3	5.9	3.9	5.9	7.6	12.8	26.7	−36.0
Oil and gas	17.4	14.1	9.4	10.1	19.1	23.2	17.4	64.0	37.7	56.4	−63.5
Personal care	10.9	9.8	20.7	20.4	15.9	14.5	27.3	38.0	28.7	−32.4	21.6
Pharmaceuticals	−26.1	−20.1	−16.4	−27.5	−16.8	−31.6	−196	NM*	43.6	153	608
Software	−8.3	−24.6	−46.8	−26.1	−3.8	−140.1	112	−49.3	−52.9	−44.8	44.4
Support services	11.5	12.0	7.6	7.9	5.7	5.1	4.5	5.1	5.8	6.6	−7.4
Telecom operators and ISPs	6.2	4.3	4.8	5.3	2.8	2.1	2.8	4.4	5.4	6.2	−7.9
Transport	4.7	3.8	3.2	2.2	4.0	1.8	3.5	3.7	4.0	7.0	−7.7
Utilities	5.0	4.3	4.7	4.8	3.1	3.0	3.1	3.3	3.5	3.6	−4.8

Source: Exane BNP Paribas.
* NM = Not meaningful.

Negative figures mean that, globally, the sector has a net cash position (as for pharmaceuticals firms). Unsurprisingly, debt service coverage ratios show that the leisure/hotels and transport sectors as largely in debt (see the above debt/EBITDA ratios).

Until around 15 years ago, the company's ability to repay its loans was evaluated on the basis of its debt-to-equity ratio, or gearing, with a 1:1 ratio considered the critical point.

Certain companies can support bank and other financial debt in excess of shareholders' equity; specifically, companies that generate high operating cash flow. KPN, the Dutch telecom operator, which generates robust cash flows from its fixed line telephony business, is an example. Conversely, other companies would be unable to support debt equivalent to more than 30% of their equity, because their margins are very thin. For example, the operating profit of Thomas Cook, the travel company, is at best only 1% of its sales revenue.

We advise against using the debt-to-equity ratio as a measure of the company's repayment capacity: shareholders' equity capital serves to repay loans only in the event of bankruptcy, not in the ordinary course of the business.

2/IS THE COMPANY RUNNING A RISK OF ILLIQUIDITY?

To understand the notion of liquidity, look at the company in the following manner: at a given point in time, the balance sheet shows the company's assets and commitments. This is what the company has done in the past. Without planning for liquidation, we nevertheless attempt to classify the assets and commitments based on how quickly they are transformed into cash. When will a particular commitment result in a cash disbursement? When will a particular asset translate into a cash receipt?

A company is illiquid when it can no longer meet its scheduled commitments.

To meet its commitments, either the company has assets it can liquidate or it must contract new loans. Of course, new loans only postpone the day of reckoning until the new repayment date. By that time, the company will have to find new resources.

Illiquidity comes about when the maturity of the assets is greater than that of the liabilities. Suppose you took out a loan, to be repaid in 6 months, to buy a machine with a useful life of 5 years. The useful life of the machine is out of step with the scheduled repayment of the loan and the interest expenses on it. Consequently, there is a risk of illiquidity in the event the investment is not very profitable. Similarly, at the current asset level, if you borrow 3-month funds to finance inventories that turn over in more than 3 months, you are running the same risk.

The risk of illiquidity is the risk that assets will become liquid at a slower pace than the rate at which the liabilities will have to be paid, because the maturity of assets is longer. In a sense, liquidity measures the speed at which assets turn over compared with liabilities.

An illiquid company is not necessarily required to declare bankruptcy, but it must find new resources to bridge the gap. In so doing, it forfeits some of its independence, because it will be obliged to devote a portion of its new resources to past uses. In times of recession, it may have trouble doing so and indeed be forced into bankruptcy.

Analysing liquidity means analysing the risk the company will have to "borrow from Peter to pay Paul". For each maturity, you must compare the company's cash needs with the resources it will have at its disposal.

We say that **a balance sheet is liquid when, for each maturity, there are more assets being converted into cash (inventories sold, receivables paid, etc.) than there are liabilities coming due.**

This graph shows, for each maturity, the cumulative amount of assets and liabilities coming due on or before that date.

If, for a given maturity, cumulative assets are less than cumulative liabilities, the company will be unable to meet its obligations unless it finds a new source of funds. The company shown in this graph is not in this situation.

What we are measuring is the **company's maturity mismatch**, similar to that of a financial institution that borrows short-term funds to finance long-term assets.

(a) Liquidity ratios

To measure liquidity, then, we must compare the maturity of the company's assets with that of its liabilities. This rule gives rise to the following ratios, commonly used in loan covenants. They enable banks to monitor the risk of their borrowers.

- **Current ratio:**

$$\frac{\text{Current assets (less than 1 year)}}{\text{Current liabilities (due in less than 1 year)}}$$

This ratio measures whether the assets to be converted into cash in less than 1 year exceed the debts to be paid in less than 1 year.

- The **quick ratio** is another measure of the company's liquidity. It is the same as the current ratio, except that inventories are excluded from the calculation. Using the quick ratio is a way of recognising that a portion of inventories corresponds to the minimum the company requires for its ongoing activity. As such, they are tantamount to fixed assets. It also recognises that the company may not be able to liquidate the inventories it has on hand quickly enough in the event of an urgent cash need. Certain inventory items have value only to the extent they are used in the production process.

The quick ratio (also called **acid test ratio**) is calculated as follows:

$$\frac{\text{Current assets (less than 1 year) excluding inventories}}{\text{Current liabilities (due in less than 1 year)}}$$

- Finally, the **cash ratio** completes the set:

$$\frac{\text{Cash and cash equivalents}}{\text{Current liabilities (due in less than 1 year)}}$$

The cash ratio is generally very low. Its fluctuations often do not lend themselves to easy interpretation.

(b) More on the current ratio

Traditional financial analysis relies on the following rule:

A company must maintain a buffer between sources and uses of funds maturing in less than 1 year to cover risks inherent in its business (loss of inventory value, deadbeat customers, decline in sales, business interruption costs that suddenly reduce shareholders' equity capital), because liabilities are not subject to such losses in value.

By maintaining a current ratio above 1 (more current assets than current liabilities), the company protects its creditors from uncertainties in the "gradual liquidation" of its current assets; namely, in the sale of its inventories and the collection of its receivables. These uncertainties could otherwise prevent the company from honouring its obligations, such as paying its suppliers, servicing bank loans or paying taxes.

If we look at the long-term portion of the balance sheet, a current ratio above 1 means that sources of funds due in more than 1 year, deemed stable,[4] are greater than fixed assets – i.e., uses of funds "maturing" in more than 1 year. If the current ratio is below 1, then fixed assets are being financed partially by short-term borrowings or by a negative working capital. This situation can be dangerous. These sources of funds are liabilities that will very shortly become due, whereas fixed assets "liquidate" only gradually on the long term.

The current ratio was the cornerstone of any financial analysis years ago. This was clearly excessive. The current ratio reflects the choice between short-term and long-term financing. In our view, this was a problem typical of the credit-based economy, as it existed in the 1970s in continental Europe. Today, the choice is more between shareholders' equity capital and banking or financial debt, whatever its maturity. This said, **we still think it is unhealthy to finance a permanent working**

4 Also called "permanent financing". They include shareholders' equity, which is never due, and debts maturing after 1 year.

capital with very short-term resources. The company that does so will be defenceless in the event of a liquidity crisis, which could push it into bankruptcy.

(c) Financing working capital

To the extent that working capital represents a permanent need, logic dictates that permanent financing should finance it. Since it remains constant for a constant business volume, we are even tempted to say that it should be financed by shareholders' equity. Indeed, companies with a high working capital are often largely funded with shareholders' equity. This is the case, for example, with big champagne companies, which often turn to the capital markets for equity funding.

Nevertheless, most companies would be in an unfavourable cash position if they had to finance their working capital strictly with long-term debt or shareholders' equity. Instead, they use the mechanism of revolving credits, which we will discuss in Chapter 27. For that matter, the fact that the components of working capital are self-renewing encourages companies to use revolving credit facilities in which customer receivables and inventories often collateralise the borrowings.

By their nature, revolving credit facilities are always in effect, and their risk is often tied directly to underlying transactions or collateralised by them (bill discounting, factoring, securitisation, etc.).

Full and permanent use of short-term revolving credit facilities can often be dangerous, because it:

• exhausts borrowing capacity;
• inflates interest expense unnecessarily;
• increases the volume of relatively inflexible commitments, which will restrict the company's ability to stabilise or restructure its activity.

Working capital is not only a question of financing. It can carry an operational risk as well. Financing through short-term borrowing solves the immediate cash management problem, but makes the company very vulnerable to any changes in its trade and financial environment. Such financing has provoked some spectacular bankruptcies or quasi-bankruptcies (i.e., Vivendi Universal). Short-term borrowing does not exempt the company from strategic analysis of how its operating needs will change over time. This is a prerequisite to any financing strategy.

Companies that export a high proportion of their sales or that participate in construction and public works projects are risky inasmuch as they often have insufficient shareholders' equity compared with their total working capital. The difference is often financed by "revolving loans" resources, until one day, when the going gets rough. ...

In sum, you must pay attention to the true nature of working capital, and understand that a short-term loan that finances a permanent working capital cannot be repaid by the operating cycle except by squeezing that cycle down, or, in other words, by beginning to liquidate the company.

(d) Companies with negative working capital

Companies with a negative working capital raise a fundamental question for the financial analyst. Should they be allowed to reduce their shareholders' equity on the strength of their robust, positive cash position?

Can a company with a negative working capital maintain a financial structure with relatively little shareholders' equity? This would seem to be an anomaly in financial theory. On the practical level, we can make two observations.

First, under normal operating conditions, the company's overall financing structure is more important and more telling than the absolute value of its negative working capital.

Let's look at companies *A* and *B*, whose balance sheets are as follows:

Company *A*			Company *B*		
Fixed assets	900	Shareholders' equity	800	Fixed assets	125	Shareholders' equity	100
Working capital	1,000	Net debt	1,100	Cash & cash equiv.	105	Neg. working capital	130

Most of company *A*'s assets – in particular, its working capital – are financed by debt. As a result, the company is much more vulnerable than company *B*, whose working capital is well into negative territory and whose fixed assets are mostly financed by shareholders' equity.

Second, a company with a negative working capital reacts much more quickly in times of crisis, such as recession. Inertia, which hinders positive working capital companies, is not as great.

Nevertheless, a negative working capital company runs two risks:

- The payment terms granted by its suppliers may suddenly change. This is a function of the balance of power between the company and its supplier, and, unless there is an outside event, such as a change in the legislative environment, such risk is minimal. On the contrary, when a company with a negative working capital grows, its position *vis-à-vis* its suppliers tends to improve.
- A contraction in the company's business volume can put a serious dent in its financial structure.

Section 12.3
CASE STUDY[5]: ERICSSON

5 The financial statements for Ericsson are on pp. 54 and 65.

2003 was clearly a turning year for Ericsson as it was able to register its first positive cash flow from operating activities since 1999. From 2000 to 2002, cumulated cash flow from operating activities reached −€2.9bn. This was mainly due to a collapse in margins and to restructuring costs (€3.8bn!) which were tending to become recurrent. Ericsson has been able to partially compensate this cash flow deficit by drastically reducing its working capital from €4.4bn at the beginning of 1999 down to €2.2bn at the end of 2002, freeing up in the process €2.2bn of cash. Sales of investments more than covered capital expenditures, so Ericsson finds itself in the nice but nonrecurring situation of getting cash from investing activities: €2.8bn from 2000 to 2002.

Even though Ericsson had stopped paying a dividend since 2002, it had to rely on external sources of financing to fill in the gap: first, financial and banking debt

6 *See p. 503 for details on ratings.*

and, then, a share issue of €3.2bn used to build up equity on the balance sheet depleted by losses and restructuring costs.

This share issue was prompted by a rating downgrade below investment grade[6] to **BB** by rating agencies which made it almost impossible for Ericsson to raise new debt, except on very expensive terms. With negative EBITDA in 2001 (−€533m) and net debt of €2.4bn, lenders were clearly wary about lending more money to Ericsson.

Even after the equity injection, 2002 EBITDA having worsened (−€1.5bn), Ericsson was not a safe play for lenders despite net cash of €0.5bn on the balance sheet.

The situation was much better in 2003 thanks to €2.7bn of cashflow from operating activities, explained by a new reduction in working capital (€3.4bn) despite a negative cash flow (−€0.7bn) sharply reduced compared to 2002 (−€2.7bn). As capital expenditures were capped at a minimum (€0.5bn) and partly financed through assets disposal, net cash (negative net debt) could be increased by €2.3bn.

Does Ericsson have liquidity problems? After having raised €3.2bn of fresh equity at the end of 2002, Ericsson has €8bn in cash and marketable securities and only €1bn in short-term financial debt. It should be able to pay off financial debts when they mature, cover losses and restructuring costs and pay for capital expenditure in 2004 and 2005, provided there is not a further collapse in its markets. So it is reasonable to say that Ericsson has no liquidity problems.

SUMMARY

download

Analysing how a company is financed can be performed either by looking at several fiscal years, or on the basis of the latest available balance sheet.

In the dynamic approach, your main analytical tool will be the cash flow statement. Cash flow from operating activities is the key metric.

Cash flow from operating activities depends on the growth rate of the business and on the size and nature of working capital. Cash flow from operating activities must cover capital expenditure, loan repayment and dividends. Otherwise, the company will have to borrow more to pay for its past use of funds.

The company uses shareholders' equity and bank or financial debts to finance its investments. These investments must gradually generate enough positive cash flow to repay debt and provide a return to shareholders.

In the static approach, analysis tries to answer the following two questions:

- Can the company repay its debts as scheduled? To answer this question, you must build projected cash flow statements, based on assumed rates of growth in sales, margins, working capital and capital expenditure. To perform a simplified analysis, you can calculate the net debt/EBITDA ratio. If the company is to have an acceptable capacity to meet its repayment commitments as scheduled, the ratio should not be in excess of 4. Similarly, the EBIT/debt service ratio should be at least equal to 3.

- Is the company running the risk of being illiquid? To answer this question, you must compare the dates at which the company's liabilities will come due and the dates at which its assets will be liquidated. Assets should mature before liabilities. If they do, the company will remain liquid.

QUESTIONS

quiz

1/ Why is it imperative to analyse the cash flow statement?

2/ Does capital expenditure depend on cash flow from operating activities?

3/ Your marketing manager suggests that you launch a marketing drive, giving some customers discounts and advantageous payment terms. State your views.

4/ Is financial expense included in cash flow from operating activities?

5/ Is a company with negative working capital illiquid?

6/ In your view, should short-term debt be separated out from medium- to long-term debt on the cash flow statement? Why?

7/ Short-term interest rates are currently very low and you are offered a 3-month loan. State your views.

8/ The debt-to-equity ratio of Allied Domecq plc (spirits group) was 2.1 mid-2004. State your views.

EXERCISES

1/ Below are the key figures for company Ivankovic over the last 5 years.

	2001	2002	2003	2004	2005
Fixed assets	100	110	120	130	140
Working capital	200	225	250	280	315
EBITDA	38	40	44	48	52
Depreciation and amortisation	10	10	11	12	13
Financial expense	14	15	17	19	22
Income tax expense	7	7.5	8	8	8.5
Dividends	5	5	5	6	6

Draw up the cash flow statement for years 2002 to 2005.
State your views.

2/ Analyse and compare the summary cash flow statements of companies A, B and C.

	A	B	C
Cash flow from operating activities	−100	50	−50
Capital expenditure	−150	−30	250
Capital increase	250	0	0
Dividends paid	0	−15	0
Decrease in net debt	0	5	200

3/ What is your view of Ringkvist AB?

Ringkvist AB	2003	2004	2005
Cash flow from operating activities	400	700	1,600
Capital expenditure	1,000	1,300	1,400
Asset disposals	0	0	0
Capital increase	300	300	0
Dividends paid	0	100	200
Decrease in net debt	−300	−400	0

4/ What is your view of Moser srl?

Moser srl	2003	2004	2005
Cash flow from operating activities	400	300	−200
Capital expenditure	1,000	1,100	300
Asset disposals	0	0	300
Capital increase	300	0	600
Dividends	0	0	0
Decrease in net debt	−300	−800	400

5/ What is your view of the liquidity of this company?

7-year fixed assets	200	Shareholders' equity	100
3-year fixed assets	200	5-year debts	200
3-month inventories	300	1-year debts	300
2-month receivables	100	1-month debts	400
1-day liquidities	200		
Total	1,000	Total	1,000

ANSWERS

Questions

1/ *In order to emphasise the dynamic of returns on investments.*
2/ *No, because financing can always be found for an investment that will bring returns, but sooner or later these returns must generate cash flows.*
3/ *This will have a double impact on cash flow from operating activities (drop in margins and increase in working capital).*
4/ *Yes, see Chapter 5.*
5/ *Normally no, as negative working capital provides the company with cash, solving any liquidity problem it may have. Nevertheless, if the company has invested this cash in fixed assets and the business is contracting, change in working capital will become a cash drain and the company may face a liquidity crisis.*
6/ *No, net decrease in debt provides more information (see Chapter 5).*
7/ *How would you pay off a loan in 3 months? You run the risk of not being able to raise new funds when your cheap loan matures.*
8/ *This level of debt can only be evaluated in relation to Allied Domecq's capacity to generate substantial cash flow. Most of the time spirits companies generate high cash flows.*

Exercises

1/ *Cash flow statement*

	2002	2003	2004	2005
Cash flow	17.5	19	21	21.5
Change in working capital	25	25	30	35
Cash flow from operating activities	−7.5	−6	−9	−13.5
Capital expenditures	20	21	22	23
Dividends paid	5	5	5	6
Decrease in net debt	−32.5	−32	−36	−42.5

The company Ivankovic is in a high-growth and high-capital-expenditure phase. Ivankovic is unable to control working capital; hence, a large cash deficit. This deficit is covered by debt, leading to a sharp rise in financial expense. The financial situation of Ivankovic is worsening and in case of a slump in the economy, Ivankovic might face bankruptcy.

2/ *Company A is probably a newly formed company – its cash flow from operating activities is still negative. It will have to make huge capital expenditures. Given the high level of risk, it finances its needs using equity exclusively. Company B has reached maturity, its operating activities generate more cash than is needed to cover its capital expenditure. The company will be able to reduce its debt. Company C is clearly in trouble. Its operations generate a large cash deficit, the company is no longer investing but is shedding assets in order to reduce debt.*

3/ *Ringkvist AB is in a virtuous circle of growth. The company is investing, the investments are generating inflows, cash from operating activities thus increases every year, and the company does not need to borrow much. In period 3, Ringkvist AB generates enough cash through operating activities to finance its capital expenditures, pay dividends and stabilise its debt level.*

4/ *Moser srl is in a vicious circle. Cash flow from operating activities declines from year to year. Moser srl thus has to borrow heavily in year 2 to finance its capital expenditure. In year 3, the company experiences serious cash shortfalls, since cash generated by operating activities is negative. The company is forced to call on its shareholders to bail it out. It also launches a programme to refocus on its core business, which leads to asset disposals. Net capital expenditures are thus nil. Moser srl must reduce its debt.*

5/ *There is no guarantee of liquidity in 1 month (shortfall of $400 - 200 = 200$), nor in 1 year (shortfall of $700 - 600 = 100$) nor in 5 years (shortfall of $900 - 800 = 100$). The company will have to restructure its debt quickly in order to postpone payment of instalments due.*

R. Elsas, M. Flannery, J. Garfinkel, *Major Investments, Firm Financing Decisions, and Long Term Performance*, working paper, EFA 2004 Maastricht meetings, May 2004,
A. Hackethal, R. Schmidt, *Financing Patterns: Measurement Concepts and Empirical Results*, University of Frankfurt, working paper 125, Department of Finance, 2004.

BIBLIOGRAPHY

Chapter 13
RETURN ON CAPITAL EMPLOYED AND RETURN ON EQUITY

The leverage effect is much ado about nothing

So far we have analysed:

- how a company can create wealth (margins' analysis);
- what kind of investment is required to create wealth: capital expenditure and increase in working capital;
- how those investments are financed through debt or equity.

We now have everything we need to carry out an assessment of the company's efficiency – i.e., its profitability.

A company that delivers returns that are at least equal to those required by its shareholders and lenders will not experience financing problems in the long term, since it will be able to repay its debts and create value for its shareholders.

Hence the importance of this chapter, in which we attempt to measure the book profitability of companies.

Section 13.1
ANALYSIS OF CORPORATE PROFITABILITY

We can measure profitability only by studying returns in relation to the invested capital. If no capital is invested, there is no profitability to speak of.

Book profitability is the ratio of the wealth created (i.e., earnings) to the capital invested. **Profitability should not be confused with margins.** Margins represent the ratio of earnings to business volumes (i.e., sales or production), while profitability is the ratio of profits to the capital that had to be invested to generate the profits.

Above all, analysts should focus on the profitability of capital employed by studying the ratio of operating profit to capital employed, which is called Return On Capital Employed (ROCE):

$$\text{Return on capital employed (ROCE)} = \frac{\text{Operating profit after tax}}{\text{Capital employed}}$$

Return on capital employed can also be considered as the **return on equity if net debt is zero.**

The operating profit figure that should be used is the one we presented in Chapter 9 – i.e., after employee profit-sharing, incentive payments and all the other revenues and charges that are assigned to the operating cycle.

Much ink has been spilled over the issue of whether opening or closing capital employed[1] or an average of the two figures should be used. We will leave it up to readers to decide for themselves. This said, they should take care not to change the method they decide to use as they go along so that comparisons over longer periods are not skewed.

Return on capital employed can be calculated by combining a margin and turnover rate as follows:

$$\frac{\text{Operating profit after tax}}{\text{Capital employed}} = \frac{\text{Operating profit after tax}}{\text{Sales}} \times \frac{\text{Sales}}{\text{Capital employed}}$$

The first ratio – i.e., Operating profit after tax/Sales – corresponds to the operating margin generated by the company, while the second – Sales/Capital employed – reflects asset turnover or capital turn (the inverse of capital intensity), which indicates the amount of capital (capital employed) required to generate a given level of sales. Consequently, a "normal" return on capital employed may result from weak margins, but high asset turnover (and thus weak capital intensity) – e.g., in mass retailing. It may also stem from high margins, but low asset turnover (i.e., high capital intensity) – e.g., whisky producers.

The following table shows the ROCE and its components achieved by some leading European groups during 2004:

2004 data	Return on capital employed after tax	=	Operating profit after tax/Sales	×	Sales/ Capital employed (asset turnover)
Nokia	77.9%		12.2%		6.4
Sap	53.6%		17.9%		3.0
Mobistar	38.7%		15.4%		2.5
Zara (Inditex)	27.6%		10.8%		2.6
Swatch	18.7%		13.5%		1.4
Nestlé	17.6%		10.0%		1.8
Ryanair	17.4%		24.8%		0.7
L'Oréal	16.6%		9.6%		1.7
Bulgari	15.6%		13.3%		1.2
BMW	14.8%		5.5%		2.7
Wolters Kluwer	12.3%		11.2%		1.1
KPN	12.1%		12.5%		1.0
Marks & Spencer	11.6%		4.8%		2.3
Tesco	11.3%		4.8%		2.3
Benetton	10.2%		9.1%		1.1
Siemens	9.7%		4.0%		2.4
Repsol YPF	8.9%		3.9%		2.3
Carlsberg	8.8%		5.2%		1.7
Rio Tinto	8.8%		15.3%		0.6
Lafarge	8.2%		11.6%		0.7
Bayer	7.6%		6.3%		1.2
Volvo	4.3%		3.9%		1.1
Tiscali	−10.7%		−8.4%		1.3

Source: Exane BNP Paribas

1 *Depending on whether capital expenditure during the period is regarded as having contributed to wealth creation or not.*

download

The first ratio derives from the various margins that we defined during our earnings statement analysis, while the second ratio reflects the asset turnover, which is a function of the sector's capital intensity and the size of the company's working capital.

Although Ryanair and Nestlé generate a similar return on capital employed, their operating margins and asset turnover are entirely different. Ryanair has a strong operating margin (25%), but a weak asset turnover of 0.7 (because it is very capital intensive) while Nestlé has a smaller operating margin (10%) but a higher asset turnover of 1.8.

These figures are calculated after tax, which means that we calculate return on capital employed after tax at the normal rate.

Analysts will have to decide for themselves whether, as we suggest here, they work on an after-tax basis. If so, they will have to calculate operating profit after theoretical tax (calculated based on the company's normalised tax rate), which is called NOPAT (Net Operating Profit After Tax).

Second, we can calculate the **Return On Equity (ROE)**, which is the ratio of net income to shareholders' equity:

$$\text{Return on equity} = \frac{\text{Net income}}{\text{Shareholders' equity}}$$

In practice, most financial analysts take goodwill amortisation or impairment losses and nonrecurring items out of net income before calculating return on equity.

Section 13.2
LEVERAGE EFFECT

1/THE PRINCIPLE

The leverage effect explains a company's return on equity in terms of its return on capital employed and cost of debt.

In our approach, we considered the total amount of capital employed, including both equity and debt. This capital is invested in assets that form the company's capital employed and that are intended to generate earnings, as follows:

download

HOW THE WEALTH CREATED IS APPORTIONED

All the capital provided by lenders and shareholders is used to finance **all the uses of funds – i.e., the company's capital employed**. These uses of funds generate operating profit, which itself is apportioned between net financial expense (returns paid to debtholders) and net income attributable to shareholders.

If we compare a company's return on equity with its return on capital employed (after tax to remain consistent), we note that the difference is due only to its financial structure, aside from nonrecurring items and items specific to consolidated accounts, which we will deal with later on.

By definition, the leverage effect is the difference between return on equity and return on capital employed.

The leverage effect explains how it is possible for a company to deliver a return on equity exceeding the rate of return on all the capital invested in the business; i.e., its return on capital employed.

Readers should pause for a second to contemplate this corporate nirvana, which apparently consists in making more money than actually generated by a company's industrial and commercial activities.

But, before getting too carried away, readers should note that the leverage effect works both ways. Although it can lift a company's return on equity above return on capital employed, it can also depress it, turning the dream into a nightmare.

The leverage effect works as follows. When a company raises debt and invests the funds it has borrowed in its industrial and commercial activities, it generates operating profit that normally exceeds the interest expense due on its borrowings. If this is not the case, it is not worth investing, as we will see at the beginning of Section II of this book. So, the company generates a surplus consisting of the difference between the return on capital employed and the cost of debt related to the borrowing. This surplus is attributable to shareholders and is added to shareholders' equity. The leverage effect of debt thus increases the return on equity. Hence its name.

Let's consider a company with capital employed of 100, which generates a return of 10% after tax, which is financed entirely by equity. Its return on capital employed and return on equity both stand at 10%.

If the same company finances 30 of its capital employed with debt at an interest rate of 4% after tax and the remainder with equity, its return on equity is:

	Operating profit after tax:	$10\% \times 100 = 10$
−	Interest expense after tax:	$4\% \times 30 = 1.2$
=	Net income after tax:	$= 8.8$

When divided by shareholders' equity of 70 $(100 - 30)$, this yields a return on equity after tax of 12.6% (8.8/70), while the after-tax return on capital employed stands at 10%.

The borrowing of 30 that is invested in capital employed generates operating profit after tax of 3 which, after post-tax interest expense (1.2), is fully attributable for an amount of 1.8 to shareholders. This surplus amount (1.8) is added to operating profit generated by equity-financed investments $(70 \times 10\% = 7)$ to give net income of $7 + 1.8 = 8.8$. The company's return on equity now stands at $8.8/70 = 12.6\%$.

The leverage effect of debt thus increases the company's return on equity by 2.6%, or the surplus generated (1.8) divided by shareholders' equity ($1.8/70 = 2.6\%$).

Debt can thus be used to boost a company's return on equity without any change in return on capital employed.

But readers will surely have noticed the prerequisite for the return on equity to increase when the company raises additional debt – i.e., **its ROCE must be higher than its cost of debt**. Otherwise, the company borrows at a higher rate than the returns it generates by investing the borrowed funds in its capital employed, giving rise to a deficit that reduces the rate of return generated by the company's equity. Its earnings decline, and the return on equity **dips below** its ROCE.

Let's go back to our company and assume that its return on capital employed falls to 3% after tax. In this scenario, its return on equity is as follows:

	Operating profit after tax:	$100 \times 3\% = \quad 3$
−	Interest expense after tax:	$30 \times 4\% = \quad 1.2$
=	Net income after tax:	$= \quad 1.8$

When divided by shareholders' equity of 70, this yields a return on equity after tax of 2.6% ($1.8/70$).

The borrowing of 30 generates, once invested in tangible assets or working capital, an operating profit after tax of 0.9, which, after deducting the 1.2 in interest charges, produces a deficit of 0.3 on the borrowed funds. This shortfall is thus deducted from net income, which will drop to $70 \times 3\% - 0.3 = 1.8$.

The original return on capital employed of 3% is thus reduced by $0.3/70 = 0.4\%$ to give a return on equity of 2.6% after tax.

When the return on capital employed falls below the cost of debt, the leverage effect of debt shifts into reverse and reduces the return on equity, which in turn falls below return on capital employed.

2/ FORMULATING AN EQUATION

Before we go any further, we need to clarify the impact of tax on this line of reasoning.

Tax reduces earnings. All revenues give rise to taxation and all charges serve to reduce the tax bite (provided that the company is profitable). Consequently, each line of the income statement can thus be regarded as giving rise to either tax expense or a theoretical tax credit, with the actual tax charge payable being the net amount of the tax expense and credits. We can thus calculate an operating profit figure net of tax, by simply multiplying the operating profit before tax by a factor of (1 − rate of corporate income tax).

As a result, we can ensure the consistency of our calculations. Throughout this chapter, we have **worked on an after-tax basis** for all the key profit indicators –

i.e., operating profit, net financial expense and net income (note that our reasoning would have been identical had we worked on a pre-tax basis).

Let's now formulate an equation encapsulating our conclusions. Net income is equal to the return on capital employed multiplied by shareholders' equity plus a surplus (or deficit) arising on net debt, which is equal to the net debt multiplied by the difference between the after-tax return on capital employed and the after-tax cost of debt.

Translating this formula into a profitability – rather than an earnings-based equation – we arrive at the following:

$$\text{Return on equity} = \text{Return on capital employed (after tax)} + \left(\text{Return on capital employed (after tax)} - \text{After-tax cost of debt} \right) \times \frac{\text{Net debt}}{\text{Shareholder's equity}}$$

or:

$$ROE = ROCE + (ROCE - i) \times \frac{D}{E}$$

Readers should not let themselves get bogged down by this equation, which is based on an accounting tautology. The leverage effect is merely a straightforward factor that is used to account for return on equity, and nothing more.

The ratio of net debt to shareholders' equity is called financial leverage or gearing. The leverage effect can thus be expressed as follows:

$$\frac{\text{Net debt}}{\text{Shareholders' equity}} \times \left(\text{Return on capital employed} - \text{After-tax cost of debt} \right)$$

Return on equity is thus equal to the return on capital employed plus the leverage effect.

Note that:

- the higher the company's return on capital employed relative to the cost of debt (e.g., if ROCE increases to 16% in our example, return on equity rises to 16% + 5.1% = 21.1%), or
- the higher the company's debt burden,

the higher the leverage effect.

Naturally, the leverage effect goes into reverse once:

- return on capital employed falls below the cost of debt;
- the cost of debt was poorly forecast or suddenly soars because the company's debt carries a variable rate and interest rates are on the rise.

The leverage effect, which is underpinned by an accounting tautology, applies even when a company has negative net debt – i.e., when its short-term financial investments exceed the value of its debt. In such cases, return on equity equates to the average of return on equity and return on short-term investments weighted by shareholders' equity and short-term investments. The leverage effect can thus be calculated in exactly the same way, with i corresponding instead to the after-tax rate of return on short-term financial investments and D showing a negative value because net debt is negative.

For instance, let's consider the case of Nokia in 2004. Its shareholders' equity stood at €14,406m and its net debt was a negative €11,308m, while its short-term financial investments yielded 2.5% after tax. Its return on capital employed after applying an average tax rate of 30.5% stood at 97% based on its operating profit of €4,330m.[2] Return on equity thus stands at:

2 $97\% =$

$$\frac{€4,330m \times (1 - 30.5\%)}{€14,406m - €11,308m}$$

$$97\% + (97\% - 2.5\%) \times \frac{-11,308}{14,406}, \quad \text{i.e. } 22.8\%$$

The reason for Nokia's ROE being lower than its ROCE is clearly not that the group's cost of debt is higher than its return on capital employed! To put things simply, Nokia is unable to secure returns on the financial markets for its surplus cash on a par with those generated by its manufacturing facilities. Consequently, it has to invest the funds at a rate below its return on capital employed, thus depressing its return on equity.

The following tables shows trends in ROE and ROCE posted by various different sectors in Europe over the 1995–2005 period.

@
download

ROE FOR LEADING LISTED EUROPEAN COMPANIES (%)

Sector	1996	1997	1998	1999	2000	2001	2002	2003	2004	2005e	2006e
Aerospace and defence	12	16	9	8	3	9	6	8	10	10	11
Automotive	16	15	13	10	9	7	10	7	10	10	12
Beverages	14	23	20	19	22	20	22	21	19	18	19
Building materials	10	13	13	13	13	12	13	12	14	14	15
Capital goods	15	14	11	14	28	10	9	4	11	13	14
Chemicals	12	14	14	11	12	10	10	8	12	13	13
Consumer goods	11	12	13	15	17	15	21	19	18	17	18
Food and home care	19	20	24	23	23	25	27	28	27	24	24
Food retail	14	14	15	15	15	14	12	15	14	14	14
General retail	16	19	15	15	15	18	17	17	17	18	18
IT hardware	10	13	8	14	16	−3	−3	6	14	13	13
IT services	9	15	16	16	13	12	10	9	9	13	14
Leisure and hotels	−11	−10	6	8	9	10	3	5	8	10	13
Luxury goods	12	13	11	11	12	10	14	15	16	17	19
Media	18	18	22	18	4	6	8	11	15	16	17
Metals and mining	5	−3	2	8	7	7	7	11	22	24	18
Oil and gas	12	13	11	13	23	20	16	17	22	22	20
Personal care	15	14	15	15	17	17	19	20	17	16	16
Pharmaceuticals	21	25	23	23	25	24	25	24	18	19	18
Software	24	29	29	28	23	31	42	25	24	23	22
Support services	19	30	30	41	22	20	19	20	19	20	21
Telecom operators and ISPs	12	6	12	4	2	2	7	11	13	14	17
Transport	14	11	10	6	11	3	10	7	8	10	11
Utilities	11	11	11	13	11	13	14	14	14	14	16

Source: Exane BNP Paribas.

ROCE FOR LEADING LISTED EUROPEAN COMPANIES (%)

Sector	1996	1997	1998	1999	2000	2001	2002	2003	2004	2005e	2006e
Aerospace and defence	9	13	11	8	6	8	7	7	11	10	10
Automotive	8	6	8	7	6	4	5	4	6	6	7
Beverages	10	16	13	13	13	12	12	13	12	12	13
Building materials	8	8	9	8	8	7	8	8	9	9	10
Capital goods	7	6	6	6	7	2	6	7	12	14	15
Chemicals	9	9	9	7	7	6	7	6	8	9	9
Consumer goods	8	7	9	11	12	11	15	15	14	13	13
Food and home care	9	10	11	11	8	8	10	11	11	11	11
Food retail	10	10	9	8	7	8	9	9	9	9	9
General retail	10	12	10	10	11	13	12	13	14	15	16
IT hardware	8	11	8	11	13	0	3	8	16	16	16
IT services	8	12	18	17	15	12	8	6	10	10	11
Leisure and hotels	2	3	4	5	5	5	3	5	7	8	14
Luxury goods	11	10	6	8	8	6	8	9	10	11	12
Media	9	10	10	7	5	6	7	7	9	9	10
Metals and mining	4	2	3	5	8	6	6	8	14	17	15
Oil and gas	9	10	6	9	17	14	9	11	16	16	14
Personal care	12	13	14	14	13	13	15	16	14	15	16
Pharmaceuticals	21	18	20	16	18	20	21	21	14	16	17
Software	65	34	58	55	36	38	50	40	52	56	63
Support services	10	13	14	15	9	9	8	8	8	9	9
Telecom operators and ISPs	11	7	10	6	4	4	5	8	9	9	9
Transport	8	7	7	5	6	3	6	5	7	8	8
Utilities	6	7	7	6	6	7	6	7	10	10	10

Source: Exane BNP Paribas.

The reader may notice, among other things, the global improvement in ROCE over the period, with stellar performances from the software industry because most of its assets are not in the balance sheet (people). Aerospace/defence and leisure/hotels have similar ROE at around 12% but very dissimilar ROCE (10% and 5%, respectively). The explanation lies in the level of debt, generally very high in the hotel and leisure business as it is a capital intensive sector, and very limited in the aerospace business. The quality of aerospace sector ROE is much better than in the leisure/hotel sector. In this sector ROCE would be worryingly low if companies in this sector were not able to regularly sell some real estate assets at profit (not included in the computation of ROCE).

3/CALCULATING THE LEVERAGE EFFECT

(a) Presentation

To calculate the leverage effect and the return on equity, we recommend using the table that starts at the bottom of this page. The items needed for these calculations are listed below. We strongly recommend that readers should use the data shown in the tables on pp. 54 and 174.

- On the income statement:
  - sales (S);
  - profit before tax and nonrecurring items (PBT);
  - financial expense net of financial income (FE);
  - operating profit $(EBIT)$.

- On the balance sheet:
  - fixed assets (FA);
  - working capital (WC) comprising both operating and nonoperating working capital;
  - capital employed – i.e., the sum of the two previous lines, as well as the sum of the two following lines, since capital employed is financed by shareholders' equity and debt (CE);
  - shareholders' equity (E);
  - net debt encompassing all short-, medium- and long-term bank borrowings and debt less marketable securities, cash and equivalents (D).

Corporate income tax is abbreviated to T_c.

download

LEVERAGE EFFECT (e.g., Ericsson)

Basic data

	€m	1999	2000	2001	2002	2003
Sales (S)		23,516	24,191	25,310	15,914	12,853
Profit before tax and nonrecurring items (PBT)		1,817	2,241	−3,105	−2,335	−1,294
+ Financial expense net of financial income (FE)		76	130	193	168	94
= Operating profit $(EBIT)$		1,893	2,371	−2,911	−2,167	−1,199
Fixed assets (FA)		4,337	4,420	3,924	2,909	2,305
+ Working capital (WC)		4,999	6,768	4,273	2,207	−1,193
= CAPITAL EMPLOYED (CE)		9,336	11,188	8,197	5,116	1,113
Shareholders' equity (E)		7,551	9,934	5,822	5,762	3,942
+ Net debt (D)		1,785	1,254	2,375	−510	−2,830
= CAPITAL INVESTED = CAPITAL EMPLOYED (CE)		9,336	11,188	8,197	5,116	1,113
Corporate income tax (T_c)		28.6%	43.9%	−33.5%	−17.7%	−14.1%

Calculations

		1999	2000	2001	2002	2003
i	After tax cost of debt $= \dfrac{FE \times (1 - T_c)}{D}$	3.0%	5.8%	10.8%	−38.8%	−3.8%
ROCE	Return on capital employed (after tax) $=$ $\dfrac{EBIT \times (1 - T_c) \text{ or } NOPAT}{CE}$	14.5%	11.9%	−47.4%	−49.9%	−122.9%
$ROCE - i$	Return on capital employed (after tax) − After-tax cost of debt	11.5%	6.1%	−58.2%	−11.1%	−119.1%
D/E	Gearing	0.24	0.13	0.41	−0.09	−0.72
	Leverage effect $= (ROCE - i) \times \dfrac{D}{E}$	2.7%	0.7%	−23.9%	1.0%	85.5%
ROE	Return on equity $= \dfrac{PBT \times (1 - T_c)}{E}$	17.2%	12.6%	−71.3%	−48.9%	−37.4%
	or $ROCE + (ROCE - i) \times \dfrac{D}{E}$	17.2%	12.6%	−71.3%	−48.9%	−37.4%

Results

		1999	2000	2001	2002	2003
× =	Operating margin after tax $(EBIT \times (1 - T_c)/S)$ Asset turnover (S/CE) **Return on capital employed (after tax)** (A)	5.7% 2.5 14.5%	5.5% 2.2 11.9%	−15.4% 3.1 −47.4%	−16.0% 3.1 −49.9%	−10.6% 11.5 −122.9%
× =	Return on capital employed − After-tax cost of debt $\quad (ROCE - i)$ Gearing (D/E) **Leverage effect** (B)	11.5% 0.24 2.7%	6.1% 0.13 0.7%	−58.2% 0.41 −23.9%	−11.1% −0.09 1.0%	−119.1% −0.72 −85.5%
=	**Return On Equity** $(A + B)$	17.2%	12.6%	−71.3%	−48.9%	−37.4%

(b) Practical problems

We recommend that readers use the balance sheets and income statements prepared during Chapters 4 and 9 as a starting point when filling in the previous table.

We cannot overemphasise the importance of the two following accounting equations:

Capital employed = Shareholders' equity + Net debt

Operating profit after tax = Net income + Net financial expense after tax.

Consequently, readers will arrive at the same return on equity figure whichever way they calculate it. It is worth remembering that using profit before tax and nonrecurring items rather than net income eliminates the impact of nonrecurring items.

Besides breaking down quasi-equity between debt or shareholders' equity, provisions for liabilities and charges between working capital or debt, etc., which we dealt with in Chapter 7, only two concrete problems arise when we calculate the leverage effect in consolidated financial statements: how to treat goodwill and associate companies.

The way goodwill is treated (see Chapter 6) has a significant impact on the results obtained. Setting off the entire amount of goodwill against shareholders' equity using the pooling of interests method caused a large chunk of capital employed and shareholders' equity to disappear from the balance sheet. As a result, the nominal returns on equity and on capital employed may look deceptively high when this type of merger accounting was used. Just because whole chunks of capital appeared to have vanished into thin air from a balance sheet perspective, this does not mean that shareholders will give up their normal rate of return requirements on the capital that has done a perfectly legitimate disappearing act under certain accounting standards. The recent abolition of the pooling of interests method in IAS[3] and US accounting standards is gradually eliminating this problem.

Likewise, goodwill amortisation when it was compulsory or impairment losses artificially reduce the capital that appears to be invested in the business. Consequently, we recommend that readers should, wherever possible, work with **gross** goodwill figures and add back to shareholders' equity the difference between gross and net goodwill to keep the balance sheet in equilibrium. Likewise, we would advise working on the basis of operating profit and net profit before goodwill amortisation or impairment losses.

By doing so, readers will be able to conduct a rigorous assessment of a company's profitability. This area is explored further in Exercise 4 at the end of this chapter.

Consolidated accounts present another problem, which is how **income from associates[4] should be treated**. Should income from associates be considered as financial income or as a component of operating profit, bearing in mind that the latter approach implies adding an income after financial expense and tax to an operating profit (which is before tax)?

- The rationale for considering income from associates as financial income is that it equates to the dividend that the group would receive if the associate company paid out 100% of its earnings. This first approach seems to fit a financial group that may sell one or other investments to reduce its debt.
- The rationale for considering income from associates as part of the operating profit is that income from associates derives from investments included in capital employed. This latter approach is geared more to an industrial group, for which such situations should be exceptional and temporary because the majority of industrial groups intend to control more than 50% of their subsidiaries.

This said, in a bid to improve the presentation of their accounts, certain groups park their least profitable assets and substantial debts in associate companies in which they own less than 40% and which are thus accounted for under the equity

3 *International Accounting Standards.*

4 *For more on income from associates see p. 79. In the Ericsson case study, the problem was disregarded as associates represented only 7% of fixed assets and their large losses in 2000 and 2001 were not recurrent.*

method. For instance, Coca-Cola boasted a headline return on capital employed of 23% in 2004. Note, however, that vital (bottling) assets worth $45bn are housed in less than 40%-owned associate companies, together with $26bn in bank and other borrowings. The return on capital employed generated by these assets stands at just 6% since internal transfer pricing keeps most of the profits within the parent company. In such situations where the letter of accounting standards is abided by, but in our opinion not the spirit, analysts would be advised to examine the profitability of the parent and associate companies separately before forming an overall assessment. Adjusted for this accounting "trick", the group's return on capital employed comes to 11.5%.[5]

Lastly, the tax rate may be affected by various deferred tax assets and liabilities arising from the restatement of individual financial statements for consolidation purposes. In practice, we recommend that readers choose an effective tax rate based on the company's average tax rate.

5 For further details concerning off-balance-sheet financing, we refer readers to Chapter 47, which explores the subject in greater depth.

4/COMPANIES WITH NEGATIVE CAPITAL EMPLOYED

Companies with negative capital employed usually have high negative working capital exceeding the size of their net fixed assets. This phenomenon is prevalent in certain specific sectors (contract catering, retailing, etc.) and this type of company typically posts a very high return on equity.

Of the two roles played by shareholders' equity – i.e., financing capital expenditure and acting as a guarantee for lenders – the former is not required by such companies. Only the latter role remains.

Consequently, return on capital employed needs to be calculated taking into account income from short-term financial investments (included in earnings) and the size of these investments (included in capital employed):

$$ROCE = \frac{(EBIT + \text{Financial income}) \times (1 - T_c)}{\text{Capital employed} + \text{Short-term financial investments}}$$

As a matter of fact, companies in this situation factor their financial income into the selling price of their products and services. Consequently, it would not make sense to calculate capital employed without taking short-term financial investments into account.

Section 13.3
USES AND LIMITATIONS OF THE LEVERAGE EFFECT

1/LIMITATIONS OF BOOK PROFITABILITY INDICATORS

Book-based return on capital employed figures are naturally of great interest to financial analysts and managers alike. This said, they have much more limited appeal from a financial standpoint. The leverage effect equation always stands up to analysis, although sometimes some anomalous results are produced. For instance, the cost of debt calculated as the ratio of financial expense net of financial income to balance sheet debt may be plainly too high or too low. This simply means that the net debt shown on the balance sheet does not reflect average debt over the year, that the company is in reality much more (or less) indebted or that its debt is subject to seasonal fluctuations.

Attempts may be made to overcome this type of problem by using average or restated figures, particularly for fixed assets and shareholders' equity. But this approach is really feasible only for internal analysts with sufficient data at their disposal.

It is thus important not to set too much store by implicit interest rates or the corresponding leverage effect when they are clearly anomalous.

For managers of a business or a profit centre, return on capital employed is one of the key performance and profitability indicators; particularly, with the emergence of economic profit indicators, which compare the return on capital employed with the weighted average cost of capital (see Chapter 19).

From a financial standpoint, however, book-based returns on capital employed and returns on equity hold very limited appeal. Since book returns are prepared from the accounts, they do not reflect risks. As such, book returns should not be used in isolation as an objective for the company because this will prompt managers to take extremely unwise decisions.

As we have seen, it is easy to boost book returns on equity by gearing up the balance sheet and harnessing the leverage effect. The risk of the company is also increased without being reflected in the accounting-based formula.

Return on capital employed and return on equity are accounting indicators used for historical analysis. In no circumstances whatsoever should they be used to project the future rates of return required by shareholders or all providers of funds.

If a company's book profitability is very high, shareholders require a lot less and will already have adjusted their valuation of shareholders' equity, whose market value is thus much higher than its book value. If a company's book profitability is very low, shareholders want much more and will already have marked down the market value of shareholders' equity to well below its book value.[6]

It is therefore essential to note that the book return on equity, return on capital employed and cost of debt do not reflect the rates of return required by shareholders, providers of funds or creditors, respectively. These returns cannot be considered as financial performance indicators because they do not take into account the two key concepts of risk and valuation. Instead, they belong to the domains of financial analysis and control. We refer readers to Chapter 19 for a more detailed analysis.

Some analysts attempt to calculate return on capital employed by using the ratio of operating profit to market capitalisation plus the market value of debt. In our view, the theoretical basis for this type of approach is very shaky because an accounting profit indicator from the past is used in conjunction with an asset valuation based on expectations of future profits.

6 *For more on this point see p. 637.*

2/USES OF THE LEVERAGE EFFECT

The leverage effect sheds light on the origins of return on equity: whether it flows from operating performance (i.e., a good return on capital employed) or from a favourable financing structure harnessing the leverage effect. Our experience tells us that, **in the long term, only an increasing return on capital employed guarantees a steady rise in a company's return on equity**.

The main point of the leverage effect is thus to show how return on equity breaks down between the profitability of a company's industrial and commercial operations and its capital structure (i.e., the leverage effect).

Consider the profitability of the following groups:

RETURN ON EQUITY (%)

	2002	2003	2004	2005
Group A	15	16	18	20
Group B	15	15	15	15
Group C	40	40	40	40

RETURN ON CAPITAL EMPLOYED (AFTER TAX) (%)

	2002	2003	2004	2005
Group A	10	8	7	7
Group B	15	15	15	15
Group C	10	10	10	10

A superficial analysis may suggest that group C is a star performer owing to its stunningly high return on equity (40%), that group A is improving and that group B is rather disappointing by comparison.

But this analysis does not even scratch the surface of the reality! C generates its very high returns through the unbridled use of the leverage effect that weakens the whole company, while its return on capital employed is average. B has no debt and carries the least risk, while its return on capital employed is the highest. A's improvement is merely a mirage because it is attributable entirely to a stronger and stronger leverage effect, while its return on capital employed is steadily declining, and so A is actually exposed to the greatest risks.

As we will see in Section III of this book, the leverage effect is not very useful in finance because it does not create any value except in two very special cases:

- in times of rising inflation, real interest rates (i.e., after inflation) are negative, thereby eroding the wealth of a company's creditors, who are repaid in a lender's depreciating currency to the great benefit of the shareholders;
- when companies have a very heavy debt burden (e.g., following an LBO,[7] see Chapter 44), which obliges management to ensure that they perform well so that the cash flows generated are sufficient to cover the heavy debt-servicing costs. In this type of situation, the leverage effect gives management a very strong incentive to do well, because the price of failure would be very high.

7 *Leveraged Buy Out.*

8 *See also pp. 54, 65 and 174.*

Section 13.4
CASE STUDY[8]: ERICSSON

Needless to say the Ericsson figures are frightening: since 2001, return on capital employed and return on equity have both been negative: between −40% and −120%. It means that Ericsson would have lost 95% of its equity in 3 years if it had not been for the end of 2002 share issue which probably saved the group from bankruptcy!

The reader would have noticed that in the table on p. 241 corporate income tax is negative in 2001, 2002 and 2003 and that the after-tax cost of debt is negative in 2002 and in 2003. This is not a mistake on our part, or undue generosity from the tax department or banks, but the result of strict application of formulas. You do not have to correct them. If you were to, there would no longer be any equality between the two formulas used to compute ROE as they are based on the fundamental accounting equation: Assets = Liabilities + Equity.

Those apparent errors have an explanation. In 2002, the after-tax cost of debt is negative because Ericsson raised new equity at the end of year which put its net debt into negative territory and time was too short for this cash to yield significant interest income to compensate for interest expense incurred over the rest of the year. Negative corporate income tax is due to the fact that accounts are consolidated on a worldwide basis but that tax is paid on a country-by-country-basis. Let us assume Ericsson is profitable in the USA. It will pay corporate income tax there even if those US profits are not enough to put the whole group in the black given its losses in other countries. Net income will be negative and the corporate income tax rate will appear to be negative on a consolidated basis.

SUMMARY

download

Return On Capital Employed (ROCE) is the book return generated by a company's operations. It is calculated as operating profit after normalised tax divided by capital employed or as the NOPAT margin (Net Operating Profit After Tax/sales) multiplied by asset turnover (sales/capital employed). Return On Equity (ROE) is the ratio of net profit to shareholders' equity.

The leverage effect of debt is the difference between return on equity and return on capital employed. It derives from the difference between return on capital employed and the after-tax cost of debt and is influenced by the relative size of debt and equity on the balance sheet. From a mathematical standpoint, the leverage effect leads to the following accounting tautology:

$$ROE = ROCE + (ROCE - i) \times \frac{D}{E}$$

The leverage effect works both ways. Although it may boost return on equity to above the level of return on capital employed, it may also dilute it to a weaker level when the return on capital employed falls below the cost of debt.

Book return on capital employed, return on equity and cost of debt do not reflect the returns required by shareholders, providers of funds and creditors. These figures cannot be regarded as financial indicators because they do not take into account risk or valuation, two key parameters in finance. Instead, they reflect the historical book returns achieved and belong to the realms of financial analysis and control.

The leverage effect helps to identify the source of a good return on equity, which may come from either a healthy return on capital employed or merely from a company's capital structure – i.e., the leverage effect. This is its only real point.

In the long run, only a healthy return on capital employed will ensure a decent return on equity. As we will see, the leverage effect does not create any value. Although it may boost return on equity, it leads to an increase in risk that is proportional to the additional profit.

QUESTIONS

quiz

1/ Why is capital employed equal to invested capital?

2/ What is the leverage effect?

3/ How is the leverage effect calculated?

4/ Why is the leverage effect equation an accounting tautology?

5/ According to the leverage effect equation, for the same after-tax ROCE of 10%, an increase in debt (costing 4% after tax) could improve the return on equity. State your views.

6/ Why is goodwill a problem when calculating ROCE?

7/ What is the basic purpose of the leverage effect?

8/ Your financial director suggests that you increase debt to increase ROE. State your views.

9/ What is the main problem with accounting profitability indicators such as ROE or ROCE?

10/ Over a given period, interest rates are low, corporation tax rates are high and the economy is doing well. What consequences will this have on the financial structure of companies?

EXERCISES

1/ Prove the leverage effect equation.

2/ A businessman is hoping to get a 20% return on equity after tax. The business generates a 3% sales margin (after-tax). Provide two possible combinations of financial structure, profitability and capital employed that could lead to the generation of a 20% return on equity (the cost of borrowing is 5% before tax, the tax rate is 40% and the company's capital employed is 1,000).

3/ Calculate the leverage effect for each year. What are your conclusions?

€m	1	2	3	4	5
Shareholders' equity	100	115	320	300	240
Long- and medium-term debt	123	180	540	640	680
Financial expense before tax	11	18.5	29	63	83
Net income	14	16	(20)	(60)	(40)
Tax rate	35%	35%	35%	35%	35%

4/ Calculate the ROCE and the ROE of Adidas Salomon. Include provisions for liabilities and charges when calculating working capital. Gross goodwill is €868m.

Consolidated income statement for Adidas Salomon (€m)	2003
NET SALES	6,267
− Cost of sales	(3,453)
= GROSS PROFIT	(2,814)
− Selling, general and administrative costs	(2,228)
= EBITDA	586
− Depreciation, amortisation and impairment losses	(96)
= OPERATING INCOME	490
− Interest and other finance charges	(49)
+ Interest, dividends and other financial income	42
= PROFIT BEFORE TAX AND NONRECURRING ITEMS	483
+ Nonrecurring items	0
+ Income from associates	0
− Income tax	(167)
= NET INCOME	316
− Goodwill amortisation	(45)
− Income attributable to minority interests	(11)
= PUBLISHED NET PROFIT (group share)	260

Consolidated balance sheet for Adidas Salomon (€m)	2003
Goodwill	592
+ Fixed tangibles and intangibles	448
+ Equity in associated companies	0
+ Other investments	193
= FIXED ASSETS	1,233
Total inventories	1,163
+ Total receivables	1,075
+ Other operating receivables	259
− Trade payables	592
− Other operating payables	751
= WORKING CAPITAL	1,154
SHAREHOLDERS' EQUITY, GROUP SHARE	1,356
Minority interests	57
Contingency and loss provisions	28
Medium- and long-term bank debts	1,225
+ Bank overdrafts and short-term borrowings	0
− Marketable securities	0
− Cash and equivalents	279
= NET DEBT	946

ANSWERS

Questions

1/ *Because accounts are balanced!*

2/ *The difference between return on equity and ROCE after tax.*

3/ *Leverage effect* $= (ROCE - i) \times \dfrac{D}{E}.$

4/ *As it is based on total assets being exactly equal to total liabilities and equity.*

5/ *That is true, but it also increases the risk to the shareholder.*

6/ *Because if it had been impaired, reducing capital employed (see Chapter 6), it would have artificially increased book returns. Our advice is to look at the gross rather than the net figures (before impairment losses on this goodwill).*

7/ *It helps to identify the source of a good return on equity.*

8/ *Is ROCE higher than the cost of debt? What is the risk for shareholders?*

9/ *They do not factor in risk.*

10/ *An increase in the leverage effect. However, see Section III of this book.*

Exercises

1/ *Where:*

$$NI = \text{Net income}$$
$$EBIT = \text{Operating profit}$$
$$T_c = \text{Tax rate}$$
$$i = \text{Cost of debt after tax}$$

$$ROE = \frac{NI}{E} = \frac{EBIT \times (1 - T_c) - i \times D}{E} = \frac{EBIT \times (1 - T_c)}{CP} - \frac{i \times D}{E}$$
$$= \frac{EBIT \times (1 - T_c) \times (E + D)}{E \times (E + D)} - \frac{i \times D}{E}$$
$$= \frac{EBIT \times (1 - T_c)}{E + D} + \frac{EBIT \times (1 - T_c)}{E + D} \times \frac{D}{E} - i \times \frac{D}{EP}$$

whereas:

$$ROCE = \frac{EBIT \times (1 - T_c)}{E + D} \qquad \text{and so} \qquad ROE = ROCE + (ROCE - i) \times \frac{D}{E}$$

2/ *Using the leverage effect equation the following can be determined:*

	Solution 1	Solution 2
Capital employed	1,000	1,000
Net borrowings	750	0
Shareholders' equity	250	1,000
Sales	1,666.7	6,666.7
Operating profit	120.8	333
Financial expense	37.5	0
Corporate income tax	33.3	133
Net income	50	200

3/

	1	2	3	4	5
ROCE after tax	9.5%	9.5%	0.7%	0.2%	3.0%
Leverage	1.23	1.57	1.69	2.13	2.83
Net cost of debt*	5.8%	6.7%	4.8%	9.7%	10.0%
Leverage effect	4.5%	4.4%	−6.9%	−20.2%	−19.7%
ROE	14%	13.9%	−6.2%	−20%	−16.7%

* Tax savings have only had a partial impact in the last 3 years.

When ROCE is above the after-tax cost of debt, debt boosts ROE and depresses it when ROCE is lower than the after-tax cost of debt. This company is on the verge of bankruptcy.

4/ *There is no one right answer. It is however important to be consistent when calculating. Special attention should be paid:*

When calculating ROCE:

○ *Our advice is to take operating income before impairment losses/amortisation on goodwill, and to use capital employed including gross goodwill (and not goodwill after impairment losses or amortisation).*

○ *If capital employed includes long-term investments and investments in associates, operating income should be restated to include income on these assets. This information was not provided, which will not have any consequences, since long-term investments represent only 16% of total fixed assets.*

When calculating ROE:

○ *ROE (group share) can be calculated by dividing net profits (group share) by shareholders' equity (group share). However, if the numerator includes minorities' shares, it will have to be divided by total shareholders' equity (including minority interests).*

Capital employed (with gross goodwill)	$1,233 - 592 + 868 + 1,154 - 28 = 2,635$
Operating income before goodwill amortisation	*490*
Tax at 34%	*167*
Return on capital employed after tax	*12.3%*
Shareholders' equity, group share	$1,356 + 868 - 592 = 1,632$
Net earnings, group share	*260*
Return on equity, group share	*15.9%*

Adidas Salomon has a satisfactory ROCE (12% is clearly above cost of capital) and a stronger ROE (16%) because the company relies on debt (leverage of 0.67) taking advantage of a low after-tax cost of debt (2.6%).

BIBLIOGRAPHY

G. Blazenko, Corporate leverage and the distribution of equity returns, *Journal of Business and Acccounting*, 1097–1120, October 1996.

M. Campello, Z. Fluck, *Market Share, Financial Leverage and the Macroeconomy: Theory and Empirical Evidence*, working paper, University of Illinois, November 2003.

V. Dimitrov, P. Jain, *The Information Content of Changes in Financial Leverage*, working paper, State University of New Jersey, 12 August 2003.

M. Dugan, D. Minyard, K. Shriver, A re-examination of the operating leverage–financial leverage tradeoff, *Quarterly Review of Economics and Finance*, 327–334, Fall 1994.

L. Lang, E. Ofek, R. Stulz, Leverage, investment and firm growth, *Journal of Financial Economics*, 3–29, January 1996.

D. Nissim, S. Penman, Financial statement analysis of leverage and how it informs about profitability and price-to-book ratios, *Review of Accounting Studies*, **8**, 531–560, 2003.

F. Reilly, The impact of inflation on ROE, growth and stock prices, *Financial Services Review*, **6**(1), 1997.

Chapter 14
CONCLUSION OF FINANCIAL ANALYSIS

As one journey ends, another probably starts

By the time they complete a financial analysis, readers must be able to answer the two following questions that served as the starting point for their investigations:

- Will the company be solvent? That is, will it be able to repay any loans it raised?
- Will it generate a higher rate of return than that required by those that have provided it with funds? That is, will it be able to create value?

Section 14.1
SOLVENCY

Here we return to the concept that we first introduced in Chapter 4.

A company is solvent when it is able to honour all its commitments by liquidating all of its assets; i.e., if it ceases its operations and puts all its assets up for sale.

Since, by definition, a company does not undertake to repay its shareholders, its equity represents a kind of life raft that will help keep it above water in the event of liquidation by absorbing any capital losses on assets and extraordinary losses.

Solvency thus depends on:

- the breakup value of a company's assets;
- the size of its debts.

Do assets have a value that is independent of a company's operations? The answer is probably yes for the showroom of a carmaker on the Unter den Linden Avenue in Berlin and probably no as far as the tools and equipment at a heavy engineering plant are concerned.

Is there a secondary market for such assets? Here, the answer is affirmative for the fleet of cars owned by a car rental company, but probably negative for the technical installations of a foundry. To put things another way: Will a company's assets fetch their book value or less? The second of these situations is the most common. It implies capital losses on top of liquidation costs (redundancy costs, etc.) that will eat into shareholders' equity and frequently push it into negative territory. In this case, lenders will be able to lay their hands on only a portion of what they are owed. As a result, they suffer a capital loss.

The solvency of a company thus depends on the level of shareholders' equity restated from a liquidation standpoint relative to the company's commitments and the nature of its business risks.

If a company posts a loss, its solvency deteriorates significantly owing to the resulting reduction in shareholders' equity and cumulative effects.

A loss-making company no longer benefits from the tax shield provided by debt.[1] As a result, it has to bear the full brunt of financial expense, which thus makes losses even greater. Very frequently, companies raise additional debt to offset the decrease in their equity. Additional debt then increases financial expense and exacerbates losses, giving rise to the cumulative effects we referred to above.

If we measure solvency using the debt/equity ratio, we note that a company's solvency deteriorates very rapidly in the event of a crisis.

Let's consider a company with debt equal to its shareholders' equity. The market value of its debt and shareholders' equity is equal to their book value because its return on capital employed is the same as its cost of capital of 10%.

As a result of a crisis, the return on capital employed declines, leading to the following situation:

Year	0	1	2	3	4	5
Book value of capital employed	100	100	100	100	100	100
= Book value of equity	=50	=50	=47	=34	=25	=25
+ Net debt (costing 6%)	+50	+50	+53	+66	+75	+75
Return on capital employed	10%	0%	−10%	−5%	5%	10%
Operating profit after tax	10	0	−10	−5	5	10
− After-tax interest expense (tax rate of 35%)	−2	−3	−3	−4	−5	−5
= Net income	=8[2]	=−3	=−13	=−9	=0	=5
Market value of capital employed[3]	100	85	55	68	85	100
= Market value of equity	=50	=38	=15	=18	=25	=30
+ Market value of net debt	+50	+47	+40	+50	+60	+70

The company's evolution does not come as a surprise. The market value of capital employed falls by 45% at its lowest point because the previously normal return on capital employed turns negative. The market value of debt declines (from 100% to 75% of its nominal value) since the risk of nonrepayment increases with the decline in return on capital employed and the growing size of its debt. Lastly, the market value of shareholders' equity collapses (by 70%).

Each year, the company has to increase its debt to cover the loss recorded in the previous year to keep its capital employed at the same level. From 1 at the start of our model, gearing soars to 3 by the end of year 5. In this scenario, its equity gets smaller and smaller, and its lenders will be very lucky to get their hands on the

1 *We disregard the impact of carrybacks here.*

2 *In year 0, since the company is profitable, financial expense is only 2 given the income tax rate of 35% (rounded figures). In addition, to keep things simple, it is assumed that the entire amount of net income is paid out as a dividend.*

3 *Market value is observed rather than calculated.*

original amounts that they invested. This scenario shows how debt can spiral in the event of a crisis! Some restructuring of equity and liabilities or, worse still, bankruptcy is bound to ensue with the additional losses caused by the disruption.

Had the same company been debt-free when the crisis began, its financial performance would have been entirely different, as shown by the following table:

Year	0	1	2	3	4	5
Book value of capital employed	100	100	100	100	100	100
= Book value of equity	=100	=100	=100	=90	=84	=88
+ Net debt	+0	+0	+0	+10	+16	+12
Return on capital employed	10%	0%	−10%	−5%	5%	10%
Operating profit after tax	10	0	−10	−5	5	10
− After tax interest expense (tax rate of 35%)	−0	−0	−0	−1	−1	−1
= Net income	=10[4]	=0	=−10	=−6	=4	=9
Market value of capital employed[5]	100	85	55	68	85	100
= Market value of equity	=100	=85	=55	=58	=68	=87
+ Market value of net debt	+0	+0	+0	+10	+17	+13

4 To keep things simple, it is assumed that the entire amount of net income is paid out as a dividend.

5 Market value is observed rather than calculated.

At the end of year 4, the company returns to profit and its shareholders' equity has hardly been dented by the crisis.

Consequently, the first company, which is comparable with the second in all respects from an economic perspective, will not be able to secure financing and is thus probably doomed to failure as an independent economic entity.

For a long time, **net assets** – i.e., the difference between assets and total liabilities or assets net of debt – was the focal point for financial analysis. Net assets are thus an indicator that corresponds to shareholders' equity and is analysed by comparison with the company's total commitments.

Some financial analysts calculate net assets by subtracting goodwill (or even all intangible fixed assets), adding back unrealised capital gains (which may not be accounted for owing to the conservatism principle), with inventories possibly being valued at their replacement cost.

Broadly speaking, calculating net assets is an even trickier task with consolidated accounts owing to minority interests (which group assets do they own?) and goodwill (what assets does it relate to and what value, if any, does it have?). Consequently, we recommend that readers should work using the individual accounts of the various entities forming the group and then consolidate the net asset figures using the proportional method.

Section 14.2
VALUE CREATION

A company will be able to create value during a given period if the return on capital employed (after tax) that it generates exceeds the cost of the capital (i.e., equity and net debt) that it has raised to finance capital employed.

Readers will have to remain patient for a little while yet because we still have to explain how the rate of return required by shareholders and lenders can be measured. This subject is dealt with in Section II of this book. Chapter 32 covers the concept of value creation in greater depth, while Chapter 19 illustrates how it can be measured.

Section 14.3
FINANCIAL ANALYSIS WITHOUT THE RELEVANT
ACCOUNTING DOCUMENTS

When a company's accounting documents are not available in due time (less than 3 months after year-end), it is a sign that the business is in trouble. In many cases, the role of an analyst will then be to assess the scale of a company's losses to see whether it can be turned around or whether their size will doom it to failure.

In this case, the analysts will attempt to establish what proportion of company's loans the lenders can hope to recover. We saw in Chapter 5 that cash flow statements establish a vital link between net income and the net decrease in debt.

It may perhaps surprise some readers to see that we have often used cash flow statements in reverse; i.e., to gauge the level of earnings by working back from the net decrease in debt.

It is essential to bear in mind the long period of time that may elapse before accounting information becomes available for companies in difficulty. In addition to the usual time lag, the information systems of struggling companies may be deficient and take even longer to produce accounting statements, which are obsolete by the time they are published because the company's difficulties have aggravated in the meantime.

Consequently, the cash flow statement is a particularly useful tool for making rapid and timely assessments about the scale of a company's losses, which is the crux of the matter.

It is very easy to calculate the company's net debt. The components of working capital are easily determined (receivables and payables can be estimated from the balances of customer and supplier accounts, and inventories can be estimated based on a stock count). Capital expenditure, capital increases in cash and asset disposals can also be established very rapidly, even in a subpar accounting system. We can thus prepare the cash flow statement in reverse to give an estimate of earnings.

A reverse cash flow statement can be used to provide a very rough estimate of a company's earnings, even before they have been reported.

In certain sectors, cash is probably a better profitability indicator than earnings.

When cash starts declining and the fall is not attributable to either heavy capital expenditure that is not financed by debt capital or a capital increase, to the repayment of borrowings, to an exceptional dividend distribution or to a change in the business environment, the company is operating at a loss, whether or not this is concealed by overstating inventories, reducing customer payment periods, etc.

If the decrease in cash cannot be accounted for by investing or financing activities, it can only come from a deterioration in the company's profitability.

Section 14.4
CASE STUDY[6]: ERICSSON

Is Ericsson solvent at the end of 2003? Yes, as it has equity of €3.9bn and intangible assets and goodwill (the value of which is open to question given the losses Ericsson has incurred) of only €1.2bn. Will it stay solvent? It will depend on the level of future losses and the willingness of shareholders to plough more money into the business if need be.

Does Ericsson create value? Clearly not! It is destroying value on a massive scale. Take as a reference the average stock price of 1997, 2 years before the beginning of the Internet bubble: SEK 27. Its March 2005 share price[7] at SEK 21 is down 22% whereas the EuroStoxx 50 index is up 32%.

Will it create value in the future? It would need to post an after-tax net income of around €1.6bn taking into account equity in the balance sheet of €12bn[8] and a cost of equity[9] of around 13%. That will certainly be a challenge.

SUMMARY

download

By the end of a financial analysis, readers must be able to answer the two following questions that served as the starting point for their investigations:

• Is the company solvent? Will it be able to repay all its creditors in full?

• Is the company creating any value for its shareholders?

A company is solvent when it is able to honour all its commitments by liquidating all of its assets; i.e., if it ceases its operations and puts all its assets up for sale. Net assets – i.e., the difference between assets and total liabilities – are the traditional measure of a company's solvency.

A company creates value if the return on capital employed (after tax) that it generates exceeds the cost of the capital (i.e., equity and net debt) that served to finance capital employed.

Lastly, we recommend that readers who need to carry out a rapid assessment of an ailing company and whose accounts are not yet available build a cash flow statement in reverse. This reverse approach starts with reduction in net debt and works back towards net income, thus gauging the scale of losses that put the company's solvency and very survival in jeopardy.

QUESTIONS

@

quiz

1/ What risks do lenders run? How can lenders protect themselves against these risks?

2/ What is the ultimate guarantee that the lenders will be repaid?

3/ What is solvency?

4/ Is an insolvent company necessarily required to declare itself bankrupt?

5/ A company goes into debt with a 1-day maturity in order to buy fixed rate bonds. Is it running a liquidity risk? And a solvency risk? In what way does the risk manifest itself? What move in interest rates does this company expect?

6/ Is a company with negative net assets illiquid? Insolvent?

7/ It has been said that a solid financial structure was a guarantee of freedom and independence for a company. Is this true?

8/ Why is it difficult to determine the exact value of net assets in consolidated financial statements?

9/ Why is the concept of net book value useful?

EXERCISES

1/ What is your view of the solvency of the following companies?

Groups	S	N	A
Intangibles	2,239	28,320	3,102
Tangibles	10,635	17,439	9,283
Working capital	−809	5,606	−532
Shareholders' equity	726	41,800	458
Net bank and other borrowings	11,041	9,743	5,763
Sales	8,136	90,333	51,044
Operating profit	94	11,202	1,394

ANSWERS

Questions

1/ *The risk of default on payment. Request guarantees or ensure a high level of solvency.*

2/ *The value of shareholders' equity.*

3/ *The ability to repay its debts in full, even in the event of bankruptcy.*

4/ *Sooner or later it will probably have to do so.*

5/ *Yes; yes; inability to obtain further loans, capital losses; decline in interest rates.*

6/ *Possibly; yes.*

7/ *Yes, except when the share price is undervalued, in which case there is a risk of takeover (see Chapter 42).*

8/ *Because of minority interests.*

9/ *Because it shows the book value of all assets and liabilities.*

Exercise

1/ *S: disastrous, lenders will only get back part of what they're owed and shareholders lose everything. These are the figures for Swissair in mid-2001, before it filed for bankruptcy in 2002.*

N: very good situation: operating profit covers net debt, shareholder's equity even after deducting 100% of intangible assets is still largely positive. These are the figures for Nestlé, one of the rare AAA corporate borrower.

A: weak situation: equity seems very limited compared with debt and intangibles. These are the figures for Ahold, the Dutch supermarket group, after it discovered accounting frauds within several of its subsidiaries.

Section II
INVESTMENT ANALYSIS

PART ONE

INVESTMENT DECISION RULES

Chapter 15
THE FINANCIAL MARKETS

A ship in a harbour is safe but is not what ships are built for

The introduction to this book discussed the role of financial securities in a market economy. This section will analyse the behaviour of the investor who buys those instruments that the financial manager is trying to sell. An investor is free to buy a security or not and, if he decides to buy it, he is then free to hold it or resell it in the secondary market.

The financial investor seeks two types of returns: the risk-free interest rate (which we call the time value of money) and a reward for risk-taking. This section looks at these two types of returns in detail, but, first, here are some general observations about capital markets.

Section 15.1
THE RISE OF CAPITAL MARKETS

The primary role of a financial system is to bring together economic agents with surplus financial resources, such as households, and those with net financial needs, such as companies and governments. This relationship is illustrated below:

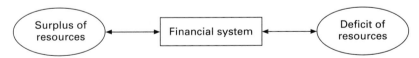

To use the terminology of John Gurley and Edward Shaw (1960), the parties can be brought together **directly** or **indirectly**.

In the first case, known as **direct finance**, the parties with excess financial resources directly finance those with financial needs. The financial system serves as a **broker**, matching the supply of funds with the corresponding demand. This is what happens when a small shareholder subscribes to a listed company's capital increase or when a bank places a corporate bond issue with individual investors.

In the second case, or **indirect finance**, financial intermediaries, such as banks, buy "securities" – i.e., loans – issued by companies. The banks in turn collect funds, in the form of demand or savings deposits, or issue their own securities that they place with investors. In this model, the financial system serves as a gatekeeper between suppliers and users of capital and performs the function of **intermediation**.

When you deposit money in a bank, the bank uses your money to make loans to companies. Similarly, when you buy bonds issued by a financial institution, you enable the institution to finance the needs of other industrial and commercial enterprises through loans. Lastly, when you buy an insurance policy, you and other investors pay premiums that the insurance company uses to invest in the bond market, the property market, etc. This activity is called "intermediation", and is very different from the role of a mere broker in the direct finance model.

With direct finance, the amounts that pass through the broker's hands do not appear on its balance sheet, because all the broker does is to put the investor and issuer in direct contact with each other. Only brokerage fees and commissions appear on a brokerage firm's profit and loss, or income, statement.

With intermediation, the situation is very different. The intermediary shows all resources on the liabilities side of its balance sheet, regardless of their nature, from deposits to bonds to shareholders' equity. Capital serves as the creditors' ultimate guarantee. On the assets side, the intermediary shows all uses of funds, regardless of their nature: loans, investments, etc. The intermediary earns a return on the funds it employs and pays interest on the resources. These cash flows appear in its income statement in the form of revenues and expenses. The difference, or spread, between the two constitutes the intermediary's earnings.

The intermediary's balance sheet and income statement thus function as holding tanks for both parties – those who have surplus capital and those who need it:

BANK BALANCE SHEET AND INCOME STATEMENT

Financial systems are experiencing **disintermediation**, a general tendency characterised by the following phenomena:

- more companies are obtaining financing directly from capital markets; and
- more companies and individuals are investing directly in capital markets.

When capital markets (primary and secondary) are underdeveloped, an economy functions primarily on debt financing. Conversely, when capital markets are sufficiently well-developed, companies are no longer restricted to debt, and they can then choose to increase their equity financing. Taking a page from John Hicks (1975), it is possible to speak of **bank-based economies** and **market-based economies**.

In a **bank-based economy**, the capital market is underdeveloped and only a small portion of corporate financing needs are met through the issuance of securities. Therefore, bank financing predominates. Companies borrow heavily from banks, whose refinancing needs are mainly covered by the central bank.

The central bank tends to have a strong influence on the level of investment and, consequently, on overall economic growth. In this scenario, interest rates represent the level desired by the government, for reasons of economic policy, rather than an equilibrium point between supply and demand for loans.

A bank-based economy is viable only in an inflationary environment. When inflation is high, companies readily take on debt because they will repay their loans with devalued currency. In the meantime, after adjustments are made for inflation, companies pay real interest rates that are zero or negative. A company takes on considerable risk when it relies exclusively on debt; however, inflation mitigates this risk. Inflation makes it possible to run this risk and, indeed, it encourages companies to take on more debt. The bank-based (or credit-based) economy and inflation are inextricably linked, but the system is flawed because the real return to investors is zero or negative. Their savings are insufficiently rewarded, particularly if they have invested in fixed-income vehicles.

The savings rate in a credit-based economy is frequently low. The savings that do exist typically flow into tangible assets and real property (purchase of houses, land, etc.) that are reputed to offer protection against inflation. In this context, savings do not flow towards corporate needs. Lacking sufficient supply, the capital markets therefore remain embryonic. As a result, companies can finance their needs only by borrowing from banks, which in turn refinance themselves at the central bank.

The lender's risk is that the corporate borrower will not generate enough cash flow to service the debt and repay the principal, or amount of the loan. Even if the borrower's financial condition is weak, the bank will not be required to book a provision against the loan so long as payments are made without incident.

In an economy with no secondary market, the investor's financial risk lies with the cash flows generated by the assets he holds and their liquidity.

In a **market-based economy**, companies cover most of their financing needs by issuing financial securities (shares, bonds, commercial paper, etc.) directly to investors. A capital market economy is characterised by direct solicitation of investors' funds. Economic agents with surplus resources invest a large portion of their funds directly in the capital markets by buying companies' shares, bonds, commercial paper or other short-term negotiable debt. They do this either directly or through mutual funds. Intermediation gives way to the brokerage function, and the business model of financial institutions evolves towards the placement of companies' securities directly with investors.

In this economic model, bank loans are extended primarily to households in the form of consumer credit, mortgage loans, etc., as well as to small- and medium-sized enterprises that do not have access to the capital markets.

The growing share of negotiable securities in financing the economy is apparent in this graph.

BANK AND CAPITAL MARKET FINANCING

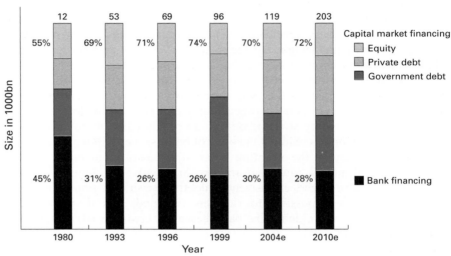

Source: McKinsey & Co., 2005.

According to Zingales and Rajan (2003), European financial markets have become more market-oriented in the last two decades. In Chapter 1, the financial manager was described as a seller of financial securities. This is the result of European economies becoming capital market economies. "Arm's length" financing, today prevalent in the USA, delivers superior results when firms are bigger, when there is stronger legal enforcement and transparency, and when innovation tends to be more dynamic. In recent decades, the globalisation of capital markets has:

- increased the need for huge amounts of capital to manage global competition;
- developed mimicry behaviour among capital markets regarding legal enforcement and transparency;
- "unified" the sources of financing of innovation.

In light of these developments, a higher degree of market orientation in Europe would clearly be a good thing.

The growing disintermediation has forced banks and other financial intermediaries to align their rates (which are the rates that they offer on deposits or charge on loans) with market rates. Slowly but surely, market forces tend to pervade all types of financial instruments.

For example, with the rise of the commercial paper market, banks regularly index short-term loans on money market rates. Medium-term and long-term lending has seen similar trends. Meanwhile, on the liabilities side, banks have seen some of their traditional, fixed rate resources dry up. Consequently, the banks have had to step up their use of more expensive, market rate sources of funds, such as certificates of deposit.

Since the beginning of the 1980s, two trends have led to the rapid development of capital markets. First, real interest rates in the bond markets have turned positive. Second, budget deficits have been financed through long-term instruments, rather than through the money market.

The risks encountered in a capital market economy are very different from those in a credit-based economy. These risks are tied to the **value of the security**, rather than to whether cash flows are received as planned. During a stock market crash, for example, a company's share price might sink even though its published earnings exceed projections.

The following graphs provide the best illustration of the rising importance of capital markets.

NUMBER OF LISTED COMPANIES IN 2002 AND 2003

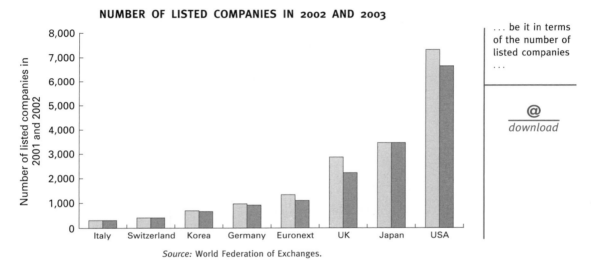

... be it in terms of the number of listed companies ...

@
download

Source: World Federation of Exchanges.

NUMBER OF TRADES IN FEBRUARY 2005

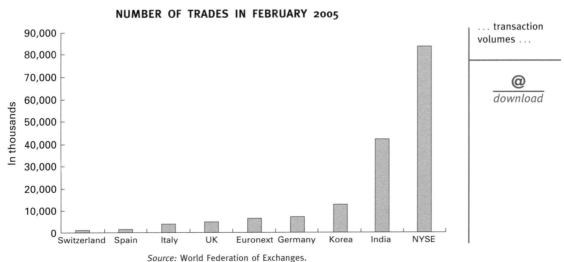

... transaction volumes ...

@
download

Source: World Federation of Exchanges.

THE 10 BIGGEST STOCK MARKETS IN THE WORLD BY MARKET CAPITALISATION 2004

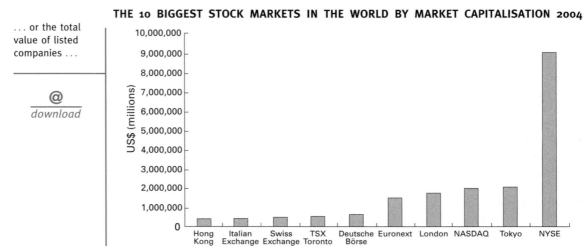

Source: World Federation of Exchanges.

Section 15.2
THE FUNCTIONS OF A FINANCIAL SYSTEM

The job of a financial system is to efficiently create financial liquidity for those investment projects that promise the highest profitability and that maximise collective utility.

However, unlike other types of markets, a financial system does more than just achieve equilibrium between supply and demand. A financial system allows investors to convert current revenues into future consumption. It also provides current resources for borrowers, at the cost of reduced future spending.

More specifically, we have three definitions of efficiency:

- **informational efficiency** refers to the ability of a market to *fully* and *rapidly* reflect new relevant information;
- **allocative efficiency** implies that markets channel resources to their most productive uses;
- **operational efficiency** concerns the property of markets to function with minimal operating costs.

Robert Merton and Zvi Bodie (2000) have isolated the **six essential functions** of a financial system:

1   means of payment;
2   financing;
3   saving and borrowing;
4   risk management;
5   information;
6   reducing or resolving conflict.

1. A financial system provides means of payment to facilitate transactions. Cheques, debit and credit cards, electronic transfers, etc. are all means of payment that individuals can use to facilitate the acquisition of goods and services. Imagine if everything could only be paid for with bills and coins!

2. A financial system provides a means of pooling funds for financing large, indivisible projects. A financial system is also a mechanism for subdividing the capital of a company so that investors can diversify their investments. If factory owners had to rely on just their own savings, they would very soon run out of investible funds. Indeed, without a financial system's support, Nestlé and British Telecom would not exist. The system enables the entrepreneur to gain access to the savings of millions of individuals, thereby diversifying and expanding his sources of financing. In return, the entrepreneur is expected to achieve a certain level of performance. Returning to our example of a factory: if you were to invest in your neighbour's steel plant, you might have trouble getting your money back if you should suddenly need it. A financial system enables investors to hold their assets in a much more liquid form: shares, bank accounts, etc.

3. A financial system distributes financial resources across time and space, as well as between different sectors of the economy. The financial system allows capital to be allocated in a myriad of ways. For example, young married couples can borrow to buy a house or people approaching retirement can save to offset future decreases in income. Even a developing nation can obtain resources to finance further development. And when an industrialised country generates more savings than it can absorb, it invests those surpluses through financial systems. In this way, "old economies" use their excess resources to finance "new economies".

4. A financial system provides tools for managing risk. It is particularly risky for an individual to invest all of his funds in a single company, because if the company goes bankrupt, he loses everything. By creating collective savings vehicles, such as mutual funds, brokers and other intermediaries enable individuals to reduce their risk by diversifying their exposure. Similarly, an insurance company pools the risk of millions of people and insures them against risks they would otherwise be unable to assume individually.

5. A financial system provides information at very low cost. This facilitates decision-making. Securities prices and interest rates constitute information used by individuals in their decisions about how to consume, save or divide their funds among different assets. But research and analysis of the available information on the financial condition of the borrower is time-consuming, costly and typically beyond the scope of the layman. Yet when a financial institution does this work on behalf of thousands of investors, the cost is greatly reduced. Unfortunately, this does not mean that financial systems always handle information perfectly. For example, herd behaviour occurs when investors move in pack-like formations and make decisions by following what everyone else is doing in the market. Such phenomenon can make the price of an asset diverge from its fundamental value. This is precisely what happened with Internet stocks in late 1999 and early 2000.

6. A financial system provides the means for reducing conflict between the parties to a contract. Contracting parties often have difficulty monitoring each other's behaviour. Sometimes conflicts arise because each party has different amounts of information and divergent contractual ties. For example, an investor gives money to a fund manager in the hope that he will manage the funds in the investor's best interests (and not the manager's!) If the fund manager does not uphold his end of the bargain, the market will lose confidence in him. Typically, the consequence of such behaviour is that he will be replaced by a more conscientious manager.

Section 15.3
THE RELATIONSHIP BETWEEN BANKS AND COMPANIES

Bank intermediation is carried out first and foremost by **commercial banks**. Commercial banks serve as intermediaries between those who have surplus funds, and those who require financing. The banks collect resources from the former and lend capital to the latter. Based on the strength of their balance sheet, commercial banks lend to a wide variety of borrowers and, in particular, to companies. Banks assume the risks related to these loans; therefore, their financial condition must be sufficiently strong to withstand potential losses. However, the larger the bank's portfolio, the lower the risk – thanks once again to the law of large numbers. After all, not every company is likely to go bankrupt at the same time!

Commercial banking is an extremely competitive activity. After taking into account the cost of risk, profit margins are very thin. Bank loans are somewhat standard products; therefore, it is relatively easy for customers to play one bank off against another to obtain more favourable terms.

Commercial banks have developed ancillary services to add value to the products that they offer to their corporate customers. Accordingly, they offer a variety of means of payment to help companies move funds efficiently from one place to another. They also help clients to manage their cash flows (see Chapter 46).

As a result, the growing importance of financial markets has changed the role of bankers. They have developed services to help their corporate clients gain direct access to capital markets, leading to the rise of **investment banking**. Investment banks offer primarily the following services:

- **Access to equity markets:** investment banks help companies prepare and carry out initial public offerings on the stock market. Later on, investment banks can continue to help these companies by raising additional funds through capital increases. They also advise companies on the issuance of instruments that may one day become shares of stock, such as warrants and convertible bonds (see Chapter 29).
- **Access to bond markets:** similarly, investment banks help large- and medium-sized companies raise funds directly from investors through the issuance of bonds. The techniques of placing securities and, in particular, the role of the investment bank in this type of transaction will be discussed in Chapter 32. The investment bank's **trading room** is where its role as "matchmaker" between the investor and the issuer takes on its full meaning.
- **Merger and acquisition advisory services**: these investment banking services are not directly linked to corporate financing or the capital markets, although a public issue of bonds or shares often accompanies an acquisition.

- **Asset management:** certain banks use their knowledge of the financial markets to offer their clientele – individuals, companies and institutions – investment products comprised of portfolios of listed or unlisted securities. These products are called mutual funds and the activity is known as asset management.

For a long time, these various lines of business were separated for regulatory reasons. Today, they coexist in all major American, European and Asian financial institutions, although not without potential conflicts of interest. A creditor is not always a disinterested party when it comes to advising a corporate client.

Section 15.4

FROM VALUE TO PRICE (1): FINANCIAL COMMUNICATION

If a company wants the financial market to fairly price its securities, it is necessary (but not sufficient) that the company provides the market with all relevant financial information about its cash flows, particularly information regarding the magnitude, the risks involved and timing of all such flows.

If the market receives inadequate information, then it will be unable to assess the real capacity of the firm to create value. Therefore, it is always necessary to communicate promptly to investors all pertinent information in order to facilitate a clear understanding of the company's value creation ability.

Financial communication serves an important economic function because it reduces the information asymmetries between market participants. Managers, for example, have more accurate information about the company they work for, compared with external investors or "outsiders". Asymmetric information may also exist among investors if some of them have access to private information.

If the market perceives that an appropriate financial communication has reduced information asymmetries, investors will accept a lower return from the company because of the lower risk of investing in the company. This in turn reduces the cost of capital. The following picture illustrates the two directions of the benefits of a higher disclosure:

The left path allows the company to reach a lower cost of equity through the reduction of the "estimation risk" of investors. If the flow of information is limited, investors will have more uncertainty about the cash flow estimates. Therefore, providers of funds will require a higher return, especially if the "information risk" cannot be diversified away.

Along the right path, the reduced information disparity among investors creates a higher liquidity of securities, which in turn leads to a lower cost of capital. Higher liquidity reduces the average transaction costs and allows the price of the securities to reach higher levels.

Botosan (2000) finds that the cost of equity is inversely related to the company's degree of disclosure. How significant is the benefit of better financial communication? According to her findings the difference of the cost of equity, for transparent companies that are closely followed by analysts, can lead to a cost reduction of up to 9 percentage points.

Section 15.5

FROM VALUE TO PRICE (2): EFFICIENT MARKETS

In addition to financial communication, the relationship between value creation and price requires another condition: the efficiency of financial markets.

An efficient market is one in which the prices of financial securities at any time *rapidly* reflect *all available relevant* information.

In an efficient (or in an equilibrium) market, prices instantly reflect the consequences of past events and all expectations about future events. As all known factors are already integrated into current prices, it is therefore impossible to predict future variations in the price of a financial instrument. Only new information can change the value of the security. Future information is by definition unpredictable, so changes in the price of a security are random. This is the origin of the **random walk** character of returns in the securities markets.

In an efficient market, competition between financial investors is so fierce that prices adjust to new information almost instantaneously. At every moment, a financial instrument trades at a price determined by its return and its risk.

Eugene Fama (1970) has developed the following **three tests** to determine whether a market is efficient.

1/ABILITY TO PREDICT PRICES

In a **weak-form** efficient market, it is impossible to predict future returns. Existing prices already reflect all the information that can be gleaned from studying **past prices** and **trading volumes**, interest rates and returns. This is what is meant by the "weak form" of efficiency.

Extra returns can be obtained only if investors have future or privileged information. According to the weak-form of efficiency, the price of an asset is the sum of three components:

1   the last available price (P_{-1});
2   the expected return from the security (see Chapter 21); and
3   a random component due to new information that might be learned during the period in question. This component of random error is independent from past events and unpredictable in the future:

$$P_0 = P_{-1} + \text{Expected return} + \text{Random error}$$

When prices follow this model, they follow a random walk.

The efficient market hypothesis says that technical analysis has no practical value[1] nor do martingales (martingales in the ordinary not mathematical sense). For example, the notion that "if a stock rises three consecutive times, buy it; if it declines two consecutive times, sell it" is irrelevant. Similarly, the efficient market hypothesis says that models relating future returns to interest rates, dividend yields, the spread between short- and long-term interest rates or other parameters are equally worthless.

1 *Investors focusing on technical analysis conduct detailed studies of trends in a stock's market value and transaction volumes in the hope of spotting short-term trends.*

2/THE MARKET RESPONSE TO SPECIFIC EVENTS

A **semi-strong** efficient market reflects all publicly available information, as found in annual reports, newspaper and magazine articles, prospectuses, announcements of new contracts, of a merger, of an increase in the dividend, etc.

Semi-strong efficiency is superior to weak-form efficiency because it requires that current prices include historical information (as assumed by the weak-form efficiency) *and* publicly available information. The latter, for example, is available in:

• financial statements;
• research on the company performed by external financial analysts;
• company announcements.

This hypothesis can be empirically tested by studying the reaction of market prices to company events (**event studies**). In fact, the price of a stock should react immediately to any announcement of relevant new information regarding a company. In an efficient market, no impact should be observable prior to the announcement, nor during the days following the announcement. In other words, prices should adjust rapidly only at the time any new information is announced.

On 28 December 2001, the Spanish cardboard manufacturer Saica announced it had purchased 22.6% of the French company La Rochette and was to launch a takeover bid at a price below €10.9 per share. The market price of La Rochette immediately moved to around €10. On 2 January 2002 the Mondi group announced a bid at €11.6. When trading resumed on 11 January, the share price stabilised at slightly over Mondi's bid price, as investors anticipated a bidding war. On 21 January Saica raised its bid to €12 per share. When trading resumed, the price stabilised at around €12.

@
download

Rules against insider-trading are becoming increasingly strict

@
download

To prevent investors with prior access to information from using it to their advantage (and so to the detriment of other investors), most stock market regulators suspend trading prior to a mid-session announcement of information that is highly likely to have a major impact on the share price. Trading resumes a few hours later or the following day, so as to ensure that all interested parties receive the information. Then, when trading resumes, no investor has been short-changed.

3/ THE IMPACT OF INSIDER INFORMATION ON THE MARKET

In a strongly efficient financial market, investors with privileged or insider information or with a monopoly on certain information are unable to influence securities prices. This is the "strong form" of efficiency.

This holds true only when financial market regulators have the power to prohibit and punish the use of insider information. In theory, professional investment managers have expert knowledge that is supposed to enable them to post better performances than the market average. However, without using any inside information, the efficient market hypothesis says that market experts have no edge over the layman. In fact, in an efficient market, the experts' performance is even slightly below the market average, in a proportion directly related to the management fees they charge!

WORLDWIDE REGULATION OF INSIDER-TRADING

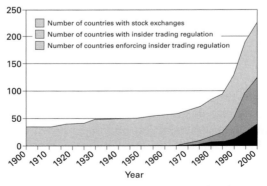

Source: based on Bhattacharya and Daouk (2002).

Actual markets approach the theory of an efficient market when:

- participants have low-cost access to all information;
- transaction costs are low;
- the market is liquid; and
- investors are rational.

Take the example of a stock whose price is expected to rise 10% tomorrow. In an efficient market, its price will rise today to a level consistent with the expected gain. "Tomorrow's" price will be discounted to today. Today's price becomes an estimate of the value of tomorrow's price.

In general, if we try to explain why financial markets have different degrees of efficiency, we could say that:

➤ **The lower transaction costs are, the more efficient a market is.** An efficient market must quickly allow equilibrium between supply and demand to be established. Transaction costs are a key factor in enabling supply and demand for securities and capital to adjust.

Brokerage commissions have an impact on how quickly a market reaches equilibrium. In an efficient market, transactions have no costs associated with them, neither underwriting costs (when securities are issued) nor trading costs (when securities are bought and sold).

When other transaction-related factors are introduced, such as the time required for approving and publishing information, they can slow down the achievement of market equilibrium.

➤ **The more liquid a market is, the more efficient it is.** The more frequently a security is traded, the more quickly new information can be integrated into the share price. Conversely, illiquid securities are relatively slow in reflecting available information. Investors cannot benefit from the delays in information assimilation because the trading and transaction volumes are low.

In general, it can be said that the less liquid a financial asset is, the higher the investor's required return is. Lower trading volume leads to greater uncertainty about the market price.

Research into the significance of this phenomenon has demonstrated that there is a statistical relationship between liquidity and the required rate of return. This indicates the existence of a risk premium that varies inversely with the liquidity of the security. The premium is tantamount to a reward for putting up with illiquidity – i.e., when the market is not functioning efficiently. We will measure the size of this premium in Chapter 22.

➤ **The more rational investors are, the more efficient a market is.** Individuals are said to be rational when their actions are consistent with the information they receive. When good and unexpected news is announced, rational investors must buy a stock – not sell it. And for any given level of risk, rational investors must also try to maximise their potential gain.

This is probably the feeblest assumption of the efficient market hypothesis, because human beings and their feelings cannot be reduced to a series of mathematical equations. It has been demonstrated that the Dow Jones

Industrial Average turns in below-average performance when it rains in Central Park, that stock market returns are lower on Monday than on Friday and so on. These phenomena have given rise to **behavioural finance**, which takes psychology into account when analysing investor decisions. This field of research provides recent evidence that investors can make systematic errors in processing new information – information that is otherwise profitably exploited by other investors.

In 1985, De Bondt and Thaler published an article presenting robust evidence that investors **overreact** to news. Today, few would disagree that financial asset prices tend to be highly volatile. Schiller (2000) went a step further and claimed that financial markets are irrationally volatile. One explanation for this behaviour is **overconfidence**, which occurs when investors believe that they have better information regarding the true state of a company's affairs than is actually the case. As the true condition of the company is revealed over time, investors' beliefs move towards a fair valuation. This tendency causes prices to reverse.

Investors can also overreact because they **mimic** other investors. Psychologists call this penchant to follow the crowd the *herding instinct*, which is the tendency of individuals to mold their thinking to the prevailing opinion. Similarly, economists call this decision-making process an *information cascade* and believe that it happens in financial markets. However, the mimicry behaviour is rational if the investor mimics someone who knows more than he does. For example, it can be rational to sell one's shares when the company's executives are selling theirs. But this rationality disappears when an investor imitates those who know no more than he does and are themselves imitating other imitators! Graham (1999) finds that several types of analysts are likely to herd on *Value Line*'s (a financial information services provider) recommendations. There are three types of mimicry:

o *Normative mimicry* – which could also be called "conformism". Its impact on finance is limited and is beyond the scope of this text.
o *Informational mimicry* – which consists of imitating others because they supposedly know more. It constitutes a rational response to a problem of dissemination of information, provided the proportion of imitators in the group is not too high. Otherwise, even if it is not in line with objective economic data, imitation reinforces the most popular choice, which can then interfere with efficient dissemination of information.
o *Self-mimicry* – which attempts to predict the behaviour of the majority in order to imitate it. The "right" decision then depends on the collective behaviour of all other market participants and can become a self-fulfilling prophecy; i.e., an equilibrium that exists because everyone thinks it will exist. This behaviour departs from traditional economic analysis, which holds that financial value results from real economic value.

At the point where these phenomena begin to occur, the market ceases to be efficient. It no longer acts in accordance with basic economic and financial data. If the "market" is a stock exchange, a speculative bubble forms that inflates the value of one or more stocks in a sector of the economy (e.g., Internet stocks in 1999). Initially, investors do not notice anything amiss. The rise in prices feeds on itself and vindicates the initial imitative behaviour. Finally comes a day when investors become conscious of the artificial nature of the trend and stop imitating each other – and begin to "rediscover" economic and financial fundamentals! The speculative bubble bursts, share prices tumble (e.g., Internet stocks in 2000), and reason and efficiency return.

Mimetic phenomena can be accentuated by **program-trading**, which is the computer programs used by some traders that rely on pre-programmed buy-or-sell decisions. For example, program-trading might automatically close out a position – i.e., sell a security – as soon as the unrealised loss grows beyond a certain threshold. However, such programs working together can lead to snowball effects as they react to information. These programs are now subject to strict controls to prevent them causing market crashes, as they are suspected to have caused the stock market crash in 1987.

Some behaviourist researchers have found that **underreaction** to new information may be the prevalent behaviour. In this case, one explanation provided by "behaviourists" is **biased self-attribution**, when investors dismiss contradictory new evidence as being random noise. This phenomenon causes investors to underreact to public information signals that contradict their existing beliefs. As Barberis explains: "Suppose a company announces earnings that are substantially higher than expected. Investors see this as good news and send the stock price higher but for some reason not high enough. This mistake is only gradually corrected; over the next six months the stock price slowly drifts upwards towards the level it should have attained at the time of the announcement. An investor buying the stock immediately after the announcement would capture this upward drift and enjoy high returns" (Barberis, 1998, p. 164).

This means that the ongoing reaction continues over the next several months after the announcement. The pattern that is established is known as **stock price momentum**, since positive initial returns are followed by the other positive returns in the mid-term.

Notwithstanding this rapidly growing field of research, financial assets prices are still largely unpredictable. Moreover, market-beating strategies generate transaction costs, which tend to cancel out the potential gains these anomalies offer. And that is good news for efficient market hypothesis and related theories!

Section 15.6
LIMITATIONS IN THE THEORY OF EFFICIENT MARKETS

1/EVIDENCE

The vast majority of evidence regarding market efficiency has concerned the weak and semi-strong forms of efficiency. The most diffuse research methodologies and their major results are illustrated hereafter.

(a) Weak-form efficiency

A widely used technique to test the weak form of efficiency is to examine the correlation of daily returns (serial correlation). The existence of a correlation – regardless of its sign – implies that the returns of one day are influenced by the returns of the previous day. This contradicts the weak form of efficiency, which states that prices follow a random walk.

The following table illustrates some examples of serial correlation with the prices (daily returns over the period April 2000–April 2005) of the top 13 European listed companies.

Ericsson	0.017	HSBC	−0.024
Novartis	−0.233	Roche	−0.047
Nestlé	−0.011	Vodafone	−0.049
BP	−0.047	ENI	−0.063
Total	−0.078	GlaxoSmithKline	−0.022
UBS	0.052	Telefónica	0.017
Royal Dutch	−0.037	**Average**	**−0.033**

The correlation coefficient can range between −1 and +1. The figures in the table show that the coefficients are negative on average but rather small in their absolute value (only −3.3%). This is the kind of evidence we would expect from efficient markets.

The absence of serial correlation is easy to describe graphically. The following example for Ericsson illustrates the point:

SERIAL CORRELATION ERICSSON (April 2000–April 2005)

The distribution of returns is random and generates a mass of chaotic points. With a serial correlation, the distribution of points would resemble a straight line. So, if there were a robust positive (or negative) relationship, the linear trend would be positively (or negatively) sloped depending upon the correlation existing among successive returns.

(b) Semi-strong efficiency

The theory of semi-strong efficiency can be measured in two ways: with event studies that examine the market's reaction to price-sensitive announcements from companies, or with the analysis of mutual funds performance.

Event studies
Event study analysis is based on the estimate of abnormal returns, which is obtained by subtracting the daily return of the market (R_M) from the return of the company (R) in the same day:

$$AR = R - R_M$$

According to the semi-strong efficiency hypothesis, the abnormal return should be observable only on the day when the information becomes public. As mentioned earlier, all previous information should have already been included in market prices. The return during the observed period is thus influenced solely by the unexpected new information. The methodology of event study has been applied to dividends, earnings announcements, mergers and acquisitions, share issues and so on.

More specifically, event studies also estimate the Cumulative Abnormal Returns (CARs), which is the sum of subsequent abnormal returns. If the market is efficient, the CAR before the announcement should be nil or very low. Thus, if abnormal returns grew during the previous period, there is good evidence that some investors might have received information before others. The analysis of *ex post* CAR is also interesting because in efficient markets abnormal returns should be zero. In short, the abnormal return should be confined to the announcement day and ideally no abnormal return should be registered before or after the announcement (Figure A):

(A) EFFICIENT MARKET

The higher the deviation from the fair market value and the more slowly it fades away, the less efficient is the financial market. In this instance we are faced with two alternative situations: the first is typical of a slow learning market and the second is characteristic of excessive reaction (market overreaction). Graphically, both situations can be represented as follows (Figures B and C):

(B) SLOW-LEARNING MARKET

(C) OVERREACTING MARKET

Cases B and C depict inefficient markets because of the way the price converges at a new equilibrium price implicit in the announcement: with a delay (case B) or by erroneously estimating the value of the new information (case C).

If there is a clear (and otherwise inexplicable) trend in prices before the announcement, then it is reasonable to assume that a few privileged investors had access to the information before the formal announcement was made to the entire market (picture D):

(D) INEFFICIENT MARKET

Mutual funds performance

The second methodology for testing semi-strong efficiency is to analyse the performance of mutual funds. In an efficient market, we would expect that their average returns would not differ systematically from the returns obtained by an average investor with a well-diversified portfolio.

The empirical evidence has been used to compare the mutual funds' results with market indexes. The results show that the managers of mutual funds tend to achieve *negative* performances compared with the market. The following graph shows this pro-efficiency result in the United States:

ANNUAL PERFORMANCE OF MUTUAL TRUST IN THE USA VS. THE MARKET INDEX (1963–1988)

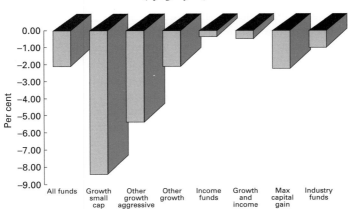

Source: Lubos Pastor and Robert Stambaugh, Mutual fund performance and seemingly unrelated assets, *Journal of Financial Economics*, **63**(3), 315–349, March 2002.

In light of this information, why do mutual funds exist? We have seen that the performance of mutual funds has been worse than the stock market index. Some may think that investors are rational if they compose their portfolio by randomly choosing stocks from a list of public companies. The major problem with this strategy is that investors may face undesired risks if the titles they choose are not consistent with their risk/return profile. The wide variety of mutual funds may help to solve this problem.

2/ANOMALIES

Although most of the available evidence confirms the efficient market hypothesis, the reader should be aware of anomalies that have arisen in the market:

1 **Dimension of companies.** There is some evidence that the compound annual return on the smallest companies is higher than on the biggest companies. Although the risk of these small stocks is also higher, it is not high enough to justify the extra return of these smaller capitalisation stocks. The reason for this excessive return is difficult to explain. Some researchers suggest that the superior historical return is a compensation for the higher transaction costs of dealing with these securities.

2 **Value vs. growth companies.** Stocks with low price-to-book and low price-to-earnings ratios are often called *value stocks*, whereas those with high values in these two ratios are called *growth stocks*. Value stocks tend to belong to oil, motor, finance and utilities. Growth stocks are in the high-tech, telecommunications and computers sectors. There is some evidence that historical returns on value stocks have exceeded those of growth stocks. A possible explanation for this anomaly is behavioural: investors can get overexcited about the growth prospects of firms with rapidly increasing earnings and, nonrationally, strongly bid for them.

3   **Calendar anomalies.** Recent research has revealed that there are predictable periods during the year when some stocks tend to outperform. Maybe the most tried and true anomaly is the outperformance of small stocks with respect to large stocks in one specific month of the year: January. As Shiller (2000) explains, the *January effect* is the most important reason that small stocks have obtained greater total returns than large stocks over the last 70 years.

Similar to the January effect, and just as inexplicably, stocks tend to do much better (a) in the first few days of a month, and (b) on Fridays rather than on Mondays (the so-called *weekend effect*). Calendar anomalies are even more puzzling because they imply that the stock market is partially predictable and therefore possible to beat.

2 *Initial Public Offerings.*

4   **Initial public offer discounts.** Year in and year out, in almost every country around the world, the very short-term returns on IPOs[2] are surprisingly high. Financial economists refer to this anomaly as *IPO underpricing*, meaning that the offer price is substantially lower than what the market is willing to pay.[3] For more details, see Chapter 31.

3 *However, the long-run performance of most IPOs fails to live up to their promise after they are issued. See Ritter (1991) and Loughran and Ritter (1995).*

Section 15.7
INVESTORS' BEHAVIOUR

At any given point in time, each investor is either:

1   a hedger;
2   a speculator; or
3   an arbitrageur.

1/HEDGING

When an investor attempts to protect himself from risks he does not wish to assume he is said to be *hedging*. The term "to hedge" describes a general concept that underlies certain investment decisions – for example, the decision to match a long-term investment with long-term financing, to finance a risky industrial investment with equity rather than debt, etc.

This is simple, natural and healthy behaviour for nonfinancial managers. Hedging protects a manufacturing company's margin – i.e., the difference between revenue and expenses – from uncertainties in areas relating to technical expertise, human resources, and sales and marketing, etc. Hedging allows the economic value of a project or line of business to be managed independently of fluctuations in the capital markets.

Accordingly, a European company that exports products to the United States may sell dollars forward against euros, guaranteeing itself a fixed exchange rate for its future dollar-denominated revenues. The company is then said to have hedged its exposure to fluctuations in currency exchange rates.

Similarly, a medium-term lender that refinances itself with resources of the same maturity has also hedged its interest rate and liquidity exposure.

Companies can also structure their operations in such a way that they are automatically hedged without recourse to the financial markets. A French company that both produces and sells in the United States will not be exposed to exchange rate risk on all of its US revenues but only on the residual flows not covered by dollar-denominated costs. This is the only portion it will have to hedge.

Keep in mind, however, that hedging techniques are not always so simple, even if they are designed to produce the same end-result.

An investor hedges when he does not wish to assume a calculated risk.

2/SPECULATION

In contrast to hedging, which eliminates risk by transfering it to a party willing to assume it, speculation is the assumption of risk. A speculator takes a position when he makes a bet on the future value of an asset. If he thinks its price will rise, he buys it. If it rises, he wins the bet; if not, he loses. If he is to receive dollars in a month's time, he may take no action now because he thinks the dollar will rise in value between now and then. If he has long-term investments to make, he may finance them with short-term funds because he thinks that interest rates will decline in the meantime and he will be able to refinance at lower cost later. This behaviour is diametrically opposed to that of the hedger.

- Traders are professional speculators. They spend their time buying currencies, bonds, shares or options that they think will appreciate in value and they sell them when they think they are about to decline. Not surprisingly their motto is *"Buy low, sell high, play golf!"*
- But small investors are also speculators most of the time. When an investor predicts cash flows, he is speculating about the future. This is a very important point, and you must be careful not to interpret "speculation" negatively. Every investor speculates when he invests, but his speculation is not necessarily reckless. It is founded on a conviction, a set of skills and an analysis of the risks involved. The only difference is that some investors speculate more heavily than others by assuming more risk.

People often criticise the financial markets for allowing speculation. Yet speculators play a fundamental role in the market, an economically healthy role, by assuming the risks that other participants do not want to accept. In this way, speculators minimise the risk borne by others.

Accordingly, a European manufacturing company with outstanding dollar-denominated debt that wants to protect itself against exchange rate risk (i.e., a rise in the value of the dollar vs. the euro) can transfer this risk by buying dollars forward from a speculator willing to take that risk. By buying dollars forward today, the company knows the exact dollar/euro exchange rate at which it will repay its loan. It has thus eliminated its exchange rate risk. Conversely, the speculator runs the risk of a fluctuation in the value of the dollar between the time he sells the dollars forward to the company and the time he delivers them – i.e., when the company's loan comes due.

Likewise, if a market's long-term financing needs are not satisfied, but there is a surplus of short-term savings, sooner or later a speculator will (fortunately) come along and assume the risk of borrowing short-term in order to lend long-term. In so doing, the speculator assumes intermediation risk.

Speculative bubbles are isolated events that should not put into question the utility and normal operation of the financial markets.

What, then, do people mean by a "speculative market"? A speculative market is a market wherein all the participants are speculators. Market forces, divorced from economic reality, become self-sustaining, because everyone is under the influence of the same phenomenon. Once a sufficient number of speculators think that a stock will rise, their purchases alone are enough to make the stock price rise. Their example prompts other speculators to follow suit, the price rises further, and so on. But at the first hint of a downward revision in expectations the mechanism goes into reverse and the share price falls dramatically. When this happens, many speculators will try to liquidate positions in order to pay off loans contracted to buy shares in the first place, thereby further accentuating the downfall.

3/ARBITRAGE

In contrast to the speculator, the arbitrageur is not in the business of assuming risk. Instead, he tries to earn a profit by exploiting tiny discrepancies that may appear on different markets that are not in equilibrium.

An arbitrageur will notice that Fortis shares are trading slightly lower in London than in Brussels. He will buy Fortis shares in London and sell them simultaneously (or nearly so) at a higher price in Brussels. By buying in London, the arbitrageur bids the price up in London; by selling them in Brussels, he drives the price down there. He or other arbitrageurs then repeat the process until the prices in the two markets are perfectly in line, or in equilibrium.

With no overall outlay of funds or assumption of risk, arbitrage consists of combining several transactions that ultimately yield a profit.

In principle, the arbitrageur assumes no risk, even though each separate transaction involves a certain degree of risk. In practice, arbitrageurs often take on a certain amount of risk as their behaviour is on the frontier between speculation and arbitrage. For arbitrage to be successful, the underlying securities must be liquid enough for the transactions to be executed simultaneously.

Arbitrage is of paramount importance in a market. By **destroying opportunities as it uncovers them**, arbitrage participates in the development of new markets by creating liquidity. It also eliminates the temporary imperfections that can appear from time to time. As soon as disequilibrium appears, arbitrageurs buy and sell assets and increase market liquidity. It is through their very actions that the disequilibrium is reduced to zero. Once equilibrium is reached, arbitrageurs stop trading and wait for the next opportunity.

Thanks to arbitrage, all prices for a given asset are equal at a given point in time. Arbitrage ensures fluidity between markets and contributes to their liquidity. It is the basic behaviour that guarantees market efficiency.

Throughout this book, you can see that financial miracles are impossible because arbitrage levels the playing field between assets exhibiting the same level of risk.

You should also be aware that the three types of behaviour described here do not correspond to three mutually exclusive categories of investors. A market participant who is primarily a speculator might carry out arbitrage activities or partially hedge his position. A hedger might decide to hedge only part of his position and speculate on the remaining portion, etc.

Moreover, these three types of behaviour exist simultaneously in every market. A market cannot function only with hedgers, because there will be no one to assume the risks they don't want to take. As we saw above, a market composed wholly of speculators is not viable either. Finally, a market consisting only of arbitrageurs would be even more difficult to imagine.

A market is fluid, liquid and displays the "right prices" when its participants include hedgers, speculators and arbitrageurs.

SUMMARY

download

The job of a financial system is to bring together those economic agents with surplus funds and those with funding needs:

- either through the indirect finance model, wherein banks and other financial institutions perform the function of intermediation; or

- through the direct finance model, wherein the role of financial institutions is limited to that of a broker.

But a financial system also provides a variety of payment means, and it facilitates transactions because:

- the funds of many investors are pooled to finance large projects; and

- the equity capital of companies is subdivided into small units, enabling investors to diversify their portfolios.

A financial system also distributes financial resources across time and space, and between different sectors. It provides tools for managing risk, disseminates information at low cost, facilitates decentralised decision-making and offers mechanisms for reducing conflict between the parties to a contract.

Financial markets are becoming more important everyday, a phenomenon that goes hand-in-hand with their globalisation. The modern economy is no longer a credit-based economy, where bank loans are the predominant form of finance. Today it is rather a capital market economy, wherein companies solicit funding directly from investors via the issuance of shares and bonds.

Alongside their traditional lending function, banks have adapted to the new system by developing advisory services to facilitate corporate access to the financial markets, be they equity markets or bond markets.

Conceptually, markets are efficient when security prices reflect all relevant, available information. It has been demonstrated that the more liquid a market is, the more readily available information is, the lower transaction costs are and the more individuals act rationally, then the more efficient the market is. The last of these factors probably constitutes the biggest hindrance to market efficiency because human beings cannot be reduced to a series of equations. Irrational human behaviour gives rise to mimicry and other anomalies, leading to speculative excesses that specialists in behavioural finance are still trying to comprehend and explain.

A financial market brings together three types of players:

● hedgers, who refuse to assume risk and instead wish to protect themselves from it;

● speculators, who assume varying degrees of risk; and

● arbitrageurs, who exploit market disequilibria and, in so doing, eliminate these discrepancies and, therefore, ensure market liquidity and efficiency.

QUESTIONS

quiz

1/ Nick Leeson bought futures betting on the Nikkei 225 index on the Osaka stock exchange, which he sold simultaneously on the Singapore stock exchange. Was this speculation, hedging or arbitrage? He lost a billion euros, plunging Baring's Bank into bankruptcy. Was this speculation, hedging or arbitrage?

2/ What is the economic function of speculation?

3/ Can you explain why an "excessive" financial manager and a narrow-minded businessman will be unable to understand each other?

4/ How can the ordinary saver reduce the risk she faces?

5/ What conditions are necessary for arbitrage to work?

6/ What is the economic function of arbitrage?

7/ Can a market in which speculators are the only traders last indefinitely?

8/ Would you be speculating if you bought so-called risk-free government bonds? And what type of risk is not present in "risk-free" bonds?

9/ Is it true that investors who lost money on Internet shares in early 2000 would not have lost anything if instead they had held onto their shares? State your views.

10/ What is a speculative market?

11/ What sort of regulatory mechanisms are in place to prevent speculative bubbles on:
   ○   derivatives markets;
   ○   secondary markets for debt securities;
   ○   equity markets?

12/ Throughout the world, financial intermediaries can be split into two groups:
   ○   brokers: they connect buyers with sellers. Trades can only be completed if the brokers find a buyer for each seller, and vice versa. Brokers work on commission.
   ○   market makers: when securities are sold to an investor, market makers buy them at a given price and try simultaneously or subsequently to sell them at

o   a higher price. Their earnings are thus the difference between the sell price and the buy price.

In your view, is the price difference earned by market makers logically equal to, higher than or lower than the commissions earned by brokers?

13/ Right or wrong?

	Right	Wrong
Provided that investors' demands are met, companies have access to unlimited funds		
The announcement of anticipated losses should impact on the share price		
Manipulating accounting indicators should have no impact on value		

14/ Which of the following statements in your view describe the inefficiency of a market?

   (a) tax-free US municipal bonds with a lower rate of return for the investor than government bonds which are taxed.
   (b) managers make higher than average profits by buying and selling shares in the company they work for.
   (c) there is some correlation between the market rate of return during a given quarter and a company's expected change in profits the following quarter.
   (d) market watchers have observed that shares that have shot up in the recent past will go up again in the future.
   (e) the market value of a company will tend to go up before the announcement of a takeover bid.
   (f) earnings on shares in a company whose profits have recently risen sharply will be high in the coming months.
   (g) on average, earnings on shares that carry a risk are higher than earnings on shares that are relatively risk-free.

15/ What is the purpose of behavioural finance?

16/ If financial markets are only occasionally efficient, is this of greater concern to small or large companies? Why?

Questions

ANSWERS

1/ *In theory, as far as his superiors were concerned, he was executing arbitrage transactions. In reality, he was speculating without his superiors being aware of his actions.*
2/ *To take risks which intermediaries do not wish to take.*
3/ *The financial manager diversifies his risk. The businessman can often not afford to do so.*
4/ *He can diversify his portfolio by buying shares in mutual funds or unit trusts.*
5/ *Trading costs must be low, all players must have access to all markets, and there must be freedom of investment.*
6/ *To ensure market equilibrium and liquidity.*

7/ *No, because it is removed from economic reality.*

8/ *Yes, on changes in interest rates. The risk of the issuer going bankrupt.*

9/ *No, because assets have a market value at any point in time.*

10/ *A market controlled solely by speculators (it is removed from economic reality).*

11/ *Delivery of the underlying security on maturity which forces equality of the trade price and the price of the underlying security. Repayment, which means that on maturity the value of the debt security will be equal to the repayment amount. Economic value of the company.*

12/ *Higher, because the risk is higher.*

13/ *Right. Wrong. Right.*

14/ *b, c, d, e, f. Inefficiency.*

15/ *It factors in the nonrational side of investors' behaviour.*

16/ *Small companies, since the limited number of investors interested in their shares means that their liquidity is low and that their share prices could shift away from a stable value for long periods.*

BIBLIOGRAPHY

For more on the macroeconomic topics covered in this chapter:

D. Farrell, *$118 Trillion and Counting: Taking Stock of the World's Capital Markets*, McKinsey Co., New York, 2005.

A. Franklin, Stock markets and resource allocation, in C. Mayer and X. Vives (eds), *European Financial Integration*, CEPR, London, 1992.

J. Gurley, E. Shaw, *Money in a Theory of Finance*, Brookings Institute Press, Washington, DC, 1960.

J.R. Hicks, *Value and Capital*, Oxford University Press, 2nd edn, 1975.

N. Naik, The many roles of financial markets, in G. Bickerstaffe (ed.), *Mastering Finance*, FT/Pitman Publishing, London, 1998.

R. Merton, Z. Bodie, *Finance*, Prentice Hall, Upper Saddle River, NJ, 2000.

L. Zingales and R. Rajan, *Banks and Markets: The Changing Character of European Finance*, working paper, January 2003.

For more about efficient markets:

U. Bhattacharya, H. Daouk, The world price of insider trading, *Journal of Finance*, **57**(1), 75–108, February 2002.

C. Botosan, Evidence that greater disclosure lowers the cost of equity capital, *Journal of Applied Corporate Finance*, **12**(4), 60–69, Winter 2000.

A. Bressand and C. Distler (eds), *Enhanced Transparency: Meeting European investors' Needs*, Standard & Poor's, 2003.

E. Dimson, M. Mussavian, A brief history of market efficiency, *European Financial Management*, **4**(1), 91–103, March 1998.

E. Dimson, M. Mussavian, *Foundations of Finance*, Darmouth Publishing Company, 2000.

E. Fama, Efficient capital markets: A review of theory and empirical work, *Journal of Finance*, 383–417, May 1970.

E. Fama, Efficient capital market II, *Journal of Finance*, 1575–1617, December 1991.

E. Fama, Market efficiency, long-term returns and behavioral finance, *Journal of Financial Economics*, **49**(3), 283–306, September 1998.

J. Fuller, M. Jensen, Just say no to Wall Street: Putting a stop to the earnings game, *Journal of Applied Corporate Finance*, **14**(4), 27–40, Winter 2002.

B. Malkiel, *A Random Walk down Wall Street*, W.W. Norton & Company, New York, 8th edn, 2003.

P. Marsh, Myths surrounding short-termism, in G. Bickerstaffe (ed.), *Mastering Finance*, FT/Pitman Publishing, London, 1998.

M. Rubinstein, Rational Markets: Yes or No? The Affirmative Case, *Financial Analysts Journal*, May/June 2001.

About empirical evidence and anomalies of efficient financial markets:

R. Banz, The relationship between return and market value of common stock, *Journal of Financial Economics*, **9**, 3–18, 1981.

M. Gibbons, H. Patrick, Day of the week effects and asset returns, *Journal of Business*, **54**, 579–596, October 1981.

R. Haugen, J. Lakonishok, *The Incredible January Effect*, Irwin, Homewood, IL, 1989.

G. Hawawini, D. Keim, *The Cross Section of Common Stock Returns: A Review of the Evidence and Some New Findings*, Warthon School, University of Pennsylvania, working paper, May 1997.

D. Keim, Size-related anomalies and stock return seasonality: Further empirical evidence, *Journal of Financial Economics*, **12**, 13–32, 1983.

T. Loughran, Book-to-market across firm size, exchange, and seasonality: Is there an effect?, *Journal of Financial and Quantitative Analysis*, **32**, 249–268, September 1997.

T. Loughran, J. Ritter, The new issue puzzle, *Journal of Finance*, **50**(1), 23–51, March 1995.

J. Ritter, The long-run performance of IPOs, *Journal of Finance*, **46**(1), 3–27, March 1991.

For those wanting to know more about behavioural finance:

N. Barberis, Markets: The price may not be right, in G. Bickerstaffe (ed.), *Mastering Finance*, FT/Pitman Publishing, London, 1998.

W. DeBondt, R. Thaler, Does the stock market overreact?, *Journal of Finance*, **49**(3), 793–805, 1985.

J. Graham, Herding among investment newsletters: Theory and evidence, *Journal of Finance*, **54**, 237–268, February 1999.

R. Shiller, A. Banjeree, A simple model of herd behavior, *Quarterly Journal of Economics*, **107**(3), 797–817, 1992.

R. Shiller, Conversation, information and herd behavior, *American Economic Review*, **85**(2), 181–185, 1995.

R. Shiller, *Irrational Exuberance*, Princeton University Press, Princeton, NJ, 2000.

H. Shefrin, *Beyond Greed and Fear, Understanding Behavioral Finance and the Psychology of Investing*, Harvard Business School Press, 2000.

R. Thaler (ed.), *Advances in Behavioural Finance*, Russell Sage Foundation, 1993.

R. Thaler, The end of behavioral finance, *Financial Analysts Journal*, 12–17, November/December 1999.

The Economist, Rethinking thinking, pp. 69–71, 18 December 1999

Websites:

www.bestcalls.com Free access to conference calls, annual statements and other documents of American companies.

www.ecgn.org Website of the European Corporate Governance network. It is possible to download international regulations, conference proceedings and other documents on corporate governance.

www.fibv.com Website of International Federation of Stock Exchanges. Free download of monthly, quarterly and annual statistics regarding stock markets.

A bird in the hand is worth two in the bush

For economic progress to be possible, there must be a universally applicable time value of money, even in a risk-free environment. This fundamental concept gives rise to the techniques of capitalisation, discounting and net present value, described below.

These are more than just tools, but actual reflexes that must be studied and acquired.

Consider an example of a businessman who invests €100,000 in his business at the end of 1995 and then sells it 10 years later for €1,800,000. In the meantime, he receives no income from his business, nor does he invest any additional funds into it. Here is a simple problem: given an initial outlay of €100,000 that becomes €1,800,000 in 10 years, and without any outside funds being invested in the €business, what is the return on the businessman's investment?

His profit after 10 years was €1,700,000 (€1,800,000 − €100,000) on an initial outlay of €100,000. Hence, his return was (1,700,000/100,000) or 1,700% over a period of 10 years.

Is this a good result or not?

Actually, the return is not quite as impressive as it first looks. To find the annual return, our first reflex might be to divide the total return (1,700%) by number of years (10) and say that the average return is 170% per year.

While this may look like a reasonable approach, it is in fact far from accurate. The value 170% has nothing to do with an annual return, which compares the funds invested and the funds recovered after 1 year. In the case above, there is no income for 10 years. Usually, calculating interest assumes a flow of revenue each year, which can then be reinvested, and which in turn begins producing additional interest.

To calculate return over a period greater than one year, we cannot simply compare the end return to the initial outlay and divide by the number of years. This is erroneous reasoning.

There is only one sensible way to calculate the return on the above investment. First, it is necessary to seek the rate of return on a hypothetical investment that would generate income at the end of each year. After 10 years, the rate of return on the initial investment will have to have transformed – €100,000 into €1,800,000. Further, the income generated must not be paid out, but rather it has to be reinvested (in which case the income is said to be **capitalised**).

Capitalising income means foregoing receipt of it. It then becomes capital and begins itself to produce interest during the following periods.

Therefore, we are now trying to calculate the annual return on an investment that grows from €100,000 into €1,800,000 after 10 years, with all annual income to be reinvested each year.

An initial attempt to solve this problem can be made using a rate of return equal to 10%. If, at the end of 1995, €100,000 is invested at that rate, it will produce 10% × €100,000, or €10,000 in interest in 1996.

This €10,000 will then be added to the initial capital outlay and begin, in turn, to produce interest. (Hence the term "to capitalise", which means to add to capital.) The capital thus becomes €110,000 and produces 10% × €110,000 in interest in 1997; i.e.. €10,000 on the initial outlay plus €1,000 on the interest from 1996 (10% × €10,000). As the interest is reinvested, the capital becomes €110,000 × €11,000, or €121,000, which will produce €12,100 in interest in 1998, and so on.

Year	Capital at the beginning of the period (€) (1)	Income (€) (2) = 10% × (1)	Capital at the end of the period (€) = (1) + (2)
1996	100,000	10,000	110,000
1997	110,000	11,000	121,000
1998	121,000	12,100	133,100
1999	133,100	13,310	146,410
2000	146,410	14,641	161,051
2001	161,051	16,105	177,156
2002	177,156	17,716	194,872
2003	194,872	19,487	214,359
2004	214,359	21,436	235,795
2005	235,795	23,579	259,374

If we keep doing this until 2005, we obtain a final sum of €259,374, as shown in the table.

Each year, interest is capitalised and itself produces interest. This is called **compound interest**. This is easy to express in a formula:

$$V_{1996} = V_{1995} + 10\% \times V_{1995} = V_{1995} \times (1 + 10\%)$$

Which can be generalised into the following:

$$V_n = V_{n-1} \times (1 + r)$$

where V is a sum and r the rate of return.

Hence, $V_{1995} = V_{1995} \times (1 + 10\%)$, but the same principle can also yield:

$$V_{1997} = V_{1996} \times (1 + 10\%)$$

$$V_{1998} = V_{1997} \times (1 + 10\%) \ldots$$

$$V_{2005} = V_{2004} \times (1 + 10\%)$$

All these equations can be consolidated into the following:

$$V_{2005} = V_{1995} \times (1 + 10\%)^{10}$$

Or, more generally:

Capitalisation formula.

$$V_n = V_0 \times (1 + r)^n$$

where V_0 **is the initial value of the investment,** r **is the rate of return and** n **is the duration of the investment in years.**

This is a simple equation that gets us from the initial capital to the terminal capital. Terminal capital is a function of the rate, r, and the duration, n.

Now it is possible to determine the annual return. In the example, the annual rate of return is not 170%, but 33.5%[1] (which is not bad, all the same!). Therefore, 33.5% is the rate on an investment that transforms €100,000 into €1,800,000 in 10 years, with annual income assumed to be reinvested every year at the same rate.

To calculate the return on an investment that does not distribute income, it is possible to reason by analogy. This is done using an investment that, over the same duration, transforms the same initial capital into the same terminal capital and produces annual income reinvested at the same rate of return. At 33.5%, annual income of €33,500 for 10 years (plus the initial investment of €100,000 paid back after the 10th year) is exactly the same as not receiving any income for 10 years and then receiving €1,800,000 vthe 10th year.

[1] $33.5\% = \left(\dfrac{1,800,000}{100,000} \right)^{1/10} - 1.$

DISCOUNTING AND CAPITALISATION AT 15%

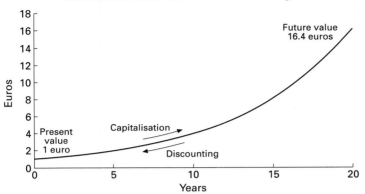

When no income is paid out, the terminal value rises considerably, quadrupling, for example, over 10 years at 15%, but rising 16.4-fold over 20 years at the same rate, as illustrated in this graph.

@
download

Over a long period of time, the impact of a change in the capitalisation rate on the terminal value looks as follows:

VALUE OF €1 CAPITALISED AT VARIOUS RATES

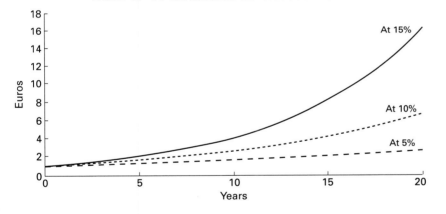

After 20 years, a sum capitalised at 15% is six times higher than a sum capitalised at one-third the rate (i.e., 5%).

@
download

This increase in terminal value is especially important in equity valuations. The example we gave earlier of the businessman selling his company after 10 years is typical. The lower the income he has received on his investment, the more he would expect to receive when selling it. Only a high valuation would give him a return that makes economic sense.

The lack of intermediate income must be offset by a high terminal valuation. The same line of reasoning applies to an industrial investment that does not produce any income during the first few years. The longer it takes it to produce its first income, the greater that income must be in order to produce a satisfactory return.

Tripling one's capital in 16 years, doubling it in 10 years or simply asking for a 7.177% annual return all amount to the same thing, since the rate of return is the same.

No distinction has been made in this chapter between income, reimbursement and actual cash flow. Regardless of whether income is paid out or reinvested, it has been shown that the slightest change in the timing of income modifies the rate of return.

To simplify, consider an investment of 100, which must be paid off at the end of year 1, with an interest accrued of 10. Suppose, however, that the borrower is negligent and the lender absent-minded, and the borrower repays the principal and the interest 1 year later than he should. The return on a well-managed investment that is equivalent to the so-called 10% on our absent-minded investor's loan can be expressed as:

$$V = V_0 \times (l + r)^2$$

$$\text{or} \quad 110 = 100 \times (1 + r)^2$$

$$\text{hence} \quad r = 4.88\%$$

This return is less than half of the initially expected return!

It is not accounting and legal appearances that matter, but rather actual cash flows.

Any precise financial calculation must account for cash flow exactly at the moment when it is received and not just when it is due.

Section 16.2
DISCOUNTING

1/WHAT DOES IT MEAN TO DISCOUNT A SUM?

To discount means to calculate the present value of a future cash flow.

Discounting into today's euros helps us compare a sum that will not be produced until later. Technically speaking, what is discounting?

To discount is to "depreciate" the future. It is to be more rigorous with future cash flows than present cash flows, because future cash flows cannot be spent or invested immediately. First, take tomorrow's cash flow and then apply to it a multiplier coefficient below 1, which is called a discounting factor. The discounting factor is used to express a future value as a present value, thus reflecting the depreciation brought on by time.

Consider an offer whereby someone will give you €1,000 in 5 years. As you will not receive this sum for another 5 years, you can apply a discounting factor to it – for example, 0.6. The present value, or today's value, of this future sum is then 600. Having discounted the future value to a present value, we can then compare it with other values. For example, it is preferable to receive 650 today than 1,000 in 5 years, as the present value of 1,000 5 years out is 600, and that is below 650.

Discounting makes it possible to compare sums received or paid out at different dates.

Discounting is based on the time value of money. After all, "time is money". Any sum received later is worth less than the same sum received today.

Remember that **investors discount because they demand a certain rate of return**. If a security pays you 110 in one year and you wish to see a return of 10% on your investment, the most you would pay today for the security (i.e., its present value) is 100. At this price (100) and for the amount you know you will receive in 1 year (110), you will get a return of 10% on your investment of 100. However, if a return of 11% is required on the investment, then the price you are willing to pay changes. In the second case, you would be willing to pay no more than 99.1 for the security because the gain would have been 10.9 (or 11% of 99.1), which will still give you a final payment of 110.

Discounting is calculated with the required return of the investor. If the investment does not meet or exceed the investor's expectations, he will forgo it and seek a better opportunity elsewhere.

Discounting converts a future value into a present value. This is the opposite result of capitalisation.

Discounting converts future values into present values, while capitalisation converts present values into future ones. Hence, to return to the example of the previous section, €1,800,000 in 10 years discounted at 33.5% is today worth €100,000. €100,000 today will be worth €1,800,000 when capitalised at 33.5% over 10 years.

CAPITALISATION

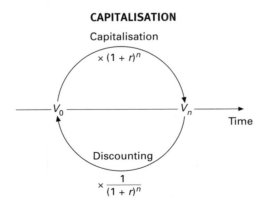

Discounting and capitalisation are thus two ways to express the same phenomenon: the time value of money.

download

2/ DISCOUNTING AND CAPITALISATION FACTORS

To discount a sum, the same mathematical formulas are used as those for capitalising a sum. Discounting calculates the sum in the opposite direction to capitalising.

To get from €100,000 today to €1,800,000 in 10 years, we multiplied €100,000 by $(1 + 0.335)^{10}$, or 18. The number 18 is the **capitalisation factor**.

To get from €1,800,000 in 10 years to its present value today, we would have to multiply €1,800,000 by $1/(1+0.335)^{10}$, or 0.056.

0.056 is the **discounting factor**, which is the inverse of the coefficient of capitalisation. The present value of €1,800,000 in 10 years at a 33.5% rate is €100,000.

More generally:

Discounting formula

$$V_0 = \frac{V_n}{(1+r)^n}$$

Which is the exact opposite of the capitalisation formula.

$1/(1+r)^n$ is the **discounting factor**, which depreciates V_n and converts it into a present value V_0. It remains below 1 as discounting rates are always positive.

Section 16.3
PRESENT VALUE AND NET PRESENT VALUE OF A FINANCIAL SECURITY

In the introductory chapter of this book, it was explained that a financial security is no more than a stream of future cash flow, to which we can then apply the notion of discounting. So, without being aware of it, you already knew how to calculate the value of a security!

1/FROM THE PRESENT VALUE OF A SECURITY ...

The Present Value (*PV*) of a security is the sum of its discounted cash flows; i.e.:

$$PV = \sum_{n=1}^{N} \frac{F_n}{(1+r)^n}$$

where F_n are the cash flows generated by the security, r is the applied discounting rate and n is the number of years for which the security is discounted.

All securities also have a **market value**, particularly on the secondary market. Market value is the price at which a security can be bought or sold.

Net Present Value (*NPV*) is the difference between present value and market value (*V_0*):

$$NPV = \sum_{n=1}^{N} \frac{F_n}{(1+r)^n} - V_0$$

If the net present value of a security is greater than its market value, then it will be worth more in the future that the market has presently valued it. Therefore, you will probably want to invest in it; i.e., to invest in the upside potential of its value.

If, however, the security's present value is below its market value, you should sell it at once, for **its market value is sure to diminish**.

2/... TO ITS FAIR VALUE

If an imbalance occurs between a security's market value and its present value, efficient markets will seek to re-establish balance and reduce net present value to zero. Investors acting on efficient markets seek out investments offering positive net present value, in order to realise that value. When they do so, they push net present value towards zero, ultimately arriving at the fair value of the security.

In efficient, fairly valued markets, net present values are zero – i.e., market value is equal to present value.

3/ APPLYING THE CONCEPT OF NET PRESENT VALUE TO OTHER INVESTMENTS

Up to this point, the discussion has been limited to financial securities. However, the concepts of present value and net present value can easily be applied to any investment, such as the construction of a new factory, the launch of a new product, the takeover of a competing company or any other asset that will generate positive and/or negative cash flows.

The **concept of net present value** can be interpreted **in three different ways**:

1 **the value created by an investment** – for example, if the investment requires an outlay of €100 and the present value of its future cash flow is €110, then the investor has become €10 wealthier;
2 **the maximum additional amount that the investor is willing to pay to make the investment** – if the investor pays up to €10 more, he has not necessarily made a bad deal, as he/she is paying up to €110 for an asset that is worth 110;
3 **the difference between the present value of the investment (€110) and its market value (€100).**

Section 16.4
THE NPV DECISION RULE

Calculating the NPV of a project is conceptually easy. There are basically two steps to be followed:

1 estimate the net cash flows that the investment will generate over its life;
2 discount these cash flows at an interest rate that reflects the degree of risk inherent in the project.

The resulting sum of discounted cash flows equals the project's net present value. The **NPV decision rule** says to invest in projects when the present value is positive (greater than zero):

$$NPV > 0 \qquad \text{Invest}$$

$$NPV < 0 \qquad \text{Do not invest}$$

The NPV rule implies that firms should invest when the present value of future cash inflows exceeds the initial cost of the project. Why does the NPV rule lead to good investment decisions? The firm's primary goal is to maximise shareholder wealth. The discount rate r represents the highest rate of return (opportunity cost) that investors could obtain in the marketplace in an investment with equal risk. When the NPV of cash flow equals zero, the rate of return provided by the investment is exactly equal to investors' required return. Therefore, when a firm finds a project with a positive NPV, that project will offer a return exceeding investors' expectations.

Although this section will highlight many of the advantageous qualities of the NPV approach, there are also a few weaknesses that bear mentioning now:

- it is less intuitive than other methodologies, such as the payback rule or the accounting return rule, which will be presented in Chapter 18;
- it does not take into account the value of managerial flexibility – in other words, the options that managers can exploit after an investment has been made in order to increase its value; and
- the NPV has a major competitor in the Internal Rate of Return (IRR), whose use seems more widespread among corporations. In most cases, the two decision rules give the same information, but the IRR is more appealing to managers because it delivers a number that is more easily interpreted.

Section 16.5
WHAT DOES NET PRESENT VALUE DEPEND ON?

While net present value is obviously based on the amount and timing of cash flows, it is worth examining how it varies with the discounting rate.

The higher the discounting rate, the more future cash flow is depreciated and, therefore, the lower is the present value. **Net present value declines in inverse proportion to the discounting rate**, thus reflecting investor demand for a greater return (i.e., greater value attributed to time).

Take the following example of an asset (e.g., a financial security or a capital investment) whose market value is 2 and whose cash flows are as follows:

Year	1	2	3	4	5
Cash flow	0.8	0.8	0.8	0.8	0.8

A 20% discounting rate would produce the following discounting factors:

Year	1	2	3	4	5
Discounting factor	0.833	0.694	0.579	0.482	0.402
Present value of cash flow	0.67	0.56	0.46	0.39	0.32

As a result, the present value of this investment is about 2.4. As its market value is 2, its net present value is approximately 0.4.

If the discounting rate changes, the following values are obtained:

Discounting rate	0%	10%	20%	25%	30%	35%
Present value of the investment	4	3.03	2.39	2.15	1.95	1.78
Market value	2	2	2	2	2	2
Net present value	2	1.03	0.39	0.15	−0.05	−0.22

Which would then look like this graphically:

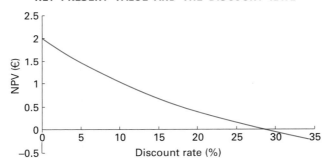

NET PRESENT VALUE AND THE DISCOUNT RATE

The higher the discounting rate (i.e., the higher the return demanded), the lower the net present value.

download

The present value and net present value of an asset vary in inverse proportion to the discounting rate.

Section 16.6
SOME EXAMPLES OF SIMPLIFICATION OF PRESENT VALUE CALCULATIONS

For those occasions when you are without your favourite spreadsheet program, you may find the following formulas handy in calculating present value.

1/THE VALUE OF AN ANNUITY F OVER n YEARS, BEGINNING IN YEAR 1:

$$PV = \frac{F}{(1+r)} + \frac{F}{(1+r)^2} + \cdots + \frac{F}{(1+r)^N}$$

or:

$$PV = F \times \left(\frac{1}{(1+r)} + \frac{1}{(1+r)^2} + \cdots + \frac{1}{(1+r)^N} \right)$$

For the two formulas above, the sum of the geometric series can be expressed more simply as:

$$PV = \frac{F}{r} \times \left[1 - \frac{1}{(1+r)^N} \right]$$

or:

$$PV = F \times \left[\frac{1}{r} - \frac{1}{r \times (1+r)^N} \right]$$

So, if $F = 0.8$, $r = 20\%$ and $N = 5$, then the present value is indeed 2.4.

Further, $(1/r) \times (1 - (1+r)^{-N})$ is equal to the sum of the first n discounting factors.

The term used to compute the value of the stream of constant payments, F, for N years is called an **annuity factor**. An example of an annuity is the coupon part of a bond with equal annual payments. The annuity factor in the current example is 2.9906. The table at the end of this book gives the value of these factors for a range of interest rates, r, and maturity dates, N.

For simplicity, we refer to the annuity factor as:

$$A_r^N$$

2/ THE VALUE OF A PERPETUITY

A **perpetuity** is a constant stream of cash flows without end. By adding this feature to the previous case, the formula then looks like this:

$$PV = \frac{F}{(1+r)} + \frac{F}{(1+r)^2} + \cdots + \frac{F}{(1+r)^n} + \cdots$$

As n approaches infinity, this can be shortened to the following:

$$PV = \frac{F}{r}$$

The present value of a €100 perpetuity discounted back at 10% per year is thus:

$$PV = 100/0.10 = €1,000$$

A €100 perpetuity discounted at 10% is worth €1,000 in today's euros. If the investor demands a 20% return, the same perpetuity is worth €500.

3/ THE VALUE OF AN ANNUITY THAT GROWS AT RATE g FOR n YEARS

In this case, the F_0 cash flow rises annually by g for n years. Thus:

$$VA = \frac{F_0 \times (1+g)}{(1+r)} + \cdots + \frac{F_0 \times (1+g)^n}{(1+r)^n}$$

or:

$$PV = \frac{F_0 \times (1+g)}{r-g} \times \left(1 - \frac{(1+g)^n}{(1+r)^n} \right)$$

Note: the first cash flow actually paid out is $F_0 \times (1+g)$.

Thus, a security that has just paid out 0.8, with this 0.8 growing by 10% each year for the four following years has, at a discounting rate of 20%, a present value of:

$$PV = (0.8 \times (1 + 10\%)/(20\% - 10\%)) \times (1 - (1.10/1.20)^4) = 2.59$$

4/THE VALUE OF A PERPETUITY THAT GROWS AT RATE g (GROWING PERPETUITY)

As n approaches infinity, the previous formula can be expressed as follows:

$$PV = \frac{F_0 \times (1 + g)}{r - g} = \frac{F_1}{r - g}$$

As long as $r > g$.

The present value is thus equal to the next year's cash flow divided by the difference between the discounting rate and the annual growth rate.

For example, a security with an annual return of 0.8, growing by 10% annually to infinity, has at a rate of 20%:

$$PV = 0.8/(0.2 - 0.1) = 8.0$$

5/WHEN CASH FLOWS RISE AT DIFFERENT RATES

This formula is useful when the growth rate is very high at the beginning of the period of projection – i.e., higher than the discounting rate – and then gradually declines. (After all, not even trees can grow for ever!)

Over three periods lasting n_1 years, n_2 years and up to infinity, cash flow rises by g_1 for $n_1 - 1$ years, then by g_2 for n_2 years and then by g_3 to infinity. Present value is then equal to:

$$= F_1 \times \left[\frac{1 - \left(\frac{1 + g_1}{1 + r}\right)^{n_1}}{r - g_1} + \frac{(1 + g_1)^{n_1 - 1}}{(1 + r)^{n_1}} \times (1 + g_2) \times \frac{1 - \left(\frac{1 + g_2}{1 + r}\right)^{n_2}}{r - g_2} + \frac{\frac{(1 + g_1)^{n_1} \times (1 + g_2)^{n_2} \times (1 + g_3)}{r - g_3}}{(1 + r)^{n_1 + n_2}} \right]$$

For example, if the first year's cash flow is 10.75, and it grows by 15% annually for the next 5 years, then by 9% annually for the five following years, and finally by 2.5% from the 11th year onwards, the value of this asset is then about 270, based on a 10% discounting rate.

The following are additional topics for consideration when calculating NPV:

(a) Capital rationing and the Present Value Index

Sometimes there is a strict capital constraint imposed on the firm, and it is faced with more NPV-positive projects than it can afford. In order to determine which project to pursue, the best formula to use is the **Present Value Index (PVI)**. This is the present value of cash inflows divided by the present value of cash outflows:

$$PVI = \frac{\text{Present value of inflows}}{\text{Present value of outflows}}$$

By using the Present Value Index, financial managers can rank the different projects and then select the investment with the highest PVI – that is, the project with the highest NPV relative to the present value of outflows. After making this selection, if the total amount of capital available has not been fully exhausted, the managers should then invest in the project with the second-highest PVI, and so on until no more capital remains to invest.[2]

2 *The PVI of excess funds, not invested in any of the projects, is always assumed to be equal to 1.0.*

More generally, the objective is to compare all combinations of x projects that meet the budget and find the one that maximises the *weighted average PVI*:

$$PVI = \frac{PV \text{ outflows of project } A}{\text{Total funds available}} \times (PVI_A) + \cdots$$
$$+ \frac{PV \text{ outflows of project } X}{\text{Total funds available}} \times (PVI_X)$$

(b) Projects with different lives

At other times, it is necessary to compare two (or more) similar projects that have positive net present values and similar PVIs but different operating costs and last for different time periods. The NPV rule would suggest undertaking the project with the lower cost. However, this conclusion could lead to the wrong decision if the lower cost project needs to be replaced before an alternative investment.

When we have to choose between two projects of two different lengths, we must reason on an equal life basis, which can be done using the **Equivalent Annual Cost** (EAC) method. This technique is based on the following steps:

3 *The EAC should not be used if the projects have different risk.*

1 calculate the present value of the costs of each of the two projects;
2 determine the equivalent annual cost of the single payment represented by the PV of the costs of the two projects. We can use the tables of the present value of an annuity; and
3 choose the project with the lower equivalent annual cost.[3]

Consider the following example. A company can undertake two (mutually exclusive) projects with different initial outlays and periodical costs. The first project (*A*) lasts for 3 years and the second project (*B*) lasts for 4 years. The discount rate is 10%.

	Initial investment	Annual costs				PV of costs
	0	**1**	**2**	**3**	**4**	
Project *A*	400	100	100	100		€590
Project *B*	500	80	80	80	80	€685

The PV of the total costs are higher for project *B*. A naive approach would be to select *A* because of the lower PV of the costs. However, project *A* has a shorter life, so perhaps it needs to be replaced earlier than project *B*.

Therefore, a different approach is required. By using annuities, and equating the PV of the total costs at date 0 with maturities of 3 years and 4 years, the following results are obtained:

PV of costs	Annuity factor	Annual equivalent cost
€590	2,4869	€237
€685	3,1699	€216

The annual equivalent cost for project *B* is €216, whereas for project *A* it is €237. Therefore, the manager should select project *B*.

The EAC converts total present value of costs to a cost per year. The reader should immediately realise that this is equivalent to a fair *rental payment* –i.e., a payment that the manager should afford periodically if he decides to rent the machine rather than buy it.

Comparing annual equivalent costs should take into account two final caveats:

1 The use of EAC for comparison of costs should always be done in *real* terms. The nominal procedure could in fact give incorrect rankings with high inflation rates.
2 The use of EAC is useless if there is no replacement expected at different future dates.

SUMMARY

Capitalisation involves forgoing immediate spending of a given sum of money. By using the interest rate at which the money will be invested, the future amounts can be calculated. Thus, the future value of a sum of money can be determined by way of capitalisation.

Discounting involves calculating today's value of a future cash flow, what is known as the present value, on the basis of rates of return required by investors. By calculating the present value of a future sum, discounting can be used for comparing future cash flows that will not be received on the same date.

Discounting and capitalisation are two ways of expressing the same phenomenon: the time value of money.

download

Capitalisation is based on compound interest. $V_n = V_0 \times (1 + r)^n$ where V_0 is the initial value of the investment, r is the rate of return, n is the duration of the investment in years, $(1 + r)^n$ is the capitalisation factor and V_n the terminal value.

Discounting is the inverse of capitalisation.

It is important to note that any precise financial calculation must account for cash flows at the moment when they are received or paid, and not when they are due.

Net Present Value (NPV) is the difference between present value and the value at which the security or share can be bought. Net present value measures the creation or destruction of value that could result from the purchase of a security or making an investment. When markets are in equilibrium, net present values are usually nil.

Changes in present value and net present value move in the opposite direction from changes in discount rates. The higher the discount rate, the lower the present value and net present value, and vice versa.

In many cases, calculating present value and net present value can be made a lot simpler through *ad hoc* formulas.

Finally, there are two special situations where the NPV framework is still valid: when projects have different lives and when there is capital-rationing. If two (or more) projects have different lives, the manager should use the equivalent annual cost; if there is capital-rationing, then it could be helpful to use the present value index.

QUESTIONS

quiz

1/ What is discounting?

2/ Why should we discount?

3/ What is the discount factor equal to?

4/ On what should you base a choice between two equal discounted values?

5/ What is the simple link between the discount factor and the capitalisation factor?

6/ Why are capitalisation factors always greater than 1?

7/ Why are discount factors always less than 1?

8/ Should you discount even if there is no inflation and no risk? Why?

9/ Why does the graph on p. 293 show curves and not lines?

10/ Esso France pays out big dividends. Should its share price rise faster or slower than the share price of Infogrames, which doesn't pay out any dividends? Why? Would it be better to have Esso France stock options or Infogrames stock options? Why?

11/ What is net present value equal to?

12/ The higher the rates of return, the larger present values will be. True of false?

13/ What mechanism pushes market value towards present value?

14/ Can net present value be negative? What does this mean?

15/ What does the discount rate correspond to in formulas for calculating present value and net present value?

16/ Are initial flows on an investment more often positive or negative? What about for final cash flows?

17/ A market is in equilibrium when present values are nil and net present values are positive. True or false?

18/ For the investment in Section 16.2, what is the maximum discount rate above which it would not be worthwhile for the investor?

19/ Can the growth rate to infinity of a cash flow be higher than the discount rate? Why?

20/ Could an investment made at a negative net present value result in the creation of value?

21/ Would you be more likely to find investments with positive present value on financial markets or on industrial markets? Why?

EXERCISES

1/ What is the present value of €100 received in 3 years at 5%, 10% and 20%?

2/ What is the present value at 10% of €100 received in 3 years, 5 years and 10 years? What are the discount factors?

3/ How much would €1,000 be worth in 5 years, invested at 5%, 10% and 20%. Why is the sum invested at 20% not double that invested at 10%?

4/ How much would €1,000 be worth in 5 years, 10 years and 20 years if invested at 8%? Why is the sum invested for 20 years not double that invested for 10 years?

5/ You are keen to obtain a helicopter pilot's licence. A club offers you lessons over two years, with a choice between the following payment terms:

   ○   you can either pay the full fees (€10,000) immediately with a 10% discount; or
   ○   you can make two equal annual payments, the first one due immediately.
   ○   At what interest rate would these two options work out at the same cost?

6/ What interest rate would turn 110 into 121 in 1 year?

7/ How much would you have to invest today to have 100 in 8 years if the interest rate was 5%? What is the capitalisation factor?

8/ At 7%, would you rather have €100 today or €131.1 in 4 years' time? Why?

9/ Show that, in order to double your money in 1 year, the interest rate would have to be around 75%/year.

10/ Show that in order to treble your money in N years, the interest rate would have to be around 125%/N.

11/ You are only prepared to forgo immediate spending if you get a 9% return on your investment. What would be the top price you would be prepared to pay for a security today that would pay you 121 in 2 years? If other investors were asking for 8%, what would happen?

12/ If instead of throwing his 30 pieces of silver away in 33 AD, Judas had invested them at 3% per annum, how much would his descendants get in 2005? Explain your views.

13/ You have the choice between buying a Francis Bacon painting for €100,000 which will be worth €125,000 in 4 years, and investing in government bonds at 6%. What would your choice be? Why?

14/ Given the level of risk, you require an 18% return on shares in Amazon.com. No dividends will be paid out for 5 years. What is the lowest price you could sell them at in 4 years' time if you bought them for $14 a share today.

15/ Ten years from now, at what price should you sell shares in Pirelli Real Estate, which pays a constant annual dividend to infinity of €9.6, in order to get a 7% return? The share price today is €137.

16/ Assume that a share in Zaleski has a market value of 897, with the following cash flow schedule:

Year	1	2	3	4	5
Cash flow	300	300	300	300	300

Calculate the NPV of the share at 5%, 10%, 20% and 25%. Plot your answers on a graph.

17/ What is the present value at 10% of a perpetual income of 100? And a perpetual income of 100 rising by 3% every year from the following year?

18/ What is the present value at 10% of €100 paid annually for 3 years? Same question for a perpetual income.

19/ An investment promises four annual payments of €52 over the next 4 years. You require an 8% return. How much would you be prepared to pay for this asset? The share is currently trading at €165. Would you be prepared to buy or to sell? Why? If you buy at that price, how much will you have gained? Will the rate of return on your investment be greater or less than 8%? Why? If you buy at €172, what will your return on this investment be? Why?

20/ Show that at 8% there is little difference between the value of a perpetual income and that of a security that offers a constant annual income equal to that of the perpetual income for only 40 years. Show that this will not be true if the rate of return is 15%.

21/ You have the opportunity to buy the right to park in a given parking place for 75 years, at a price of €300,000. You could also rent a parking place for €2,000 a year, revised upwards by 2% every year. If the opportunity cost is 5%, what would you choose?

22/ You are the proud owner of the TV screening rights of the film *Singing in the Rain*. You sell the rights to screen the film on TV once every 2 years, for €0.8m. What is the value of your asset? The film has just been screened. You make the assumption that screenings will be possible for 30 years or in perpetuity. The discount rate is 6%.

23/ You have found your dream house and you have the choice between renting it with a lease in perpetuity for €12,000 or buying it. At what purchase price would you be better off renting, if the loan you needed to buy the house costs you 7%, and the rent increases by 3% per year?

24/ Your current after-tax annual income is €50,000, which should increase by 4% per year until you retire. You believe that if you interrupt your professional career for 2

/years to do an MBA, you could earn €65,000 after tax per year, with an annual increase of 5% until you retire. What is your present value if you retire in 40 years' time, and the discount rate is 4%. If the total cost of the MBA is €50,000 payable immediately, what is the net present value of this investment? Is it worth doing an MBA?

Questions

1/ *Converting a future value into a present value.*
2/ *So as to be able to compare a future value and a present value of a future inflow.*
3/ $1/(1+r)^n$.
4/ *If the present values are equal, it makes no difference.*
5/ *One is the opposite of the other.*
6/ *Because interest rates are positive.*
7/ *Because interest rates are positive.*
8/ *Yes, because discounting is used to factor in an interest rate which remunerates the forgoing of immediate spending. Discounting is thus unrelated to inflation or risk.*
9/ *Because of capitalisation, which every year adds interest earned over the past year to the principal, and interest is earned on this interest in the future. This is called compound interest.*
10/ *The Infogrames' share price will have to rise more than that of Esso France in order to make up for the lack of dividends. As stock options are options to buy shares at a fixed exercise price, their value will increase if the share price rises. So it would be better to have Infogrames' stock options.*
11/ *To the difference between the present value and the market value of an asset.*
12/ *False, the opposite is true.*
13/ *Arbitrage.*
14/ *Yes. The asset has been overvalued.*
15/ *To the required return on this asset.*
16/ *Negative, positive.*
17/ *False, the opposite is true. NPV = 0 and PV > 0.*
18/ *Around 28%.*
19/ *No, because growth is not a process that can continue endlessly!*
20/ *No, unless you've made an error in your calculations of the cash flows or under-estimated them.*
21/ *In industrial markets because arbitrage operations take longer to execute than in financial markets (building a factory takes longer than buying a share) and, therefore, disequilibrium is more frequent.*

Exercises

1/ $100/1.05^3 = €86.4$; $100/1.1^3 = €75.1$; $100/1.2^3 = €57.9$.
2/ €75.1; €62.1; €38.6; 0.751; 0.621; 0.386.
3/ €1,276, €1,611, €2,488. *Because the principal (€1,000) remains the same and interest more than doubles as a result of the process of compound interest.*
4/ €1,469, €2,159 and €4,661. *Because the principal (€1,000) remains the same and interest more than doubles as a result of the process of compound interest.*
5/ 11.55% *per year.*
6/ 10% (121/110 − 1).

7/ €67.7; €1.48.

8/ It makes absolutely no difference, because €100 capitalised at 7% a year would be worth €131.1 in 4 years.

9/ This is a good estimate. Over 5 years, a sum doubles at 14.87%, and 75%/5 = 15%.

10/ This is a good estimate. Over 5 years, a sum trebles at 24.57%, and 125%/5 = 25%.

11/ At 101.8. Other investors are prepared to pay 103.7 and you cannot buy this security.

12/ 6.2×10^{26} pieces of silver (0.62 billion billion billion pieces of silver!). Although mathematically possible, Judas's descendants would be unlikely to get anything at all, given the wars, revolutions, periods of inflation, state bankruptcies, etc. that have occurred since 33 AD!

13/ €100,000 at 6% will be worth €126,248 in 4 years, which is more than €125,000, but if you're an art lover it might be worth forgoing €1,248 for the pleasure of admiring a Francis Bacon in the comfort of your own home for 4 years. There's more to life than money!

14/ $14 \times 1.18^4 =$ €27.

15/ €137, because the whole of the return on this share is in the dividend. 7% × €137 = €9.6.

16/ 402; 240; 109; 0; −90.

17/ 1,000; 1,429.

18/ €248.7; €1,000.

19/ €172. Buy, because its present value is higher than its market value. €7. Greater than 8%, because at 8% it is worth €172; so if I buy at €165, I'll earn more. 8%.

20/ With income of 100, you get 1,250 and 1,192, a difference of 5%. At 15%: 666.7 and 664.2 – a difference of 0.4%. Barring other factors, income over a period exceeding 40 years no longer has a significant impact on present value.

21/ €2,000 over 75 years growing at 2% would be worth €59,086, so it would be better to buy.

22/ €5.34m, €6.47m.

23/ €288,767.

24/ €1,923,077, €662,470, yes.

BIBLIOGRAPHY

The pioneering works on the net present value rule are:

I. Fisher, *The Theory of interest*, Augustus M. Kelley, New York, 1965. Reprinted from the 1930 edition.

J. Hirshleifer, On the theory of optimal investment decision, *Journal of Political Economy*, **66**, 329–352, August 1958.

F. Lutz, V. Lutz, *The Theory of the Investment of the Firm*, Princeton University Press, Princeton, NJ, 1951.

J. Tobin, Liquidity preference as behaviour towards risk, *Review of Economic Studies*, February 1958.

There are a number of financial calculation workbooks available which will help you get to grips with discounting calculations. You can also read:

T. Copeland, F. Weston, *Financial Theory and Corporate Finance*, Addison Wesley, New York, 1987.

You could finally consult:

E. Fama, M. Miller, *The Theory of Finance*, Rinehart and Winston, New York, 1972.

Chapter 17
THE INTERNAL RATE OF RETURN

A whimsical "nugget"

If net present value is inversely proportional to the discounting rate, then there must exist a discounting rate that makes NPV equal to zero.

The discounting rate that makes net present value equal to zero is called the "internal rate of return (IRR)" or "yield to maturity".

To apply this concept to capital budgeting, simply replace "yield to maturity" by "IRR", as the two terms mean the same thing. It is just that one is applied to financial securities (yield to maturity) and the other to capital expenditure (IRR).

Section 17.1
HOW IS INTERNAL RATE OF RETURN DETERMINED?

To calculate IRR, make r the unknown quantity and simply use the NPV formula again. The rate r is determined as follows:

$$VAN = 0, \qquad \text{or} \quad \sum_{n=1}^{N} \frac{F_n}{(1+r)^n} = V_0$$

To use the same example from the previous chapter:

$$\frac{0.8}{(1+r)} + \frac{0.8}{(1+r)^2} + \cdots + \frac{0.8}{(1+r)^5} = 2$$

In other words, an investment's internal rate of return is the rate at which its market value is equal to the present value of the investment's future cash flows.

It is possible to use trial-and-error to determine IRR. This will result in an interest rate that gives a negative net present value and another that gives a positive net present value. These negative and positive values constitute a range of values, which can be narrowed until the yield to maturity is found, which in this case is about 28.6%.[1]

1 *See figure on p. 299.*

Obviously, this type of calculation is time-consuming. It is much easier to just use a calculator or spreadsheet program with a function to determine the yield to maturity.

INTERNAL RATE OF RETURN AS AN INVESTMENT CRITERION

Internal rate of return is used frequently in financial markets because it immediately tells the investor the return to be expected for a given level of risk. The investor can then compare this expected return with his required return rate, thereby simplifying the investment decision.

The decision-making rule is very simple: if an investment's internal rate of return is higher than the investor-required return, he will make the investment or buy the security. Otherwise, he will abandon the investment or sell the security.

In our example, since the internal rate of return (28.6%) is higher than the return demanded by the investor (20%), he should make the investment. If the market value of the same investment were 3 (and not 2), the internal rate of return would be 10.4%, and he should not invest.

An investment is worth making when its internal rate of return is equal to or greater than the investor's required return. An investment is not worth making it when its internal rate of return is below the investor's required return.

THE LIMITS OF THE INTERNAL RATE OF RETURN

With this new investment decision-making criterion, it is now necessary to consider how IRR can be used *vis-à-vis* net present value. It is also important to investigate whether or not these two criteria could somehow produce contradictory conclusions.

If it is a simple matter of whether or not to buy into a given investment, or whether or not to invest in a project, the two criteria produce exactly the same result.

If the cash flow schedule is the same, then calculating the NPV by choosing the discounting rate or calculating the internal rate of return (and comparing it with the discounting rate) are two sides of the same mathematical coin.

1/THE REINVESTMENT RATE AND THE MODIFIED IRR (MIRR)

Consider two investments *A* and *B*, with the following cash flows:

Year	1	2	3	4	5	6	7
Investment *A*	6	0.5					
Investment *B*	2	3	0	0	2.1	0	5.1

At a 5% discount rate, the present value of investment A is 6.17 and that of investment B 9.90. If investment A's market value is 5, its net present value is 1.17. If investment B's market value is 7.5, its net present value is 2.40.

Now calculate their yield to maturity. It is 27.8% for investment A and 12.7% for investment B. Or, to sum up:

	NPV at 5%	IRR (%)
Investment A	1.17	27.8
Investment B	2.40	12.7

Investment A delivers a rate of return that is much higher than the required return (27.8% vs. 5%) during a short period of time. Investment B's rate of return is much lower (12.7% vs. 27.8%), but still higher than the 5% required return demanded, and it is delivered over a far longer period (7 years vs. 2). Our NPV and internal rate of return models are telling us two different things. So should we buy investment A or investment B?

At first glance, investment B would appear to be the more attractive of the two. Its NPV is higher and it creates the most value: 2.40 vs. 1.17.

However, some might say that investment A is more attractive, as cash flows are received earlier than with investment B and therefore can be reinvested sooner in high-return projects. While that is theoretically possible, it is the strong (and optimistic) form of the theory because competition among investors and the mechanisms of arbitrage tend to move net present values towards zero. Net present values moving towards zero means that exceptional rates of return converge toward the required rate of return, thereby eliminating the possibility of long-lasting high-return projects.

Given the convergence of the exceptional rates toward required rates of return, it is more reasonable to suppose that cash flows from investment A will be reinvested at the required rate of return of 5%. The exceptional rate of 27.8% is unlikely to be recurrent. And this is exactly what happens if we adopt the NPV decision rule. The NPV in fact assumes that the reinvestment of interim cash flows is made at the required rate of return (k):

$$\left[\sum_{n=1}^{N} F_n \times (1+r)^{N-n} \right] \times (1+r)^{-N} - F_0 = \sum_{n=1}^{N} \frac{F_n}{(1+r)^n} - F_0$$

If we apply the same equation to the IRR, we observe that the reinvestment rate is simply the IRR again. However, in equilibrium, it is unreasonable to think that the company can continue to invest at the same rate of the (sometimes) exceptional IRR of a specific project. It is instead much more reasonable to assume that, at best, the company can invest at the required rate of return.

However, a solution to the reinvestment rate problem of IRR is the **Modified IRR (MIRR)**.

The MIRR is the rate of return that yields an NPV of zero when the initial outlay is compared with the terminal value of the project's net cash flows reinvested at the required rate of return.

Determining the MIRR requires two stages:

1   calculate forward until the end of the project to determine the terminal value of the project by compounding all intermediate cash flows at the required rate of return; and

2   find the internal rate of return that equates the terminal value with the initial outlay.

So by capitalising cash flow from investments A and B at the required rate of return (5%) up to period 7, we obtain from investment A in period 7: $6 \times 1.005^6 + 0.5 \times 1.05^5$, or 8.68. From investment B we obtain: $2 \times 1.05^6 + 3 \times 1.05^5 + 2.1 \times 1.05^2 + 5.1$, or 13.9. The internal rate of return is 8.20% for investment A and 9.24% for investment B.

We have thus reconciled the NPV and internal rate of return models.

Others might say that it is not consistent to expect investment A to create more value than investment B, as only 5 has been invested in A vs. 7.5 for investment B. Even if we could buy an additional "half-share" of A, in order to equalise the purchase price, the NPV of our new investment in A would only be $1.17 \times 1.5 = 1.76$, which would still be less than investment B's NPV of 2.40. For reasons discussed above, it is unlikely to find another investment with a return identical to that of investment A.

Instead, we should assume that the 2.5 in additional investment would produce the required rate of return (5%) for 7 years. In this case, NPV would remain by definition at 1.17, whereas the internal rate of return of this investment would fall to 11%. NPV and the internal rate of return would once again lead us to conclude that investment B is the more attractive investment.

2/MULTIPLE OR NO IRR

Consider the following investment:

Year	0	1	2
Cash flow	−1	7.2	−7.2

There are two annual rates of return! Which one should we choose? At 10%, the NPV of this investment is −0.40. So it is not worth realising, even though its internal rate of return is higher than the required rate of return.

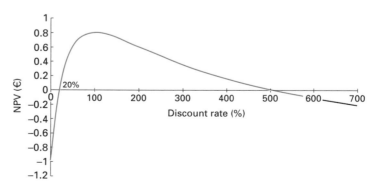

The project has two IRRs, and we do not know which one is the right one. There is no good reason to use one over the other. Investments with "unconventional" cash

flow sequences are rare, but they can happen. Consider a firm that is cutting timber in a forest. The timber is cut, sold and the firm gets an immediate profit. But, when harvesting is incomplete, the firm may be forced to replant the forest at considerable expense.

Another example may be a strip-mining project, which normally requires a final investment to reclaim the land and satisfy the requirements of environmental legislation.

Consider now the following investment:

Year	0	1	2
Cash flow	3.2	−7.1	4.0

There is no internal rate of return that makes NPV zero! At 10%, the NPV of this investment is 0.05 and it is worth buying.

A project like this has no IRR. Thus, we have no benchmark for deciding if it is a good investment or not. Although the NPV remains positive for all the discount rates, it remains only *slightly* positive and the company may decide not to do it.

3/ INVESTING OR FINANCING?

Consider two projects with the following flows:

Project	F_0	F_1	IRR	NPV (15%)
A	−100	120	20%	€4.35
B	100	−120	20%	−€4.35

The flows are exactly the same but with opposite signs. The IRR of the two projects is the same (20%) but the NPV is positive for project A and negative for project B (both with a discount rate of 15%). According to the IRR rule, projects A and B have the same value; on the other hand, the NPV says that project A is preferable to project B.

Although an investment project with the cash flows of B may seem quite unusual, there are some situations where it is possible. For example, consider a business school conducting seminars and courses whereby the participants pay in advance. Large expenses (travelling expenses of external teachers, materials and salaries of teachers, etc.) are incurred at the seminar date or later on: thus, cash inflows precede cash outflows.

Consider our trial-and-error method to calculate the IRR of project B:

F_0	F_1	k	NPV
100	−120	15%	−€4.35
100	−120	20%	€0.00
100	−120	30%	€7.69

The reader will surely have noticed that the net present value of project B is *negative* when the discount rate is below 20%. Conversely, the NPV is positive when the discount rate is above 20%.

The decision rule for this kind of project is exactly the opposite to the "traditional" IRR rule. In fact, you should **accept the project when IRR is less than the discount rate and reject the project when IRR is greater than the discount rate**.

Why has the rule ended up being inverted like this? The reason is clearly shown in the graph of the NPV profile of project B. The curve is upward sloping (similar to a loan), implying that NPV is *positively related* to the discount rate.

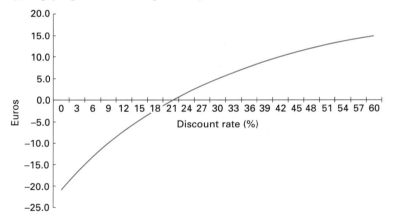

Intuitively, the "inverted IRR" rule makes sense. If the firm wants to obtain €100 immediately, it can either invest in project B or *borrow €100* from a bank, which will have to be repaid in the following period with an interest rate of 20%. Thus, the project is actually a substitute for borrowing.

When we compare two projects like A and B we need to adopt two different decision rules, which is clearly unacceptable.

4/CHANGING DISCOUNT RATES

It is common to discount cash flows at a constant rate throughout a project's life. However, this may not be appropriate under certain circumstances. In fact, the required rate of return is a function of interest rates and of the uncertainty of cash flows, both of which can change substantially over time.

The necessity of using different discount rates can be easily overcome with the NPV criteria, whereby different discount rates can be set for each period. Conversely, the IRR method can only be compared with a single rate of return and cannot cope with changing discount rates.

5/PROBLEMS SPECIFIC TO MUTUALLY EXCLUSIVE PROJECTS

Further problems may arise when a choice must be made among several investments (or securities), as is often the case in reality. Investments have different cash flow timetables that are all equally attractive. In this case, the investment decision is not about whether to invest or not, but rather it is about *which* investment to make. This situation refers to **mutually exclusive investments.** This occurs when there are two projects, *A* and *B*, and you can either accept *A*, accept *B*, or reject both projects, *but it is impossible to accept both of them simultaneously.*

Why would a company decide to abandon one or more viable projects? Typically, the dilemma arises from **capital rationing**. Capital rationing may arise for two reasons:

- Because a firm cannot obtain funds at market rates of return (**hard rationing**). Hard rationing implies market imperfections, transaction costs and agency costs arising from the separation of ownership and management.
- Or because of internally imposed financial constraints by management (**soft rationing**). Soft rationing may arise when:
  - there are maximum limits on borrowing and shareholders are reluctant to inject additional equity;
  - the management intends to pursue a steady growth strategy, avoiding exceptional growth rates; and
  - there are divisional ceilings imposed through annual capital budgets.

Mutually exclusive projects may give rise to two problems: the **scale problem** and the **timing problem**, both of which will be examined next.

To understand the **scale problem**, consider two projects of different dimensions, one of which can be defined as a small-scale project, and the other as a large-scale project:

Project	F_0	F_1	IRR	NPV (10%)
Small-scale	−10	15	50%	€3.64
Large-scale	−100	120	20%	€9.09

The point of this example is that when considering two mutually exclusive investments, the financial manager typically concludes that the one offering the highest IRR is necessarily the one that should be chosen. If in this case we had to choose only one project, and we rank them based on their IRRs, we would choose to invest in the small-scale project. However, the large-scale project generates a much higher NPV; this project thus creates more wealth for shareholders. The NPV would tell us to undertake the large-scale project.

Why is there this conflict? The large-scale project is ten times bigger than the small-scale project. Even though the latter provides a higher rate of return, the opportunity of making a much larger investment seems more attractive for shareholders.

For managers who continue to prefer to use the IRR method, there is a solution to the scale problem. The approach is to calculate the IRR for an imaginary project with cash flows equal to the difference in cash flows between the large-scale and small-scale investments. This difference is defined as the *incremental project*.

The financial manager can use the incremental project's cash flows to determine the **incremental IRR** – i.e., the incremental return from choosing the large project instead of the small project:

	F_0	F_1	**Incremental IRR**	NPV (10%)
Incremental (large- to small-scale)	−90	105	17%	€5.45

If, as in this example, the incremental project's IRR is higher than the required rate of return, then the large-scale investment is definitely the best choice. If the inverse is true, then we should accept the small-scale project.

The logic of this approach works because both projects exceed the required rate of return. Therefore, this method is like equating the bigger scale project to be the sum of the small-scale project and the incremental project. Then it is possible to examine the incremental project's cash IRR, and, if it also exceeds the required rate of return, we can accept the bigger project. If not, then we should prefer the small-scale project.

Why is this? If we accept the large-scale investment we are in fact making two investments, not just one. We are accepting one project with cash flows identical to those of the small-scale project and another with cash flows equal to those of the incremental project. Since both projects (small-scale and incremental) exceed the required rate of return, we may conclude that we are happy to undertake the incremental project *and* the small-scale project. The only way to do both is to accept the large-scale project.

The same decision obtained by comparing the incremental IRR with the required rate of return could also be obtained by:

- simply comparing the NPV of the two projects. The large-scale project has a higher NPV and is the preferred project according to the NPV rule; and
- estimating the incremental NPV. If it is positive, then the large-scale project is preferable. Vice versa, the smaller project is more attractive if the incremental NPV is negative.

In order to understand the **timing problem**, consider two projects with the same initial amount (ergo, no problem of scale). Project A is a marketing campaign that could push the sales of existing products. The cash inflows are immediate but disappear progressively. This can be defined as the "short-sighted" project. Project B is a new product development with big, positive cash inflows expected at the end of the development process. This will be defined as the "far-sighted" project:

	0	1	2	3	IRR (%)
Project A (marketing campaign)	−10,000	8,000	3,000	1,000	14
Project B (new product development)	−10,000	0	2,000	11,500	11

According to the IRR method, project *A* is more attractive because it has a higher IRR (14% vs. 11%). The NPV profile of the two alternatives is:

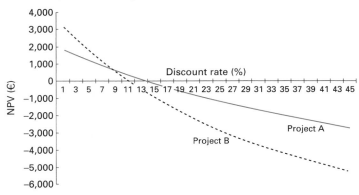

In the graph above, it can be seen that the NPV of project *B* is higher if the discount rate is low – say, below 8%. When the discount rate is low, *B* has the higher NPV; when the discount rate is high, *A* has the higher NPV. If the discount rate is above 8% then the NPV of project *A* exceeds that of project *B*. The NPV of project *B* declines more rapidly than the NPV of project *A*. This occurs because the cash flows of *B* occur later.

In order to determine which project is more attractive, a comparison should be made between the NPVs of the two projects. The decision will then be a function of the discount rate.[2]

A naive reliance on the IRR method can lead to decisions that favour investments with short-term payoffs. Perhaps this is one of the reasons behind the frequent criticism regarding managers of public corporations and their supposed "short-termism".

Section 17.4

SOME MORE FINANCIAL MATHEMATICS: INTEREST RATE AND YIELD TO MATURITY

2 *Alternatively, we could subtract the cash flows of A from the cash flows of B, and then calculate the incremental IRR: if the discount rate is lower than the incremental IRR we should accept project B.*

1/NOMINAL RATE OF RETURN AND YIELD TO MATURITY

Having considered the yield to maturity, it is now important to examine interest rates; for example, on a loan that you wish to take out. Where does the interest rate fit in this discussion?

Consider someone who wants to lend you €1,000 today at 10% for 5 years. 10% means 10% **per year** and constitutes the **nominal rate of return** of your loan. This rate will be the basis for calculating interest, proportional to the time elapsed and the amount borrowed. Assume that you will pay interest annually.

The first problem is how and when will you pay off the loan?

Repayment terms constitute the method of amortisation of the loan. Take the following example:

(a) Bullet repayment

The entire loan is paid back at maturity.

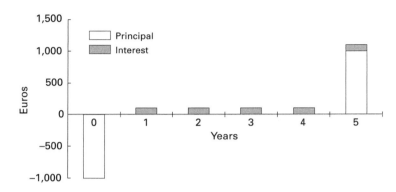

The cash flow table would look like this:

Period	Principal still due	Interest	Amortisation of principal	Annuity
1	1,000	100	0	100
2	1,000	100	0	100
3	1,000	100	0	100
4	1,000	100	0	100
5	1,000	100	1,000	1,100

Total debt service is the annual sum of interest and principal to be paid back. This is also called debt servicing at each due date.

(b) Constant amortisation

Each year, the borrower pays off a constant proportion of the principal, corresponding to $1/n$, where n is the initial maturity of the loan.

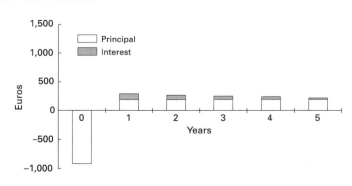

The cash flow table would look like this:

Period	Principal still due	Interest	Amortisation of principal	Annuity
1	1,000	100	200	300
2	800	80	200	280
3	600	60	200	260
4	400	40	200	240
5	200	20	200	220

(c) Equal instalments

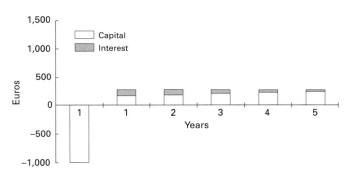

The borrower may wish to pay off his loan by constant annuities – i.e., allocate a constant sum to interest and amortisation payments.

In the above cases, the borrower paid off either a constant sum in interest or a declining sum in interest. The principal was paid off in equal instalments.

Based on the discounting method described previously, consider a constant annuity A, such that the sum of the five discounted annuities is equal to the present value of the principal, or €1,000:

$$1,000 = \frac{A}{1.10} + \frac{A}{(1.10)^2} + \cdots + \frac{A}{(1.10)^5}$$

This means that **the NPV of the 10% loan is nil; in other words, the 10% nominal rate of interest is also the internal rate of return of the loan.**

Using the formula from Chapter 16, the previous formula can be expressed as follows:

$$1,000 = \frac{A}{0.10} \times \left(1 - \frac{1}{(1.10)^5}\right)$$

$A = $€263.80. Hence, the following repayment schedule:

Period	Principal still due	Interest	Amortisation of principal	Annuity
1	1,000	100	163.80	263.80
2	836.20	83.62	180.18	263.80
3	656.02	65.60	198.20	263.80
4	457.82	45.78	218.02	263.80
5	239.80	23.98	239.80	263.80

In this case, the interest for each period is indeed equivalent to 10% of the remaining principal (i.e., the nominal rate of return), and the loan is fully paid off in the 5th year. Internal rate of return and nominal rate of interest are identical, as calculation is on an annual basis and the repayment of principal coincides with the payment of interest.

Regardless of which side of the loan you are on, both work the same way. We start with invested (or borrowed) capital, which produces income (or incurs interest costs) at the end of each period. Eventually, the loan is then either paid back (leading to a decline in future revenues or in interest to be paid) or held onto, thus producing a constant flow of income (or a constant cost of interest).

(d) Interest and principal both paid when the loan matures

In this case, the borrower pays nothing until the loan matures.

The sum that he will have to pay at maturity is none other than the future value of the sum borrowed, capitalised at the interest rate of the loan.

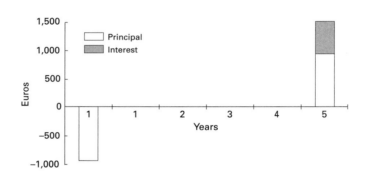

$$V = 1,000 \times (1 + 10\%)^5 \quad \text{or} \quad V = 1,610.5$$

This is how the repayment schedule would look:

Period	Principal and interest still due	Amortisation of principal	Interest payments	Annuity
1	1,100	0	0	0
2	1,210	0	0	0
3	1,331	0	0	0
4	1,464.1	0	0	0
5	1,610.51	1,000	610.51	1,610.51

This is a zero-coupon loan.

2/EFFECTIVE ANNUAL RATE, NOMINAL RATES AND PROPORTIONAL RATES

This section will demonstrate that discounting has a much wider scope than might have appeared in the simple financial mathematics presented previously.

(a) The concept of effective annual rate

What happens when interest is paid not once per year, but several times per year?

Suppose that somebody lends you money at 10% but says (somewhere in the fineprint at the bottom of the page) that interest will have to be paid on a half-yearly basis. For example, suppose you borrowed €100 on 1 January and then had to pay €5 in interest on 1 July and €5 on 1 January of the following year, as well as the €100 in principal at the same date.

This is not the same as borrowing €100 and repaying €110 one year later. The nominal amount of interest may be the same ($5 + 5 = 10$), but the repayment schedule is not. In the first case, you will have to pay €5 on 1 July (just before leaving on summer holidays), which in the second case you could have kept until the following 1 January. In the first case you pay €5 instead of investing it for 6 months, as you could have done in the second example.

As a result, the loan in the first case costs more than a loan at 10% with interest due annually. Its effective rate is not 10%, since interest is not being paid on the benchmark annual terms.

To avoid comparing apples and oranges, a financial officer must take into account the effective date of disbursement. We know that €1 today is not the same as €1 tomorrow. Obviously, the financial officer wants to postpone expenditure and accelerate receipts, thereby having the money work for him. So, naturally, the repayment schedule matters when calculating the rate.

Which is the best approach to take? If the interest rate is 10%, with interest payable every 6 months, then the interest rate is 5% **for 6 months**. We then have to calculate **an effective annual rate** (and not for 6 months), which is our point of reference and our constant concern.

In our example, the lender receives €5 on 1 July, which, compounded over 6 months, becomes $5 + (10\% \times 5)/2 = €5.25$ on the following 1 January, the date on which he receives the second €5 interest payment. So, over 1 year he will have received €10.25 in interest on a €100 investment.

So the effective annual rate is 10.25%. This is the real cost of the loan, since the return for the lender is equal to the cost for the borrower.

If the nominal rate (r_a) is to be paid n times per year, then the effective annual rate (t) is obtained by compounding this nominal rate n times:

$$(1 + t) = (1 + r_a/n)^n$$

where n is the number of interest payments in the year and r_a/n the proportional rate during one period, or $t = (1 + r_a/n)^n - 1$.

In our example:

$$t = (1 + 10\%/2)^2 - 1 = 10.25\%$$

Formula for converting nominal rate into effective annual rate.

The effective interest rate is thus 10.25%, while the nominal rate is 10%.

It should be common sense that an investment at 10% paying interest every 6 months produces a higher return at year-end than an investment paying interest annually. In the first case, interest is compounded after 6 months and thus produces interest on interest for the next 6 months. So, obviously, a loan on which interest is due every 6 months will cost more than one on which interest is charged annually.

It is essential to first calculate the effective annual rate before comparing investments (or loans) with different cash flow streams. The effective annual rate measures returns on the common basis of a year, thus making meaningful comparisons possible. This is not possible with nominal rates.

The table below gives the returns produced by an investment (a loan) at 10% at varying instalments:

Interest-compounding period	Initial sum	Sum after 1 year	Effective annual rate (%)
Annual	100	110,000	10,000
Half-year	100	110,250	10,250
Quarterly	100	110,381	10,381
Monthly	100	110,471	10,471
Bimonthly	100	110,494	10,494
Weekly	100	110,506	10,506
Daily	100	110,516	10,516
Continuous[3]	100	110,517	10,517

3 *The formula for continuously compounded interest is:* $t = e^k - 1.$

Effective annual rate can be calculated on any time scale. For example, a financial officer might wish to use continuous rates. This might mean, for example, a 10% rate producing €100, paid out evenly throughout the year on principal of €1,000. The financial officer will use the annual equivalent rate as his reference rate for this investment.

(b) The concept of proportional rate

In our example of a loan at 10%, we would say that the 5% rate over 6 months is **proportional** to the 10% rate over 1 year. More generally, two rates are proportional if they are in the same proportion to each other as the periods to which they apply.

10% per year is proportional to 5% per half-year or 2.5% per quarter, but 5% half-yearly is not equivalent to 10% annually. **Effective annual rate and proportional rates are therefore two completely different concepts that should not be confused.**

Proportional rates are of interest only in calculating the interest actually paid. In no way can they be evaluated with other proportional rates, as they are not comparable.

Proportional rates serve only to simplify calculations, but they hide the true cost of a loan. Only the effective annual rate (10.25%/year) gives the true cost, unlike the proportional rate (10%/year).

When the timespan between two interests payment dates is less than 1 year, the proportional rate is lower than the effective annual rate (10% is less than 10.25%).

To avoid error, use the effective annual rate.

As we will see, the bond markets can be misleading since they reason in terms of nominal rate of return: paper is sold above or below par value, the number of days used in calculating interest can vary, there could be original issue discounts and so on. And, most importantly, on the secondary market a bond's present value depends on fluctuations in market interest rates.

In the rest of this book, unless otherwise specified, an interest rate or rate of return is assumed to be an effective annual rate.

SUMMARY

download

In this section we learned about the theoretical foundations of interest rates, which force financial managers to discount cash flows; i.e., to depreciate the flows in order to factor in the passage of time.

This led us to a definition of present value, the basic tool for valuing a financial investment, which must be compared with its market value. The difference between present value and the market value of an investment is net present value.

In a market in equilibrium the net present value of a financial investment is nil because it is equal to its present value.

As the value of an investment and the discount rate are fundamentally linked, we also looked at the concept of yield to maturity (which cancels out NPV). Making an investment is only worth it when the yield to maturity is equal to or greater than the investor's required return. At fair value, internal rate of return is identical to the required return rate. In other words, net present value is nil.

Internal rate of return should be handled with care, as it is based on the implicit assumption that cash flows will be reinvested at the same rate. It should only be relied on for an investment decision concerning a single asset and not for choosing from among several assets, whether they are financial (e.g., an investment) or industrial (e.g., a mine, a machine, etc.). NPV should be used for such decisions.

Finally, some financial mathematics helped us look at the link between the nominal interest rate and the yield to maturity of an operation. The nominal (annual) rate of a loan is the rate used to calculate interest in proportion to the period of the loan and the capital borrowed. However, one must use the yield to maturity, which may differ from the apparent nominal rate, when interest is not paid on an annual basis.

QUESTIONS

quiz

1/ Why can the internal rate of return not be used for choosing between two investments?

2/ Does the interest rate depend on the terms of repayment of a loan or an investment?

3/ Does the interest rate depend on when cash flows occur?

4/ What are proportional rates?

5/ What is internal rate of return?

6/ What are proportional rates used for? And internal rate of return?

7/ On the same loan, is the total amount of interest payable more if the loan is repaid in fixed annual instalments, by constant amortisation or on maturity?

8/ If you believe that interest rates are going to rise, would you be better off choosing loans that are repayable on maturity or in fixed annual instalments?

9/ If the purchase price of an investment is positive and all subsequent cash flows are positive, show how there can only be a single yield to maturity.

10/ Is it better to make a small percentage on a very large amount or a large percentage on a small amount? Does this bring to mind one of the rules explained in this chapter?

11/ A very high yield to maturity over a very short period is preferable to a yield to maturity that is 2% higher than the required rate of return over 10 years. True or false?

EXERCISES

1/ What interest rate on an investment would turn 120 into 172.8 over 2 years? What is the yield to maturity? What is the proportional rate over 3 months?

2/ What is the terminal value on an initial investment of 100, if the investor is seeking a 14% yield to maturity after 7 years?

3/ For how many years will 100 have to be invested to get 174.9 and a yield to maturity of 15%?

4/ You invest €1,000 today at 6% with interest paid on a half-yearly basis for 4 years. What is the yield to maturity of this investment? How much will you have at the end of the 4-year period?

5/ Investment A can be bought for 4 and will earn 1 per year over 6 years. What is the yield to maturity? Investment B costs 6 and earns 2 over 2 years, then 1.5 over 3 years. What is the yield to maturity? Which investment would you rather have? Why? Do you need to know what the minimum rate of return is in order to make a decision?

6/ A company treasurer invests 100 for 18 months. The first bank he approaches offers to reinvest the funds at 0.8% per quarter, and the second bank at 1.6% per half-year. Without actually doing the calculation, show how the first bank's offer would be the best option. What are the two yields to maturity?

7/ A company treasurer invests €10,000,000 on the monetary market for 24 days. He gets back €10,019,745. What is the rate of return over 24 days? What is the yield to maturity?

8/ Draw up a repayment schedule for a loan of 100, with a yield to maturity of 7% over 4 years, showing repayment in fixed annual instalments and constant amortisation.

9/ Draw up a repayment schedule for a loan of 400, with a yield to maturity of 6.5% over 7 years with repayment deferred for 2 years, showing repayment in fixed annual instalments and constant amortisation.

10/ A bond issued at 98% of the nominal value is repaid at maturity at 108% after 10 years. Annual interest paid to subscribers is 7% of the nominal value. What is the yield to maturity of this bond? And what if it had been issued at 101%? So, what is the rule?

11/ What is the discounted cost for the issuer of the bond described in question 10 if we factor in a 0.35% placement commission, an annual management fee of 2.5% of the coupon, a closing fee of 0.6% of the amount paid and an issue price of 98%.

12/ You sell your flat valued at €300,000 for a down payment of €100,000 and 20 monthly payments of €11,000. What is the monthly interest rate for this transaction? What is the yield to maturity?

13/ Calculate the yield to maturity of the following investment, which can be purchased today for 1,000:

Year	1	2	3	4	5
Cash flow	232	2,088	232	−232	−927

Questions

ANSWERS

1/ *Because it does not measure the value created.*
2/ *No.*
3/ *Yes.*
4/ *Rates that have a proportional relationship with the periods to which they relate.*
5/ *Rates that apply to different periods, but which transform the same sum in an identical manner over the same period.*
6/ *For calculating the interest that is paid out/earned. For calculating the yield to maturity.*
7/ *On maturity, because the principal is lent in full over the whole period.*
8/ *On maturity, so that you can take advantage for as long as possible of a low interest rate on the maximum amount of principal oustanding.*
9/ *At a discount rate equal to the yield to maturity, the present value of future cash flows is equal to the purchase price of the investment. If the discount rate increases, present value will drop and will never again be equal to the market price of the investment. If the discount rate decreases, present value will rise and will never again be equal to the market price of the investment. Accordingly, there is only a single yield to maturity.*
10/ *A small percentage on a very large amount. NPV is preferable to yield to maturity.*
11/ *False, because an investment with an acceptable yield to maturity over a long period creates more value than an investment with a very high yield to maturity but which is of little significance given the short period of the Investment.*

Exercises

1/ *44% over 2 years. 20%. 5% over 3 months.*
2/ *250.*
3/ *4 years.*
4/ *6.09%, €1,266.8.*

5/ *13%, 13.8%, a choice between these two securities cannot be based on yield to maturity. Only NPV can be relied on. Yes, you have to know what the required rate of return is.*

6/ *As the rates are proportional (0.8% over 3 months and 1.6% over 6 months), the first offer is better, since interest is capitalised after 3 months and not 6. 3.24% and 3.23%.*

7/ *0.1975% over 24 months, 3.05%.*

8/ *Fixed annual instalments of 29.53, constant amortisation of 25/year and interest of 7, 5.25, 5 and 1.75.*

9/ *Fixed annual instalments of 109.2, constant amortisation of 90.74/year and interest of 29.5, 23.6, 17.7, 11.8 and 5.9.*

10/ *7.85% (don't forget interest for year 10), 7.42%, value and rates vary in opposite directions.*

11/ *8.12%.*

12/ *0.925%; 11.7%.*

13/ *There are 2: 15.1% and 48.3%.*

BIBLIOGRAPHY

If you wish to learn more about internal rate of return and financial mathematics, you can consult:

T. Copeland, F. Weston, *Financial Theory and Corporate Policy*, Addison Wesley, 1987.

E. Pilotte, Evaluating mutually exclusive projects of unequal lives and differing risks, *Financial Practice and Education*, **10**(2), 69–77, Fall/Winter 2000.

S. Ross, R. Westerfield, J. Jaffe, *Corporate Finance*, McGraw-Hill, 2002.

S. Smart, W. Megginson, L. Gitman, *Corporate Finance*, Thomson South Western 2004.

On capital rationing:

R. Brealey, S. Myers, *Principles of Corporate Finance*, 6th edn, McGraw-Hill, 2002.

T. Mukherjee, H. Kent Baker, R. D'Mello, Capital rationing decisions of 'Fortune 500' firms: Part II, *Financial Practice and Education*, **10**(2), 69–77, Fall/Winter 2000.

H.M. Weingartner, Capital rationing: Authors in search of a plot, *Journal of Finance*, **32**, 1403–1432, December 1977.

Chapter 18
INCREMENTAL CASH FLOWS AND OTHER INVESTMENT CRITERIA

Back to flows and financial analysis

The "mathematics" we studied in Chapter 16, dealing with present value and internal rate of return, can also be applied to investment decisions and financial securities. When dealing with financial securities, we calculate the yield to maturity. The same approach holds for analysing industrial investments, whereby we calculate a rate that takes the present value to zero. This is called the Internal Rate of Return (IRR). Internal rate of return and yield to maturity are thus the same.

Net Present Value (NPV) measures the value created by the investment and is the best criteria for selecting or rejecting an investment, be it industrial or financial. When it is simply a matter of deciding whether or not to make an investment, NPV and IRR produce the same outcome. However, if the choice is between two mutually exclusive investments, net present value is more reliable than the internal rate of return.

This chapter will discuss:

* the cash flows to be factored into investment decisions, which are called **incremental cash flows**; and
* **other investment criteria** that are less relevant than NPV and IRR and have proven disappointing in the past. As future financial managers, you should nevertheless be aware of them, even if they are more pertinent to accounting than financial management.

Section 18.1
THE PREDOMINANCE OF NPV AND THE IMPORTANCE OF IRR

Each investment has a Net Present Value (NPV), which is equal to the amount of value created. Remember that the net present value of an investment is the value of the positive and negative cash flows arising from an investment, discounted at the rate of return required by the market. The rate of return is based upon the investment's risk.

From a financial standpoint and if forecasts are correct, an investment with positive NPV is worth making since it will create value. Conversely, an investment with negative NPV should be avoided as it is expected to destroy value. Sometimes investments with negative NPV are made for strategic reasons, such as to protect a position in the industry sector or to open up new markets with strong, yet hard to quantify, growth potential. It must be kept in mind that if the NPV is really negative, it will certainly lead to the destruction of value. Sooner or later, projects with negative NPV have to be offset by other investments with positive NPV that create value. Without doing so, the company will be headed for ruin.

The Internal Rate of Return (IRR) is simply the rate of return on an investment. Given an investment's degree of risk, the investment is financially worthwhile if the IRR is higher than the required return. However, if the IRR is lower than the risk-based required rate of return, the investment will serve no financial purpose.

Graham and Harvey (2001) conducted a broad survey of corporate and financial managers to determine which tools and criteria they use when making financial decisions. They asked them to indicate how frequently they used several capital budgeting methods by ranking them on a scale ranging from 0 (never) to 4 (always). The findings showed that net present value and internal rate of return carry the greatest weight, and justifiably so. Some 75% of financial managers systematically value investments according to these two criteria.

Interestingly, large firms apply these criteria more often than small- and medium-sized companies and MBA graduates use them systematically, while older managers tend to rely on the payback ratio.

A 25-year-old study by Gitman and Forrester (1977) found that only 9.8% of large firms used NPV as their primary capital budgeting tool. By comparing those results with the more up-to-date work of Graham and Harvey, it is apparent that the popularity of the NPV method has grown significantly over time.

The third most frequently used decision criterion is the payback method, which is particularly popular among small firms. This and other criteria will be discussed later on in Section 18.4.

Bruner et al. (1998) surveyed 27 significant corporations and 10 financial advisers. 89% of corporations and 100% of advisors confirmed that they always use NPV as a primary tool in evaluating investment opportunities.

Dallocchio and Salvi (2000) conducted a survey of 56 CFOs and treasurers of multinational companies. When asked about the criteria they choose for valuing the M&A transactions of their company, 75% of respondents ranked NPV and IRR as the most popular approaches. These were followed by the payback method (20%) and economic value added (5%).

The strong popularity of NPV is widespread globally, as shown by other studies. Hall (2000) and Lumby (1991) have illustrated the diffusion of the NPV technique in South Africa and the United Kingdom, respectively.

Section 18.2
THE MAIN LINES OF REASONING

Any well-advised investment decision must respect the following six principles that:

1 consider cash flows rather than accounting data;
2 reason in terms of incremental cash flows, considering only those associated with the project;
3 reason in terms of opportunity;
4 disregard the type of financing;
5 consider taxation;

and is, above all, **consistent**.

1/CONSIDER CASH FLOWS

We have already seen that the return on an investment is assessed in terms of the resulting cash flows. One must therefore analyse the negative and positive cash flows, and not the accounting income and expenses. These accounting measures are irrelevant because they do not take into account working capital generated by the investment and include depreciation which is a noncash item.

As a result, only cash flows are relevant in the financial analysis of investments.

2/REASON IN TERMS OF INCREMENTAL FLOWS

When considering an investment, one must take into account all the flows it generates, and nothing else but these flows. It is crucial to assess all the consequences of an investment upon a company's cash position. Some of these are self-evident and easy to measure, and others are less so.

A theatre group plans to launch a new complex and substantial costs have already been incurred in its design. Should these be included in the investment programme's cash flows? The answer is no, since the costs have already been incurred regardless of whether or not the complex is actually built. Therefore, they should not be considered part of the investment expenditure.

It would be absurd to carry out an investment simply because the preparations were costly and one hopes to recoup funds that, in any case, have already been spent. The only valid reason for pursuing an investment is that it is likely to create value.

Now, if the personnel department has to administer an additional 20 employees hired for the new complex (e.g., 5% of its total workforce), should 5% of the department's costs be allocated to the new project? Again, the answer is no. With or without the new complex, the personnel department is part of overhead costs. Its operating expenses would only be affected if the planned investment generates additional costs – for example, recruitment expenses.

However, design and overheads will be priced into the ticket charged for entry to the new complex.

A perfume company is about to launch a new product line that may cut sales of its older perfumes by half. Should this decline be factored into the calculation of the investment's return? Yes, because the new product line will prompt a shift in consumer behaviour: the decline in cash flow from the older perfume stems directly from the introduction of this new product.

When estimating cash flows on an incremental basis, one only considers the future cash flows arising from the investment. Our objective is to calculate the investment's marginal contribution to the company's profitability.

3/REASON IN TERMS OF OPPORTUNITY

For financial managers, an asset's value is its market value, which is the price at which it can be bought (investment decision) or sold (divestment decision). From this standpoint, its book or historic value is of no interest whatsoever, except for tax purposes (taxes payable on book capital gains, tax credit on capital losses, etc.).

The opportunity principle boils down to some very simple rules:

- if a company decides to hold on to a business, this implies that it should be prepared to buy that business (it did not already own it) in identical operating circumstances; and
- if a company decides to hold on to a financial security that is trading at a given price, this security is identical to one that it should be prepared to buy (if it did not already own it) at the same price.

Financial managers are in effect "asset dealers". They must introduce this approach within their company, even if it means standing up to other managers who view their respective business operations as essential and viable. Only by systematically confronting these two viewpoints can a company balance its decision-making and management processes.

For example, if a project is carried out on company land that was previously unused, the land's after-tax resale value must be considered when valuing the investment. After all, in principle, the company can choose between selling the land and booking the after-tax sales price, or using the land for the new project. Note that the book value of the land does not enter into this line of reasoning.

Theoretically, a financial manager does not view any activity as essential, regardless of whether it is one of the company's core businesses or a potential new venture. The CFO must constantly be prepared to question each activity and reason in terms of:

- buying and selling assets; and
- entering or withdrawing from an economic sector of activity.

If we push our reasoning to the extreme, one could say that for financial managers an investment is never a necessity, but simply a "good or bad" opportunity.

4/Disregard the type of financing

When comparing an investment's return with its cost of financing (what we will call weighted average cost of capital in Chapter 23), the two items must be considered separately.

In practice, since the discount rate is the cost of financing the investment (weighted average cost of capital), interest expense, repayments or dividends should not be included in the flows. **Only operating and investment flows are taken into account, but never financing flows. This is the same distinction that was made in Chapter 2.** Failure to do so would skew the project's net present value. This would also overstate its IRR, since the impact of financing would be included twice:

- first, within the weighted average cost of capital for this investment which is its cost of financing; and
- second, at the cash flow level.

Consider, for example, an investment with the following flows:

Year	0	1	2	3
Investment flows	−100	15	15	115

The NPV of this investment is 7.2 (if cash flows are discounted at 12%) and its IRR is 15%. Now, assume that 20% of the investment was financed by debt at an annual after-tax cost of 6%. Then it is possible to deduct the debt flows from the investment flows and calculate its NPV and IRR:

Year	0	1	2	3
Investment flows	−100	15.0	15.0	115.0
Debt-financing flows	20	−1.2	−1.2	−21.2
Net flows	−80	13.8	13.8	93.8

With a rate of 12%, the NPV is 10.1 and IRR is 17.2%. Now, if 50% of the investment were financed by debt, NPV would rise to 14.4 and the IRR to 24%. At 80% debt-financing, NPV works out to 18.7 and the IRR 51%.

This demonstrates that by taking on various degrees of debt, it is possible to manipulate NPV and IRR This is the same as using the financial leverage that was discussed in Chapter 12. However, this is a slippery slope. It can lead unwary companies to invest in projects whose low industrial profitability is offset by high debt, which in fact increases the risk considerably.

As common sense tells us, when debt increases so does the required return on equity as the risk increases for shareholders. It is not correct to continue valuing NPV at a constant discount rate of 12%. The discount rate has to be raised in conjunction with the level of debt. This corrects our reasoning and NPV remains constant. The IRR is now higher, but the minimum required return has risen aswell to reflect the greater degree of risk of an investment financed by borrowings.

It would be absurd to believe that one can undertake an investment because it generates an IRR of 10% whereas the corresponding debt can be financed at a rate of 7%. In fact, the debt is only available because the company has equity that acts as collateral for creditors. Equity has to be remunerated, and this is not reflected in the 7% interest on the debt. No company can be fully financed by debt, and it is therefore impossible to establish a direct comparison between the cost of debt and the project's return.

5/CONSIDER TAXATION

Clearly, taxation is an issue because corporate executives endeavour to maximise their after-tax flows. Consider that:

- additional depreciation generates tax savings that must be factored into the equation;
- the cash flows generated by the investment give rise to taxes, which must be included as well; and
- certain tax shields offer tax credits, rebates, subsidies, allowances and other advantages for carrying out investment projects.

In practice, it is better to value a project using after-tax cash flows and an after-tax discount rate in order to factor in the various tax benefits from an investment. Therefore, the return required by investors and creditors is calculated after tax.

In cases where cash flows are discounted before tax, it is important to ascertain that all flows and components of weighted average cost of capital are considered before taxes as well.

When considering an investment, it is also necessary to look at the tax implications.

6/BE CONSISTENT!

Finally, the best advice is to always be consistent.

- If the base of valuation is on constant euro values – that is, excluding inflation – be sure that the discount rate excludes inflation as well. We recommend using current euro values, because the discount rate already includes the market's inflation expectations.
- If it is a pre-tax valuation, make sure the discount rate reflects the pre-tax required rate of return. We recommend using after-tax valuations because a world without taxes only exists in textbooks!
- And if flows are denominated in a given currency, the discount rate must correspond to the interest rates in that currency as well.

Section 18.3
WHICH CASH FLOWS ARE IMPORTANT?

In practice, three types of cash flow must be considered when assessing an investment: **operating flows, investment flows and extraordinary flows**. Financial managers try to plan both the amount of a cash flow and its timing. In other words, they draw up projections of the cash flows on the investment.

Where the investment has a limited life, it is possible to anticipate its cash flows over the entire period. But, in general, the duration of an investment is not predetermined, and one assumes that at some point in the future it will be either wound up or sold. This means that the financial manager has to forecast all cash flows over a given period with an explicit forecast period, and reason in terms of *residual (or salvage) value* beyond that horizon. Although the discounted residual value is frequently very low since it is very far off in time, it should not be neglected. Its book value is generally zero, but its economic value may be quite significant since accounting depreciation may differ from economic depreciation. The residual value reflects the flows extending beyond the explicit investment horizon, and on into infinity. If some of the assets may be sold off, one must also factor in any taxes on capital gains.

1/OPERATING FLOWS

The investment's contribution to total Earnings Before Interest, Taxes, Depreciation and Amortisation (EBITDA) must be calculated. It represents the difference between the additional income and expenses arising from the investment, excluding depreciation and amortisation.

Then, from EBITDA the **theoretical tax** on the additional operating profit must be deducted. The actual tax is then calculated by multiplying the effective tax rate with the differential on the operating profit, taking into account any tax loss carryforwards.[1]

In other words:[1]

$$\text{Operating flows} = EBITDA - EBIT \times T_C$$

where T_C is the corporate tax rate.

2/INVESTMENT FLOWS

As in Chapter 21, the definition of investment is quite inclusive, ranging from investments in working capital to investments in fixed assets.

It is essential to deduct changes in working capital from EBITDA. Unfortunately, some people tend to forget this. In most cases, working capital is just a matter of a timelag. It builds up gradually, grows with the company and is retrieved when the business is discontinued. A euro capitalised today in working capital can be retrieved in 10 years' time, but it will not be worth the same. Money invested in working capital is not lost. It is simply capitalised until the investment is

1 *The same result can be obtained with the following formula:*

Operating flows
$= EBIT$
$\times (1 - T_C) +$
Depreciation and amortisation

discontinued. However, this capitalisation carries a cost, which is reflected in the discounted amount.

Investment in fixed assets includes investment in production capacity and growth, whether in the form of tangible assets (machinery, land, buildings, etc.) or intangible assets (research and development, patents and licenses, etc.) or financial assets (shares in subsidiaries) for external growth.

The calculation must be made for each period, as the investment is not necessarily restricted to just 1 year, nor spread evenly over the period. Once again, remember that our approach is based on cash and not accounting data. The investment flows must be recognised when they are paid, not when the decisions to make them were incurred. And, finally, do not forget to reason in terms of net investment – that is, after any disposals, investment subsidies and other tax credits.

3/ EXTRAORDINARY FLOWS

It may seem surprising to mention extraordinary items when projecting estimated cash flows. However, financial managers frequently know in advance that certain expenses that have not been booked under EBITDA (litigation, tax audits, etc.) will be disbursed in the near future. These expenses must all be included on an after-tax basis in the calculation of estimated free cash flow.

Extraordinary flows can usually be anticipated at the beginning of the period since they reflect known items. Beyond a 2-year horizon, it is generally assumed that they will be zero.

This gives us the following cash flow table:

Periods		0	1	. . .	n
Incremental EBITDA		+	+	+	
−	Incremental tax on operating profit		−	−	−
−	Change in incremental working capital R		− −	−	+ +
−	Investments	− − −	−	−	
+	Divestments after tax	+	+	+	+ +
−	Extraordinary expenses		−		
=	Cash flow to be discounted	− −	+	+	+ +

Section 18.4
OTHER INVESTMENT CRITERIA

1/ THE PAYBACK PERIOD

The payback period is the time necessary to recover the initial outlay on an investment.

Where annual cash flows are identical, the payback period is equal to:

$$\frac{\text{Investment}}{\text{Annual cash flow}}$$

For the following investment:

Period	0	1	2	3	4	5
Cash flows	−2.1	0.8	0.8	0.8	0.8	0.8

The payback period is $2.1/0.8 = 2.6$ years.

Where the annual flows are not identical, the cumulative cash flows are compared with the amount invested, as below:

Period	0	1	2	3	4	5
Cash flows	−1	0.3	0.4	0.4	0.5	0.2
Cumulative cash flows		0.3	0.7	1.1	1.6	1.8

The cumulative flow is 0.7 for period 2 and 1.1 for period 3. The payback period is thus 2–3 years. A linear interpolation gives us a payback period of 2.75 years.

Once the payback period has been calculated, it is compared with an arbitrary cutoff date determined by the financial manager. If the payback period is longer than the cutoff period, the investment should be rejected. Clearly, when the perceived risk on the investment is high, the company will look for a very short payback period in order to get its money back before it is too late!

The payback ratio is used as an indicator of an investment's risk and profitability. However, it can lead to the wrong decision, as shown in the example below of investments *A* and *B*.

	Flows in period 0	Flows in period 1	Flows in period 2	Flows in period 3	Recovery within	20% NPV
Investment *A*	−1,000	500	400	600	2 years and 2 months	42
Investment *B*	−1,000	500	500	100	2 years	−178

The payback rule would prompt us to choose investment *B*, even though investment *A* has positive NPV, but not *B*. The payback rule can be misleading because it does not take all flows into account. It emphasises the liquidity of an investment rather than its value.

Moreover, because it considers that a euro today is worth the same as a euro tomorrow, the payback rule does not factor in the time value of money. To remedy this, one sometimes calculates a discounted payback period representing the time needed for the project to have positive NPV. Returning to the example, it then becomes:

Year	0	1	2	3	4	5
Cumulative present values	−2.1	−1.43	−0.88	−0.41	−0.03	0.29

The discounted payback period is now 4 years compared with 2.6 years before discounting. Discounted or not, the **payback period is a risk proxy**, since the shorter it is, the lower the risk of the investment. **That said, it ignores the most fundamental aspect of risk: the uncertainty of estimating liquidity flows.** Therefore, it is just an approximate indicator since it only measures the liquidity risk.

However, the payback ratio is fully suited to productive investments that affect neither the company's level of activity nor its strategy. Its very simplicity encourages employees to suggest productivity improvements that can be seen to be profitable without having to perform lengthy calculations. It only requires common sense. However, calculating flows in innovative sectors can be something of a shot in the dark. Also, the payback rule tends to favour investments with a high turnover rate. As a result, it has come under quite a bit of criticism because it can only compare investments that are similar.

2/RETURN ON CAPITAL EMPLOYED

The Return On Capital Employed (ROCE) represents wealth created over the year divided by capital employed. Wealth created is equal to after-tax operating profit, while the capital employed is the sum of fixed assets and the working capital generated by the investment:

$$ROCE = \frac{\text{Operating income after tax}}{\text{Net average fixed assets} + \text{Net average working capital}}$$

This ratio has a strong accounting bias, and is frequently just a comparison between the project's operating profit and the average book value of fixed assets and working capital. One can then calculate the average accounting return, which is the annual ROCE over the life of the investment. The computation of ROCE takes into account the after-tax operating profit and capital employed (working capital plus the residual investment after depreciation).

Depreciation plays a detrimental role, as shown in the example below of an initial investment of 500 generating annual EBITDA of 433 for 5 years. With stable working capital of 500 and a 40% tax rate, the free cash flow projection is as follows:

	31/12/y	y + 1	y + 2	y + 3	y + 4	y + 5
EBITDA		433	433	433	433	433
Tax		−133	−133	−133	−133	−133
Changes in working capital	−500	0	0	0	0	+500
Investment	−500					
Free cash flow	−1,000	+300	+300	+300	+300	+800

The investment's IRR works out to 23.75%. What is its return on capital employed? Assuming **the asset is depreciated on a straight-line basis** over 5 years then gives:

	$y + 1$	$y + 2$	$y + 3$	$y + 4$	$y + 5$
After-tax operating profit	200	200	200	200	200
Average Net Asset Value (NAV) of investment	400	300	200	100	0
Average working capital	500	500	500	500	500
ROCE	22%	25%	29%	33%	40%

If the **declining balance method of depreciation** is used (40%, 30%, 20%, 5% and 5%), this yields:

	$y + 1$	$y + 2$	$y + 3$	$y + 4$	$y + 5$
After-tax operating profit	140	170	200	245	245
Average NAV of investment	300	150	50	25	0
Average working capital	500	500	500	500	500
ROCE	17%	26%	36%	47%	49%

So, what is the return on capital employed? In the first case, it averages at 29.8% and in the second case it is 35%. Do you really believe that just changing an accounting method can influence the intrinsic profitability of a project? Of course not, and this example clearly illustrates the flaw inherent in the criteria.

Although the highest returns are usually realized on projects with the longest durations, accounting rates of return do not take into account the date of the flow. Hence, they generally tend to overstate returns. Another drawback with accounting rates of return is that they maximise rates without considering the corresponding risk.

On the surface, it may seem that there is no connection between return on capital employed and the internal rate of return. The first discounts flows while the second calculates book wealth. And yet, taken over a year, their outcomes are identical. An amount of 100 that increases to 110 a year later has an IRR of $100 = 110/(1 + r)$, so $r = 10\%$ and an ROCE of 10/100, or 10%.

ROCE and IRR are equal over a given period of time. ROCE is therefore calculated by period, while IRR and NPV are computed for the entire life of the investment.

Although accounting rates of return should not be used as investment or financing criteria, they can be useful financial control tools.

Sooner or later, a discounted return has to be translated into an accounting rate of return. If not, the investment has not generated the anticipated *ex post* return and has not achieved its purpose. We strongly advise you to question any differences between IRR and ROCE. That is, are income flows distributed or retained, do profits arise unevenly over the period (starting out slowly or not at all and then gathering momentum), what is the terminal value, etc.?

SUMMARY

The criteria with which investment decisions are based include:

- first and foremost, Net Present Value (NPV), which is the best criteria because it measures the value creation of the investment;

- the Internal Rate of Return (IRR), which measures the yield to maturity of the investment; and

- if necessary and to simplify calculations, the payback ratio, which measures the amount of time needed to pay back the investment, and the return on capital employed (operating profit after tax for the period divided by capital employed for the period), which is more of a financial control tool.

The flows that are used for calculating NPV and IRR are free cash flows:

- EBITDA on the investment;

- corporate income tax calculated on the operating income of the investment;

- change in working capital created by the investment;

- capital expenditure (including any divestments).

To avoid making errors, it is necessary to:

- reason only in terms of cash flow, not charges and revenues;

- reason in terms of incremental flows – i.e., consider the cash flows arising on the investment, all the cash flows arising on the investment and only the cash flows arising on the investment. This involves calculating the investment's marginal contribution to the company's cash flows;

- reason in terms of opportunity – i.e., in financial values and not in book values;

- disregard the way in which the investment was financed – flows used in the calculations never include financial income and expenditure, new loans and repayment of loans, capital increases and capital reductions, or dividends;

- consider ordinary taxation (on operating profits) or exceptional taxes (on capital gains, subsidies, etc.); and

- finally, the best advice is to **be consistent!**

In the business world, the differences between practice and theory in investment decisions are diminishing. Financial managers now look increasingly at NPV and IRR when making investment decisions.

QUESTIONS

quiz

1/ When making an investment decision, should you reason:

- in terms of cash flow?
- marginally?
- without regard to the type of financing?
- with consideration for taxation?

2/ Define the payback ratio.

3/ What are the drawbacks of the payback ratio?

4/ Define return on capital employed.

5/ Can an investment decision be based on return on capital employed?

6/ What purpose does the return on capital employed serve?

7/ What roles do depreciation and amortisation play in the calculation of cash flows to be discounted?

8/ What is the optimal depreciation method for a company that is not taxed? What about for a company that pays tax at the standard rate?

9/ A company is planning to build a new plant to replace an older one that is to be demolished. What are the most important flows to consider?

- (a) market value of the land and the older plant;
- (b) demolition costs;
- (c) costs of building an access road the previous year;
- (d) production losses while an old plant is demolished and a new one is being built;
- (e) depreciation of the plant;
- (f) tax credits on the investment;
- (g) part of the salary of the managing director;
- (h) constitution of working capital?

10/ When can investment in working capital be neglected?

11/ Provide examples of investments where residual value must under no circumstances be neglected.

12/ In Germany, profits for 2000 were taxed at 40% if they were paid out and 30% if reinvested. What rate should be used when making an investment decision?

13/ In an inflationary environment, how should you reason in evaluating an investment?

14/ When operating cash flow is negative, should IRR and NPV be calculated including the interest expense on loans used to finance it?

15/ Should an investment subsidy be included in investment flows or by reducing the discount rate?

EXERCISES

1/ The following investment project is submitted to you:

- project: extension of an industrial plant;
- purchase of equipment €20m;
- setup costs €1.5m;

- useful life 8 years;
- residual value 0;
- increase in working capital €2.5m.

The project will result in an increase in EBITDA of €3m per year, over the 8 years during which the new asset is used. The equipment is depreciated over 5 years. The corporate income tax rate is 40%:

(a) Draw up the cash flow schedule for the project, on the basis of straight-line depreciation.
(b) Calculate each of the two cases:
- net present value at 10%;
- the internal rate of return of the project.

2/ A company is planning to replace a machine with a new, better performing one. The figures for the investment are as follows:

- Purchase of new machine:
- cost €2m;
- useful life 5 years, residual value nil;
- linear depreciation over 5 years;
- savings on charges €0.8m per year.
- Sale of second-hand machine:
- purchase cost €1.5m (machine bought the previous year);
- linear depreciation over 5 years (residual value is nil);
- net book value today €1.2m;
- potential sale price €1.0m.

If the tax rate on profits and capital gains/losses is 40%, what is the "value" for the company of the new machine the company is planning to buy (this company's required rate of return is 12%)?

Calculate the net present value and the internal rate of return of the planned investment.

3/ Take the following project:

Period	0	1	2	3	4	5
Cash flow	−100	110	−30	25	50	100

What problem do you come up against when calculating the payback ratio? What is the NPV of this project at 10%? What is the internal rate of return?

4/ The Catalonia Region is prepared to pay €2m to a private company prepared to run a bus service three times a day between Lérida and Tarragona, for a period of 10 years. The initial outlay for the project is estimated at €0.8m, but annual operating losses (excluding depreciation) will amount to €0.2m. What is the NPV for this investment. If the private company's required rate of return is 10%, will it take up the contract? And if it is 15%?

5/ Industrial Electric plc estimates its needs for a component used in its products at 7,000 units per year for the next 10 years. A subcontractor offers to supply the parts at €5 per unit.

Industrial Electric can make the part in its own workshops for €3 per unit, if it buys a new machine. A new machine would cost €78,000, have a useful life of 10 years and a residual value of nil. The company generally gets a 10% return (after tax) on its capital expenditure. It depreciates machinery on a straight-line basis and tax is levied at a rate of 35%.

Should the company accept the subcontractor's offer?

6/ A large oil company has been invited to get involved in a project to build a parking facility in the centre of Frankfurt. The project includes a 450-car public parking lot, a 200-car garage and a petrol station covering 1,000 m². It will take 1 year to build, and a 30-year concession to run the facility will be granted by the municipality (after construction has been completed). Total capital expenditure will be €8,400,000 and working capital will be nil. The annual income statement for the project after the construction looks like this:

Charges		Revenues	
Operating	670,000	Parking places	1,680,000
Depreciation and amortisation	280,000	Garage	770,000
Income tax expense	1,000,000	Petrol station	800,000
Net profits	1,300,000		
	3,250,000		3,250,000

Calculate the average accounting return on the project, the payback ratio, the net present value at 10% and the internal rate of return. Is the average accounting return equal to the average of the annual returns on the project?

7/ A year ago, Robin plc invested in a machine to improve the manufacturing of one of its products. It has just discovered that a new machine has come onto the market which would improve performance more than the one it bought. That machine cost €8,000 a year ago, and is depreciated on a straight-line basis over 8 years (the same period as its useful life after which it will be scrapped). If it were sold now, the company would get around €5,000 (tax credit on the capital loss would be 40%).

The new machine costs €11,000 and would be depreciated for €10,500 on a straight-line basis over its useful life, estimated at 7 years. It could be sold at the end of its useful life for €500 which is what its book value would be.

The company is hoping to produce 100,000 units of its product annually for the next 7 years. With the equipment currently in use, the company's per-unit cost price breaks down as follows: €0.14 per unit in direct labour costs, €0.10 for raw materials and €0.14 in general costs. The new machine will enable the company to cut direct labour costs to €0.12 per unit produced. The cost of raw materials will drop to €0.09 per unit thanks to a reduction in waste. General costs will remain €0.14 per unit. All other factors will remain unchanged – in particular, supplies, energy consumed and maintenance costs. Profits are taxed at 40%.

(a) Draw up the cash flow schedule for the contemplated investment.
(b) Calculate the payback ratio on this investment.

8/ Pincer plc is hoping to increase sales by granting its customers longer payment periods. Its annual sales currently stand at €1m and it gives its customers an average of 30 days to pay.

(a) The company made the following assumptions when defining its customer credit policy.

Extension of payment period (days)	Increase in sales (€)
15	400,000
30	600,000
45	700,000
60	750,000

The sales price of a manufactured unit is €4 and the cost price is €3.2, including €1 in fixed costs. What policy should the company introduce if it requires a 20% return (before tax) on its capital invested (its inventories are financed through supplier credit)?

(b) Pincer has also made the following forecasts for bad debts:

Extension of payment period (days)	Bad debts (sales, %)
15	2
30	4.5
45	7
60	12

Bad debts currently only account for 1.2% of debts. Which policy should the company introduce?

9/ In the summer of 2001, the UK advertising group WPP got involved in a stock market battle with Havas Advertising for Tempus, a company listed on the London Stock Exchange. Havas Advertising offered shareholders 541 pence per share, before WPP increased its offer to 555 pence per share. WPP's offer was accepted.

Tempus's share capital was divided into 77 million shares. Before the takeover bid, WPP held 17 million Tempus shares (22% of the company's share capital) that it had bought up on the market over the years at an average price of 240 pence per share.

(a) How much did WPP pay for Tempus (the total price for 100% of the shares)?
(b) How much did Havas Advertising and WPP value the shareholders' equity of Tempus at?
(c) Do you think that the fact that WPP already held 22% of the share capital of Tempus which it had acquired relatively cheaply gave it the option of paying more for the rest of the shares?

Questions

1; 2; 3; 4; 5 and 6.

7/ *In calculating tax.*

8/ *It makes no difference. Depreciation is quicker.*

9/ *(a) yes; (b) yes; (c) no; (d) yes; (e) tax point of view; (f) yes; (g) no; (h) yes.*

10/ *When it is negligible!*

11/ *Investment in real estate.*

12/ *30%.*

13/ *In current euro values.*

14/ *No, never; negative flows are part of capital expenditure in finance just as the purchase of a fixed asset is.*

15/ *In investment flows, because it is deducted from the flows to be invested and not from the risk, which remains the same.*

Exercises

1/

Year	0	1	2	3	4	5	6	7	8
− Investment flows	−21.5								
+ ΔEBITDA		3	3	3	3	3	3	3	3
− ΔWorking capital		2.5							−2.5
− ΔTaxes		−0.4	−0.4	−0.4	−0.4	−0.4	1.2	1.2	1.2
= Cash flows	−21.5	0.9	3.4	3.4	3.4	3.4	1.8	1.8	4.3

NPV= 6.9; IRR = 0.9%.

2/

Year	0	1	2	3	4	5
− Purchase of new machine	−2					
+ Sale of old machine	1					
+ Tax credit on capital loss	−0.2 × 40%					
+ Cost savings after tax		0.8 − 60%	0.48	0.48	0.48	0.48
+ Tax savings on incremental depreciation and amortisation		0.1 − 40%	0.04	0.04	0.04	0.04
= Cash flows to be discounted	−0.92	0.52	0.52	0.52	0.52	0.64

NPV= 1; IRR = 50%.

3/ *Difficult to calculate payback period as investment is made in two phases.*
NPV = 67.7. IRR = 42.64%.

4/ *At 10% no, at 15% yes.*

5/ *Yes, because the NPV on the investment is − €5,310.*

6/ *1.58/(8.4 − 0)/2 = 38%, 7 years and 9 months. NPV at 10% = €6.5m. IRR = 16%. No,
it is 60% and heavily influenced by the rate of the last year which is very high
(464%) because the asset is practically fully depreciated.*

7/ *Figures for year 0: 5,000 (sale of old machine) − 11,000 (purchase of new
machine) + 800 (tax credit at 40% of capital loss on sale of old machine) = 5,200.
Years 1 to 7: (100,000 × 0.03 − (8,000/8 − 10,500/7)) × 60% + (8,000/8 − 10,500/
7) = 2,000. Year: 500. Payback ratio: around 3 years.*

8/ *(a) Extend the period to 15 because NPV would then be the highest at €25,260 for
1 year.*

(b) The 15-day period is the only one for which NPV is positive.

9/ *(a) £373m.*

(b) £427m for WPP and £417m for Havas Advertising.

*(c) No, because if WPP had not bought, it could have sold its shares (for 541 pence
per share at least). In terms of opportunity costs, WPP paid more than £425m for
Tempus's shareholders' equity.*

BIBLIOGRAPHY

For more on techniques used for making investment decisions:

H. Bierman, S. Smidt, *The Capital Budgeting Decision*, Macmillan, New York, 1992.
T. Copeland, T. Koller, J. Murrin, *Valuation. Measuring and Managing the Value of Companies*, 3rd
edn, John Wiley & Sons, 2000.
A. Damodaran, *Corporate Finance. Theory and Practice*, 2nd edn, John Wiley & Sons, 2002.

Surveys regarding the popularity of capital budgeting techniques:

R. Bruner, K. Eades, R. Harris, R. Higgins, Best practice in estimating the cost of capital: Survey and
synthesis, *Financial Practice and Education*, 13–28, Spring/Summer 1998.
M. Dallocchio, A. Salvi, *La Funzione Finanziaria nel Nuovo Millennio*, working paper, Bocconi
University, 2000.
L. Gitman, J.R. Forrester, A survey of capital budgeting techniques used by major US firms, *Financial
Management*, **6**, 66–71, 1977.
J. Graham, C. Harvey, The theory and practice of corporate finance: Evidence from the field, *Journal
of Financial Economics*, **60**, 187–243, May 2001.
J.H. Hall, *An Empirical Investigation of the Capital Budgeting Process*, working paper, University of
Pretoria, 2000.
L. Lumby, *Investment Appraisal and Investment Decision*, 4th edn, Chapman & Hall, London, 1991.
E. Trahan, L. Gitman, Bridging the theory–practice gap in corporate finance: A survey of chief
financial officers, *Quarterly Review of Economics and Finance*, **1**, Spring 1995, 73–87.

Chapter 19
MEASURING VALUE CREATION

Separating the wheat from the chaff

Creating value has become such an important issue in finance that a host of indicators have been developed to measure it. They come under a confusing array of acronyms – TSR, MVA, EVA, CFROI, ROCE–WACC – but most of these will probably be winnowed out in the years to come. Ultimately, they should be reduced to those few that best mirror and address the recent developments in cash flow statements.

The current profusion of indicators has its advantages, as normally we expect only the most reliable to survive. However, in practice, some companies use the lack of clear guidelines and standards to choose indicators that best serve their interests at a given time, even if this involves the laborious task of changing indicators on a routine basis.

The table below should help you find your way through the maze of indicators. It charts the chronological appearance of value measures according to three criteria: ease of manipulation, sensitivity to financial markets and category (accounting, economic or stock market indicators).

EVOLUTION OF FINANCIAL INDICATORS

Accounting criteria, economic criteria and stock market criteria.

@
download

Predictably, the indicators cluster around a diagonal running from the upper left-hand corner down to the lower right-hand: this reflects the companies' diminished ability to manipulate the indicators over time. Gradually, investors become more experienced and financial markets become more influential, and so less prone to misinterpreting company data.

Value creation indicators fall into three categories:

➢ **Accounting indicators.** Until the mid-1980s, companies mainly communicated their **net profit/loss** or **Earnings Per Share (EPS)**. Regrettably, this is a key accounting parameter that is also very easy to manipulate. This practice of massaging EPS is called "window-dressing", or improving the presentation of the accounts by adjusting exceptional items, provisions, etc. The growing emphasis on operating profit or EBITDA represents an improvement because it considerably reduces the impact of exceptional items or noncash expenses.

The second-generation accounting indicators appeared as investors began to reason in terms of **profitability** – i.e., **efficiency** – by comparing return with the equity used. This ratio is called *Return On Equity*, or **ROE**. However, it is possible to leverage this value as well, since a company can boost its ROE by skilfully raising its debt level. Even though ROE might look more attractive, no "real" value has been created since the increased profitability is cancelled out by higher risk not reflected in accounting data.

Since the Return On Capital Employed (**ROCE**) indicator avoids this bias, it has tended to become the main measure of economic performance. Only in a few sectors of activity is it meaningless to use ROCE (such as in banking or insurance). In those industries, return on equity is still widely used.

While NPV and other economic indicators represent valuable tools for strategic analysis and a good basis for estimating the market value of companies, they are based on projections that are frequently difficult to assess. Unfortunately, the cash flow for one, single year is easy to manipulate and meaningless. Indeed, it is not intuitively interpretable. At the same time, we know that the major drivers of cash flows are the *growth of earnings and revenues* of the company and ROCE. By focusing attention on ROCE, there is a better intuitive grasp of how the company is performing. It is then easier to assess the firm's growth both over time and relative to its industry.

➢ **Economic indicators** emerged with the realisation that profitability *per se* cannot fully measure value because it does not factor in risks. To measure value, returns must also be compared with the cost of capital employed. Using the cost of financing of a company, called the Weighted Average Cost of Capital or WACC, it is possible to assess whether value has been created (i.e., when return on capital employed is higher than the cost of capital employed) or destroyed (i.e., return on capital employed is lower than the cost of capital employed).

However, some companies restrict their disclosures to just this ratio. For example, the French company Suez's objective is to realise a return on capital employed that is at least 3% higher than its cost of capital. But companies can also go one step further by applying the calculation to capital employed at the beginning of the year in order to measure the value created **over the period**. The difference can then be expressed in currency units rather than as a percentage.

This popular measure of value creation has been most notably developed in the **EVA model**, or *Economic Value Added*. It is also known as **economic profit**.

Yet the best of all indicators is undoubtedly *Net Present Value* (see **NPV** in Chapter 16), which provides the exact measure of value created. It has been repeatedly demonstrated that intrinsic value creation is the principal driver of *companies' market value*. But NPV has one drawback because it must be computed over several periods. For the external analyst who does not have access to all the necessary information, the NPV criterion becomes difficult to handle. The quick and easy solution is to use the above-mentioned ratios. It is important to remember that, while the other ratios are simpler to use, they are also less precise and may prove misleading when not used with care.

➤ **Market indicators**: *Market Value Added* (**MVA**) and *Total Shareholder Return* (**TSR**) are highly sensitive to the stock market. MVA represents the difference between the value of equity and net debt, and the book value of capital employed. It is expressed in currency units. TSR is expressed as a percentage and corresponds to the addition of the return on the share (dividends/value of the share) and the capital gains rate (capital gains during the period divided by the initial share value). It is the return earned by a shareholder who bought the share at the beginning of a period, earned dividends and then sold the share at the end of the period.

A major weakness with these two measures is that they may show destruction in value because of declining investor expectations about future profits, even though the company's return on capital employed is higher than its cost of capital. This happened to Bic, which saw its share price halved from 1998 to 2004. However, during this time its ROCE was consistently above 10% per year whereas its cost of capital was only about 8.5%. Conversely, in a bull market a company with mediocre economic performances may have flattering TSR and MVA. In the long term, these highs and lows are smoothed out and TSR and MVA eventually reflect the company's modest performances. Yet, in the meantime there may be some major divergences between these indicators and company performance.

These considerations prompted some stock exchange authorities to recommend making a clear distinction between economic indicators and measures of stock market value creation (TSR and MVA). The former measure the past year's performance, and the latter tend to reflect anticipations of future value creation. The measures of stock market value creation take into account the share price, which reflects these anticipations. Yet the different measures of economic performance and stock market value are complementary, rather than contradictory.

➤ Aside from accounting, economic and market indicators, companies frequently adopt a fourth category of performance variables known as **value drivers**. These are measured with a class of associated metrics called **Key Performance Indicators (KPIs)**.

Value drivers are at the root of business performance because they are frequently **leading indicators** of performance, while financial results (such as ROCE, for example) are lagging indicators. Management has a strong need to understand where their company is going in the future. KPIs can be either *operating* or *strategic* measures, for example in:

○ pharmaceutical companies ⇒ value driver: R&D pipeline;
○ packaged food division ⇒ market share; and
○ retailers ⇒ number of stores opened in a given year or number of new product categories introduced.

It is frequent among practitioners to undertake value driver analysis by breaking down ROCE into its elementary financial components (EBIT, capital employed). Although this is a good starting point, the "real" value drivers can be found by further disaggregating the factors that drive each kind of revenue and costs. This in turn allows for analysing concrete improvement actions.[1]

While it is worthwhile to mention value drivers at this juncture, the rest of this chapter will continue to focus on accounting, economic and market criteria. The reasons for leaving behind the discussion of value drivers are:

○ value drivers are highly company- and industry-specific. They are also innumerable. It would be highly impractical to try and dedicate appropriate attention to all of them here; and
○ value drivers are normally identified and adopted on a business-unit-by-business-unit basis. The scope of this text is more concerned with detailed examinations of corporate- and company-wide measures at a higher level.

1 *For example, retailers of durable goods may break down the cost side of EBIT margin into trip per transactions, cost per trip and number of transactions.*

Section 19.1
ACCOUNTING CRITERIA

Certain accounting indicators like net profit, shareholders' equity and cash flow from operations are more representative of a firm's financial strength. However, they are flawed and not appropriate for the purposes of financial analysis, mainly because:

• accounting items can be manipulated;
• they may not consider the time value of money and the opportunity cost of capital.

The same could be said of the criteria presented next in this section – Earnings Per Share (**EPS**), the Accounting Rate of Return (ARR) and equity per share. However, they are systematically used as analytical criteria for all financial decisions, even at the board level.

Even so, are they really of any practical use?

Although EPS, the accounting rate of return and equity per share are primarily of an accounting nature and generally tend to ignore risks, they do have a few saving graces. As will be demonstrated, these criteria do have some merit and can impart useful information.

However, it is inappropriate to believe that by artificially boosting them you have created value. Nor is it correct to assume that there is a constant and automatic link between improving these criteria and creating value. In order to maximise value, it is simply not enough to maximise these ratios, even if they are linked by a coefficient to value or the required rate of return.

1/EARNINGS PER SHARE

Notwithstanding the comments just made about Earnings Per Share (EPS), many financial managers continue to favour using it. Despite its limitations, it is still the most widespread multiple because it is directly connected to the share price via the price–earnings ratio. EPS's popularity is rooted in three misconceptions:

- the belief that earnings per share factors in the cost of equity and, therefore, the cost of risk;
- the belief that accounting data influence the value of the company. Changing accounting methods (for inventories, depreciation, goodwill, etc.) will not modify the company's value, even if it does change earnings per share; and
- the belief that any financial decision that lifts EPS will change value as well. This would imply that the P/E ratio[2] remains the same before and after the financial decision, which is frequently not the case. Thus, value is not a direct multiple of earnings per share, because the decision may affect investors' assessment of the company's risks and growth potential.

2 *The P/E ratio is equal to Price/ Earnings per share. It measures the relative dearness of a share.*

Consider company *A* which, based upon its risks, and growth and profitability prospects, has a P/E ratio of 20. Its net profit is 50. Company *B* has equity of 450 with net profit of 30, giving it a P/E of 15. Company *A* decides to acquire a controlling interest in company *B*, paying a premium of 33% on *B*'s value; i.e., a total of 600. Company *A* finances the acquisition entirely by taking on debt at an after-tax cost of 3%. Both companies *A* and *B* are fairly valued with regards to their risk exposure. There are no industrial or commercial synergies that could increase the new group's earnings, and no goodwill.

Company *A*'s net profit is thus:

	Former net profit of *A*:	50
+	Net profit of *B*:	30
−	Cost of financing:	18 = 600 × 3%
=	New net profit of *A*:	62, or +24%

Since *A* financed its acquisition of *B* entirely through debt, it still has the same number of shares. The increase in earnings per share is therefore equal to that in net profit – that is, 24%. This certainly seems like an extraordinary result! But has *A* really created value by buying *B*? The answer is no, since there are no synergies to speak of between *A* and *B*. Keep in mind that *A* paid 33% more than *B*'s equilibrium price. In fact, company *A* has destroyed value in proportion to this premium – i.e., 150 – because it cannot be offset by synergies.

In fact, the explanation for the – apparent – paradox of a 24% rise in earnings per share matched by a destruction of value is that **the buyer's EPS has increased, because the P/E of the company bought by means of debt is higher than the after-tax cost of the debt.** Here, *B* has a P/E of 20 given the 33% premium paid by *A* on the acquisition. The inverse of 20 (5%) is much higher than the 3% after-tax cost of the debt for A.

At present low interest rates (4% net of taxes), an acquisition paid in cash must be based on a P/E ratio of more than 25 to have a negative impact on the EPS of the buyer. Such a situation leaves plenty of margin to manoeuvre.

Consider now company C, which has equity of 1,400 with net profit of 140 – i.e., a P/E of 10. It merges with company D, which has the same risk exposure, equity of 990 and a P/E of 18 (net profit of 55), with no control premium. Thanks to very strong industrial synergies, C is able to boost D's net profit by 50%. Without doubt, value has been created. And, yet, it is not difficult to prove (see Exercise 1) that C's EPS dropped 7% after the merger. This is a mechanical effect due simply to the fact that D's P/E of 18 is higher than C's P/E of 10, because D has better earnings prospects than C.

At the risk of being repetitious, a word of warning about the widespread fallacy that EPS growth equals value creation. This has led to the misconception that, accordingly, EPS dilution means that value has been destroyed. This is a myth. EPS is an accounting metric, not a measure of value.

So, what was the net result of company C's acquisition of company D? **The question is not whether company C's EPS has been enhanced or diluted, but whether it paid too much for D.** In fact, it did not, since there was no control premium paid and industrial synergies were created. After the operation, C's shares will trade at a higher P/E, as it should enjoy greater earnings growth thanks to the contribution from D's higher growth businesses. In the end, the higher P/E ratio should more than compensate for the diluted EPS, lifting the share price. This is only logical considering that the industrial synergies created value.

In fact, EPS can be a reliable indicator of value creation under three conditions only:
- the risk on capital employed remains the same from one period to the next, or before and after operations such as mergers, capital increases or share buybacks, investments, etc.;
- earnings' growth remains the same before and after any given operation; and
- the company's financial structure remains the same from one period to the next, or before and after a given operation.

If these three conditions are met, we can assume that EPS growth reflects the creation of value, and EPS dilution the destruction of value.

If just one of these conditions is lacking, there is no way to effectively evaluate EPS. It is not possible to infer that any increase in EPS reflects the creation of value, nor that a decrease is a destruction of value. In our example of a combination between A and B financed by debt, although A's EPS rose 24% its risk increased sharply. Its position is no longer directly comparable with that before the acquisition of B.

Similarly, C's post-merger EPS cannot be compared with its EPS prior to the merger. While the merger did not change its financial structure, C's growth rate after the merger with D is different from what it was beforehand.

2/ACCOUNTING RATES OF RETURN

Accounting rates of return comprise:

- Return On Equity: R_{CE} (**ROE**);
- Return On Capital Employed (**ROCE**), which was earlier described in Chapter 13.

The main drawback of accounting rates of return on equity or capital employed is precisely that they are accounting measures. As will be demonstrated below, these have their dangers.

Consider[3] company X, which produces a single product and generates a return of 30% on capital employed amounting to 100. X operates in a highly profitable sector and is considering diversifying. Should it expect the present 30% rate of return to be generated on other possible projects? If it does, X will never diversify because it is unlikely that any other investments will meet these criteria.

3 *To simplify the discount calculation, we assume that the planned investments will generate a return to infinity.*

How can this problem be rationally approached? The company generates an accounting return of 30%. Suppose its shareholders and investors require a 10% return. Its market value is thus 30/10%, or 300.

The proposed investment amounts to 100 and generates a return of 15% on identical risks. The required rate of return is constant at 10%. We see that:

	Present operating profit	30% × 100 = 30
+	Operating profit on new investment	15% × 100 = 15
=	Total	45

This yields an enterprise value of $45/10\% = 450$ (+150), with a return on capital employed of $45/200 = 22.5\%$.

The value of the capital employed has increased by more than the amount invested (150 vs. 100) because the profitability of company X's investment is higher than the rate required by its shareholders and investors. Value has been created, and X was right to invest. And, yet, the return on capital employed fell by 30% to 22.5%, demonstrating that this criterion is not relevant.

In general, if the investment yields more than the required rate of return, the increase in the value of the company will exceed that of the sums invested.

The inverse example is company Y, which has a return of 5% on capital employed of 100. Assuming the shareholders and investors require a 10% return as well, the value of Y's capital employed is $5/10\% = 50$.

The proposed investment amounts to 25 and yields a return of 8%. Since we have the same 10% required return, we get:

	Present operating profit	$5\% \times 100 = 5$
+	Operating profit of new investment	$8\% \times 25 = 2$
=	Total	7

This results in capital employed being valued at $7/10\% = 70$ (+20), with a return of $7/125 = 5.6\%$.

The value of Y's capital employed has indeed increased by 20, but this is still less than the increase of 25 in capital invested. Value has been destroyed. The return on the investment is just 8%, whereas the required rate is 10%. The company has lost money and should not have made the investment. And, yet, the return on capital employed rose from 5% to 5.6%.

Similarly, one could demonstrate that ROE increases after an acquisition funded by a share issue, when the target company's reverse $1/(P/E)$ is higher than the buyer's current ROE.

Financial managers should approach book rates of return with caution. These ratios are accounting measures, not external measures. They assume that the company is operating in a closed system! The minimum criterion should be the return required by the financial system.

Setting aside all these accounting concepts (R), what are the implications for the financial concepts (k)?

Unfortunately, investors and corporate managers continue to view decision-making in terms of the impact on accounting measures, even though it has just been demonstrated that these criteria have little to say about the creation of value. True, accounting systems are a company's main source of information. However, financial managers need to focus first and foremost on how financial decisions affect value.

3/EQUITY PER SHARE

Equity per share is one way of measuring shareholder value. It therefore seems logical to assume that there is a coefficient linking the price of the share with equity per share. This is called the **Price-to-Book Ratio (PBR)**. However, the warnings against the P/E ratio apply to the PBR as well.

Bear in mind that if equity has been correctly valued in the accounts – that is, if it includes unrealised capital gains on assets – the price-to-book ratio will be:

- lower than 1 if the expected return on equity is lower than the return required by shareholders; and
- higher than 1 if the expected return is higher than that required by the shareholders.

Section 19.2
ECONOMIC CRITERIA

1/NET PRESENT VALUE

It should now be clear that the concept of value corresponds perfectly to the measure of **net present value**. Financial management consists of constantly measuring the net present value of an investment, project, company or source of financing. Obviously, one should only allocate resources if the net present value is positive; in other words, if the market value is lower than the present value. **Net present value reflects how allocation of the company's resources has led to the creation or destruction of value.** On the one hand, there is a constant search for anticipated financial flows – while keeping in mind the uncertainty of these forecasts. On the other hand, it is necessary to consider the rate of return (k) required by the investors and shareholders providing the funds.

The value created is thus equal to the difference between the capital employed and its book value. Book value is the amount of funds invested in the company's operations.

> Creation of value = Enterprise value – Book value of capital employed

The creation of value reflects investors' expectations. Typically, this means that, over a certain period, the company will enjoy a rent with a present value allowing its capital employed to be worth more than its book value!

The same principle applies to choosing a source of financing for allocating resources. To do so, one must disregard the book value and determine instead the value of the financial security issued and deduct the required rate of return. This approach represents a shift from the explicit or accounting cost to the **financial cost, which is the return required on this category of security**. By minimising the cost of a source of financing one is actually minimising the overall financial cost.

On its own, the concept of cost may be insufficient when analysing certain very complex products. In such cases, one must resort to the concept of present value. This is particularly true of hybrid securities.

A source of financing is considered cheap **only** if its net present value is negative.

Once again, the only reliable financial criterion is net present value.

2/ECONOMIC PROFIT OR ECONOMIC VALUE ADDED (EVA)

Economic profit is less ambitious than net present value. It only seeks to measure the wealth created by the company in each financial year. EVA factors in not just the cost of debt, such as in calculating net profit, but it also accounts for the cost of equity.

The innovative aspect of EVA is that it identifies the income level at which value is created. This is because EVA is calculated after deducting the capital charge – i.e., the remuneration of the funds contributed by creditors and shareholders.

Economic profit or EVA first measures the excess of ROCE over the weighted average cost of capital. Then, to determine the value created during the period, the ratio is multiplied by the book value of the capital employed at the start of the reporting period. Thus, a company that had an opening book value of capital employed of 100 and an after-tax return on capital employed of 12% with a WACC of only 10% will have earned 2% more than the required rate. It will have created a value of 2 on funds of 100 during the period.

$$\text{Economic profit} = \text{Capital employed} \times (ROCE - WACC)$$
$$EVA = \text{Capital employed} \times (ROCE - WACC)$$

Economic profit is related to net present value, because NPV is the sum of the economic profits discounted at the weighed average cost of capital:

$$NPV = \sum_{i=0}^{\infty} \frac{\text{Economic profit}_i}{(1 + \text{Weighted average cost of capital})^i} = \sum_{i=0}^{\infty} \frac{EVA_i}{(1 + WACC)^i}$$

4 *The table shows the EVAs of some European firms.*

Company[4]	2004 EVA (in €m)
Shell	13,319
Novartis	5,942
Nestlé	2,757
Telecom Italia	2,057
AstraZeneca	1,977
Arcelor	1,538
Ericsson	1,339
SAP	1,127
Carrefour	1,049
BASF	910
L'Oréal	526
Zara	519
Porsche	466
Heineken	362
Italcementi	213
Michelin	209
ABB	194
Swatch	159
Antena 3 de Televisión	84
Bulgari	62
Bic	59
Aguas de Barcelona	13
easyJet	−95
Carlsberg	−118
Vodafone	−154
British Airways	−299
Fiat	−1,794
DaimlerChrysler	−4,289

Source: computed from annual reports.

To calculate EVA, it is necessary to switch from an accounting to an economic reading of the company. This is done by restating certain items of capital employed as follows:

- The research and development costs expended by the company during the past 5–10 years must be capitalised and added to fixed assets if they contributed to the development of the business for more than 1 year.
- The exceptional losses of previous years must be restated and added to capital employed insofar as they artificially reduce the company's capital.
- The goodwill recorded in the balance sheet must be taken as gross – i.e., corrected for cumulative amortisation. The badwill must be deducted from assets.

Of course, the profit and loss account (operating profit/loss and taxes) must be restated to ensure consistency with the capital employed calculated previously.

The firms that develop economic profit tools for companies generally have a long list of accounting adjustments that attest to their expertise. Such accounting expertise typically represents a barrier to entry for others seeking to perform the same analyses.

EVA's novelty also lies in its scope of application, since it enables a company to measure performance at all levels by applying an individual required rate of return to various units. It is a decentralised financial management tool.

A study by Kleineman, published in the *Journal of Applied Corporate Finance* (JACF) in 1999, reports that US companies adopting EVA during the period 1987–1996 outperformed median firms in the same industry. During the 4-year period covered by the study, firms using EVA posted results that were 28.8% better than those that did not.

Conversely, Biddle et al. (1999), in the same issue of the JACF, examined the claim that EVA, rather than net income, is more closely associated with stock returns and firm value. Yet their evidence indicates that EVA does not dominate net income in relationship to stock returns and firm value. But the debate is still open. Feltham et al. (2004) have claimed, in fact, that EVA has greater power than earnings in explaining market-adjusted stock returns.

Keep in mind these words of warning about EVA:

- If managers are judged based on EVA they will have a strong incentive to reduce invested capital. However, it can happen that the reduction in the invested capital is purely cosmetic.
- If managers are judged according to the current year's EVA, they will have a bias towards assets-in-place. As a result, they may be induced to abandon high-growth investments. Such behaviour in turn reduces the long-term economic value added that such investments may have otherwise added to the value of the company. A company can be tempted to maximise its EVA for a single year, at the cost of future EVA, by underinvesting or artificially reducing its working capital. In general, it is very difficult to find an annual measure of performance that truly reflects the creation of value. The only real measure of a company's ability to create value in the long term is the net present value of all future flows.

- If management's compensation is based on short-term EVA, managers may sacrifice future growth for current EVA.
- EVA will be overestimated for companies' divisions that are underallocated capital, and underestimated for those divisions or business units that are overallocated capital.
- Companies that undertake value-adding projects may end up with a lower value if the new projects increase the operating and financial risk and, thus, the cost of capital.
- Above all, EVA is an example of successful marketing and communication. Its promoters have taken a financial concept that has been around for a long time and reformulated it in easy-to-understand terms that can be explained at all organisational levels.

In short, we think there are good reasons for agreeing with Damodaran's opinion on EVA, "economic value added is an approach skewed toward assets-in-place and away from future growth" (Damodaran, 2001, p. 821).

3/CASH FLOW RETURN ON INVESTMENT (CFROI)

The original version of Cash Flow Return On Investment (**CFROI**) corresponds to the average of the internal rates of return on the company's existing investments. It measures the IRR earned by a firm's existing projects.
    CFROI is the internal rate of return and it is equal to:

1   the company's **Gross Capital Employed (GCE)** – i.e., before depreciation and adjusted for inflation. GCE is computed by adding depreciation back to the book value of the assets to arrive at an estimate of the original investment in the assets. The gross investment must then be converted into current value by reflecting the inflation incurred since the asset was purchased; *and*
2   the **current year *EBIT*** $\times$ **(1 − Tax rate) + Depreciation and amortisation**. We define this measure as Gross Cash Flow (GCF). GCF is then considered as an annuity with the same length as the expected life of the assets (N); *and*
3   the expected value of the assets at the end of their life, in current values. This is defined as the SV (**Salvage Value**):

Analytically, CFROI is the result of:

$$GCF(PV \text{ of an annuity, } N \text{ years, } CFROI) + SV/(1 + CFROI) - GCE = 0$$

CFROI is then compared with the weighted average cost of capital. If CFROI is higher than WACC the company is creating value, and if it is lower then the firm is destroying value.
    There are two major differences between the CFROI and the "traditional" IRR:

1   the internal rate of return is based on incremental *future* cash flows. Conversely, the CFROI reconstructs an asset using both cash flows that have already occurred and cash flows that are yet to occur; and

2   CFROI holds gross cash flows constant over a project's life and considers them as an annuity with a length of N years and a rate equal to CFROI. IRR does not assume that after-tax cash flows are constant over time.

The CFROI is complex to calculate, and even more difficult to explain to nonfinancial managers than ROCE. As is the case with EVA, the series of accounting adjustments required to calculate CFROI seem designed to convince users to call on the services of its creators, in this case the Holt firm, to implement the system. As a result, a simplified version of CFROI is frequently used, one which is more of an accounting measure than a financial one.

In general, there can be relevant differences between ROCE and CFROI when companies:

- have very long-lived fixed assets;
- have a high incidence of fixed assets vs. working capital;
- have very old or very new fixed assets; and/or
- have irregular capital expenditure patterns.

However, it is possible to demonstrate that an increase in CFROI does not necessarily indicate a higher value of the firm because such a result may have come at the expense of lower growth and higher risk.

Section 19.3
MARKET CRITERIA

1/CREATING STOCK MARKET VALUE (MARKET VALUE ADDED)

For listed companies, *Market Value Added (MVA)* is equal to:

$$MVA = \text{Market capitalisation} + \text{Net debt} - \text{Book value of capital employed}$$

In most cases, if no other information is available, we assume that net debt corresponds to its book value. Thus, the equation becomes simpler:

$$\text{Value created} = \text{Market capitalisation} + \text{Book value of net debt}$$
$$- (\text{Book value of equity} + \text{Book value of debt})$$
$$= \text{Market capitalisation} - \text{Book value of equity}$$

So, market value added is frequently considered to be the difference between market capitalisation and the book value of equity. This is the equivalent of the Price-to-Book Ratio (PBR) discussed in Chapter 28.[5]

The following table shows the MVA of a few big European groups as of April 2005:

5 *The market-to-capital ratio is a variation of MVA expressed as a ratio rather than a unit amount, because it is obtained by dividing the market capitalisation of debt and equity by the amount of capital invested.*

Company	MVA (in €)
Sanofi	89,559,750
Total	85,532,690
Royal Dutch	64,445,650
ENI	55,434,690
Telefónica	50,229,740
Nokia	41,540,550
France Telecom	41,111,920
Banco Santander	40,346,824
Telecom Italia Mobile	36,873,090

MVA, and particularly any change in MVA, constitutes a more relevant measure of value than just developments in share price. MVA assesses the increase in value with regard to the capital invested.

Inversely, MVA can raise measurement problems due to the use of accounting data.

It is easy to demonstrate the relationship between market value added and intrinsic value creation in equilibrium markets, since:

$$\text{Market value added} = \sum_{t=0}^{\infty} \frac{\text{Economic profit}_t}{(1 + WACC)^t}$$

Economic profit being equal to Capital employed $\times (ROCE - WACC)$. This is also equivalent to:

$$\text{Enterprise value} = \text{Book value of assets} + \sum_{t=0}^{\infty} \frac{\text{Economic profit}_t}{(1 + WACC)^t}$$

However, those who do not believe in market efficiency contend that MVA is flawed because it is based on market values that are often volatile and out of the management's control. Yet this volatility is an inescapable fact for all, as that is how the markets function.

2/TOTAL SHAREHOLDER RETURN (TSR)

TSR is the return received by the shareholder who bought the share at the beginning of a period, earned dividends (which are generally assumed to have been reinvested in new shares) and values his portfolio with the last share price at the end of the period. In other words:

$$TSR = \frac{\text{Share appreciation} + \text{Dividends}}{\text{Price}}$$

at the beginning of the period.

In order for it to be meaningful, the TSR ratio is calculated on a yearly basis over a fairly long period of, say, 5–10 years. This smoothes out the impact of erratic market movements; e.g., the tech, media and telecom stock bubble of 2000.

Below is a table of the total shareholder returns of the 24 largest European groups from 1991 to 2004:

UPDATE

Company	TSR (%)
Nokia	68
Ericsson	29
Royal Bank of Scotland	28
Telefónica	27
BBV Argentaria	24
Banco Santander	24
Vodafone	23
ING	22
ENI	21
Roche	20
HSBC	20
BNP Paribas	19
Total	19
UBS	17
Siemens	17
Credit Suisse	16
Deutsche Telekom	15
BP	15
GlaxoSmithKline	14
EON	14
Nestlé	14
Royal Dutch	13
Shell	13
Novartis	−2

Since markets are not always in equilibrium, there may be times when the creation of both intrinsic value and market value are not automatically correlated. This is particularly true during bust (or boom) periods, when a company may earn more than the cost of its capital and yet still see the market value of its capital employed collapse.

Section 19.4
PUTTING THINGS INTO PERSPECTIVE

1/IN SUMMARY

As long as performance measures and their implementation remain so diversified, it is vital to have a good understanding of their respective flaws. By choosing one or another measure, companies can present their results in a more or less flattering light. Financial managers typically choose those measures that will demonstrate the creation, rather than the destruction, of value.

Ratio	Economic criteria			Market criteria		Accounting criteria		
	Net present value	Economic profit	Cash flow return on investment	Market value added	Total shareholder return	Earning per share	Accounting rates of return	Equity per share
Acronym	NPV	EVA	CFROI	MVA	TSR	EPS	ROE,	ROCE
Strengths	The best criterion	Simple indicator leading to the concept of weighted average cost of capital	Not restricted to just 1 year	Astoundingly simple. Reflects the total rather than annual value created	Represents shareholder return in the medium to long term	Historical data. Simple	Simple concepts	
Weaknesses	Difficult to calculate for an external analyst	Restricted to 1 year. Difficult to evaluate changes over a period of time	Complex calculations	Subject to market volatility. Difficult to apply to unlisted companies	Calculated over too short a period. Subject to market volatility	Does not factor in risks. Easily manipulated. Does not factor in the cost of equity	Accounting measures; thus, do not factor in risks. Restricted to 1 year. To be significant, must be compared with the required rate of returns	Little connection with value creation

2/CREATING VALUE OR VALUES?

Over the past 10 years, the concept of value creation has spread rapidly, to the point where no corporate communication can afford to disregard it. Increasingly, value is assessed not just as it pertains to shareholders, but to all the stakeholders in the company: shareholders, employees and clients alike.

Managers now talk of stakeholder value, customer capital and human capital just as they do of financial capital.

While these concepts are certainly very appealing, we believe they are rooted in two misconceptions:

➤ The creation of value is sometimes rather hastily accused of leading to layoffs, plant closures, drastic cost reductions or disregard for environmental protection, labour law and human dignity. In fact, the opposite is true! A look at groups that have created sustainable value for their shareholders, frequently over long periods, shows that these same companies are at the forefront of innovation, constantly creating new markets, meeting new needs, hiring and training employees, inspiring loyalty and strong customer relationships. Just a few examples are l'Oréal, General Electric, Sony, Nokia, Nestlé and BMW.

Cost-cutting strategies can only be temporary and they cannot durably create shareholder value. Cost-cutting only works in the short-term and only if it gives rise to a strategy of profitable growth.

➤ Shareholders entrust their money to managers whose task is to multiply it. Financial directors must operate within the framework of a given corporate mission and with the shareholders' best interests in mind. When managers pursue other objectives, they betray the basic tenet upon which this pact is founded. More importantly, they are sure to fall short of all their objectives.

Only by creating sustainable value can a company ensure that it has the means to finance growth, train and pay its employees properly, produce quality goods or services, and respect the environment.

Fortunately, there is more to life than finance. Yet, in finance there is just one, overriding objective – creating value – and only by meeting this objective can one achieve all the others.

3/MORE ON THE REQUIRED RATE OF RETURN

Shareholders cannot demand more from their investments than is warranted by the degree of risk. We refer here to the mythical figure of 15%, which is frequently proclaimed to be the minimum return required. In our view, this is a pipedream.

Under current market conditions, a return of about 9% on a share with average risk seems reasonable. This corresponds to the 10-year government bond rate of about 5%, plus a risk premium of 4%.[6] Expecting 15% is too demanding and completely unjustified, unless the company has a beta of at least 2.5. And, in reality, less than 0.2% of large, listed European companies fall into this category!

6 *See Chapter 22.*

How can a company achieve these returns of 15% **in the long term**?

➤ **Debt leverage.** Using debt, the company can have a book return on equity that is higher than its return on capital employed. This can only be achieved if the return on capital is higher than its net debt charge. For a company with average risk to achieve a return on equity of 15%, its debt would probably have to represent 200% of equity. This is pretty much the case of France Télécom, but most companies do not have the luxury of its recurring cash flows! Fundamentally, leveraging debt to achieve 15% ROE significantly increases the risk for both investors and the company.

Is this really what investors demanding 15% returns want?

➤ **Increasing operational risks.** To take an exaggerated example, a company could decide to expand in risky, developing markets. In these nations, the normal returns are much higher than in the euro area because the risks are much higher as well.

Is this really what investors demanding 15% returns want?

➤ **Creative accounting.** Two ways of accomplishing this are by employing the *pooling of interests* technique and using substantial asset writedowns. These two stratagems have roughly the same effect and both eliminate vast swathes of equity, thereby making it easier to achieve 15% book returns. These practices were used massively by groups like AOL, Time Warner, Vivendi Universal. Obviously, these are just accounting tricks, and neither will last much longer in Europe.[7] Shareholders will always demand their share of the returns on equity, regardless if some legal sleight of hand has eliminated some of the shareholders' equity from the balance sheet.

7 See Chapters 6 and 7.

Is this really what investors demanding 15% returns want?

8 See Chapter 47.

➤ **Off-balance-sheet financing.**[8] This is achieved when a company spins off its unprofitable assets to an unconsolidated entity, thus apparently improving its profitability. In fact, this is just another way of distorting reality and misleading the financial community, as was shown with the example of Coca-Cola in Chapter 13.

Is this really what investors demanding 15% returns want?

In the first two cases, the managers increase the risk for shareholders, who may thus expect to earn a 15% book or discounted return. But the price is that risk will increase accordingly. In the last two cases, corporate managers play with appearances and manipulate accounting rates of return. As is only logical, the impact on discounted rates of return is nil, but there will always be blind or naive investors who fall for these ploys.

In fact, as the preceding chapter discussed, economic theory in the medium term (and plain common sense!) tells us that the return corresponds to the normal rate of return required, given the risk incurred. This is reinforced by deregulation and technological advances, which have eroded the barriers to entry protecting economic rents. Many large groups like Saint-Gobain, Michelin, Air Liquide and even Coca-Cola, all worldwide market leaders in their sectors, with patents, big name brands and powerful distribution networks in mature sectors, can either barely manage to cover, or earn just slightly more than, their cost of capital.

Today, companies create value when their investments yield 7–9% returns at average risk levels, and this is clearly well below the "magical" 15%. To demand 15% is to miss many investment opportunities that could create value.

In Europe, 15% returns at average risk levels are both unsustainable and unwarranted from a theoretical point of view. Practically speaking, such expectations on the part of the investor reflect wishful thinking. This type of attitude can lead to dangerous behaviour that encourages excessive debt levels and aggressive off-balance-sheet accounting. It is hoped that managers aiming for 15% do so only after having deducted exceptional writedowns or goodwill from their capital. In reality, that would yield an overall return of 9% on the total equity contributed by shareholders. Under these circumstances, such behaviour and results would then be quite pardonable.

Shareholders can only expect returns compatible with the risks incurred. If they earn more, good for them, but this does mean they can systematically require more.

SUMMARY

download

The tools used for measuring creation of value can be classified under three headings:

- **Economic tools,** which yield the best results since they factor in returns required by investors (the weighted average cost of capital) and do not depend directly on the sometimes erratic price movements of markets. NPV is the most important of these. EVA, the popular term for economic profit, measures how much the shareholder has increased his wealth over and above standard remuneration. However, EVA has the drawback of being restricted to the financial period in question; EVA can thus be manipulated to yield maximum results in one period at the expense of subsequent periods.

- **Market tools,** which measure MVA (Market Value Added), or the difference between the company's enterprise value, its book value, and TSR (Total Shareholder Returns). TSR is the rate of shareholder returns given the increase in the value of the share and the dividends paid out. These market tools are only useful over the medium term, because to be meaningful they should avoid the market fluctuations that can distort economic reality.

- **Accounting indicators,** which have the main drawback of being designed for accounting purposes; i.e., they do not factor in risk or return on equity. They include Earnings Per Share (EPS) linked to the value of the share by the Price/Earnings ratio (P/E), shareholders' equity linked to the value of the share by the Price/Book Ratio (PBR), accounting profitability indicators (shareholders' equity, Return On Equity – ROE, Return On Capital Employed – ROCE) to be compared with the cost of equity (or the Weighted Average Cost of Capital, WACC).

A thorough understanding of the weaknesses of all of these tools is vital. Given the lack of a generally accepted standard measure for value creation, companies quite naturally rely on those criteria that show them off in the best light.

QUESTIONS

quiz

1/ What is the main drawback of accounting profitability indicators?

2/ Why do EVA adversaries describe it as a great marketing stunt?

3/ Why is a TSR calculated over 1 year?

4/ Will a company that is making losses record positive economic profits or EVA?

5/ Can a company with a positive net profit show a negative economic profit?

6/ What is the sum of future EVA discounted to the cost of capital equal to?

7/ Subject to what conditions is it possible to compare EPS before and after a deal?

8/ What is your view of this quotation: "A series of positive EVA can only be a sign of two things: either of a monopoly that is more or less temporary (for example, a high-tech development) or a poor estimation of the cost of capital"?

9/ Is a drop in return on equity synonymous with a value destruction? Why?

10/ Is a drop in Return On Capital Employed (ROCE) synonymous with a value destruction? Why?

11/ Can a company create value and have a negative TSR over 1 year? And over 10 years?

12/ What does TSR correspond to in terms of investment choice?

13/ If you were stranded on a deserted island with only one criterion for measuring value creation, which would you want to use? Why?

14/ If EPS drops after a deal, does this necessarily imply value destruction?

15/ If EPS rises after a deal, does this necessarily imply value creation?

16/ Why does an accurate calculation of EVA or profitability mean that the balance sheet will have to be restated?

17/ What is the drawback of company rankings based on EVA?

18/ Do layoffs systematically lead to value creation?

19/ Can value be created by developing new products and new markets or by reducing costs?

20/ The hotel chain CIGA provides information to the market on value creation, measured by a ROCE calculated as the ratio between EBITDA and the historic value (i.e., gross before depreciation and amortisation) of capital employed. State your views.

21/ The group Lagardère states in its annual report that, "the rate used to measure the cost of capital is the discount rate which is equal to the flow of net future dividends (excluding tax credits) at the average share price." State your views. What assumption must be made for this statement to be true?

EXERCISES

1/ Show that, in the example on p. 349, *C*'s EPS drops by 7% after the company merges with *D*.

2/ Use the figures provided in Section I of this book (Chapters 10 to 12) and calculate the EVA and the MVA of Bic. The weighted average cost of capital of Bic is 8.5% and it has a market capitalisation of €2.1bn.

Questions

1/ The very fact that they are accounting indicators and not part of the realm of value, since they do not factor in risk or the cost of equity.

2/ Take a concept that has existed for years, give it a new trendy name and the full media treatment and you've got EVA.

3/ Intellectual trickery! TSR only means something if it is calculated over at least 5 years in order to eliminate extreme market movements.

4/ No, because, since it is making losses, it does not cover the cost of equity.

5/ Yes, if net profits do not cover the cost of equity.

6/ To NPV.

7/ Subject to the risk of capital employed, the capital structure and the growth rate remaining the same before and after the operation.

8/ It is quite true given the pressure from the competition.

9/ Not necessarily if there is a simultaneous drop in risk (capital employed, capital structure) and an improvement in growth prospects. If not, then yes.

10/ Same answer as for question 9 above.

11/ Over 1 year, yes. Much less likely over 10 years, since sudden fluctuations in prices that are not linked to the company's economic performance are set off against each other.

12/ The Internal Rate of Return (IRR).

13/ Net present value, which is the best criterion.

14/ Not necessarily, if the growth rate after the deal is higher than before or if the risk related to capital structure and capital employed is reduced. If not, then yes.

15/ Not necessarily, if the growth rate after the deal is lower than before or if the risk related to capital structure and capital employed is increased. If not, then yes.

16/ In order to get away from the formal constraints of accounting which are heavily influenced by the principle of conservatism and to think more in terms of economic value.

17/ It focuses on an annual indicator and does not factor in an investment policy which could take over a year to yield results.

18/ No; on the contrary, the creation of value is built on the development of new products and new markets, which leads to an increase in headcount.

19/ In theory, by creating new products and markets, because the sky is the limit! Reducing costs is less effective as all possible cost-cutting options are soon exhausted.

20/ ROCE is usually calculated on the basis of operating profit/capital employed (in net book value – i.e., after depreciation and amortisation). CIGA calculates the numerator and the denominator after depreciation and amortisation, which is explained by the highly asset-based nature of its activity – a hotel is not written down economically even if it has been fully amortised.

21/ Equalising the flow of dividends and share prices does not give the cost of capital but the cost of equity. That said, in the case of XYZ, a group which carries no debt, the two are equal.

Exercises

1/ Profits rise from 140 to $140 + 55 + 27.5 = 222.5$, or a multiplication by $222.5/140 = 1.59$. The number of C's shares increases by $990/1,400 = 70.7\%$, since D is paid in C's shares, or a multiplication by 1.707. EPS is multiplied by $1.59/1.707 = 93\%$, or a drop of 7%.

$2/\ EVA\ 2001 = 2001\ operating\ profits \times (1-tax) - capital\ employed \times 8.5\% = 232 \times (1-35\%) - 1,199 \times 8.5\% = €49m.\ MVA\ 2001 = 2,100 - 1,155 = €945m$

BIBLIOGRAPHY

For a general overview of value creation indicators:

G. Biddle, R. Bowen, J. Wallace, Evidence on EVA, *Journal of Applied Corporate Finance*, **12**(2), 69–79, Summer 1999.

T. Copeland, What do practitioners want? *Journal of Applied Finance*, **12**(1), 5–11, Spring/Summer 2002.

T. Copeland, T. Koller, J. Murrin, *Valuation*, 3rd edn, John Wiley & Sons, 2000.

A. Damodaran, Value creation and enhancement: back to the future, *Contemporary Finance Digest*, **2**, 5–51, Winter 1998.

A. Damodaran, *Corporate Finance: Theory and Practice*, 2nd edn, John Wiley & Sons, 2001.

R. Kleineman, Some new evidence on EVA companies, *Journal of Applied Corporate Finance*, **12**(2), 80–91, Summer 1999.

B. Madden, *CFROI: A Total System Approach to Valuing a Firm*, Butterworth-Heinemann, 1998.

For more on EVA and economic profit:

R. Bernstein, An empirical analysis of EVA as a proxy for market value added, *Financial Practice and Education*, **7**, 41–49, 1997.

G. Feltham, G. Isaac, C. Mbagwa, G. Vaidyanathan, Perhaps EVA does beat earnings: Revisiting previous evidence, *Journal of Applied Corporate Finance*, **10**(1), 83–88, Winter 2004.

G. Stewart, *The Quest for Value*, Harper Business, 1991.

The reader can also consult an interesting monographic issue on "Eva and incentive compensation" in the *Journal of Applied Corporate Finance*, **12**(2), Summer 1999.

A history of return on investment and the cost of capital in the USA:

E. Fama, K. French, The corporate cost of capital and the return on corporate investment, *Journal of Finance*, **54**, 1939–1967, December 1999.

The impact of EPS accretion and dilution on stock prices:

G. Andrade, *Do Appearances Matter? The Impact of EPS Accretion and Dilution on Stock Prices*. Harvard Business School, Working Paper 00-007.

Chapter 20
RISK AND INVESTMENT ANALYSIS

When uncertainty creates value ...

Valuing an investment by discounting future flows at the weighted average cost of capital can provide some useful parameters for making investment decisions, but it does not adequately reflect the investors' exposure to risk. On its own, this technique does not take into account the many factors of uncertainty arising from industrial investments. Attempting to predict the future is too complicated (if not impossible!) to be done using mathematical criteria alone.

Accordingly, investors have developed a number of risk analysis techniques whose common objective is to *know more about a project* than just the information provided by the Net Present Value (NPV). In fact, these techniques allow the investor to:

1   *know* the most important *sources of uncertainty* of a project and the quantitative impact of each of them. With this information, a manager can decide if it is necessary to conduct additional analysis, such as market research, product testing, logistics alternatives and so on; and
2   *identify* a project's *key value drivers* so that the manager can accurately monitor these factors before, during and after an investment is made.

Nonetheless, these traditional approaches to risk analysis suffer from an important shortcoming: they don't consider *the value of flexibility*. Recently, options theory of investment decisions has begun to allow investors to assess some new concepts that are crucial to investment analysis.

The reader must realise that the business plan is the first stage in assessing the risks related to an investment. The purpose of the business plan is to model the firm's most probable future, and it helps to identify the parameters that could significantly impact on a project's value. For example, in certain industries where sales prices are not very important, the model will be based on gross margins, which are more stable than turnover.

Establishing a business plan helps to determine the project's dependence upon factors over which investors have some influence, such as costs and/or sales price. It also outlines those factors that are beyond investors' control, such as raw material prices, exchange rates, etc. Obviously, the more the business plan depends upon exogenous factors, the riskier it becomes.

1/BREAKEVEN ANALYSIS

Managers often want to know what *quantity* of a particular product has to be sold in order to break even or produce a specific profit. Similarly, they may want to know the level of *sales* the new product must reach in order to break even.

The breakeven methodology divides costs into fixed and variable components, and seeks to find the minimum level of output that balances sales with fixed costs. As already discussed (Chapter 10), fixed costs are constant and independent of the quantity produced. It is the variable costs that depend upon production levels.

Suppose a company has an investment opportunity with the following characteristics:

Initial date	JAN 06
Initial investment	€2,000,000
Initial sales price per unit (P)	€60
Annual price change	−2%
Initial cost per unit	−40
Annual cost improvement	5%
Interest rate on debt	6%
Project life	5 years

The model assumes changing sales volumes and price erosion during the time period. Yet the company can benefit from a decreasing cost per unit over the period. Selling and administration costs also vary each year, but in a way unrelated to sales output. Therefore, they are considered as fixed cost. The model's inputs are:

	Jan-06	Jan-07	Jan-08	Jan-09	Jan-10	Jan-11
Sales volume		50,000	55,000	45,000	35,000	30,000
Price per unit		60.00	58.80	57.62	56.47	55.34
Sales revenues		3,000,000	3,234,000	2,593,080	1,976,503	1,660,263
Variable costs						
Annual cost per unit		40.00	38.00	36.10	34.30	32.58
Manufacturing cost		(2,000,000)	(2,090,000)	(1,624,500)	(1,200,325)	(977,408)
Contribution margin		**1,000,000**	**1,144,000**	**968,580**	**776,178**	**682,855**
Fixed costs						
Selling and admin. costs		(30,000)	(40,000)	(50,000)	(70,000)	(70,000)
Other		(400,000)	(400,000)	(400,000)	(400,000)	(400,000)
Total fixed costs		**(430,000)**	**(440,000)**	**(450,000)**	**(470,000)**	**(470,000)**
EBIT		**570,000**	**704,000**	**518,580**	**306,178**	**212,855**
Interest expenses		120,000	79,800	14,964	—	—

The breakeven formula is:

$$\text{Breakeven } Q = F/(P - V)$$

where Q is the quantity produced and sold, V the variable cost per unit, F the fixed cost and P the selling price per unit.

The revenue breakeven point can be obtained by multiplying:

$$\text{Breakeven } Q \times P$$

In our example, the two breakeven measures are:

Breakeven volume	21,500	21,154	20,907	21,194	20,649
Breakeven revenues	1,290,000	1,243,846	1,204,739	1,196,834	1,142,736

A better alternative is to calculate the **financial breakeven point**, which includes interest expenses in fixed costs. The breakeven will then become higher:

Financial breakeven volume	27,500	24,990	21,602	21,194	20,649
Financial breakeven revenues	1,650,000	1,469,435	1,244,800	1,196,834	1,142,736

Breakeven analysis is very popular among managers because it gives them very clear targets. In fact, they can specify targets for different areas of the firm (sell 20,000 units, keep variable costs below 50% of the selling price, etc.).

2/OPERATING AND FINANCIAL LEVERAGE

Operating leverage is the variability of earnings to corresponding changes in revenues. A firm that has high fixed costs relative to total costs will have a high operating leverage, because the cyclicality of operating income will change proportionally more than when sales change:

$$\text{Operating leverage} = \Delta\% EBIT / \Delta\% \text{Sales}$$

A firm with a high operating leverage experiences higher variability in EBIT than companies with lower operating leverage. Other things being equal, a higher operating leverage will lead to greater risk for the company (as measured by beta, see Chapter 21).

Although it is difficult for a company to change the incidence of fixed costs, companies can follow some strategies that may lead to a lower operating leverage, such as:

- negotiating higher labour flexibility and increasing the percentage of remuneration linked to the financial success of the company;
- creating alliances and joint ventures, with the aim of sharing the fixed costs of new initiatives; or
- subcontracting and outsourcing, which reduce the amount of fixed assets and annual depreciation.

The **unlevered beta**, or **asset beta** (see Chapter 23), and the operating leverage are linked because the unlevered beta is determined by both the business in which the firm operates and the operating leverage of the firm.

Financial leverage is the change in the earnings per share relative to changes in the operating profit. It is affected by the capital structure policy of the company and thus is highly firm-specific:

$$\text{Financial leverage} = \Delta\%EPS/\Delta\%EBIT$$

Other things being equal, an increase in financial leverage increases the risk (and the beta) of the equity in a firm. Why? Because fixed interest payments on debt will result in high net income in good times and very low net income in bad times.

The **levered (or equity) beta** reflects both the operating and financial risk of a company.

Combined leverage is the product of operating and financial leverage. It is a proxy for the total risk of a company.

$$\text{Combined leverage} = \text{Operating leverage} \times \text{Financial leverage}$$

$$= \Delta\%EPS/\Delta\%\text{Sales}$$

The combined leverage represents an important principle of finance. As it is the product of financial leverage and the operating leverage, companies should be reluctant to increase the financial leverage if the operating leverage is already high. Conversely, companies with low operating leverage (and therefore operating a stable business) can afford to have a higher debt/equity ratio.

In the previous example, if there is additional information that the tax rate is 33% and the number of shares is 10,000, then the three types of leverage are:

		Jan-07	Jan-08	Jan-09	Jan-10	Jan-11
Sales		3,000,000	3,234,000	2,593,080	1,976,503	1,660,263
EBIT		570,000	704,000	518,580	306,178	212,855
Interest expenses		(120,000)	(79,800)	(14,964)	—	—
Earnings before tax		450,000	624,200	503,616	306,178	212,855
Tax		(148,500)	(205,986)	(166,193)	(101,039)	(70,242)
Earnings After Tax (EAT)		301,500	418,214	337,423	205,139	142,613
Earnings Per Share (EPS)		30.15	41.82	33.74	20.51	14.26
Operating leverage						
Change in EBIT			23.51	(26.34)	(40.96)	(30.48)
Change in sales			7.80	(19.82)	(23.78)	(16.00)
Degree of Operating Leverage (DOL)	EBIT/Sales		3.01	1.33	1.72	1.90
Financial leverage						
Change in EPS			38.71	(19.32)	(39.20)	(30.48)
Change in EBIT			23.51	(26.34)	(40.96)	(30.48)
Degree of Financial Leverage (DFL)	EPS/EBIT		1.65	0.73	0.96	1.00
Combined leverage						
Change in EPS			38.71	(19.32)	(39.20)	(30.48)
Change in sales			7.80	(19.82)	(23.78)	(16.00)
Degree of combined leverage	EPS/Sales		4.96	0.97	1.65	1.90

3/SENSITIVITY ANALYSIS

An important risk analysis consists in determining how sensitive the investment is to different economic assumptions. This is done by *holding all other assumptions fixed* and then applying the present value to each different economic assumption. It is a technique that highlights the consequences of changes in *prices, volumes, rising costs* or *additional investments* on the value of projects.

To perform a sensitivity analysis, the investor:

1 fixes a base case set of assumptions and calculates the NPV; and
2 allows one variable to change while holding the others constant, and recalculates the NPV based on these assumptions. Usually, analysts develop both pessimistic and optimistic forecasts for each assumption, and then move to a more complete range of possible values of the key drivers (see the figure below for an example).

The sensitivity analysis requires a good understanding of the sector of activity and its specific constraints. The industrial analysis must be rounded off with a more financial analysis of the investment's sensitivity to the model's technical parameters, such as the discount rate or terminal value (exit multiple or growth rate to infinity).

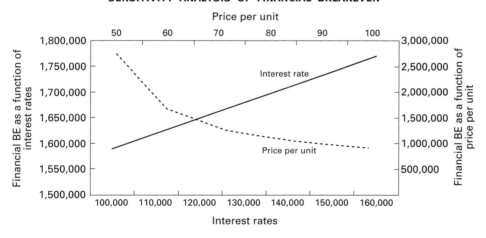

SENSITIVITY ANALYSIS OF FINANCIAL BREAKEVEN

Practitioners usually build a sensitivity matrix, which offers an overview of the sensitivity of the investment's NPV to the various assumptions.

4/SCENARIO ANALYSIS AND MONTE CARLO SIMULATION

With a **scenario analysis**, the analyst calculates the project NPV assuming a whole set of new assumptions, rather than adjusting one assumption at a time. For example, the analyst may foresee that if production volume falls short of expectations, operating costs per unit may also be higher than anticipated. In this case, two variables change at the same time. But, as the reader can easily understand, in reality the situation may be much more complex.

Although scenario analysis is appealing, it can be very difficult to understand how different variables are related to each other. The problem is two-sided:

• What are the assumptions that move together?
• What is the strength of their relationships?

As with sensitivity analysis, companies often build a base case scenario and then move to optimistic and pessimistic scenarios. In our example, the two alternative scenarios lead to the following results:

SCENARIO SUMMARY

	Current values	Best case	Worst case
Volume	50,000	55,000	46,000
Price × unit	60.00	63.00	58.00
Cost × unit	40.00	38.00	41.00
Interest expenses	120,000	110,000	130,000
Result cells:			
Financial breakeven	1,650,000	1,360,800	1,910,588

An even more elaborate variation of scenario analysis is the **Monte Carlo simulation**, which is based on sophisticated mathematical tools and software. It consists of isolating a number of the project's key variables or value drivers, such as turnover or margins, and allocating a probability distribution to each. The analyst enters all the assumptions about distributions of possible outcomes into a spreadsheet. The model then randomly samples from a table of predetermined probability distributions in order to identify the probability of each result.

Assigning probabilities to the investment's key variables is done in two stages:

1 First, influential factors are identified for each key variable. For example, with turnover, the analyst would also want to evaluate sales prices, market size, market share, etc.
2 It is then important to look at available information (long-run trends, statistical analysis, etc.) to determine the uncertainty profile of each key variable using the values given by the influential factors.

Generally, there are several types of key variables, such as simple variables (e.g., fixed costs), compound variables (e.g., turnover = market × market share), or variables resulting from more complex, econometric relationships.

The investment's net present value is shown as an uncertainty profile resulting from the probability distribution of the key variables, the random sampling of groups of variables and the calculation of net present value in this scenario. Repeating the process many times gives us a clear representation of the NPV risk profile.

Once the uncertainty profile has been created, the question is whether to accept or reject the project. The results of the Monte Carlo method are not as clearcut as present value, and a lot depends upon the risk/reward tradeoff that the investor is willing to accept. One important limitation of the method is the analysis of interdependence of the key variables; for example, how developments in costs are related to those in turnover, etc.

Moreover, the major problem in applying the Monte Carlo simulation lies in its possible misuse. Although it is not universally practised, the Monte Carlo simulation should *discount cash flows at the risk-free rate*. With traditional NPV analysis, the use of the cost of capital means that the uncertainty of expected cash flows can be considered. However, when plotting an entire distribution of NPVs and looking at the mean and the variance of the distribution, there is a risk of double-counting if the cash flows have been discounted at the cost of capital: "A distribution of NPVs generated by discounting at the risk-free rate is free of any prior risk adjustment, so the volatility of that distribution to some degree measures the risk of the project" (Smart et al., 2003, p. 321).

A consequent problem is that it is difficult to interpret a distribution of NPVs calculated using the risk-free rate. The analysis of risk by looking at the variance of the distribution ignores the fact that shareholders may eliminate some of the risk through diversification. There is a solution to the problem. It can be solved if the cost of capital is used because it includes a measure of the systematic risk, the beta of equity.

Section 20.2
THE CONTRIBUTION OF REAL OPTIONS

1/THE LIMITS OF CONVENTIONAL ANALYSIS

Do not be confused by the variety of risk analysis techniques presented in the preceding section. In fact, all of these different techniques are based on the same principle. In the final analysis, simulations, the Monte Carlo or the certainty equivalent methods are just complex variations on the NPV criteria presented in Chapter 16.

Like NPV, conventional investment risk analyses are based on two fundamental assumptions:

- the choice of the anticipated future flow scenario; and
- the irreversible nature of the investment decision.

The second assumption brings up the limits of this type of analysis. Assuming that an investment is irreversible disregards the fact that corporate managers, once they get new information, generally have a number of options. They can abandon the investment halfway through the project if it does not work out, they can postpone part of it or extend it if it has good development prospects or use new technologies. The teams managing or implementing the projects constantly receive new information and can adapt to changing circumstances. In other words, **the conventional approach to investment decisions ignores a key feature of many investment projects: flexibility**.

It might be argued that the uncertainty of future flows has already been factored in via the mathematical hope criteria and the discount rate, and therefore this should be enough to assess any opportunities to transform a project. However, it can be demonstrated that this is not necessarily so.

The discount rate and concept of mathematical hope quantify the direct consequences of random events. However, they do not take into account the managers' ability to change strategies in response to these events.

2/REAL OPTIONS

Industrial managers are not just passively exposed to risks. *In many cases, they are able to react to ongoing events.* They can increase, reduce or postpone their investment, and they exercise this right according to ongoing developments in prospective returns.

In fact, the industrial manager is in the same situation as the financial manager who can increase or decrease his position in a security given predetermined conditions.

Industrial managers who have some leeway in managing an investment project are in the same position as financial managers holding an option. [1]

The flexibility of an investment thus has a value that is not reflected in conventional analysis. **This value is simply that of the attached option.** Obviously, this option does not take the form of the financial security with which you have already become familiar. It has no legal existence. Instead, it relates to industrial assets and is called a **real option**.

1 *If you are not familiar with options, we advise you to read Chapter 29 before reading the rest of this chapter.*

Real options relate to industrial investments. Real options offer the right, but not the obligation, to change an investment project and, in particular, when new information on its prospective returns becomes available.

The potential flexibility of an investment, and therefore of the attached real options, is not always easy to identify. Industrial investors frequently do not realise or do not want to admit (especially when using a traditional investment criterion) that they do have some margin for manoeuvre. This is why it is often called a **hidden option.**

3/REAL OPTIONS CATEGORIES

The theory of real options is complex, but, like any conceptual universe, it helps us to discuss and analyse problems.

Given the potential value of hidden options, it is tempting to consider all investment uncertainties as a potential source of value. But the specific features of option contracts must not be overlooked. The following three factors are necessary to ensure that an investment project actually offers real options:

- the project must have a degree of **uncertainty**. The higher the underlying volatility, the greater the value of an option. If the standard deviation of the flows on a project is low, the value of the options will be negligible;
- investors must be able to get **more information** during the course of the project, and this information must be sufficiently precise to be useful; and
- once the new information has been obtained, it must be possible to change the project **significantly and irrevocably**. If the industrial manager cannot use the additional information to modify the project, he does not really have an option but is simply taking a chance. In addition, the initial investment decision must also have a certain degree of irreversibility. If it can be changed at no cost, then the option has no value. And, lastly, since the value of a real option stems from the investor's ability to take action, any increase in **investment flexibility generates value**, since it can give rise to new options or increase the value of existing options.

Real options apply primarily to decisions to invest or divest, but they can appear at any stage of a company's development. As a result, the review in this text of options theory is a broad outline, and the list of the various categories of real options is far from exhaustive.

The option to launch a new project corresponds to a call option on a new business. Its exercise price is the startup investment, a component that is very important in the valuation for many companies. In these cases, they are not valued on their own merits, but according to their ability to generate new investment opportunities, even though the nature and returns are still uncertain.

A good example of this principle is television channels currently using analog broadcasting. Since the business model of digital broadcasting is still uncertain and the corresponding development costs are high, the value of a television channel is partly based on anticipated changes in the market in which the channel operates. But the value also includes an option to develop in the new digital market, which still remains to be defined.

Similarly, R&D departments can be considered to be generators of real options embedded within the company. Any innovation represents the option to launch a new project or product. This is particularly true in the pharmaceutical industry. If the project is not profitable, this does not mean that the discovery has no value. It simply means that the discovery is out-of-the-money. Yet, this situation could change with further developments.

The option to develop or extend the business is comparable with the launch of a new project. However, during the initial investment phase decisions have to be made, such as whether to build a large factory to meet potentially strong demand or just a small plant to first test the waters.

A real options solution would be to build a small factory with an option to extend it if necessary. Flexibility is just as important in current operations as when deciding on the overall strategy of a project. Investments should be judged by their ability to offer recurring options throughout their lifecycle. Certain power stations, for example, can easily be adapted to run on coal or oil. This flexibility enhances their value, because they can be easily switched to a cheaper source of energy if prices fluctuate. Similarly, some auto plants need only a few adjustments in order to start producing different models.

The option to reduce or contract business is the opposite of the previous example. If the market proves smaller than expected, the investor can decide to cut back on production, thus reducing the corresponding variable costs. Indeed, he can also decide not to carry out part of the initial project, such as building a second plant. The implied sales price of the unrealised portion of the project consists of the savings on additional investments. This option can be described as a put option on a fraction of the project, even if the investment never actually materialised.

The option to postpone a project. The initial investment in the rights of an oilfield is minimal in comparison with prospecting and extraction costs. It can thus be quite useful to defer the start of the project; for example, until the business environment becomes more propitious (oil prices, operating costs, etc.). To a certain extent, this is similar to holding a well-known but not fully exploited brand.

There is a certain time value in delaying the realisation of a project, since in the meantime better information about the project's income and expenses may become available. This enables a better assessment of the potential for value creation.

Nonetheless, the option to defer the project's start is valid only if the investor is able to secure ownership of the project from the outset. If not, his competitors may take on the project. In other words, the advantage of deferring the investment could be cancelled out by the risk of new market entrants.

Looking beyond the investment decision itself, **option models can be used to determine the optimal date for starting up a project**. In this case, the waiting period is similar to holding an American option on the project. The option's value corresponds to the price of ensuring future ownership of the project (land, patents, licence, etc.).

The option to defer progress on the project is a continuation of the previous example. Some projects consist of a series of investments rather than just one initial investment. Should investors receive information casting doubt on a project that has already been launched, they may decide to put subsequent investments on hold, thus effectively halting further development. In fact, investors hold an option on the project's further development at every call for more financing.

The option to abandon means that the industrial manager can decide to abandon the project at any time. Thus, hanging on to it today means keeping open the option to abandon at a later date. However, the reverse is not possible. This asymmetry is reflected in options theory, which assumes that managers can sell their project at any time (but they might not be able to buy it back once a project is sold).

Such situations are analogous to the options theory of equity valuations that we will examine in Chapter 35. If the project is set up as a levered company, the option to abandon corresponds to shareholders' right to default. The value of this option is equal to that of equity, and it is exercised when the amount of outstanding debt is greater than the value of the project.

In the example below, the project includes an option to defer its launch (wait and see), an option to expand if it proves successful and an option to abandon it completely:

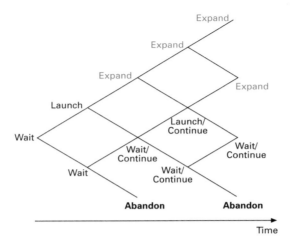

4/THE EXPANDED NET PRESENT VALUE

Since options allow us to analyse the various risks and opportunities arising from an investment, the project can be assessed as a whole. This is done by taking into account its two components – anticipated flows and real options. Some authors call this the **Expanded Net Present Value (ENPV)**, which is the opposite of the "passive" NPV of a project with no options. Based on the preceding pages, this gives:

$$ENPV = NPV + \text{Real option value}$$

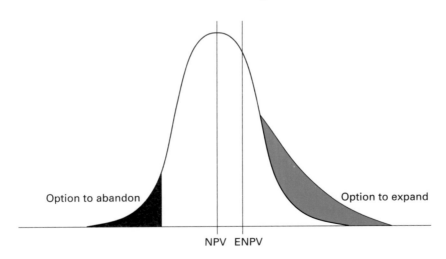

When a project is very complex with several real options, the various options cannot be valued separately since they are often conditional and interdependent. If the option to abandon the project is exercised, the option to reduce business obviously no longer exists and its value is nil. *As a result, there is no additional value on options that are interdependent.*

5/EVALUATING REAL OPTIONS

Option theory sheds light on the valuation of real options by stating that uncertainty combined with flexibility adds value to an industrial project. How appealing! It tells us that the higher the underlying volatility, and thus the risk, the greater the value of an option. This appears counterintuitive compared with the net present value approach, but remember that this value is very unstable. The time value of an option decreases as it reaches its exercise date, since the uncertainty declines with the accumulation of information on the environment.

> The uncertainty inherent in the flexibility of an industrial project creates value, because the unknown represents risk that has a time value. As time passes, this uncertainty declines as the discounted cash flows are adjusted with new information. The uncertainty is replaced with an intrinsic value that progressively incorporates the ever-changing expectations.

Consider the case of a software publisher who is offered the opportunity to buy a licence to market cellphone software for €50m. If the publisher does not accept the deal right away, the licence will be offered to a rival. The software can be produced on the spot at a cost of €500m.

If the software is produced immediately, the company should be able to generate €20m in cash flows over the next year. The situation the following year, however, is far more uncertain, since one of the main telephone carriers is due to choose a new technological standard. If the standard chosen corresponds to that of the licence offered to our company, it can hope to generate a cash flow of €90m per year. If another standard is chosen, the cash flows will plunge to €10m per year. The management of our company estimates there is a 50% chance that the "right" standard will be chosen. As of the second year, the flows are expected to be constant to infinity.

The present value of the immediate launch of the product can easily be estimated with a discount rate of 10%. The anticipated flows are $0.5 \times 90 + 0.5 \times 10 = €50m$ from the 2nd year on to infinity. Assuming that the first year's flows are disbursed (or received) immediately, the present value is $50/0.1 + 20 = €520m$ for a total cost of $500 + 50 = €550m$. According to the NPV criteria, the project destroys €30m in value and the company should reject the licensing offer. And, yet, this would be a serious mistake!

If it buys the licence, the company can decide to produce the software whenever it wants to and can easily wait a year before investing in production. While this means giving up revenues of €20m the first year, the company will have the advantage of knowing which standard the telephone operator will have chosen. It can thus decide to produce only if the standard is suited to its product. If it is not, the company abandons the project and saves on development costs. The licence offered the company thus includes a real option: the company is entitled to earn the flows on the project in exchange for investing in production.

The NPV approach assumes that the project will be launched immediately. That corresponds to the immediate exercise of the call option on the underlying instrument. This exercise destroys the time value. To assess the real value of the licence, we have to work out the value of the corresponding real option: i.e., the option of postponing development of the software.

When a company has a real option, using NPV or any other traditional investment criteria implies that it will exercise its option immediately. It is important to keep in mind that this is not necessarily the best solution or the only reality that the company/investor faces.

The value of an option can be determined by the binomial method, which will be described in greater detail in Section 29.5.

Imagine that the company has bought the licence and put off producing the software for a year. It now knows what standard the carrier has chosen. If the standard suits its purposes, it can immediately start up production at an NPV of $90 \times (1 + 1/0.1) - 500 = €490$m at that date. If the wrong standard was chosen, the NPV of developing the software falls to $10 \times (1 + 1/0.1) - 500 = -€390$m, and the company drops the project (this investment is irreversible and has no hidden options). The value of the real option attached to the licence is thus €490m for a favourable outcome and 0 for an unfavourable outcome. Using a risk-free discount rate of 5%, the calculation for the initial value of the option is €207m, since:

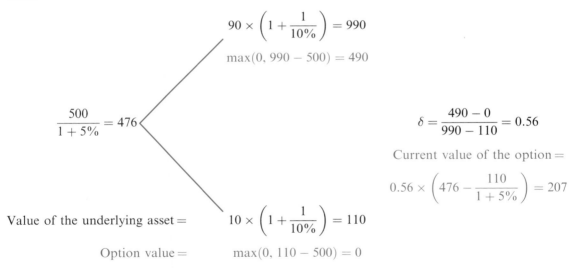

$$90 \times \left(1 + \frac{1}{10\%}\right) = 990$$

$$\max(0,\ 990 - 500) = 490$$

$$\frac{500}{1 + 5\%} = 476$$

$$\delta = \frac{490 - 0}{990 - 110} = 0.56$$

Current value of the option =

$$0.56 \times \left(476 - \frac{110}{1 + 5\%}\right) = 207$$

Value of the underlying asset = $\quad 10 \times \left(1 + \frac{1}{10\%}\right) = 110$

Option value = $\quad \max(0,\ 110 - 500) = 0$

Here is another look at the licensing offer. The licence costs €50m and the value of the real option is €207m assuming development is postponed 1 year. With this proviso, the company has been offered the equivalent of an immediate gain of $207 - 50 = €157$m.

In this example, the difference between the two approaches is considerable. Legend has it that when an oil concession was once being auctioned off, one of the bidding companies offered a price that was less than a tenth that of its competitor, quite simply because he had "forgotten" to factor in the real options!

This example assumed just one binomial alternative but, when attempting to quantify the value of real options in an investment, one faces a myriad of alternatives. More generally, the binomial model uses the **replicating portfolio**

approach: suppose that we know the value of the option at the end of the period, both in the up and in the down state. We could simply obtain the value by discounting the expected value of the two returns at an appropriate discount rate. Although correct, this approach suffers two limitations:

- we do not know the probability of the up and down scenario. This problem can be overcome; and
- the discount rate is not the cost of capital we use in estimating the NPV of the project without flexibility. A real option has different payouts and different risk than the underlying project. Thus, the cost of capital inappropriately reflects the riskiness of the cash flows of the project with flexibility.

It is sometimes possible to choose δ shares of a "traded" or twin (of the project with flexibility!) security (an asset named S, which is perfectly correlated with the option) and B euros of risk-free debt. Suppose that if the price goes up, the twin security price will be S_U (supposedly known), while if it goes down will be S_D (also known). In the up state, the project with flexibility will return P_U (a figure that we are able to estimate as we will see later on) while in the down state it will return P_D (also estimatable). The result is two equations and two unknowns (B and δ):

$$\delta \times S_U + B \times (1 + r_f) = P_U$$

$$\delta \times S_D + B \times (1 + r_f) = P_D$$

The solution of this simple system is:

$$\delta = (P_U - P_D)/(S_U - S_D)$$

$$B = (P_U - \delta \times S_U)/(1 + r_f)$$

In each node, the present value of the project with flexibility is:

$$\delta \times PV \text{ of the project at the node} \pm B$$

We then work backward, node-by-node and in a similar way, to arrive at the present value of the project with real options – i.e., the expanded net present value.

The reader should be aware that the expanded net present value cannot be lower than the "passive" NPV.

But what is this security that is perfectly correlated (the twin!) with a project with real options? The trick is to use the project itself, taking the present value without flexibility, as the twin security. In other words, we use the present value of the "passive" project as an estimate of the price it would have if it were traded on the market. This solution is extremely reasonable and useful because, after all, the project with flexibility has the highest asset correlation with the no-flexibility project.

It is now possible to take all of these tools and create some order out of this line of reasoning. The approach for option valuation is a five-step process. Discussion of the process provides an opportunity to analyse a few other important concepts.

Step 1   Calculate the "passive" present value of the project, using the traditional discounted cash flow methods.

Step 2   Build a so-called **event tree** – i.e., the lattice that models the values of the "passive" investment. This tree does not contain decision nodes and simply models the evolution of the present value of the project.

The up and down movements can be determined by the following formulae:[2]

$$\text{Up movement} = U = e^{\sigma\sqrt{T}}$$

$$\text{Down movement} = D = e^{-\sigma\sqrt{T}}$$

Step 3   Turn the event tree into a **decision tree**, by identifying the managerial flexibility and building it into the *appropriate* nodes of the tree – i.e., when the flexibility is effectively possible. For example, suppose that it is possible to expand the project and its payouts by 15% by spending an additional €10 at any time. Wherever the exercise of this option is possible in the event tree, multiply by 15% and reduce by €10 the corresponding node on the original tree. For each node, then choose the maximum value between the original event tree and the tree with the incorporated flexibility.

Step 4   Use the replication portfolio approach to value the **present value of the project with flexibility**. Then the entire decision tree can be solved by working from the final branches backward through time:

$$\delta \times PV \text{ of the no-flexibility project at the node} \pm B$$

Step 5   Calculate the **expanded net present value** by subtracting the initial investment from the present value of the project with flexibility.

Real options are calculated using quite sophisticated mathematical tools, which iterate the option's flows by a portfolio of financial assets – i.e., the foundation of the binomial method. Estimating volatility is always the most problematic issue regarding the concrete application of this methodology.

In practice, the information derived from the quantification of real options is frequently not very significant when compared with a highly positive NPV in the initial scenario. However, when NPV is negative at the outset, one always has to consider the flexibility of the project by *resorting* to real options.

In general, Copeland, Koller and Murrin sum up the practice quite succinctly: "For practitioners to use the option pricing approach, it must be relatively transparent and easy to understand" (Copeland et al., 2000, p. 411). Likewise, so too should the reader avoid using extremely complicated valuation tools if they hamper an appropriate understanding of the value added by real options.

6/CONCLUSION

The predominant appeal of real options theory is its factoring of the value of flexibility that the traditional approaches ignore. The traditional net present value approach assumes that there is only one possible outcome. It does not take

2 *If we build the event tree with these up and down movements we are building a geometric tree. The main characteristic is that it has multiplicative up and down movements that model a log-normal distribution of outcomes – whose returns can go to infinity on the up side and to zero on the down side.*

into account possible adaptive actions that could be taken by corporate managers. Real options fill this gap.

But do not get carried away, as applying this method can be quite difficult because:

- not everyone knows how to use the mathematical models. This can create problems in communicating findings; and
- estimating some of the required parameters, such as volatility, opportunity costs, etc., can be complicated.

If not properly applied, real options can give very high values. In turn, these can be used to justify the unjustifiable: e.g., stock prices during the Internet bubble in 2000 or UMTS licences in 2001.

Their main advantage is that they force users to reason "outside of the box" and come up with new ideas.

SUMMARY

download

Traditional risk analysis methods are all based on the principle of net present value. They are applicable when all investment decisions are irreversible and projects have no flexibility.

With breakeven analysis, the manager or the analyst tries to understand the level of output and revenues that must be reached in order to break even. It is an important tool for a manager because it can set very clear targets. It is convenient to use this method by considering all fixed costs, including financial expenses.

Sensitivity analysis allows the manager to understand how sensitive the NPV is to changes in assumptions on key value drivers, while holding everything else constant.

Scenario analysis changes multiple assumptions simultaneously. In this manner, the analyst must make some effort in estimating which variables move together as well as the intensity of their relationship. Using the Monte Carlo method, a better idea of the prospects of flows can be obtained by allocating a probability distribution to each of them. Although powerful, the method is not so easy to interpret and can be misused.

The limitations of all these methods become evident when project managers are able to use new information to modify a project that is already under way; i.e., when there is a certain amount of flexibility. In such cases, the industrial manager is in the same situation as the financial manager who can increase or decrease his position in a security given predetermined conditions. The industrial manager can also be compared with a financial manager who holds an option. Flexibility of an investment has a value – the value of the option attached to it. This concrete property of a flexible investment is a real option.

Three factors are necessary to ensure that an investment project actually offers real options:

- there is some uncertainty surrounding the project;

- there is additional information arriving over the course of time; and

- it must be possible to make significant changes to the project on the basis of this information.

A number of different types of real options can be present in investment projects:

- the option to launch a new project;

- the option to expand, reduce or abandon the project; or

- the possibility to defer the project or delay the progress of work.

The study of investments on the basis of their net present value can be expanded, thanks to the concept of the real option. The result we obtain by including real options in the analysis is known as expanded net present value. This is the sum of the net present value of the project and the real options attached to the project. The uncertainty inherent in the flexibility of an industrial project creates value, but this uncertainty declines as time goes by. The uncertainty is replaced by the intrinsic value arising from the discounted flows adjusted for the new information.

QUESTIONS

@
_____
quiz

1/ How does using different scenarios differ from simple cash flow discounting?

2/ In a simplified form, can the Monte Carlo method be implemented without a computer?

3/ What does the theory of options contribute to the valuing of an investment?

4/ Is the theory of options opposed to the theory of efficient markets?

5/ Can a project that contains significant real options be valued properly by the NPV criteria? By the construction of scenarios? By the Monte Carlo method? By the certainty equivalent method?

6/ Provide an example of a project where there is an option to abandon.

7/ Provide an example of a project where there is an option to expand.

8/ In practice, what is the most serious problem raised by real options?

9/ What makes the contribution of real options attractive for operations managers?

EXERCISES

1/ An Internet portal aimed at pet owners has just developed a nuclear sewing machine and offers you the opportunity to invest in the industrialisation of this product. The project will last 5 years, and for 4 years you will not be paid a dividend. But if the company is floated on the stock exchange after 5 years (which is the plan) you will get €5m. The founders of the portal estimate that your initial investment will be about €2.5m.

What return will this project bring you?

Given the project's risk, you decide that you require a return of more than 20%. What investment do you offer?

The founders, keen to obtain the €2.5m in question and believing firmly in the success of their project, offer you the following arrangement: you give them €2.5m and, if all goes well, you'll get €5m after 5 years. If the project fails, then they'll give you €1m after 5 years out of the €2.5m you invested. They believe that this reduces your risk considerably. How would you go about tackling this problem (without doing any calculations)?

ANSWERS

Questions

1/ *The assumptions are obvious.*
2/ *No.*
3/ *The valuation of management's margin for manoeuvre.*
4/ *No.*
5/ *No, no, no, no.*
6/ *Definitive closure of a mine.*
7/ *Buy a plot of land that is too big for the plant to be constructed, in order to be able to cater for a growing market.*
8/ *Valuing the alternatives.*
9/ *They highlight flexibility and the ability to adapt to a new environment.*

Exercise

1/ *IRR = 14.87%. Around €2m. The founders' offer could be compared with a put option on the project with a strike price of €1m. The whole problem lies in the valuation of this option (the volatility of the value of the project must be appreciated). The founders value it at €0.5m. The option that they're "offering" you does in fact reduce your risk, since your loss is now limited to €1.5m compared with €2.5m previously.*

BIBLIOGRAPHY

For more about sensitivity and simulations:

S. Benninga, *Financial Modelling*, 2nd edn, MIT Press, 2000.
A. Day, *Mastering Financial Modelling*, Financial Times/Prentice Hall, 2001.
S. Smart, W. Megginson, L. Gitman, *Corporate Finance*, Thomson Southwestern, 2003.

For more about real options:

M. Amra, N. Kulatilaka, *Real Options*, Harvard Business School Press, 1999.
T. Copeland, V. Antikov, *Real Options*, Texere, New York, 2001.
T. Copeland, T. Koller, J. Murrin, *Valuation*, 3rd edn, John Wiley & Sons, 2000.
J. Cox, M. Rubinstein, S. Ross, Option pricing: A simplified approach, *Journal of Financial Economics*, 229–263, September 1979.
A. Dixit, R. Pindyck, *Investment under Uncertainty*, Princeton University Press, 1994.
A. Dixit, R. Pindyck, The option approach to capital investment, *Harvard Business Review*, May/June 1995.
L. Trigeorgis, *Real Options*, Praeger, 1994.
L. Trigeorgis, A conceptual options framework for capital budgeting, *Advances in Futures and Options Research*, **3**, 145–167, 1998.
www.real-options.com, website entirely dedicated to real options.

After having covered the basics of finance (discounting, capitalisation, value and interest rates), it is time to delve deeper into another fundamental concept: risk. Risk is the uncertainty over future asset values and future returns. For better or for worse, without risk, finance would be quite boring!

Risk means uncertainty today over the cash flows and value of an asset tomorrow. Of course, it is possible to review all the factors that could have a negative or positive impact on an asset, quantify each one and measure the total impact on the asset's value. In reality, it is infinitely more practical to boil all the risks down to a single figure.

Chapter 21
RISK AND RETURN

It takes two to tango.

Investors who buy financial securities face risks because they do not know with certainty the future selling price of their securities, nor the cash flows they will receive in the meantime. This chapter will try to understand and measure this risk, and also examine its repercussions.

Section 21.1
SOURCES OF RISK

First, it is useful to begin by explaining the difference between **risk** and **uncertainty**. This example, adapted from Bodie and Merton (2000), describes it quite nicely:

RISK AND UNCERTAINTY

Suppose you would like to give a party, to which you decide to invite a dozen friends. You think that 10 of the 12 invitees will come, but there is some *uncertainty* about the real number of people that will eventually show up – 8. This situation can be risky only if the uncertainty affects your plan for the party.

For example, in providing for your guests, suppose you have to decide how much food to prepare. If you knew for sure that 10 people will show up, then you would prepare exactly enough for 10 – no more and no less. If 12 actually show up, there will not be enough food, and you will be displeased with that outcome because some guests will be hungry and dissatisfied. If 8 actually show up, there will be too much food, and you will be displeased with that too because you will have wasted some of your limited resources on surplus food. Thus, the uncertainty matters and, therefore, there is risk in this situation.

On the other hand, suppose that you have told your guests that each person is to bring enough food for a single guest. Then it might not matter in planning the party whether more or fewer than 10 people come. In that case, there is uncertainty but no risk.

There are various risks involved in financial securities, including:

➤ **Industrial, commercial and labour risks, etc.**

There are so many types of risks in this category that we cannot list them all here. They include: lack of competitiveness, emergence of new competitors, technological breakthroughs, an inadequate sales network, strikes and others. These risks tend to lower cash flow expectations and thus have an immediate impact on the value of the stock.

➤ **Liquidity risk**

This is the risk of not being able to sell a security at its fair value, as a result either of a liquidity discount or the complete absence of a market or buyers.

➤ **Solvency risk**

This is the risk that a creditor will lose his entire investment if a debtor cannot repay him in full, even if the debtor's assets are liquidated. Traders also call this **counterparty risk**.

➤ **Currency risk**

Fluctuations in exchange rates can lead to a loss of value of assets denominated in foreign currencies. Similarly, higher exchange rates can increase the value of debt denominated in foreign currencies when translated into the company's reporting currency base.

➤ **Interest rate risk**

The holder of financial securities is exposed to the risk of interest rate fluctuations. Even if the issuer fulfils his commitments entirely, there is still the risk of a capital loss or, at the very least, an opportunity loss.

➤ **Political risk**

This includes risks created by a particular political situation or decisions by political authorities, such as nationalisation without sufficient compensation, revolution, exclusion from certain markets, discriminatory tax policies, inability to repatriate capital, etc.

➤ **Regulatory risk**

A change in the law or in regulations can directly affect the return expected in a particular sector. Pharmaceuticals, banks and insurance companies, among others, tend to be on the frontlines here.

➤ **Inflation risk**

This is the risk that the investor will recover his investment with a depreciated currency – i.e., that he will receive a return below the inflation rate. A flagrant historical example is the hyperinflation in Germany in the 1920s.

➤ **The risk of fraud**

This is the risk that some parties to an investment will lie or cheat – i.e., by exploiting asymmetries of information in order to gain unfair advantage over other investors. The most common example is insider-trading

➤ **Natural disaster risks**

They include storms, earthquakes, volcanic eruptions, cyclones, tidal waves, etc., which destroy assets.

➤ **Economic risk**

This type of risk is characterised by bull or bear markets, anticipation of an acceleration or a slowdown in business activity, or changes in labour productivity.

The list is nearly endless, however at this point it is important to highlight two points:

- most financial analysis mentioned and developed in this book tends to generalise the concept of risk, rather than analysing it in depth. So, given the extent to which markets are efficient and evaluate risk correctly, it is not necessary to redo what others have already done; and
- risk is always present. The so-called risk-free rate, to be discussed later, is simply a manner of speaking. **Risk is always present, and to say that risk can be eliminated is to be excessively confident or to be unable to think about the future – both of which are very serious faults for an investor.**

Obviously, any serious investment study should begin with a precise analysis of the risks involved.

The knowledge gleaned from analysts with extensive experience in the business, mixed with common sense, allow us to classify risks into two categories:

- economic risks (political, natural, inflation, swindle and other risks), which threaten cash flows from investments and which come from the "real economy"; and
- financial risks (liquidity, currency, interest rate and other risks), which do not directly affect cash flow, but nonetheless do come under the financial sphere. These risks are due to external financial events, and not to the nature of the issuer.

Section 21.2
RISK AND FLUCTUATION IN THE VALUE OF A SECURITY

All of the aforementioned risks can penalise the financial performances of companies and their future cash flows. Obviously, if a risk materialises that seriously hurts company cash flows, investors will seek to sell their securities. Consequently, the value of the security falls.

Moreover, if a company is exposed to significant risk, some investors will be reluctant to buy its securities. Even before risk materialises, investors' perceptions that a company's future cash flows are uncertain or volatile will serve to reduce the value of its securities.

Most modern finance is based on the premise that investors seek to reduce the uncertainty of their future cash flows. By its very nature, risk increases the uncertainty of an asset's future cash flows, and it therefore follows that such uncertainty will be priced into the market value of a security.

Investors consider risk only to the extent that it affects the value of the security. Risks can affect value by changing anticipations of cash flows or the rate at which these cash flows are discounted.

To begin with, it is important to realise that in corporate finance no fundamental distinction is made between the risk of asset revaluation and the risk of asset devaluation. That is to say, whether investors expect the value of an asset to rise or decrease is immaterial. It is the fact that risk exists in the first place that is of significance and affects how investors behave.

All risks, regardless of their nature, lead to fluctuations in the value of a financial security.

Consider for example a security with the following cash flows expected for years 1 to 4:

Year	1	2	3	4
Cash flow (in €)	100	120	150	190

Imagine the value of this security is estimated to be €2,000 in 5 years. Assuming a 9% discounting rate, its value today would be:

$$\frac{100}{1.09} + \frac{120}{1.09^2} + \frac{150}{1.09^3} + \frac{190}{1.09^4} + \frac{2,000}{1.09^5} = €1,743$$

If a sudden sharp rise in interest rates raises the discounting rate to 13%, the value of the security becomes:

$$\frac{100}{1.13} + \frac{120}{1.13^2} + \frac{150}{1.13^3} + \frac{190}{1.13^4} + \frac{2,000}{1.13^5} = €1,488$$

The security's value has fallen by 15%. However, if the company comes out with a new product that raises projected cash flow by 20%, with no further change in the discounting rate, the security's value then becomes:

$$\frac{100 \times 1.20}{1.13} + \frac{120 \times 1.20}{1.13^2} + \frac{150 \times 1.20}{1.13^3} + \frac{190 \times 1.20}{1.13^4} + \frac{2,000 \times 1.20}{1.13^5} = €1,786$$

The security's value increases for reasons specific to the company, not because of a rise of interest rates in the market.

Now, suppose that there is an improvement in the overall economic outlook that lowers the discounting rate to 10%. If there is no change in expected cash flows, the stock's value would be:

$$\frac{120}{1.10} + \frac{144}{1.10^2} + \frac{180}{1.10^3} + \frac{228}{1.10^4} + \frac{2,400}{1.10^5} = €2,009$$

Again, there has been no change in the stock's intrinsic characteristics and yet its value has risen by 12.5%.

If there is stiff price competition, then previous cash flow projections will have to be adjusted downward by 10%. If all cash flows fall by the same percentage and the discounting rate remains constant, the value of the company becomes:

$$2,009 \times (1 - 10\%) = €1,808$$

Once again, the security's value increases for reasons specific to the company, not because of a rise in the market.

In the previous example, a European investor would have lost 10% of his investment (from €2,009 to €1,808). If, in the interim, the euro had fallen from $1 to $0.86, a US investor would have lost 23% (from $2,009 to $1,555).

Closer analysis shows that some securities are more volatile than others; i.e., their price fluctuates more widely. We say that these stocks are "riskier". **The riskier a stock is, the more volatile its price is, and vice versa.** Conversely, the less risky a security is, the less volatile its price is, and vice versa.

In a market economy, a security's risk is measured in terms of the volatility of its price (or of its rate of return). The greater the volatility, the greater the risk, and vice versa.

Volatility can be measured mathematically by **variance** and **standard deviation**.

MONTHLY RETURNS OF SOME FINANCIAL SECURITIES

Source: Datastream.

Typically, it is safe to assume that risk dissipates over the long term. The erratic fluctuations in the short term give way to the clear outperformance of equities over bonds, and bonds over money market investments. The chart below tends to back up this point of view. It presents data on the **Path Of Wealth** (POW) for the three asset classes. The POW measures the growth of €1 invested in any given asset, assuming that all proceeds are reinvested in the same asset.

NOMINAL RETURNS IN THE UK

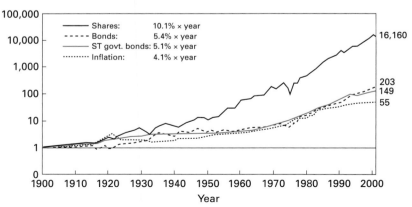

Source: Dimson et al. (2002).

Since 1900, UK stocks have risen 16,160-fold; hence, an average annual return of 10.1% vs. 5.4% for bonds, 5.1% for money market funds and average inflation of just 4.1%.

As is easily seen from the chart, risk does dissipate, but only over the long term. In other words, an investor must be able to invest his funds and then do without them during this long-term timeframe. It sometimes requires strong nerves not to give in to the temptation to sell when prices collapse, as happened with stock markets in 1929, 1974 and September 2001.

Since 1900, UK stocks have delivered an average annual return of 10.1%. Yet, during 33 of those years the returns were negative; in particular, in 1974 when investors lost 57% on a representative portfolio of UK stocks.

If you are statistically inclined, you will recognise the "Gaussian" or "normal" distribution in this chart, showing the random walk of share prices underlying the theory of efficient markets.

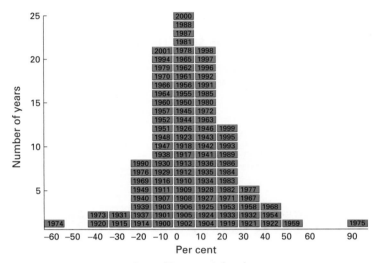

Source: Dimson et al. (2002).

And in worst case scenarios, it must not be overlooked that some financial markets vanished entirely, including the Russian equity market after the First World War and the 1917 Revolution, the German bond market with the hyperinflation of 1921–23, and the Japanese and German equity markets in 1945. Over the stretch of one century, these may be exceptional events, but they have enormous repercussions when they do occur.

The degree of risk depends on the investment timeframe and tends to diminish over the long term. Yet, rarely do investors have the means and stamina to think only of the long term and ignore short- to medium-term needs. Investors are only human, and there is definitely risk in the short and medium terms!

Section 21.3
TOOLS FOR MEASURING RETURN AND RISK

1/EXPECTED RETURN

To begin, it must be realised that a security's rate of return and the value of a financial security are actually two sides of the same coin. The rate of return will be considered first.

The **holding-period return** is calculated from the sum total of cash flows for a given investment – i.e., income – in the form of interest or dividends earned on the funds invested and the resulting capital gain or loss when the security is sold.

If just one period is examined, the return on a financial security can be expressed as follows:

$$F_1/V_0 + (V_1 - V_0)/V_0 = \text{Income} + \text{Capital gain or loss}$$

where F_1 is the income received by the investor during the period, V_0 is the value of the security at the beginning of the period and V_1 is the value of the security at the end of the period.

In an uncertain world, investors cannot calculate their returns in advance, as the value of the security is unknown at the end of the period. In some cases, the same is true for the income to be received during the period.

Therefore, investors use the concept of **expected return**, which is the average of possible returns, weighted by their likelihood of occurring. Familiarity with the science of statistics should aid in understanding the notion of expected outcome.

Given security A with 12 chances out of 100 of showing a return of -22%, 74 chances out of 100 of showing a return of 6% and 14 chances out of 100 of showing a return of 16%, its expected return would then be:

$$-22\% \times \frac{12}{100} + 6\% \times \frac{74}{100} + 16\% \times \frac{14}{100}, \quad \textit{or about 4\%}$$

More generally, expected return or expected outcome is equal to:

$$E(r) = \sum_{t=1}^{n} r_t \times p_t = \bar{r}$$

Expected return formula.

where r_t is a possible return and p_t the probability of it occurring.

2/VARIANCE, A RISK ANALYSIS TOOL

Intuitively, the greater the risk on an investment, the wider the variations in its return and the more uncertain that return is. While the holder of a government bond is sure to receive his coupons (unless the government goes bankrupt!), this is far from true for the shareholder of an offshore oil-drilling company. He could either lose everything, show a decent return or hit the jackpot.

Therefore, the risk carried by a security can be looked at in terms of the dispersion of its possible returns around an average return. Consequently, risk can be measured mathematically by the variance of its return; i.e., by the sum of the squares of the deviation of each return from expected outcome, weighted by the likelihood of each of the possible returns occurring, or:

$$V(r) = \sum_{t=1}^{n} p_t \times (r_t - \bar{r})^2$$

Risk formula.

Standard deviation in returns is the most often used measure to evaluate the risk of an investment. Standard deviation is expressed as the square root of the variance:

$$\sigma(r) = \sqrt{V(r)}$$

The variance of investment A above is therefore:

$$\frac{12}{100} \times (-22\% - 4\%)^2 + \frac{74}{100} \times (6\% - 4\%)^2 + \frac{14}{100} \times (16\% - 4\%)^2$$

where $V(r) = 1\%$, which corresponds to a standard deviation of 10%.

In sum, to formalise the concepts of risk and return:
- expected outcome $E(r)$ is a measure of expected return; and
- standard deviation $\sigma(r)$ measures the average dispersion of returns around expected outcome – in other words, risk.

Section 21.4
HOW DIVERSIFICATION REDUCES RISK

Typically, investors do not concentrate their entire wealth in only one financial asset, because they prefer to hold well-diversified portfolios. We can liken this behaviour to the old saying, "Don't put all your eggs in one basket".

The following table contains evidence of an interesting phenomenon, which gives the standard deviation for the monthly return of 13 European companies and the EuroStoxx 50 Index from April 2000 to April 2005 (% values):

Ericsson	37.14	Roche	25.25
Novartis	33.37	Vodafone	43.49
Nestlé	27.02	ENI	26.70
Total	27.05	GlaxoSmithKline	29.05
UBS	30.62	Telefónica	36.43
Royal Dutch	27.27	Deutsche Telekom	47.04
HSBC	26.00	EuroStoxx 50	23.57

The standard deviation of single assets is higher than the standard deviation of the entire market (as given by the market index)! If investors buy portfolios of assets, instead of single assets, they can reduce the overall risk of their entire portfolio because asset prices move independently. They are influenced differently by macroeconomic conditions.

This suggests that adding securities to a portfolio makes it possible to reduce the idiosyncratic influence that single securities have on the total return of the portfolio. This "diversification effect" is due to:

- the reduced weighting of single securities on the portfolio performance; and
- the higher balance that occurs between favourable and unfavourable securities.

When choosing securities, investors should evaluate the *marginal contribution* that each additional asset brings to the variance of the entire portfolio.

Fluctuations in the value of a security can be due to:

- fluctuations in the entire market. The market could rise as a whole after an unexpected cut in interest rates, stronger than expected economic growth figures, etc. All stocks will then rise, although some will move more than others (see the figure below). The same thing can occur when the entire market moves downward; or
- factors specific to the company that do not affect the market as a whole, such as a major order, the bankruptcy of a competitor, a new regulation affecting the company's products, etc.

These two sources of fluctuation produce two types of risk: market risk and specific risk.

➤ **Market, systematic or undiversifiable risk** is due to trends in the entire economy, tax policy, interest rates, inflation, etc., and affects all securities. Remember, this is the risk of the security **correlated** to market risk. To varying degrees, market risk affects all securities. For example, if a nation switches to a 35-hour working week with no cut in wages, all companies will be affected. However, in such a case it stands to reason that textile makers will be affected more than cement companies.

➤ **Specific, intrinsic or idiosyncratic risk** is independent of market-wide phenomena and is due to factors affecting just the one company, such as mismanagement, a factory fire, an invention that renders a company's main product line obsolete, etc. (in the next chapter, it will be shown how this risk can be eliminated by diversification).

Market volatility can be economic or financial in origin, but it can also result from anticipations of flows (dividends, capital gains, etc.) or a variation in the cost of equity. For example, overheating of the economy could raise the cost of equity (i.e., after an increase in the central bank rate) and reduce anticipated cash flows due to weaker demand. Together, these two factors could exert a double downward pressure on financial securities.

WHAT DIVERSIFICATION DOES

It is now possible to partition risk typologies according to their nature. There are some risks that only impact a small number of companies: e.g., project risk, competitive risk and industry risk. The latter refers to the impact that industrial policy can have on the performance of a specific industry.

Conversely, there are other risks that impact a much larger number of companies: e.g., interest rate risk, inflation risk and external shock risks. By their nature, these types of risk influence almost all companies in a country. Consider interest rate risk. It is reasonable to assume that an increase in interest rates will diminish the investments in fixed assets of *all* companies, because it affects different sectors and companies with varying levels of intensity.

Finally, there are some risks that lie between the two extremes. Their impact differs substantially among industries. A good example is currency risk, which is important particularly for companies that have a significant proportion of their sales in foreign currencies.

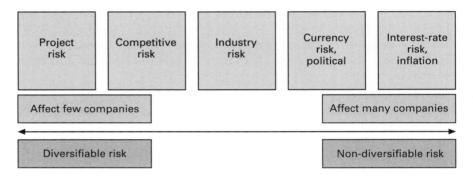

When an investor wants to know the contribution of risk to the portfolio, rather than the total risk of an asset, what is the appropriate risk measure he should use? The standard deviation of a single asset is not the correct measure, because standard deviation measures the risk in isolation without considering the correlation with other assets. A better measure would be the **covariance** between the returns of the assets included in the portfolio.

Section 21.5
PORTFOLIO RISK

1/THE FORMULA APPROACH

Consider the following two stocks, Air Liquide (*AL*) and Philips (*P*), which have the following characteristics:

	Philips (*P*, %)	Air Liquide (*AL*, %)
Expected return: $E(r)$	6	13
Risk: $\sigma(r)$	10	17

As is clear from this table, Air Liquide offers a higher expected return while presenting a greater risk than Philips. Inversely, Philips offers a lower expected return but also presents less risk.

These two investments are not directly comparable. Investing in Air Liquide means accepting more risk in exchange for a higher return, whereas investing in Philips means playing it safe.

Therefore, there is no clearcut basis by which to choose between Air Liquide and Philips. However, the problem can be looked at in another way: **would buying a combination of Air Liquide and Philips shares be preferable to buying just one or the other?**

It is likely that the investor will seek to diversify and create a **portfolio** made up of Air Liquide shares (in a proportion of X_{AL}) and Philips shares (in a proportion of X_P). This way, he will expect a return equal to the weighted average return of each of these two stocks, or:

$$E(r_{AL,P}) = X_{AL} \times E(r_{AL}) + X_P \times E(r_P)$$

where $X_{AL} + X_P = 1$.

Depending on the proportion of Air Liquide shares in the portfolio (X_{AL}), the portfolio would look like this:

X_{AL} (%)	0	25	33.3	50	66.7	75	100
$E(r_{AL,P})$ (%)	6	7.8	8.3	9.5	10.7	11.3	13

The portfolio's variance is determined as follows:

$$\sigma^2(r_{AL,P}) = X_{AL}^2 \times \sigma^2(r_{AL}) + X_P^2 \times \sigma^2(r_P) + 2X_{AL} \times X_P \times \text{cov}(r_{AL}, r_P)$$

$\text{Cov}(r_{AL}, r_P)$ is the covariance between Air Liquide and Philips. It measures the degree to which Air Liquide and Philips fluctuate together. It is equal to:

$$\text{Cov}(r_{AL}, r_P) = E[(r_{AL} - E(r_{AL})) \times (r_P - E(r_P))]$$

$$= \sum_{i=1}^{n} \sum_{j=1}^{m} p_{i,j} \times (r_{AL_i} - \bar{r}_{AL}) \times (r_{P_j} - \bar{r}_P)$$

$$= \rho_{AL,P} \times \sigma(r_{AL}) \times \sigma(r_P)$$

p_{ij} is the probability of joint occurrence and $\rho_{AL,P}$ is the correlation coefficient of returns offered by Air Liquide and Philips. The correlation coefficient is a number between -1 (returns 100% inversely proportional to each other) and 1 (returns 100% proportional to each other). Correlation coefficients in the stock market are usually positive, as most stocks rise together in a bullish market and most fall together in a bearish market.

By plugging the variables back into our variance equation above, we obtain:

$$\sigma^2(r_{AL,P}) = X_{AL}^2 \times \sigma^2(r_{AL}) + X_P^2 \times \sigma^2(r_P) + 2X_{AL} \times X_P \times \rho_{AL,P} \times \sigma(r_{AL}) \times \sigma(r_P)$$

Given that:

$$-1 \leq \rho_{AL,P} \leq 1$$

It is therefore possible to say:

$$\sigma^2(r_{AL,P}) \le X_{AL}^2 \times \sigma^2(r_{AL}) + X_P^2 \times \sigma^2(r_P) + 2X_{AL} \times X_P \times \sigma(r_{AL}) \times \sigma(r_P)$$

or:

$$\sigma^2(r_{AL,P}) \le (X_{AL} \times \sigma(r_{AL}) + X_P \times \sigma(r_P))^2$$

As the above calculations show, the overall risk of a portfolio consisting of Air Liquide and Philips shares is less than the weighted average of the risks of the two stocks.

Assuming that $\rho_{AL,P}$ is equal to 0.5 (from the figures in the above example), we obtain the following:

X (%)	0	25	33.3	50	66.7	75	100
$\sigma(r_{AL,P})$ (%)	10.0	10.3	10.7	11.8	13.3	14.2	17.0

Hence, a portfolio consisting of 50% Air Liquide and 50% Philips has a standard deviation of 11.8% or less than the average of Air Liquide and Philips, which is $(50\% \times 10\%) + (50\% \times 17\%) = 13.5\%$.

On a chart, it looks like this:

Although fluctuations in Air Liquide and Philips stocks are positively correlated with each other, having both together in a portfolio creates a less risky profile than investing in them individually.

Only a correlation coefficient of 1 creates a portfolio risk that is equal to the average of its component risks.

CORRELATION BETWEEN DIFFERENT MARKETS

Globalisation has increased correlation among Western markets. The lowest correlation coefficient is just 0.75.

	France	Germany	Italy	Netherlands	Spain	Switzerland	UK	USA
France	1	0.96	0.96	0.98	0.78	0.76	0.75	0.90
Germany	0.96	1	0.95	0.97	0.86	0.82	0.80	0.88
Italy	0.96	0.95	1	0.97	0.86	0.87	0.82	0.90
Netherlands	0.98	0.97	0.97	1	0.86	0.84	0.85	0.93
Spain	0.78	0.86	0.86	0.86	1	0.85	0.92	0.88
Switzerland	0.76	0.82	0.87	0.84	0.85	1	0.86	0.80
UK	0.75	0.80	0.82	0.85	0.92	0.86	1	0.92
USA	0.90	0.88	0.90	0.93	0.88	0.80	0.92	1

download

However, sector diversification is still highly efficient thanks to the low correlation coefficients among different industries:

CORRELATION BETWEEN EUROPEAN STOCKS IN DIFFERENT SECTORS

	Oil and gas	Basic manu-facturing	Industrial stocks	Cyclical consumer goods	Non-cyclical consumer goods	Cyclical services	Non-cyclical services	Utilities	Finance	IT
Oil and gas	1	0.39	0.56	−0.09	0.26	0.36	0.39	−0.10	0.26	0.03
Basic manufacturing	0.39	1	0.51	0.76	0.12	0.58	0.32	0.33	0.13	−0.07
Industrial stocks	0.56	0.51	1	0.28	0.21	0.91	0.88	0.26	−0.20	−0.47
Cyclical consumer goods	−0.09	0.76	0.28	1	0.08	0.50	0.14	0.57	−0.09	−0.30
Noncyclical consumer goods	0.26	0.12	0.21	0.08	1	0.25	0.27	0.63	−0.66	−0.90
Cyclical services	0.36	0.58	0.91	0.50	0.25	1	0.91	0.56	−0.58	−0.81
Noncyclical services	0.39	0.32	0.88	0.14	0.27	0.91	1	0.43	−0.80	−0.91
Utilities	−0.10	0.33	0.88	0.14	0.27	0.91	1	0.43	−0.80	−0.95
Finance	0.26	0.13	−0.20	−0.09	−0.66	−0.58	−0.80	−0.80	1	0.77
IT	0.03	−0.07	−0.47	−0.30	−0.90	−0.81	−0.91	−0.95	0.77	1

There are some negative correlation coefficients, due in part to the 2000 bubble, during which technology, media and telecom stocks performed well, to the detriment of other stocks.

download

Diversification can:

- either reduce risk for a given level of return; and/or
- improve return for a given level of risk.

2/ THE MATRIX APPROACH

It is possible to use matrices that contain all the elements of the variance of a portfolio in order to visually assess the elements of variance. The previous example yields the following table:

	AL	P
AL	$X_{AL}^2 \times \sigma_{AL}^2$	$X_{AL} \times X_P \times \sigma_{AL,P}$
P	$X_P \times X_{AL} \times \sigma_{P,AL}$	$X_P^2 \times \sigma_P^2$

The variance of a two-asset portfolio is the sum of the four elements contained in the matrix. Since the order in which we sum the assets is irrelevant, we may simply double the cell that contains the covariance, because they are exactly the same.

The matrix approach is a useful tool when the investor manages a portfolio of many assets. Consider the following example, with N assets that result in the following matrix:

Assets	A	B	C	$\cdots$	N
A	$X_A^2 \times \sigma_A^2$	$X_A \times X_B \times \sigma_{A,B}$	$X_A \times X_C \times \sigma_{A,C}$	$\cdots$	$X_A \times X_N \times \sigma_{A,N}$
B	$X_B \times X_A \times \sigma_{B,A}$	$X_B^2 \times \sigma_B^2$	$X_B \times X_C \times \sigma_{B,C}$	$\cdots$	$X_B \times X_N \times \sigma_{B,N}$
C	$X_C \times X_A \times \sigma_{C,A}$	$X_C \times X_B \times \sigma_{C,B}$	$X_C^2 \times \sigma_C^2$	$\cdots$	$X_C \times X_N \times \sigma_{C,N}$
$\vdots$	$\vdots$	$\vdots$	$\vdots$	$\vdots$	$\vdots$
N	$X_N \times X_A \times \sigma_{N,A}$	$X_N \times X_B \times \sigma_{N,B}$	$X_N \times X_C \times \sigma_{N,C}$	$\cdots$	$X_N^2 \times \sigma_N^2$

Following the diagonal cells from the top left to the bottom right, it should be noted that the number of terms in the diagonal is always identical to the number of assets included in the portfolio. Consequently, the "group" of variances that can have an impact on the risk of the portfolio equals the number of assets included in the portfolio. The number of covariances is much more numerous, which rapidly increases as we add assets to the portfolio.

What exactly does this result mean?

As with a portfolio of two assets, the variance of a portfolio of N assets is the sum of all the cells of the matrix. Thus, the variance of the portfolio is mostly influenced by covariances because their higher number exceeds that of variances.

Suppose that there is an equal weight for each asset included in the portfolio; i.e., each asset has a weight of $1/N$. Then there will be N elements on the diagonal of variances and $N(N-1)$, or $N^2 - N$, terms in the other cells. The portfolio variance will then be given by:

$$\sigma_P^2 = N \times \left(\frac{1}{N}\right)^2 \overline{\text{var}} + (N^2 - N) \times \left(\frac{1}{N}\right)^2 \overline{\text{cov}}$$

where $\overline{\text{var}}$ and $\overline{\text{cov}}$ indicate the average variance and covariance, respectively. It can then be simplified to:

$$\sigma_P^2 = \left(\frac{1}{N}\right) \overline{\text{var}} + \left(\frac{N^2 - N}{N^2}\right) \overline{\text{cov}}$$

$$\sigma_P^2 = \left(\frac{1}{N}\right) \overline{\text{var}} + \left(1 - \frac{1}{N}\right) \overline{\text{cov}}$$

This equation highlights the importance of the matrix approach because, if we increase the number of assets included in the portfolio, the variance of the portfolio converges towards the average covariance of the assets.

Ideally, if the covariance were zero we could eliminate all risk from our portfolio. Unfortunately, financial assets tend to move together, thus the average covariance is positive.

Yet, it is now possible to understand the real meaning of what was previously defined as "market risk". This is the risk measured by the covariance, and it represents the portion of risk that cannot be eliminated even after having taken advantage of diversification.

Section 21.6
MEASURING HOW INDIVIDUAL SECURITIES AFFECT PORTFOLIO RISK: THE BETA COEFFICIENT

1/THE BETA AS A MEASURE OF THE MARKET RISK OF A SINGLE SECURITY

Following is a brief summary of topics covered so far in this chapter:

- the risk of a well-diversified portfolio is solely a function of the market risk of the securities it contains; and
- the contribution of a single asset to the risk of portfolio is measured by its covariance with the returns of the portfolio. This sensitivity measure is called the **beta** (β) of a financial asset.

Since market risk and specific risk are independent, they can be measured independently and we can apply the Pythagorean theorem (in more mathematical terms, the two risk vectors are orthogonal) to the overall risk of a single security:

$$(\text{Overall risk})^2 = (\text{Market risk})^2 + (\text{Specific risk})^2 \qquad (21.1)$$

The systematic risk presented by a financial security is frequently expressed in terms of its sensitivity to market fluctuations. This is done via a linear regression between periodic market returns (r_{M_t}) and the periodic returns of each security J: (r_{J_t}). This yields the regression line expressed in the following equation:

$$r_{J_t} = \alpha_J + \beta_J \times r_{M_t} + \varepsilon_{J_t}$$

β_J is a parameter specific to each investment J and it expresses the relationship between fluctuations in the value of J and the market. It is thus a coefficient of volatility or of sensitivity. **We call it the beta coefficient.**

A security's total risk is reflected in the standard deviation of its return $\sigma(r_J)$.

A security's **market risk** is therefore equal to $\beta_J \times \sigma(r_M)$, where $\sigma(r_M)$ is the standard deviation of the market return. Therefore, it is also proportional to the beta – i.e., the security's market-linked volatility. The higher the beta, the greater the market risk borne by the security. If $\beta > 1$, the security magnifies market fluctuations. Conversely, securities whose beta is below 1 are less affected by market fluctuations.

The chart shows that the β of Philips is higher than that of Air Liquide.

download

COMPARED EVOLUTION OF EUROSTOXX 50 INDEX, AIR LIQUIDE AND PHILIPS (INDEX = 100)

Source: Datastream.

The **specific risk** of security J is equal to the standard deviation of the different residues ε_{J_t} of the regression line, expressed as $\sigma(\varepsilon_J)$; i.e., variations in the stock that are not tied to market variations.

In summation, proposition (21.1) can be expressed mathematically as follows:

$$\sigma^2(r_J) = \beta_J^2 \times \sigma^2(r_M) + \sigma^2(\varepsilon_J)$$

2/ CALCULATING BETA

β measures a security's sensitivity to market risk. For security J, it is mathematically obtained by performing a regression analysis of security returns vs. market returns.

Hence:

$$\beta_J = \frac{\text{Cov}(r_J, r_M)}{V(r_M)}$$

where $\text{Cov}(r_J, r_M)$ is the covariance of the return of security J with that of the market and $V(r_M)$ is the variance of the market return. This can be represented as:

$$\beta_J = \frac{\displaystyle\sum_{i=1}^{n}\sum_{k=1}^{n} p_{i,k} \times (r_{J_i} - \bar{r}_J) \times (r_{M_t} - \bar{r}_M)}{\displaystyle\sum_{i=1}^{n} p_i \times (r_{M_i} - \bar{r}_M)^2}$$

More intuitively, β corresponds to the slope of the regression of the security's return vs. that of the market. The line we obtain is defined the **characteristic line** of a security. As an example, we have calculated the β for Philips. It is 1.78, subverting the conclusion that might be drawn from a glance at the previous chart.

BETA OF PHILIPS

$y = 1.7877x + 0.0071$
$R^2 = 0.7546$

Philips daily returns (%)

EuroStoxx50 returns (%)

The interpretation of beta from the figure is readily apparent. The graph tells us that the returns of Philips are magnified 1.78 times over those of the market. When the market does well, Philips is expected to do even better. When the market does poorly, Philips is expected to do even worse. As Philips' β is over 1, it is more volatile than the market and thus riskier.

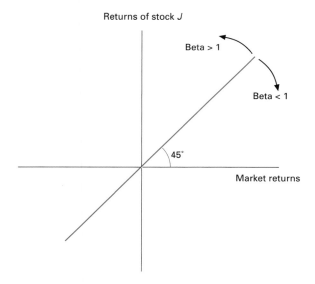

Now consider an investor who is debating whether or not to add Philips to his portfolio. Given that Philips has a magnification effect of 1.78, his reasoning will be affected by the fact that this stock will increase the risk of the portfolio.

3/PARAMETERS BEHIND THE BETA

By definition, the market β is equal to 1. Why? The β of fixed income securities ranges from about 0 to 0.5. The β of equities is usually higher than 0.5, and normally between 0.5 and 1.5. Very few companies have negative β, and a β greater than 2 is quite exceptional. To illustrate, the table below presents betas, as of April 2005, of the EuroStoxx 50 component stocks:

Sanofi-Synthélabo	0.3	Repsol	0.8	Deutsche Telekom	1.1	LVMH	1.6
RWE	0.4	Unilever	0.8	PPR	1.1	Siemens	1.6
E-ON	0.4	BASF	0.8	AXA	1.2	Philips	1.7
Air Liquide	0.4	Mun-Re	0.8	San Paolo IMI	1.2	Alcatel	1.8
ENI	0.5	Bayer	0.9	BNP Paribas	1.2		
TotalFinaElf	0.5	L'Oréal	1.0	Société Générale	1.3		
Suez	0.5	Fortis	1.0	Nokia	1.3		
Danone	0.5	Volkswagen	1.0	DaimlerChrysler	1.3		
Ahold	0.7	Allianz	1.0	Telefónica	1.3		
Aventis	0.7	BHV	1.0	ABN Amro	1.3		
Generali	0.7	Vivendi Universal	1.0	ING	1.3		
Carrefour	0.7	Unicredito	1.0	Deutsche Bank	1.3		
Endesa	0.7	Telecom Italia	1.1	Santand. Cent. Hisp.	1.4		
Royal Dutch	0.7	TIM	1.1	BBV Argentaria	1.4		
Saint-Gobain	0.8	Aegon	1.1	France Télécom	1.4		

For a given security, the following parameters explain the value of beta:

(a) Sensitivity of the sector to the state of the economy

The greater the effect of the state of the economy on a business sector, the higher is its β – temporary work is one such highly exposed sector. Another example is automakers, which tend to have a β close to 1. There is an old saying in North America, "As General Motors goes, so goes the economy". This serves to highlight how GM's financial health is to some extent a reflection of the health of the entire economy. Thus, beta analysis can show how GM will be directly affected by macroeconomic shifts in the economy.

(b) Cost structure

The greater the proportion of fixed costs to total costs, the higher the breakeven point and the more volatile the cash flows. Companies that have a high ratio of fixed costs (such as cement makers) have a high β, while those with a low ratio of fixed costs (like mass-market service retailers) have a low β.

(c) Financial structure

The greater a company's debt, the greater its financing costs. Financing costs are fixed costs which increase a company's breakeven point and, hence, its earnings volatility. The heavier a company's debt or the more heavily leveraged the company is, the higher is the β of its shares.

(d) Visibility on company performance

The quality of management and the clarity and quantity of information the market has about a company will all have a direct influence on its beta. All other factors being equal, if a company gives out little or low-quality information, the β of its stock will be higher as the market will factor the lack of visibility into the share price.

(e) Earnings growth

The higher the forecasted rate of earnings growth, the higher the β. Most of a company's value in cash flows are far down the road and thus highly sensitive to any change in assumptions.

Section 21.7
CHOOSING AMONG SEVERAL RISKY ASSETS AND THE EFFICIENT FRONTIER

This section will address the following questions: Why is it correct to say that the beta of an asset should be measured in relation to the market portfolio? Above all, what is the market portfolio?

To begin, it is useful to study the impact of the correlation coefficient on diversification. Again, the same two securities will be analysed: Air Liquide (AL) and Philips (P). By varying $\rho_{AL,P}$ between -1 and $+1$, we obtain (in %):

Proportion of P shares in portfolio (X_{AL})		0	25	33.3	50	66.7	75	100
Return on the portfolio: $E(r_{AL,P})$		6.0	7.8	8.3	9.5	10.7	11.3	13.0
Portfolio risk $\sigma(r_{AL,P})$	$\rho_{AL,P} = -1$	10.0	3.3	1.0	3.5	8.0	10.3	17.0
	$\rho_{AL,P} = -0.5$	10.0	6.5	6.2	7.4	10.1	11.7	17.0
	$\rho_{AL,P} = 0$	10.0	8.6	8.7	9.9	11.8	13.0	17.0
	$\rho_{AL,P} = 0.3$	10.0	9.7	10.0	11.1	12.7	13.7	17.0
	$\rho_{AL,P} = 0.5$	10.0	10.3	10.7	11.8	13.3	14.2	17.0
	$\rho_{AL,P} = 1$	10.0	11.8	12.3	13.5	14.7	15.3	17.0

Note the following caveats:

- if Air Liquide and Philips were perfectly correlated (i.e., the correlation coefficient is 1), diversification would have no effect. All possible portfolios would lie on a line linking the risk/return point of Philips with that of Air Liquide. Risk would increase in direct proportion to Air Liquide's stock added;
- if the two stocks were perfectly inversely correlated (correlation coefficient −1), diversification would be total. However, there is little chance of this occurring, as both companies are exposed to the same economic conditions; and
- generally speaking, Air Liquide and Philips are positively, but imperfectly, correlated and diversification is based on the desired amount of risk.

With a fixed correlation coefficient of 0.3, there are portfolios that offer different returns at the same level of risk. Thus, a portfolio consisting of two-thirds Philips and one-third Air Liquide shows the same risk (10%) as a portfolio consisting of just Philips, but returns 8.3% vs. only 6% for Philips.

As long as the correlation coefficient is below 1, diversification will be efficient.

IMPACT OF THE CORRELATION COEFFICIENT ON RISK AND RETURN

There is no reason for an investor to choose a given combination if another offers a better (efficient) return at the same level of risk.

Efficient portfolios (such as a combination of Air Liquide and Philips shares) offer investors the best risk–return ratio (i.e., minimal risk for a given return).

Efficient portfolios fall between *Z* and Air Liquide. The portion of the curve between *Z* and Air Liquide is called the efficient frontier.

EFFICIENT FRONTIER

For any portfolio that does not lie on the **efficient frontier**, another can be found that, given the level of risk, offers a greater return or that, at the same return, entails less risk.

All subjective elements aside, it is impossible to choose between portfolios that have different levels of risk. There is no universally optimum portfolio and, therefore, it is up to the investor to decide, based upon his appetite for risk. However, given the same level of risk, some portfolios are better than others. These are the efficient portfolios.

With a larger number of stocks – i.e., more than just two – the investor can improve his efficient frontier, as shown in the chart below:

EFFICIENT FRONTIER

Section 21.8
CHOOSING BETWEEN SEVERAL RISKY ASSETS AND A RISK-FREE ASSET: THE CAPITAL MARKET LINE

1/RISK-FREE ASSETS

By definition, **risk-free assets are those whose returns**, the risk-free rate (r_F), **is certain.** This is the case with a government bond, assuming of course that the government does not go bankrupt. The standard deviation of its return is thus zero.

If a portfolio has a risk-free asset F in proportion $(1 - X_P)$ and the portfolio consists exclusively of Philips shares, then the portfolio's expected return $E(r_{P,F})$ will be equal to:

$$E(r_{P,F}) = (1 - X_P) \times r_F + X_P \times E(r_P) = r_F + (E(r_P) - r_F)) \times X_P \quad (21.2)$$

The portfolio's expected return is equal to the return of the risk-free asset, plus a risk premium, multiplied by the proportion of Philips shares in the portfolio. The risk premium is the difference between the expected return on Philips and the return on the risk-free asset.

How much risk does the portfolio carry? Its risk will simply be the risk of the Philips stock, commensurate with its proportion in the portfolio, expressed as follows:

$$\sigma(r_{P,F}) = X_P \times \sigma(r_P) \tag{21.3}$$

If the investor wants to increase his expected return, he will increase X_P. He could even borrow money at the risk-free rate and use the funds to buy Philips stock, but the risk carried by his portfolio would rise commensurately.

By combining equations (21.2) and (21.3), we can eliminate X_P, thus deriving the following equation:

$$E(r_{P,F}) = r_F + \frac{\sigma(r_{P,F})}{\sigma(r_P)} \times [E(r_P) - r_F]$$

This portfolio's expected return is equal to the risk-free rate, plus the difference between the expected return on Philips and the risk-free rate. This difference is then weighted by the ratio of the portfolio's standard deviation to Philips' standard deviation.

Continuing with the Philips example, and assuming that r_F is 3%, with 50% of the portfolio consisting of a risk-free asset, the following is obtained:

$$E(r_{P,F}) = 3\% + (6\% - 3\%) \times 0.5 = 4.5\%$$

$$\sigma(r_{P,F}) = 0.50 \times 10\% = 5\%$$

Hence:

$$E(r_{P,F}) = 3\% + (5\%/10\%) \times (6\% - 3\%) = 4.5\%$$

For a portfolio that includes a risk-free asset, there is a linear relationship between expected return and risk. To lower a portfolio's risk, simply liquidate some of the portfolio's stock and put the proceeds into a risk-free asset. To increase risk, it is only necessary to borrow at the risk-free rate and invest in a stock with risk.

2/RISK-FREE ASSETS AND EFFICIENT FRONTIER

The risk–return profile can be chosen by combining risk-free assets and a stock portfolio (the alpha portfolio in the chart at the top of the next page). This new portfolio will be on a line that connects the risk-free rate to the efficient portfolio that has been chosen. In the chart, the portfolio located on the efficient frontier, M, maximises utility. The line joining the risk-free rate to portfolio M is tangent to the efficient frontier.

Investors' taste for risk can vary; yet, the above graph demonstrates that the shrewd investor should be invested in portfolio M. It is then a matter of adjusting the risk exposure by adding or subtracting risk-free assets.

If all investors acquire the same portfolio, this portfolio must contain all existing shares. To understand why, suppose that stock i was not in portfolio M. In that case, nobody would want to buy it, since all investors hold portfolio M. Consequently, there would be no market for it and it would cease to exist.

The "market portfolio" includes all stocks at their market value. The market portfolio is thus weighted proportionally to the market capitalisation of a particular market.

The weighting of stock i in a market portfolio will necessarily be the value of the single security divided by the sum of all the assets. As we are assuming fair value, this will be the fair value of i.

3/CAPITAL MARKET LINE

The expected return of a portfolio consisting of the market portfolio and the risk-free asset can be expressed by the following equation:

$$E(r_P) = r_F + \frac{\sigma_P}{\sigma_M} \times [E(r_M) - r_F]$$

where $E(r_P)$ is the portfolio's expected return, r_F the risk-free rate, $E(r_M)$ the return on the market portfolio, σ_P the portfolio's risk and σ_M the risk of the market portfolio.

This is the equation of the **capital market line**, which is graphically tangent to the efficient frontier containing the portfolio M. The reason is that if there was a more efficient combination of risk-free and risky assets, the weighting of the risky assets would depart from that of the market portfolio, and supply and demand for these stocks would seek a new equilibrium.

The most efficient portfolios in terms of return and risk will always be on the capital market line. The tangent point at M constitutes the optimal combination for *all* investors. If we introduce the assumption that all investors have

homogeneous expectations – i.e., that they have the same opinions on expected returns and risk of financial assets – then the efficient frontier of risky assets will be the same for all of them. The capital market line is the same for all investors and each of them would thus hold a combination of the portfolio M and the risk-free asset.

With the assumption of homogeneous expectations, it is reasonable to say that the portfolio M includes all the assets weighted for their market capitalisation. This is defined as the **market portfolio**.[1] The market portfolio is the portfolio that all investors hold a fraction of, proportional to the market's capitalisation.

1 *In practice, investors use global capitalisation market indexes as a proxy for the market portfolio.*

The *capital market line* links the market portfolio M to the risk-free asset. For a given level of risk, no portfolio is better than those located on this line.

These portfolios consist of two types of investments:

- an investment in the risk-free rate and in the market portfolio, between $\sigma = 0$ and $\sigma = \sigma_M$; and
- an investment in the market portfolio financed partly by debt at the risk-free rate, beyond σ_M.

A rational investor will not take a position on individual stocks in the hope of obtaining a big return, but rather on the market as a whole. He will then choose his risk level by adjusting his debt level or by investing in risk-free assets. This is the **separation theorem**. According to this theorem the financial decision of an investor requires "two steps":

1   first, collect data and information on financial assets, estimate the expected risk and return for each of them, simulate sets of combinations of assets, build the efficient frontier of risky assets, link the risk-free asset with the efficient frontier, delineate the market portfolio (*M*); and then
2   choose how to allocate wealth between *M* and the risk-free assets. This decision is a function of personal preferences and attitude toward risk.

Only portfolios located on a line passing through *M* and on tangent to the efficient frontier are optimal. The others, such as portfolio *Z*, are suboptimal.

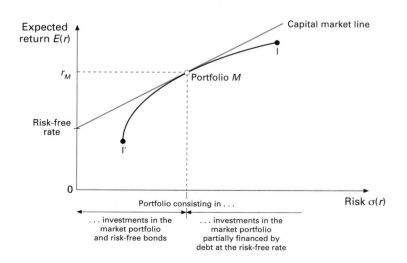

With this understanding of what a market portfolio is, it is now possible to answer the initial question of Section 21.7: Why can we say that the beta of an asset should be measured in relation to the market portfolio? The answer is because all investors have a certain fraction of their wealth invested in the market portfolio. The additional risk of a new title should be computed measuring the covariance of that asset with the market portfolio.

Section 21.9
HOW PORTFOLIO MANAGEMENT WORKS

The financial theory described so far seems to give a clear suggestion: invest only in highly diversified mutual funds and in government bonds. However, not all investors subscribe to this theory. Some take other approaches, herein described below. Sometimes, investors combine different approaches.

First, we will consider the difference between a **top-down** and a **bottom-up** approach. In a top-down approach, investors focus on the asset class (shares, bonds, money market funds) and the international markets wherein they wish to invest (i.e., the individual securities chosen are of little importance). In a bottom-up approach (commonly known as stock-picking), investors choose stocks on the basis of their specific characteristics, not the sector wherein they belong. The goal of the bottom-up approach is to find that rare pearl.

The strategy that is closest to portfolio theory is clearly index management, which seeks to replicate the performance of a market index. **Index trackers** seek to replicate an index as closely as possible. This is the preferred investment of those who believe in efficient markets. Index funds have developed as the general public has become more acquainted with portfolio theory. Index funds were created about 30 years ago and have since grown in value from €6m to more than €2,500bn today.

There are two types of stock-pickers:

➤ **Investors who focus on fundamental analysis and seek to determine the intrinsic value of a stock. They believe that, sooner or later, market value will approach intrinsic value.** These investors believe that all other price changes are temporary phenomena. Intrinsic value is what financial analysts seek to measure. A fundamental investor seeks to invest over the medium or long term and like Warren Buffet, who is the most famous of them all, wait patiently for the market value to converge towards the intrinsic value – i.e., for the market to agree with them; and

➤ **Investors who focus on technical analysis, the so-called chartists, who do not seek to determine the value of a stock. Instead, these investors conduct detailed studies of trends in a stock's market value and transaction volumes in the hope of spotting short-term trends.** Chartists prefer to analyse how the market perceives intrinsic value rather than looking at the stock's actual intrinsic value.

Chartists believe the market is predictable in the very short term, and this is often the attitude of traders and banks who take positions for very short periods, from a few hours to a few days.

Technical analysis is not based directly on any theory. It is based more on psychology than mathematics. Chartists believe that, while investors are not perfectly rational, they at least are fixed in their way of reasoning, with predictable reactions to certain situations. Chartists look for these patterns of behaviour in price trends.

One method consists in calculating a moving average of prices over a certain number of days (generally 20). Chartists look for a price to break through its moving average, either upward or downward.

Another method is based on comparing a stock's prices with its highs and lows over a given period. This is used in identifying support and resistance levels:

- a support is a level that the price has very little chance of falling below; and
- a resistance is a level that the price has very little chance of rising above.

The fundamental investor believes that markets are predictable in the medium or long term, but certainly not in the short term. Chartists believe they are predictable in the short term, but not in the medium or long term. Believers in efficient markets espouse the notion that markets are never predictable.

2 *Stocks that exhibit low price-to-book and low price-to-earnings ratios are value stocks, whereas those with high P/E and price-to-book ratios are called growth stocks.*

Some fundamental investors seek out **growth stocks** (companies in sectors offering sustainable growth[2]), while others seek out **value stocks** (companies in more mature sectors that provide long-term performance). At the end of the spectrum, investors choose **income stocks** whose prices are relatively stable and provide the bulk of their returns from dividends. Asset managers have developed several types of funds targeted specifically at these types of investors: growth funds, value funds and mixed funds. These last, mixed funds, are actually a combination of the first two.

Another type of fund management has arisen recently, so-called **alternative management**, which is based on market declines, volatility, liquidity, time value and abnormal valuations, rather than on rising prices. An example of alternative management is the **hedge fund**, which is a speculative fund seeking high returns and relying heavily on derivatives, and options in particular. Hedge funds use leverage and commit capital in excess of their equity. Hedge funds offer additional diversification to "conventional" portfolios, as their results are in theory not linked to the performances of equity and bond markets. Short-seller funds, for example, bet that a stock will fall by borrowing shares at interest and selling them, then buying them back after their price falls and returning them to the borrower.

Institutional investors are taking a growing interest in hedge funds. 6,000 hedge funds were active as of mid-2001, with about €500bn under management.

In recent years, hedge funds' risk-adjusted performance has been above that of traditional management. From 1990 to 2001, the average performance of a basket of hedge funds was 11.6%, vs. 7.9% for a basket of shares and 7.0% for bonds. It is important to note, however, that this greater return is in compensation for these funds' greater risk exposure.

There are various risks involved in financial securities. There are economic risks (political, inflation, etc.) which threaten cash flows from financial securities and which come from the "real economy", and there are financial risks (liquidity, currency, interest rate and other risks) which do not directly affect cash flow and come under the financial sphere.

All risks, regardless of their nature, lead to fluctuations in the value of a financial security.

In a market economy, a security's risk is measured in terms of the volatility of its price (or of its rate of return). The greater the volatility, the greater the risk, and vice versa.

We can break down the total risk of a financial security into the market-related risk (market or systematic risk) and a specific risk that is independent of the market (intrinsic or diversifiable risk). These two risks are totally independent.

The market risk of a security is dependent on its β coefficient, which measures the correlation between the return on the security and the market return. Mathematically, this is the regression line of the security's return vs. that of the market.

The β coefficient depends on:

- the sensitivity of the company's business sector;

- the economic situation;

- the company's operating costs structure (the higher the fixed costs, the higher the β);

- the financial structure (the greater the group's debts, the higher the β);

- the quality and quantity of information provided to the market (the greater visibility there is over future results, the lower the β); and

- earnings growth rates (the higher the growth rate, the higher the β).

Although the return on a portfolio of shares is equal to the average return on the shares within the portfolio, the risk of a portfolio is lower than the average risk of the shares making up that portfolio. This happens because returns on shares do not all vary to exactly the same degree, since correlation coefficients are rarely equal to 1.

As a result, some portfolios will deliver better returns than others. Those portfolios that are located on the portion of the curve known as the efficient frontier will deliver better returns than those portfolios that are not. However, given portfolios located on the efficient frontier curve, it is impossible to choose an optimal portfolio objectively from among them. The choice then becomes an individual one, and every investor chooses the portfolio according to his personal appetite for (or aversion to) risk.

By including risk-free assets – i.e., assets on which the return is guaranteed such as government bonds – it is possible to obtain portfolios that are even more efficient.

The inclusion of a risk-free asset in a portfolio leads to the creation of a new efficient frontier which is the line linking the risk-free asset to the market portfolio in the risk/ returns space. This new line is called the capital market line. Investors are well advised to own shares in this market portfolio and to choose the level of risk that suits them by investing in risk-free assets or by going into debt. On this line, no portfolio could perform better; i.e., no portfolio could offer a better return for a given level of risk, or a lower risk for a given return. Portfolio theory is generally applied in varying degrees, as demonstrated by the existence of investment strategies that favour certain securities rather than market portfolios.

QUESTIONS

quiz

1/ How is risk measured in a market economy?

2/ What does the β coefficient measure?

3/ In the graph on p. 402, which is the most volatile asset? What motivates investors to enter this asset?

4/ The β coefficient measures the specific risk of a security. True of false?

5/ Is the Air Liquide share more or less risky than the whole of the market? Why?

6/ Upon what is the β coefficient dependent?

7/ Why are market risk and specific risk totally independent?

8/ Will an increase in a company's debt reduce or increase the volatility of its share price?

9/ As a result of a change in the nature of its business, there is a relative rise in the proportion of fixed costs in group A's total costs. Will this affect the risk attached to its share price? If so, how?

10/ Explain why it is unhealthy for a company to invest its cash in shares.

11/ Is the β of a diversified conglomerate close to 1? Why?

12/ Internet companies have low fixed costs and low debt levels, yet their β coefficients are high. Why?

13/ Is the β coefficient of a group necessarily stable over time? Why?

14/ You buy a lottery ticket for €100 on which you could win €1,000,000, with a probability rate of 0.008%. Is this a risky investment? Could it be even riskier? How could you reduce the risk? Would this be a good investment?

15/ Why is standard deviation preferable to variance?

16/ What law of statistics explains that, in the long term, risk disappears? State your views.

17/ You receive €100,000, which you decide to save for your old age. You are now 20. What sort of investment should you go for? Perform the same analysis for if it happened when you are 55 and 80.

18/ Do shares in Internet companies carry a greater or smaller risk than shares in large retail groups? Why?

19/ There are some sceptics who claim that financial analysis serves no purpose. Why? State your views.

20/ Why are negative β coefficients unusual?

21/ What can you say about a share for which the standard deviation of the return is high, and the β is low?

22/ Must the values of financial assets fluctuate in opposite directions in order to reduce risk? Why?

23/ What other concept does the capital market line bring to mind?

24/ Why does the market portfolio include all high-risk assets in order to achieve maximum diversification?

25/ Security A carries little risk and security B has great risk. Which would you choose if you wanted to take the least risk possible?

26/ The correlation coefficient between French equities and European equities developed as follows:

Years	1970–1979	1980–1989	1990–1999	2000–2002
Coefficient	0.43	0.42	0.73	0.86

Are you surprised by the table above? Does it prove that there is nothing to gain by geographic diversification? Does it reduce the importance of geographic diversification?

27/ Use the table on p. 399 to determine which industrial sector makes the greatest contribution to reducing the risk of a portfolio.

28/ What is the only asset that can be used to precisely measure the levels of risk of a portfolio?

29/ What conditions are necessary for a risk-free asset to be free of risk? Provide an example. Is it really risk-free?

30/ Show that the market portfolio must be on the capital market line and on the portion of the curve called the efficient frontier in Section 21.2.

31/ Why does this chapter provide an explanation of the development of mutual funds?

32/ Can the risk of a portfolio be greater than the individual risk of each of the securities it contains? Under what circumstances?

33/ Under which circumstances can the risk of a portfolio be less than the individual risk of each of the securities it contains?

34/ The greater the number of shares in a portfolio, the less the marginal contribution to diversification of an additional security will be. True or false?

35/ Will very wide diversification eliminate specific risk? And market risk?

EXERCISES

1/ Calculate the return on the Fiat share and on the Italian index over 13 months until 1 July 2002. To help you, you have a record of the share price and of the general index. What is the total risk of the Fiat share? What is the β coefficient of Fiat? What portion of the total risk of the Fiat share is explained by market risk?

Period	Jul-01	Aug-01	Sep-01	Oct-01	Nov-01	Dec-01	Jan-02	Feb-02	Mar-02	Apr-02	May-02	Jun-02	Jul-02
Fiat	24.8	25.6	25.3	18.5	17.1	17.9	17.8	17.3	14.8	16	13.1	12.9	12.9
Italian index	1650	1611	1509	1256	1342	1400	1433	1437	1426	1503	1462	1371	1285

2/ A portfolio gives a 10% return with a standard deviation of 18%. You would like the standard deviation to drop to 14%. What should you do? What should you do if you want the standard deviation to rise to 23%?

3/ Calculate the risk and returns of portfolio Z in Section 21.2. What is the proportion of Air Liquide shares and Philips shares in this portfolio?

4/ A portfolio gives a 10% return for a standard deviation of 18%. The shares in companies C and D have the following returns and standard deviations:

	C	D
Expected return (%)	10	20
Standard deviation (%)	15	30

The correlation between the return on these two shares is 25%.

(a) Calculate the expected return and the standard deviation for each of the following portfolios:

α: 100%C; β: 75%C + 25%D; σ: 50%C + 50%D; δ: 25%C + 75%D; ε: 100%D

(b) Plot your results on a graph. What are your conclusions?

ANSWERS

Questions

1/ *The volatility of the value of the asset is measured by the standard deviation of its rate of return.*
2/ *The correlation between the return on the security and the market return, the market risk of the security, the line of the regression of the security's return vs. that of the market.*
3/ *Philips' shares carry the most risk, but they will also bring the highest returns.*
4/ *False, it measures the market risk of a security.*
5/ *It is difficult to give a very accurate answer, without knowing what the share's specific risk is. Disregarding this, the Air Liquide stock carries less risk than the market since its β coefficient is less than 1.*
6/ *On the company's operating cost structure, its financial structure, its information policy and the growth rate of its earnings.*
7/ *One has an impact on all securities, the other on a given security.*
8/ *Yes, it will increase volatility due to the leverage effect, see Chapter 18.*
9/ *Yes, it will increase volatility due to the effect of breakeven point, see Chapter 15.*
10/ *Because cash by definition should be available at all times, and share prices are very volatile.*
11/ *Usually, yes, because conglomerates are highly diversified and are a bit like "mini-markets" in their own right.*
12/ *Because of the very poor visibility we currently have over what is going to happen to Internet stocks.*
13/ *No, as the group's business and financial structure can change over the course of time, which will have a knock-on effect on the β.*
14/ *Yes, very risky, because you have a 99.992% chance of losing your €100. Yes, it could, if you used debt to finance the €100. If you bought all of the lottery tickets you would be sure of winning the €1,000,000, but that would cost you €100/ 0.008% = €1,250,000, which wouldn't be a very good investment.*
15/ *Because it's around 1, like returns, unlike variance which is around 2.*
16/ *The law of large numbers. The risk is never completely eliminated.*

17/ *Equities, bonds, money market investments.*
18/ *A greater risk as the outlook is very uncertain, whereas the visibility over the earnings of large retail groups is very good.*
19/ *Financial analysis contributes very little, as it must be acted upon immediately and the results seen in the share price–financial analysis kills financial analysis. Financial analysis is necessary for market equilibrium (rationality) but can only be "disinterested".*
20/ *Because if they weren't, when markets went up, the price of most securities making up these markets would fall, which would be absurd.*
21/ *That it carries a specific risk that is very high.*
22/ *Of course not. The correlation must just not be equal to 1.*
23/ *The leverage effect.*
24/ *By definition.*
25/ *A combination of A and B, and not only security A, so that $\rho \neq 1$.*
26/ *No, because it reflects advances in European integration and globalisation, which both increase the synchronisation of economies. No, as long as correlation coefficients remain lower than 1, although they are now very close. Yes.*
27/ *The IT sector, because correlation coefficients with the other sectors are lower.*
28/ *A risk-free asset.*
29/ *There must be no doubts about the solvency of the issuer, no risk vis-à-vis the rate at which the coupons can be reinvested, and protection against inflation. A zero-coupon government bond indexed to inflation. No, because there will always be a risk that the price will fluctuate before maturity.*
30/ *By construction, on the capital market line because this line is constructed from 2 points – itself and the risk-free asset. It is on the efficient frontier in Section 21.2 because, given its high level of diversity, risk is reduced to a minimum.*
31/ *Because a mutual fund is a reduced model of market portfolio, which would be difficult to compile at an individual level.*
32/ *Yes, it is financed by debt.*
33/ *If it includes a large percentage of risk-free assets.*
34/ *True, because the portfolio is already very diversified.*
35/ *Yes, by definition. No, this would be impossible.*

Exercises

1/ *Returns on the Fiat share: $12.9/24.8 - 1 = -48\%$. Returns on the Italian index: $1,285/1,650 - 1 = -22\%$. Fiat risk $\sigma = 10.25\%$. Index risk $\sigma = 6.55\%$; $\beta = 0.82$; $53\% = (0.82 \times 6.55\%)/10.25\%$.*

2/ *Add more risk-free assets until they account for 4/18 of the portfolio. Use debt to finance an increase in the size of this portfolio by 5/18.*

3/ *83% of Air Liquide shares and 17% of Philips shares. $E(r) = 7.19\%$ and $\sigma = 9.57\%$.*

4/

	Expected return (%)	Standard deviation (%)
α	10.00	15.00
β	12.50	15.00
σ	15.00	18.37
δ	17.50	23.72
ε	20.00	30.00

BIBLIOGRAPHY

To learn more about the history of risk analysis:

N. Barberis, Asset allocation: Have investors got it wrong? *Financial Times*, 30 June 1997.
E. Dimson, P. Marsh, M. Staunton, *The Triumph of the Optimist: 101 Years of Global Investment Returns*, Princeton University Press, 2002.
P. Bernstein, *Against the Gods: The Remarkable Story of Risk*, Flammarion, 1997.

To learn more about the theoretical analysis of risk:

N. Barberis, Investing for the long run when returns are predictable, *Journal of Finance*, **55**, 225–264, February 2000.
Z. Bodie, R. Merton, *Finance*, Prentice Hall, 2000.
E. Fama, M. Miller, *Theory of Finance*, Holt, Rinehart & Winston, 1971.
D. Hirshleifer, Investor psychology and asset pricing, *Journal of Finance*, **56**, 1533–1597, August 2001.

For more about asset management and investment strategies:

A. Damodaran, *Style Investing*, John Wiley & Sons, 2003.

Index-based Investing, *Financial Times Survey*, 18 July 2001.

Chapter 22
THE COST OF EQUITY

There's no gain without pain

The previous chapter described the important concepts of risk, return and market portfolio. It also highlighted the notion of risk premium (i.e., the difference between the risk-free rate and the return on the market portfolio), and this chapter continues to explore the risk premium in greater depth.

By seeking to systematically estimate the risk premium – i.e., in a fairly valued market – the question arises: What risk premium must be added to the risk-free rate to determine the required rate of return?

Investors must look at the big picture, first by investing in the market portfolio, then by borrowing or by investing in risk-free instruments commensurate with the level of risk they wish to assume. This approach allows them to assess an investment by merely determining the additional return and risk it adds to the market portfolio.

Investment risk is often broken down into its component parts, not necessarily in economic and financial terms, but rather into the volatility of the security itself and the volatility of the market as a whole.

We want to know how to get from r (the historical rate of return on invested capital) to k (the expected return required by investors on a specific security).
Remember that this approach applies only if the investor owns a perfectly diversified portfolio. Here is why: the greater the risk assumed by the financial investor, the higher his required rate of return. However, if he makes **just one** investment and that turns out to be a failure, his required rate of return will matter little, as he will have lost everything.
With this in mind, it is easier to understand that risk premium is relevant only if the financial investor manages not a single investment, but a diversified portfolio of investments. In this case, the failure of one investment should be offset by the return achieved by other investments, which should thereby produce a suitable return for the portfolio as a whole.

The concept of risk premium only makes sense when risk is spread over many investments.

Look at it this way:

- What is a bank if not a portfolio of loans and financial resources?
- What is a financial group if not a portfolio of industrial investments?
- What is a mutual fund if not a portfolio of securities?
- What is an insurance company if not a portfolio of statistical risks?

"Portfolio" and "diversification" are fundamental concepts in finance.

This is the main difference between an industrial investment and a financial investment.

An entrepreneur who sets up his own company does not act like a financial investor, as he owns just one investment. As his assets are not diversified, it is a matter of "life or death" for the firm that the investment succeed. The law of averages in risk diversification does not apply to him.[1]

The financial investor, on the other hand, needs portfolio management tools to estimate the risk–return on each of his investments. Portfolio theory is not *the* main objective here, but it *is* useful to introduce some basic notions with which financial managers must be familiar.

1 *However, the very fact that he does not diversify his portfolio means that he must achieve strong performances in managing the company, as he has everything to lose. So he's likely to take steps to reduce risk.*

2 *See also Appendix 22.A for a formal derivation of the CAPM.*

Section 22.1
RETURN REQUIRED BY INVESTORS: THE CAPM[2]

The CAPM (Capital Asset Pricing Model) was developed in the late 1950s and 1960s, based on the work of Harry Markowitz, William Sharpe, John Lintner and Jack Treynor, and it is now universally applied.

The CAPM is based on the assumption that investors act rationally and have at their disposal all relevant information on financial securities (see "efficient markets" in Chapter 21). Like the investor in Chapter 27, they seek to maximise their return, at a given level of risk.

From portfolio selection, we know that the investor:

1   considers the efficient portfolios – that is, the portfolios that offer the highest return for a given level of risk (measured by the standard deviation);
2   introduces the risk-free asset. The tangent point between the risk-free asset and the efficient frontier is the portfolio with the highest ratio of risk premium to standard deviation; and
3   holds the same portfolio as everybody else as long as there are **homogeneous expectations** among investors. This portfolio is the **market portfolio**.

From the analysis of risk of individual securities, it has been shown that:

1   the contribution of a stock to a portfolio depends on the stock's sensitivity to the returns of the portfolio; and
2   the sensitivity to the returns of the market portfolio is known as **beta** (β).

The CAPM says that if all investors hold the market portfolio, the risk premium they will demand is proportional to market beta.

The expected return of an asset will then be a linear function of beta:

$$\begin{array}{c} \text{Expected return on} \\ \text{a financial asset} \end{array} = \begin{array}{c} \text{Risk-free} \\ \text{rate} \end{array} + \beta \times \left(\begin{array}{c} \text{Expected return of} \\ \text{market portfolio} \end{array} - \begin{array}{c} \text{Risk-free} \\ \text{rate} \end{array} \right)$$

Remember that, in order to minimise total risk, investors seek to reduce that component which can be reduced – i.e., the specific risk. They do so by diversifying their portfolios.

As a result, when stocks are fairly valued, investors will receive a return only on the portion of risk that they cannot eliminate – the market risk, or the nondiversifiable risk. Indeed, in a market in which arbitrage is theoretically possible, they will not be amply remunerated for a risk that they could otherwise eliminate themselves by simply diversifying their portfolios.

Portfolio theory's essential contribution is to show that an investor's required rate of return is not linked to total risk, but solely to market risk. Conversely, in a fairly valued market, intrinsic, or diversifiable, risk is not remunerated.

This means that the required rate of return (k) is equal to the risk-free rate r_F,[3] plus the risk premium for the nondiversifiable risk; i.e., the market risk.

This can be expressed as follows:

> Required rate of return = Risk-free rate + $\beta \times$ Market risk premium
>
> or $\quad k = r_F + \beta \times (k_M - r_F)$

3 *For the risk-free rate, k_F is equal to r_F. The required rate of return is equal to the return that is actually received, as the asset has no risk.*

where k_M is the required rate of return for the market and β the sensitivity coefficient described previously.

Note that the coefficient β measures the nondiversifiable risk of an asset and not its total risk. So it is possible to have a stock that is, on the whole, highly risky, but with a low β if it is only loosely correlated with the market.

The difference between the return expected on the market as a whole and the risk-free rate is called the **equity risk premium**. This averages 3–5% in developed economies, but is higher in emerging markets.

The pattern of excess returns for equity holdings is observed in every country with a significant capital market. The US, along with the UK, Japan, Germany and France, account for more than 85% of the capitalised global equity value. According to the excellent retrospective of Mehra and Prescott (2003), the annual return on the British stock market was 5.7% over the post-war period, which is an impressive 4.6% premium over the average bond return of 1.1%. Similar statistical differentials are documented for France, Germany and Japan. The table below illustrates the equity premium in the post-war period for these countries.

Country	% real return on a market index	% real return on a relatively riskless security	% equity premium
UK (1947–1999)	5.7	1.1	4.6
Japan (1970–1999)	4.7	1.4	3.3
Germany (1978–1997)	9.8	3.2	6.6
France (1973–1998)	9.0	2.7	6.3

1/THE EXPECTED RISK PREMIUM OVER TIME

MARKET RISK PREMIUM IN EUROPE

Source: Associés en Finance.

MARKET RISK PREMIUM IN THE USA

Source: BNP Paribas.

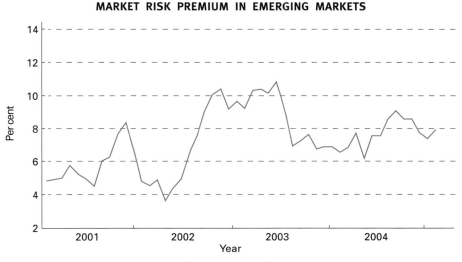

MARKET RISK PREMIUM IN EMERGING MARKETS

Source: Crédit Lyonnais Asset Management.

Over the very long term (104 years!), the historical risk premium is as follows:

Germany (excluding 1922 and 1923)	5.2%
Belgium	2.4%
US	4.6%
France	3.7%
Italy	4.2%
Japan	5.6%
The Netherlands	3.7%
UK	4.0%
Switzerland (since 1911)	1.6%

Source: Dimson et al. (2005).

A distinction must be made between **historical equity risk premium** and **expected equity risk premium**. The historical risk premium is based on a comparison of annual performance of equity markets (including dividends) vs. the long-term risk-free rate. Expected risk premium is not directly observable. However, it can be calculated by estimating the future cash flows of all the companies, and then finding the discount rate that equates those cash flows with current share prices. It is this expected risk premium that is used in the CAPM.

To determine the risk premium for each stock, simply multiply the market risk premium by the stock's beta coefficient.

Hence, if the risk-free rate is 5.0% and the expected risk premium is 4.5%, the Philips' shareholder will expect a return of $5.0\% + 1.78 \times 4.5\% = 13.01\%$, if Philips' β is 1.78, while the Air Liquide shareholder will expect: $5.0\% + 0.42 \times 4.5\% = 6.89\%$, as Air Liquide's β is 0.44.

A final remark. In the CAPM, the equilibrium risk premium is equal to the variance of the market portfolio times a weighted average of the degree of risk aversion of the holders of wealth (A):

$$E(r_M) - r_F = A \times \sigma_M^2$$

A should be considered as an index of the degree of risk aversion prevailing in the economy.

Section 22.2
PROPERTIES OF THE CAPM

4 *It differs from the capital market line, which has the total risk σ of the security on the X-axis, not the β coefficient.*

1/THE SECURITY MARKET LINE

The French organisation Associés en Finance publishes the securities market line[5] for the entire euro zone. It is calculated on the basis of the **expected return** on the Y-axis and the **beta coefficient of each stock** on the X-axis.[4]

Example from early 2005.

download

SML FOR THE EUROZONE

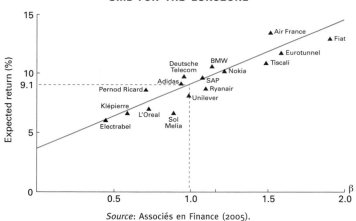

Source: Associés en Finance (2005).

Chapter 40 examines how the value of a stock can be expressed in terms of the flow of future dividends that it is expected to pay. These dividends are discounted at the rate required by the shareholder. The expected return is thus calculated by equating the current price of the stock to the discounted sum of dividends paid out to the company to infinity.

The securities market line is quite instructive. It helps determine the required rate of return on a security on the basis of the only risk that is remunerated – i.e., the market risk.

Shifts in the securities market line itself characterise the nature of changes in the markets and make it easier to understand them:

- a parallel shift, with no variation in slope (i.e., risk premium) reflects a change in the market brought on by a change in interest rates. For example, a cut in interest rates normally leads to a downward shift and thus a general appreciation of all stocks;
- a nonparallel shift (or pivoting) reflects a change in the risk premium and thus in the remuneration of risk. In this case, the riskiest stocks will move the most, whereas the least risky stocks may not be significantly affected.

In addition, the position of points *vis-à-vis* the market line serves as a decision-making tool. The above chart tells us that Bongrain offers too high an expected return for its risk. Investors will realise this and buy it, thus raising its price and lowering expected return. A stock that is "above" the securities market line is thus undervalued, while a stock that is "below" the securities market line (like Unilever) is overvalued.

But do not rush to place an order. Since this chart was printed, prices have had plenty of time to adjust.

2/LINEARITY

An important property of CAPM is that the measure of risk for individual assets is proportional to the weight of each security when the assets are combined into a portfolio.

Thus, for example, if an investor buys $a\%$ of asset X that has a systematic risk of β_X and $1 - X$ of the total wealth into asset Y with a systematic risk of β_Y, then the beta of the portfolio would simply be the weighted average of the betas of single securities.

This property is extremely useful if we want to compute the beta of a diversified company. We could in fact consider the beta of single operating businesses and then weight each of them according to their relative market capitalisation (alternatively, we could use sales or other dimensions).

Section 22.3
THE LIMITS OF THE CAPM MODEL

The CAPM model assumes that markets are efficient and it is without a doubt the most widely used model in modern finance. But financial analysts are always quick to criticise and, thus, this section merits appeasing the critics by summarising how the CAPM presents some problems in practice.

1/THE LIMITS OF DIVERSIFICATION

The CAPM model is a development of portfolio theory and is based on the assumption that diversification helps reduce risk (to the nondiversifiable risk). A study by Campbell et al. (2001) shows that diversification is increasingly complex and that, whereas in the 1970s a portfolio of 20 stocks reduced risk significantly, today at least 50 are required to achieve the same result.

This is due, among other things, to the greater volatility of individual stocks, although markets as a whole are no more volatile. Other reasons for this phenomenon are the arrival to market of riskier companies, such as biotechnology, Internet and younger companies, and the dwindling prominence of conglomerates, which, by nature, provided some diversification in and of themselves.

Meanwhile, the correlation between market return and return on individual stocks is falling. This may undermine the relevance of the CAPM model. Statistically, the beta is becoming less and less relevant.

2/DIFFICULTIES IN PRACTICAL APPLICATION OF THE CAPM

The first difficulty one encounters when using the CAPM is determining the risk-free rate, which, all things considered, is just a theoretical concept.

The term "risk-free" means no risk of default and no coupon reinvestment risk. Zero-coupon government bonds come the closest to meeting this definition. However:

1   While governments' power to mint currency means that their risk of default is low, they still have some risk (the Argentine default in 2002 is one illustration).
2   In order to have zero reinvestment risk on the coupon, the reference period must be known.

In the case of an asset paying a return only once in 5 years it may be easy to use the zero-coupon rate produced by the yield curve as a risk-free rate (see Chapter 29). However, the single-period CAPM model is often used to value assets whose cash flows are spread out over time. So, theoretically, we would have to use a different discounting rate for each of the periods. Each of these rates would have to be calculated with a different risk-free rate, thus complicating the use of the CAPM model. In practice, this is done only to value bonds (see Chapter 31). For other assets, the risk-free rate, at best, reflects no more than the asset's duration.

Richard Roll has pointed out that determining a market portfolio is not as easy as one would like to think. In theory, the market portfolio is not made up solely of stocks nor even just financial assets, but of all the assets that can be acquired. It is therefore impossible, in practice, to come up with a true market portfolio, especially when looking at it from an international point of view.

However, this is not an insurmountable obstacle. Indeed, in a portfolio already containing a large number of assets, the marginal contribution to return of a new asset is low. Portfolio diversification makes return and risk approach a limit – the return offered by a theoretically ideal market portfolio. So the market portfolio can be approximated with a portfolio containing "only" a large number of assets. Unfortunately, recent studies have shown that more and more assets must be included in a portfolio for it to be considered highly diversified.

However, we would still have to determine the return expected from the market portfolio. As the CAPM model is used for making forecasts, it can also be used to calculate the return expected from a security based upon the return expected from the market portfolio, as well as the security's anticipated risk (its β). However, "anticipated" data cannot be observed directly in the market, and so forecasts must be done on the basis of historical data and macroeconomic data. For some countries, such as emerging nations, this is not easy!

3/THE INSTABILITY OF THE β

The main criticism of the beta is its instability over time. It boils down a large amount of information into a single figure, and this strength becomes its weakness.

The CAPM model is used to make forecasts. It can be used to calculate expected return on the basis of anticipated risk. Therefore, it would be better to use a forecast β rather than a historical value, especially when the coefficient is not stable over time.

For this reason, calculations must often be adjusted to reflect the regularity of earnings and dividends, and visibility on the sector. Some studies (e.g., Blume, 1975) have sought to demonstrate a convergence of the β towards 1. However, this looks counterintuitive, as some sectors will always be riskier than the market.

4/RISK PREMIUM ESTIMATE AND TIME DIVERSIFICATION

To many, the size of the equity premium is a mystery. The figures that have been calculated seem to imply that investors historically required a high degree of compensation to invest in stocks rather than government bonds. Financial economists refer to the surprisingly high equity premium in the United States as the **equity premium puzzle**.

Equity premiums are a function of the volatility of the economy and of the risk associated with that particular market.[5] Keeping this in mind, here are a few hints for the reader who wants to estimate his own "home-made" equity premium:

1 the risk premium should be measured over the longest period possible. Since stock returns are volatile, it is possible to obtain premiums with large standard errors only if short-time periods are used;

2 the type of average to be used is of importance. Assuming the returns being averaged are largely independent and that the future is like the past, arithmetic average is the best estimate of expected returns over a given future holding period. On the other hand, if our goal is to estimate returns over the next 10 or 30 years and returns are not independent, then geometric average is a better choice;

3 the equity risk premium can be measured by using any treasury security; however, in practice only two securities are used. The first is short-term government bonds, which are sometimes preferred because they are the closest thing there is to a risk-free security. The second is the long-term government bond rates, chosen by those whose time horizon in financial analysis tends to be long-term. Long-term government bonds raise some questions because, although free from default, they are not entirely risk-free securities;

4 the possibility of reducing the historical rate of return downward by $1\frac{1}{2}$ to 2% as a consequence of the **survivorship bias**. Brown et al. (1995) stated that survival imparts a bias to *ex post* returns. A substantial upward bias would

[5] *Thus we would expect riskier markets to have larger premiums than other financial markets that are perceived as less risky.*

exist on markets that survive over a century without going bankrupt. Goetzmann and Jorion (1999) find that over a very long period (1926–1996), the performance of the US market – during which time it did not experience an interruption in trading – exceeded the median return on a set of 11 countries with continuous histories by 1.9% in real terms or 1.4% in nominal terms.

The term "risk premium" implies that stocks are riskier than bonds. Is this conclusion always valid? Generally speaking, the differences in volatility between stocks and other investments depend on the holding period assumptions used to do the mathematics. The risk premium is normally calculated using the annual total returns of financial securities. By extending the holding period (2 years, 5 years and so on), it is possible to see that standard deviation decreases substantially for stocks, and to a lower extent for bonds and other less volatile securities. This effect is called **time diversification**.

STANDARD DEVIATION OF RANDOM RETURNS FOR DIFFERENT HOLDING PERIODS

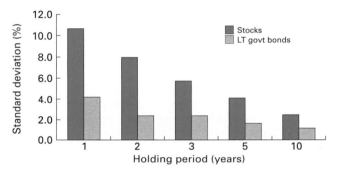

The phenomenon shown in the picture above was created with a simulation of random numbers for stocks and bonds. Assuming a 1-year holding period, the standard deviation of stocks is two to three times greater than the standard deviation of long-term government bonds. As the holding period increases, the standard deviation declines more rapidly for stock than for bonds. Using a 10-year holding period return the two assets have nearly identical riskiness. In conclusion, although stocks are surely riskier in the short run than bonds, in the long term this evidence tends to disappear.

Are long holding period horizons relevant to investors? Yes, and much more so than investors realise. As Siegel highlights, "one of the greatest mistakes that investors make is to underestimate their holding period. This is so because many investors think about the holding periods of a particular stock, bond, or mutual fund. But the holding period that is relevant for portfolio allocation is the *length of time the investors hold any stocks or bonds*, no matter how many changes are made among the individual issues in their portfolio" (Siegel, 2002, p. 29).

4/THE THEORETICAL LIMITS OF CAPM AND MARKETS AT FAIR VALUE

The CAPM assumes markets are fairly valued. But markets are not necessarily always at fair value. The fact that technical analysis has become so prominent on

Ibbotson Associates has broken down the NYSE stock returns into deciles by size, as measured by the aggregate market value of the common equity. The results show that the excess returns over the basic general equity risk premium increase with decreasing size, as shown in the table below (Pratt, 2003, p. 91):

Decile	Beta	Arithmetic mean return (%)	Realised return in excess of r_F (%)	Estimated return in excess of r_F (%)	Size premium (return in excess of CAPM) (%)
Mid-cap, 3rd–5th decile	1.12	14.46	9.23	8.65	0.58
Low-cap, 6th–8th decile	1.22	15.75	10.52	9.45	1.07
Micro-cap, 9th–10th decile	1.36	18.41	13.18	10.56	2.62

If we expand CAPM to also reflect the size effect, we can expand the cost of equity capital formula to add this factor:

$$k = r_F + \beta \times (k_M - r_F) + \text{Size premium}$$

Hamon and Jacquillat (1999) have demonstrated the existence of a liquidity premium in Europe, which is nil for large caps and significant for small caps. The liquidity premium should be added to the return derived from the CAPM model to arrive at the total return expected by the shareholder. Hamon and Jacquillat use the term "market plane" (instead of securities market line). Under their model, expected return on a security is a linear equation with two parameters: the market premium and the liquidity premium. What is λ? Let us report the definition from the original article:

$$k = r_F + \beta \times (k_M - r_F) + \lambda \times \text{Liquidity premium}$$

In March 2005, Associés en Finance estimated the market plane parameters for eurozone stocks at:

$$k = 3.00\% + \beta \times 5.63\% + \lambda \times 0.47\%$$

The liquidity premium, which is expected in addition to the required rate of return, finds its opposite number in the notion of "liquidity discount".

LIQUIDITY PREMIUM IN EUROPE

Source: Associés en Finance.

There is some evidence that the cost of equity goes up where insider-trading laws are not enforced and legal protection of minorities is flawed. The legal system governing investors and markets in a given country *can influence systematic risk* because it determines the level of protection given to minority shareholders and other financial claimants.

LaPorta et al. (1999) report that companies in common law countries have higher valuations than do companies in civil law countries. These results are consistent with the prediction that better shareholder protection is associated with higher corporate valuation. At the same time, the growth rate in sales is also higher for common law countries, suggesting that companies in those countries may face better investment opportunities.

Section 22.5
THE COST OF EQUITY BASED ON HISTORICAL RETURNS

The easiest and most intuitive way to estimate the cost of equity is to look at the past! If investors have rational expectations – i.e., if they think that on average they get what they expect – we may reasonably assume that future returns will replicate past returns. Of course, this can only occur if the risk profile of the company in the past does not change significantly now or in the future.

Historical returns may refer to two types:

- market rate of returns; or
- accounting rate of returns.

1/MARKET RATE OF RETURNS

The holding period return is the sum of two components: periodic dividends and the price appreciation over the single period. We may then assume that:

$$k_E \text{ is the average of the stream of } \frac{P_t - P_{t-1} + \text{Div}_t}{P_{t-1}}$$

Two comments:

1   length of the observation period. In principle, the longer the observed period, the higher the credibility of the average value. However, if we extend the length too much there is the risk that the company's risk profile will have changed in the meanwhile. Thus, the historical average may not entirely reflect the investor's expected rate of return.

2   nominal vs. real rate of return. It is usually better to estimate real rate of returns rather than the nominal ones. Inflation rates change each year and expected inflation may not coincide with the historical inflation rate. A solution to this problem is to use a two-step procedure to take inflation into account. First, the average real return is calculated. We can use the Fisher formula to obtain holding period return on a security net of inflation:

$$r_{\text{real}} = \frac{1 + r_{\text{nominal}}}{1 + \text{Annual inflation}} - 1$$

where r indicates the annual rate of return.

Given an estimate of the historical real return, the future long-run expected nominal return – our k_E – can be calculated by considering an estimate of long-run expected inflation:

$$k_E = (1 + \text{Average } r_{\text{real}}) \times (1 + \text{Expected inflation})$$

2/ACCOUNTING RATES OF RETURN

The fluctuations of market prices in inefficient markets may imply a low significance for the results obtained with the analysis of historical market returns. Or, historical market returns may be impossible to calculate for unlisted companies.

In these cases, we can use accounting rates of return, which implies a two-step formula. First, we compute the after-tax *ROI* that we call k_E(unlevered):[6]

$$k_E(\text{unlevered}) = ROI \times (1 - T_C)$$

6 T_C is the corporate tax rate.

Then we compute the "final" or levered k_E, using the target debt/equity ratio:

$$k_E = k_E(\text{unlevered}) + [k_E(\text{unlevered}) - k_D] \times (1 - T_C) \times \frac{D}{E}$$

However, we have some doubts about the validity of this methodology given that accounting data can be easily manipulated.

THE COST OF EQUITY BASED ON CURRENT MARKET PRICES

The cost of equity can also be estimated by looking at current market prices. In this case, the analyst tries to extrapolate – through appropriate formulas – the cost of equity implicit in the stock prices. There are two alternative techniques that can be used to deduct the expected returns:

- the Dividend Discount Model (DDM); or
- the P/E model.

1/THE DIVIDEND DISCOUNT MODEL (DDM)

7 The reader has two alternatives: the arithmetic and the geometric average. Some textbooks suggest the arithmetic average (Brealey and Myers, 2000; Pratt, 2003) while others the geometric (Copeland et al., 2000). Consider the following example: you invest €1,000 in a stock whose annual returns are +50% in t_1 and −50% in t_2. At the end of the 1st year the price of the share will be €1,500; at the end of the second €750. The arithmetic average is 0; the geometric average is −13.4%. Mathematically, the geometric average is always lower than the arithmetic unless all observations are equal and the difference is a function of the volatility of returns.

The DDM is based on the assumption that the value of a company is given by the stream of dividends the investor expects to receive over a period of time. Assuming that:

- the growth rate of dividends and the cost of equity are constant from 0 to ∞; and
- the growth rate of dividends cannot exceed the cost of equity. Then, we can say – rewriting the Gordon formula (p. 301) – that the cost of equity is:

$$P_0 = \frac{\text{Div}_0 \times (1 + g)}{k_E - g}$$

$$\text{i.e.} \quad k_E = \frac{\text{Div}_0 \times (1 + g)}{P_0} + g$$

What if there are no dividends? In Chapter 38 it is shown that many companies around the world do not distribute dividends. One statistic provides valuable insight to help the reader understand the importance of this fact: 80% of the 5,000 listed US companies in 2003 did not pay cash dividends! Fama and French (2001) report that the percentage of firms paying cash dividends fell from 66.5% in 1978 to 20.8% in 1999.

However, if the company pays dividends, there are two basic methodologies for estimating the growth rate, or g:

1   The historical growth rate of dividends. To apply this methodology a time series of dividends is necessary. The growth rate of dividends is calculated from period to period to determine the *average*.[7] This number is the growth rate of dividends;

2   The "internal" growth rate formula. According to this methodology, the growth of dividends is given by reinvesting cash flows in new projects, according to the following formula (see Sidenote 8 at the top of the next page):

$$g = ROE \times (1 - \text{Payout})$$

2/THE P/E MODEL

The Gordon formula can be rearranged in order to express the cost of capital as a function of the P/E ratio:

$$k_E = \frac{\text{Div}_0 \times (1+g)}{P_0} + g = \frac{\text{Payout} \times EPS_0 \times (1+g)}{P_0} + g = \frac{\text{Payout} \times (1+g)}{P_0/EPS_0} + g$$

The assumptions are the same as for the DDM model. The growth rate of earnings can be estimated with the historical growth rate we described for the DDM. The P/E ratio is the "trailing ratio".

The main difference between the DDM and the P/E model is that the former is based on the growth of dividends while the latter on the growth of earnings. For this reason, the P/E model can be particularly useful when the company does not distribute dividends.

8 *If we want to measure the change in value of our investment by looking at the past, we should prefer the geometric average. Conversely, if we want a standardised measure of performance, we should choose the arithmetic average. The arithmetic average assumes that returns are independent while the geometric average assumes serial correlation among successive periods.*

This chapter has shown how to work out the cost of equity; i.e., the rate of return required on equity capital. The investor's required rate of return is not linked to total risk, but solely to market risk. Conversely, in a market in equilibrium, intrinsic, or diversifiable, risk is not remunerated.

The CAPM (Capital Asset Pricing Model) is used to determine the rate of return required by an investor:

$$\text{Risk-free rate} + \beta \times \text{Market risk premium}$$

$$\text{or} \quad k = r_F + \beta \times (k_M - r_F)$$

Although the CAPM is used universally, it does have drawbacks that are either practical (for reliable determination of beta coefficients) or fundamental in nature (since it supposes that markets are in equilibrium). This criticism has led to the development of new models, such as the Arbitrage Pricing Theory (APT), and has highlighted the importance of the liquidity premium for groups with small freefloats. Like the CAPM, the APT assumes that the required rate of return no longer depends on a single market rate; however, it considers a number of other variables too, such as the difference between government bonds and Treasury bills, unanticipated changes in the growth rate of the economy or the rate of inflation, etc.

Two more techniques for estimating the cost of equity were discussed:

- the historical return method, where the cost of equity equals either the historical total market return or the accounting rate of return; and

- the current market price method, where the cost of equity can be extrapolated from current stock prices through appropriate formulae.

SUMMARY

download

QUESTIONS

quiz

1/ Explain in a few lines why diversifiable risk cannot be remunerated on markets in equilibrium?

2/ Given that diversifiable risk is not remunerated, would it be worthwhile to diversify an investment?

3/ What is the rate of return required by the shareholder equal to?

4/ What is the drawback of the β coefficient?

5/ A shareholder requires a rate of return that is twice as high on a share with a β coefficient that is twice as high as that of another share. True of false?

6/ What does a low risk premium indicate?

7/ On the graph on p. 424 does the Nokia share seem undervalued or overvalued to you? What about the France Télécom share?

8/ What is the strong point of the APT compared with the CAPM? And the weak point?

9/ Will liquidity premiums tend to rise or fall during a crash? Why?

10/ What does a negative liquidity premium indicate?

11/ The standard deviation of the earnings on Bouygues shares is 40%, while for Metaleuropa it is only 28%. However, Bouygues has a β of 1.13 and Metaleuropa one of 1.7. Explain how this is possible.

12/ Explain why an investor would be prepared to require a lower return on a risk-free share for a share with a negative β.

13/ How do you explain the fact that rates of return required by investors may be identical for two groups of totally different activities (oil and IT services, for example) as long as they have the same β?

14/ An experiment was recently carried out where a child, an astrologer and a financial analyst were each given €10,000 to invest for 8 years. Who do you think achieved the best results?

EXERCISES

1/ What rate of return should be required on the Aventis share, which has a β of 0.7, if the Pinault Printemps Redoute share, which has a β of 1.1, returns 10% and is correctly valued, and the rate of a risk-free asset is 5%?

2/ Are the following shares undervalued, correctly valued or overvalued. The rate for a risk-free asset is 5.5% and the market risk premium is 4%.

Share	Air Liquide	Carrefour	Volkswagen	ING	Alcatel
β	0.4	0.7	1	1.3	1.8
Rate of return	9%	8.3%	9%	10%	15%

3/ You think that the Alboni.com share will be worth €40 in 1 year. What price would you be prepared to pay today if the no-risk cash rate is 5%, the market rate of return is 9% and the β is 2.7?

4/ Your portfolio has a β of 1.2, the no-risk cash rate is 5.6% and the risk premium is 3%. In this chapter you learned about the APT and were told that the two V factors are growth of GDP and unanticipated inflation. The equation for the model is: $r_j = 5.6\% + b_{j_1} \times 2\% + b_{j_2} \times 5\%$. Suppose that the sensitivity of your portfolio to GDP growth is −0.4, what is your portfolio's sensitivity to unanticipated inflation? You believe that a recession is looming and you wish to eliminate your portfolio's sensitivity to GDP growth but you still want to get the returns you expected. What happens to your portfolio's sensitivity to unanticipated inflation?

5/ The Treasury bill rate is 5% and the market portfolio return is expected to be 13%.

   a   What is the market risk premium?
   b   What is the required rate of return on an investment which has a beta of 1.6?
   c   If the expected return on Pippus Corporation is 17%, what is its beta?
   d   If an investment with a beta of 1.8 were expected to give a return of 19%, would it be convenient?

6/ What would the slope of the CML be if the degree of risk aversion increased from 2 to 3?

Questions

ANSWERS

   1/ *Because, if it were remunerated, this would be an "unwarranted" gain.*
   2/ *Yes, in order to eliminate it, given that it is not remunerated.*
   3/ *Risk-free rate + Market risk premium.*
   4/ *Its instability.*
   5/ *No, because this would be forgetting the constant (the no-risk cash rate) in the equation for the required rate of return.*
   6/ *That the market may be about to take a steep dive because risk is not being adequately rewarded.*
   7/ *Overvalued, because the required rate of return, given the risk, is too low. It will thus rise, causing the share price to fall. France Télécom is on the "securities market line" and is therefore correctly valued.*
   8/ *Analysis of the market return in different components. The degree of precision required, because risk premiums by factor and the associated betas are difficult to estimate.*
   9/ *To rise, because investors will only wish to invest in very liquid shares that they can sell immediately.*
   10/ *A good thing for small companies, generally growing rapidly, which are in fashion at the time.*
   11/ *The standard deviation is explained both by the market risk and the specific risk of the share, while the β only reflects the market risk of the share. Bouygues thus has a very high specific risk.*
   12/ *These types of shares are very rare and very valuable, because they go up when the market falls! Their marginal contribution to the reduction of a portfolio's risk is thus strong.*
   13/ *Because what is important in the CAPM is not the specific risk but the market risk of each security.*
   14/ *The child. If markets are really efficient, the answer is completely random.*

Exercises

1/ *Risk premium: $(10\% - 5\%)/1.1 = 4.54\%$. $k = 5\% + 0.7 \times 4.54\% = 8.2\%$.*

2/ *Undervalued: Air Liquide, Alcatel. Correctly valued: Carrefour. Overvalued: Volkswagen, ING.*

3/ *€40/(5\% + 2.7 \times (9\% - 5\%) + 1) = €34.5.*

4/ *$r = 5.6\% + 1.2 \times 3\% = 9.2\%$. $(9.2\% - 5.6\% + 2\% \times 0.4)/5\% = 0.88(9.2\% - 5.6\%)/5\% = 0.72$.*

5/ *(a) Market risk premium is $13 - 5 = 8\%$. (b) Required rate of return for an investment of beta of $1.6 = 5 + 1.6(13 - 5) = 17.8\%$. (c) Return $= 5 + \beta(8) = 17$, $\beta = (17 - 5)/8 = 1.5$. (d) Required rate of return $= 5 + 1.8(8) = 19.4\%$. The investment return is less than the required rate of return. Hence, its NPV will be negative.*

6/ *If the risk aversion increases from 2 to 3, the risk premium on the market portfolio would increase from 0.08 to 0.12, and the slope of the CML would increase from 0.4 to 0.6.*

BIBLIOGRAPHY

To read articles by the economists who developed the CAPM:

J. Lintner, The valuation of risk assets and the selection of risky investments in stock portfolios and capital budgets, *Review of Economics and Statistics*, **47**, 13–37, February 1965.

H. Markowitz, Portfolio selection, *Journal of Finance*, **7**, 77–91, March 1952.

W. Sharpe, Capital asset prices: A theory of market equilibrium under conditions of risk, *Journal of Finance*, **19**, 425–442, September 1964.

For an overview of the CAPM:

T. Copeland, F. Weston, *Financial Theory and Corporate Policy*, Addison-Wesley, 1984.

E. Fama, M. Miller, *The Theory of Finance*, Holt, Rinehart Winston, 1972.

For criticism on the limitations of the CAPM:

M. Blume, Betas and their regression tendencies, *Journal of Finance*, **30**, 785–795, June 1975.

J. Campbell, M. Lettau, B. Malkiel, Y. Xu, Have individual stocks become more volatile? An empirical exploration of idiosyncratic risk, *Journal of Finance*, **56**, 1–43, February 2001.

E. Fama, K. French, Size and book-to-market factors in earnings and returns, *Journal of Finance*, **50**, 131–155, 1995.

N. Groenewold, P. Fraser, Forecasting beta: How does the "five-year rule of thumb" do?, *Journal of Business & Accounting*, **27**, 953–982, September/October 2000.

R. Roll, A critique of the asset pricing theory's tests, Part I: On past and potential testability of the theory, *Journal of Financial Economics*, **4**, 129–179, March 1997.

For a deeper analysis of the CAPM:

R. Brealey, S. Myers, *Principles of Corporate Finance*, 6th edn, McGraw-Hill, 2000.

R. LaPorta, F. Lopez-de-Silanes, A. Shleifer, R. Vishny, *Investor Protection and Corporate Valuation*, working paper, National Bureau of Economic Research, October 1999.

S. Roll, S. Ross, An empirical investigation of the Arbitrage Pricing Theory, *Journal of Finance*, **35**, 1073–1103, December 1980.

S. Ross, The arbitrage theory of capital asset pricing, *Journal of Economic Theory*, **13**, 341–360, December 1976.

J. Siegel, *Stocks for the Long Run*, 3rd edn, McGraw-Hill, 2002.

For an overview of the APT:

R. Roll, S. Ross, The Arbitrage Pricing Theory approach to strategic portfolio planning, *Financial Analysts' Journal*, 14–26, May/June 1984.

For articles derived from the APT, excluding the Fama–French work already cited:

M. Brennan, T. Chordia, A. Subrahmanyam, Alternative factor specifications, security characteristics, and the cross section of expected stock returns, *Journal of Financial Economics*, **49**, 345–373, 1998.

E. Fama, K. French, The cross section of expected stock returns, *Journal of Finance*, **47**, 427–465, June 1992.

G. Hawawini, D. Keim, *The Cross Section of Common Stock Returns: A Review of the Evidence and Some New Findings*, working paper, Wharton, May 1998.

http://mba.tuck.darmouth.edu/pages/faculty/ken.french/data_library.html is the website where it is possible to download the parameters of the Fama–French model.

http://www.associes-finance.com is the website where two graphs of this chapter (pp. 424 and 432) were downloaded.

On the liquidity premium:

J. Hamon, B. Jacquillat, Is there value-added information in liquidity and risk premiums?, *European Financial Management*, **5**, 369–393, 1999.

H. Mendelson, Y. Amihud, Asset pricing and the bid–ask spread, *Journal of Financial Economics*, **17**, 223–249, December 1986.

H. Mendelson, Y. Amihud, The liquidity route to a lower cost of capital, *Journal of Applied Corporate Finance*, **17**, 223–249, Winter 2000.

For a comprehensive review of risk premiums:

B. Cornell, *The Equity Risk Premium*, John Wiley & Sons, 1999.

R. Mehra, E. Prescott, *The Equity Premium in Retrospect*, Working Paper #9525, National Bureau of Economic Research, February 2003.

J. Siegel, *Stock for the Long Run*, 3rd edn, McGraw-Hill, 2002.

On risk premiums:

R. Arnott, P. Bernstein, What risk premium is "normal"? *Financial Analysts' Journal*, 65–87, March/April 2002.

S. Brown, W. Goetzmann, S. Ross, Survivorship bias, *Journal of Finance*, 853–873, July 1995.

J. Claus, J. Thomas, Equity premia as low as three percent? Evidence from analysts' earnings forecasts for domestic and international stock markets, *Journal of Finance*, **56**, 1629–1666, October 2001.

B. Cornell, *The Equity Risk Premium: The Long-run Future of the Stock Market*, John Wiley & Sons, 1999.

E. Dimson, P. Marsh, M. Staunton, *The Triumph of the Optimists: 101 Years of Investment Returns*, Princeton University Press, 2002.

F. Fama, K. French, The equity premium, *Journal of Finance*, **57**, 637–659, April 2002.

W. Goetzmann, P. Jorion, *Global Stock Markets in the Twentieth Century*, working paper, Yale School of Management, 1999.

R. Ibbotson, P. Chen, Long-run stock returns: Participating in the real economy, *Financial Analysts' Journal*, 88–103, January/February 2003.

M. Kritzman, *Puzzles of Finance: Six Practical Poblems and Their Remarkable Solutions*, John Wiley & Sons, 2000.

R. Mehra, The equity premium: why is it a puzzle? *Financial Analysts' Journal*, 54–69, January/February 2003.

R. Mehra, E. Prescott, *The Equity Premium in Retrospect*, Working Paper #9535, National Bureau of Economic Research, February 2003.

For alternative techniques – DDM and P/E model:

A. Abrahms, *Quantitative Business Valuation*, McGraw-Hill, 2001.

T. Benninga, S. Sarig, *Corporate finance: A Valuation Approach*, McGraw-Hill, 1997.

T. Copeland, T. Koller, J. Murrin, *Valuation*, John Wiley & Sons, 2000.

E. Fama, K. French, Disappearing dividends: Changing firm characteristics or lower propensity to pay?, *Journal of Financial Economics*, **60**, 3–43, April 2001.

S. Pratt, *Cost of Capital: Estimation and Applications*, John Wiley & Sons, 2003.

On chaos theory:

E. Peters, *Chaos and Order in Capital Markets*, John Wiley & Sons, 1999.

Appendix 22.A
A FORMAL DERIVATION OF THE CAPM

The figure below shows the expected return and standard deviation of the market portfolio, M, the risk-free asset, r_f, and a generic risky asset I. The line connecting the risk-free asset and the market portfolio is the *capital market line*.

We know that when markets are in equilibrium the prices of all financial assets must adjust until there is no excess demand. Prices, in other words, must be fixed at a level where the supply of assets equals their demand. Therefore, the market portfolio for market in equilibrium includes all marketable assets held in proportion to their value weights. The proportion of a single asset in the market portfolio is given by:

$$w_i = \frac{\text{Market value of a single asset}}{\text{Market value of all assets}}$$

Thus, a generic portfolio (P) consisting of $a\%$ invested in the single (risky) asset I and ($1 - a\%$) in the market portfolio will have the following mean and standard deviation:

$$E(r_P) = aE(r_i) + (1 - a)E(r_M)$$

$$\sigma(r_P) = [a^2\sigma_i^2 + (1 - a)^2\sigma_M^2 + 2a(1 - a)\sigma_{iM}]^{1/2}$$

A crucial point is that the market portfolio already contains asset I held according to its market value weight because the market portfolio includes all assets held according to their market value weights.

The change in the mean and standard deviation with respect to the % of the portfolio, a, invested in asset I is determined as follow:

$$\frac{\partial E(r_P)}{\partial a} = E(r_i) - E(r_M)$$

$$\frac{\partial \sigma(r_P)}{\partial a} = \frac{1}{2}[a^2\sigma_i^2 + (1 - a)^2\sigma_M^2 + 2a(1 - a)\sigma_{i_m}]^{-1/2}$$

$$\times [2a\sigma_i^2 - 2\sigma_M^2 + 2a\sigma_M^2 + 2\sigma_{iM} - 4a\sigma_{iM}]$$

Sharpe and Treynor's insight is that $a\%$ is the excess demand for an individual risky asset. And we know that in equilibrium the excess demand for any asset must be zero. Therefore, if we evaluate the two equations above where excess demand equals zero, *we can then determine he equilibrium price at point M (i.e., the only point where there is no excess demand)*. We obtain:

$$\frac{\partial E(r_P)}{\partial a}\bigg|_{a=0} = E(r_i) - E(r_M)$$

$$\frac{\partial \sigma(r_P)}{\partial a}\bigg|_{a=0} = \frac{1}{2}(\sigma_M^2)^{-1/2}(-2\sigma_M^2 + 2\sigma_{iM}) = \frac{\sigma_{iM} - \sigma_M^2}{\sigma_M}$$

The slope of the risk–return tradeoff evaluated at M is:

$$\frac{\partial E(r_P)/\partial a}{\partial \sigma(r_P)/\partial a}\bigg|_{a=0} = \frac{E(r_i) - E(r_M)}{(\sigma_{iM} - \sigma_M^2)/\sigma_M}$$

The final step is to recognise that the slope of the opportunity set IMI' must also be equal to the slope of the capital market line $r_f M$. Since the slope of the capital market line is:

$$\frac{E(r_M) - r_f}{\sigma_M}$$

If we equate the slope of the risk–return tradeoff evaluated at M with the slope of the capital market line, we obtain:

$$\frac{E(r_M) - r_f}{\sigma_M} = \frac{E(r_i) - E(r_M)}{(\sigma_{iM} - \sigma_M^2)/\sigma_M}$$

Finally, we appropriately rearrange the equation by solving for $E(r_i)$:

$$E(r_i) = r_f + [E(r_M) - r_f] \frac{\sigma_{iM}}{\sigma_M^2}$$

This is the final equation of the **capital asset pricing model**: It states that the required rate of return on *any* asset is equal to the risk-free rate of return plus a risk premium. The latter is the *price* of the risk $[E(r_M) - r_f]$ multiplied by the quantity of risk (σ_{iM}/σ_M^2).

When shown graphically, this equation is also called the **security market line**.

Chapter 23
FROM THE COST OF EQUITY TO THE COST OF CAPITAL

Mirror, mirror on the wall ...

Determining the cost of capital, or the weighted average cost of capital, is not a simple task. Of course, it is one of the fundamentals of finance. The cost of capital has to be factored into investment decisions because it is the rate used for discounting cash flows for NPV[1] or that is compared with the IRR.[2] Cost of capital is also used to determine enterprise value (see Chapter 40). Truly, its importance can hardly be understated.

But, before reading on, it is imperative to understand the distinction between cost of capital, which is the weighted average cost of the capital contributed to the firm, and the cost of equity, which is just one component of the weighted average of the cost of capital.

1 *Net Present Value.*

2 *Internal Rate of Return.*

Section 23.1
THE COST OF CAPITAL AND THE β OF ASSETS

The cost of capital is the minimum rate of return on the company's investments that can satisfy both shareholders (the cost of equity) and debtholders (the cost of debt). The cost of capital is thus the company's total cost of financing.

When markets are in equilibrium, any investor with a perfectly diversified portfolio holds a fraction of both the company's equity and its debt. This is known as the CAPM that was discussed in Chapter 22. In other words, each investor holds a share of the company's operating assets, since this is equal to the sum of equity and net debt. Accordingly, each investor has some exposure to the risk arising from the company.

The cost of equity required by investors thus depends on just one factor: **the risk arising from the assets-in-place**. This means that the cost of the company's financial resources – its cost of capital – is none other than the rate of return required by investors, which is a function of the risk on capital employed.

The cost of capital depends solely on the risk of the assets-in-place, specifically its systematic risk, since unsystematic or specific risks are not remunerated.

The cost of capital is thus shaped by the economic characteristics of each sector of activity. It rises when fixed costs are high or the business is cyclical, and falls when the business operates more on variable costs or is easily predictable.

Modigliani and Miller (1958, 1977)[3] were the first to state that the company's cost of capital is not a function of its capital structure. If the risk on capital employed is such that it requires a 12% rate of return, and if it is fully equity-financed, shareholders will expect a minimum 12% return. On the other hand, if it is fully debt-financed, creditors will again require a 12% rate of return since they incur the same risk with the operating assets as the shareholders in the previous example. Lastly, suppose financing is *equally* divided between debt and equity. If the cost of debt is 10%, then shareholders will require a 14% return on equity to achieve a weighted average of 12% – i.e., the remuneration justified by the 12% risk for capital employed or the cost of capital.

Assume that in a perfect market the company changes its capital structure – for example, by buying back some of its equity via the issue of new debt. In this case, an investor with a perfectly diversified portfolio who holds 1% of the company's equity and 1% of its debt and thus 1% of its capital employed will continue to hold 1% of capital employed, though now with a lower amount of equity because of the share buyback and a higher % of net debt. The transaction is thus totally neutral for the investor. It will not affect the cost of capital, even if it is now divided between the cost of debt and the cost of equity, because the risk on capital employed remains unchanged.

As we have already discussed, the cost of capital is equal to the weighted average costs of net debt and of net equity. This will be examined in greater detail in the next section.

The cost of capital is not the weighted average of two separate costs. The overall riskiness of the company is represented by the cost of capital, whose two key components are debt and equity. The costs of equity and debt are a function of the risk of the assets, the cost of overall capital and the respective weighting of each.

For purely practical reasons, however, the cost of capital is calculated by taking the costs of debt and equity together.

Section 23.2
ALTERNATIVE METHODS FOR ESTIMATING THE COST OF CAPITAL

The cost of capital can be calculated in three ways: directly, indirectly or via enterprise value.

1/DIRECT CALCULATION VIA THE β OF ASSETS

Since a company's liabilities merely provide a "screen" between the asset side of the company and the financial market, the rate of return required to satisfy investors is equal to the risk-free rate plus a risk premium related to the company's activity.

Applying the CAPM gives us:

$$k = r_F + \beta_A \times (r_M - r_F)$$

where k is the weighted average cost of capital, r_F the risk-free rate, r_M the market rate of return and β_A the **beta of assets** or **unlevered beta** – that is, the β of a debt-free company.

Just as the beta of a security measures the deviation between its returns and those of the market, so too does the beta of an asset measure the deviation between its future cash flows and those of the market. Yet these two betas are not independent. A firm that invests in projects with a high β_A – in other words, projects that are risky – will have a high β_E on its shares because its profitability will fluctuate widely.

	Asset beta
Construction materials	0.71
Capital goods	0.66
Car manufacturers	0.56
Chemical	0.82
Consumer goods	0.71
Distribution	0.75
Electronic	1.60
Energy	0.82
Food	0.44
Tourism and recreation	0.91
Media and entertainment	1.37
Metal and steel	1.34
Other public utilities	0.69
Other services	0.65
Paper	0.57
Pharmacy and cosmetics	0.62
Real estate	0.42
Telecommunications	1.15
IT services	1.41
Transports	0.72
All sectors	**0.84**[4]

Source: BNP Paribas, Business Valuation Team.

It is also possible to calculate the beta of an asset using the following formula:

$$\beta_A = \frac{\left[\beta_E + \beta_D \times (1 - T_C) \times \dfrac{V_D}{V_E}\right]}{\left[1 + (1 - T_C) \times \dfrac{V_D}{V_E}\right]}$$

4 *This figure is lower than 1 because it is the β of all shares on the market that – gross of the impact of net debt – average 1.*

where V_D is the market value of net debt, V_E the market value of equity and T_C the corporate tax rate.

β_D corresponds to the beta of net debt. For groups with low net debt, β_D is frequently approximated to zero, thereby simplifying the formula. It now becomes:

$$\beta_A = \frac{\beta_E}{\left[1 + (1 - T_C) \times \dfrac{V_D}{V_E}\right]}$$

It is not recommended to assume that $\beta_D = 0$ for companies with a higher net debt. The greater a company's debt, the less it depends on interest rates and the more it is a function of the specific features of the company itself (i.e., fixed vs. variable costs) and its sector of activity. Debt then begins to behave more like equity.

The beta of debt is calculated in the same way as that of equity by regressing the returns on listed debt against market returns of the debt of the same credit quality.

2/INDIRECT CALCULATION

In practice, to determine the rate of return required by all of the company's providers of funds, it is necessary to **calculate the cost of capital by valuing the various securities issued by the company**.

THE WEIGHTED AVERAGE COST OF CAPITAL

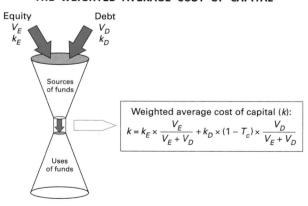

The cost of capital is related to the value of the securities and represents the amount the company would have to pay to refund all its liabilities, regardless of the cost of its current resources. As such, it symbolises the application of financial market logic to the corporation.

To calculate a company's cost of capital, we determine the rate of return required of each type of security and weight each rate according to its relative share in financing. This is none other than the WACC[5] formula:

5 *Weighted Average Cost of Capital.*

$$k = k_E \times \frac{V_E}{V_E + V_D} + k_D \times (1 - T_C) \times \frac{V_D}{V_E + V_D}$$

Thus, a company with equity financing of 100 at a rate of 15.7%, and debt financing of 50 at a pre-tax cost of 7%, has a cost of capital of 12% (with a 35% tax rate, T_C).

This is the most frequently used method to calculate the cost of capital. Nevertheless, beware of relying too much on spreadsheets to calculate the cost of capital, instead of getting your hands dirty by working on some examples yourself.

When performing simulations, it is all too tempting to change the company's capital structure while forgetting that the cost of equity and the cost of debt are not constant: they are a function of the company's structure. It is all too easy to reduce the cost of capital on paper by increasing the relative share of net debt, because debt is always cheaper than equity!

In the preceding example, if the share of debt is increased to 80% without changing either the cost of debt or equity, then the cost of capital works out to 5.1%. **While the arithmetic may be correct, this is totally wrong financially.**

Do not forget that higher debt translates into a higher cost of both equity and net debt, as shown in the graph.

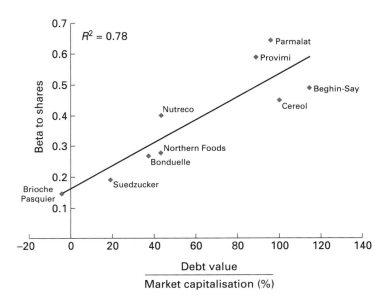

3/THE IMPLICIT CALCULATION BASED ON ENTERPRISE VALUE

The cost of capital can be estimated based on enterprise value and a projection of anticipated future free cash flows, since:

$$V = V_E + V_D = \sum_{t=0}^{\infty} \frac{FCF_t}{(1+k)^t}$$

It is then necessary to solve the equation with k as the unknown factor. However, this calculation is rarely used because it is difficult to determine the market consensus for free cash flows.

4/THE PITFALLS OF THE INDIRECT COST-OF-CAPITAL CALCULATION

(a) Expected rate of return or effective rate of return?

The cost of capital is a financial concept reflecting the *expected* rate of return **required or expected** by investors at a given point in time. It is not an accounting concept and should not be confused with the *ex post* return on capital employed, which is the **effective** rate of return.

Since it is not an accounting concept, calculation of the cost of capital should be based on market rather than accounting data.

The cost of capital is neither an inverted P/E, nor the return on equity (R_E), nor the rate of return. Instead, it is the rate of return currently required by shareholders as measured by the CAPM:

$$k_E = r_F + \beta_E \times (r_M - r_F)$$

The cost of debt is not the cost of debt contracted 10 years, 1 year or 3 months ago. Nor is it the company's average cost of debt or the ratio of financial expenses to average debt for the year, which covered the nominal cost of debt.

The cost of net debt is the rate at which the company could refinance its existing debt given its present economic position. It cannot be lower than the risk-free rate.

The tax savings generated by debt are represented by the factor $(1 - T_C)$ as applied to the cost of debt. Remember that cash flow was originally calculated at a marginal tax rate based on operating profit.

It is possible to estimate the rate at which the company can refinance its existing debt using two alternatives:

- use the official rating of the company. If the company has a rating given by one of the recognised rating agencies (Standard & Poor's, Moody's, etc.), the analyst should simply use the Yield To Maturity (YTM) required by financial markets at the time of the valuation for similar securities belonging to that class of rating; or

- create an implicit or synthetic rating. In the case where the company has not got an official rating, then the analyst proceeds by giving the company an **implicit** (or **synthetic rating**). The idea is very simple (albeit difficult when applied!): the analyst tries to replicate the style of analysis performed by rating agencies in order to arrive at a reasonable approximation of the rating that the company could have received from such an agency. Once we have the implicit rating, the analyst uses the yield to maturity required on financial markets for the obtained class of rating.

(b) Accounting or market values of equity and debt?

Shareholders base their required rate of return on the market value of equity – that is, the amount at which equity can be bought or sold – rather than using book values. The same reasoning applies to debtholders.

The choice of weighting is based on market values rather than book values.

This is consistent with the idea of selecting the required rate of return rather than the book rate of return. Using the book value of liabilities can be very misleading because it may significantly differ from the market value of equity and debt.

The yield to maturity shown in bond quotations in the financial press is based on the closing market price of a bond, not on its face value. Similarly, the implied cost of equity for a company's cost should be based on the market price per share at which it trades.

For example, the L'Oréal shareholder does not require a 17%[6] return on book equity of €7.5bn, but an 8% return on market capitalisation of €53bn! Similarly, an investor buying Eurotunnel bonds with a nominal yield of 5% at a price of 60% of the nominal amount does not require a 5% return. Instead, he is looking for 9%.[7]

The market value of debt can be estimated without too much difficulty. The process is as follows:[8]

Step 1   Identify the annual contract payments.

Step 2   Determine the credit quality of debt. Credit ratings may be estimated from bond-rating models that mimic the behaviour of rating agencies (i.e., an implicit rating).

Step 3   Estimate the yield to maturity for which debt would trade, by reference to current market yields with similar *ratings, maturity and coupons*.

Step 4   Calculate the present value of financing payments, discounting each annual, promised payment with the estimated yield to maturity: The result should approximate the market value of debt.

6 *Book rate of return on 2001 equity.*

7 *Discounted rate of return on a borrowing listed at 60%.*

8 *This approach is inadequate if debt has options features like caps, floors, call provisions, convertibility options and so on. In these cases we should use the option framework in order to value these derivatives (see Garbade, 2002).*

Two comments:

1   This process can be readily applied to just single debt instruments and not only to the entire amount of debt;
2   Step 4 calculations can be simplified if contract payments are constant over time, in which case we can use the following formula:

Estimated market value of debt

$$= \text{Annual interest expenses} \times \frac{(1 - 1/(1 + \text{Current } YTM)^{\text{maturity of debt}})}{\text{Current } YTM}$$

Section 23.3
SOME PRACTICAL APPLICATIONS

When making an investment decision, and even if using the indirect method, it is not particularly difficult to calculate the cost of capital. If the company is publicly listed, the calculation is based on readily available market data. Average prices are often used to smooth out any erratic market swings. If the company is not listed, the calculation is based on the cost of capital of companies of comparable size and risk operating in the same sector of activity. If the peer sample has been well-chosen, the resulting cost of capital will be the same as that of the unlisted company.

The indirect method is less adapted to valuations, because to determine the value of equity one needs the cost of capital, and to calculate the cost of capital one needs the cost of equity! However, there are two ways to solve this dilemma:

●   use the parameters associated with a target capital structure, while being careful to use the costs of equity and net debt **that correspond to the target capital structure**, and not the present costs;
●   use the direct method. The advantage of this alternative is that one avoids the frequent mistake of using costs of equity and debt that do not correspond to the capital structure in question.

1/DIVERSIFIED COMPANIES

The overall cost of capital of a diversified company can be calculated similarly to a company with a single business. Conversely, the analyst should be cautious if the divisions do not show the same risk profile. In these cases, each division should be analysed separately according to its cost of capital; the weighted average costs of capital of different divisions would then represent the overall cost of capital for the company. As shown in Chapter 22, diversification does not reduce the cost of capital because it only considers systematic risk. As unsystematic risk can be eliminated by diversification, it does not affect the required rate of return.

2/MULTINATIONAL COMPANIES

A similar logic applies to companies operating in different countries. A British company investing in Russia, for example, should not use a discount rate based on British data just because its suppliers of funds are British. After all, the project's flows are affected by Russian systematic risks (inflation, taxation, exchange rates, etc.), rather than British systematic risk. Therefore, the company should correctly apply a beta reflecting the project's sensitivity to Russian systematic risk.

After the West-based company has invested in Russia, its cost of capital will probably be higher. The difference would be made up of two costs, a lower one for western Europe and a higher one for Russia reflecting the different levels of systematic risk (political and macroeconomic) in the two regions.

This approach avoids the frequent error of discounting flows denominated in one currency using discount rates denominated in another currency.

3/EMERGING MARKETS

In developing countries, calculating the cost of capital of an investment raises some practical problems. The risk-free rate of local government bonds is often just wishful thinking, since these countries have little solvency. The local risk-free rate and betas of local peer groups are rarely measured, let alone significant, given the limited size of financial markets in these countries.

We suggest Bancel and Perrotin's (1999) system for calculating the cost of capital in such cases:

	Government bond rate of the eurozone
+	Sovereign spread
+	$\beta_E \times$ European risk premium
=	Cost of capital in an emerging market

The sovereign *spread* represents the difference between bond yields issued on international markets (in euros or dollars) by the country in question vs. those offered by eurozone or dollarzone bonds. This yield represents the political risk in the emerging country. When the developing nation has not made any international issues, it is possible to use a bond issue by another state with the same credit rating as a benchmark.

β_E is the beta coefficient of the sector of activity calculated in developed financial markets. This parameter measures the sensitivity of an industry's flows to the overall economic environment. It is shaped by the sector of activity, not the country.

Obviously, this rate must be applied to flows that have been converted from their local currencies into euros. If the flows are denominated in dollars, then remember to apply a USD rather than an EUR benchmark.

For example, it is possible to calculate the cost of capital of a Chilean investment project based on the following assumptions: $\beta_E = 0.82$, r_F in the US $= 5\%$, a Chilean government bond rate of 7.5% and a US risk premium of 4%:

> 5%
> + 7.5% − 5%
> + 0.82 × 4%
> = 10.78% on flows denominated in dollars.

If the project's flows are denominated in Chilean pesos, the cost of capital is converted from dollars into pesos as follows:

$$\text{Cost of capital in pesos} = \frac{1 + \text{Cost of capital in US\$}}{\dfrac{1 + \text{Inflation rate in US}}{1 + \text{Inflation rate in Chile}}} - 1$$

4/COMPANIES WITH NEGATIVE NET FINANCIAL DEBT

For the purposes of this discussion, disregard negative net debt situations that occur when a company has sold a major asset in order to use the proceeds for another investment – such as the buyback of shares, etc. – since such a situation is temporary.

Consider a group that, for structural reasons, has net cash of 2 with no banking or financial debt, and equity of 9.

Assume that the shareholders buying these shares understand that they are buying both operating assets with a given risk level and have a cash situation with virtually no risk. In other words, the risk on the share is lower than the risk on the company given the structurally positive net cash balance.

The cost of capital of this company can be estimated using the indirect method applying a **negative value** for V_D. So, in this example, if the cost of equity is 7% and net cash generates 2% after taxes:[9]

$$k = 7\% \times \frac{9}{9 - 2} + 2\% \times \frac{-2}{9 - 2} = 8.4\%$$

To offer the 7% return required by shareholders, the company would have to invest in projects yielding at least 8.4%. The 7% cost of equity is the weighted average of the required 8.4% return on capital employed and the 2% on net cash.

The company's cost of capital is thus 8.4%.

The cost of capital for a company with a structurally positive cash balance does not differ from that of a company with the same capital employed but no cash. The cost of equity changes, but the cost of capital remains the same.

5/PRIVATE COMPANIES

In order to examine the cost of capital of private or unlisted firms, well-diversified investors make underlying assumptions about the CAPM that are less defensible. The owner of a private firm may be willing (or even have to) invest the bulk of his wealth in the business. In this case, he will be concerned with the total risk for the firm, rather than just the market risk.

9 *Alternatively, we could say that:* $2\% \times \frac{2}{9} + k \times \frac{7}{9} = 7\%$.

With undiversified investors, there are two basic ways to add the discount for *lack of marketability* in the cost of equity of a private firm:

- Add a premium to the cost of equity to reflect the higher risk created by the owner's inability to diversify. In this case, one can use the returns demanded by venture capitalists on their investments in fledgling businesses. The problem with this approach is it is impossible to know how much of their required rate of return – which can range between 30% and 50% on their portfolios – is for lack of marketability.
- Adjust the beta to reflect total risk rather than market risk. This adjustment is relatively simple, since the R^2 of the regression measures the proportion of risk that is the market risk:

$$\text{Total beta} = \frac{\text{Total risk}}{\text{Systematic risk}} \times \beta = \frac{1}{R^2} \times \beta$$

Section 23.4
CAN CORPORATE MANAGERS INFLUENCE THE COST OF CAPITAL?

Chapter 34 demonstrates why there is little point in using debt and its tax advantages to lower the cost of capital. While net debt costs less than equity, it tends to increase the risk to shareholders, who retaliate by raising the required rate of return and consequently the cost of equity. Debt works to the advantage of the company, because the interest on the net debt can be deducted from its tax base (which it cannot do for dividends). The opposite tends to apply to investors.

In short, in a perfect world in which investors had diversified portfolios, one man's gain would be another man's loss.

Moreover, if debt really did reduce the cost of capital, one would have to wonder why highly efficient companies, such as L'Oréal, Nestlé, BMW or Heineken, are not levered, given that they have no reason to fear bankruptcy?

Since the cost of capital depends on the risk to the company, the only way it can be lowered is through risk-reducing measures, such as:

- Lowering the breakeven point by shifting from fixed to variable costs – i.e., subcontracting, outsourcing, etc. Unfortunately, the margins will probably decline accordingly.
- Improving the business's visibility and smoothing its cyclical nature – i.e., wining medium-term supply contracts with important clients. Here, too, however, margins may be affected since, in exchange, the clients will demand price concessions.
- Diversifying the business does not help as it does not reduce market risk, but rather specific risk, which is the only one to be remunerated.
- Shifting from a risky activity (e.g., a biotech startup) in a high-risk country like Pakistan to a safer business in a more stable country (cheese production in Switzerland) will no doubt cut the cost of capital, but it will also lower

profitability. In addition, it would have no impact on value, since it is simply a lateral move in the market.

In conclusion, managers have virtually no means of lowering the cost of capital while simultaneously creating value. Their only viable strategy is to improve the return on capital employed by increasing flows and reducing the amount of capital employed.

Similarly, increasing the risk for capital employed increases the cost of capital, but value will not be destroyed if profitability improves at the same time.

The cost of capital and the beta of the Bouygues Group have declined from 2002 to 2005 thanks to the expansion in the telecom and media segments.

BETA OF BOUYGUES 1992 (MONTHLY DATA)

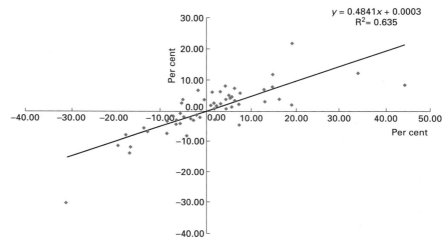

$y = 0.4841x + 0.0003$
$R^2 = 0.635$

BETA OF BOUYGUES 2005 (MONTHLY DATA)

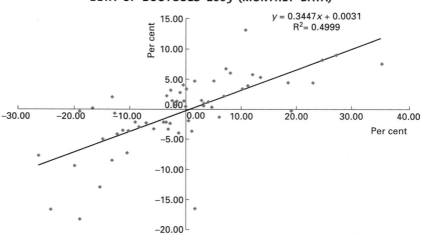

$y = 0.3447x + 0.0031$
$R^2 = 0.4999$

COST OF CAPITAL: A LOOK AT THE EVIDENCE

A study by Gitman and Vandenberg (2000) compares the cost of capital method-ologies of major US corporations in 1997 and 1980. The results show that practitioners have substantially changed their practices for computing the cost of capital.

There is robust evidence that the gap between theory and practice is rapidly narrowing. Firms that use the required return from investors as the primary procedure for the cost of equity capital have increased from 35.6% to 70.3%. Conversely, the use of historical dividend yields has a lower relevance. It is also important to note that 93% of firms estimating required shareholders' return (64.9% ÷ 70.3%) use CAPM as the preferred cost-of-equity capital techniques.

Procedure	1980 (%)	1997 (%)
Historical dividend yield plus estimate of growth	3.40	4.50
Return required by investors	35.60	70.30
APT	NA	0.90
CAPM	NA	64.90
Other	NA	4.50
Current dividend yield plus estimate of growth	26.00	9.00
Dividend yield estimate only	1.70	0.00
Cost of debt plus a risk premium for equity	13.00	17.10
Earnings/Price (E/P) ratio	15.80	2.70
Market return adjusted for risk	22.60	14.40
*Totals**	*118.10*	*118.00*

*Response totals greater than 100% because of multiple responses.

These results are consistent with those obtained by Graham and Harvey (2001), shown below. Their survey provides further evidence of the increasing popularity of the CAPM method to calculate the cost of capital:

Cost of equity capital method	Percentage of CFOs who use a given method
CAPM	72
Arithmetic average historical return	48
Multibeta CAPM	33
Dividend Discount Model (DDM)	15
Investor expectations	13
Regulatory decisions	6

Using a scale with 2% intervals, Gitman and Vandenberg (2000) asked firms to detail their firm's approximate overall cost of capital. The following table compares the results from two different years, 1980 and 1997:

Range of overall cost of capital (%)	October 1980 (%)	April 1997 (%)
Less than 5	1.70	0.00
5–7	0.60	0.90
7–9	3.40	5.50
9–11	10.10	43.60
11–13	20.90	28.20
13–15	21.50	14.50
15–17	22.60	3.60
17–19	12.30	2.70
19–21	4.00	0.90
21–23	0.60	0.00
23–25	0.60	0.00
Greater than 25	1.70	0.00
Approximate mean	*14.25*	*11.53*

The most frequent response in 1997 was between 9 and 11%, well below the corresponding response in 1980 (15–17%). The difference between the two values results mainly from the decline in interest rates in the United States. It may also be attributable to a reduction in average risk faced by responding firms.

Finally, it is interesting to examine the frequency of cost of capital revision:

Frequency of revision	1980 (%)	1997 (%)
Annually	21.50	27.12
When environmental conditions change sufficiently to warrant it	50.30	49.20
Quarterly or semiannually	4.00	5.10
Less frequently than annually	13.00	8.50
Each time a major project is evaluated	11.20	10.20
Totals	*100.00*	*100.00*

The answers indicate that the majority of respondents revise their cost of capital when environmental conditions change sufficiently to warrant it. The frequency of revisions of the cost of capital has increased over time, and is recently done on a yearly basis.

A final study by Bruner et al. (1998) yielded results that are also consistent with previous ones. Here are the main results of their findings:

1   there are different alternatives in the risk-free rates choice. An almost equal percentage of analysts use 10- and 30-year Treasuries, while a lower percentage use 3-month T-bills;

2   the majority of corporations use published sources for the beta estimation while around 30% of respondents estimate it themselves;

3   around 40% of firms use a fixed rate of 5–6% for the market risk premium, while a lower percentage (around 10%) use a value between 4% and 4.5%. Around 50% of financial advisors who were interviewed claim to use a much higher rate of between 7% and 7.5%.

SUMMARY

download

The cost of capital or the Weighted Average Cost of Capital (WACC) is a fundamental concept in corporate finance. It is relied on for making investment decisions and for the valuation of businesses.

The cost of capital is not just the risk of capital employed. It exists before the capital structure is even fully assembled or finalised. In fact, creditors and shareholders will determine the rate of return they require on debt and equity on the basis of the capital structure and of the risk of capital employed.

Only for calculation purposes is the cost of capital often calculated as the weighted average cost of equity and debt.

The cost of capital can be calculated either:

●   using a direct method on the basis of the β of the capital employed; or

●   using an indirect method where it is equal to the weighted average of the values of the cost of equity and the cost of net debt; or

●   by observing the value of capital employed, when this figure is available.

For a diversified company, there are as many costs of capital as there are sectors in which it operates. Similarly, every country or economic area has its own specific cost of capital, which is dependent upon the political landscape and macroeconomic risks.

For emerging countries, the methodology must be adapted to factor in both the lack of certain data (risk-free interest rate) and international parameters (the industry's β).

A company's negative net debt structure brings down the cost of its equity, but has no impact on the cost of capital, even if the company has no cash.

QUESTIONS

quiz

1/ When is the cost of capital equal to the cost of equity? Can the cost of capital be equal to the cost of debt?

2/ Why does the cost of capital constitute a direct link between return on capital expenditure and the returns required by capital investors?

3/ Why is the cost of capital not an accounting concept?

4/ What is the cost of capital equal to?

5/ Is the cost of equity equal to the return on the shares?

6/ What is the cost of reserves equal to? And the cost of depreciation?

7/ How many costs of capital are there in a company that has diversified into different (business) sectors but not geographic areas? What about if it has done so within each of the company's divisions?

8/ Can a company that invests in projects on which the returns are lower than its cost of capital continue to obtain resources through cash flow? Through debt? Through capital increases?

9/ A listed company launches a takeover bid on another company at a price that is far too high. According to the cost of capital theory, what should the sanction be?

EXERCISES

1/ What is the cost of equity of a company whose shares are trading at 30.2 and which pays a dividend of 5 over 5 years and 6 after 5 years?

2/ What is the cost of debt for a company whose debt at 11% has a nominal value of 1,000, is trading at 1,037.9 and has a life of 5 years (redemption at maturity)?

3/ Use the answers to Questions 1 and 2 and calculate the cost of capital of this company. The company has issued 1,000 shares.

4/ Calculate the cost of capital of a company for which the key figures are as follows:

	Equity	Debt
Book value	10,000	1,000
Value	12,000	1,000
Perpetual remuneration	1,800	100

5/ What is the net present value of the following perpetual investment before and after tax?

Cost: 100
Cash flow before tax: 26
Tax rate: 50%
Capital structure:

	Percentage (%)	Cost before tax (%)	Cost after tax (%)
Equity	60	24	24
Debt	40	16	8

Cyclone case study

The Cyclone Group operates in three sectors: the sale of commercial shipping equipment, shipping of goods by sea between mainland France and Réunion (the group owns two container ships) and a small shipyard which oversees the careenage of most of the boats in Réunion.

The three divisions are listed on the *Second Marché* or on the *Marché Libre* of the Euronext Paris Stock Exchange.

	Equipment sales division	Maritime shipping division	Shipyard
Market capitalisation	2,160	18,520	632
Shareholders' equity	1,580	10,512	824
Net debt (estimated value)	812	−12	1,356
Sales	22,210	23,724	701
EBIT	405	1,625	82
Net income	226	1,057	−24
β_E observed	0.8	0.5	1.2
β_D estimated	0.1	0	0.3
Tax rate	35%	35%	35%

(a) What is your view of the financial health of this group (very simple financial analysis)?

(b) The required return for a risk-free investment is around 6.5% (before tax) and the average required return for the market portfolio is 11% (before tax). Calculate the overall cost of capital for this group.

Questions

1/ *When debt is zero. Yes, but only if the company is carrying very heavy debts.*
2/ *By definition.*
3/ *Because it is the cost at which the company could reconstitute its liabilities today.*
4/ *To the required return on the capital employed.*
5/ *No, it is generally much higher.*
6/ *Cost of reserves: cost of capital increase; cost of depreciation: company's cost of capital.*
7/ *As many as there are divisions. Only one.*
8/ *Yes, unfortunately using cash flow. Yes, using debt if its debts are still low. With difficulty through a capital increase.*
9/ *Its value drops.*

Exercises

1/ *18.00%.*
2/ *10.00%.*
3/ *17.74%.*
4/ *14.62%.*
5/ *Before tax: k = 20.8%; NPV = 25; after tax: k = 17.6%; NPV = −26.*

Cyclone case study

(a) *The group is economically cohesive (it is not a conglomerate). The shipping and equipment sales divisions are profitable, although the shipyard is not; however, it is a small division compared with the others. Overall, the group is profitable and carries very little debt. There is the possibility that the current capital allocation may not be optimal, given the co-existence of profitable divisions and a nonprofitable division.*

(b)

	Equipment sales division (%)	Maritime shipping division (%)	Shipyard (%)	Group (%)
k_E	10.10	8.75	11.90	8.98
k_D after tax	4.52	4.23	5.10	4.89
K	8.57	8.75	7.26	8.60

BIBLIOGRAPHY

Y. Amihud, H. Mendelson, The liquidity route to a lower cost of capital, *Journal of Applied Corporate Finance*, **12**(4), 8–25, Winter 2000.

F. Bancel, Th. Perrotin, Le coût du capital dans les pays émergents, *Analyse Financière*, **119**, 76–88, June 1999 [in French].

S. Benninga, *Corporate Valuation: A Valuation Approach*, McGraw-Hill, 1997.

C. Botosan, Evidence that greater liquidity lowers the cost of capital, *Journal of Applied Corporate Finance*, **12**(4), 8–25, Winter 2000.

E. Fama, K. French, The corporate cost of capital and the return on corporate investment, *Journal of Finance*, **54**(6), 1939–1967, December 1999.

K. Garbade, *Fixed Income Analytics*, MIT Press, 2002.

F. Modigliani, M. Miller, The cost of capital corporation finance and the theory of investment, *American Economic Review*, 261–297, June 1958.

S. Myers, Interactions of corporate financing and investment decisions: Implication for capital budgeting, *Journal of Finance*, **29**(1), 1–25, March 1974.

S. Pratt, *Cost of Capital: Estimation and Applications*, 2nd edn, John Wiley & Sons, 2003.

R. Schramm, H. Wang, Measuring the cost of capital in an international CAPM framework, *Journal of Applied Corporate Finance*, **12**(3), 63–72, Autumn 1999.

R. Stulz, Globalisation, corporate finance and the cost of capital, *Journal of Applied Corporate Finance*, **12**(3), 8–25, Autumn 1999.

For more on the evidence coming from the practice:

R. Bruner, K. Eades, R. Harris, R. Higgins, Best practices in estimating the cost of capital: Survey and synthesis, *Financial Practice and Education*, 13–29, Spring/Summer 1998.

L. Gitman, P. Vandenberg, Cost of capital techniques used by major US firms: 1997 vs. 1980, *Financial Practice and Education*, 54–68, Fall/Winter 2000.

J. Graham, C. Harvey, The theory and practice of corporate finance: Evidence from the field, *Journal of Financial Economics*, 187–243, May 2001.

The following websites provide information on the cost of capital:

Europe – *www.associes-finance.fr*
USA – *www.ibbotson.com, www.stern.nyu.edu/~adamodar*

Chapter 24
THE TERM STRUCTURE OF INTEREST RATES

Here comes a curveball[1]

1 *A baseball term used when the pitcher's delivery causes the ball to deviate from a straight line by imparting spin.*

2 *Capital Asset Pricing Model.*

Conventional financial theory, portfolio theory and the CAPM,[2] which were presented in Chapter 21, are concerned with the notion of interest rates and reducing them to the level of a factor that is exogenous to their models – namely, the risk-free rate. But the risk-free rate is by no means a given variable, and no financial instrument in existence allows investors to completely escape risk.

Moreover, because it is a single-period model, the CAPM draws no distinction between short-term and long-term interest rates. As has been discussed, a money market fund does not offer the same annual rate of return as a 10-year bond. An entire body of financial research is devoted to understanding movements in interest rates and, in particular, how different maturities are linked. This is the study of how the yield curve is formed.

Section 24.1
FIXED INCOME SECURITIES AND RISK

Investing in debt securities is not risk-free, although it is much less risky than options or even stocks. There are at least three risks involved in debt securities:

- inflation risk;
- the risk of a change in interest rates if the security's maturity is different from the investment horizon; and
- counterparty (or default) risk.

Counterparty risk is ignored in yield curves, because they are generally based on government debt; therefore, the risk is considered to be negligible. Two other risks play a more important part in the interest rate structure.

1/FIXED INCOME INSTRUMENTS AND INFLATION

When an investor buys an Italian government zero-coupon bond and keeps it until maturity, he has sure and advance knowledge of the sum he will receive when the bond is redeemed (assuming that the state does not go bankrupt). However, he is not certain of that sum's future purchasing power.

Let us take the example of a zero-coupon bond redeemable for €1,000 in September 2022. If you had paid €377 for this bond in September 2002, your return will be 5% per year if you keep the bond until maturity. In 2002, the market was pricing in long-term inflation at about 1.5%. This means that the price of an asset worth €1 in 2002 (equivalent to the value of a subway ticket) should be worth €1.35 in 2002.[3] So you invested €377 today in your zero-coupon bond believing that you will be able to buy 741 subway tickets (1,000/1.35) in 2022.

Unfortunately, if between 2002 and 2022 inflation is not 1.5% per year, but 4% per year, you will be able to buy just 456 tickets,[4] not 741. By investing in a long-term bond, you have frozen your nominal interest rate (5%), but not the interest rate after inflation that you will ultimately receive. This rate is called the "real interest rate".

The relationship between nominal interest rate and real interest rate can be expressed as follows:

$$\text{Real interest rate} = \frac{1 + \text{Nominal interest rate}}{1 + \text{Inflation rate}} - 1$$

If inflation is not too high, the equation can be simplified as follows:

$$\text{Real interest rate} = \text{Nominal interest rate} - \text{Inflation rate}$$

2/ FIXED INCOME SECURITIES AND THE TIMEFRAME FOR INVESTMENT

An investor who does not want to get trapped by an unexpected upturn in inflation can invest his €377 for 1 year, and then repeat the transaction every year. He will thus be sure that the rate at which he invests will reflect anticipations of inflation. Hence, if the 1-year nominal rate is 3% (composed of a real rate of 2% and inflation of 1%) and if inflation rises to 2.5%, short-term rates will probably move to 4.5%. Repeated investment in short-term, fixed income securities limits the risk of an unexpected upturn in inflation. Hence, our investor, with his €377 invested at 3% and with inflation of 1%, can buy 558 subway tickets in 20 years. This is true even if inflation rises to 2.5%, as the short-term rate would then be 4.5%, with the real long-term rate unchanged at 2%.

However, this strategy exposes the investor to trends in real short-term interest rates. It is possible that, with constant 1% inflation, real interest rates will move to 1%. The investor's nominal rate would then be 2% and in 20 years, even without any change in inflation, he would only be able to buy 459 subway tickets and not the 558 he was expecting.

Investors also choose their investment timeframe on the basis of liquidity preferences. Repeated short-term investments secure a certain measure of liquidity in exchange for uncertainty about the ultimate rate of return. To secure a guaranteed return, an investor in long-term bonds must keep her bonds until maturity.

3 $1.35 = 1 \times (1 + 1.5\%)^{20}$.

4 $456 = 1,000 / (1 + 4\%)^{20}$.

3/CHOOSING RISK

Thus, it can be seen that investors must choose their type of risk. They can elect to have the maturity of their investment coincide with their investment timeframe, and thus expose themselves to inflation risk (but not interest rate risk), or they can choose a short-term timeframe and renew their investment on a regular basis, and thus expose themselves to interest rates (but not inflation).

Depending upon the timeframe chosen, an investor will not consider short-term and long-term rates in the same way:

- The long-term investor is willing to receive a lower yield to maturity than a short-term investor who will have to renew constantly, considering that "normally" long-term rates are below short-term rates.
- The short-term investor, on the other hand, will consider it "normal" that short-term rates should be below long-term rates.

Only a bond with a redemption value and interest rate indexed to inflation can protect against unexpected changes in inflation and ensure a fixed annual rate, as long as the issuer does not go bankrupt and the bond's maturity is the same as the investment timeframe.

Section 24.2
THE DIFFERENT INTEREST RATE CURVES

1/HOW A BOND BREAKS DOWN

Consider a bond issued by the Scania Group on 27 March 2002 paying 6% annual interest on a €1,000 face value and a 5-year maturity.

Like any financial security, the Scania bond is a cash flow timetable. But, in another light, it can also be thought of as a **portfolio of zero-coupon bonds**.[5] This "portfolio" is based on a zero-coupon bond that matures 27 March 2003 with a redemption value of €60, a zero-coupon bond that matures 27 March 2004 with a redemption value of €60, and so on, concluding with a zero-coupon bond that matures 27 March 2007 with a redemption value of €1,060.

5 *For example, this is the case with French OAT government bonds.*

Each of these zero-coupon bonds can be valued individually. The sum of the values is equal to the value of the Scania bond (otherwise arbitrage traders would quickly re-establish the equilibrium). The present value of our Scania bond can thus be calculated as follows:

$$PV = \sum_{t=1}^{5} \frac{F_t}{(1 + r_t)^t}$$

where F_t is the cash flows of year i (€60 the first 4 years and €1,060 the 5th year) and r_t is the market rate for zero-coupon bonds with a maturity of N years. The single rates of interest on zero-coupon bonds are named **spot rates**. The series of spot rates r_1, r_2, etc. is *one* way of expressing the **term structure** of interest rates.

Rather than discounting each of the payments at a different rate of interest, it could be possible to find a single rate of discount that would produce the same result. This rate is defined as **yield to maturity**, and it is in fact exactly the same as the internal rate of return, but masqueraded under another name!

The reader, however, should be aware that it could be not entirely correct to use the yield to maturity to determine bond prices. Why?

1   Because the bondholder may demand different rates of return for different periods. Unless the two bonds offer exactly the same set of cash flows, they will probably have different yields to maturity. The yield to maturity thus represents only a rough guide to the appropriate yield on another bond.
2   Because the yield to maturity does not determine bond prices. Actually, it is the other way round. The value of any package of cash flows is determined by discounting each cash flow at the appropriate spot rate. Then, *given the value*, we could compute the yield to maturity that, like all averages, summarizes the relevant information contained in the term structure of interest rates.

Forward rates are implicit in the spot rate curve. In general, if we are given spot rates, r_1 and r_2 for years 1 and 2, we can determine the forward rate f_2, such that:

$$(1 + r_2)^2 = (1 + r_1) \times (1 + f_2)$$

We solve for f_2, yielding:

$$f_2 = \frac{(1 + r_2)^2}{(1 + r_1)} - 1$$

As previously discussed, one important characteristic of financial securities is maturity. Clearly, an investor will not demand the same return on a 5-year investment as he would on a 1-year one, because he does not expose himself to the same risk. What return should he demand for the short, medium and long term and, more generally, for each possible maturity?

2/CURVE OF ZERO-COUPON RATES AND SWAP CURVE

By charting the interest rate for the same categories of risk at all maturities, the investor obtains the yield curve that reflects anticipations of all financial market operators.

However, if bond market data were used to calculate yields to maturity, then the coupons would introduce a bias. The yield curve shows the interest rate on instruments with different maturities and different coupons. Using a zero-coupon curve allows one to track overall changes in yields to maturity, while offering the advantage of describing more precisely the changes caused by market anticipation.

Zero-coupon bonds for each maturity have recently developed very quickly, although they are rarely listed, and when there are they are too illiquid for their yield to maturity to be significant. So a zero-coupon yield curve is only based on listed and liquid bonds (such as government bonds). One common method is commonly obtained with the **bootstrapping model**, which first studies bonds maturing in 1 year. Their yield to maturity is necessarily a zero-coupon yield (as there is only one cash flow, 1 year out). Then, by observing the price of a 2-year bond, we can figure the yield to maturity of a 2-year zero-coupon bond. The entire curve is obtained by repeating the calculation for each maturity.[6]

With the development of inflation-indexed government bonds, it should soon be possible to estimate the real yield curve on zero-coupon bonds. Inflation-indexed bonds are a financial innovation that dissociates two risks that had been intertwined: the coupon reinvestment risk and the inflation risk.

Interest rate swaps[7] allow banks to trade fixed-rate-based interest streams for variable-rate ones among themselves or with clients. This development has led to a much larger market than the one for government bonds, as many governments are seeking to reduce their debt. More and more often, yield curves are calculated on the basis of interest rate swaps, and they are becoming the benchmark.

6 That is, the bond has only one final stream with both capital and capitalised interest.

7 See Chapter 48.

3/THE VARIOUS YIELD CURVES

The concept of premium helps explain why the interest rate of any financial asset is generally proportional to its maturity.

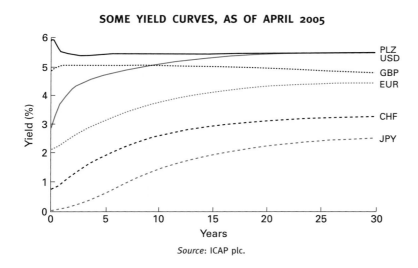

SOME YIELD CURVES, AS OF APRIL 2005

Source: ICAP plc.

Hence, the so-called yield curve should have a configuration of the Swiss or eurozone yield curve in the chart to the right.

download

Generally speaking, the yield curve reflects the market's anticipation about:

•   long-term inflation;
•   the central bank's monetary policy; and
•   the country's issuing debt management policy.

Hence, during a period of economic recovery, the yield curve tends to be "normal" (i.e., long yields are higher than short yields). The steepness of the slope depends on:

•   how strong an expected recovery is;
•   what expectations the market has about the risk of inflation; and
•   the extent to which the market expects a rapid tightening in central banks' intervention rates (to calm inflationary risks).

Based on the chart above, it is clear that the market expects a strong recovery in 2003. The curve's upward slope is also due to the extremely low levels reached by short-term rates in the US, following central bank intervention in late 2001 to support the economy.

In contrast, when a recession follows a period of growth, the yield curve tends to reverse itself (with long-term rates falling below short-term rates). The steepness of the negative slope depends on:

- how strong expectations of recovery are;
- how credible the central bank's policy is (i.e., how firm the central banks are in fighting inflation); and
- the extent to which inflationary trends appear to be diminishing (despite the recession, if inflationary trends are very strong then long-term rates will tend to remain stable, and the curve could actually be flat for some time).

Lastly, when rates are low, the curve cannot remain flat for any length of time because investors will buy fixed rate bonds. As long as investors expect that their capital gain, which is tied to falling long-term rates, is more than the cost of short-term financing, then they will continue to purchase fixed rate bonds. However, when long-term rates seem to have reached a lower limit, these expectations will disappear because investors will demand a differential between long-term and short-term rate yields on their investment. This results in:

- either a rebound in long-term rates;
- or stable long-term rates if short-term rates fall because of central bank policies; and
- a steepening in the curve, the degree of which will depend on the currency.

The shape of the yield curve can also depend upon anticipation of political events. Hence, the downward slope in the Polish yield curve is clearly due to market anticipation of Poland's entry into the European Union, leading to a convergence in long-term rates.

Section 24.3
RELATIONSHIP BETWEEN INTEREST RATES AND MATURITIES

1/RELATION BETWEEN INTEREST RATE AND RISK-FREE MATURITIES

By no means are short-term and long-term rates completely disconnected. In fact, there is a fundamental and direct link between them.

About 20 years ago, this relationship was less apparent and common consensus favoured the **theory of segmentation**, which said that supply and demand balanced out across markets, with no connection between them – e.g., the long-term bond market and the short-term bond market.

As seen above, this theory is generally no longer valid, even though each investor will tend to focus on his own timeframe. It is worthwhile to review the basic mechanisms. For example, an investor who wishes to invest on a 2-year time basis has two options:

- he invests for 2 years at today's fixed rate, which is the interest rate for any 2-year investment; or
- he invests the funds for 1 year, is paid the 1-year interest rate at the end of the year and then repeats the operation.

In a risk-free environment, these two investments would produce the same return, as the investor would already know the return that he would be offered on the market in 1 year for a 1-year bond. As he also knows the current 1-year rate, he can determine the return on a 2-year zero-coupon bond:

$$(1 + {}_0r_2)^2 = (1 + {}_0r_1) \times (1 + {}_1r_1)$$

where ${}_0r_2$ is the current 2-year rate, ${}_1t_1$ the 1-year rate in 1 year and ${}_0r_1$ the current 1-year rate.

The formula can be generalised for all 1-year rates:

$$(1 + {}_0r_N)^N = \prod_{t=0}^{N-1}(1 + {}_ir_1)$$

The long-term rate (*N* years) in a risk-free environment is thus the geometric average of *n* 1-year interest rates.

2/RELATION BETWEEN INTEREST RATES AND MATURITIES IN A RISK-FREE ENVIRONMENT AND WITH NO RISK-AVERSION

If it cannot be assumed that the investor knows the 1-year rate in advance, but only that he anticipates this rate and is adopting a neutral attitude to risk, the result still produces the same type of equation.

The investor does not know with certainty the short-term rate that he will be offered in 1 year. He will therefore choose between the two options above, depending on his expectations about rates.

For example, if he believes that the short-term rate will fall sharply, he will choose the first option, in order to receive a high return for 2 years.

If, on the contrary, he believes that the short-term rate will rise, he will choose the second option, in order to receive a higher return beginning the 2nd year.

Thanks to arbitrage, the investor's hopes are the same in both options. However, this does not mean that the investor's gain will be the same after 2 years, regardless of the option chosen. Otherwise, all investors would choose the investment offering the higher return. This would raise its price and thus lower its yield, until equality between the two investments was re-established.

So, at equilibrium, this is expressed as follows:

$$(1 + {}_0r_2)^2 = (1 + {}_0r_1) \times (1 + E({}_1r_1))$$

where ${}_0t_2$ is the current 2-year rate and $E({}_1t_1)$ is the 1-year rate that is currently expected in 1 year's time.

Hence:

$$(1 +_0 r_2) = \sqrt{(1 +_0 r_1) \times (1 + E(_1 r_1))}$$

The 2-year rate is thus the geometric average of the current 1-year rate and current expectation of the 1-year rate a year from now.

If the current 1-year rate is 3% and the 2-year rate is 4%, the market is anticipating a 5% 1-year rate in 1 year. This is expressed as follows:

$$1.04 = \sqrt{1.03 \times (1 + E(_1 r_1))}$$

$$\text{i.e.,} \quad E(_1 t_1) = \frac{1.04^2}{1.03} - 1 \approx 5\%$$

Therefore, the market anticipates a rise in short-term rates. This implicit rate is called the forward–forward rate. This formula is applied across any number of n periods:

The long-term rate is a geometrical average of short-term rates anticipated for future periods.

Mathematically, this is expressed as follows:

$$(1 +_0 r_N) = \sqrt{(1 +_0 r_1) \times (1 + E(_1 r_1)) \times (1 + E(_2 r_1)) \times \cdots \times (1 + E(_{N-1} r_1))}$$

where $_0 r_N$ is the current rate at N year(s) and $E(_x r_1)$ is the currently expected 1-year rate in x year(s).

The shape of the yield curve provides valuable information. For example, if long-term yields are higher than short-term ones, investors are anticipating a hike in short-term interest rates.

Based on this theory, the investor must be risk-neutral. In other words, he has no preference (unlike the investors in Section 24.1) between a long-term investment or repeated short-term investments. As we saw in Section 24.1, this can happen because it is not easy to say whether the long-term or short-term renewed investment strategy is riskier.

3/INITIAL THEORIES OF RISK

The first theories to highlight the existence of a premium to reflect the relative lack of liquidity of long-term investments was the market **preferred habitat theory** and the **liquidity preference theory**.

In the mid-1960s, Modigliani and Sutch advanced the theory of preferred habitat, which says that investors prefer certain investment timeframes. Companies that wish to issue securities whose timeframe is considered undesirable, will thus have to pay a premium to attract investors.

The theory of liquidity preference is based on the same assumption, but goes further in assuming that the preferred habitat of all investors is the short term. Investors preferring liquidity will require a liquidity premium if they are to invest for the long term. Hence, long-term rates will necessarily be higher than the geometric average of anticipations of short-term rates. Even if investors anticipate fixed short-term rates, the yield curve will slope upward.

Section 24.4
THE STOCHASTIC APPROACH TO MODELLING THE
RATE STRUCTURE

A more sophisticated mathematical theory consists in saying that bond prices depend on a certain number of factors called state variables, which are subject to a diffusion process. Thus, in noting $P(x_1, x_2, \ldots, x_n, t)$ a bond price where x_i are variables of state:

$$dP(x_1, \ldots, x_N, r) = P_r + \sum_n P_{x_i} \, dx_i + \frac{1}{2} \sum_i P_{x_i x_i} \sigma_{x_i}^2 \, dr + \sum_{i \neq j} P_{x_i x_i} \rho_{ij} \sigma_i \sigma_j \, dr$$

And the yield of the bond is thus equal to:

$$\frac{dP}{P} = E(x_1, x_2, \ldots, x_N, r) + \sum_n V_n(x_1, x_2, \ldots, x_N, r) \, dr$$

As the number of variables is chosen arbitrarily, the major task is to determine the variables and the random processes that they follow. The first models developed under this methodology assumed that there was only one variable of state, the short-term interest rate.

Two approaches are possible. The first consists in presenting the price of zero-coupon bonds as the solution to a differential equation. The second approach, often called "probabilistic", is based on an explicit calculation of conditional expected return under a risk-neutral probability. These methods assume that it is possible to adjust risk by adjusting probability. In this new universe, based on this different probability, all prices discounted at the risk-free rate are winners and it is enough to discount cash flow at the risk-free rate (i.e., at the very short-term rate). The second method can be used to define some requirements that the risk premium must meet, whereas in the first model it could be chosen arbitrarily.

Section 24.5
A FLASHBACK

After having studied the yield curve, it is easier to understand that the discounting of all the cash flows from a fixed income security at a single rate, regardless of the period when they are paid, is an oversimplification. Although this is the method that will be used throughout this text for stocks and capital expenditure, it is an oversimplification. It would be wrong to use it for fixed income securities.

In order to be more rigorous, it is necessary to discount each flow with the interest rate of the yield curve corresponding to its maturity: the 1-year rate for next year's income stream, the 3-year rate for flows paid in 3 years, etc. Ultimately, yield to maturity is similar to an average of these different rates.

SUMMARY

download

The most prevalent risks associated with an investment in a debt security include the risk of default, the coupon reinvestment risk and the risk of inflation. Relying on financial analysis, the risk of default can be isolated and analysed separately. However, the other two risks lie at opposite ends of the risk scale. Investors factor them into the risk equation through a liquidity premium, which depends on the maturity of the debt security.

Rates of return on bonds with different maturity dates can be plotted on a graph known as the "yield curve". In order to avoid distortions linked to coupon rates of bonds, it is better to analyse zero coupon curves that can be reconstituted on the basis of the yield curve.

The shape of the yield curve depends on changes in expectations about short-term rates and the liquidity premium that investors will require for making a long-term investment. In a risk-free environment, the long-term rate at *n* years is a geometrical average of short-term rates anticipated for future periods. Generally, there is a positive link between the interest rate of a financial asset and its duration, which is where the rising yield curves come from. However, the yield curve can also slope the other way, especially during a recession.

Different mathematical models are now seeking to model and anticipate the shape of yield curves and how they will change on the basis of simple parameters.

QUESTIONS

quiz

1/ What is the difference between the zero-coupon curve and the yield curve?

2/ Why is a yield curve showing higher long-term interest rates than short-term rates (rising curve) called a normal curve?

3/ What risk are we talking about when we say that government bonds are risk-free?

4/ What is the "reinvestment risk"?

EXERCISES

1/ You observe the following prices for different bonds (note that the coupons on all of them have just been paid)

Bond	Maturity (years)	Annual coupon (%)	Price
1	1	7	99
2	2	9	99
3	3	8	95
4	4	7	89
5	5	10	97

(a) Calculate the return on each of these bonds.
(b) Reconstruct the zero coupon curve at 5 years.

2/ In 2004 you notice that the yields to maturity of the same company's two bonds, 5% of 2008 and 9% of 2008 are selling at 87.44 and 100.71, respectively, and the resulting yield to maturity is 8.87 and 8.78%. You are wondering as to why two bonds issued by the same company with the same maturity do not offer the same yield to maturity. What could be a reasonable answer?

Questions

1/ The yield curve is drawn directly, taking into account the maturity but without adjusting the coupon of each bond. The zero-coupon curve is recalculated and can be used directly for valuing a security.

2/ The preference for liquidity means that in normal circumstances (i.e., when anticipated changes in the inflation rate do not interfere) that long-term rates are higher than short-term rates.

3/ There is no economic risk of the issuer going bankrupt.

4/ The risk of reinvesting coupons and changes in the rate of inflation (risk of losing purchasing power).

Exercises

1/ (a) 8.08%; 9.57%; 10.01%; 10.51%; 10.81%.
   (b) 8.08%; 9.64%; 10.09%; 10.62%; 11.01%.

2/ The answer needs an estimation of the spot rates for the remaining years and the present value of the payments to be received. That is to say, that each year's coupon and the principal payments must be discounted using the appropriate spot rates, not the yield to maturity. By doing so, we would discover that the two bonds are valued correctly by the market. Thus, the yield to maturity is different because the two bonds have different time profiles of cash flow patterns: the 5% coupon bond has more cash flows coming later; the opposite occurs for the 9% bond. Yield to maturity is only a measure of convenience frequently used for the sake of simplicity – not the one that actually gets into the discounted cash flow of the bonds.

Period	Spot rate r_t	Coupon	PV at r_t	Coupon	PV at r_t
2005	0.06	50	47.17	90	84.91
2006	0.07	50	43.67	90	78.61
2007	0.08	50	39.69	90	71.44
2008	0.09	1,050	743.85	1,090	772.18
			€874.38		€1,007.14

P. Abken, Innovations in modeling the term structure of interest rates, *Federal Reserve Bank of Atlanta Economic Review*, 222–247, July/August 1990

D. Backus, S. Foresi, C. Telmer, Discrete-time models of bond pricing, *National Bureau of Economic Research*, September 1998.

F. Black, E. Derman, W. Toy, A one-factor model of interest rates and its application to treasury bond options, *Financial Analysts' Journal*, **46**, 33–39, January/February 1990.

M. Brennan, E. Schwartz, Bond pricing and market efficiency, *Financial Analysts' Journal*, **38**, 49–56, September/October 1982.

G. Costantinides, A theory of the nominal term structure of interest rates, *Review of Financial Studies*, **5**(4), 531–552, 1992.

J. Cox, J. Ingersoll, S. Ross, A reexamination of traditional hypothesis about the term structure of interest rates, *Journal of Finance*, **36**, 769–799, September 1981.

P. Dybvig, J. Ingersoll, S. Ross, Long forward and zero-coupon rates can never fall, *Journal of Business*, **1**, 1–25, 1996.

D. Heath, R. Jarrow, A. Morton, Bond pricing and the term structure of interest rates, *Econometrica*, **60**, 225–262, March 1992.

J. Hicks, *Value and Capital*, 2nd edn, Oxford University Press, 1946.

T. Ho, S. Lee, Term structure movements and pricing interest rate contingent claims, *Journal of Finance*, 1011–1029, December 1986.

R. Jarrow, *Modelling Fixed Income Securities and Interest Rate Options*, McGraw-Hill, 1996.

F. Lutz, The structure of interest rates, *Journal of Economics*, **55**, 36–63, November 1940.

D. Meiselman, *The Term Structure of Interest Rates*, Prentice Hall, 1962.

F. Modigliani, R. Sutch, Innovations in interest rate policy, *American Economic Review*, **56**, 178–197, May 1966.

B. Tuckman, *Fixed Economic Securities*, John Wiley & Sons, 1995.

Section III
CORPORATE FINANCIAL POLICIES

PART ONE
FINANCIAL SECURITIES

We wrote in the first chapter that a financial manager helps secure a company's financing needs by selling securities to his investor clients. In the following chapters, you will learn more about such securities – debt, equity, options and hybrids – as well as how they are valued and sold to investors.

Chapter 25
ENTERPRISE VALUE AND FINANCIAL SECURITIES

Getting back to basics

- Valuing a financial security.
- Determining its required rate of return, which is linked directly to its present value.
- And calculating the cost of financing of this security.

These are three different ways of looking at the same thing.
   This is fundamental.

Valuing a security and calculating a company's financing costs are two ways of looking at the same problem. Once you've figured out one, you've figured out the other.

That is why we wish to discuss valuation of financial securities a little further.

Section 25.1
A COMPLETELY DIFFERENT WAY OF LOOKING AT THINGS

While accounting looks at a company by examining its past and by focusing on its costs, finance is mainly a projection of the company into the future. Finance reflects not only risk, but also, and above all, the value that results from the perception of risk and future returns.

In finance, everything is about the future – return, risk and value.

We will thus speak constantly of **value**. As we saw previously, by "value" we mean **the present value of future cash flows discounted at the rate of return required by investors**:

- equity (E) will be replaced by the **value of equity** (V_E);
- net debt (D) will be replaced by the value of net debt (V_D);
- capital employed (CE) will be replaced by enterprise value (EV), or firm value.

We will speak in terms of a financial assessment of the company (rather than the accounting assessment provided by the balance sheet). Our financial assessment will include only the market values of assets and liabilities:

	VALUE OF NET DEBT (V_D)
ENTERPRISE VALUE or FIRM VALUE (EV)	EQUITY VALUE (V_E)

As operating assets are financed by equity and net debt (which are accounting concepts), a company's enterprise value will consist of the market value of net debt and the market value of equity (which are financial concepts). This chapter therefore reasons in terms of:

> Enterprise value = Value of net debt + Equity value

Important: Enterprise value is sometimes confused with equity value. Equity value is the enterprise value remaining for shareholders after creditors have been paid. To avoid confusion, remember that **enterprise value is the sum of equity value and net debt value**.

In this book we refer to the market value of operating assets (industrial and commercial) as "enterprise value", which is the sum of the market value of equity (i.e., the company's market capitalisation if it is publicly traded) and the market value of net debt. Enterprise value and firm value are synonyms.

Similarly, in this chapter we will reason not in terms of return on equity, but rather required rate of return, which was discussed in depth in Chapter 28. In other words, the accounting notions of **ROCE (Return On Capital Employed)**, **ROE (Return On Equity)** and i **(cost of debt)**, which are based on past observations, will give way to **WACC**[1] or k **(required rate of return on capital employed)**, k_E **(required rate of return on equity)** and k_D **(required rate of return of net debt)**, which are the returns required by investors who are financing the company.

1 *Weighted Average Cost of Capital.*

Section 25.2
DEBT AND EQUITY

We will see later (Part Two of this section) why a firm seeks to adjust debt and equity levels, as well as the repercussions on company financing of doing so. At this point, you should recognise the basic differences between debt and equity.

➤ **Debt**:

  ○ has a remuneration which is independent of the company's results and is contractually set in advance. Except in some extreme cases (a missed payment, or bankruptcy), the lender will receive the interest due to him regardless of whether the company's results are excellent, average or poor;

○ always has a repayment date, however far off, that is also set contractually. We will set aside, for the moment, the rare case of perpetual debt;

○ is paid off ahead of equity when the company is liquidated and its assets sold off. The proceeds will first be used to pay off creditors, and only when they have been fully repaid will any surplus be paid to shareholders.

➤ **Equity**:

○ has a remuneration which depends on company earnings. If those earnings are bad, there is no dividend or capital gain;

○ carries no guarantee of repayment at any date, however distant into the future. The only "way out" for an equity investor is to sell to another equity investor, who thus takes over ownership;

○ is remunerated last, in the event of bankruptcy, only after the creditors have been paid off. As you know, in most cases, the liquidation of assets is not enough to fully pay off creditors. Shareholders then have no recourse, as the company is no longer solvent and equity is negative!

In other words, shareholders are fully exposed to company risk, as creditors have the first claim on revenue streams generated by operating assets (free cash flows) and only once they have been paid what is owed to them will the rest be paid to shareholders.

In light of the above, it is natural that shareholders alone should have voting rights and thus the right to appoint management. They have a very direct interest in the operating assets being managed as efficiently as possible – i.e., in having cash flow as high as possible – so that there is something left over after the creditors have been paid off (interest and principal).

Voting rights are not a fourth difference between debt and equity. Rather, they are the logical continuation of the three differences listed above. **Shareholders come after creditors in their claim on cash flow and are thus exposed to company risk. They therefore have voting rights.**

Hence, the higher the enterprise value, the higher the equity value. As debt is not exposed to company risk (except in the event of bankruptcy), its value will be much less sensitive to variations in enterprise value. Here we find the concept of leverage, which means that a slight change in enterprise value can have a proportionally significant impact on equity value.

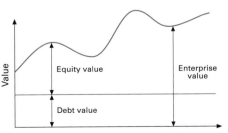

For investors, equity is naturally riskier than debt.

download

Section 25.3
OVERVIEW OF HOW TO COMPUTE ENTERPRISE VALUE

There are three basic ways of valuing operating assets, and, more generally, any financial security:

1 **the discounted cash flow model** values enterprise value on the basis of its ability to generate free cash flows, which will be discounted at a rate that reflects the risk carried by the operating assets;

2 **the comparables model**, which compares the observable values of assets that are as comparable as possible – i.e., which have the same level of risk and growth. This is a highly pragmatic and simple model, as its mathematical basis is solving the unknown by setting two ratios equal to each other. It does not lack a theoretical basis, in that, if markets are efficient, a company's value ought to be comparable with others. Please go to Chapter 40 if you want to read more about this model;

3 **the option model** is much more complex, and we will discuss it in Chapter 35 after having first presented options in Chapter 20. The option model is quite rich in concepts, but difficult to apply.

Section 25.4
VALUATION BY DISCOUNTING FREE CASH FLOWS

Let's review some basic concepts already discussed in the previous chapters regarding the discounted cash flow methodology. The reader will forgive us but these concepts will be constantly recalled in this section of the book. The reason is quite simple: *(almost) all financial securities* can be valued with the discounted free cash flows methodology.

As we saw in Chapter 24, the value of securities is equal to cash flow discounted at a rate that reflects risk – i.e., volatility in cash flow. Valuing operating assets by Discounted Cash Flow (DCF) is thus the basic model used in valuing a company and financial securities.

1/FREE CASH FLOWS TO FIRM

After-tax free cash flow measures the cash flow generated by operating assets. It is calculated as follows:

Calculation basis	Explanations
Earnings Before Interest, Tax, Depreciation and Amortisation (EBITDA)	We are looking only at the operating level
— Corporate income tax on Earnings Before Interest and Taxes (EBIT)	Equal to the operating profit multiplied by the corporate income tax rate
— Change in working capital	Here we move from an accounting concept to a cash flow basis, thus we subtract the working capital needs
— Net capital expenditure (Capex)	Companies live and breathe, after all . . .
= **Free Cash Flow to Firm (FCFF)**	

Free Cash Flows to Firm (FCFF) belong to the investors funding the company's operating assets – i.e., its shareholders and creditors. Creditors receive interest and debt repayments; shareholders primarily receive dividends and sometimes their shares are bought back by their company.

Free cash flowss to firm can be obtained in the following way, entirely equivalent to the previous one:

Calculation basis
EBIT × (1 − Tax rate)
+   Depreciation
−   Change in working capital
−   Net capital expenditure (Capex)
=   **Free Cash Flow to firm (FCFF)**

2/THE DISCOUNTING RATE

As you know, the discounting rate of any asset depends on the risk it carries. It can be calculated on the basis of the CAPM[2] and is equal to the risk-free rate, plus a premium proportional to the market risk (or systematic risk) of the asset (see Chapter 22).

2 *Capital Asset Pricing Model.*

It can also be calculated indirectly, as free cash flow belongs to shareholders and creditors, each of whom has a required rate of return based on the risk that they are exposed to. Shareholders and creditors share the risk of operating assets unequally. Shareholders demand a higher rate of return than creditors, as they are exposed to more risk, as we have seen.

Free cash flows will be discounted at the return required by all of the company's investors – i.e., its shareholders and creditors. This is what we call the **Weighted Average Cost of Capital**, or **WACC** (k), or, simply, the **cost of capital**. In practical terms, WACC is based on the average of the return required by shareholders (k_E) and the after-tax return demanded by creditors (k_D), weighted by the respective portions of equity and debt in enterprise value (see also Chapter 23).

3/MORE ON HOW ENTERPRISE VALUE IS CALCULATED

Generally speaking, a company's enterprise value is equal to the sum of its after-tax free cash flows discounted at the return required by shareholders and creditors (k or WACC):

$$EV = \sum_{t=0}^{\infty} \frac{FCFF_t}{(1+k)^t}$$

This formula assumes that free cash flows have been determined each year to perpetuity. Doing this would be a highly difficult task and you will very often go on simpler assumptions for each asset. There are three main assumptions possible.

(a) Zero growth in free cash flows

In this exceptional case, we assume constant free cash flows to perpetuity:

$$EV = \frac{FCFF}{k}$$

If free cash flow is 10 annually to perpetuity and investors require a 10% return, enterprise value is equal to 100.

(b) Constant growth in free cash flows

Let's say that free cash flow increases each year at a rate of g. In this case, it is not difficult to demonstrate (see Section 16.6) that enterprise value would then be equal to:

$$EV = \frac{FCFF_1}{k - g} = \frac{FCFF_0 \times (1 + g)}{k - g}$$

If free cash flow is currently 9.35 and rising by 7% annually, and investors require 10%, enterprise value will be 333.

The risk here is in overvaluing growing companies by extrapolating a strong growth rate to perpetuity. The risk is all the greater as assumptions for the distant future are often just an extrapolation of the present or immediate past.

Moreover, a constant growth rate in free cash flows can only be assumed when that rate is below WACC. If the growth rate is above WACC, be careful. Trees don't grow to the sky, after all. Sooner or later, a company's growth will slow and end up, at best, at the level of the economy in general, or even below it. We can then apply the third model.

(c) Cash flow rising at different rates over three periods

Refer to Section 16.6 for the formula used in modelling increasing flows at different rates over three different periods.

4/A LITTLE BACKGROUND

As we have seen, because of the mechanism of discounting, cash flow that is far into the future accounts for only a small portion of the present value of operating assets. Let's now calculate the present value of free cash flows of 10 for 5, 10 and 20 years:

Present value of a cash flow of 10 for ...	5 years	10 years	20 years	To perpetuity
At 15%	33.5	50.2	62.6	66.7
At 10%	37.9	61.4	85.1	100
At 5%	43.3	77.2	124.6	200

We see that the 5, 10 and 20 years account for respectively about 50% (33.5/66.7), 75% (50.2/66.7) and 94% (62.6/66.7) of the enterprise value discounted to perpetuity at 15%.

At 10%, they account for 38%, 61% and 85%, respectively. The proportion of the 5, 10 and 20 years in total value is linked directly to the discounting rate.

The valuation of the first 5, 10 and 20 years is thus decisive in calculating enterprise value.

Some remarks, to conclude:

- The main attraction of these models is their **simplicity**, since they **apparently** require no internal financial analysis of the company. Remember, however, that cash flow growth depends on the return on reinvested capital, as we will see in Chapter 48. The lack of internal financial analysis is thus only apparent.
- These models are somewhat abstract. They consider the purchase of an operating asset as an investment whose monetary payoff is free cash flows. This is a purely financial point of view, which may not be necessarily in line with the other considerations (strategic, operational, political, organisational, etc.) that may drive the final decision regarding an investment. When used in a multi-period framework, this model often produces lower values than the other models.

SUMMARY

download

The value of a group's equity and debt lies in the value of its operating assets. Since operating assets are financed exclusively by means of shareholders' equity and net debt, we get:

Value of operating assets = Value of net debt + Equity value

By definition, debts are remunerated independently of the company's results, they always have a repayment date and, in the event of bankruptcy, they get priority for repayment over shareholder's equity. On the basis of these three features, debts can be distinguished from shareholders' equity which is remunerated on the basis of the company's results, repayment is never guaranteed and, in the event of bankruptcy, shareholders are repaid after creditors, which more often than not means they never get anything!

There are three ways of valuing operating assets:

- by discounting cash flows – i.e., the flows on cash generated by operating assets at the rate of return required by investors;

- by using methods which compare the operating assets of companies with similar levels of risk, earnings and growth. The valuation ratios of these comparable companies, preferably the EV/EBIT and EV/NOPAT ratios, can be determined and then be applied to the parameters of the company to be valued;

- by the option model, which is rich in concepts but hard to apply practically.

QUESTIONS

quiz

1/ Why should enterprise value not be confused with the value of shareholders' equity?

2/ What are the three methods used for valuing operating assets?

3/ What is a perpetual zero-coupon bond?

4/ Why are voting rights attached to shareholders' equity?

EXERCISES

1/ QDSL is expected to pay dividends of €1, €2 and €3 for the next 3 years. Thereafter, the dividends are expected to grow at a constant rate of 4%. If the required rate of return is 11%, what will be the current stock price? What will be the stock price next year and at the end of 3 years?

2/ PEP Corp. is expected to pay a dividend of €3 a share next year. The dividends are expected to grow at the rate of 4% annually. If the current stock price is €25, what is the implied market capitalisation rate?

ANSWERS

Questions

1/ *Because we would be forgetting debt.*

2/ *The Discounted Cash Flow (DCF) method, the comparative multiples method and the option model.*

3/ *The dream of every issuer! No payments will ever have to be made which means that it is worth nothing and cannot exist.*

4/ *Because since the shareholders are the ones with the most at stake, they should be able to choose the managers who they think will be best able to manage the operating assets.*

Exercises

1/ $P_0 = DIV_1/(1 + k) + DIV_2/(1 + k)^2 + DIV_3/(1 + k)^3 + P_3/(1 + k)^3$, *where* $P_3 = DIV_4/(k - g) = 3 \times 1.04/(0.11 - 0.04) = €32.6$; $P_0 = (1/1.11) + (2/1.11^2) + (3 + 32.6)/1.11^3 = €37.3$; $P_1 = (2/1.11) + (3 + 32.6)/1.11^2 = €37$

2/ $k = (DIV_1/P) + g = (3/25) + 0.04 = 16\%$.

BIBLIOGRAPHY

On valuation techniques:

J. Abrams, *Quantitative Business Valuation*, McGraw-Hill, 2001.

T. Copeland, T. Koller, J. Murrin, *Valuation. Measuring and Managing the Value of Companies*, 3rd edn, John Wiley & Sons, 2000.

B. Cornell, *Corporate Valuation Tools for Effective Appraisal and Decision Making*, Irwin, 1993.

A. Damodaran, *Damodaran on Valuation: Security Analysis for Investment and Corporate Finance*, John Wiley & Sons, 1994.

A. Damodaran, *The Dark Side of Valuation: Valuing Old Tech, New Tech, and New Economy Companies*, Financial Times/Prentice Hall, 2001.

A. King, *Valuation: What Assets Are Really Worth*, John Wiley & Sons, 2002.

M. Mard (ed.), *Valuation for Financial Reporting: Intangible Assets, Goodwill, and Impairment Analysis*, SFAS 141 and 142, John Wiley & Sons, 2002.

G. Norton, *Valuation: Maximizing Corporate Value*, John Wiley & Sons, 2003.

R. Reilly, *Handbook of Advanced Business Valuation*, McGraw-Hill, 2000.

G. Smith, *Valuation of Intellectual Property and Intangible Assets*, 3rd edn, John Wiley & Sons, 2000.v

Chapter 26
DEBT SECURITIES

Or "rendering what is fixed, volatile, and what is volatile, fixed"

A debt security is a financial instrument representing the borrower's obligation to the lender from whom he has received funds.

This obligation provides for a schedule of cash flows defining the **terms of repayment** of the funds and the **lender's remuneration** in the interval. The remuneration may be fixed during the life of the debt or floating if it is linked to a benchmark or index.

Most debt securities began as regular loans or credits, evolving into **bonds** with the development of financial markets and **disintermediation** in the 1960s.

Unlike conventional bank loans, debt securities can be traded on secondary markets (stock exchanges, money markets, mortgage markets and interbank markets). Debt securities are bonds, commercial papers, treasury bills and notes, certificates of deposit and mortgage-backed bonds or mortgage bonds. Furthermore, the current trend is to securitise loans to make them negotiable.

Disintermediation was not the only factor fuelling the growth of bond markets. The increasing difficulty of obtaining bank loans was another, as banks realised that the interest margin on such loans did not offer sufficient return on equity. This pushed companies to turn to bond markets to raise the funds banks had become reluctant to advance.

The Directorate-General for Economic and Financial Affairs of the European Union produces a monthly note on developments in the euro-denominated bond markets (*http://europa.eu.int/comm/economy_finance/publications_en.htm*). Here is a graph that shows the recent evolution of this market by the type of issuer:

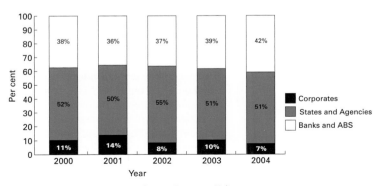

Companies accounted for 7% of euro-denominated issues in 2004.

Source: European Union.

Lastly, investors have welcomed the emergence of corporate bonds offering higher yields than government bonds. Of course, these higher returns came at the cost of higher risks.

The following picture illustrates the market value of bonds listed at the end of 2003.[1]

1 *The graph includes only markets with the highest market value for which a breakdown for the typology of issuer (private, public, foreign) was available.*

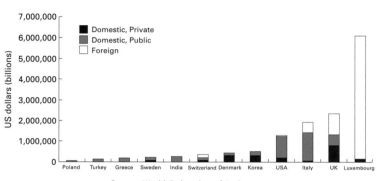

Source: World Federation of Exchanges.

Many of the explanations and examples offered in this chapter deal with bonds, but they can easily be applied to all kinds of debt instruments. We shall take the example of the Scania March 2002 bond issue with the following features.

SCANIA CV AB – 6% MARCH 2002 BOND ISSUE	
Amount:	€500,000,000
Denomination:	€1,000
Issue price:	99.863% or €998.63 per bond, payable in one instalment on the settlement date
Date of issue:	27 March 2002
Settlement date:	27 March 2002
Maturity:	5 years
Annual coupon:	6% – i.e., €60 per bond payable in one instalment on March 27 of each year, with the first payment on 27 March 2003
Yield to maturity for the subscriber:	On the settlement date
Average life:	5 years
Normal redemption date:	The bonds will be redeemed in full on 27 March 2007 at par value
Guarantee:	The borrowing is unconditionally and irrevocably guaranteed by Scania AB
Further issues (fungibility):	The issuer may, without prior permission from the bondholders, create and issue new bonds with the same features as the present bonds with the exception of the issue price and the first coupon payment date. The present bonds could thus be exchanged with the new bonds
Rating:	A – (S&P)
Listing:	Luxembourg Stock Market

Section 26.1

BASIC CONCEPTS

1/THE PRINCIPAL

(a) Nominal or face value

Loans that can be publicly traded are divided into a certain number of units giving the same rights for the same fraction of the debt. This is the nominal, face or par value, which for bonds like Scania is generally €1,000.

The nominal value is used to calculate the interest payments. In the simplest cases, it equals the amount of money the issuer received for each bond and that the issuer will repay upon redemption.

(b) Issue price

The issue price is the price at which the bonds are issued – that is, the price investors pay for each bond. *The Scania bond was issued on 27 March 2002 at a price of €998.63 – i.e., 99.86% of its face value.*

Depending on the characteristics of the issue, the issue price may be higher than the face value (issued at a premium), lower than the face value (issued at a discount) or equal to the face value (at par).

(c) Redemption

When a loan is amortised, it is said to be redeemed. In Chapter 25 we looked at the various ways a loan can be repaid:

- redemption at maturity, or on a bullet repayment basis. *This is the case with the Scania issue*;
- redemption in equal slices (or series), or constant amortisation;
- redemption in fixed instalments.

Other methods exist, such as determining which bonds are redeemed by lottery ... there is no end to financial creativity!

A **deferred redemption period** is a grace period, generally at the beginning of the bond's life, during which the issuer does not have to repay the principal.

The terms of the issue may also include provisions for **early redemption** (call options) or retraction (put options). A call option gives the issuer the right to buy back all or part of the issue prior to the maturity date, while a put option allows the bondholder to demand early repayment.

No such options are included in the Scania issue.

(d) Maturity of the bond

The life of a bond extends from its issue date to its final redemption date. Where the bond is redeemed in several instalments, the **average maturity** of the bond corresponds to the average of each of the repayment periods.

$$\frac{Average}{maturity} = \frac{Average}{life} = \frac{\displaystyle\sum_{t=1}^{N} t \times \text{Number of bonds redeemed during year } t}{\text{Total number of shares to be redeemed}}$$

where t is the variable for the year and N the total number of periods.

The Scania bonds have a maturity of 5 years.

(e) Guarantees

Repayment of the principal (and interest) on a bond borrowing can be guaranteed by the issuer, the parent company, collaterals, pledges or warranties. Bonds are rarely secured, while commercial paper and certificates of deposit can in theory be secured but in fact never are.

The bonds issued by Scania CV AB are guaranteed by the parent company, Scania AB.

2/INCOME

(a) Issue date

The issue date is the date on which interest begins to accrue. It may or may not coincide with the **settlement date**, when investors actually pay for the bonds purchased.

Interest on the Scania bond begins to accrue on the settlement date.

(b) Interest rate

The coupon or nominal rate is used to calculate the interest (or coupon in the case of a bond) payable to the lenders. Interest is calculated by multiplying the nominal rate with the nominal or par value of the bond.

On the Scania issue, the coupon rate is 6% and the coupon payment €60.

In addition to coupon payments, investors may also gain an additional remuneration if the issue price is lower than the par value. *On the Scania issue, investors paid €998.63 for each bond, whereas interest was based on a par value of €1,000 and the bond will be redeemed at €1,000.* In this case, the bond sold at a **discount**.

When the issue price is higher than the par value, the bond is said to sell at a **premium**.

A **redemption premium or discount** arises where the redemption value is higher or lower than the nominal value.

(c) Periodic coupon payments

Coupon payments can be made every year, half-year, quarter, month or even more frequently. On certain borrowings, the interval is even longer, since the total compounded interest earned is paid only upon redemption. Such bonds are called **zero-coupon bonds**.

In some cases, the interest is **prepaid**; that is, the company pays the interest at the beginning of the period to which it relates. In general, however, the **accrued** interest is paid at the end of the period to which it relates.

The Scania issue pays accrued interest on an annual basis.

Section 26.2
THE YIELD TO MATURITY

The actual return on an investment (or the cost of a loan for the borrower) depends on a number of factors: the difference between the settlement date and the issue date, the issue premium/discount, the redemption premium/discount, the deferred redemption period and the coupon payment interval. As a result, the nominal rate is not very meaningful.

We have seen that the **yield to maturity** (see Chapter 25) cancels out the bond's net present value – that is, the difference between the issue price and the present value of future flows on the bond. **Note that for bonds the yield to maturity (y) and the internal rate of return are identical.** This yield is calculated on the settlement date, when investors pay for their bonds, and is always indicated in the prospectus for bond issues. The yield to maturity takes into account any timing differences between the right to receive income and the actual cash payment.

In the case of the Scania bond issue:

$$99.863\% - \left(\sum_{t=1}^{5} \frac{6\%}{(1+y)^t} + \frac{100\%}{(1+y)^5} \right) = 0 \qquad \text{i.e., } y = 6.033\%$$

The yield to maturity, before taxation and intermediaries' fees, represents:

- **for investors**, the rate of return they would receive by holding the bonds until maturity, assuming that the interest payments are reinvested at the same yield to maturity, which is a very strong assumption;
- **for the issuer**, the pre-tax actuarial cost of the loan.

From the point of view of the investor, the bond schedule must take into account intermediation costs and the tax status of the income earned. For the issuer, the gross cost to maturity is higher because of the commissions paid to intermediaries. This increases the actuarial cost of the borrowing. In addition, the issuer pays the intermediaries (**paying agents**) in charge of paying the interest and reimbursing the principal. Lastly, the issuer can deduct the coupon payments from its corporate income tax, thus reducing the actual cost of the loan.

The yield to maturity on a security is the *ex ante* **promised rate** at a moment in time. The lender will obtain this rate if he keeps the security till the maturity *and the security doesn't default*. Thus, the promised rate is not necessarily the rate actually realised if the bond is held to maturity. The **realised rate** is the rate of discount that equates all payments actually received by investors, including the final principal payment, with the market price of the security at the time the security was purchased. The difference between the two rates is known as the **loss rate** attributable to default. If default probability is a positive number, the **expected yield** on a security will be less than the promised one.

1/SPREADS

The spread is the difference between the rate of return on a bond and that on a benchmark used by the market. Spreads are commonly expressed in basis points: 100 b.p. = 1%. In the euro area, the benchmark can be:

- a short-term rate, the 3- or 6-month Euribor, for variable rate debt;
- the Interest Rate Swap (IRS) rate or government bond yields for long-term fixed rate debt.

2 *An interesting study on yield spreads in major financial areas is periodically published by the International Monetary Fund and can be freely obtained at http:// www.imf.org/ external/pubs/ft/ weo/2003/01/ index.htm*

The Scania bond was issued with a spread of 139 basis points (1.39%), meaning that Scania had to pay 1.39% more than Swedish government bond yields per year to raise funds.

The spread is a key parameter for valuing bonds, in particular at the time of issue. It depends on the perceived credit quality of the issuer and the maturity of the issue, which are reflected in the credit rating and the guarantees given. Spreads are, of course, a relative concept, depending on the bonds being compared. The stronger the creditworthiness of the issuer and the market's appetite for risk, the lower the margin will be.[2]

Spreads tend to widen during a crisis, both in absolute terms and relative to each other.

EU: YIELD DIFFERENTIALS WITH 10-YEAR GOVERNMENT BONDS

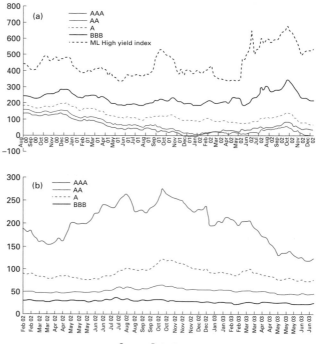

Source: Datastream.

Spreads are so important that they have become the key criteria for both issuers and investors when they want to issue, sell or buy bonds.

2/ The secondary market

Once the subscription period is over, the price at which the bonds were sold (their issue price) becomes a thing of the past. The value of the instrument begins to fluctuate on the secondary market. Consequently, the yield to maturity published in the prospectus applies only at the time of issue; after that, it fluctuates in step with the value of the bond.

Theoretically, changes in the bond's yield to maturity on the secondary market do not directly concern the borrower, since the cost of the debt was fixed when it was contracted.

For the borrower, the yield on the secondary market is merely an **opportunity cost** – that is, the **cost of refunding** for issuing new bonds. It represents the "real" cost of debt, but is not shown in the company accounts where the debt is written at its historical cost, regardless of any fluctuations in its value on the secondary market.

3/ LISTING TECHNIQUES

The price of bonds listed on stock markets is expressed as a percentage of the nominal value. In fact, they are treated as though the nominal value of each bond were €100. Thus, a bond with a nominal value of €5,000 will not be listed at €4,950 but at 99% (4,950/5,000 × 100). Similarly, a bond with a nominal value of €10,000 will be listed at 99%, rather than €9,900.

This makes it easier to compare bond prices.

For the comparison to be relevant, the prices must not include the fraction of annual interest already accrued. Otherwise, the price of a bond with a 15% coupon would be 115 just before its coupon payment date and 100 just after. This is why bonds are quoted **net of accrued interest**. Bond tables thus show both the price expressed as a percentage of the nominal value and the fraction of accrued interest, which is also given as a percentage of the nominal value.

The table below indicates that on July 10, 2003, the Scania bond traded at 108.950% with an accrued interest of 1.803%. This means that at that date the bond costs €1.107,53 – i.e., €1.000 × (108.950% + 1.803%).

Price	Bond ticker	Gross YTM	Maturity	Maturity date	Duration	Accrued interest	Next coupon payment
108.95%	014536736	3.173%	3.7 years	03/27/07	3.391	1.803%	27/03/04

Certain debt securities, mainly fixed rate Treasury notes with annual interest payments, are quoted at their yield to maturity. The two listing methods are rigorously equivalent and require just a simple calculation to switch from one to the other.

By now, you have probably realised that the price of a bond does not reflect its actual cost. A bond trading at 105% may be more or less expensive than a bond trading at 96%. **The yield to maturity is the most important criterium allowing investors to evaluate various investment opportunities according to the degree of risk they are willing to accept and the length of their investment.** However, it merely offers a temporary estimate of the **promised** return which may be different from the **expected** return which incorporates the probability of default of the bond.

4/FURTHER ISSUES AND ASSIMILATION

Having made one bond issue, the same company can later issue other bonds with the same features (time to maturity, coupon rate, coupon payment schedule, redemption price and guarantees, etc.) so that they are interchangeable. This enables the various issues to be grouped as one, for a larger total amount. This offers two advantages:

- administrative expenses are reduced, since there is just one issue;
- more importantly, the bonds are more liquid and therefore more easily traded on the secondary market. Their price is accordingly lower, as investors are willing to accept slightly lower interest rates on securities that are more liquid.

Bonds assimilated are issued with the same features as the bonds with which they are interchangeable. The only difference is in the issue price,[3] which is shaped by market conditions that are very likely to have changed since the original issue.

The Scania bond provides for further (future fungible) issues.

3 *In some cases, the first coupon payment is different while the issue price is identical: the bonds only become fungible after the first coupon payment.*

Section 26.3
FLOATING RATE BONDS

So far we have looked only at fixed income debt securities. The cash flow schedule for these securities is laid down clearly when they are issued, whereas the securities that we will be describing in this section give rise to cash flows that are not totally fixed from the very outset, but follow preset rules.

EURO-DENOMINATED ISSUES BY TYPE OF COUPON

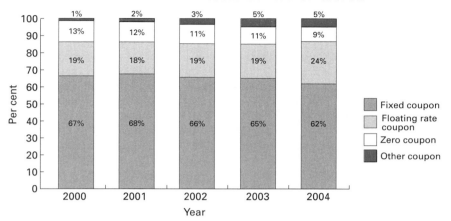

In 2004, floating rate debt securities accounted for 24% of euro issues.

1/THE MECHANICS OF THE COUPON

The coupon of a floating rate bond is not fixed, but is indexed to an observable market rate, generally a short-term rate, such as the 6-month Euribor. In other words, the coupon rate is periodically reset based on some reference rate plus a spread. When each coupon is presented for payment, its value is calculated as a function of the market rate, based on the formula:

$$\text{Coupon}_t = (\text{Market rate}_t + \text{Spread}) \times \text{Par value}$$

This cancels out interest rate risk since the issuer of the security is certain of paying interest at exactly the market rate at all times. Likewise, the investor is assured at all times of receiving a return in line with the market rate. Consequently, there is no reason for the price of a variable rate bond to move very far from its par value unless the issuer's solvency becomes a concern.

Let's take the simple example of a fixed rate bond indexed to the 1-year rate that pays interest annually. On the day following payment of the coupon and in the year prior to its maturity date, the price of the bond can be calculated as follows (as a percentage of par value):

$$V = \frac{100 + r_1 \times 100}{1 + r_1} = 100$$

where r_1 is the 1-year rate.

Here the price of the bond is 100% since the discount rate is the same as the rate used to calculate the coupon. Likewise, we could demonstrate that the price of the bond is 100% on each coupon payment date. The price of the bond will fluctuate in the same way as a short-term instrument in between coupon payment dates.

If the reference rate covers a period that is not the same as the interval between two coupon payments, the situation becomes slightly more complex. This said, since there is rarely a big difference between short-term rates the price of the bond will clearly not fluctuate much over time.

The main factor that can push the price of a variable rate bond well below its par value is a deterioration in the solvency of the issuer.

Consequently, floating rate bonds are not highly volatile securities, even though their value is not always exactly 100%.

Three final points about the mechanics of the coupon of floating rate securities:

- there is a distinction between a floating rate security and what is sometimes referred to as a **variable rate** (or **adjustable rate**) **security** and the *frequency* at which the coupon rate is reset and the *reference rate*. A floating rate security resets more than once a year, and the reference rate is a short-term rate. In contrast, a variable rate security does not reset more than once a year, and the reference rate is a long-term interest rate;
- there are some issues whose coupon rate moves in the *opposite direction* to the interest rate change. They are called **inverse floaters**;
- there are some securities whose coupon rate is equal to the reference rate as long as the reference rate is within a contractually specified range. If, at the reset rate, the reference rate is outside this range, the coupon rate is zero for that single period. These securities are called **range notes**.

2/The spread

Like those issuing fixed rate securities, companies issuing floating rate securities need to pay investors a return that covers the counterparty (credit) risk. Consequently, a fixed margin (**spread**) is added to the variable percentage when the coupon is calculated. For instance, a company may issue a bond at 3-month Euribor + 0.45% (or 45 basis point). The size of this margin basically depends on the company's financial creditworthiness.

The spread is set once and for all when the bond is issued, but of course the company's risk profile may vary over time. This factor, which does not depend on interest rate trends, slightly increases the volatility of variable debt securities.

The issue of credit risk is the same for a fixed rate security as for a variable income security.

3/Index-linked securities

Floating rates, as we described them in the first paragraph of this section, are indexed to a market interest rate. Broadly speaking, however, a bond's coupons may be indexed to any index or price, provided that it is clearly defined from a contractual standpoint. Such securities are known as **index-linked securities**.

For instance, most European countries have issued bonds indexed to inflation. The coupon paid each year and the redemption price are reset to take into account the rise in the price index since the bond was launched. As a result, the investor benefits from complete protection against inflation. With the advent of the euro, for example, the UK government issued a bond indexed to the rate of inflation in the United Kingdom. Likewise, Mexican companies have brought to market bonds linked to oil prices, while other companies have issued bonds indexed to their own share price.

To value this type of security, projections need to be made about the future value of the underlying index, which is never an easy task.

The following table shows the main reference rates in Europe.

REFERENCE RATES IN EUROPE

Reference rate	Definition
EONIA (Euro Over Night Index Average)	European money market rate. This is an average rate weighted by overnight transactions reported by a representative sample of 64 European banks. Published by the European Banking Federation.
EURIBOR (European Inter Bank Offered Rate)	European money market rate corresponding to the arithmetic mean of offered rates on the European banking market for a given maturity (between 1 week and 12 months). Published by the European Central Bank based on daily quotes provided by 64 European banks.
LIBOR (London Inter Bank Offered Rate)	Money market rate observed in London corresponding to the arithmetic mean of offered rates on the London banking market for a given maturity (between 1 and 12 months) and a given currency (euro, sterling, dollar, etc.).
Interest Rate Swap (IRS)	The Interest Rate Swap (IRS) rate indicates the fixed interest rate that will equate the present value of fixed rate payments with the present value of floating rate payments in an interest rate swap contract. The convention in the market is for the swap market makers to set the floating leg – normally at Euribor – and then quote the fixed rate that is payable for that maturity.

Section 26.4
OTHER DEBT SECURITIES

There are two important classes of debt that deserve some attention.

1/EUROBONDS

The **Eurobond** segment of the international bond market consists of bonds that are predominantly placed outside the country of the currency in which the securities are denominated. Eurobonds are marketed internationally; i.e., they are offered in several different markets at the same time, although the bond is denominated in a single currency.[4]

4 *A **swap-driven Eurobond** issue is a bond arranged in the currencies in which the issuer maintains a comparative advantage, and converted in other currencies which are equally advantageous to the borrowers.*

A Eurobond is different from a **foreign bond**, which is a bond issued by a foreign government or corporation *in a single market* under the security regulations of that country.[5]

The Eurobond market, a truly international market, is essentially unregulated. So, the principal difference between a "Yankee" bond and a Eurobond is that the former are SEC[6]-registered and trade like any other US domestic bond.

Because of investors' exchange rate sensitivities, Eurobond maturities are usually shorter, and issue sizes generally smaller, than in the domestic market.

The coupon payment is normally made once per year. Because domestic bonds generally pay interest semiannually, domestic bonds and Eurobonds must be compared based on their effective annual yields.

The fact that most of the trades take place in an over-the-counter market hampers the transparency on the secondary market quite a lot.

Fees charged by banks to place them range from 0.25% to 0.90% of the nominal of an issue. Higher fees may be charged for small issues.[7]

Eurobonds are generally bearer bonds.[8] This makes it more difficult to refund them prior to maturity, because most buyers can be contacted directly only when they claim their interest payments from the paying agent. This behaviour may be due to the fact that European investors are accustomed to the privacy provided by bearer bonds.

(a) Reasons for issuing Eurobonds

Sometimes it is more advantageous for a borrower to raise funds outside its domestic market, due to the effects of tax or regulatory rules. National governments often impose tight controls on foreign issuers of securities denominated in the local currency and sold within their national boundaries. However, governments in general have less stringent limitations for securities denominated in foreign currencies and sold within their markets to holders of those foreign currencies.

Eurobonds offer tax anonymity and flexibility. Interest paid in Eurobonds is generally not subject to an income-withholding tax.

International markets are very competitive in terms of using intermediaries, and a borrower may well be able to raise cheaper funds in the international markets. Other reasons are:

- a desire to diversify sources of long-term funding;
- the prestige associated with an issue of bonds in the international market;
- the flexibility of Eurobonds compared with domestic bonds issues.

(b) Market statistics

According to Claes et al. (2002), the Eurobond market is geographically concentrated. Europe has always been the most intensive user of the Eurobond market.

The majority of Eurobonds are issued by the financial industry. Taken together, financial services companies and financial corporates have issued nearly 70% of all the Eurobonds.

---

5 For example, **Yankee bonds** are issued by non-Americans in the US market; **samurai bonds** are issued by non-Japanese in the Japanese market. Try to imagine the market to which the following denominations refer: **bulldog bonds**, **matador bonds**, **Rembrandt bonds**.

6 Securities and Exchange Commission.

7 Unfortunately for bankers, fees sharply went down in recent years.

8 A **bearer bond** is a bond for which physical possession of the certificate is proof of ownership. The issuer does not know the identity of the bondholder. A **registered bond** is a bond for which the issuer keeps a record (register) of its owners. Transfer of ownership must be notified and recorded in the register.

About 50% of the issues have at least one rating at launch. Investment grade bonds cover 95–97% of the entire market; approximately 40% of the issues are AAA and 30% are AA. Only 5% are in the lowest investment grade category (BBB).

Eurobonds are not necessarily syndicated. The lead managers place the issue in 17.4% of the cases on their own. For 90.6% of Eurobonds, the issue is coordinated by a single book runner.

36% of the bonds are issued in USD; if we consider JPY and DEM they covered almost 60% of both the number of issues and the total nominal value.

The 10% and 90% percentile of nominal values are US$28.6m and US$352.5m. The overall mean size of the issues is US$167.

About the maturities, starting from the last decade the importance of issues with a 1–5-year maturity has increased. Eurobonds with maturities longer than 10 years represent between 10% and 15% of the market.

Finally, two other important aspects:

- only 7.8% of issues are subordinated;
- 71.4% of issues have no guarantee given to the investors.

2/ MEDIUM TERM NOTES (MTNs)

A medium term note is essentially a plain vanilla debt security (generally) with a fixed coupon and maturity date. MTNs are generally *noncallable, unsecured, senior debt securities* with *investment grade* ratings. Notes can be issued either as bearer or registered securities

There are two important differences between MTNs and corporate bonds:

- the distribution process: MTNs are normally sold on a *best efforts basis* by financial intermediaries. Therefore, the borrowing company is not guaranteed to place all its paper;[9]
- MTNs are usually sold in relatively small amounts on a *continuous basis*. This is actually a unique characteristic of MTNs: they are offered to investors continually over a period of time as part of an *MTN programme*.

Companies with MTN programmes have great flexibility in the types of securities they may issue. This flexibility concerns the coupon (fixed vs. floating), the embedded options and the maturities.

Despite their denomination, MTNs are not necessarily medium-term. The single bonds issued in a programme can in fact range in maturity from 9 months to 30 years or more.

The total amount of debt issued in a MTN programme generally ranges from €100m to €1bn. The single issue size can be rather small and some issues have been for as little as €5m!

9 *Certain MTN issues are underwritten by investment banks, making them indistinguishable from conventional corporate bonds.*

(a) Reasons for issuing MTNs

A MTN programme is a series of issues over time, matching the issuer's funding requirement, and therefore should be preferred over a "traditional" bond by companies that do not need all the funding at once, nor for the full duration of the programme.

However, corporate bonds continue to be preferred when:

10 *Rule 415*
(March 1982)
permits delayed or
continuous
issuance of so-
called shelf-
registered
corporate
securities. Issuers
register securities
that may be sold
for 2 years after
the effective date
of the registration
without the
requirement of
another
registration
statement each
time new offerings
are made. Thus,
shelf registration
enables issuers to
take advantage of
brief periods of
low interest rates
by selling
previously
registered
securities at a
moment's notice.

- funds are required immediately;
- issuers expect interest rates to rise in the near future and they want to lock in a fixed rate for all the funding required;
- issuers want to minimise the cost of the issue. The all-in cost of a straight bond issue is in fact generally lower than the all-in cost of an MTN programme. This reflects the economies of scale that may be achieved when issuing big amounts at once, as well as the greater secondary market liquidity of larger sized issues. The liquidity premium associated with large-volume issues is not known with certainty, but is estimated at around 5–10 basis points (Kitter, 1999).

Three major advantages can be reached through MTN programmes:

1   High financial flexibility. This frequently is the most important reason behind the corporate treasury's decision to use this funding instrument, notwithstanding the interest cost advantage of straight bonds. The major flexibility is with regard to the term to maturity of the issues. It is not rare to see issues with unconventional maturities, like 15 months, 4.5 years and so on. This makes MTNs the preferred instrument when the primary need of the issuer is to **match exactly the duration of assets with the duration of liabilities**.
2   A fast issue process of single issues, often less than a day.
3   Avoiding publicity, since the distribution method frequently is the private placement. This characteristic is particularly relevant in times of turbulent markets, high volatility and financial distress of the company.

COMPARATIVE CHARACTERISTICS OF BOND ISSUES IN THE INTERNATIONAL BOND MARKET

	Domestic markets	US market (Yankee bonds)	Eurobond market
Regulatory bodies	Official agency approval	SEC	Minimum regulatory control
Disclosure requirements	Variable	More detailed: • High initial and ongoing expense • Onerous to non-US firms	Determined by market prices
Issuing costs	Variable up to 4%	0.75%–1.00%	0.2–0.5%
Rating requirements	Usually not	Yes	No, but commonly done
Exchange listing	Usual	Usual	Usual
Queuing	Queuing is common	Queuing is not common	No formal process
Currency of denomination restrictions	Part of queuing (many countries have in the past or now restrict use of currency)	US does not restrict the use of $US	No restrictions
Speed of issuance	Variable	Relatively slow until Rule 415 *shelf registration*[10]	Usually fast (bought deal leads to fast issuance)

COMPARATIVE CHARACTERISTICS OF BOND ISSUES IN THE INTERNATIONAL BOND MARKET (cont.)

	Pros	Cons	Pros	Cons	Pros	Cons
Issuer incentives	+ Local visibility, diversification of funding sources	− Market may be small, queuing may prevail	+ Large market, great depth	− Disclosure is costly to foreigners, speed	+ Lower annual interest expenses, speed of placement	− Cannot sell issue in US until seasoned
Lender incentives	+ Diversified currency portfolio	− Reporting to tax authorities, withholding tax may apply	+ Great depth and liquidity, appeal of standardised information	− Reporting to tax authorities	+ Diversified currency portfolio, bearer bonds, no withholding tax	− Less liquidity and information disclosures

Section 26.5
THE VOLATILITY OF DEBT SECURITIES

The holder of a debt security, who may have regarded himself to be protected having chosen this type of security, actually faces three types of risk:

- **interest rate risk** and **coupon reinvestment risk**, which affect almost solely fixed rate securities;
- **credit risk**, which affects fixed rate and variable rate securities alike. We will consider this at greater length in the following section.

1/CHANGES IN THE PRICE OF A FIXED RATE BOND CAUSED BY INTEREST RATE FLUCTUATIONS

(a) Definition

What would happen if, at the end of the subscription period for the Scania 6% bond, the market interest rate rose to 7% (scenario 1) or fell to 5% (scenario 2). In the first scenario, the bondholder would evidently attempt to sell the Scania bond to buy securities yielding 7%. The price of the bond will fall such that the bond offers its buyer a yield to maturity of 7%. Conversely, if the market rate falls to 5%, holders of the Scania bond will hold onto their bonds. Other investors will attempt to buy them, and the price of the bond will rise to a level at which the bond offers its buyer a yield to maturity of 5%.

An upward (or downward) change in interest rates therefore leads to a fall (or rise) in the present value of a fixed rate bond, irrespective of the issuer's financial condition.

The value of a fixed rate debt instrument is not fixed. It varies inversely with market rates: if interest rates rise, its value declines; if interest rates fall, its value appreciates.

As we have seen, if the yield on our Scania bond rises to 6.033%, its price will move to 99.863.

But if its yield to maturity rises to 6.533% (a 0.5-point increase), its price will change to:

$$V = \sum_{t=1}^{5} \frac{6\%}{(1 + 6.533\%)^t} + \frac{100\%}{(1 + 6.533\%)^5} = 97.79\% \qquad \text{i.e., a decrease of 2.08}$$

This shows that holders of bonds face a risk to their capital, and this risk is by no means merely theoretical given the fluctuations in interest rates over the medium term.

GERMANY: LONG- AND SHORT-TERM INTEREST RATES SINCE 1981

Source: Datastream.

(b) Measures: modified duration and convexity

The modified duration of a bond measures the percentage change in its price for a given change in interest rates. The price of a bond with a modified duration of 4 will increase by 4% when interest rates fall from 7% to 6%, while the price of another bond with a modified duration of 3 will increase by just 3%.

From a mathematical standpoint, modified duration can be defined as the absolute value of the first derivative of a bond's price with respect to interest rates, divided by the price:

$$Modified\ duration = \frac{1}{V} \times \sum_{t=1}^{N} \frac{t \times F_t}{(1 + r)^{t+1}}$$

where r is the market rate and F_t the cash flows generated by the bond.

Turning back to the example of the Scania bond at its issuance date, we arrive at the following:

$$Modified\ duration = \frac{1}{99.863\%} \times \left[\frac{1 \times 6\%}{(1 + 6.033\%)^2} + \frac{2 \times 6\%}{(1 + 6.033\%)^3} \right.$$
$$\left. + \frac{3 \times 6\%}{(1 + 6.033\%)^4} + \frac{4 \times 6\%}{(1 + 6.033\%)^5} + \frac{5 \times 106\%}{(1 + 6.033\%)^6} \right] = 4.$$

Modified duration is therefore a way of calculating the percentage change in the price of a bond for a given change in interest rates. It simply involves multiplying the change in interest rates by the bond's modified duration. A rise in interest rates from 6.033% to 6.533% therefore leads to a price decrease of 0.5% × 4.210 = 2.105%; i.e., from 99.863 to 99.863 × (1 − 2.105%) = 97.76%.

We note a discrepancy of 0.03% with the price calculated previously (97.79%). Modified duration is valid solely at the point where it is calculated (i.e., 6.033% here). The further we move away from this point, the more skewed it becomes. For instance, at a yield of 6.533% it is 4.18 rather than 4.21. This will skew calculation of the new price of the bond, but the distortion will be small if the fluctuation in interest rates is also limited in size. From a geometrical standpoint, the modified duration is the first derivative of price with respect to interest rates and it reflects the slope of the tangent to the price/yield curve. Since this forms part of a hyperbolic curve, the slope of the tangent is not constant and moves in line with interest rates.

(c) Parameters influencing modified duration

Let's consider the following three bonds:

Bond	A	B	C
Coupon	5%	5%	0%
Price	100	100	100
Yield to maturity	5%	5%	5%
Redemption price	100	100	432,2
Residual life	5 years	15 years	30 years

How much are these bonds worth in the event of interest rate fluctuations?

Market interest rates	A	B	C
1%	119.4	155.5	320.7
5%	100	100	100
10%	81.0	62.0	24.8
15%	66.5	41.5	6.5

Note that *the longer the maturity of a bond, the greater its sensitivity to a change in interest rates*.

Modified duration is primarily a function of the maturity date. **The closer a bond gets to its maturity date, the closer its price moves towards its redemption value and the further its sensitivity to interest rates decreases.** Conversely, the longer it is until the bond matures, the greater its sensitivity to interest rate fluctuations.

Modified duration also depends on two other parameters, which are nonetheless of secondary importance to the time to maturity factor:

- **the bond's coupon rate**: the lower the coupon rate, the higher its modified duration;
- **market rates**: the lower the level of market rates, the higher a bond's modified duration.

Modified duration represents an investment tool used systematically by fixed income portfolio managers. If they anticipate a decline in interest rates, they opt for bonds with a higher modified duration – i.e., a longer time to maturity and a very low coupon rate – or even zero-coupon bonds, to maximise their capital gains.

Conversely, if portfolio managers expect a rise in interest rates, they focus on bonds with a low modified duration (i.e., due to mature shortly and carrying a high coupon) in order to minimise their capital losses.

Convexity is the second derivative of price with respect to interest rates. **It measures the relative change in a bond's modified duration for a small fluctuation in interest rates.** Convexity expresses the speed of appreciation or the sluggishness of depreciation in the price of the bond if interest rates decline or rise.

2/ COUPON REINVESTMENT RISK

As we have seen, the holder of a bond does not know at what rate its coupons will be reinvested throughout the life of the bond. Only zero-coupon bonds afford protection against this risk simply because they do not carry any coupons!

First of all, note that this risk factor is the mirror image of the previous one. If interest rates rise, the investor suffers a capital loss, but is able to reinvest coupon payments at a higher rate than the initial yield to maturity. Conversely, a fall in interest rates leads to a loss on the reinvestment of coupons and to a capital gain.

Intuitively, it seems clear that for any fixed income debt portfolio or security, there is a period over which:

- the loss on the reinvestment of coupons will be offset by the capital gain on the sale of the bond if interest rates decline;
- the gain on the reinvestment of coupons will be offset by the capital loss on the sale of the bond if interest rates rise.

All in all, once this period ends, the overall value of the portfolio (i.e., bonds plus reinvested coupons) is the same, and the investors will have achieved a return on investment identical to the yield to maturity indicated when the bond was issued.

In such circumstances, the portfolio is said to be **immunised**; i.e., it is protected against the risk of fluctuations in interest rates (capital risk and coupon reinvestment risk).

This time period is known as the **duration** of a bond. It may be calculated at any time, either at issue or throughout the whole life of the bond.

For instance, an investor who wants to be assured of achieving a certain return on investment over a period of 3 years will choose a portfolio of debt securities with a duration of 3 years.

Note that the duration of a zero-coupon bond is equal to its remaining life.

In mathematical terms, duration is calculated as follows:

$$\text{Duration} = \frac{\displaystyle\sum_{t=1}^{N} \frac{t \times F_t}{(1+r)^t}}{\displaystyle\sum_{t=1}^{N} \frac{F_t}{(1+r)^t}}$$

download

Duration can be regarded as being akin to the discounted average life of all the cash flows of a bond (i.e., interest and capital). The numerator comprises the discounted cash flows weighted by the number of years to maturity, while the denominator reflects the present value of the debt.

The Scania bond has a duration of 4.46 years at issue.

Duration is linked to modified duration by a very simple equation, since:

$$\text{Duration} = (1 + r) \times \text{Modified duration}$$

We can see that 4.21 × (1 + 6.033%) = 4.46 years.

Turning our attention back to modified duration, we can say that it is explained by the duration of a bond, which brings together in a single concept the various determinants of modified duration – i.e., time to maturity, coupon rate and market rates.

Note, however, that duration is **barely used in practice** owing to the constant fluctuations in market rates and the constant shifts in investors' investment horizons.

Section 26.6
DEFAULT RISK AND THE ROLE OF RATING

1/RATING AND DEFAULT RISK

Default risk can be measured on the basis of a traditional financial analysis of the borrower's situation, or by using credit-scoring, as we saw in Chapter 8. Specialised agencies, which analyse the risk of default, issue ratings which reflect the quality of the borrower's signature. There are three agencies that dominate the market: Standard & Poor's (*www.standardandpoors.com*), Moody's (*www.moodys.com*) and Fitch (*www.fitch.com*).

A number of scholars have investigated the main determinants of rating opinions. For corporate debt, higher ratings are generally associated with:

1 larger companies;
2 lower debt ratios;
3 higher ROA;[11]
4 lower variation in earnings;
5 higher interest coverage ratios;
6 lack of subordination.[12]

11 *Return On Assets.*

12 *Overall, these studies were able to explain from 60% to 90% of the ratings assigned by the rating agencies.*

Although rating services have existed in the USA since the beginning of the 20th century, they are a more recent development in Europe (1980s and 1990s) and are expected to increase even faster with the new Basle 2 banks' capital requirements (see *www.bri.org*).

Rating agencies provide ratings for companies, banks, sovereign states and municipalities. They can decide to rate a specific issue or to give an absolute rating for the issuer (rating given to first-ranking debt). Rating agencies also distinguish between short- and long-term prospects.

Some examples of long-term debt ratings:

Moody's	Standard & Poor's and Fitch	Definition	Examples (April 2005)
Aaa	AAA	Best quality, lowest risk	Austria, City of Paris, General Electric, Germany, Nestlé, Spain
Aa	AA	High quality. Very strong ability to meet payment obligations	City of Rome, ENI, Microsoft, Transport for London, Total
A	A	Upper- to medium-grade obligations. Issuer has strong capacity to meet its obligations	3i, Autostrade, Banesto, Carrefour, Coca-Cola, Endesa, Iberdrola, Nokia, Sony, Telefónica, Vodafone
Baa	BBB	Medium grade. Issuer has satisfactory capacity to meet its obligations	Accor, DaimlerChrysler, Ericsson, Mattel, Mitsubishi, Motorola, Philips, Romania, Telecom Italia, Vivendi Universal
Ba	BB	Speculative. Uncertainty of issuer's capacity to meet its obligations	Alcatel, Japan Airlines, Nikon
B	B	Issuer has poor capacity to meet its obligations	Amazon, Bolivia, City of Istanbul, Lucent, Ukraine
Caa	CCC	Poor standing. Danger with respect to payment of interest and return of principal	Ecuador, Telefónica de Argentina
Ca	CC	Highly speculative. Often in default	
C	C	Close to insolvency	
	D or SD	Insolvent!	Enron, Iridium

Short-term debts:

Moody's	Standard & Poor's and Fitch	Definition	Examples (July 2003)
Prime 1	A-1	Superior ability to meet obligations	BMW, Danone, ENI, Pfizer, Procter & Gamble, Unilever
Prime 2	A-2	Strong ability to repay obligations	Aeroporti di Roma, DaimlerChrysler, Pepsi, Pinault Printemps
Prime 3	A-3	Acceptable ability to repay obligations	Alcatel, Toshiba
Not Prime	B	Speculative	Bulgaria, Fiat
	C	Vulnerable	Lucent
	D	Insolvent	

Short-term rating is not independent of long-term rating, as seen in the diagram below:

CORRELATION

Long-term rating   Short-term rating

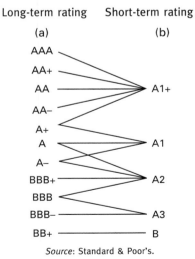

Source: Standard & Poor's.

Rating services also add an **outlook** to the rating they give – stable, positive or negative – which indicates the likely trend of the rating over 2–3 years ahead.

Short- and medium-term ratings may be modified by a + or a − or a numerical modifier, which indicates the position of the company within its generic rating category.

The **watchlist** alerts investors that an event (acquisition, disposal, merger), once it has been weighed into the analysis, is likely to lead to a change in the rating. The company on the watchlist is likely to be upgraded when the expected outcome is positive, downgraded when the expected outcome is negative and, when the agency is unable to determine the outcome, it indicates an unknown change.

During the last two decades, the number of downgrades of corporate bond ratings has exceeded the number of upgrades. Blume et al. (1998) have demonstrated that this is mainly the effect of ever-more-stringent standards used by agencies in assigning ratings.

Ratings between AAA and BBB are referred to as **Investment Grade**, and those between BB and D as **Speculative Grade** (or *Non Investment Grade*). The distinction between these two types of risk is important to investors, especially institutional investors, which are often not permitted to buy risky, speculative grade bonds!

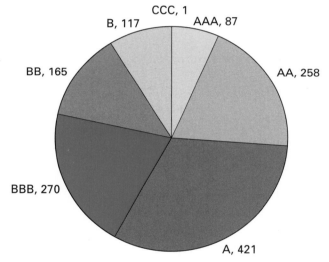

RATING CLASSIFICATION OF NEW EU ISSUERS (1981–2004)

Source: Standard & Poor's.

The reader should avoid considering speculative grade bonds as a synonym of "junk bonds". The term "junk" originated in the mid-1970s to describe those corporate securities that lost their investment grade status due to a fundamental deterioration in the quality of their operating and financial performance (so-called "fallen angels").

Since the late-1970s, this market began to include more newly issued or original issues that represented a source of capital for emerging or continuing growth companies, and those other companies which previously relied on private placements.

EU CUMULATIVE AVERAGE DEFAULT RATES (1981–2004)

Source: Standard & Poor's.

From the sample of international issuers rated by Standard & Poor's over 5 years, 0.46% of issuers rated AA failed to pay an instalment on a loan, while 24.6% of issuers rated B defaulted.

In Europe, financial rating agencies generally rate companies at their request, which enables them to access privileged information (medium-term plans, contacts with management). Rating agencies very rarely rate companies without management cooperation. When they do, the accuracy of the rating given depends on the quality of the information on the company available on the market. If the company does not require a public rating immediately, it may ask to keep it **confidential**, and is then referred to as a *shadow rating*.

Because the rating agencies work independently, they sometimes attach different ratings to a bond issue; this phenomenon is known as a **split rating**. The yield on a split-rated bond tends to be an average of yields for the higher and lower rating categories.

RATING PROCESS

With the disappearance of exchange fluctuation exposure in Europe thanks to the introduction of the euro, investors no longer shy away from bonds issued in other eurozone countries, making it easier for them to diversify their portfolios. However, given that they are relatively less well-informed about the financial situation of these new investment targets, investors now rely on rating agencies much more than they did before the advent of the euro.

Moreover, the current opening up of the bond market to new issuers that are smaller and more of an unknown quantity has led to an increase in this trend, which has long been established practice in the USA, where the spectre of issuers' ratings looms large.

As shown in the diagram below, the rating given to a company has a direct impact on the cost of the debt it has to pay. On average, in October 2004, compared with risk-free rates (government bond rates or swap curves), an *industrial* company rated AAA would have to pay 0.10% more to issue a 1-year bond and 0.52% for a 30-year bond, while an issuer rated BBB would have to pay between 1% and 1.8% more, depending on the maturity date.

SPREADS AS A FUNCTION OF RATING AND MATURITY FOR INDUSTRIAL COMPANIES (APRIL 2005)

Not surprisingly, the longer the maturity, the higher the cost of risk. Spreads are substantially higher for below investment grade loans.

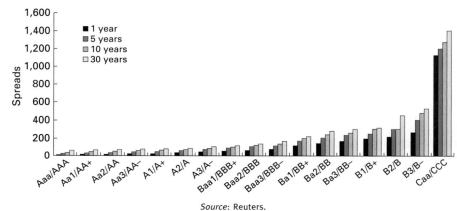

Source: Reuters.

A final comment. Academic research demonstrates that bond ratings can be predicted with a high degree of accuracy with publicly available data, leading some to question what value the agencies add beyond certification. However, it is true that bond yields are more and more associated with ratings than publicly available data alone, implying that the agencies seem to provide additional information, perhaps as a result of their contacts with management.

2/ EXPLAINING THE SPREAD ON CORPORATE BONDS

Is the relation between rating and corporate spread so strongly influenced by the default probability signalled by the class of rating of companies? The evidence is not so unanimous. An article by Elton et al. (2001) has explored the relative importance of the following factors in explaining corporate spreads in the USA:

1   expected default loss, because investors require a higher promised payment to compensate for the expected loss from defaults;
2   tax premium, because interest payments on corporate bonds are taxed in the USA at the state level whereas interest payments on government bonds are not;
3   risk premium, because a portion of the risk on corporate bonds is systematic rather than diversifiable.

Why should a systematic risk exist also for bonds? There are basically two reasons, as the authors point out:

- If expected default loss were to move with equity prices – while stock prices rise default risk goes down and vice versa – it would introduce a systematic factor. However, the relationship between the economic cycle and yield spread is not always the same, depending on the sector to which the issuer belongs. Athanassakos and Carayannopoulos (2002) have demonstrated that while in the industrial and transportation sectors bond premia are generally higher during recessionary periods, the opposite is true for utilities. This may be the result of investors decreasing their demand for bonds in highly cyclical industries, while at the same time increasing the demand for instruments less affected by general economic conditions such as bonds issued by utilities.
- The compensation for risk required in capital markets changes over time. If changes in the required compensation for risk affect both corporate bonds and equities, then this would introduce a systematic factor.

A debt security is a financial instrument representing the borrower's obligation to the lender from whom he has received funds. This obligation provides for a schedule of financial flows defining the terms of repayment of the funds and the lender's remuneration in the interval.

The price of a bond does not reflect its actual cost. The yield to maturity (which cancels out the bond's NPV – that is, the difference between the issue price and the present value of future flows) is the only criterium allowing investors to evaluate the various investment opportunities (according to risk and length of investment). On the secondary market, the yield to maturity is merely an opportunity cost for the issuer – i.e., the cost of refunding today.

The basic parameters for bonds are as follows:

- Nominal or face value.

- Issue price, with a possible premium on the nominal value.

- Redemption: redemption at maturity (known as a bullet repayment), constant amortisation or fixed instalments. The terms of the issue may also include provisions for early redemption (call options) or retraction (put options).

- Average life of bond: Where the bond is redeemed in several instalments, the average life of the bond corresponds to the average of each of the repayment periods.

- Nominal rate: also known as the coupon rate and used to calculate interest payable.

- Issue/redemption premium/discount: the difference between the issue premium/discount and the nominal value and the difference between the redemption premium/discount and the nominal value.

- Periodic coupon payments: frequency at which coupon payments are made. We talk of zero-coupon bonds when total compounded interest earned is paid only upon redemption.

SUMMARY

download

The diversity of these parameters explains why the yield to maturity may differ from the coupon rate.

Floating rate debt securities are exposed to the risk of interest rate fluctuations: the value of a fixed rate debt security increases when interest rates fall, and vice versa. This fluctuation is measured by:

- The modified duration, which measures the percentage change in the price of a bond for a small change in interest rates. Modified duration is a function of the maturity date, the nominal rate and the market rate.

- Convexity, the second derivative of price with respect to interest rates, which expresses the speed of appreciation or the sluggishness of depreciation in the price of the bond if interest rates decline or rise.

- Coupon reinvestment risk There is a time period over which the portfolio is said to be immunised; i.e., it is protected against the risk of fluctuations in interest rates (capital risk and coupon reinvestment risk). This period is known as the duration of the bond, and is equal to the ratio of the discounted cash flows weighted by the number of years to maturity and the present value of the debt.

Fixed rate securities have a coupon that is not fixed but indexed to an observable market rate (with a fixed margin that is added to the variable rate when the coupon is calculated). Variable rate bonds are not very volatile securities, even though their value is not always exactly 100% of the nominal.

All debt securities are exposed to default risk that are assessed by rating agencies on the basis of ratings (AAA, AA, A, BBB, etc.) which depend on the volatility of the economic assets and the financial structure of the issuer. The result is a *spread* which is the difference between the bond's yield to maturity and that of a no-risk loan over an identical period. Obviously, the better the perceived solvency of the issuer, the lower the spread.

QUESTIONS

quiz

1/ Why is bond-rating important?

2/ What is the default risk?

3/ What is the "character" of a bond issuer?

4/ What should a credit analyst consider as the drivers of credit risk?

ANSWERS

1/ *Because bonds with lower ratings tend to have higher interest costs.*

2/ *Default risk is the risk that the issuer will fail to meet its obligation to make timely payment of interest and principal.*

3/ *Character relates to the ethical reputation as well as the business qualifications and operating record of the board of directors, management and others responsible for the use of the borrowed funds.*

4/ *A credit analyst should consider the "four Cs of credit": character, capacity, collateral and covenants.*

BIBLIOGRAPHY

E. Altman, S.A. Nammacher, *Investing in Junk Bonds*, John Wiley & Sons, 1987.

T.J. Andersen, *Euromarket Instruments: A Guide to the World's Largest Debt Markets*, New York Institute of Finance, 2000.

G. Athanassakos, P. Carayannopoulos, An empirical analysis of the relationship of bond yield spreads and macro-economic factors, *Applied Financial Economics*, **11**, 197–207, 2002.

M. Blume, F. Lim, C. MacKinlay, The declining credit quality of US corporate debt: Myth or reality? *Journal of Finance*, **53**, 1389–1413, August 1998.

R. Cantor, F. Packer, The credit rating industry, *Journal of fixed income*, **5**, 10–34, December 1995.

M. Choudry, *The Bond and Money Markets: Strategy, Trading and Analysis*, Butterworth-Heinemann, 2002.

A. Claes, M.J. De Ceuster, R. Polfliet, Anatomy of the Eurobond market: 1980–2000, *European Financial Management*, **8**(3), 373–386, 2002.

A. Diaz, E. Navarro, Yield spread and term to maturity: Default vs. liquidity, *European Financial Management*, **8**(4), 449–478, December 2002.

D.K. Eiteman, A. Stonehill, M. Moffett, *Multinational Business Finance*, Addison-Wesley, 1999.

E. Elton, M. Gruber, D. Agrawal, C. Mann, Explaining the rate spread on corporate bonds, *Journal of Finance*, **56**(1), 247–278, February 2001.

F. Fabozzi, *The Handbook of Fixed Income Securities*, 5th edn, Irwin, 1997.

J. Finnerty, D. Emery, *Debt management: A Practitioner's Guide*, Harvard Business School Press, 2001.

D. Guha, L. Hiris, The aggregate credit spread and the business cycle, *International Review of Financial Analysis*, **11**, 219–227, 2002.

J. Hand, R. Holthausen, R.W. Leftwich, The effect of bond rating agency announcements on bond and stock prices, *Journal of Finance*, **47**, 733–752, June 1992.

J. Jewell, M. Livingston, Split ratings, bond yields and underwriter spreads, *Journal of Financial Research*, **21**, 185–204, Summer 1998.

R. Leftwich, Evaluating the bond-rating agencies, in G. Bickerstaffe (ed.), *Mastering Finance* (p. 217), Financial Times/Pitman Publishing, 1998.

A. Shivdasani, M. Zenner, How to choose a capital structure: Navigating the debt–equity decision, *Journal of Applied Corporate Finance*, **17**(1), 26–35, Winter 2005.

R. Smith, I. Walter, *Global Banking*, 2nd edn, Oxford University Press, 2003.

B. Tuckman, *Fixed Income Securities*, 2nd edn, John Wiley & Sons, 2003.

J. Van Horne, *Financial Market Rates and Flows*, 6th edn, Prentice Hall, 2001.

Chapter 27
Managing net debt

Pay now, play later; play now, pay later

Deciding on an absolute level of net debt – that is, of debt vs. equity – is a capital structure issue. Once this ratio has been decided, it is up to the CFO and the corporate treasurer to lower the cost of debt and monitor the return on investments. At the same time, treasurers must ensure that the company can meet its debt obligations and that the liquidity of the investments is adapted to the company's development needs. This means choosing between the various financial products available and evaluating banks vs. other investors.

Before plunging headfirst into a discussion of existing products, we will examine their general features and the investment selection criteria applied by corporate treasurers. We will see further on that financing can be far more than just a financial resource and that it can raise quite complex issues. This is especially true with structured financing, which has shaken the foundations of capital structure policies. We will end the chapter with a roundup of investment products.

Section 27.1
General features of corporate financing

Corporate managers have a wide range of products at their disposal for financing or investing cash surpluses. These products differ in terms of type of counterparty, maturity and seniority of redemption rights as well as the existence of collateral or accounting, legal and tax advantages. However, this wealth of options can become confusing when trying to compare the actual cost of the various products.

We therefore distinguish between:

- bank and market products (or intermediated vs. market financing);
- short-, medium- or long-term borrowings;
- loans backed by collateral, unsecured senior loans and subordinated loans

Each of these distinctions is not enough to characterise a loan *per se*: financing can take the form of a bank loan or a listed issue, it can be secured or unsecured, short or medium term, etc. In addition, lines have blurred as the inventors of new financial products endeavour to combine the advantages of the various types of financing already available. Our classification is thus simply a framework designed to help you evaluate the products presented in the following sections.

	Bank financing		Market financing	
	Short-term	Long-term	Short-term	Long-term
Asset-backed	Factoring (invoice discounting)	Collateralised bank loan Sale/leaseback	Securitisation (asset-backed commercial paper)	Securitisation (asset-backed securities)
Unsecured	Bank overdraft Credit facility	Senior bank loan Subordinated bank loan	Commercial paper	Bonds

1/BANK VS. MARKET FINANCING

Bank financing is a question of **negotiation and intermediation** whereas primary market financing is governed by **market forces**. Market financing allows the firm to call directly on financial investors without transiting through a financial institution's balance sheet.

For small- and medium-sized companies, the choice between bank financing (bank loans) and market financing is skewed in favour of bank financing.

The main differences between these two general financing categories are:

- cost;
- volume;
- flexibility.

The nature of the costs of intermediated borrowing differs significantly from that of market debt. At first sight, it may seem that the only difference is the bank's intermediation fees but, in fact, the interest rates agreed in Continental Europe between a company and its bank generally do not correspond to the actual cost of the funds. In a highly competitive environment, banks may offer clients very attractive terms that do not entirely reflect the level of counterparty risk. They make up for the lost revenue by charging for other services (investment bank services, cash management, . . .).

Conversely, they take advantage of the sectors or geographical zones in which there is little competition to overstate lending rates. Lastly, the amount banks may lend is a function of their financial position. Prudential regulations set a limit on the risk-weighted credit exposure allowed each financial institution according to its capital base. This is the famous capital adequacy ratio also known as the **Cooke ratio**.[1] As a result, when pricing the credit, banks include the opportunity cost of the capital immobilised by the credit as well as direct and fixed costs and the risk provision.

1 *To be replaced by the McDonough ratios in 2005.*

The Basel Committee on Banking Supervision released the final version of the new **Basel II framework** at the end of June 2004. The new rules, however, will not be in effect in any single country until the end of 2006 at the very earliest, and national implementation will take place in stages over several years.

The Basel II agreement retains a single measure of risk-weighted assets that serves as the denominator for the calculation of a single regulatory capital ratio. Total Risk Weighted Assets (RWAs) is the sum of RWA for credit risk, market risk and operational risk. The mechanical calculation of RWA for market risk and operational risk, which are not asset-based requirements, is to multiply the regulatory capital requirements for each by 12.5, the reciprocal of the minimum capital ratio of 8%.

The Standardised Approach (SA) builds on the work of ratings agencies – called External Credit Assessment Institutions (or ECAIs) – and specifically uses ratings from ECAIs to measure and differentiate credit risk. It includes 13 separate asset classes, and several of the 13 classes themselves have differentiated weightings. The SA also proscribes risk-weighting adjustments for high-risk categories, and for maturity. Lastly, the SA includes extensive rules for credit mitigation. The risk weights for corporates under the SA range from 20% to 150%, compared with the 100% weight for essentially all corporate exposures under the current accord. The differentiation is clearly superior to Basel I, but remains limited: corporates rated in the BBB and BB rating categories have the same 100% weight, and those in the B and CCC categories have the same 150% weight

RISK WEIGHTINGS UNDER STANDARDISED APPROACH OF BASEL II: CORPORATES

	AAA to AA−	A+ to A−	BBB+ to BB−	Below BB−	Unrated
Claims on corporates	20.0	50.0	100.0	150.0	100.0

When resorting to market financing, the issue costs are proportional to the funds raised. One or more banks may form an underwriting syndicate to buy the securities issued and endeavour to resell them immediately on the market (**firm underwriting**). They thus accept the risk that they may not be able to sell the securities. Banks can also simply act as agents selling the securities to investors without taking any responsibility (**best efforts**). A company that resorts to market financing usually has to set up specific services to keep investors constantly informed of the company's plans and prospects. In general, it also has to have the company or issue rated (see Chapter 26). However, since the market already values the debt, the company may consider that the rate offered reflects the actual cost of financing, since, as we explained above, bank lending rates are usually lower.

One advantage of bank credit is that companies can borrow the exact amount they need while financial markets impose specific constraints in terms of issue volumes. To be listed, a security has to be sufficiently liquid, and the minimum liquidity required is usually measured in units of hundreds of thousands of euros. This means that companies cannot issue "small" debt volumes, which considerably restricts their access to the listed debt market. It rules out small- and medium-sized companies as well as larger firms that have only limited or temporary borrowing requirements.

These listing constraints in terms of volume apply to the availability of funds as well. **Whereas bank loans can be obtained fairly rapidly, the preliminaries for floating an issue take several weeks (especially if it is the first time that the company has issued bonds), with no guarantee of success.** These preparations concern chiefly the rating and the information that must be provided to investors. Moreover, market volatility means that the success of the issue may be uncertain. A company that launches an issue while a major strategic operation (acquisition, restructuring, etc.) is underway may find it difficult to sell its securities in a market disconcerted by the rapid changes in the company's situation. Funds are easier to obtain through intermediated transactions. In the same vein, a company can renegotiate the terms of its bank credit if its situation changes, which of course is out of the question for listed debt securities, since their characteristics are determined once and for all upon issuance.

All these reasons explain why, in Continental Europe, bank loans account for the lion's share of the financing of small- and medium-sized firms. Market financing continues to be the preserve of large groups or investment funds that apply the necessary discipline and deal in volumes that are sufficiently large to ensure that the securities issued are liquid.

Corporate treasurers allocate the cheapest resources to the more predictable portion of their borrowing requirements. They then adjust their credit levels using the financing that is easily available (bank loans for large groups, overdrafts in the case of SMEs[2]) as new information emerges. When unexpectedly faced with large funding requirements, they call on the resources immediately available, which are then gradually replaced by less costly or better structured resources (term loans, guarantees, etc.) Bear in mind as well that **corporate treasurers have to diversify their sources of funds to avoid becoming dependent on the specific features of a given category of financing**.

So, even if the nominal cost of bond borrowings is marginally higher, the bond market enables companies to remain more independent *vis-à-vis* banks and avoid excessively constraining covenants. **Bank loans impose greater constraints on the company with covenants and guarantees to their loans.** In that respect bond issues are easier to manage for the treasurer once issued.

2 Small- and Medium-sized Enterprises.

2/Financial planning

The information provided by cash projections allows corporate treasurers to obtain better financing conditions than when they have no idea what the future holds. Suppose the treasurer knows for certain that he will have to invest €100m during the year and that the company will not generate positive cash flow until its 3rd year. His best option would be to use financing for which no reimbursements are necessary during the first 2 years, such as a bank credit with deferred repayment or a bullet 5-year bond borrowing (i.e., redeemable in one shot after 5 years).

In addition, the potential gains for the company, such as greater visibility and lower financing or transaction costs, depend on the size of the amounts mobilised for each maturity.

The distinction between long-, medium- and short-term financial resources reflects the treasurer's main forecast horizons and, accordingly, the type of information at his disposal.

As a result, treasurers deal with these issues separately by setting up a financing plan with various maturities. Afterwards, of course, they may switch between short-, medium- and long-term financing as opportunities arise.

Depending on the treasurer's anticipations regarding interest rate, he can use derivatives to swap long-term interest rates for floating rates even if he decides to borrow long-term money.

3/Guarantees

For a long time, financing products were classified in a given credit category according to the collateral[3] or guarantees given to protect creditors, since these guarantees directly impact the cost of the borrowing. They are usually divided into two categories:

- **business loans**, guaranteed solely by the prospects of the lending company, in other words, by its financial health (general balance sheet financing);
- **loans granted for a specific purpose and secured by the transaction or asset that they have helped finance.** Collateralised loans are probably the oldest and most significant in this category. In general, the amount of credit granted does not exceed the value of the asset pledged by the borrower.

The concept of lending for specific purposes has come under attack for being contrary to the financial logic according to which financing contributes to the cash position, which is the result of a company's overall operational decisions rather than of specific transactions. While the distinction between business loans and specific purpose, secured credit may sometimes be blurred, **using collateral definitely reduces the cost of a loan and may sometimes allow a company to obtain financing that is not necessarily justified by its intrinsic qualities**. This is the case, for example, of securitisation and finance leases.

The borrower identifies the assets pledged in order to segregate them and obtain better financing terms. Using collateral based on a given transaction makes it possible to isolate the various economic risks. Since investors' perception of these risks differs according to their respective resources and preferences, the cost of financing the various components may be cheaper than that of the whole.

4/Debt redemption priority rights

Contrary to the secured creditor, the unsecured creditor is said to be a **chirographic creditor**. Legal or contractual provisions may rank certain creditors behind chirographic creditors, thus making them **subordinated creditors**. This means that if the company is wound up, they are paid after the preferred creditors but before

3 *An asset pledged to ensure payment of a debt is called "collateral".*

the shareholders. The **debt held by creditors with either a security claim *or* a priority claim on repayment of the principal and the interest** is generally called **senior debt**.

Subordinated debt is repaid after the claims of the other creditors – in particular, the senior creditors – have been settled.

Subordinated creditors represent a guarantee for the other creditors because, by increasing the assets, they contribute to the company's solvency.

In exchange for taking on a greater risk, subordinated creditors demand a higher interest rate than the holders of less risky debt – in particular, the senior creditors. The rating of the subordinated debt depends on its level of subordination.

Subordinated debt allows creditors to choose the level of risk they are willing to accept, ensuring a better distribution of risks and remuneration.

When setting up financing for a leveraged buyout (see Chapter 44) the *highly* subordinated debt that fits between subordinated debt and equity is called **mezzanine debt**. Mezzanine investors are repaid only after all other subordinated debt claims have been settled. Being far riskier, mezzanine financing also carries a higher rate of return, generally accompanied by a *warrant kicker* or *conversion option* to increase its yield. The equity kicker component usually regards the equity of the issuing company.

In short, corporate treasurers create as many financial products with varying risk/reward profiles as needed according to their debt repayment priorities.

5/ACCOUNTING, LEGAL AND TAX FEATURES

Certain types of financing are based on using a tax advantage at a given time (finance leases or perpetual subordinated notes), off-balance-sheet financing (securitisation, sale/leasebacks) or legal protection (e.g., nonrecourse borrowing). In such cases, the emphasis is on achieving a specific objective and the cost of credit becomes less important.

Section 27.2
MARKETABLE DEBT SECURITIES

At a given risk level, market-financing vehicles are relatively homogenous. We have classified them by maturity.

1/MEDIUM- TO LONG-TERM DEBT SECURITIES

Bonds are the main medium-term market-financing vehicles used by corporations, particularly in the 5–10-year segment. Bonds can be subordinated, convertible or redeemable in shares; in short, they are the answer to investors' dreams!

Bonds can be issued in a currency other than that of the issuer. The most liquid currencies are the euro, the dollar, sterling and the Swiss franc.

VALUE OF BONDS LISTED (DOMESTIC AND FOREIGN) (1990–2003)

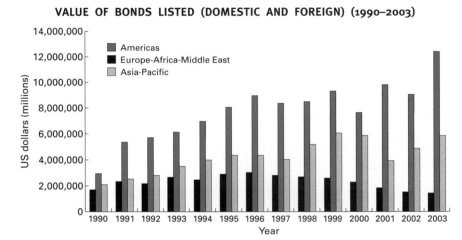

Source: World Federation of Exchanges.

High-yield bonds are generally subordinated debt, typically taking the form of 5-, 6- or 10-year bonds. These bonds are issued by companies in the process of being turned around or with a weak financial base – in particular, LBOs. Their high yields match the level of risk involved, making them a very speculative investment. The holders of these bonds enter into a debt subordination agreement whereby, in the event of bankruptcy proceedings (whether court-ordered or amicable), their claims are not settled until all claims held by traditional bank lenders have been fully repaid.

HIGH-YIELD BOND MARKET NEW ISSUANCE

Source: Standard & Poor's.

Medium-term notes are negotiable notes with a maturity of more than 1 year. The market for medium-term notes is still in its infancy and, as in the case of the bond market, investors in Continental Europe would rather entrust their medium-term funds to institutional investors such as insurance companies and financial institutions than to medium-sized industrial companies. In any event, the issuing of both negotiable medium-term notes and high-yield bonds is virtually impossible without a credit rating. This product can be issued continuously within a Euro Medium Term Notes programme using the same documentation.

2/ COMMERCIAL PAPER

Commercial paper is negotiable debt securities issued on the money market by companies for periods ranging from 1 day to 1 year. In practice, the average maturity of commercial paper is very short, between 1 and 3 months. They are issued in minimum denominations of €150,000 at fixed or variable rates. Issuers can also launch variable rate commercial paper linked with a variable rate/fixed rate swap or paper denominated in US dollars with a euro swap, allowing them to separate the company's financing from interest or exchange rate risk management.

Commercial paper enables companies to borrow directly from other companies without going through the banking system at rates very close to those of the money market.

Obtaining at least a short-term credit rating for a commercial paper issue is optional, but implicitly recommended since companies are required to indicate whether they have called on a specialised rating agency and, if so, must disclose the rating given. Moreover, any issuer can ask a bank for a commitment to provide financing should the market situation make it impossible to renew the note. These backup lines came into their own in 2001 when the US commercial paper market for nonfinancial issuers contracted by 40%. Companies have to have such lines if they want their commercial paper issues to get an investment grade rating. Certain credit-rating agencies, for example, will only keep their short-term rating of outstanding commercial paper at A1+ if 70% of the paper is covered by a backup line.

Two markets are active on the European level:

- The ECP (European Commercial Paper) market is based in London and not regulated. In March 2003, volume outstanding from corporate issues on this market was €57bn (excluding banks and securitisation).
- The French TCN (*Titres de Créances Négociables*) on which French but also other European corporates issue. This market is regulated, more secured and has flexible transactions (spot and overnight delivery). This market is regulated and under the supervision of French market authorities. In March 2003, volume outstanding from corporate issues on this market reached €54bn (excluding banks and securitisation).

Continental European central banks are currently trying to unify the European market and create the Short Term European Paper (STEP).

In addition to lower issue costs, commercial paper gives the company some autonomy *vis-à-vis* its bankers. It is very flexible in terms of maturity and rates, but less so in terms of issue amounts.

The interest rates on commercial paper have decreased from 8% to 1% over the last 14 years.

download

COMMERCIAL PAPER RATES

Source: World Federation of Exchanges.

Lastly, regardless of their country of origin, companies can issue American commercial paper. Such issues are governed by Regulation 144A defining the terms and conditions of securities issues by foreign companies in the US.

In addition to straight commercial paper, companies can use the commercial paper market for securitisation transactions. A vehicle is then created to receive trade receivables from one or several corporates (usually the vehicle is kept alive and "refilled" by the corporates); the vehicle is financed on the commercial paper market. This specific market segment called Asset Backed Commercial Paper (ABCP) had outstanding issues of €85bn in 2003 (€59bn for the European market and €26bn for domestic markets).

Section 27.3
BANK DEBT PRODUCTS

Banks have developed a number of credit products that, contrary to market financing, are tailored to meet the specific needs of their clients. We will first take a look at business loans before moving on to discuss the various types of specific purpose, secured financing. Because of the numbers of loans, we will only describe their general features and the main products.

1/BUSINESS LOANS

(a) Features of business loans

Business loans have two key characteristics: they are based on interest rates and take into account the overall risk to the company.

Business loans are based on **interest rates** and the cheapest usually wins. They rarely come with ancillary services, such as debt recovery, and are determined according to the maturity schedule and margin on the market rate.

These loans take into account **corporate risk**. The bank lending the funds agrees to take on the company's overall risk as reflected in its financial health. A profitable company will always obtain financing as long as it adopts a sufficiently prudent capital structure. In fact, the financial loan is guaranteed by the corporate manager's explicit compliance with a certain number of criteria, such as ratios, etc.

Financial loans are a type of credit that is repaid by the cash flow generated by the company.

They are business loans because they are not granted for a specific purpose (investments, trade payables, inventories, etc.). There is no connection between the funds advanced and the company's disbursements. They can even be used to finance an investment already made.

This translates into two possible approaches:

- The company calculates how much it needs and negotiates with its bank to obtain the corresponding credit – for example, a credit line even if no investment is explicitly planned during the period.
- The bank determines the overall amount of financing required by the company based on investment volumes and changes in investment as well as working capital requirements and grants an overall loan to cover these requirements.

For companies, these loans are often a backup mechanism to meet any kind of cash payment.

Syndicated loans are typically set up for facilities exceeding €100m that a single bank does not want to take on alone. The **lead bank** (or banks depending on the amounts involved) is in charge of arranging the facility and organising a syndicate of 5–20 banks that will each lend part of the amount.

A syndicated loan (or credit facility) is a relatively large loan to a single borrower structured by a lead manager(s) and the borrower. Funds are provided by a group of banks (rather than a single lender).[4]

There are four types of credit or lending facilities:

1 **Committed facilities**, a legally enforceable agreement that binds bank to lend up to stated amounts.

2 **Revolving credits.** In this case, the borrower has the right to borrow or "draw down" on demand, repay and then draw down again The borrower is charged a commitment fee on unused amounts. Options include:

   o multi-currency option: right to borrow in several currencies;

4 A good website giving useful information on syndicated loans is: www. loanpricing.com

○ competitive bid option: solicit best bid from syndicate members;

○ swingline: overnight lending option from lead manager.

3 **Term loans.**

4 **Letters of credit, equipment lines,** ...

Once lending terms are set, pieces of the loan are sold to other banks. Some bank lenders are members of the syndicate while others are not, and buy only "participations". A borrower pays a fee to a manager to structure and sell the loan. Fees increase with the complexity of the loan, and the risk of the borrower.

What is the borrowers' rationale for using this instrument?

*   The potential to raise larger amounts than from a single bank.
*   The possibility of doing few visits to the market. This in turn determines lower fixed costs and scale economies.
*   Enhanced visibility among a larger group of lenders.
*   The tradability of syndicated loans. Their high liquidity determines lower rates.

The lenders' rationale belongs to the following factors:

*   Diversification of bank loan portfolios.
*   Reduced risk of default against syndicate vs. a single bank.
*   Access to deals/credits not otherwise available to some banks.
*   Upfront fee income (to managers) + loan trading and derivative sales potential.

Below is the single-sided, secondary trading volume for 1991–2003 subdivided into par and distressed volume.

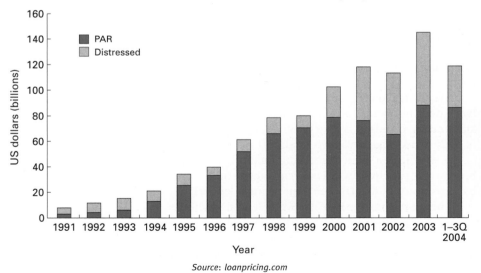

US SECONDARY LOAN MARKET VOLUME ($BN)

Source: loanpricing.com

The lead bank receives a commission of between 0.15% and over 1% of the loan. The size of the commission depends on the borrower's rating, the lead bank's level of commitment (whether it is underwriting the loan or not) and the size of the loan.

(b) Types of business loans

Overdrafts on current accounts are the corporate treasurer's means of adjusting to temporary cash shortages, but given their high interest charges they should not be used too frequently or for too long. Small enterprises can only obtain overdrafts against collateral, making the overdraft more of a secured loan.

Commercial loans are short-term loans that are easy to set up, which is why they are very popular.

The bank provides the funds for the period specified by the two parties. The interest rate is the bank's refinancing rate plus a margin negotiated between the two parties. It generally ranges from 0.10% to 1.50% per year depending on the borrower's creditworthiness since there are no other guarantees.

Commercial loans can be made in foreign currencies either because the company needs foreign currencies or because the lending rates are more attractive.

The repeated use of commercial loans may result in a **short- or medium-term confirmed credit line**. When the credit facility is confirmed, an **engagement or confirmation commission** amounting from 1/16% to 1/18% is paid. The commission is based on the borrower's creditworthiness and the duration of the credit and allows the company to discount the commercial paper as and when needed.

Extending this concept leads us to the **master credit agreement**, which is a confirmed credit line between several banks offering a group (and by extension its subsidiaries) a raft of credit facilities ranging from overdrafts, commercial credit lines, backup lines, foreign currency advances or guarantees for commercial paper issues (see above). These master agreements take the form of a contract and give rise to an engagement commission on all credits authorised, in addition to the contractual remuneration of each line drawn down. Large groups use such master agreements as multi-currency and multi-company backup lines and umbrella lines, and secure financing from their usual banks according to market conditions. Smaller companies sometimes obtain similar financing from their banks. Engagement commissions are usually paid on these credit lines.

Master agreements take into account the borrower's organisation chart by organising and regulating its subsidiaries' access to the credit lines. At the local level, the business relationship between the company's representatives and the bank's branches may be based on the credit conditions set up at group level. Subsidiaries in other countries can draw on the same lines on the same conditions. Centralising credit facilities in this manner offers a number of advantages by:

- pooling cash between subsidiaries in different countries to minimise cash balance differentials;
- harmonising the financing costs of subsidiaries or divisions;
- centralising administrative and negotiating costs to achieve real economies of structure.

Master agreements are based on a network of underlying guarantees between the subsidiaries party to the agreement and the parent company. In particular, the parent company must provide a letter of comfort for each subsidiary.

(c) Covenants

Banks include a certain number of covenants in the loan agreements, chiefly regarding accounting ratios, financial decisions and share ownership. These covenants fall into four main categories:

- **Positive or affirmative covenants** are agreements to comply with certain capital structure or earnings ratios, to adopt a given legal structure or even to restructure.
- **Negative covenants** can limit the dividend payout, prevent the company from pledging certain assets to third parties (negative pledges) or from taking out new loans or engaging in certain equity transactions, such as share buybacks.
- *Pari passu* clauses are covenants whereby the borrower agrees that the lender will benefit from any additional guarantees it may give on future credits.
- **Cross default** clauses specify that, if the company defaults on another loan, the loan which has a cross default clause will become payable even if there is no breach of covenant or default of payment on this loan.

2/SPECIFIC PURPOSE, SECURED LENDING

When specific purpose, secured lending takes the form of a bank loan, it is perfectly suited to cash management or investment plans. Such loans can be used to:

- accelerate collection of receivables;
- finance or defer an expense.

The actual use of such lending has diverged from its theoretical definition. For companies of a certain size, specific purpose, secured loans form part of their overall financial resources and usually serve more to raise working capital in general than finance the specific underlying operations.

Banks, too, no longer respect the main principles of this lending category. Before granting a loan, banks analyse the applicant's finances and look at its overall debt level. Any decision to grant a loan is based on an overall assessment of the company.

We will take a quick survey of the main types of conventional credit instruments and recommend you turn to specialised textbooks for a more detailed examination.

(a) Financing accounts receivable

This short-term financing technique bridges the cash flow gap between invoicing and collection and is backed by the corresponding trade receivable. It is the counterpart to trade credit (inter-company credit), which is widely used in Continental Europe.

Suppose, for example, that a company sold a product with a delayed settlement period. This means, of course, that it has not yet received the proceeds of the sale. It will therefore turn to a credit institution to refinance the receivable; that is, it assigns its claim on its customers to the credit institution at its nominal value less a discount representing the remuneration of the service rendered. The credit institution is repaid when the receivable falls due. If the customer defaults on the payment, the credit institution returns the claim to the company, which bears the consequences of its customer's default,

Factoring is a credit transaction whereby a company holding an outstanding trade bill transfers it to its bank or a specialised financial institution in exchange for the payment of the bill, less interest and commissions. We discussed this off-balance-sheet financing technique in greater detail in Chapter 7.

Factoring companies or factors specialise in buying a given portion of a company's trade receivables at a discount on the face value The factoring company then collects the invoice payment directly from the debtors.

Banks increasingly offer nonrecourse discounting services, which consist in an outright purchase of the trade receivables without recourse in the event of default. This technique removes contingent liabilities from the bank's on- and off-balance-sheet accounts.

Specific products exist to finance receivables arising from exporting. A **promissory note** is a physical proof of the existence of a receivable in the accounts of an exporter. Promissory notes are negotiable and therefore allow financing of the receivable.

(b) Loans to finance or defer an expense

Customers use these loans to finance an asset or to bridge the time gap between payments to suppliers and settlements. The object of the financing thus plays a twofold role: on the one hand, it represents a guarantee for the creditor and, on the other, it is used to repay the credit. It is thus self-liquidating.

Bridge loans are set up to provide funds until permanent financing is raised that will be used to repay them, such as capital increases, bond borrowings or the disposal of a subsidiary. Bridge loans are of short duration, expensive and frequently used for large amounts. They have developed in step with financial transactions – in particular, mergers and acquisitions. They can take the form of an overdraft or a spot loan that is repaid by means of an asset disposal or the issue of financial securities.

Loans secured by inventory are used to finance inventories arising on the seasonal nature of the activities of certain companies. Sugar beet producers, for example, process their crops in October and November but sell their produce throughout the year. To finance their inventories, they can deposit a portion in public bonded warehouses. In exchange, they receive a warehouse warrant giving the holder title to the merchandise. This receipt enables the producer to pledge the goods after endorsing the receipt and registering the transaction in the books of the warehouse.

The sugar beet producer can then sell the warrant to obtain working capital. When it matures, the warrant is either reimbursed and the producer regains control over the goods, or it is not repaid and the holder sells the goods.

Bank guarantees are not real cash loans, since the bank advances the funds only if the client defaults. They are therefore recorded as off-balance-sheet commitments by the financial institutions.

For companies, bank guarantees can ease cash shortages by enabling them to delay payment of amounts due, **collect** advances immediately or avoid payments – for example, of lease deposits.

They also make it easier to obtain financing from other banks or institutions, or on better terms, or allow the company to win a contract it might not have got without the bank guarantee. This said, the obligation arising on the guarantee may not be greater than that of the main debtor.

The three main types of guarantees are documentary credit, customs guarantees and buyer's credit.

Documentary credit (or Letter of Credit – L/C) ensures the performance and settlement of trade contracts between importers and exporters of different nationalities. The banks of the two parties to the contract guarantee their respective clients, thus limiting the risk that goods will be delivered but not paid, or paid but not delivered.

When a contract is signed between an importer/buyer and an exporter/seller, the importer takes the initiative for the documentary credit by contacting his bank, which informs the exporter's bank that it has opened a documentary credit payable on its accounts. Payment is effected upon successful presentation of the required documents to the importer's bank.

Documentary credit can be revocable or irrevocable and payment procedures vary (documents vs. payment or documents vs. acceptance), but they all have the same purpose: to establish a relationship based on trust between two trade partners who do not know each other.

Note, too, that the International Chamber of Commerce has standardised the trade terms used in import/export contracts (incoterms).

Buyer's credit or **export credit** is used to finance export contracts of goods and/ or services between an exporter and the buyer importing the goods/services. The banks granting the buyer's credit undertake to provide the borrower with the funds needed to pay the supplier directly according to the terms specified by contract.

The borrower in turn gives the bank an irrevocable mandate to pay the funds only to the supplier. The agreement stipulates the interest rates, duration and repayment conditions of the loan, and any bank fees or penalties that may arise in the event the borrower does not meet its obligations.

The credit agreement also specifies that the transaction is purely financial, since the borrower must repay the funds notwithstanding any disputes that may arise in the course of its business with the exporter. The advantages to the supplier are:

- insurance against payment default;
- the cost of the credit is not deducted from the contract while the risk level remains acceptable to the bank;
- the portion of the contract that must be paid upon maturity is not on the balance sheet.

Moreover, in most cases the first payments can be made before completion of the contract. There is thus less need to resort to cash or pre-financing loans. And, lastly, if the sale is denominated in a foreign currency there is no need to worry about hedging the foreign exchange risk while the borrower makes his repayments.

Certain types of buyer's credit can also be used to finance major projects and thus resemble project financing, which we will discuss below.

Section 27.4

LEASING

1/TYPES OF LEASES

In a lease contract the firm (lessee) commits itself to making fixed payments (usually monthly or semiannually) to the owner of the asset (lessor) for the right to use the asset. These payments are either fully or partially tax-deductible, depending on how the lease is categorised for accounting purposes. The lessor is either the asset's manufacturer or an independent leasing company.

If the firm fails to make fixed payments it normally results in the loss of the asset and even in bankruptcy, although the claim of the lessor is normally subordinated to other lenders.

The lease contract may take a number of different forms, but normally is categorised as either an operating or a financial lease.

For **operating leases**, the term of the lease contract is *shorter* than the economic life of the asset. Consequently, the present value of lease payments is normally lower than the market value of the asset. At the end of the contract the asset reverts back to the lessor, who can either offer to sell it to the lessee or lease it again to somebody else. In an operating lease, the lessee has generally the right to cancel the lease and return the asset to the lessor. Thus, the lessee bears little or no risk if the asset becomes obsolete.

A **financial (or capital) lease** normally lasts for the entire economic life of the asset. The present value of fixed payments tends to cover the market value of the asset. At the end of the contract, the lease can be renewed at a reduced rate or the lessee can buy the asset at a favourable price. This contract cannot be cancelled by the lessee.[5]

From an accounting point of view, leasing an asset rather than buying it substitutes lease payments as a tax deduction for the payments that the firm would have claimed if it had owned the asset: depreciation and interest expenses on debt.

SIC-15 clarifies the recognition of incentives related to operating leases by both the lessee and lessor. SIC 17 "Leases" has been effective for annual financial statements since 1999. According to these principles:

- Finance leases are those that transfer substantially all risks and rewards to the lessee.
- Lessees should capitalise a finance lease at the lower of the fair value and the present value of the minimum lease payments.
- Rental payments should be split into (i) a reduction of liability, and (ii) a finance charge designed to reduce in line with the liability.
- Lessees should calculate depreciation on leased assets using useful life, unless there is no reasonable certainty of eventual ownership. In the latter case, the shorter of useful life and lease term should be used.
- Lessees should expense operating lease payments.

5 *There are two other typologies of financial leases. The **sale-and-leaseback** lease occurs when a company sells an asset it owns to another firm and immediately leases it back. **Leveraged leases** are a three-sided arrangement among the lessor, the lessee and the lenders. The principal difference with other leases is that the lender supplies a percentage of the financing to the lessor – who will use this amount to co-finance the acquisition of the asset – and receive interest payments from the lessor.*

2/REASONS FOR LEASING

There are different reasons a firm can prefer leasing.

1   The firm may not have the borrowing capacity to purchase an asset.
2   Operating leases provide a source of off-balance-sheet financing for heavily leveraged firms. However, this opportunity does not reduce the firm's financial risk. Lenders are in fact careful in considering the cash flow effects of lease payments.
3   The firm may want to avoid bond covenants.

3/TO LEASE OR BUY?

The analysis regarding whether firms should buy or lease follows the same principles so far illustrated of investment analysis. Thus, we have basically three alternatives in valuing the relative convenience of leases:

1   The decisions can be based according to the present value of incremental after-tax cash flows of the two alternatives. In computing the present value of a lease's cash flows, we should use the after-tax cost of borrowing, since we are comparing two borrowing alternatives. A lease payment is like the debt service on a secured bond issued by the lessee, and the discount rate should be approximately the same as the interest rate on such debt.
2   Alternatively, we can compare the IRR of the two alternatives and choose the one with the lower rate.
3   Finally, we could compute the difference between the two cash flows (buying and leasing) and compute the internal rate of return on these differential cash flows. This rate should then be compared with the after-tax cost of debt to determine which alternative is more attractive.

Suppose an airline company needs a new airplane with an economic life of 5 years. The company is considering two alternative sources of financing: a fixed rate loan and a financial leasing. The following table shows the general financial information about the plane and the two alternatives:

LEASE OR PURCHASE OF A BUSINESS JET, INPUT VARIABLES

		5 years
General information	Monthly payments in year 1	12
	Discount rate	5.00%
	Marginal tax rate	35.00%
Purchase information	Total number of monthly loan payments	60
	Purchase price, before sales/use taxes	€51,000,000
	Downpayment, if purchased	€5,100,000
	Interest rate, if financed	6.00%
Lease information	Total number of monthly lease payments	60
	Fair market value, if leased	€51,000,000
	Monthly lease payment, from Boeing, before sales/use tax	€597,721
	Downpayment, if leased	€5,100,000
	Residual value after 10 years	90.51%
	Security deposit (refunded at end of lease, escrowed at discount rate)	€5,100,000

The following table reports the NPV[6] of the two alternatives:

6 *Net Present Value.*

LEASE OR PURCHASE OF A BUSINESS JET

Discount rate	5.00%						
Marginal tax rate	35.00%						
Downpayment/Security deposit	€5,100,000						
Interest rate, if financed	6.00%						
Residual value	90.51%						
Lease payment	€597,721						

If purchased:

Purchase price, including sales/use taxes	€51,000,000						
Sales price at end of holding period	€46,160,100						
Monthly payment computed, includes sales/use taxes	−€887,376						
Total number of monthly payments	60						

Year:	1	2	3	4	5	6	Totals
Cash outflow	€15,748,507	€10,648,507	€10,648,507	€10,648,507	€10,648,507	€0	€58,342.535
Cash inflow/Tax savings	−€3,437,400	−€5,082,913	−€3,647,422	−€2,557,459	−€35,698,758	€0	−€50,423,952
Net cash flow	€12,311,107	€5,565,594	€7,001,085	€8,091,048	−€25,050,251	€0	€7,918,583
Annual present values	€12,311,107	€5,300,565	€6,350,190	€6,989,351	−€20,608,903	€0	€10,342,311

Net present value of cash flows, if purchased	**€10,342,311**						

If leased:

Monthly lease payment	−€597,721						
Total number of monthly lease payments	60						

Year:	1	2	3	4	5	6	Totals
Cash outflow	€17,372,652	€7,172,652	€7,172,652	€7,172,652	€7,172,652	€0	€46,063,260
Cash inflow/Tax savings	−€4,295,428	−€2,510,428	−€2,510,426	−€2,510,428	−€8.324,831	€0	−€20,151,544
Net cash flow	€13,077,224	€4,662,224	€4,662,224	€4,662,224	−€1,152,179	€0	€25,911,716
Annual present values	€13,077,224	€4,440,213	€4,228,774	€4,027,404	−€947,901	€0	€24,825,715

Net present value of cash flows, if leased	**€24,825,715**						
Difference in cash flows (Purchase − Lease)	−**€14,483,404**						

The NPV of the purchase alternative is around €10m while the NPV of the lease alternative is around €24m. Thus, from a financial standpoint, the company should prefer the lease alternative.

A banker's imagination knows no bounds when creating specialised bank financing packages that combine funding with accounting, tax, legal or financial advantages. We develop different products with off-balance-sheet features in Chapter 47. This section will therefore be focused on project financing.

1/PRINCIPLE AND TECHNIQUES

Project financing is used to raise funds for large-scale projects with costs running into hundreds of million of euros, such as oil extraction, mining, oil refineries, purchase of methane tankers, the construction of power plants, works of art.

Lenders base their decision to extend such financing on an assessment of the project itself rather than the borrower, and on the projected cash flows generated by the project that will repay the credit. They rely on the project's assets as collateral for the debt.

This type of financing was first used in the early 1930s by American banks to extend financing to oil prospectors who could not offer the guarantees required for standard loans. The banks drew up loan contracts in which a fraction of the oil still in the ground was given as collateral and part of the future sales were set aside to repay the loan.

With this financial innovation, bankers moved beyond their traditional sphere of financing to become more involved, albeit with a number of precautions, in the actual risk arising on the project.

But it is all too easy to become intoxicated by the sophistication and magnitude of such financial structures and their potential returns. Remember that the bank is taking on far more risk than with a conventional loan, and could well find itself at the head of a fleet of superoiltankers or the owner of an amusement park of uncertain market value ... And, lastly, the parent company cannot completely wash its hands of the financial risk inherent to the project, and banks will do their best to ensure it gives financial security, just in case ...

When considering project financing, it is essential to look closely at the professional expertise and reputation of the contractor. The project's returns and thus its ability to repay the loan often depend on the contractor's ability to control a frequently long and complex construction process in which cost overruns and missed deadlines are far from rare. Project financing is not just a matter of applying a standard technique. Each individual project must be analysed in detail to determine the optimal financing structure so that the project can be completed under the best possible financial conditions.

The financiers, the future manager of the project and the contractor(s) are grouped in a pool taking the form of a company set up specifically for the project. This company is the vehicle for the bank financing.

Clearly, project financing cannot be applied to new technologies, which have uncertain operating cash flows, since the loan repayment depends on these cash flows. Similarly, the operator must have acknowledged expertise in operating the project, and the project's political environment must be stable to ensure that operations proceed smoothly. Only thus can investors and banks be assured that the loan will be repaid as planned.

In addition to investors and banks, two other players can take on an important role in project finance:

- international financial organisations such as the World Bank and regional development banks like the EBRD,[7] especially if the project is located in a developing country. These institutions may lend funds directly or guarantee the loans extended by the other banks;
- export facilitating organisations like COFACE[8] in France, EBRD in the UK or SACE[9] in Italy, which underwrite both the financial and the commercial risks arising on the project.

7 European Bank for Reconstruction and Development.

8 Compagnie Française d'Assurance pour le Commerce Extérieur.

9 Società per l'Assicurazione Commercio con l'Estero.

2/RISKS AND HOW THEY ARE HEDGED

The risks on large projects arise during three quite distinct stages:

- when the project is being set up;
- during construction;
- during operations.

Contrary to appearances, risks arise as soon as the project is in the planning stage. Analysing a major project can take up to several years and requires considerable expertise and numerous technical and financial feasibility studies. All this can be quite costly. At this stage, no one is sure that the project will actually materialise. Moreover, when there is a call for tenders, the potential investors are not even sure that their bid will be retained.

But, of course, the greatest risk occurs during construction, since any loss can only be recouped once the facilities are up and running!

Some of the main risks incurred during the construction phase are:

- Cost overruns or delays. These are par for the course on large projects that are complex and lengthy. Such risks can be covered by a specific insurance that can make up for the lack of income subject to the payment of additional premiums. Any claims for benefits are paid directly to the lenders of the funds, or to both borrowers and lenders. Another method is for the contractor to undertake to cover all or part of any cost overruns and to pay an indemnity in the event of delayed delivery. In exchange, the contractor may be paid a premium for early completion.
- Noncompletion of work, which is covered by performance bonds and contract guarantees, which unconditionally guarantee that the industrial unit will be built on schedule and with the required output capacity and production quality.
- "Economic upheavals" imposed by the government (e.g., car factories in Indonesia, dams in Nigeria) and arbitrary acts of government, such as changes in regulations.
- Natural catastrophes that are not normally covered by conventional insurance policies.
- Etc.

As a result, financing is released according to expert assessments of the progress made on the project.

Risk exposure culminates between the end of construction and the start of operations. At this point, all funds have been released but the activity that will generate the flows to repay them has not yet begun and its future is still uncertain. Moreover, a new risk emerges when the installations are delivered to the client, since they must be shown to comply with the contract and the client's specifications. Because of the risk that the client may refuse to accept the installations, the contract usually provides for an independent arbitrator, generally a specialised international firm, to verify that the work delivered is in conformity with the contract.

Once the plant has come onstream, anticipated returns may be affected by:

➤ **Operating risks** *per se*: faulty design of the facilities, rising operating or procurement costs. When this occurs, the profit and loss account diverges from the business plan presented to creditors to convince them to extend financing. Lenders can hedge against this risk by requiring long-term sales contracts, such as:

    o *take or pay*: these contracts link the owner of the facilities (typically for the extraction and/or transformation of energy products) and the future users whose need for it is more or less urgent. The users agree to pay a certain amount that will cover both interest and principal payments, irrespective of whether the product is delivered and of any cases of *force majeure*;

    o *take and pay*: this clause is far less restrictive than take or pay, since clients simply agree to take delivery of the products or to use the installations if they have been delivered and are in perfect operating condition.

➤ **Market risks.** These risks may arise when the market proves smaller than expected, the product becomes obsolete or the conditions in which it is marketed change. They can be contained, although never completely eliminated, by careful study of the sales contracts; in particular, the revision and cancellation clauses, which are the linchpin of project financing, as well as detailed market research.

➤ **Foreign exchange risks** are usually eliminated by denominating the loan in the same currency as the flows arising on the project or through swap contracts (see Chapter 48).

➤ **Abandonment risk** arises when the interests of the industrial manager and the bankers diverge. For example, the former may want to bail out as soon as the return on capital employed appears insufficient, while the latter will only reach this conclusion when cash flow turns negative. Here again, the project-financing contract must lay down clear rules on how decisions affecting the future of the project are to be taken.

➤ **Political risks**, for which no guarantees exist but which can be partly under-written by state agencies.

Section 27.6
INVESTMENT OF CASH

Financial novices may wonder why debt-burdened companies do not use their cash to reduce debt. There are two good reasons for this:

- paying back debt in advance can be costly because of early repayment penalties or unwise, if the debt was contracted at a rate that is now lower than prevailing rates;
- keeping cash on hand enables the company to seize investment opportunities quickly and without constraints or to withstand changes in the economic environment. Some research papers (Opler et al., 1999) have demonstrated that companies with strong growth or volatile cash flows tend to have more free cash than average. Conversely, companies that have access to financial markets or excellent credit ratings have less cash than average.

Obviously, all financing products used by companies have a mirror image as investment products, since the two operations are symmetrical. The corporate treasurer's role in investing the company's cash is nevertheless somewhat specific because the purpose of the company is not to make financial profits by engaging in risky investments. This is why specific products have been created to meet this criteria.

First of all, remember that all investment policies are based on anticipated developments in the bank balances of each account managed by the company or, if it is a group, on consolidated, multi-currency forecasts. The treasurer cannot decide to make an investment without first estimating its amount and the duration. Any mistake and the treasurer is forced to choose between two alternatives:

- either having to resort to new loans to meet the financial shortage created if too much cash was invested, thus generating a loss on the difference between lending and borrowing rates (i.e., the interest rate spread);
- or having to retrieve the amounts invested and incur the attendant penalties, lost interest or, in certain cases such as bond investments, risk of a capital loss.

Since corporate treasurers rarely know exactly how much cash they will have available for a given period, their main concern when choosing an investment is its liquidity – that is, how fast can it be converted back into cash. **For an investment to be cashed in immediately, it must have an active secondary market or a redemption clause that can be activated at any time.**

The corporate treasurer's first concern in investing cash is preserving liquidity.

Of course, if an investment can be terminated at any time, its rate of return is uncertain since the exit price is uncertain. A 91-day Treasury bill at a nominal rate of 4% can be sold at will, but its actual rate of return will depend on whether the bill was sold for more or less than its nominal value. However, if the rate of return is set in advance it is virtually impossible to exit the investment before its maturity since there is no secondary market or redemption clause, or else only at a prohibitive cost.

The treasurer's second concern – security – is thus closely linked to the first. Security is measured in terms of the risk on the interest and principal.

When making this tradeoff between liquidity and security, the treasurer will, of course, try to obtain the **best return** taking into consideration the **variable tax rates**, since various investment products may be subject to different tax regimes.

1/INVESTMENT PRODUCTS WITH NO SECONDARY MARKET

Interest-bearing current accounts are the simplest way to earn interest on cash. Nevertheless, interest paid by banks on such accounts is usually limited and significantly lower than what the money market offers. It should be noted that regulations in some countries (e.g., France) do not allow current accounts to pay interest.

Time deposits are fixed term deposits on an interest-bearing bank account that are governed by a letter signed by the account holder. The interest on deposits with maturity of at least 1 month is negotiated between the bank and the client. It can be at a fixed rate or indexed to the money market. No interest is paid if the client withdraws the funds before the end of the fixed term.

Cash certificates are time deposits that take the physical form of a bearer or registered certificate.

Repos (repurchase agreements) are agreements whereby institutional investors or companies can exchange cash for securities for a fixed period of time (a securities for cash agreement is called a reverse repo). At the end of the contract, which can take various legal forms, the securities are returned to their initial owner. All title and rights to the securities are transferred to the buyer of the securities for the duration of the contract.

The remuneration of the buyer of the securities can be determined at the outset according to how the contract will be unwound, and it can be adapted to various requirements. The only risk is that the borrower of the cash (the repo seller) will default.

Repo sellers hold equity or bond portfolios, while repo buyers are looking for cash revenues. From the buyer's point of view, a repo is basically an alternative solution when a time deposit is not feasible – for example, for periods of less than 1 month. A repo allows the seller to obtain cash immediately by pledging securities with the assurance that it can buy them back.

Since the procedure is fairly unwieldy, it is only used for large amounts, well above €2m. This means that it competes with negotiable debt securities, such as commercial paper. The development of money market mutual funds investing in repos has lowered the €2m threshold and opened up the market to a larger number of companies.

The principle of **securities lending** is similar to that of repurchase agreements. It enables a company with a large cash surplus or listed investments to improve the yield on its financial instruments by entrusting them to institutional investors. These investors use them in the course of forward transactions and pay the income arising on the securities and a borrowing fee to the original owner (the company). No cash changes hands in the course of the transaction. The incremental return thus stems from the remuneration of default risk on the part of the institutional investors borrowing the securities.

2/ SECONDARY MARKET INVESTMENT PRODUCTS

Marketable Treasury bills and notes are issued by governments at monthly or weekly auctions for periods ranging from 2 weeks to 5 years. They are the safest of all investments given the creditworthiness of the issuer (governments), but their other features make them less flexible and competitive. However, the substantial amount of outstanding negotiable Treasury bills and notes ensures sufficient liquidity, even for large volumes. These instruments can be a fairly good vehicle for short-term investments.

Certificates of deposit are quite simply time deposits represented by a dematerialised negotiable debt security in the form of a bearer certificate or order issued by an authorised financial institution. Certificates of deposit are issued in minimum amounts of €150,000 for periods ranging from 1 day to 1 year with fixed maturity dates. In fact, they are a form of short-term investment. CDs are issued by banks, for which they are a frequent means of refinancing, on a continuous basis depending on demand. Their yield is very close to that of the money market, and their main advantage is that they can be traded on the secondary market, thus avoiding the heavy penalties of cashing in time deposits before their maturity date. The flipside is that they carry an interest rate risk..

Money market or cash mutual funds are funds that issue or buy back their shares at the request of investors at prices that must be published daily. The return on a money market capitalisation mutual fund arises on the daily appreciation in net asset value that is similar to that of the money market. Depending on the mutual fund's stated objective, the increase in Net Asset Value (NAV) is more or less steady. A very regular progression can only be obtained at the cost of profitability.

In order to meet its objectives, each cash mutual fund invests in a selection of Treasury bills, certificates of deposit, commercial paper, repos, variable rate or fixed rate bonds with a short residual maturity. Its investment policy is backed by quite sophisticated interest rate risk management. The management fees of cash mutual funds are paid out of the fund's net asset value (there is no direct entry or exit fee).

Securitisation vehicles are special purpose vehicles created to take over the claims sold by a credit institution or company engaging in a securitisation transaction. In exchange, they issue units that the institution sells to investors.

In theory, **bond** investments should yield higher returns than money market or money market indexed investments. However, interest rate fluctuations generate capital risks on bond portfolios that must be hedged, unless the treasurer has opted for variable rate bonds. Investing in bonds therefore calls for a certain degree of technical know-how and constant monitoring of the market. Only a limited number of institutional investors have the resources to invest directly in bonds, and then only using cash that is available for longer periods of time.

The high yields arising on investing surplus cash in the **equity** market over long periods become far more uncertain on shorter horizons, when the capital risk exposure is very high, well above that of a bond investment. Treasurers must keep a constant eye on the secondary market, and sharp market swings have rendered the few treasurers still positioned on the market extremely cautious. However, they may be responsible for monitoring portfolios of equity interests.

SUMMARY

download

Deciding on an absolute level of net debt – that is, of debt vs. equity – is a capital structure issue. Once this ratio has been decided, it is up to the CFO and the corporate treasurer to lower the cost of debt and monitor the return on investments. At the same time, treasurers must ensure that the company can meet its debt obligations and that the liquidity of the investments is adapted to the company's development needs. This means choosing between the various financial products available and playing off banks against investors. These products differ in terms of type of counterparty, maturity and seniority of redemption rights as well as the existence of collateral or accounting, legal and tax advantages. However, this wealth of options can become confusing when trying to compare the actual cost of the various products. We therefore distinguish between:

- bank and market products;
- short-, medium- or long-term borrowings;
- loans backed by collateral, unsecured senior loans and subordinated loans.

For small- and medium-sized companies, the choice between bank financing (bank loans) and market financing is skewed in favour of bank financing as their needs do not correspond to the size and liquidity required by financial markets.

The distinction between long-, medium- and short-term financial resources reflects the treasurer's main forecast horizons and, accordingly, the type of information at his disposal.

Giving guarantees or seniority to a loan often allows interests paid to be lowered but limits the financial flexibility of the firm.

Debt market products include long-term financing: **bonds** (investment grade or high yield depending on the rating of the company) and short-term financing: **commercial paper**.

Bank debt products include loans for general purpose financing (business loans) for which agreements include standard covenants (positive covenants to comply with certain requirements; negative covenants to limit the financial flexibility of the company; *pari passu* clauses; cross default clauses). Specific purpose financing is backed by assets (factoring, export credit, loans on inventories, . . .).

The corporate treasurer's first concern in investing cash is liquidity. The treasurer's second concern – security – is thus closely linked to the first. Security is measured in terms of the risk on the interest and principal. Products he can use can be split between products with a secondary market (Treasury bills, money market funds, . . .) or without (time deposit, repos, . . .).

1/ Should the analysis of covenants in high-yield corporate issues be analysed separately from other characteristics?

2/ In an article in a popular daily publication, a statement similar to the following was made: "Repurchase agreements are extremely risky vehicles." Explain why this statement is ambiguous.

3/ Is project financing based on the personal and real guarantees of the sponsors?

ANSWERS

1/ *Covenants in high-yield corporate bond issues should be reviewed in conjunction with the issuer's overall strategy.*

2/ *When a repurchase agreement is used to create leverage (i.e., when it is used as a financing vehicle), it is a risky vehicle because of the risk associated with leverage. In contrast, when it is used as a vehicle in which to invest funds on a short-term basis, if properly structured it is a high-quality money market instrument.*

3/ *No, one of the main features of project financing is that the feasibility of the project is mainly – if not exclusively – based on the cash flows of the project.*

BIBLIOGRAPHY

Th. Barnhill, W. Maxwell, M. Shenkman, *High Yield Bonds: Market Structure, Valuation and Portfolio Strategies*, McGraw-Hill, 1999.

M. Crouhy, D. Galai, T. Mark, *Risk Management*, McGraw-Hill, 2001.

F.J. Fabozzi, *The Handbook of Fixed Income Securities*, 6th edn, McGraw-Hill, 1997.

B. Esty, Petrozueta: A case study on the effective use of project finance, *Journal of Applied Corporate Finance*, 26–37, Autumn 1999.

T. Opler, L. Pinkowitz, R. Stulz, R. Williamson, The determinants and implications of corporate cash holding, *Journal of Financial Economics*, 3–46, April 1999.

S. Mian, C. Smith, Accounts receivable management policy: Theory and evidence, *Journal of Finance*, 169–200, March 1992.

Chapter 28
SHARES

One of a kind, or one of many?

A share or a stock is a security that is not redeemed – the investment can only be realised through a disposal – and whose revenue flows are uncertain. It is in compensation for these two disadvantages that shareholders have a say in managing the company via the voting rights attached to their shares.

The purpose of this chapter is to present the key parameters used in analysing stocks and to show how the stock market operates. In the previous chapters, you learned that the easiest and most efficient way to determine equity value is to subtract the value of net debt from enterprise value (i.e., the value of its operating assets):

Equity value is equal to enterprise value minus net debt value.

To determine the value of a share, simply divide equity value by the number of shares.

Section 28.1
BASIC CONCEPTS

This section presents the basic concepts for analysing the value of stocks, whether listed or not. To familiarise ourselves with basic stock information, let's use the example of Nestlé. On April 23, 2005, Datastream reported the following facts about Nestlé's stock:

1 *Return On Equity.*

2 *Earnings Per Share.*

3 *Price/Earnings ratio.*

Latest price SF317.7		1-month change +0.7%		Volume 1,224,000	ROE[1] 18.21%
				Dividend yield 2.52%	Market to book value 3.06
Year's high/low 279.75–341.0	EPS[2] 17.3	P/E[3] 18.4		Market cap SF109,089.4m	Beta 0.495

1/VOTING RIGHTS

Shares are normally issued with one voting right each. For our purposes, this is more of a compensation for the risk assumed by the shareholder than a basic characteristic of stock.

A company can issue shares with limited or without voting rights. These are known under different names, including preference shares, savings shares or, simply, nonvoting shares.

At the other extreme, companies in some countries, such as the Netherlands and Sweden, issue several types of shares ("A" shares, "B" shares, etc.) having different numbers of voting rights. Some shareholders use this to strengthen their hold on a company, as we will see in Chapters 42 and 43.

2/EARNINGS PER SHARE (EPS)

EPS is equal to net attributable profit divided by the total number of shares in an issue. EPS reflects the theoretical value creation during a given year, as net profit belongs to shareholders.

There is no absolute rule for presenting EPS. However, financial analysts generally base it on restated earnings, as shown below:

> Net attributable profit:
> — Exceptional (after-tax) profit
> — Other nonrecurring items not included in exceptional profit
> + Depreciation and goodwill amortisation

Nestlé's 2004 EPS is SF17.3.

Some companies have outstanding equity-linked securities, such as convertible bonds, warrants and stock options. In this case, analysts calculate, in addition to standard EPS, **fully diluted EPS**.

3/DIVIDEND PER SHARE (DPS)

Dividends are generally paid out from the net earnings for a given year but can be paid out of earnings that have been retained from previous years. Companies sometimes pay out a quarterly or half-year dividend.

European company dividends can come with a tax credit. The dividend and tax credit taken together constitute the gross dividend. The tax credit is a way of totally or partially returning to shareholders some of the tax that the company has already paid and thus avoiding the double taxation of both the company and its shareholders.

In 2004 Nestlé paid a SF8.0 dividend per share.

Some shares – like preference shares – pay out higher dividends than other shares or have priority in dividend payments over those other shares. They are generally nonvoting shares.

4/DIVIDEND YIELD

Dividend yield per share is the ratio of the last dividend paid out to the current share price:[4]

$$\text{Dividend yield} = \frac{\text{Dividend per share}}{\text{Share price}} = \frac{DPS_0}{P_0}$$

Yield is either gross (including the tax credit) or net (without the tax credit).

The net dividend yield on Nestlé is 2.52%.

Yield is based on market value and never on book value.

4 *The average yield on stocks listed on Western stock markets is currently about 3%.*

DIVIDEND YIELD (%)

	UK	Germany	France	Italy	Spain	Netherlands	Belgium	Switzerland	USA	Japan
1989	1.40	1.65	1.76	1.78	1.12	1.35	1.16	1.43	1.94	3.53
1990	1.33	2.07	1.90	1.97	1.09	1.47	1.21	1.34	1.92	2.97
1991	1.59	1.78	1.51	1.27	1.11	1.39	0.31	1.26	2.23	2.52
1992	1.73	1.71	1.54	1.12	1.07	1.43	0.36	1.18	2.55	1.77
1993	1.84	1.58	1.44	1.18	1.37	1.36	0.26	1.34	2.63	2.03
1994	2.07	1.85	1.66	1.54	1.40	1.71	0.34	1.75	2.46	2.11
1995	1.98	1.63	1.50	1.18	1.23	1.62	0.38	1.72	2.49	1.74
1996	2.45	1.88	1.59	1.46	1.32	1.90	0.46	2.11	2.86	2.16
1997	2.72	2.26	1.74	1.61	1.81	2.19	0.52	2.67	3.08	1.93
1998	3.55	3.13	2.47	2.80	3.08	3.14	1.02	3.81	4.24	1.80
1999	3.05	2.55	2.44	2.58	2.86	2.75	2.07	2.95	4.60	2.00
2000	2.38	3.09	3.00	2.89	3.00	3.08	1.45	2.93	4.52	2.42
2001	2.55	2.25	2.68	2.52	2.55	2.98	1.33	2.78	3.48	2.04
2002	2.40	2.22	2.56	2.27	2.69	3.16	1.66	3.14	3.26	1.44
2003	1.81	1.32	1.62	1.57	2.06	1.79	1.12	2.02	2.39	0.90
2004	2.13	1.69	2.00	1.90	2.62	2.14	1.60	2.51	2.74	1.44

Source: Datastream.

download

5/PAYOUT RATIO

The payout ratio is the percentage of earnings from a given year that is distributed to shareholders in the form of dividends. It is calculated by dividing dividend by earnings for the given year:

$$\text{Payout ratio} = d = \frac{\text{Cash dividend}}{\text{Net income}}$$

When the payout ratio is above 100%, a company is distributing more than its earnings; it is tapping its reserves. Conversely, a payout close to 0% indicates that the company is reinvesting almost all its earnings into the business.

In 2002, European companies paid out an average of about 45% of their earnings.

It will be clear that the higher the payout ratio, the weaker future earnings growth will be. The reason for this is that the company will then have less funds to invest. As a result, fast-growing companies such as Amgen[5] and Gene Logic[6] pay out little or none of their earnings, while a mature company will pay out a higher percentage of its earnings. Mature companies are said to have moved from the status of a **growth stock** to that of an **income stock**.

The dividend is legally drawn on parent company profits. However, it should be assessed on the basis of consolidated net attributable profit – the only meaningful figure, as in most cases the parent company is merely a holding company.

5 *Amgen is the world's largest biotechnology company.*

6 *Gene Logic is a company dedicated to empowering life science research.*

6/CASH FLOW PER SHARE

Cash flow per share has no theoretical basis, in that it does not constitute true creation of value.

Cash flow per share is nonetheless used for two reasons:

- when EPS is very low, it can be used for comparisons where EPS cannot;
- one of its components, depreciation, in some cases has little connection to real wear and tear and instead results from a tax strategy. Consolidated accounts fortunately offset this drawback.

Such calculations assume that cash flow provides a better picture of real earnings than reported earnings do. However, cash flow is not equal to real earnings, only proportional to them.

When the expression "price to cash flow" is mentioned, it is best to check what exactly is included in the vague term "cash flow".

7/EQUITY VALUE (BOOK VALUE OR NET ASSET VALUE) PER SHARE

Equity value (book value or net asset value) per share is the accounting estimate of the value of a share. While book value may appear to be directly comparable with equity value, it is determined on an entirely different basis – it is the result of strategies undertaken up to the date of the analysis and corresponds to the amount invested by the shareholders in the company (i.e., new shares issued and retained earnings).

Book value may or may not be restated. This is generally done only for financial institutions and holding companies.

8/COST OF EQUITY (EXPECTED RATE OF RETURN)

According to the CAPM (see Chapter 22), the cost of equity is equal to the risk-free rate plus a risk premium that reflects the stock's market (or systematic) risk:

$$K_E = r_f + \beta \times (r_M - r_f)$$

9/SHAREHOLDER RETURN (HISTORICAL RATE OF RETURN)

In a given year, shareholders receive a return in the form of dividends (dividend yield) and the increase in price or market value (capital gain):

$$\frac{P_1 - P_0}{P_0} + \frac{\text{Div}_1}{P_0}$$

Total Shareholder Return (TSR) is calculated in the same way, but over a longer period.

10/LIQUIDITY

A security is said to be liquid when it is possible to buy or sell a large number of shares on the market without too great an influence on the price. Liquidity is a typical measure of the relevance of a share price. It would not make much sense to analyse the price of a stock that is traded only once a week, for example.

A share price is relevant only if the stock is sufficiently liquid.

A share's liquidity is measured mainly in terms of free float and trade volumes.

(a) Free float

The free float is the proportion of shares available to purely financial investors, to buy when the price looks low and sell when it looks high. Free float does not include shares that are kept for other reasons – i.e., control, sentimental attachment or "buy and hold" strategies. A skyrocketing share price could make sellers out of loyal shareholders, thus widening the free float.

Free float can be measured either in millions of euros or in percentage of total shares. It is becoming more common to use free-float based indexes – i.e., indexes composed of the relative free float value of each company. The free float factor is normally given by the percentage of shares remaining after the block ownership and restricted shares adjustments are applied to the total number of shares:

> Free float factor (%)
>   = 100% − [Larger of block ownership and restricted shares adjustments (%)]

Free float market capitalisation is the portion of a stock's total market capitalisation that is available for trading:

> Free float market capitalisation
>   = Capitalisation free float factor × Total market

Thus, it may happen that a company with a high total market value has a lower percentage in the free float index because the percentage of shares "free to float" is low. At the same time, mid-caps could increase their relevance in the indexes if relevant shareholders hold a low portion of the entire equity.

Dow Jones (DJ) was the first institution to create free float indexes. The indexes offered by DJ are free float market capitalisation weighted to reflect the portion of a stock's shares that is available for trading. This is achieved by adjusting a stock's shares by the shares held in strategic holdings – i.e., block ownership. This block ownership adjustment is applied if blocks of at least 5% of a stock's total number of shares are held by private, cross or government ownership (see also *http://www.dowjones.com/index_aboutdow.htm*).

Block ownership is not applied if:

- blocks are less than 5% of the total number of shares;

- blocks are held by custodian nominees, trustee companies, mutual and pension funds, investment companies with short-term investment strategies.

(b) Volumes

Liquidity is also measured in terms of volumes traded daily. Here again, absolute value is the measure of liquidity, as a major institutional investor will first try to determine how long it will take to buy (or sell) the amount it has targeted. But volumes must also be expressed in terms of a percentage of the total number of shares and even as a percentage of free float.

11/MARKET CAPITALISATION

Market capitalisation is the market value of company equity. It is obtained by multiplying the total number of shares outstanding by the share price. However, rarely can the majority of the shares be bought at this price at the same time – for example, in an attempt to take control and appoint new management. A premium most often must be paid (see Chapter 40).

All too often, only the shares in free float are counted in determining market capitalisation. All shares must be included, as market cap is the market value of company equity and not of the free float.

On April 23, 2005, Nestlé had a market cap of SF128bn.

12/PRICE TO BOOK RATIO (PBR)

PBR (*Price to Book Ratio*) measures the ratio between market value and book value:

$$PBR = \frac{\text{Price per share}}{\text{Book value per share}} = \frac{\text{Market capitalisation}}{\text{Book value of equity (net worth)}}$$

PBR can be calculated either on a per-share basis or for an entire company. Either way, the result is the same.

It may seem surprising to compare book value with market value, which, as we have seen, results from a company's future cash flow. Even in the event of liquidation, equity value can be below book value (due, for example, to restructuring costs, accounting issues, etc.).

There is no direct link between book value and market value.

However, there is an economic link between book value and market value, as long as book value correctly reflects the market value of assets and liabilities.

It is not hard to show that a stock's *PBR* will be above 1 if its market value is above book value, when return on equity (r_E) is above the required rate of return (k_E). The reason for this is that, if a company consistently achieves 15% *ROE*, whereas shareholders require only 10%, a book value of 100 would mean an equity value of 150, and the shareholders will have achieved their required rate of return:

$$\frac{15\% \times 100}{150} = 10\%, \quad \text{and} \; PBR = 1.5$$

However, PBR will be below 1 if ROE (r_E) is below the required rate of return (k_E).

A sector cannot long show equity value below book value, as sector consolidation will soon intervene and re-establish balance, assuming that markets are efficient. Nor can a sector long have equity value higher than book value, as new entrants will be attracted to the sector and will bring down the abnormally high returns. Market equilibrium will thus have been re-established.

As an illustration, here are the PBRs seen on the main world markets since 1989:

PBR

	UK	Germany	France	Italy	Spain	Netherlands	Belgium	Switzerland	USA	Japan
1989	1.8	4.2	2.1	2.8	3.4	1.8	3.1	4.1	1.9	6.6
1990	2.1	5.1	2.9	3.0	3.1	2.1	2.9	3.7	2.6	7.0
1991	1.7	5.1	2.1	2.1	2.2	1.8	2.0	1.9	2.0	3.8
1992	2.0	5.1	1.8	1.8	2.4	2.2	1.8	2.0	2.5	3.7
1993	2.2	4.2	1.6	1.6	1.6	2.1	1.6	2.1	2.7	2.7
1994	2.0	2.4	1.9	1.7	1.5	1.7	1.9	1.8	1.9	5.7
1995	2.3	4.2	1.8	1.5	2.1	2.5	1.7	2.4	2.5	3.2
1996	2.4	3.8	1.8	1.5	1.9	2.8	1.7	2.8	2.8	3.1
1997	2.4	4.3	2.0	1.6	2.3	3.3	1.8	2.6	2.9	2.9
1998	2.7	2.4	2.5	2.0	3.2	3.2	2.2	2.2	3.4	2.6
1999	2.1	2.8	3.1	2.1	3.0	2.9	2.3	2.5	3.1	1.4
2000	3.0	3.3	4.0	4.4	3.6	3.4	3.1	4.7	4.1	3.2
2001	3.2	2.8	4.3	4.7	3.4	3.9	2.0	5.1	3.6	2.1

Section 28.2
Price/Earnings ratio

1/Principle

Most market operators now value shares based on Earnings Per Share (EPS) multiplied by the Price/Earnings (P/E) ratio. P/E is equal to:

$$P/E = \frac{\text{Price per share}}{EPS}$$

Another way to put this is to consider the aggregate values:

$$P/E = \frac{\text{Market capitalisation}}{\text{Net income}}$$

EPS reflects theoretical value creation over a period of 1 year. Unlike a dividend, EPS is not a revenue stream:

As an illustration, here are the P/E ratios of the main markets since 1988:

P/E

	UK	Germany	France	Italy	Spain	Netherlands	Belgium	Switzerland	USA	Japan
1988	12.0	10.0	10.0	12.0	14.0	10.0	10.0	10.0	13.0	54.0
1989	12.2	13.7	11.7	15.3	12.7	12.2	13.4	12.3	13.0	58.2
1990	11.6	15.2	10.3	16.7	9.3	10.9	11.2	11.3	14.1	46.1
1991	13.9	16.1	11.0	16.1	9.7	11.5	12.0	13.5	16.3	41.8
1992	16.4	16.3	11.7	14.3	9.2	12.9	13.1	14.2	20.0	36.1
1993	18.1	20.9	15.0	18.4	12.4	15.3	16.1	16.3	19.9	53.6
1994	17.1	18.6	14.4	23.3	14.5	16.5	17.5	17.2	17.9	66.3
1995	15.2	16.0	12.1	18.2	12.2	13.2	13.8	17.3	16.8	58.9
1996	15.7	16.5	14.8	15.6	12.8	16.1	15.5	19.2	19.0	61.4
1997	17.2	19.7	17.1	18.1	18.6	21.9	15.8	23.6	21.7	49.0
1998	19.9	21.2	18.6	25.8	22.9	22.8	19.9	25.1	25.3	44.1
1999	23.7	20.1	20.6	25.0	21.8	27.9	20.0	21.3	29.5	67.8
2000	24.2	23.1	24.3	31.9	23.2	27.6	15.4	20.3	29.7	80.4
2001	21.0	21.1	19.3	22.4	19.1	22.1	12.3	19.9	25.3	49.7
2002	19.9	18.2	18.0	16.6	15.1	16.1	11.2	20.7	27.8	40.8
2003	14.9	10.3	11.8	16.9	13.0	13.2	8.8	NA	NA	NA

NA = Not available.

While there is no obligation to do so, P/E is based on estimated earnings for the current year. However, forward earnings are also considered; for example, $N + 1$ expresses the current market value of the stock vs. estimated earnings for the following year. For fast-growing companies or companies that are currently losing money, P/E_{N+1} or P/E_{N+2} are sometimes used, either to give a more representative figure (and thus to avoid scaring the investor!) or because, in the case of loss-making companies, it is impossible to calculate P/E for year N.

The widespread use of P/E (which is implicitly assumed to be constant over time!) to determine equity value has given rise to the myth of *EPS* as a financial criterium to assess a company's financial strategy. Such or such decision might or might not be taken on the basis of its positive or negative impact on *EPS*. This is why P/E is so important, but it also has its limits, as we will demonstrate (see Chapter 40).

P/E is conceptually similar to the $NOPAT$[7] multiple. The latter is the division of enterprise value by after-tax operating profit, while P/E is the division of equity market value by net profit.

Hence, many of the things we have said about the $NOPAT$ multiple also apply to P/E:

7 *Net Operating Profit After Tax.*

- Another way of understanding P/E is to note that it expresses market value on the basis of the number of years of earnings that are being bought. Thus an equity value of 100, with earnings of 12.5 is valued at eight times these earnings. The P/E is thus 8. This means that, if *EPS* remains constant, the investor will have to wait 8 years to recover his investment, while ignoring the residual value of the investment after 8 years, while omitting the discount and while assuming that the investor receives all of the *EPS*. If the *EPS* rises (falls), the investor will have to wait less (more) than 8 years.

- In an efficient market, the greater EPS growth is, the higher the *P/E*, and vice versa.
- *P/E* is inversely proportional to interest rates: all other factors being equal, the higher the interest rates the lower the *P/Es* and vice versa, again assuming efficient markets:

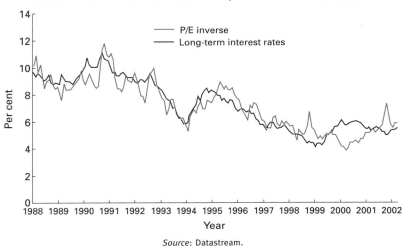

INTEREST RATES AND INVERSE OF P/E FOR THE EURO MARKET

Source: Datastream.

The looser correlation seen in 2000 is due to the speculative bubble on Internet, tech and media stocks.

- the greater the perceived risk, the lower the *P/E*, and vice versa.

P/E is used in the same way as the *NOPAT* multiple. To value a company, it is useful to set it alongside other companies as comparable as possible in terms of activity, growth prospects and risk, and then apply their *P/E* to it.

P/E reflects a risk that the *NOPAT* multiple does not, that of financial structure, which comes on top of the risk presented by the operating assets.

P/E can only be used for valuation purposes if the comparable companies have the same *EPS* growth and the same risks on both the operating and financial levels.

2/P/E AND INVESTORS' REQUIRED RATE OF RETURN

Inverse *P/E*, also called earnings yield, is often mistakenly used in approximating investors' required rates of return. This should only be done in those very rare cases where earnings growth is nil and the company pays out 100% of its earnings. Here is our reasoning:

$$P = \frac{DPS}{k_E} = \frac{EPS}{k_E}$$

Then:

$$\frac{P}{E} = \frac{P}{EPS} = \frac{1}{k_E} \qquad \text{and, thus,} \qquad \frac{1}{\frac{P}{E}} = k_E$$

In most cases, companies are growing, and the inverse P/E is below the required rate of return. Using the inverse P/E to approximate required rate of return would seriously underestimate the latter – a big mistake.

The P/E of a company with an EPS of 12 that is trading at 240 would then be:

$$\frac{240}{12} = 20$$

The inverse P/E is just 5%, whereas the required return nowadays is probably about 10%.

For a mature company, the inverse P/E is above the shareholders' required rate of return. Using the inverse P/E to approximate required rate of return would overestimate the rate of return – another big mistake.

All in all, the inverse P/E reflects only an immediate accounting return for a new shareholder who has bought the share for V and who has a claim on EPS:

$$\text{Accounting rate of return} = \frac{EPS}{V} = \frac{1}{P/E}$$

- a very low return means that shareholders expect EPS growth to be strong enough to ultimately obtain a return commensurate with their required rate of return;
- a very high rate means that immediate return is uncertain and shareholders expect negative EPS growth to ultimately bring accounting return closer to their required rate of return;
- a normal rate – i.e., in line with the required rate of return means that EPS growth is expected to be nil, and the investment is considered a perpetual annuity.

Section 28.3
KEY MARKET DATA

We are now able to fill in the blanks of the chart on the next page, but the chart will only make sense if you have first assessed the company's strategy and finances.

We have filled in the data for Nestlé, whose ROE (18.21%) surpasses the rate of return required by its shareholders. Hence, equity value (SF128bn) is greater than book value (SF33.7bn), and PBR is greater than 1.

Strong earnings growth and low risk explain why Nestlé's P/E is so high. At 40%, its payout is average, as Nestlé has no difficulty in financing its investments.

At 100%, Nestlé's free float is very high, and the market for the stock is thus liquid and meaningful. So the above comments apply here.

KEY MARKET DATA ON NESTLÉ

In SF

	2000	2001	2002	2003	2004
Adjusted share price					
High	387.5	386.5	389.5	313.5	346.0
Low	254.2	301.5	348.0	237.0	279.8
Average or last	330.5	354.9	389.5	285.6	316.8
Absolute data					
Number of fully diluted shares[8] (m)	386.5	381.4	395.9	404	404
Market capitalisation (bn)	127.7	135.4	195.9	109.6	136.8
Equity, less minority interests (bn)	29.9	33.7	35.4	36.8	39.2
Value of net debt (bn)	7.7	27.8	27.8	13.6	9.6
Multiples					
Fully diluted EPS	14.91	17.25	17.56	15.58	16.05
EPS growth	+22%	+16%	+2%	−11%	+3%
P/E	22.2	20.6	22.2	17.8	21.1
After-tax operating profit (m)	6,935	6,960	7,479	6,000	5,551
Price/Book Ratio (PBR)	4.27	4.02	3.28	2.91	3.35
Dividend					
Dividend Per Share (DPS)	5.5	6.4	7.0	7.0	7.2
DPS growth	+28%	+16%	+9%	+6%	+3%
Payout	37%	37%	40%	45%	46%
Return					
Beta (β)	0.88	0.74	0.65	0.90	0.90
Risk premium: $r_M - r_F$	4.10%	4.45%	3.88%	4.85%	5.23%
Risk-free rate: r_F	3.83%	2.80%	3.38%	2.46%	2.61%
Return on equity (ROE)	19.3%	19.8%	27.34%	22.5%	17.84%
Free float	99%	99%	99%	99%	99%

8 *See Section 28.6.*

Section 28.4
ADJUSTING PER-SHARE DATA FOR TECHNICAL FACTORS

1/REWRITE HISTORY, IF NECESSARY

"Let's not mix apples with oranges." This old saying applies to the adjustment of per-share data after the detachment of rights and for free share awards and rights issues, which, **from a technical point of view**, can modify the value of a stock.

Studying past share prices only makes sense if they are comparable – that is, if they have been adjusted for variations that are due solely to technical factors. Prices prior to the detachment of a right are adjusted by multiplying them by what is called the "adjustment coefficient".

(a) Free share awards

Suppose a company decides to double its equity by incorporating its reserves, and issues one new share for each existing share. Each shareholder is then the owner of twice as many shares without having paid in additional funds and with no change to the company's financial structure. The unit value of the shares has simply been divided into two.

Naturally, the company's equity value will not change, as two shares will be equal to one previously existing share. However, the share price before and after the operation will have to be adjusted to obtain a comparable series.

In this case, simply divide the shares existing after the free share award by 2. The adjustment coefficient is $\frac{1}{2}$.

More generally, if N' new shares are issued for N already existing shares, the adjustment coefficient is as follows:

$$\frac{N}{N + N'}$$

(b) A rights issue with an exercise price below the current share price

This is the second reason we might have to adjust past per-share data. We will go into further detail in Chapter 31, which deals with share offerings.

To subscribe the new shares, investors must first buy one or more rights detached from previously existing shares and whose price is theoretically such that it doesn't matter whether investors buy previous existing shares or use the rights to buy new ones. The detachment of the right from the existing shares makes an adjustment necessary.

For a rights issue (in which the company is raising additional funds instead of simply incorporating its reserves, as in the example above), the adjustment coefficient is:

$$\frac{\text{Share price after detachment}}{\text{Share price before detachment}} = \frac{\text{Share price after detachment} - \text{Rights}}{\text{Share price before detachment}}$$

If P is the price of the already-existing share, K the issue price of the new shares, N' the number of new shares and N the number of already existing shares, the adjustment coefficient will be equal to:

$$\frac{N \times P + N' \times K}{(N' + N) \times P}$$

More generally, the adjustment coefficient is equal to the price after detachment of the right (either the right to receive a free share or the right to buy a new one) divided by the price before detachment of the right. Henceforth, we will assume all prices to have been adjusted.

To make the adjustment, simply multiply all the share data (e.g., price, EPS, DPS) before the detachment by this coefficient.

As you have seen, the adjustment consists in rewriting past stock performance to make it comparable with today and tomorrow, and not the reverse.

2/THE IMPACT OF FUTURE TRANSACTIONS

When equity-linked securities (convertible bonds, mandatory convertibles, bonds with warrants attached, stock options, etc.) have been issued, financial managers must factor these potential new shares into their per-share data. Here again, we must adjust to obtain an average number of outstanding shares.

As there is at least potential dilution, we have to assume full conversion in calculating the per-share data on a **fully diluted basis**. This is easy to do for Convertible Bonds (CBs). Simply assume that the CBs have been converted. This increases the number of shares but lowers financing costs as interest is no longer paid on the CBs.

For warrants, two methods can be used. The **first method**, called the "**investment of funds method**", assumes that all investors will exercise their warrants and that the company will place the proceeds in a financial investment.

Take the following example. Let's assume two companies, A and B, which are in the same sector, offer the same prospects on revenue and earnings, and have the same equity value and financial structure.

In euros	Company A	Company B
Number of shares	1,000,000	1,000,000
Share price	2,000	2,000
Equity value	2,000,000,000	2,000,000,000
Net profit	100,000,000	100,000,000
EPS	100	100

On 1 September 2004, company A decides to issue 100,000 bonds with warrants attached at a €1,000 nominal value and 2% nominal interest rate, maturing on 1 September 2008, with the warrants being exercisable from 1 January 2005 to 1 January 2007 at one share at €2,400 for each warrant. The issue's first purpose

is to refinance existing debt, whose pre-tax cost is 5%. Annual after-tax savings in financing costs (at 34.43%) until the bond matures will be:

$$(5\% - 2\%) \times 100{,}000 \times 1{,}000 \times (1 - 34.43\%) = €\,1{,}967{,}100$$

Hence:

In euros	Company A	Company B
Net profit	101,967,100	100,000,000
EPS	102.0	100

The reader shouldn't be too impressed by this improvement in *EPS* because it means that 100,000 new shares could be issued from 2005 to 2007. This is an additional risk for company *A* shareholders. Let's assume that all the warrants are exercised at once and that the proceeds are invested at 3% after taxes[9] pending use in the company's industrial projects. Fully diluted *EPS* would be as follows:

$$EPS = \frac{100{,}000 \times 2{,}400 \times 3\% + 101{,}967{,}100}{1{,}000{,}000 + 100{,}000} = €\,99.24$$

9 Depending on the case, we can assume either the company's average rate on short-term investment or the weighted average cost of capital.

Comparing *A* and *B*, we obtain:

In euros	Company A	Company B
Net profit	109,167,100	100,000,000
EPS	99.24	100

The commonly used **second method**, called the **treasury method**, consists in assuming that investors will exercise their warrants but that the company does not invest the proceeds, but uses them, rather, to buy back some of its shares on the market. The company thus offsets some of the dilution caused by the exercise of the warrants. This is the method recommended by the IASB.[10]

10 International Accounting Standards Board.

Let's go back to that last example and use this method. The apparent savings in financing costs is obviously the same, and we apparently end up with net profit of €101,967,100 and an *EPS* of €101.9.

100,000 new shares will be issued at first. The exercise of the warrants raises the following sum for the company:

$$100{,}000 \times €\,2{,}400 = €\,240{,}000{,}000$$

The company could use this sum to buy back 120,000 of its own shares at a price of €2,000 (at the moment when the warrants are exercised, and at a different price afterwards).

Fully diluted *EPS* would then be:

$$EPS = 101{,}967{,}100 / (1{,}000{,}000 + 100{,}000 - 120{,}000) = €\,104.05$$

As can be seen, the two methods produce different results. In our example, the first method produces dilution, while the second produces accretion.

The treasury method can be considered to be the closest to the financial markets, as the main figure it uses is the company's share price. However, the treasury method assumes that the best investment for a company is to buy back its own shares.

Share analysis is centred on changes in stock market prices, multiples (especially P/E), dividends and returns, compared with required returns.

Dividends are analysed by looking at returns (dividend on the share price) and the payout ratio (dividend on net profit).

The P/E (Price/Earnings ratio) is the ratio of the value of the share to EPS (Earnings Per Share). Changes in P/E follow future EPS growth and move in the opposite direction to interest rates and risk (financial and operational).

It is only when the company pays out all of its profits and when financial and industrial markets are in equilibrium that inverse P/E (also called earnings yield) is equal to shareholders' required rates of return. Generally, the inverse P/E criteria results in an underestimation of shareholders' required rates of return.

We'll be looking at P/E, which is more of a valuation instrument than an instrument used in financial policy, in greater detail in the following chapters.

SUMMARY

download

1/ Why is adjustment necessary?

2/ Define growth stock and yield stock.

3/ What are the growth prospects for a company that pays out all of its profits?

4/ Does a "high" P/E necessarily mean that the company is experiencing high growth?

5/ What assumptions must be made for inverse P/E to provide an approximate estimate of required rate of return?

6/ Will a change in required rate of return have a greater impact on a company that pays out 75% of its profits than a company that has a payout ratio of 5%, but which should increase to 75% in 25 years?

7/ Will a share with a higher than average required rate of return for the same risk be undervalued or overvalued?

8/ What is dividend growth that is higher per share than for the total amount of dividends paid out a sign of? What is dividend growth that is higher for the total amount of dividends paid out than the payout per share a sign of? What are your conclusions?

9/ Is a company's earnings growth the most important criterium defining a growth stock?

10/ What does a PBR that is much higher than 1 mean?

QUESTIONS

quiz

1/ You buy a stock which has the following features:

- o   price: €500;
- o   EPS: €33.3;
- o   payout ratio: 25%;
- o   projected EPS growth: 15%.

What will EPS have to be equal to in year 3 for you to get a 12% return on your investment? What will the share be worth then?

EXERCISES

2/ What is your view of the following companies?

Company	Share price	EPS (€)			Payout	Yield	EPS growth 2000–2003	BV/S	P/R 2002	β
		2001	2002	2003						
Danone	147	5.52	5.99	6.39	56%	2.1%	24%	57.4	24.5	0.5
M6	27.25	0.81	0.75	0.95	72%	2.1%	20%	2.5	36.3	1.5
Thyssen-Krupp	16.79	1.29	0.34	1.35	39%	3.0%	32%	26.2	49.4	1.0

The risk-free rate is 5.3%. The market premium is 3.9%.

3/ For each of the following shares, provide an approximation of the missing figure (?) and then give your view of each share:

	Share A	Share B	Share C	Share D
P/E	10	25	7	50
Payout ratio d	95	20	20	?
Annual EPS growth after 5 years: g	?	30%	5%	30%
Long-term debt/Shareholders' equity	0.15	0.20	0.25	8
r_E	10	30	?	90%
PBR	1	?	0.4	45

ANSWERS

Questions

1/ *Because a share is no longer the same after a right has been detached.*
2/ *Growth stock: a stock which does not pay out much but is likely to in the future (high expectations of capital gains). Yield stock: stock that pays out a high dividend given the lack of investment opportunities (low expectations of capital gains).*
3/ *Zero, unless there is an improvement in productivity or an upturn in the economy.*
4/ *Generally, yes, but not if the company is experiencing problems (drop in profits, anticipated restructuring).*
5/ *That the company will pay out all of its profits in dividends, that profits will be constant and that the markets will be in equilibrium.*
6/ *No, on the contrary, the latter will be more sensitive as a result of the long period that will elapse before any inflows are received.*
7/ *Undervalued.*
8/ *Capital reductions. Capital increases.*
9/ *Yes, along with the rate of return on shareholders' equity.*
10/ *That the rate of return on shareholders' equity is much higher than that required by shareholders.*

Exercises

1/ $P/E = 13.1 V = €665$.

2/ Danone is a company with average growth and a low risk. Accordingly, its P/E is higher than the market average. Return on shareholders' equity (10%) is higher than the required rate (7.2%), which explains why its PBR (2.6), is higher than 1. M6 is growing briskly with a high PBR (11!). The company is very profitable (30%) and pays out a large amount of its profits. Thyssen-Krupp has a very cyclical activity and is in a turnaround phase, but returns on shareholders' equity fall below the rate required by shareholders (PBR of 0.68). The company has continued to pay a dividend, even in years when profits fell sharply.

3/ The g of A is very low at around 100%. PBR of $B = P/E \times r_{SE} = 7.5$. r_{SE} of $C = PBR/P/E = 5.7\%$. The d of D: probably very low, given the amount of debt and the very high growth rate. A is very close to returning a profit, without growing. B is growing briskly with excellent returns. The returns achieved by C will not meet the requirements of its shareholders and will have to pay out much more (see Chapter 44). D's returns on shareholders' equity are exceptional, which is explained by a very high leverage effect.

For institutional aspects regarding stock markets see the www.fibv.com website, where the reader can find the links of the stock exchanges belonging to the International Federation of Stock Exchanges.

BIBLIOGRAPHY

Chapter 29
OPTIONS

Or, how to pay for being frightened!

In the previous chapters, we saw that when calculating net present value the required rate of return includes a risk premium that is added to the time value of money. The study of options is useful from a purely financial point of view, as it highlights the notion of remuneration of risk.

True, options are more complex than shares or bonds. Moreover, in their daily use they have more to do with financial management than finance. However, we will see that many financial assets (contingency value rights, warrants and stock options) can be analysed as options or as the combination of an option and a less risky asset.[1]

Why do we place a chapter on options here, right in the middle of the financial securities a company can use to finance itself?

- Some securities are de facto financial options. For example, we will show that a warrant can be compared with a call option.
- Some securities have embedded options – i.e., options *incorporated* in the main contract. As we will see in Chapter 30, a convertible bond can be seen as a combination of a conventional bond and an option.
- Some securities can be usefully interpreted with the options framework. For example, equity capital can be conceptually analysed as a call option on the value of the firm, while a long-term loan is the sum of several short-term debts and an option on future trends in the yield curve.

We will also examine how options theory can be applied to major financial strategy decisions within a company.

Options are an effective tool of analysis whose applications are limited only by financial managers' imaginations.

This is why we have included them in our discussion of the basic concepts of finance.

The purpose of this chapter is not to make you a wizard in manipulating options or to teach you the techniques of speculation or hedging on options, but merely to show you how they work in practice.

Section 29.1
DEFINITION AND THEORETICAL FOUNDATION OF OPTIONS

An option gives you the right to buy or sell an asset at a predetermined price during a predetermined period.

1/SOME BASIC DEFINITIONS

There are **call** (buy) **options** and **put** (sell) **options**. The asset that can thereby be bought or sold is called the underlying asset. This can be either a financial asset (stock, bond, Treasury bond, forward contract, currency, stock index, etc.) or a physical one (a raw material or mining asset, for example).

The price at which the underlying asset can be bought or sold is called the **strike price**. The holder of an option may exercise it (i.e., buy the underlying asset if he holds a call option or sell it if he holds a put option) either at a given date (**exercise date**) during a period called the **exercise period**.

A distinction is made between "**US-style options**" (the holder can exercise his right at any moment during the exercise period) and "**European-style options**" (the holder can only exercise his right on a given date, called the exercise date). Most listed options are "US-style" options, and they are found on both sides of the Atlantic, whereas most over-the-counter options are "European-style".

Call options are, legally speaking, a promise to sell made by the seller of the call option to the buyer of the call option.

Two examples:

Let's say Peter sells Helmut a call option on the insurance company Allianz having an €85 strike price and maturing in 9 months. For 9 months (US-style option) or after 9 months (European-style option), Helmut will have the right to buy one Allianz share at a price of €85, regardless of Allianz's share price at that moment. Helmut is not required to buy a share of Allianz from Peter but, if Helmut wants to, Peter must sell him one for €85.

Obviously, Helmut will exercise his option only if Allianz's share price is above €85. Otherwise, if Helmut wants to buy an Allianz share, he will simply buy it on the market for less than €85.

Now let's say that Paul buys from Clara put options on $1m in currency at an exchange rate of €1.1/$, exercisable 6 months from now. Paul may, in 6 months' time (if it's a European-style option) sell $1m to Clara at €1.1/$, regardless of the dollar's exchange rate at that moment. Paul is not required to sell dollars to Clara but, if he wants to, Clara must buy them from him at the agreed-upon price.

Obviously, Paul will only exercise his option if the dollar is trading below €1.1.

Put options are, legally speaking, a promise to buy made by the seller of the put option to the buyer of the put option.

The above examples highlight the fundamentally asymmetric character of an option. An option contract does not grant the same rights or obligations to each side. **The buyer of any option has the right but not the obligation, whereas the seller of any option is obliged to follow through if the buyer requests.**

The value at which an option is bought or sold is sometimes called the **premium**. It is obviously paid by the buyer to the seller, who thereby obtains some financial compensation for a situation in which he has all the obligations and no rights. Hence, a more precise definition of an option:

An option is a contract between two sides, under which one side gives the other side the right (but not the obligation) to buy from him (a call option) or to sell to him (a put option) an asset, in exchange for the payment of a premium.

This asset will be bought (or sold) at a predetermined price called the strike price, during a period of time (the exercise period for US-style options), or at a precise date (the exercise date for European-style options).

When the option matures, we can diagram the payouts for the buyer and the seller of the call option in the following way:

CALL OPTION

At maturity, if Allianz is trading at €90, Helmut will exercise his option, buy his Allianz share at €85 and sell it again, if he wishes, and make €5 in profit (minus the premium he paid for the option).

Similarly, for the put option:

PUT OPTION

This diagram highlights the **asymmetry of risk** involved: the buyer of the option risks only the premium, while his profit is almost unlimited, while the seller's gain is limited, but his loss is potentially unlimited.

2/THE THEORETICAL BASIS OF OPTIONS

In a risk-free environment, where it was possible to know today with certainty what will happen tomorrow, options would not exist, as they would be completely unnecessary.

For if the future is known with certainty there would be no risk and all financial assets would bring in the same return – i.e., the risk-free rate. What purpose would an option have – i.e., the right to buy or sell – if we already knew what the price will be at maturity? What purpose would a call option on Siemens serve, at a strike price of €170, if we already knew that Siemens' share price will be below €160 at maturity and that the option will therefore not be exercised? And if we knew that, at maturity, Siemens' share price would be €250, the price of the option would be such that it would offer the risk-free rate, just like Siemens' shares, since the future would be known with certainty.

Options would not exist if the future were known with certainty.

In a risky environment, options remunerate the risk of an uncertain future.

The basis of an option is therefore the remuneration of risk.

Options might therefore be called pure financial products, as they are merely remuneration of risk. There is no other basis to the value of an option.

More generally, all risk premiums are a sort of option.

Section 29.2
MECHANISMS USED IN PRICING OPTIONS

Let's suppose that Felipe buys a call option on Solvay at a €50 strike price maturing in 9 months and, simultaneously, sells a put option on the same stock at a €50 strike maturing in 9 months. Assume the funds paid for the call option are largely offset by the funds received for the sale of the put option. What will happen at maturity?

If Solvay is trading at above €50, Felipe will exercise his call option and pay €50. The put option will not be exercised, as his counterparty will prefer to sell Solvay at the market price.

If Solvay is trading below €50, Felipe will not exercise his call option, but the put option that he sold will be exercised and Felipe will have to buy Solvay at €50.

Hence, regardless of the price of the underlying asset, buying a call option and selling a put option on the same underlying asset, at the same maturity and at the same strike price, is the same thing as a forward purchase of the underlying asset at maturity at the strike price.

In other words:

Buying a call option and selling a put option is a forward purchase of the underlying asset, or a put–call parity.

Assuming fairly valued markets, we can thus deduce that at the maturity of the exercise period:

Value at maturity of a call option − Value at maturity of a put option

= Value at maturity of the underlying asset − Strike price

It looks like this on a chart:

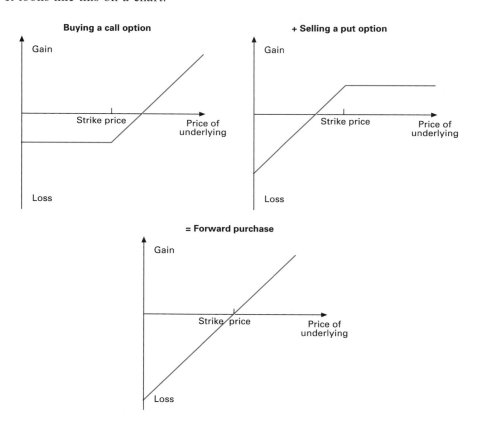

We can see that the profit (or loss) of this combination is indeed equal to the difference between the price of the underlying asset at maturity and the strike price.

Let's now consider the following transaction: Eugueni wants to buy Solvay stock, but does not have the funds necessary at his immediate disposal. However, he will be receiving €50 in 9 months, enough to make the purchase. He can thus borrow the present value of €50, 9 months out, and buy Solvay.

At maturity, the profit (or loss) on this transaction will thus be equal to the difference between the value of the Solvay shares and the repayment of the €50 loan.

So we are back to the previous case and can thus affirm that in value terms:

Buying a call option and selling a put option on the same underlying asset, at the same strike price and at the same maturity, is like buying the underlying asset by borrowing the present value of the strike price, as long as the two options are European-style options and as long as there is no dividend payout in the interim.

We have used a stock for the underlying asset, but the above statement applies to any underlying asset (currencies, bonds, raw materials, etc.).

We can express this in eight different ways, which are all equivalent:

1 Buying a call option and selling a put option is like buying the underlying asset and borrowing at the risk-free rate.
2 Buying a call option and selling the underlying asset is like buying a put option and borrowing at the risk-free rate.
3 Buying a call option and investing in a risk-free asset is like buying the underlying asset and buying the put option.
4 Buying a put option and selling a call option is like investing in a risk-free asset and selling the underlying asset.
5 Buying a put option and buying the underlying asset is like buying a call option and investing in a risk-free asset, and we are back to Item 3 in our list.
6 Buying a put option and borrowing at the risk-free rate is like buying a call option and selling the underlying asset, and we are back to Item 2 in our list.

Also:

7 Buying a put option is like buying a call option and selling the underlying asset and investing in a risk-free asset.
8 Buying a call option is like buying a put option and buying the underlying asset and borrowing at the risk-free rate.

Items 7 and 8 show that we can "manufacture" a synthetic call option based on a put option and vice versa.

When we have three investment opportunities on an underlying asset, we can always recreate the fourth, as long as we can borrow and invest in the risk-free asset!

Section 29.3
ANALYSING OPTIONS

1/INTRINSIC VALUE

Intrinsic value is the difference (if it is positive) between the price of the underlying asset and the option's strike price. For a put option, it's the opposite. In the rest of this chapter, unless otherwise mentioned, we will use call options as examples.

By definition, intrinsic value is never negative.

Let's take a call option on sterling, with a strike price of €1.5/£ and maturing in end-December. Let's say that it is now June and that the pound is trading at €1.6.

What is the option's value? The holder of the option may buy a pound for €1.5, while the pound is currently at €1.6.

This immediate possible gain is none other than the option's intrinsic value, which will be billed by the seller of the option to the buyer. The option will be worth at least €0.1.

Technically, a call option is said to be:

- **out-of-the-money** when the price of the underlying asset is below the strike price (zero intrinsic value);
- **at-the-money** when the price of the underlying asset is equal to the strike price (zero intrinsic value);
- **in-the-money** when the price of the underlying asset is above the strike price (positive intrinsic value).

2/TIME VALUE

Now let's imagine that sterling is trading at €1.4 in October. The option would be out-of-the-money (€1.4 is less than the €1.5 strike price) and the holder would not exercise it. Does this mean that the option is worthless? No, because there is still a chance, however slight, that sterling will move over €1.5 by the end of December. This would make the option worth exercising. So the option has some value, even though it is not worth exercising right now. This is called **time value**.

For an in-the-money option – i.e., whose strike price (€1.5) is below the value of the underlying asset (let's now assume that £1 = €1.7), intrinsic value is €0.2. But this intrinsic value is not all of the option's value. Indeed, we have to add time value, which ultimately is just the anticipation that intrinsic value will be higher than it is currently. For there is always a probability that the price of the underlying asset will rise, thus making it more worthwhile to wait to exercise the option.

The anticipation of an even greater intrinsic value is called the time value of an option.

In more concrete terms, time value represents "everything that could happen" from now until the option matures.

Hence:

$$\text{An option's value} = \text{Intrinsic value} + \text{Time value}^2$$

2 *The reader might remark that there is always a probability that the price of the underlying asset may decrease and that the time value could be negative as well. This cannot happen for it would imply that the option price may be lower than its intrinsic price which, as we have seen above, is impossible.*

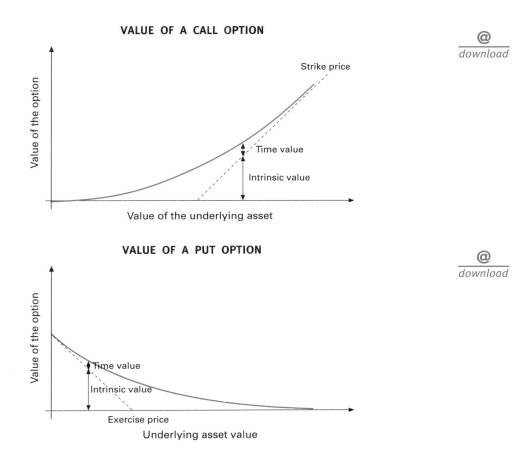

VALUE OF A CALL OPTION

VALUE OF A PUT OPTION

Time value diminishes with the passage of time, as the closer we get to the maturity date, the less likely that the price of the underlying asset will exceed the strike price by that date. Time value vanishes on the date the option expires.

This means that an option is worth at least its intrinsic value. But is there an upper limit on the option's value?

In our example, the value **at maturity** of the call option on sterling is as follows:

- If sterling is trading above €1.5, the option is worth the current price of sterling less €1.5 – i.e., its intrinsic value – which is below the value of the underlying asset.
- If sterling is below or equal to €1.5, the option will be worthless (i.e., no intrinsic value) and, thus, even further below the price of the underlying asset.

This means that if the option's value is equal to the price of the underlying asset, all operators will sell the option to buy the underlying asset, as their gain will be greater in any case.

The value of a call option is always above its intrinsic value, as it possesses time value, but it is always below the value of the underlying asset.

There are six criteria in determining the value of an option. We have already discussed one of them, the price of the underlying asset. The other five are:

- the strike price;
- the volatility of the underlying asset;
- the option's maturity;
- the risk-free rate;
- the dividend or coupon, if the underlying asset pays one out.

1/STRIKE PRICE

Assuming the same value of the underlying asset, the higher the strike price, the lower the value of a call option.

Hence, and again assuming the same value for the underlying asset, the higher the strike price, the greater the value of a put option.

This is just common sense: the higher a call option's strike price, the less chance the price of the underlying asset will exceed it. It is thus normal that the value of this call option is lower. However, the price of the put option will rise, as the underlying asset can be sold at a higher price.

The value of a call option (*call*) is inversely proportional to the strike price.

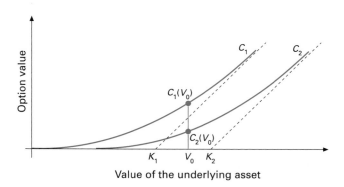

2/VOLATILITY IN THE VALUE OF THE UNDERLYING ASSET

The value of both a call and a put option rises with the volatility in the value of the underlying asset.

Here again, this is easy to understand: the more volatile the underlying asset, the more likely it is to rise and fall sharply. In the first case, the return will be greater for the holder of a call option; in the second, it will be greater for the holder of a put option. As an option is nothing more than pure remuneration of risk, the greater that risk is, the greater the remuneration must be, and thus the option's value.

Time value rises with the volatility of assets.

3/THE TIME TO MATURITY

The further away maturity is, the greater the value of both a call and a put option.

You can easily see that the further away maturity is, the greater the likelihood of fluctuations in the price of the underlying asset. This raises the option's value.

The further away maturity is, the greater time value is.

4/THE RISK-FREE RATE

We have seen that the passage of time has a cost: the risk-free rate. The further away the maturity date on an option, the further away the payment of that cost. The holder of a call (put) option will thus have a cash advantage (disadvantage) that depends on the level of the risk-free rate.

The value of a call option increases with the risk-free rate, while the value of a put option is an inverse function of the risk-free rate.

The buyer of the call option pays the premium, but pays the strike price only when exercising the option. Everything happens as if he was buying on credit until "delivery". The amount borrowed is in fact the present value of the strike price discounted at the risk-free rate, as we have seen previously.

Interest rates have much less influence on the value of an option than the five other factors.

5/DIVIDENDS OR COUPONS

When the underlying asset is a stock or bond, the payment of a dividend or coupon lowers the value of the underlying asset and, thus, lowers the value of a call option and raises the value of a put option. This is why some investors prefer to exercise their calls (on US-style options) before the payment of the dividend or coupon.

Section 29.5
METHODS FOR PRICING OPTIONS

1/REASONING IN TERMS OF ARBITRAGE (BINOMIAL METHOD)

To model the value of an option, we cannot use traditional discounting of future cash flow at the required rate of return as we have for other financial securities, because of the risk involved. For cash flow depends on whether or not the option will be exercised and the risk varies constantly. Hence, the further the option is into the money, the higher its intrinsic value and the less risky it is.

Cox et al. (1979) thus had the idea of using arbitrage logic in comparing the profit generated with options, *compared taking a direct position on the underlying asset.*

Let's take the example of a call option with a €105 strike price on a given stock (currently trading at €100) and for a given maturity.

Let's also assume that there are only two possibilities at the end of this period: either the stock is at €90, or it is at €110. At maturity, our option will be worth its intrinsic value – i.e., either €0 or €5, or €0 or €20 for the four options.

We can try to obtain the same result (€0 or €20) in the same conditions using another combination of securities (a so-called **replicating portfolio**). If we achieve this result, the four call options and this other combination of securities should have the same value. If we can determine the value of this other combination of securities, we will have succeeded in valuing the call option.

To do so, let's say you borrow (at 5%, for example) a sum whose value (principal and interest) will be €90 at the end of the period concerned, and then buy a share for €100 today.

At the end of the period:

- either the share is worth €110, in which case the combination of buying the share and borrowing money is worth €110 − €90 = €20;
- or the share is worth €90, in which case the replicating portfolio is worth 90 − 90 = 0.

Since the two combinations – the purchase of four call options, on the one hand, and borrowing funds and buying the share directly, on the other – produce the same cash flows, regardless of what happens to the share price, their values are identical. Otherwise, arbitrage traders would quickly intervene to re-establish the balance. So what is the original value of this combination? Let's look at it this way:

Purchase of a share: €100
−   Borrowing of a sum that at maturity would be worth €90, hence, at 5%, 90/1.05
=   85.7
=   Value: €14.3

€14.3 corresponds also to the value of the four call options. We thus deduce that the call option at a €105 strike is worth €3.58. We have valued the option using arbitrage theory.

"Delta" is the number of shares that must be bought to duplicate an option. In our example, four calls produce a profit equivalent to the purchase of one share. The option's delta is therefore 1/4, or 0.25.

More generally, delta is defined as the ratio between the variation in the option's value, and the variation in the price of the underlying asset.

Hence:

$$\delta = \frac{5 - 0}{110 - 90} = 0.25$$

We can therefore conclude that:

Value of a call option
$$= \delta \times (\text{Price of the underlying asset} - \text{PV of capital borrowed})$$

Our example above obviously oversimplifies in assuming that the underlying asset can only have two values at the end of the period. However, now that we have understood the mechanism, we can go ahead and reproduce the model in backing up two periods (and not just one) before the option matures. This is called the binomial method, as there are two possible states at each step. But multiplying the number of periods or subdividing each period into subperiods, we can obtain a very large number of very small subperiods until we have a very large number of values for the stock at the option's maturity date, which is more realistic than the simplified schema that we developed above.

Here is what it looks like graphically:

VALUE OF THE UNDERLYING ASSET
OPTION VALUE

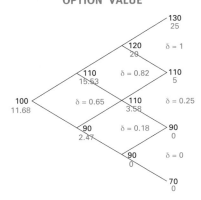

2/The Black and Scholes model

In a now famous article, Fisher Black and Myron Scholes in 1972 presented a model for pricing European-style options that is now used very widely. It is based on the construction of a portfolio composed of the underlying asset and a certain number of options such that the portfolio is insensitive to fluctuations in the price of the underlying asset. It can therefore return only the risk-free rate.

The Black and Scholes model is the continuous time (the period approaches 0) version of the discrete time binomial model. The model calculates the possible prices for the underlying asset at maturity, as well as their respective probabilities of occurrence, based on the fundamental assumption that this is a random variable with a log-normal distribution.

For a call option, the Black and Scholes formula is as follows:

$$\text{Value of the call option} = N(d_1) \times V - N(d_2) \times K \times e^{-T \times r_F}$$

with:

$$d_1 = \frac{\ln\left(\dfrac{V}{K}\right) + \left(r_F + \dfrac{\sigma^2}{2}\right) \times T}{\sigma \times \sqrt{T}} \qquad \text{and} \qquad d_2 = d_1 - \sigma \times \sqrt{T}$$

where V is the current price of the underlying asset, $N(d)$ is a cumulative standard normal distribution (average $= 0$, standard deviation $= 1$), K the option's strike price, e the exponential function, r_F the continual annual risk-free rate, σ the instantaneous standard deviation of the return on the underlying asset, T the time remaining until maturity (in years) and ln the Naperian logarithm.

In practice, the instantaneous return is equal to the difference between the logarithm of the share price today and yesterday's share price:

$$r = \ln V_1 - \ln V_0$$

To cite an example, the value of a European-style 9-month call, with a strike price of €100, while the share price is today at €90, with a 3.2% risk-free rate and a 20% standard deviation of instantaneous return, is €3.3.

Comparing the model equation formula from p. 567, you will see that $N(d_1)$ is the option's delta, while $Ke^{-T \times r_F}$ represents the present value of the strike price. Hence:

$$\text{Call option's value} = V \times \delta - N(d_2) \times \text{Present value of the strike price}$$

The model confirms that the value of a call option:

- rises with the current price of the underlying asset (V);
- falls with the strike price's net present value, which depends on the risk-free rate (r_F) and the time remaining till maturity $\sqrt{T}$;
- rises with volatility σ multiplied by the amount of time remaining till maturity.

The Black and Scholes model was initially designed for European-style stock options. The developers of the model went on the following assumptions:

- no dividend payout throughout the option's life;
- constant volatility in the underlying asset over the life of the option, as well as the interest rate;

- liquidity of the underlying asset so that it can be bought and sold continuously, with no intermediation costs; and
- that market participants behave rationally!

More complex models have been derived from Black and Scholes to surmount these practical constraints. The main ones are those of Garman and Kohlhagen (1983) for currency options and R. Merton (1976), which reflects the impact of the payment of a coupon during the life of a European-style option.

US-style options are more difficult to analyse, and depend on whether the underlying share pays out a dividend or not:

- If the share pays no dividend, the holder of the option has no reason to exercise it before it matures. He will sell his option rather than exercise it, as exercising it will make it lose its time value. In this case, the value of the US-style call option is thus identical to the value of a European-style call option.
- If the share does pay a dividend, the holder of the call may find it worthwhile to exercise his option the day before the dividend is paid. To determine the precise value of such an option, we have to use an iterative method requiring some calculations developed by R. Roll. However, we can simplify for a European-style call option on an underlying share that pays a dividend: the Black and Scholes model is applied to the share price minus the discounted dividend.

The formula for valuing the put option is as follows:

download

$$\text{Value of the put option} = N(-d_1) \times V - N(-d_2) \times K \times e^{-T \times r_F}$$

Value of the put option.

Of the six criteria of an option's value, five are "given" (price of the underlying asset, strike price, maturity date, risk-free rate and, where applicable, the dividend); only one is unknown: volatility.

From a theoretical point of view, volatility would have to be constant for the Black and Scholes model to be applied with no risk of error; i.e., historical volatility (which is observed) and anticipated volatility would have to be equal. In practice, this is rarely the case: market operators adjust upward and downward the historical volatility that they calculated (over 20 days, 1 month, 6 months, etc.) to reflect their anticipations on the future stability or instability of the underlying asset. However, several classes of options (same underlying, but different maturity or strike price) can be listed for the same underlying asset. This allows us to observe the implied volatility of their quoted prices and thus value the options of another class.

This is how anticipated volatility is obtained and is used to value options. This practice is so entrenched that options market traders trade anticipations of volatility directly.

Anticipated "vol" (volatility) is then applied to models to calculate the value of the premium.

The Black and Scholes model can thus be used "backwards"; i.e., by taking the option's market price as a given and then calculating implied volatility. The operator can then price options by tweaking the price on the basis of his own anticipations. He then buys options whose volatility looks too low and sells those whose implied volatility looks too high.

To illustrate, here is the average volatility on European stocks since 1990:

STOCK INDEX VOLATILITY OF MAJOR EUROPEAN MARKETS

Source: Datastream.

It is interesting to note that, despite these simplifying assumptions, the Black and Scholes model has been de facto adopted by market operators, each of them adapting it to the underlying asset concerned.

Section 29.6
TOOLS FOR MANAGING AN OPTIONS POSITION

Managing a portfolio of options (which can also be composed of underlying assets or the risk-free asset) requires some knowledge of four parameters of sensitivity that help us measure precisely the risks assumed and develop speculative, hedging and arbitrage strategies.

1/THE IMPACT OF FLUCTUATIONS IN THE UNDERLYING ASSET: DELTA AND GAMMA

We have already discussed the delta, which measures the sensitivity of an option's value to fluctuations in the value of the underlying asset.

Mathematically, the delta is derived from the option's theoretical value *vis-à-vis* the price of the underlying asset and is thus always between 0 and 1, either positive or negative. Whether it is positive or negative depends on the type of option.

The delta of a call option is positive, since an increase in the price of the underlying asset increases the option's value.

The delta of a put option is negative, since a decrease in the price of the underlying asset lowers the option's value.

We have seen that, when using the Black and Scholes formula, the delta of a call option is equal to $N(d_1)$. The delta of a put option is equal to $N(d_1) - 1$. This index is prized by managers of options portfolios, as it links the option's value and the value of the underlying asset directly. Indeed, we have seen that the delta is above all an underlying equivalent: a delta of 0.25 tells us that a share is equivalent to four options. But managers use the delta above all as an indicator of sensitivity: How much does the option's value vary in euros when the underlying asset varies by €1?

The delta can also express probability of expiration in-the-money: a delta of 0.80 means that there is an 80% probability that the option will expire in-the-money.

Unfortunately, the delta itself varies with fluctuations in the underlying asset and with the passing of time.

The delta of a call option far in-the-money is very close to 1, as any variation in the underlying asset will show up directly in the option's value, which is essentially made up of intrinsic value.

Similarly, a call option that is far out-of-the-money is composed solely of its time value and a variation in the underlying asset has little influence on its value. Its delta is thus close to 0.

The delta of an at-the-money call option is close to 0.5, indicating that the option has as much chance as not of being exercised.

This is expressed in the following table:

	Out-of-the-money	At-the-money	In-the-money
Call option	$0 < \delta < 0.5$	$\delta = 0.5$	$0.5 < \delta < 1$
Put option	$-0.5 < \delta < 0$	$\delta = -0.5$	$-1 < \delta < -0.5$

Hence, the idea of measuring the sensitivity of delta to variations in the value of the underlying asset: **this is what gamma does**. Mathematically, it is none other than a derivative of the delta *vis-à-vis* the underlying asset, and is often called the delta of the delta!

A zero-gamma options position is completely immune against fluctuations in the value of the underlying asset.

2/THE IMPACT OF TIME: THETA

Options are like people: they run down with time. Even if there is no change in the underlying asset price, the passage of time alone shows up in gains or losses for the holder of an option.

Mathematically speaking, the theta is equal to the opposite of the derivative of the theoretical value of the option with respect to time.

3/THE IMPACT OF VOLATILITY: VEGA

The vega can be defined as the rate of change in derivative of the theoretical value of the option *vis-à-vis* implied volatility. Vega is always positive for a call option, as for a put option, as we have seen that the time value of an option is an increasing function of volatility.

All other factors being equal, the closer an option is to being in-the-money (with maximum time value), the greater the impact of an increase in volatility.

While each of the tools presented here is highly useful in and of themselves, combining them tells us even more. In practice, it is impossible to create a position that is neutral on all criteria at once. No return is possible when taking no risk. No pain, no gain! Hence, a delta-neutral position and a gamma-negative position must necessarily have a positive theta to be profitable.

Most operators visualise their positions by drawing up a chart that gives the value of theta for various prices of the underlying asset.

4/MODEL RISK

Options markets, whether organised (listed) or not (over the counter), have developed considerably since the mid-1970s, owing to the needs for hedging (of currency risks, interest rates, share prices, etc.), an appetite for speculation (an option allows its holder to take a position without having to advance big sums) and the increase in arbitrage trading.

In these conditions, a new type of approach to risk has developed on trading floors: model risk. The notion of model risk arose when some researchers noticed that the Black and Scholes model was biased, since it (like many other models) models share prices on the basis of a log-normal distribution. We have seen empirically that this type of distribution significantly minimised the impact of extreme price swings.

Recent studies have shown that the distribution of return has a configuration something like this:

To simplify, we can say that the Black and Scholes model does not reflect the risk of a market crash.

This has given rise to the notion of model risk, as almost all banks use the Black and Scholes model (or a model derived from it). Financial research has uncovered risks that had hitherto been ignored.

An anomaly in the options market highlights the problems of the Black and Scholes model. When we determine the implied volatility of an underlying asset (the only factor not likely to be observed directly) based on the price of various options having the same underlying asset, we can see that we do not find a single figure. Hence, the implied volatility on options far out-of-the-money or far in-the-money is higher than the implied volatility recalculated on the basis of at-the-money options. This phenomenon is called the volatility smile (because when we draw volatility on a chart as a function of strike price, it looks like a smile).

We will see in the following chapters the many applications of options in corporate finance:

* to raise financing (see Chapter 30);
* to resolve conflicts between management and ownership or between ownership and lenders (see Chapter 35);
* to hedge risks and invest (see Chapter 48);
* to choose investments (see Chapter 20);
* to take over a company (see Chapter 42).

This gives you an idea of how important options are.

SUMMARY

download

Options are very useful financial products to analyse complex corporate finance problems. You will soon see that the number of ways in which they can be used continues to grow! This is why this chapter is so important.

An option is a contract between two sides, under which one side gives the other side the right (but not the obligation) to buy from him (a call option) or to sell to him (a put option) an asset, in exchange for the payment of a premium. This asset will be bought (or sold) at a predetermined price called the strike price, during a period of time (the exercise period for US-style options), or at a precise date (the exercise date for European-style options).

The basis of an option is the remuneration of risk. The option cannot exist in a risk-free environment and it thrives on risk.

The value of an option (call or put) can be broken down into an intrinsic value and a time value. Intrinsic value is the difference between the price of the underlying asset and the option's strike price. It can only be zero or positive. Time value is the premium on the intrinsic value, which remunerates passing time.

There are six criteria for determining the value of an option:

* the price of the underlying asset;
* the strike price;
* the volatility of the underlying asset;
* the option's maturity;
* the risk-free rate; and, if applicable,
* the dividend or the coupon if the underlying asset is a share or a bond that pays one or the other during the life of the option.

Models have been developed for valuing options, the main ones being the Black and Scholes model and the binomial model. They have been adapted over time to make them less restrictive and capable of factoring specific features.

Lastly we looked at tools for managing an option's position.

QUESTIONS

quiz

1/ Define a call or put option.

2/ What are the six criteria for determining the value of an option?

3/ What does the delta of an option indicate?

4/ What impact will a rise in volatility have on the value of a call option? And a drop in interest rates? And payment of a dividend? And the extension of the maturity of an option? And an upward revision of the strike price? And on the value of a call option?

5/ Can you set the sale of a call option off against the purchase of a put option on the same underlying asset at the same maturity?

6/ How would this investor find counterparties?

7/ Show how, in the end, the investor always pays too much for the option. Why is this statement absurd?

8/ Of the following four transactions, which carries the most risk:

  ○   purchase of a call option;
  ○   sale of a call option;
  ○   purchase of a put option;
  ○   sale of a put option. Why?

9/ Time value is the anticipation of intrinsic value being stronger than it is now. However, intrinsic value can drop. Why then can time value not be negative?

10/ In concrete terms, what does the difficulty in valuing an option boil down to?

11/ Why are options particularly well suited to arbitrage strategies? And speculation?

12/ Show how the purchase of an option and the sale of another option can protect you against the risk of a drop in the value of the underlying share, without costing you anything if you give up the profit on a possible rise in the value of the underlying asset over a given threshold.

13/ If you hold stock options on the shares in your company, would you be pleased to see the company paying out large dividends? Why?

14/ In your view, what is the main contribution of the Black and Scholes model?

EXERCISES

1/ The Schauspielhaus in Berlin sells tickets 30 minutes before the start of every concert that has been sold out, known as *Nacheinlasskarten*.

Holders of these tickets are entitled to occupy any free seat in the concert hall 30 seconds before the concert starts. Buyers of these tickets wait at the doors giving access to the various categories of seats in the concert hall. Thirty seconds before the concert starts, they are allowed in and can occupy any free seat. If there are no free seats they have to leave the hall and are not allowed to try again for a different category of seat (in any event, the conductor has already raised his baton). If the legitimate ticket holder for the seat arrives before the concert starts, the holder of the *Nacheinlasskart* must give up his/her seat and leave the hall.

What is your view of this type of ticket? Be as specific as possible. Careful! This is a lot more complicated than you probably think it is.

2/ You wish to value a call option on the Atari share (which does not pay dividends) after 6 months with a strike price of €35 and a 6-month duration. You do not know what volatility to factor in. Fortunately, 3-month options are listed at €3 for a strike price of €31. What is the implicit volatility of these options? The interest rate is 3% and the Atari share is trading at €32. What is the value of this first option?

3/ Redo the exercise above, assuming in the first case that the Atari share rises to €40 or falls to €25. What is the impact on the value of the option? What basic feature of the option have you highlighted?

Questions

1/ An option is a promise to buy for a call and to sell for a put.
2/ The strike price, the value of the underlying share, volatility, the interest rate, the maturity of the option and any dividend or coupon.
3/ The hedge ratio and the probability that the option will expire in-the-money.
4/ Rise, fall, fall, rise, fall. Rise, rise, rise, rise, rise.
5/ No. The position obtained in this way would correspond to the sale, on maturity of the option, of the underlying asset.
6/ By going onto the futures market.
7/ See Section 29.1.
8/ Sale of a call option (unlimited losses as the value of the asset is unlimited). The purchase of a put option is also very risky (but the loss is limited to the value of the underlying share minus the strike price).
9/ Because, in this case, the value of the option would be lower than the intrinsic value, resulting automatically in arbitrage (purchase of the option, exercise of the option, sale of the underlying share obtained).
10/ To determining the volatility to be used.
11/ Because, by combining them, you can reconstitute an underlying asset, as a result of their strong leverage effect.
12/ Sale of a call option with a strike price of 120, and using the price obtained on this option to purchase a put option at say 100. You will then be protected against a drop below 100, but will not benefit from a rise above 120.
13/ No, not at all, as this would reduce the value of the stock options.
14/ The method for calculating conditional assets, which enabled the "industrialisation" of options.

Exercises

1/ This is a call option at a zero strike price combined with a put option at a zero strike price, the value of which depends on how many people arrive in time for the concert.
2/ 37.3%, €2.39.

3/ €7.27, €0.42, the risk! Because a 25% rise in the value of the Atari share will lead to a 204% rise in the value of the option and a 22% drop in the value share, it will lead to an 82% fall in the value of the option.

BIBLIOGRAPHY

Read the articles written by the founders of option valuation:

F. Black, M. Scholes, The valuation of option contracts and a test of market efficiency, *Journal of Finance*, **27**, 399–417, May 1972.
F. Black, M. Scholes, The pricing of options and corporate liabilities, *Journal of Political Economy*, **18**, 637–654, May/June 1973.
J. Cox, S. Ross, M. Rubinstein, Option pricing: A simplified approach, *Journal of Financial Economics*, **7**, 229–263, September 1979.
M. Garman, S. Kohlhagen, Foreign currency option values, *Journal of International Money and Finance*, December 1983.
R. Merton, Theory of rational option pricing, *Bell Journal of Economics and Management Services*, **4**, 637–654, Summer 1976.
R. Merton, Options pricing when underlying stock returns are discontinuous, *Journal of Financial Economics*, **3**, 125–144, January/March 1973.
R. Roll, An analytic valuation formula for unprotected American call options on stocks with known dividends, *Journal of Financial Economics*, 251–258, November 1977.

To find out more about options:

J. Cox, M. Rubinstein, *Options Markets*, Prentice Hall, 1985.
S. Figlewski, W. Silber, M. Subrahmanyam, *Financial Options: From Theory to Practice*, Irwin, 1990.
J. Hull, *Options, Futures and Other Derivatives*, 4th edn, Prentice Hall, 2000.

To learn more about the mechanics of option trading:

L. McMillan, *Options as a Strategic Investment*, 4th edn, New York Institute of Finance, 2002.

Chapter 30
HYBRID SECURITIES

A bit of magic, or Houdini in the land of financial assets

In the early 1980s many new types of securities made their first appearance in Europe, products of a fertile imagination that drew on parallels in US and other international financial markets.

Before we begin the study of these different products, we caution the reader to bear in mind the following points.

- Some types of securities, by offering a lower interest rate in exchange for other advantages to the holder, give the impression of lowering the cost of financing to the company. It is an error to think this way. **In markets in equilibrium, all sources of financing have the same cost if one adjusts for the risk borne by the investor.** To know whether a source of financing is cheap or dear, one must consequently look past the apparent cost to the overall valuation of the financing. **Only if securities have been issued at prices higher than market value can one say that the cost of financing is indeed lower.**
- With the exception of products that exactly match a particular market demand, these sophisticated hybrid securities are costly to issue and sell. As such, they are a signal to investors that the company, or its majority shareholder, is having trouble attracting investors, perhaps because it is experiencing other difficulties.
- Agency theory and signalling theory, by emphasising the fundamental asymmetry of information between issuer and investor, are both very useful for explaining the appeal of products of this kind.
- Lastly, it must not be forgotten that corporate finance is not immune to fashion. Investors have a great appetite for novelty, especially if it gives them the feeling of doing high finance!

Hybrid instruments – *essentially bonds with an equity component or "nonordinary" shares* – are found in a multitude of guises. This generic heading encompasses a seemingly endless array of finance instruments, including convertible bonds, mandatory convertibles, reverse convertibles, preferred shares, LYONs.[1] Within each one of these instruments are found a wide range of variations and features. These include reset, negative pledge, screw and forced conversion clauses, as well as stepup coupons, call schedules, call options with soft and hard protection, etc,

The range of possibilities can seem bewildering, but it is this very flexibility that proves a huge attraction for investors, issuers and financial institutions. On the sell

1 *Liquid Yield Option Notes.*

side companies issue these securities and corporate service departments advise on the type of options to include in them. On the buy side, investment managers seek to build portfolios with limited risk exposure using these securities, and hedge funds utilise arbitrage opportunities between the convertible bond and the common share. Sometimes (more often than we may think) investors simply hedge part of the features of these products and turn them back to bonds or shares.

We will look first at products with embedded options (warrants, convertible bonds, mandatory convertibles), then at products that offer a preferential return (preference shares, bonds redeemable in shares, investment certificates) and, lastly, at exchangeable bonds.

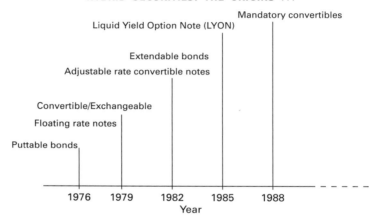

HYBRID SECURITIES: THE ORIGINS ...

Section 30.1
WARRANTS

1/DEFINITION

A **warrant** is a security that allows the holder to subscribe to another newly issued security (share, bond or even another warrant) during a given period, in a proportion and at a price fixed in advance.

Subscription warrants may be attached to an issue of shares or bonds, in which case the issue is said to be one of "shares cum warrants" or "bonds cum warrants". Attached warrants to buy shares may be called an "equity sweetener" or "equity kicker". Warrants can also be issued and distributed to existing shareholders at no charge. Once securities with attached warrants have been issued, the whole is split into its two component parts: the shares or bonds become traditional securities, and the warrants take on a life of their own. **The warrants are traded separately after issue.**

By way of illustration, Lafuma[2] issued shares with attached equity subscription warrants in January 2002. Each warrant in that issue allows the holder to subscribe

2 *Lafuma is a French group specialised in "sports and nature" equipment. It develops three activity divisions: hiking–camping; technical–mountaineering; hunting–fishing–riding.*

to one Lafuma share at €52 until December 2004. In June 2002 the Lafuma warrants were trading at €3.5, whereas Lafuma shares were trading at €50.

As liquidity in the stock and bond markets has increased, financial institutions have taken the opportunity to issue warrants on existing securities independently of the company that issued the underlying shares. These securities are also called **covered warrants** because the issuing institution covers itself by buying the underlying securities on the market.

Warrants ordinarily involve only a transaction between one investor and another and therefore play no direct role in financing a business. There being no limits to the imagination, some players have not hesitated in creating warrants on baskets of existing securities (such as indexes). Thus, a warrant on a basket of different shares gives one the right to acquire during a given period of time a lot consisting of those shares, in proportions and at an overall price fixed in advance.

2/Value

Conceptually, a warrant is similar to a call option sold by a company on shares in issue or to be issued. The exercise price of this option is the price at which the holder of the warrant can acquire the underlying security; the expiry date of the option is the same as the expiry date of the warrant.

A warrant, however, has a few particular characteristics that must be taken into account in its valuation:

➤ It normally has a long life (typically 2–3 years[3]), which increases its time value and makes it more difficult to accept the assumption of constant interest rates used in the Black and Scholes model.

➤ The underlying asset is more likely to pay a periodic return during the time the warrant is held:

○ for an equity warrant, the payment of dividends on the underlying share lowers the value of that share and thereby reduces the value of the warrant. More generally, any transaction that changes the value of the share affects the value of the warrant;

○ for a debt warrant, the price of the underlying bond varies over time, and the closer a bond comes to maturity, the more its market price tends towards its redemption price. Its volatility gradually declines, making the Black–Scholes model, which assumes constant volatility, inapplicable as stated.

➤ Lastly, in the case of subscription warrants, the dilution associated with exercise of the warrants entails a gradual change in the value of the underlying security. When investors exercise warrants, the number of outstanding shares increases, and the issuing firm receives the strike price as a cash inflow. When investors exercise call options, no change in outstanding shares occurs, and the firm receives no cash.[4]

To get round these difficulties, traders use models derived from the binomial and Black–Scholes models, taking into account the fact that the exercise of warrants can create more shares and thus affect the stock price. This is the case with

3 *But perpetual warrants are not unknown.*

4 *Warrants and convertible bonds also affect accounting numbers because of the increase in the number of shares. This causes the firm's net income to be spread over a larger number of shares, thereby decreasing earnings per share. For this reason, firms capitalised with these instruments must report earnings on a primary basis and a fully diluted basis.*

5 *How do we obtain the dilution factor? If the warrants are exercised, equity value will increase by the amount of the exercise money to $E + N_2 K$. So the share price after the warrants exercise will be:*

Share price after exercise =

$$\frac{E + N_2 K}{N_1 + N_2}$$

warrants, management options and convertible bonds. As a general rule, using an unadjusted option-pricing model to value these options will overstate their value.

Fortunately, there is a simple and reasonable solution if we want to continue to use the Black–Scholes formula. We must:

1   value a "traditional" call option similar to those of a warrant;
2   then multiply the call value times an adjustment factor for dilution.

If N_1 represents the number of "old shares" outstanding and N_2 represents the number of new shares issued as a result of the warrant being exercised, then the price of the warrant equals the price of an identical call option, C, multiplied by the dilution factor $N_1/(N_1 + N_2)$:[5]

$$\text{Value of a warrant} = C \times \frac{N_1}{N_1 + N_2}$$

Here is an application to Edison, a key player in the Italian energy sector (and the only Italian company that deals in both the production and sale of electric power and natural gas) as of July 11, 2003.

6 *Volatility has been estimated on daily trading data over the preceding 3 months. There is no rule about how much data to gather, or about the frequency with which returns should be measured. Daily returns probably portray better the current state of the company and the market, but they may be subject to measurement problems if the stock does not trade frequently. Weekly or monthly returns solve the measurement problem, but require 60 observations so that they may no longer reflect the company's current situation. The returns we have used are continuously compounded returns $(\ln(P_t/P_{t+1}))$ because the B–S formula assumes continuous compounding.*

WARRANT EDISON 04/03–12/07

Amount issued:	1,094,831,000
Number of outstanding shares:	4,079,070,000
Current price of the warrant:	€0.390
Date of issue:	April 2003
Date of maturity:	December 2007
Life to final date:	4.46 years
Risk-free rate:	3.05%
Equity price:	€1.134
Strike price:	€1
Volatility (annualised standard deviation):	43.72%[6]

$$C = 1.134 \times (0.771\,916\,36) - 1 \times (2.718^{-(3.34\% \times 4.46)}) \times (0.429\,322\,16) = €0.501$$

$$\text{Dilution factor} = \frac{4,079,070,000}{4,079,070,000 + 1,094,831,000} = 0.788$$

$$\text{Warrant} = €0.501 \times 0.788 = 0.395$$

Agency theory offers an almost "psychological" approach to these hybrid securities. They are seen as a preferred means of resolving conflicts between shareholders, creditors and managers.

At maturity, the value of the warrants will either be the share price minus the exercise price or zero, whichever is higher. Thus, analytically:

$$\text{Warrant value at maturity} = \max\left(\frac{E + N_2 K}{N_1 + N_2} - K, 0\right)$$

$$\text{Warrant value at maturity} = \max\left(\frac{E + N_2 K}{N_1 + N_2} - \frac{(N_1 + N_2)K}{N_1 + N_2}, 0\right)$$

$$\text{Warrant value at maturity} = \max\left(\frac{E + N_2 K - N_1 K - N_2 K}{N_1 + N_2}, 0\right)$$

$$\text{Warrant value at maturity} = \frac{N_1}{N_1 + N_2}\max\left(\frac{E}{N_1} - K, 0\right)$$

Take a bond with an attached equity warrant as an example. A hybrid security of this kind may seem unnatural since it combines a low-risk asset (bond) with a high-risk asset (share). However, there is something in it for each of the parties.

The company's **managers** benefit from the flexibility that warrants provide, since the company can set bounds on the date of the capital increase (by setting the subscription period of the warrant) and the amount of funds that will be raised (by setting the exercise price and the number of warrants per bond at appropriate levels). The amount of funds raised in the form of bonds can be completely different from the amount potentially raised later in the form of shares. Furthermore, the company may be able to have the use of funds from both sources for several years, since the warrants may be exercised before the bonds are paid off.

A company that wants to accomplish the capital increase part of the issue quickly will set an exercise price barely above, or even below, the current value of the share. If it chooses, it can also move up the beginning of the subscription period. If it prefers to bring in a greater amount of funds, it will increase the number of warrants per bond (which must then have a lower yield to maturity if equilibrium is to be maintained) and/or raise the exercise price of the warrants.

Because it entails selling an option, though, the opportunity cost of a warrant can be substantial. Take the case of a company that has sold for €10 the right to buy one share at €100. Suppose that at the time this warrant becomes exercisable, the shares are trading at €210. A straight capital increase without a rights issue at a very slight discount to the share price would bring in, say, €205 per share, whereas exercise of the warrants will bring in €110 per share all told. The opportunity cost is €95 per share.

Lastly, stock market history has shown that exercise of warrants can never be taken for granted. In the euphoria of the speculative bubble, many Internet companies issued warrants with high exercise prices that were never exercised.

The **holders** of bonds with attached equity warrants, if they keep both securities, are both creditors and potential shareholders. As creditors, they benefit from a small but relatively certain yield; as potential shareholders, they have hope of realising a capital gain.

In a context of rising interest rates and falling share prices, however, holders of bonds cum warrants suffer the downside risks of both debt and equity securities instead of combining their advantages.

On the other hand, the holders of the bonds may be different from the holders of the warrants. The bonds may end up with investors preferring a fixed rate security, while the warrants go to investors seeking a more volatile security.

In appearance only, **existing shareholders** retain their proportionate equity stake in the company. The warrant mechanism makes for gradual dilution over time. An issue of bonds with equity warrants allows existing shareholders to maintain their control over the company with a smaller outlay of funds, since they can buy the warrants and resell the bonds. If they do this, the securities they will end up holding will be much riskier overall because the bonds will no longer be there to cushion fluctuations in the value of the warrants.

The dilution problem is postponed but, when the warrants are exercised, they may have risen in value to such an extent that existing shareholders can pay for virtually all of their proportionate share of the capital increase by selling their warrants.

4/PRACTICAL USES

Warrants are increasingly widely used in corporate finance. They are frequently issued in connection with capital increases. They may be distributed free of charge in a number of different situations.

- **A company in difficulty that wants to raise fresh capital.** Before going ahead with a capital increase, the company decides to make a bonus distribution of warrants to existing shareholders. In practice, the shareholders are giving themselves these warrants. They can then speculate more readily on the company's turnaround.
- **When creditors are cancelling debts due to them**, shareholders may give them equity warrants in return. The value of these warrants is virtually nil at the start but, if the company regains its footing, the warrants will rise in value and make up for some or all of the loss on the cancelled debts. A deal of this kind is the way to reconcile the normally divergent interests of creditors and shareholders. In modern finance, this technique replaces the "return to better fortune" clause in loan agreements.
- **In a tender offer** for shares of company *A* in exchange for shares of company *B*, shareholders of *A* may be offered not only shares of *B* but also warrants for shares of *B*.
- **In a Leveraged Buy Out** (LBO, see Chapter 44), warrants may be used to offer an additional reward to holders of mezzanine debt or even to management (another instance of an "equity kicker").

The reader must nevertheless be wary of the fetish of throwing in "free" equity warrants as a miracle remedy to ensure the success of a deal. It must not be forgotten that warrants entail potential dilution and that in finance nothing is ever free!

Section 30.2
CONVERTIBLE BONDS

1/DEFINITION

A **convertible bond** is like a traditional bond except that it also gives the holder the right to exchange it for one or more shares of the issuing company during a conversion period set in advance. A convertible bond is similar to a bond cum warrant. The most important difference is that warrants can be separated into distinct securities and a convertible cannot[7] directly, but investors can hedge part of the product; in practice, the two products are therefore very similar.

This is a financial product of considerable flexibility in use. The interest rate can be fixed, variable, indexed, floating, adjustable or determined in some other way (also under the form of a zero coupon), and any amortisation schedule can be specified for return of principal.

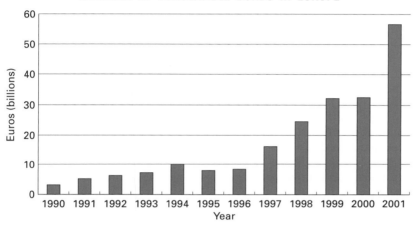

ISSUANCE OF CONVERTIBLE BONDS IN EUROPE

Source: BondWare Capital Data.

As an example, in April 2002 ABB issued a convertible bond with the following characteristics:

ABB APRIL 2002 CONVERTIBLE BOND ISSUE ($968m)	
Issue price:	$1,000
Face value:	$1,000
Issue date:	29 April 2002
Maturity:	16 May 2007
Interest rate:	4.625% ($46.25 coupon)
Redemption price:	$1,000
Conversion ratio:	87.7489 shares for 1 bond
Conversion period:	From 29 April 2002 to 16 May 2007
ABB share price at the time of issue:	SF14.218 ($8.77)

The **conversion period** is specified in the bond indenture or issue contract. It may begin on the issue date or at a later date. It may run to the maturity date, or a decision may be forced if the company calls the bonds before maturity, in which case investors must choose between converting or redeeming them.

The bond may be convertible into one or more shares (87.7489 shares for each bond in our example). This ratio, called the **conversion ratio**,[8] is set at the time of issue. The conversion ratio is adjusted for any capital increases or decreases, mergers, asset distributions or distributions of bonus shares in order to preserve

7 *A convertible preferred stock can be converted into common stocks. The only difference with a convertible bond is that normally it has an infinite maturity.*

The flexibility of convertible bonds explains their great success in Europe.

download

8 *Bond traders also speak of the conversion price of a convertible bond, which is calculated as the ratio of the face value of the bond to the conversion ratio.*

the rights of holders of the convertibles as if they were shareholders at the time of issue.

The **conversion premium** is the amount by which the conversion price exceeds the current market price of the share. The conversion premium is typical. In our ABB example, the conversion premium is 30%.[9] Since ABB offered no redemption premium, ABB shares must rise 30% by the maturity date of the bonds for investors to be willing to convert their bonds into shares rather than redeem them for cash. The calculation is slightly different when a redemption premium is involved.

Some convertible bonds are issued with a **call provision** that allows the issuer to buy them back at a predetermined price. Holders must then choose between redeeming for cash or converting into shares. The indenture may provide for a minimum period of time during which the call provision may not be exercised ("hard noncall" period) and/or set a condition for exercising the call provision, such that the share price has exceeded the conversion price for more than 20 or 30 days ("soft call" provision).

In some cases, the issuer may at conversion provide either newly issued shares or existing shares held in a portfolio – for example, following a share buyback (see Chapter 38).

Convertible bonds must not be confused with the similar-sounding **exchangeable bonds**, which are pure debt securities from the point of view of investors, but not from the investor's.

10 *One complication in determining the value of a convertible bond is the call feature, typical of nearly all convertibles. The issuer retains the right to redeem the bonds early, either to refinance its debt more cheaply or, more commonly, to force early conversion of an in-the-money convertible. If the issuer calls, bondholders can convert to equity or accept the call price. The right to call starts some years after issue and often is allowed only if the underlying share is significantly in-the-money (for example, 30%).*

2/VALUE

The value of a convertible bond during its life is the sum of three components:[10]

1   the value of the straight bond alone is called the **investment value** (or just the **bond value**) of the convertible bond. It is calculated by discounting the future cash flows on the bond at the market interest rate, assuming no conversion;
2   the **conversion value**, which is what the bonds would be worth if they were immediately converted in the stock at current market price;
3   the **option value**. The value of convertible generally exceeds both the straight bond and the conversion value because holders of convertibles have the option to wait and convert later on (time value of the option). The option to take advantage of whichever is greater in the future – the straight bond value or the conversion value – raises the value of the convertible over both the straight bond and the conversion value.

Value of a convertible bond
    = The greater of (Straight bond or Conversion value) + Option value

When the value of the firm is low, the value of the convertible tends to be mostly influenced by the value of the straight debt. The opposite happens when the value of the firm is very high: the value is mostly influenced by the conversion value. Graphically, we have:

VALUE OF A CONVERTIBLE BOND

@
download

The attractiveness of convertible bonds to some investors is given by its "defensive" quality, since the bond value provides a *floor* to the price of the security while giving the opportunity for price appreciation if the underlying stock rises. The bond value thus represents a minimum value: the convertible will never be worth less than this floor value, even if the share price falls significantly. It also cushions the impact of a falling share price on the price of the convertible. Bear in mind, though, that investment value is not a fixed number but one that varies as a function of changes in interest rates.

11 An investment holding company listed on the Main Board of the Kuala Lumpur Stock Exchange, Faber Group Berhad (Faber) has interests in property development, hotels and hospital support services.

EXAMPLE OF A CONVERTIBLE BOND – FABER GROUP[11] ZERO COUPON 10/05

The convertible issued by Faber Group in December 2000 behaved like a bond when first issued, but by the end of August 2002 it had become virtually indistinguishable from the share.

Whenever the share price is well above the redemption value of the convertible, as in the "share" zone of the chart above, the convertible behaves more and more like the share because the probability that it will be converted into shares is very high.

In the "bond" zone, the convertible behaves essentially like a bond because, given the level and trend of the share price, the probability of conversion is low. The price of the convertible is close to its investment value.

In the "hybrid" zone, the value of the convertible reflects the simultaneous influence of both the level of interest rates and the price of the underlying security.

There can also be a high-risk zone for the convertible if the share price has fallen sharply. Grave doubts appear as to the company's ability to repay its debts. The price of the convertible adjusts downward accordingly, until it offers a yield to maturity consistent with the risk of default by the issuer.

3/THEORETICAL ANALYSIS

Unlike a bond with attached equity warrants, a convertible bond is an indivisible product. The straight bond cannot be sold separately from the call option.

For the investor, the convertible bond is often presented as a miracle product, with downside protection by virtue of its debt component and upside potential by virtue of its equity component.

In much the same fashion, the convertible bond is pitched to issuers as the panacea of corporate finance. Initially, it enables the company to issue debt at an interest rate lower than the normal risk-adjusted rate; at a later point, it may enable the company to issue fresh equity at a price higher than the current share price.

No, there are no miracles in finance. At best, one can find mirages, and this is one. If the company is able to issue bonds at an interest rate below its normal cost of debt, it is because it has agreed to issue shares in the future at a price (SF18.48 in our ABB example) *below* the share value at that time – necessarily below, or conversion would not take place. *Current shareholders will therefore be diluted on poor terms for them.*

Similarly, if the investor is getting a call option on the share, it is because in return he accepts a lower rate of return on the bond than the issuer-specific risk would justify, because in return he is getting a call option on the share.

The apparent cost of the convertible bond is low only because its true cost is partly hidden. The company is selling investors call options, which they pay for by accepting a lower interest rate on the bonds than the company could normally obtain given its risk.

The cost of a convertible bond may be calculated in intuitive fashion as a weighted average of the cost of equity and the cost of debt. The weighting corresponds to the probability that the convertible will actually be converted. This probability is not hard to estimate if one assumes that returns on the share are normally distributed.

Equilibrium market theory is not of much help in explaining why convertible bonds, which are no more than a combination of two existing products, should themselves exist. Unsurprisingly, agency theory and signalling theory – together with the "matching hypothesis" – are far more useful in understanding the importance of convertibles.

➤ According to **agency theory**, a convertible bond is a mode of **resolving conflicts between shareholders and creditors**. The temptation of managers of leveraged companies is to undertake risky investments that increase shareholder wealth at the creditors' expense. With this fear in mind, creditors refuse to finance the company except via convertible bonds. Creditors will then have some protection, since the convertible gives them the option of becoming shareholders if there are transfers of value working against them as creditors. A heavily indebted company may have to pass up highly profitable investment projects if it cannot obtain bank financing that would not put too great a strain on its cash flow at the start. With its low apparent interest cost, the convertible bond is an attractive alternative. A convertible bond also helps in **resolving conflicts between shareholder-managers and outside shareholders**. A shareholder-manager of a company with convertible bonds outstanding will hesitate to divert company resources to private use at the expense of other shareholders, since he knows that would increase the probability of having to redeem the convertibles in cash. If the company is already carrying a sufficiently high debt load, redemption could put it in difficulty and threaten the manager's position, so he is deterred from taking such action.

➤ The **"matching" hypothesis** provides another contribution to the explanation of why convertible bonds exist. A young, fast-growing company or one with limited financial resources will avoid taking on too much debt, as its cash flow is likely to be highly variable and its cost of debt, given its short history, likewise high. In these cases, it makes sense to issue securities whose cash flows *match* those of the firm.

➤ A fast-growing company will have little inclination to issue more shares, either because it believes its shares are undervalued or because it **fears sending out a negative signal**. That leaves only convertible bonds. Investors, relieved that the signal associated with a capital increase has not been sent, will welcome an issue of convertibles. This is what the **signalling theory** assumes.

Taken together, these three explanations provide good reasons for issues of convertible bonds by smaller companies that are growing rapidly, are already heavily indebted or have assets that are quite risky. We could also add another explanation, which is commonly known as the **"backdoor equity" hypothesis**. Young, growing firms cannot usually issue debt because of high financial distress costs. At the same time, they may be unwilling to issue equity if current stock prices are too low. Thus, convertible bonds could offer a good compromise solution. Convertible bonds cause expensive dilution, but it occurs when the firm can afford it![12]

The market for convertibles is also supplied by large groups, which use it to raise funds from specialised investors that invest only in convertible bonds. For these large groups, convertibles offer **a way of diversifying the investor base** and raising money in large quantities more easily. Lastly, groups in financial difficulty will resort to issuing convertibles when the equity market is closed to them, as was the case for ABB.

4/TAXATION

The tax treatment of convertible bonds favours the investor since it is the same as for other bonds. As well as this tax advantage, convertibles offer a means of rewarding financial investors when shareholders are unwilling to have the company pay dividends.

With those convertibles (such as a French *Océane*) for which the issuer can provide either new or existing shares, a tax problem may arise when the latter are

12 If a company has many real options it needs the capital in "two stages": the first stage is used to prove that real investment options may be worth pursuing; the second, to exploit effectively the option. Corporations may prefer to use convertible debt because it can be designed in such a way that investors can "exercise" (or be "forced" to exercise through call options) their real options only if they turn out to be valuable, or abandon the conversion option if the real option disappears (thus avoiding the overinvestment problem of companies with high liquidity and no good investment opportunities).

used. The "sale" of shares held on the company's balance sheet is considered a disposition for tax purposes, and the company will owe tax on any capital gain. If the company issues new shares, no tax is owed.

Section 30.3
PREFERENCE SHARES

The securities called **preference shares** (a definition prevailing in the United Kingdom) or **preferred shares** (a definition prevailing in the United States) enjoy economic advantages over ordinary shares, typically in return for a total or partial absence of voting rights.

1/DEFINITION

Preference shares are created on the occasion of a capital increase by decision of the shareholders at an (extraordinary where applicable) general meeting.

The advantages conferred on preference shares may include:

- a claim to a higher proportion of earnings than is paid out on other shares;
- priority in dividend distributions, meaning the dividend on preference shares must be paid before any ordinary dividend is paid on other shares;
- a cumulative dividend, so that if earnings are insufficient to pay the preference dividend in full, the amount not distributed becomes payable from future earnings;
- a firm cannot go in default if it misses paying some dividends;
- rating agencies and financial analysts consider preference shares as a part of equity (thus improving the rating of the company).

At the same time, there are two important disadvantages in issuing preference shares:

- for the issuer – because the dividends are generally not tax-deductible;[13]
- for the investors – because they have limited voting rights.

We should note here that the term "preferred securities", often shortened to just "preferreds", is much broader in scope and may encompass convertible bonds and subordinated debt securities as well as preference shares without voting rights. The reader is advised to look closely at the detailed characteristics of any security called a "preferred" and not to assume that it is necessarily a preference share.

Special features can be added to preference shares to make them more attractive to investors or less risky to issuers:

- **adjustable rate preference share**: the dividend rate is pegged to an index rate, such as a Treasury bill or Treasury bond;
- **participating preference share**: the dividend is divided in a fixed and a variable component. The latter is generally set as a function of earnings.
- **trust preference share**: the dividend on these stocks is tax deductible like interest

13 *This is not always true. In the United States, for example, companies do not have to pay taxes on 70% of the preferred dividends they receive on preference shares investment they have made in other firms. This tax saving might then be "shared" with the issuing company, enabling the company to bring the preferred dividend rate down.*

expenses. Firms issuing this security get the tax shield of debt and keep leverage low (because preference shares are treated like equity by analysts and rating agencies).

2/Value

Valuation of preference shares follows the same principles as valuation of ordinary shares (cf. Chapter 40), but the flow of dividends is greater and more certain.

Let's suppose we want to calculate the value of a *perpetual preferred stock*. The formula is similar to that of a perpetuity (see Chapter 16):

$$V_{\text{preferred}} = \frac{\text{Annual dividend rate}}{\text{Expected dividend yield}}$$

An approach of this kind will normally give a higher market value for the preference share than for the ordinary share. What is frequently observed, however, is a discount in the value of the preference share compared with the ordinary share. The origins of this discount are the lesser liquidity of the secondary market in preference shares and the limited voting rights belonging to this category of shareholders.

3/Theoretical analysis

(a) For the company

Preference shares can enable a company in difficulty, but with good chances of recovering, to attract investors by granting them special advantages.

Banks are often issuers of preference shares because these securities are classified by central banks as part of the bank's own funds for the purpose of determining its net capital. This is so even though the preference share pays a constant annual dividend expressed as a percentage of par value, which gives it a strong resemblance to a debt security. Analysts are not fooled; for their purpose, preference shares are reclassified as debt.

Against these advantages, preference shares also present several drawbacks:

1　They cost more than a traditional capital increase: the preference dividend is higher than the ordinary dividend, whereas the preference share itself is usually worth less than the ordinary share because of its lesser liquidity.
2　Their issuance entails complications that are avoided with an ordinary capital increase, such as calling a special shareholders' meeting.
3　Furthermore, understanding such issues can be quite difficult. Preference shares frequently trade at a steep discount to theoretical value because holders demand a big premium over market value before they will sell or exchange them.

(b) For current shareholders

For current shareholders, issuing preference shares makes sense only if those shares have no voting rights. When this is true, a capital increase can be accomplished without diluting their control of the company. A company with family shareholders may issue preference shares in order to attract outside financial investors without putting the family's power over the company in jeopardy.

But this advantage brings with it an additional cost for current shareholders, and so appears to us quite illusory over the long term. It is just as if the company's cost of equity had been raised.

In France, for example, one finds a class of securities called nonvoting **priority dividend shares** (*Actions à Dividende Prioritaire* or ADP) that must obey some very specific restrictions: they can represent no more than one-quarter of the company's authorised capital; their voting rights must be restored after 3 years with no dividend; and the issuer must have the right to buy them back. Similar characteristics are shared by Italian *azioni privilegiate* and, partially, by the *azioni di risparmio* (saving shares).

Today this product has virtually disappeared from stock markets, which prefer to see a single quoted share class for each company traded in substantial volume. These securities cease to exist either when the issuing company is taken over by another or when it offers to exchange the priority dividend shares for ordinary shares.

On the other hand, preference shares remain useful as a vehicle for financial investments in unlisted companies or, in cross-border business combinations, as a means of equalising dividend flows between different shareholders in dual-listed companies, as in the case of Reed-Elsevier.

4/ BETWEEN PREFERENCE SHARES AND CONVERTIBLE DEBT: CONVERTIBLE PREFERRED STOCKS

Recent financial innovation has introduced a new, distinct class of securities – convertible preferred securities – which are designed to provide issuers with the dual benefits of maintaining the dilution-limiting benefits of convertible debt while providing significant rating agency, balance sheet and (in limited cases) regulatory equity content. In addition, all classes of convertible securities can be structured such that issuer interest payments are tax-deductible.

Their main characteristics are: (1) deep subordination; (2) long-dated maturity; (3) multi-year dividend/interest deferral; (4) various common stock conversion features.[14]

Within the convertible preferred stock category, there are two primary security types:

14 *Given these features, the after-tax cost of these securities tends to be higher than "normal" convertible debt.*

- **Conventional convertible preferred.** Typically structured as either perpetual or 30-year preferred stock.
- **Mandatory convertible preferred stock.** Short-maturity preferred securities that automatically convert into common stock at maturity.

An important attribute of these securities is the amount of "equity" that rating agencies assign to the product. S&P tends to view this equity in percentage terms while Moody's assigns content in distinct groupings. The factors that influence the "amount" of equity are the following:

- the type of equity-linked product being used;
- the amount of other hybrid equity products on the issuer's balance sheet;
- the industry or sector of the issuer;
- management credibility.

Here is a spectrum of convertible alternatives:

EQUITY							DEBT
	←						→
Products	Common stock	Mandatory convertible	Convertible preferred	Hybrid preferred securities	Convertible debt	Moderate, high-premium convertible debt	Zero-coupon convertible debt	Straight debt
Certainty of conversion	Certain	Certain/High		High		Medium	Very low	None
Rating agency equity treatment	100%	Partial equity treatment			0%			

Section 30.4
OTHER HYBRID SECURITIES

Financial innovation has reduced the difference between the investment characteristics of debt and equity. Firms are able to issue securities that function very much like equity although are frequently treated as debt for tax purposes. Much of this innovation represents "equity in drag" (Bulow et al., 1990). Innovation has in fact eroded each of the traditional tests used for distinguishing debt and equity.

The criteria by which we can show the disappearing distinction between debt and equity are the following:

1 **Debt–equity ratios.** It can be observed that high-yield (or speculative) debt – i.e., debt issued by companies with very high leverage and a rating below BBB – has a strong positive correlation with equity while the correlation is very low or even negative with government bonds:[15]

15 The correlation coefficients have been calculated using monthly returns over the preceding 5 years.

	EMU government bond indexes (%)			European DJ EuroStoxx indexes (%)		
High-yield European issuers	3–5 years	10+ years	All maturities	EuroStoxx 50	EuroStoxx	EuroStoxx small
High yield (all)	−1.4	7,6	2.2	47	50	59
European high-yield BB	−11	−15	−12	59	63	73
European high-yield B	−16	−18	−17	61	66	78

Correlation coefficients consistently show that straight noninvestment-grade bonds trade nearly as much like stocks as pure debt instruments. From the investor's standpoint, this evidence implies that there is a sizable equity component in high-yield debt.

2   **Subordination.** The seniority hierarchy has become less clear with leveraged buyout operations, where numerous levels of seniority can be used.

3   **Unconditional promise to make fixed money payments.** Recent innovations in the debt market (pay-in-kind securities,[16] zero-coupon bonds, etc.) have circumvented an important characteristic of "traditional debt" – that is, the promise to make regular cash payouts, the omission of which would trigger a default.

4   **Convertibility into the stock of the corporation.** The conversion option introduces a crucial element of equity-type into debt contracts.

5   **Relationship between holding of the stock and the debt security.** The key distinction between debt and equity is that creditors should have interests that diverge from those of equity holders. However, some placement techniques – like so-called "strip-financing" – reduce this distinction because each financial claimant of a company holds a portion both of debt and equity.

16 Pay-in-kind securities give the issuer the option either of paying interest in cash or in additional securities, valued at par.

1/MANDATORY CONVERTIBLES

Unlike convertible bonds, for which there is always some risk of nonconversion, **mandatory convertibles** are **necessarily** transformed into equity capital (unless the issuing company goes bankrupt in the meantime) since the issuer redeems them by delivering shares; no cash changes hands at redemption.

Mandatory convertibles are hybrid securities, which automatically convert into a predetermined number of shares dependent on the stock price at the time of conversion. They are closer to equity than debt because they redeem in shares instead of cash, and provide little downside protection (just the coupon payments). In addition, mandatory convertibles are often treated as equity on the balance sheet and regarded as equity by the rating agencies.

Mandatory convertibles are more established in the US than in Europe. Since the beginning of 2002, €8.5bn of mandatory convertibles have been issued in

Europe compared with $16.3bn (€14.7bn) of US deals of at least $100m. They have emerged primarily as an opportunistic response to uninviting market conditions for direct equity issuance and have helped companies de-leverage their balance sheets.

Mandatory convertibles appeal to investors looking for high yield and capital appreciation, although they have less downside protection than standard convertible bonds. As a result, we see interest from equity funds and outright investors but the main investors are hedge funds because they are able to significantly offset stock exposure.

In view of the ongoing pressure on corporates' balance sheets and the need to refinance upcoming redemptions, it is reasonable to expect further interest in mandatory convertible securities.

The value of a bond redeemable in shares is the present value of the interest payments on it plus the present value of the shares received upon redemption. In pure theory, this is equal to the value of the share increased by the present value of the interest and decreased by the present value of the dividends that will be paid before redemption. The discount rate for the interest is the required rate of return on a risky debt security, while the discount rate for the dividends is the company's cost of equity.

For tax purposes, bonds redeemable in shares are treated as bonds until they are redeemed and subsequently as shares.

There has been in recent years a revival for mandatory convertibles and new features have been added to make this product more attractive for investors.

Mandatory convertibles are equity-linked hybrid securities such as PERCS (Preferred Equity Redemption Cumulative Stock) or DECS (Debt Exchangeable for Common Stock, or Dividend Enhanced Convertible Securities), which automatically convert to common stock on a prespecified date.

Mandatory convertibles have been designed with a variety of payout structures, and carry different names depending on their payout structure and the investment bank underwriting their issue: examples are Morgan Stanley's PERCS, PEPS[17] and Salomon Brothers' DECS.

They have been issued by a number of companies, large and small, to raise capital: these include Texas Instruments, General Motors, Citicorp, Sears, Kaiser Aluminium, Reynolds Metals, American Express, First Chicago, Boise Cascade and All State. Two recent issuers were AT&T and Motorola, which raised $900m and $1.2bn, respectively, in 2001 by selling mandatory convertibles. In Europe, Lafarge[18] used a similar product, a bond redeemable either in shares or in cash, when it acquired Blue Circle. This issue was in reality a capital increase conditional on the success of its bid for the target company. Legally, capital increases can never be conditional. This is also the structure used by AXA in 2003.

17 *Personal Equity Plans.*

18 *Lafarge holds top-ranking positions in each of its four divisions: cement, aggregates and concrete, roofing and gypsum.*

2/INVESTMENT CERTIFICATES

Investment certificates are created by a capital increase that results in stripping of the shares. On one side, there are investment certificates with the pecuniary rights of the new shares; these are subscribed by new investors. On the other side, there are voting rights certificates in nominative form; the investment certificates are freely negotiable.

3/TRACKING STOCKS

A **tracking stock** is an issue of shares for which performance is indexed to the earnings of a subsidiary or division. Tracking stock is technically a class of the parent company's shares. It confers no right to vote on the decisions of the subsidiary that it supposedly represents. If the business is sold, however, the holder of shares of tracking stock has the right to receive a portion of the capital gain.

There are three main reasons for issuing tracking stocks:

1   they allow investors to buy only those portions of the firm that they feel have the greatest potential or value;
2   they provide more transparency to investors on how well the firm is doing in different businesses;
3   they enable a company to retain full control of a subsidiary while allowing the market to establish a value for it, thereby providing a ready currency for acquisitions.

This type of security is relatively well developed in the United States but extremely rare in Europe. To date, only Alcatel has issued tracking shares, on its optronics division; in 2 years, they have lost 98% of their value – they have now been cancelled as Alcatel has sold this division.

The value of a share of tracking stock is theoretically equal to what a share of the subsidiary would be worth if it were publicly traded. However, in the absence of effective control over the subsidiary, the legal complexity and the often low liquidity generally result in a sharp discount to the theoretical value.

However, while the positive announcement returns of tracking stocks are well-documented, an examination of their post-issue market performance is lacking. Billett and Vijh (2000) document three key results:

1   tracking stocks earn significantly negative buy-and-hold excess returns during the 3-year period following the issue date. The authors find significantly negative returns surrounding the earnings announcements during this period. This evidence contrasts with the post-issue returns of spinoffs, which are known to be positive, and of carveouts, which are known to be insignificant.
2   contrary to a common justification given to adopt tracking stocks, they do not increase the transparency of firm earnings.
3   there is a large positive announcement period for returns to events resulting in the elimination of the tracking stock structure.[19]

It is no surprise that this type of security came into being during a period of bull market euphoria. A tracking stock is often the precursor of a spinoff or de-merger (see Chapter 43).

From a conceptual viewpoint, one might well ask whether shares of tracking stock represent minority interests or whether they are just another means of financing for the parent company, like ordinary shares or bonds. Although, legally,

19 *Clayton and Qian (2003) have found less pessimistic evidence. Overall their study suggests that the wealth gains due to the announcement effect are permanent and underestimate the total wealth gains from the issue of tracking stock. The evidence is that the parent stock and the combined firm perform better in the 3 years following a tracking stock issue than the 3 years prior to the announcement.*

the securities are issued by the parent company, we think tracking stock has more to do with minority interests than with direct financing instruments. However, a proposition of this kind must be nuanced according to the particular characteristics of each issue.

Amid claims of better performance and higher market value, tracking stocks also raise an important ethical question because one board of directors controls both the parent company and the parent stock. But will it always act in the best interest of the tracking stock? Allocation of capital is an important conflict of interest that may arise with tracking stocks. The high-growth unit with the tracking stock may need a lot of capital. In case of external capital rationing, should the capital come from the slower growing but cash-rich, more mature company? Investors typically value cashcow divisions and companies on the basis of their cash flows. If these flows were diverted to other divisions, investors could be justifiably upset.

4/EXCHANGEABLE BONDS

An **exchangeable bond** is a bond issued by one company that is redeemable in the shares of a second company in which the first company holds an equity interest. Thus, while a convertible bond can be exchanged for specified amounts of common stock in the issuing firm, an exchangeable bond is an issue that can be exchanged for the common stock of a company other than the issuer of the bond.

At maturity, two cases are possible. If the price of the underlying shares has risen sufficiently, holders will exchange their bonds for the shares; the liability associated with the bonds will disappear from the first company's balance sheet, as will the asset associated with the shares. If the price has not raised enough, holders will redeem their bonds for cash, and the first company will still have the underlying shares. In neither case will there be any contribution of equity capital. An exchangeable bond is therefore like a collateralised loan with a call option for the holder on securities held in the company's portfolio.

For the investor, a bond issued by company X that is exchangeable for shares of company Y is very close to a convertible bond issued by Y. The only thing separating these two financial instruments is the default risk of X vs. that of Y.

By way of example, in May 2002 Lagardère issued a bond exchangeable for shares in T-Online, a telecom access provider in which Lagardère held a stake of about 9%. This issue raised €700m for the group at an apparent interest rate of just 3%. The quid pro quo is obviously twofold: for one thing, Lagardère cannot be sure of having unloaded its holding in T-Online; for another, if it does succeed in disposing of that stake, it will have let it go at a price below its market value.

Exchangeable bonds, like convertibles, can have a behaviour divided in "zones" (bond, hybrid and equity) according to the price evolution of the underlying asset. See, for example, the exchangeable bond issued by Intel, which is convertible in Samsung shares:

EXAMPLE OF A CONVERTIBLE BOND – INTEL CV ZERO 01/02/04

The convertible issued by Intel in 2001 behaved like a bond when first issued, but by end-2001 it had become virtually indistinguishable from the Samsung stock price.

SUMMARY

download

Hybrid securities often seem to be equity, but that is not always the case. A convertible bond that is not converted remains a debt; a bond with attached warrants is likewise still a debt.

Many of these hybrids give the impression of lowering the company's cost of financing. Do not believe it! In markets in equilibrium, all sources of financing have the same cost when adjusted for the risk taken by the investor. It is not enough to look only at the apparent cost; the full cost of any source of financing must be understood and taken into account.

Similarly, these securities give the impression of belonging to the world of high finance. More often than not, though, their use is a sign that the issuer is in trouble or is having difficulty placing ordinary equity or debt securities with investors.

Agency theory explains the existence of these products by showing their usefulness in resolving potential conflicts between shareholders and creditors or between shareholder-managers and outside shareholders. Signalling theory sees in them the mark of an undervalued, heavily indebted company that is unwilling to finance itself through a traditional capital increase.

A convertible bond is like a traditional bond, generally one bearing a fixed rate, except that it also gives the holder the right to exchange it for one or more shares (depending on the conversion ratio) of the issuing company during a conversion period set in advance. Its value is analysed as the sum of the value of the traditional bond and the value of a call option on the shares with an exercise price equal to the conversion price.

Convertible bonds are issued at lower coupon rates than traditional bonds. This is not an advantage for the issuing company but merely the compensation for the call option it has granted the investor "at no charge". A subscription warrant is a security that allows the holder to subscribe during a given period, in a proportion and at a price fixed in advance, to another security.

A subscription warrant may be attached to an issue of shares or bonds or distributed by itself "at no charge". Conceptually, a warrant is a form of call option sold by the company on shares to be issued. Issuing warrants enables a company to accomplish a capital increase by a process of gradual dilution.

Preference shares, bonds redeemable in shares, investment certificates and tracking stocks are other categories of hybrid securities.

QUESTIONS

quiz

1/ Can any financial product normally make it possible to obtain resources at below market cost?

2/ Define a convertible bond, bond with equity warrants, preference share, investment certificate and bond redeemable in shares.

3/ The bond market yield is 7%. A company issues a bond with equity warrants at a gross yield to maturity of 3% assuming the warrants are not exercised. What is the cost of this product? What is the breakdown of that cost?

4/ Is a convertible bond more costly to the issuing company than a bond with equity warrants?

5/ Which is (are) the most appropriate financial product(s) for the following companies:

○ a company that wants to raise fresh equity capital immediately but does not want to risk losing control;

○ a company that wants to raise fresh equity capital immediately in which the state is the majority shareholder;

○ a company with a very volatile share price that wants to gradually broaden its shareholder base;

○ a company emerging from a period of difficulties whose future is still perceived by investors to be risky.

6/ Rank convertible bonds, investment certificates, bonds with equity warrants, preference shares and new ordinary shares in terms of:

○ actual or potential dilution;
○ achieved rate of return;
○ potential capital gain;
○ cost to the issuing company.

7/ Which product would *appear* to be a case of "tails I win, heads you lose"?

8/ Show that, if managers think their company's shares are undervalued, there is a better product to issue than a convertible bond.

9/ Show that, if managers think their company's shares are overvalued, there is a better product to issue than a convertible bond.

10/ Given your answers to Questions 8 and 9, how do you explain the existence of convertible bonds?

11/ True or false:

(a) The higher the conversion premium, the higher the yield on a convertible bond.
(b) The higher the volatility of the underlying share, the higher the conversion premium.
(c) A rise in the payout ratio on the underlying share increases the probability of conversion before a convertible bond matures.
(d) A convertible bond does not offer the same percentage of upside participation in the share price as the share itself, but in return it offers downside protection.

12/ Why isn't a bond redeemable in shares attractive to financial investors?

13/ Why is there a good chance that preference shares will be worth less than the same issuer's ordinary shares, despite the preferences accorded to them?

EXERCISE

1/ Company X has capital of 2 million shares that are currently trading at €2,000 per share. On its balance sheet it has a liability for an issue of convertible bonds with the following characteristics:

- ○ nominal value: €500m (500,000 convertible bonds of face value €1,000 each);
- ○ interest rate: 5%;
- ○ conversion ratio: 1 for 1.

Company X expects to have net profit of €300m next year.

(a) Calculate X's *fully diluted* earnings per share. The corporate income tax rate is 36.7%.

(b) Redo the same exercise, replacing the convertible bond with a bond with attached warrants to subscribe to one share of X at €2,100. Assume the pre-tax rate of return on short-term investments is 8%. Use two different methods to make your calculations.

(c) What would be the result of the calculation in (b) above if X issued the bond with warrants to pay off another borrowing at a pre-tax interest rate of 8%? Assume that the expected net profit is after interest expense on the previous borrowing.

ANSWERS

Questions

1/ *Normally, no.*

2/ *See definitions in this chapter.*

3/ *One cannot say what the cost of this product is; the most one can say is that the cost consists of a minimum rate plus an option.*

4/ *There is no basis for affirming that either one is more costly than the other.*

5/ *Preference shares (but no one is fooled); investment certificates; convertible bonds; convertible bonds.*

6/ *In descending order of dilution: preference shares, investment certificates, ordinary shares, convertible bonds, bonds with equity warrants. In descending order of return: convertible bonds, bonds with equity warrants, preference shares, investment certificates, ordinary shares. In descending order of potential capital gain: ordinary shares, preference shares, investment certificates, bonds with equity warrants, convertible bonds. The cost to the company depends on the pricing!*

7/ *Convertible bond.*

8/ *Traditional bond that will be paid off by a capital increase once the share price has risen.*

9/ *Ordinary shares that will never have to be redeemed.*

10/ *By agency theory and signalling theory.*

11/ *True: b and d; false: a and c.*

12/ *Because it is simply a forward purchase of shares, payable immediately.*

13/ *Because of their lower liquidity; there are considerably fewer of them than there are of the ordinary shares.*

Exercise

1/ (a) *Saving on interest costs (after tax at 36.7%): €15.83m. Fully diluted EPS = €126.3.*
   (b) *Invest proceeds at short term: fully diluted EPS = €141.3. Use proceeds to buy back shares: fully diluted EPS = €151.9.*
   (c) *Gain on interest expense: $(8\% - 5\%) \times 0.6333 \times 500 = €9.50m$; by the short-term investment method: fully diluted EPS = €145.1; by the share buyback method: fully diluted EPS = €156.7.*

BIBLIOGRAPHY

General:

N. Doherty, *Integrated Risk Management: Techniques and Strategies for Reducing Risk*, McGraw-Hill, 2000.

On convertible bonds:

E. Arzac, PERCS, DECS and other mandatory convertibles, in D. Chew (ed.), *The New Corporate Finance: Where Theory Meets Practice*, 2nd edn, McGraw-Hill, 1999.
M. Brennan, E. Schwartz, The case for convertibles, *Journal of Applied Corporate Finance*, **1**, 55–64, 1988.
R. Burlacu, *The Probability of Conversion as a Measure of the Equity and Bond Component of Convertible Bonds*, research document, Affi Congress, 1999.
T. Chemmanur, D. Nandy, A. Yan, Why issue mandatory convertibles? Theory and empirical evidence, downloadable from *www.ssrn.com*, July 2003.
K. Connolly, *Pricing Convertible Bonds*, John Wiley & Sons, August 1998.
T. Ganshaw, D. Dillon, Convertible securities: A toolbox of flexible financial instruments for corporate issuers, *Journal of Applied Corporate Finance*, **13**(1), 22–30, Spring 2000.
F. Jen, D. Choi, S.H. Lee, Some new evidence on why companies use convertible bonds, *Journal of Applied Corporate Finance*, **10**(1), 44–53, Summer 1997.
C. Lewis, R. Rogalski, J. Seward, Understanding the design of convertible debt, *Journal of Applied Corporate Finance*, **11**(1), 45–53, Summer 1998.
D. Mayers, Why firms issue convertible bonds: The matching of financial and real investment options, *Journal of Financial Economics*, **47**, 83–102, 1998.
J. McConnell, E. Schwarz, The origin of LYONs: A case study in financial innovation, in D. Chew (ed.), *The New Corporate Finance: Where Theory Meets Practice*, 2nd edn, McGraw-Hill, 1999.
K. Nyborg, Rationale for convertible bonds, in G. Bickerstaffe (ed.), *Mastering Finance*, Financial Times/Pitman Publishing, 1998.
J. Stein, Convertible bonds as backdoor equity financing, *Journal of Financial Economics*, **32**, 1992.

On tracking stocks:

M. Billett, A. Vijh, *The Market Performance of Tracking Stocks*, working paper, NBER, 2000.
M. Clayton, Y. Qian, *Wealth Gains from Tracking Stocks: Long-run Performance and Ex-date Returns*, working paper, National Bureau of Economic Research, 2003.
S. Langner, *Tracking Stocks*, working paper, National Bureau of Economic Research, 2002.
D. Tompkins, Are tracking stocks on track? *Business Horizons*, 73–78, November/December 2000.

On exchangeable bonds:

F. Fabozzi, *The Handbook of Fixed Income Securities*, 7th edn, Irwin, 1997.
J.D. Finnerty, D.R. Emery, *Debt Management. A Practitioner's Guide*, Harvard Business School Press, 2001.

On hybrid securities and equity "in drag" :

F. Black, M. Scholes, The pricing of options and corporate liabilities, *Journal of Political Economy*, 637–654, May/June 1973.

J. Bulow, L.H. Summers, V.P. Summers, Distinguishing debt from equity in the junk bond era, in J. Shoven and J. Waldfogel (eds), *Debt, Taxes and Corporate Restructurings*, Brooking Institute Press, 1990.

M. Fridson, Do high-yield bonds have an equity component? *Financial Management*, 82–84, Summer 1994.

M. Jensen, W. Meckling, The theory of the firm: Managerial behavior, agency costs, and capital structure, *Journal of Financial Economics*, **3**, 305–360, 1976.

S. Myers, N. Majluf, Corporate financing and investment decisions when firms have information that investors do not have, *Journal of Financial Economics*, **13**, 187–221, 1984.

I. Nelken I. (ed.), *Handbook of Hybrid Instruments: Convertible Bonds, Preferred Shares, LYONs, ELKS, DECS and other Mandatory Convertible Notes*, John Wiley & Sons, 2000.

C. Smithson, D. Chew, The use of hybrid debt in managing corporate risk, in J. Stern and D. Chew (eds), *The Revolution in Corporate Finance*, 4th edn, McGraw-Hill, 2003.

Chapter 31
SELLING SECURITIES

Get 'em while they're hot!

Now that we have studied the properties of the various financial securities, let's see how companies sell them to investors. Bank finance was beautiful in its simplicity – whenever a company needed funds, it turned to its bank. Now that direct financing has become more common, companies can raise funds from a great many investors whom it does not necessarily know. That means they have to market their financing!

Section 31.1
GENERAL PRINCIPLES IN THE SALE OF SECURITIES

1/THE PURPOSE OF OFFERINGS

The company's main goal in selling its securities to investors is to obtain the highest possible price.

For the sale to be successful, the company must offer investors a return or a potential capital gain. Otherwise, it will be harder to gain access to the market in the future.

The offering must be in line with this objective. The price of a security is equal to its present value, as long as all publicly available information has been priced in. This is the very basis of market efficiency. Conversely, asymmetric information is the main factor that can keep a company from selling an asset at its fair value.

Investors must therefore be given the information they need to make an investment decision. The company issuing securities and the bank(s) handling the offerings must provide investors with information. Depending on the type of offering, this can be in the form of:

- a mandatory legal written documentation called a "prospectus";
- presentations by management via meetings/conference calls with investors, or electronic road shows;

- valuations and comments by financial professionals on the deal and the issuer via notes by financial analysts and presentations to the bank's salesteams, for example.

A firm underwriting commitment by the bank(s) handling the transaction can provide additional reassurance to investors because, if the bank is willing to arrange and underwrite the offering, it must believe that the offering will succeed and that the price is "fair". After all, investors are also clients to whom the bank regularly offers shares.

In any offering the bank's exact positioning is always ambiguous. In theory, it is mandated by the company that is issuing securities and must therefore defend that company's interests to the fullest. But, to do so, it must persuade the investors, who are its regular customers, to subscribe. It cannot afford to lead its clients astray. Ultimately, it defends the interests of both sides, not to mention its own!

Investor information needs and the complexity of the deal depend on the following:

- The amount of information that is already available on the issuing company itself. Clearly, an initial public offering of shares in a company unknown to the market will require a big effort to educate investors on the company's strategy, business, financial profile and perhaps even the sector on which it operates. This information is already contained in the share price of a publicly traded company, as that price reflects investor anticipations. This is why it is generally easier to offer shares in a company that is already listed.
- Investor risk. Investors need more information for shares than for bonds, which are less risky.
- The type and number of investors targeted. In addition to regulatory restrictions, it is generally more difficult for a European company to sell its securities in the US than in Europe, especially if the company and its industry are not known outside its home country (sometimes the opposite can occur, as in the oil services sector, for example). Meanwhile, a private placement with a few investors is simpler than a public offering:

The type of offering will depend on the complexity and risk involved.

Complexity of the deal →

Initial public offering

Secondary share offerings

Bond issues

Convertible bond issues

Block trades

2/THE ROLE OF BANKS

The bank(s) in charge of an offering have four roles, whose complexity depends on the type of offering:

- **arranging the deal** – i.e., choosing the type of offering on the basis of the goal sought: volume of securities to offer and in what form and timetable, choosing the market for the offering, contacts with market authorities, preparation of legal documents in liaison with specialised attorneys;
- **information**: an offering is often an opportunity for an issuer to report on its recent activity, prospects and strategy. The consistency of this information is checked by the bank and the lawyers in charge of the deal during a phase called "due diligence", which consists of interviews with the company's management. Information is also gathered by the brokerage arm of the bank and then put out in research notes written by the bank's financial analysts. The bank also organises meetings between the issuer and investors in one or more markets (road shows or one-on-one meetings);
- **distribution**: the bank's salesteams approach their regular clients, the investors, to market the securities and take investors' orders. The issue price is then set by the bank in liaison with the issuer or seller, and the securities are allocated to investors. An equilibrium price is established in the "after-market" phase. In the days after that, the bank may intervene on the market in order to facilitate exchanges of blocks among investors;
- **underwriting**: in some cases the bank provides the issuer (or seller) with a guarantee that the securities will find buyers at the agreed-upon price. The strength and timing of the guarantee varies with the deal. The bank thus assumes a certain market risk.

Most offerings, especially public offerings,[1] require a **syndicate** made up of several banks. Depending on how involved it is in the deal, and in particular the degree of guarantee, any one bank may play the role of:

1 *That is, for a flotation on a regulated market or a public retail offer.*

- **Global coordinator**, who coordinates all aspects of an offering; global coordinators usually serve as lead manager and book-runner, as well. For fixed income issues, the global coordinator is called the **arranger**.
- The **lead manager** is responsible for preparing and executing the deal. The lead helps choose the syndicate. One (or two) leads also serve as book-runners. The lead also takes part in allocating the securities to investors.
- **Joint-leads** play an important role, but do not usually serve as book-runners.
- **Co-leads** underwrite a significant portion of the securities but have no role in structuring the deal.
- **Co-managers** play a more limited role in the transaction, normally just underwriting a small portion of securities.

For some transactions (a block trade of already-existing shares or a bond issue), the banks may buy the securities from the seller (or issuer) and then sell them to investors. This is called a **bought deal**. Unsold securities go onto the bank's balance sheet.

A **firm underwriting** agreement carries less of a commitment than a bought deal. A firm underwriting is a commitment by the bank to buy the securities only if the offering fails to attract sufficient investor interest. In some cases, the bank may be released from its commitment in the event of *force majeure*.

Before agreeing to underwrite more complex deals, banks may wish to have some idea of investors' intentions. They do so via a process called **book-building**, which occurs at the same time that information is sent out and the securities are marketed. Volumes and prices from potential investors are listed in the book. This helps determine if the transaction is feasible and, if so, at what price. Only after the book-building process do banks choose or not to underwrite the deal. Book-building allows the banks running the transaction to limit their risk, by ensuring them that investors are willing to buy the securities.

Book-building helps determine, at a given moment, the best price for the seller and/or company and to allocate the securities on a more or less discretionary basis.

In some cases, the bank does not pledge that the transaction will go through successfully, only that it will make its best efforts to ensure that this happens. This is rare in a formal documented offer, as investor confidence could be sapped if there is no formal pledge that the deal will go through. As a result, best efforts is the rule only in offerings by smaller companies or in very special cases (companies in difficulty, for example).

In some transactions, the bank's commitment is halfway between an initial bought deal and a post-book-building bought deal. When a block of existing shares is being sold, a bank may make a "backstop" or floor underwriting commitment; i.e., go through the book-building process but guarantee the seller a minimum price.

There are two techniques for adjusting the offering to anticipations of investor behaviour, as well as to their actual behaviour: **greenshoe** and **clawback**.

To stabilise the price after the transaction, the issuer or seller may give the bank the option of buying a number of shares over and above the shares offered to investors (as many as 15% more in a capital increase and 25% for block trades of existing shares). This is called a greenshoe (named after the first company to use it). The bank allocates all the securities to investors, including the greenshoe shares – i.e., more than the official offering. These additional shares are borrowed by the bank:

- If the price falls after the offering, the bank buys shares on the market up to the limit of the greenshoe. This supports the price. It then has 30 days to resell these shares if the price moves back up. If the price doesn't rise, the bank repays the loan using the shares it bought to support the price. In this case the greenshoe is not exercised.
- If the price moves up, the bank can resell the shares or, if the price rises immediately after the transaction, the bank no longer has the shares, so it will pay back the loan by exercising the greenshoe. The company will thus have sold more shares than originally planned.

Greenshoes are used for secondary offerings (i.e., sale of existing shares), new share issues (the lead bank receives, free of charge, warrants that it may or may not exercise), or convertible bond issues (when it takes the form of a simple extension of the issue, decided 2 or 3 days after its launch).

An offering targeted at several categories of investors (institutional, retail, employees, etc.) will be split into several tranches reserved for each of them. The *clawback* clause guarantees the company some flexibility in the size of each tranche. Hence, if institutional demand is very heavy and retail demand very light, the *clawback* allows the shares initially allocated to retail investors to be reallocated to institutional investors.

To simplify the transaction, the bank may advise the company to target a limited number of investors, thus avoiding the rules governing a public offering, including supervision by market authorities, obligation to present information, etc. This is called a **private placement** and is possible on all types of products. Private placements are often used in offerings to US investors (generally under Rule 144-A), as the offering would otherwise be subject to extremely strict restrictions.

3/ISSUE DISCOUNTS

Studies show that when a company is floated its stock normally rises by an average of about 10 to 15% over its issue price, depending on the country, the timing (and how the rise is calculated!). Meanwhile, shares in a company that is already listed are usually offered at a discount ranging from 2 to 5% although the range varies profoundly according to different countries.

Country	Period	Sample size	Mean underpricing (%)
Australia	1976–1994	328	+15.2
Austria	1984–1996	67	+6.5
Belgium	1984–1990	28	+10.1
Brazil	1979–1992	66	+74.1
Canada	1971–1992	258	+5.4
Chile	1982–1997	55	+8.8
China	1990–1996	226 (A-shares)	+388.0
	1987–1995	57 (B-shares)	+37.1
Denmark	1989–1997	29	+8.0
	1984–1992	76	+3.9
Finland	1984–1997	102	+9.9
France	1984–1995	228 (Second Marché)	+20.9
	1992–1998	264	+13.2
Germany	1970–1993	180	+9.2
Greece	1987–1994	129	+51.7
Hong Kong	1980–1996	334	+15.9
India	1992–1994	386	+72.3
Indonesia	1989–1994	106	+15.1
Israel	1993–1994	28	+4.5
Italy	1985–1998	135	+20.3
Japan	1970–1996	975	+24.0
	1989–1995	456 (OTC market)	+15.7
Korea	1980–1990	347	+78.1
Malaysia	1990–1994	220	+72.6

Country	Period	Sample size	Mean underpricing (%)
Mexico	1987–1990	37	+33.0
Netherlands	1982–1991	72	+7.2
	1984–1994	64	+4.0
New Zealand	1979–1991	149	+28.8
Nigeria	1989–1993	63	+19.1
Norway	1984–1996	68	+12.5
Philippines	1987–1997	104	+22.7
Poland	1991–1998	149	+35.6
Portugal	1992–1998	21	+10.5
Singapore	1973–1992	128	+31.4
Spain	1985–1990	71	+10.8
Sweden	1979–1997	233	+29.3
Switzerland	1985–1994	55	+34.6
Taiwan	1971–1990	168	+45.0
Thailand	1988–1989	32	+56.73
Turkey	1990–1995	138	+13.6
UK	1959–1990	2,133	+12.0
	1989–1996	385	+10.1
USA	1960–1997	13,910	+13.7

Source: Paleari (2000).

This discount is theoretically due to the asymmetry of information between the seller and the investors or intermediaries. One side knows more about the company's prospects, while the other side knows more about market demand. The transaction is therefore possible. Selling securities generally sends out a negative signal, so the seller has to price his securities slightly below their true value to ensure the deal goes off and that investors are satisfied.

Some authors suggest that the discount is due to the "**winners' curse**", the curse that pursues the winner of an auction. The winner in fact shouldn't be (economically) pleased about the win because it is clear that everybody else participating at the auction apparently thought the object's value was less than the price paid by the winner!

IPOs after all are similar to auctions. The IPO discount could then be due to the fact that there are both informed and uninformed investors. Uninformed investors cannot distinguish which issues are really attractive and thus are exposed to the winners' curse. This is why an average discount is offered, to guarantee an appropriate return for uninformed investors who will be receiving many shares of a "bad deal" and few shares of a "good deal".

Others suggest that the discount is a way of remunerating the banks underwriting the deal. The discount makes the issue easier to market, reduces their risk and allows them to meet institutional client demand.

The issue discount is another way to persuade investors to invest in a transaction that appears to carry some risk.

The greater the asymmetry in information between an issuer and investors and the lower the liquidity of the security, the greater is the issue discount. The issue discount will thus be high for an initial public offering, less for the sale of shares in an already listed company, low or nonexistent for convertible bonds and totally absent for bonds.

So much for the major principles. Let's look now at how the main types of securities are offered. As you will see, the methods converge towards two main techniques: bought deals and book-building.

Section 31.2
INITIAL PUBLIC OFFERINGS (IPOs)

1/HOW AN IPO WORKS

The purpose of this section is not to analyse the motivations, strategic or otherwise, of an initial public offering, or IPO, but simply to describe how it works.

IPOs are surely the most complex of transactions. They involve selling securities, on which prior information is extremely limited, to a large number of investors, including institutional and retail investors and employees.

An IPO can include a primary tranche (i.e., shares newly issued by the company) and/or a secondary tranche (i.e., existing shares). The techniques are the same for both tranches, and, in fact, existing shares and new shares are bundled up in the same lot of shares to be offered.

However, the techniques vary depending on whether the shares are being offered to institutional investors, retail investors or employees.

2/HOW IPOs ARE DONE

A number of techniques exist for floating a company. However, in the past few years, IPOs on regulated markets have almost all been in the same form: that of an **underwritten deal** with institutional investors and a **retail public offering** with retail investors.

(a) Underwriting

Offerings of securities to institutional investors are often underwritten. This is the main tranche in almost all IPOs. Under this system, one or more banks organise the marketing and sale of securities to investors via a phase of book-building. The price set after book-building will serve as a basis for setting the price of the retail public offering. Other techniques are used for the other tranches (employees and retail investors, in particular).

IPOs that make use of book-building take place in several phases.

The initial **review phase** is handled by the banks. This consists in assessing and preparing the legal and regulatory framework of the deal (choice of market for listing, whether to offer shares in the US, etc.); structuring the deal; supervising documentation (due diligence, prospectus), as well as underwriting and execution of agreements; preparing financial analysis reports; designing a marketing campaign (i.e., the type and content of management presentations, programme of meetings between management and investors).

Then comes the **execution phase**, with the publishing of financial analysis notes by syndicate banks. This is a pre-marketing period lasting 1–2 weeks prior to the effective launch of the operation. The notes are presented to investors during "warmup" meetings, which help test investor sentiment. Analysts' research notes cannot be published during the blackout period that precedes the launch. The terms of the transaction and, in particular, the price range are set on the basis of conclusions from this pre-marketing exercise.

The marketing campaign itself then begins, and the offering is underway. During this period, full information is distributed via draft prospectuses (certified by market authorities), which may be national or international in scope. The prospectus includes all information on the company and the transaction. The offering is marketed within a price range of about 15%. Company managers are mobilised during this period for numerous meetings with investors (roadshows) or for one-on-one meetings. The information given to investors is mainly on company results, markets and strategy.

In the meantime, investor intentions to subscribe in terms of volumes and prices are recorded in an order book, on the basis of the preliminary price range.

After this period, which can last 5–15 days, the sale price of the existing shares and/or newly issued shares is set. The price reflects market conditions, overall demand as reflected in the order book and the price sensitivity that investors may have expressed.

Not until after this phase might banks enter into a firm underwriting agreement. The shares are then immediately allocated, thus limiting the bank's risk. After allocation, investors are theoretically committed. However, up to the actual settlement and delivery of the shares (3 days after the transaction), banks still face counterparty risk. There is also business risk, in that an institutional investor may decide he does not wish to take delivery of the shares after all. In sum, the only risks the syndicate takes is that of a market crash between the moment the price is set and the moment when the shares are allocated, and that of stabilising the price for around a month after the transaction by buying shares on the market.

The guarantee given by the bank to the company is also implicitly a guarantee for the market. The bank determines a value after review of internal information. This partly resolves the problem of asymmetry of information. The signal is no longer negative, because a bank with access to internal information is taking the risk of buying the shares at a set price if the market does not.

The final prospectus (with the issue price) is sent out after the price is set and the subscription period is closed. The lead bank knows the quantity and quality of demand. The book-runner allocates the new shares to investors in concert with the issuer and/or seller, who can thus "choose" his shareholders to a certain extent.

The shares are allocated on the basis of certain criteria determined in advance. Allocation is discretionary but not arbitrary. The goal may be to favour US, European or local investors. Generally, the main goal in allocation is to favour "quality" investors – i.e., those who are unlikely to sell their shares in the immediate after-market. The banks may steer the issuer to what it believes are quality investors, thus limiting excessive **flowback** – i.e., the massive sale of securities immediately after the offering.

Book-building offers several advantages, including greater flexibility. For one thing, the price can be adjusted as necessary during the marketing phase, which can sometimes last several weeks. Moreover, shareholders can still be chosen via a discretionary allocation of shares.

BOOK-BUILDING

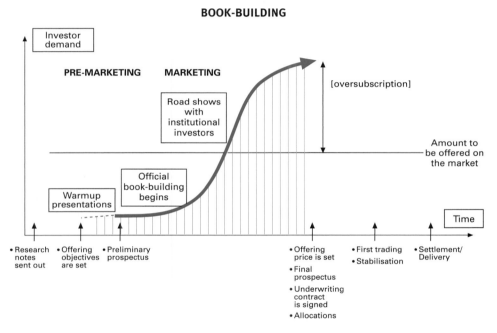

Book-building also has a cost. According to Ljungqvist et al. (2000), the direct costs of book-building are typically twice as large as direct costs for fixed price offers. However, book-building leads to less issue-underpricing.

(b) How shares are offered to retail investors

In an underwritten deal, shares are allocated at the discretion of the lead, based on the order book, as well as on criteria announced in advance. However, when shares are being sold to retail investors, the issue is centralised by the market itself.

➢ **The retail public offering**

In a retail public offering, a price range is set before the offering, but the exact price is set after the offering. The final price reflects market demand. French market authorities, for example, require a marketing period lasting at least 3 days, after which a draft prospectus is issued with the characteristics of the deal. Based on a price range, financial intermediaries collect orders from investors. The issue price is set jointly by the issuer and the syndicate lead and is generally equal to the underwriting price.[2] The final prospectus is then approved by the market authorities.

With the agreement of the market authorities, the banks can adjust the price if they have previously reserved the right to do so, but, in general, they must begin the process anew if the new price is outside the initial range. Shares are allocated on the basis of orders if supply is equivalent to demand and can be reduced on the basis of predetermined criteria. Allocation of shares to the various categories of buyers is done on the same basis as the fixed price offer.

Orders are filled on the basis of a percentage resulting from the comparison of supply and demand. Normally, at least 1% of the order is filled, but there may be provision for a minimum number of shares per order, so that broker fees do not end up swallowing up any potential gain. Similarly, there are sometimes several categories of orders with different allocation priorities.

➤ **Fixed price offering**

Under a fixed price offering, a certain number of shares are offered to the public at a preset price, which is generally identical to the price offered to institutional investors. The price is set after the book-building phase and is independent of market conditions. It is applied regardless of the number of shares requested. If it is far below what the market is willing to pay, the price will rise sharply in the days after the IPO and primary market buyers will have a capital gain to show for their initiative.

The only difference between a fixed price offering and a retail public offering is how the price is set.

➤ **Minimum price offering**

Under this technique, a number of shares is offered to the public at a certain price, under which they will not be sold. The local Securities Centralised Administration centralises orders, in which buyers must specify a floor price, and tries to find a sufficiently wide price range at which orders can be allocated in a certain proportion (about 6%) if there is sufficient demand.

In a minimum price offering, some orders may be shut out entirely, and orders at very high prices are paradoxically eliminated. This explains why the first quoted price is above the preset minimum price. If demand is too strong to quote the shares, trading is declared "limit up" and resumes at a higher price or another technique is used for the initial quotation.

➤ **An ordinary full listing**

The principle of an ordinary full listing is simple: the shares are offered on the basis of the market's normal trading and quoting conditions. A minimum sale price is set, but buy orders are not centralised by the local Securities Centralised Administration. Quotation is possible at a price normally no higher than 110% of the minimum price; at least 6% of the buy orders are filled (4% in exceptional cases). As in a minimum price offering, trading may be suspended "limit up" and resumed at a higher price. In addition, orders may have to be covered by sufficient funds (the goal being to discourage speculation).

3/US listings for non-US companies

Companies normally list their shares on their domestic stock market, where they are better known. However, they may wish to tap foreign investors to widen their shareholder base and could thus seek a foreign listing.

As can be seen from the table below, this decision is not so rare!

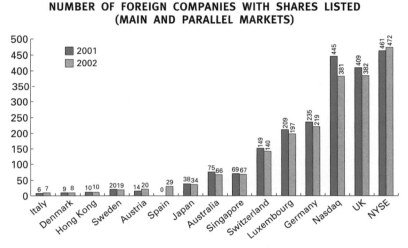

NUMBER OF FOREIGN COMPANIES WITH SHARES LISTED (MAIN AND PARALLEL MARKETS)

Source: International Federation of Exchanges.

Since the American markets (NYSE and NASDAQ) are by far the preferred alternative for companies that want to list, we focus our attention on US listing.

A company can list its shares on the US market via (1) a private placement, (2) American depositary receipts or (3) full listing.

(a) Private placements

Under Rule 144A, companies may opt for private placement of their shares, but they may only do so with US **Qualified Institutional Buyers** (QIBs). QIBs are then prohibited from selling their shares on the open market for 2 years, but can trade with other QIBs via the PORTAL system. Private placements are simply a means to gain access to US investors, but do not allow a company to register its shares with the Securities Exchange Commission (SEC) or to quote them in the US.

This is the least restrictive way to raise capital on US markets, as private placements are not registered with the SEC. All the issuing company has to do is translate the information that it has provided to its domestic market.

(b) Indirect listing via American Depositary Receipt (ADR)

3 *American Depositary Receipts may be also called – generically – Depositary Receipts (DRs), or Rule 144A Depositary Receipts or Global Depositary Receipts (GDRs), which are the "private placement" discussed above in the text. However, different names typically identify the market in which the depositary receipts are available: **ADRs** are publicly available to US investors on a national stock exchange or in the over-the-counter market; **Rule 144A ADRs** are privately placed and resold only to Qualified Institutional Buyers (QIBs) in the US QIB PORTAL market; and **GDRs** are generally available in one or more markets outside the foreign company's home country, although these may also be known as ADRs.*

ADRs, also known as DRs or GDRs,[3] are negotiable instruments issued by a US bank and representing the shares that it has acquired in a foreign company listed on a non-US market, something like tracking stocks, except they are not issued by the company itself. ADRs are traded on a regulated market or an Over The Counter (OTC) market.

ADR shares can be established either for existing shares already trading in the secondary market of the home country, or as part of a global offering of new shares.

There are several types of ADR:

- Level 1 ADRs are not traded on an organised market but only over the counter. They do not allow companies to raise funds on the US market, but nor do they require any particular information to be put out.
- Level 2 ADRs are listed on an organised market. This attracts some US pension funds, but requires the companies to publish a 20-F report every year. The 20-F is a more extensive document than a typical European annual report (it includes, for example, a table for converting from the company's accounting principles to US GAAP). Companies are not allowed to raise funds with Level 2 ADRs.
- Level 3 ADRs provide the company with a listing (via its ADR) on an organised market, and also allow it to raise funds via a public offering. Level 3 accordingly requires full registration with the SEC (F-1). Moreover, the company is subject to strict obligations on information (based on the 20-F and 6-K). The published documents must list, among other things, plans for acquisitions or reorganisation, as well as a partial reconciliation of company accounts to US GAAP. Companies usually go this route when they have significant commercial interests in North America.

More than 3,000 ADRs are listed from 50 different countries, including AXA, LVMH, Alcatel, Ilog, Luxottica, Telefónica, Korea Telecom, Nokia, BP-Amoco and many others.

The establishment of a depositary receipt programme should offer numerous advantages to non-US companies. Advantages may include:

- Expanded market share through broadened and more diversified investor exposure with potentially greater liquidity, which may in turn reduce the cost of capital and increase the share price.
- Enhanced visibility and image for the company's products, services and financial instruments in a marketplace outside its home country.
- Flexible mechanism for raising capital and a vehicle or currency for mergers and acquisitions.

The empirical evidence is generally consistent with the idea that US listing could be advantageous to companies. Here is a summary of the major results (Karolyi, 1998):

1 Share prices react favourably to corporate decisions to list abroad, particularly in the case of US listing. The average positive abnormal return is 0.4% during the 1st week after listing (about 12% annualised).

2   Significant reductions in risk measures (as measured by betas) are observed following cross-border listings.

3   There are significant liquidity effects for firms that list their shares abroad.

4   There is a significant price decline during the post-listing period. Companies experience a decline of 12–19% in the year following listing. This decline is generally large enough to erase the price increase that occurs immediately after the listing (see Item 1, above). This evidence represents a **puzzle** for financial economists since no robust explanation has been found to explain this phenomenon.[4]

(c) Full listing

Companies can also list their ordinary shares in both their home countries and directly in the US. This gives them access to institutional investors whose by-laws do not allow them to buy shares outside the US.

The main difference between ordinary registered shares and ADRs is that ordinary registered shares carry lower transaction costs, as there is no depositary. They are also more liquid and are less subject to arbitrage trading between domestic shares and ADRs.

Full listing is a relatively long and complex process that is meant only for very large companies (UBS Warburg, Deutsche Telekom, DaimlerChrysler, Repsol YPF, etc.). US market authorities require more complete documents than the French Commission des Opérations de Bourse.

Section 31.3
CAPITAL INCREASES

1/THE DIFFERENT METHODS

The method chosen for a capital increase depends:

1   first of all on whether the company is listed or not;
2   then on how eager current shareholders are to subscribe.

(a) Listed companies

When the large majority of current shareholders are expected to subscribe to the capital increase and it is not necessary or desirable to bring in new shareholders, the transaction comes with pre-emptive subscription rights (the transaction is then called a "rights issue"). The issue price of the new shares is set and announced in advance and the offering then unfolds over several days. The price is set at a significant discount to the market price, so that the transaction will go through even if the share price drops in the runup to the listing of new shares. To avoid penalising existing shareholders, the issue comes with pre-emptive subscription rights, which are negotiable throughout the transaction period.

However, when current shareholders are not expected to subscribe or when the company wants to widen its shareholder base, no pre-emptive subscription rights

4 *Reese and Weisbach (2002) suggest the hypothesis that non-US firms cross-list in the United States to increase protection of their minority shareholders. Cross-listing on the NYSE or NASDAQ in fact subjects a non-US firm to a number of provisions of US securities' law, and requires the firm to conform to US GAAP. It therefore increases the expected cost to managers of extracting private benefits, and commits the firm to protect minority shareholders' interests.*

are issued. The issue price is then not set until a marketing and pre-placement period has been completed, with a very slight discount to the share price at the end of this period. There are no pre-emptive subscription rights, but there may be a period during which current shareholders are given priority in subscribing.

(b) Unlisted companies

In this case, the issue price's discount will not be dictated by the fear that the share price will fluctuate during the operation (as the company is not listed), but rather by the wish of current shareholders to raise cash by selling the subscription rights they may have received.

If current shareholders do not wish to raise cash, the company will issue pre-emptive subscription rights at a price about equal to the share price, or may issue shares to identified investors that have been found via a private placement.[5]

Which method should be used for a capital increase?

Rights issue subscribed mainly by:	Listed company	Unlisted company
Current shareholders	Pre-emptive subscription rights Steep discount to the market price	Pre-emptive subscription rights with a steep discount if current shareholders wish to raise cash; pre-emptive subscription rights with no discount or no pre-emptive rights if current shareholders do not want to raise cash
New shareholders	Offer without pre-emptive subscription rights (at a slight discount to the current share price) In some cases, a reserve rights issue	Pre-emptive subscription rights with a steep discount if shareholders want to raise cash; reserved rights issue if shareholders do not want cash

Shares cannot be issued below par value (this is also the case for listed companies). Book value or an expert appraisal constitutes a floor value.

2/RIGHTS ISSUE

A fixed price rights issue with pre-emptive subscription rights (also called *privileged subscription*, or *rights issues*) is the traditional issue preferred by small investors (or their representatives). Such issues acknowledge their loyalty or, conversely, allow them to raise a little cash by selling their subscription rights.

In some countries, such as the United States and Japan, rights issues are quite rare while in Continental Europe they must generally be sold by rights.

Such issues remain open for at least 10 trading days. Banks underwrite them at a price well below the current share price, generally at a discount of 15–30%. No bank will guarantee a price near the current market price, because the longer the subscription period, the greater the risk of a drop in price. It is at this price that the banks will buy up any shares that have not found takers.

A steep discount would be a considerable injustice to existing shareholders as the new shareholders could buy shares at 20% below the current market price. Rights issues resolve this problem by allowing existing shareholders to buy a number of shares proportional to the number they already have. If existing shareholders use all their pre-emptive rights – i.e., buy the same proportion of new shares as they possess of existing shares – they should not care what price the new shares are offered at.

The price of the new shares plus the value of the pre-emptive subscription rights is equivalent to the stock's current market value (i.e., its share price if it is listed), even if the price of the new shares is below the current share price.

Even when existing shareholders do not wish to subscribe, the pre-emptive subscription rights keep them from being penalised, as they can sell the right on the first day it is detached.

(a) Definition

The subscription right is a right attached to each existing share allowing its holder to subscribe to the new share issue.

The subscription right offers the existing shareholder:

- the certainty of being able to take part in the capital increase in proportion with his current stake;
- the option of selling the right (which is listed separately for listed companies) throughout the operation. This negotiable right adjusts the issue price to the current share price.

The subscription right is similar to a call option whose underlying is the share, whose strike price is the issue price of the new shares and whose exercise period is that of the capital increase. Hence, its theoretical value is similar to that of a call option whose time value is very low, given its short maturity.

If the issue price and the current share price are the same, the subscription right's market value will be zero and its only value will be the priority it grants.

If the share price falls below the issue price, the rights issue will fail, as nobody will buy a share at more than its market price. The right then loses all value. Fortunately, the reverse occurs more frequently.

(b) Calculating the theoretical value of the subscription right

Let's take a company that has 1,000,000 shares outstanding, trading at €50 each. The company issues 100,000 new shares at €40 each, or one new share for each 10 existing ones. Each existing share will have one subscription right, and to buy a new share for €40, 10 subscription rights and €40 will be required.

After the new shares have been issued, an existing shareholder who holds one share and has sold his pre-emptive subscription rights must be in the same situation as an investor who has bought 10 pre-emptive subscription rights and one new share. So the share price after the deal should be equal to:

Pre-deal price − 1 pre-emptive right

but also:

Issue price + 10 pre-emptive subscription rights

In our example:

€50 − 1 pre-emptive right = €40 + 10 pre-emptive rights

Hence:

The value of the right = €0.91

The post-deal share price should be equal to:

€50 − €0.91 = €40 + 10 × €0.91 = €49.09

It is easy to calculate the theoretical value of the subscription right:

$$\text{Subscription right} = \frac{\text{Value of the existing share} - \text{Issue price}}{1 + \text{Subscription parity}}$$

as it should make no difference to an investor whether he buys an existing share minus the right or buys the necessary number of rights plus one new share.

Mathematically, the value of the subscription right looks like this:

$$(V - K) \times \frac{N'}{N + N'}$$

where V is the pre-issue share price, K the issue price of the new shares, N' the number of new shares issued and N the number of existing shares.

We can see that this formula can be used to find the previous result.

The detachment of subscription rights is conceptually similar to a bonus share award. Hence the existing shareholder may, if he wishes, sell some pre-emptive rights and use the cash and remaining rights to subscribe new shares, without laying out new cash (see the exercise at the end of this chapter).

(c) Advantages and drawbacks of pre-emptive rights

The subscription right is valid for at least 10 days – a relatively lengthy amount of time. The issue price therefore has to be well below the share price, so that if the share price does fall during the period the deal can still go through. The value of the right (i.e., the difference between the share price and the issue price) will fall but will remain positive, as long as the share price, ex-rights, is above the issue price.

This is a double-edged sword, as, once the deal is launched and the rights issued, nothing can delay the capital increase, even if the share price drops significantly during the deal. This is why the initial discount is so significant.

Complicating the transaction further is the fact that shareholders who do not possess a number of shares divisible by the subscription parity must sell or buy rights on the market, so that they will. This can be difficult to do on international markets.

The fixed price offer with subscription rights is poorly suited to current, strong market volatility. That's why it is meant mainly for existing shareholders and is not feasible in transactions equal to a large portion of market cap, because the new shares must be marketed aggressively to new shareholders.

Another potential complication is the large proportion of US investors among current shareholders and they are sometimes unable to exercise their pre-emptive subscription rights.

3/Capital increases without pre-emptive subscription rights

In rights issues without pre-emptive subscription rights, the company also turns to a bank or a banking syndicate for the issue. But their role is more important in this case, as they must market the new shares to new investors. They generally underwrite the issue, as described above for IPOs. A retail public offering can be undertaken simultaneously. Alternately, the bank can simply launch the transaction and centralise orders without having gone through a book-building phase. The company may issue 10–15% more shares than expected, via a *greenshoe*, under which warrants are issued to the banks (see above).

Local regulations tend to limit the flexibility to issue shares without subscription rights so that the shareholder will not be diluted at an absurd price. Therefore, in most countries regulation fixes a maximum discount to the last price or a minimum issue price as a reference to a price average.

When new shares are issued with no preset price, current shareholders can be given first priority without necessarily receiving pre-emptive rights. Indeed, such a priority period is the rule when pre-emptive rights are not issued. However, unlike pre-emptive rights, the priority period cannot be bought or sold. However, priority periods have the disadvantage of lengthening the total transaction period, as they generally last 3 trading days.

Legally speaking, a public issue of new shares, with or without pre-emptive rights, is considered to have been completed when the banks have signed a contract on a firm underwriting of the transaction, regardless of whether or not the shares end up being fully subscribed.

4/Equity lines

The way an equity line works is that a company issues warrants to a bank which exercises them at the request of the company when it needs to raise equity. Equity lines smooth the impact of a capital increase over time. The shares issued when the warrants are exercised are immediately resold by the bank.

The strike price is the average price over a short period (5 days in recent operations), less a discount of about 10%. The number of warrants that can be issued at any one time depends on the stock's liquidity (equivalent to a fraction of the number of shares traded over the 5 previous days), thus partly preventing the problem of overhang (i.e., the fear that the arrival of a large number of shares on the market will depress the share price).

Equity lines are suitable for young businesses whose stock performance history does not allow conventional rights issues. However, it opens the way to many uncertainties – in particular, on the terms imposed on the banks in exercise warrants and reselling the shares.

Equity lines may be less convenient for low-liquidity shares and low market capitalisation because there could be a strong pressure to reduce the price of the shares. This phenomenon has been defined as the "death spiral" in the US because it has determined the end of various new-economy companies.

5/THE NEW-EQUITY (OR ISSUES) PUZZLE

A study by Ritter and Loughran (1995) has compared how an investor would have fared buying stock in a company that made a seasoned equity offering vs. buying stock in similarly capitalised nonissuing firms (**Seasoned Equity Offerings**, or SEOs, simply refer to a sale of additional stock by a company whose shares are already publicly traded.)

The authors studied 2,680 companies that sold additional shares from 1970 to 1990. Each company that issued shares was compared with a company of equal market capitalisation that did not. As a result, two portfolios were created, each with the same number of companies and a similar market capitalisation. The only difference was that one portfolio was made up of stock-issuing companies, while the other, the reference portfolio, consisted only of nonissuing companies.

The average annual return of the issuing companies was a measly 7% a year. The nonissuing companies averaged a return of 15.3% annually. In each case, the timeframe studied was the 5 years following the date of the seasoned offering.

Other researchers have shown that many IPOs and SEOs start out well. Their stock prices rise, but, then, over the following period (3–5 years) they perform far worse than the average stock. In fact, they underperform the rest of the market by around 30%. In academic circles this phenomenon is known as the "new-equity puzzle".

Playing devil's advocate with their own study, Ritter and Loughran wondered if the poor performance of the issuing companies could have been due to something other than the fact that they had issued more stock. After all, the stock issuers' share prices had run up about 72%, on average, in the year preceding the second stock offering. Perhaps the subsequent slump merely evened out their returns.

Section 31.4
BLOCK TRADES OF SHARES

A block is a large number of shares that a shareholder wishes to sell on the market. Normally, only a small fraction of a company's shares are traded during the course of a normal day. Hence, a shareholder who wants to sell, for example 5% of a company's shares, cannot do so directly on the market. If he did, he could only do so over a long period and with the risk of driving down the share price. They are sold via book-building and/or bought deals, which were described above.

1/BOOK-BUILDING AND ACCELERATED BOOK-BUILDING

Like a rights issue, a block trade is done via book-building. However, while rights issues allow companies to raise significant funds for investment, a block trade does not raise any new capital or have any direct impact on the company's business.

Moreover, fewer shares are usually involved in a block trade than in a capital increase. Block trades are thus "simpler" deals than capital increases and require less marketing. Book-building is faster, top management is less involved or not involved at all and the deal can sometimes be done within a few hours.

EDF'S SALE OF 7.8% OF PECHINEY (€368m)

Accelerated book-building takes just a few hours.

@
download

Bigger transactions involving a strategic shift (exit by a controlling shareholder, etc.), may require an intense marketing campaign, and the deal will be managed as if it were a rights issue.

Book-building can come with a public offer of sale when the company wants to allow retail investors to acquire shares, but only for the larger issues. For companies list on the Euronext, for example, a retail offering is possible only if it involves at least 10% of the total outstanding shares or at least 20 times the average daily volumes during the previous 6 months.

Block trades use methods similar to those of IPOs, particularly in price-setting. For example, prices can be set in advance or on the basis of terms set when the offering begins. However, in the latter case, no price range is required (but the price-setting mechanism and the maximum price must be spelled out). In the requisite filings with Euronext, the initiator may reserve the right to withdraw the offer if takeup is insufficient or increase the number of shares on offer as much as 25% if demand is greater than expected.

2/BOUGHT DEALS

When the seller initiates book-building or accelerated book-building, he has no guarantee that the transaction will go through. Nor does he know at what price the deal will be done. To solve this problem, he can ask the bank to buy the shares itself. The bank will then sell them to investors. This is called a "bought deal".

The bank is then taking a significant risk and will only buy the shares at a discount to the market price. In recent bought deals involving liquid stocks, this discount has ranged from 2% to 5%.

The way it works is this: the seller contacts a few banks one evening after the markets close. He may have mentioned to some banks a few days or weeks beforehand that it might be selling shares, thus ensuring better quality replies. The seller asks each bank the price it is willing to offer for the shares. Bids must be submitted within a few hours. The seller chooses the bank solely on the basis of price, and the shares are sold that very night. The bank must then organise its salesteams to resell the shares during the night in North America or Asia, taking advantage of the time difference, and then the following morning in Europe.

For the seller, bought deals offer the advantage of being certain that the deal will go through and at the price stated at the moment when it decides whether to sell. There are some disadvantages, however:

- the deal will generally be at a greater discount than in accelerated book-building;
- share performance can suffer, as the bank that has acquired the shares will want to sell them as quickly as possible, even if that means making the price fall.

Section 31.5
BONDS

As the bond market develops and becomes more international, investors need benchmarks to measure the risk of default by issuers they do not always know very well. Ratings have thus become crucial in bond offerings. Companies that do not have a rating from at least one agency are finding it increasingly difficult to issue bonds.

The corporate bond market can be separated between companies having a rating of at least **BBB** (investment grade) and companies rated **BB** or lower (below investment grade). The latter, when they want to issue bonds, must offer higher interest rates. Such bonds are called "high-yield". The investment grade and high-yield markets are separate, not just for the issuers, but also for investors and for the investment banks handling the offering.

The graph shows the average amount of issues for each class of rating, in €m (year 2004).

download

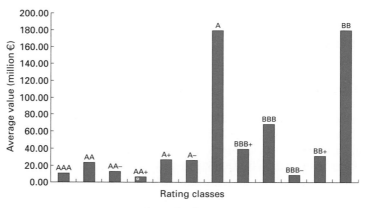

AVERAGE VALUE OF ISSUES PER RATING CLASS

Source: Bondsware.

1/INVESTMENT GRADE BONDS

The euro switchover has naturally given rise to a pan-European bond market, and has allowed much larger issues than were previously possible on national markets. €1bn issues are no longer rare, and only issues of €10bn or more are exceptional. France Telecom, for example, issued €16.4bn in one go in 2001.

Bond-offering techniques have thus evolved towards those used for shares, and market regulations have followed suit. For example, **competitive bidding** has gradually given way to book-building. The alternative technique (i.e., competitive bidding) consists in a tender from banks. The issuer chooses the bank that will head up the offering on the basis of the terms offered (mainly price). It thus takes the risk of giving the lead mandate to a bank that is overly aggressive on price. The reason this is risky is that prices of bonds on the secondary market may fall after the operation begins as the bonds were issued at too high a price (hence at an excessively low rate). Buyers will not like this and will demand a higher interest rate the next time the issuer comes to the primary market. Competitive bidding is similar to a bought deal and is often used by state-owned companies, as well as companies that have already tapped the bond markets.

Corporate bonds are generally placed via book-building.

Book-building helps avoid price weakness after launch, as the issue price (or spread) is not preset. The lead bank suggests a price range and sounds out investors to see what price they are willing to pay. Presentations to investors, one-on-one meetings and electronic road shows over the Internet or Bloomberg allow management to present its strategy.

The lead then "builds a book" of volumes and prices (either rate or spread) offered by each investor interested in the issue. There is little risk of miscalculation, as the issue price is set by the market. The period between when the price is set and the effective delivery of the shares is called the **grey market** (as well as for IPOs and rights issues). Shares are traded on the grey market without, technically, even existing. Transactions on the grey market are unwound after settlement and delivery and the first official quotations. The lead intervenes on the grey market to maintain the spread at which the issue has been priced. This is especially useful when an issue requires intense marketing or would benefit from it. Companies wishing to market investors aggressively (notably to return to the market when they wish) will use book-building.

So there are some similarities between share and bond offerings. *However, the process is much shorter for bonds and can even be extremely short, especially if a company is a frequent issuer, and if the issue is on its local market.* The process is longer for a first issue or if the company is targeting a large proportion of international investors.

A sample timetable for an issuer who has issued bonds in the past is given in the following diagram:

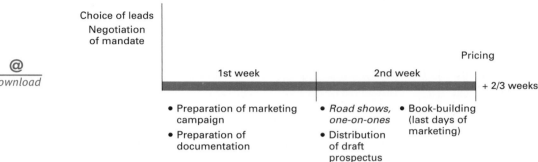

The role of the lead is not just to market the paper, but to advise the client, where applicable, for the obtaining of a rating. It determines the spread possible through comparisons with issuers having a similar profile and chooses the members of the syndicate to help sell the bonds to the largest possible number of investors.

When the company plans several issues in the medium term, it can put out an umbrella prospectus to cover all of them, under an issue of **EMTNs** (**Euro Medium Term Notes**). This allows the company to tap the markets very rapidly, when it needs to or when the market is attractive.

Underwriting syndicates routinely stabilise the secondary market price for poorly received initial public offerings. Few debt IPOs suffer sharp price declines during the first few days of trading, in part because the syndicate imposes so-called "penalty bids" whose common aim is to discourage investors from immediately reselling their shares.

A number of studies have examined the determinants of the at-issue yield spread, which is an increasing function of the issue costs (the at-issue yield is measured by equating the net proceeds, after deducting the issue costs, with the present value of the coupon and principal payments). Datta et al. (1999), for example, have documented that the at-issue yield spread is *negatively* related to credit rating and *positively* related to bond maturity. As issue costs are an important determinant of the at-issue yield spread, these findings imply similar relations for the issue costs.

Several studies have investigated the determinants of direct issue costs, which consist primarily of underwriter fee (e.g., Lee et al., 1996; Altinkilic and Hansen, 2000). These studies generally find that direct issue costs are positively related to bond maturity and are negatively related to issue size and credit quality. There is also weak evidence that bond issues are underpriced. Wasserfallen and Wydler (1988) and Helwege and Kleiman (1998) report results that indicate slight underpricing, but Fung and Rudd (1986) find "no clear evidence of underpricing".

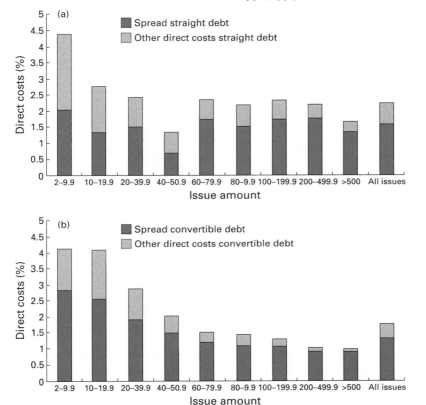

Source: Lee et al. (1996).

The two graphs show, respectively, the direct costs of straight and convertible debt (in % of the issue size). Underpricing is not included.

2/HIGH-YIELD BONDS

The high-yield bond market has developed in Europe only since the late-1990s. Until then, the financing needs of risky companies were covered exclusively by equity or bank loans.

By definition, high-yield, or noninvestment grade bonds, are risky products.

High-yield issues take longer and require more aggressive marketing than a standard issue, as there are fewer potential buyers.

See how much more risky they are! Look at the annual default rates provided by Altman (2002):

HISTORICAL DEFAULT RATES – 1971/2001 ($m)

In 2001, a record $63.61bn of developed nation high-yield straight bond defaulted or restructured under distressed conditions. The 2001 rate is considerably higher than the 2000 rate, well above the historic weighted average annual rate 1971–2001 of 4.32% per year. However, it is important to remark that the probability of default in the high-yield category is not irrelevant and should be included in the estimation of expected returns.

Melnik and Nissim (2003) investigate the pricing of initial offerings of public debt, using trader quotes of high-yield corporate bonds and risk-adjusted benchmarks. They find underpricing averaging only 39 basis points, which is sharply lower than previous research indicates. Moreover, they find that underpricing is not related to the degree of information problems, such as how long the company has been public, its bond rating or size of the offering.

Their most interesting result is the tradeoff between the cost components. Underwriters appear to set the two cost components (fee and spread) so that one offsets the other. Fang (2005) suggests that reputable underwriting banks obtain lower yields and charge higher fees, but issuers' net proceeds are higher. These findings suggest that banks' underwriting decisions reflect reputation concerns, and are thus informative of issue quality.

3/RULE 144A

As already explained in the preceding sections, the US SEC approved Rule 144A in April 1990, an initiative that allowed for the immediate resale of private placements *among* **Qualified Institutional Buyers (QIBs)**.[6] Rule 144A facilitates the resale of privately placed debt and equity securities and thus increases secondary trading among institutional investors.

Under this ruling, it is possible to resale privately placed bond securities to QIBs. Thus, large financial institutions can sell previously acquired private

6 *A QIB, broadly defined, is a financial institution that owns and manages $100m ($10m in the case of a registered broker-dealer) or more in qualifying securities. For a banking institution to qualify as a QIB, a $25m minimum net worth test must also be satisfied.*

placements without having to register the securities or hold the securities for 2 years. The SEC rule has modified the 2-year holding period requirement on privately placed securities by permitting QIBs to trade these positions among themselves.

Thus, Rule 144A issues do not require SEC registration. By lifting the registration requirements for purchasers of 144A, the SEC sought to reduce regulatory costs and create a more liquid market for these restricted securities.

Rule 144A imposes less stringent disclosure and reporting requirements than a registered issue entails, so issuers can complete the offering fairly quickly. On the other hand, Rule 144A bonds have limited liquidity because only qualified institutional investors can buy and sell them. Despite this drawback, more companies have warmed up to Rule 144A. The annual volume of bonds issued under the rule increased from $3.39bn in 1990 to $235.17bn in 1998, and they have been as much as 80% of the high-yield bond market.

Rule 144A is particularly important for foreign issuers. Under this rule, in fact, these firms have gained access to institutional investors without having to meet the strict disclosure standards required of US public companies. The Rule 144A market is evolving rapidly and now closely resembles the SEC-registered market in terms of underwriting practices, marketing, disclosure and credit-rating requirements.

	Rule 144A offering	Public offering
Size	$250m–$1,000m	$250m–$1bn
Rating	Two ratings are required	Two ratings are required
Spread	Credit spread usually slightly higher than public	Lowest credit spread
Syndicate composition	Usually three or more underwriters, depending on deal	Usually three or more underwriters, depending on deal
Covenants	Covenants similar to those required for a public issue	Loosest covenant structure
	Long preparation time needed before accessing the market	Long preparation time needed before accessing the market

Source: Adapted from Johnson (2000, p. 91)

Given the growing "convergence" between the two forms, why should a company choose one form or the other? There are basically two reasons: (1) different average sizes and (2) the desire not to report to the SEC on an ongoing basis.

While Rule 144A permits issuers to raise debt and equity capital, the total amount of capital raised via debt is nearly eight times the amount raised via equity.

Debt issuers pay a price – in the form of higher yields – for the convenience associated with Rule 144A offerings (Livingston and Zhou, 2002). Rule 144A issues, particularly those of private companies that do not file financial statements with the SEC, have substantially higher yields than their SEC-registered counterparts. Overall, they yield 19 basis points more than public bonds and 54 basis points more than private debt offerings. Investors apparently regard the lack of information about the issue as a risk factor and demand higher yields in return for the added uncertainty, which more dramatically affects private companies without SEC-mandated transparency.

Section 31.6
CONVERTIBLE AND EXCHANGEABLE BONDS

Convertible and exchangeable bonds are issued via accelerated book-building or bought deals.

Convertible Bonds (CBs) (examined in Chapter 30) are a very specific product. They are first of all bonds paying interest and redeemed in cash at maturity. They are called convertibles, as the investor has the right to ask that the bond be redeemed not in cash but in shares, based on a parity set at issue, if the share price has risen enough by then. Holders of convertible bonds are entitled to all information put out by the issuer to its shareholders, while the share price tells them precisely how much the CB's option component is worth.

There is little problem of asymmetry of information between the investor and issuer in the case of a convertible bond, as the convertible's bond component protects the investor.

The only factor that could make an investor hesitate to invest in a convertible bond is the product's complexity. However, CBs are now well known to professional investors, and are sold mainly to specialised investors or *hedge funds*.

Section 31.7
SYNDICATED LOANS

Syndicated loans are not securities in their own right, but merely loans made to companies by several banks. A syndicated loan offering is nonetheless similar to a bond issue. The company first chooses the bank that will arrange the deal. This bank may do a bought deal of the entire loan and then syndicate it afterwards. The arranger is paid specifically for its advisory and placement role.

The main terms are negotiated between the arranger and the company and are put into a **term sheet**. Meanwhile, the bank and company choose a syndication strategy, as well as the banks (or financial institutions) that will be members of the syndicate.

After meetings with the company and a memorandum of information, the banks contacted will decide whether or not to take part in the syndicated loan. Once the syndicate is formed, the legal documentation is finalised. The entire process can take 2 months, between the choice of arranger to the delivery of funds.

Syndicated loans are closely dependent on the quality of the company's relationship with its banks. Syndicated loans do not often make much money for the banks when they are not the arranger, and they take part only as they wish to develop or maintain good relations with a client, to whom they can later market more lucrative transactions. Membership in a syndicate sometimes even comes with the stipulation that it will be remunerated through an implicit or explicit pledge from the company to choose the bank as the lead at its next market transaction or as advisory for its next M&A deal.

TOP 10 BOOKRUNNERS OF INVESTMENT-GRADE SYNDICATED LOANS (JANUARY TO MARCH 2005)

Position	Bookrunner	Value (US$m)	Deals	Share (%)
1	Citigroup Inc.	39,356	126	9.5
2	JP Morgan	34,101	126	8.2
3	Bank of America	26,031	139	6.3
4	BNP Paribas	25,058	89	6.1
5	Sumitomo Mitsui Banking Corp.	24,446	233	5.9
6	Mizuho Financial Group Inc.	20,948	212	5.1
7	Mitsubishi Tokyo Financial Group Inc.	19,654	239	4.8
8	Barclays	19,285	69	4.7
9	Royal Bank of Scotland	18,453	63	4.5
10	HSBC	17,593	72	4.3
Total		*413,745*	*1,102*	*100*

Source: Euromoney.

Syndication forms of a loan can be of three types:

1 **Underwritten deal**, whose major characteristics are:

  a The lead manager(s) guarantee that funds will be provided.

  b The commitment of lenders can be of two types: *full commitment* or committed for the entire amount and *partial commitment*, in which some commitment is contingent on market interest. Full commitment is an important competitive tool for lenders and it usually requires higher fees from the borrower.

2 **Best efforts deal.** The commitment is only of the lead manager(s). The remainder of funds is contingent on sufficient market interest. However, best efforts deals are quite rare because the commitment of lenders is a major value of the syndicated loan.

3   **Club deal.** This is typical of smaller deals (<$250m). They are pre-marketed within a group of relationship banks.

The members of a syndicate can have the following titles:

➤   **Lead manager/Arranger/Book-runner.** This is the bank that handles the loan design and the structuring of the syndicate. Thus: it maintains contact with the borrower; structures the credit terms so they meet the borrower's requirements; assists in preparing an information memorandum; provides counsel in preparing the credit agreement and related documents; arranges the bank syndicate.

➤   **Agent bank.** Often the lead bank or a co-lead manager bank that maintains the fiduciary relationship with the lending participants and coordinates two functions:

a   administrative functions – loan service payments;

b   coordination functions – when changes in terms are requested or when trouble looms.

➤   **Manager and co-managers.** The managing banks are appointed by the lead bank to help identify and organise a wider contingent of participating banks (*participants*) as the final bank lenders. Some of the lending banks participating with major amounts are referred to as *co*-managers; however, none of the responsibilities of the arranging and managing banks falls to them.

➤   **Participants (or selling group).** *Other* lenders who supply funds for pieces of the loan. In order to avoid confusion, it is useful to specify that all intermediaries that make up the syndicate participate in the funding, but they must also accomplish other tasks, while the selling group is engaged exclusively in the selling activity.

Although the final structure of the bank syndicate can vary substantially – depending on the type of finance it tries to accommodate – a typical bank syndicate could be structured as follows:[7]

7 *In the simplest transactions, called "club loans", there are only two layers of intermediaries: the lead-managing and the participating banks.*

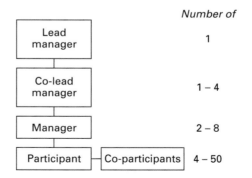

	Number of
Lead manager	1
Co-lead manager	1 – 4
Manager	2 – 8
Participant — Co-participants	4 – 50

The syndication process normally generally develops in three steps:

1   **Preliminary contacts**: the borrower contacts the lender and gets the syndication mandate (sets pricing, terms, fees of loan, etc.).

2   **General syndication**: the lead manager canvasses the market for commitments and closes the phase once all funds are committed.

3   **Secondary syndication**: the lead manager prepares an information memorandum and a term sheet on loan. Managers above the "hold target" sell off the excess loan commitment to "participants".

The "fee system" of a syndicated loan is:

➤   **Management fee.** This is a *front-end*, flat percentage (e.g., 1%) fee, determined as a percentage of loan proceeds.[8] It is usually sized in categories by giving more fee to banks that underwrite a higher amount. This fee is divided in:

> 8 *This is an important difference from public bonds for which fees are "discounted" from the selling prices of the securities (gross spread).*

1   *praecipium*. This is the part of the management fee that the lead manager reserves for its remuneration.

2   *underwriting fee*. The remaining management fee is then distributed among underwriting banks. The agreement may discipline an equal treatment between all participants or a differentiation in function of the efforts of each bank.

3   *residual pool*. This is the management fee net of the praecipium and of the underwriting. It normally pertains to the lead and the co-lead managers (if any).

➤   **Agent fee.** Annual fee due in order to administer the loan.

There may be two additional fees if the borrower can draw funds when necessary:

➤   **Commitment fee.** This is a flat percentage (e.g., $\frac{1}{2}$%) per annum on the undrawn portion of the loan.

➤   **Facility fee.** This is paid on the entire committed amount, annually, regardless of the amount drawn. This fee may replace the commitment fee for investment grade borrowers, or when a competitive bid option is used (a syndicate member may have some unused commitment).

Let's consider this example. Suppose a fully committed syndicated loan of $100,000,000, lead-managed by a single bank. Suppose these are the following agreements regarding the fees:

•   1% management fee on the $100m = $1,000,000 in fees divided as follows:

  ◦   lead bank retains of the *total* amount $\frac{1}{4}$% as *praecipium*;
  ◦ $\frac{3}{4}$% of the *amount raised by each bank* is distributed among managers at the $10m level;
  ◦ $\frac{1}{2}$% of the *amount raised by each bank* is distributed among managers at the $5m level;
  ◦ $\frac{1}{4}$% is for participants;
  ◦   the remaining amount of the total fee is distributed discretionarily between the lead and co-manager.

The result is the following:

EXAMPLE OF FEES IN A SYNDICATED LOAN

	No. of banks	Amount raised per bank	Total amount raised	Praecipium	Participation fees	Pool share	Total fees
Lead manager	1	15,000,000	15,000,000	250,000	112,500	40,909	403,409
Co-managers	4	10,000,000	40,000,000		300,000	109,091	409,091
	6	5,000,000	30,000,000		150,000		150,000
	15	1,000,000	15,000,000		37,500		37,500
			100,000,000	250,000	600,000	150,000	1,000,000

SUMMARY

download

The aim of all types of equity offerings is to sell the shares to investors at the highest price at any given time.

To achieve this, the large gap in the quantity and quality of information available to the issuer compared with that available to the investor must be reduced. One of the roles of banks in equity offerings is to inform investors by passing on information obtained from the issuer. The bank has three other roles. It must structure the deal, distribute the securities and generally provide the issuer with a guarantee at a given level.

There are two main types of equity placements:

- book-building;
- bought deals.

Book-building means that the bank or the banking syndicate will only commit itself to the deal if it knows that there is investor appetite for the shares. Following a phase of dissemination of information to investors, investor intentions to subscribe are recorded in an order book. It is only at this stage that the banks will sign a firm underwriting agreement, thus limiting the risk taken. For a bought deal, the banks will buy the securities from the issuer, and it is up to the banks to place the securities with investors as quickly as possible in order to limit the risk.

Initial public offerings are very complex transactions and involve the dissemination of appropriate information to a variety of investors. Two types of offering exist side by side. The underwritten deal, when the banking syndicate places the securities with institutional investors on the basis of the orders recorded in the order book. Generally, a retail public offering is made to retail investors at the same time. In a retail public offering, a price range is set before the offering, but the exact price is set after the offering. The final price reflects market demand. When the offer to retail investors is a fixed price offer, the issue price is preset. Generally identical to the price offered to institutional investors, it is totally independent of the market. Minimum price offerings and full listings using standard market procedures are rarely used these days.

There are two techniques for carrying out capital increases of companies that are already listed, depending on how eager existing shareholders are to subscribe new shares. There is the fixed price capital increase with pre-emptive subscription rights, or a capital increase without pre-emptive subscription rights but possibly with a period during which existing shareholders are given priority to subscribe.

For the former, the issue price is set at a significant discount to the market price. In addition, in order to avoid penalising existing shareholders, the issue comes with pre-emptive subscription rights, which are negotiable. Accordingly, the price of the new shares is equivalent to the stock's current market value even if the price of the new shares is below the current share price. A pre-emptive subscription right is akin to a call option.

A capital increase without a pre-emptive subscription right, for which shareholder approval is required, is an underwritten deal. The issue price is close to the market price. For unlisted companies, capital increases are carried out with or without pre-emptive subscription rights, with defined investors who have been identified following a private placement.

Block trades and issues of convertible bonds are carried out via book-building (or accelerated book-building which takes only a few hours) or via a bought deal.

The procedure a company uses to issue bonds depends first and foremost on the company's rating (whether the stock is investment grade – i.e., rated BBB or higher – or noninvestment grade – i.e.. lower than BBB). A company whose stock is rated as investment grade can invite banks to bid for the opportunity to carry out a bought deal, or opt for book-building. Whatever procedure is chosen, the deal is completed within a shortened timeframe.

For noninvestment grade companies, the placement procedure is closer to the capital increase procedure via book-building.

Convertible bonds, despite their apparent complexity, are products that are relatively easy to place as they offer substantial guarantees. They can be sold to investors within a relatively short period.

The procedure for placing a syndicated loan is similar to that for placing a bond issue with a limited number of investors. The banks that are involved are generally keen to develop a business relationship with the borrower.

QUESTIONS

quiz

1/ What is a prospectus used for?

2/ Why does it take longer to set up a share issuance than a bond issue?

3/ What financial product can a greenshoe be compared with?

4/ Why is the timetable for a first issue for a company issuing a high-yield bond much longer than for the issue of a standard bond?

5/ Which placement procedure carries the most risk for a bank? Why?

6/ Describe two different methods used for calculating the value of a subscription right.

7/ Will a shareholder that subscribes a capital increase with a pre-emptive subscription right become poorer if the share price drops after the operation? Why?

8/ Which party is the bank that places the shares working for – the issuer or the investor subscribing the shares?

9/ Which is more costly for an issuer – an underwritten deal or a bought deal? Why?

10/ Why can convertible bonds be placed so quickly?

11/ Immediately after bonds are placed on the market, the price rises. What is the good news for the issuer? And the bad news? Which is the most important?

EXERCISE

1/ In June 2001, Marionnaud Parfumeries carried out a capital increase with subscription rights. 1,225,479 new shares were issued at a price of €99. Before the capital increase, the company's share capital was made up of 6,127,395 shares, which meant that one new share was being issued for five existing shares. Before the capital increase, the share was trading at €125.70.

(a) Calculate the theoretical value of the Pre-emptive Subscription Right (PSR).

(b) Calculate the theoretical share price after the capital increase.

(c) If you own 28 Marionnaud shares, what should you do before and after the capital increase so that your portfolio remains more or less as it is.

ANSWERS

Questions

1/ *For providing investors with a description of the company and the deal which will assist them in making a decision as to whether to invest or not.*

2/ *Because investors are taking a greater risk by investing in shares than in bonds. Further and better information is needed because of this risk.*

3/ *A call option held by the banks and sold by the company.*

4/ *Because a bond issued by a below-investment grade company carries much more risk than a standard bond. The investor thus needs a lot more information on which to base an investment decision.*

5/ *A bought deal, as a risk is taken that the market will change before the shares can be sold.*

6/ *The equation described in the chapter and application of the Black–Scholes equation which we studied in Chapter 33.*

7/ *No, because the shareholder was able to acquire shares with a discount to the share price.*

8/ *For the issuer, but the bank must also ensure that investors are satisfied with the deal, or it may lose its clients!*

9/ *Usually a bought deal, because it transfers the risk of the deal failing to the bank, and this has a cost.*

10/ *Because a convertible bond provides the same guarantees as a bond, along with the possibility of making the same gains as a share. Investors buying them are thus taking a limited risk.*

11/ *Investors will be happy. A lower interest rate could have been paid. If the rise remains reasonable, the former, because it will be possible to retain an open financial market.*

Exercise

1/ (a) *€4.45.*

(b) *€121.25.*

(c) *Sell 23 PSRs for €102.35, buy one share with the five remaining PSRs plus €99. I would then own 29 shares worth €121.25 each (or €3,516) and €3 in cash, compared with €3,519 for 28 shares before the capital increase.*

On book-building and IPOs:

L. Benveniste, W. Busaba, Bookbuilding versus fixed price: An analysis of competing strategies for marketing IPOs, *Journal of Financial and Quantitative Analysis*, **32**, 383–403, December 1997.

F. Cornelli, D. Goldreich, Bookbuilding and strategic allocation, *Journal of Finance*, **56**, 2,337–2,370, December 2001.

F. Cornelli, D. Goldreich, *Bookbuilding: How Informative Is the Order Book?*, working paper, London Business School, 2001.

F. Derrien, K. Womack, Auction vs. book-building and the control of underpricing in hot IPO markets, *Review of Financial Studies*, forthcoming.

A. Ljungqvist, T. Jenkinson, W. Wilhelm, *Has the Introduction of Bookbuilding Increased the Efficiency of International IPOs?*, working paper, 2000.

S. Paleari, M. Giorgino, G. Giudici, *L'Esame delle Matricole: Le Nuove Quotazioni sulla Borsa Italiana dal 1985 al 2000*, Bancaria Editrice, 2001 [in Italian].

On IPO underpricing:

P. Dechow, A. Hutton, R. Sloan, Solving the new equity puzzle, in G. Bickerstaffe (ed.), *Mastering Finance*, Financial Times/Pitman publishing, 1998.

T. Loughran, J. Ritter, Why don't issuers get upset about leaving money on the table in IPOs?, *Review of Financial Studies*, **15**, 413–444, July 2002.

J. Ritter, I. Welch, A review of IPO activity, pricing, and allocations, *Journal of Finance*, August 2002.

K. Rock Why new issues are underpriced, *Journal of Financial Economics*, **15**, 187–212, January 1986.

Websites:

www.adrbny.com
www.hoovers.com/global/ipoc/index.xhtml
www.ipoworld.it
www.nasdaq.com/about/going_public.stm
www.unibg.it/sige/iposineurope/europa.htm

On ADR:

Bank of New York, *Global Offerings of Depositary Receipts: A Transaction Guide*, February 1997.

D. Ely, M. Salehizadeh, American depositary receipts: An analysis of international stock price movements, *International Review of Financial Analysis*, **10**, 243–363, 2001.

A. Karolyi, Sourcing equity internationally with Depositary Receipt Offerings: Two exceptions that prove the rule, *Journal of Applied Corporate Finance*, **10**(4), 90–101, Winter 1998.

A. Karolyi, DaimlerChrysler AG: the truly global share, *Journal of Corporate Finance*, **9**, 409–430, 2003.

D. Miller, The market reaction to international cross-listings: Evidence from Depositary Receipts, *Journal of Financial Economics*, **52**, 103–123, 1999.

W. Reese, M. Weisbach, Protection of minority shareholder interests, cross-listings in the United States, and subsequent equity offerings, *Journal of Financial Economics*, **66**, 65–104, 2002.

On share issues:

P. Chollet, E. Ginglinger, The pricing of French unit seasoned equity offerings, *European Financial Management*, **7**(1), 23–38, March 2001.

B. Eckbo, R. Masulis, O. Norli, Seasoned public offerings: Resolution of the new issues puzzle, *Journal of Financial Economics*, **56**(2), 251–291, May 2000.

J. Ritter, T. Loughran, The new issues puzzle, *Journal of Finance*, **50**(1), March 1995.

On debt issues:

O. Altinkilic, R.S. Hansen, Are there economies of scale in underwriting fees? Evidence of rising external financing costs, *Review of Financial Studies*, **13**, 191–218, 2000.

E. Altman, P. Arman, Defaults and returns on high yield bonds: Analysis through 2001, *Journal of Applied Finance*, **12**(1), Spring/Summer 2002.

H. Bouhuys, S. Jaeger, Recent developments in the high yield market, *Journal of Applied Corporate Finance*, **12**(1), Spring 1999.

R. Cantor, F. Packer, F., The credit rating industry, *Journal of Fixed Income*, **5**, 10–34, 1995.

C.L. Courtadon, *The Competitive Structure of the Eurobond Underwriting Industry*, Salomon Center Monograph, New York University, 1985.

S. Datta, M. Datta, A. Patel, The market pricing of debt IPOs, *Journal of Applied Corporate Finance*, **12**(1), Spring 1999.

B. Emerick, W. White, The case for private placements: How sophisticated investors add value to corporate debt issuers, in D. Chew (ed.), *The New Corporate Finance: Where Theory Meets Practice*, 2nd edn, McGraw-Hill, 1999.

L. Fang, Investment bank reputation and the price and quality of underwriting services, *Journal of Finance*, forthcoming, 2005.

J. Helwege, P. Kleiman, The pricing of high-yield debt IPOs, *Journal of Fixed Income*, **8**(2), 61–68, September 1998.

I. Lee, S. Lochhead, J. Ritter, Q. Zhao, The cost of raising capital, *Journal of Financial Research*, **19**, 59–74, 1996.

A. Melnik, D. Nissim, Debt issue costs and issue characteristics on the market for US solar denominated international bonds, *European Finance Review*, **7**, 277–296, 2003.

R. Taggart, The growing role of junk bonds in corporate finance, in D. Chew (ed.), *The New Corporate Finance: Where Theory Meets Practice*, 2nd edn, McGraw-Hill, 1999.

On Rule 144A:

G. Johnson, Yankee bonds and cross-border private placements: An update, *Journal of Applied Corporate Finance*, **13**(3), 80–91, Fall 2000.

M. Livingston, L. Zhou, The impact of Rule 144A debt offerings upon bond yields and underwriter fees, *Financial Management*, 5–27, Winter 2002.

PART TWO
CAPITAL STRUCTURE POLICIES

This part presents the concepts and theories that underpin all important financial decisions. In particular, we will examine their impact on value, keeping in mind that basically to maximise a value, we must minimise a cost. You will see that we have travelled far from the world of accounting, since cost is the one parameter that should not affect the choice of capital structure. The chapters of this part will introduce you to the many considerations involved when a company chooses its:

- Capital structure policy. Don't forget that "capital structure" is the mixture of debt and equity resulting from decisions on financing operations.
- Dividend (or, more generally) equity policy.

Chapter 32
VALUE AND CORPORATE FINANCE

No, Sire, it's a revolution!

Section 32.1
THE PURPOSE OF FINANCE IS TO CREATE VALUE

1/INVESTMENT AND VALUE

The accounting rules we looked at in Section I of the book showed us that an investment is a use of funds, but not a reduction in the value of assets. We will now go one step further and adopt the viewpoint of the financial manager for whom a profitable investment is one that increases the value of capital employed.

We will see that a key element in the theory of markets in equilibrium is the market value of capital employed. This theory underscores the direct link between the return on a company's investments and that required by investors buying the financial securities issued by the company.

The true measure of an investment policy is the effect it has on the value of capital employed. This concept is sometimes called "enterprise value", a term we would prefer to avoid because it can easily be confused with the value of equity (capital employed less net debt). The two are far from the same!

Hence the importance of every investment decision, as it can lead to three different outcomes:

- Where the expected return on an investment is higher than that required by investors, the value of capital employed rises instantly. An investment of 100 that always yields 15% in a market requiring a 10% return is worth 150 (100 × 15%/10%). The value of capital employed thus immediately rises by 50.
- Where the expected return on the investment is equal to that required by investors, there is neither gain nor loss. The investors put in 100, the investment is worth 100 and no value has been created.
- Where the expected return on an investment is lower than that required by investors, they have incurred a loss. If, for example, they invested 100 in a project yielding 6%, the value of the project is only 60 (100 × 6%/10%), giving an immediate loss in value of 40.

Value remains constant if the expected rate of return is equal to that required by the market.

- An immediate loss in value results if the return on the investment is lower than that required by the market.
- Value is effectively created if the expected rate of return is higher than that required by the market.

The resulting gain or loss is simply the positive or negative net present value that must be calculated when valuing any investment. All this means, in fact, that, if the investment was fairly priced, nothing changes for the investor. If it was "too expensive", investors take a loss, but if it was a good deal, they earn a profit.

The graph below shows that value is created (the value of capital employed exceeds its book value) when the economic return exceeds the weighted average cost of capital – i.e., the rate of return required by all suppliers of funds to the company.

VALUE CREATION FOR THE LARGEST EUROPEAN LISTED GROUP (2005)

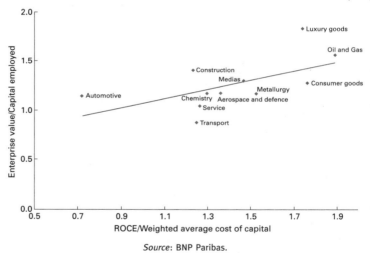

Source: BNP Paribas.

2/THE RELATIONSHIP BETWEEN COMPANIES AND THE FINANCIAL WORLD

In the preceding chapters we examined the various financial securities that make up the debt issued by a company from the point of view of the investor. We will now cross over to the other side to look at them from the issuing company's point of view:

- each **amount** contributed by investors represents a **resource** for the company;
- the financial securities held by investors as assets are recorded as liabilities in the company's balance sheet; and, most importantly,
- the **rate of return** required by investors represents a financial cost to the company.

At the financial level, a company is a portfolio of assets financed by the securities issued on financial markets. Its liabilities – i.e., the securities issued and placed with investors – are merely a financial representation of the industrial or operating assets. The financial manager's job is to ensure that this representation is as transparent as possible.

What is the role of the investor?

Investors play an active role when securities are issued, because they can simply refuse to finance the company by refusing to buy the securities. In other words, if the financial manager cannot come up with a product offering a risk/reward tradeoff acceptable to the financial market, the lack of funding will eventually push the company into bankruptcy.

We will see that when this happens it is often too late. However, the financial system can impose a sanction that is far more immediate and effective: the valuation of the securities issued by the company.

The investor has the power not just to provide funds, but also to value the company's capital employed through the securities already in issue.

Financial markets continuously value the securities in issue. In the case of debt instruments, rating agencies assign a credit rating to the company, thus determining the value of its existing debt and the terms of future loans. Similarly, by valuing the shares issued, the market is, in fact, valuing the company's equity.

So how does this mechanism work?

If a company cannot satisfy investors' risk/reward requirements, it is penalised by a lower valuation of its capital employed and, accordingly, its equity. Suppose a company offers the market an investment of 100 that is expected to yield 10 every year over a period long enough to be considered to perpetuity.[1] However, the actual yield is only 5. The disappointed investors who were expecting a 10% return will try to get rid of their investment. The equilibrium price will be 50, because, at this price, investors receive a return of 10% (5/50) and it is no longer in their interests to sell. But by now it is too late ...

Concretely, investors who are unhappy with the offered risk/reward tradeoff sell their securities, thus depressing the value of the securities issued and of capital employed, since the company's investments are not profitable enough with regard to their risk. True, the investor takes a hit, but it is sometimes wiser to cut one's losses ...

In doing so, he is merely giving tit for tat: an unhappy investor will sell off his securities, thus lowering prices. Ultimately, this can lead to financing difficulties for the company.

The "financial sanction" affects first and foremost the valuation of the company via the valuation of its shares and debt securities.

As long as the company is operating normally, its various creditors are fairly well protected.[2] Most of the fluctuation in the value of its debt stems from changes in interest rates, so changes in the value of capital employed derive mainly from changes in the value of equity. We see why the valuation of equity is so important for any normally developing company. This does not apply just to listed

1 We have applied this strong assumption to simplify the calculation, but it does not modify the reasoning.

2 Since there is always a risk, their required rate of return comprises a risk premium.

companies: unlisted companies are affected as well whenever they envisage divestments, alliances, transfers or capital increases.

The role of creditors looms large only when the company is in difficulty. The company then "belongs" to the creditors, and changes in the value of capital employed derive from changes in the value of the debt, by then generally lower than its nominal value. This is where the creditors come into play.

The valuation of capital employed and, therefore, the valuation of equity are the key variables of any financial policy, regardless of whether the company is listed or not.

3/IMPLICATIONS

Since we consider that creating value is the overriding financial objective of a company, it ensues that:

- A financial decision harms the company if it reduces the value of capital employed.
- A decision is beneficial to the company if it increases the value of capital employed.

A word of caution, however! Contrary to appearances, this does not mean that every good financial decision increases earnings or reduces costs.

Financial shortsightedness consists in failing to distinguish between cost and reduction in value, or between income and increase in value.

As can be seen, we are not in the realm of accounting, but in that of finance – in other words, value. An investment financed by cash from operations may increase earnings, but could still be insufficient with regard to the return expected by the investor, who as a result has lost value.

Certain legal decisions, such as restricting a shareholder's voting rights, have no immediate impact on the company's cash and yet may reduce the value of the corresponding financial security and thus prove costly to the holder of the security.

We cannot emphasise this aspect enough and would insist that you adopt this approach before immersing yourselves further in the raptures of financial theory.

Section 32.2
VALUE CREATION AND MARKETS IN EQUILIBRIUM

Corporate financial policy consists first and foremost of a set of principles necessary for taking decisions designed to maximise value for the providers of funds, in particular shareholders.

1/A CLEAR THEORETICAL FOUNDATION

We have just said that a company is a portfolio of assets and liabilities, and that the concepts of cost and revenue should be seen within the overall framework of value. Financial management consists of assessing the value created for the company's fund providers.

Can the overall value of the company be determined by an optimal choice of assets and liabilities? If so, how can you be sure of making the right decisions to create value?

You may already have raised the following questions:

- Can the choice of financing alone increase the value of the firm, in particular when certain investors, such as banks, have allowed the company to incur more debt than would have been wise?
- Is capital employed financed half by debt and half by equity worth more than if it were financed wholly through equity?
- More generally, can the entrepreneur increase the value of capital employed – that is, influence the market's valuation of it – by either combining independent industrial and commercial investments or implementing a shrewd financing policy?

If your answer to all these questions is yes, you attribute considerable powers to financial managers. You consider them capable of creating value independently of their industrial and commercial assets.

And yet, the equilibrium theory of markets is very clear:

When looking at valuations, financial investors are not interested in the underlying financial engineering, because they could duplicate such operations themselves. This is called the value additivity rule.

We now provide a more formal explanation of the above rule, which is based on arbitrage. To this end, let us simplify things by imagining that there are just two options for the future: either the company does well, or it does not. We will assign an equal probability to each of these outcomes. We will see how the free cash flow of three companies varies in our two states of the world:

Company	Free cash flow	
	State of the world: bad	State of the world: good
A	200	1,000
B	400	500
G	600	1,500

3 *We are assuming that companies A, B and G have the same number of shares.*

Note that the sum of the free cash flows of companies A and B is equal to that of company G. We will demonstrate that the share price of company G is equal to the sum of the prices of shares B and A.[3] To do so, let us assume that this is not the case, and that $V_A + V_B > V_G$ (where V_A, V_B and V_G are the respective share prices of A, B and G).

You will see that no speculation is necessary here to earn money. Taking no risk, you sell short one share of A and one share of B and buy one share of G. You immediately receive $V_A + V_B - V_G > 0$; yet, regardless of the company's fortunes, the future negative flows of shares A and B (sold) and positive flows of share G (bought) will cancel each other out. You have realised a gain through arbitrage.

The same method can be used to demonstrate that $V_A + V_B < V_G$ is not possible in a market that is in equilibrium. We therefore deduce that: $V_A + V_B = V_G$. It is thus clear that a diversified company, in our case G, is not worth more than the sum of its two divisions A and B.

Let us now look at the following three securities:

Company	Free cash flow	
	State of the world: bad	State of the world: good
C	100	1,000
D	500	500
E	600	1,500

According to the rule demonstrated above, $V_C + V_D = V_E$. Note that security D could be a debt security and C share capital. E would then be the capital employed. The value of capital employed of an indebted company ($V_{(C+D)}$) can be neither higher nor lower than that of the same company if it had no debt (V_E).

The additivity rule is borne out in terms of risk: if the company takes on debt, financial investors can stabilise their portfolios by adding less risky securities. Conversely, they can go into debt themselves in order to buy less risky securities. So why should they pay for an operation they can carry out themselves at no cost?

This reasoning applies to diversification as well. If its only goal is to create financial value without generating industrial and commercial synergies, there is no reason why investors should entrust the company with the diversification of their portfolio.

2/ILLUSTRATION

Are some asset combinations worth more than the value of their individual components, regardless of any industrial synergies arising when some operations are common to several investment projects? In other words, is the whole worth more than the sum of its parts?

Or, again, is the required rate of return lower simply because two investments are made at the same time? Company managers are fuzzy on this issue. They generally answer in the negative, although their actual investment decisions tend to imply the opposite. Take Gucci, for example, which was taken over in 2002 by the Pinault Printemps Redoute Group. If financial synergies exist, one would have to conclude that the required rate of return in the luxury segment differs depending on whether the company is independent or part of a group. Gucci would therefore appear to be worth more as part of the Pinault Group than on a standalone basis.

The question is not as specious at it seems. In fact, it raises a fundamental issue. If the required return on Gucci has fallen since it became part of the Pinault Group, its financing costs will have declined as well, giving it a substantial, permanent and possibly decisive advantage over its competitors.

Diversifying corporate activities reduces risk, but does it also reduce the rate of return required by investors?

Suppose the required rate of return on a company producing a single product is 10%. The company decides to diversify by acquiring a company of the same size on which the required rate of return is 8%. Will the required rate of return on the new group be lower than $(10\% + 8\%)/2 = 9\%$ because it carries less risk than the initial single-product company?

We must not be misled into believing that a lower degree of risk must be always matched by a lower required rate of return. On the contrary: **markets only remunerate systematic or market risks – i.e., those that cannot be eliminated by diversification.** We have seen that unsystematic or specific risks, which investors can eliminate by diversifying their portfolios, are not remunerated. Only non-diversifiable risks related to market fluctuations are remunerated. This point was discussed in Chapter 22.

Since diversifiable risks are not remunerated, **a company's value remains the same whether it is independent or part of a group.** Gucci is not worth more, now that it has become a division of the Pinault Group. All else being equal, the required rate of return in the luxury sector is the same whether the company is independent or belongs to a group.

On the other hand, Gucci's value will increase if, and only if, Pinault's management allows it to improve its return on capital employed.

Purely financial diversification creates no value.

Value is created only when the sum of cash flows from the two investments is higher because they are both managed by the same group. This is the result of **industrial synergies** $(2 + 2 = 5)$, **and not financial synergies**, which do not exist.

The large groups that indulged in a spate of financial diversifications in the 1960s have since realised that these operations were unproductive and frequently loss-making. Diversification is a delicate art that can only succeed if the diversifying company already has expertise in the new business. Combining investments *per se* does not maximise value, unless industrial synergies exist. Otherwise, an investment is either "good" or "bad" depending on how it stacks up against the required rate of return.

In other words, managers must act on cash flows; **they cannot influence the discount rate applied to them** unless they reduce their risk exposure.

There is no connection between the required return on any investment and the portfolio in which the investment is held.

Unless it can draw on industrial synergies, the value of a company remains the same whether it is independent or part of a large group. The financial investor does not want to pay a premium in the form of lower returns for something he can do himself at no cost by diversifying his portfolio.

3/A FIRST CONCLUSION

The value of the securities issued by a company is not connected to the underlying financial engineering. Instead, it simply reflects the market's reaction to the perceived profitability and risk of industrial and commercial operations.

The equilibrium theory of markets leads us to a very simple and obvious rule, that of the additivity of value, which in practice is frequently neglected. Regardless of developments in financial criteria, in particular earnings per share, value cannot be created simply by adding (diversifying) or reducing value that is already in equilibrium.

To ensure a flow of financing, financial managers have to transform their industrial and commercial assets into financial assets. This means that they have to sell the very substance of the company (future risk and returns) in a financial form.

Financial investors evaluate the securities offered or already issued according to their required rate of return. By valuing the company's share, they are, in fact, directly valuing the company's operating assets.

The valuation of the different securities has nothing to do with financial engineering; it is based on a valuation of the company's industrial and commercial assets.

We emphasise that this rule applies to listed and unlisted companies alike, a fact that the latter are forced to face at some point. Capital employed always has an equilibrium value, and the entrepreneur must ultimately recognise it.

This approach should be incorporated into the methodology of financial decision-making. Some strategies are based on maximising other types of value – for example, nuisance value. They are particularly risky and are outside the conceptual framework of corporate finance. The first reflex when faced with any kind of financial decision is to analyse whether it will create or destroy value. If values are in equilibrium, financial decisions will be immaterial.

Does this mean that, ultimately, financing or diversification policies have no impact on value?

On the contrary, the equilibrium theory of markets represents a kind of ideal that is very useful for the financial professional but, like all ideals, it tends to remain out of reach. In a way, it is the paradise that all financial managers strive for, while secretly hoping never to reach such a perfect state of boredom ...

Our aim is not to encourage nihilism, merely a degree of humility.

Section 32.3
VALUE AND ORGANISATION THEORIES

1/LIMITS OF THE EQUILIBRIUM THEORY OF MARKETS

The equilibrium theory of markets offers an overall framework, but it completely disregards the immediate interests of the various parties involved, even if their interests tend to converge in the medium term.

Paradoxically, the neoclassical theory emphasises the general interest while completely overlooking that of the individual parties.

We cannot rely on the equilibrium theory alone to explain corporate finance.

Since the equilibrium theory demonstrates that finance cannot change the size of the capital employed, but only how it is divided up, it ensues that many financial problems stem from the struggle between the various players in the financial realm.

First and foremost, we have the various parties providing funding to the company. To simplify, they can be divided into two categories: shareholders and creditors. But we will soon see that, in fact, each type of security issued gives rise to its own interest group: shareholders, preferred creditors, ordinary creditors, investors in hybrid products, etc. Further on in this chapter, we will see that interests may even diverge within the same funding category.

One example should suffice to convince you. According to the equilibrium theory of markets, investing at the required rate of return does not change the value of capital employed. But if the investment is very risky and, therefore, potentially very profitable, creditors, who earn a fixed rate, will only see the increased risk without a corresponding increase in their return. The value of their claims thus decreases to the benefit of shareholders, whose shares increase by the same amount, the value of capital employed remaining the same. And, yet, this investment was made at its equilibrium price.

This is where the financial manager comes into play! His role is to distribute value between the various parties involved. **In fact, the financial manager must be a negotiator at heart.**

But let's not forget that the managers of the company are stakeholders as well. Since portfolio theory presupposes good diversification, there is a distinction between investors and managers, who have divergent interests with different levels of information (internal and external). This last point calls into question one of the basic tenets of equilibrium theory, which is that all parties have access to the same information.

2/SIGNALLING THEORY AND ASYMMETRIC INFORMATION

Signalling theory is based on two basic ideas:

- the same information is not available to all parties: the managers of a company may have more information than investors;
- even if the same information were available to all, it would not be perceived in the same way, a fact frequently observed in everyday life.

Thus, it is unrealistic to assume that information is fairly distributed to all parties at all times – i.e., that it is symmetrical as in the case of efficient markets. On the contrary, **asymmetric information** is the rule.

In short, perfect and equally shared information is at best an objective, and most often an illusion.

This can clearly raise problems. Asymmetric information may lead investors to undervalue a company. As a result, its managers might hesitate to increase its capital because they consider the share price to be too low. This may mean that profitable investment opportunities are lost for lack of financing, or that the existing shareholders find their stake adversely diluted because the company launched a capital increase anyway.

This is where the **communication policy** comes into its own: basing financial decisions on the financial criteria alone is not enough: managers also have to convince the markets that these decisions are wise.

As a result, pure financial expertise does not suffice if it is not matched by an ability to communicate and to shape market sentiment.

The cornerstone of the financial communications policy is the **signal** the managers of a company send to investors. Contrary to what many financial managers and CEOs believe, the signal is neither an official statement or a confidential tip. **It is a real financial decision, taken freely, and which may have negative financial consequences for the decision-maker if it turns out to be wrong.**

After all, investors are far from naive and they take each signal with the requisite pinch of salt. Three points merit attention:

➤ **Investors' first reaction is to ask themselves why the signal is being sent, since nothing comes for free in the financial world.** The signal will be perceived negatively if the issuer's interests are contrary to those of investors. For example, the sale of a company by its majority shareholder would, in theory, be a negative signal for the company's growth prospects. Managers must therefore pursuade the buyer of the contrary or provide a convincing explanation for the disposal.

Similarly, owner-managers cannot fool investors by praising the merits of a capital increase without subscribing to it!

However, the market will consider the signal to be credible if it deems that it is in the issuer's interest that the signal be correct. This would be the case, for example, if the managers reinvest their own assets in the company ...

➤ **The reputation of management and its communications policy** certainly play a role, but we must not overestimate their importance or lasting impact.

➤ **The market supervisory authorities stand ready to impose penalties** on the dissemination of misleading information or insider-trading. If investors, particularly international investors, believe that supervision is effective, they will factor this into their decisions. This said, some managers may be tempted to send incorrect signals to obtain unwarranted advantages. For example, they could give overly optimistic guidance on their company's prospects in order to push up share prices. However, markets catch on to such misrepresentations quickly and react to incorrect signals by piling out of the stock.

In such a context, the "watchdog" role played by the market authorities is crucial and the recent past has shown that the authorities intend to assume it in full. Such rigour is essential if we are to have the best possible financial markets and the lowest possible financing costs.

Financial managers must therefore always consider how investors will react to their financial decisions. They cannot content themselves with wishful thinking, but must make a rational and detailed analysis of the situation to ensure that their communication is convincing.

Signalling theory says that corporate financial decisions (e.g., financing, dividend payout) are signals sent by the company's managers to investors. It examines the incentives that encourage good managers to issue the right signals and discourage managers of ailing companies from using these same signals to give a misleading picture of their company's financial health.

In sum, information asymmetry may lead to a share being priced at less than its objective value, with two consequences:

* investments are not maximised because the cost of financing is too high;
* the choice of financing is skewed in favour of sources (such as debt) where there is less information asymmetry.

Stephen Ross initiated the main studies in this field in 1977.

3/AGENCY THEORY

Agency theory says that a company is not a single, unified entity. It considers a company to be a legal arrangement that is the culmination of a complex process in which the conflicting objectives of individuals, some of whom may represent other organisations, are resolved by means of a set of contractual relationships.

On this basis, a company's behaviour can be compared with that of a market, insofar as it is the result of a complex balancing process. Taken individually, the various stakeholders in the company have their own objectives and interests that may not necessarily be spontaneously reconcilable. As a result, conflicts may arise between them, especially since our modern corporate system requires that the suppliers of funds entrust managers with the actual administration of the company.

Agency theory analyses the consequences of certain financial decisions in terms of risk, profitability and, more generally, the interests of the various parties. It shows that some decisions may go against the simple criteria of maximising the wealth of all parties to the benefit of just one of the suppliers of funds.

To simplify, we consider that an agency relationship exists between two parties when one of them, the agent, carries out an activity on behalf of the other, the principal. The agent has been given a mandate to act or take decisions on behalf of the principal. This is the essence of the agency relationship.

This very broad definition allows us to include a variety of domains such as the resolution of conflicts between:

* executive shareholders/nonexecutive shareholders;
* nonshareholder executives/shareholders;
* creditors/shareholders.

Thus, shareholders give the company executives a mandate to manage the funds that have been entrusted to them to the best of their ability. However, their concern is that the executives could pursue other objectives than maximising the value of the equity, such as increasing the company's size at the cost of profitability, minimising the risk to capital employed by rejecting certain investments that would create value, but could put the company in difficulty if they fail, etc.

One way of resolving such conflicts of interest are stock options or linking management compensation to share performance. This gives managers a financial incentive that coincides with that of their principal, the shareholders. Since stock options give the holders the right to buy or subscribe to shares at a fixed price, the managers have a financial incentive to see the price of their company's shares rise so that they receive significant capital gains. It is then in their interests to make the financial decisions that create the most value. In France over half of listed companies have set up stock option plans.

In France, one-third of management compensation in industrial firms with turnover of over US$500m is based on the economic performance of the company and its share price. In the US, the proportion is two-thirds..

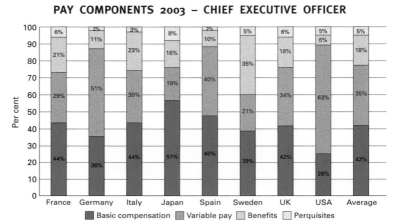

PAY COMPONENTS 2003 – CHIEF EXECUTIVE OFFICER

Debt plays a role as well since it has a constraining effect on managers and encourages them to maximise cash flows so that the company can meet its interest and principal payments. Failing this, the company risks bankruptcy and the managers lose their jobs. Maximising cash flows is in the interests of shareholders as well, since it raises the value of shareholders' equity. Thus, the interests of management and shareholders converge. Maybe debt is the modern whip!

The diverging interests of the various parties generate a number of costs called agency costs. These comprise:

- the cost of monitoring managers' efforts (control procedures, audit systems, performance-based compensation) to ensure that they correspond to the principal's objectives. Stock options represent an agency cost since they are exercised at less than the going market price for the stock;
- the costs incurred by the agents to vindicate themselves and reassure the principals that their management is effective, such as the publication of annual reports;
- residual costs.

Ang et al. (2000) have shown that the margins and asset turnover rates of small- and medium-sized American firms tend to be lower in companies managed by nonshareholding CEOs, in which managers have little stake in the capital, and that have many nonexecutive shareholders.

The main references in this field are Jensen and Meckling (1976), Grossman and Hart (1980), and Fama (1980). Their research aims to provide a scientific explanation of the relationship between managers and shareholders and its impact on corporate value.

Their main contribution is thus the endeavour to compare financial theory and organisational theory.

This research forms the intellectual foundation on which the concept of **corporate governance** was built. Corporate governance attempts to regulate the decision-making power of executives to ensure that they do not serve their own vested interests to the detriment chiefly of shareholders, but also of creditors, employees and the company in general.

These developments have caused Treasury shares, cross-shareholdings and voting right restrictions to be called into question. More board of director meetings are being held and a percentage of listed companies have set up committees to monitor internal auditing, compensation and the re-election of executives or directors. The proportion of directors with no links to company executives or large shareholders has increased as well to 27% in France. In the US, where capital ownership tends to be more widely dispersed, this proportion is 80%. Similarly, the number of directorships held by the same person has been limited to five,[4] executive compensation is now routinely disclosed and the accounts are released more rapidly. All these measures are designed to give shareholders more control over managers.

4 *Not including directorships in controlled, unlisted companies.*

4/Free rider problem

We saw above that the interests of the different types of providers of funds may diverge, but so may those of members of the same category.

The term "free rider" is used to describe the behaviour of an investor who benefits from transactions carried out by other investors in the same category without participating in these transactions himself.

This means, first, that there must be several – usually, a large number – of investors in the same type of security and, second, that a specific operation is undertaken implying some sort of sacrifice, at least in terms of opportunity cost, on the part of the investors in these securities.

As a result, when considering a financial decision, one must examine whether free riders exist and what their interests might be.

Below are two examples:

- Responding to a takeover bid: if the offer is motivated by synergies between the bidding company and its target, the business combination will create value. This means that it is in the general interest of all parties for the bid to succeed and for the shareholders to tender their shares. However, it would be in the individual interest of these same shareholders to hold on to their shares in order to benefit fully from future synergies.
- Bank *A* holds a small claim on a cash-strapped company that owes money to many other banks: it would be in the interests of the banks as a whole to grant

additional loans to tide the company over until it can pay them back, but the interest of our individual bank would be to let the other banks, which have much larger exposure, advance the funds themselves. Bank A would thus hold a better valued existing claim without incurring a discount on the new credits granted.

Section 32.4
HOW CAN WE CREATE VALUE?

Before we begin simulating different rates of return, we would like to underscore once again that a project, investment or company can only realise extraordinary returns if it enjoys a strategic advantage. The equilibrium theory of markets tells us that, under perfect competition, the net present value of a project should be nil. If a financial manager wants to advise on investment choices, he will no doubt have to make a number of calculations to estimate the future return of the investment. But he will also have to look at it from a strategic point of view, incorporating the various economic theories he has learned.

A project's real profitability can only be explained in terms of economic rent – that is, a position in which the return obtained on investments is higher than the required rate of return given the degree of risk. The essence of all corporate strategies is to obtain economic rents – that is, to generate imperfections in the product market and/or in factors of production, thus creating barriers to entry that the corporate managers strive to exploit and defend.

The purpose of a financial strategy is to try to "skew" market mechanisms in order to secure an economic rent.

But don't fool yourself, economic rents do not last for ever. Returns that are higher than the required rate, taking into account risk exposure, inevitably attract the attention of competitors or of the antitrust authorities, as in the case of Microsoft. Sooner or later, deregulation and technological advances put an end to them. There are no impregnable fortresses, only those for which the right angle of attack has not yet been found.

We insist on the consequences of a good strategy. When based on accurate forecasts, it immediately boosts the value of capital employed and, accordingly, the share price. This explains the difference between the book value of capital employed and its market value, which may vary by a factor of 1–10, and sometimes even more.

Rather than rising gradually as the returns on the investment accrue, the share price adjusts immediately so that the investor receives the exact required return, no more, no less. And if everything proceeds smoothly thereafter, the investment will generate the required return until expectations prove too optimistic or too pessimistic.

Section 32.5
VALUE AND TAXATION

Depending on the company's situation, certain types of securities may carry tax benefits. You are certainly aware that tax planning can generate savings, thereby creating value or at least preventing the loss of value. Reducing taxes is a form of value creation for investors and shareholders. All else equal, an asset with tax-free flows is worth more than the same asset subject to taxation.

Better to have a liability with cash outflows that can be deducted from taxes than the same liability with outflows that are not deductible.

This goes without saying, and any CFO worthy of his title will do his best to reduce tax payments.

However, tax optimisation should not merely endeavour to reduce costs if this leads to higher risks. Financial managers must think in terms of value.

They must carefully examine the impact each financial decision will have on taxes. The main issues we will be addressing in the following chapters are:

- taxation of debt vs. equity;
- taxation of accelerated depreciation and one-off writedowns;
- taxation of capital gains vs. ordinary income (dividends or coupons);
- taxation of financial income and expenses;
- usable or unusable tax loss carryforwards.

SUMMARY

download

From a financial point of view, a company's aim is to create value; i.e., it should be able to make investments on which the rate of return is higher than the required rate of return, given the risk involved. If this condition is met, the share price or the value of the share will rise. If not, it will fall.

The theory of markets in equilibrium teaches us that it is very difficult to create lasting value. Rates of return actually achieved tend over the medium term to meet required rates of return, given technological progress and deregulation, which reduce entry barriers and economic rents that all managers must strive to create and defend, even if sooner or later they will be eliminated. Similarly, diversification or debt cannot create value for the investor who can, at no cost on an individual level, diversify his portfolio or go into debt. Finally, **there is no connection between the required return on any investment and the portfolio in which the investment is held** – value can only be created by industrial synergies. **Financial synergies do not exist.**

It is important to understand that the creation of value is not just the outcome of a calculation of returns. It has an economic basis which is a sort of economic rent that comes out of a strategy, the purpose of which is to "skew" market mechanisms. Accordingly, the conceptual framework of the theory of markets in equilibrium alone fails to explain corporate finance.

Signal and agency theory were developed to make up for the shortcomings of the theory of markets in equilibrium.

Signal theory is based on the assumption that information is not equally available to all parties at the same time, and that information asymmetry is the rule. This can have disastrous consequences and result in very low valuations or a suboptimum investment policy. Accordingly, certain financial decisions, known as signals, are taken to shake up this information asymmetry. These signals can however have a negative financial impact on the party who initiates them if they turn out to be unfounded.

Agency theory calls into question the claim that all of the stakeholders in the company (shareholders, managers, creditors) have a single goal – to create value. Agency theory shows how, on the contrary, their interests may differ and some decisions (related to borrowing, for example) or products (stock options) come out of attempts at achieving convergence between the interests of managers and shareholders or at protecting creditors. Agency theory forms the intellectual basis of corporate governance.

QUESTIONS

quiz

1/ Take the example on p. 641 and give a probability of 50% to the two states of the world. Calculate the value of *A*, *B* and *G*. Calculate the value of *C*, *D* and *E*. What are your conclusions?

2/ You offer investors the opportunity to invest 100, financed solely with equity. Assuming that no taxes are payable, projected constant annual profits to perpetuity are 25 (we assume that necessary capital expenditure is equal to depreciation, that change in WCR is nil and that all profits are paid out).

   (a)   What is the rate of return required by the market on this investment?

   (b)   The return on this investment only comes to 10 per year. If the required rate of return is not modified, what will the value of this share be on the secondary market?

   (c)   Same question if the return on the investment is 50 per year? And if profits are nil?

   (d)   What impact will all of the above scenarios have on the company?

   (e)   Is it possible to define a simple rule on the creation and destruction of value?

3/ What does it mean when a source of financing is cheap?

4/ When is value created:

     ○   in the choice of investment?
     ○   in the choice of financing?

5/ You are required to analyse a number of decisions and establish whether or not they will create value. You then have to decide whether value was in fact created or transferred on a general level, and if so, who were the winners and who were the losers.

	Creation of value	Transfer of value
Set up an oligopoly		
Innovate		
Secure loans at a lower rate than the market rate		
Improve productivity		
Reduce income tax		

6/ Analyse the following financial decisions. Do they send out positive, negative or neutral signals?

Signal	+	−	=
Sale of company by managing shareholder			
Sale of company by non-managing shareholder			
Failure of a managing shareholder who has invested most of his wealth in the company to subscribe to a capital increase			
Failure of a capital investor to subscribe to a capital increase			
Increase the Dividend Per Share (DPS)			
A family-run company running up excessive debts			
Giving out free shares in order to maintain the dividend per share			
Giving subscription rights to all shareholders at a strike price that is twice the price at which the share is currently trading			

7/ What is synergy?

8/ Can we talk about financial synergy?

9/ What is a conglomerate discount? How can it be avoided?

10/ Show how the share price of a very profitable company which invests at a rate of return that is higher than the required rate of return can still drop.

11/ Should an investment have a higher expected rate of return than required rate of return? Generally will value always be created?

12/ Show how the conglomerate discount leads to an increase in the cost of equity.

13/ Can a signal be sent if there is no cash flow?

14/ What is an economic rent? What is it based on?

15/ A company that is close to insolvency carries out a capital increase. Is this a signal? Why? What criteria can you identify as being necessary for a decision to be described as a signal?

16/ An increasing number of large groups now ask their top managers to invest a large amount of their personal wealth (often more than 40%) in company shares. What is the theory behind this type of behaviour? Why?

17/ Can you explain why the behaviour described in Question 17 could have the secondary effect of encouraging managers to diversify their groups' activities?

1/ A company has two divisions, A and B, for which the figures are as follows:

	Division A	Division B
Capital employed	1,000	1,000
Expected return	15%	15%
Net operating income	50	300

(a) What are the values for divisions A and B if you assume, for calculation purposes, that operating income is constant to perpetuity?

(b) The company pays out 50 and so finances its investments for 300. The company invests everything in division B at the same return on capital employed (30%). How much value is created?

(c) Same question if the 300 is invested in division A at the average rate of return of A (5%).

(d) Same question if the 300 is divided equally between A and B.

(e) What are your conclusions?

Questions

1/ $V_A = 600$, $V_B = 450$, $V_G = 1,050$, $V_C = 550$, $V_D = 500$, $V_E = 1,050$, $V_A + V_B = V_G$, $V_E - V_D = V_C$.

2/ *(a)* 25%.

(b) 40.

(c) 200; 0.

(d) None.

(e) Value is created when the return is higher than the required rate of return; and vice versa.

3/ That the risk is underestimated by providers of funds.

4/ In the choice of investment: when an investment is made with a return that is higher than the required rate of return. In the choice of financing: when a company can finance its operations at a lower rate of return than usually required by the market for the same risk.

5/ Transfer of client value to shareholders. Creation of value. Transfer of creditors' value to shareholders. Creation of value. Creation of value.

6/ Signal: Negative. Neutral. Neutral. Negative. Positive. Positive. Positive. Neutral.

7/ Synergy results from a reduction in charges or an improvement in products that leads to the value of the whole being greater than the sum of the values of the parts.

8/ No.

9/ The fact that a conglomerate is worth more than the parts of which it is made up. By dismantling conglomerates.

10/ This is possible because of an error in anticipation (which was too high at the outset).

11/ This is the strength of a good corporate strategy, but obviously, if industrial markets are efficient, it is impossible. Macroeconomically, this could be a simple transfer of value between the customers and the shareholders.

12/ If a conglomerate raises funds of 100 to invest in various assets, and if a discount of 25% is applicable, the 100 will only be worth 75 and it is at this price that new shares will be issued and not 100. This is where the higher cost of equity comes from.

13/ *No, because a decision based on financial policy is only a signal if it has negative financial consequences for the management which took the decision, if the signal turns out to be wrong.*

14/ *An economic rent is a situation in which it is possible to obtain a higher return on capital employed than the required rate of return given the risk, on the basis of a special strategic advantage. It is based on a (temporary) lack of equilibrium of the market.*

15/ *This cannot be interpreted as a signal because the company has no other choice than to carry out a capital increase if it wishes to avoid bankruptcy. A decision can only be qualified as a signal if it is taken freely and if there is a viable alternative.*

16/ *Agency theory, in order to reconcile management's financial criteria with those of the shareholders who have appointed them as managers.*

17/ *Because this severely limits the diversification of the personal portfolios of managers, who may wish to make up for this by diversifying the activities in which their groups are involved.*

Exercise

1/ (a) $V_A = 50/0.15 = 333.3$; $V_B = 300/0.15 = 2,000$.
 (b) V_A unchanged; $V_B = 390/0.15 = 2,600$; for 300 reinvested, creation of value $= 300$.
 (c) V_B unchanged; $V_A = 65/0.15 = 433.33$; for 300 reinvested, destruction of value $= 200$.
 (d) $V_A = 57.5/0.15 = 383.33$; $V_B = 345/0.15 = 2,300$; for 300 reinvested, creation of value $= 50$.
 (e) Tendency within conglomerates to spread the investment budget. This does not make for optimal returns.

BIBLIOGRAPHY

For more on signal and agency theories:

A. Alchian, H. Demsetz, Production, information costs and economic organization, *American Economic Review*, 777–795, 1972.
J. Ang, R. Cole, J. Wuhkin, Agency costs and ownership structure, *Journal of Finance*, 81–106, February 2000.
E. Fama, Agency problems and the theory of the firm, *Journal of Political Economy*, 288–307, April 1980.
S. Grossman, O. Hart, Takeover bids, the free-rider problem and the theory of the corporation, *Bell Journal of Economics*, 42–64, Spring 1980.
M. Jensen, W. Meckling, Theory of the firm: Managerial behavior, agency costs and ownership structure, *Journal of Financial Economics*, 305–360, October 1976.
S. Ross, The determination of capital structure: Incentive signalling approach, *Bell Journal of Economics*, 23–40, Summer 1977.
S. Ross, Some notes on financial incentive signalling models, activity choice and risk preferences, *Journal of Finance*, 777–792, June 1978.

For more on corporate governance:

www.ecgn.org, the website of European Corporate Governance, an Institution which monitors the corporate governance practices in the world.

Stock options and, more generally, other forms of variable compensation:

A. Morgan, A. Poulser, Linking pay to performance–compensation proposal in the S&P 500, *Journal of Financial Economics*, 489–523, December 2001.

An interesting website on the remuneration process is:

www.towersperrin.com

For more on all of the topics covered in this chapter:

K. Ward, *Corporate Financial Strategy*, Macmillan, 2001.

Chapter 33
CAPITAL STRUCTURE AND THE THEORY OF PERFECT CAPITAL MARKETS

Does paradise exist in the world of finance?

The question that lies at the heart of this chapter is whether there is an optimal capital structure, one in which the combination of net debt and equity maximises enterprise value. In other words, is there a capital structure in which the Weighted Average Cost of Capital (WACC, as defined below) is the lowest possible?

This question may come as a surprise considering that in Chapter 13 we demonstrated the effect of leverage on accounting parameters, but bear in mind that we have left the world of accounting to enter into the realm of finance.

In fact, if we were to skip directly to our conclusion, we could have called this chapter "The futility of accounting leverage in finance".

Note that we consider the weighted average cost of capital (or cost of capital), denoted k or WACC, to be the rate of return required by all the company's investors either to buy or to hold its securities. **It is the company's cost of financing and the minimum return its investments must generate in the medium term. If not, the company is heading for ruin.**

k_D is the rate of return required by lenders of a given company, k_E is the cost of equity required by the company's shareholders and k is the weighted average rate of the two types of financing, equity and net debt (from now on referred to simply as debt). The weighting reflects the breakdown of equity and debt in enterprise value.

With V_D, the market value of net debt, and V_E the market value of equity, we get:

$$k = k_D \times \left(\frac{V_D}{V_D + V_E} \right) + k_E \times \left(\frac{V_E}{V_D + V_E} \right)$$

or, since the enterprise value is equal to that of net debt plus equity ($V = V_E + V_D$):

$$k = k_D \times \left(\frac{V_D}{V} \right) + k_E \times \left(\frac{V_E}{V} \right)$$

If, for example, the rate of return required by the company's creditors is 5% and that required by shareholders 10% and the value of debt is equal to that of equity, the return required by all of the company's sources of funding will be 7.5%. Its weighted average cost of capital is thus 7.5%.

Example: Recent
developments in
the cost of capital
of the largest
listed European
groups.

WEIGHTED AVERAGE COST OF CAPITAL OF THE MOST IMPORTANT LISTED EUROPEAN GROUPS

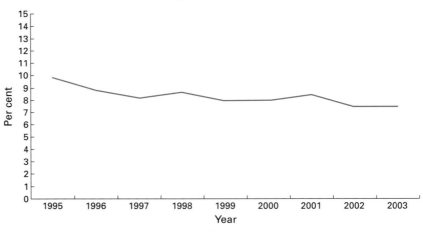

Source: BNP Paribas.

To simplify our calculations and demonstrations in this chapter, we will assume infinite durations for all debt and investments. This enables us to apply perpetual bond analytics and, more importantly, to assume that the company's capital structure remains unchanged during the life of the project, income being distributed in full.

The assumption of an infinite horizon is just a convention designed to simplify our calculations and demonstrations, but they remain accurate within a limited time horizon (say, for simplicity, 15–20 years!).

We will start by assuming a tax-free environment, both for the company and the investor, in which neither income nor capital gains are taxed. In other words, heaven! Concretely, the optimal capital structure is one that minimises k – i.e., that maximises the enterprise value (V). Remember that the enterprise value results from discounting free cash flow at rate k. However, free cash flow is not related to the type of financing. The demonstrations below endeavour to measure and explain changes in k according to the company's capital structure.

Section 33.1
THE EVIDENCE FROM THE REAL WORLD

According to conventional wisdom, there is an optimal capital structure that maximises enterprise value by the judicious use of debt and the leverage it offers. This enables the company to minimise its weighted average cost of capital – that is, the cost of financing.

Why do we say that? Because there is enough evidence showing that the leverage of companies is not highly volatile. If the leverage doesn't change so often it means that companies are generally satisfied with the level of debt they have in their capital structure.

We know that *ex ante* debt is always cheaper than equity ($k_D < k_E$) because it is less risky. Consequently, a moderate increase in debt will help reduce k, since a more expensive resource, equity, is being replaced by a cheaper one, debt. This is the practical application of the preceding formula and the use of leverage.

However, any increase in debt also increases the risk for the shareholder. Markets then demand a higher k_E the more debt we add in the capital structure. The increase in the expected rate of return on equity cancels out part (or all, if the firm becomes highly leveraged!) of the decrease in cost arising on the recourse to debt. More specifically, the traditional theory claims that a certain level of debt gives rise to a very real risk of bankruptcy. Rather than remaining constant, shareholders' perception of risk evolves in stages.

The risk accruing to shareholders increases in step with that of debt, prompting the market to demand a higher return on equity. This process continues until it has cancelled out the positive impact of debt financing.

At this level of financial leverage, the company has achieved the optimal capital structure ensuring the lowest weighted average cost of capital and thus the highest enterprise value. Should the company continue to take on debt, the resulting gains would no longer offset the higher return required by the market.

Moreover, the cost of debt increases after a certain level because it becomes more risky. At this point, not only has the company's cost of equity increased, but also that of its debt.

In short, the evidence from the "real world" shows that an optimal capital structure can be achieved – let's say – with some, but not too much leverage.

REAL WORLD APPROACH TO OPTIMAL CAPITAL STRUCTURE

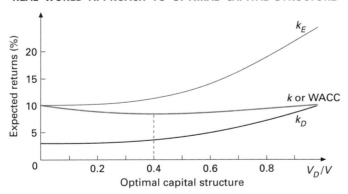

According to the traditional approach, an optimal capital structure can be achieved where the weighted average cost of capital is minimal.

In this example, the debt-to-equity ratio that minimises k is 0.4. The optimal capital structure is thus achieved with 40% debt financing and 60% equity financing.

The evidence from the capital structure can be explained with a theoretical model. This is a success. Why? Because if we have a model that explains the determinants of an optimal capital structure policy we can:

- *explain* and interpret the behaviour of companies;
- *predict* where companies should position themselves and *suggest* these positions and an appropriate "convergence path".

The common name of the model we are talking about is the (static) "**tradeoff model**". It simply states that the optimal capital structure of a company is where benefits and costs of debt are best balanced.

This "thriller solution" – a startlingly simple conclusion – has been the result of the long evolution of financial theory, a story that started out with Franco Modigliani and Merton Miller in 1958 with a totally different result compared with "real world" wisdom.

Section 33.2
THE CAPITAL STRUCTURE POLICY IN PERFECT FINANCIAL MARKETS

The perfect markets theory of capital structure contradicts the "real world" approach. It states that, barring any distortions, there is *no one* optimal capital structure.

We will demonstrate this proposition by means of an example given by Franco Modigliani and Merton Miller (MM), who showed that in a perfect market and without taxes, the traditional approach is incorrect. **If there is no optimal capital structure, the overall cost of equity (k or WACC) remains the same regardless of the firm's debt policy.**

The main assumptions behind the theorem are:

1 companies can issue only two types of securities: risk-free debt and equity;
2 financial markets are frictionless;
3 there is no corporate and personal taxation;
4 there are no transaction costs;
5 firms cannot go bankrupt;
6 *insiders* and *outsiders* have the same set of information;
7 management acts on the exclusive behalf of shareholders.

According to MM, investors can take on debt just like companies. So, in a perfect market they have no reason to pay companies to do something they can handle themselves at no cost.

Imagine two companies that are completely identical except for their capital structure. The value of their respective debt and equity differs, but the sum of both – i.e., the enterprise value of each company – is the same. If the reverse were true, equilibrium would be restored by arbitrage.

We will demonstrate this using the examples of companies X and Y, which are identical except that X is unlevered and Y carries debt of 80,000 at 5%. If the traditional approach were correct, Y's weighted average cost of capital would be lower than that of X and its enterprise value higher:

	Company X	Company Y
Operating profit: OP	20,000	20,000
Interest expense (at 5%): IE	0	4,000
Net profit: NP	20,000	16,000
Dividend: $DIV - NP$20,000 16,000		
Cost of equity: k_E	10%	12%
Equity: $V_{CP} = DIV/k_E$	200,000	133,333
Debt: $V_D = IE/k_D$	0	80,000
Enterprise value: $V = V_E + V_D$	200,000	213,333
Weighted average cost of capital: $k = OP/V$	10%	9.4%
Gearing: V_D/V_E	0%	60%

Y's cost of capital is higher than that of X since Y's shareholders bear both the operating risk and that of the capital structure (debt), whereas X's shareholders incur only operating risk.

Modigliani and Miller demonstrated that Y's shareholders can achieve a higher return on their investment by buying shares of X, at no greater risk.

Thus, if a shareholder holding 1% of Y shares (equal to 1,333) wants to obtain a better return on investment, he must:

- sell his Y shares ...
- ... **replicate** Y's debt/equity structure in proportion to his 1% stake – that is, borrow $1,333 \times 60\% = 800$ at 5% ...
- ... invest all this $(800 + 1,333 = 2,133)$ in X shares.

The shareholder's risk exposure is the same as before the operation: he is still exposed to operating risk, which is the same on X and Y, as well as to financial risk, since his exposure to Y's debt has been transferred to his personal borrowing. However, the personal wealth invested by our shareholder is still the same (1,333).

Formerly, the investor received annual dividends of 160 from company Y (12% × 1,333 or 1% of 16,000). Now, his net income on the same investment will be:

	Dividends (company X)	2,133 × 10%	=	213
−	Interest expense	800 × 5%	=	40
=	Net income		=	173

He is now earning 173 every year instead of the former 160, *on the same personal amount invested and with the same level of risk.*

Y's shareholders will thus sell their Y shares to invest in X shares, reducing the value of Y's equity and increasing that of X. This arbitrage will cease as soon as the enterprise values of the two companies come into line again.

Thus, barring any distortions, the enterprise value of a company must be independent of its financing policy.

Investing in a leveraged company is neither more expensive nor cheaper than in a company without debt; in other words, the investor should not pay twice, once when buying shares at enterprise value and again to reimburse the debt. The value of the debt is deducted from the price paid for the equity.

While obvious, this principle is frequently forgotten. And, yet, it should be easy to remember: the value of an asset, be it a factory, a painting, a subsidiary or a house, is the same regardless of whether it was financed by debt, equity or a combination of the two. As Merton Miller explained when receiving the Nobel Prize for economics, "it is the size of the pizza that matters, not how many slices it is cut up into."

Or, to restate this: the weighted average cost of capital does not depend on the sources of financing. True, it is the weighted average of the rates of return required by the various providers of funds, but this average is independent of its different components, which adjust to any changes in the financial structure.

Let's look at a more practical implication. Suppose a company with an invested capital (working capital and fixed assets) of €500,000. The investments can generate a constant (and perpetual) operating income of €120,000. Suppose also that:

- annual depreciation equals the new investments of each period;
- the annual variation of working capital is approximately zero;
- the payout ratio is 100%.

Let us limit the analysis to a range of leverage values between 0% and 25%. The cost of debt is 8%.

The following table shows the effects of debt on net income and on total cash flows (dividends + interest expenses), *when there is no taxation and no other distortions:*

$V_D/(V_D + V_E)$ **market values**	0%	5%	10%	15%	20%	25%
Operating income	120,000	120,000	120,000	120,000	120,000	120,000
Interest expenses	0	(4,000)	(8,000)	(12,000)	(16,000)	(20,000)
Operating income before taxes	120,000	116,000	112,000	108,000	104,000	100,000
Tax rate	0%					
Taxes	0	0	0	0	0	0
Net income	120,000	116,000	112,000	108,000	104,000	100,000
Dividends	120,000	116,000	112,000	108,000	104,000	100,000
Total cash flows	120,000	120,000	120,000	120,000	120,000	120,000

The total cash flows remains constant, regardless of the level of debt. In a *perfect* MM world, if we increase the proportion of debt in the capital structure the only effect we obtain is a redistribution of the slices of the "pizza" from shareholders to creditors. The total value of the "pizza" doesn't change. That is:

$$V_L = V_U$$

This is the **first proposition** of the MM theorem in absence of taxation. It simply states that, *in perfect financial markets*, the value of a levered company is exactly the same as an unlevered company.

The absence of any effect produced by changing leverage on total cash flows implies that the weighted average cost of capital (k) doesn't change, whatever the leverage.

How is it possible to obtain a constant k if k_D is constant too (due to the absence of financial distress costs) and, thus, if we increase the leverage we would expect a continuously decreasing k? The answer must be searched in the **second proposition** of MM (with no taxes) according to which the cost of equity must be computed as follows:

$$k_E = k_{EU} + (k_{EU} - k_D) \times \frac{V_D}{V_E}$$

The above equation is the equation of a line with an intercept equal to $\boldsymbol{K_{EU}}$ – **cost of equity of a company all equity-financed (or unlevered)** – and an angular coefficient ($K_{EU} - K_D$). Since K_{EU} is influenced by the operating risk of the company – a kind of risk basically uninfluenced by the capital structure policy – the positive inclination of the line reflects the fact that, by incrementing the debt/equity ratio, the shareholder is charged with an increasing financial risk in exchange for which he will ask for a higher remuneration.

The following picture illustrates this circumstance. As can be seen, the cost of debt is represented by a horizontal line, since there are no financial distress costs. Since K is also uninfluenced by the degree of leverage, it results that the cost of equity line must have the values shown in the picture so that K can remain unchanged.

In a perfect market, the rise in expected returns related to leverage is cancelled out by the rise in risk, so that the share's value remains the same.

When debt increases, so does the risk to shareholders, and the cost of equity. As a result, total shareholder wealth does not change.

SUMMARY

Is there such a thing as an optimal capital structure – i.e., a way of splitting the financing of operating assets between debt and equity which would enhance the value of the operating assets and minimise the company's cost of capital? This is the central question that this chapter attempted to answer.

The real world camp says yes, but without being able to prove it, or to set an ideal level of net debt and equity.

Modigliani and Miller said no in 1958, and showed how, if it were so, there would be arbitrages that re-established the balance.

For an investor with a perfectly diversified portfolio, and in a tax-free universe, there is no optimal capital structure. The following rules can be formed on the basis of the above:

● for any given investment policy and if no taxes are levied, value cannot be instantly created by the choice of a "good" capital structure;

● whether a given company is sold and the deal is paid in shares only, or whether the deal is paid in a whole range of different securities (shares, debt, hybrid shares), this will not change the value of its operating assets (excluding tax);

● in a world without taxes, the expected leverage effect is an illusion. The cost of capital (excluding tax) is linked to the company's assets and is independent of the method of financing.

But a world without taxes is a utopia, which is why the next chapter brings tax and other "distortions" into the equation.

QUESTIONS

1/ Why is the cost of equity for a company with no debt equal to the average weighted cost of capital?

2/ What is the cost of capital equal to?

3/ What are the two risks for a shareholder of an indebted company?

4/ Of the following decisions, which is the most important: An investment decision? A financing decision? Why?

5/ Explain what impact an increase in debt will have on the β of shares.

6/ What are Modigliani and Miller's theories based on?

7/ The fact that shareholders' expected returns rise with the level of debt does not run contrary to the approach taken by Modigliani and Miller. Why?

8/ Is the cost of capital an accounting or financial concept?

9/ Why can it be dangerous to use a spreadsheet to create simulations of the cost of capital?

10/ Can a company create value by going into debt?

11/ What is the cost of net debt of a company that has no more shareholders' equity equal to? And the cost of capital?

12/ What are we forgetting when we say that by increasing return on equity, the leverage effect of debt cannot increase value?

13/ True of false? "By reducing financial leverage, we reduce the cost of debt and the cost of equity, and, accordingly, the weighted average cost of capital?" Why?

14/ True of false? "The more debt we incur, the higher the interest rate we are charged. Our shareholders also require a higher return. Additionally, if we want a low cost of capital, we have to have a low level of debt." Why?

EXERCISES

1/ 60% of company A's needs are equity-financed – at a cost of 9% – and 40% debt-financed at 5%. Excluding tax, what is the weighted average cost of capital of this company?

2/ In a tax-free world, two companies A and B are similar in every respect, except their capital structures. B has no debts while C has debts of 24,000 at 5%. The companies have been valued as follows:

	Company B	Company C
Operating income	10,000	10,000
Financial expense	0	1,200
Net income	10,000	8,800
k_E	8%	11%
V_E	125,000	80,000
V_D	0	24,000
V	125,000	104,000
K	8%	9.62%
$V_D/(V_E + V_D)$	0%	23%
Payout	100%	100%

You own 1% of company B's shares. How much will you receive every year? Show how you can increase this amount without altering the amount of your investment or increasing the level of risk. When will arbitrage cease? What will the P/E be for companies B and C?

3/ A company with no debts has a weighted average cost of capital of 8%.

(a) What is the cost of equity for this company?

(b) It decides to borrow 33.5% of the value of its operating assets at a rate of 5%, in order to finance a capital reduction of 33.5%. What is the cost of equity now?

(c) If the market risk premium is 4% and the β of the company's shares before it goes into debt was 1.2, what is the new β of shares after the capital reduction?

(d) What is the β of the debt, if the β of the capital employed is equal to the average β of the capital employed and the debt weighted by the relative share of debt and equity in financing the capital employed:

$$\left(\beta = \beta_E \times \frac{V_E}{V_E + V_D} + \beta_D \times \frac{V_D}{V_D + V_E} \right)$$

4/ Deutsche Telekom and France Telecom have a similar economic risk. The beta of France Telecom shares is 1.4 and 1.1 for Deutsche Telekom. If the no-risk cash rate is 5.5% and the risk premium is 4%, what are the shareholders' required returns? If the net/debt shareholders' equity ratio is 1.5 in value for France Telecom, what is it for Deutsche Telekom which has debts of 7% compared with 7.5% for France Telecom (imagine that this is a tax-free world)?

ANSWERS

Questions

1/ *Because shareholders' equity alone bears the risk of capital employed.*
2/ *To the average weighted by the values of the cost of equity and the cost of net debt.*
3/ *The risk of capital employed and the risk of capital structure.*
4/ *Investment, because it is easier to create value by making a good investment, and we learned in this chapter that there is no such thing as good financing.*
5/ *Debt capital, by increasing the risk of shares, increases the β.*
6/ *Arbitrage.*
7/ *Because the risk also increases.*
8/ *Financial, because only market values (rates and values) come into the calculation of the cost of capital.*
9/ *Because by modifying the relative weights of debt/shareholders' equity, we often forget that the cost of shareholders' equity and debt depends on this relative weight, and that they are not constant, no matter what the capital structure.*
10/ *No, this would be too good to be true and all companies would have huge debts.*
11/ *To the cost of shareholders' equity of a debt-free company in the same sector. Ditto.*
12/ *The risk of shareholders' equity increases and, accordingly, the returns required by shareholders increases at the same time.*
13/ *False, by reducing leverage, an "expensive" resource (shareholders' equity, the cost of which is reduced) is replaced with a "cheap" resource (debt, the cost of which is reduced). In sum, the weighted average cost of capital remains constant.*
14/ *False, the company is replacing an "expensive" resource (shareholders' equity) with a "cheap" resource (debt) even though the cost will rise. In sum, the weighted average cost of capital remains constant.*

Exercises

1/ $k = 7.4\%$.
2/ *A shareholder of 1% of company B will receive the following sum every year: $1\% \times 125,000 \times 8\% = 100$. He sells his shares in company B and buys shares in company C. However, because the company is indebted, as a shareholder, he carries a higher risk than before. If he wants to keep the same level of risk, he must put an equivalent amount into the debt underlying the shares he has bought in company C. Accordingly, if n is the percentage of 1,250 paid for the shares in company C, $n \times 23.1\% = 1 - n$. The solution to this equation is $n = 1/(1 + 23.1\%) = 81\%$. Or, for assets totalling 1,250: 19% is lent at 5% and 81% is invested in company C shares. Which is an income of $19\% \times 1,250 \times 5\% + 81\% \times 1,250 \times 11\% = 123$,*

more than the initial income of 100. Arbitrage will cease when the value of the capital employed of companies B and C is equal – for example, 111,400 – which gives an equity value for company C of 114,000 – 24,000 = 90,000 and a P/E of 10.2 for company C and 11.4 for company B.

3/ *(a)* $k_E = 8\%$.

  (b) $k_E = 9.5\%$.

  (c) $\beta = 1.57$.

  (d) $\beta_D = 0.45$.

4/ *Deutsche Telekom:* $k_E = 9.9\%$; *France Telecom:* $k_E = 11.1\%$; $V_D/V_E = 0.49$.

BIBLIOGRAPHY

For a classic example of a real world point of view:

B. Graham, L. Dodd, *Security Analysis*, 3rd edn, McGraw-Hill, 1951.

To read the seminal article by Modigliani and Miller:

F. Modigliani, M. Miller, The cost of capital, corporation finance and the theory of investment, *American Economic Review*, **47**, 261–297, June 1958.

F. Modigliani, M. Miller, Corporate income taxes and the cost of capital, *American Economic Review*, 433–443, June 1963.

M. Miller, Debt and taxes, *Journal of Finance*, 261–275, May 1977.

For a general overview on capital structure that is still interesting to read:

J. Stiglitz, On the irrelevance of corporate financial policy, *American Economic Review*, **47**, 851–866, December 1974.

Chapter 34
THE TRADEOFF MODEL

There's no gain without pain

In the previous chapter we saw that the value of a firm is the same whether or not it has taken on debt. True, investors will pay less for the shares of a levered company, but they will have to pay back the debt (or buy it back, which amounts to the same) before obtaining access to the enterprise value. In the end, they will have paid, directly or indirectly, the same amount (value of equity plus repayment of net debt) – that is, the enterprise value.

Now, what about the financial manager who must issue securities to finance the creation of enterprise value? It does not matter whether he issues only shares or a combination of bonds and shares, since the proceeds will be the same, again, the enterprise value.

Enterprise value depends on future flows and how the related, nondiversifiable risks are perceived by the market.

But if that is the case, why diversify sources of financing? The preceding theory is certainly elegant, but it cannot fully explain how things actually work in real life.

In this chapter we look at **two basic explanations of real life happenings**. First of all, within the same market logic, biases occur which may explain why companies borrow funds, and why they stop at a certain level. The fundamental factors from which these biases spring are *taxes* and *financial distress* and *agency costs*. **Their joint analysis will give birth to the "tradeoff model".**

But there are costs of debt that can modify the optimal capital structure:

- **information asymmetries**;
- **the disciplining role of debt**;
- **financial flexibility**.

Traditional tradeoff models generally limit their attention on the pros and cons of tax shield and financial distress costs. We believe that the elements of the balance are more numerous than these two factors. Two other factors may also be added:

- the business sector;
- the lifecycle of the company.

To this end, Chapter 35 will discuss a more complete view of capital structure choice that tries to include all the factors mentioned above.

Maybe the main reasons for the interference between capital structure and investment are the divergent interests of the various financial partners regarding value creation and their differing levels of access to information. This lies at the core of the manager/shareholder relationship we will examine in this chapter. Chapter 35 is devoted to an analysis of the capital structure as resulting from a compromise between creditors and shareholders.

Rather than being simply a search for value, the choice of financing is far more an endeavour to reduce conflicts of interest between shareholders and managers or shareholders and lenders, as well as the information asymmetry between management and investors.

Section 34.1
THE BENEFITS OF DEBT

1/CORPORATE INCOME TAXES

Up to now, our reasoning was based on a tax-free world, which, of course, does not exist. The investor's net return can be two-to-five times (or more) lower than the pre-tax cash flows of an industrial investment.

It would therefore be foolhardy to ignore taxation, which forces financial managers to devote a considerable amount of their time to tax optimisation.

For financial managers, this chapter will cover familiar ground and our insistence on the importance of tax aspects in every financial decision will seem obvious.

But we should not go to the other extreme and concentrate solely on tax variables. All too many decisions based entirely on tax considerations lead to ridiculous outcomes, such as insufficient earnings capacity. Tax deficits alone are no reason to buy a company!

In 1963, F. Modigliani and M. Miller pushed further their initial demonstration, but this time they factored in corporate income tax (*but no other taxes*) in an economy in which companies' financial expenses are tax-deductible, but not dividends. This is pretty much the case in most countries.

The conclusion was unmistakable: once you factor in corporate income tax, there is more incentive to use debt rather than equity financing.

Interest expenses can be deducted from the company's tax base, so that creditors receive their coupon payments before they have been taxed. Dividends, on the other hand, are not deductible and are paid to shareholders after taxation.

Thus, a debt-free company with equity financing of 100 on which shareholders require a 10% return will have to generate profit of at least 15.4 in order to provide the required return of 10 after a 35% tax.

If, however, its financing is equally divided between debt at 5% interest and equity, a profit of 12.4 will be enough to satisfy shareholders despite the premium for the greater risk to shares created by the debt (e.g., 12.9%).

Operating profit	12.4
− Interest expense	2.5
= Pre-tax profit	9.9
− 35% tax	3.5
= Net profit	6.4 or 12.9% of 50

Allowing interest expenses to be deducted from companies' tax base is a kind of subsidy the state grants to companies with debt. *But to benefit from this tax shield, the company must generate a profit.*

When corporate income taxes are levied, the enterprise value of the levered company is equal to that of an unlevered company plus the present value of the tax savings arising on the debt.

Take, for example, a company with an enterprise value of 100, of which 50 is financed by equity and 50 by perpetual debt at 5%. Interest expenses will be 2.5 each year. Assuming a 35% tax rate and an operating profit of more than 2.5 regardless of the year under review (an amount sufficient to benefit from tax savings), the tax savings will be $35\% \times 2.5$ or 0.88 for each year. The present value of this perpetual bond increases shareholders' wealth by $0.88/12.9\% = 6.8$ if 12.9% is the cost of equity. Taking the tax savings into account increases the value of equity by 12% to 56.8 $(50 + 6.8)$.

TAX SAVINGS AS A PERCENTAGE OF EQUITY

The longer the maturity of the debt and the larger the amount, the greater the present value of the tax savings.

V_n/V	K_F	Maturity of debt		
		5 years	10 years	Infinity
0	10.0[1]	0	0	0
25	11.0	2.1	3.3	5.1
33	11.4	3.1	4.8	7.0
50	12.9	5.8	8.7	12.0
66	15.6	10.1	14.3	17.9

1 *Based on a β of 1.1, a 4% risk premium and a risk-free rate of 5.6%.*

2 *This is the basis of the APV method (Adjusted Present Value).*

The value of a levered company is equal to what it would be without the debt, plus the amount of savings generated by the tax shield.[2]

The question now is what discount rate should be applied to the tax savings generated by the deductibility of interest expense? Should we use the cost of debt, as Modigliani and Miller did in their article in 1963, the weighted average cost of capital or the cost of equity?

Using the cost of debt is justified if we are certain that the tax savings are permanent. In addition, this allows us to use a particularly simple formula:

$$\text{Value of the tax savings} = \frac{T_C \times K_D \times V_D}{K_D} = T_C \times V_D$$

Nevertheless, there are good reasons to prefer to discount the savings at the cost of equity, since it would be difficult to assume that the company will continually carry the same debt, generate profits and be taxed at the same rate. Moreover, the tax savings accrue to the shareholders, so it should be reasonable to discount them at the rate of return required by those shareholders.

Bear in mind that these tax savings only apply if the company has sufficient earnings power and does not benefit from any other tax exemptions, such as tax loss carry forwards, etc.

Let's discuss in more detail the implication of interest deductibility. To this end, we use the example used at the end of Chapter 33 in which a company with an invested capital of €500,000 generates a constant (and perpetual) operating income of €120,000.

Let's limit the analysis to a range of leverage values between 0% and 50%. The cost of debt is still 8%. Now we introduce a corporate tax rate of 35%.

The following table shows the effects of a debt tax shield on net income and on total cash flows (dividends + interest expenses), *when there are no other distortions*:

$V_D/(V_D + V_E)$ **market values**	0.00%	7.49%	14.60%	21.35%	27.78%	33.90%
Operating income	120,000	120,000	120,000	120,000	120,000	120,000
Interest expenses	0	(4,000)	(8,000)	(12,000)	(16,000)	(20,000)
Operating income before taxes	120,000	116,000	112,000	108,000	104,000	100,000
Tax rate	35%					
Taxes	(42,000)	(40,600)	(39,200)	(37,800)	(36,400)	(35,000)
Net income	78,000	75,400	72,800	70,200	67,600	65,000
Dividends	78,000	75,400	72,800	70,200	67,600	65,000
Total cash flows	78,000	79,400	80,800	82,200	83,600	85,000

Total cash flows increase together with the increase of debt in the capital structure. When corporate taxes are introduced in the analysis, the "pizza" of the firm value must be divided in three parts: shareholders, creditors and the state (cash outflows for taxes). One goal of the shareholders is to *reduce the state's slice* because the cash outflow subtracted to the state accrues to them (a similar privilege does not belong to creditors for which the dimension of their slice is fixed!).

To achieve this result, shareholders – and the management acting on behalf of them – prefer to increase the percentage of debt in the capital structure in order to exploit as much as possible the deductibility of interest expenses, and reduce the outflows for taxes (in short: they act to reduce the slice of the state).

The value of the levered company is always higher than the value of the unlevered firm. The **first proposition of Modigliani–Miller (MM) with corporate taxes** then transforms into:

$$V_L = V_U + T_C \times V_D$$

Correspondingly, the cost of equity becomes:

$$K_E = K_{EU} + (K_{EU} - K_D) \times (1 - T_C) \times \frac{V_D}{V_E}$$

The cost of equity is similar to the one we saw in Chapter 33, while the weighted average cost of capital decreases constantly. Graphically, we can represent this new situation as follows:

MM WITH CORPORATE TAXES

The reader is surely thinking that something in the reasoning above is not completely clear. How can we say that shareholders improve their financial situation by increasing debt if the dividends they get continue to decrease (see the second-last line of the last table)? The answer is that the debt increase is obtained by substituting debt with shares (through, for example, leveraged share repurchase). True that the total market value of equity decreases but it now must be divided by a lower number of shares. The net result is an increase in the value of *each share*; that is the figure the reader should always focus attention on:

$V_D/(V_D + V_E)$	0.00%	7.49%	14.60%	21.35%	27.78%	33.90%
No. of shares	5,000	4,513	4,053	3,612	3,141	2,630
Price × Share	130.0	136.8	144.3	153.0	165.6	185.4

3/INTRODUCING PERSONAL TAXES, A POSSIBLE RESTRICTION TO OUR REASONING

The personal taxes paid by investors can *reduce* and even *cancel out* the advantages of deducting interest payments on corporate debt.

Let us return to the simple example of the company at the beginning of the chapter. Assume now that the dividends are not taxed at the personal investor's level but that – for the sake of simplicity – the interest income is taxed 70% at the creditors' level.

If the company has no debt financing, it will still have to generate a pre-tax profit of at least 15.4 to satisfy shareholders' required rate of return. However, if its financing is 50 debt and 50 equity, the company will need to turn in a minimum profit before taxes and interest of 18.2. This will allow it to pay 8.3 interest to its creditors, leaving them with a net return of 5%[3] after the 70% tax. The shareholders get 6.4 (equivalent to 12.9% return) after a tax of 3.5 ($3.5 = 35\% \times (18.2 - 8.3)$). If, on the contrary, the company cannot get 18.2 but only 15.4 there is a subtraction of value from shareholders to creditors (shareholders would get 4.6, equivalent to 9.2% return compared with 6.4 net profit – and 12.9% return – of a world with only corporate taxes).

> Given the net expected return required by creditors – the introduction of the tax rate on interest income increases the total amount of money necessary to pay debt and subtracts resources to shareholders.

If the personal tax rate on interest income is cut to 30%, thus lower than the tax rate on corporate income, debt becomes cheaper, giving rise to (low) tax savings, although still less than MM found in their article published in 1963.

In 1977, Miller released a new study in which he revisited the observation made in 1958 with Modigliani that there is no one optimal capital structure. This time, however, he factored in both corporate **and personal taxes**.

Miller claimed that the taxes paid by investors can cancel out those paid by companies. This would mean that the value of the firm would remain the same regardless of the type of financing used. Again, there should be no optimal capital structure.

Miller's objective was to demonstrate that real life is far more complicated than the simplified assumptions applied in the theories and models. The value of the tax shield is not so big as the 1963 article would induce to conclude. Suppose that, in addition to the corporate income tax (T_C) that there are also two other tax rates:

- T_D = personal tax rate on interest income;
- T_E = personal tax rate on dividends.

If we:

1. consider the cash flows net of all taxes that shareholders and creditors must pay to tax authorities;
2. sum them; and
3. rearrange terms,

3 *5% of 50 is 2.5. This is net return. The gross return is 8.3.*

then the "complete" tax shield (G) is:

$$G = \left[1 - \frac{(1 - T_C) \times (1 - T_E)}{(1 - T_D)} \right] \times V_D$$

The reader will immediately notice that if $T_E = T_D$ the tax shield turns back to the "original" $T_C \times V_D$.

In our last example, if T_E is zero, $T_D = 30\%$ and $T_C = 35\%$, G is still positive but much lower than the world with no personal taxes because it equals only 0.0714 (or 7.14%).

If we include T_E into the analysis two alternatives may be possible:

- if $T_E = T_D$ the tax shield is equal to the basic case (i.e., the case with only corporate taxes);
- if $T_E > T_D$ the tax shield is bigger than the basic case;
- if $T_E < T_D$ the tax shield tends to be smaller than the basic case. If the personal income tax on stocks is lower than the tax on income from bonds, the before-tax return on bonds has to be high enough to offset this disadvantage – otherwise, no investor would hold bonds and companies couldn't exploit the interest tax shield. In other words, the advantage of interest deductibility of debt is counterbalanced by the fact that the required interest payments have already been "grossed up" by any differential that bondholders must pay on interest income. Thus, the advantage of debt financing may be lost.

When personal taxes are introduced in the analysis, the firm's objective is no longer to minimise the corporate tax bill; the firm should minimise the present value of *all* taxes paid on corporate income (those paid by bondholders and shareholders).

Once we factor in the tax credit granted before shareholders are taxed, the tax benefits on debt disappear, although since not all earnings are distributed not all give rise to tax credits. Say a company has an enterprise value of 1,000. Regardless of its type of financing, investors require a 6% return after corporate **and** personal income taxes. Bear in mind that this rate is not comparable with that determined by the CAPM, which is calculated **before** personal taxation.

In France, for example, the main tax rates applied in 2004 were:

- corporate tax: 34.43%;
- tax on dividends: marginal income tax rate of 50%;
- capital gains tax: 26% including social contributions;
- tax on interest income: 25% including a flat tax of 15% and social contributions.

Many listed and unlisted companies distribute one-third of their profits in the form of dividends. The average holding period of shares is estimated to be 3 years. This means that only one-third of corporate net profits are taxed immediately at the shareholder level (at 50%). The remainder is taxed only when the capital gains are realised – i.e., after 3 years – at a rate of 26%, of which the present value (at 6% discount rate) is 22%. In other words, the tax rate on equity held by shareholders is $\frac{1}{3} \times 50\% + \frac{2}{3} \times 22\% = 31\%$.

Now let us assume that the company has operating profit of 127 and a cost of equity of 6% if it is entirely equity-financed.

Enterprise value	1,000	1,000	1,000	1,000
Equity	1,000	750	500	250
Debt	0	250	500	750
Interest rate	–	6%	7%	8%
Operating profit	127	127	127	127
– Interest expense	0	15	35	60
= Pre-tax profit	127	112	92	67
– Corporate income tax	44	39	32	23
= Net profit	83	73	60	44
Income tax:				
On dividends/capital gains (31%)	26	23	19	14
On interest (25%)	0	4	9	15
Shareholder's net income	57	50	41	30
Shareholder's net return	6%	7%	9%	13%
Creditor's net income	0	11	26	45
Creditor's net return	–	4%	5%	6%
Net income for investors	57	62	67	75
Total taxes	70	65	60	52

The net return of the investor, who is both shareholder and creditor of the firm, can be calculated depending on whether net debt represents 0%, 33.3%, 100% or 3 times the amount of equity.

The value created by debt must thus be measured in terms of the increase in net income for investors (shareholders and creditors). Our example shows that flows increase significantly only when the debt level is particularly high, well above the French average (15% market value).

Miller's reasoning now becomes clearer. The table below shows that in certain countries, such as Morocco, the tax savings on corporate debt are more than offset by the personal taxes levied.

TAX RATES IN VARIOUS COUNTRIES (%)

Country	On dividends	On capital gains	On interest	On earnings
Germany	25.0	0.0[4]	30.0	38.36
Belgium	15.0 or 25.0	0.0	15.0	40.17
Spain[5]	25–48.0	20.0–48.0	20–48.0	35.0
France	50[6]	26.0	25.0	35.43
Italy	12.5	12.5 or 27.0	12.5	40.25
Netherlands	25.0	0.0[7]	30.0	34.5
UK	40.0	40.0	20.0	30.0
USA	38.6	20.0	38.6	35.0
Morocco	10.0	10.0	44.0	35.0
Tunisia	0.0	35.0	35.0	35.0

4 Excluding capital gains on speculative transactions or on substantial equity stakes.

5 Nonflatrate-withholding taxes plus regular taxation. 20% on capital gains on assets held more than 2 years.

6 At the highest marginal rate and taking into account the tax credit and CSG tax.

7 Unless stake exceeds 5%.

Bear in mind, too, that companies do not always use the tax advantages of debt since there are other options, such as accelerated depreciation, provisions, etc.

In the study mentioned above, Graham (2000) shows that if we take into account the personal taxes paid by the investor, the value created by debt falls from 9.7% to 4.3% of the firm's value. And we haven't even factored in the present value of bankruptcy costs yet!

De Angelo and Masulis (1980) have extended Miller's work by analysing the effect of tax shields other than interest payments on debt – e.g., noncash charges such as depreciation and investment tax credits. Their model predicts that firms' debt will be negatively related to the level of available tax shield substitutes.

Graham et al. (2004) find that employee stock option deductions lead to large aggregate tax savings and also affect corporate marginal tax rates. Their evidence suggests that option deductions substitute for interest deductions in corporate capital structure decisions, explaining in part why some firms use so little debt.

What all this amounts to is that, while interest tax shield is certainly a key parameter in absolute terms, it is unlikely to be the determinant of capital structure.

3/INFORMATION ASYMMETRIES AND THE PECKING ORDER THEORY

The analysis of the impact of informational asymmetries on capital structure decisions requires the introduction of two new concepts: internal capital and external capital. **Internal capital** is represented by the cash flows generated internally or, more generically, by periodical income which is nondistributed among shareholders; **external capital** is raised outside the firm, and can either be financial debt or equity from new shareholders.

The categories that operate within the company (directors, management, major shareholders, employees – in short, the "insiders") normally know more about the company than all other stakeholders ("outsiders"). These asymmetries tend to penalise the company when it needs to raise funds outside. External creditors have a smaller set of information and do not believe that insiders have convenience to spread all the information they have. This in turn may have two forms:

1   a higher cost of capital;
2   a smaller amount of capital raised (capital rationing).

It is reasonable to assume that informational asymmetries are more relevant:

• for small companies;
• in startup phases;
• when control of the company is in the hands of a few shareholders.

Internal capital doesn't penalise the company neither in terms of cost nor in terms of quantity. However, the use of excess liquidity and of the residual borrowing capacity determines a lower **financial flexibility** and may hamper the future financial equilibrium of the company.

The major disadvantages of external capital are the additional cost of informational asymmetries and the dilution of control (that happens if shares are sold at a "bargain price" to new shareholders or if debt contracts introduce covenants and guarantees).

It is well documented that the additional cost of informational asymmetries are higher if the new external capital is a share issue. All other things being equal, new debt thus may have the comparative advantage of a lower cost and volume penalisation.

The evidence shows that the reaction of the market to the announcement of bond issues is:

- not necessarily negative;
- of limited amount;
- not always statistically significant, when the reaction is negative.

The reaction of share prices can even be positive if the company announces the use of additional bank debt.[8] The reason may lie in the arm's length relationship that banks keep with companies which should signal a higher quality of information. The bank may know confidential information regarding its clients, control its liquidity, be part of their board of directors, all elements that justify a higher quality of companies that prefer to raise funds through the bank channel.

8 *See, for example, James and Smith (2003).*

A totally different result is obtained when firms announce the issue of equity capital to new shareholders. These announcements are in fact generally viewed by the market as a bad signal and the evidence shows that market negative reaction tends to be statistically significant.

Debt may be raised through a public offer or a private placement. It is reasonable to say that debt raised through private placements – which is by definition more concentrated than the public – has two important additional advantages:

1   increase the control of outsiders in the company;
2   is more flexible if the contract needs to be amended or restructured.

This is why companies with lower informational asymmetry "problems" tend to use more frequently public issues; vice versa, there is a more frequent use of intermediated debt by small, young and family-controlled companies.

Having established that information asymmetry carries a cost, our next task is to determine what type of financing carries the lowest cost in this respect. The uncontested champion is, of course, internal financing, which requires no special procedures. Its advantage is simplicity.

Debt comes next, but only low-risk debt with plenty of guarantees (pledges) and covenants restricting the risk to creditors and thus making it more palatable to them.

This is followed by riskier forms of debt and hybrid securities.

Capital increases come last, because they are automatically interpreted as a negative signal. To counter this, information asymmetry must be reduced by means of roadshows, one-to-one meetings, prospectuses and advertising campaigns. Investors have to be persuaded that the issue offers good value for money!

In an article published in 1984, Myers elaborates on a theory initially put forward by Donaldson in 1961, stating that, according to the **pecking order theory**, companies prioritise their sources of financing:

- internal financing heads their list of preferences. Companies adjust their dividend payout objectives to their investment opportunities;

- since earnings and investment opportunities vary from year to year, companies may have to draw down their cash balances;
- if this is not enough and external financing becomes necessary, they issue risk-free debt. Credit lines are kept open to ensure that they can do so as needed;
- when a company cannot resort to traditional borrowings, it issues securities, starting with the least risky type and gradually moving up the scale;
- lastly, when all else fails, the company issues equity.

As can be seen, although the corporate manager does not choose the type of financing arbitrarily, he does so without great enthusiasm, since they all carry the same cost relative to their risk.

The pecking order is determined by the law of least effort. Managers do not have to "raise" internal financing, and they will always endeavour to limit intermediation costs, which are the highest on share issues.

Let's take a look at what happens in the real world of companies to see if they really privilege internal capital. The following picture shows the evolution of the breakdown of financing of 274 multinational companies belonging to three different geographical areas (Europe, USA, Japan) between 1993 and 2001.

The histograms represent the percentage of internal capital (self-financing) and of the external capital (new equity and the variation of the stock of debt).

SOURCE OF FINANCE FOR 274 MULTINATIONAL ENTERPRISES

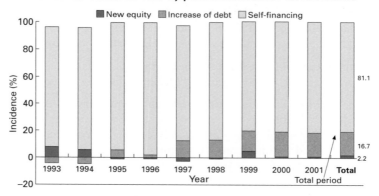

Source: Mediobanca – R&S.

The picture suggests three major comments:

➢ Internal financing has always represented the major source of companies' financing. The average incidence (80%) of internal capital is consistent with the findings of Donaldson, who suggested that the behaviour of management is driven by two important factors:

    a   firm's survival. The need for preserving the life of the company induces the management to accumulate liquidity in excess and to keep the residual borrowing capacity unchanged;

    b   independence and self-sufficiency. Management prefers to be free to decide, regardless of external influences, even that of capital markets. An appropriate reserve of liquidity could ease achievement of this objective.

➤ Internal financing has not covered the entire amount of funds required by new investments. Each period thus shows a "financial gap" that needs to be filled with external capital.

➤ The financial gap has been mostly covered with debt and, if necessary, equity capital. However, the latter resource assumes a marginal role, consistent with the predictions of the pecking order model.

The evidence shown in the above picture seems to confirm the existence of a pecking order of financing choices.

A word of caution, however. The reader should never forget that internal capital has a cost like all other sources of financing, which can be estimated with the models presented in the chapters where we have discussed the cost of equity capital (Chapters 22 and 23). So, it is important to pay attention to avoid the illusion of considering internal capital as zero-cost or discretionary-cost capital. The cost of capital is always an *opportunity cost of capital*, and should be estimated by looking at the expected returns required (or obtained) by shareholders of similar (in terms of risk and duration) investments and companies.

Finally, it is interesting to note that, although the general preference for internal capital is common to all three areas, there also exist some differences in each of them, as shown by the next picture.

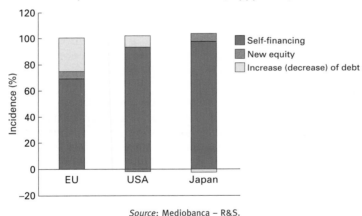

COMPOSITION OF FINANCING DIVIDED BY GEOGRAPHICAL AREA (INDUSTRIAL SECTOR ONLY, 1999–2001)

Source: Mediobanca – R&S.

4/CORPORATE MANAGERS CONTROL

Now let us examine the interests of nonshareholder executives. They may be tempted to shun debt in order to avoid the corresponding constraints, such as a higher breakeven threshold, interest payments, principal repayments. Corporate managers are highly risk-averse and their natural inclination is to accumulate cash rather than resort to debt to finance investments. Debt financing avoids this trap, since the debt repayment prevents surplus cash from accumulating. Shareholders encourage debt as well because it stimulates performance. The more debt a company has, the higher its risk. In the event of financial difficulties, corporate executives may lose their jobs and the attendant compensation package and remuneration in kind. This threat is considered to be sufficiently dissuasive to encourage sound management, generating optimal liquidity to service the debt and engage in profitable investments.

> The explicit cost of debt is a simple yet highly effective means of controlling a firm's management team. Large groups are well aware of the leverage this gives them and require the executives of their main subsidiaries to carry a level of "incentive debt" that is charged to the subsidiary.

Given that the parameters of debt are reflected in a company's cash situation while equity financing translates into capital gains or losses at shareholder level, management will be particularly intent on the success of its debt-financed investment projects. This is another, indirect, limitation of the perfect markets theory: **since the various forms of financing do not offer the same incentives to corporate executives, financing does indeed influence the choice of investment.**

This would indicate that a levered company is more flexible and responsive than an unlevered company. This hypothesis was tested and proven by Ofek, who showed that the more debt they carry, the faster listed US companies react to a crisis, either by filing for bankruptcy, curtailing dividend payouts or reducing the payroll.

Debt is thus an internal means of controlling management preferred by shareholders. In Chapter 42 we will see that another is the threat of a takeover bid.

However, the use of debt has its limits. When a group's corporate structure becomes totally unbalanced, debt no longer acts as an incentive for management. On the contrary, the corporate manager will be tempted to continue expanding via debt until his group has become too big to fail, as did the Korean groups at the end of the 1990s. This risk is called "moral hazard".

The field of research with more empirical evidence has examined if the companies which have experienced a fast increase of leverage have become more efficient, as measured by profit margins and the return on invested capital.

This is the case of **Leveraged Buy Outs or LBOs**. An LBO is the acquisition, generally by management (MBO), of all a company's shares using borrowed funds. It becomes a leveraged buildup if it then uses debt to buy other companies in order to increase its standing in the sector. The 1980s were the heyday of funds dedicated to such LBOs.

It is generally thought that the purpose of the funds devoted to LBOs is to use accounting leverage to obtain better returns. In fact, the success of LBOs cannot be attributed to accounting leverage, since we have already seen that this alone does not create value.

The real reason for the success of LBOs is that when it has a stake in the company, management is far more committed to making the company a success. With management most often holding a share of the equity, resource allocation will be designed to benefit shareholders. Executives have a twofold incentive: to enhance their existing or future (in the case of stock options) stake in the capital and to safeguard their jobs and reputation by ensuring that the company does not go broke. It thus becomes a classic case of the carrot and the stick!

The results reported by Palepu (1990) show in fact an improvement – although quite limited – of the operating efficiency of companies subjected to leveraged buyouts. Similar results are discussed in Kaplan (1989) and Smith (1990).

Mature, highly profitable companies with few investments to make are the most likely candidates for an LBO. Jensen demonstrated that, in the absence of heavy debt, the executives of such companies will be strongly tempted to use the substantial free cash flow to grow to the detriment of profits by overinvesting or diversifying into other businesses, two strategies that destroy value.

The only value created by debt is the fact that it forces managers to improve enterprise value.

Similar circumstances characterise **leveraged recapitalisations** (commonly obtained by a share repurchase funded with new debt). Denis and Denis (1993) report a relevant improvement of the operating efficiency (return on the assets increased by 21.5%) of the 29 companies included in the sample.

Section 34.2
THE COSTS OF DEBT

1/COSTS OF FINANCIAL DISTRESS

We have seen that the more debt a firm carries, the greater the risk that it will not be able to meet its commitments. If worst comes to worst, the company files for bankruptcy which, in the final analysis, simply means that assets are reallocated to more profitable ventures.

In fact, the bankruptcy of an unprofitable company strengthens the sector and improves the profitability of the remaining firms and therefore their value. Bankruptcy is a useful mechanism which helps make the market stay healthier by eliminating the least efficient companies.

The public authorities would do well to apply this reasoning. Better to let a troubled sector rid itself of its lame ducks than to keep them artificially afloat, which in turn creates difficulties for the healthy, efficient firms to the point where they, too, may become financially distressed.

For investors with a well-diversified portfolio, the cost of the bankruptcy will be nil, since when a company is discontinued, its assets (market share, customers, factories, etc.) are taken over by others who will manage them better. One man's loss is another man's gain! If the investor has a diversified portfolio, the capital losses will be offset by other capital gains.

In practice, however, markets are not perfect and we all know that even if bankruptcies are a means of reallocating resources they carry a very real cost to those involved. These include:

➢ Direct costs:
   ○ redundancy payments;
   ○ lawyers' fees;
   ○ administrative costs;
   ○ shareholders' efforts to receive a liquidation dividend.
➢ Indirect costs:
   ○ order cancellations (for fear they will not be honoured);
   ○ less trade credit (because it may not be repaid);
   ○ reduced productivity (strikes, underutilisation of production capacity);
   ○ no more access to financing (even for profitable projects); as well as
   ○ incalculable human costs.

From this point of view, one could say bankruptcy occurs when shareholders refuse to inject more funds once they have concluded that their initial investment is lost. In essence, they are handing the company over to its creditors, who then become the new shareholders. The creditors bear all the costs of the malfunctioning company, thus reducing their chances of getting repaid even more.

The following table reports the major results of some studies regarding direct and indirect costs in the USA:

	Direct costs	Indirect costs	Sample	Period
Altman (1984)	4.3	8.7	18 companies	1970–78
Ang et al. (1982)	7.5	NA	55 companies	1963–78
Betker (1995)	3.9	NA	75 companies	1986–93
Cutler and Summers (1988)	3.0	9.0	Case study	
Warner (1977b)	5.3	NA	11 railway companies	1933–55
Weiss (1990)	3.1	NA	37 companies in U.S. Chapter 11	1980–86
White (1983)	6.0	NA	96 companies	1978–79

Even without going to the extremes of bankruptcy, a highly levered company faces certain costs for its financial distress that reduce its value. It may have to cut back on R&D expenditure, maintenance, training or marketing expenses in order to meet its debt payments and will find it increasingly difficult to raise new funding, even for profitable investment projects.

After factoring all these costs into the equation, we can say that:

Value of levered firm	=	Value of unlevered firm	+	Present value of the tax shield arising on debt	−	Present value of bankruptcy costs and malfunction costs

Because of tax deduction, debt can, in fact, create value. A levered company may be worth more than if it had only equity financing. However, there are two good reasons why this advantage should not be overstated. First, when a company with excessive debt is in financial distress, its tax advantage disappears, since it no longer generates sufficient profits. Second, the high debt level may lead to restructuring costs and lost investment opportunities if financing is no longer available. As a result, debt should not exceed a certain level.

In practice, the *total* tax savings arising on debt are considered to represent 10–15% of the firm's value. This compares with direct and indirect bankruptcy costs, which various studies have estimated at between 5% and 15% of the market value of the defaulting companies. However, this figure needs to be weighted by the probability that the firm will default.

As can be seen, the magnitude of bankruptcy costs vs. tax savings are quite similar, making it difficult to determine just whether value is created by debt at all.

The same reasoning applies to the weighted average cost of capital. When a company borrows funds, its cost of capital declines thanks to the tax savings on the interest payments, but if there is a risk of default, shareholders factor the bankruptcy costs into the cost of equity.

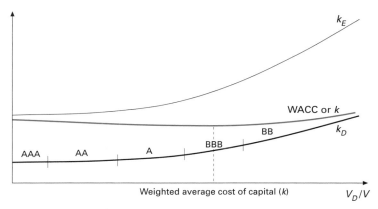

This relationship can be observed by charting a given industry's cost of capital according to its credit rating.

Paradoxically, this long detour brings us back to our starting point, the real world approach which says: "Some debt is fine, but not too much."

The theoretical optimal debt ratio appears to be when the present value of the tax savings arising on additional borrowing is offset by the increase in the present value of financial distress and bankruptcy costs.

One concern of shareholders is that they want to estimate the *expected* costs of financial distress. They are not satisfied with the estimation of distress costs, because these costs must be "weighted" with the probability that they will actually occur.

If we define *CFD* as the costs of financial distress and π the probability of financial distress or bankruptcy, the expected costs of financial distress are the result of:

$$\text{Expected costs of financial distress} = \pi \times CFD^9$$

The probability of bankruptcy (we use bankruptcy and financial distress synonymously for the sake of simplicity) is given by the probability that, internally, cash flows could be insufficient to face the contractual commitments of creditors.

9 *The reader should consider that, by calculating the expected financial distress costs as a percentage of the unlevered value of the firm, we are already including their present value into the analysis (since the unlevered value of the firm is the present value of cash flows).*

This probability is a function of:

- the ratio between the operating cash flows and the cash flow of debt (interests and principal repayment). The higher this ratio, the lower is the probability of default;
- the volatility of operating cash flows. The probability of default is directly linked to cash flow volatility.

A direct approach for the estimation of the probability of default is the use of historical default rates produced by rating agencies, major investment banks and research centres, which comes under the form of cumulated percentage of insolvencies occurred along different time horizons.

In practice, the reader should use the time horizon consistent with that of the average life (or duration) of the company debt. The following table illustrates the cumulative default rates of US companies over 1, 5 and 10 years. Thus, the cumulative probability of default (π) of an A-rated company with a debt with an average life of 10 years should be around 0.45%.

	1 year (%)	5 years (%)	10 years (%)
AAA	0.00	0.04	0.04
AA	0.00	0.56	0.62
A	0.00	0.15	0.45
BBB	0.07	1.43	2.45
BB	0.71	7.69	14.25
B	1.58	19.17	27.15
CCC	1.63	36.07	48.38

2/AGENCY COSTS

The conflicts of interest between shareholders and creditors reach their apex when the company is in financial distress. In these circumstances, in fact, shareholders may be tempted to use three types of actions for damaging creditors' interests:

1　Investing in high-risk projects ("**risk shifting**"), whose return distribution is wider than the average. The hope of shareholders is to increase the chance of exploiting the positive side of the probability distribution, since their responsibility (and their potential loss) is limited to the capital invested in the company, regardless of the risk of the operating activity.
2　**Underinvesting.** The management of a highly indebted company could refuse to invest in a project with a positive NPV, but insufficient to restore the financial equilibrium of the company. This of course may happen if shareholders contribute to finance the project. In this case, the value created could be used to repay debt, thus leaving the wealth of shareholders unchanged.
3　**Milking the property.** Shareholders could distribute high ordinary dividends and even extraordinary dividends, by selling part of the assets-in-place.

The most important consequence of agency conflicts is that the relative costs could be paid by shareholders! Let's see why: creditors know that shareholders can adopt one or more of the three strategies described above. Their *ex ante* reaction is to increase the required remuneration on new funds, charging shareholders of the likelihood of opportunism.

What are the possible solutions to the agency problems? There are basically four answers to this question:

➤ Introduce contractual provisions (**covenants**) that discipline the role of management and major shareholders.

➤ Increase the **degree of concentration of debt**. This is equivalent to saying that it is necessary to reduce the number of creditors of the company. By so doing, the cost of debt renegotiation should decrease, should the company incur financial distress.

➤ Use appropriate **placement techniques**. Take, for example, the so-called "strip financing", a technique by which all lenders "buy" simultaneously portions of all the *tranches* of the issuing securities. Needless to say, the conflicts of interests between classes of claimants tend in this case to vanish rapidly.

➤ Raise **guaranteed debt** and **leasing**. In both cases, the value of debt tends to be correlated to the value of fixed assets. Hence:

1   the losses suffered by creditors are limited by the liquidation value of the assets over which they have a privilege;
2   monitoring costs may be lower because the borrower cannot sell the assets used as collaterals or simply possessed thanks to a leasing contract.

Agency and financial distress costs are detrimental to shareholders. Now we will discuss two alternatives that can be used to estimate this value destruction effect.

The first methodology is based on an explicit estimate of financial and distress costs. The value obtained must then be subtracted from the value of the company (inclusive of the tax shield):

$$\text{Value of a levered company} = V_L = V_U + G - (\pi \times CFD)$$

This technique – known as the **Adjusted Present Value**, APV – enlightens the three major sources of value creation and destruction. At the same time, the APV suffers the important limitations related to the uncertainty surrounding the estimate of parameters (π and CFD) for which there still isn't robust nor well-detailed evidence.

The second technique is to rectify the cost of debt (K_D) and the cost of equity (K_E). However, in order to use this methodology we must be able to identify firms with a similar risk profile. Two major advantages:

•   examine simultaneously the effects of both financial distress and agency cost;
•   it is easier to apply and to collect appropriate information.

3/LOSS OF FINANCIAL FLEXIBILITY

Having and retaining flexibility is a strong concern of finance directors. They know that choice of financing is a problem to be evaluated over time, not just at a given moment; a choice today can reduce the spectrum of possibilities for another choice to be made tomorrow.

Thus, taking on debt now will reduce borrowing capacity in the future, when a major investment – perhaps foreseeable, perhaps not – may be needed. If borrowing capacity is used up, the company will have no choice but to raise fresh equity. From time to time, though, the primary market in equities is closed for reason of depressed share prices. If that should be the case when the company needs funds, it may have to forgo the investment.

The equity capital market may not be open for new business during a crisis, when investors prefer to stick with safer debt securities. Debt markets stay open regardless of economic conditions.

True, the markets for high-yield debt securities react as the equity markets do and may at times be closed to new issues. There are periods such as the second half of 2001 and first half of 2002 when the number of issues of shares and high-yield bonds has been extremely small.

Raising money today with a share issue, however, does not foreclose another capital increase at a later time. Moreover, an equity financing today will increase the borrowing capacity that can be mobilised tomorrow.

A sharp increase in debt reduces the company's financial flexibility, whereas a capital increase augments its borrowing capacity.

The desire to retain flexibility prompts the company to carry less debt than the maximum level it deems bearable, so that it will at all times be in a position to take advantage of unexpected investment opportunities. Here, again, we find the option concept applied to corporate finance.

In addition, the finance director will have taken pains to negotiate unutilised lines of credit with the company's bank; to have in hand all the shareholder authorisations needed to issue new debt or equity securities; and to have effective corporate communication on financial matters with rating agencies, financial analysts and investors. Brounen et al. (2004) have found that financial flexibility appears to be the most important factor in determining the corporate debt policies of European firms.

Going beyond the debt–equity dichotomy, the quest for financial flexibility will require the finance director to open up different capital markets to the company. A company that has already issued securities on the bond market and keeps a dialogue going with bond investors can come back to this market very quickly if an investment opportunity appears.

The proliferation of financing sources – bilateral or syndicated bank loans, securitised receivables, bonds, convertibles, shares, and so on – allows the company to enhance its financial flexibility even further. But this strategy faces two limitations:

• issues on different markets have to be big enough to ensure sufficient liquidity for investors;

- multiple disparate sources of financing (possibly at different levels with a group structure) make the capital structure more complex and harder to manage (especially during liquidity crises).

Financial flexibility has a value, although difficult to estimate. We should bear in mind that the value of financial flexibility is reasonably linked to the number and the dimension of investment projects. If the company has a lot of investment opportunities and the average value of the investments is high, it should also have a high financial "reserve".

Section 34.3
THE TRADEOFF MODEL

Let us continue with the example used throughout the chapter by introducing the costs of debt into the analysis: financial distress costs and agency costs.

Debt disadvantages determine a crucial consequence: the cost of debt is no longer a horizontal line. It becomes a convex curve. The reader can go back to Chapter 23, where we discussed the estimate of K_D and concluded that the cost of debt reflects financial distress costs and agency costs.

The following table shows the effects of debt on net income and on total cash flows (dividends + interest expenses), *when the cost of debt is an increasing function of leverage*:

$V_D/(V_D + V_E)$ **market values**	0%	8%	15%	23%	31%	41%
Operating income	120,000	120,000	120,000	120,000	120,000	120,000
Interest expenses	0	(4,125)	(8,750)	(14,625)	(22,000)	(31,250)
Operating income before taxes	**120,000**	**115,875**	**111,250**	**105,375**	**98,000**	**88,750**
Tax rate	35%					
Taxes	(42,000)	(40,556)	(39,938)	(36,881)	(34,300)	(31,063)
Net income	**78,000**	**75,319**	**72,313**	**68,494**	**63,700**	**57,688**
Dividends	78,000	75,319	72,313	68,494	63,700	57,688
Total cash flows	**78,000**	**79,444**	**81,063**	**83,119**	**85,700**	**88,938**

The cost of equity line, already positive, steepens even further because it follows the evolution of the line of the cost of debt.

The weighted average cost of capital is a typical U-shaped curve: it decreases at the beginning thanks to the increasing weight of the cheaper "ingredient" and it increases when leverage is "not so small". The increase of leverage pushes the cost of debt *and* the cost of equity rapidly up. The final result is that – starting from a certain degree of leverage – the weighted average cost of capital begins to increase:

TRADEOFF MODEL

According to the extended tradeoff model, optimal leverage is obtained where the weighted average cost of capital reaches the minimum point (k^*). This is also the point where the value of the company is maximised.

In our example, this value is around 11.9% while the optimal leverage ranges between 15% and 25%. As always, a word of caution. The reader should in fact think that the optimal leverage and the minimum cost of capital are best represented by ranges of values rather than single points. A point estimation is not reasonable in the day-by-day activity of companies.

The graph also illustrates the positive line of the value of the firm under the hypothesis that tax advantages are progressively offset by financial distress costs. The difference between the values of this line and the curve of the effective value of the company indicates the eroded value of debt costs: financial distress costs, agency costs and loss of flexibility.

The existence of an optimal capital structure implies that financial management shouldn't base a company's financial policies only opportunistically, but rather they should devote themselves to understand the determinants of their company's temporary optimal financial ratio.

Above all, the finance manager should be aware that there are at least three important things that can add value:

- adopt an appropriate tax planning, with the major goal of exploiting as much as possible the additional value that the "complete" tax shield can bring to the company;
- try to match assets with liabilities – i.e., match the duration of assets with the duration of liabilities;
- write financial contracts that minimise the conflict of interest between financial claimants.

The finance function contributes to create value by setting optimal financial policies. In this regard, the optimal leverage policy is a crucial step because it represents the "place" where the company maximises its value.

The tradeoff model allows for different leverages among different industries. Companies belonging to sectors with high and stable operating income and a high percentage of fixed assets are those with an expected high leverage. Vice versa, those with an unsatisfactory profitability and a high incidence of intangible assets should have a lower debt level.

The model explains that it is possible to seek a "convergence path" towards optimal leverage. If the financial manager believes that his company is not at the optimal point he may choose the best alternatives which can bring the company to the desired leverage.

Finally, as we will see in Chapter 35, the model teaches us not to give too much importance to Earnings Per Share (EPS). The typical attitude of examining alternative financial policies according to their result on EPS could be weak. What matters is not only earnings per share: it is price (or value) per share! The two things may not always give the same results. EPS focalisation catches the "return" aspects of financial policies but it neglects the "risk" profile of the available alternatives. And our reader perfectly knows that financial decisions should always consider the entire risk/return profile!

Notwithstanding the importance of the extended tradeoff model some questions are still looking for an answer:

- Is the optimal capital structure influenced by the lifecycle stage the company is going through?
- Is there a role for competitors in determining the optimal capital structure of the firm?
- Why do managers sometimes prefer to use funding as a way to send "signals" to financial markets?
- What is the optimal maturity structure of debt? And the optimal percentage of floating debt? How much debt issued in different currencies should a company have?
- When a company wants to move towards an appropriate debt/equity mix, should it reach that leverage rapidly or gradually?

In Chapter 35, we will focus on these issues to illustrate how to reach an appropriate **design** for the capital structure of a company. After having explored the bulk of the theory, the time will come to examine "*details*".

SUMMARY

download

In this chapter we went beyond the simplified structure of perfect markets and looked at a number of different factors (tax, bankruptcy costs, information asymmetry, conflicts of interest) which make analysis more complex, but also more relevant.

Modigliani and Miller demonstrated how, when corporate tax is included in the equation (financial expenses are tax-deductible whereas dividends are not), debt financing becomes an attractive option. The optimal capital structure is thus one which includes a maximum amount of debt, and the value of a levered company is equal to what it would be without the debt, plus the amount of savings generated by the tax shield.

There are, however, two major drawbacks to this approach. First, the higher a company's debts, the greater the probability of bankruptcy and attendant costs, whether direct or indirect (profitable investments that are not made). Second, if the personal tax situation of the investor is taken into account, this offsets the tax shield that debt enjoys at a corporate level. For individual taxpayers, the tax breaks on income from equity are better than they are for debt.

Problems stemming from information asymmetry between shareholders and investors have an obvious impact on the choice of capital structure. Managers believing that their companies are undervalued would prefer to increase debt levels than to issue new shares at a low price, and possibly carry out a capital increase once the share price has gone up. Similarly, a decision to use debt finance for a project is a sign of management's confidence of its ability to meet payments on the debt and an indirect sign that the project is likely to be profitable.

Pushing the information asymmetry problem to the limit brings us to the pecking order theory which holds that managers choose sources of financing on the basis of the amount of intermediation costs and agency costs, cash flow, debt and only then a capital increase.

Finally, according to agency theory, debt is analysed as an internal means of controlling management, which has to work hard to ensure that debt repayments are met. For a mature company making healthy profits, but without major growth prospects, incurring large debts is a way for its managers to avoid spending its cash on risky diversification projects or rash expansion projects, which both destroy value. The LBO, an innovation of the 1980s, is what has come out of this theory. LBOs create value, not on the basis of the accounting illusion of the leverage effect, but thanks to the high motivation of managers who are under pressure to repay debts, and who have a financial incentive to work harder as a result of the potentially very lucrative profit-sharing schemes that have been set up.

This takes us a long way from the simplistic assumptions made in the first models designed by Modigliani and Miller!.

QUESTIONS

quiz

1/ According to the new approach by Modigliani and Miller (1963), how does the value of a levered company differ from the value of an unlevered company?

2/ What are the two drawbacks to Modigliani and Miller's 1963 theory?

3/ What is Modigliani and Miller's 1977 theory based on and what conclusions do they draw?

4/ Describe the tax breaks for debt financing and for equity financing.

5/ What are the latest tax trends with regard to sources of financing?

6/ Why are holding companies keen to have stakes that are larger than 5%?

7/ What is the value of a levered company when there is a strong likelihood that it will file for bankruptcy?

8/ What is your view of the following statement: "X went bankrupt because its financial expenses amounted to 13% of its sales?"

9/ Why do managers tend to be wary of debt?

10/ Why is it a good thing for a highly profitable company that has reached maturity to carry a lot of debt?

11/ Over the 1990s, interest rates in Europe were generally revised downwards. If Modigliani and Miller's 1963 theory was right, should debt levels of companies have increased or decreased? Debt levels actually fell. State your views.

12/ According to signal theory, should undervalued companies carry more or less debt than other companies? Why?

13/ If Modigliani and Miller's 1963 theory had been right, how much corporate income tax would the state have collected every year?

14/ In your view, after a failed takeover bid, will the debt-to-equity ratio of the target tend to rise or fall? Why?

15/ In your view, can the theories of capital structure described in this chapter be proven with as much certainty as say the put/call parity described in Chapter 33 that deals with options? Why?

16/ Is it better to calculate book value or the value of leverage (debt-to-equity ratio) in order to assess the level of risk taken by a company?

17/ Does the pecking order theory imply that the company has an optimal capital structure? What are the criteria for determining capital structure according to this approach?

18/ If there was an optimal debt-to-equity ratio, should it be stable over time? Why?

19/ An LBO fund is prepared to pay 3,000 for operating assets if the financing is split equally between debt and equity, and 35,000 if the split is 75% debt and 25% equity. State your views.

EXERCISES

1/ 70% of company A's needs are equity-financed at a cost of 10%, and 30% debt-financed at 6%. What is the weighted average cost of capital of this company if the tax rate is 20%, 50% and 80%?

2/ A company is totally financed by equity capital for a market value of 200 million. The only tax it has to pay is corporate income tax at a rate of 40%. Calculate the value of this company if it borrows 50 million at 6% to perpetuity, to be used to repay a part of shareholders' equity. Shareholders would then require an 11% return.

3/ Company C is financed by equity for a market value of 40 and by debt for a market value of 30. This debt is perpetual and its interest rate is 6%. The corporate income tax rate is 40%:

(a) How much of C's enterprise value is due to debt? The shareholders' required rate of return is 11%.

(b) By how much will the enterprise value increase if the company borrows 5 on the same terms as previously (assume a required rate of return of 11% to simplify calculations)?

(c) By how much will the enterprise value fall if there is a change in the tax laws and in 4 years' time financial expenses will no longer be tax-deductible.

4/ Redo the table on p. 675 for the Netherlands and Morocco. State your views.

ANSWERS

Questions

1/ Difference: present value of tax saving due to the fact that financial expenses are tax-deductible.

2/ The cost and disruption of bankruptcy and individual income tax.

3/ The individual tax payable by the investor cancels out the impact of the corporate tax payable. Conclusion: no optimal capital structure.

4/ Financial expenses are tax-deductible. Tax credit.

5/ More favourable treatment for equity due to the drop in the corporate income tax rate, and heavier taxes on debt income for creditors.

6/ So that they can enjoy a more favourable tax regime (the "parent company" regime, under which dividends received from subsidiaries in which they have a stake of more than 5% are exempt from corporate income tax).

7/ Value of unlevered company + Present value of tax saving − Present value of cost of filing for bankruptcy.

8/ This line of reasoning is false. A company goes bankrupt because its present and expected profits are inadequate compared with its risk, and not because it is carrying too much debt. If it is carrying too much debt, this is because its profits are too low, and not the other way round.

9/ Because, by increasing the risk to which their companies are exposed, they increase their chances of losing their jobs.

10/ Because it can avoid using its free cash flows, it will not destroy value by diversifying or making unprofitable investments.

11/ Debt levels should have risen to set off the drop in interest rates so that tax-deductible financial expenses at least remain constant. Conclusion: either this theory does not stand up or there are other factors which explain the situation.

12/ More debt, because they are not keen to issue new equity while the value of their shareholders' equity is undervalued.

13/ Zero, since all companies would incur sufficient debts to reduce their tax bills to zero.

14/ It should go up, because shareholders will put pressure on management to achieve better results.

15/ No, because we are not dealing with mathematical certainties but with behaviour.

16/ Value, because if the company is very profitable its equity capital will be worth much more than its book value. A more accurate assessment of the company's ability to meet its debt repayments will then be possible.

17/ No, because financial resources are used in a given order in line with requirements. The difference between operating inflows and investment outflows.

18/ No, because interest rates, tax rates, risk aversion, volatility of operating assets, the maturity of a sector, etc., change over time.

19/ A difference in this amount cannot simply be due to the tax break on debt. It is also difficult to believe that management would be more motivated by the higher level of debt (50/50 is already a high level). This can only be some sort of trap.

Exercises

1/ 8.44%; 7.9%; 7.36%.

2/ $200 + 50 \times 40\% \times 6\% / 11\% = 210.9$.

3/ (a) $(30 \times 6\% \times 40\%)/11\% = 6.5$.

(b) The value increases by 1.1.

(c) Reduction of the value by 5.

4.

	Italy		Morocco	
	$D = 0$	$D = 500$	$D = 0$	$D = 500$
Operating income	146	146	100	100
− Interest expense	0	35	0	35
= Pre-tax profit	146	111	100	65
− Income tax expense	59	45	35	23
= Net earnings	87	66	65	42
Income tax: on dividends/capital gains on interest	17^{10} 0	13^{10} 4	6.5^{11} 0	4.2^{11} 15.8
Investors' net income	70	85	58.5	57
Total taxes	76	61	41,5	43

10 *10%, the rate is identical for capital gains and dividends.*

11 *At 19.3% = 1/3 × 12.5% + 2/3 × 22.7% = 27% (paid over 3 years).*

In Italy, debt receives more favourable tax treatment, while in Morocco, equity enjoys better tax breaks.

BIBLIOGRAPHY

Modigliani and Miller's main work on capital structure:

M. Miller, Debt and taxes, *Journal of Finance*, **32**, 261–276, May 1977.
M. Miller, The M&M proposition 40 years later, *European Financial Management*, **4**(2), 113–120, July 1998.
F. Modigliani, M. Miller, Corporate income taxes and the cost of capital: A correction, *American Economic Review*, **53**, 433–443, June 1963.

Following on the above work, on the problems of capital structure and taxes:

H. DeAngelo, R. Masulis, Optimal capital structure under corporate and personal taxation, *Journal of Financial Economics*, **8**(1), 3–29, March 1980.
E. Fama, K. French, Taxes, financing decisions and firm value, *Journal of Finance*, **53**(3), 819–843, June 1998.
D. Galai, Taxes, M&M propositions and government's implicit cost of capital in investment project in the private sector, *European Financial Management*, **4**(2), 143–157, July 1998.
J. Graham, How big are the tax benefits of debt? *Journal of Finance*, **55**(5), 1901–1941, October 2000.
J. Graham, M. Lang, D. Shackelford, Employee stock options, corporate taxes and debt policy, *Journal of Finance*, **59**(4), 1585–1618, August 2004.

On the disciplining role of debt:

D. Denis, D. Denis, Leveraged recaps in the curbing of corporate overinvestment, *Journal of Applied Corporate Finance*, **6**(1), 60–71, 1993.
E. Fama, What's different about bank loans? *Journal of Monetary Economics*, **35**, 1985.
M. Jensen, Agency costs of free cash flows, corporate finance and takeovers, *American Economic Review*, **76**, 323–329.
S.N. Kaplan, Campeau's acquisition of Federated: Value destroyed or value added?, *Journal of Financial Economics*, **25**, 191–212, 1989.

K.G. Palepu, Consequences of LBO, *Journal of Financial Economics*, **26**, 247–262, 1990.
C. Smith, Corporate ownership structure and performance: The case of management buyouts, *Journal of Financial Economics*, **27**, 143–164, 1990.

On financial asymmetries and pecking order theory:

D. Brounen, A. De Jong, K. Koedijk, Corporate finance in Europe: Confronting theory with practice, *Financial Management*, Winter 2004.
G. Donaldson, *Corporate Debt Capacity: A Study of the Corporate Debt Policy and Determination of Corporate Debt Capacity*, Harvard Graduate School of Business Administration, 1961.
G. Donaldson, *Strategy for Financial Mobility*, Graduate School of Business Administration, 1969.
G. Donaldson, *Managing Corporate Wealth: The Operations of a Comprehensive Financial Goals System*, Praeger, 1984.
C. James, D.C. Smith, Are banks still special? New evidence on their role in the corporate capital-raising process, in J. Stern and D. Chew (eds), *The Revolution in Corporate Finance*, Blackwell, 2003.
S. Myers, Determinants of corporate borrowing, *Journal of Financial Economics*, **5**, 146–175, 1977.
S. Myers, The capital structure puzzle, *Journal of Finance*, **12**, 1984.

On the costs of financial distress:

E. Altman, *Default and Returns on High Yield bonds: Analysis through 1999 and Default Outlook for 2000–2002*, working paper, New York University/Salomon Center, 2000.
E. Altman, A further empirical investigation of the bankruptcy costs question, *Journal of Finance*, **39**(4), 589–609, September 1984.
G. Andrade, S. Kaplan, How costly is financial (no economic) distress? Evidence from highly leveraged transactions that became distressed, *Journal of Finance*, October 1998.
N. Baxter, Leverage risk of ruin and the cost of capital, *Journal of Finance*, **22**, 322–403, September 1967.
E.H. Kim, A mean-variance theory of optimal capital structure and corporate debt capacity, *Journal of Financial Economics*, 83–110, March 1979.
A. Kraus, R. Litzenberger, A state-preference model of optimal financial leverage, *Journal of Finance*, 911–922, September 1973.
A. Shapiro, *Modern Corporate Finance*, Macmillan, 1989.
J. Stiglitz, Some aspects of the pure theory of corporate finance: Bankruptcies and takeovers, *Bell Journal of Economics and Management Science*, 458–482, Autumn 1972.
S. Titman, The effect of capital structure on a firm's liquidation decision, *Journal of Financial Economics*, **13**, 1351–1371, 1984.

On the application of agency theory to problems relating to capital structure:

Ph. Berger, E. Ofek, D. Yermack, Why CEOs use insufficient debt, *Financial Times, Mastering Finance*, **3**, 27, May 1997.
M. Jensen, The agency costs of free cash flow, corporate finance, and takeovers, *American Economic Review*, **76**, 323–329, May 1986.
M. Jensen, W. Meckling, Theory of the firm: Managerial behavior, agency costs and ownership structure, *Journal of Financial Economics*, **3**, 305–360, October 1976.
E. Ofek, Capital structure and firm response to poor performance: An empirical investigation, *Journal of Financial Economics*, **34**, 3–30, August 1993.

Some articles that summarise the topics covered in this chapter:

Bank of America roundtable on "The link between capital structure and shareholder value", in D. Chew (ed.), *The New Corporate Finance: Where Theory Meets Practice*, 2nd edn, McGraw-Hill, 1999.

An interesting issue of the *Journal of Applied Corporate Finance*, **17**(1), Winter 2005, contains various interesting articles on "capital structure, payout policy and the IPO process".

J. Ang, J. Chua, J. McConnell, The administrative costs of corporate bankruptcy: A note, *Journal of Finance*, **37**(1), 219–226, 1982.

M. Barclay, C. Smith, The capital structure puzzle: Another look at the evidence, *Journal of Applied Corporate Finance*, **12**(1), 8–20, Spring 1999.

B. Betker, Management's incentives, equity's bargaining power, and deviations from absolute priority in Chapter 11, *Journal of Business*, **68**, 1995.

D. Cutler, L. Summers, The costs of conflict and financial distress: Evidence from Texaco—Perinzoil litigation, *RAND Journal of Economics*, **19**, 157–172, Summer 1988.

J. Warner, Bankruptcy, absolute priority and the pricing of risky debt claims, *Journal of Financial Economics*, 239–276, May 1977.

L. Weiss, Bankruptcy resolution: Direct costs and violations of absolute priority of claims, *Journal of Financial Economics*, **27**, 285–314, October 1990.

M. White, Bankruptcy costs and the new bankruptcy code, *Journal of Finance*, **36**, 477–496, 1983.

Appendix 34A
THE CAPITAL STRUCTURE CHOICE: THE ENDESA CASE

Endesa is the leading utility in the Spanish electricity system and the number one private sector multinational electricity utility in Latin America; it is a major operator in the Mediterranean region, particularly in Italy; it has a growing presence in the various natural gas market segments in Spain and Portugal; its business in the renewable energies field is well-consolidated; and it has equity interests in companies in the telecommunications industry and in other services that complement and contribute value to its core business.

Endesa has total installed capacity of 41,800 MW and 20.9 million customers. It controls about 45% of Spain's electricity production and distribution. This strong domestic position is one of the main rating supports. Spanish operations provide about 60–65% of both total revenues and EBITDA, and will remain the major contributor in the future.

The group is implementing a strategy focused on consolidating its electricity business and strengthening its financial position through debt reduction. Consolidated gross debt (including preferred stock) declined by 17% year on year in 2003, to €19.7bn, thanks to €2.4bn in asset disposals, depreciation of the US dollar against the euro, and an $800m capital increase at Endesa. As a result, debt to capital at year-end 2003 shrank to 62%, from 68% in 2002. Further debt reduction may be constrained by the substantial investments planned both in new generation capacity and to improve the reliability and quality of supply.

The ratings of A assigned by S&P reflect Endesa's strong position as the largest vertically integrated electric utility in Spain, one of Europe's fastest growing electricity markets. In addition, Spain's regulatory regime has become more transparent and supportive since the publication of the tariff-setting methodology at the end of 2002. These strengths are partially offset by a financial profile that is still below par for the rating category, a large capital expenditure programme and the company's considerable exposure to investments in Latin America.

Determination of the tradeoff model for the optimal capital structure of Endesa has been made using the following data and assumptions as of 30 October 2004:

ENDESA

Capital structure		Financial market		Income statement	
Current MV of equity	€16,827.51	Current beta for stock	1.11	Current EBITDA	€5,121.00
MV of interest-bearing debt	€18,112.00	Current bond rating	A	Current depreciation	€2,051.00
No. of shares outstanding	1,059			Current tax rate	35.00%
Debt value of operating leases (if any)	€0.00	Long-term government bond ratio	3.92%	Current capital spending	€2,050.00
Risk premium	4.00%	Pre-tax cost of debt	4.32%	Current interest expense	€1,484.00

The coverage ratios have been reconstructed using – as a reference point – the aggregate ratios regarding utilities included in the Standard & Poor's publication *Corporate Ratings Criteria 2003*. Moreover, the spread for the same class of companies has been obtained from the website *www.bondsonline.com* (go to: "utility spreads").

IF THE INTEREST COVERAGE RATIO IS

>	≤	Rating is	Spread is (%)
−100,000	0.2	D	20.00
0.2	0.5	C	15.00
0.501	0.7	CC	12.00
0.701	0.85	CCC	8.55
0.8501	1.15	B−	7.10
1.151	1.4	B	6.05
1.41	1.7	B+	5.55
1.701	2	BB	3.75
2.01	2.5	BB+	3.70
2.501	3	BBB	0.74
3.01	3.25	A−	0.40
3.2501	3.5	A	0.27
3.501	3.9	A+	0.25
3.901	5.5	AA	0.16
5.50	100,000	AAA	0.03

The basic steps for obtaining the k (or WACC) and the firm value for different leverage ratios are the following:

1   estimate the rating of debt for different levels of leverage;
2   estimate the (after-tax) cost of debt for different levels of leverage by summing the spread for the specific class of rating to the risk-free rate;
3   estimate the levered beta and the cost equity for each level of leverage;
4   estimate the k and the firm value for each level of leverage;
5   choose the leverage that minimises the k: that is, the optimal leverage according to the prescriptions of the tradeoff model.

The results obtained with Endesa are reported in the following table:

ENDESA TRADEOFF MODEL

Debt ratio (%)	Beta	Cost of equity (%)	Bond rating	Interest rate on debt (%)	Tax rate (%)	Cost of debt (after tax) (%)	WACC (or k) (%)	Firm value (%)
0	0.65	6.53	AAA	3.95	35.00	2.57	6.53	€35,425.29
10	0.70	6.72	AAA	3.95	35.00	2.57	6.31	€36,909.00
20	0.76	6.96	AAA	3.95	35.00	2.57	6.08	€38,521.31
30	0.84	7.26	AAA	3.95	35.00	2.57	5.85	€40,279.68
40	0.94	7.66	AAA	3.95	35.00	2.57	5.63	€42,204.92
50	1.08	8.23	AA	4.08	35.00	2.65	5.44	€43,911.53
60	1.29	9.08	BB	7.67	35.00	4.99	6.62	€34,864.23
70	1.64	10.49	BB	7.67	35.00	4.99	6.64	€34,772.42
80	2.35	13.32	B+	9.47	35.00	6.16	7.59	€29,824.56
90	4.47	21.81	B+	9.47	35.00	6.16	7.72	€29,245.58

The results suggest that the optimal capital structure of Endesa should be around a debt ratio of 50%. The current debt ratio of this company is around 52%, which means that the company has already adopted a capital structure policy close to the optimal. The final table reports the expected changes that could occur if the company decides to converge toward the optimal ratio:

	Current	Optimal	Change
$V_D/(V_D + V_E)$ ratio	51.84%	50.00%	−1.84%
Beta for the stock	1.11	1.08	−0.03
Cost of equity	8.36%	8.23%	−0.13%
After-tax interest rate on debt	2.81%	2.65%	−0.16%
WACC (or k)	5.48%	5.44%	−0.04%

Chapter 35
DEBT, EQUITY AND OPTIONS THEORY

Light too bright to see by

The theories of corporate finance examined so far may have given the impression that the only difference between debt and equity is the required rate of return. However, **there is a big difference between the 10% return required by creditors and that required by shareholders.**

Shareholders simply hope to achieve this rate, which forms an average of rates that can be either positive or negative. The actual return can range from 0% to 100%, with the entire gamut of variations in between!

Creditors are far more assured of receiving the required rate, but never more. They can only hope to earn the 10% return but, with a few exceptions, this hope is almost always fulfilled. So here we have the first distinction between creditors and shareholders: the probability distribution of their remuneration is completely different.

This said, although the creditor's risk is very low, it is not nil. Capitalism is built on the concept of corporation, which legally **restricts shareholders' liabilities with respect to creditors'**. When a company defaults, shareholders hold a "trump card" that allows them to hand the company, or rather, its liabilities, over to the lenders.

The main financial innovation of the 19th century is the corporation.

In the rest of this chapter, *we will concentrate on the valuation of companies in which shareholder responsibility is limited to the amount they have invested.* This applies to the vast majority of all companies in modern capitalism, be they corporations, limited liability companies or sole ownerships with limited liability.

This is the fundamental difference between shareholders and creditors: the former can lose their entire investment, but also hope for unlimited gains, while the latter will at best earn the flows programmed at the beginning of the contract. A central assumption of option pricing models is that prices are distributed log-normally: there is no limit to the positive side that may be realised, while the minimum value is zero. It can be demonstrated that the fact that prices are log-normally distributed underlies the normal distribution of returns.

Keep this in mind as we use options to analyse corporate structure and, more importantly, the relationship between shareholders and creditors.

Section 35.1
ANALYSING THE FIRM IN LIGHT OF OPTIONS THEORY

To keep our presentation simple, we will take the example of a joint stock company in which the market value of the firm is divided between debt (V_D) and equity (V_E).

We will also assume that the company has issued only one type of debt – zero-coupon bonds – redeemable upon maturity at full face value (principal and interest) for 100.

1/EQUITY AND DEBT IN TERMS OF OPTIONS

Depending on the market value of the firm when the debt matures, two outcomes are possible.

- The value of the firm is higher than the amount of debt to be redeemed (e.g., 120). In this case, the shareholders let the company repay the lenders and take the residual value of 20.
- The value of the firm is lower than the amount of debt to be redeemed (e.g., 70). The shareholders may then invoke their limited liability clause, forfeiting only their investment, and transfer the company to the lenders who will bear the difference between the value of the firm and their claim.

Now let us analyse this situation in terms of options. From an economic standpoint, shareholders have a call option, known as a European call if it can only be exercised at the end of its life, on the firm's assets. Its features are:

- **Underlying asset** = market value of the firm.
- **Exercise price** = amount of debt to be reimbursed (100).
- **Volatility** = volatility of the underlying assets; i.e., the capital employed.
- **Maturity** = expiration date.
- **Interest rate** = risk-free rate corresponding to the maturity of the option.

At the expiration date, shareholders exercise their call option and repay the lenders, or they abandon it. The value of the option is no other than the value of equity (V_E).

From the shareholder's point of view, when a company borrows funds, it is selling its "enterprise value" to its creditors, but with an option to buy it back (at the exercise price) when the debt matures. The shares of a levered company thus represent call options on the capital employed.

The lender, on the other hand, who has invested in the firm at no risk, *has sold the shareholders a put option on the capital employed.* We have just seen that in the event of default the creditors may find themselves the unwilling owners of the company. Rather than recouping the amount they lent, they get only the value of the company back. In other words, they have "bought" the company in exchange for the outstanding amount of debt.

The features of the put option are:

- **Underlying asset** = market value of the firm.
- **Exercise price** = amount of debt redeemable upon maturity (100).
- **Volatility** = volatility of the underlying asset.
- **Maturity** = maturity of the debt.
- **Interest rate** = risk-free rate corresponding to the maturity of the option.

The sale of this (European-style) put option results in additional remuneration for the debtholder which, together with the risk-free rate, constitutes the total return. This is only fair, since the debtholder runs the risk that the shareholders will exercise their put option – in other words, that the company will not pay back the debt.

The value of this option is equal to the difference between the value of the loan discounted at the risk-free rate and its market value (discounted at a rate that takes into account the default risk – i.e., the cost of debt k_D). This is the risk premium that arises between any loan and its risk-free equivalent.

All this means is that the debtholder has lent the company 103 at an interest rate equal to the risk-free rate. The company should have received 103, but the value of the loan is only 100 after discounting the flows at the normal rate of return required in view of the company's risk, rather than the risk-free rate.

The company uses the balance of 3, which represents the price of the credit risk, to buy a put option on the value of the firm. In short, the company received 100 while the bank paid 100 for a risky claim since it sold a put option on the value of the firm that the company, and therefore the shareholders, will exercise if its value is lower than that of the outstanding date at maturity. By exercising the option, the company, and thus its shareholders, discharge their debt by transferring ownership of the capital employed to the creditors.

Lending to a company is a means of investing in its assets at no risk. The lender sells the shareholders a put option at an exercise price that is equal to the debt to be repaid.

In conclusion, we see that, depending on the situation at the redemption date, one of the following two will apply:

- if $V_D < V$ the value of the call option is higher than 0, the value of the put option is zero and equity is positive;
- if $V_D > V$ the value of the call option is 0, the value of the put option is higher than 0, and the equity is worthless.

2/AN OPTIONS APPROACH TO FINANCIAL SECURITIES

We have already seen that the additivity rule for equity and debt applies and that there is no connection between enterprise value and the type of financing:

$$\text{Value of the firm} = \text{Equity} + \text{Debt}$$

Based on the preceding developments, we deduce that:

> Value of equity = Value of the call option on firm value
> Value of debt = Present value of debt at the risk-free rate
> — Value of the put option
> Firm value = Value of the call option
> + Present value of debt at the risk-free rate
> — Value of the put option

This brings us back to the fundamental equality between put and call options:

> Buying a call option + Selling a put option
> = Buying the underlying asset + Borrowing at the risk-free rate

This underscores the relationship between the value of a call on capital employed and the value of a put on the same capital employed:

> Value of equity = Firm value − Present value of debt at the risk-free rate
> + Value of the put

Section 35.2
CONTRIBUTION OF THE OPTIONS THEORY TO THE VALUATION OF EQUITY

We have demonstrated that the value of a firm's equity is comparable with the value of a call option on the value of the firm. The option's exercise price is the amount of debt to be repaid at maturity, the life of the option is that of the debt and its underlying asset is the firm's value.

This means that, at the valuation date, the value of equity is made up of an intrinsic value and a time value. The intrinsic value of the call option is the difference between the present value of capital employed and the debt to be repaid upon maturity. The time value corresponds to the difference between the total value of equity and the intrinsic value.

The main contribution of options theory to corporate finance is the concept of a time value for equity.

Take, for example, a company where the return on capital employed is lower than that required by investors in view of the related risk. The market value is thus lower than the book value.

If the debt were to mature today, the shareholders would exercise their put option since the capital employed is worth only 70 while the outstanding debt is 80.

The company would have to file for bankruptcy. Fortunately, the debt is not redeemable today, but only in, say, 2 years' time. By then, the firm value may have risen to over 80. In that case, equity will have an intrinsic value equal to the difference between the firm value at the redemption date and the amount to be redeemed (in our case, 80).

Today, however, the intrinsic value is zero (we know that it cannot be negative) and the present value of equity (8) can only be explained by the time value, which represents the hope that, when the debt matures 2 years hence, enterprise value will have risen enough to exceed the amount of debt to be repaid, giving the equity an intrinsic value.

As seen in the graphs on this and the following page, a company's financial position can be considered from either the shareholders' or the creditors' standpoint.

By now you must be eager to apply your new-found knowledge of options to corporate finance!

(a) The time value of an option increases with the volatility of the underlying asset

The more economic or industrial risk on a company, the higher the volatility of its capital employed and the higher the time value of its equity. The options method is thus used to value large, risky projects financed by debt, such as the Channel Tunnel, leisure parks, etc., or those with inherent volatility, such as biotech startups.

(b) The time value of an option depends on the position of the exercise price relative to the market value of the underlying asset

When the call option is out-of-the-money (firm value lower than outstanding debt), the company's equity has only time value. Shareholders hope for an improvement in the company, whose equity has no intrinsic value.

A DECOMPOSITION OF THE UNDERLYING ASSET VALUE

Decomposition of the value of the firm.

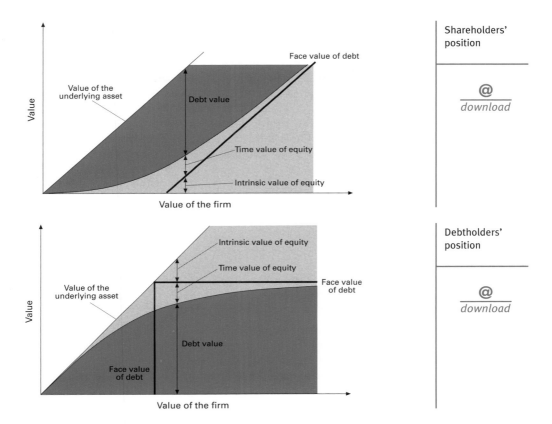

When the call option is at-the-money (firm value equal to debt at maturity), the time value of equity is at its highest and anything can happen. Using the options method to value equity is now particularly relevant, since it can quantify shareholders' anticipations.

When the call option is in-the-money (firm value higher than outstanding debt at maturity), the intrinsic value of equity quickly outweighs the time value. The risk on the debt held by the lenders decreases and becomes nearly nonexistent when the enterprise value tends towards infinity. This brings us back to the traditional idea that the higher the enterprise value, the less risk creditors have of a default, and the more the cost of debt approaches the risk-free rate.

Using options theory to analyse liabilities is particularly helpful when a company is in financial distress.

The options method is therefore applied to companies that carry heavy debt or are very risky.

(c) The time value of an option increases with its maturity

This is why it is so important for companies in distress to reschedule debt payments, preferably at very long maturities.

The example below illustrates the use of options to value equity.

Example   Take a company that has both debt and equity financing and let us assume its debt is 100, redeemable in 1 year. If, based on its degree of risk, the debt carries 6% interest, the amount to be repaid to creditors 1 year later is 106.

Traditional theory tells us that if the firm's value is 150 at the time of calculation, the value of equity – defined as the difference between firm value and the value of debt – will be $150 - 100 = 50$.

What happens if we apply options theory to this value?

We will assume the risk-free rate is 5%. The discounted value of the debt + interest payment at the risk-free rate is $106/1.05$, or 100.95.

The value of debt can be expressed as:

Value of debt = Value of debt at the risk-free rate − Value of a put

i.e., value of the put $= 100.95 - 100 = 0.95$.

We know that the value of equity breaks down into its intrinsic and time value:

	Value of equity	=	50
−	Intrinsic value $= 150 - 106$	=	44
=	Time value	=	6

You see that, for this company with limited risk, the time value measuring the actual risk is far lower than the intrinsic value. Similarly, the value of the put, which acts as a risk premium, is very low as well.

Now, let's increase the risk to the capital employed and assume that the cost of equity required by the creditors is 15% rather than 6%, corresponding to a 10% risk premium. The amount to be repaid in 1 year is thus 115.

The value of the debt discounted at the risk-free rate is $115/1.05$, or 109.52. The value of the put is thus $= 109.52 - 100 = 9.52$.

Note that the risk premium for this company is much higher than in the preceding example, reflecting the increasing probability that the company will default on its debt.

The value of equity, which is still 50, breaks down into intrinsic value of 35 $(150 - 115)$ and a time value of 15 $(50 - 35)$. Since there is more risk than in our previous example, the time value accounts for a higher portion of the equity value.

Section 35.3
USING OPTIONS THEORY TO ANALYSE A COMPANY'S FINANCIAL DECISIONS

Options theory helps us understand how major, corporate financial decisions (choice of capital structure, dividend payout, investment decisions, etc.) affect shareholders and creditors differently, and how they can result in a transfer of value between the two.

Example   Take the example of a holding company Holding SA, which owns 100 ordinary shares of Fille SA, listed at €2,230. We will assume that the liabilities of

Holding SA comprise 100 shares and 300 bonds. Each of the latter is a zero-coupon bond with a redemption value of €1,000 in 3 years' time. The creditors do not expect any coupon payments or changes in the capital structure before the debt redemption date.

The table below lists the closing prices for a call option on a Fille SA share at various exercise prices:

Exercise price (€)	Value of a 3-year call option on Fille SA (€)
2,600	130
2,800	80
3,000	45
3,200	32

The firm value of Holding SA is equal to the number of Fille SA shares multiplied by their closing price – i.e., €223,000.

Consider each of the 100 shares booked under liabilities at Holding SA as being an option on its value employed (the shares of Fille SA) – i.e., €223,000 – with an exercise price that is equal to the amount of Holding SA debt outstanding, giving 300 bonds × €1,000 = €300,000.

Each Holding SA share can thus be considered to be a call option with an exercise price of: €300,000/100 shares = €3,000, and a maturity of 3 years.

According to the table above, Holding SA's equity value is thus €45 × 100 shares = €4,500.

MARKET VALUE BALANCE SHEET OF HOLDING SA

The value of debt is equal to the difference between the firm value (€223,000) and that of equity (€4,500) – i.e., €218,500.

download

One bond is therefore worth €728.3 (€218,500/300), corresponding to an implied yield of 11.1% (in fact: $728.3 = 1,000/(1 + 0.111)^3$).

We will now discuss a few major financing or investment decisions in a context of **equilibrium** – that is, where the debt, shares and assets held are bought or sold at their fair value, **without the market having anticipated the decision**.

1/INCREASING DEBT

Suppose the shareholders of Holding SA decide to issue 20 additional bonds and use the proceeds to reduce the company's equity by distributing an exceptional dividend. The overall exercise price corresponding to the redemption value of the debt at maturity is:

$$320 \text{ bonds} \times €1,000 = €320,000, \quad \text{or } €3,200 \text{ per share}$$

A look at the listed prices of the options shows us that at an exercise price of €3,200, Holding SA's equity is valued €32 × 100 shares = €3,200, indicating that the value of its debt at the same date is: €219,800 (223,000 − 3,200).

The new bondholders will thus pay €13,737 (20 bonds × €219,800/320 bonds), which will go to reduce the equity of Holding SA.

The shareholders consequently have €13,737 in cash and €3,200 in shares – i.e., a total of €16,937 compared with the previous €4,500. They have gained €12,437 to the detriment of the former creditors, who have seen the value of their claim fall from €218,500 to: 300 bonds × €219,800/320 bonds, or €206,063.

Their loss (218,500 − 206,063 = €12,437) exactly mirrors the shareholders' gain.

The implicit yield to maturity has risen to 13.3%, reflecting the fact that the borrowing has become riskier, since it now finances a larger share of the same amount of capital employed.

Increasing the risk to creditors has enhanced the value of the shares, thereby reducing that of the bonds. The existing creditors have lost out because they were not able to anticipate the change in corporate structure and have been harmed by the dividend distribution.

Common (accounting) sense seems to indicate that distributing €13,737 in cash to shareholders should translate into an equivalent decrease in the value of their Holding SA shares. According to this reasoning, after the buyback Holding SA's shares should have been revalued at −€9,237 (€4,500 − €13,737), but that cannot be!

Options theory solves this apparent paradox. It shows that when new debt is issued to reduce equity, the time value of the shares decreases less than the amount received by shareholders and remains positive. True, the likelihood that the value of Fille SA shares will be higher than that of the redeemable debt upon maturity has lessened (since debt has increased), but it is still not nil, giving a time value that, while lower, is still positive.

Of course, this example is exaggerated. Such a decision would have catastrophic consequences for shareholders who would be taken to court by the creditors and lose all credibility in the eyes of the market. But it effectively illustrates the contribution of options theory to equity valuations.

Increasing debt increases the value of shareholders' investment to the detriment of the claims held by existing creditors. Thus value is transferred from creditors to shareholders.

Conversely, when debt is reduced by a capital increase, the overall value of shares does not increase by the value of the shares issued. The old debt, which has become less risky, has in fact "confiscated" some of the value to the benefit of creditors and to the detriment of shareholders.

2/THE INVESTMENT DECISION

Now let us return to our initial scenario and assume that Holding SA manages to exchange the 100 shares of Fille SA for 100 shares of a company with a higher risk profile called Risk SA, for €223,000 (100 × €2,230).

Each share of Holding SA is equal to a call option on a Risk SA share with an exercise price of €3,000 (300 × 1,000/100).

Suppose the value of a call option on a Risk SA share is €140 with an exercise price of €3,000 and an exercise date in 3 years' time.

The Holding SA shares are consequently worth €14,000.

Exchanging a low-risk asset (Fille SA) for a highly volatile asset (Risk SA) has redistributed value to the benefit of shareholders, whose gain is €9,500 (14,000 − 4,500).

Their gain is offset by an equivalent loss to creditors, since the value of the debt has fallen from 218,500 to 223,000 − 14,000 = €209,000; i.e., a €9,500 decline.

The higher risk led to an increase in the implicit yield to maturity of the bonds from 11.1% to 12.8%.

As in our previous examples, the transfer of value was only possible because creditors underestimated the power shareholders have over the company's investment decisions.

3/RENEGOTIATING THE TERMS OF DEBT

What if we now return to our initial situation and imagine that the company is able to reschedule its debt? This happens when creditors prefer to let a company in financial distress attempt a turnaround rather than precipitate its demise.

So let's assume the debt is due in 4, rather than the initial 3 years. A look at our options price list for Fille SA shares with a 4-year maturity shows us that they carry a higher premium.

Exercise price (€)	Value of put on Fille SA shares in 3 years (€)
2,600	140
2,800	89
3,000	53
3,200	40

This, of course, comes as no surprise to our attentive readers who remember learning in Chapter 29 that the value of an option increases with the length of its life.

The value of equity is thus €53 × 100 shares = €5,300. A bond is therefore worth €725.7 (€217,700/300). Without having abandoned any flows, creditors' generosity will have cost them €800.

To sum up:

- Leveraging a company either to distribute dividends, reduce capital or to invest tends to increase the risk to creditors, transferring value from them to shareholders. The value of the shares diminishes less than the dividend payout and increases when the debt is used for investment purposes.
- Similarly, replacing nonrisky with risky assets does not change enterprise value, but it does transfer value from creditors to shareholders.
- Lastly, rescheduling debt transfers value from creditors to shareholders, even if the interest rate remains the same.

This is called the expropriation effect, where some of the value of the claims is confiscated without any exchange of flows.

Section 35.4
RESOLVING CONFLICTS BETWEEN SHAREHOLDERS AND CREDITORS

Creditors have a number of means at their disposal to protect themselves and overcome the asymmetry from which they suffer. They can be grouped under two main headings:

- hybrid financial securities;
- restrictive covenants.

1/HYBRID FINANCIAL SECURITIES

Hybrid financial securities combining features of both debt and equity – such as convertible bonds, bonds with equity warrants, participating loan stock, etc. – would not be necessary in a perfect market. By issuing such hybrid securities, shareholders are in effect giving creditors a call option on equity which neutralises the call option on equity creditors have granted shareholders.

In fact, should shareholders make investment or financing decisions that are detrimental to creditors, the latter can exercise their warrants or convert their bonds into shares, thus becoming shareholders themselves and, if all goes well, recouping in equity what they have lost in debt!

Jensen and Meckling (1976) have demonstrated that the issue of convertible bonds reduces the risk of the firm's assets being replaced by more risky assets that increase volatility and thus the value of the shares. The same reasoning is applied when "free" warrants are granted to creditors who agree to waive some of their claims during a corporate restructuring plan.

2/RESTRICTIVE COVENANTS

We will discuss the four main types of covenants, but our list is far from comprehensive. They can concern:

- corporate investment and production policies;
- dividend payments;
- net debt and subsequent debt issues;
- early redemption provisions.

(a) Corporate investment and production policies

The purpose of such covenants is chiefly to protect debtholders against the possibility that the firm will substitute more risky assets for the existing ones. Any investment in other companies, mergers, absorption or asset disposals are either restricted or subject to approval by the debtholders.

In some cases, the securities of certain subsidiaries or the equipment the issue served to finance are given as collateral. This restricts the possibility of asset substitution.

The company may also be obliged to invest in certain projects, to continue holding certain assets, maintain its working capital or raise it above a certain threshold.

(b) Dividend payments

These covenants are designed to avoid the massive dividend distributions financed by increases in debt or asset disposals we discussed previously.

For example, they can link dividend distribution to a minimum level of equity during the life of the debt. Similarly, they frequently restrict or rule out the distribution of reserves or share buybacks.

These clauses have the added advantage of imposing a minimum level of investment on shareholders in order to utilise the cash that cannot be distributed, thus reducing the risk of underinvestment.

(c) Net debt and subsequent debt issues

Any unforeseen, subsequent issue of equal or higher ranking debt reduces value for existing debtholders. And yet, it would not be in the interests of either the current bondholders or the shareholders to rule out any further debt issues. To protect themselves against a reduction in the value of their claims, debtholders can impose limits on the amount of net debt and the nature of the new debt issued based on certain ratios:

$$\frac{\text{Net financial debt}}{\text{Equity}}, \frac{\text{Operating income}}{\text{Interest expenses}}, \frac{\text{Net financial debt}}{EBITDA^1}, \frac{\text{Receivables}}{\text{Payables}}, \text{etc.}$$

When these ratios exceed the predefined threshold, the debt immediately falls due.

It can also become payable when the ratios exceed these thresholds because of deteriorating corporate results rather than new borrowings.

In practice, these are chiefly *rendez-vous* clauses that force the company to arrange a restructuring plan with its creditors to contain the risk to the latter, which increases with the financial distress of the company.

1 *Earnings Before Interest, Taxes, Depreciation and Amortisation.*

(d) Early redemption clauses for all or part of the debt

In a context of information asymmetry, early redemption clauses are a means of dealing with the problem of overinvestment and asset substitution. Analysing equity as an option on the firm's value shows that paying a coupon or an annuity before the final repayment offers some protection to creditors and thus reduces share value.

In short, covenants are affirmative or negative pledges that entail the immediate repayment of the debt when not respected.

The main contribution of options theory to corporate finance is the concept of the time value of equity. The options approach is predicated on the physical separation of shareholders and debtholders, which has become standard practice, even in Europe.

You will have realised that this is very different from the simple accounting leverage effect that seemed to show that shareholders create wealth by investing at a higher rate than the cost of debt. The shareholder/debtholder relationship takes on an entirely different meaning where value is concerned. When risks change, the interests of the two parties may diverge radically without any exchange of flows between them or change in the overall value of the firm.

We hope to have impressed on you the importance of reasoning in terms of value and assessing all decisions not just on the basis of profits, but also risk. The use of options may now seem blindingly obvious to you, and we hope you always keep in mind the notion of risk transfers.

Please don't be discouraged by the difficulty of applying these formulas to real life. They are very efficient qualitative tools that will enable you to tackle the financial re-engineering of a group with more imagination and creativity.

SUMMARY

download

It seems like stating the obvious when we say that the status of the creditor differs radically from that of the shareholder. The shareholder stands to gain a potentially unlimited amount and his risk is limited to his investment, while the creditor, who can also lose his investment, can only expect a return that is fixed.

This asymmetry brings options to mind. This chapter showed that there is more than one similarity.

The shareholders' equity of a levered company can be seen as a call option granted by creditors to shareholders on the company's operating assets. The strike price is the value of the debt and the maturity is the date on which the debt is payable. When the debt falls due, if the value of the operating assets is higher than the amount of the debt to be repaid, the shareholders exercise their call option on the operating assets, and pay the creditors the amount of the debt outstanding. If, however, the value of the operating assets is lower than the amount of the debt to be repaid, the shareholders decline to pay off the debt, and the creditors appropriate the operating assets.

Similarly, we can show that lending to a company is a means of investing in its assets at no risk. The lender sells the shareholders a put option at a strike price that is equal to the debt to be repaid.

Using this options-based approach we can break down the value of equity into intrinsic value and time value. Intrinsic value is the difference between the present value of capital employed and the debt to be repaid upon maturity. Time value is the hope that, when the debt matures, enterprise value will have risen to exceed the amount of the debt to be repaid.

This leads to a better understanding of the impact of certain decisions on the financial situation of creditors and shareholders:

- a dividend payout financed by the sale of assets will increase creditors' risk, reduce the value of the debt owed to them and, at the same time, increase the value of shareholders' equity;

- investing in high-risk projects (but for which the net value at the required rate of return is nil) does not result in an immediate change in enterprise value, but increases creditors' risk, reduces the value of debt and increases the value of shareholders' equity by the same amount;

- by financing its own investments (or carrying out a capital increase), the company increases enterprise value by this amount (if the return on the investment is equal to the required rate of return). Part of this additional value will go to the creditors, whose risk is reduced, to the detriment of shareholders, as the overall value of their shares will not rise by the amount of the funds invested or the capital increase.

All financial decisions must be examined not only from an overall point of view, but also in terms of the creation or destruction of value for the various stakeholders. A given financial decision could be neutral in terms of overall value, but could enhance the value of some financial securities at the expense of others.

QUESTIONS

quiz

1/ When making a comparison with options, what does shareholders' equity correspond to?

2/ When making a comparison with options, what does a credit risk correspond to?

3/ For what type of company can we apply the options theory for the valuation of shareholders' equity?

4/ According to this theory, can the value of a company's equity be nil?

5/ Why is the application of this theory more advantageous for companies in difficulty?

6/ Is this view of the company opposed to the theory of markets in equilibrium?

7/ Give an example of a decision where creditors are "expropriated" by shareholders, without the debt agreement being renegotiated. Explain.

8/ Is the effect of expropriation a result of market inefficiency?

9/ A company is in trouble as a result of low profits and excessive debts.

   (a) Do you think that the creditors and the shareholders have the same concerns? More specifically, in the event of the following:
   ○   massive new investments carrying a very high risk but that will possibly lead to high returns which will enable the company to get back on its feet with a low level of profits;
   ○   an increase in debt;
   ○   an increase in shareholders' equity.

(b) Would your answer be different if the company were profitable and carrying very little debt?

(c) What financial product do these examples of creditor–shareholder relationships bring to mind?

10/ What is a covenant? Provide a theoretical example of the usefulness of covenants.

11/ Does a covenant represent a prevention against issuing new debt or does it ensure that shareholders/management will enter into discussions with creditors.

12/ Can you give an example of a group where shareholders' equity is made up of pure time value?

13/ What is the role of debt in the management/shareholder relationship?

EXERCISES

1/ The investment firm Verfinance owns 5,000 shares in Uninet, a group involved in the maintenance products sector, worth 10 million. This is what Verfinance's simplified balance sheet looks like:

Uninet shares $V = 10$	Shareholders' equity
	Debt

The debt is a 5-year zero coupon bond (issued today). Its redemption value is 6 million.

The following table relating to the Uninet share appears in the financial press in the section on European call options:

Strike price	5-year option	7-year option
1,200	1,010	1,085
1,600	731	832
2,000	510	627
2,400	348	468

(a) Does the above table seem consistent to you?

(b) Can you value the shareholders' equity and the debt of Verfinance with the data you have?

(c) What could you do to increase the value of the company's shareholders' equity? Make several suggestions. Which would seem to be the most realistic to you? Why? Would you be creating value? Why? All in all, have you created value or transferred value?

2/ Companies A and B each have to pay 100 to their creditors in 1 year. The risk-free rate is 5% per year. Below are the key figures for companies A and B, before and after a capital increase of 50 that they are planning for the purpose of financing new investments:

	A		B	
	Before	After	Before	After
Enterprise value	100	150	100	150
Volatility of capital employed	10%	10%	40%	40%
Equity value	7	?	18	?
Value of debt	93	95.1	82	92.1
Implicit interest rate on debt	7.5%	5.2%	22%	8.6%

What is the equity value of A and B after the capital increase? Show that it is not in the interests of the shareholders of A or B to carry out a capital increase to finance investments. Does the capital increase create value? Show that, nevertheless, shareholders' wealth is increased. Do you think that the creditors would agree to finance new investments? Why? How do you explain this paradox?

3/ Take the figures for Holding SA and assume that the shareholders in the company decide to pay out a cash dividend of €13,380 totally financed by the sale of 63 shares in Daughter plc (€13,380/€2,230).

(a) What is the new value of Holding plc's equity, according to the options theory?
(b) What is the value of Holding plc's debt, according to the options theory? What is the yield to maturity?
(c) What is the result of the operation?

Questions

ANSWERS

1/ *To a call option on the operating assets, the strike price of which is the amount of debt to be repaid.*
2/ *To the risk-free assets minus a put option, the strike price of which is the amount of debt to be repaid.*
3/ *Companies in difficulty and high-risk companies.*
4/ *No, because there is always some hope, no matter how little, that the enterprise value will rise before the debt must be repaid, to above the amount to be repaid.*
5/ *Because the time value of their equity is higher.*
6/ *No, it is not incompatible.*
7/ *Investing at a fair price, but in a much more risky venture.*
8/ *No, only the lack of anticipation.*
9/ *(a) No, better for the shareholder, better for the shareholder, better for the shareholder.*
   (b) Fundamentally no, but the problem is considerably reduced.
   (c) Options.
10/ *A restriction that the creditors place on shareholders so that they cannot increase their risk.*
11/ *Covenants force management/shareholders to approach creditors to renegotiate loan agreements if they wish to exceed the limits set in these covenants.*
12/ *Philip Holzmann, Lucent, Mobilcom.*
13/ *Control.*

Exercises

1/ (a)   The table is consistent.

  (b)   The shares can be compared with options on the assets (i.e., the Uninet shares). Strike price = 6m/5,000 = 1,200, maturity = same as debt = 5 years. Value of these options = 1,010. Value of Verfinance's shareholders' equity = 1,010 × 5,000 = 5.05m. Value of debt = 4.95m.

  (c)   Capital reduction. "Exchange" Uninet shares for much more volatile shares. There would also be a transfer of value from creditors to shareholders, but no creation of net value.

2/ 54.9; 57.9. The capital increase of 50 will only increase the value of shareholders' equity by 47.9 for A and 39.9 for B. The capital increase creates value for the creditors (2.1 for A and 10.1 for B), but destroys the same amount of shareholder value. Accordingly, this is not a simple transfer of value. No, because, unlike the capital increase, an increase in debt level will reduce the value of the debt.

3/ (a)   Shareholders have a call option on 94 Daughter plc shares (100 − 6) with a strike price of 300,000 (300 bonds × 1,000). This option is equal to 94% of an option of an asset made up of 100 Daughter plc shares (94/94%) and the strike price is equal to 319,149 (300,000/94%). The new value of shareholders' equity is thus: 94% × 32.55 × 100 shares = 3,060. The value of the option – 32.22 – is calculated by linear interpolation on the basis of the table provided.

  (b)   The value of the debt will then be 94 × 2,230 − 3,060 = 206,560, a decrease of 11,940. The yield to maturity on the debt rises to 13.2%, which means an increase in the risk on Holding plc's debts. The shareholders will have 3,060 worth of Holding plc shares and 13,380 in cash (dividends paid), a total of 16,440 compared with 4,500 initially. Their gain of 11,940 (16,440 − 4,500) is made at the expense of the creditors, who lose: 218,500 − 206,560 = 11,940.

BIBLIOGRAPHY

Black, Scholes and Merton were the first to analyse the value of shares and debts using options as a reference:

F. Black, M. Scholes, The pricing of options and corporate liabilities, *Journal of Polical Economy*, **81**, 637–654, May/June 1973.

R. Merton, On the pricing of corporate debt: The risk structure of interest rates, *Journal of Finance*, **29**(2), 449–470, May 1974.

For an overall view of options theory applied to capital structure see:

M. Chesney, R. Gibson-Asner, The investment policy and the pricing of equity in a levered firm: A re-examination of the contingent claim's "valuation approach", *European Journal of Finance*, **5**, 95–107, June 1999.

T. Copeland, F. Weston, *Theory of Finance and Business Finance*, Addison-Wesley, 1987.

A. Damodaran, *Valuation*, John Wiley & Sons, 1994.

D. Galai, R. Masulis, The option pricing model and the risk factor of stock, *Journal of Financial Economics*, **33**, 53–81, 1976.

K. Garbade, *Pricing Corporate Securities as Contigent Claims*, unpublished manuscript, Stern School of Business, 1999.

R. Geske, H. Johnson, The valuation of corporate liabilities as compound options: A correction, *Journal of Financial and Quantitative Analysis*, **7**, 63–81, March 1979.

C. Hsia, Coherence of the modern theories of finance *Financial Review*, Winter 1999.

M. Jensen, W. Meckling, Theory of the firm: Managerial behavior, agency costs and ownership structure, *Journal of Financial Economics*, **3**, 305–360, October 1976.

J. Kalotay, Valuation of corporate securities: Applications of contingent claim analysis, in E. Altman and M. Subrahmanyam (eds), *Recent Advances in Corporate Finance*, Richard Irwin, 1985.

S. Mason, R. Merton, The role of contingent claims analysis in corporate finance, in E. Altman and M. Subrahmanyam (eds), *Recent Advances in Corporate Finance*, Richard Irwin, 1985.

R. Merton, On the pricing of corporate debt: The risk structure of interest rates, *Journal of Finance*, **29**, 449–470, 1974.

J. Ogden, Determinants of the ratings and yields on corporate bonds: Tests of the contingent claim model, *Journal of Financial Research*, **10**, 329–340, 1986.

S. Y. Park, M. Subrahmanyam, Option features of corporate securities, in S. Figlewski, W. Silber and M. Subrahmanyam (eds), *Financial Options: From Theory to Practice*, Richard Irwin, 1990.

C. W. Smith, Applications of option pricing analysis, in J. Bicksler (ed.), *Handbook of Financial Economics*, North Holland, 1979.

Chapter 36
WORKING OUT DETAILS: THE DESIGN OF THE CAPITAL STRUCTURE

Steering a course between Scylla and Charybdis

By way of conclusion to the part on capital structure policy, we would like to reflect once again on the thread that runs throughout this set of chapters: the choice of a source of financing.

We begin by restating for the reader an obvious truth too often forgotten:

If the objective is value creation, the choice of investments is much more important than the choice of capital structure. Because financial markets are liquid, situations of disequilibrium on them do not last. Arbitrages inevitably occur to erase them. For this reason, it is very difficult to create value by issuing securities at a price higher than their value. In contrast, industrial markets are much more "viscous". Regulatory, technological and other barriers make arbitrages – building a new plant, launching a rival product, and so on – far slower and harder to implement than on a financial market, where all it takes is a telephone call or an online order.

An industrial business can therefore hope to find a strategy that secures it an economic rent – that is, a strategy that enables it to earn a return on investment higher than the required return adjusted for risk. If it can do so, it will create value. **But let it harbour no illusions as to permanence: sooner or later, that rent will erode and disappear.**

In other words, a company that has made investments at least as profitable as its providers of funds require will never have insurmountable financing problems. If need be, it can always restructure the liability side of its balance sheet and find new sources of funds. Inversely, a company whose assets are not sufficiently profitable will sooner or later have financing problems, even if it initially obtained financing on very favourable terms. How fast its financial position deteriorates will depend simply on the size of its debt.

Good financing can never make up for a bad investment.

Section 36.1
THE MAJOR CONCEPTS

1/COST OF A SOURCE OF FINANCING

Several simple ideas can be stated in this context.

1. The cost of all sources of financing is given by the risk profile and the required return of the investment. Thus, a cement plant in Russia might require a 25% rate of return, and this will be the case whether it is financed by equity or debt and whether the investor is Russian, Swiss or Indonesian.

The required rate of return is basically independent of the method of financing and the nationality of the investor. It depends solely on the risk of the investment itself.

   The following consequences ensue:

- It is generally not possible to link the financing to the investment.
- No "portfolio effect" can reduce this cost.
- Only the bearing of systematic risk will be rewarded.

It is therefore shortsighted to choose a source of financing based on what it appears to cost. To do so is to forget that all sources of financing will **cost the same, given the risk**.

2. For the purpose of managing the liability side of the company's balance sheet, **it is a great mistake to take the apparent cost of a source of financing as its true cost**.

We have too often heard it said that the cost of a capital increase was low because the yield on the shares was low, that internal financing costs nothing, that convertible bonds can lower a company's cost of financing and so on. Statements of this kind confuse the accounting cost with the true financial cost.

   A source of financing is a bargain only if, for whatever reason, it brings in more than its market value. A convertible bond is a good deal for the issuer not because it carries a low coupon rate, but only if the option embedded in it can fetch more than its market value.

   Let us dwell briefly on the error one commits by confusing apparent cost and true financial cost.

- The difference is minor for debt. It may arise from changes in market interest rates or, more rarely, from changes in default risk. In matters of financial organisation, debt has the merit that its accounting cost is close to its true cost; furthermore, that cost is visible on the books, since interest payments are an accounting expense.
- The error is greater for equity, inasmuch as the yield on the share needs to be augmented for prospective growth.
- The error is extreme for internal financing, where, as we have seen, the apparent cost of reinvested cash flow is nil.

• The error is hard to evaluate for all forms of hybrid securities – and this is often the explanation for their success. But let the reader beware: the fact that such securities carry low yields does not mean their financial cost is low. As we have shown in the foregoing chapters, an analysis of the hybrid security using both present value and option valuation techniques is needed to identify the true cost of this financing source.

> 3. When it comes to a company's financing policy, the immediate direct consequences of its sources of financing cannot be neglected.

Debt, by virtue of the liability that it represents for timely payments of interest and principal, has a direct consequence on the company's cash flow. Debt can plunge the company into the ditch if it runs into difficulties; on the other hand, it can turn out to be a turbocharger that enables the company to take off at high speed if it is successful.

| Source | Instrument | Theoretical cost to be taken for investment valuation | Cost according to financial theory | Apparent or explicit cost (accountability, cash flow) | Difference | Determinants of the difference |
			(A)	(B)	(A) − (B)	
Debt			Market rate to which the company can refinance	Contractual rate	Weak	Evolution of market interest rates; evolution of default risk
Equity	**Shares increase**	The same for all products, it is a function of the system-atic (non-diversifiable) risk of the investment	Expected return required by the market on shares with the same risk profile	Nil in income statement; apparent cost measured by the return	Important	Expected dividend growth rate
	Self-financing			Nil in the income statement; no apparent cost	Relevant	Total absence of apparent cost
Hybrid products	**Convertible bonds**		Yield to maturity + Value of the convertible option	Low yield to maturity	Medium	Value of convertible option
	Preference shares		Return should be slightly lower than the ordinary shares	Higher than ordinary shares and fixed throughout the life of the instrument	Weak	They are shares for which a part of the value is guaranteed (present value of fixed dividends)
	Income bonds		Rate higher than the cost of debt	Mostly linked to the periodical income	Variable, according to results	Variability of results

If a company is successful, the cost of a capital increase will appear to be much higher. On the one side, we have a fixed cost (the cost of debt); on the other, we have a variable cost that can even be negative *ex post*. An issue of new shares at a very high price followed by a crash on the stock market produces a negative rate of return for the investor, and thus a negative cost. (With debt, negative cost can occur only in the case of extreme difficulties in which creditors cancel a portion of their claims.)

2/IS THERE A "ONCE-AND-FOR-ALL" OPTIMAL CAPITAL STRUCTURE?

The answer is clear: no, the optimal capital structure is a firm-specific policy and changes across time.

At the same time, there are a few loose ideas on the subject that the reader will have absorbed. Otherwise, how could one explain why the notion of what constitutes a "good" or "balanced" capital structure should have changed so much, and so often, over the course of time?

➢ In the 1950s and 1960s, a good capital structure was one with little debt. Against a backdrop of economic stability, the accent was on securing the company's industrial and financial autonomy.

➢ In the 1970s, a good capital structure needed to show a "normal" level of debt – that is, (just) not excessive relative to equity. In a context of strong economic growth and low or even negative real (inflation-adjusted) interest rates, the accent was on taking advantage of the financial leverage that debt provides.

➢ In the 1980s, a good capital structure needed to reflect a rebalancing of the structure of the business, characterised by gradual diminution of debt, improved profitability and heightened reliance on internal financing.

➢ In the early 1990s, in an environment of low investment and high real interest rates, there was no longer a choice: being in debt was not an option. A new "pecking order" (see Chapter 34) appeared. A company with cash but without opportunities to invest it at a high enough return would choose:

  ○ first to pay down its debt;
  ○ then to buy back its shares;
  ○ lastly, to raise its payout ratio. This move was last on the list because it mortgages the company's future: a rise in the dividend, unlike a share buyback, implies a commitment of prospective earnings – the "ratchet" effect of the dividend.

➢ In the late 1990s, though, debt was back in grace if used either to finance acquisitions or to reduce equity. The reason: nominal interest rates at their lowest level in 30 years. But the euphoric climate of real growth and low inflation gave way in the early 2000s to an economic crisis coupled with equity markets virtually closed to new issues, making it hard for companies that had just finished borrowing heavily to quickly rebalance their capital structure.

The great majority of companies, though, had been paying down their debt for more than 10 years, thereby giving them considerable borrowing capacity they could use to get them through a difficult period.

NET DEBT/SHAREHOLDERS' EQUITY OF MOST IMPORTANT EUROPEAN AND AMERICAN GROUPS

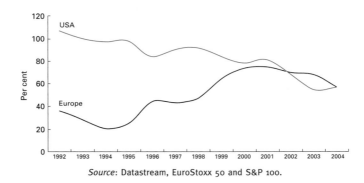

Source: Datastream, EuroStoxx 50 and S&P 100.

NET DEBT/MARKET VALUE OF EQUITY OF MOST IMPORTANT EUROPEAN AND AMERICAN GROUPS

Shareholders' position

download

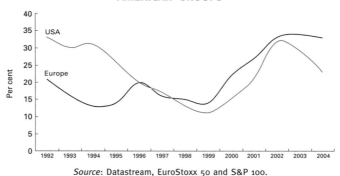

Source: Datastream, EuroStoxx 50 and S&P 100.

NET DEBT/EBITDA OF MOST IMPORTANT EUROPEAN AND AMERICAN GROUPS

Debtholders' position

@
download

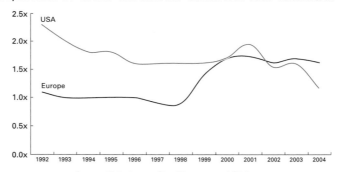

Source: Datastream, EuroStoxx 50 and S&P 100.

3/ CAPITAL STRUCTURE, INFLATION AND GROWTH

Because inflation is always a disequilibrium phenomenon, it is quite difficult to analyse from a financial standpoint. We can observe, however, that, during a period of inflation and negative real interest rates, overinvestment and excessive borrowing leads to a general degradation of capital structures. Companies that invest reap the benefit of inflated profits: adjusted for inflation, the cost of financing is low. Shareholders can benefit from this phenomenon as well: a low rate of return on investment will be offset by the low cost of financing.

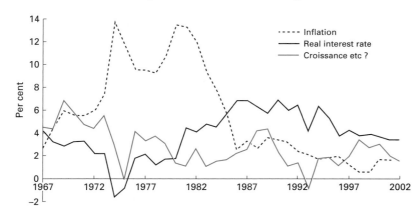

Companies' inclination to take on debt depends a great deal on the real interest rate and the real growth rate of the economy.

download

When inflation is accompanied by low real interest rates, companies are tempted to overinvest and pay for it by borrowing, thereby unbalancing their capital structure.

Disinflation leads to exactly the opposite behaviour: high real interest rates encourage companies to get rid of debt, all the more so that high rates are usually accompanied by anaemic economic activity and a business climate not conducive to borrowing.

4/ WHAT IS EQUITY FOR?

Let us begin by recalling the three fundamental differences between equity capital and debt capital.

*   There is no commitment to pay a periodic return on equity, whereas there is such a commitment on debt. The shareholder's reward depends solely on how well the business does, unlike the creditor's.
*   There is no commitment to pay back the funds raised from shareholders, whereas there is such a commitment on funds borrowed from lenders.[1]
*   If the company is liquidated, creditors will be paid in full before shareholders receive anything.

1 *Except for perpetual notes, which are extremely rare.*

Equity capital thus plays two roles. Its first function is of course to finance part of the investment in the business. The more important purpose, though, is to serve as a guarantee to the company's creditors that finance the other part of the investment. For this reason, the cost of equity includes a risk premium.

Whence the insurance aspect of equity capital (cf. discussion in Chapter 35 of equity as an option): like insurance, equity financing always costs too much until the accident crisis happens, in which case one is happy to have a lot of it. When a crisis does come, having considerable equity on the balance sheet gives a company time – time to survive and restructure when earnings are depressed, to introduce new products, to seize opportunities for external growth and so on. By comparison, a company with considerable debt suffers greatly because it has fixed expenses (interest payments) and fixed maturities (principal repayment) that will drag it down further.

The amount of equity capital in a business is also an indicator of the level of risk shareholders are willing to run. In a crisis, the companies with the most leverage are the first to disappear.

5/WHAT IF IT WERE ALL MERELY HERITAGE FROM THE PAST?

One simple idea is that a company's capital structure today is the result, not of any conscious choice of a target debt–equity ratio, but of a series of decisions taken in the past based on the financial context of the moment: issuing shares when the stock market was booming and valuations were high, issuing debt and buying back shares when the market was in a slump and share prices were low.

If its managers had in mind a target debt–equity ratio, any company that raised fresh equity would, in the wake of the capital increase, go out and borrow more in order to move its capital structure back towards the target ratio. This is not what we observe. The companies with little debt are the ones that have capital increases when their relative valuation (measured by the price-to-book ratio) is generous, and vice versa. Similarly, the current capital structure is explained by decisions taken a long time ago and thus by relative valuation levels at the time.

Research by Malcolm Baker and Jeffrey Wurgler (2002) supports the theory that this is indeed the principal determinant of current capital structure, given the highly pragmatic, opportunistic attitude of corporate finance directors – which corresponds entirely to the motivations of investors: issue shares when prices are high, issue debt and buy back shares when prices are low.

Section 36.2
COMPETITORS, LIFECYCLE AND OTHER CAPITAL STRUCTURE DETERMINANTS

Graham and Harvey (2004) surveyed top executives and finance directors at 392 public groups to determine which criteria they use in taking a financing decision. According to their study – which will be further examined in Section 36.6 – the tax saving on debt was not an essential criterion in the choice of capital structure, nor was fear of substantial bankruptcy costs. Rather, concern about downgrading of the company's credit rating came top of the list. It is reassuring to see that the conclusions of the second Modigliani–Miller article (1963) are not prompting companies to focus on tax considerations in deciding whether or not to take on debt.

Even if companies say they have a fairly precise target for the level of their debt, more than half of all finance directors base their choice of financing also on preserving

flexibility. The reader should recall that loss of flexibility is one of the costs of debt discussed in Chapter 35. The existence of a long-term optimal ratio and the temporary divergences that frequently can choose to follow could be consistent with the term **dynamic tradeoff theory** (Hovakimian et al., 2002, p. 25). This theory says that "although many companies allow their leverage ratios to drift away from their targets for a time, when the distance becomes large enough managers take steps to move their companies back toward the targets." Yes, description effectively suggests that, whereas the tradeoff theory explains observed corporate debt *level*, the pecking order (see Chapter 34) offers an apparently superior explanation for capital structure *changes*, especially those involving security issues.

The reader should be aware that capital structure is the result of complex compromises *also* determined by:

- **the capital structure of competitors**;
- **the lifecycle of the company**;
- **shareholder preferences**;
- **market opportunities or constraints**;
- **signalling policies**.

1/CAPITAL STRUCTURE OF COMPETITORS

- To have higher net debt than one's rivals is to bet heavily on the company's future profitability – that is, on the economy, the strategy and so forth.
- To have higher net debt than one's rivals, other things equal, is to be more vulnerable to a cyclical downturn, one that could lead to a shakeout in the sector and extinction of the weakest.

There is good evidence that the average capital structure of the sector is an important benchmark for management when setting capital structure policies. Experience shows that business leaders are loath to imperil an industrial strategy by adopting a financing policy substantially different from their competitors'. If they have to take risks, they want them to be industrial or commercial risks, not financial risks. The rationale of this behaviour is clear: since all companies behave similarly, the average leverage indicates the sustainable level of financial risk belonging to the same sector!

Our opinion is that benchmarking on competitors is not contradictory with the precepts of the tradeoff model. Companies within the same sector – and in the same stage of the lifecycle – share the same basic economic and financial characteristics. Hence, financial policies shouldn't be so different.

Industries with high volatility of cash flows and low tangible assets are those where we expect leverage to be lower. On the contrary, in sectors where flows are stable and companies can provide high collaterals, the use of debt should be higher.

The choice of capital structure is not absolute but *relative*: the real question is how to finance the business compared with the industry average – that is, compared with the company's competitors.

However, there are at least two situations where the simple replica of what competitors do could be erroneous:

- when the sector is made up of highly heterogeneous companies;
- when the sector is going through a restructuring phase.

With the analyses in hand, the person or body taking the financing decision will be able to do so with full knowledge of the facts. The investor will bear in mind that, statistically (and, thus, for his diversified portfolio), his dream of multiplying his wealth through judicious use of debt will be the nightmare of the company in financial difficulty.

The financial success of a few tends to make one forget the failure of companies that did not survive because they were too much in debt.

2/LIFECYCLE OF THE COMPANY

It is a mistake if the reader thinks that the *tradeoff* model helps us to discover an optimal leverage that doesn't change across time. The optimal capital structure is a concept that evolves from sector to sector – as discussed above – and from firm to firm.

Let's think about startup companies. They normally:

➤ Have a high need of equity capital because of their:

- o lower tax shield capacity;
- o high financial distress costs (low tangible assets);
- o short history.

➤ Need additional resource for new investments whose amount normally exceeds annual depreciation.

The necessity of funding with external resources is in this case quite high since internal sources (self-financing and liquidity) are insufficient to cover the amount of new investments in fixed assets and working capital.

At the same time, they must keep an adequate level of financial flexibility for facing the uncertain competitive dynamics of evolving sectors like, for example, advanced technologies. The capital structure of startup companies must then:

- try to match assets and liabilities;
- give the company a financial reserve for absorbing an unfavourable reduction of cash flows;
- allow them to exploit real market opportunities.

Furthermore, it is reasonable to assume that the information asymmetries in the initial phases are high and that the use of external equity capital could dilute excessively the shares' value.

A startup will have a hard time getting any debt financing. It has no past and thus no credit history, and it probably has no tangible assets to pledge as security. The technological environment around it is probably quite unsettled, and its free cash flow is going to be negative for some time. For a lender, the level of specific risk is very high. The startup consequently has no choice but to seek equity financing.

At the other extreme, an established company in a market that has been around for years and is reaching maturity will have no difficulty attracting lenders. Its credit history is there, its assets are real, and it is generating free cash flows (predictable with low forecast error) which are all the greater if the major investments have already been made. In short, it has everything a creditor craves. In contrast, an equity investor will find little to be enthusiastic about: not much growth, not much risk, thus not much profitability.

The evidence shows that bigger companies – living their maturity phase – tend to have higher leverage ratios, which confirms their high capacity of lowering the costs of debt thanks to their stability and higher fixed assets.

Here we see the lifecycle of financing sources. An industrial venture is initially financed with equity. As the company becomes institutionalised and its risk diminishes, debt financing takes over, freeing up equity capital to be invested in emerging new sectors.

Similarly, in an industry with high fixed costs, a company will seek to finance itself mostly with equity, so as not to pile the fixed costs of debt (interest payments) on top of its fixed operating costs and to reduce its sensitivity to cyclical downswings. But sectors with high fixed costs – steel, cement, paper, energy, telecoms, etc. – are generally highly capital-intensive and thus require large investments, inevitably implying borrowing as well.

An industry such as retailing with high variable costs, on the other hand, can make the bet that debt will follow, as the fixed costs of borrowing come on top of low fixed operating costs.

Lastly, the nature of the asset can influence the availability of financing to acquire it. A highly specific asset – that is, one with little value outside of a given production process – will be hard to finance with debt. Lenders will fear that if the company goes under, the asset's market value will not be sufficient to pay off their claims.

THE LIFECYCLE OF A COMPANY AND THE TRADEOFF MODEL

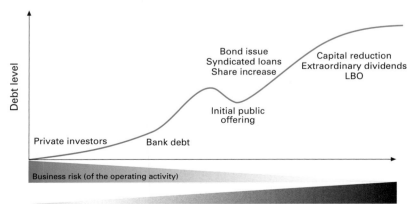

	Startup	Growth	Maturity
Tax shield	Zero	Increases with earnings	High
Disciplining role of debt	Low, shareholder-managers	Increases, new external shareholders	Decreases, little new investments
Information asymmetries	High, business only an idea	Decreases, track record and credibility	Decrease, higher transparency
Financial distress costs	Very high	High	Declining
Agency costs	Very high	High	Declining
Financial flexibility (need of)	Very high	High	Low
Tradeoff	**Costs of debt > Benefits**	**Relevant benefits from debt**	**Benefits of debt > Costs**

Section 36.3
OTHER FACTORS AFFECTING THE CAPITAL STRUCTURE CHOICE

Three other factors can help us to explain the optimal capital structure, on one side, and temporary divergences from it, on the other:

- **shareholder preferences** in terms of risk aversion and willingness to cede control;
- **opportunities** or **constraints** in the capital markets at a given moment;
- the willingness of the company to send "**signals**" to the market.

Which of these factors is the most important? Is there a ranking among them?

Our idea in this regard is quite simple. These factors explain *temporary* differences between the optimal capital structure of a company according to the precepts of the "tradeoff model" and its current capital structure.

Thus, there is no specific ranking between the factors. Given the fact that the "extended tradeoff" model should be the prominent interpreting model, the idea that companies' choices may diverge from the predictions of this model can be imputable to one of the abovementioned factors.

However, the reader should bear in mind that it is difficult to imagine a company systematically diverging from the long-term optimal capital structure; this is because persisting differences may be the cause of financial disequilibrium.

1/SHAREHOLDER PREFERENCES

If the company's shareholder base is made up of influential shareholders, majority or minority, their viewpoints will certainly have an impact on financing choices.

Some holders will block capital increases that would dilute their stake because they are unable to take up their share of the rights. A company in this situation must then go deeply in debt. Others may have a marked aversion to debt because they have no desire to increase the level of risk they are bearing.

The choice of capital structure is also the choice of a level of risk that shareholders are willing to incur.

2/OPPORTUNITIES AND CONSTRAINTS

Since markets are not systematically in equilibrium, opportunities can arise at a given moment. A steep runup in share prices will enable a company to have a capital increase on the cheap (sell shares at a very high price). The folly of a bank that says yes to every loan application and the sudden infatuation of investors for a particular kind of stock (Internet companies in early 2000) are other examples. Lastly, loopholes in tax regulations may create financing opportunities (think of subordinated perpetual notes in the 1980s), but, unfortunately, the tax administration never stays duped for long.

Let the reader not be intoxicated by opportunities. It is hard to base a financing policy on a succession of opportunities, which are by definition unpredictable. They can happen only on margin.

Furthermore, if the company at some point in time is enjoying exceptionally low-cost financing, investors, for their part, will have made a bad mistake. In their fury, they risk tarnishing the company's image, and it will be a long time before they can be counted on to put up new money. The startup that went public at the peak of the "new economy" boom on the stock market will surely have raised money at low cost, but how will it raise more capital a year later, after its share price has fallen by 70%?

On the contrary, the company may suffer **capital rationing** – that is, a situation in which capital markets cannot satisfy all the financing the companies ask. This may be due to credit restrictions that may occur in turbulent periods as a consequence of authorities' decisions or of bank systems' policies.

3/SIGNALLING AND DEBT POLICY

The signalling theory is based on the strong assumption that corporate managers are better informed about their companies than the suppliers of funding. This means that they are in a better position to foresee the company's future flows. As seen in our example in Chapter 35, they know what state of nature their company is in. Consequently, any signal they send indicating that flows will be better than expected or that risks will be lower may enable the investor to create value. Investors are therefore constantly on the watch for such signals. But, for the signals to be credible there must be a penalty for the wrong signals in order to dissuade companies from deliberately misleading the market.

In the context of information asymmetry, markets would not understand why a corporate manager would borrow to undertake a very risky and unprofitable venture. After all, if the venture fails, he risks losing his job or worse if the venture causes the company to fail. So, debt is a strong signal for profitability, but even more for risk. It is unlikely that a CEO would resort to debt financing if he knows that in a worst case scenario he will not be able to repay the debt.

Ross (1977) has demonstrated that any change in financing policy changes investors' perception of the company and is therefore a market signal.

It is thus obvious that an increase in debt increases the risk on equity. The managers of a company that has raised its gearing rate are, in effect, signalling to the markets that they are aware of the state of nature, that it is favourable and that they are confident that the company's performances will allow them to pay the additional financial expenses and pay back the new debt.

This signal carries its own penalty if it is wrong. If the signal is false – i.e., if the company's actual prospects are not good at all – the extra debt will create financial difficulties that will ultimately lead, in one form or another, to the dismissal of its executives.[2] In this scheme, managers have a strong incentive to send the correct signal by ensuring that the firm's debt corresponds to their understanding of its repayment capacity.

Ross (1977) has shown that, assuming managers have privileged information about their own company, they will send the correct signal on condition that the marginal gain derived from an incorrect signal is lower than the sanction suffered if the company is liquidated.

"*They put their money where their mouths are.*" This explains why debt policies vary from one company to the other: they simply reflect the variable prospects of the individual companies.

The actual capital structure of a firm is not necessarily a signal, but any change in it certainly is.

When a company announces a capital increase, research has shown that its share price generally drops by an average 3%. The market reasons that corporate managers would not increase capital if, based on the inside information available to them, they thought it was undervalued, since this would dilute the existing shareholdings in unfavourable conditions. If there is no pressing reason for the capital increase, investors will infer that, based on their inside information, the managers consider the share price to be too high and that this is why the existing shareholders have accepted the capital increase. On the other hand, research has shown too that the announcement of a bond issue has no material impact on share prices.

It ensues that the sale of a manager's stake in the company is a very negative signal. It reveals that he has internal information indicating that the value of future flows, taking risk into account, is lower than the proceeds he expects from the sale of his investment. Conversely, any increase in the stake, especially if financed by debt, constitutes a very positive signal for the market.

This explains why financial investors prefer to subscribe to capital increases rather than buy from existing shareholders. It is also the reason why every year in the US and the UK, all directors must disclose the number of shares they hold or control in the companies of which they are board members.

2 Note that a bad manager whose forecast of future flows was unintentionally wrong will be sanctioned just as much as one who deliberately sent the wrong signal.

Section 36.4
EFFECTS OF THE FINANCING CHOICE ON ACCOUNTING AND FINANCIAL CRITERIA

With this description of the key ideas borne in mind, the time has come for the reader to implement a choice of capital structure as part of a financing plan. To this end, we suggest that the following documents be on hand:

1   past financial statements: income statements, balance sheets, cash flow statements;
2   forecast financial statements and financing plan, constructed in the same form as past cash flow statements. These can be either mean forecasts or simulations based on several assumptions; the latter strikes us as the better solution. A simulation model will be very useful for establishing the probable future course of the company's capital structure, profitability, business conditions and so on, given a set of assumptions. This kind of exercise is facilitated by using spreadsheet software and simulation assumptions that allow for a dynamic analysis;
3   to be fully prepared, the analyst will also want to have sector average ratios, which can be obtained from various industry studies.

An important task is then to study the consequences of a financing choice on pre-tax earnings. This traditional yardstick is not sufficient, though, if the financing plan calls for issuing new shares. When that is the case, the analyst will need to look at earnings per share and book value per share.

1/IMPACT ON BREAKEVEN POINT[3]

3 *See also Chapter 10.*

Other things equal, debt raises the company's breakeven point.

This is obvious inasmuch as interest payments constitute a *fixed cost* that cannot be reduced except by renegotiating the terms of the loan or filing for bankruptcy. Take as an example a company with fixed costs of 40 and variable costs of 0.5 per unit sold. If the selling price is 1, the breakeven point is 80 units. If the company finances an investment of 50 with debt at 6%, the breakeven point rises to 86 units because fixed costs have increased by 3 (interest expense on the borrowing). If the investment is financed with equity, the breakeven point stays at 80.

The problem is trickier when the interest rate is indexed to market rates but the interest payments are still a fixed cost in the sense of being independent of the level of activity. Typically, interest rates rise when general economic activity is weakening. In such a case, it is important to test the sensitivity of the company's earnings to changes in interest rates. Take the previous example but suppose that the debt bears a floating rate. If the interest rate rises to 10%, the breakeven point goes to 90 units; if it rises to 15%, breakeven does to 95.

In a period of difficult economic conditions and rising interest rates, the company's interest expense increases, raising its breakeven point and worsening its problems.

2/Impact on return on equity

For a company with no debt, the Return On Equity (ROE) is equal to the rate of Return On Capital Employed (ROCE). For a company with debt, one must add to the former a supplement (sometimes negative) for the effect of financial leverage (difference between ROCE and cost of debt, multiplied by the debt–equity ratio).

The analysis of the return on equity must therefore distinguish the part due to the economic return on capital employed from the part due to leverage. However, a static analysis is not sufficient. What is needed is to determine the sensitivity of return on equity to any change in financial leverage, cost of debt or return on capital employed.

3/Impact on earnings per share

An investment financed by debt increases the company's net profit, and thus earnings per share, only if the after-tax return generated by its investments is greater than the after-tax cost of debt. If this is not the case, the company should not make the investments. If an investment is particularly sizeable and long-term, it may happen that its rate of return is less than the cost of debt for a period of time, but this must be a temporary situation.

To study these phenomena, companies are accustomed to analysing changes in earnings per share relative to operating profit (EBIT[4]).

4 *Earnings Before Interest and Taxes.*

Example   Consider the example of a company, which makes an investment of 200 in period 0 that will become fully operational in period 2. This investment is financed by a call to shareholders (case *A*) or by borrowing (case *B*). A simulation of the main parameters of profitability gives the results shown below:

	Period 0	Period 1		Period 2	
		Case *A*	Case *B*	Case *A* (Equity)	Case *B* (Debt)
Operating profit (EBIT)	300	300	300	370	370
— Interest expense at 6%	0	0	12	0	12
= Pre-tax profit	300	300	288	370	358
— Income tax at 35%	105	105	101	130	125
= Net profit	195	195	187	242	233
Number of shares	100	120	100	120	100
Earnings per share	1.95	1.62	1.87	1.85	2.33

In period 2, earnings per share will be greater if the investment is financed by debt. In case B, the interest expense reduces EPS, but by less than the dilution due to the capital increase in case A.

This conclusion cannot be generalised, however. The chart below simulates various levels of EPS as a function of operating profit in period 2.

FINANCING ALTERNATIVES AND THEIR IMPACT ON EPS

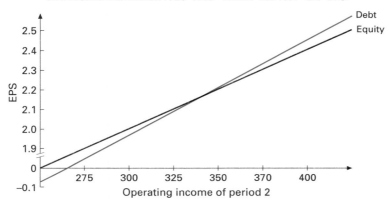

The reader will be able to verify that, if operating profit is less than 340, the preceding assertion is reversed. However, a steep decline in earnings is required to produce this result.

Let's now discuss the limitation of the EPS analysis in more detail. We know that – as a first approximation – P/EPS can be considered as a proxy of the reciprocal of the cost of equity. We also know that the price of a share is the result of earnings per share (measure of return) times the reciprocal of the cost of equity (measure of risk):

$$P = EPS \times \frac{P}{EPS}$$

Capital structure policies should then always be examined considering their impact on *price and value* rather than earnings per share. In a no-growth world, price is the result of earnings per share *and* perceived risk.

Let's continue to use the numerical example we showed in Chapters 33 and 34 regarding – the reader will surely remember – a no-growth company with an invested capital of €500,000. The investments generate a constant (and perpetual) operating income of €120,000. The company distributes 100% of net income. The cost of debt is 8%.

The following picture examines the EPS "myopia" regarding, respectively, three cases:

A The "basic'" MM: EPS have an upward trend, while P/EPS a slight downward trend. The result is an increase in price for each debt level.
B MM with corporate taxes (and no other imperfections). EPS are always lower than under case A, but continue to have an upward trend. The reciprocal of the cost of equity isn't changed. The net result is a lower price per share for each debt level, but the price continues to be an increasing function of debt level.
C The tradeoff model. In this case, the EPS have a lower inclination than before while the reciprocal of the cost of capital has a stronger negative inclination due to the higher financial risk weighing on shareholders. The net result is an upside-down U-shaped curve: the price starts rising for low debt levels, but it

decreases when leverage becomes remarkable. The major implication of this example is that financial managers shouldn't give excessive emphasis to earnings per share, *especially if the different mixes of financing they are considering alter the financial risk of the company and its cost of equity.*

4/EPS "MYOPIA"

(A) MM with no taxes and other imperfections.

(A) MM WITH NO TAXES, NO BANKRUPTCY AND AGENCY COSTS

(B) MM with corporate taxes, no other imperfections.

(B) MM WITH CORPORATE TAXES, NO BANKRUPTCY AND AGENCY COSTS

(C) Tradeoff model

(C) TRADEOFF MODEL

In short: beware! The faster growth of EPS with debt financing is a purely arithmetic result; it does not indicate greater value creation. It is due simply to the leverage effect, the counterpart of which is a higher level of risk for the shareholder.

An investment financed by debt increases EPS in year N if the company's marginal return on capital employed in year N is greater than the after-tax cost of debt.

An investment financed by equity in year N increases EPS in year $N + 1$ if the company's marginal return on capital employed in year $N + 1$ is greater than the reciprocal of P/E in year N.

5/IMPACT ON SOLVENCY

Debt increases the company's risk of becoming insolvent. We refer the reader to the development of this topic in Chapter 12.

6/IMPACT ON LIQUIDITY

The liquidity of the company is its ability to meet its financial obligations on time in the ordinary course of business, obtain new sources of financing and thereby ensure balance at all times between its income and expenditure.

In a truly serious financial crisis, companies can no longer obtain the financing they need, no matter how good they are. This is the case in a crash brought on by a panic. It is not possible to protect oneself against this risk, which fortunately is altogether exceptional. The more common liquidity risk occurs when a company is in trouble and can no longer issue securities that financial markets or banks will accept; investors have no confidence in the company at all, regardless of the merit of its investment projects.

Liquidity is therefore related to the term structure of financial resources. It is analysed both at the short-term level and at the level of repayment capacity for medium- and long-term debt. This leads to the use of the traditional concepts and ratios that we have already seen: working capital, equity, debt, current assets/current liabilities and so on.

For analysing the impact on liquidity, the simulation must bear on free cash flows. The analyst will need to simulate different levels of debt and repayment terms and test whether free cash flows are sufficient to pay off the borrowings without having to reschedule them.

Section 36.5
WORKING OUT THE DETAILS OF THE CAPITAL STRUCTURE

The capital structure policy is ideally a three-step process:

Step 1   The financial manager must decide the desired mix of debt and equity. This is the choice between the debt/equity mix.

Step 2   A firm that is not positioned at its optimal debt ratio, should decide (if) and how to reach the optimal level.

Step 3   The financial manager is called to decide about the most appropriate financing vehicle for raising capital.

So far we have discussed thoroughly only the first step which, however, is the most important because it underlies the financial equilibrium of the company. We will now dedicate some attention to the other two steps.

1/THE CONVERGENCE PATH

This second-step decision – the decision regarding if and how to get to the optimal level – involves the analysis of two joint aspects:

- The *speed* of convergence toward the optimal ratio. This decision is strictly firm-specific because different circumstances may influence it.
- The *alternative methods* that the company can use to achieve the desired result.

We will now first discuss the reasons for which a company may decide *not to move* to the optimal debt ratio. Let's start our analysis with underlevered firms because this is the less problematic situation for a company (after all, it doesn't risk going bankrupt!). Companies may prefer to neglect the value-maximising objective – which underlies the extended tradeoff model and optimal leverage – because the finance function may have different objectives. If the company prefers to increase income as much as possible or to maintain a high bond rating, the financial manager will try to keep the company underlevered. In this regard, Kigsen (2005) has examined to what extent credit ratings directly affect capital structure decisions. Firms near a credit rating upgrade or downgrade issue less debt relative to equity than firms not near a change in rating.

Regarding the maximisation of net income, the rationale is quite clear: a company which carries low debt has a limited amount of interest expenses and thus a higher net income.

Less obvious is the emphasis that a company may put on maintaining a high rating. Rather than a lot of words, the reader would surely prefer to read the words of the treasurer of Pepsi who said:[5] "One of our financial aims at Pepsi is to minimise the amount of cash on our books. More precisely, our objective is to have zero excess cash on the books [...] *At the same time, we try to have the maximum amount of debt that we can while still maintaining our single-A credit rating*."

Why? It is the treasurer once again who provides us with an excellent rationale: "We want to be single-A because that gives us immediate access, under almost any conditions, to large amounts of cash at best rates from all the commercial paper markets in the U.S., Europe and Japan." So, companies with a huge need of short-term debt and financial flexibility could decide to remain underlevered in order to keep its rating unchanged.

5 *Chew et al. (2003, p. 214).*

If a company raises a lot of funds from the commercial paper market, a lowering of the credit rating could imply two unpleasant consequences:

1   the total size of the market is lower and thus the firm may incur capital rationing in periods of market uncertainty;
2   the average number of issues shrinks dramatically and thus bigger firms may not collect all the money they need.

A look at the following table will convince the reader:

COMMERCIAL PAPER MARKET IN 2002

Rating class	Total market size ($tn)	Average issue size ($tn)
A1/P1	1.2	60–80
A2/P2[6]	180	2

Source: Bondware.

6 *A2/P2 is a category roughly equivalent to a BBB long-term rating.*

However, we think that maintaining a high-grade rating doesn't necessarily conflict with the tradeoff objective. After all, it seems that these companies have a maximum leverage represented by the amount of debt they can raise without seeing their rating being lowered. Let's ask for some additional help from our treasurer: "We do have a capital structure or leverage target. And we arrive at that target by determining the largest leverage ratio consistent with our desired credit rating. Once we get to that leverage target, we try to stay there. How do we stay there? Mainly by using our excess cash to buy back stocks."[7]

A final reason that may be suggested to explain the underlevered choice is the desire of firms to avoid debt covenants that come with debt. Covenants tend to restrict managerial flexibility and the degrees of freedom in exploiting the investment opportunities that may arise in the future.

7 *Chew et al. (2003, p. 214).*

More problematic is the opposite case, regarding overlevered firms, because these firms face a high probability of default and bankruptcy. The "bankruptcy fear" may be overcome only if there is a counterbalancing force which may justify excessive debt ratios. This counterforce may be represented by governments and local authorities who may decide to shield firms from the costs associated with default or to back up loans made by banks to companies. In these cases, companies may decide voluntarily to remain overlevered.[8]

If the firm is aware that it is far from optimal leverage and decides that it doesn't want to stay away from that point, the first important decision is the **speed of change**: gradual vs. immediate.

8 *This reason helps us to explain the undoubtedly excessive debt ratios of Korean firms during the 1990s and the reluctance of local companies to decrease leverage.*

The most important advantage of moving rapidly toward the optimal point is that it is possible to benefit immediately from a lower cost of capital and a higher value. But the company must be sure of the calculation. In fact, the worst signal the management can send to the market is to discover that the optimal ratio was not exactly the one toward which the company has converged, but a different one. If management are not so confident about the optimal leverage of the firm, they had better move slowly and discover step by step the degree of precision of their calculations.

Underlevered firms (Palepu, 1986) may decide to change the capital structure rapidly if takeover threat is high. In fact, many hostile acquisitions are financed with unused debt capacity. Thus, firms with excess capacity tend to adapt to the optimal rapidly in order to reduce the probability of takeover.

There are five **alternative methods** that can be used to change the debt–equity mix:

1 **recapitalisation**. This alternative is done by using new equity to retire debt (reduce leverage) or new debt to buy back equity (or paying a large dividend). This alternative is frequently a necessity for companies under takeover threat. Recapitalisations aimed at increasing the debt ratio in a fast and substantial way are called *leveraged recapitalisations*. On the contrary, *equity-for-debt swaps* are designed to reduce leverage with debt agreements by which lenders take an equity stake in the firm in exchange for a portion of debt in their possession.

2 **divestitures**. The firm can change its debt ratio by selling part of the assets and using the proceeds of the sale to pay off debt or to reduce equity. Naturally, if the firm chooses this alternative it needs to select the assets to be divested with extreme attention. On one side, companies should in principle sell assets earning less than the cost of capital; on the other side, the assets must also be attractive for potential buyers and the amount they are willing to pay for those assets. The recent move of Vivendi Universal to reduce debt through disposal is a good example.

3 **sale and leaseback**. This solution allows the company to sell assets to a leasing company, collect money, repay debt or equity while maintaining possession of the assets by retaking them with a lease from the leasing company. The company can thus reduce the capital employed and modify the debt/equity ratio with the proceeds of the sale. But it usually corresponds more to window-dressing than a real reduction of debt.

4 **use of a different mix of financing for the new investments**. In this case, the company will change its leverage ratio *gradually*. The speed of change will be related to the amount of new investments, the incidence of their value on the existing investments, and the difference between the debt ratio chosen for the new investment and the current debt ratio of the company.

5 **changing the amount of cash returned to shareholders**. This means that a new dividend policy may alter the debt ratio of the company. If the firm uses earnings and cash flows to increase the dividend payout ratio or distributes extraordinary dividends the debt ratio will go up because the company takes cash out of the firm and the firm becomes less valuable. This method normally implies a *gradual* change in debt ratios.

The reader is surely aware that the five alternatives satisfy different needs. For the sake of simplicity, we can say that the first three methods are useful if there is an urgency of change because, for example, the company is under takeover threat or it is in serious financial distress.

If the company is neither under bankruptcy or takeover threat, alternatives 3 and 4 could be preferred because they leave the management the flexibility of deciding along the way if the optimal debt ratio is exactly what they calculated at the beginning of the changing process.

2/THE MATURITY, BASIS AND THE CURRENCY STRUCTURE OF DEBT

Once the company has decided the amount of optimal debt, many other decisions are still to be taken. They basically concern the **design of debt**. Here we want to focus the attention on three important aspects of the design:

1   **The maturity structure of debt** – that is, the amount of short- and long-term debt.

2   **The basis structure of debt** – that is, the incidence of fixed vs. floating rate debt. Companies can choose to undergo interest rate risk:

  o   either through the income statement, under the form of higher interest rates, if the debt is floating rate; or
  o   through the balance sheet, under the form of a lower value of debt, if the debt is fixed rate.

3   **The currency structure of debt** – that is, the amount of debt issued in foreign currencies. If the company has part of its revenues or cash flows in foreign currencies it should decide if it wants to issue some debt in the same foreign currencies. By so doing, the company matches inflows with outflows and avoids currency risk.

Let's examine the basic "coordinates" of the problem. We know that the value of a firm is given by the present value of the cash flows generated by its assets and that this value changes cyclically over time. If we assume that the company is financed only with short-term debt which is not influenced by changes in macroeconomic variables, the situation would be the following:

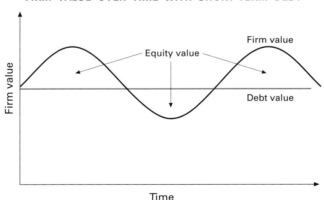

FIRM VALUE OVER TIME WITH SHORT-TERM DEBT

In some periods the company may suffer a serious bankruptcy problem, since the value of debt is higher than the value of the firm (and thus the equity value is negative). A company facing such a situation will surely try to borrow less and abandon the tax shields and the other advantages of debt.

If the firm can design financial debt so that the cash outflows of the service of debt match exactly the cash inflows, debt and equity value would follow a completely different dynamics:

FIRM VALUE OVER TIME WITH LONG-TERM DEBT

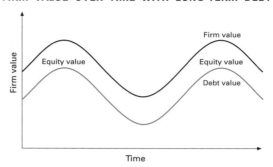

The debt value can be designed so that it moves accordingly to the enterprise value. If the firm is successful in doing so, the equity value remains constantly positive. The bankruptcy probability is then reduced substantially and the company can have a higher debt capacity and a higher optimal debt ratio.

> There is a simple (but strong!) principle that the financial manager can use if he wants to avoid additional risks: match as close as possible cash outflows (due to the service of debt) with cash inflows. This principle can be termed the "matching principle" or the "hedging principle".

Perfect matching is of course not always achievable as desired, but the financial manager should do his best to inspire financial policies with this principle in mind if he wants to minimise credit and financial risks.

We will now provide the reader with a basic "toolbox" that can help him to satisfy the "hedging principle".

(a) Debt maturity structure

The application of this principle to financing maturity choice requires matching the *duration of assets* with the *duration of liabilities*. This is the **cash-flow-matching approach**. While there are no particular difficulties in estimating the duration of debt, we could have problems in defining the duration of assets.

In this regard, the estimate of the duration of a project or assets can be done using the sequence of expected operating cash flows (CF_t):

$$\text{Duration of assets} = \frac{dPV}{dr} = \frac{\left[\displaystyle\sum_{t=1}^{N} \frac{t \times CF_t}{(1+r)^t} + \frac{N \times TV}{(1+r)^N} \right]}{\left[\displaystyle\sum_{t=1}^{N} \frac{CF_t}{(1+r)^t} + \frac{TV}{(1+r)^N} \right]}$$

where r is the market (free-risk) interest rate, TV is the terminal value and N the horizon of analysis.

The duration of assets can be alternatively interpreted as:

1 a measure of *when*, on average, the cash flows on the assets come due;
2 a measure of the *sensitivity* of asset value to a 1% change in interest rates.

An alternative – and conceptually better – measure of duration can be obtained regressing the changes in asset value (for listed companies) or in operating income (for listed, unlisted and short-lived companies) on interest rate changes:

$$\Delta \text{Asset value}_t = a + b \times \Delta \text{Interest rate}_t$$

If we adopt this methodology, coefficient b is a proxy of the duration of the assets (or of the operating income). The "regression methodology" is based on historical data and should always be used after controlling the significance of the t-test of coefficient b.

Conceptually, this methodology could be acceptable if we consider that the one based on the explicit duration formula keeps cash flows fixed while interest rates change. In practice, cash flows can be affected by interest rate changes – if interest rates rise, cash flows usually decrease – and the link between the two variables is basically a function of the business the firm operates. Thus, the duration formula tends to underestimate the actual one. The regression methodology should help to overcome this problem.

However, once the appropriate duration of the assets has been calculated the company should try to have a maturity structure of its debt with a similar (*average*) duration.[9]

The most important consequence is that – no matter the direction of interest rates changes – the value of assets and liabilities will go up or down for the same amount. Equity value will then be unaffected by interest rates.

The strong interdependence between investments and liabilities has also been examined by the **"incentive contracting"** or **"agency costs" hypothesis** (Myers, 1977). According to this second approach, the optimal leverage of a company is a function of the growth opportunities that companies have in the different stages of their lifecycle. The agency cost hypothesis argues that shortening the effective maturity of debt can mitigate conflicts of interests. Using shorter term debt forces managers to periodically generate information for investors to evaluate return and risk of major operating decisions. Investors will thus reprice the debt upon maturity based on new information. This approach mitigates asset substitution and underinvestment problems. Furthermore, short-term debt triggers effective monitoring by requiring periodic repayments of principal.

According to this approach, companies with high-growth opportunities should:

- use a higher amount of equity capital (to avoid the underinvestment problem);
- have a higher percentage of short-term debt, since the agency costs are higher for longer maturities. If the company wants to avoid the underinvestment problem it could be more appropriate to raise debt which will mature before the companies exercise their growth option.

The empirical evidence on the incentive contracting hypothesis is not univocal. Barclay and Smith (1995, 1996) and Guedes and Opler (1996) have obtained results consistent with the hypothesis that companies with higher growth opportunities have a higher incidence of short-term debt. On the contrary, Stohs and Mauer (1996) and Scherr and Hulburt (2001) haven't found statistically robust evidence between the market-to-book ratio (a proxy of growth opportunities) and the debt maturity structure.

9 *The reader should also recall that duration is a linear operator – i.e., the average duration of two assets simply is a weighted average of the single durations.*

The third approach to the maturity choice is a **tax-based explanation** (Brick and Ravid, 1985). If the term structure of interest rates is not flat then long-term debt could be a better solution because coupons on long-term bonds are higher than coupons on short-term bonds and the tax benefit of debt is accelerated.

(b) Fixed vs. floating rate

The second important choice is whether the debt should be fixed or floating rate. Generally speaking, it seems reasonable to see a higher percentage of floating rate debt if:

1   there is high uncertainty about the duration of future investments. If the firm is restructuring itself or the industry to which it belongs is undergoing profound transformations, the estimate of duration of assets may be difficult to do. In these cases, the firm may prefer to use short-term or floating rate debt until the uncertainty fades away.
2   the cash flows of the company are affected by the inflation rate. When operating income has a positive covariance with interest rates the company should consider using floating rate debt. Floating rate debt, in fact, has interest payments that increase when market rates increase and vice versa. The "cross-hedging" argument assumes that the company reduces the risk of bankruptcy, increases its debt capacity and gets greater value from leverage. The regression methodology examined above (with the interest rate as the independent variable) can also give some indications regarding the choice of the optimal basis structure of debt.

In addition to the changes in interest rates, we may also use the changes in inflation rate as the independent variable:

$$\Delta \text{Asset value}_t = a + b \times \Delta \text{Inflation rate}_t$$

10 *Earnings tend to grow with inflation when companies have high-pricing power over its products. This power may be the result of external regulation, the uniqueness of its products and leadership in their industries.*

Coefficient b is a proxy of the sensitivity of the asset (or the operating income) value to the inflation rate. The inflation rate is a crucial determinant of interest rates: they tend to increase when inflation is high and decrease when inflation is low. If earnings and cash flows follow the same dynamics (i.e., earnings increase when inflation is high and decrease when inflation is low) the firm should predominantly use floating rate debt.[10]

(c) Currency structure

The hedging principle also applies to currency structure. The idea is that if companies have cash inflows from operating assets denominated in foreign currencies the liabilities should be issued in the same proportion in the foreign currencies. Thus, a European company that expects 30% of its cash flows to be in US dollars should try to mitigate the currency risk issuing 30% of debt in US dollars.

Section 36.6
CAPITAL STRUCTURE POLICIES: A LOOK AT THE EVIDENCE

It is now time to discover if the principles and the guidelines discussed in these chapters are consistent with the behaviour of financial management.

In this regard, we compare the Graham and Harvey survey (2001) with the survey of Bancel and Mittoo (2002). We have already mentioned the Graham and Harvey article. The Bancel and Mittoo study is basically a "replica" of Graham and Harvey's but applied to European companies. The authors have surveyed managers in 16 European countries to examine the link between the theory and practice of capital structure across countries of different legal systems.

Generally speaking, it is surprising to discover extreme similarities between the two geographical areas. In most of the cases, the answers given by the financial managers in the EU and the USA tend to be the same.

This is in fact the case regarding the most important factors affecting the amount of debt: financial flexibility is the key issue in determining the capital structure choice in both areas. Similarly, the necessity of maintaining the credit rating unchanged is the second most important factor while the tax shield ranks third in Europe and fourth in the USA. There is little evidence about the influence of the bankruptcy costs and industry norms of capital structure.

1/EVIDENCE ON CAPITAL STRUCTURE

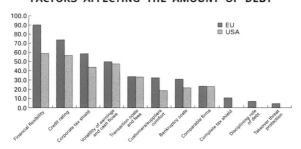

FACTORS AFFECTING THE AMOUNT OF DEBT

(A) Capital structure choice is primarily driven by financial flexibility, credit rating and corporate tax shield.

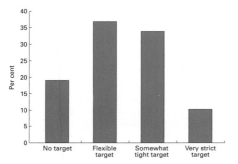

DO FIRMS HAVE TARGET DEBT RATIOS?

(B) The % of companies that do not have a target leverage are a minor fraction. It is however important to observe that the bulk of the answers regard a less flexible leverage target.

Source: Graham and Harvey (2001).

(C) The maturity structure decision is mainly driven by the matching principle and the will to avoid the refinancing risk that may occur if the company should raise debt in "bad times".

download

FACTORS AFFECTING THE CHOICE BETWEEN SHORT- AND LONG-TERM DEBT

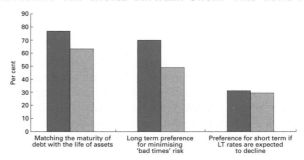

The similarities between the capital structure determinants are consistent with the recent findings on capital structure of companies belonging to different countries and economic systems. Common wisdom has long held that, in relationship-based economies like, for example, Germany, Italy and Japan, companies have higher leverage than companies in market-oriented economies, like that of the US and the UK. The higher leverage should in turn reduce the weighted average cost of capital and increase the competitiveness of companies.

The "folklore" of higher borrowing capacity comes from the strong relationship with banks. These institutions support companies when they are close to distress and exercise some control over investment policies to make sure they do not go awry. As a consequence, the costs of debt tend to disappear while the benefits remain. In short, companies in these countries tend to have a higher borrowing capacity.

This "folklore" has recently been questioned. According to Zingales and Rajan (1998), Japanese and German companies do not borrow more than US companies, and, in fact, German companies (as well as UK companies) seem to borrow less than their international competitors.

SUMMARY

download

Whereas frequent disequilibria in industrial markets allow hope of creating value through judicious investment, the same cannot be said of choosing a source of financing. Financial markets are typically close to equilibrium, and all sources of financing have the same cost to the company given their risk.

The cost of financing to buy an asset is equal to the rate of return required on that asset, regardless of whether the financing is debt or equity and regardless of the nationality of the investor.

It follows that the choice of source of financing is not made on the basis of its cost (since all sources have the same risk-adjusted cost!). Apparent cost must not be confused with financial cost (the true economic cost of a source of financing). The difference between apparent cost and financial cost is low for debt; it is attributable to the possibility of changes in the debt ratio and default risk. The difference is greater for equity owing to growth prospects; greater still for internal financing, where the explicit cost is nil; and difficult to evaluate for all hybrid securities. Lastly, a source of financing is cheap only if, for whatever reason, it has brought in more than its market value.

Because there is no optimal capital structure, the choice between debt and equity will depend on a number of considerations:

- Macroeconomic conditions. High real (inflation-adjusted) interest rates and low activity growth will prompt companies to deleverage. Inversely, rapid growth and/or low real interest rates will favour borrowing.

- The desire to retain a degree of financial flexibility so that any investment opportunities that arise can be quickly seized. To this end, equity financing is preferred because it creates additional borrowing capacity and does not compromise future choices. Inversely, if current borrowing capacity is used up, the only source of financing left is equity; its availability depends on share prices holding up, which is never assured.

- The maturity of the industry and the capital structure of competitors. A startup will get no financing but equity because of its high specific risk, whereas an established company with sizeable free cash flows but little prospect of growth will be able to finance itself largely by borrowing. Companies in the same business sector often mimic each other (what matters is to be no more foolish than the next guy!).

- Shareholder preferences. Some will favour borrowing so as not to be diluted by a capital increase in which they cannot afford to participate. Others will favour equity so as not to increase their risk. It is all a question of risk aversion.

- Financing opportunities. These are by definition unpredictable, and it is hard to construct a rigorous financing policy around them. When they occur, they make it possible to raise funds at less than the normal cost – but at the expense of the investors who have deluded themselves.

The reader who performs simulations of the principal financial parameters, differentiating according to whether the company is using debt or equity financing should be fully aware that such simulations mainly show the consequences of financial leverage:

- raising the breakeven point;

- accelerating EPS growth;

- increasing the rate of return on book equity;

- degrading solvency;

- affecting liquidity in a way that varies with the term of the debt.

Once the company has decided about the debt/equity mix, the financial manager should focus his attention on the other elements that define the "design" of the capital structure. Design of a capital structure is somehow similar to the definition of "financial architecture" used by S. Myers (1999, p. 138): "financial architecture means the entire financial design of the business, including ownership (e.g. concentrated vs. dispersed), the legal form of organization (e.g. corporation vs. limited-life partnership), incentives, financing and allocation of risk."

The most important factors determining the design of the capital structure are the maturity, basis and currency structure. The choices regarding these three aspects can be done following the same principle – the "matching principle" or the "hedging principle" – according to which the optimal design of debt is the one that perfectly matches cash inflows and cash outflows.

QUESTIONS

quiz

1/ Can a good financing plan make up for a mediocre investment?

2/ What disorder afflicts the investor who mistakes the coupon rate on a convertible bond for its financial cost?

3/ A 17% rate of return is required on a certain asset. The acquisition of that asset is financed entirely by equity. What rate of return do shareholders require on it? If the asset were financed entirely by debt, what rate of return would lenders require on it?

4/ What is the source of financing for which the difference between financial cost and apparent cost is greatest?

5/ Would you advise a startup to seek debt financing? If yes, could it get it?

6/ Is there an optimal capital structure?

7/ Equity capital has two roles in a financing plan. What are they?

8/ Free subscription warrants are distributed to all the shareholders on a one-for-one basis. The value of each warrant is b. What is the value of the share after the warrant is detached, other things equal?

9/ If a shareholder sells the warrant, what is he actually selling?

10/ What difference is there between a big dividend payout and a share buyback of the same amount (a) for the company? (b) for the shareholders?

11/ What is the fundamental journal article on the subject of capital structure?

12/ In the final analysis, isn't the cheapest financial resource short-term borrowing?

13/ How do you reconcile these two statements: "You can't make money without borrowing money" and "Borrowing can't create value".

14/ Will a company with ample growth opportunities tend to issue short-term, medium-term or long-term debt? Why?

15/ Give two examples of inflation profits. Under what conditions can they occur?

16/ If you believe a finance director's main concern is financial flexibility, would you expect a company ever to use up its borrowing capacity?

17/ Is a company destined always to be financed with equity capital?

18/ Why do startups go through several rounds of financing before they reach maturity? Couldn't they do it with a single big round?

19/ Can an entrepreneur with an industrial strategy be opportunistic in his financing choices over time?

20/ Why did European companies rid themselves of so much debt in 1980–1998? Why did they stop doing it in 1998–2002?

EXERCISE

1/ A company is considering the following investment:

Year	0	1	2	3	4	5
Cash flow	−100	−10	0	0	10	150

which can be financed either with equity:

Year	0	1	2	3	4	5
Debt/Equity	30%	22%	22%	22%	22%	22%
EPS	10	8.25	9.1	10.3	11.8	13.6
EPS growth rate		−17.5%	+10%	+13%	+15%	+15%
Rate of return on equity	15%	11%	11%	11.4%	11.6%	12%

or with debt:

Year	0	1	2	3	4	5
Debt/Equity	30%	67%	67%	67%	67%	67%
EPS	10	9.3	10.4	12	14.1	16.5
EPS growth rate	−7%	+12%	+15%	+17%	+17%	+17%
Rate of return on equity	15%	14%	17%	18%	21%	22%

If the cost of capital is 10%, the shareholder-required rate of return is 12% and the cost of debt is 5%, do you think this investment should be financed with equity or with debt? Isn't there another question that should be asked first?

Questions

1/ *No, because it is very difficult to create value at the level of the financing plan.*
2/ *Myopia, because he is not noticing that holders of convertible bonds expect the share price to rise so that they can convert them.*
3/ *17%, 17%.*
4/ *Internal financing.*
5/ *No, because it would be far too risky for a startup, requiring certain outflows from uncertain inflows. Probably not.*
6/ *No!*
7/ *Providing part of the financing and providing security to lenders.*
8/ *Value of the share less b. The warrant is therefore not free.*
9/ *A share of the value above the exercise price, and of course a time value as well.*
10/ *(a)   For the company, none.*
    (b)   For the shareholder, the individual freedom to receive or not to receive funds from the share buyback, whereas all shareholders receive the dividend.
11/ *Modigliani–Miller (1958).*
12/ *No, no and no!*
13/ *"You can't make money without borrowing money": this statement applies to an investor with a poorly diversified portfolio; it's all or nothing if he goes into debt to leverage it. "Borrowing can't create value": this statement applies to a perfectly diversified portfolio.*
14/ *Short-term, so as to be able to refinance on better terms as growth opportunities become profitable investments.*
15/ *Inventory profits and opportunity profits on investment realised sooner than expected. Provided the inflation rate is higher than the interest rate.*

16/ No, because the finance director will always want to retain some room to manoeuvre, just in case.

17/ No, the less risky it becomes, the more readily it can be financed with debt.

18/ In order to profit from a valuation that rises between each round. No, because, between each round, investors want to be sure that the business plan is panning out.

19/ No, because an industrial strategy can't wait for opportunities to arrive.

20/ High real interest rates and low investment. Because virtually all their debt had already been paid off, they could not go on deleveraging.

Exercise

1/ The IRR on the investment is 8%, less than the cost of capital. The investment should not be made; the question of how to finance it is academic.

BIBLIOGRAPHY

F. Bancel, U. Mittoo, The determinants of capital structure choice: A survey of European firms, *Financial Management*, Winter 2004.

M. Barclay, C. Smith, The capital structure puzzle: Another look at the evidence, *Journal of Applied Corporate Finance*, **12**(1), 8–20, Summer 1999.

M. Baker, J. Wurgler, Market timing and capital structure, *Journal of Finance*, **57**(1), 1–32, February 2002.

D. Chew et al., Stern Stewart roundtable on capital structure and stock repurchase, in J. Stern and D. Chew (eds), *The Revolution in Corporate Finance*, 4th edn, Blackwell, 2003.

J. Graham, C. Harvey, The theory and practice of corporate finance: Evidence from the field, *Journal of Financial Economics*, **63**, 187–243, May 2001.

B. Grundy, Merton H. Miller: His contribution to financial economics, *Journal of Finance*, **56**(4), 1183–1206, August 2001.

A. Hovakimian, T. Opler, S. Titman, The capital structure choice: New evidence from a dynamic trade-off model, *Journal of Applied Corporate Finance*, **15**(1), 24–30, Spring 2002.

D. Kigsen, Credit rating and capital structure, *Journal of Finance*, forthcoming, 2005.

P. MacKay, G. Phillips, *Is There an Optimal Industry Financial Structure?*, working paper, University of Maryland, 2001.

A. de Miguel, J. Pindado, Determinants of capital structure: New evidence from Spanish panel data, *Journal of Corporate Finance*, **7**, 77–99, 2001.

F. Modigliani, M. Miller, Taxes and the cost of capital: A correction, *American Economic Review*, 433–443, June 1963.

S. Myers, Determinants of corporate borrowing, *Journal of Financial Economics*, 147–176, November 1977.

S. Myers, Still searching for optimal capital structure, *Journal of Applied Corporate Finance*, **6**(1), 4–14, Spring 1993.

S. Myers, Financial architecture, *European Financial Magazine*, **5**(2), 133–141, 1999.

S. Myers, Capital structure, *Journal of Economic Perspectives*, **15**(2), 81–102, Spring 2001.

K. Palepu, Predicting takeover targets: A methodological and empirical analysis, *Journal of Accounting and Economics*, **8**(1), 3–35, 1986.

P. Vernimmen, Politique financière de l'entreprise, *Encyclopédie de Gestion*, Vol. 2, pp. 2325–2356, 2nd edn, Economica, 1997 [in French].

L. Zingales, In search of new foundations, *Journal of Finance*, **55**(4), 1623–1653, August 2000.

L. Zingales, R. Rajan, Debt, folklore and cross-country differences in financial structure, *Journal of Applied Corporate Finance*, **10**(4), 102–107, Winter 1998.

On maturity, basis and currency structure:

M. Barclay, C. Smith, The maturity stucture of corporate debt, *Journal of Finance*, **50**, 609–631, 1995.

M. Barclay, C. Smith, On financial architecture: Leverage, maturity and priority, *Journal of Applied Corporate Finance*, **8**, 4–17, 1996.

I. Brick, A. Ravid, On the relevance of debt maturity structure, *Journal of Finance*, **40**(5), 1985.

A. Damodaran, Financing innovations and capital structure choices, *Journal of Applied Corporate Finance*, **12**, 28–39, 1999.

J. Guedes, T. Opler, The determinants of the maturity of corporate debt issues, *Journal of Finance*, **51**, 1809–1833, 1996.

G. Jun, F. Jen, Trade-off model of debt maturity structure, *Review of Quantitative Finance and Accounting*, **20**, 5–34, 2003.

J.R. Morris, On corporate debt maturity strategies, *Journal of Finance*, 29–37, March 1976.

J.R. Morris, On corporate debt maturity strategies, *Journal of Financial and Quantitiative Analysis*, 339–357, September 1976.

F. Scherr, H. Hulburt, The debt maturity structure of small firms, *Financial Management*, **30**(1), 85–112, 2001.

C. Smithson, C. Smith, D. Wilford, *Managing Financial Risk*, Richard Irwin, 1995.

M. Stohs, D. Mauer, Determinants of corporate debt maturity, *Journal of Business*, **69**, 279–312, 1996.

On the application of the theory of signals to capital structure:

G. Donaldson, *Corporate Debt Capacity: A Study of Corporate Debt Policy and the Determination of Corporate Debt Capacity*, Harvard University Division of Research, 1961

H. Leland, Agency costs, risk management and capital structure, *Journal of Finance*, **53**(4), 1213–1243, August 1998.

S. Myers, The capital structure puzzle, *Journal of Finance*, **39**, 575–592, July 1984.

S. Myers, N. Majluf, Corporate financing and investment decisions when firms have information investors do not have, *Journal of Financial Economics*, **13**, 187–222, June 1984.

S. Ross, The determination of capital structure: The incentive signaling approach, *Bell Journal of Economics*, **8**, 23–40, Summer 1977.

Appendix 36A
CAPITAL STRUCTURE DESIGN: THE ALITALIA CASE

The Alitalia Group – the Italian national airline carrier – has revenues of about €5,000m and carries 22 million passengers a year, thanks to a fleet of around 180 aircraft and 22,000 employees in Italy and abroad.

The business model adopted is centred on core business passengers and cargo, and is increasingly oriented towards efficient operation and the optimal use of resources. It seeks to offer a solid basis for the company's development programmes, while at the same time ensuring competitive service and top quality.

The image of the Alitalia Group is deeply linked to its history, or rather to the interaction between the development of Alitalia and the growth of Italy over a period of more than 50 years. Attention to the customer, which is at the centre of Alitalia's strategy, inspired the company's entrance into SkyTeam in 2001, one of the largest international alliances, that placed the company on a par with other prestigious companies such as Air France, Delta Air Lines, AeroMexico, Korean and CSA.

More than 8,000 flights a day to 512 destinations in 114 countries – these are the salient figures of the great SkyTeam challenge that renews itself every day on the wings of Alitalia by offering millions of passengers throughout the world a unique, instantly recognisable travel experience based on quality and attention to detail.

The Alitalia Group is made up of Alitalia–Linee Aeree Italiane S.p.A. and of companies operating essentially in the air transport sector and/or related areas.

The aim of Alitalia's new business organisation is to focus on the core business (passengers and cargo) and to give high priority to customers' needs by tightly coordinating all operations that increase the efficiency and quality of service provided.

In line with the strategic aims of its 2004–2006 business plan, this formula sets out to relaunch the offer (using marketing and network tools, advertising campaigns, direct and indirect sales) backed up by a completely redesigned cost structure.

Alitalia's new entrepreneurial model is divided into a corporate area (which covers all functions of management and strategic planning) and into business areas corresponding to the activities that Alitalia carries out in its role as a domestic and international airline.

A quantitative approach can be used to estimate Alitalia's sensitivity to changes in a number of macroeconomic variables using two measures: Alitalia's firm value (the book value of debt and the market value of equity) and its operating income.

1/Value and cash flow sensitivity to macroeconomic factors

The value of a firm is a reasonable choice if we want to measure its sensitivity to changes in interest rates, inflation rates and other macroeconomic variables because firm value reflects the effect of these variables on cash flows (as well as on discount rates). However, in many cases it could be reasonable to estimate the sensitivity of operating cash flows against the same variables mentioned above. This is particularly the case when it is necessary to design interest payments on debt, since these payments are primarily made out of operating income.

The first step is to collect past data on firm value, operating income and specific macroeconomic variables against which we want to measure its sensitivity. We have chosen four macroeconomic measures:

- *Long-term treasury bond rates*, as a measure of the sensitivity of firm value and cash flows to changes in interest rates and of investment duration.
- *Real GDP*, as a measure of the sensitivity to the economic cycle.
- *Currency rate*, since the sensitivity to the currency rate provides a measure of exposure to the currency rate risk. We have analysed the €/$ currency rate.
- *Inflation rate*, since sensitivity to the inflation rate helps determine whether the interest rate on financial debt should be fixed or floating.

The second step is to estimate the sensitivity of firm value to changes in macro-economic variables by regressing changes in firm value each year against changes in each of the individual variables.

ALITALIA'S FIRM VALUE AND MACROECONOMIC VARIABLES, 1988–2003 (%)

Period	Change in operating income	Change in firm value	Change in LT bond rate	Change in GDP	Change in inflation	Change in currency
1988	−35.4	−0.89	−5.82	3.13	7.88	−2.49
1989	−188.5	22.29	12.36	4.05	33.27	7.39
1990	−18.5	−11.63	−4.42	2.89	−7.31	−13.39
1991	86.9	3.02	−3.49	1.91	6.08	2.61
1992	−117.3	41.06	8.85	1.40	−18.11	−4.35
1993	−663.7	41.02	−35.62	0.69	−20.04	10.62
1994	−149.1	41.02	36.78	−0.88	−6.86	−1.35
1995	−226.8	12.12	0.46	2.30	36.29	−9.15
1996	−93.3	−31.41	−32.58	2.95	−28.12	3.05
1997	−1206.8	−41.30	−24.80	1.02	−53.63	11.92
1998	328.4	−30.18	−28.26	2.05	−3.91	1.24
1999	−244.4	−12.36	26.94	1.74	−5.23	5.03
2000	43.2	125.11	−1.21	1.65	54.60	15.45
2001	−8.1	23.16	−12.94	3.16	11.11	3.17
2002	−20.0	38.69	−0.80	1.67	−13.57	−5.21
2003	83.1	17.25	−9.34	0.37	2.07	−16.55

Step 1 *Sensitivity to changes in long-term interest rates*   The regression of changes in firm value and operating income against changes in interest rates over the period gives the following results (with *t*-statistics in parentheses):

Dependent variable	Intercept	Coefficient	R^2
Change in firm value	0.18 (1.75)	0.62 (1.23)	9.7%
Change in operating income	−1.29 (−1.51)	3.53 (0.80)	4.1%

These results suggest that Alitalia's firm value and operating income are unaffected by changes in interest rates. However, the results of the regression could also be used to understand whether the firm should use fixed or floating rate debt: a firm whose operating income doesn't move with interest rates should in fact consider using a certain number of fixed rate loans.

Step 2 *Sensitivity to changes in the economy (real GDP)*   Is Alitalia a cyclical firm? One way of answering this question is to measure the sensitivity of firm value and operating income to changes in economic growth as measured by real GDP. The result is the following:

Dependent variable	Intercept	Coefficient	R^2
Change in firm value	0.11 (0.53)	4.58 (0.39)	1.3%
Change in operating income	−2.13 (−1.15)	31.4 (0.30)	0.1%

These results suggest that Alitalia seems to be mildly sensitive to cyclical movements in the economy. This is quite surprising especially if we consider that the air transport industry is "very sensitive to the macroeconomic fluctuation and extremely vulnerable when critical geopolitical events and are reflected on the demand with dramatic multiplicative effect" (Alitalia's *Annual Report 2003*, p. 29, downloadable from *www.alitalia.com*). The low *t*-statistics suggest that the statistical significance is irrelevant.

Step 3 *Sensitivity to changes in the inflation rate*   Firms whose value tends to move with inflation should be more likely to issue floating rate debt. The analysis of the relationship between firm value and operating income leads to the following results:

Dependent variable	Intercept	Coefficient	R^2
Change in firm value	0.15 (1.81)	0.91 (2.77)	35.3%
Change in operating income	−1.31 (−1.73)	6.18 (2.09)	22.4%

Alitalia's firm value and operating income is positively affected by changes in the inflation rate, and the relationship is significant. Other things being equal, Alitalia should be using floating rate debt rather than fixed rate debt.

Step 4 *Sensitivity to changes in the currency*   If we look at the relationship between the firm value and operating income and the €/$ rate we obtain the following results:

Dependent variable	Intercept	Coefficient	R^2
Change in firm value	0.14 (1.41)	0.96 (0.81)	4.5%
Change in operating income	−1.44 (−1.75)	−16.83 (−1.78)	18.2%

The firm's operating income has been very sensitive to changes in the exchange rate over the last 15 years. In particular, a stronger euro seems to benefit Alitalia's operating income. If this pattern continues, Alitalia might consider issuing some debt denominated in dollars.

2/FINAL RECOMMENDATIONS

Based upon the above analysis, the quantitative approach suggests two conclusions:

- The debt issued should be primarily floating rate debt.
- The debt should be a mix of euro and dollar currencies; the exact choice of currencies will depend upon the makeup of revenues on international routes. An extension of this analysis could include the sensitivity of firm value and operating income to other foreign currencies.

Part Three
Equity capital and dividend policies

Equity capital and dividend policies are of such importance in corporate finance that they must of necessity be addressed in depth. The chapters in this part deal in turn with internal financing, dividends and share buybacks, and capital increases.

Chapter 37
INTERNAL FINANCING: REINVESTING CASH FLOW

It's all grist to the mill

An often-heard precept in finance says that a company ought to fund its development solely through internal financing – that is, by reinvesting its cash flow in the business. This position seemingly corresponds to the interests of both its managers and its creditors, and indirectly to the interests of its shareholders.

Indeed:

- For shareholders, reinvesting cash flow in the business ought to translate into an increase in the value of their shares and thus into capital gains on those shares. In virtually all of the world's tax systems, capital gains are taxed less heavily than dividends. Other things equal, shareholders will prefer to receive their returns in the form of capital gains. They will therefore look favourably on retention rather than distribution of periodic cash flows.
- By funding its development exclusively from internal sources, the company has no need to go to the capital markets – that is, to investors in shares or corporate bonds – or to banks. For this reason, its managers will have greater freedom of action. They, too, will look favourably on internal financing.
- Lastly, as we have seen, the company's creditors will prefer that it rely on internal financing because this will reduce the risk and increase the value of their claims on the company.

This precept is not wrong, but here we must emphasise the dangers of taking it to excess. A policy of *always* or *only* reinvesting internally generated cash flow postpones the financial reckoning that is indispensable to any policy. It is not good for a company to be cut off from the capital markets or for capital mobility to be artificially reduced, allowing investments to be made in unprofitable sectors. The company that follows such a policy in effect creates its own *internal capital market* independent of the outside financial markets. On that artificial market, rates of return may well be lower, and resources may accordingly be misallocated.

The sounder principle of finance is probably the one that calls for distributing all periodic earnings to shareholders and then going back to them to request funding for major projects. In the real world, however, this rule runs up against practical considerations – substantial tax and transaction costs, and shareholder control issues – that make it difficult to apply.

In short, internal financing enjoys an extraordinarily positive image among those who own, manage or lend to the company. However, although internally generated cash flow belongs fundamentally to the shareholders, they have very little control over it. The result is that a policy of reinvesting cash flow can prove to be a timebomb for the company.

Section 37.1
REINVESTED CASH FLOW AND THE VALUE OF EQUITY

1/INTERNAL FINANCING AND VALUE CREATION

We begin by revisiting a few truisms.

➤ Does the reader fully appreciate that, given unchanged market conditions, the value of the company must increase by the amount of profit that it reinvests? This much occurs almost automatically, one might say. The performance of a strategy that seeks to create "shareholder value" is measured by the extent to which it **increases the value of shareholders' equity by more than the amount of reinvested earnings**.

➤ **The apparent cost of internal financing is nil.** This is certainly true in the short term, but what a trap it is in the long term to think this way! Does the reader know of any good that is free, except for things available in unlimited quantity, which is clearly not the case with money? Reinvested cash flow indeed has a cost, and, as we have learned from the theory of markets in equilibrium, that cost has a direct impact on the value of the company. It is an **opportunity cost**. Such a cost is, by nature, not directly observable – unlike the cost of debt, which is manifested in an immediate cash outflow. As we explained previously, retaining earnings rather than distributing them as dividends is financially equivalent to paying out all earnings and simultaneously raising new equity capital. **The cost of internal financing is therefore the same as the cost of a capital increase: to wit, the cost of equity.**

➤ Does this mean the company ought to require a rate of return equal to the cost of equity on the investments that it finances internally? No. As we saw in Chapter 23, it is a mistake to link the cost of any source of financing to the required rate of return on the investment that is being financed. Whatever the source or method of financing, the investment must earn at least the cost of capital.[1] By reinvesting earnings rather than borrowing, the company can reduce the proportion of debt in its capital structure and thereby lower its cost of debt. In equilibrium, this cost saving is added on top of the return yielded by the investment, to produce the return required by shareholders. Similarly, an investment financed by new debt needs to earn not the cost of debt, but the cost of capital, which is greater than the cost of debt. The excess goes to increase the return to the shareholders, who bear additional risk attributable to the new debt.

[1] *At the same level of business risk as for the company's existing operating assets.*

➤ **Retained earnings add to the company's financial resources**, but they increase shareholder wealth only if the rate of return on new investments is greater than the weighted average cost of capital. If the rate of return is lower, each euro invested in the business will increase the value of the company by less than one euro, and shareholders will be worse off than if all the earnings had been distributed to them. This is the market's sanction for poor use of internal financing.

Consider the following company. The market value of its equity is 135, and its shareholders require a rate of return of 7.5%.

Year	Book value of equity	Net profit	Dividend (Div)	Market value of equity (V) P/E = 9	Gain in market value (ΔV)	Rate of return (ΔV + Div)/V
1	300.0	15.0	4.5	135.0		
2	310.5	15.6	4.7	140.4	5.4	7.2%
3	321.4	16.2	4.9	145.8	5.4	7.1%
4	332.7	16.8	6.7	151.2	5.4	8.0%

Annual returns on equity are close to 7.5%. Seemingly, shareholders are getting what they want. But are they?

To measure the harm done by ill-advised reinvestment of earnings, one need only compare the change in the book value of equity over 4 years (+32.7) with the change in market value (+16.2). For each €1 the shareholders reinvested in the company, they can hope to get back only €0.50. Of what they put in, fully half was lost – a steep cost in terms of forgone earnings.

Think of reinvesting cash flow (internal financing) as a machine to transform energy (money) into work (value). When the return on reinvested cash flow is equal to the cost of capital, this machine has an energy yield of 1. Its energy yield falls below 1 whenever the return on incremental investment is below the required return. When that happens, there is a loss of energy; in other words, value is destroyed, not created.

Beware of "cathedrals built of steel and concrete" – i.e., companies that have reinvested to an extent not warranted by their profitability!

Reinvesting earnings automatically causes the book value of equity to grow. It does not cause growth in the market value of the company unless the investments it finances are sufficiently profitable – that is, unless those investments earn more than the required rate of return given their risk. If they earn less, shareholders' equity will increase but shareholders' wealth will not. Shareholders would be better off if the funds that were reinvested had instead been distributed to them.

In our example, the market value of equity (151) is only about 45% of its book value (333). True, the rate of return on equity (5%) is in this case far below the cost of equity (7.5%).

More than a few unlisted mid-sized companies have engaged in excessive reinvestment of earnings in unprofitable endeavours, with no immediate visible consequence on the valuation of the business.

The owner-managers of such a company get a painful wakeup call when they find they can sell the business, which they may have spent their entire working lives building, only for less than the book value (restated or not) of the company's assets. The sanction imposed by the market is severe.

Only investment at least at the cost of capital can maintain the value of reinvested cash flow.

2/INTERNAL FINANCING AND TAXATION

From a tax standpoint, reinvestment of earnings has long been considered a panacea for shareholders. It ought to translate into an increase in the value of their shares and thus into capital gains when they liquidate their holdings. Generally, capital gains are taxed less heavily than dividends.

Other things equal, then, shareholders will prefer to receive their income in the form of capital gains and will favour reinvestment of earnings. Since the 1990s, however, as shareholders have become more of a force and taxes on dividends have been reduced in most European countries, this form of remuneration has become less attractive.

Within a corporate group, the parent company rarely requires its subsidiaries to distribute all their earnings, except perhaps if they do so in the form of share dividends. This is surprising because receiving a dividend and then participating in a capital increase amounts, on the parent's books, to the same thing as revaluing the investment in the subsidiary – thereby reducing the amount of tax that will be due when that asset is sold.

A simple example should suffice to convince the sceptical reader. Consider a mini-group made up of a company and its wholly owned subsidiary, which it acquired at a cost of 100 and which has a net book value of 100. Suppose this subsidiary pays no dividend for 5 years but generates and retains cumulative earnings of 60 over that period.

On the consolidated balance sheet, the subsidiary will account for shareholders' equity of 160, but in the parent's individual company (i.e., unconsolidated) accounts, the investment in the subsidiary will still be carried at 100.

If the subsidiary had distributed all its earnings and also made capital increases in the same amount, the subsidiary would represent consolidated shareholders' equity of 160, and the carrying value of the investment on the parent's balance sheet would also be 160.

Suppose the subsidiary is sold at the end of the period at a price of 180. The capital gains tax liability would be calculated on a basis of 80 (180 − 100) in the first case but only 20 (180 − 160) in the second case.

Within a consolidated group, reinvestment of earnings at the subsidiary level leads to a divergence in values for tax purposes and values for financial reporting purposes, and consequently to a higher effective tax rate. Tax is assessed on the gain realised against the value carried on the parent's unconsolidated balance sheet. If we assume a capital gains tax of 20% and therefore a tax liability of 16 in the first case, the effective tax rate will be 80% (16/20), since the consolidated basis is 160 and the apparent gain is 20.

Section 37.2

INTERNAL FINANCING AND THE VARIOUS STAKEHOLDERS

1/SHAREHOLDERS AND LENDERS

We have seen (cf. the discussion of options theory in Chapter 28) that, whenever a company becomes more risky, there is a transfer of value from creditors to shareholders. Symmetrically, whenever a company pays down debt and moves into a lower risk class, shareholders lose and creditors gain.

Reinvestment of earnings can be thought of as a capital increase in which all shareholders are forced to participate.

This capital increase tends to diminish the risk borne by creditors and thus, in theory, makes them better off by increasing the value of their claims on the company.

The same reasoning applies in reverse to dividend distribution. The more a company pays out in dividends, the greater the transfer of value from creditors to shareholders. This is to be expected, since a high-dividend policy is the inverse of a high-earnings-retention policy.

2/SHAREHOLDERS AND MANAGERS

Under the agency theory approach, creditors and managers are seen as having a common interest in favouring reinvestment of earnings. When profits are not distributed, "the money stays in the business", whereas shareholders "always want more".

There is a sanction, however, for taking reinvestment to excess: the takeover bid or *tender offer* in cash or shares, as we will see in Chapter 42.

If a management team performs poorly, the market's sanction will sooner or later take the form of a decline in the share price. If it lasts, the decline will expose the company to the risk of a takeover. Assuming the managers themselves do not hold enough of the company's shares to ensure that the tender offer succeeds or fails, a change of management may enable the company to get back on track, by once again making investments that earn more than the cost of capital, and thereby lead to a rise in the share price.

A formalisation of agency theory as applied to tender offers has been made by Michael Jensen (1986). The key to Jensen's approach is the notion of *free cash flow*.

If the manager directs free cash flow into unprofitable investments, his ego may be gratified by the size of the investment budget, or his position may become more secure if those investments carry low risk, but in no case will the shareholder be happy with the result. The sanction, according to Jensen, is a takeover bid. Tender offers constitute the market for corporate control, a market in which management teams compete to run companies.

Jensen defines the difference between the acquisition price and the new market value of the company as the value of supervision provided by outside firms.

Retained earnings, on the other hand, are one source of financing about which not much disclosure is necessary. The cost of any informational asymmetry having to do with internal financing is therefore very low. It is not surprising that, as predicted by Jensen and observed in a study conducted by Harford (1999), companies that have cash available make less profitable investments than other companies. Money seems to burn a hole in managers' pockets.

We should also point out the pernicious relation between stock options held by management and the company's free cash flow. For managers that have call options on the company's shares, retained earnings are a costless resource that can be applied to enhance their personal wealth by boosting valuation of the shares.

Section 37.3
INTERNAL FINANCING AND RETURN CRITERIA

1/INTERNAL FINANCING AND ORGANIC GROWTH

A company with a book value of equity of 100 and return on equity of 15% will make a profit of 15. If its payout ratio is 33.3%, it will retain two-thirds of its earnings – that is, 10. The book value of equity will increase from 100 to 110, an increase of 10%, in year 1. If these rates are maintained, the results will be as shown in the table opposite.

Year	Book value of equity at beginning of year	Net profit (15% of equity)	Retained earnings	Book value of equity at end of year
1	100.0	15.0	10.0	110.0
2	110.0	16.5	11.0	121.0
3	121.0	18.2	12.1	133.1
4	133.1	20.0	13.3	46.4

The book value of a company that raises no new money from its shareholders depends on its rate of return on equity and its dividend payout ratio.

The growth rate of book value is equal to the product of the rate of return on equity and the earnings retention ratio, which is the complement of the payout ratio.

We have:

$$g = ROE \times (1 - d)$$

where g is the rate of growth of shareholders' equity,[2] ROE (Return On Equity) is the rate of return on the book value of equity and d is the dividend payout ratio.

This is merely to state the obvious, as the reader should be well aware.

In other words, given the company's rate of return on equity, the company's reinvestment policy determines the growth rate of the book value of its equity.

2 *Note that in this section, since no new shares are issued, the growth rate of book value per share is always equal to the growth rate of book value.*

2/MODELS OF INTERNAL GROWTH

If capital structure is held constant, growth in equity allows parallel growth in debt and thus in all long-term funds required for operations. We should make clear that here we are talking about book values, not market values. In effect, the model assumes that there is a direct and systematic relation between the accounting value of shareholders' equity and the market value thereof; that is, the price-to-book ratio is constant.

At constant capital structure, growth in book equity determines growth in capital employed.

The preceding model can be generalised to companies with debt as well as equity capital. To do so, we need only recall that the rate of return on book value of equity is equal to the rate of return on capital employed adjusted for the positive or negative effect of financial leverage (gearing) due to the presence of debt.

$$ROE = ROCE + (ROCE - i) \times D/E$$

or:

$$g = \left[ROCE + (ROCE - i) \times \frac{D}{E}\right] \times (1 - d)$$

where g is the growth rate of a company's capital employed at a constant capital structure and a constant rate of Return On Capital Employed ($ROCE$).

This is the **internal growth model**.

It is clear that the rates of growth of revenue, production, $EBITDA$[3] and so on will be equal to the rate of growth of book equity if the following ratios stay constant:

$$\frac{Revenue}{Capital\ employed}, \frac{Production}{Capital\ employed}, \frac{EBITDA}{Capital\ employed}$$

3 *Earnings Before Interest, Taxes, Depreciation and Amortisation.*

Through the internal growth model, we establish a direct link between the rate of growth of the business and the rate of growth of capital employed.

To illustrate this important principle, we consider a company whose assets are financed 50% by equity and 50% by debt, the latter at an after-tax cost of 5%. Its after-tax return on capital employed is 15%, and 80% of earnings are re-invested. Accordingly, we have:

Period	Book equity at begining of period	Net debt	Capital employed	Operating profit after tax	Interest expenses after tax	Net profit	Dividends	Retained earnings	Book equity at end of period
1	100	100	200	30	5	25	5	20	120
2	120	120	240	36	6	30	6	24	144
3	144	144	288	43.2	7.2	36	7.2	28.8	172.8

This gives us an average annual growth rate of book equity of:

$$g = [15\% + (15\% - 5\%) \times 1] \times 80\% = 20\%$$

The reader can verify that, if the company distributes half its earnings in dividends, the growth rate of the book value of equity falls to:

$$g = [15\% + (15\% - 5\%) \times 1] \times 50\% = 12.5\%$$

The growth rate of capital employed thus depends on:

- The rate of **return on capital employed**: the higher it is, the higher the growth rate of financial resources.
- The **cost of debt**: the lower it is, the greater the leverage effect, and thus the higher the growth rate of capital employed.
- The **capital structure**.
- The **payout ratio**.

For the shareholder, the growth rate of capital employed by the company corresponds to the growth rate of book value per share, provided there are no capital increases. The same is true of the growth rate of Earnings Per Share (EPS) and dividend per share.

In a situation of equilibrium, then, shareholders' equity, debt, capital employed, net profit, book value per share, earnings per share and dividend per share all grow at the same pace, as illustrated in the example above. This equilibrium growth rate is commonly called the company's **growth potential**.

We confide to the reader, however, that this model is today somewhat old-fashioned. It lends itself to analysis of growth in earnings per share, and for this reason it was particularly relevant when equity valuation focused on EPS.

Furthermore, the gearing or financial leverage ratio (debt/equity) that this model strives to keep constant in the name of preserving the capital structure is no longer the principal analytical tool for evaluating capital structure. For one thing, market values can vary relative to book values; for another, ratios such as net debt/EBITDA or operating profit/interest expenses have largely supplanted debt/equity.

Another model has been proposed by Mottura (1987). The objective of this model is twofold:

1. to understand if the internal financing is adequate to guarantee a certain growth rate (*expressed in terms of revenue growth*);
2. to discover the amount of external financing needed by the company, in case internal financing is insufficient.

The answer to the first point is given by:[4]

$$\frac{\text{Capital employed}}{\text{Sales}} \times \Delta\text{Sales} \gtrless \frac{\text{Retained earnings}}{\text{Sales}}$$

There can be three possible results:

1. if there is a perfect equivalence of the two terms, the growth rate of the company can be completely financed with internal resources;
2. if the left side is lower than the right side, the company generates internally an amount of resources that exceed the financial needs for financing growth. The

4 The ratio Capital employed/Sales is also called the "capital intensity".

company can then decide: to grow at a higher rate, distribute extraordinary dividends or increase liquidity;

3   if the left side is higher than the right side, the excepted growth rate cannot be financed entirely internally. The company has basically two alternatives: reduce the growth rate or raise external capital. In this case, the amount needed is given by:

$$\text{External financing} = \text{Retained earnings} - \Delta\text{Sales} \times \frac{\text{Capital employed}}{\text{Sales}}$$

Example   A simple example will help to understand the model. Suppose a company at time 0 (today) and 2 years later with these characteristics:

	Sales	Capital employed	Retained profits	$\frac{\text{Capital employed}}{\text{Sales}}$	ΔSales	$\frac{\text{Retained earnings}}{\text{Sales}}$
t_0	500	700	150	1.4		0.3
t_1	700	980	210	1.4	40%	0.3
t_2	1,400	1,960	420	1.4	100%	0.3

In t_1, the above inequality is:

$$1.4 \times 0.4 = 0.56 > 0.3$$

Internal resources cannot entirely satisfy the company needs. External financing needed by the company is:

$$\text{External financing} = 150 - (200 \times 1.4) = -130$$

Similarly, in t_2, the figures are:

$$1.4 \times 1.0 = 1.4 > 0.3$$

Again, internal resources are inadequate. External financing will be higher:

$$\text{External financing} = 210 - (700 \times 1.4) = -770$$

We can also use the above inequality for determining the maximum growth rate of sales. We must solve the inequality for ΔSales. In our example, the answer will be 21.43%.[5]

3/ADDITIONAL ANALYSIS

The first of the models above – the internal growth model – assumes all the variables are growing at the same pace and also that returns on funds reinvested by organic growth are equal to returns on the initial assets. These are very strong assumptions.

A policy of reinvesting cash flow can be analysed only in terms of the *marginal* rate of return on reinvested earnings.

Suppose a company reinvests two-thirds of its earnings in projects that yield no return at all.

5 *Since Capital employed/Sales and Retained Earnings/Sales do not change in both periods, 21.43% is simply the result of 0.3/1.4.*

We would observe the following situation:

Period	Book equity at beginning of period	Net profit	Return on equity	Dividends	Retained earnings	Book equity at end of period
1	100	15	15.0%	5	10	110 (+10.0%)
2	110	15 (+0%)	13.6%	5 (+0%)	10	120 (+9.1%)
3	120	15 (+0%)	12.5%	5 (+0%)	10	130 (+8.3%)

We see that, if net profit and earnings per share do not increase, growth of shareholders' equity slows, and return on equity declines because the incremental return (on the reinvested funds) is zero.

If, on the other hand, the company reinvests two-thirds of its earnings in projects that yield 30%, or double the initial rate of return on equity, all the variables are now rising.

Period	Equity at beginning of period	Net profit	Rate of return on equity	Dividends	Retained earnings	Equity at end of period
1	100	15	15.0%	5	10	110 (+10.0%)
2	110	18 (+20%)	16.4%	6 (+20%)	12	122 (+10.9%)
3	122	21.6 (+20%)	17.7%	7.2 (+20%)	14.4	136.4 (+11.8%)

Although the rate of growth of book equity increases only slightly, the earnings growth rate immediately jumps to 20%. The rate of growth of net profit (and earnings per share) is linked to the *marginal* rate of return, not the *average*.

Here we see that there are multiplier effects on these parameters, as revealed by the following relation:

$$\frac{\text{Change in net profit}}{\text{Net profit}} = \frac{\text{Change in net profit}}{\text{Change in book equity}} \times \frac{\text{Change in book equity}}{\text{Net profit}}$$

This means that, barring a capital increase, the rate of growth of earnings (or earnings per share) is equal to the marginal rate of return on equity multiplied by the earnings retention ratio (1 − Dividend payout ratio).

In a similar way, it can be shown that the rate of growth of free cash flow can be deduced from the rate of growth of net profit:

$$\text{Change in net profit} = \text{Growth of free cash flow} \times \left(\frac{V_D}{V_E}\right)$$

This is another manifestation of the leverage effect.

Internal financing by reinvestment of cash flow enjoys an excellent image: it reduces risk for the creditor and results in capital gains rather than more heavily taxed dividends for the shareholder. For managers, it is a resource they can mobilise without having to go to third parties; as such, it reduces the company's risk and increases the value of their stock options.

For the same reason, though, systematic reinvestment of cash flow can be dangerous. It is not appealing from a financial standpoint if it allows the company to finance investments that bring in less than the rate of return required given their risk. To do so is to destroy value. If the penalty for value destruction is delayed, as it often is because companies that reinvest excessively are cut off from the capital markets, the eventual sanction is all the harsher.

The trap for the unwitting is that internal financing has no explicit cost, whereas its true cost, which is an opportunity cost, is quite real.

Reinvesting cash flow makes possible organic growth at a rate equal to the rate of return on equity multiplied by the earnings retention ratio (1 minus the payout ratio). With constant financial leverage and a constant rate of return on capital employed, the organic growth rate is the same as the growth rate of book equity and capital employed. Lastly, the rate of growth of earnings per share is equal to the marginal rate of return on book equity multiplied by the earnings retention ratio.

SUMMARY

download

1/ Why does internal financing enjoy such a positive image?

2/ Why is a policy of sticking strictly to internal financing unsound?

3/ What determines the rate of growth of capital employed?

4/ What should a company do if its rate of return on reinvested earnings is below the weighted average cost of capital?

5/ By what criterion should a policy of reinvesting cash flow be judged?

6/ In your opinion, which theory best explains the interest of internal financing from an overall standpoint?

7/ Show with an example why reinvestment of earnings by the company has no cost for a holder of options on the company's shares.

8/ What is the market's sanction for over-reliance on internal financing?

9/ What kind of companies rely heavily on internal financing? What kind do not?

10/ Can internal financing lower the cost of capital?

11/ What are the advantages and drawbacks of 100% internal financing for family shareholders?

12/ Why is internal financing the financial resource with the lowest implementation cost?

13/ Under what conditions is the dividend growth rate at least equal to the growth rate of free cash flow?

QUESTIONS

quiz

EXERCISES

1/ An entrepreneur is determined to retain control of his company and refuses to accept any outside investors. The company's return on capital employed is 10% after tax. He wishes to achieve growth of 25% a year. The cost of debt is 7% before tax, and the tax rate is 40%.

(a) If he has no earnings distribution policy, what capital structure is he choosing implicitly?

(b) If instead he has to pay out one-third of the company's earnings, what capital structure is he choosing?

(c) If he chooses financial leverage (debt/equity) equal to 1, what is the implied normal growth rate of the company?

(d) Which other parameters can he play with?

2/ Choose an example of "death spiral" deterioration of capital structure, with an initial positive leverage effect and then a negative leverage effect. Construct tables like those presented in this chapter.

ANSWERS

Questions

1/ *Because it reduces risk to creditors, it results in capital gains rather than more heavily taxed dividends, and increases the value of managers' stock options.*

2/ *It isolates the company from the capital markets.*

3/ *The rate of return on capital employed, the capital structure and the interest rate on debt.*

4/ *Pay out all its earnings.*

5/ *The marginal rate of return on investment.*

6/ *Agency theory.*

7/ *Holders of options get no benefit from earnings paid out as dividends, but retained earnings increase the value of the shares and therefore the value of their options (assuming they are call options, of course).*

8/ *A takeover bid.*

9/ *Growth companies with high rates of return. Mature companies that generate cash.*

10/ *No. Unless it changes the risk on capital employed, it has no impact on the cost of capital.*

11/ *Capital increases that could dilute the family's shareholding are avoided, but potential dividends are reduced.*

12/ *Because nobody else's agreement need be sought before going ahead with it.*

13/ *When the company has positive net debt.*

Exercises

1/ (a) $D/E = [(g/(1-d)) - r_{ce}]/(r_{ce} - i(1-40\%)) = 2.6$;

(b) $D/E = 4.7$;

(c) $g = 15.8\%$ if he pays no dividend, $g = 10.5\%$ if he pays out one-third of earnings;

(d) *He can try to improve his rate of return on capital employed.*

2/ *Moulinex is a good example of a death spiral with a high-leverage effect. This group financed fast growth mainly with debt. When interest rates rose sharply in the late 1970s, its difficulties accelerated. Consider the following example of a company for which the leverage effect changes sign in year 4.*

	Equity	Debt	Capital employed	Operating earnings after tax	Interest expenses after tax	Net profit	Divi-dends	Rein-vested earnings	Equity at end of period
1	100	100	200	20	8	12	2	10	110
2	110	140	250	25	12	13	1	12	122
3	122	190	312	28	17	11	0	11	133
4	133	258	391	31	26	5	0	5	138
5	138	350	488	34	35	−1	0	−1	137
6	137	474	611	43	47	−4	0	−4	133

BIBLIOGRAPHY

M. Jensen, Agency costs of free cash flow, corporate finance and takeovers, *American Economic Review*, **76**(2), 323–329, May 1986.
J. Harford, Corporate cash reserves and acquisitions, *Journal of Finance*, **56**(6), December 1999.
P. Mottura, Condizioni di equilibrio finanziario della strategia d'impresa, *Finanza Marketing e Produzione*, **1**, 1987 [in Italian].

Chapter 38
RETURNING CASH TO SHAREHOLDERS: DIVIDEND POLICIES

To each his own habit

The topics addressed in this chapter are the logical complement of the preceding chapter, since there are only two possible destinations for net earnings: either they are reinvested in the business, or they are distributed to shareholders as dividends or through share buybacks.

We pursue our inquiry by looking this time at the external aspect of distribution policy and how the value of the share is directly linked to the dividend.

We will also deal in this chapter with share buybacks, which are an alternative means for the company to return excess cash to its shareholders.

Section 38.1
DIVIDENDS AND MARKET VALUE

1/DIVIDENDS AND EQUILIBRIUM MARKETS

In markets in equilibrium, payment of a dividend has no impact on the shareholder's wealth, and the shareholder is indifferent about receiving a dividend of €1 or a capital gain of €1.

At equilibrium, by definition, the company is earning its cost of equity. Consider a company, Equilibrium plc, with share capital of €100 on which shareholders require a 10% return. Since we are in equilibrium, the company is making a net profit of €10. Either these earnings are paid out to shareholders in the form of dividends, or they are reinvested in the business at Equilibrium plc's 10% rate of return. Since that rate is exactly the rate that shareholders require, €10 of earnings reinvested will increase the value of Equilibrium plc by €10 – neither more nor less. Thus, either the shareholders collectively will have received €10 in cash, or the aggregate value of their shares will have increased by the same amount.

If Equilibrium plc now wishes to increase its payout ratio without disposing of assets or cutting back its investment programme, it will have to raise new money to finance the higher dividends. It has two choices:

* It can issue new shares. If it raises only as much new money as it has just paid out in dividends, the value of its equity capital will be unchanged. The old shareholders (who received cash) will own less of the company, and the new shareholders (who subscribed to the rights issue) will own more.
* It can borrow. The increase in the dividend will then be offset by a reduction in the value of equity capital due to the increase in debt.

In markets in equilibrium, there are no good or bad dividend policies.

If the company pays out a high proportion of its earnings, its shares will be worth less but its shareholders will receive more cash. If it distributes less, its shares will be worth more (provided that it reinvests in projects that are sufficiently profitable) and its shareholders will receive less cash – but the shareholder, if he wishes, can make up the difference by selling some of his shares.

The chart below plots the share price of Legris Industrie, which paid a special dividend of €19 on 21 September 2001. The price of the shares adjusted immediately. Legris Industrie's shares fell by €19 but shareholder wealth was unchanged.

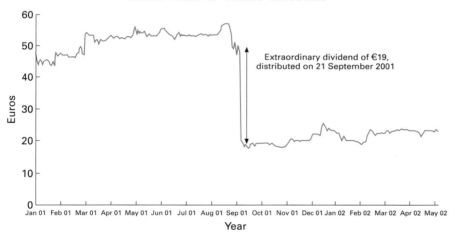

In a universe of markets in equilibrium, paying out more or less in dividends will have no effect on shareholder wealth. Companies should thus not be concerned about dividend policy and should treat dividends as an adjustment to cash flow. This harks back to the Modigliani–Miller approach to financial policy: there is no way to create lasting value with merely a financing decision.

2/ DIVIDENDS AND SIGNALLING THEORY

Equilibrium market theory has a hard time finding any good reason for dividends to be paid at all. Since they do exist in the real world, new explanations must be sought for the earnings distribution problem.

A justification for the existence of dividends is proposed by the theory of signalling, around which an entire literature devoted to the dividend problem developed, mainly during the 1980s.

> The dividend is a means of communication between the company and the market.

The financial information that investors get from companies may be biased by selective disclosure or even manipulative accounting. Managers are naturally inclined to present the company in the best possible light, even if the image they convey does not represent the exact truth. Companies that really are profitable will therefore seek to distinguish themselves from others that are not, through policies that the latter cannot imitate because they lack the resources to do so. Paying dividends is one such policy because it requires the company to have cash. A company that is struggling is not able to imitate a company that is prospering.

For this reason, dividend policy is a means of signalling that cannot be faked, and managers use it to convince the market that the picture of the company they present is the true one.

Dividend policy is also a way for the company's managers to show the market that they have a plan for the future and are anticipating certain results. If a company maintains its dividend when its earnings have decreased, that signals to the market that the decline is only temporary and earnings growth will resume.

Dividends are paid a few months after the close of the year, therefore the level of the dividend depends on earnings during both the past and the current period. That level thus provides information – a signal – about expected earnings during the current period.

> A dividend reduction, though, is not necessarily bad news for future earnings. It might also indicate that the company has a new opportunity and need to invest.

Thus, during the 1990s we saw a number of groups traditionally positioned in mature industries reorient themselves towards businesses with faster growth. Examples in France include Bouygues, Vivendi (formerly Générale des Eaux) and Mannesmann (before being taken over and split by Vodafone). With the wave of privatisation in slow-growth industries such as electricity and gas, growth opportunities abroad also revitalised companies in those sectors. On the other side some sectors reached some kind of maturity and in companies like Microsoft dividend policy changed.

The strategic communication aspect of dividend policy is of crucial importance, especially when there is a change in policy. One trap to be avoided is having a dividend rise interpreted as signalling a scarcity of investment opportunities. A dividend cut can be justified to investors by a strategy of renewed growth. Telefónica, for example, eliminated its dividend altogether to finance part of its expansion in Latin America.

3/ DIVIDENDS AND AGENCY THEORY

By requiring managers to pay out a fraction of the company's earnings to share-holders, dividend policy is a means of imposing "discipline" on those managers and forcing them to include in their reckoning the interest of the company's owners. A generous dividend policy will have the consequence of increasing the company's dependence on either shareholders or lenders to finance the business.

In either case, those putting up the money have the power to say no. In the extreme, shareholders could demand that all earnings be paid out in dividends in order to reduce managers' latitude to act in ways that are not in the shareholders' interest. The company would then have to have regular rights issues, to which shareholders would decide whether to subscribe based on the profitability of the projects proposed to them by the managers. This is the virtuous cycle of finance.

Although attractive intellectually because it greatly reduces the problem of asymmetric information, this solution runs up against the high costs of carrying out a capital increase – not just the direct costs, but the cost in terms of management time as well.

Bear in mind also that creditors watch out for their interest and tend to oppose overly generous dividends that could increase their risk, as we saw in Chapter 37.

Even though the dividend is often quite small in relation to the value of equity capital (a few percent at most), it plays an important role. It is a signal from the company to the financial markets. It is an instrument for control of managers by the market, in that it deprives the company of some of the cash the managers would have been able to invest as they saw fit. If the managers still wish to invest that much cash, they will have to borrow; and because debt imposes a discipline of its own (repayment), this pushes them to be more efficient.

4/ ASSESSING DIVIDEND POLICY

The criterion for assessing a dividend policy is the marginal rate of return on capital employed. If that rate is higher than the weighted average cost of capital, the company will create value by reinvesting its earnings. If this is the case, the share-holder will want the payout ratio to be low or even zero. This is why a fast-growing, highly profitable company such as Deutsche Telekom pays no dividend. Sooner or later, though, growth will slow and, with help from competition, profitability will decline. The situation will return to equilibrium, and the company will be more inclined to pay a dividend.

At the opposite extreme, a company that can no longer find any investment projects that will earn at least its cost of capital will have to pay out all its earnings in dividends. If it does not, it will destroy value.

Over the life of the company, the payout ratio follows a path determined by the cycle in the company's marginal rate of return on capital employed.

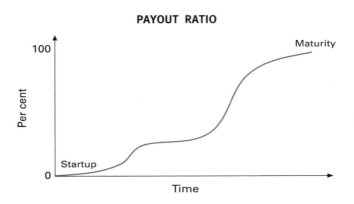

Section 38.2
DIVIDEND DISTRIBUTION IN PRACTICE

1/PAYOUT RATIO AND DIVIDEND GROWTH RATE

In practice, when dividends are paid, the two key criteria of analysis are:

➤ The **payout ratio** (*d*), represented by:

$$d = \frac{\text{Dividend}}{\text{Net profit}}$$

➤ The rate of growth of dividends per share.

All other criteria are irrelevant, frequently inaccurate and possibly misleading. For example, it is absurd to take the ratio of the dividend to the par value of the share since par value often has little to do with equity value.

Hence the difficulty for a company of meeting a dividend yield objective. It is the shareholder who, when evaluating the company, determines the desired yield, not the other way round.

In this regard, numerous tests have been performed to show that investors systematically re-evaluate a company when the amount of the dividend is made public.

In Europe, a payout ratio no greater than 20% is considered to be a low-dividend policy, whereas one greater than 60% is deemed high. The average in 2003 was about 58%.

0% < d < 20%		21% < d < 30%		31% < d < 40%		41% < d < 50%		51% < d < 100%	
Continental	0%	Tietoenator	21%	Edison	31%	Volkswagen	41%	Unicredito Italiano	54%
Elan	0%	TPG NV	21%	Telecom Italia	31%	Carrefour	41%	San Paolo IMI	54%
Epcos	0%	OMV	21%	France Telecom	31%	Publicis Groupe	41%	Bayer	55%
Grafton Group	0%	Altana	22%	Finmeccanica	32%	Merck KGAA	43%	Alleanza	57%
Hannover Ruck.	0%	Medion	22%	Promotora de Infmcs	32%	Linde	43%	AEM SpA	58%
Mobistar	0%	Gucci Group	22%	Henkel	32%	Thyssenkrupp	43%	Royal Dutch	58%
Qiagen	0%	Alstom	23%	Solvay	32%	Banca Antonveneta	44%	Lafarge	59%
Ryanair	0%	Banco de Valencia	23%	Titan Cmt.	32%	BIC	44%	Banco Santander Cen.	62%
T-Online	0%	Celesio	23%	Schering (XET)	33%	DaimlerChrysler	44%	Ote-Hellenic Telc.	62%
Telefónica	0%	Fresenius Med. Care	23%	Dassault Systèmes	34%	L'Oréal	45%	ENI	63%
Telefónica Móviles	0%	Suedzucker	24%	Essilor Intl.	34%	Sanofi-Synthélabo	45%	Red Eléc. de España	66%
Telekom Austria	0%	Fondiaria-Sai	24%	Banca Naz. Lavoro	34%	Valeo	45%	Total	67%
Thomson SA	0%	Luxottica	24%	Beiersdorf	35%	BASF	45%	Mediaset	67%
Zeltia	0%	Autogrill	25%	Nokia	35%	Pinault Printemps	46%	Air Liquide	67%
Altran Tech.	2%	UCB	25%	Banca Intesa	35%	Zodiac	47%	Lagardère Groupe	69%
Repsol	8%	Sacyr Vallehermosa	25%	Petróleos	36%	Bca Mte dei Paschi	47%	Atos Origin	70%
Puma	8%	Mediobanca	26%	Euronext	36%	Bco Pop. Español	47%	Mediolanum	71%
STMicroelectronics	9%	Grupo Ferrovial	26%	Air France	36%	Metro	48%	Christian Dior	74%
Allianz	10%	Erste Bank	26%	Bouygues	36%	DSM	49%	Bank of Piraeus	76%
Deutsche Börse	11%	Dexia	26%	Generali	36%	Casino Guichard-P	49%	EFG Eurobank Ergasias	76%
Neopost	12%	Bulgari	28%	Aventis	36%	CSM Cert.	49%	Mondadori	76%
BMW	14%	Gas Natural SDG	28%	Siemens	37%	BNP Paribas	49%	SNAM Rete Gas	79%
Inditex	16%	Cosmote Mobile	28%	Bca Pop. Milano	38%	Pernod-Ricard	50%	Banca Fideuram	85%
Agfa-Gevaert	19%	Italcementi	29%	Hermes Intl	38%	Akzo Nobel	50%	Accor	86%
Heineken	20%	Saipem	29%	Michelin	39%	Allied Irish Banks	50%	RCS Mediagroup	97%
Celanese	20%	Peugeot SA	29%	Deutsche Post	39%	Bco Espírito Santo	50%	ENEL	100%

Source: Datastream.

In 2003, around 10% of the 300 largest listed companies in Europe had paid no dividend. In the United States the proportions are quite different. Fama and French have established that although 66% of listed US companies were paying a dividend in 1978, only 21% were doing so in 1999. To be sure, the increase in the number of young, listed technology and Internet companies explains part of this trend. But even companies that pay dividends had declining payout ratios, because profitable investment opportunities abounded during the period and shareholders became convinced that increasing the retention ratio was a good choice. The growing popularity of stock option plans gave beneficiaries of those plans no incentive to have their company pay out more in dividends, since a high-payout ratio reduces the value of stock options.

The trend away from dividends has had a sharp reversal starting in 2000 (Julio and Ikenberry, 2004). A confluence of events has conspired of late to make bosses and investors think again about dividend policies. Investors have noticed the minimal amounts of cash they were earning from their shares. They have grown more sceptical about accounting profits in the wake of Enron and WorldCom and now wonder if evidence of profitability in the form of a dividend cheque might help them to sleep more easily. Some big firms have piled up so much cash that it seems to burn a hole in their pockets.

The now-passing unfashionability of dividends was most pronounced in America, where technology firms have seized on the idea that paying a dividend would indicate weakness, telling investors that they could not find profitable growth opportunities to use the money. As a result, maturing technology firms have come to own large cash piles: by 2004 Microsoft had $49bn, Cisco $8.5bn and Dell $5.4bn, for example. One of Europe's cash hoarders is Nokia, with over €12.1bn.

Reduced transaction costs mean shareholders who want cash can get it by selling shares; the cost of this alternative to receiving a dividend is no longer prohibitive. The current tax treatment, as we will see in Section IV of this book, does not encourage the payment of dividends. Lastly, the sharp rise in share prices over the past 20 years has made the returns from dividends seem insignificant in comparison with those realised from capital gains – another incentive for managers not to focus on an aggressive payout policy.

For these reasons, the payout ratio and the dividend growth rate (per share) are the only concrete parameters that are useful in analysing dividend policy.

As John Lintner (1956) has established, managers have a payout ratio target expressed in terms of future earnings, an absolute reference. For example, managers set an objective of distributing 45% of the company's earnings and try to keep fluctuations in the unit dividend as small as possible in the face of significant variations in earnings.

Thus, in 1993, payout ratios in Europe and the United States were quite high (60%), but the explanation has more to do with poor earnings than with any change in dividend policy. To avoid a cut in dividend per share, managers allowed the payout ratio to rise temporarily. The same phenomenon explains the rise in payout ratios in 2002.

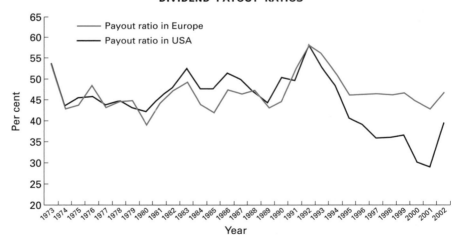

Some degree of regularity is desirable, either in earnings growth or in dividends paid out, so the company must necessarily choose an objective for the profile of dividends over time. For this purpose, dividend profiles can be classified in the following three categories:

- If earnings growth is regular, dividend policy is of lesser importance and the company can cut its payout ratio without risk.

- If earnings are cyclical owing to the nature of the business sector, it is important for the dividend to be kept steady. The company needs to retain enough manoeuvring room to ensure that phases of steady dividends are followed by phases of rising dividends.
- Lastly, a dividend that varies frequently conveys no useful information to the investor and may even suggest to him that the company's management has no coherent strategy for doing business in its sector. A profile of this kind can hardly have any beneficial effect on the share price.

A dividend policy must be credible – that is, consistent with the earnings that the company achieves. In the long term, no dividend profile, regardless of how smooth it is, can have favourable effects unless it appears sustainable. In other words, it must not be inconsistent or incompatible with the earnings profile.

In this regard, Koch and Sun (2004) have investigated whether a change in dividends alters investors' assessments about the valuation implications of part earnings. Results confirm the hypothesis that changes in dividends cause investors to revise their expectations about the persistence of part earnings changes.

Compare, for example, the dividend and earnings profiles since 1980 of two industrial groups: one, Nestlé, a growth company and the other, FIAT, a cyclical:

NESTLÉ (a) and FIAT (b)

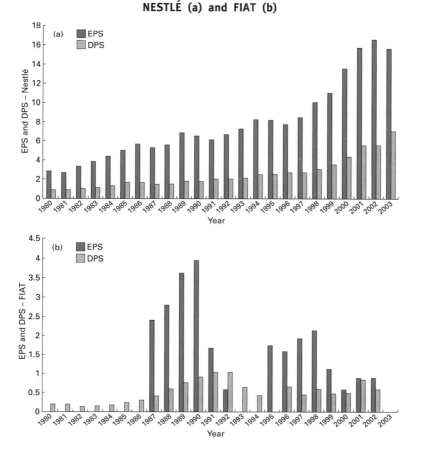

On the stock market, a high-payout ratio implies low-price volatility, *ceteris paribus*. This is easily demonstrated with the dividend discount valuation model. The share price of a company that pays out all its earnings in dividends will behave much like the price of a bond.

Here we re-encounter the concept of *duration*. The security with the highest duration will also have the highest volatility. A high-payout ratio tends to reduce duration and thereby makes the share price less volatile.

To be sure, the payout ratio is not the only determinant of a share's volatility.

For a company, paying out little or none of its earnings translates into growth in book value, an increase in market value and thus eventually into capital gains. To realise those gains, though, the shareholder has to sell. If selling the company's shares is a "crime" – and some managers come close to regarding it as one – then a low-dividend policy is an inducement to crime. A family-owned company that pays low dividends risks weakening its control.

A high-dividend policy, on the other hand, is certainly one way of retaining the loyalty of shareholders that have got used to the income and forget about the value. This tends to be particularly true of family shareholders without management roles in the company.

A financial holding company that wishes to pay dividends must either have received dividends itself from the companies in which it holds stakes or have realised potential capital gains by selling off some assets. A euro of dividends received goes directly onto the income statement and can therefore be redistributed. A euro of capital gain, in contrast, must be realised before it can go into earnings. There has to be a sale.

Brav et al. (2003) have surveyed 384 CFOs and Treasurers, conducting in-depth interviews with an additional two dozen, to determine the key factors that drive dividend and share repurchase policies. They have found that managers are very reluctant to cut dividends, that dividends are smoothed through time, and that dividend increases are tied to long-run sustainable earnings but much less so than in the past. Rather than increasing dividends, many firms use repurchases as an alternative. Paying out with repurchases is viewed by managers as being more flexible than using dividends, permitting a better opportunity to optimise investment. Managers like to repurchase shares when they feel their stock is undervalued and in an effort to affect EPS.[1] Dividend increases and the level of share repurchases are generally paid out of residual cash flow, after investment and liquidity needs are met. Financial executives believe that retail investors have a strong preference for dividends, in spite of the tax disadvantage relative to repurchases. In contrast, executives believe that institutional investors as a class have no strong preference between dividends and repurchases. In general, management views provide at most moderate support for agency, signalling and clientele hypotheses of payout policy. Tax considerations play only a secondary role.

1 *Earnings Per Share.*

2/HOW DIVIDENDS ARE PAID

(a) Advance dividend

This practice consists in paying a fraction of the forthcoming dividend in advance, whence the name. The decision is taken by the board of directors or the executive board and need not be approved by the AGM. An advance dividend offers a way of smoothing cash inflows to shareholders and cash outflows from the company. The advance is typically paid in December or January (midway between two annual dividend dates) and represents between a quarter and a half of the annual dividend.

In the United States, Canada and the United Kingdom, infra-annual dividends are common.

(b) Dividend paid in shares

Companies may offer shareholders a choice of receiving dividends in cash or in shares of the company.[2] The decision is taken by shareholders at the ordinary general meeting at which the accounts of the year are approved. However, the company's by-laws must specifically allow such a choice.

Paying the dividend in shares allows the company to make a distribution of earnings while retaining the corresponding cash funds.

There is no tax advantage for shares issued in payment of dividends. The value of the shares received is taxed as if it were paid in cash. A shareholder who chooses to be paid in the form of shares must therefore pay tax on the dividend without having received any cash, which may present a problem.

Offering to pay dividends in shares may lead to some limited redistribution of ownership among the shareholders, since some will accept and others will decline.

A share dividend represents no special financial advantage for shareholders other than the ability to reinvest dividends at no charge and generally at a slight discount to the market price (at most 10%). Some investors have no compunctions about taking payment of their dividends in shares and immediately selling those shares in order to pocket the discount. Manipulation of this kind drives down the price. For this reason, the practice, although quite popular in the early 1990s, has practically disappeared.

2 If its by-laws allow, a company may distribute shares that it holds in portfolio in place of a cash dividend. This is not the same as paying the dividend in its own shares.

(c) Preferential dividend

To reward loyal shareholders that have held their shares for more than 2 years, some companies (among them, for example, Air Liquide) have instituted the practice of paying a preferential dividend.

A preferential dividend can be established only by decision of an extraordinary general meeting and only when the company has issued securities such as convertible bonds or warrants that could give rise to new shares.

Lastly, we should mention once again preference shares (see Chapter 30), which have a higher dividend than ordinary shares.

A company may in certain circumstances buy back its own shares and either keep them on the balance sheet or cancel them, in which case there is said to be a **capital decrease** or **capital reduction**. Even when shares are repurchased but not cancelled, analysts will (in their own calculations) reduce the number of shares in circulation by the quantity of shares bought back.

Neglecting taxes, if one supposes that the company buys back shares from all shareholders in proportion to their holdings and then cancels those shares, the resulting capital decrease is strictly identical to the payment of a dividend. Cash is transferred from the company to the shareholders with no change in the structure of ownership.

As we will see below, however, an actual capital decrease cannot be egalitarian in this way. Furthermore, a capital decrease is likely to be a more exceptional event than payment of dividends.

We know that no earnings retention policy is attractive unless the company can invest its funds at a rate of return greater than or equal to the weighted average cost of capital. Let us take the reasoning here to its logical extreme. Every euro re-invested by the company must earn at least the rate of return required by providers of funds; if it does not, value will be destroyed. Rather than destroy value, it is better to return that euro to the owners. We can call this "decapitalisation".

From a theoretical viewpoint, when a business no longer has any investment projects that are sufficiently profitable, it should not only pay out all its earnings but also return all or part of its equity capital.

Equity capital is also needed to finance the risk of the business. Without it, the company could find itself in a serious cash crisis at the first downturn in the economy. On the other hand, when the company has acquired a strategic position in its market strong enough to ensure continued profitability and value, the normal course of action is to reduce equity financing and increase debt. Free cash flow has become sure enough to support the regular fixed repayments required on borrowings.

Equity capital serves to bear business risk. When that risk appears under control, equity can normally be replaced in part by debt capital.

1/DESCRIPTION

We will not be talking here of capital decreases that occur following an accounting determination that the book value of equity is insufficient. A capital reduction in this context may be required by law or undertaken voluntarily (to lower the par value of the share and make possible a new issue of shares as part of a recapitalisation). Since capital decreases of this kind do not result in an outflow of cash, they are altogether different, a matter of law and accounting rather than finance.

Our attention will be focused on capital decreases that correspond to an actual distribution of cash and subsequent cancellation of shares. From an economic standpoint, this is analysed as a reduction in equity capital, although from a tax standpoint, as we will see, it is treated as a distribution of assets.

A capital decrease corresponding to a distribution of cash can be accomplished in a number of ways:

➤ By reducing the par value of all shares, thereby automatically reducing authorised capital.

➤ For listed companies only, by buying back shares on the **open market**. In France and Italy, such repurchases are limited to 10% of the share capital and must be made as part of an authorised share buyback programme. The company must have published an information document about the programme approved by stock exchange authorities prior to its release. The programme may last no longer than 18 months. The shares acquired may be cancelled (up to a limit of 10% of the capital every 24 months) and the purchase cost deducted from the par value of the repurchased shares, with any excess cost charged against distributable reserves. The repurchased shares may also be kept in treasury by the company to serve as acquisition currency or to fulfil the exercise of stock options held by employees. Lastly, they can be sold on the open market for the purpose of stabilising the share price. If the shares are not cancelled, however, the repurchases cannot really be described as a capital decrease.

On the company's books, repurchased shares appear on the consolidated balance sheet as marketable securities if they were acquired for the purpose of stabilising the share price or fulfilling employee stock options. In all other cases, the purchase cost is subtracted from shareholders' equity. Under IASB[3] and US accounting standards, repurchased shares are always deducted from consolidated equity.

3 *International Accounting Standards Board*

➤ By **tender offer**. For a listed company in France, for example, this takes the form of a public share repurchase offer by the company for its own shares. In practice, the board of directors, using an authorisation that must have been granted to it at an extraordinary general meeting, makes an offer to all share-holders to buy all or part of their shares at a certain price during a certain period (usually about 1 month). If too many shares are tendered under the offer, the company scales back all the surrender requests in proportion. If too few are tendered, it cancels the shares that are tendered. If a management decides on a tender offer, it has the option of considering the traditional fixed price offering or the *Dutch auction method*. In Dutch auctions, the firm no longer offers to repurchase shares at a single price, but rather announces a *range* of prices. Each shareholder thus must specify an acceptable selling price within the prescribed range set by the company. If he chooses a high selling price, he will increase the proceeds provided the shares are accepted by the company, but he reduces the probability that shares will be accepted for repurchase. At the end of the offer period, the firm tabulates ''the book'' of received offers, and determines the lowest price that allows repurchasing the desired number of shares.

In some other European countries, a share buyback can be accomplished by issuing **put warrants** to each shareholder, each warrant giving the holder the right to sell one share to the company at a specified price. Such a warrant is a put option issued by the company. This technique has never been used in France, mainly for tax reasons.

A capital decrease changes the capital structure and thereby increases the risk borne by creditors. To protect the latter, the law generally allows creditors to require additional guarantees or call their loans early, although they cannot block the operation outright.

2/THEORETICAL ANALYSIS

Jagannathan et al. (2000) have measured the growth in open market stock repurchases and the manner in which stock repurchases and dividends are used by US corporations. Stock repurchases and dividends are used at different times from one another, by different kinds of firms. Stock repurchases are very pro-cyclical, while dividends increase steadily over time. Dividends are paid by firms with higher "permanent" operating cash flows, while repurchases are used by firms with higher "temporary", nonoperating cash flows.

4 However, Grullon and Michaely (2004) have recently found that repurchasing firms experience a significant reduction in systematic risk and cost of capital.

Repurchasing firms also have much more volatile cash flows and distributions.[4] Finally, firms repurchase stock following poor stock market performance and increase dividends following good performance. These results are consistent with the view that the flexibility inherent in repurchase programmes is one reason why they are sometimes used instead of dividends.

Several different considerations might explain why a company would buy back its own shares:

- Absence of opportunities to invest at the required rate of return. Managers therefore pass the funds to shareholders, who take it upon themselves to find investments elsewhere that meet their requirements.
- Signalling good news (managers believe the shares are undervalued).
- Increasing financial leverage, to take fuller advantage of the corresponding tax break.
- Direct tax incentive: if the object is to transfer cash from the business to shareholders, it is more tax-efficient to buy back shares than to pay a dividend.
- Hurting creditors: buying back shares increases the risk of the business and therefore diminishes the value of its debt (cf. Chapter 35). Creditors may try to block it.
- Transferring value between shareholders who decline the offer for reasons of power (they want to increase their stake in the company) and shareholders who agree to sell back their shares at a price exceeding their value.

Empirical analysis confirms that share buybacks are mainly undertaken for signalling purposes. On this point, Jagannathan et al. have established that, compared with dividends, share buybacks give little indication of future earnings. Companies that raise their dividends do in fact see their earnings increase, but this is not the case when companies buy back shares. In a way, declaring a dividend represents an undertaking by the company's managers to maintain that dividend, whereas a share buyback entails no such moral commitment. Thus, cyclical businesses are more likely to use share buybacks than businesses with steady growth.

Dittmar (2000) has investigated the relation between stock repurchases and distribution, investment, capital structure, corporate control and compensation policies over the 1977–1996 period. He finds that firms repurchase stock to take advantage of potential undervaluation and, in many periods, to distribute excess capital. However, firms also repurchase stock during certain periods to alter their leverage ratio, fend off takeovers and counter the dilution effects of stock options.

Grullon and Ikenberry (2000) argue that repurchases add value in two main ways:

1 for the tax efficiency in returning excess capital to shareholders;
2 for the signal managers send to investors about their belief that the company is undervalued.

If stock repurchase and dividends serve the same economic function, why is repurchasing popularity growing more rapidly? Basically for two reasons:

- they are a more efficient way of distributing excess capital taxwise;
- they provide corporate managers the flexibility to make small adjustments in the capital structure, in order to correct perceived undervaluation of the firm's shares.

We frequently see it argued that a capital decrease, by replacing a more costly form of financing (equity) with a less costly one (debt), lowers the weighted average cost of capital. The reader who has absorbed the lessons of Chapters 22 and 23 and understands that cost of capital is independent of capital structure (remember "the size of a pizza is the same no matter how you slice it"?) may be indulgent. To err is human; only to persist in error is diabolical!

A capital decrease by itself does not reduce a company's cost of capital and thus cannot create value. At best, it can avoid value destruction by preventing the company from investing cash at less than the cost of equity.

Only if the company managed to buy back its shares at less than they are worth could it hope to create value. The theory of markets in equilibrium leaves little hope of being able to do this.

A share buyback should nowadays be regarded as a normal transaction. The message that it "signals" is this: the company's managers take the shareholders' interest to heart and exceptionally, for want of adequate investment opportunities, they are paying out part of a large cash flow to avoid destroying value.

Because the announcement of a share buyback draws media attention, it probably has more impact than an increase in the dividend – even one that might signal a lasting change in the company's dividend policy.

Share buybacks are becoming a normal way of reallocating cash from mature businesses to newer sectors or faster growing companies.

3/SHARE BUYBACKS IN PRACTICE

Consider a company with a book value of equity of €400m, one million shares outstanding and earnings of €20m. Suppose that it reduces its share capital by 20% by buying back its own shares at their market value, in one case at €200 per share and in another case at €800 per share. It pays for the buyback by borrowing at 3% after tax (or by liquidating short-term investments earnings 3%, which amounts to the same thing).

BEFORE

Price per share	Book value of equity	Market value of equity	Earnings	Book value per share	EPS	P/E
€200	€400m	€200m	€20m	€400	€20	10
€800	€400m	€800m	€20m	€400	€20	40

AFTER

Price per share	Book value of equity	Market value of equity	Earnings	Book value per share	EPS	P/E
€200	€360m	€160m	€18.8m	€450 +12.5%	€23.5 +17.5%	8.5
€800	€240m	€640m	€15.2m	€300 −25%	€19 −5%	42.1

After the transaction, the book value of equity has decreased by the amount of funds spent on the repurchase – €40m in one case, €160m in the other – and so has the market value. Going forward, earnings are reduced by the additional interest charges. The relevant analysis, however, is at the per-share level. The repurchase is made at the current share price (or at current value, if the company is not quoted), possibly increased by a premium of 5% or 10% to induce holders to tender their shares under the offer.

With repurchase at €200, earnings per share increase by 17.5%, whereas book value per share increases by 12.5%. With repurchase at €800, earnings per share decrease by 5% whereas book value per share decreases by 25%.

More generally, repurchase of shares by the company results in:

- an increase in earnings per share (accretion) whenever the reciprocal of P/E is greater than the after-tax rate of interest paid on incremental debt (or earned on short-term debt securities). If E/P is less than the rate of interest, there is a decrease in earnings per share (dilution);
- an increase in the book value of equity per share whenever book value per share before the purchase is greater than the purchase price per share.

The transaction is thus the inverse of a capital increase, which should come as no surprise to the reader.

Bear in mind that, although the calculation of the change in earnings per share is of interest, it is not an indicator of value creation. The real issue is not whether a capital decrease will mechanically dilute earnings per share, but:

- whether the price at which the shares are repurchased is less than their estimated value;
- whether the increase in the debt burden will translate into better performance by management; and
- whether the marginal rate of return on the funds returned to shareholders by the buyback was less than the cost of capital.

These are the three sources of value creation in a capital decrease.

Section 38.4
TAXATION OF DIVIDENDS, SHARE BUYBACKS AND CAPITAL REDUCTION

1/TAXATION OF DIVIDENDS

(a) Dividend tax credit

As we have seen, the income tax borne by investors can reduce, eliminate or even reverse the advantage of debt financing conferred by the deductibility of interest expenses against the income tax borne by the company. Being nondeductible, dividends are taxed once by the corporate income tax on the company and a second time by the personal income tax on the shareholder. To avoid this double taxation, some countries have instituted an offsetting mechanism called the **dividend tax credit**, which is intended to neutralise the effect of corporate income tax at the level of the investor.

For certain categories of shareholders, therefore, there is no tax friction when dividends are paid, and this is important.

Lastly, when dividends are paid out of earnings that are either not subject to corporate income tax or taxed at a rate lower than the normal rate (such as capital gains), the company must pay a special equalisation tax. This tax is equal to 50% of the amounts paid (and thus offsets the dividend tax credit). It is payable only on distributions eligible for dividend tax credit. Equalisation tax is also owed when dividends are paid out of the earnings of accounting periods closed more than 5 years before.

2/TAXATION OF SHARE BUYBACKS

The way dividends are taxed can have wide-ranging consequences for how a firm is run. For an individual investor, the tax treatment depends on how his shares were sold. If they were bought back from him as part of a share buyback programme, the tax he must pay is the capital gains tax, as in a normal share sale. It may be remarked that, since the company bought the shares on the open market, it would be a complicated matter to subject the investor to any tax treatment different from that which would apply if he had sold to another investor. If the capital decrease was accomplished by a public share repurchase offer (not part of a buyback programme) or by reduction of the par value, the difference between the repurchase price and the investor's original acquisition price is deemed a dividend (without dividend tax credit, of course) and is taxed at the investor's marginal income tax rate.

Taxes largely explain the growing popularity of share buybacks compared with dividends. The firm may be indifferent between dividends and buybacks as a means of distributing profits, but many investors are not. In America and many other countries, dividends received by investors are taxed at a higher rate than capital gains, such as those created by share repurchases.

In most countries, tax rules allow firms to treat interest payments on debt as a tax-deductible expense, whereas cash payments to equity holders in the form of dividends or share repurchases come out of after-tax income. All else being equal, therefore, the tax system typically makes debt a cheaper source of finance for a firm at the margin rather than equity.

In recent years, governments almost everywhere have become increasingly concerned about the impact of taxation on companies. By and large, they have favoured tax reforms that are intended to boost business activity, such as cutting marginal tax rates – though in practice their reforms have often had unpredictable results.

Removing the tax disadvantage of paying dividends may force managers to find other plausible excuses for holding on to cash – or else to pay it out. This may make it harder for them to squander cash on ill-advised ventures such as, say, Microsoft's costly move into cable television.

Lastly, we note that the company may offer its shareholders cash or securities that it holds in portfolio. In the latter case, the company will owe capital gains tax on the difference between the value of the securities distributed and its tax basis for those securities (initial acquisition cost).

SUMMARY

download

Within the framework of equilibrium market theory, dividend policy has little importance. The shareholder is indifferent between receiving a dividend and letting the company reinvest the cash in assets that will earn the rate of return he requires. His wealth is the same in either case.

Signalling theory interprets dividends as information communicated by managers to investors about future earnings. A rise in the dividend signals good news, a cut signals bad news.

Agency theory interprets dividends as a means of mitigating conflicts between owners and managers. Paying a dividend reduces the amount of cash that managers are able to invest without much control on the part of shareholders. On the other hand, paying a dividend aggravates conflicts between owners and lenders when the amount of that dividend is significant.

All things considered, dividend policy should be judged on the basis of the company's marginal rate of return on capital employed. If that rate is above the weighted average cost of capital, the dividend can be low or nil because the company is creating value when it reinvests its earnings. If the marginal rate of return is below the cost of capital, shareholders are better off if the company distributes all its earnings to them.

As long as the company has opportunities to invest at a satisfactory return, managers set a target dividend payout ratio that will be higher or lower depending on whether the company has reached maturity or is still growing. Fluctuations in net earnings can be smoothed over in the per-share dividend so that it does not move erratically and send the wrong signal to investors.

The reader should not forget that, to some extent, dividend policy determines the composition of the shareholder body: paying no dividends leads to low loyalty on the part of shareholders, who must regularly sell shares to meet their needs for cash.

A capital decrease can take the form of either a reduction in the par value of all shares via distribution to shareholders of the corresponding amount of cash, or a buyback of shares in which shareholders are free to participate or not as they see fit.

A capital decrease may be undertaken for several different purposes: to return funds to shareholders when managers are unable to find investment projects meeting the shareholders' return requirements; to signal an undervalued share price; as an indirect means of increasing the percentage of control held by shareholders that do not take part in the buyback; or to distribute cash to shareholders at a lower tax cost than by paying a dividend.

The reduction in equity capital produces an increase in earnings per share if the reciprocal of the share's P/E ratio is higher than the after-tax interest rate paid on incremental debt (or forgone on short-term investments). But, make no mistake, this has only a remote association with value creation.

Debt-financed capital decreases are economically sound when they allow equity capital to be reallocated away from companies that have reached maturity and achieved predictable cash flows, towards newer companies that are still growing. They are a means of preventing overinvestment and haphazard diversification. However, they lead to value creation only if one or more of the following hold: the added debt burden constrains managers to achieve better performance; the shares are bought back at a price below their true value; or the funds returned to shareholders would have earned less than the cost of capital if kept in the company.

1/ What are the two criteria by which a dividend policy should be judged?

2/ Does an increase in the dividend result in an increase in the value of the share?

3/ Given tax neutrality, would you prefer to receive dividends or realise capital gains? Same question given the French tax system.

4/ According to signalling theory, what is indicated by maintaining the per-share dividend following a capital increase by incorporation of reserves?

5/ Is there a cost to the company of issuing bonus shares? Does such an issue change shareholder wealth? What purpose does it serve?

6/ Does a high dividend provide assurance of a stable share price? Why or why not?

QUESTIONS

quiz

7/ Can a company have a target dividend yield for its shareholders? Why or why not?

8/ On the record date of the dividend, the value of the share decreases instantly by the amount of the dividend. Is the shareholder worse off?

9/ What is the natural temptation of a company that is required to pay out 100% of its earnings, in terms of how much earnings it records?

10/ On what condition would you invest in a company that pays no dividend?

11/ A company that has not been paying dividends announces that it will pay one. How would you interpret this news according to (a) equilibrium market theory, (b) agency theory and (c) signalling theory?

12/ Is a manager who holds stock options in favour of a high-dividend policy? Why or why not?

13/ Do tobacco companies in Western countries have high-payout ratios? Why or why not?

14/ What signal is sent by paying a dividend in shares?

15/ Explain why a sharp increase in dividend often results in a decrease in the value of the company's borrowings.

16/ What is the impact of a debt-heavy capital structure on the payout ratio?

17/ In what circumstances does a company have good reason to have a capital decrease?

18/ Neglecting tax considerations, can a capital decrease enhance the value of the company's operating assets? The value of its shares?

19/ What difference do you see between payment of dividends and capital reduction?

20/ What is the necessary condition for a share buyback to increase earnings per share? To increase the book value of equity capital per share?

21/ What does a share buyback programme mean for the company's creditors?

22/ Under what conditions might a fast-growing company with opportunities to invest at a rate of return higher than its cost of capital have a capital decrease?

23/ Does a manager who holds stock options in the company prefer buybacks or dividends? Why?

EXERCISES

1/ On 24 May 2002, you observe the following data on Yahoo! Finance:

- ○   TotalFinaElf share price: €168.2
- ○   Net dividend per share: €3.8
- ○   Earnings per share: €10.82

Calculate TotalFinaElf's payout ratio and the gross yield and net yield on the company's shares. What do you think?

2/ What do you think of the dividend policies of the following companies.

		1997	1998	1999	2000	2001	2002	2003
A	EPS	100	115	131	150	160	165	167
	DPS	20	23	26	30	35	41	60
B	EPS	350	402	458	524	559	577	584
	DPS	70	80	92	105	112	115	117
C	EPS	100	50	0	−50	−50	0	50
	DPS	5	5	5	5	5	5	6
D	EPS	500	520	550	600	500	400	300
	DPS	100	80	70	100	120	150	200

3/ Gassoumi plc has the following characteristics:

- ○ Net earnings: €100m
- ○ Number of shares: 1,000,000
- ○ Market price per share: €1,000
- ○ Book value of equity: €1,200m
- ○ EPS: €100
- ○ Book value per share: €1,200

The company decides to take advantage of a sudden stock market slump by buying back a quarter of its shares at a price of €500 per share. Its after-tax cost of debt is 5%.

Calculate EPS and book value per share. Same question if the buyback price is €1,500 per share. What do you conclude?

4/ Rowak plc is a Syldavian industrial company listed on the Klow Stock Exchange. The number of shares in issue has been constant over the period at one million. The corporate income tax rate is 33%.

(a) Calculate Rowak's after-tax ROCE and ROE in each year. What do you think?
(b) What do you think of the fact that Rowak has never paid a dividend?
(c) In early September 2000, the company's market capitalisation is 200 million, and its managers believe the shares are worth 150 each. Rowak's chairman proposes to the board of directors that 50 million be devoted to buying back (and cancelling) outstanding shares. The programme is to be financed by borrowing at 10% before tax. The board of directors refuses. Why, in your opinion?
(d) In December 2002, the company's market capitalisation has fallen to 90 million (still with the same number of shares in issue) and the estimated value of the share is 120. Rowak's chairman puts forward his proposal again. What do you think now?

(figures in millions)	Revenue	Net profit	Pre-tax interest expenses	Book value of equity	Net debt	Market capitalisation
1997	170	8	9	50	60	55
1998	130	10	10	60	70	90
1999	170	11	10	71	75	152
2000	220	13	9	84	76	195
2001	230	13	7	97	70	210
2002	240	13	6	110	65	90

ANSWERS

Questions

1/ Dividend growth rate and payout ratio.

2/ Not according to equilibrium market theory, but it could be a positive signal.

3/ According to equilibrium market theory, you should not care; according to agency theory, you should prefer dividends. If your marginal income tax rate is more than 44%, you should prefer capital gains.

4/ The company expects to maintain its profitability.

5/ The company does not gain or lose. An issue of bonus shares does not increase shareholder wealth. It can improve liquidity by increasing the number of shares in circulation. It can be a positive signal if the dividend per share is maintained.

6/ A high dividend helps to ensure stability of the share price but in no way guarantees it.

7/ No, because the shareholder determines what yield he chooses to receive.

8/ No. The shares are worth less, but the shareholder receives the difference in cash. If this were not the case, there would be arbitrage opportunities.

9/ Conceal earnings to avoid having to pay them out in dividends and thereby maximise internal financing.

10/ If the marginal rate of return on capital employed is greater than the weighted average cost of capital.

11/ (a) Indifferent.

(b) Agency costs are reduced because managers will have less opportunity for uncontrolled investment.

(c) Growth is slowing.

12/ No, because high dividends hold down the price of the shares on which the manager holds stock options.

13/ Yes, because their growth prospects are weak (and also to get their shareholders addicted, like their customers!).

14/ The company does not have the cash to pay a cash dividend!

15/ Because there is a transfer of value from creditors, whose claims on the company become riskier, to shareholders.

16/ Reduces the payout ratio because there are periodic interest and principal payments to be made.

17/ Whenever the marginal rate of return on its investments is less than the rate of return required by its shareholders.

18/ There will be a reduction in the informational asymmetry and a consequent increase in value.

19/ *Fundamentally, the two are the same, but the dividend goes to all shareholders whereas the capital reduction may be reserved for only some of them. The tax treatment may also be different.*

20/ *EPS increase whenever the reciprocal of P/E is higher than the after-tax interest rate on debt (or short-term investments). Depends on the ratio of price to book value (PBR).*

21/ *An increase in risk borne by them.*

22/ *If its shares are particularly undervalued.*

23/ *He prefers buybacks because paying a dividend reduces the value of the shares and therefore the value of his stock options.*

Exercises

1/ *d = 3.8/10.8 = 35%; gross yield: 3.8 = 1.5/168.2 = 3.4%; net yield: 2/160 = 1.25%. Average dividend level is that of a company approaching maturity.*

2/ *A: fast growth has been slowing, payout ratio increasing. This is fairly logical. B: same growth pattern, but payout ratio is constant. This is surprising because the marginal rate of return has become very low (1.6% in 2003) and is surely below the cost of capital. C: cyclical company that keeps its dividend per share steady. Payout ratio is very low at the top of the cycle (5%) and very high at the bottom (>100%). D: No coherent dividend policy at all.*

3/ *At a cost of €500 per share: repurchase amount is €125m. Associated interest costs =€6.25m. EPS after the repurchase =€125. Book value per share =€1,433. At a cost of €1,500 per share: EPS =€108.3; book value per share =€1,100.*

4/ *(a)*

	1997	1998	1999	2000	2001	2002
ROE	12.7	12.8	12.1	11.9	10.6	9.7
ROCE	16	16.7	15.5	15.5	13.4	11.8

Returns on equity and capital employed have declined, reducing the leverage effect and the company's financial risk.

(b)

	1998	1999	2000	2001	2002
ΔEarnings/ΔEquity	20%	9.1%	15.4%	0	0

The dividend policy Rowak has been following (no dividend) was consistent with its situation until 2000 since it was getting adequate returns on reinvested earnings. This is no longer the case. Earnings are not growing, and shareholders are becoming relatively poorer.

(c) Why would you want to pay 200 for shares that you believe are worth 150?

(d) The proposal makes sense now because a gross disequilibrium in the market means the shares can be bought back at a price below their estimated value.

Overview of the dividend policy problem:

F. Black, The dividend puzzle, *Journal of Portfolio Management*, 634–639, Summer 1976.

L. Brav, J. Graham, C. Harvey, R. Michaely, *Payout Policy in the 21st Century*, working paper, National Bureau of Economic Research, April 2003.

BIBLIOGRAPHY

R. Lease, K. John, A. Kalay, U. Loewenstein, O. Sarig, *Dividend Policy*, Harvard Business School Press, 2000.

Equilibrium markets:

M. Miller, F. Modigliani, Dividend policy, growth, and the valuation of shares, *Journal of Business*, **34**, 411–433, January 1961.

M. Miller, M. Scholes, Dividends and taxes, *Journal of Financial Economics*, **6**, 332–364, December 1978.

Empirical studies:

P. Asquith, D. Mullins, The impact of initiating dividend payments on shareholders' wealth, *Journal of Business*, 77–96, January 1983.

F. Black, M. Scholes, The effect of dividend yield and dividend policy on common stock prices and returns, *Journal of Financial Economics*, 1–22, May 1974.

The Economist, The dividend puzzle, 9 January 2003.

E. Fama, K. French, Disappearing dividends: Changing firm characteristics or lower propensity to pay? *Journal of Financial Economics*, **60**, 3–43, April 2001.

B. Julio, D. Ikenberry, Reappearing dividends, *Journal of Applied Corporate Finance*, **16**(4), 89–100, Fall 2004.

J. Lintner, Distribution of incomes of corporations among dividends, retained earnings and taxes, *American Economic Review*, **46**(2), 97–116, May 1956.

Signalling theory:

J. Baskin, Dividend policy and the volatility of common stocks, *Journal of Portfolio Management*, **15**, 19–25, Summer 1989.

S. Benartzi, R. Michaely, R. Thaler, Do changes in dividends signal the future or the past? *Journal of Finance*, **52**(3), 1007–1034, July 1997.

A. Koch, A. Sun, Dividend changes and the persistence of part earnings changes, *Journal of Finance*, **49**(5), 2093–2118, October 2004.

M. Miller, The information content of dividends, in J. Bossons, R. Dornbush, S. Fisher (eds), *Macroeconomics: Essays in Honor of Franco Modigliani*, MIT Press, 1987.

A. Ofer, D. Siegel, Corporate financial policy, information and market expectations: An empirical investigation of dividends, *Journal of Finance*, 889–911, September 1987.

Agency theory:

S. Bhattacharya, Imperfect information, dividend policy and the bird in the hand fallacy, *Bell Journal of Economics*, 259–270, Summer 1979.

F. Easterbrook, Two agency-cost explanations of dividends, *American Economic Review*, **74**, 650–659, September 1984.

P. Healy, G. Paloque, Earnings information conveyed by dividend initiations and omissions, *Journal of Financial Economics*, **21**, 149–176, September 1988.

M. Jensen, W. Meckling, A theory of the firm: Managerial behavior, agency cost and ownership structure, *Journal of Financial Economics*, **3**, 305–360, October 1976.

R. La Porta, F. Lopez-de-Silanes, A. Shleifer, Agency problems and dividend policies around the world, *Journal of Finance*, **55**(1), 1–33, February 2000.

S. Myers, Outside equity, *Journal of Finance*, **55**(3), 1005–1037, June 2000.

M.S. Rozeff, Growth, beta, and agency costs as determinants of dividend payout ratios, *Journal of Financial Research*, **5**, 249–259, Autumn 1982.

Share buybacks:

L. Dann, Common stock repurchases: An analysis of returns to bondholders and stockholders, *Journal of Financial Economics*, **9**, 113–138, June 1981.

A. Dittmar, Why do firms repurchase stocks? *Journal of Business*, **73**(3), 331–355, July 2000.

G. Grullon, D. Ikenberry, What do we know about stock repurchases? *Journal of Applied Corporate Finance*, **13**(1), 31–51, Spring 2000.

G. Grullon, R. Michaely, The information content of share repurchase programs, *Journal of Finance*, **59**(2), 651–680, April 2004.

B. Hausch, D. Logue, J. Seward, Dutch auction share repurchases: Theory and evidence, in D. Chew (ed.), *The New Corporate Finance: Where Theory Meets Practice*, 2nd edn, McGraw-Hill, 1999.

M. Jagannathan, C. Stephens, M. Weisbach, Financial flexibility and the choice between dividends and stock repurchases, *Journal of Financial Economics*, **57**, 355–384, September 2000.

R. Masulis, Stock repurchase by tender offer: An analysis of the cause of common stock price changes, *Journal of Finance*, **35**(2), 305–319, May 1980.

W. McNally, Open market stock repurchase signaling, *Financial Management*, **28**(2), 55–67, Summer 1999.

B. Soter, E. Brigham, P. Evanson, The dividend cut "heard 'round the world": The case of FPL, in D. Chew (ed.), *The New Corporate Finance: Where Theory Meets Practice*, 2nd edn, McGraw-Hill, 1999.

T. Vermaelen, Repurchases, tender offers, signaling and managerial incentives, *Journal of Financial and Quantitative Analysis*, **19**(2), 163–181, June 1984.

Other articles:

T. Koller, S. Foushee, Much ado about dividends, *McKinsey Quarterly*, **2**, 157–159, 2003.

Chapter 39
CAPITAL INCREASES

There are no victories at bargain prices

The previous chapters have already begun our study of equity financing. This chapter analyses the consequences for the shareholder of a capital increase via an issue of new shares for cash. Capital increases resulting from mergers and acquisitions will be dealt with in Chapters 42 and 43.

Section 39.1
A DEFINITION OF CAPITAL INCREASE

1/A CAPITAL INCREASE IS A SALE OF SHARES . . .

A capital increase is first of all a **sale of shares**. But who is the seller? The **current shareholder**. The paradox is that the seller receives no money. As we will see in this chapter, **to avoid diluting his stake in the company at the time of a capital increase, the shareholder must subscribe to the same proportion of the new issue that he holds of the pre-existing shares.** Only if he subscribes to more than that is he (from the standpoint of his own portfolio) buying additional control; if less, he is selling control.

To this point, we have presented market value as a sanction on the company's management, an external judgement that the company can ignore so long as its shareholders are not selling out and it is not asking them to stump up more money. A capital increase, which conceptually is a sale of shares at market value, has the effect of reintroducing this value sanction via the company's treasury – i.e., its cash balance. **For the first time, market value, previously an external datum, interferes in the management of the company.**

2/ . . . THE PROCEEDS OF WHICH GO TO THE COMPANY, AND THUS INDIRECTLY TO ALL OF ITS INVESTORS . . .

This may seem paradoxical, but it is not. The proceeds of the capital increase indeed go to the company. Shareholders will benefit to the extent that the additional funds enable the company to develop its business and thereby increase its earnings. Creditors will see their claims on the company made less risky and therefore more valuable.

3/... WHICH IMPLIES SHARING BETWEEN OLD AND NEW SHAREHOLDERS

When a company issues bonds or takes out a loan from a bank, it is selling a "financial product". It is contracting to pay interest at a fixed or indexed rate and repay what it has borrowed on a specified schedule. As long as it meets its contractual obligations, the company does not lose its *autonomy*.

In contrast, when a company issues new shares, the old shareholders are agreeing to share their rights to the company's equity capital (which is increased by the proceeds of the issue), their rights to its future earnings and their control over the company itself with the new shareholders.

A capital increase is simply a sale of shares. It implies sharing the parameters of the company. The magnitude of this sharing depends on the market value of the equity capital, but it applies to a cake made larger by the proceeds of the capital increase.

To illustrate, consider a company E with equity capital worth €1,000m split between two shareholders, F (80%) and G (20%).

If G sells his entire shareholding (€200m) to H, neither the value nor the proportion of F's equity in the company is changed. If, on the other hand, H is a new shareholder brought in by means of a capital increase, H will have to put in €250m to obtain a 20% interest, rather than €200m as previously, since the value of equity after a capital increase of €250m is €1,250m (1,000 + 250). The new shareholder's interest is indeed 20% of the larger amount. **Percentage interests should always be reckoned on the value including the newly issued shares.**

After this capital increase has been made to the €1,000m base, the value of F's shareholding in the company is the same as it was (€800m) but his ownership percentage has decreased from 80% to 64% (800/1,250), while G's has decreased from 20% to 16%.

We see that if a shareholder does not participate in a capital increase, his percentage interest declines. This effect is called **dilution**.

In contrast, if the capital increase is reserved entirely for F, his percentage interest in the company rises from 80% to 84% (1,050/1,250), and the equity interest of all other shareholder(s) is necessarily diluted.

Lastly, if F and G each take part in the capital increase in exact proportion to their current shareholding, **the market value of equity no longer matters** in this one particular case. Their ownership percentages remain the same, and each puts up the same amount of funds for new shares regardless of the market value. This is illustrated in the table[1] at the top of the next page for equity values of €500m, €1,000m and €2,000m. In effect, F and G are selling new shares to themselves.

1 *The figures in parentheses indicate cash flows: positive means an inflow, negative an outflow.*

(€ million)	Value of equity in E	Value of shares held by F	Value of shares held by G	Value of shares held by H
Before capital increase	1,000	800 or 80%	200 or 20%	
G sells 20% of the shares to H for 200	1,000	800 or 80%	0 or 0% (+200)	200 or 20% (−200)
H subscribes to a cash capital increase of 250	1,250	800 or 64%	200 or 16%	250 or 20% (−250)
G sells 20% of the shares to F for 200	1,000	1,000 or 100% (−200)	0 or 0% (+200)	
F subscribes to a cash capital increase of 250	1,250	1,050 or 84% (−250)	200 or 16%	
F and G subscribe to a cash capital increase of 250 in proportion to their ownership percentage at different initial values of equity (1,000, 2,000 and 500, respectively)	1,250 2,250 750	1,000 or 80% (−200) 1,800 or 80% (−200) 600 or 80% (−200)	250 or 20% (−50) 450 or 20% (−50) 150 or 20% (−50)	

Section 39.2
CAPITAL INCREASES AND FINANCE THEORY

1/CAPITAL INCREASES AND MARKETS IN EQUILIBRIUM

A capital increase is analysed first and foremost as a sale of new shares at a certain price. If that price is equal to the true value of the share, there is no creation of value, nor is any current shareholder made worse off. This is an obvious point that is easily lost sight of in the analysis of financial criteria that we will get to later on.

If the new shares are sold at a high price (more than their value), the company will have benefited from a low-cost source of financing to the detriment of its most recent shareholders. The Internet companies that were able to raise money on very advantageous terms until early 2000 can be cited as an example.

Recall that the cost entailed by a capital increase is neither the immediate return on the stock nor the accounting rate of return on equity. It is the rate of return required by shareholders given the market valuation of the stock (see Chapter 22 for determination of the cost of equity).

As we have seen, however, this cost is eminently variable. The sanction for not meeting it is that, other things equal, the value of the share will decline. The company will be worth less, but in the short term there will be no impact on its treasury.

2/TAXATION

A cash capital increase generally results in immediate de-leveraging, making the capital structure less advantageous from a tax standpoint. But the equity injection is usually part of a plan to achieve a new capital structure. For this reason, the tax factor is not a fundamental parameter of a capital increase.

3/SHAREHOLDERS AND CREDITORS

For a company in financial difficulty, a capital increase results in a transfer of value from shareholders to creditors, since the new money put in by the former enhances the value of the claims held by the latter. According to the contingent claims model, the creditors of a "risky" business are able to appropriate most of the increase in the company's value due to an injection of additional funds by shareholders. The value of the put option sold by creditors to shareholders has a lower value. This is the reason that recovery plans for troubled companies always link any new equity financing to prior or concomitant concessions on the part of lenders.

Recapitalisation increases the intrinsic value of the equity and thereby reduces the riskiness of the company, thus increasing the value of its debt as well. Creditors run less risk by holding that debt. This effect is perceptible, though, only if the value of debt is close to the value of operating assets – that is, only if the debt is fairly high-risk.

4/SHAREHOLDERS AND MANAGERS

A capital increase is generally a highly **salutary** thing to do because it helps to reduce the asymmetry of information between shareholders and managers. A call on the market for fresh capital is accompanied by a series of disclosures on the financial health of the company and the profitability of the investments that will be financed by the capital increase. This practice effectively clears management of suspicion and reduces the agency costs of divergence between their interest and the interest of outside shareholders. A capital increase thus encourages managers to manage in a way that maximises shareholders' interest.

The reader will already have applied the line of reasoning above – so familiar has it become by now. What is new here is the conflict between old and new shareholders, under the cover of the oft-repeated hypocrisy that "we are all partners" in the same company.

5/CAPITAL INCREASE AS A SIGNAL

If one assumes that managers look out for the interests of current shareholders, it is hard to see how they could propose a capital increase when the share price is undervalued.

If one believes in asymmetry of information, a capital increase ought to be a signal that the share price is overvalued. A capital increase may be a sign that managers believe the company's future cash flows will be less than what is reflected in the current share price. The management team takes advantage of the overvaluation by issuing new shares. The funds provided by the capital increase will then serve not to finance new investments but to make up for the cash shortfall due to lower-than-expected operating cash flows.

Furthermore, as we have already noted, a capital increase implies a change in capital structure. Following the injection of new funds, financial leverage is appreciably decreased. The company's risk diminishes, and there is a transfer of value from shareholders to creditors; the value of the company's shares does not increase by the full value of the funds that are raised.

In practice, the announcement of a capital increase produces a downward adjustment of 3–5% in the share price. Only the old shareholders suffer this diminution of value. Three major explanations have been proposed for this regularity:

- Some claim that this effect is due to the negative consequences of the capital increase on the company's accounting ratios. We do not think so.
- Others explain it by invoking a market mechanism: a product sells for a bit less when there is a larger quantity of it; "you catch more flies with honey than with vinegar".
- Lastly, still others explain it as being due to the negative signal that a capital increase sends. The reader who wants to raise fresh capital for his company should take this effect into account and be able to respond in advance to the criticisms.

download

CAPITAL INCREASES IN 2002 (US$000,000)

Source: World Federation of Exchanges.

Section 39.3
OLD AND NEW SHAREHOLDERS

1/DILUTION OF CONTROL

Returning to the examples given above, we see that there is dilution of control – that is, reduction in the percentage equity interest of certain shareholders, whenever those shareholders do not subscribe to an issue of new shares in proportion to their current shareholding.

The dilution is greatest for any shareholder that does not participate at all in the capital increase. It is nil for any shareholder that subscribes in proportion to his holding. By convention, we will say that:

Dilution of control is the reduction of rights in the company sustained by a shareholder for which the capital increase entails neither an outflow nor an inflow of funds.

Recall that if new shares are issued at a price significantly below their value, current shareholders will usually have pre-emptive subscription rights that enable them to buy the new shares at that price. This right of first refusal is itself tradable and can be acquired by investors that would like to become shareholders on the occasion of the capital increase.

In the absence of subscription rights, the calculation of dilution of control by a capital increase is straightforward:

$$\frac{\text{Number of new shares}}{\text{Number of old shares} + \text{Number of new shares}}$$

When the capital increase is made with an issue of pre-emptive subscription rights, this calculation no longer holds.

With a rights issue of this kind, we have to distinguish between three measures of dilution. *The most important of these is **real dilution**, which is equivalent to what we just now called dilution (with no modifier) in the absence of pre-emptive subscription rights.*

(a) Apparent dilution

Any capital increase with subscription rights gives rise to **apparent dilution** (sometimes called "overall dilution"), which is expressed by the ratio:

$$\frac{\text{Number of new shares}}{\text{Number of old shares} + \text{Number of new shares}} = \frac{N'}{N + N'}$$

In the case of a rights issue, this degree of dilution is only apparent because it is the result of two distinct transactions:

- a capital increase in the strict sense; and
- a detachment of subscription rights, which is analysed as a distribution of bonus shares.

As we saw in Chapter 34, subscription rights enable current shareholders to participate partially in the capital increase with no outlay of funds. As a result, the dilution of their ownership is not as great as the apparent dilution would make it appear.

We therefore need to calculate only the dilution due solely to the capital increase, independently of the subscription rights mechanism. This degree of dilution is called **real dilution** and, in the analysis of the capital increase, real dilution is what we are interested in knowing.

(b) Real dilution

Real dilution is the dilution of control that occurs when the capital increase is cash-neutral for a shareholder that, on balance, neither pays nor receives any funds: the shareholder sells a portion of his subscription rights in order to buy new shares.

Method 1   The simplest way to calculate real dilution is to reckon on an aggregate basis rather than per share. Real dilution is then calculated as follows:

$$\text{Real dilution} = \frac{\text{Proceeds of capital increase}}{\text{Value of equity before capital increase} + \text{Proceeds of capital increase}}$$

Method 2   Regardless of the formal issue price, the existence of subscription rights ensures that the capital increase will always be subscribed at the company's market value. Every new shareholder will have to pay the issue price and the price of one or more rights in order to obtain one new share. Therefore, to calculate real dilution eliminating the bias due to subscription rights, one need only assume that the issue price is equal to the market value of the shares.

The theoretical number n' of shares that would have been issued under these conditions is:

$$n' = \frac{\text{Proceeds of the issue}}{\text{Market value of each share}}$$

Real dilution is then equal to $n'/(N + n')$ where n' is the number of shares that would have brought in the same funds if the issue price had been equal to the market value.

(c) Technical dilution

Technical dilution is apparent dilution less real dilution. It is due to the distribution of "free" bonus shares that automatically accompanies any capital increase via a rights issue.

Technical dilution represents the additional dilution attributable to the sale of subscription rights by shareholders who take the occasion of the capital increase to reduce their investment in the company.

As with any distribution of bonus shares, the various parameters of the company – earnings per share, dividend per share, value of the share – must be adjusted to correct for this technical aspect of the operation, which in no way changes the value of the company.

2/ ANTICIPATION MECHANISM

Take the example of a highly profitable company, entirely equity-financed, that now has investments of 100. With these investments, the company is on track to be worth 400 in 4 years, which corresponds to an annual rate of return on equity of 41.4%. Suppose that this company can invest an additional 100 at a rate of return similar to that on its current investments. To finance this additional capital requirement, it must sell new shares. Suppose also that the shareholder-required rate of return is 10%.

Before the company announces the capital increase and before the market anticipates it, the value of its equity capital 4 years hence is going to be 400, which, discounted at 10%, is 273 today.

If, upon the announcement of the capital increase, management succeeds in convincing the market that the company will indeed be worth 800 in 4 years, which is 546 today, the value accruing to current shareholders is $546 - 100 = 446$. There is thus instantaneous value creation of 173 $(446 - 273)$ for the old shareholders.

The anticipation mechanism operates in such a way that new shareholders will not receive an excess rate of return. They will get only the return they require, which is 10%. If the intended use of funds is clearly indicated when the capital increase is announced, the share price *before* the capital increase will reflect the investment opportunities, and only the old shareholders will benefit from the value creation due to future investments.

Some share prices that show very high P/E ratios are merely reflecting anticipations of exceptional investment opportunities. The 400 of added value in this example is already priced in. The reader will even be able to observe companies whose share prices are at times so high that they cannot correspond to growth opportunities financed in the traditional way by operating cash flow and borrowing. The shareholders of these companies have placed a bet on the internal and external growth opportunities the company may be able to seize, as it may have done in the past, financed in part by issuing new shares.

Section 39.4
CAPITAL INCREASES AND FINANCIAL CRITERIA

In this section, we reckon only in terms of adjusted figures. The example we use is the capital increase by Pierre & Vacances in early 2002.

PIERRE & VACANCES CAPITAL INCREASE

Pre-increase data

Number of shares:	7,651m
Share price:	€68.45
Market capitalisation:	€524m
Book value of equity:	€133m
Earnings per share, 2002 estimate:	€3.87

Post-increase data

Number of new shares issued:	850,000
Issue price:	€67.5
Proceeds of the issue:	€57.375m
Pre-emptive subscription right:	Not applicable
Offer period:	11 March to 20 March 2002
Eligibility date of new shares:	1 October 2001

NB. The reader must not confuse the amount of the capital increase in the financial sense – that is, the amount of funds raised – which is €57.375m for Pierre & Vacances in the legal and accounting sense of the term.

Accountants and lawyers are accustomed to apportioning the proceeds of a capital increase between the increase in authorised capital (the number of new shares issued multiplied by the par value of the share; for Pierre & Vacances, the par value is €3.05, and the increase in authorised capital is therefore €2.592m) and the increase in the share premium account (the remainder). Since the reader knows how to distinguish between the €2.6m and the €57.4m, we are confident he will know how to distinguish between the two meanings of "capital increase".

1/CAPITAL INCREASE AND EARNINGS PER SHARE

A capital increase will change earnings per share instantaneously. If EPS decreases, there is said to be **dilution** of earnings; if it increases, there is said to be **accretion** (or the operation is said to be "earnings-enhancing", which may sound better). This dilution has nothing in common with the dilution of Part One of this section other than the name, and is calculated differently. The one has to do with a shareholder's percentage of ownership, the other with earnings per share.

Consider Pierre & Vacances, whose shares carry a mid-range P/E (17.4) warranted by the company's moderate risk and reasonable growth prospects, and company A, whose very weak prospects of EPS growth justify a low P/E (8.0). For both companies, shareholders require an after-tax rate of return on equity of 9%, and we will assume that both Pierre & Vacances and company A invest the funds raised by a capital increase at 9%; there is neither creation nor destruction of value on this occasion. For both, the value of equity capital therefore increases by the amount of the capital increase.

Pierre & Vacances and company A each increase the number of shares by 10% and raise €57.4m, which, invested at 9%, will increase their net earnings by 5. The impact of the capital increase will be as shown in the table below.

	Before capital increase					After capital increase			
	Book value of equity	P/E	Earnings	Number of shares	EPS	Book value of equity	Earnings	Number of shares	EPS
Pierre & Vacances	€524m	17.4	€29.6m	7,651m	€3.87	€581m	€34.8m	8,501m	€4.09 (+6%)
Company A	€524m	8	€65.5m	7,651m	€8.56	€581m	€70.7m	8,501m	€8.32 (−3%)

Pierre & Vacances's EPS increases by 6% but the operation does not create value. Similarly, company A's EPS decreases by 3% but the operation does not destroy value. This demonstrates once again that earnings per share are not a reliable indicator of value creation or destruction. These changes are merely mechanical and depend fundamentally on:

- the company's P/E ratio; and
- the rate of return on the investments made with the proceeds of the capital increase.

More generally, the rule the reader will want to retain is that any capital increase will:

- **dilute** EPS whenever the reciprocal of P/E is greater than the rate of return on the investments financed by the capital increase;
- **be neutral** whenever the reciprocal of P/E is equal to this incremental ROCE;[2] and
- increase or "**enhance**" EPS whenever the reciprocal of P/E is less than incremental ROCE.

2 *Return On Capital Employed.*

It can easily be demonstrated that the earnings dilution occasioned by a capital increase at the market price is equal to:

$$\text{Change in } EPS = P/E \times \frac{\text{Capital raised}}{\text{Market capitalisation after capital increase}}$$
$$\times \left(\text{After-tax rate of return} - \frac{E}{P} \right)$$

For Pierre & Vacances, any investment that generates a return per year greater than 5.7% (the reciprocal of P/E of 17.4) will increase earnings per share, whereas for company *A* the bar is set higher at 12.5% (reciprocal of 8). Hence the appeal of issuing new shares when P/Es are high, even though no value is created.

In the short term, it is rare for funds raised by a capital increase to earn the required rate of return immediately, either because they are sitting in the bank waiting for the investments to be made or because some period of time must elapse before the achieved rate of return reaches the required level. Consequently, it is not rare for EPS to decrease following a capital increase – but this does not necessarily mean that value is being destroyed.

Three measures of EPS dilution might be distinguished here:

1   Instantaneous dilution with no reinvestment of the funds raised. This is seldom calculated because it holds no interest.
2   Dilution assuming investment of the funds at the risk-free rate of interest. This is the measure that financial analysts generally calculate.
3   Dilution with reinvestment of the funds. This is obviously the measure of most interest, but it is difficult to get hold of because it requires forecasting the rate of return on future investments.

In the long term, EPS dilution should normally be offset by the earnings generated by the investment financed by the capital increase. It is therefore necessary to study the expected rate of return on that investment, for it will determine the future course of the company's value.

With the wisdom that derives from experience, and notwithstanding what any theory might indicate, we could almost say that whenever P/Es are high, it is a crime for a company not to issue new shares!

2/CAPITAL INCREASE AND VALUE OF EQUITY CAPITAL

To say that the book value of a company's equity increases after a capital increase is to state the obvious, since the proceeds of the share issue are included in that book value.

It is of more interest to compare the percentage increase in book value with the ratio of the proceeds of the capital increase to the market value of equity and to calculate the growth in value per share.

Let us go back to the example of Pierre & Vacances and make several different assumptions about market value (only the last of which is true). In all cases, we set the proceeds of the capital increase at the actual percentage level, which is 11% of the group's market capitalisation before the operation.

	Case 1	Case 2	Case 3 (real)
Book value of equity	€133m	€133m	€133m
Market value of equity	€100m	€133m	€524m
Capital increase	€11m	€15m	€57m
Dilution	10%[3]	10%	10%
Increase in book value	+8%	+11%	+43%

3 $0.85/(0.85 + 7.651)$.

At constant capital structure, the increase in equity allows a parallel increase in debt and thus in the company's overall financial resources. This phenomenon is all the more important when the company is profitable and its market value is greater than its book value. Here we link up again to the PBR (Price-to-Book Ratio) notion that we examined in Chapter 28.

A capital increase may increase a company's financial power considerably, with relatively little dilution of control.

- If the market value of equity coincides with book value, the dilution of control will be accompanied by a similar increase in the company's overall financial resources.
- If the market value is greater than book value, the dilution of control will be countered by a greater increase in financial resources.
- If the market value is less than book value, the dilution of control will be accompanied by a lesser increase in financial resources.

3/BOOK VALUE PER SHARE

Let us continue with the example of Pierre & Vacances, this time changing the issue price of the new shares but keeping the size of the issue at 850,000 shares.

Issue price	€12.9	€17.4	€67.5
Book value per share before capital increase	€17.4	€17.4	€17.4
Book value per share after capital increase	€16.9 (−3%)	€17.4 (0%)	€22.4 (+29%)

At the time of a capital increase, book value per share increases if the share price is greater, and decreases if the share price is less, than book value before the capital increase. This is self-evident since in the one case the issue price is higher than book value per share and in the other case it is lower.

This increase or decrease also applies to the rights of the old shareholders in respect of the book value of equity.

Consider a fast-growing company worth €40m whose book value is €1m. If it carries out a €40m capital increase that doubles its market value, the old shareholders' equity rights are multiplied by 20.5 (from €1m to €20.5m)! For them, the capital increase locks in what was previously just a potential. If the company were to be wound up right after the capital increase, the old shareholders would have a right to €20.5m when they had put in only €1m, whereas the new shareholders would have a right to €20.5m when they had put in €40m. In a way, this imbalance is the "price of admission" when investing in such a profitable company – but also one entailing high risk, as shown, for example, by the Internet companies.

Book value per share is diluted for old shareholders if the market value of the company's shares is less than the book value (*PBR* < 1). It is increased if market value is greater than book value (*PBR* > 1).

QUESTIONS

quiz

1/ What is important in a capital increase where each shareholder takes his proportionate share of the issue?

2/ What is dilution of control?

3/ When are there three different measures of dilution of control? What are they?

4/ What is the purpose of subscription rights? What is their theoretical value?

5/ At what price is a capital increase effected when made with an issue of subscription rights? When made without?

6/ How can a company be sold by means of a capital increase?

7/ What is the consequence of a capital increase on EPS in the short term? In the long term?

8/ Should there be an issue of new shares whenever the share price is overvalued?

9/ Why are the most profitable companies the ones that gain the most by issuing new shares?

10/ When an investment bank underwrites an issue of new shares, it charges the issuing company a commission. How is this commission analysed using options theory?

11/ Does a capital increase with pre-emptive subscription rights signal overvaluation of the shares more strongly than one without?

EXERCISES

1/ (a) A company has a market value of €100m divided into 1 million shares. It proposes to raise funds equivalent to 25% of its value by issuing new shares at €75. Calculate the value of the right subscription, the apparent, technical and real dilutions, the adjustment coefficient and the subscription ratio.

(b) A shareholder holds 90 shares of the company above. Show the bonus share aspect inherent in a capital increase of this kind.

(c) If the shareholder does not subscribe to the new issue, what is his new ownership percentage? Calculate it in two different ways.

(d) Show that if all shareholders subscribe to the capital increase, the issue price does not matter.

(e) What is EPS after the capital increase if previously it was €10?

(f) If the book value of equity was €80m before the capital increase, what is the percentage increase in it? What is the book value per share before the operation? What is it after the operation?

(g) Answer questions (a) through (f) again assuming that, after a sharp runup in share prices, the market value of the company has doubled. The amount of the capital increase is still €25m, but the issue price rises to €150. What conclusions do you draw?

2/ Case study: Ixo capital increase

> Issue of 45,395,820 new shares, or 9 new for every 2 old, with pre-emptive subscription rights
> Number of shares before the capital increase: 10,087,960
> Issue price: €0.48
> Eligibility date of new shares: 1 January 2001
> Subscription period: from 17 December 2001 to 10 January 2002
> Listing exchange: Nouveau Marché
> Six-month high/low: €1.25/€0.40
> Latest price: €0.61
> The company has never paid a dividend
> Issue proceeds (gross):   €21.79m
> Stated purpose: restore financial balance, strengthen resources for growth
> Intention of principal shareholders: I-Partners and XK Interactive, which own 52.22% of Ixo, have indicated that they intend to subscribe for at least 34 million new shares (75% of the issue).

(a) What do you think of Ixo? (financial analysis, analysis of share price)

(b) Compare consolidated shareholders' equity with the amount of the capital increase, the amount of the latter to market capitalisation before the operation and consolidated shareholders' equity after the operation with net debt. What do you conclude?

(c) Calculate the real dilution entailed by the capital increase.

(d) Calculate the value of the pre-emptive subscription right.

(e) What do you think of the majority shareholders' intention?

Condensed income statement

€ million	1999	2000	6 months 2001
Revenue	65.6	79.6	45.7
Operating profit	(1.2)	(17.3)	(8.7)
Interest expense	(1.0)	(1.0)	(1.0)
Exceptional items and other	7.1	(41.7)	(4.7)
Tax	(2.1)	1.5	0.0
Net profit	2.8	(58.5)	(14.4)

Condensed balance sheet

€ million	2000	06/01	€ million	2000	06/01
Intangible assets	40.4	35.4	Shareholder equity	13.7	(1.0)
Investments	5.3	2.0	Debt	27.1	30.3
Tangible fixed assets	2.5	2.4	Current liabilities	42.3	41.6
Receivables and inventories	26.7	27.3			
Marketable securities and cash	8.2	3.8			

Questions

1/ *Not much.*
2/ *Reduction in the equity rights of shareholders that do not subscribe to the capital increase in proportion to their current shareholding.*
3/ *When there is a capital increase along with an issue of pre-emptive subscription rights. Apparent dilution (ignoring the value of the rights), real dilution (the one that matters) and technical dilution (solely attributable to the rights).*
4/ *Subscription rights ensure that the old shareholders can take part in the capital increase if they wish.*
5/ *At market value. At the price guaranteed by the bank underwriting the share issue.*
6/ *By having a very large capital increase with a very small issue premium.*
7/ *Generally, dilution. It depends on the returns generated by the projects that are financed.*
8/ *In theory, yes. In practice, this is quite difficult to do.*
9/ *Because this is the virtuous circle of the capital increase.*
10/ *The commission represents the price of the put option that the company buys from the bank. In effect, the company is buying the right to sell the newly issued shares to the bank at the guaranteed price.*
11/ *Yes, because the substantial discount provides a cushion against a sharp drop in the market price and because the banks were unwilling to get caught up in a process that would have led to them guaranteeing a price close to the market price.*

Exercises

1/ (a) *Subscription right = 6.25, apparent dilution = 25, real dilution = 20, technical dilution = 5, adjustment coefficient = 0.9375, subscription ratio = 1 new for 3 old.*
(b) *The shareholder has 90 subscription rights. If he sells 72 of them and keeps 18, he will be able to buy 6 new shares without expending any cash. This is equivalent to receiving 6 bonus shares.*
(c) $(90 + 6)/(1,000,000 + 333,333) = 0.0072 = (90/1,000,000) \times (1 - 20).$
(d) *Since the control percentages are unchanged and the amount of the increase is fixed, the price has no effect.*
(e) *Before the funds raised are invested, EPS falls to 7.5.*
(f) *Book value of equity increases by 31.25%. Book value per share drops from €80 before to €78.75 after.*
(g) *Subscription right = 7.14, apparent dilution = 14.3, real dilution = 11.1, adjustment coefficient = 0.9643, subscription ratio = 1 new for 6 old. Book value per share after: €90.*

2/ *Ixo case study*
(a) *Ixo is in serious financial difficulty. Although revenue has been growing, its operating loss has been widening. The big losses are knocking the capital structure out of balance: equity is going negative, and debt is increasing rapidly. The company is on the verge of bankruptcy.*
(b) *Book value of equity before capital increase = −€1m. Amount of capital increase = −€22m. Market capitalisation before capital increase = €6m. Although the dilution is steep, the company's financial capacity will be restored on the basis of a share price greater than zero (not a foregone conclusion given its financial situation).*

(c) Real dilution is 79%.

(d) €0.11.

(e) A positive signal, but in truth it is hard to see how the rescue operation could succeed without such a commitment.

BIBLIOGRAPHY

P. Asquith, D. Mullins, Equity issues and offering dilution, *Journal of Financial Economics*, **15**(1), 61–89, January/February 1986.

A. Kalay, A. Shimrat, Firm value and seasoned equity issues: Price pressure, wealth redistribution, or negative information, *Journal of Financial Economics*, **19**(1), 109–126, September 1987.

T. Loughran, J. Ritter, The new issues puzzle, *Journal of Finance*, **50**, 23–51, March 1995.

R. Masulis, A. Korwar, Seasoned equity offerings: An empirical investigation, *Journal of Financial Economics*, **15**(1), 91–118, January/February 1986.

S. Myers, N. Majluf, Corporate financing and investment decisions when firms have information that investors do not have, *Journal of Financial Economics*, **13**(2), 187–221, June 1984.

Section IV
FINANCIAL MANAGEMENT

PART ONE
VALUATION AND FINANCIAL ENGINEERING

In this Part, we will first see that valuing a company is a risky but necessary undertaking for all financial decision-making. We will then examine the issues an investment banker deals with on a daily basis when assisting a company in its strategic decisions:

- organise a group;
- launch an IPO;[1]
- sell assets, a subsidiary or the company;
- merge or demerge;
- asset-based financing and more.

In short, the stuff that all-nighters are made of!

1 *Initial Public Offering.*

Chapter 40
VALUATION

Just how rosy is the future?

In Chapter 25 we reviewed the major principles of valuation and saw that equity value is not the primary focus of the valuation exercise even if it is often its ultimate goal. This chapter contains a more in-depth look at the concepts introduced in Chapter 25 and presents the problems you will probably encounter when using different valuation techniques.

Section 40.1
OVERVIEW OF THE DIFFERENT METHODS

Generally, we want to value a company in order to determine the value of its shares or of its equity capital.

Broadly speaking, there are two methods for valuing equity capital, the direct method and the indirect method. In the direct method, obviously, we value equity capital directly. In the indirect method, we first value the firm as a whole (what we call "enterprise" or "firm" value), then subtract the value of net debt.

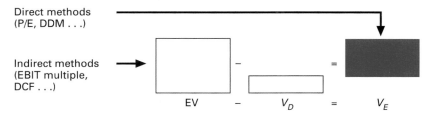

Direct methods (P/E, DDM . . .)

Indirect methods (EBIT multiple, DCF . . .)

$$EV \quad - \quad V_D \quad = \quad V_E$$

In addition, there are two basic approaches, independent of whether the method is "direct" or "indirect".

➤ The fundamental approach of valuing either:

  ○ a stream of dividends, this is the **Dividend Discount Model (DDM)**; or
  ○ free cash flows, this is the **Discounted Cash Flow (DCF) method**.

This approach attempts to determine the company's intrinsic value, in accordance with financial theory, by discounting cash flows to their present value using the required rate of return.

➤ The "pragmatic" approach of valuing the company by analogy with other assets or companies of the same type. This is the **peer comparison** method. Assuming markets are efficient, we should be able to measure the value of one company by reference to another's value.

	Indirect approach	Direct approach
Discounted present value of financial flows (intrinsic value method)	Present value of free cash flows discounted at the weighted average cost of capital (k) — Value of net debt	Present value of dividends at the cost of equity capital: k_E
Multiples of comparable companies (peer comparison method)	$EBIT^2$ multiple $\times EBIT -$ Value of net debt	Multiple (P/E^3) $\times$ Net income

2 Earnings Before Interest and Taxes.

3 Price/Earnings ratio.

Next you will see that the **sum-of-the-parts method** consists in valuing the company as the sum of its assets less its net debt. However, this method is more a combination of the techniques used in the direct and indirect methods rather than a method in its own right.

Lastly, we mention the use of options theory, whose applications we saw in Chapter 35. In practice, nearly no one values equity capital by analogy to a call option on the assets of the company. The concept of real options, however, had its practical heyday in early 2000 when it was used to explain the market values of "new economy" stocks. Needless to say, this method has since fallen out of favour ...

If you remember the efficient market hypothesis, you are probably asking yourself why market value and discounted present value would ever differ. In this chapter we will take a look at the origin of the difference (if any!) and try to understand the reason for it and how long we think it will last. Ultimately, market values and discounted present values should converge.

Section 40.2
PREMIUMS AND DISCOUNTS

A newcomer to finance might think that the market for the purchase and sale of companies is a separate market with its own rules, its own equilibria, its own valuation methods and its own participants.

In fact, nothing could be further from the truth. The market for corporate control is simply a segment of the financial market. **The valuation methods used in this segment are based on the same principles as those used to measure the value of a financial instrument.** Experience has proven that the higher the stock market, the higher the price for an unlisted company.

Participants in the market for corporate control think the same way as investors in the financial market. Of course, the smaller the company is, the more tenuous is the link. The value of a butcher shop or a bakery is largely intangible and hard to measure, and thus has little in common with financial market values. But, in reality, only appearances make the market for corporate control seem fundamentally different.

1/STRATEGIC VALUE AND CONTROL PREMIUM

There is no real control value other than strategic value. We will develop this concept hereafter. For a long time, the **control premium** was a widely accepted notion that was virtually a pardon for dispossessing minority shareholders. When a company was valued at 100 and another company was willing to pay a premium of 20 to the controlling shareholder (holding 50.01%, for example), minority shareholders were excluded from this advantageous offer.

The development of financial markets and financial market regulations has changed this. The current philosophy is that all shares have the same value. Regulated markets have made equality among shareholders a sacrosanct principle in most countries. Recent changes in stock market regulation (Germany, European directive) show clearly a trend in that direction. The Netherlands are becoming more and more peculiar in this regard in the European environment.

Shareholder agreements have become a common method for expressing this principle in unlisted companies.

When control of a listed company changes hands, minority shareholders receive the same premium as that paid to the majority shareholder.

We subscribe fully to this concept, so long as protecting minority shareholders does not hinder value-oriented restructuring. Nevertheless, entrepreneurs we have met often have a diametrically opposed view. For them, minority shareholders are passive beneficiaries of the fruits of all the personal energy the managers/majority shareholders have invested in the company. It is very difficult to convince entrepreneurs that the roles of manager and shareholder can be separated and that they must be compensated differently and, especially, that risk assumed by all types of shareholders must be rewarded.

What, then, is the basis for this premium, which, in the case of listed companies, can often lift a purchase price to 20% or 30% more than current market price? The premium is still called a "control premium" even though it is now paid to the minority shareholders as well as to the majority shareholder.

If we assume that markets are efficient, the existence of such a premium can be justified only if the new owners of the company obtain more value from it than did its previous owners. A control premium derives from the **industrial, commercial or administrative synergies** the new majority shareholders hope to unlock. They hope to improve the acquired company's results by managing it better, pooling resources, combining businesses or taking advantage of economies of scale. These value-creating actions are reflected in the buyer's valuation. The trade buyer (i.e., an acquirer which already has industrial operations) wants to acquire the company so as to change the way it is run and, in doing so, create value.

The company is therefore worth more to a trade buyer than it is to a financial buyer (i.e., usually a venture capitalist fund which has no operations in the industry), who values the company on a **standalone** basis, as one investment opportunity among others, **independently of these synergies**.

The peculiarity of the market for corporate control is the existence of synergies that give rise to strategic value.

In this light, we now understand that the trade buyer's expectations are not the same as those of the financial investor. This difference can lead to a different valuation of the company. We call this **strategic value**.

Strategic value is the value a trade buyer is prepared to pay for a company. It includes the value of the projected free cash flows of the target on a standalone basis, plus the value of synergies from combining the company's businesses with those of the trade buyer. It also includes the value of expected improvement in the company's profitability compared with the business plan provided, if any.

We previously demonstrated that the value of a financial security is independent of the portfolio to which it belongs, but now we are confronted with an exception. Depending on whether a company belongs to one group of companies or another, it does not have the same value. Be sure you understand why this is the case. The difference in value derives from different cash flow projections, not from a difference in the discount rate applied to them, which is a characteristic of the company and identical for all investors. **The principles of value are the same for everyone, but strategic value is different for each trade buyer, because each of them places a different value on the synergies it believes it can unlock and on its ability to manage the business better than current management.**

For this reason, a company's strategic value is often higher than its standalone value.

Consider a company that earns Net Operating Profit After Tax (NOPAT) of 10 and whose value, based on a multiple of 20, is estimated at 200. Now suppose an industrial group thinks it can buy the company and increase its NOPAT by 2 and that these synergies have a value of 20. For this potential acquirer, the strategic value of the company is $200 + 20 = 220$. This is the maximum price the group will be willing to pay to buy the company.

As the seller will also hope to benefit from the synergies, negotiation will focus on how the additional profitability the synergies are expected to generate will be shared between the buyer and the seller.

But some industrial groups go overboard, buying companies at twice their standalone value on the pretext that its strategic value is high or that establishing a presence in such-and-such geographic location is crucial. They are in for a rude awakening. Sometimes the market has already put a high price tag on the target company. Specifically, when the market anticipates merger synergies, speculation can drive the share price far above the company's strategic value, even if all synergies are realised. In other cases, a well-managed company may benefit little or even be hurt by teaming up with another company in the same industry, meaning either that there are no synergies to begin with or, worse, that they are negative!

The following table shows the premia (bid price compared with share price 1 month before) of public deals in Europe.

	1998–2004 (%)	2002–2004 – transactions above €100m (%)
France	12.3	21.0
Germany	9.9	16.3
UK	19.5	13.3
Italy	14.6	15.4
Spain	7.5	18.2
Northern Europe	17.0	16.6
Benelux	20.9	7.7
Total Europe	**16.6**	**16.1**

Source: Mergermarket.com

2/MINORITY DISCOUNTS AND PREMIUMS

We have often seen minority holdings valued with a discount, and you will quickly understand why we believe this is unjustified. A "minority discount" would imply that minority shareholders have less of a claim on the cash flows generated by the company than the majority shareholder. False!

Whereas a control premium can (and must) be justified by subsequent synergies, there is no basis for a minority discount.

In fact, a shareholder who already has the majority of a company's shares may be forced to pay a premium to buy the shares held by minority shareholders. On average in Europe, the premium paid to buy out minorities is in the region of 25%, equivalent to that paid to obtain control. Indeed, majority shareholders may be willing to pay such a premium if they need full control over the acquired company to implement certain synergies. As an example, the minorities of StudioCanal were bought back by the Canal+ Group with a 26% premium over the last market price. In 2003 the offer to buy back Pizza Express minority shareholders at a 16% premium failed to convince two large shareholders and the company was delisted with these institutional investors keeping 10% of capital.

This said, the lack of liquidity associated with certain minority holdings, either because the company is not listed or because trading volumes are low compared with the size of the minority stake, can justify a discount. In this case, the discount does not really derive from the minority stake *per se*, but from its lack of liquidity.

Lack of liquidity may increase volatility of the share price. Therefore, investors will discount an illiquid investment at a higher rate than a liquid one. The difference in values results in a liquidity discount.

The Discounted Cash Flow (DCF) method consists in applying the techniques of the investment decision (see Chapter 16) to the calculation of the value of the firm. We will focus on the **present value** of the cash flows from the investment. This is the **fundamental valuation method**. Its aim is to value the company as a whole (i.e., to determine the value of the capital employed, what we call "enterprise value"). After deducting the value of net debt, the remainder is the value of the company's shareholders' equity.

As we have seen, the cash flows to be valued are the after-tax amounts produced by the firm. They should be discounted out to infinity at the company's weighted average cost of capital (see Chapter 23).

In practice, we project specific cash flows over a certain number of years. This period is called the **explicit forecast period**. This length of this period varies depending on the sector. It can be as short as 5–7 years for a consumer goods company and as long as 20–30 years for a utility. For the years beyond the explicit forecast period, we establish a **terminal value**.

The value of the firm is the sum of the present value of after-tax cash flows over the explicit forecast period and of the net present value of the terminal value at the end of the explicit forecast period.

1/SCHEDULE OF CASH FLOWS OVER THE EXPLICIT FORECAST PERIOD

As we saw in Chapter 25, free cash flow measures the cash-producing capacity of the company. Free cash flow is calculated as follows:

Operating income (EBIT)
—   Normalised tax on operating income
+   Depreciation and amortisation
—   Capital expenditure
—   Change in working capital
=   Free cash flow after tax

You buy a company for its future, not its past, no matter how glorious it was. Consequently, future cash flows are based on projections. As they will vary depending on growth assumptions, the most cautious approach is to construct several scenarios. But, for starters, are you the buyer or the seller? The answer will influence your valuation. The objective of negotiation being to reconcile the buyer's and seller's points of view, we have found in our experience that discounted cash flow analysis is an extremely useful discussion tool.

It is alright for a business plan to be optimistic – our bet is that you have never seen a pessimistic one – the important thing is how it stands up to scrutiny. It should be assumed that competition will ultimately eat into margins, that increases in profitability will not be sustained indefinitely without additional investment or additional hiring, etc. Quantifying these crucial future developments means entering the inner sanctum of the company's strategy.

How long the explicit forecast period is will depend on the company's "visibility" – i.e., the period of time over which is it reasonable to establish projections. This period is necessarily limited. In 10 years' time, for example, probably only a small portion of the company's profits will derive from the production facilities it currently owns or from its current product portfolio. The company will have become a heterogeneous mix of the assets it has today and those it will have acquired over the next 10 years.

The forecast period should therefore correspond to the time during which the company will live off its current configuration. If it is too short, the terminal value will be too large and the valuation problem will only be shifted in time. Unfortunately, this happens all too often. If it is too long (more than 10 years), the explicit forecast is reduced to an uninteresting theoretical extrapolation.

Let's look at Fralia, an unlisted company, the 7-year business plan of which looks like this:

(in €m)	2004	2005e	2006e	2007e	2008e	2009e	2010e	2011e
Profit and loss statement								
Turnover	5 000	5,250	5,513	5,788	5,962	6,141	6,325	6,420
EBITDA[4]	700	788	882	984	1,094	1,212	1,340	1,477
— Depreciation and amortisation	−238	−250	−255	−261	−270	−280	−295	−310
= EBIT	462	538	627	723	824	932	1,045	1,167
Balance sheet								
Fixed assets	2,500	2,550	2,610	2,680	2,759	2,801	2,840	2,850
+ Working capital	500	525	551	579	596	614	632	642
= Capital employed	3,000	3,075	3,161	3,259	3,355	3,415	3,472	3,492
Operating margin after 35% tax	6.0%	6.7%	7.4%	8.1%	9.0%	9.9%	10.7%	11.8%
ROCE[5] after 35% tax	10.0%	11.4%	12.9%	14.4%	16.0%	17.7%	19.6%	21.7%

4 *Earnings Before Interest, Taxes, Depreciation and Amortisation.*

5 *Return On Capital Employed.*

The least we can say about the business plan is that it is ambitious. The operating margin, after taxes of 35%, rises from 6.0% to 11.8%. Asset turnover improves significantly enough that investment in fixed assets and working capital does not need to grow as fast as turnover. After-tax return on capital employed rises from 10.0% in 2004 to 21.7% in 2011! This business plan deserves a critical analysis, including a comparison with analysts' projections for listed companies in the same sector.

Projected after-tax free cash flows are as follows:

(in €m)	2005e	2006e	2007e	2008e	2009e	2010e	2011e
EBIT	538	627	723	824	932	1,045	1,167
− Corporate income tax	(188)	(219)	(253)	(288)	(326)	(366)	(408)
+ Depreciation and amortisation	250	255	261	270	280	295	310
− Capital expenditure	(300)	(315)	(331)	(349)	(322)	(334)	(320)
− Changes in working capital	(25)	(26)	(28)	(17)	(18)	(18)	(10)
= Free cash flow	275	321	372	439	546	622	739

Using a weighted average cost of capital of 10%, the end-2004 present value of the after-tax free cash flows generated during the explicit forecast period works out to €2,164m.

2/TERMINAL VALUE

It is very difficult to estimate a terminal value, because it represents the value at the date when existing business development projections will no longer have any meaning. Often analysts assume that the company enters a phase of maturity after the end of the explicit forecast period. **In this case, the terminal value can be based either on the capital employed or on the free cash flow in the last year of the explicit forecast period.**

In the first case, we establish a value based on capital employed, revalued or not, in the last year of the explicit forecast period. This is the method of choice in the mining industry, for example, where we estimate a liquidation value by summing the scrap value of the various assets – land, buildings, equipment, less the costs of restoring the site.

Remember that if you assume terminal value greater than book value, you are implying that the company will be able to maintain a return on capital employed in excess of its Weighted Average Cost of Capital *WACC*). If you choose a lower value, you are implying that the company enters a phase of decline after the explicit forecast period. Lastly, if you assume that terminal value is equal to book value, you are implying that the company's economic profit[6] falls immediately to zero! You must be careful to be consistent with the explicit forecast period, which might have ended with a year of high economic profit.

Fralia's capital employed totals €3,492m in 2011. Discounted over 7 years at 10%, this is equivalent to €1,792m at the end of 2004. Fralia's end-2004 value is therefore €2,164m + €1,792m, or €3,956m.

The second method consists in estimating terminal value based on a multiple of a measure of operating performance. This measure can be, among other things, turnover, EBITDA or EBIT. Generally, this "horizon multiple" is lower than an equivalent, currently observable multiple. This is because we assume that, all other things equal, prospects for growth decrease with time, warranting a lower multiple.

6 *NOPAT (EBIT after tax) − WACC × Capital employed.*

Nevertheless, since using this method to assess the terminal value implies mixing intrinsic values with comparative values, we do not advise to use it.

You could also call upon the most commonly used terminal value formula, which consists of a normalised cash flow, or annuity, that grows at a rate (g) out to infinity. This is the Gordon–Shapiro formula:

Value of the company at the end of the explicit forecast period

$$= \frac{\text{Normalised cash flow}}{k - g}$$

The difficulty, of course, is in choosing the normalised cash flow value and the perpetual growth rate. **The normalised cash flow** must be consistent with the assumptions of the business plan. It depends on long-term growth, the company's investment strategy and the growth in the company's working capital. Lastly, normalised cash flows may be different from the cash flow in the last year of the explicit forecast period, because normalised cash flow is what the company will generate after the end of the explicit forecast period and will continue to generate to infinity.

Concerning the growth rate to infinity, do not get carried away:

- Apart from the normalised cash flow's growth rate to infinity, you must take a cold hard look at your projected long-term growth in return on capital employed. How long can the economic profit it represents be sustained? How long will market growth last?
- Most importantly, the company's rate of growth to infinity cannot be significantly greater than the long-term growth rate of the economy as a whole. For example, if the anticipated long-term inflation rate is 1% and real GDP growth is expected to be 2%, then if you choose a growth rate g that is significantly greater than 3%, you are implying that the company will not only outgrow all of its rivals but also will eventually take control of the economy of the entire country or indeed of the entire world (trees do not grow to the sky)!

In the case of Fralia, the normalised cash flow must be calculated for the year 2012, because we are looking for the present value at the end of 2011 of the cash flows expected in 2012 and every subsequent year to infinity. Given the necessity to invest if growth is to be maintained, you could use the following assumptions to determine the normalised cash flow:

Normalised cash flow	
Normalised 2012 EBIT	1,185
$-$ Corporate income tax	(415)
$+$ Depreciation and amortisation	315
$-$ Capital expenditure	(315)
$-$ Change in working capital	(10)
$=$ Normalised 2012 free cash flow	760

Using a rate of growth to infinity of 1.5%, we calculate a terminal value of €8,941m. Discounted over 7 years, this gives us €4,588m at end-2004. The value of Fralia is therefore €4,588m + €2,164m, or €6,752m. Note that the terminal value of €8,941m at end-2011 corresponds to a multiple of 7.5 times the 2012 EBIT. This means that choosing a multiple of 7.5 is theoretically equivalent to applying a growth rate to infinity of 1.5% to the normalised cash flow and discounting it at the required rate of return of 10%.

Our experience tells us that no economic profit can be sustained for ever. The company's expected return on capital employed must gradually converge towards its cost of capital. Regardless of the calculation method, the terminal value must reflect this. To model this phenomenon, we recommend using "cash flow fade". In this approach, you define a time period during which a company's return on capital employed diminishes, either because its margins contract or because asset turnover declines. Ultimately, the ROCE falls to the weighted average cost of capital. At the end of this time period, the enterprise value is equal to the book value of capital employed.

3/CHOOSING A DISCOUNT RATE

As we have seen above, the discount rate is the **Weighted Average Cost of Capital (WACC)** or simply, the cost of capital. Estimating it is one of the most sensitive aspects of the discounted cash flow approach.

Certain industrial companies use normative discount rates; for example, we have come across some groups for which all investments had to have a 15% return (no matter what the characteristics of the target were). Beware of such rates that do not yield market values. These rates might lead either to destroy value in buying too expensive or to miss some opportunities because the discount rate is too high compared with market practice.

The weighted average cost of capital is the minimum rate of return required by the company's sources of funding – i.e., shareholders and lenders.

It is the overall cost of financing a company's activities that must be estimated.

The difficulty is in estimating the weighted average cost of capital in real-world conditions. You may want to turn back to Chapter 23 for a more detailed look at this topic.

4/THE VALUE OF NET DEBT

Once you obtain the enterprise value using the above methodology, you must remove the value of net debt to derive equity value. Net debt is composed of financial debt net of cash: i.e., of all bank borrowings, bonds, debentures and other financial instruments (short-, medium- or long-term), net of cash, cash equivalents and marketable securities.

Theoretically, the value of net debt is equal to the value of the future cash outflows (interest and principal payments) it represents, discounted at the market cost of similar borrowings. When all or part of the debt is listed or traded over the counter (listed bonds, syndicated loans), you can use the market value of the debt. You then subtract the market value of cash, cash equivalents and marketable securities. To illustrate this point remember that, prior to its restructuring (see Chapter 45), Marconi debt was trading at 35% of its face value!

Often the book value of net debt is used as a first approximation of its present value. This approach makes sense especially when the debt was not contracted very long ago, or when the debt carries a variable rate and the company's risk profile has not fundamentally changed. If interest rate or the risk of the company has significantly changed from when the debt has been issued then the market value of net debt is different from its book value.

When the company's business is seasonal, year-end working capital may not reflect average requirements, and debt on the balance sheet at the end of the year may not represent real funding needs over the course of the year (see Chapter 11). Some companies also perform year-end "window-dressing" in order to show a very low level of net debt. In these cases, if you notice that interest expense does not correspond to debt balances,[7] you should restate the amount of debt by using a monthly average, for example.

[7] The interest rate calculated as interest in the income statement/net debt in the closing balance sheet does not reflect the actual interest rates paid on the ongoing debt during the year.

5/OTHER VALUATION ELEMENTS

(a) Provisions

Provisions must be treated in a manner consistent with cash flow. If the business plan's EBIT does not reflect future charges for which provisions have been set aside – such as for restructuring, site closures, etc. – then the present value of the corresponding provisions on the balance sheet must be deducted from the value of the company.

Pension liabilities are a sticky problem (this is further developed in Chapter 7). How to handle them depends on how they were booked and, potentially, on the age pyramid of the company's workforce. You will have to examine the business plan to see whether it takes pension payments into account and whether or not a large group of employees are to retire just after the end of the explicit forecast period.

Normally, pension liabilities should be treated as debt. Present value of future outflows for pension should be subtracted from the enterprise value.

With rare exceptions, deferred taxes generally remain relatively stable. In practice, they are rarely paid out. Consequently, they are usually not considered as debt.

(b) Unconsolidated or equity-accounted investments

Naturally, if unconsolidated or equity-accounted financial investments are not reflected in the projected cash flows (via dividends received), you should add their value to the value of discounted cash flows. In this case, use the market value of these assets, including, if applicable, tax on capital gains and losses.

For listed securities, use the listed market value. Conversely, for minor, unlisted holdings, the book value is often used as a shortcut. However, if the company holds a significant stake in the associated company – this is sometimes the case for holdings booked using the equity method – you will have to value the affiliate separately. This may be done rapidly, applying, for example, a sector average P/E to the company's pro rata share of the net income of the affiliate. It can also be more detailed, in valuing the affiliate with a multi-criteria approach if the information is available.

(c) Tax loss carryforwards

If tax loss carryforwards are not yet included in the business plan, you will have to value any tax loss carryforward separately, discounting tax savings until they are exhausted. We advise to discount savings at the cost of equity capital as they are directly linked to the earnings of the company and are as volatile (if not more).

(d) Minority interests

Future free cash flow calculated on the basis of consolidated financial information will belong partly to the shareholders of the parent company and partly to minority shareholders in subsidiary companies if any.

   If minority interests are significant, you will have to adjust for them by either:

- including only the pro rata portion of the cash flows in the group cash flows when you perform the valuation of the group;
- performing a separate DCF valuation of the subsidiaries in which some minority shareholders hold a stake and subtract from the enterprise value the minority share of the subsidiary.

Naturally, this assumes you have access to detailed information about the subsidiary.

   You can also use a multiple approach. Simplifying to the extreme, you could apply the group's implied P/E multiple to the minority shareholders' portion of net profit to give you a first-blush estimate of the value of minority interests. Alternatively, you could apply the group's price-to-book ratio to the minority interests appearing on the balance sheet. In either case, we would recommend against valuing minority interests at their book value.

(e) Dilution

You might be wondering what to do with instruments that give future access to company equity, such as convertible bonds, warrants and stock options. If these instruments have a market value, your best bet will be to subtract that value from the enterprise value of the company to derive the value of equity capital, just as you would for net debt. The number of shares to use in determining the value per share will then be the number of shares currently in circulation. This is tantamount to the company buying back all of these instruments on the open market, then cancelling them. Potential dilution would then fall to zero, but net debt would increase.

   Alternatively, you could adjust the number of shares used to calculate value per share. This is the treasury stock method (see p. 552).

6/PROS AND CONS OF THE CASH FLOW APPROACH

The advantage of the discounted cash flow approach is that it quantifies the often implicit assumptions and projections of buyers and sellers. It also makes it easier to keep your feet on the ground during periods of market euphoria, excessively high valuations and astronomical multiples. It forces the valuation to be based on the company's real economic performance.

Nevertheless, as satisfying as this method is in theory, it presents three major drawbacks:

- it is very sensitive to assumptions and, consequently, the results it generates are very volatile. It is a rational method, but the difficulty in predicting the future brings significant uncertainty;
- it sometimes depends too much on the terminal value, in which case the problem is only shifted to a later period. Often the terminal value accounts for more than 50% of the value of the company, compromising the method's validity. However, it is sometimes the only applicable method, such as in the case of a loss-making company for which multiples are inapplicable;
- lastly, it is not always easy to produce a business plan over a sufficiently long period of time. The external analyst often finds he lacks critical information.

7/THE LOGIC BEHIND THE CASH FLOW APPROACH

You might be tempted to think this method works only for estimating the value of the majority shareholder's stake and not for estimating the discounted value of a flow of dividends. You might even be tempted to go a step further and apply a **minority discount** to the present value of future cash flows for valuing minority holding.

This approach is generally erroneous! Applying a **minority discount** to the discounted cash flow method implies that you think **the majority shareholder is not managing the company fairly**. A discount is justified only if there are "losses in transmission" between free cash flow and dividends. This can be the case if the company's strategy regarding dividends, borrowing and new investment is unsatisfactory or oriented towards increasing the value of some other assets owned by the majority shareholder.

Minority discounts are inconsistent with the discounted cash flow method. Similarly, increasing the cash-flow-based value can be justified only if the investor believes he can unlock synergies that will increase free cash flows.

8/DISCOUNTING CASH FLOW AND DISCOUNTING DIVIDENDS

Another approach consists in discounting the flow of future dividends. The concept is simple. The value of a share, like that of any other financial security, is equal to the present value of all the cash flows that its owner is entitled to receive – namely, the dividends. We are now putting ourselves in the position of the shareholder, so the discount rate to be used is the cost of equity (k_E).

This method is little used today, because it is extremely complicated to implement. The critical variable is the rate of growth in dividends: this rate depends on numerous factors: marginal rate of return, payout ratio, gearing, etc.

This method is still used in very specific cases, such as companies in mature sectors with very good visibility and high payout ratios. Examples of such industries are utilities, concessions and real estate companies.

Section 40.4
MULTIPLE APPROACH OR PEER GROUP COMPARISONS

1/PRESENTATION

Peer comparison or the multiples approach is based on three fundamental principles:

- the company is to be valued in its entirety;
- the company is valued at a multiple of its profit-generating capacity. The most generally used is the P/E, EBITDA and EBIT multiples;
- markets are efficient and comparisons are therefore justified.

The approach is global, because it is based not on the value of operating assets and liabilities *per se*, but on the overall returns they are expected to generate. The value of the company is derived by applying a certain multiplier to the company's profitability parameters. As we saw in Chapter 25, multiples depend on expected growth, risk and interest rates.

Higher expected growth, low risk in the company's sector and low interest rates will all push multiples higher.

The approach is comparative. At a given point in time and in a given country, companies are bought and sold at a specific price level, represented by an EBIT multiple. These prices are based on internal parameters and by the overall stock market context. Prices paid for companies acquired in Europe in 2004, for example, when EBIT multiples were still high (ten times on average) were not the same as for those acquired in 1980 when multiples hovered around five times EBIT, nor for those bought in 1990, when multiples were near long-term averages (around seven times).

Multiples can derive from a sample of comparable, listed companies or a sample of companies that have recently been sold. The latter sample has the virtue of representing actual transaction prices for the equity value of a company. These multiples are respectively called **market multiples** and **transaction multiples**, and we will look at them in turn. As these multiples result from comparing a market value with accounting figures, keep in mind that the two must be consistent. The enterprise value must be compared with an operating datum, such as turnover, EBITDA or EBIT. The value of equity capital must be compared with a figure after interest expense, such as net profit or cash flow.

2/BUILDING A SAMPLE OF COMPARABLE COMPANIES OR COMPARABLE TRANSACTIONS

For market multiples, a peer group comparison consists in setting up a sample of comparable, listed companies that have not only similar sector characteristics, but also similar operating characteristics, such as ROCE and expected growth rates. Given that the multiple is usually calculated on short-term projections, you should choose companies whose shares are liquid and are covered by a sufficient number of financial analysts.

For transaction multiples you should use transactions in the same sector as the company you are trying to value. The transactions should not be too old; if they were not recent, they would reflect different market conditions. In addition, the size and geographical characteristics of the deals should be similar to the one contemplated. There is often a tradeoff between retaining a sufficient number of transactions and having deals that can be qualified as similar.

3/THE MENU OF MULTIPLES

There are two major groups of multiples: those expressing the enterprise value (i.e., the value of capital employed) and those expressing the value of equity capital.

Multiples expressing the value of capital employed are multiples of operating balances before subtracting interest expense. As we discussed in Chapter 25, we believe NOPAT is the best denominator – i.e., EBIT less corporate income taxes. We recognise, however, that those most commonly used in the financial community are EBIT and EBITDA.

Multiples expressing the value of equity capital are multiples of operating balances after interest expense, principally net income (P/E multiple), as well as multiples of cash flow and multiples of underlying income – i.e., before exceptional items. For an analysis of the P/E multiple, refer to Chapter 25.

4/ENTERPRISE VALUE MULTIPLES

Whichever multiple you choose, you will have to value the capital employed for each listed company in the sample. This value is the sum of the company's market capitalisation (or transaction value of equity for transaction multiples) and value of its net debt at the valuation date, plus minority interests and the nonrecurring portion of provisions for risks and contingencies. As in the DCF method, if the charges corresponding to the provisions for nonrecurring risks and contingencies are not reflected in the benchmark figure (EBIT, EBITDA, etc.) you will have to add those provisions to net debt in order to remain consistent (for further analysis of provisions for pensions see Chapter 7).

You will then calculate the multiple for the comparable companies over three fiscal years: the current year, last year and next year. Note that we use the same value of capital employed in all three cases, as current market values should reflect anticipated changes in future operating results.

(a) EBIT multiple

Our preference clearly goes to the multiple of Earnings Before Interest and Taxes (EBIT), because it enables us to compare the genuine profit-generating capacity of the various companies. The numerous possible definitions of "genuine profit-generating capacity" all have advantages and disadvantages. We do not intend to examine each of them, only to emphasise the notion implicit in all of them.

A company's genuine profit-generating capacity is the normalised operating profit-ability it can generate year after year, excluding exceptional gains and losses and other nonrecurring items.

You may have to perform a series of restatements in order to derive this operating income (see Chapter 3 for a more detailed discussion). You will have to deduct from operating income certain expenses wrongly attributed to other fiscal years or capitalised when they should not have been. Same treatment must be applied to expenses that have been booked below the operating line but which are really of an operating nature. In theory, this operating income figure used should be after-tax so as to correct for differences in effective tax rates among the companies in the sample, particularly if they operate in different countries. But financial analysts often ignore these differences and use a pre-tax operating figure.

The EBIT multiple is the ratio of the value of capital employed to EBIT (operating income).

Consider Analogous plc, a listed company comparable with Fralia the characteristics of which in 2004 were as follows:

€m	2004
Market capitalisation (value of equity capital)	9,000
+ Value of debt	500
= Value of capital employed (A)	9,500
Operating income (EBIT) (B)	780
EBIT multiple (A/B)	12.2×

The 2004 pre-tax operating income (EBIT) multiple is 12.2 times. Applied to Fralia's 2004 operating income of €462m, Analogous' multiple would value Fralia's enterprise at €5,636m.

The table at the top of the next page shows the EBIT multiple for European companies in different sectors.

Sector	Multiple of 2005 EBIT (e)	Multiple of 2006 EBIT (e)
Oil and gas	6.2	—
Mining	6.9	7.2
Automotive	7.9	6.4
Capital goods	9.7	—
Construction and building materials	9.9	8.9
Telecoms	9.9	8.9
Chemicals	10.3	9.8
Aerospace and defence	10.3	—
Industry services	10.5	9.4
Electronics	10.8	10.3
Food retail	10.9	10.1
Other retail	11	—
Media	11.2	10.2
Food and beverage	11.5	10.5
Luxury	12	10.2
Utilities	12.1	—
Pharmaceuticals	12.2	10.9
Transportation	12.8	11.4
Cosmetic	14.1	12.4
All sectors	*9.3*	—

Source: Exane BNP Paribas.

(b) EBITDA multiple

The EBITDA multiple follows the same logic as the EBIT multiple. It has the merit of eliminating the sometimes significant differences in depreciation methods and periods. It is very frequently used by stock market analysts for companies in capital-intensive industries.

Be careful when using the EBITDA multiple, however, especially when the sample and the company to be valued have widely disparate levels of profitability. In these cases, the EBITDA multiple tends to overvalue companies with low profitability and undervalue companies with high profitability, independently of depreciation policy. Situated further upstream from EBIT, EBITDA does not capture certain (other) elements of profitability. Applying the sample's multiple therefore introduces a distortion.

(c) Other multiples

Operating multiples can also be calculated on the basis of other measures, such as turnover. Some industries have even more specific multiples, such as multiples of the number of subscribers, number of visitors or page views for Internet companies, tonnes of cement, etc. These multiples are particularly interesting when the return on capital employed of the companies in the sample is standard. Otherwise, results will be too widely dispersed.

These multiples are generally used to value companies that are not yet profitable. They have been widely used during the Internet bubble. They tend to ascribe far too much value to the company to be valued and we recommend avoiding them.

5/ EQUITY VALUE MULTIPLES

You may also decide to choose multiples based on operating balances after interest expense. These multiples include the price to book ratio, the cash flow multiple and the P/E multiple, as discussed in Chapter 25. All these multiples use market capitalisation at the valuation date (or price paid for the equity for transaction multiples) as their numerator. The denominators are book equity, cash flow and net profit, respectively. For the P/E, the net profit used by analysts is the company's bottom line restated to exclude exceptional items and the amortisation of goodwill, so as to put the emphasis on recurrent profit-generating capacity. You can also choose to calculate a multiple of dividends if the company to be valued has a consistently high payout ratio.

These multiples indirectly value the company's financial structure, thus creating distortions depending on whether the companies in the sample are indebted or not.

Consider the following two similarly sized companies, Ann and Valeria, operating in the same sector and enjoying the same outlook for the future, with the following characteristics:

Company	Ann	Valeria
Operating income	150	177
− Interest expense	30	120
− Corporate income tax (40%)	48	23
= Net profit	72	34
Market capitalisation	1,800	?
Value of debt (at 10% p.a.)	300	1,200

Ann's P/E multiple is 25 (1,800/72). As the two companies are comparable, we might be tempted to apply Ann's P/E multiple to Valeria's bottom line to obtain Valeria's market capitalisation – i.e., the market value of its shares – or $25 \times 34 = 850$.

Although it looks logical, this reasoning is flawed. Applying a P/E of 25 to Valeria's net income is tantamount to applying a P/E of 25 to Valeria's NOPAT ($177 \times (1 - 40\%) = 106$) less a P/E of 25 applied to its after-tax interest expense ($120 \times (1 - 40\%) = 72$). After all, net income is equal to net operating profit after tax less interest expense after tax.

The first term ($25 \times NOPAT$) should represent the enterprise value of Valeria; i.e., $25 \times 106 = 2,650$.

The second term (25 × after-tax interest expense) should represent the value of debt to be subtracted from capital employed to give the value of equity capital that we are seeking. However, 25 × interest expense after tax is 1,800, whereas the value of the debt is only 1,200.

In this case, this type of reasoning would cause us to overstate the value of the debt (at 1,800 instead of 1,200) and to understate the value of the company's equity.

The proper reasoning is as follows: we first use the multiple of Ann's NOPAT to value Valeria's capital employed. If Ann's market capitalisation is 1,800 and its debt is worth 300, then its capital employed is worth $1,800 + 300$, or 2,100. As Ann's NOPAT is $150 \times (1 - 40\%) = 90$, the multiple of Ann's NOPAT is 2,100/90 = 23.3. Valeria's capital employed is therefore worth 23.3 times its NOPAT, or $23.3 \times 106 = 2,470$. We now subtract the value of the debt (1,200) to obtain the value of equity capital, or 1,270. This is not the same as 850!

These distortions are the reason why financial analysts use multiples of operating income or of operating income before depreciation and amortisation. This approach removes the bias introduced by different financial structures.

6/TRANSACTION MULTIPLES

The approach is slightly different, but the method of calculation is the same. The sample is composed of information available from recent transactions in the same sector, such as the sale of a controlling block of shares, a merger, etc.

If we use the price paid by the acquirer, our multiple will contain the **control premium** the acquirer paid to obtain control of the target company. As such, the price includes the value of anticipated synergies. Using listed share prices leads to a so-called minority value, which we now know is nothing other than the standalone value. In contrast, transaction multiples reflect majority value – i.e., the value including any control premium for synergies. For listed companies it has been empirically observed that control premiums are around 20% (see p. 817) of pre-bid market prices (i.e., prices pre announcement of the tender offer).

You will find that it is often difficult to apply this method, because good information on truly comparable transactions is often lacking.

In sum, the peer group or multiple method is a broad, comparative method, which predicts that a company should be worth x times its profit-generating capacity; i.e., its recurrent, underlying profit.

7/MEDIANS, MEANS AND REGRESSIONS

People often ask if they should value a company by multiplying its profit-generating capacity by the mean or the median of the multiples of the sample of comparable companies.

Our advice is to be wary of both means and medians, as they can mask wide disparities within the sample, and sometimes may contain extreme situations that should be excluded altogether. Try to understand why the differences exist in the first place rather than to bury them in a mean or median value that has little real significance. For example, look at the multiples of the companies in the sample as a function of their expected growth. Sometimes this can be a very useful tool in positioning the company to be valued in the context of the sample.

Some analysts perform linear regressions to find a relationship between, for example:

- the EBIT multiple and expected growth in EBIT;
- the multiple of turnover and the operating margin;
- the price to book ratio and the return on equity (in particular, when valuing a bank).

This method allows us to position the company to be valued within the sample. The issue still pending is to find the most relevant criterion. R^2, which indicates the significance of the regression line, will be our guide in determining which criteria are the most relevant in the industry in question.

Section 40.5
THE SUM-OF-THE-PARTS METHOD AND RESTATED NET ASSET VALUE (RNAV)

The sum-of-the-parts method consists in valuing the company's different assets and liabilities separately and then adding them together.

The sum-of-the-parts method is simple. It consists in systematically studying the value of each asset and each liability on the company's balance sheet. For a variety of reasons – accounting, tax, historical – book values are often far from reality. They must therefore be restated and revalued before they can be assumed to reflect a true net asset value. The sum-of-the-parts method is an **additive method**. Revalued assets are summed, and the total of revalued liabilities is subtracted.

To apply this method properly, therefore, we must value each asset and each liability. Estimates must be consistent, even though the methods applied might be different.

1/TYPE OF APPROACH

(a) General philosophy

Without waxing philosophical, we can say that there are two basic types of value used in the sum-of-the-parts method:

- **market value**: this is the value we could obtain by selling the asset. This value might seem indisputable from a theoretical point of view, but it virtually assumes that the buyer's goal is liquidation. This is rarely the case. Acquisitions are usually motivated by the promise of industrial or commercial synergies.

- **value in use**: this is the value of an asset that is used in the company's operations. It is a kind of market value at replacement cost.

The sum-of-the-parts method is the **easiest to use** and the values it generates are the least **questionable** when the assets have a value on a market that is **independent of the company's operations**, such as the property market, the market for airplanes, etc. It is hard to put a figure on a new factory in a new industrial estate. The value of the inventories and vineyards of a wine company is easy to determine and relatively undisputed.

We have a wide variety of values available when we apply the sum-of-the-parts method. Possible approaches are numerous. We can assume discontinuation of the business, either sudden or gradual – or keep a going concern basis, for example. The important thing is to be consistent, sticking to the same approach throughout the valuation.

(b) Tax implications

The acquirer's objectives, the "philosophy" as we named it, will influence the way taxes are included (or not) in the sum-of-the-parts approach.

- If the objective is to liquidate or break up the target company into component parts, the acquirer will buy the assets directly, giving rise to capital gains or losses. The taxes (or tax credits) theoretically generated will then decrease (increase) the ultimate value of the asset.
- If the objective is to acquire some assets (and liabilities), and to run them as a going concern, then the assets will be revalued through the transaction. Increased depreciation will then lower income tax compared with liquidation or the breakup case above.[8]
- If the objective is to acquire a company and maintain it as a going concern (i.e., not stopping the activities) and a separate entity, the acquiring company buys the shares of the target company rather than the underlying assets. It cannot revalue the assets on its books and will depreciate them from a lower base than if it had acquired the assets directly. As a result, depreciation expense will be lower and taxes higher.

The theoretical tax impact of a capital gain or loss must be taken into account if our objective is to break up the company.

[8] *Acquisition of assets will most often generate deductible depreciation whereas acquisition of shares of a company will generate goodwill, which in most European countries does not give rise to tax-deductible amortisation.*

2/TANGIBLE ASSETS

Production assets can be evaluated on the basis of replacement value, liquidation value, going concern value or still other values.

We do not intend to go into great detail here. Our main point is that in the sum-of-the-parts method it is important to determine an overall value for productive and commercial assets. Rather than trying to decompose assets into small units, you should reason on a general basis and consider sufficiently large groups of assets that have a standalone value (i.e., for which a market exists or that can operate on a standalone basis).

For example, it makes no sense to value the land on which a warehouse has been built. It makes more sense to value the combination of the land and the buildings on it. An appraiser will value the combination based on its productive potential, not on the basis of its individual components. Of course, this is not the case if the objective is to reuse the land for something else, in which case you will want to deduct the cost of knocking down the warehouse.

3/INVENTORIES

For industrial companies, valuing inventories usually does not pose a major problem, unless they contain products that are obsolete or in poor condition. In this case, we have to apply a discount to their book value, based on a routine inventory of the products.

In some situations, you will have to revalue the inventories of companies with long production cycles; the revaluation can lead to gains on inventories. This is often the case with champagne, cognac, whisky and spirits in general. Here again, revaluation will have an impact on income taxes. Remember that when you revalue inventories, you are **decreasing future profits**.

4/INTANGIBLE ASSETS

It might seem paradoxical to value intangible assets, since their liquidation value has for a long time been considered to be low. It is now widely acknowledged, however, that the value of a company is partly determined by the very real value of its intangible assets, be they brand names, a geographical location or other advantages.

The sum-of-the-parts approach makes no sense unless it takes into account the company's intangible assets.

Some noteworthy examples:

- **Lease rights**: the present value of the difference between market rental rates and the rent paid by the company.
- **Brands**: particularly hard to value. The importance of brands in valuation is growing.

In general, there are three methods for valuing brands.

Method 1   The first method asks how much would have to be spent in advertising expense, after tax, to rebuild the brand. Using this method, some consumer products groups value their brands based on a 4-year series of advertising and promotional budgets. Clearly, this is a totally empirical method.

Method 2   The second method calculates the present value of all royalty payments that will be or could be received from the use of the brand by a third party.

Method 3   The third method consists in analysing the brand's fundamental utility. After all, the brand's *raison d'être* is to enable the company to sell more and at higher prices than would otherwise be possible without the brand name. Discounting this "excess profit" over a certain period of time should yield, after subtracting the related higher costs, an estimate of the value of the brand. Users of this method discount the incremental future operating income expected from the use of the brand and subtract the additional operating expense, working capital and investments, thereby isolating the value of the brand. We will not hide the fact that this approach, while intellectually appealing, is very difficult to apply in practice, because often there is no generic "control" product to use as a benchmark.

Lease rights and brands are difficult, but not impossible to value.

5/ USEFULNESS OF SUM-OF-THE-PARTS VALUES

Sum-of-the-parts values are akin to book values (and therefore to net asset value), and, as such, can be deceptive. Many people think they imply safe or reliable values. In fact, when we say that a company has a high restated net asset value, it means that from a free cash flow point of view, the company's terminal value – to be obtained through liquidation, for example – is high compared with the value of intermediate cash flows. Consequently, the more "restated net asset value" a company has, the more speculative and volatile its value is. Granted, its industrial risk may be lower, but most of the value derives from speculation about resale prices.

For this reason, the sum-of-the-parts method is useful for valuing small companies with no particular strategic value. The sum-of-the-parts method is particularly applicable for companies, such as airlines, whose assets can be sold readily on a secondary market.

As a final note, financial analysts often use the sum-of-the-parts method to value diversified groups. They sum the values of the group's various activities, with each piece calculated by the DCF method or through the use of multiples. Analysts then subtract head office costs and consolidated net debt.

Section 40.6
EXAMPLE: VALUATION OF ERICSSON

The information presented below aims at giving a real example of valuation of a listed company. It represents for a large part abstracts from brokers' notes on Ericsson. Alongside brokers, we aim at benchmarking the market value of the Ericsson share.

1/DCF

One of the brokers you read provides the following estimates (in SEKm).

	2005e	2006e	2007e	2008e	2009e	2010e	2011e	2012e	2013e
Revenues	142,825	150,472	153,107	157,700	165,585	175,521	186,930	198,145	208,053
Revenue growth	*11.4%*	*5.4%*	*1.8%*	*3.0%*	*5.0%*	*6.0%*	*6.5%*	*6.0%*	*5.0%*
EBIT		29,828	29,882	29,096	28,864	29,147	29,666	30,660	30,712	31,208
EBIT margin	*20.9%*	*19.9%*	*19.0%*	*18.3%*	*17.6%*	*16.9%*	*16.4%*	*15.5%*	*15.0%*
+ Depreciation	4,246	4,713	5,188	5,051	5,304	5,622	5,987	6,347	6,664
− Capex	4,428	4,664	4,746	4,101	4,306	4,563	4,860	5,152	5,410
− Change in working capital	−1,292	−3,928	−4,224	505	868	1,093	1,255	1,234	1,090
− Tax	7,299	7,071	6,721	6,639	6,703	6,824	7,052	7,064	7,178
Free cash flow	*23,639*	*26,787*	*27,042*	*22,670*	*22,574*	*22,808*	*23,479*	*23,609*	*24,195*

Assuming a risk-free rate of 5%, a beta of assets of 1.1 and a risk premium of 5%, we find a WACC of 10.5%. You may also assess that the long-term growth rate of cash flows will be a bit higher than the economy in general, let us say 3% (at least that is the common view of a lot of brokers).

Then, the present value of cash flows over the period 2005–2013 (valued as at 01/01/2005) is SEK136,954m. The terminal value is SEK333,272m; with a present value of SEK135,280m. The enterprise value of Ericsson is hence SEK299,232m.

Ericsson has a net cash position as at 31/12/2003 of SEK42,911m. Therefore, the equity value of the group will be higher than its enterprise value at SEK315,145m. With 15,861 million shares, the value per share comes out at SEK19.9. This value is close to the market price (at the time of the valuation, of course).

2/COMPARABLE COMPANIES' MULTIPLES

As Ericsson is listed we are very reluctant in applying multiples of other companies to derive a fair valuation; we prefer computing the multiples of the group and of competitors and then benchmarking the multiple and trying to assess if the differences are justified.

Brokers show different comparable panels: some include the large US players (Cisco, Lucent, Motorola) and some have a portfolio reduced to European players. For illustrative purposes we show here the multiples of European comparables.

	EV/Revenues		EV/EBITDA		P/E	
	2004	2005	2004	2005	2004	2005
Alcatel	1.0×	0.9×	6.3×	6.2×	19.3×	17.8×
Ericsson	2.4×	2.3×	10.4×	8.8×	18.1×	16.1×
Nokia	1.3×	1.3×	7.7×	8.2×	16.6×	17.4×

Ericsson's multiples are clearly on the top of the range. In other words, if Ericsson was valued by applying competitors' multiples, value would be significantly lower than the actual market value. The question then is: Are these multiples (in particular, EV/EBITDA) justified by either higher growth or lower risk compared with the two other groups?

Although brokers recognise the fact that Ericsson has demonstrated higher growth in the past, some brokers doubt the capacity of Ericsson to sustain the growth it has performed in the past and therefore qualify the multiples as demanding (nice way of saying too high).

Section 40.7
COMPARISON OF VALUATION METHODS

1/RECONCILING THE DIFFERENT METHODS OF VALUATION

If markets are efficient, all of the valuation methods discussed so far should lead to the same valuation. In reality, however, there are often differences among the sum-of-the-parts value, the DCF-based value and the peer comparison value. You must analyse the source of these differences and **resist the temptation to average them**!

(a) Analysing the difference between sum-of-the-parts value and discounted cash flow value

If the sum-of-the-parts value is higher than the DCF value or the value derived from a comparison of multiples, then the company is being valued more for its past, its revalued equity capital, than for its outlook for future profitability. In this case, the company should not invest, but divest, liquidating its assets to boost profitability and improve the allocation of its resources.

This strategy had its heyday in the 1980s. Companies were bought up on the open market, and then sold off piecemeal. The buyer realised a gain because the parts were worth more than the company as a whole. Far from a return to un-bridled, 19th-century capitalism, these purely financial transactions represented a better allocation of resources as well as punishment for bad management.

If the sum-of-the-parts value is lower than the DCF value or the value derived from multiples, which is the usual case in an economy where companies have a lot of intangibles, then the company is very profitable and invests in projects with expected profitability greater than their cost of capital. The company has real expertise, a strong strategic positioning and enjoys high barriers to entry. But the chances are that it will not escape competitive pressure for ever.

For a long time, **goodwill** was a favoured tactic for adjusting sum-of-the-parts values for the company's expected return on capital employed, particularly with respect to its weighted average cost of capital. It was a quick way of valuing all of the company's **intangible capital**.

The starting point of these mixed methods is capital employed as analysed in Chapter 4, adjusted for capital gains and losses, if any.

A normalised operating income is then calculated, applying a required rate of return on capital employed. The difference between the operating income projected in the business plan and the normalised operating income is then deemed goodwill, if it is positive, and negative goodwill if it is negative. Conceptually, this "excess profit" is the income stream the acquiring company is prepared to buy. This income stream is then discounted over a certain period of time. Note that if we discount the excess profit at the weighted average cost of capital, we come back to the notion of economic profit and its present value. This converges with the fundamental concept of valuation of cash flows – i.e., the difference between economic profitability and the discount rate – in this case, the weighted average cost of capital.

(b) Comparison values versus DCF values

If the value obtained via peer comparison is greater than the DCF-based value (and if all the calculations are correct!), then the company's managers should be thinking about floating the company on the stock exchange without further ado, because financial investors have a more favourable view of the company's risk profile and profitability outlook than its current management or shareholders. Conversely, if the value obtained by comparison is lower than the DCF value and if the business plan is reliable, it would be wiser to wait until more of the long-term growth potential in the company's business plan feeds through to its financial statements before launching an IPO; and maybe do a public to private[9] if the company is already listed.

9 See p. 916.

If transaction multiples generate a higher value than market multiples or the DCF model, then it would be better to organise a trade sale by soliciting bids from several industry participants. In short, look before you leap!

2/THE LIFECYCLE THEORY OF COMPANY VALUE

Companies that have achieved a certain level of success will see their sum-of-the-parts and cash flow values differ throughout their "lifecycle". Lifecycle is an important factor in determining the value of companies, like it was in determining the optimal capital structure and financing policies (see Section III, Part Two).

When the company is founded, its restated net asset value and cash flow value are identical; the company has not yet made any investments. After the first year or two of operations, restated net asset value may dip because of startup losses. Cash flow value meanwhile is greater, because it anticipates hopefully positive future profitability.

During the growth phase, restated net asset value will rise as all or part of the company's profits are reinvested and the company builds a customer base (the value of which does not appear in the accounts, however). Cash flow value also continues to rise and remains above the restated net asset value. The company's expertise has not yet become a tangible asset. It is still associated with the individuals who developed it.

At maturity, cash flow value will start growing more slowly or stop growing altogether, reflecting a normal profit trend. Nonetheless, the restated net asset value continues to grow, but more slowly because the company increases its payout ratio. Broadly speaking, restated net asset value and cash flow value are very close.

If the company then enters a phase of decline, its profits decline and the cash flow value slips below the restated net asset value. The latter continues to grow but only very slowly, until the company starts posting losses. The restated net asset value falls. As for the cash flow value, it is already very low. **The restated net asset value then becomes particularly speculative.**

THE LIFECYCLE OF VALUE

Restated net asset value and cash flow value evolve differently throughout the life of the company.

At any given point in time, it is very important to understand the reasons for the difference between the restated net asset value and the cash flow value, because this understanding gives important clues as to the situation and future prospects of the company.

You might now be thinking that our kaleidoscope of methods leads to as many values as there are images of the company:

- sum-of-the-parts, or restated net asset value;
- peer comparison value;
- intrinsic value (i.e., DCF), etc.

We advise against calculating a wide variety of valuations, unless it is to show that you can prove anything when it comes to valuation. But you must not throw up your hands in despair, either. Instead, try to understand each type of value, which corporate circumstances it applies to and what its implicit assumptions are. It is more important to determine ranges than to come up with precise values. Precision is the domain of negotiation, whose goal is to arrive at an agreed **price**.

Lastly, remember that valuing a company means:

- taking a speculative stance not only on the future of the company, but also on its market conditions. The cash flow and comparison methods demonstrate this;
- implicitly extrapolating past results or expected near-term results far into the future, opening the door to exaggeration;
- sometimes forgetting that restated net asset values is not a good reference if the profitability of the company differs significantly from its investors' required return.

Shareholders' decision to sell all or part of a company is based on the price they believe they can obtain compared with their set of calculated valuations.

To the financial manager, the market for corporate control is nothing but a segment of the broader capital market. From this principle it follows that there is no such thing as control value other than the strategic value deriving from synergies.

SUMMARY

@

download

Industrial synergies generally make a company's strategic value higher than its financial or standalone value. The essence of negotiation lies in determining how the strategic value pie will be divided between the buyer and the seller, with both parties trying, not surprisingly, to obtain the largest possible share.

The value of a company's equity capital is the difference between the enterprise value (value of the invested capital) and the value of its net debt.

The first company valuation method – Discounted Cash Flow, or DCF – is based on the notion that the value of the company is equal to the amount of free, after-tax cash flows generated by the company and discounted at a rate commensurate with its risk profile. The discount rate applied is the Weighted Average Cost of Capital (WACC). DCF calculation is performed as follows:

- the flow of free, after-tax cash flows is discounted over the explicit forecast period – i.e., the period over which there is visibility of the company's operations;

- a discounted terminal value is calculated on the basis of an estimated growth rate carried to infinity;

- the value of equity capital is the difference between the value of the company obtained above and the value of the company's debt.

The peer group or multiples method is a comparative approach that sets the company to be valued off against other companies in the same sector. In this approach, the enterprise value of the company is estimated via a multiple of its profit-generating capacity before interest expense. The EBIT and EBITDA multiples are among those commonly used. The multiple used in the comparison can be either a market multiple or a transaction multiple.

Using direct methods the value of equity capital can be computed in discounting dividends or applying P/E to the net result.

The sum-of-the-parts method of valuation consists in valuing each of the company's assets and commitments separately, then subtracting the latter from the former. There are several types of restated net value, from liquidation value to going concern value, and there are important tax considerations. Either capital gains or losses will be subject to tax, or depreciable assets will be undervalued and yearly taxes higher. Calculating restated net asset value makes sense only if it includes the company's intangible assets, which can be particularly difficult to value.

No company valuation is complete without an analysis of the reasons for the differences in the results obtained by the various valuation methods. These differences give rise to decisions of financial engineering and evolve throughout the life of the company.

QUESTIONS

quiz

1/ What is the most relevant cash flow when valuing a company using the discounted cash flow method?

2/ What sort of a discount can a minority shareholder get compared with a financial value? Show how the situation differs between a listed company and an unlisted company.

3/ What is a synergy?

4/ Logically, should a foreign investor with little knowledge of the country pay more or less for a company? Explain why foreign investors often offer the highest price. What is the role of the investment bank?

5/ Should the buyer's costs be separated from the target company's costs in the cost savings that come out of a merger of two companies?

6/ Describe the type of company that has a financial value that is higher than its strategic value.

7/ Which method in your view would be best suited for valuing:

- ○ a property management company;
- ○ a holding company;
- ○ a mutual fund;
- ○ a company in the aeronautics sector;
- ○ a bicycle factory;
- ○ a portfolio of movies.

8/ Can an asset have several values? Why?

9/ Is a valuation of a cinema theatre or a chemist shop in terms of a number of weeks' sales a result of the sum-of-the-parts or the cash flow method?

10/ What are the two determining factors when valuing a wine estate?

11/ Which method should be used for estimating the value of a company in decline?

12/ When a company is bought, is there a control premium?

13/ Name the types of companies for which cash flow value is much higher than restated net asset value.

14/ Can the purchase of a company by venture capitalists create value? And by trade buyers?

EXERCISES

1/ Megabyte plc is a high-tech company experiencing transitional problems. To get through this difficult period, management has decided on a €150m recapitalisation. In 5 years' time, the company should make net profits of €21m, and be valued at 30 times its profits. Assume that the discount rate is 25% and that there will be no cash flows generated for 5 years.

- ○ What is the present value of shareholders' equity?
- ○ What is the present value of shareholders' equity if profits of only €14m are expected in 5 years?
- ○ What do you conclude from the above?

2/ The table below shows the forecasts for Management plc (in €m):

Year	1	2	3	4	5
Sales	3,960	4,080	4,200	4,326	4,458
Cost of good sold	1,782	1,794	1,806	1,860	1,917
Marketing costs	870	897	924	996	1,026
Administrative costs	396	408	420	432	447
Depreciation and amortisation	330	315	300	300	300
EBIT (operating income)	582	666	750	738	768

The company is expecting annual capital expenditure of 300 per year over the next 5 years; working capital requirements will increase by 50 in years 1 and 2, and stabilise thereafter. The following information is also available:

- The company has net debts today of €2,250m.
- The company's cost of equity is estimated at 10%, and the cost of debt at 6% (before tax).
- Financing is split 2/3 equity and 1/3 debt.
- The tax rate is 37%.
- An increase in inflows of 2% to infinity can be expected from year 6.

Work out the value of Management plc using the DCF method.

3/ The mean multiple for the 2004 operating profits of comparable peers is 15, and the mean 2004 P/E is 25. Calculate the equity value of Pixi Spa. Key figures for the company are set out below.

	€m
Net debt at 31 December 2002	100
2004e operating profits	60
2004e net profits	32

ANSWERS

Questions

1/ *Free cash flows.*
2/ *A liquidity discount only. For a private company the liquidity issue for a minority shareholder will be much more important as probably no one will be buyer of its minority stake (apart maybe from the majority shareholder!). Stock market for a minority shareholder provides some (if not perfect) liquidity.*
3/ *See chapter.*
4/ *He should pay less because information asymmetry works against him. There is a price to be paid for strategic reasons (e.g., to enter a market). This is where the advisory banks come in – their role is to reduce information asymmetry.*
5/ *No. At the end of the day it will be a value creation for the new group, who gets it (the acquirer or the target's shareholders) is a negotiation question.*
6/ *A company with a large market share that is very well run and in a high-growth nonstrategic market segment.*

7/ DCF value, sum-of-the parts value, sum-of-the parts value, sum-of-the parts value, DCF value, DCF value.

8/ Yes, because an asset can have a value for an investor or a trade buyer that differs from its value within the company it currently forms part of.

9/ It looks like the sum-of-the-parts method but it is actually the normalised cash flow method.

10/ Valuation of inventories, quality of the estate's land.

11/ Sum-of-the-parts value.

12/ Synergy gains are important here, not a majority control premium compared with the minority.

13/ Consulting services, advertising and Internet companies.

14/ Yes, for an LBO[10] (see Chapter 44). Yes. Improved management, more efficient allocation of resources and better sharing of information.

10 *Leveraged Buy Out.*

Exercises

1/ Present value with profits of 21: €86.4m. Present value with profits of 14: €17.6m. A one-third drop in profits reduces the value by more than 80% – very high volatility of value.

2/ Cost of capital 7.9%. Enterprise value = €6,967m. Equity value = €4,730m.

Years	1	2	3	4	5	Terminal value
EBITDA	912	981	1,050	1,038	1,068	
– Corporate income tax	216	246	279	273	285	
– Change in working capital	50	50	0	0	0	
– Capital expenditure	300	300	300	300	300	
= Free cash flows	346	385	471	465	483	8,307

3/ Equity value = €800m.

BIBLIOGRAPHY

A. Cheng, R. McNamara, *The Valuation Accuracy of the Price-Earnings and Price-Book Benchmark Valuation Methods*, working paper, 1998.

T. Copeland, T. Koller, J. Murrin, *Valuation: Measuring and Managing the Value of Companies*, 3rd edn, John Wiley & Sons, 2000.

A. Damodaran, *Investment Valuation*, 2nd edn, John Wiley & Sons, 2002.

A. Damodaran, *The Dark Side of Valuation*, Financial Times/Prentice Hall, 2001.

L. Kruschwitz, A. Löffler, *DCF*, working paper, 2003.

B.J. Madden, *CFROI Valuation*, Butterworth-Heinemann Finance, 1999.

A. Rappaport, *Creating Shareholder Value*, Free Press, 1997.

G.B. Stewart, J. Stern, *The Quest for Value*, Harpers, 1991.

Chapter 41
CHOICE OF CORPORATE STRUCTURE

What a cast of characters!

Section 41.1
SHAREHOLDER STRUCTURE

Our objective in this section is to demonstrate the importance of a company's shareholder structure. While the study of finance generally includes a clear description of why it is important to value the company and its equity, analysis of who owns the stock and how shareholders are organised is often neglected. Yet, in practice, this is where financial analysts often look first.

There are several reasons for looking precisely at the shareholder base of a company. First, the shareholders theoretically determine the company's strategy, but we must understand who really wields power in the company, the shareholders or the managers. You will undoubtedly recognise the watermark of "agency theory". This theory provides a theoretical explanation of shareholder-manager problems and stands in opposition to the efficient market hypothesis.

Second, we must know the objectives of the shareholders when they are also the managers. Wealth? Power? Fame? In some cases, the shareholder is also a customer or supplier of the company. In an agricultural cooperative, for example, the shareholders are upstream in the production process. The cooperative company becomes a tool serving the needs of the producers, rather than a profit centre in its own right. This is probably why many agricultural cooperatives are not very profitable.

Lastly, disagreement between shareholders can paralyse a company – in particular, a family-owned company.

Studies have demonstrated that control blocks were much more frequent in Continental European countries than in the UK or the US (Becht and Mayers, 2000, argue that more than 50% of European listed companies are controlled by a single block of voting shareholders). Some have linked this fact with the level of minority protection the law provides. In countries with strong legislation on protection of minority shareholders there will be a larger number of companies not controlled by a single shareholder.

1/DEFINITION OF SHAREHOLDER STRUCTURE

The shareholder structure is the percentage ownership and the percentage of voting rights (see Chapter 6) held by different shareholders. When a company issues shares with multiple voting rights or nonvoting preference shares or represents a cascade of holding companies, these two concepts are separate and distinct. A shareholder having 33% of the shares with double-voting rights will have more control over a company the remaining shares of which are widely held than will a shareholder with 45% of the shares with single-voting rights if two other shareholders hold 25% and 30%. A shareholder who holds 20% of a company's shares directly and 40% of the shares of a company that holds the other 80% will have rights to 52% of the company's earnings but will be in the minority for decision-taking. In the case of companies that issue equity-linked instruments (convertible bonds, warrants, stock options) attention must be paid to the number of shares currently outstanding vs. the fully diluted number of potential shares.

Shareholder structure is the study of how power is distributed among the different shareholders, potential shareholders and managers.

Lastly, without placing much importance on them, we should mention **nominee** (warehousing) **agreements**. Under a nominee agreement, the "real" shareholder sells his shares to a "nominee" and makes a commitment to repurchase them at a specific price, usually in an effort to remain anonymous. A shareholder may enter into a nominee agreement for one of several reasons: transaction confidentiality, group restructuring or deconsolidation, etc. Conceptually, the nominee extends credit to the shareholder and bears counterparty and market risk. If the issuer runs into trouble during the life of the nominee agreement, the original shareholder will be loath to buy back the shares at a price that no longer reflects reality. As a result, nominee agreements are difficult to enforce. Moreover, they can be invalidated if they create an inequality among shareholders. We do not recommend the use of nominee agreements.

2/GENERAL FRAMEWORK

Theoretically, in all jurisdictions, the shareholders of a company ultimately hold the decision power. They exercise it through the assembly of shareholders (AGM). Nevertheless, the types of decisions reserved to the general meeting can differ from one country to another. Generally, shareholders decide on:

- appointment of board members;
- appointment of auditors;
- approval of annual accounts;
- distribution of dividends;
- change in by-laws;
- mergers;
- capital increase and share buyback;
- dissolution.

In most European countries – depending on the type of decision – there are two types of meetings at which shareholders vote: ordinary or extraordinary.

At the Ordinary General Meeting (OGM) of shareholders, shareholders vote on matters requiring a simple majority of voting shares. These include decisions regarding the ordinary course of the company's business such as approving the financial statements, payment of dividends, appointment and removal of members of the board of directors.

At the Extraordinary General Meeting (EGM) of shareholders, shareholders vote on matters that require a change in the company's operating and financial policies: changes in the articles of association, capital increases, mergers, asset contributions, demergers, capital decreases, etc. These decisions require a qualified majority. Depending on the country and on the legal form of the company this qualified majority is generally two thirds or three quarters of outstanding voting rights.

The main levels of control of a company are as follows:

% of voting rights	Power
< Blocking minority	Virtually no control
Between blocking minority and 50%	Veto extraordinary meeting decisions
50%	Veto ordinary meeting decisions
Between 50% and qualified majority	Approve ordinary meeting decisions
≥ Qualified majority	Approve ordinary and extraordinary meeting decisions

	Super-majority	Type of decision
Austria	3/4	Changes in the articles of association Exclusion of subscription rights in the course of capital increase Liquidation
Belgium	3/4	Changes in the articles of association (80% majority for the changes in the purpose)
Denmark	2/3	Changes in the articles of association (90% majority for resolutions which limit dividends, transferability of shares and voting rights)
Finland	2/3	Changes in the articles of association
France	2/3	Merger, demerger Capital increase and decrease Dissolution Changes in the articles of association
Germany	3/4	Reduction and increase of capital Major structural decisions Merger or transformation of the company Changes in the articles of association

	Super-majority	Type of decision
Greece	2/3	Issuance of a loan by means of debt securities Mergers Dissolution of the company Appointment of liquidators Changes in the articles of association
Ireland	3/4	Changes in the articles of association Purchase of own shares Giving of financial assistance for the purchase of own shares Restructuring of the company (may also require court approval) Winding up of the company
Italy	—	Defined in the articles of association
Luxembourg	2/3	Changes in the articles of association
Netherlands	2/3	Restrictions in pre-emption rights Capital reduction
Norway	2/3	Changes in the articles of association (90% for resolutions which limit dividends, transferability of shares and voting rights)
Portugal	2/3	Changes in the articles of association Merger Dissolution
Russia	2/3	Changes in the articles of association Reorganisation of the company Liquidation Capital increase Purchase of own shares Approval of the deal representing more than 50% of the company's assets
Spain	—	Defined in the articles of association
Sweden	2/3	Changes in the articles of association Purchase of own shares
Switzerland	2/3	Changes in the purpose Issue of shares with increased voting powers Limitation of pre-emption rights Change of location Dissolution
UK	3/4	Altering the articles of association Disapplying members' statutory pre-emption rights on issues of further shares for cash Capital decrease Approving the giving of financial assistance/purchase of own shares by a private company, or, off market, by a public company Procuring the winding up of a company by a court Voluntarily winding up a company

(a) Minority shareholders

Shareholders holding less than the blocking minority (if such a concept exists in the country) of a company that has another large shareholder have a limited number of options open to them. They cannot change the company's purpose or the way it is managed. At best, they can force compliance with disclosure rules, call for an audit or an EGM.

Their power is most often limited to that of a naysayer. In other words, a small shareholder can be a thorn in management's side, but no more. Nevertheless, we can observe that their voice has recently become more and more heard, and they have formed some associations defending their interest. Shareholder activism has become a defence tool where the law was not providing one.

It should be noted that in some countries (Sweden, Norway, Portugal) minority shareholders can force the payment of a minimum dividend.

A minority shareholder can protect his interests by concluding a **shareholders' agreement** with other shareholders. Under these contracts, divestment of one shareholder will be coordinated with the others (pre-emptive rights, call/put agreements, ...). In the strongest form of agreement, the block will act as one shareholder both on the board and at the shareholders' meeting (see Section 41.3).

As you will see below, the stock exchange probably offers the minority shareholder the best protection.

(b) Blocking minorities

A shareholder who holds a blocking minority (one-quarter or one-third of the shares plus one share depending on the country and the legal form of the company) can veto any decision taken at an extraordinary shareholders' meeting that would change the company's by-laws, corporate purpose or called-up share capital.

A blocking minority is in a particularly strong position when the company is in trouble, because it is then that the need for operational and financial restructuring is the most pressing. The power of blocking minority shareholders can also be large in periods of rapid growth, when the company needs additional capital.

The notion of a blocking minority is closely linked to exerting control over changes in the company's by-laws. Consequently, the more specific and inflexible the by-laws are, the more power the holder of a blocking minority wields.

A blocking minority does not give its holder control over decisions taken in ordinary shareholders' meetings (dividend payout, etc.). It gives veto power, not direct power.

(c) Joint ventures

Most technological or industrial alliances take place through **joint ventures**, often held 50/50, or through joint partnerships that perform services at cost for the benefit of their shareholders.

These often-ephemeral companies can easily fall victim to boardroom paralysis. When business is booming, one or both of the partners may want to take it over entirely. Conversely, when the joint venture's fortunes are fading, both partners may be looking for an exit.

Preparing the potential future exit of one partner is key when creating a joint venture. Joint venture agreements often have **exit clauses** intended to resolve conflicts. Some examples are:

- a buy–sell provision, also called a **Dutch clause** or a **shotgun clause**. For example, shareholder A offers to sell his shares at a price X to shareholder B. Either B agrees to buy the shares at price X or, if he refuses, he must offer his stake to A at the same price X. Another form calls for a simple auction among shareholders;
- an appraisal clause, which states that the price of a transaction between shareholders will be determined by independent appraisal.

In sum, the joint venture company – like any company – must have a coherent strategy and set of objectives. A 50/50 sharing arrangement injects numerous difficult-to-resolve problems into the management equation.

(d) Employee-shareholders

Many companies have invited their employees to become shareholders. In most of these cases, employees hold a small proportion of the shares and, in a few cases, the majority. This shareholder group, loyal and nonvolatile, lends a degree of stability to the capital and, in general, strengthens the position of the majority shareholder, if any, and of the management.

The main schemes to incentivise employees are:

- **Direct ownership.** Employees and management can invest directly in the shares of the company. In LBOs[1] venture capitalists bring the management into the shareholding structure to minimise agency costs.
- **Employee Stock Ownership Programmes (ESOPs).** ESOPs consist in granting shares to employees as a form of compensation. Alternatively, the shares are acquired by shareholders but the firm will offer free shares so as to encourage employees to invest in the shares of the company. The shares will be held by a trust (or employee savings plan) for the employees. Such programmes can include lockup clauses to maintain the incentive aspect and limit flowback (see Chapter 31). In that case the shares allocated to each employee will vest (i.e., become available) gradually over time.
- **Stock options.** Stock options are a right to subscribe to new (or existing) shares at a certain point in time.

1 *Leveraged Buy Outs.*

For service companies and fast-growing companies, it is key to incentivise employees and management with shares or stock options. For other companies, offering stock to employees can be part of a broader effort to improve employee relations (all types of companies).

For **service companies**, employees arguably constitute their most important asset, so the advantages of making them shareholders are clear. Employees must be in agreement with company policy; if they are not they will leave to join rival firms or start their own. Thus, the employee–management balance of power is very different from the one in industrial companies. This dynamic has given rise to the many forms of partnership commonly used by law firms, investment banks or other companies heavily dependent on human capital.

The wealth-creating capacity of **fast-growing companies** often constitutes an effective source of motivation for middle and upper management, whose personal motivations then contribute directly to the development of the company. For these companies, making managers and other employees shareholders not only generates additional motivation for old employees in the company, but also motivates the new and potential employee-shareholders, who hope to reap a significant capital gain. **Stock options** are the main vector for this policy.

The main challenge of stock option plans is to achieve a soft landing once the company runs out of hypergrowth. The additional motivation the options generate can condemn the company to seeking growth at all costs, while the excess cash should in principle be returned to shareholders. Management will focus on short-term share price growth rather than on long-term value creation.

Lastly, a company may wish to encourage employees to become shareholders as part of a human resources policy aimed at promoting the company's image internally. The success of such a policy largely depends on the overall corporate mood. In large companies, employees can hold up to 10% (Diageo 1%, Bayer 2.1%, Saint-Gobain 6.3%, Société Générale 7.65%, BSCH 10%). Steria, the IT services company, is one of the listed companies with the largest employee shareholding (ca 30%).

Regardless of the type of company and its motivation for making employees shareholders, you should keep in mind that the special relationship between the company and the employee-shareholder cannot last for ever. Prudent investment principles dictate that the employee should not invest too heavily in the shares of the company that pays their salaries, because in so doing they in fact compound the "everyday life" risks they are running. Basically, the company should be a particularly fast-growing and safe one before the employee agrees to a long-term participation in the fruits of its expansion. Most often, this condition is not met. Moreover, just because employees hold stock options does not mean they will be loyal or long-term shareholders. The LBO models we will study in Chapter 44 become dangerous when they make a majority of the employees shareholders. In a crisis, the employees may be keener to protect their jobs than to vote for a painful restructuring. When limited to a small number of employees, however, LBOs create a stable, internal group of shareholders.

(e) The family-owned company

By "family-owned" we mean that the shareholders have been made up of members of the same family for several generations and, often through a holding company, exert a significant influence on management. This is still the dominant model in Europe. Faccio and Lang have analysed the ultimate ownership of 5,232 firms across Western Europe and conclude that still over 44% of the firms are family-owned. British firms are mostly widely held (63% widely held vs. 24% family-owned) and Continental Europe firms are in the majority family-owned (except in northern Europe where ownership is more balanced).

	Europe (%)	France (%)	Germany (%)	UK (%)	Italy (%)	Spain (%)
Spread	37	14	10	63	13	26
Family and nonlisted shareholder	44	65	65	24	60	56
State	4	5	6	0	10	4
Another listed company	2	4	4	1	3	2
Financial institution	9	11	9	9	12	12
Cross-shareholding	1	1	3	0	1	0
Other	3	0	3	3	1	0
By size (% with spread shareholding)						
20 largest	45	60	45	90	35	45
50 mid-sized	29	14	10	65	8	34
50 smallest	25	8	14	42	14	36

Source: Faccio and Lang (2003).

However, this type of shareholder structure is on the decline for several reasons:

- some new or capital-intensive industries, such as telecoms, media and energy/utilities, require so much capital that a family-owned structure is not viable. Indeed, family ownership is more suited to consumer goods, retailing, services, processing, etc.;
- financial markets have matured and financial savings are now properly rewarded, so that, with rare exception, diversification is a better investment strategy than concentration on a specific risk (see Section II of this book);
- increasingly, family-owned companies are being managed on the basis of financial criteria, prompting the family group either to exit the capital or to dilute the family's interests in a larger pool of investors that it no longer controls.

Lastly, there are generally no tax incentives for a company to remain family-owned. In fact, family members who are passive investors in the company are in Europe penalised though inheritance taxes and wealth taxes.

In the EuroStoxx 50 very few companies have controlling shareholders or minority shareholders with a stake above 20%:

- LVMH is still family-controlled. The founding families (together with the Spanish group March) still hold c. 20% stake in Carrefour.
- L'Oréal is held at 27% by the Bettencourt family and 26% by Nestlé.
- Olympia holds c. 21% of Telecom Italia.
- The French state owns (as we write) the majority of the capital of France Telecom, the Italian state holds 30% in ENI and 31% in ENEL (which should be lowered to 20%), and the German state 26% in Deutsche Telekom.

- Regional banks (caisses régionales) hold 52% of Crédit Agricole SA.
- Unicredito is held at over 20% by Italian foundations.
- Management holds nearly 40% of the capital of SAP.

(f) Financial investors, investment funds and financial holding companies

The term "financial investors" regroups entities with a wide variety of investment objectives and approaches. Some are passive investment funds that do not participate in the management of the company. Others constitute the largest single shareholder in a company, with 20–40% of the capital, and hold seats on the board of directors. Financial investors holding a significant stake will then participate in defining the company's strategy. Finally, some financial investors, holding more than 50% of the capital, control the company. They determine strategy and appoint senior executives.

There has recently been considerable change in Continental Europe in this regard. Only a few years ago, large financial holding companies, such as Deutsche Bank, Paribas, Mediobanca, Société Générale de Belgique, Investor (the Wallenbergs), etc., played a major role in managing companies. In most cases these holdings were linked to a large banking group which financed them and helped them set up industrial empires through cross-shareholdings. In a sense, they played the role of (then-deficient) capital markets. Although their orientation was fundamentally financial, with financial returns their primary objective, they held their investments for a very long time. Their gradual disappearance or mutation has led to the breakup of core shareholder groups and cross-shareholdings.

Today, private equity funds, financed by insurance companies, pension funds or other investors, play a major role. In most cases these funds specialise in a certain type of investment vehicle: LBO funds, mezzanine funds, venture capital funds, "vulture" funds that purchase the debt of a struggling company in order to take it over, and so on. They invest in companies put on the block (i.e., put up for sale) by a group looking to refocus on its core business or by a family-held group faced with succession problems. These private equity funds can also give an acquisitive company in a consolidating market the resources it needs to achieve its goals. Finally, the funds may help a company whose shares are depressed (in the opinion of the management) to delist itself in a **public to private** (P to P) transaction.

Managed by teams of investment professionals whose compensation is linked to performance, these funds have a limited lifespan (no more than 10 years). Before the closing of the fund, the companies that the fund has acquired are resold, floated on the stock exchange or the fund's investments are taken over by another fund.

Before concluding, a note about corporate governance. In companies not controlled by dominant shareholders, you must scrutinise the composition of the board of directors and how it functions, even as closely as the shareholder structure. Certain investors can take de facto control of the board without having control in terms of number of shares or voting rights.

Section 41.2
Initial Public Offerings (IPOs) and corporate governance

Theoretically, the principles of financial management that we have developed throughout this book find their full expression in the share price of the company. They apply to unlisted companies as well, but for a listed company market approval or disapproval, expressed through the share price, is immediate. Today, a stock exchange listing offers distinct benefits: **it enables a financial manager to access capital markets and obtain a market value for his company**.

When you see that several billion euros can change hands on financial markets in the course of a few hours (few days if you take into account the preparation of the transaction), you can understand that markets constitute a very different means than the complex negotiations necessary to obtain private financing.

"Paper" – i.e., financial securities – can be placed on financial markets so quickly because:

* financial analysts periodically publish studies reviewing company fundamentals, reinforcing the market's efficiency (see Chapter 15);
* listing on an organised market enables financial managers to "sell" the company in the form of securities that are bought and sold solely as a function of profitability and risk. Poor management is punished by poor share price performance, or worse – from management's point of view – by a takeover offer;
* listed companies must publish up-to-date financial information and file an annual report (or equivalent) with the market authority.

1/The decision to list a company

Whether or not to float a company on the stock exchange is a question that **concerns** first and foremost **the shareholders** rather than the company. But, technically, it is the company that requests a listing on the stock exchange.

When a company is listed, its shareholders' investments become more **liquid**, but the difference for shareholders between a listed company and an unlisted company is not always that significant. Companies listed on the market gain liquidity at the time of the listing, since a significant part of the equity is floated. But, thereafter, only a few shares are usually traded every day, unless the market "falls in love" with the company and a long-term relationship begins.

An IPO is always to the advantage of minority shareholders.

In addition to real or potential liquidity, a stock market listing gives the minority shareholder a level of protection that no shareholders' pact can provide. The company must publish certain information, and the market expects a consistent dividend policy. In the event the majority shareholders sell their stake, the rights of minority shareholders are protected (see Chapter 42).

Conversely, a listing complicates life for the majority shareholder. Liquidity gives him the opportunity to sell some of his shares in the market without losing control of the company. Listing can also allow a majority shareholder to get rid of a bothersome or restless minority shareholder by providing a forum for the minority shareholder to sell his shares in an orderly manner. But, in return, the majority shareholder will no longer be able to ignore financial parameters such as P/E multiples, EPS, dividends per share, etc. (see Chapter 28) when determining his strategy.

Once a majority shareholder has taken his company public, investors will judge his company on its ability to create value and communicate financial information properly. As we will see in Chapter 42, delisting a company to take it private again is a long, drawn-out process.

For the company, a stock market listing presents several advantages:

- the company becomes widely known to other stakeholders (customers, suppliers, etc.). If the company communicates well, the listing constitutes a superb form of "free" advertising, on an international scale;
- the company can tap the financial markets for additional funding and acquire other companies, using its shares as currency. This constitutes invaluable flexibility for the company;
- the company finds it easier to incentivise employees to the success of the company through stock options, stock-based bonuses, etc.;
- in a group, a mother company can obtain a market value for a subsidiary by listing it, in the hope that the value will be high enough to have a positive impact on the value of the parent company's shares;

Now for the warning flags: a stock market listing does not guarantee happy shareholders. If only a small percentage of the shares are traded, or if total market capitalisation is low – i.e., less than €200m, large institutional investors will not be interested, especially if the company is not included in a benchmark index (see Chapter 15). Volatility on the shares will be relatively high because the presence of just a few buyers (or sellers) will easily drive up (down) the share price significantly. The French and UK governments have stepped in to create tax or regulatory incentives (for insurance companies) to invest in such "small-cap" companies. In Section 41.4 we will look at the different types of discounts that can affect a listed stock.

A listing can also be virtual, as it is in a tracking stock (see p. 594).

2/IPO TECHNIQUES

See Chapter 31.

3/CHOOSING A MARKET FOR THE IPO

One of the essential choices to be made in an IPO is on which market the stock will be listed.

(a) Principles

With rare exception, the natural market for the listing is the company's home country. This is where the company is best known to local investors, who are the most likely to accord it the highest value. Only a very small number of companies from major European countries are not listed in their home country.

The next question is whether there should be a second listing on a foreign market. In the 1970s and 1980s, European companies sought to free themselves from the constraints of their domestic market and create a broader shareholder base. This desire led to a trend of simultaneous listings on several exchanges, essentially in Europe: Belgium, Germany, Switzerland, the United Kingdom.

Beginning in the mid-1980s, many companies felt that an additional listing was unnecessary because European markets were becoming increasingly integrated. Conversely, a listing on a US market started to become attractive.

Listing on a foreign market generally constitutes a constraint on a company, because it requires additional financial reporting. With a listing on a foreign market therefore come direct and indirect costs. We see three justifications for bearing these costs:

- financial: facilitate capital increases through access to a larger pool of investors, enable share-based takeovers of foreign companies, reduce the cost of equity capital or, equivalently, increase the value of the company's shares;
- commercial: make the company and its brands more widely known internationally, thereby facilitating the relationship with customers and suppliers;
- social: create a new type of compensation (stock options) for the employees of foreign subsidiaries.

Reducing the cost of capital is the most intellectually valid reason. It is based on the observation that international markets remain segmented. Domestic investors still have strong incentives – legal, tax or cultural – for investing in securities listed on their home markets. Multiple listings enable a company to access a greater pool of investors. Listing on a foreign exchange will also allow reducing information asymmetry because the company must comply with the same stringent disclosure rules as other companies, the securities of which are traded in the market in question. Finally, foreign listings put the company in a more favourable light back home. A company that has successfully run the SEC[2] gauntlet will command more respect in its home market as US regulation is considered by investors as a reference (although this might be less true since the issues faced by Enron and WorldCom).

2 *Securities and Exchange Commission.*

This said, statistical analysis has not shown that multiple listings significantly lower the cost of capital. Experience shows that liquidity begets liquidity and that transaction volume gravitates very quickly and virtually irreversibly to the most liquid market.

The current transaction volumes of three companies listed both in Europe and the United States are shown at the top of the next page.

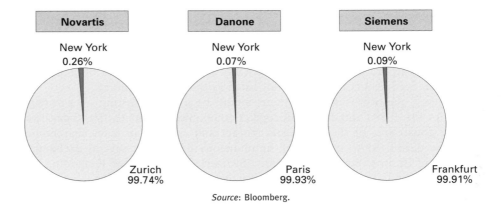

Source: Bloomberg.

Institutional investors buy and sell shares in the most liquid market, which in the vast majority of cases is the company's home market.

The only real advantages for listing in a country other than a company's home country are that the company can use its shares to pay for acquisitions in the foreign country and provide stock-based incentives to local employees. But, obviously, fashion can also influence the listing choices.

(b) In Europe

Traditionally, national European stock markets offered firms a choice of two market segments (one for large and one for small capitalisations).

In the mid-1990s national stock markets created segments dedicated to young and fast-growing companies (*Nouveau Marché* in France, *Neuer Markt* in Germany, *NMAX* in the Netherlands, *Euro.NM* in Belgium, *Nuovo Mercato* in Italy, . . .). These markets had great success in the listing of TMT[3] companies in the 1999–2001 years but most of these segments did not survive the bursting of the Internet bubble. One after the other the new markets closed and it was proposed to the companies still listed on those markets to join traditional market segments.

Euro NM[4] (a grouping of the abovementioned national new markets) and its competitor NASDAQ[5] Europe (or EASDAQ) also disappeared.

The globalisation of financial markets has prompted the Paris, Brussels, Amsterdam and Lisbon Stock Exchanges to join together to form Euronext. Euronext is now a leading stock exchange in Europe alongside Frankfurt, London, Milan and Zurich. Consolidation in European stock exchanges is expected to continue (with the London Stock Exchange likely to consolidate with either the Deutsche Börse or Euronext).

Besides national stock exchange segments, Euronext has developed two additional segments (NextPrime for old-enconomy firms and NextEconomy for new-technology firms) with specific information requirements (publish financial information in English, have information available on the company website, use IASBs[6], release quarterly financial information).

In 2005, Euronext stock exchanges (Belgium, France, the Netherlands and Portugal) merged their national market segments to form Eurolist. In this single list, companies are assigned a capitalisation indicator (A for a market cap above

3 *Telecom Media Technology*.

4 *Euro New Market*.

5 *National Association of Securities Dealers Automatic Quotation system*.

6 *International Accounting Standard Board standards*.

€1bn, B for a market cap between €150m and €1bn, and C for a market cap below €150m).

Beyond the segment where the company is listed, more important are the indices to which it belongs. Each country has its famous traditional indices (FTSE 100 in the UK, MIB 30 in Italy, CAC 40 in France, etc.); in addition, some pan-European indices have been developed (EuroStoxx 50, Euronext 100). Being part of an index will bring liquidity and therefore a better valuation to the share. Some funds called "tracking funds" aim at replicating the exact performance of an index. We can observe that when a company is included in an index its share price goes up.

(c) US markets

There are two principal markets, the New York Stock Exchange (NYSE) and National Association of Securities Dealers Automated Quotation system (NASDAQ).

- The NYSE was founded in 1792 and remains the largest stock exchange in the world both in transaction volumes and market capitalisation. It attracts the largest companies in its market: 2,800 companies are listed on the NYSE, including 470 non-US companies.
- Founded in 1971, NASDAQ is the electronic quotation system behind the eponymous market for innovative American SMEs.[7] Around 3,600 stocks are listed on NASDAQ. It has been so successful that certain companies listed on it have become large groups in their own right, such as Microsoft, Intel, Apple, and have remained listed on NASDAQ. In fact, NASDAQ includes two market segments: the NASDAQ National Market, where the most active stocks are traded, and the NASDAQ Small Cap Market, where the shares of smaller companies are traded.

7 *Small- and Medium-sized Enterprises.*

Criteria for admission to the US stock exchanges include profitability at the time of the IPO, minimum capital requirements and corporate governance criteria, such as number of independent board members. Disclosure requirements are more numerous than on European markets and include, for example, quarterly financial statements in compliance with US GAAP.[8] For this reason, many non-US companies list their shares in the form of American Depositary Receipts (ADR).[9]

8 *Generally Accepted Accounting Principles.*

9 *See p. 612.*

Section 41.3
HOW TO STRENGTHEN CONTROL OVER A COMPANY

Defensive measures for maintaining control of a company always carry a cost. From a purely financial point of view, this is perfectly normal: there are no free lunches!

> Measures to preserve control are not only costly to put in place but also effectively preclude the company from accessing certain financial instruments. These costs are borne by current shareholders and, ultimately, by the company itself in the form of a higher cost of capital.

With this in mind, let us now take a look at the various takeover defences at the disposal of a European company. We will see that they vary greatly depending on the country, on the existence or absence of a regulatory framework and on the powers granted to companies and their executives. Certain countries, such as the UK, and to a lesser extent, France and Italy, regulate anti-takeover measures strictly, while others, such as Germany and the Netherlands, allow companies much more leeway.

Broadly speaking, countries where financial markets play a significant role in evaluating management performance, because companies are more widely held, have more stringent regulations. This is the case in the UK and France.

Conversely, countries where capital is concentrated in relatively few hands have either more flexible regulation or no regulation at all. This goes hand-in-hand with the by-laws of the companies, which ensure existing management a high level of protection. In Germany, half of the seats on the board of directors are reserved for employees, and board members can be replaced only by a 75% majority vote. Similarly, in the Netherlands and Switzerland, the supervisory board has extensive powers, and boards can issue a large number of shares without prior approval of the EGM.

Paradoxically, when the market's power to inflict punishment on companies is unchecked, companies and their executives may feel such insecurity that they agree to protect themselves via the by-laws. Sometimes this contractual protection is to the detriment of the company's welfare and of free market principles. This practice is common in the US.

The extremely long discussions on the European directive on public offers (which has finally been adopted in 2004) demonstrate precisely this difficulty: how to coax very different stock market regulations from one country to another toward a common standard. In the UK, the sanctity of the market is the rule, whereas Germany prizes its respect for employee rights. France stands somewhere between the two. The directive attempts to generalise certain guiding principles. In particular, it states that management should have only limited ability to implement defensive measures without prior consulting with shareholders. The directive also states that the acquisition of a listed company should be made through launching a public offer on 100% of capital.

Defensive measures fall into four categories:

➢ Separate management control from financial control:

- o different classes of shares – shares with multiple voting rights and nonvoting shares;
- o holding companies;
- o limited partnerships.

- ➤ Control shareholder changes:
  - ○ right of approval;
  - ○ pre-emption rights.
- ➤ Strengthen the position of loyal shareholders:
  - ○ reserved capital increase;
  - ○ share buyback and cancellation;
  - ○ mergers and other tie-ups;
  - ○ employee shareholdings;
  - ○ warrants.
- ➤ Exploit legal and regulatory protection:
  - ○ regulations;
  - ○ voting caps;
  - ○ strategic assets.

1/SEPARATING MANAGEMENT CONTROL FROM FINANCIAL CONTROL

(a) Different classes of shares: shares with multiple voting rights and nonvoting shares

As an exception to the general rule, under which the number of votes attributed to each share must be directly proportional to the percentage of the capital it represents (principle of one share, one vote), companies have in some countries the right to issue multiple voting shares or nonvoting shares.

In the Netherlands, and the Scandinavian countries, dual classes of shares are commonplace. The company issues two (or more) types of shares (generally named A shares and B shares) with the same financial rights but with different voting rights.

French corporate law provides for the possibility of double-voting shares but, contrarily to dual-class shares, all shareholders can benefit from the double-voting rights if they hold the shares for a certain time.

Multiple voting shares can be particularly powerful, as the following example will illustrate: Trader Classified Media is a Dutch-listed company which is a leader in the classified advertising sector worldwide. Trader Classified Media has two classes of shares. The 39.6 million A shares bear one voting right each whereas the 51.6 million B shares bear 12 voting rights each. The controlling shareholder (Groupe MacBain) holds mainly B shares having 67.6% of voting rights but only 47.3% of capital.

These dual-class shares can appear as unfair and opposite to the principle that the person who brings the capital gets the power in a company. Some countries (Italy, Spain, UK and Germany) have outlawed dual-class shares.

Issuing nonvoting shares is similar to issuing dual-class shares because some of the shareholders will bring capital without getting voting power. Nevertheless, issuing nonvoting shares is a more widely spread practice than issuing dual-class shares across Europe. Actually, as a compensation for giving up their voting rights, holders of nonvoting shares usually get a preference treatment regarding dividends (fixed dividend, increased dividend) compared with ordinary shareholders ....

Therefore, nonvoting (preference) shares are not perceived as unfair but as a different arbitrage from the investor between return, risk and power in the company.

(b) Holding companies

Holding companies can be useful but their intensive use leads to complex, multi-tiered shareholding structures. As you might imagine, they present both advantages and disadvantages.

Suppose an investor holds 51% of a holding company, which in turn holds 51% of a second holding company, which in turn holds 51% of an industrial company. Although he holds only 13% of the capital of this industrial company, the investor uses a cascade of holding companies to maintain control of the industrial company.

A holding company allows a shareholder to maintain control of a company, because a structure with a holding disperses minority shareholders. Even if the industrial company were floated on the stock exchange, the minority shareholders in the different holding companies would not be able to sell their stakes.

Maximum marginal personal income tax is generally higher than income taxes on dividends from a subsidiary. Therefore, a holding company structure allows the controlling shareholder to draw off dividends with a minimum tax bite and use them to buy more shares in the industrial company.

Technically, a holding company can "trap" minority shareholders; in practice, this situation often leads to an ongoing conflict between shareholders. For this reason, holding companies are usually based on a group of core shareholders intimately involved in the management of the company.

A two-tiered holding company structure often exists where:

- a holding company controls the operating company;
- a top holding company holds the controlling holding company. The shareholders of the top holding are the core group. This top holding's main purpose is to buy back the shares of minority shareholders seeking to sell some of their shares.

Often, a holding company is formed to represent the family shareholders prior to an IPO. For example, Profesa Investment BV and Portman Baela SL are holding companies formed to hold the del Pino family's stakes in Ferrovial.

(c) Limited Share Partnerships (LSPs)

A limited share partnership introduces a complete separation between management and financial ownership of the company.

A limited share partnership is a company the share capital of which is divided into shares, but with two types of partners:

- several limited partners with the status of shareholders, whose liability is limited to the amount of their investment in the company. A limited share partnership is akin to a public limited company in this respect;

- one or more general partners, who are jointly and severally liable, to an unlimited extent, for the debts of the company. Senior executives of the company are usually general partners, with limited partners being barred from the executive suite.

The company's by-laws determine how present and future executives are to be chosen. These top managers have the most extensive powers to act on behalf of the company in all circumstances. They can be fired only under the terms specified in the by-laws. The general partners can limit their financial liability by setting up a (limited liability) family holding company. In addition, the LSP structure allows a change in management control of the operating company to take place within the holding company. As an example, a father can hand over the reins to his son, while the holding company continues to perform its management functions.

Thus, theoretically, the chief executive of a limited share partnership can enjoy absolute and irrevocable power to manage the company without owning a single share. Management control does not derive from financial control, as in a public limited company, but from the stipulations of the by-laws, in accordance with applicable law. Limited share partnerships have recently gained renewed attractiveness because the general partners can be legal entities, which limit their liability by circumventing the spirit of the law ... for now. Several large, listed, French and Swiss companies have adopted limited share partnership form, including Merck, Michelin and Lagardère (Pirelli until 2003).

2/CONTROLLING SHAREHOLDER CHANGES

(a) Right of approval

The right of approval, written into a company's by-laws, enables a company to avoid "undesirable" shareholders. This clause is frequently found in family-owned companies or in companies with a delicate balance between shareholders. The right of approval governs the relationship between partners or shareholders of the company; be careful not to confuse it with the type of approval required to purchase certain companies (see below).

Technically, the right-of-approval clause requires every partner to obtain the approval of the company prior to selling any of his shares. The company must render its decision within a specified time period. If no decision is rendered, the approval is deemed granted.

If it refuses, the company, its board of directors, executive committee, senior executives or a third party must buy back the shares within a specified period of time, or the shareholder can consummate the initially planned sale.

The purchase price is set by agreement between the parties or, in the event that no agreement is reached, by independent appraisal.

Right-of-approval clauses might not be applied when shares are sold between shareholders or between a shareholder, his spouse or his ascendants and descendants.

(b) Pre-emption rights

Akin to the right of approval, the pre-emption clause gives a category of shareholders or all shareholders a priority right to acquire any shares offered for sale. Companies whose existing shareholders want to increase their stake or control changes in the capital use this clause. The board of directors, the chief executive or any other authorised person can decide how shares are divided amongst the shareholders.

Technically, pre-emption rights procedures are similar to those governing the right of approval.

Most of the time, pre-emption rights do not apply in the case of inherited shares, liquidation of a married couple's community property or if a shareholder sells shares to his spouse, ascendants or descendants.

Right-of-approval and pre-emption right clauses constitute a means for controlling changes in the shareholder structure of a company. If the clause is written into the by-laws and applies to all shareholders, it can prevent any undesirable third party from obtaining control of the company. These clauses cannot block a sale of shares indefinitely, however. The existing shareholders must always find a solution that allows a sale to take place in the event they do not wish to buy.

3/ STRENGTHENING THE POSITION OF LOYAL SHAREHOLDERS

(a) Reserved capital increases

In some countries, such as the Netherlands, a company can issue new shares at terms that are highly dilutive for the existing shareholders. For example, to fend off a rampant takeover by LVMH, the Italian group Gucci[10] issued a large block of shares to the PPR Group through a reserved capital increase, which left LVMH with a highly diluted stake.

The new shares can be purchased either for cash or for contributed assets. For example, a family holding company can contribute assets to the operating company to strengthen its control over this company.

In the strongest form of poison pill, shares can be issued at a discount to share price.

(b) Mergers

Mergers are first and foremost a method for achieving strategic and industrial goals. As far as controlling the capital of a company is concerned, a merger can have the same effect as a reserved capital increase, by diluting the stake of a hostile shareholder or bringing in a new, friendly shareholder. We will look at the technical aspects in Chapter 43.

The risk, of course, is that the new shareholders, initially brought in to support existing management, will gradually take over control of the company.

(c) Share buybacks and cancellations

This technique, which we studied in Chapter 38 as a financial technique, can also be used to strengthen control over the capital of a company. The company offers to

10 *Gucci was then listed in the Netherlands and in the US through a Dutch holding company.*

repurchase a portion of outstanding shares with the intention of cancelling them. As a result, the percentage ownership of the shareholders who do not subscribe to the repurchase offer increases. In fact, a company can regularly repurchase shares. For example, Peugeot regularly uses this method for strengthening the control of the family shareholders.

(d) Employee shareholdings

Employee-shareholders generally have a tendency to defend a company's independence when there is a threat of a change in control. A company that has taken advantage of the legislation favouring different employee share ownership schemes can generally count on a few percentage points of support in its effort to maintain the existing equilibrium in its capital. In 1999, for example, the employee-shareholders of Société Générale rallied behind management in its effort to see off BNP's takeover bid. The various forms of employee share ownership include profit-sharing plans, stock option plans, capital increases reserved for employees and stock-based company pension plans. Employee savings plans almost always enjoy favourable tax treatment.

(e) Warrants

The company issues warrants to certain investors. If a change in control threatens the company, investors exercise their warrants and become shareholders. This issue of new shares will make a takeover more difficult, because the new shares dilute the ownership stake of all other shareholders.

For example KLM has issued an option to the Dutch government such that if its flight authorisations are challenged by another country[11] the Dutch government can take 50.1% of the capital of KLM.

This type of provision is very common in the Netherlands (Ahold is another Dutch example) and in the US.

11 *In the current state of regulation each airline must be controlled by investors of the home country to keep its authorisations.*

4/LEGAL AND REGULATORY PROTECTION

(a) Regulations

Certain investments or takeovers require approval from a government agency or other body with vetoing power. In most countries, sectors where there are needs for a specific approval are:

* media;
* financial institutions;
* activities related to national defence (for national security reasons).

Golden shares are special shares that enable governments to prevent another shareholder from increasing its stake above a certain threshold in some recently privatised companies (the Spanish government used it for Telefónica, Repsol and Endesa; the Italian one for Enel and Telecom Italia). The legitimacy of golden shares is being questioned by EU authorities.

(b) Voting caps

In principle, the very idea of limiting the right to vote that accompanies a share of stock contradicts the principle of "one share, one vote". Nevertheless, companies can limit the vote of any shareholder to a specific percentage of the capital. In some cases, the limit falls away once the shareholder reaches a very large portion of the capital (e.g., 50% or 2/3).

For example, Danone's by-laws stipulate that no shareholder may cast more than 6% of all single-voting rights and no more than 12% of all double-voting rights at a shareholders' meeting, unless he owns more than two-thirds of the shares. It is commonly used in Europe, specifically in Switzerland (12 firms out of the 50 largest use it), Germany, Belgium, the Netherlands and Spain. BASF, Bayer, Deutsche Bank, Nestlé, Total, Alcatel and Novartis use voting caps.

This is a very effective defence. It prevents an outsider from taking control of a company with only 20% or 30% of the capital. If he truly wants to take control, he has to "ante up" and bid for all of the shares. We can see that this technique is particularly useful for companies of at least a certain size. It makes sense only for companies that do not have a strong core shareholder.

(c) Strategic assets (poison pills)

Strategic assets can be patents, brand names or subsidiaries comprising most of the business or generating most of the profits of a group. In some cases the company does not actually own the assets but simply uses them under licence. In other cases these assets are located in a subsidiary with a partner who automatically gains control should control of the parent company change hands. Often contested as misuse of corporate property, poison pill arrangements are very difficult to implement and, in practice, are generally ineffective.

As a general matter, change of control provisions on key contracts can play the role of poison pills. These contracts can be joint venture agreements, distribution contracts or even bank debt contract.

5/THE LESSONS OF THE PAST

Anti-takeover measures are difficult to implement once a company is in the thick of a takeover battle. Most often, they force the bidder to sweeten his offer, but rarely to abandon it. In so doing, however, a hostile offer sometimes becomes a friendly one (e.g., Vodafone/Mannesmann, Lafarge/Blue Circle).

Whether a hostile offer is successful or a white knight (i.e., a counter-bidder welcomed by the management of the target company) comes to the rescue, events invariably lead to the loss of the target company's independence.

Which, then, are the most effective defensive measures?

In recent bids involving large companies, those that have taken the initiative far upstream have been at a clear advantage. An integral part of a good defence is being in a position to seize opportunities. Moreover, a company must anticipate potential threats and be in a position to strike first if necessary.

Loyal shareholders can be the best defence. What makes them loyal?

* good financial performance;
* crystal-clear financial communication;
* a share price that reflects the company's value; and
* skilled management, who respect the principles of shareholders' value and corporate governance.

Section 41.4
FINANCIAL SECURITIES' DISCOUNTS

When a financial security trades at a discount – i.e., when the market value of the security is less than the value as we have defined it throughout this book – the market is inefficient. For example, if you cannot sell a bond, the discounted present value of which is 100 for more than 80, the market is inefficient.

When a security sells at a discount, the market is inefficient.

With this definition in mind, we examine below the different types of discounts on equities.

1/IPO OR "LIQUIDITY" DISCOUNTS

When a company is first floated on the stock market, its share price generally rises (see Chapter 31). Statistics show, for example, an average rise of 9% in the UK, and 15–16% in the US and France. The discount reflects the fact that sellers, on the one hand, and investors or intermediaries, on the other, have different information. The former have more information on the company's prospects, while the latter have a good idea of market demand. A deal is therefore possible, but price is paramount. In this asymmetrical situation, signal theory says that the sale of shares by the shareholders is a negative signal, so the seller is obliged to "leave some money on the table" in return for ensuring that the IPO goes off smoothly and to investors' satisfaction.

In an unlisted company, a minority shareholder who wants to sell his stake will suffer a liquidity discount. He knows the value of the shares he wants to sell, but cannot obtain that value unless the majority shareholder also decides to sell. We find the same phenomenon in a listed company with a narrow **free float** and whose capital is controlled by one or a few shareholders. A minority shareholder can only exit at the listed, market price, which depends on the principal shareholder's financial communication policy. Many small- and medium-sized listed companies are chronically undervalued because of insufficient liquidity of their shares.

In a widely held listed company, things are different. Minority shareholders are to a large extent protected by the regulatory authorities, which watch out for their interests. This brings us back to the debate in Chapter 40 over control premiums.

2/ HOLDING COMPANY DISCOUNTS

A holding company owns minority or majority investments in listed or unlisted companies either for purely financial reasons or for the purpose of control.

A holding company trades at a discount when its market capitalisation is less than the sum of the investments it holds. This is usually the case: for example, the holding company holds assets worth 100, but the stock market values the holding company at 80 only. Consequently, the investor who buys the holding company's stock will think he is buying something "at a discount", because he is paying 80 for something that is worth 100. But he knows that the holding company will always sell at a discount. The market value of the holding will never reach 100 unless something happens to eliminate the discount, such as a merger between the holding company and its operating subsidiary.

The size of the discount varies with prevailing stock market conditions. In bull markets holding company discounts tend to contract, while in bear markets they can widen to more than 30%. Some investors speculate on these changes as a function of index performance.

Here are three reasons for this phenomenon:

- the free float of the holding company is usually smaller than that of the companies in which it is invested, making the holding's shares less liquid;
- tax inefficiencies. Capital gains on the shares held by the holding are taxed twice: first at the holding company level, then at the level of the shareholders. Moreover, it takes time for the flow of dividends to come from the operating company up to the ultimate holding company;
- administrative inefficiencies: the holding company has its own administrative costs, which, discounted over a long period, constitute a liability to be subtracted from the value of the investments it holds. Imagine a holding company valued at €2bn with administrative costs of €10m p.a. If those costs are projected to infinity and discounted at 8% p.a., their present value is €125m before tax, or 6.25% of the value of the holding company.

These factors can generally explain a statistical discount up to the 15–25% range. Beyond that, the discount is probably more indicative of a power struggle between investors and holding companies. The former want to get rid of the latter and finance the operating assets directly. The disappearance of many listed holding companies over the last few years, such as Olivetti and IFI in Italy, Marine Wendel and Eurafrance in France, Cobepa and Electrabel in Belgium or Companie Financière Michelin in Switzerland, has demonstrated how effective investor pressure can be.

3/ CONGLOMERATE DISCOUNTS

A conglomerate is an industrial group active in several, diverse businesses. Whether the group combines water and telecoms or missiles and magazines, the market value of the conglomerate is usually less than the sum of the values of the assets the conglomerate holds. The difference, the conglomerate discount, generally reflects investors' fears that resources will be poorly allocated. In other words, the group might de-emphasise profitable investments in order to support ailing divisions, the profitability of which is mediocre or below their cost of capital.

Moreover, investors now want "pure play" stocks and prefer to diversify their holdings themselves. In a conglomerate, investors cannot select the company's portfolio of assets; investors are in fact stuck with the holding company's choice. As in the case of holding companies, head office costs absorb some of the value of the conglomerate. Finally, a company can suffer both a conglomerate and a holding company discount if some of the company's activities are lodged in a listed subsidiary.

A persistent conglomerate discount usually leads to a spinoff[12] or a hostile takeover bid.[13]

12 *See Chapter 43.*

13 *See Chapter 42.*

Section 41.5
ORGANISING A DIVERSIFIED GROUP

Imagine you were suddenly at the helm of a diversified industrial group. What sort of organisation should you choose? Should you set up a separate company for each major business unit, with a holding company overseeing them or a single legal entity with several divisions?

1/SUBSIDIARIES OR DIVISIONS?

If your group is built around a parent company that owns virtually all of its different subsidiaries, the "one-to-many" or "flat" model presents several organisational advantages. The senior management of each subsidiary has more autonomy. Profitable companies shine and are not damaged by money-losing operations, making the group as a whole more transparent.

Does the choice of structure have an impact on the value of diversified groups? The efficient market hypothesis says no, there should be no significant difference between the two models.

If in fact there is a difference, it is most often a result of taxes, even if it is becoming easier and easier to build a tax consolidation group wherein the losses of some companies can be offset against the taxable profits of the others. The flat organisational structure is often composed of a cash-poor parent and cash-rich subsidiaries, and managing the resulting cash flows is often complex. Lastly, shareholders are one step removed from the 99.99%-owned subsidiaries, which are managed by the holding company, not the shareholders.

Listing certain subsidiaries brings in minority shareholders and increases the capital available to the group while offering investors a slice of the assets that interest them the most. The same reasoning holds for bringing financial investors into the capital of the subsidiaries.

Opinions vary widely on this topic. The company gains access to equity financing without fundamentally changing the capital structure of the group. Carried too far, however, the parent company becomes a financial holding company with the problem of the holding company discount.

We note, however, that in certain sectors of the economy legislation requires the presence of a financial partner or a public listing. In Luxembourg, for example, a shareholder may not hold more than 25% of the capital of a radio station; in France no one may own more than 49% of a free-to-air TV channel. A recent study has shown that the share price performance of the subsidiary improves when the parent company's stake falls below 50%! A company that creates a new subsidiary and sells a stake on the stock exchange is said to perform a **carveout**.

Depending on market conditions, valuations and strategies, sometimes it will be advantageous to list subsidiaries and bring in minority shareholders and sometimes it will be better to do the opposite and delist a subsidiary. Many companies – Telefónica, France Télécom, Deutsche Telekom, Dixon's, to name a few – listed their Internet or similar subsidiaries in 2000. This was to take advantage of the high multiples the market was ascribing to the sector in the hope of paying for future acquisitions with the shares of their newly listed subsidiaries rather than with cash. This strategy works well when valuations are high because, when acquisitions are paid in paper, the question of price becomes one of parity. At the same time, many "old-economy" companies – Lafarge, Saint Gobain and Kingfisher stand out as examples – bought out minority shareholders in their listed subsidiaries, as the market had virtually forgotten their existence. Moral: nothing is irreversible. Vodafone demonstrated it in 2003 when it bought back the minority shareholders of several European-listed subsidiaries. France Telecom did the same in 2004.

2/CASCADE STRUCTURE

As a newly minted CEO, you may be tempted to structure your group as a Russian Matryushka doll, like Groupe Arnault and LVMH or Olivetti and Telecom Italia, or like the current Albert Frère Group:

Although the group controls a quarter of Bertelsmann and 7% of Suez, the Frère family's financial interest in the two groups is only 1% and 0.3%, respectively.

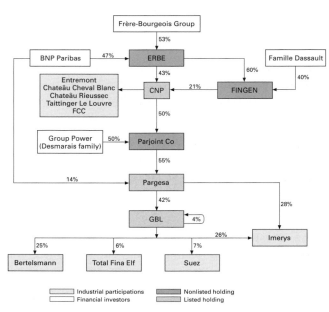

Source: company reports.

At each level, it makes sense to create a new company only if it will house different businesses. The most profitable activities must be as close as possible to the controlling holding company. Otherwise, if it is the company at the bottom of the "cascade", cash flow will have trouble reaching the controlling holding company, and the shareholder will have the impression his money is working for free!

What are the advantages and disadvantages of such a cascade structure?

The **multiplier effect** is maximised. With capital of 100, you can control a set of businesses with a capital of 2,500! Even more leverage can be obtained if intermediate structures borrow, but we strongly recommend against this practice. As they do not hold the operating assets directly and depend solely on dividends for their livelihood, borrowing would make the intermediate structures even more fragile. Remember that a chain is only as strong as its weakest link.

These cascade companies generally trade with a deep discount (between 20% and 50%). If a parent company wants to participate in its subsidiary's capital increase in order to maintain control over it, it must in turn carry out a capital increase. But, because of the holding discount, the new shares of the holding will be issued at a heavy discount, increasing its cost of capital. In effect, the cost of capital for a parent holding company which has stock that trades at a 50% discount is twice the cost of capital of the operating subsidiary.

These structures have fallen a bit out of fashion. Investors are afraid of being caught on the least liquid and most fragile rung on the ladder and of suffering an accumulation of discounts.

SUMMARY

download

Shareholder structure explains how power is distributed among a company's different shareholders or groups of shareholders. Major shareholder categories are as follows:

- minority shareholders, for whom the stock market offers the best protection. A blocking minority gives them a certain degree of control over the company because it allows vetoing certain corporate decisions;

- a 50/50 split, the structure of choice in a joint venture;

- employee-shareholders. Normally these shareholders are loyal and nonvolatile, lending a degree of stability to the capital;

- family shareholders. This model is in decline. New industries require too much capital for a family-owned structure to be viable. Funding requirements make capital markets become increasingly important;

- financial investors and investment funds, whose objectives vary.

Listing a company on the stock market enables majority shareholders to increase the liquidity of their shares but, in return, it requires them to tie their strategy to the scrutiny of the financial community. Defensive measures for maintaining control of a company's capital carry a cost, because they prevent investors from taking advantage of the potential opportunities a takeover might offer.

These measures include:

- separating management control from financial control through double-voting shares, holding companies, limited share partnerships, investment certificates and nonvoting shares;

- controlling shareholder changes through right-of-approval clauses, or pre-emption rights;

- strengthening the position of loyal shareholders by carrying out reserved capital increases, buying back shares, merging, encouraging employees to become shareholders and issuing warrants;

- exploiting legal and regulatory opportunities: specific regulations, voting rights limitations and poison pills.

Tax considerations aside, whether a group is made up of subsidiaries or divisions depends on control and organisational factors. Listing certain subsidiaries gives the group access to additional equity capital without changing the shareholder structure of the group. But such carveouts risk transforming the parent company into a financial holding company.

Lastly, remember that shares with low market liquidity, shares of a holding company or conglomerate, or shares without voting rights often trade at discounted values. These discounts increase the cost of capital.

QUESTIONS

quiz

1/ What techniques can be used for choosing shareholders?

2/ What sort of general meeting must be held to approve capital transactions?

3/ What power does a shareholder with a blocking minority have?

4/ What purpose does a "Dutch clause" serve?

5/ Why can management compensation in the form of stock create value?

6/ How would compensating employees in stock run contrary to financial theory?

7/ Are there any voting rights attached to a tracking stock?

8/ What advantages are there in buying 100% of the capital of a limited share partnership?

9/ Why do so many conglomerates continue to survive, despite the loss of value they generate? Can this situation last?

10/ What is the advantage of cascade structures for the majority shareholder? And for other shareholders?

11/ What is the difference between a holding company discount and a conglomerate discount?

12/ A company manager has a 55% stake in his unlisted company, in which a competitor also has a 32% stake. The former is keen to dilute the shareholding of the latter, without diluting his own stake at the same time. What should he do?

13/ Why is the shareholding of a family-run business unstable in the long term? What is the likely future of such a business? How can this process be slowed down?

14/ Two managers have a 25% and 75% stake, respectively, in a company. They are keen to bring in a capital investor with the minimum dilution to their shareholdings. How should they go about solving this difficult problem?

15/ Why would a company with an 85% stake in a subsidiary launch a takeover bid for the remaining 15%?

1/ Provide a description of the shareholdings and management in the following situations:

- ○ company 1: capital split between two investors each holding the blocking minority;
- ○ company 2: large group holding absolute majority, rest widely held;
- ○ company 3: no shareholder has more than 5% of shareholders' equity;
- ○ company 4: trade buyer with blocking minority, capital investor with share-holding significant but below blocking minority, rest widely held;
- ○ company 5: trade buyer just below simple majority, rest widely held.

Questions

1/ *Approval, pre-emption, A and B shares, etc.*
2/ *Extraordinary General Meeting (where applicable).*
3/ *Blocking decisions at EGMs.*
4/ *Use dissuasion to limit strategic divergence among shareholders.*
5/ *Because it permits reduction of agency costs.*
6/ *Their risks are not diversified.*
7/ *No, only in very limited circumstances.*
8/ *None, see chapter.*
9/ *It is in the interest of management – power, prestige. No, because sooner or later there will be pressure from shareholders.*
10/ *Secure control with limited resources. None.*
11/ *See chapter.*
12/ *Reserved capital increases if some minority shareholders vote with him so as to get the EGM's approval, contribution of assets, etc.*
13/ *The principle of portfolio diversification renders the principle of a family shareholding structure unstable. It will be sold to pay taxes (wealth and inheritance taxes). Provide them with tax breaks.*
14/ *By creating a holding company or issuing convertible bonds.*
15/ *In order to get rid of minority shareholders and unlock sought-after group synergies.*

Exercises

1/ *Stable shareholding structure – companies 2, 4 and 5. Unstable shareholding structure – companies 1 and 3. Managers: 1 – highly controlled. 3 – only risk is risk of a takeover bid. 4 – stable (but risk of takeover bid could exist, depending on relationship with capital investor. 5 – stable (risk of takeover bid not excluded).*

On group structure:

BIBLIOGRAPHY

M. Becht, C. Mayer, *Corporate Control in Europe*, working paper, ECARES and Said Business School, 2000.
B. Cornell, Q. Liu, The parent company puzzle: When is the whole worth less than one of the parts? *Journal of Corporate Finance*, **7**, 341–366, December 2001.
M. Faccio, L. Lang, The ultimate ownership of Western European corporations, *Journal of Financial Economics*, **65**(3), 365–395, September 2003.
D. Miller, The market reaction to international cross-listings: Evidence from depositary receipts, *Journal of Financial Economics*, **51**, 103–123, January 1999.

P. Dussauge, B. Garrette, *Cooperative Strategy: Competing Successfully through Strategic Alliances*, John Wiley & Sons, 1999.

On shareholding structure:

K. Rydqvist, Dual-class shares: A review, *Oxford Review of Economic Policy*, **8**, 45–57, 1992.

On IPO:

A. Subrahmanyam, S. Titman, The going public decision and the development of financial markets, *Journal of Finance*, **54**(3), 1045–1082, June 1999.

Chapter 42
TAKING CONTROL OF A COMPANY

A peek behind the scenes of investment banking

At any given time, a company can have several valuations, depending on the point of view of the buyer and the seller and their expectations. This variety sets the stage for negotiation, but, needless to say, a transaction will take place only if common ground can be found – i.e., if the seller's minimum price does not exceed the buyer's maximum price.

The art of negotiation consists in allocating the value of the anticipated synergies between the buyer and the seller, in finding an equilibrium between their respective positions, so that both come away with a good deal. The seller receives more than the value for the company on a standalone basis because he pockets part of the value of the synergies the buyer hopes to unlock. Similarly, the buyer pays out part of the value of the synergies, but has still not paid more than the company is worth to him.

Transactions can also result from erroneous valuations. A seller might think his company has reached a peak, for example, and the buyer that it still has growth potential. But, generally, out-and-out deception is rarer than you might think. It's usually only in hindsight that we say we made a killing and that the party on the other side of the transaction was totally wrong!

In this chapter we will focus on the acquisition of one company by another. We will not consider industrial alliances – i.e., commercial or technology agreements negotiated directly between two companies and that do not involve a transaction on the equity of either of them. Before examining the various negotiating tactics and the purchase of a listed company, let us first take a look at the merger and acquisition phenomenon and the economic justification behind a merger.

Section 42.1
THE RISE OF MERGERS AND ACQUISITIONS

1/MERGER AND ACQUISITION WAVES

Acquisitions can be paid for either in cash or in shares. Generally speaking, share transactions predominate when corporate valuations are high, as they were in 1999–2000, because they avoid having to determine absolute values.

Conversely, when the market is bearish, cash payments are more attractive to both parties. The seller receives cold, hard cash which will not lose value as shares might, while the buyer is reluctant to issue new shares at prices he considers to be a discount to the intrinsic value of the buyers' shares.

WORLDWIDE MERGER ACTIVITY

* Six months.

As shown in the above graph, mergers and acquisitions tend to come in waves:

- in the 1960s conglomerates were all the rage. ITT, Gulf & Western, Fiat, Schneider and many others rose to prominence during this period. The parent company was supposedly able to manage the acquired subsidiaries better, plus meet their capital needs. Most transactions were paid for with shares;
- in the 1980s most acquisitions were paid for in cash. Many of the big conglomerates formed in the 1960s were broken up. They had become less efficient, poorly managed and valued at less than the sum of the values of their subsidiaries;
- in the 1990s companies within the same sector joined forces, generally in share transactions: Total–Fina-Elf, Glaxo Wellcome–SmithKlineBeecham, Tabacalera–Seita, Veba–Viag, etc.

Shleifer and Vishny (2001) explain this phenomenon by saying that, on a given market at a given time, there are overvalued and undervalued companies. The former bid to acquire the latter. The bid depresses the acquirer's valuation but also keeps this overvalued firm from falling too far or too fast when investors realise that the company is overvalued. AOL's acquisition of Time Warner was a case in point. The merger wave ends when there are no more undervalued firms left, because they have all been bought up (end of the 1980s) or because there are no more overvalued firms (2000, 2001).

Putting the purely financial elements aside, the determinants of mergers and acquisitions can be macroeconomic, microeconomic or human factors, as we will now see.

2/MACROECONOMIC FACTORS

Periods of innovation and technological change are often followed by merger waves. During the innovation period (railways yesterday, Internet today), many new companies are founded. Inevitably, however, the outlook for the growth and survival of these startups dim, leading to a period of consolidation (Tiscali buys WorldOnline). Moreover, startups' heavy financing needs may prompt them to seek the support of a major group that, in turn, can take advantage of the growth in a startup's business (France Telecom buys Orange).

Many companies are undergoing a change in market scope. Twenty years ago, their market was national; now they find they must operate in a regional (European) or more often worldwide context (Danone is an example). Adapting to this change requires massive investment, in both physical and human capital, leading to much higher financing needs (pharmaceuticals). Lastly, as competition increases, companies that have not yet merged must grow rapidly in order to keep up with their now larger rivals. Critical mass becomes important (e.g., Rhône-Poulenc–Hoechst, and then Aventis–Sanofi-Synthélabo).

Legislative changes have fostered restructuring in many industries. A broad trend towards deregulation began in the 1980s in the US and the UK, profoundly changing many sectors of the economy, from air transport to financial services to telecommunications. In Europe, a single market is being implemented in conjunction with a policy of deregulation in banking, energy and telecommunications. European governments further scale back their presence in the economy by privatising many publicly held companies. In many cases, these companies then become active participants in mergers and acquisitions (Suez, ENI, Tabacalera, Deutsche Telekom).

The increasing importance of financial markets has played a fundamental role in corporate restructuring. In the space of 20 years, European economies have evolved from primarily credit-based systems, where banks were the main suppliers of funds, to financial market systems, characterised by disintermediation (see Chapter 15). Not surprisingly, this structural change was accompanied by a shift in power from banks and other financial companies (Paribas, Mediobanca, Deutsche Bank, etc.) to investors. Accordingly, shareholders are exerting pressure on corporate managers to produce returns commensurate with shareholders' expectations:

- in the event of disappointing performance, shareholders can sell their shares. In so doing, they depress the share price. Ultimately, this can lead to a restructuring (Edison) or a takeover (Paribas);
- conversely, companies must convince the market that their acquisitions (Danone/Quaker-Oats) are economically justified.

In conclusion, the financial and regulatory environment is a determining factor in economic consolidation. Industrial and technological changes naturally prompt companies to merge with each other. The decline in real growth in Europe has made it more difficult for firms to grow organically. In response, managers in search of new-growth drivers try to combine with another company.

3/ Microeconomic factors

By increasing their size and production volumes, companies reduce their unit costs. A rule of thumb says that, when production volume for manufacturing companies doubles, the unit price declines by around 20%. On this basis, an acquisition constitutes a shortcut to economies of scale – in particular, in R&D and administrative costs (DaimlerChrysler). Moreover, higher volume puts a company in a better position to negotiate lower costs with its suppliers (Carrefour-Promodès).

Mergers can increase a company's market share and boost its revenues dramatically. To the extent that companies address complementary markets, merging will enable them to broaden their overall scope. Complementarity comes in two forms:

* geographic (WalMart–ASDA). The two groups benefit from their respective presence in different regions;
* product (JP Morgan–Chase). The group can offer a full palette of services to its customers, ranging from traditional financing to specific advisory services.

Although riskier than organic growth, mergers and acquisitions allow a company to save valuable time. In growing sectors of the economy, speed – the first-mover advantage – is often a critical success factor. Once the sector matures, it becomes more difficult and more costly to chip away at competitors' market shares, so acquisitions become a vector of choice (Alcan–Pechiney). When a company is expanding internationally or entering a new business, acquiring an existing company is a way to circumvent barriers to entry, both in terms of market recognition and expertise (Wal-Mart in Germany, UGC in the UK).

By gaining additional stature, a company can more easily take new risks in a worldwide environment. The transition from a domestic market focus to worldwide competition requires that companies invest much more. The financial and human risks become too great for a medium-sized company (oil and gas exploration, pharmaceutical research). An acquisition instantly boosts the company's financial resources and reduces risk, facilitating decisions about the company's future.

4/HUMAN FACTORS

In addition to the economic criteria prompting companies to merge, there is also the human factor. Many companies founded between 1945 and 1970, and often controlled by a single shareholder-manager, are now encountering, not surprisingly, problems of succession. In some cases, another family member takes over (BMW, Fiat, Lagardère). In other cases, the company must be sold if it is to survive.

5/THE LARGER CONTEXT

Mergers and acquisitions, although tricky to manage, are part of the lifecycle of a company and are a useful growth tool.

THE LIFECYCLE OF THE FIRM

Mergers are no panacea, however. Approximately two out of three fail because the promised synergies never materialise.

Synergies are often overestimated, their cost and time to implement underestimated. For example, making information systems compatible or restructuring staff can be notoriously difficult.

Let us now take a look at the various techniques for buying or selling a company.

Section 42.2
CHOOSING A NEGOTIATING STRATEGY

A negotiating strategy aims at achieving a price objective set in accordance with the financial value derived from our valuation work in Chapter 40. But price is not everything. The seller might also want to limit the guarantees he grants, retain managerial control, ensure that his employees' future is safe, etc.

Depending on the number of potential acquirers, the necessary degree of confidentiality, the timing and the seller's demands, there is a wide range of possible negotiating strategies. We present below the two extremes: private negotiation and auction.

1/PRIVATE NEGOTIATION

The seller or his advisor contacts a small number of potential acquirers to gauge their interest. After signing a confidentiality agreement, the potential acquirers might receive an information memorandum describing the company's industrial, financial and human resource elements. Discussions then begin. It is important that each potential acquirer believe he is not alone, even if in reality he is. In principle, this technique requires extreme confidentiality. Psychological rather than practical barriers to the transaction necessitate the high degree of confidentiality.

For this confidentiality reason, the seller often prefers to hire a specialist, most often an investment banker, to find potential acquirers and keep all discussions under wraps. Such specialists are usually paid a success fee that can be proportional to the size of the transaction. Strictly speaking, there are no typical negotiating procedures. Every transaction is different. The only absolute rule about negotiating strategies is that the negotiator must have one.

The advantage of private negotiation is a high level of confidentiality. In many cases, there is no paper trail at all.

The discussion focuses on:

- how much control the seller will give up (and the status of any remaining minority shareholders);
- the price;
- the payment terms;
- any conditions precedent;

- representations and warranties; and
- any contractual relationship that might remain between the seller and the target company after the transaction.

As you might expect, price remains the essential question in the negotiating process. Everything that might have been said during the course of the negotiations falls away, leaving one all-important parameter: price. We now take a look at the various agreements and clauses that play a role in private negotiation.

(a) Memorandum Of Understanding (MOU) or Letter Of Intent (LOI)

When a framework for the negotiations has been defined, a memorandum of understanding is often signed to open the way to a transaction. A memorandum of understanding is a moral, not a legal obligation. Often, once the MOU is signed, the management of the acquiring company presents it to its board of directors to obtain permission to pursue the negotiations.

The memorandum of understanding is not useful when each party has made a firm commitment to negotiate. In this case, a memorandum of understanding slows down the process rather than accelerates it.

(b) Agreement in principle

The next step might be an agreement in principle, spelling out the terms and conditions of the sale. The commitments of each party are irrevocable, unless there are conditions precedent, such as approval of the regulatory authorities. The agreement in principle can take many forms.

(c) Financial sweeteners

In many cases, specific financial arrangements are needed to get over psychological, tax, legal or financial barriers. These arrangements do not change the value of the company.

These arrangements cannot transform a bad transaction into a good one. They serve only to bring the parties to the transaction closer together.

Sometimes, for psychological reasons, the seller refuses to go below some purely symbolic value. If he draws a line in the sand at 200, for example, whereas the buyer does not want to pay more than 190, a schedule spreading out payments over time sometimes does the trick. The seller will receive 100 this year and 100 next year. This is 190.9 if discounted at 10%, but it is still 200 to his way of thinking. Recognise that we are out of the realm of finance here and into the confines of psychology, and that this arrangement fools only those who ... indeed want to be fooled.

This type of financial arrangement is window-dressing to hide the real price. Often companies build elaborate structures in the early stages of negotiation, only to simplify them little by little as they get used to the idea of buying or selling the company. Far from a magical solution, such sweeteners give each party time to gravitate towards the other. In these cases it is only a stage, albeit a necessary one.

The following techniques are part of the investment banker's stock in trade:

- set up a special purpose holding company to buy the company, lever up the company with debt, then have the seller reinvest part of the funds in the hope of obtaining a second gain (this is an LBO,[1] see Chapter 44);
- have the buyer pay for part of the purchase price in shares, which can then be sold in the market if the buyer's shares are listed;
- pay for part of the purchase price with convertible bonds;
- link part of the purchase price to the sale price of a nonstrategic asset the buyer does not wish to keep;
- an earnout clause, which is more complicated and presents a number of dangers.

An earnout clause links part of the transaction price to the acquired company's future financial performance. The clause can take one of two forms:

- either the buyer takes full control of the target company at a minimum price, which can only be revised upwards; or
- he buys a portion of the company at a fixed price and the rest at a future date, with the price dependent on the company's future profits. The index can be a multiple of EBIT, EBITDA[2] or pre-tax profit.

Earnout provisions are very common in transactions involving service companies and were one of the causes of the distress of the UK advertising agencies (Saatchi & Saatchi, WPP) at the end of the 1980s.

1 Leveraged Buy Out.

2 Earnings Before Interest, Taxes, Depreciation and Amortisation.

2/AUCTION

In an auction, the company is offered for sale, under a predetermined schedule, to several potential buyers, who are competing with each other. The objective is to choose the one offering the highest price. An auction is often private, but it can also be announced in the press or by a court decision.

Private auctions are run by an investment bank in the following manner. Once the decision is taken to sell the company, a brief summary of the company is prepared (a "teaser"). It is sent, together with a confidentiality agreement, to a large number of potentially interested companies and financial investors.

In the next stage (often called "phase I"), once the potentially interested buyers sign the confidentiality agreement, they receive additional information, gathered in an information memorandum. Then they submit a nonbinding offer indicating the price, any conditions precedent and eventually their intentions regarding the future strategy for the target company.

At that point of time ("phase II") either:

- a "shortlist" of around half a dozen candidates allowed in phase II is drawn up. They receive still more information and possibly a schedule of visits to the company's industrial sites and meetings with management. Often a **data room** is set up, where all economic, financial and legal information concerning the target company is available for perusal. Access to the data room is very restrictive, no photocopies can be made, etc. At the end of this stage, potential investors submit binding offers; or

- **exclusive negotiations** are opened. For a given period of time, the potential buyer is the only candidate. At the end of the exclusive period, the buyer must submit a binding offer or withdraw from the negotiations.

Together with the binding offers, the seller will ask the bidder(s) to propose a markup (comments) to the disposal agreement (called a Share Purchase Agreement, SPA) previously provided by the seller. The ultimate selection of the buyer depends not only, naturally, on the binding offer, but also on the buyer's comments on the share purchase agreement.

An auction leads to a high price because buyers are in competition with each other. In addition, it makes it easier for the seller's representatives to prove that they did everything in their power to obtain the highest possible price for the company, be it:

- the executive who wants to sell a subsidiary;
- a majority shareholder whose actions might be challenged by minority shareholders; or
- the investment banker in charge of the transaction.

Moreover, an auction is faster, because the seller, not the buyer, sets the pace. Competition sometimes generates a price that is well in excess of expectations.

However, the auction creates confidentiality problems. Many people have access to the basic data, and denying rumours of a transaction becomes difficult. So the process must move quickly. Also, as the technique is based on price only, it is exposed to some risks, such as several potential buyers teaming up with the intention of splitting the assets among them. Lastly, should the process fail, the company's credibility will suffer. The company must have an uncontested strategic value and a sound financial condition.

3/THE OUTCOME OF NEGOTIATIONS

In the end, whatever negotiating method was used, the seller has a single potential buyer, who can then impose certain conditions. Should the negotiations fall apart at this stage, it could spell trouble for the seller because he would have to go back to the other potential buyers, hat in hand. So the seller is in a position of weakness when it comes to finalising the negotiations. The principal remaining element is the representations and warranties clause.

Representations and warranties ("reps & warranties") are particularly important because they give confidence to the buyer that the profitability of the company has not been misrepresented. It is a way to secure the value of assets and liabilities of the target company as the contract cannot provide a detailed valuation.

Representations and warranties are not intended to protect the buyer against an overvaluation of the company. They are intended to certify that **all of the means of production are indeed under the company's control and that there are no hidden liabilities**.

Well-worded representations and warranties clauses should guarantee to the buyer:

- the substance of fixed assets (and not their value);
- the real nature and the value of inventories (assuming that the buyer and the seller have agreed on a valuation method);
- the real nature of other elements of working capital;
- the amount and nature of all of the company's other commitments, whether they are on the balance sheet, such as debts, or not.

The representations and warranties clause is generally divided into two parts.

In the first part (representations), the seller makes commitments related to the **substance** of the company that is to be sold.

The seller generally states that the target company and its subsidiaries are properly constituted, that all the fixed assets on the balance sheet, including brands and patents, or used by the company in the ordinary course of business actually exist. As such, representations and warranties do not guarantee the book value of the fixed assets, but their existence.

The seller declares that inventories have been booked in accordance with industry standards and the demands of the tax authorities, and that depreciation and provisions have been calculated according to GAAP.[3] The seller declares that the company is up to date in tax payments, salaries and other accruals and that there are no prejudicial contracts with suppliers, customers or employees. All elements already communicated to the buyer – in particular, exceptional items such as special contracts, guarantees, etc. – are annexed to the clause and excluded from it because the buyer is already aware of them.

Lastly, the seller guarantees that during the transitional period – i.e., between the last statement date and the sale date – the company was managed in a prudent manner. In particular, he certifies that no dividends were distributed or assets sold, except for those agreed with the buyer during the period, that no investments in excess of a certain amount were undertaken, nor contracts altered, etc.

In the second part of the clause (warranties), the seller guarantees the amount of the company's equity capital as of the most recent statement date (statements annexed to the agreement). The seller agrees to indemnify the buyer against any decrease caused by events that took place prior to the sale date. The guarantee remains in effect for a given period of time and is capped at a specified amount. This clause is often accompanied by a holdback (part of the purchase price is put in an escrow account) on part of the purchase price or a bank guarantee.

The representations and warranties clauses are the main addition to the sale agreement, but, depending on the agreement, there may be many other additions, so long as they are legally valid – i.e., not contrary to company law, tax law or stock market regulations requiring equal treatment of all shareholders. A nonexhaustive list would include:

- means of payment;
- status and future role of managers and executives;
- agreements with majority shareholders;
- audit of the company's books. On this score, we recommend against realising a full audit before the two parties have reached an agreement. An audit often

3 *Generally Accepted Accounting Principles.*

detects problems in the company, poisoning the atmosphere, and can serve as a pretext to abandon the transaction.

Of course, the parties to the contracts should also call upon legal experts to ensure that each clause is legally enforceable.

The final step is the actual consummation of the deal. It often takes place at a later date, because certain conditions first must be met: accounting, legal or tax audit, restructuring, regulatory approval for a foreign group, approval of domestic or European competition commissioners, etc.

Section 42.3
TAKING OVER A LISTED EUROPEAN COMPANY

For a public company, the negotiation cannot take place between two parties in the same way as for a private company. The transaction has to include a number of minority shareholders who had invested in the company.

Local regulations aim at protecting minority shareholders in order to develop financial markets. The main target of these regulations is to guarantee a transparent and equal treatment of all shareholders.

In order to acquire a listed company, the acquirer needs to acquire shares from a large number of minority shareholders. It would be most often very difficult and take a long time to acquire shares on the open market little by little; therefore, the acquirer usually makes a public offer (takeover bid) to all shareholders to buy their shares.

Each European country has regulations governing takeovers of companies listed on domestic stock exchanges. The degree of constraints varies from one country to another.

1/STAKE-BUILDING

To succeed in acquiring a listed company the first step can be to start building a block in the company. This can be done on the open market by buying shares.

In order to prevent the acquirer from taking control of a company in that way, most European market regulations require investors in a listed company to publicly declare when they pass certain thresholds in the capital of a company. If the acquirer fails to declare, his shares lose voting rights.

The first threshold is most often 5% (Belgium, France, Germany, Poland, Spain, . . .).

Regulatory disclosure requirements allow minority shareholders to monitor stake-building and prevent an acquirer from getting little by little control of a company. These requirements are also helpful for the management of the company to monitor the shareholder structure of the company. By-laws can set additional thresholds to be declared (generally lower thresholds than required by law).

Regulatory threshold disclosure requirements are the following:

Belgium	5% and multiples (cannot be below 3% in by-laws)
England	NA
France	5%, 10%, 20%, 33.33%, 50% (cannot be below 0.5% in by-laws)
Germany	5%, 10%, 25%, 50%, 75%
Netherlands	5%, 10%, 25%, 66.66%, 75% (but not through stake-building)
Poland	5%, 10% and each 2% afterwards, 25%, 50%, 75%
Spain	5% and multiples (cannot be below 3% in by-laws)
US	5%

2/TYPE OF OFFER

It is very unusual for an acquirer to gain control of a public company without launching a public offer on the target. Such offers are made to all shareholders over a certain period of time (2–10 weeks depending on the country). Public offers can be split between:

- Share offers or cash offers.
- Voluntary or mandatory offers.
- Hostile or recommended offers.

(a) Cash and share offers

The table below (continued at top of next page) summarises the criteria relevant to assess if a bidder wants to propose shares or cash in a public offer:

	Payment in cash	Payment in shares	Comments
Signal from buyer's point of view	Positive: buyer's stock is undervalued. Debt financing: positive signal	Negative: buyer's stock is overvalued	
Signal from seller's point of view	None	Positive: the seller is taking some of the risk	
Allocation of synergies	Target company's shareholders benefit from synergies only via the premium they receive	Target company's shareholders participate fully in future synergies	In a friendly share exchange offer, the premium might be minimal if the expected synergies are high
Psychological effects	Cash lends credibility to the bid and increases its psychological value	Payment in shares has a "friendly" character	

	Payment in cash	Payment in shares	Comments
Purchaser's financial structure	Increases gearing	Decreases gearing	The size of the deal sometimes requires payment in shares
Impact on purchaser's share price	After the impact of the announcement, no direct link between the purchaser's and target's share price	Immediate link between purchaser's and target's share price, maintained throughout the bid period	A share exchange offer gains credibility when the two companies' share prices align with the announced exchange ratio
Accounting effects	Increases EPS and its growth rate if the inverse of the target's P/E including any premium is greater than the after-tax cost of debt of the acquirer	Increases EPS if the purchaser's P/E is higher than the target's, premium included	EPS is not a real indicator of value creation
Purchaser's tax situation	Interest expense deductible	No impact, except capital gain if treasury shares are used	Taxation is not a determining factor
Seller's tax situation	Taxable gain	Gain on sale can be carried forward	
Index weighting	No change	Higher weighting in index (greater market capitalisation)	In the case of a share exchange, possible rerating owing to size effect

In practice, the choice is not so black and white. The purchaser can offer a combination of cash and shares (mixed offers), cash as an alternative to shares or contingent value rights. The purchaser's investment banker plays a key role in choosing the type of bid, the premium offered, how the bid is communicated to investors, etc.

(b) Voluntary and mandatory offers

The concept of a mandatory offer does not exist in every country. Nevertheless, in most countries, when an acquirer passes a certain threshold or acquires the control of the target, he is required by stock exchange regulation to offer to buy back the shares of all shareholders.

This is one of the founding rules of stock exchange regulations. In Russia, where the concept of a public offer is not materialised in any regulation, a shareholder acquiring over 30% of the capital of a listed company has to offer to buy back all minority shareholders.

It should be noted that in the US and in the Netherlands, there is no mandatory offer and an acquirer can buy a majority of the capital of a listed company without having to launch an offer for the minority shareholders.

Generally, the constraints for a mandatory offer are tighter than for a voluntary offer. For example, in England and France the mandatory offer will be in cash or provide at least a cash alternative.

Obviously the conditions to realisation of the offer that the acquirer is allowed to set in a mandatory offer are limited. In a voluntary offer there is more flexibility as the acquirer has already gained control over a large part of the capital of the target.

In Spain, the mandatory offer can be only on part of the capital and depends on the stake that the acquirer has bought. For example, an acquirer who has bought 25% of capital has to launch an offer on an additional 10%.

Spain has peculiar rules in terms of mandatory offers: in all other countries where mandatory offers exist, the mandatory offer has to be on 100% of capital.

(b) Hostile and recommended offers

The success or failure of an offer largely depends on the attitude of the management of the target towards the offer.

To maximise the chances of success, the terms of an offer are generally negotiated with the management prior to the announcement, and then recommended by the board of the company. The offer is then qualified friendly or recommended.

In some cases, the management of the target is not aware of the launch of an offer; it is then called an unsolicited offer. Facing this sudden event the board has to convene and to decide whether the offer is acceptable or not. If the board rejects the offer, it becomes hostile. This does not mean that the offer will not succeed but just that the bidder will have to fight against management during the offer period to convince shareholders.

3/ CERTAINTY OF THE OFFER

It would be very disruptive for the market if an acquirer could launch an offer and withdraw it a few days later. All market regulations try to ensure that, when a public offer is launched, shareholders are actually given the opportunity to tender their shares.

Therefore, market regulation requires that the offer is funded when it is launched. Full funding ensures that the market does not run the risk of a buyer falling short of financing when the offer is a success! This funding usually takes the form of a guarantee by a bank (generally the bank presenting the offer commits itself to pay for the shares, should the acquirer not have the funds).

Another principle is that offers should be unconditional. In particular, the bidder cannot set conditions to the execution of the offer that remains in his hands (as an example an offer cannot be conditional upon board approval of the acquirer). Nevertheless, in most countries, the offer can be subject to a minimum acceptance (which generally cannot be too high) and regulatory approvals

4 *That is,
possibility for the
majority
shareholder to
force the buyback
of minority
shareholders and
delist the company
if minority
shareholders
represent only a
small part of the
capital.*

5 *Bundesanstalt
für Finanz-
dienstleistungs-
aufsicht.*

6 *Comisión
Nacional de los
Mercados de
Valores.*

(including anti-trust). In a few countries (the UK, the Netherlands, the US), the offer can be subject to a material adverse change clause.

4/DOCUMENTATION AND MARKET AUTHORITY ROLE

The main role of market authorities is to guarantee the equal treatment of all shareholders and the transparency of the process.

In that regard, market authorities will have a key role in public offers:

- They set (and often control) the standard content of the offer document. This document will contain all relevant information allowing the target's shareholder to take a proper decision.
- They supervise the process timetable.
- Their green light is in most countries necessary for the launch of the offer (they therefore control the price offered).

5/SUMMARY OF NATIONAL REGULATIONS

The table below (and continued at the top of the next page) summarises the principal rules applicable to takeover bids in Europe:

Country	Regulator	Threshold for mandatory bid	Minimum percentage mandatory bid must encompass	Bid conditions allowed?	Bid validity after approval	Squeezeout[4] possible?
Germany	BAFin[5]	30% of voting rights	100%	None, if mandatory bid	4–10 weeks	Yes, if more than 95% of shares
Belgium	Commission Bancaire et Financière	No specific threshold, mandatory bid if change of control	100% of shares	Under rare circumstances	10–20 trading days	Yes, if more than 95% of voting shares
Spain	CNMV[6]	25% of shares, 6% p.a. if between 25% and 50%. 50% of shares	At least 10% of all votes, warrants and convertible bonds. On 75% of capital if the 50% threshold is passed	Yes. Participation can be limited to 75%	None specified, but delisting possible	

Country	Regulator	Threshold for mandatory bid	Minimum percentage mandatory bid must encompass	Bid conditions allowed?	Bid validity after approval	Squeezeout possible?
France	AMF[7]	33.3% of shares or voting rights, 2% p.a. between 33.3% and 50% of shares or voting rights	100% of shares and equity-linked securities	Under rare circumstances	25–35 trading days	Yes, if more than 95% of voting rights
Italy	CONSOB[8]	30% of shares, 3% p.a. beyond 30%	100% of voting shares	Under some circumstances	15–35 trading days	Yes, if more than 98% of voting rights
Netherlands	SER[9]	None[10]	100% of shares and equity-linked securities	Yes	More than 20 trading days	Yes, if more than 95% of voting rights
UK	Takeover Panel	30% of voting rights	100% of shares and all instruments convertible or exchangeable into shares	Must be approved by regulator	Less than 60 trading days	Yes, if more than 90% of the shares
Switzerland	COPA[11]	33.3% of voting rights[12]	100% of shares	Yes	20–40 trading days	Yes, if more than 98% of voting rights
Poland	Securities commission	50%	100% of shares	Minimum acceptance. Regulatory clearance	7–90 days	Yes, if more than 90%

6/EUROPEAN DIRECTIVE ON PUBLIC OFFERS

Cross-border takeovers are becoming more common in Europe, particularly in the form of share exchange offers. This trend has lead the EU to issue a directive on public offers. Europe had been working on this directive for 15 years before it was finally voted for in 2004.

The text is rather general in nature and leaves considerable flexibility for translation into national legislation. As a result, only relatively minor amendments may be necessary in national regulations in most European countries. Moreover,

7 *Autorité des Marchés Financiers formed from the merger of COB and CMF in 2003.*

8 *Commissione Nazionale per le Società e la Borsa.*

9 Sociaal-
Economische
Raad.

10 It should be
noted that given
specific corporate
governance rules
acquiring over
50% of capital in
the Netherlands
does not mean
having control
over the company.

11 Commission
des offres
publiques d'achat.

12 Or a threshold
up to 49% if the
by-laws of the
target company
permit.

13 In Spain, the
mandatory
takeover bid is
allowed to cover
only a portion of
the shares.

European countries will have a 2-year transition period for adapting their legislation to the new texts.

The directive first sets forth some basic principles:

- Shareholders in the same category must be treated equally.
- Shareholders must have enough time and information to decide whether the takeover bid is well-founded.
- Management of the target company must act in the interests of the company and allow shareholders the opportunity to make up their own minds on the takeover bid.
- Manipulation of share prices is naturally banned.
- A bid must have secured financing before being announced.
- The bid must not keep the target company from operating properly.

In addition to basic principles, the directive sets precise rules in certain areas. Here are the main subjects:

- the principle of a mandatory takeover bid;
- the principle of mandatory buyout and mandatory squeezeout;
- anti-takeover defences;
- available information;
- takeover law.

(a) Mandatory takeover bids

The directive lays down the principle that a shareholder that has assumed effective control over a company must bid for all equity-linked securities. It is up to individual countries to set a threshold of voting rights that constitutes effective control.

This article in the directive is unlikely to have a major impact on most national takeover rules, but it will result in significant changes in the spirit of Dutch law, as well as changes in Spanish law[13] (Spain abstained from the Commission vote on the text). The principle of effective control will guide new national regulations in countries that will soon join the European Union and whose financial markets are in the process of assuming a European identity that will differ in this point from US regulations. For example, in the US (as in the Netherlands currently), an investor can take effective control of a company without offering an exit for minority shareholders. A public listing does not offer minorities the same protection as in France or the UK.

The directive states very specifically the floor price of a mandatory bid: the highest price paid by the new controlling shareholder in the 6–12 months prior to the bid (the exact period is set by national regulations).

A mandatory bid can be in either cash or shares (if the shares are listed and are liquid).

(b) Squeezeouts and mandatory buyouts

Article 14 of the directive lays down the principle of the right to make squeezeout offers (up to national legislation to decide):

- having obtained at least 90% of a company's shares (as is currently the case in Italy and the UK), individual countries have the option of raising the threshold to 95% (as is currently the case in Germany, France and the Netherlands); or
- having obtained at least 90% of the shares in the course of a bid for all the shares.

Interestingly, the fair price for such an offer is, here again, stated very precisely. The price of a squeezeout can be the same as that of the mandatory bid or of a voluntary bid that has obtained more than 90% of the shares. Would this mean the end of the multi-criteria valuations at this point in the takeover? It would appear so.

In parallel, the text also allows minority shareholders to demand a buyout (in the same circumstances that allow a squeezeout).

It is worth pointing out that the directive does not require countries to enact a squeezeout/buyout mechanism for all cases, but only in the event of a public bid.

(c) Anti-takeover defences

The issue of limiting anti-takeover defences, poison pills and the like, has been more controversial. This is one of the reasons the European Parliament voted down the previous version of the directive. Some countries opposed this article, as they feared that, by limiting anti-takeover defences, Europe would be at a disadvantage to the US, which does allow such practices.

The directive bans the boards of target companies from taking anti-takeover defences during the bid – such as poison pills, massive issuing of shares, etc. – without approval from an extraordinary general meeting.

The directive requires clear transparency on the control structure (restrictions in voting rights, multiple voting rights, shareholder pacts, etc.), as well as defence measures (contracts with change-of-control clauses, option of issuing shares without AGM approval, golden parachutes, etc.).

Multiple voting rights and/or restrictions on voting rights are valid as of the first general shareholders' meeting after a bid that has given a bidder a qualified majority of the company. This does not apply to golden shares that have been deemed compatible with European law.[14]

The European Parliament left open the option on whether to enforce articles on poison pills and on the principle of "one share, one vote". The mechanism here is especially complex: choice of governments to include it in law or not, then choice of companies to opt in or not (with specific rules if the bidder is not European).

(d) Available information

The contents of the takeover prospectus is specified. It includes information on the bid, the bidder and the bidder's intentions with the target's business and employees. Requirements by other national authorities in Europe are similar.

More generally, the directive frames the procedures for public takeover bids in order to give the shareholder enough time and information to decide on whether the bid is well-founded. Hence, the bid must normally last between 2 and 10 weeks.

The final text of the directive is disappointing. In particular, the tight restrictions on anti-takeover defences, which became optional in the last version

14 *European law strictly limits national government leeway on golden shares in privatised companies. Golden shares are nonetheless still possible in some sectors and special cases, such as the defence industry.*

of the text (under German insistence) will hinder harmonisation of national regulations on this point.

But let's look on the bright side. Even though the directive is unlikely to have any fundamental impact on most national regulations (France, UK, etc.), it is one step in the right direction, as it generalises the notions of mandatory takeover bids, squeezeouts, etc. A clause providing for review 5 years after the directive enters force will be a clear opportunity to update the text in the direction of a more integrated European market.

6/CONTINGENT VALUE RIGHTS

A company seeking to acquire another company faces two contradictory constraints. On the one hand, it wants to offer a sufficiently high price so as to ensure the success of its bid. On the other hand, it does not want to overpay. The purchaser can solve this dilemma by using a financial instrument that serves as a compromise: the Contingent Value Right (CVR). A CVR can be defensive or attractive.

A defensive CVR is used in a cash bid. A cash bid can turn out to be expensive if all of the target's shareholders tender their shares. For this reason, the acquirer might want to dissuade shareholders from tendering some of their shares by guaranteeing the future performance of their target company shares – in particular, with respect to the bid price. In this case, the CVR guarantees a price at a given maturity date on the untendered shares of the target company.

An attractive CVR is used in share exchange offers. It represents a portion of the premium offered to the target company's shareholders and is intended to encourage them to tender their shares. For example, in July 1999, the Paribas shareholders who tendered their shares to BNP received a CVR guaranteeing them a specified return on BNP shares until July 2002 (with a limit of €20 per CVR).

CVRs are listed financial instruments that can be sold by the shareholders who receive them. For the issuer, it constitutes a commitment.

CVRs have been used in a number of transactions with different features including the acquisition of Equant by France Telecom, the acquisition of the Pillsbury Company by General Mills from Diageo or the acquisition of AGF by Allianz.

This technique was quite popular in the late 1990s, giving rise to a lively debate among specialists as to the theoretical value of CVRs and, by extension, the value of the advantage offered to shareholders. Empirical evidence, however, shows that CVRs tend to trade at a discount to theoretical value (based on option-pricing models).

SUMMARY

download

The art of negotiation consists in allocating the value of the synergies expected from a merger or acquisition between the buyer and the seller. For an unlisted company, there are two basic methods of conducting the negotiations:

- private negotiation, which preserves a high level of confidentiality, while excluding offers that might have been received had the process been wider;

- a private auction, which heightens the competition between buyers, but is more restrictive for the seller.

Regardless of the chosen procedure, certain elements are common to every deal:

- memorandums of understanding and agreements in principle serve to describe the general agreement found between the parties and are a milestone along the path to full commitment of the parties to the deal;

- representations and warranties guarantee to the buyer that all of the means of production belong to the company and that there are no hidden liabilities;

- many agreements now also include clauses wherein the seller certifies substantive aspects of the company and the amount of equity capital;

- in some cases, earnout clauses link a portion of the purchase price to the company's future profits.

Stake-building can be the first step to acquiring control over a listed company. But it can only be slow and faces the requirement of declaring the crossing of thresholds. A public offer is the usual way to acquire a listed company. It is based on two fundamental principles: transparency and equal treatment of shareholders. It can be in cash or in shares, hostile or friendly, voluntary or mandatory.

Contingent Value Rights (CVRs) are financial instruments issued during an acquisition to persuade shareholders to tender (or dissuade them from tendering) their shares to the bid.

1/ What are the advantages and drawbacks of private negotiation?

2/ What are the advantages and drawbacks of a private sale by auction?

3/ Do CVRs encourage or dissuade shareholders from tendering their shares to a bid?

4/ Does the buyer send a positive signal to the market when issuing a CVR? A negative signal?

5/ What is the advantage of a public purchase or share exchange offer for a minority shareholder?

6/ What advantages does a public offer have for the acquirer over an acquisition on the market? What are the drawbacks?

7/ Can a company launch an offer to buy another company that is for sale, without having any real intention of closing the deal? Why? What protection is there for the seller?

8/ How can differences between buyers and sellers that are rooted in psychological issues be settled?

9/ Why are earnout clauses so popular with companies in the service sector?

10/ All things being equal, what is the downside of a deal being kept highly confidential?

11/ When is it a good idea to go for a private auction?

QUESTIONS

quiz

12/ How can a buyer be protected against any hidden liabilities and debts that the target may have?

13/ What is the purpose of representations and warranties? What are the limits of such clauses?

14/ What is the logical result of a successful hostile buyup of shares on the market?

15/ What major practical restriction does the private sale of blocks of shares get round?

16/ Why do market authorities ask for the suspension of trading at the announcement of a public offer?

17/ Why are defence mechanisms against hostile takeover bids very strictly regulated?

18/ On the basis of financial theory, how can the role of an investment bank in a deal be summarised?

ANSWERS

1/ *Advantage: negotiations are kept confidential. Drawback: potential candidates may be left out.*

2/ *Advantage: organisation of a market. Drawback: lack of confidentiality*

3/ *Both are possible: see chapter.*

4/ *Yes. No.*

5/ *The minority shareholder is protected as he will be able to sell his shares at the same price as the majority shareholder.*

6/ *The acquirer does not cause the share price to rise. The drawback is that, if a stock market battle unfolds, he will not be in such a good position.*

7/ *Yes. To obtain information. Memorandums of understanding and of agreement, confidentiality agreements.*

8/ *Through the use of financial sweeteners.*

9/ *The deal itself can have an unpredictable impact on human resources – the company's main assets.*

10/ *The sale price will probably be lower.*

11/ *When the business for sale is very profitable, and attractive to both trade buyers and financial investors.*

12/ *General warranties.*

13/ *It provides a guarantee for the assets and liabilities of the company. Under no circumstances can such a clause guarantee the fairness of the price paid for the business.*

14/ *A takeover bid.*

15/ *The illiquidity of blocks of securities and centralisation of the market.*

16/ *To allow fair and equal dissemination of information.*

17/ *Anti-takeover measures can deprive shareholders of the capital gains that come out of the free process of auctions.*

18/ *Manage information asymmetry.*

BIBLIOGRAPHY

G. Emery, J. Switzer, Expected market reaction and the choice of method of payment for acquisitions, *Financial Management*, **28**, 73–86, Winter 1999.

G. Hubbard, P. Darius, A reexamination of the conglomerate merger wave in the 1960s, *Journal of Finance*, **54**, 1131–1152, June 1999.

M.C. Jensen, R.S. Ruback, The market for corporate control: The scientific evidence, *Journal of Financial Economics*, **11**, 5–50, April 1983.

G. Schwert, Hostility in takeovers: In the eyes of the beholder? *Journal of Finance*, **55**, 2599–2640, December 2000.

M. Sirower, A. Rappaport, Stock of cash, *Harvard Business Review*, **77**, 147–158, November/December 1999.

A. Shleifer, R. Vishny, Stock market driven acquisition, *Journal of Financial Economics*, **70**(3), 295–311, 2003.

J. Weston, B. Johnson, J. Siu, *Takeovers, Restructuring and Corporate Governance*, 3rd edn, Prentice Hall, 2000.

www.euronext.fr

Chapter 43
MERGERS AND DEMERGERS

When the financial manager celebrates a wedding (or a divorce!)

At first glance, this chapter might seem to repeat the previous ones in that selling a company almost always leads to linking it up with another. In everyday language we often talk of the merger of two companies, when in reality one company typically takes control of the other, using the methods described in Chapter 42. In fact, all that we have previously said about synergies and company valuations will be used in this chapter. **The only fundamental difference we introduce here is that 100% of the seller's consideration will be in shares of the acquiring company and not in cash.**

In addition, because markets nowadays prefer "pure play" companies, demergers have come back into fashion. We will take a look at them in Section 43.3.

Section 43.1
ALL-SHARE DEALS

In this section, we will examine the general case of two separate companies that decide to pool their operations and redistribute roles. Before the business combination can be consummated, questions of valuation and power-sharing among the shareholders of the new entity must be resolved. Financially, the essential distinguishing feature among mergers and acquisitions is the nature of the consideration paid: 100% cash, a combination of cash and shares, or 100% shares. Our discussion will focus on the last of these forms. Finally, we will not address the case of a company that merges with an already wholly owned subsidiary, which raises only accounting, tax and legal issues and no financial issues.

1/THE DIFFERENT TECHNIQUES

(a) Legal merger

A legal merger is a transaction, by which two or more companies combine to form a single legal entity. In most cases, one company absorbs the other. The shareholders of the acquired company become shareholders of the acquiring company and the acquired company ceases to exist as a separate legal entity.

A legal merger is a combination of the assets and liabilities of two or more companies into a single legal entity.

From legal and tax points of view, this type of business combination is treated as a contribution of assets and liabilities, paid in new shares issued to the ex-shareholders of the acquired company.

 For example, in 2002, Dexia merged its Belgian bank business (including the recently acquired Artesia). Through that transaction, four legal entities (Dexia Bank, Artesia Banking Corporation, Bacob and Artesia Services) merged to form one single entity renamed Dexia Bank Belgium.

 This type of transaction is often used in group restructuring. It is rare to see two listed companies merge.

(b) Contribution of shares

Consider the shareholders of companies A and B. Shareholders of company B, be they individuals or legal entities, can enter into a deal with company A wherein they **exchange their shares** of B for shares of A. In this case, companies A and B continue to exist, with B becoming a subsidiary of A and the shareholders of B becoming shareholders of A.

 Financially and economically, the transaction is very close to the sale of all or part of company B funded by an equivalent issue of new company A shares, reserved for the shareholders of company B.

 In 1999, Richemont contributed its 15% stake in Canal+ to Vivendi and received in exchange a 2.9% interest in Vivendi.

 For listed companies, the most common approach for achieving this result is a share exchange offer as described in Chapter 42.

(c) Asset contribution

In a **contribution** (or transfer) **of assets**, company B contributes a portion of its assets (and liabilities) to company A in return for shares issued by company A.

 In a legal merger, the shareholders of company B receive shares of company A. In a transfer of assets, however, company B, not the shareholders thereof, receives the shares of company A. The position of company B shareholders is therefore radically different, depending on whether the transaction is a legal merger or a simple transfer of assets. In the transfer of assets, company B remains and becomes a shareholder of company A. Shareholders of B do not become direct shareholders of company A. In the legal merger, shareholders of B become direct shareholders of company A.

 If company B contributes all of its assets to A, B becomes a holding company and, depending on the amount of the assets it has contributed, can take control of

A. This procedure is often used in corporate restructurings to spin off certain activities.

Economically, there is no difference between these transactions. The group created by bringing together *A* and *B* is economically identical regardless of how the business combination is effected.

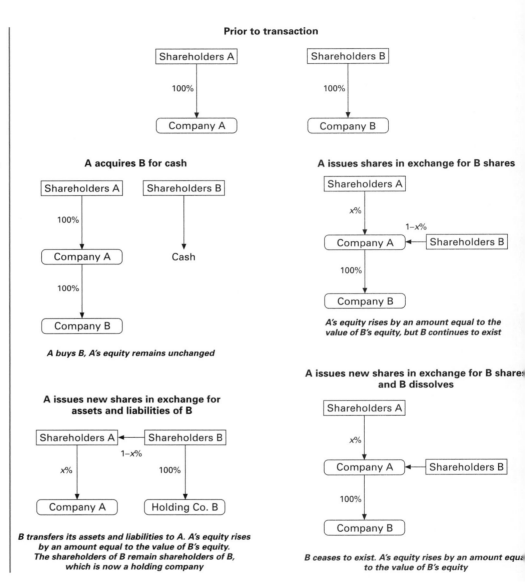

Prior to transaction

A acquires B for cash

A buys B, A's equity remains unchanged

A issues shares in exchange for B shares

A's equity rises by an amount equal to the value of B's equity, but B continues to exist

A issues new shares in exchange for assets and liabilities of B

B transfers its assets and liabilities to A. A's equity rises by an amount equal to the value of B's equity. The shareholders of B remain shareholders of B, which is now a holding company

A issues new shares in exchange for B shares and B dissolves

B ceases to exist. A's equity rises by an amount equal to the value of B's equity

As an example of asset contribution you can have a look at the NBC-VU transaction in 2003. VU contributed its entertainment assets (VUE: cinema, TV channels) to NBC in exchange for 20% of the new NBC-Universal. General Electric which was the 100% shareholder of NBC prior to the transaction retained control and 80% of the capital.

2/ANALYSIS OF THE DIFFERENT TECHNIQUES

For simplicity's sake, we will assume that the shares of both companies are fairly priced and that the merger does not create any industrial or commercial synergies. Consequently, there is no value creation as a result of the merger.

(a) From the point of view of the company

Companies *A* and *B* have the following characteristics:

(in €m)	Value of capital employed	Value of shareholders' equity agreed in the merger
Company A	900	450
Company B	1,000	750

Depending on the method used, the post-transaction situation is as follows:

(in €m)	A acquires B shares for cash[1]	A issues new shares in exchange for B shares and dissolves B	A issues new shares in exchange for B shares and B becomes a 100% subsidiary of A	A issues new shares in exchange for assets and liabilities of B
Value of A's new capital employed (now A + B)	1,900	1,900	1,900	1,900
Value of A's shareholders' equity	450	1,200	1,200	1,200
Percentage of A held by A shareholders	100%	37.5%	37.5%	37.5%
Percentage of A held by B shareholders	—	62.5%	62.5%	62.5%[2]

1 The acquisition of B is financed by debt, not a capital increase.

2 In fact, company B, not its shareholders, holds 62.5% of A.

The value of capital employed and consolidated operating income are the same in each scenario. Economically, each transaction represents the same business combination of companies *A* and *B*.

Financially, however, the situation is very different, even putting aside accounting and revaluation questions. If *A* pays for the acquisition in shares, the shareholders' equity of *A* is increased by the shareholders' equity of *B*. If *A* purchases *B* for cash, the value of *A*'s shareholders' equity does not increase.

It can be noted that when the target is a listed company, a 100% successful share exchange offer is financially equivalent to a legal merger.

We reiterate that our reasoning here is strictly arithmetic and we are not taking into account any impact the transaction may have on the value of the two companies. If the two companies were already correctly priced before the transaction and there are no synergies, their value will remain the same. If not, there will be a change in value. **The financial mechanics (sale, share exchange, etc.) have no impact on the economics of a business combination.**

This said, there is one important financial difference: an acquisition paid for in cash does not increase a group's financial clout (i.e., future investment capacity), but an all-share transaction creates a group with financial means which tend to be the sum of that of the two constituent companies.

From the point of view of the acquiring company, the only difference between a share exchange and a cash acquisition is in the financial clout of the new group.

In terms of value creation, our rules still hold, unless there are synergies or market inefficiencies.

(b) From the point of view of shareholders

A **cash acquisition** changes the portfolio of the acquired company's shareholders, because they now hold cash in place of the shares they previously held.

Conversely, it does not change the portfolio of the acquiring company's shareholders, nor their stake in the company.

An **all-share transaction** is symmetrical for the shareholders of A and B. No one receives any cash. When the dust settles, they all hold claims on a new company born out of the two previous companies. Note that their claims on the merged company would have been exactly the same if B had absorbed A. In fact, who absorbs whom is not so important: it is the percentage ownership the shareholders end up with that is important. Moreover, it is common for one company to take control of another by letting itself be "absorbed" by its "target".

Merger synergies are not shared in the same way. In a cash acquisition, selling shareholders pocket a portion of the value of synergies immediately (depending on the outcome of the negotiation). The selling shareholders do not bear any risk of implementation of the synergies. In an all-share transaction, however, the value creation (or destruction) of combining the two businesses will be shared according to the relative values negotiated by the two sets of shareholders.

In a cash acquisition, shareholders of the acquiring company alone assume the business risks. In an all-share transaction, the risks are shared by the two groups of shareholders.

For the shareholders of company B, a **contribution of shares**, with B remaining a subsidiary of A, has the same effect as a legal merger of the two companies. An **asset contribution** of company B to company A is also very similar to a legal merger. The only difference is that, in an asset contribution, the claim of company B ex-shareholders on company A is via company B, which becomes a holding company of company A.

3/PROS AND CONS OF PAYING IN SHARES

In contrast to a cash acquisition, there is no cash outflow in an all-share deal, be it an exchange of shares, an asset contribution in return for shares or a demerger with a distribution of shares in a new company. The transaction does not generate any cash that can be used by shareholders of the acquired company to pay capital gains taxes. For this reason, it is important for these transactions to be treated as "tax-free".

What is the advantage of paying in shares? The efficient markets hypothesis, which analyses a merger as an acquisition followed by a capital increase, does not provide a satisfactory answer. Sometimes company managers want to change the ownership structure of the company so as to dilute an unwelcome shareholder's stake, constitute a group of core shareholders or increase their power by increasing the company's size or prestige. More importantly, paying in shares enables the company to skirt the question of financing and merge even with very large companies. Some critics say that companies paying in shares are paying for their acquisitions with "funny money"; we think that depends on post-merger ownership structure and share liquidity. And, most importantly, it depends on the ability of the merged company to harness anticipated synergies and create value. We provide on p. 883 of Chapter 42 a table setting out the pros and cons of payment in shares vs. cash.

Section 43.2

THE MECHANICS OF ALL-SHARE TRANSACTIONS

1/RELATIVE VALUE RATIO AND EXCHANGE RATIO

In practice, a noncash merger requires first that the target company be valued. Then the acquiring company must be valued, since it must issue new shares to the target's shareholders. The ratio of shareholders' equity value of company A/ shareholders' equity value of company B is called **relative value**. To determine relative values, a full valuation of the two companies to be merged is generally performed, according to the methods described in Chapter 40. Such valuation is usually done on a standalone basis, with synergies valued separately.

Let us take another look at companies A and B, with the following key figures:

(in €m)	Value of shareholders' equity[3]	Value of shareholders' equity agreed in the merger
A (acquirer)	450	450
B (target)	680	750

3 *Market capitalisation if the companies are listed.*

The difference between the 750 agreed and the 680 is nothing but the result of a negotiation. *B* has succeeded in convincing *A* that either its market valuation underestimated its intrinsic value or, contrarily, that *A*'s market cap was overoptimistic. Remember that during the negotiation of the relative value ratio, the companies will usually gather much more information than what has been made public.

In our example, the relative value ratio is 1.67 (750/450). In other words, B is deemed to be worth 1.67 times A. The agreed relative value ratio gives the ex-shareholders of A $1/(1 + 1.67)$ or 37.5% of the shares of the new company and the ex-shareholders of B $1.67/(1 + 1.67)$ or 62.5%.

If the relative value ratio were 1.5 – i.e., close to the ratio of the market capitalisation of the two companies, the ownership structure of the two shareholder groups would be different (40%/60%).

The relative value agreed between the two companies determines who will own how much of the new company. As a result, this ratio will define the power each shareholder will wield after the transaction.

Once relative values have been determined, often after long, protracted negotiations, the **exchange ratio** is a direct result thereof. It is the ratio of the number of shares of company A to be tendered for each company B share received.

Once again, let's assume the following characteristics for companies A and B:

	Value of shareholders' equity agreed in merger (€)	Number of shares	Value per share (€)
A (acquirer)	450m	4,500,000	100
B (acquiree)	750m	3,750,000	200

In exchange for contribution of capital of €750m, A issues 7,500,000 (=€750m/€100) new shares to the shareholders of B. Company B's 3,750,000 outstanding shares will be exchanged for the 7,500,000 newly issued A shares. The exchange ratio is therefore 1 B share for 2 A shares (or 1 for 2).

Once relative values are determined, calculating the exchange ratio is a simple matter:

$$\text{Exchange ratio} = \text{Relative value ratio} \times \frac{\text{Premerger number of } A \text{ shares}}{\text{Premerger number of } B \text{ shares}}$$

(... A shares for one B share)	(B is worth ... times A)	
2	=	1.67	× 4,500,000/3,750,000

The difficulty is not so much in determining the per-share value of the acquired company as in establishing the **relationship that will serve as the basis for the exchange**. There is flexibility for the parties to set the value of shares as long as the exchange ratio is kept. We're not interested in calculating absolute shareholder equity values, but relative values. We often observe that the parties will both inflate values of their companies, but at the end of the negotiation all that matters is the relative value!

It is customary in the mergers and acquisitions business to examine what would be the exchange ratio based on the performance metrics generally monitored by the market. The most frequently used measures are net income, cash flow, dividends, market capitalisation and book value[4] ...

4 *Some analysts look at the ratio based on sales, EBITDA (Earnings Before Interest, Taxes, Depreciation and Amortisation) or EBIT. We think these are inappropriate because they do not take account of the company's relative debt burden (i.e., relative weight of debt in the overall financing of the company).*

2/DILUTION OR ACCRETION CRITERIA

To help refine our analysis, let us suppose companies *A* and *B* have the following key financial elements:

(in €m)	Sales	Net income	Book equity	Value of shareholders' equity
A	1,500	15	250	450
B	5,000	35	450	680

Putting aside for one moment potential industrial and commercial synergies, the financial elements of the new company *A* + *B* resulting from the merger with *B* are as follows:

(in €m)	Sales	Net income	Book equity	Value of shareholders' equity
Group A + B	6,500	50	700	1,130

In theory, the value of the new entity's shareholders' equity should be the sum of the value of the shareholders' equity of *A* and *B*. In practice, it is higher or lower than this amount, depending on how advantageous investors believe the merger is.

Using the agreed relative value ratio of 1.67, our performance measures for the new group are as follows:

(in €m)	Group net income	Group book equity	Theoretical value of group shareholders' equity
The ex-shareholders of A have a claim on:	18.75	262.5	423.75
vs. before the transaction:	15	250	450
The ex-shareholders of B have a claim on:	31.25	437.5	706.25
vs. before the transaction:	35	450	680
TOTAL Before transaction	50	700	1,130
After transaction	50	700	1,130

As a result of the agreed relative value ratio, the ex-shareholders of *B* suffer a **dilution** (reduction) in book equity, as their portion declines from €450m to €437.5m, and in their share of the net income of the new entity. At the same time, they enjoy an **accretion** in their share of the new group's theoretical market capitalisation from €680m to €706.25m. Naturally, the situation is the opposite for the ex-shareholders of *A*.

When *A* absorbs *B* via a share exchange, if the relative value *B/A* is less than the relative ratio calculated for a given reference metric (value of shareholders' equity, book value, net income, etc.), the ex-shareholders of *A* enjoy an accretion in value with respect to that metric.

In contrast, when the agreed relative value (*B/A*) is higher than the reference metric, *A* shareholders will suffer dilution with regards to that metric.

Turning our attention now to the earnings per share of companies *A* and *B*, we observe the following:

5 *Price/Earnings ratio.*

	Value of shareholders' equity (€m)	Net income (€m)	P/E[5]	Number of shares (million)	Earnings per share (€)
Company *A*	450	15	30	4.5	3.33
Company *B*	680	35	19.4	3.75	9.33

6 *Before goodwill.*

On the basis of the relative value ratio agreed in the merger (750/450), the earnings per share[6] of the new group *A* now stand at $(15 + 35)/(4.5 + 7.5)$ or €4.17 per share. EPS have risen from €3.33 to €4.17, representing an increase of more than 25%. The reason is that the portion of earnings deriving from ex-company *B* is purchased with shares valued at *A*'s P/E multiple of 30 (450/15), whereas *B* is valued at a P/E multiple of 21 (750/35). Company *A* has issued a number of shares that is relatively low compared with the additional net income that *B* has contributed to *A*'s initial net income.

Earnings per share (before goodwill) automatically increase when the P/E of the acquiring company is greater than the P/E of the acquired company (and vice versa).

The reasoning is similar for other performance metrics, such as cash flow per share.

3/SYNERGIES

As an all-share merger consists conceptually of a purchase followed by a reserved capital increase, the sharing of synergies is a subject of negotiation just as it is in the case of a cash purchase.

In our example, let us suppose that synergies between *A* and *B* will increase the after-tax income of the merged group by €10m from the 1st year onwards.

The big unknown is the credit and the value investors will ascribe to these synergies:

- €300m – i.e., a valuation based on *A*'s P/E multiple of 30;
- €194m – i.e., a valuation based on *B*'s P/E multiple of 19.4;
- €226m – i.e., a valuation based on a P/E multiple of 22.6, the average of the P/Es of *A* and *B*;
- some other value.

Two factors lead us to believe that investors will attribute a value that is lower than these estimates:

➤ The amount of synergies announced at the time of the merger is only an estimate and the announcers have an interest in maximising it to induce shareholders to approve the transaction. In practice, making a merger or an acquisition work is a managerial challenge. You have to motivate employees who may previously have been competitors to work together, create a new corporate culture, avoid losing customers who want to maintain a wide variety of suppliers, etc. Experience has shown that:

   ○ more than half of all mergers fail on this score;
   ○ actual synergies are slower in coming;
   ○ the number of synergies is lower than originally announced.

➤ Sooner or later, the company will not be the only one in the industry to merge. Because mergers and acquisitions tend to come in waves, rival companies will be tempted to merge for the same reasons: unlock synergies and remain competitive. As competition also consolidates, all market participants will be able to lower prices or refrain from raising them, to the joy of the consumer. As a result, the group that first benefited from merger synergies will be forced to give back some of its gains to its customers, employees and suppliers.

A study of the world's largest mergers and acquisitions since 1998 shows that the P/E multiples, at which the market values synergies when they are announced, are well below P/Es of both the acquiring company and the target.

Based on this information, let's assume that the investors in our example value the €10m p.a. in synergies at a P/E of 12, or €120m.

The value of shareholders' equity of the new group is therefore:

$$450 + 680 + 120 = €1,250m$$

Value is created in the amount of $1,250 - 1,130 = €120m$. This is not financial value creation, but the result of the merger itself, which leads to cost savings or revenue enhancements. The €120m synergy pie will be shared between the shareholders of A and B.

In the extreme, the shareholders of A might value B at €800m. In other words, they might attribute the full present value of the synergies to the shareholders of B. The relative value ratio would then be at its maximum, 1.78.[7] Note that in setting the relative value ratio at 1.67, they had already offered the ex-shareholders of B 84%[8] of the value of the synergies!

The relative value ratios of 1.19[9] and 1.78 constitute the upper and lower boundaries of the negotiable range. If they agree on 1.19, the shareholders of A will have kept all of the value of the synergies for themselves. Conversely, at 1.78, all of the synergies accrue to the shareholders of B.

The relative value choice determines the relative ownership stake of the two groups of shareholders, A's and B's, in the post-merger group, which ranges from 45.6%/54.4% to 36%/64%. The difference is significant!

Determining the value of potential synergies is a crucial negotiating stage. It determines the maximum merger premium that company A will be willing to pay to the shareholders of B:

7 *(680 + 120)/450.*

8 *(62.5% × 1,250 − 680)/120.*

9 *680/(450 + 120).*

- large enough to encourage shareholders of B to approve the merger;
- small enough to still be value-creating for A shareholders.

4/THE "BOOTSTRAP GAME"

Until now, we have assumed that the market capitalisation of the new group will remain equal to the sum of the two initial market capitalisations. In practice, a merger often causes an adjustment in the P/E, called a **rerating** (or eventually derating!). As a result, significant transfers of value occur to and between the groups of shareholders. These value transfers often offset a sacrifice with respect to the post-merger ownership stake or a post-merger performance metric.

If we assume that the new group A continues to enjoy a P/E multiple of 30 (ignoring synergies), as did the pre-merger company A, its market capitalisation will be €1,500m. The ex-shareholders of A, who appeared to give up some relative value with regard to the post-merger market cap metric, see the value of their share of the new group rise to 562.5m,[10] whereas they previously owned 100% of a company that was worth only €450m. As for the ex-shareholders of B, they now hold 62.5% of the new group, a stake worth €937.5m, vs. 100% of a company previously valued at only €680m.

Whereas it seemed A shareholders came out losing, in fact it's a win–win situation. The transaction is a money machine! The limits of this model are clear, however. A's pre-merger P/E of 30 was the P/E multiple of a growth company. Group A will maintain its level of growth after the merger only if it can light a fire under B and convince investors that the new group also merits a P/E multiple of 30.

This model works only if company A keeps growing through acquisition, "kissing" larger and larger "sleeping beauties" and bringing them back to life. If not, the P/E multiple of the new group will simply correspond to the weighted average of the P/E multiples of the merged companies.[11]

You have probably noticed by now that it is advantageous to have a high share price, and hence a high P/E multiple. They allow you to issue highly valued paper to carry out acquisitions at relatively low cost, all the while posting automatic increases in earnings per share. You undoubtedly also know how to recognise an accelerating treadmill when you see one ...

The higher a company's P/E multiple, the more attractive it is for the company to make acquisitions.

The potential immediate rerating after the merger does not guarantee creation of shareholder value. In the long run, only the new group's economic performance will enable it to maintain its high P/E multiple.

10 *37.5% × 1,500.*

11 *This is a variant of the tale Warren Buffett told Berkshire Hathaway shareholders in his February 1982 letter to shareholders. http://www. berkshire hathaway.com/ letters/1981.html*

Section 43.3
DEMERGERS AND SPLITOFFS

Demergers are common in the United States and the United Kingdom. In Continental Europe, legislation and taxation were very unfavourable until the

1990s, severely limiting the number of demergers until then. Now, more appropriate tax treatment has since come into effect, and the technique has gained popularity.

1/PRINCIPLES

The principle of a demerger is simple. A group with several divisions, in most cases two, decides to separate them into distinct companies. The shares of the newly created companies are distributed to the shareholders in exchange for shares of the parent group. The shareholders, who are the same as the shareholders of the original group, now own shares in two or more companies and can buy or sell them as they see fit.

There are two basic types of transactions, depending on whether, once approved, the transaction applies to all shareholders or gives shareholders the option of participating.

- Separation of the activities of a group. The original shareholders become the shareholders of the separated companies. | **Demerger.**
- The transaction can be carried out by distributing the shares of a subsidiary in the form of a dividend (a spinoff), or by dissolving the parent company and distributing the shares of the ex-subsidiaries to the shareholders (a splitup).
- Immediately after the transaction, the shareholders of the demerged companies are the same, but ownership evolves very quickly thereafter.

- In a splitoff, shareholders have the option to exchange their shares in the parent company for shares in a subsidiary. To avoid unnecessary holdings of treasury shares, the shares tendered are cancelled. | **Splitoff.**
- A splitoff is a share repurchase paid for with shares in a subsidiary rather than in cash.
- If all shareholders tender their shares, the splitoff is identical to a demerger. If the offer is relatively unsuccessful, the parent company remains a shareholder of a now-listed subsidiary.

2/WHY DEMERGE?

Broadly speaking, studies on demergers have shown that the shares of the separated companies outperform the market, both in the short and long term.

In the context of the efficient markets hypothesis and agency theory, demergers are an answer to conglomerate discounts (see Chapter 41). In this sense, a demerger creates value, because it solves the following problems:

- Allocation of capital within a conglomerate is suboptimal, benefiting divisions in difficulty and penalising healthy ones, making it harder for the latter to grow.
- The market values primary businesses correctly but undervalues secondary businesses.
- The market has trouble understanding conglomerates, a problem aggravated by the fact that virtually all financial analysts are specialised by industry. With the number of listed companies constantly growing and investment possibilities therefore expanding, investors prefer simplicity. In addition,

large conglomerates communicate little on smaller division increasing therefore the information asymmetry.
- The conglomerate has operating costs that add to the costs of the operating units without creating value.

Demergers can also reduce creditor protection. The transaction can be structured in such a way that one of the new companies carries all the debt, while the other is financed by equity capital only. In this case, the creditors bear much more risk than they did before because their loans are backed up by fewer assets. The value of the debt decreases, and the value of equity capital increases by an equivalent amount. Value has been transferred from debtholders to shareholders.

In practice, however, debtholders are rarely spoiled that way. Loan agreements and bond indentures generally stipulate that in the event of a demerger the loan or the bonds become immediately due and payable. Empirical studies have shown that, on average, demergers lead to no transfer of value from creditors to shareholders. In most jurisdictions, creditors can veto a demerger if the demerged companies are not liable for each other's debts and can demand repayment if provided for in their contracts.

Lastly, we note that demergers expose the newly created companies to potential takeovers. Prior to the demerger, the company might have been too big or too diverse. Potential acquirers might not have been interested in all its businesses. And the process of acquiring the entire company, then selling off the unwanted businesses is cumbersome and risky. A demerger creates smaller, pure play companies, which are more attractive in the takeover market. Empirically, it has been shown that demerged subsidiaries not always outperform. This is the case when the parent company has completely divested its interest in the new company or has itself become subject to a takeover bid.

Because of their complexity and the detailed preparation they require, demergers are rare. Examples include Chargeurs, demerged into Chargeurs International (textiles) and Pathé (cinema); Hillsdown Holdings plc and Terranova plc; Burton Group plc and Debenhams; Novartis AG and Ciba Specialty Chemicals Inc.; Eridania Beghin Say, demerged into Beghin Say, Céréol, Provimi and Cérestar, and the following splitoffs: Ixo/Infosources, General Motors/Delphi and AT&T/Lucent.

In a study published in 2004, Veld and Veld-Merkoulova show evidence on a European sample that demergers do create value. As demonstrated in some US studies, the abnormal returns following the announcement of a demerger are on average ca 2–4% (depending on the sample retained).

Demerging is not a panacea. If one of the demerged businesses is too small, its shares will suffer a deep liquidity discount. And not all conglomerates are financial failures: General Electric and Bouygues are two prominent, contrary examples.

If we wanted to be cynical, we might say that demergers represent the triumph of sloth (investors and analysts do not take time to understand complex groups) and selfishness (managers want to finance only the high-performance businesses).

But it's also the triumph of modern financial theory, which says that enterprises that bring together unrelated businesses without creating value will not stay as a group indefinitely.

Business combinations, commonly referred to as mergers and acquisitions, can take many forms. The most important distinction among them is the method of payment: (i) cash, or cash and shares, or (ii) 100% in shares.

All-share deals can take several forms:

- **legal merger**: two or more companies are combined to form a single company. In general, one company is dissolved and absorbed into the other;

- **contribution of shares**: the shareholders of company *B* exchange their shares for shares of company *A*;

- **asset contribution**: company *B* transfers a portion of its assets to company *A* in exchange for shares issued by company *A*.

The economics of the business combination are independent of the financial arrangements. This said, in an all-share deal the resources of the two entities are added together, increasing the merged company's financial capacity, compared with what it would have been after the conclusion of a cash deal. Also, in an all-share deal, all the shareholders of the resulting group share the risks of the merger. When the deal is negotiated, the companies are valued and the **relative value ratio** and **exchange ratio** are set. The exchange ratio is the number of shares of the acquiring company that will be exchanged for the tendered shares of the acquired company. The relative value ratio determines the position of each group of shareholders in the newly merged group.

The higher a company's P/E multiple, the more tempted it will be to carry out acquisitions by issuing shares, because its earnings per share will automatically increase. But be careful! No value is created. The increase in EPS is only a mathematical result deriving from the difference between the P/E multiples of the acquirer and the acquiree. At the same time, the P/E multiple of the new entity declines, because the market capitalisations of the new group should theoretically correspond to the sum of the market capitalisation of the two companies prior to the merger. Sometimes the new company's P/E multiple stays the same as the acquiring company's P/E multiple. We call this the "magic kiss" effect, because it implies that the company has only to "wake up" the "sleeping beauty" it has acquired. In each case, the value of the merger synergies is added to the value of the new company. How they are shared by the two groups of shareholders determines the premium the acquiring company will pay to the target's shareholders to persuade them to participate in the deal.

Lastly, recent amendments to tax laws in Europe make it feasible to **demerge** companies. A demerger is a simple concept. A diversified group decides to separate several business divisions into distinct companies and to distribute the shares of the new companies to shareholders in return for shares of the parent group.

The value created by a demerger can be analysed as follows:

- unlocking the value trapped in the conglomerate discount (efficient markets hypothesis);

- an increase in risk borne by creditors if one of the companies keeps all of the debt (rare in practice).

A demerger results in companies being more exposed to takeover bids.

SUMMARY

@
download

1/ What is the fundamental difference between a merger and a sale

- for the shareholder of the acquired company?
- for the acquiring company?
- for the shareholder of the acquiring company?
- for the acquired company?

2/ Unlike what happens when a company is sold, when companies merge, their shareholders' equity is added together. Why?

3/ In your view, what are the possible reasons behind a merger? And a demerger?

4/ Ignoring tax issues, would a shareholder with a 51% controlling interest in a company be better off buying another company or merging with it?

5/ Is the dilution of EPS that follows all mergers generally greater or less than that which follows a standard capital increase?

6/ Why is determination of the exchange parity important?

7/ What is the difference between the relative value ratio and the exchange ratio?

8/ When negotiating, is agreement first reached on the relative value or on the calculation method?

9/ Why do shareholders in an acquired company agree to the dilution of their shareholdings after completion of the merger?

10/ Where does the creation of value lie in a merger?

11/ Why are the legal procedures related to mergers so onerous?

12/ In what circumstances can a demerger lead to creation of shareholder value? And value for creditors?

13/ Can the success of a merger be judged by comparing the market performance of the new entity with that of the reference index?

14/ Can the success of a merger be judged by looking at the change in share price of the companies when the merger is announced?

EXERCISES

1/ Alpha AG is wholly owned by Mr Alpha and Beta AG is wholly owned by Mr Beta. The key figures for the two companies are as follows:

€m	Net profit	Equity value	Book equity
Alpha	60	750	800
Beta	30	1,500	400

Alpha acquires Beta. Calculate the shareholdings (as a percentage) of Mr Alpha and Mr Beta using net profits, equity value and book equity. What are your conclusions?

2/ Below are the key figures for Gamma plc and Delta plc:

€m	Net profit	Book equity	P/E	Number of shares
Gamma	20	60	50	2,000
Delta	40	300	8	1,000

(a) Gamma acquires Delta. The criterion selected for calculation purposes is equity value. Calculate the old and new EPS, equity per share and the percentage of the shareholdings of the former shareholders of Gamma in the new entity.

(b) Redo the calculations with a P/E for Gamma of only 15, and then 6.

(c) What are the minimum and maximum relative values if the synergies that come out of the merger increase the profits of the new group by 10, and if the new group is valued on the basis of a P/E of 21? What would the ratios be then?

(d) What is the value of Epsilon, the new name for the merged Gamma and Delta (still with synergies of 10) if it is valued on the basis of a P/E of 50.

(e) What is the value created and what does it represent?

Questions

1/ *The shareholder of the acquired company receives shares instead of cash. The acquiring company issues shares instead of reducing cash (or incurring debt), its shareholding structure is modified. The shareholder of the acquiring company loses some control, but the risk is shared. The acquired company no longer exists as a separate legal entity.*

2/ *By definition.*

3/ *Synergies. Conglomerate discounts.*

4/ *Buying it, so as not to lose his controlling interest in it.*

5/ *This isn't where the problem lies. What's important is to know whether the merger will create value and not whether EPS will be diluted.*

6/ *Because it is the basis for sharing the creation of value and provides shareholders with protection.*

7/ *Relative value is the value of one of the companies compared with the other. Exchange ratio is the number of shares in the acquiring company that are exchanged for one share in the acquired company.*

8/ *On relative value and then on the calculation methods which would lead to determination of the agreed relative value. On the surface, it looks like the opposite is true.*

9/ *Because they form part of a larger whole that is likely to generate synergies and because the merger could result in the P/E of the new entity being revalued.*

10/ *In the synergies created.*

11/ *In order to ensure the equal treatment of shareholders – the rights of all shareholders should be respected.*

12/ *When there is a conglomerate discount. Rarely for creditors.*

13/ *Not only. The initial business plans drawn up by companies should be taken into account.*

14/ *Yes, thanks to the efficiency of markets.*

Exercises

1/

	Net profits	Value	Shareholders' equity
Mr Alpha's share	2/3	1/3	2/3
Mr Beta's share	1/3	2/3	1/3

The criteria selected are crucial.

2/ *(a) and b)*

	Old (for Gamma)	New ($P/E = 50$)	New ($P/E = 15$)	New ($P/E = 6$)
EPS	0.01	0.0227	0.0145	0.0082
Equity per share	0.03	0.136	0.087	0.049
% of control held by Gamma shareholders	100% of Gamma	75.8	48.4	27.3

The higher a company's P/E, the more it will get out of a merger.

(c) *If Gamma shareholders get all of the synergies: relative value of 3.59 and exchange ratio of 0.557 Gamma shares for 1 Delta share. If Gamma shareholders sell all of the synergies: relative value of 2.13 and exchange ratio of 0.940 Gamma shares for 1 Delta share.*

(d) *Value of the whole = $50 \times (40 + 20 + 5) = 3{,}250$.*

(e) *Wealth created = 2,180. The wealth created is a result of synergies (500) and the revaluation of Delta (1,680).*

BIBLIOGRAPHY

On value creation and mergers:

J. Ang, Y. Cheng, *Direct Evidence on the Market Driven Acquisitions Theory*, EFMA 2003 Helsinki meetings, European Financial Management Association.

M. Bradley, A. Desai, E. Kim, Synergetic gains from corporate acquisitions and their division between the stockholders of target and acquiring firms, *Journal of Financial Economics*, **21**, 3–40, February 1988.

Z. Fluck, A. Lynch, Why do firms merge and then divest? A theory of financial synergy, *Journal of Business*, **72**(3), July 1999.

A. Ghosh, Does operating performance really improve following corporate acquisitions, *Journal of Corporate Finance*, forthcoming.

P. Healy, K. Palepu, R. Ruback, *Does Corporate Performance Improve after Mergers*, working paper, National Bureau of Economic Research, May 1990.

I. Loughran, A. Vijh, Do long-term shareholders benefit from corporate acquisitions?, *Journal of Finance*, **52**(5), 1765–1790, December 1997.

W. Megginson, A. Morgan, L. Nail, *The Determinants of Positive Long-term Performance in Strategic Mergers: Corporate Focus and Cash*, working paper, June 2002.

M. Rhodes-Kropf, S. Viswanathan, Market valuation and merger waves, *Journal of Finance*, **59**(6), 2685–2718, December 2004.

M. Sirower, *The Synergy Trap*, Free Press, 1997.

M. Walker, Corporate takeovers, strategic objectives and acquiring firm shareholder wealth, *Financial Management*, 53–66, Spring 2000.

On demergers:

P. Anslinger, S. Klepper, S. Subramaniam, Breaking up is good to do, *McKinsey Quarterly*, **1**, 16–27, 1999.

T. Chemmanur, A. Yan, *Corporate Control and Disciplining Effect of Spin-offs: A Theory of Performance and Value Improvements in Spin-offs*, working paper, Boston College, January 2002.

P. Cusatis, J. Miles, J. Woolridge, Restructuring through spin-offs, *Journal of Financial Economics*, **33**, 293–311, June 1993.

S. Gilson, P. Healy, C. Noe, K. Palepu, *Information Effects of Spin-offs, Equity Carve-outs, and Targeted Stock Offerings*, working paper, Harvard University, November 1997.

S. Krishnaswami, V. Subramaniam, Information asymmetry, valuation, and the corporate spin-off decision, *Journal of Financial Economics*, **53**(1), July 1999.

W. Maxwell, R. Rao, Do spin-offs expropriate wealth from bondholders?, *Journal of Finance*, **58**(5), 2087–2108, October 2003.

M. McKenna, *Methods of Divesting Assets: Straight Sales, Carve-outs, Spin-offs, Tracking Stocks and Hybrid Divestitures*, working paper, Stern School of Business, April 1999.

J.D. Rosenfeld, Additional evidence on the relation between divestiture announcements and shareholder wealth, *Journal of Finance*, **39**, 1437–1448, December 1984.

C. Veld, Y. Veld-Merkoulova, Do spin-offs create value? The European case, *Journal of Banking & Finance*, **28**, 1111–1135, 2004.

Chapter 44
LEVERAGED BUYOUTS (LBOS)

Use management as a lever and lean on it!

Leveraged Buy Outs (LBOs) are a form of corporate acquisition. Equity capital is reduced by the increase of financial leverage. There is usually a concomitant change in control. This technique is very popular in English-speaking countries and has found favour in Continental Europe as well.

Why are financial investors willing to pay more for a company than a trade buyer investor? Are they miracle workers? Watch out for smoke and mirrors. Value is not always created where you think it will be.

In the course of this chapter we will use the leveraged buyout of Weetabix, bought by Hicks, Muse, Tate & Furst, as an example.[1]

1 *We have based this example on publicly available information, and have for some of the figures either simplified the reality or made some estimates. It should be considered as illustrative and does not intend to reflect the reality or the exact state of the company.*

Section 44.1
LBO STRUCTURES

1/PRINCIPLE

The basic principle is to create a holding company, the sole purpose of which is to hold financial securities. The holding company borrows money to buy another company, often called the "target". The holding company will pay interest on its debt and pay back the principal from the cash flows generated by the target. In LBO jargon, the holding company is often called *NewCo* or *HoldCo*.

Operating assets are the same after the transaction as they were before it. Only the financial structure of the group changes. Equity capital is sharply reduced and the previous shareholders sell part or all of their holding.

From a strict accounting point of view, this setup makes it possible to benefit from the effect of financial gearing (see Chapter 13).

Obtaining tax consolidation between the holding company and the target is one of the drivers of the overall structure.

Now let us take a look at the example of Weetabix, sold in November 2003 by Sir Richard George and Weetabix's other minority shareholders for £642m (we will assume for illustrative purposes that this represents the value of equity and the enterprise value – in fact, Weetabix had cash on its balance sheet at the time of the acquisition). Weetabix generated annual operating profit of £44m.

A holding company is created and buys Weetabix, financing the purchase with £192m in equity and £450m in debt.

We assume that the pre-tax cost of debt is 7.5% (5% plus a 2.5% margin). The balance sheets are as follows:

Target's revalued balance sheet		Holding company's unconsolidated balance sheet		Group's consolidated balance sheet	
Assets £642m	Shareholders' equity £642m	Shares of target company £642m	Debt £450m	Assets £642m	Debt £450m
			Shareholders' equity £192m		Shareholders' equity £192m

Note that consolidated shareholders' equity, on a revalued basis, is now 65% lower than it was prior to the LBO.

The profit and loss statement, meanwhile, is as follows:

€m	Weetabix	Holding company	Consolidated
Earnings before interest and tax	44	31[2]	44
− Interest expense	0	−34	−34
− Income tax at 30%	−13	0[3]	−3[4]
= Normalised net income	31	(3)	7

2 *Assuming 100% payout.*

3 *The holding company benefits from tax exemption.*

4 *Assuming tax consolidation treatment.*

2/TYPES OF LBO TRANSACTIONS

Leveraged Buy Out or *LBO* is the term for a variety of transactions in which an external financial investor uses leverage to purchase a company. Depending on how management is included in the takeover arrangements, LBOs fall into the following categories:

- a *(Leveraged) Management Buy Out* or *(L)MBO* is a transaction undertaken by the existing management together with some or all of the company's employees;
- when outside managers are brought in, the transaction is called a *BIMBO* – i.e., a combination of a *buyin* and a management *buyout*. This is the most common type of LBO in the UK;
- finally, the term *Leveraged Build Up (LBU)* is used to describe an LBO in€which the new group continues to acquire companies in its sector so as to create industrial synergies. These acquisitions are financed primarily with debt.

3/EXIT STRATEGIES

The average LBO lifetime is becoming shorter and shorter. Financial investors now€generally keep the investment for 3–5 years. There are several exit strategies:

- sale to a trade buyer. Our general comment here is that in most cases financial investors bought the company because it had not attracted trade buyers. When time for the exit of the financial buyer has arrived, either the market or the company will have had to change for a trade buyer to be interested;
- stock market flotation. This strategy must be implemented in stages, and it does not allow the sellers to obtain a control premium. It is more attractive for senior management;
- sale to another financial investor, who in turn sets up another LBO. These "secondary" LBOs are becoming more and more common.

If the company has grown or become more profitable on the financial investors' watch, it will be easier for them to exit. Improvement may take the form of a successful redundancy or cost-cutting plan or a series of bolt-on acquisitions in the sector. Size is important if flotation is the goal, because small companies are often undervalued on the stock market, if they manage to get listed at all.

The problem emerges when the target company's profits do not allow a large enough dividend payment to the parent company, which is then unable to pay its bank interest charges or repay in a timely fashion its debt. Apart from recapitalising the company, several options exist, two of which are not very viable:

- borrow at the subsidiary level, and lend to the parent company. This would constitute an intra-group transfer for purely financial reasons and could be challenged, depending on national corporate law, as misuse of corporate property;

• merge the two entities.

Renegotiate with creditors is the traditional solution, but in some countries creditors cannot secure their loans with the assets of the subsidiary so long as the loans are extended to the holding company.

Section 44.2
THE PLAYERS

1/POTENTIAL TARGETS

The transactions we have just examined are feasible only with certain types of target companies. Companies for which income streams are volatile by nature, such as trading companies, do not have access to LBO financing. The same is true for companies requiring heavy capital expenditure, such as certain high-tech companies.

The target company must generate profits and cash flows that are sufficiently large and stable over time to meet the holding company's interest and debt payments. The target must not have burdensome investment needs. Mature companies that are relatively shielded from variations in the business cycle make the best candidates: food, retail, building materials, real estate, cinema theatres, yellow pages are all prime canididates.

The group's LBO financing already packs a hefty financial risk, so the industrial risks had better be limited. Targets are usually drawn from sectors with high barriers to entry and minimal substitution risk. Targets are often positioned on niche markets and control a significant portion of them.

Traditionally, LBO targets are "cash cows", but, more recently, there has been a movement towards companies exhibiting higher growth or operating in sectors with opportunities for consolidation.

2/THE SELLERS

Around half of all LBOs are carried out on family-owned companies. An LBO solves the succession problem. In 40% of cases, a large group wishing to refocus on a core business sells a subsidiary or a division via an LBO. The larger transactions fall into the latter category (Houghton Mifflin sold by Vivendi Universal, Provimi sold by Edison, Seat PG by Telecom Italia, Rexel sold by PPR).

Finally, some listed companies that are undervalued (often because of liquidity issues or because of lack of attention from the investment community because of their size) sometimes opt for "**public-to-private**" (**P to P**) LBOs. In the process, the company is delisted from the stock exchange. Despite the fact that these transactions are complex to structure and generate high execution risk, they are becoming more and more common thanks to the drop in market values. The LBO on the Irish packaging group Jefferson Smurfit in 2002 has been one of the largest European P to Ps (€5.6bn in enterprise value).

3/LBO FUNDS ARE THE EQUITY INVESTORS

Setting up an LBO requires specific expertise, and certain investment funds specialise in them. These are called *private equity sponsors*, because they invest in the equity capital of unlisted companies, or *venture capitalists*, because they venture into risky territory!

LBOs are particularly risky because of their high gearing. Investors will therefore undoubtedly require high returns. Indeed, required returns are often in the region of 25% p.a. In addition, in order to eliminate diversifiable risk, these specialised investment funds often invest in several LBOs.

The US and UK LBO markets are more mature than those of Continental Europe. For this reason, Anglo-Saxon funds such as BC Partners, Candover, Carlyle, Cinven, CVC, Hicks Muse and KKR dominate the market, particularly when it comes to large transactions. In the meantime, the purely European funds, such as Eurazeo, Industrie Kapital and PAI, are holding their own, generally specialising in certain sectors or geographic areas.

To reduce their risk, LBO funds also invest alongside another LBO fund or an industrial company (sometimes the seller) with a minority stake. In this case, the industrial company contributes its knowledge of the business and the LBO fund its expertise in financial engineering, the legal framework and taxation.

4/THE LENDERS

For smaller transactions (less than €10m), there is a single bank lender, often the target company's main bank.

For larger transactions, debt financing is more complex. The high degree of financial gearing requires not only traditional bank financing, but also subordinated lending and **mezzanine debt**, which lie between traditional financing and shareholders' equity. This results in a four-tier structure: traditional, secured loans called **senior debt**, to be repaid first; **subordinated** or **junior debt** to be repaid after the senior debt; mezzanine financing, the repayment of which is subordinated to the repayment of the junior and senior debt; and, last in line, shareholders' equity.

These borrowings can be complemented by seller financing, wherein the seller of the target company does not receive full payment immediately, and by securitisation.[5]

5 *See p. 961.*

LBO FINANCING EXAMPLE: WEETABIX

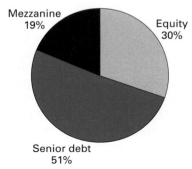

Mezzanine 19%

Equity 30%

Senior debt 51%

(a) Senior debt

Senior debt generally totals four to five times the target's EBITDA.[6] It is composed of several tranches, from least to most risky:

* tranche A is repaid in equal instalments over 3–5 years;
* tranches B and C are repaid over a longer period (5–7 years) after the A tranche has been amortised.

Each tranche has a specific interest rate, depending on its characteristics (tranches B and C will be more expensive than tranch A because they are repaid after and are therefore more risky). The cost of senior LBO financing is 200 to 300 basis points[7] over government bond yields.

When the debt amount is high, the loan will be "syndicated" to several banks (see Chapter 27). Some banks have launched "Collateralised Debt Obligation" (CDO) funds, specialised in senior LBO financing.

(b) Junior or subordinated bonds

High-yield bond issues are sometimes used to finance LBOs, but this technique is reserved for the largest transactions so as to ensure sufficient liquidity. In practice, the lower limit is around €100m.

An advantage of this type of financing is that it carries a bullet repayment and a maturity of 8–10 years. In accordance with the principle of subordination, the bonds are repaid only after the senior debt is repaid.

Given the associated risk, high-yield LBO debt offers investors, as the name suggests, high interest rates. They can be as much as 800 basis points over government bond yields.

In addition, senior debt may include:

* a revolving credit facility to finance working capital seasonality; and
* an acquisition facility to allow the target company to make a small acquisition without having to refinance the whole transaction.

These additional financings at the target level are provided by the same bank(s) as the bank(s) senior financing the acquisition at the holding level.

(c) Mezzanine debt

Mezzanine debt also comes under the heading of (deeply) subordinated debt, but is unlisted and provided by specialised funds.

Returns on mezzanine debt take two forms: a relatively low interest rate and a share in any capital gain when the LBO fund sells its stake.

As we saw in Chapter 30, certain instruments accommodate this financing need admirably. These "hybrid" securities include convertible bonds, mandatory convertibles, warrants, bonds with warrants attached, etc.

Most of the time, mezzanine debt is made of bullet bonds[8] with warrants attached.

6 *Earnings Before Interest, Taxes, Depreciation and Amortisation.*

7 *100 basis points = 1%.*

8 *See p. 318.*

Mezzanine financing is a true mixture of debt and shareholders' equity. Indeed, mezzaniners demand returns more akin to the realm of equity investors, often approaching 15% p.a.

Given the associated risk, investors in mezzanine debt – "mezzaniners" – demand not only a high return, but also a say in management. Accordingly, they are sometimes represented on the board of directors.

Subordinated and mezzanine debt offer the following advantages:

- they allow the company to lift gearing beyond the level acceptable for bank lending;
- they are longer term than traditional loans and a portion of the higher interest rate is paid through potential dilution. The holders of mezzanine debt often benefit from call options or warrants on the shares of the holding company;
- they make upstreaming of cash flow from the target company to the holding company more flexible. Mezzanine debt has its own specific terms for repayment, and often for interest payments as well. Payments to holders of mezzanine debt are subordinated to the payments on senior and junior debt;
- they make possible a financing structure that would be impossible by using only equity capital and senior debt.

LBO financing spreads the risk of the project among several types of instruments, from the least risky (senior debt) to the most risky (common shares). The risk profile of each instrument corresponds to the preferences of a different type of investor.

download

(d) Securitisation

Increasingly, LBOs are partly financed by securitisation (see Chapter 47). Securitised assets include receivables and/or inventories, when there is a secondary market for them.

A new technique, the securitisation buyout, has arisen in the UK. It is similar to the standard securitisation of receivables, but aims to securitise the cash flows from the entire operating cycle.

5/EUROPEAN ENVIRONMENT

In a survey led in 2004, the European Private Equity and Venture Capital Association (EVCA) benchmarked European national tax and legal environments for financial buyers. The main issues covered in this study are:

*   fund structures and pension funds incentive to invest in private equity;
*   merger regulation (private equity funds do not bear competition issues; therefore, a specific simplified anti-trust clearance procedure should exist);
*   company and capital gain tax rate;
*   taxation of stock options;
*   entrepreneurial environment;
*   bankruptcy and insolvency process.

Based on these criteria, the scores of the different countries are the following (1 being the most attractive and 3 the least attractive):

Country	Score	Country	Score
UK	1.26	France	1.89
Luxembourg	1.49	Spain	1.96
Ireland	1.53	**Total average**	**1.97**
Greece	1.75	Sweden	2.05
Netherlands	1.76	Czech Republic	2.12
Portugal	1.81	Finland	2.30
Belgium	1.82	Germany	2.37
Italy	1.86	Austria	2.42
Hungary	1.86	Denmark	2.46

Source: EVCA, selected data.

The UK still represents the bulk of the LBO market with 686 transactions in 2003 compared with 563 for the rest of Europe! In value terms, the UK market accounted for €23.5bn compared with €39.7bn for the rest of Europe. Larger transactions are becoming more common outside the UK (Legrand for €4.9bn, Jefferson Smurfit for €3.2bn, Seat PG for €5.65bn ...).

Section 44.3
LBOs AND FINANCIAL THEORY

LBOs have gained considerable popularity since the mid-1980s, even though the market is cyclical and experienced a dry spell in the early 1990s.

BUYOUTS AND BUYINS IN CONTINENTAL EUROPE

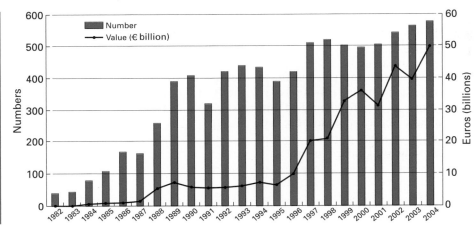

9 *Centre for Management Buy Out Research.*

Source: CMBOR[9]/Barclays Private Equity/Deloitte & Touche.

Experience has shown that LBOs are often done at the same price or at an even higher price than the price a trade buyer would be willing to pay. Yet the trade buyer, assuming he plans to unlock industrial and commercial synergies, should be willing to pay more. How can we explain the widespread success of LBOs? Do they create value? How can we explain the difference between the pre-LBO value and the LBO purchase price?

At first, we might be tempted to think that there is value created because increased leverage reduces tax payments. But the efficient markets hypothesis casts serious doubts on this explanation, even though financial markets are not in reality always perfect. To begin with, the present value of the tax savings generated by the new debt service must be reduced by the present value of bankruptcy costs. Second, the arguments in Chapter 34 have led us to believe that the savings might not be so great after all. Hence, the attractions of leverage are not enough to explain the success of the LBO.

We might also think that a new, more dynamic management team will not hesitate to restructure the company to achieve productivity gains and that this would justify the premium. But this would not be consistent with the fact that LBO transactions in which pre-LBO management stays in place create as much value as the others.

Agency theory provides a credible explanation. The high debt level prompts shareholders to keep a close eye on management. Shareholders will closely monitor operating performance and require monthly in-depth reporting. Management is put under pressure by the threat of bankruptcy if the company does not generate enough cash flow to rapidly pay down debt. At the same time, the managers often become – either directly or potentially – shareholders themselves via their stock options, so they have incentive to manage the company to the best of their ability.

Management, motivated by a potentially big payoff and frightened by a heavy debt burden, will manage the company in the most efficient manner possible, increasing cash flows and hence the value of the company. It's the carrot-and-stick approach!

Kaplan has demonstrated through the study of many LBOs that their operating performance compared with that of peer companies are much better. This is one example where there is a clear interference of financial structure with operating performance.

LBO transactions greatly reduce agency problems and, in so doing, create value.

However, LBOs that allow the former managers to "liquidate" the majority of their holdings and invest only a small portion as part of a core group of shareholders while remaining in their management positions are particularly dangerous. Management's motivation in these cases is not increased but, on the contrary, significantly decreasing!

SUMMARY

download

A leveraged buyout is a transaction wherein the purchase of a company is financed primarily with borrowed funds. A holding company contracts the debt and purchases the target company. The company's cash flow is regularly funnelled upstream to the holding company via dividends to enable the latter to pay interest and reimburse the loans.

An LBO is often a solution in a family succession situation or when a large group wants to sell off a division. It can also be a way for a company to delist itself when it is undervalued in the market.

The target company in an LBO may keep the current management in place or hire a new management team. Equity capital is provided by specialised funds. The structure depends on several layers of debt – senior, junior, mezzanine – with different repayment priority. As priority declines, risk and expected returns increase.

Increased gearing and the deductibility of interest expense do not satisfactorily explain why value is created in an LBO. Instead, it appears that the heavier debt burden motivates management to do a better job managing the company, of which they are often destined to become shareholders themselves. This is agency theory in action.

QUESTIONS

quiz

1/ Explain why an LBO is a type of capital reduction.

2/ What risks are involved in an LBO?

3/ Can mezzanine financing in the context of an LBO be compared with equity or debt?

4/ In the context of an LBO, does the holder of senior debt take more or less risk than the holder of junior debt?

5/ Can an LBO be carried out on an Internet company?

6/ Can an LBO be carried out on a cereals trader?

ANSWERS

Questions

1/ *Because debt is replaced with shareholders' equity.*
2/ *The risk that debts will outweigh cash flows generated.*
3/ *With debt because sooner or later it has to be repaid.*
4/ *Less risk because the holder of senior debt is repaid before the holder of junior debt.*
5/ *No, because an Internet company's cash flows are much too volatile to allow it to carry debt.*
6/ *No, because a cereal trader's cash flow is much too volatile to allow it to carry high fixed financial costs.*

BIBLIOGRAPHY

P. Halpern, R. Kieschnick, W. Rotenberg, *An Examination of Agency Costs in Firms which Subsequently Engage in an LBO*, working paper, University of Toronto, 1999.

M. Jensen, Corporate control and the politics of finance, *Journal of Applied Corporate Finance*, **4**(2), 13–33, 1991.

S. Kaplan, The effects of management buy-outs on operating performance and value, *Journal of Financial Economics*, **24**, 217–254, October 1989.

S. Kaplan, *The Staying Power of Leveraged Buyouts*, working paper, University of Chicago, 1992.

EVCA, *Benchmarking European Tax and Legal Environments*, benchmark paper, European Private Equity and Venture Capital Association, 2004.

www.evca.com, site of the European Private Equity and Venture Capital Association.

www.nottingham.ac.uk/business/cmbor, the Centre for Management Buy-out Research's website.

Chapter 45
BANKRUPTCY AND RESTRUCTURING

Women and children first!

Every economic system needs mechanisms to ensure the optimal utilisation of resources. Bankruptcy is the primary instrument for reallocating means of production from inefficient to efficient firms.

Theoretically, bankruptcy shakes out the bad apples from sectors in difficulty and allows profitable groups to prosper. Without efficient bankruptcy procedures, financial crises are longer and deeper.

The bankruptcy process can allow a company to reorganise, often requiring asset sales, a change in ownership and partial debt forgiveness on the part of creditors. In other cases, bankruptcy leads to liquidation, the death of the company.

Generally speaking, bankruptcy is triggered when a company can no longer meet its short-term commitments and thus faces a liquidity crisis. Nevertheless, the exact definition of financial distress leading to file for bankruptcy may differ from one jurisdiction to an other.

Bankruptcy is a critical juncture in the life of the firm. Not only does bankruptcy require that each of the company's stakeholders make specific choices, but the very possibility of bankruptcy has an impact on the investment and financing strategies of healthy companies.

Section 45.1
CAUSES OF BANKRUPTCY

Companies do not encounter financial difficulties because they have too much debt, but because they are not profitable enough. A heavy debt burden does no more than hasten the onset of financial difficulties.

The problems generally stem from a ill-conceived strategy, or because that strategy is not implemented properly for its sector (costs are too high, for example). As a result, profitability falls short of creditor expectations. If the company does not have a heavy debt burden, it can limp along for a certain period of time. Otherwise, financial difficulties rapidly start appearing.

Generally speaking, financial difficulties result either from a market problem, a cost problem or a combination of the two. The company may have been caught unaware by market changes and its products might not suit market demands (e.g., Swissair, Boo.com). Alternatively, the market may be too small for the number of companies competing in it (e.g., online book sales, satellite TV platforms in various European countries, etc.). Ballooning costs compared with these of rivals can also lead to bankruptcy. Moulinex, for example, was uncompetitive against South-East-Asian-manufactured products. ISMM, meanwhile, paid dearly for the rights to the 2002 and 2006 Football World Cups.

Nevertheless, a profitable company can encounter financial difficulties, too. For example, if a company's debt is primarily short-term, it may have trouble rolling it over if liquidity is lacking on the financial markets. In this case, the most rational solution is to restructure the company's debt.

One of the fundamental goals of financial analysis as it is practised in commercial banks, whose main business is making loans to companies, is to identify the companies most likely to go belly up in the near or medium term and not lend to them. Numerous standardised tools have been developed to help banks identify bankruptcy risks as early as possible. This is the goal of credit-scoring, which we analysed in Chapter 8.

Rating agencies also estimate the probability that a company will go bankrupt in the short or long term (bankruptcies as a function of rating were presented in Chapter 26). When US energy giant Enron filed for bankruptcy at the end of 2001, rating agencies were criticised for not anticipating financial difficulties and warning creditors. In this case, the rating system did not work properly.

BANKRUPTCY RATE OF COMPANIES RATED BY MOODY'S

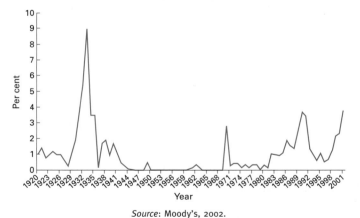

Source: Moody's, 2002.

2/THE DIFFERENT EUROPEAN BANKRUPTCY PROCEDURES

The bankruptcy process is one of the legal mechanisms that is the least standardised and homogenised around the world. Virtually all countries have different systems. In addition, legislation is generally recent and evolves rapidly.

The European Union regulation (issued 29 May 2000) on bankruptcy merely defines the competence of the different jurisdictions rather than effectively setting a bankruptcy procedure applicable all across Europe.

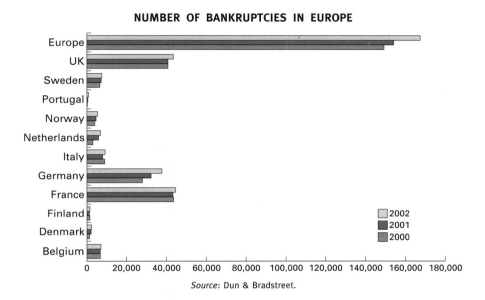

NUMBER OF BANKRUPTCIES IN EUROPE

Source: Dun & Bradstreet.

The number of bankruptcies has significantly increased in 2002 with Germany being specifically impacted.

Nevertheless, among the different procedures, some patterns can be found. In a nutshell, there are two different types of bankruptcy procedure. The process will be either "creditor-friendly" or "debtor- (company-) friendly". But, all processes have the same ultimate goals although they might rank differently:

- pay down the liabilities of the firm;
- minimise the disruptive impact on the industry;
- minimise the social impact.

A creditor-oriented process sets clearly the reimbursement of creditors as the main target of the bankruptcy process. In addition, the seniority of debt is of high importance and is therefore recognised in the procedure. In this type of procedure, creditors gain control or at least retain a great deal of power in the process. That type of process results most likely in the liquidation of the firm. The bankruptcy procedure in the United Kingdom clearly falls into that definition.

Such a regulation may seem unfair and too tough but it aims at preventing financial distress more than solving it in the less disturbing way for the whole economy. There is some kind of self-discipline of firms in those countries whereby firms will keep their level of debt reasonable to avoid financial distress. As a counterpart, creditors are more confident to grant loans, and money is less scarce for companies. For those supporting this type of process, the smaller number of bankruptcies in countries with stringent regulation (and an efficient judicial system) is evidence that this self-regulation works.

At the other end of the spectrum, some jurisdictions will give the maximum chance to the company to restructure. These procedures will generally allow management to stay in place and give sufficient time to elaborate a restructuring plan. Among countries with that approach we note the US (the Chapter 11 procedure) and France.

To summarise, the following criteria help to define a bankruptcy procedure:

- Does the procedure allow restructuring or does it systematically lead to liquidation (most jurisdictions design two distinct procedures)?
- Does the management stay in place or not?
- Does the procedure include secured debts? In some countries, secured debts (i.e., debts that are guaranteed by a specific asset) and related assets are excluded from the process and treated separately allowing greater certainty of repayment. In such countries, securing a debt by a pledge on an asset gives strong guarantees.
- Do creditors take the lead, or at least have a word in the outcome of the process? In most jurisdictions, creditors vote for the plan that is proposed to them as the outcome of the bankruptcy process. Sometimes they even have greater power and are allowed to name a trustee who will liquidate the assets to pay down debt. But in some countries (e.g., France) they are not even consulted.

	UK	France	Germany	Sweden	Spain	Italy
Type	Creditor-(lender-)friendly	Debtor-(borrower-)friendly	Creditor-(lender-)friendly	Creditor-(lender-)friendly	Creditor-(lender-)friendly	Debtor-(borrower-)friendly
Possible restructuring	Rare after opening of a proceeding	Yes	Yes (rare)	No	Yes	Yes
Management can stay in place	No	Yes*	Yes*		Yes*	***
Creditors vote on restructuring/liquidation plan	Yes	No	Yes	Yes	Yes	Yes**
Priority rule	Proceeding charges; secured debts on specific assets; tax and social security; other secured debts; other debts	Salaries; tax, other social liabilities; part of secured debts; proceeding charges; other secured debts; other debts	Proceeding charges; secured debts; other debts	Secured debts; proceeding charges; unpaid secured debts; tax and social liabilities; other debts	Secured debts; salaries; tax and social liabilities; creditor initiating procedure (25%); unsecured debts; subordinated debts	Proceeding charges; preferential creditors (inc. tax and social) and secured creditors; unsecured creditors

*   Assisted by court-designated trustee.
**   Yes, in case of restructuring (pre-emptive arrangement) but only consultative committee in case of liquidation (fallimento).
*** No, in case of liquidation (fallimento).

3/Potential inefficiencies in the bankruptcy procedure

Depending on the severity of the bankruptcy process and, in particular, whether it allows and promotes restructurings or not, two opposite inefficiencies can be thought of:

• allow restructuring of an inefficient firm, which destroys value. This could be an issue because such restructuring may destabilise the whole industry;
• lead to liquidation of efficient companies. A firm can be caught in a bankruptcy procedure because of a liquidity problem. In that case, liquidation could be value-destroying.

4/Restructuring plans

It is important to understand that not all financial difficulties lead to voluntary or court-mandated reorganisation or liquidation, which is often costly, lengthy and sometimes ineffective. The first step is usually private negotiation between the company (shareholders and/or managers) and its creditors. The more numerous the company's sources of funding – common shareholders, preferred shareholders, convertible bond holders, creditors, etc. – the more complex the negotiations.

Barring private negotiation, the potential conflicts between the various parties necessitate the intervention of a judge.

The business plan submitted by a company in financial distress is a key element in estimating the company's ability to generate the cash flows to pay off creditors.

A restructuring plan requires sacrifices from all of the company's stakeholders. It generally includes a recapitalisation, often funded primarily by the company's existing shareholders, and renegotiation of the company's debt. Creditors are often asked to give up some of their claims, accept a moratorium on interest payments and/or reschedule principal payments.

Creditors and shareholders are naturally at odds with each other in a restructuring. To bring them all on board, renegotiated debt agreements sometimes include clawback provisions, whereby the principal initially foregone will be repaid if the company's future profits exceed a certain level. Alternatively, creditors might be granted share warrants. If the restructuring is successful, warrants enable the creditors to reap part of the benefits.

To succeed, financial restructuring must be accompanied by business restructuring. Only such restructuring will enable the company to return to profitability. As part of the effort to improve productivity, operational restructuring is very likely to involve staff reductions. Certain businesses might be sold or discontinued. Note that restructuring a company in difficulty can sometimes be a vicious circle. Faced with a liquidity crisis, the company must sell off its most profitable operations. But, as it must do so quickly, it sells them for less than their fair value. The profitability of the remaining assets is therefore impaired, paving the way to new financial difficulties.

Section 45.2
BANKRUPTCY AND FINANCIAL THEORY

1/THE EFFICIENT MARKETS HYPOTHESIS

In the efficient markets hypothesis, bankruptcy is nothing more than a reallocation of assets and liabilities to more efficient companies. It should not have an impact on investor wealth, because investors all hold perfectly diversified portfolios. Bankruptcy, therefore, is simply a recomposition of the portfolio.

The reality of bankruptcy is, however, much more complicated than a simple redistribution. Bankruptcy costs amount to a significant percentage of the total value of the company. By bankruptcy costs, we mean not only the direct costs, such as the cost of court proceedings, but also the indirect costs. These include loss of credibility *vis-à-vis* customers and suppliers, loss of certain business opportunities, etc. Economists have tried to measure these costs but, because of the complexity of the task, their results have been applicable only in isolated cases and are not statistically meaningful. According to these researchers (in particular, Warner, 1977; Stanley and Girth, 1971; Weiss, 1989), bankruptcy costs range from 3% to 15% of the enterprise value of the company.

Bankruptcy costs have an impact on a company's choice of financial structure. A company that takes on a lot of debt increases its risk of going bankrupt, and investors will discount the value of its assets by the present value of the bankruptcy costs. Potential bankruptcy costs thus reduce the tax advantage of borrowing that stems from the deductibility of interest expense.

2/SIGNAL THEORY AND AGENCY THEORY

The possibility of bankruptcy is a key element of signalling theory. An aggressive borrowing strategy sends a positive signal to the market, because company managers are showing their belief that future cash flows will be sufficient to meet the company's commitments. But this signal is credible only because there is also the threat of sanctions: if managers are wrong, the company goes bankrupt and incurs the related costs.

Moreover, conflicts between shareholders and creditors, as predicted by agency theory, appear only when the company is close to the financial precipice. When the company is in good health, creditors are indifferent to shareholder decisions. But any decision that makes bankruptcy more likely, even if this decision is highly likely to create value overall for the company, will be perceived negatively by the creditors.

Let's look at an example. Rainbow Ltd manufactures umbrellas and is expected to generate just one cash flow. To avoid having to calculate present values, we assume the company will receive the cash flow tomorrow. Tomorrow's cash flow will be one of two values, depending on the weather. Rainbow has borrowings and will have to pay 50 to its creditors tomorrow (principal and interest).

Weather	Rain	Shine
Cash flow	50	50
Payment of principal and interest	−50	−50
Shareholders' portion of cash flow (equity)	50	0

Rainbow now has an investment opportunity requiring an outlay of 40 and returning cash flow of 100 in case of rainy weather and −10 in case of sunny weather. The investment project appears to have a positive net present value. Let's see what happens if the investment is financed with additional borrowings.

Weather	Rain	Shine
Cash flow	200	40
Payment of principal and interest	−90	−40 (whereas 90 was due)
Shareholders' portion of cash flow (equity)	110	0

Even though the investment project has a positive net present value, Rainbow's creditors will oppose the project because it endangers the repayment of part of their loans. Shareholders will of course try to undertake risky projects as it will more than double the value of the equity.

It can be demonstrated that when a company is close to bankruptcy all financial decisions constitute a potential transfer of value between shareholders and creditors. Any decision that increases the company's overall risk profile (risky investment project, increase in debt coupled with a share buyback) will transfer value from creditors to shareholders. Decisions that lower the risk of the company (e.g., capital increase) will transfer value from shareholders to creditors. As we showed in Chapter 35, these value transfers can be modelled using options theory.

Conflicts between shareholders and creditors and between senior and junior creditors also influence the decisions taken when the company is already in bankruptcy. On one hand, creditors want to accelerate the procedure and liquidate assets quickly, because the value of assets rapidly decreases when the company is "in the tank". On the other hand, shareholders and managers want to avoid liquidation as long as possible because it signifies the end of all hope of turning the company around, without any financial reward. For managers, it means they will lose their jobs and their reputations will suffer. At the same time, managers, shareholders and creditors would all like to avoid the inefficiencies linked with liquidation. This common objective can make their disparate interests converge.

The table at the top of the next page shows what is the average hope for repayment in case of bankruptcy depending on the ranking of the debt.

Whereas senior creditors get on average 60% of their money back, most junior creditors will receive less than 25% of their initial lending.

	Average recovery (%)			
	1982–2002	1982–2000	2001	2002
Secured bank loans	61.6	67.3	64.0	51.0
Equipment trust	40.2	65.9	NA	38.2
Senior secured	53.1	52.1	57.5	48.7
Senior unsecured	37.4	43.8	35.5	30.0
Senior subordinated	32.0	34.6	20.5	26.6
Subordinated	30.4	31.9	15.8	24.4
Junior subordinated	23.6	22.5	NA	NA
All bonds	37.2	39.1	34.7	34.3

Source: Moody's. NA = Not available.

3/FREE RIDERS

Lastly, a company in financial difficulties gives rise to the free rider problem (see Chapter 32). For example, a small bank participating in a large pool of banks may prefer to see other banks renegotiate their loans, while the terms of its loan remain unchanged.

Free rider problems will often arise when creditors are in different situations, in terms of commitment or of ranking of their debt.

It has been observed that the number of bankruptcies is greater in countries with long-developed financial markets. The proposed explanation is that in those countries, the companies are more likely to have public or syndicated debt and therefore a large number of creditors. In addition, with sophisticated markets, firms are more likely to have several types of debt: secured loans, senior debt, convertibles, subordinated,... In this context it may appear to be very difficult to restructure the firm privately (i.e., to find an agreement with a large number of parties with often-conflicting interests); hence, the bankruptcy process is the favoured route.

In bank-financing-based countries firms have strong relations with banks. The latter are likely to organise privately the restructuring in case of financial distress. This is often the case in Germany or in France where bilateral relationships between banks and corporates are stronger than in the Anglo-Saxon world.

3/THE LIMITS OF LIMITED LIABILITY

Modern economies are based largely on the concept of limited liability, under which a shareholder's commitment can never exceed the amount he invested in the company. It is this rule that gives rise to the conflicts between creditors and shareholders and all other theoretical ramifications of this theme (agency theory).

In bankruptcy, managers can be required to cover liabilities in the event of gross negligence. In such cases, they can be forced to pay back creditors out of their own pockets, once the value of the company's assets is exhausted. So, when majority shareholders are also the managers of the company, their responsibility is no longer limited to their investment. Such cases are outside the framework of the pure financial decision situations we have studied here.

Section 45.3

AN ILLUSTRATIVE EXAMPLE OF FINANCIAL RESTRUCTURING

We have chosen to illustrate the process of financial restructuring with the financial distress that Marconi, the British telecom equipment group, experienced in 2002.[1]

Marconi, like many telecom groups, had developed in the late 1990s an ambitious end-to-end global strategy implying significant internal and external growth. Following the downturn of the telecom market, Marconi was left with a large third-party financial debt burden of ca £4bn and insufficient cash flows to meet its commitments.

At the end of 2001, Marconi conducted a strategic review that led to a complete change of the group strategy and an operating restructuring (reducing overheads, selling assets). In 2002, Marconi initiated a negotiation process with banks and bondholders in order to emerge from financial distress.

An agreement was reached in March 2003 whereby claim holders, in exchange for the ca £4bn financial and bank debt, would receive – on a pro rata basis – of their initial claim:

- £340m cash distribution;
- £450m senior secured notes maturing April 2008;
- £304m junior secured notes maturing October 2008. The junior notes are secured on the US assets of the group (i.e., proceeds from the disposal of the US assets will be first applied to pay down junior notes);
- 99.5% of the equity of the restructured group.

Marconi's shareholders will receive:

- 0.5% of the equity of the restructured group;
- warrants allowing them to acquire up to 5% of the equity with an exercise price implying a post-restructuring market capitalisation of £1.5bn.

New corporate goverance rules are also proposed in the restructuring plan:

- board with a majority of nonexecutive independent members;
- new incentivisation plan for management and employees.

Basically banks and bondholders give up most of their claim to become owners of the group. A small incentive is left for the shareholders so that they accept the restructuring plan!

Prior to the plan, the debt was trading at ca 35% of face value. The new bonds are trading close to 100% of face value. Before restructuring market capitalisation of Marconi plc was £25m (2.8bn shares at 0.8 pence/share); after restructuring the market capitalisation of the new Marconi Corporation plc was ca £540m (200,000

1 *The case and figures have been voluntarily simplified and could therefore appear as altered.*

shares at £2.97/share). For the shareholders and creditors the financial impact of the plan was the following:

	Before restructuring (May 2003)	After restructuring (May 2003)
Financial creditors	£4bn × 35% = £1.4bn	1.1 × 100% = £1.1 bn (cash and notes) + 99.5% × 0.54 = £0.54bn (share of market cap.) = £1.64bn
Shareholders	2,800 × 0.008 = £0.025bn	Value of the shares: 0.5% × 0.540 = £0.003bn + value of warrants: £0.014bn = 0.017bn

This example illustrates how shareholders' limited liability gives them the ability to give up the assets to banks when they realise that the value of the assets falls below the commitments of the firm. At the end of the day creditors have increased the value of their claims, shareholders are left with almost no value but some hope given by the warrants.

SUMMARY

download

Bankruptcy is triggered when a company can no longer meet its short-term commitments and thus faces a liquidity crisis. This situation does not arise because the company has too much debt, but because it is not profitable enough. A heavy debt burden does no more than hasten the onset of financial difficulties.

The bankruptcy process is one of the legal mechanisms that is less standardised and homogenised around the world. Virtually all countries have a different system. Depending on the country, the process will be either "creditor-friendly" or "debtor- (company-) friendly". But all processes have the same goals although they might rank differently:

● pay down the liabilities of the firm;

● minimise the disruptive impact on the industry;

● minimise the social impact.

The bankruptcy process can generate two types of inefficiencies:

● allow restructuring of an inefficient firm, which destroys value;

● lead to liquidation of efficient companies.

Prior to court proceedings, a company experiencing financial difficulties can try to implement a restructuring plan. The plan generally includes recapitalisation and renegotiation of the company's debt.

Bankruptcy generates both direct (court proceedings, lawyers, . . .) and indirect costs (loss of credibility *vis-à-vis* customers and suppliers, loss of certain business opportunities, etc.). These costs have an impact on a company's choice of financial structure.

Financial distress will generate conflict between shareholders and creditors (agency theory), and conflict among creditors (free rider issues).

1/ Why do companies go bankrupt?

2/ What risks do you take if you buy a subsidiary of a group that you know is in financial distress?

3/ Do the same types of conflict arise in the event of the bankruptcy of a partnership and that of a limited company? Why?

4/ How can bankruptcy play a role in the survival of the company?

5/ How do bankruptcy costs impact on the tax breaks available on debt?

6/ Why are companies that are emerging from bankruptcy proceedings often strong competitors?

7/ Why are companies in France that are emerging from bankruptcy proceedings rarely strong competitors?

8/ Can a company with no debts go bankrupt? Can it destroy value?

9/ Why is a company able to get back on its feet financially during the bankruptcy period?

10/ Why do creditors agree to grant loans to companies during the bankruptcy period?

11/ What are for shareholders the pros of the creditor-friendly bankruptcy procedure?

12/ Give countries which have creditor-friendly bankruptcy procedures.

1/ Company *A* will be shutting down tomorrow after having generated a final cash flow. It has debts of 500 used to finance its activities. Depending on whether the economic situation is good or bad (there is an equal probability of either), the flows are as follows:

Economic situation	−	+
Operating cash flow	500	1,000
Payment of debt	−500	−500
Shareholders' portion of cash flow	0	500

The company is offered an investment yielding 0 if things go badly (−) and 300 if things go well (+).
(a) What is the initial value of the debt? And of shareholders' equity?
(b) What is the objective value of the investment project? At what price would investors be prepared to invest? Does your answer depend on the way this investment is financed?
(c) What conditions would new creditors set for financing this new investment?
(d) Are conflicts that arise between shareholders and creditors a result of the way in which the company finances investments?

2/ JNH is a high-tech group that is in financial distress. Its key financials are as follows:

In €m	2002	2003	2004
Sales	8,026	5,208	3,018
Operating income	130	(168)	(100)
Financial expense	(330)	(144)	(62)
Restructuring costs	(1,020)	(314)	
Net income	(1,220)	(626)	(162)
Fixed assets		122	72
Working capital		614	330
Shareholders' equity		(620)	(784)
Subordinated debt		616	616
Senior debt		740	570

The JNH share is trading at €24. The company's share capital is divided into 8,910,000 shares. The value of the senior debt can be estimated at half of its face value and the value of the subordinated debt at 21% of its face value. The following rescue plan has been submitted to all of the investors in the company:

○ Shareholder subscription to a capital increase of 15,500,000 new shares at a price of €20 per share, totalling €310m.
○ Partial repayment and conversion of the subordinated debt into capital: issue of 3,850,000 new shares and repayment of €36.96m.
○ Waiver of €160m of debts by senior creditors. In exchange, 1,250,000 warrants entitling holders to subscribe after 3 years to one share per warrant at a price of €25 per share. The value of these warrants is estimated at €4 per warrant. The

proceeds of the capital increase that are left over after partial repayment of the subordinated debt will be used to repay the senior creditors.

(a) What is your view of the financial health of this company?
(b) Calculate the value of the different securities used to finance the capital employed.
(c) Calculate how much the various lenders will have before and after the rescue plan. Assume the negotiated amount of the face value of the senior debt will be 80% after the plan.
(d) Who is the key beneficiary of this plan?

ANSWERS

Questions

1/ *Because their return on capital employed is too low.*
2/ *The risk that the sale will be declared invalid as it took place during the period immediately preceding the bankruptcy.*
3/ *No, because in partnerships, partners' liability is not limited to their contributions.*
4/ *It puts the counter back to zero for all contracts.*

5/ *The present value of the cost of bankruptcy is deducted from the enterprise value. The more debts a company has, the higher the bankruptcy costs.*

6/ *Because a portion of their charges may have been renegotiated and revised downwards (rent, personnel expense, miscellaneous charges).*

7/ *Because in France public policy is weighted heavily in favour of job preservation, and the recovery plan that saves the largest number of jobs is likely to be the one selected by the bankruptcy courts, even if in the long term it leads to the demise of the company.*

8/ *No, since it doesn't owe anything (or practically anything). Yes, if it invests at a rate of return higher than that required by shareholders.*

9/ *Because in most jurisdictions repayments on old debts are frozen, and customers continue to pay their debt.*

10/ *Because their new debts will be paid off before the old debts if the company is liquidated.*

11/ *Managers will try to postpone bankruptcy as much as possible.*

12/ *US, France.*

Exercises

1/ (a) $V_d = 500$, $V_e = 250$.

(b) *150, nearly 300 if it is debt-financed, 150 if it is equity-financed.*

(c) *If they are certain that they will be reimbursed first (if their credit is ranked higher than that of existing creditors).*

(d) *Yes, but only because the company was close to bankruptcy at the outset.*

2/ (a) *The group is in very poor shape financially, and its returns are far too low. The disposal of the most attractive assets that became necessary to meet cash needs merely served to accelerate the group's plunge into bankruptcy. The business is shrinking away.*

(b) *Value of shareholders' equity* $=€213.84m$.
   Value of subordinated debt $=€129.36m$.
   Value of senior debt $=€285m$.
   Value of capital employed $=€628.2m$.

(c) *Value of senior creditors' assets* $= (310 - 36,94) + (570 - 160 - 310 + 36.94) \times 80\% + 1.25 \times 4 = €387.61m$.
   Value of shareholders' equity $= 628.2 - (570 - 160 - 310 + 36.94) \times 80\% -1.25 \times 4 = €513.65$.
   Value of a share $= 513.65/(8,91 + 15.5 + 3.85) = €18.2$
   Shareholders wealth without capital increase $=€162.2m$ *(compared with €213.83m before plan).*
   Subordinated creditors' assets $= 36.94 + 3.85 \times 18.2 = €107m$ *(compared with €129.36m before).*
   Wealth of shareholders who subscribed to the capital increase $= 15.5 \times 18.2 = €282.1m$ *(for €310m invested).*

(d) *The creditors.*

BIBLIOGRAPHY

E. Altman, Financial ratios, discriminant analysis and the prediction of corporation bankruptcy, *Journal of Finance*, **23**, 589–609, September 1968.

E. Altman, *Corporate Financial Distress and Bankruptcy: A Complete Guide to Predicting and Avoiding Distress and Profiting for Bankruptcy*, John Wiley & Sons, 1993.

E. Altman, *Bankruptcy, Credit Risk and High-yield Junk Bonds*, Blackwell, 2001.

E. Berkovitch, R. Israel, Optimal bankruptcy laws across different economic systems, *Review of Financial Studies*, **12**(2), 347–377, Summer 1999.

S. Claessens, L. Klapper, *Bankruptcy Around the World: Explanation of its Relative Use*, World Bank Development Research Group, July 2002.

S. Davidenko, J. Franks, *Do Bankruptcy Codes Matter? A Study of Defaults in France, Germany, and the UK*, working paper, London Business School, June 2004.

I. Hashi, The economics of bankruptcy, reorganization, and liquidation: Lessons for East European transition economies, *Russian and East European Finance and Trade*, **33**(4), 6–34, July/August 1999.

U. Hege, Workouts, court-supervised reorganization and the choice between private and public debt, *Journal of Corporate Finance*, **9**, 233–269, 2003.

Moody's, *Bankruptcy and Ratings: A Leveraged Finance Approach for Europe – UK versus France and Germany*, Moody's Global Credit Research, March 2000.

D. Stanley, M. Girth, *Bankruptcy: Problems, Process, Reform*, Brooking Institute Press, 1971.

J. Warner, Bankruptcy costs: Some evidence, *Journal of Finance*, **32**, 337–347, May 1977.

L. Weiss, Bankruptcy resolution, direct costs and violation of priority of claims, *Journal of Financial Economics*, **27**, 285–314, October 1990.

M. White, The corporate bankruptcy decision, *Journal of Economic Perspective*, **3**(2), 129–151, October 1989.

PART TWO
MANAGING NET DEBT AND FINANCIAL RISKS

In this part, we aim to analyse the day-to-day management of a company's financial resources in terms of:

- management of cash flows and treasury, which we will examine in Chapter 46; and
- management of financial risks, particularly interest rate, exchange rate, liquidity, credit risks and the risk of fluctuations in raw materials prices, which is described in Chapter 48.

These components were traditionally managed by distinct corporate functions – i.e., treasury and risk management. This said, they have now generally been pooled under the responsibility of the corporate treasurer given the interlinkage between them. His or her role is to oversee:

- a centralised treasury unit responsible for managing cash flows;
- a financing unit responsible for securing funds and negotiating borrowing terms with banks; and
- a front-office unit handling market transactions as well as interest rate and exchange rate risks;
- in large groups, a joint administrative unit ("back office") that processes transactions for all units.

We will also cover a particular aspect of debt financing, which is closely linked with the management of risk: Chapter 47 details how the company can finance itself by giving in guarantee some of its assets. Asset-based financing is often linked to off-balance-sheet financing, although tighter accounting rules make it now harder to achieve.

Chapter 46
MANAGING CASH FLOWS

A balancing act ...

Cash flow management is the traditional role of the treasury function. It handles cash inflows and outflows, as well as intra-group fund transfers. With the development of information systems, this function is usually automated. As a result, the treasurer merely designs or chooses a model, and then only supervises the day-to-day operations. Nonetheless, we need to take a closer look at the basic mechanics of the treasury function to understand the relevance and the impact of the different options.

Sections 46.1 and 46.2 explain the basic concepts of cash flow management, as well as its main tools. These factors are common to both small companies and multinational groups. Conversely, the cash-pooling units described in Section 46.3 remain the sole preserve of groups. In Section 46.4 we describe the products that the treasurer may use to invest the firm's residual cash in hand.

Section 46.1
BASIC TENETS

1/VALUE DATING

From the treasurer's standpoint, the balance of cash flows is not the same as that recorded in the company's accounts or that shown on a bank statement. An example can illustrate these differences.

Example BigA, a company headquartered in Toulouse, issues a cheque for €1,000 on 15 April to its supplier SmallB in Nice. Three different people will record the same amount, but not necessarily on the same date:

* BigA's accountant, for whom the issue of the cheque theoretically makes the sum of €1,000 unavailable as soon as the cheque has been issued;
* BigA's banker, who records the €1,000 cheque when it is presented for payment by SmallB's bank. He then debits the amount from the company's account based on this date;
* BigA's treasurer, for whom the €1,000 remains available until the cheque has been debited from the relevant bank account. The date of debit depends on

when the cheque is cashed in by the supplier and how long the payment process takes.

There may be a difference of several days between these three dates, which determines movements in the three separate balances.

1 Note that the concept of value date exists only in Continental Europe.

Cash management based on value dates[1] is built on an analysis from the treasurer's standpoint. The company is interested only in the periods during which funds are actually available. Positive balances can then be invested or used, while negative balances generate real interest expense.

The date from which a bank makes incoming funds available to its customers does not correspond exactly to the payment date. As a result, a **value date** can be defined as follows:

- **for an interest-bearing account**, it represents the date from which an amount credited to the account bears interest following a collection of funds; and the date from which an amount debited from the account stops bearing interest following a disbursement of funds;
- **for a demand deposit account**, it represents the date from which an amount credited to the account may be withdrawn without the account holder having to pay overdraft interest charges (in the event that the withdrawal would make the account show a debit balance) following a collection, and the date from which an amount debited from the account becomes unavailable following a disbursement.

Under this system, it is therefore obvious that:

- a credit amount is given a value date after the credit date for accounting purposes;
- a debit amount is given a value date prior to the debit date for accounting purposes.

Let us consider, for example, the deposit of the €1,000 cheque received by SmallB when the sum is paid into an account. We will assume that the cash in process is assigned a value date three calendar days later and that on the day following the deposit SmallB makes a withdrawal of €300 in cash, with a value date of 1 day.

VALUE DATES

Although the initial account balance is zero, SmallB's account is in debit on a value date basis and in credit from an accounting standpoint.

	€1,000 cheque paid in ←	€1,000 in cash withdrawn	Value date
	D	D + 1	D + 3
Account balance	1,000 ←	700 ←	
Balance on a value date basis	−300 ←		700 ←

Although the account balance always remains in credit from a accounting standpoint, the balance from a value date standpoint shows a debit of €300 until $D + 3$. The company will therefore incur interest expense, even though its financial statements show a credit balance.

Consequently, a payment transaction generally leads to a debit for the company on a value date basis several days prior to the date of the transaction for accounting purposes. Value dates are thus a **way of charging for banking services** and covering the corresponding administrative costs. Nonetheless, value dates penalise large debits, the cost of which is no higher from an administrative standpoint than that of debit transactions for smaller amounts.

2/ Account balancing

Company bank current accounts are intended simply to cover day-to-day cash management. They offer borrowing and investment conditions that are far from satisfactory:

- the cost of an overdraft is much higher than that of any other type of borrowing;
- the interest rate paid on credit balances is low or zero and is well below the level that can be obtained on the financial markets.

It is therefore easy to understand why it makes little sense for the company to run a permanent credit or debit balance on a bank account. **A company generally has several accounts with various different banks.** In some cases, an international group may have several hundred accounts in numerous different currencies, although the current trend is towards a reduction in the number of accounts operated by businesses.

In the account-balancing process, cash surpluses are pooled on a daily basis into a concentration account through interbank transfers and are used to finance accounts in debit.

One of the treasurer's primary tasks is to avoid financial expense (or maximise financial income) deriving from the fact that some accounts are in credit while others show a debit balance. The practice of **account-balancing** is based on the following two principles:

- avoiding the simultaneous existence of debit and credit balances by transferring funds from accounts in credit to those in debit;
- channelling cash outflows and cash inflows so as to arrive at a balanced overall cash position.

Although the savings achieved in this way have been a decisive factor in the emergence of the treasury function over the past few decades, only small companies still have to face this type of problem. Banks offer account balancing services, whereby they automatically make the requisite transfers to optimise the balance of company accounts.

3/ Bank charges

The return on capital employed[2] generated by a bank from a customer needs to be analysed by considering all the services, loans and other products the bank offers, including some:

2 *When a bank lends some money, it "uses part of the bank equity" because it has to constitute a minimum solvency ratio (equity/ weighted assets).*

- not charged for and thus representing unprofitable activities for the bank (e.g., cheques deposited by retail customers);
- charged for over and above their actual cost, notably using charging systems that do not reflect the nature of the transaction processed.

The banking industry is continuously reorganising its system of bank charges. The current trend is for it to cover its administrative processing costs by charging fees and to establish the cost of money (i.e., the cost of the capital lent to customers) by linking interest rates to financial markets. Given the integration between banking activities (loans, payment services and investment products), banks generally apply **flat rate charges** (i.e., not linked to the amount borrowed).

Transfers between Eurozone banks have been made much easier and automated to a great extent under the aegis of the European Central Bank. As a result, the traditional practice of value-dating has been called into question. Nonetheless, it remains the **cornerstone** of the system of bank charges in various different Continental European countries, and particularly France, Italy, Spain and Portugal.

Section 46.2
CASH MANAGEMENT

1/CASH BUDGETING

The cash budget shows not only the cash flows that have already taken place, but also all the receipts and disbursements that the company plans to make. These cash inflows and outflows may be related to the company's investment, operating or financing cycles.

The cash budget, showing the amount and duration of expected cash surpluses and deficits, serves two purposes:

- to ensure that the credit lines in place are sufficient to cover any funding requirements;
- to define the likely uses of loans by major categories (e.g., the need to discount based on the company's portfolio of trade bills and drafts).

Planning cash requirements and resources is a way of adapting borrowing and investment facilities to actual needs and, first and foremost, of managing a group's interest expense. It is easy to see that a better rate loan can be negotiated if the need is forecast several months in advance. Likewise, a treasury investment will be more profitable over a predetermined period, during which the company can commit not to use the funds.

The cash budget is a **forward-looking management chart showing supply and demand for liquidity within the company**. It allows the treasurer to manage interest expense as efficiently as possible by harnessing competition not only among different banks, but also with investors on the financial markets.

2/FORECASTING HORIZONS

Different budgets cover different forecasting horizons for the company. Budgets can be used to distinguish between the degree of accuracy users are entitled to expect from the treasurer's projections.

Companies forecast cash flows by major categories over long-term periods and refine their projections as cash flows draw closer in time. Thanks to the various services offered by banks, budgets do not need to be 100% accurate, but can focus on achieving the relevant degree of precision for the period they cover.

An annual cash budget is generally drawn up at the start of the year based on the management control budget. The annual budgeting process involves translating the expected profit and loss account into cash flows. The top priority at this point is for cash flow figures to be consistent and material in relation to the company's business activities. At this stage, cash flows are classified by category rather than by type of payment.

These projections are then refined over periods ranging from 1 to 6 months to yield rolling cash budgets, usually for monthly periods. These documents are used to update the annual budgets based on the real level of cash inflows and outflows, rather than using management accounts.

Day-to-day forecasting represents the final stage in the process. This is the basic task of a treasurer and the basis on which his or her effectiveness is assessed. Because of the precision required, day-to-day forecasting gives rise to complex problems:

- it covers all movements affecting the company's cash position;
- each bank account needs to be analysed;
- it is carried out on a value date basis;
- it exploits the differences between the payment methods used;
- as far as possible, it distinguishes between cash flows on a category-by-category basis.

The following table summarises these various aspects.

BANK No. 1

Account value dates

	Monday	Tuesday	Wednesday	Thursday	Friday
Bills presented for payment Cheques issued Transfers issued Standing orders paid Cash withdrawals Overdraft interest charges paid Sundry transactions					
(1) TOTAL DISBURSEMENTS					

BANK No. 1 (*cont.*)

Account value dates

	Monday	Tuesday	Wednesday	Thursday	Friday
Customer bills presented for collection Cheques paid in Standing orders received Transfers received Interest on treasury placements Sundry transactions					
(2) TOTAL RECEIPTS					
(2) − (1) = DAILY BALANCE ON A VALUE DATE BASIS					

Day-to-day forecasting has been made much easier by IT systems.

3 *Enterprise Resources Planning.*

Thanks to the ERP[3] and other IT systems used by most companies, the information received by the various parts of the business is processed directly and can be used to forecast future disbursements instantaneously. As a result, cash budgeting is linked to the availability of information and thus of the characteristics of the **payment methods** used.

3/THE IMPACT OF PAYMENT METHODS

The various payment methods available raise complex problems and may give rise to uncertainties that are inherent in day-to-day cash forecasting. There are two main types of uncertainty:

- **Is the forecast timing of receipts correct?** A cheque may have been collected by a sales agent without having immediately been paid into the relevant account. It may not be possible to forecast exactly when a client will pay down its debt by bank transfer.
- **When will expenditure give rise to actual cash disbursements?** It is impossible to say exactly when the creditor will collect the payment that has been handed over (e.g., cheque, bill of exchange or promissory note).

From a cash-budgeting standpoint, payment methods are more attractive where one of the two participants in the transaction possesses the initiative both in terms of **setting up the payment and triggering the transfer of funds**. Where a company has this initiative, it has **much greater certainty** regarding the value dates for the transfer.

The following table shows an analysis of the various different payment methods used by companies from this standpoint. It does not take into account the risk of nonpayment by a debtor (e.g., not enough funds in the account, insufficient account details, refusal to pay). This risk is self-evident and applies to all payment methods.

	Initiative for setting up the transfer	Initiative for completing the fund transfer	Utility for cash budgeting
Cheque	Debtor	Creditor	None
Paper bill of exchange[4]	Creditor	Creditor	Helpful to both parties insofar as the deadlines are met by the creditors
Paper promissory note[5]	Debtor	Creditor	
Electronic bill of exchange[6]	Creditor	Creditor	
Electronic promissory note[7]	Debtor	Creditor	
Transfer[8]	Debtor	Debtor	Debtor
Debit[9]	Creditor	Creditor	Creditor

From this standpoint, establishing the actual date on which cheques will be paid represents the major problem facing treasurers. Postal delays and the time taken by the creditor to record the cheque in its accounts and to hand it over to its bank affect the debit date. Consequently, treasurers endeavour to:

- process cheques for small amounts globally, to arrive at a statistical rule of thumb for collection dates, if possible by periods (10th, 20th, end-of-month);
- monitor large cheques individually to get to know the collection habits of the main creditors – e.g., public authorities (social security, tax, customs, etc.), large suppliers and contractors.

Large companies negotiate with their banks so that they are debited with a value date of $D + 1$ for their cheques, where D is the day on which the cheques arrive at the clearinghouse. As a result, they know in the morning which cheques will be debited with that day's value date.

Although their due date is generally known, domiciled bills and notes can also cause problems. If the creditor is slow to collect the relevant amounts, the debtor, which sets aside sufficient funds in its account to cover payment on the relevant date, is obliged to freeze the funds in an account that does not pay any interest. Once again, it is in the interests of the debtor company to work out a statistical rule of thumb for the collection of domiciled bills and notes and to get to know the collection habits of its main suppliers.

The treasurer's experience is invaluable, especially when it comes to forecasting the behaviour of customers (payment dates) and of creditors (collection dates for the payment methods issued).

Aside from the problems caused by forecasting uncertainties, payment methods do not all have the same flexibility in terms of domiciliation – i.e., the choice of account to credit or debit. The customer cheques received by a company may be paid into an account chosen by the treasurer. The same does not apply to standing orders and transfers, where the account details must usually be agreed in advance and for a certain period of time. This lack of flexibility makes it harder to balance

4 *Written document, in which the supplier asks the customer to pay the amount due to its bank on the due date.*

5 *Written document, in which the customer acknowledges its debt and undertakes to pay the supplier on the due date.*

6 *Electronic bill of exchange on a magnetic strip.*

7 *Electronic promissory note on a magnetic strip.*

8 *Order given by the customer to its bank to debit a sum from its account and to credit another account.*

9 *Payment method, whereby a debtor asks its creditor to issue standing orders and its bank to pay the standing orders.*

accounts. Lastly, the various payment methods have different value dates. The treasurer needs to take the different value dates into account very carefully in order to manage his or her account balances on a value date basis.

4/OPTIMISING CASH MANAGEMENT

Our survey of account balancing naturally leads us to the concept of **zero cash**, the nirvana of corporate treasurers, which keeps interest expense down to a bare minimum.

Even so, this aim can never be completely achieved. A treasurer always has to deal with some unpredictable movements, be they disbursements or collections. The greater the number or the volume of unpredictable movements, the more imprecise cash budgeting will be and the harder it is to optimise. This said, several techniques may be used to improve cash management significantly.

(a) Behavioural analysis

The same type of analysis as performed for payment methods can also yield direct benefits for cash management. The company establishes collection times based on the habits of its suppliers. A statistical average for collection times is then calculated. Any deviations from the normal pattern are usually offset where an account sees a large number of transactions. **This enables the company to manage cash balance on each account to "cover" payments forecast with a certain delay** of up to 4 or 5 days **for value date purposes**.

Optimising forecasts using behavioural studies directly leads to the optimisation of cash flow management.

In any case, payments will always be covered by the overdraft facilities agreed with banks, the only risk for the company being that it will run an overdraft for some, but over a limited period and thus pay higher interest expense.

(b) Intercompany agreements

Since efficient treasury management can unlock tangible savings, it is only normal for companies that have commercial relationships with each other to get together to maximise these gains. Various types of contract have been developed to facilitate and increase the reliability of payments between companies. Some companies have attempted to demonstrate to their customers the mutual benefits of harmonisation of their cash management procedures and have negotiated special agreements with customers in certain cases. In a bid to minimise interest expense attributable to the use of short-term borrowings, others offer discounts to their customers for swift payment. Nonetheless, this approach has drawbacks because for obvious commercial reasons it is hard to apply the stipulated penalties when contracts are not respected.

(c) Lockbox systems

Under the lockbox system, the creditor asks its debtors to send their payments directly to a PO box that is emptied regularly by its bank. The funds are immediately paid into the banking system, without first being processed by the creditor's accounting department.

When the creditor's and debtor's banks are located in the same place, cheques can easily be cleared on the spot. Such clearing represents another substantial time saving.

(d) Checking bank terms

The complexity of bank charges and the various different items on which they are based makes them hard to check. This task is thus an integral part of a treasurer's job.

Companies implement systematic procedures to verify all the aspects of bank charges. In particular, treasurers are keen to get their banks to ensure that all payments are credited or debited with a value date of $D + 1$, with any gains or losses being set off against the corresponding cash volumes on a monthly or quarterly basis. The conditions used to calculate interest payments and transaction charges may be verified by reconciling the documents issued by the bank (particularly interest rate scales and overdraft interest charges) with internal cash monitoring systems. Flat rate charges may be checked on a test basis. The most common bank errors occur when standard conditions are applied rather than the specific terms negotiated. In addition, failure to meet the counter opening times (which determine the day on which a transaction is deemed to have been executed) and mistakes in credit and debit interest are also the source of potential bank errors.

Section 46.3
CASH MANAGEMENT WITHIN A GROUP

Managing the cash positions of the subsidiaries of a group is akin to managing the individual bank accounts held by each subsidiary. Prior to any balancing between subsidiaries at group level, each subsidiary balances its own accounts. Consequently, managing the cash position of a group adds an additional tier of data-processing and decision-making based on principles that are exactly the same as those explained in Sections 46.1 and 46.2 for individual companies (i.e., group subsidiaries or SMEs[10]).

10 *Small- and Medium-sized Enterprises.*

1/CENTRALISED CASH MANAGEMENT

The methods explained in the previous sections show the scale of the task facing a treasury department. It therefore seems natural to centralise cash management on a groupwide basis, a technique known as cash pooling, since it allows a group to take responsibility for all the liquidity requirements of its subsidiaries.

The cash positions of the subsidiaries (lenders or borrowers) can thus be pooled in the same way as the various accounts of a single company, thereby creating a genuine internal money market. The group will thus save on all the additional costs deriving from the inefficiencies of the financial markets (bank charges, brokerage fees, differences between lending and borrowing rates, etc.). In particular, cash pooling enables a group to hold onto the borrowing/lending margin that banks are normally able to charge.

Cash pooling balances the accounts of a group's subsidiaries, thereby saving on the interest expense deriving from the market's inefficiencies.

This is not the only benefit of pooling. It gives a relatively big group comprising a large number of small companies the option of tapping financial markets. Information-related costs and brokerage fees on an organised market may prevent a large number of subsidiaries from receiving the same financing or investment conditions as the group as a whole. With the introduction of cash pooling, the corporate treasurer satisfies in the markets the financing needs of the group. The treasurer then organises an internal refinancing of each subsidiary on the same financing terms as the group receives.

Cash pooling has numerous advantages. The manager's workload is not proportional to the number of transactions or the size of the funds under management. Consequently, there is no need to double the size of a department handling the cash needs of twice the number of companies. The skills of existing teams will nevertheless need to be enhanced. Likewise, investment in systems (hardware, software, communication systems, etc.) can be reduced when they are pooled within a single central department. Information-gathering costs can yield the same type of saving. Consequently, cash pooling offers scope for genuine "industrial" economies of scale.

The compelling logic of having such a unit sometimes masks its *raison d'être* because although the creation of a cash-pooling unit may be justified by very good reasons, it may also lead to an unwise financial strategy and possibly even management errors. Notably, cash pooling will give rise to an internal debt market totally disconnected from the assets being financed. Certain corporate financiers may still be heard to claim that they have secured better financing or investment terms by leveraging the group's size or the size of the funds under management. But such claims do not stand up to analysis because the level of risk associated with investments alone determines their financing cost in a market economy. If the integration of a company within a larger group enables it to secure better financing terms, this improvement will be to the detriment of the overall entity's borrowing costs. We recommend that any readers still tempted to believe in financial economies of scale take another look at the analysis in Chapter 35.

In theory, once a company has achieved the critical mass needed to give it access to the financial markets, any economies of scale generated by cash pooling are "industrial" rather than financial.

This said, we concede that cash pooling may create a mass effect leading certain banks concerned solely with their market share to overlook the link between risk and profitability!

A prerequisite for cash pooling is the existence of an efficient system transmitting information between the parent company and its subsidiaries (or between the head office and decentralised units). The system requires the subsidiaries to send their forecasts to the head office in real time. The rapidity of fund movements – i.e., the unit's efficiency – depends on the quality of these forecasts, as well as on that of the corporate information system.

Lastly, a high degree of centralisation reduces the subsidiaries' ability to take initiatives. The limited responsibilities granted to local cash managers may not encourage them to optimise their own management, when it comes to either conducting behavioural analysis of payments or controlling internal parameters. Local borrowing opportunities at competitive rates may therefore go begging. To avoid demotivating the subsidiaries' treasurers, they may be given greater responsibility for local cash management.

2/THE DIFFERENT TYPES AND DEGREES OF CENTRALISATION

Looking beyond its unifying nature in theory, there are many different ways of pooling a group's cash resources in practice, ranging from the outright elimination of the subsidiaries' cash management departments to highly decentralised management. There are two major types of organisation, which reflect two opposite approaches:

- Most common is the centralisation of balances and liquidity, which involves the groupwide pooling of cash from the subsidiaries' bank accounts. The group balances the accounts of its subsidiaries just as the subsidiaries balance their bank accounts. There are various different variations on this system.
- Significantly rarer is the centralisation of cash flows, under which the group's cash management department not only receives all incoming payments, but may also even make all the disbursements. The department deals with issues such as due dates for customer payments and customer payment risks, reducing the role of any subsidiary to providing information and forecasting. This type of organisation may be described as hypercentralised.

The centralisation of cash balances can be dictated from above or carried out upon the request of the subsidiary. In the latter case, each subsidiary decides to use the group's cash or external resources in line with the rates charged, thereby creating competition between the banks, the market and internal funds. This flexibility can help alleviate any demotivation caused by the centralisation of cash management.

In addition, coherent cash management requires the definition of uniform banking terms and conditions within a group. In particular, fund transfers between subsidiaries should not be subject to value dating.

NOTIONAL POOLING AND THE RISK OF BANKRUPTCY

Notional pooling may be dangerous for banks when the subsidiary of a globally healthy group is threatened with bankruptcy.

Notional pooling provides a relatively flexible way of exploiting the benefits of cash pooling. With notional pooling, subsidiaries' account balances are never actually balanced, but the group's bank recalculates credit or debit interest based on the fictitious balance of the overall entity. This method yields exactly the same result as if the accounts had been perfectly balanced, **but the fund transfers are never carried out in practice**. As a result, this method leaves subsidiaries' some room for manoeuvre and does not impact their independence.

A high-risk subsidiary thus receives financing on exactly the same terms as the group as a whole, while the group can benefit from limited liability from a legal standpoint by declaring its subsidiary bankrupt. Notional pooling prevents a bank from adjusting its charges, thus introducing additional restrictions and setting reciprocal guarantees between each of the companies participating in the pooling arrangements. This network of contracts may prove to be extremely hard and complex to manage.

Consequently, cash balances are more commonly pooled by means of the daily balancing of the subsidiaries' positions. The **Zero Balance Account (ZBA)** concept requires subsidiaries to balance their position (i.e., the balance of their bank accounts) each day by using the concentration accounts managed at group or subgroup level. The banks offer automated balancing systems and can perform all these tasks on behalf of companies.

To sum up, the degree of centralisation of cash management and the method used by a group do not depend on financial criteria only. The three key factors are as follows:

- the group's managerial culture – e.g., notional pooling is more suited to highly decentralised organisations than daily position balancing;
- regulations and tax systems in the relevant countries;
- the cost of banking services. While position balancing is carried out by the group, notional pooling is the task of the bank.

3/INTERNATIONAL CASH MANAGEMENT

The problems arising with cash pooling are particularly acute in an international environment. This said, international cash management techniques are exactly the same as those used at national level – i.e., pooling on demand, notional pooling, account balancing.

Regulatory differences make the direct pooling of account balances of foreign subsidiaries a tricky task. Indeed, many groups find that they cannot do without the services of local banks, which are able to collect payments throughout a given zone. Consequently, multinational groups tend to apply a two-tier pooling system. A local concentration bank performs the initial pooling process within each country, and an international banking group, called an overlay bank, then handles the international pooling process.

INTERNATIONAL CASH POOLING

International cash pooling

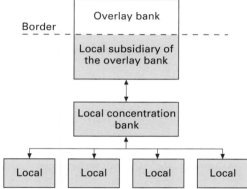

The international bank sends the funds across the border, as shown in the above chart, which helps to dispense with a large number of regulatory problems.

At local level, centralisation can be tailored to the specific regulatory requirements in each country, while at the higher level the international bank can carry out both notional pooling and daily account balancing. Lastly, it can manage the subsidiaries' interest and exchange rate risks (see Chapter 48) by offering exchange rate and interest rate guarantees. The structure set up can be used to manage all the group's financial issues rather than just the cash management aspects.

Within the Eurozone, the interconnection of payment systems under the aegis of the European Central Bank has made it possible to carry out fund transfers in real time, more cheaply and without having to face the issue of value dating. In the Eurozone, cash pooling may thus be carried out with the assistance of a single concentration bank in each country with cross-border transfers not presenting any problems.

Section 46.4
INVESTMENT OF CASH

Financial novices may wonder why debt-burdened companies do not use their cash to reduce debt. There are two good reasons for this:

- Paying back debt in advance can be costly because of early repayment penalties or unwise, if the debt was contracted at a rate that is lower than rates prevailing today.

- Keeping cash on hand enables the company to seize investment opportunities quickly and without constraints or to withstand changes in the economic environment. Some research papers[11] have demonstrated that companies with strong growth or volatile cash flows tend to have more free cash than average. Conversely, companies that have access to financial markets or excellent credit ratings have less cash than average.

11 *T. Opler, L. Pinkowitz, R. Stulz and R. Williamson.*

Obviously, all financing products used by companies have a mirror image as investment products, since the two operations are symmetrical. The corporate treasurer's role in investing the company's cash is nevertheless somewhat specific because the purpose of the company is not to make profits by engaging in risky financial investments. This is why specific products have been created to meet this criterion.

Remember that all investment policies are based on anticipated developments in the bank balances of each account managed by the company or, if it is a group, on consolidated, multicurrency forecasts. The treasurer cannot decide to make an investment without first estimating its amount and the duration. Any mistake and the treasurer is forced to choose between two alternatives:

- either having to resort to new loans to meet the financial shortage created if too much cash was invested, thus generating a loss on the difference between lending and borrowing rates (i.e., the interest rate spread);

- or having to retrieve the amounts invested and incur the attendant penalties, lost interest or, in certain cases such as bond investments, risk of a capital loss.

Since corporate treasurers rarely know exactly how much cash they will have available for a given period, their main concern when choosing an investment is its liquidity – that is, how fast can it be converted back into cash. **For an investment to be cashed in immediately, it must have an active secondary market or a redemption clause that can be activated at any time.**

The corporate treasurer's first concern in investing cash is liquidity.

Of course, if an investment can be terminated at any time, its rate of return is uncertain since the exit price is uncertain. A 91-day Treasury bill at a nominal rate of 4% can be sold at will, but its actual rate of return will depend on whether the bill was sold for more or less than its nominal value. However, if the rate of return is set in advance it is virtually impossible to exit the investment before its maturity since there is no secondary market or redemption clause, or else, only at a prohibitive cost.

The treasurer's second concern – security – is thus closely linked to the first. Security is measured in terms of the risk to the interest and principal.

When making this tradeoff between liquidity and security, the treasurer will, of course, try to obtain the **best return** taking into consideration **tax issues**, since various investment products may be subject to different tax regimes.

1/INVESTMENT PRODUCTS WITH NO SECONDARY MARKET

Interest-bearing current accounts are the simplest way to earn interest on cash. Nevertheless, interest paid by banks on such accounts is usually significantly lower than what the money market offers.

Time deposits are fixed term deposits on an interest-bearing bank account that are governed by a letter signed by the account holder. The interest on deposits with maturity of at least 1 month is negotiated between the bank and the client. It can be at a fixed rate or indexed to the money market. No interest is paid if the client withdraws the funds before the agreed maturity date.

Repos (repurchase agreements) are agreements whereby institutional investors or companies can exchange cash for securities for a fixed period of time (a securities for cash agreement is called a reverse repo). At the end of the contract, which can take various legal forms, the securities are returned to their initial owner. All title and rights to the securities are transferred to the buyer of the securities for the duration of the contract.

The remuneration of the buyer of the securities can be determined at the outset according to how the contract will be unwound. The agreement can be adapted to various requirements. The only risk is that the borrower of the cash (the repo seller) will default.

Repo sellers hold equity or bond portfolios, while repo buyers are looking for cash revenues. From the buyer's point of view, a repo is basically an alternative solution when a time deposit is not feasible – for example, for periods of less than 1 month. A repo allows the seller to obtain cash immediately by pledging securities with the assurance that it can buy them back.

Since the procedure is fairly unwieldy, it is only used for large amounts, well above €2m. This means that it competes with negotiable debt securities, such as commercial paper. However, the development of money market mutual funds investing in repos has lowered the €2m threshold and opened up the market to a larger number of companies.

The principle of **securities lending** is similar to that of repurchase agreements. It enables a company with a large cash surplus or listed investments to improve the yield on its financial instruments by entrusting them to institutional investors. These investors use them in the course of forward transactions while paying to the original owner (the company) the income arising on the securities and a borrowing fee. No cash changes hands in the course of the transaction. The incremental return thus stems from the remuneration of default risk on the part of the institutional investors borrowing the securities.

2/SECONDARY MARKET INVESTMENT PRODUCTS

Marketable Treasury bills and notes are issued by governments at monthly or weekly auctions for periods ranging from 2 weeks to 5 years. They are the safest of all investments given the creditworthiness of the issuer (governments), but their other features make them less flexible and competitive. However, the substantial amount of outstanding negotiable Treasury bills and notes ensures sufficient liquidity, even for large volumes. These instruments can be fairly good vehicles for short-term investments.

Certificates of deposit (CDs) are quite simply time deposits represented by a dematerialised negotiable debt security in the form of a bearer certificate or order issued by an authorised financial institution. Certificates of deposit are issued in minimum amounts of €150,000 for periods ranging from 1 day to 1 year with fixed maturity dates. In fact, they are a form of short-term investment. CDs are issued by banks, for which they are a frequent means of refinancing, on a continuous basis depending on demand. Their yield is very close to that of the money market, and their main advantage is that they can be traded on the secondary market, thus avoiding the heavy penalties of cashing in time deposits before their maturity date. The flipside is that they carry an interest rate risk.

We described the main characteristics of commercial paper and medium-term negotiable notes on pp. 497 and 519.

Money market or cash mutual funds are funds that issue or buy back their shares at the request of investors at prices that must be published daily. The return on a money market capitalisation mutual fund arises on the daily appreciation in Net Asset Value (NAV). This return is similar to that of the money market. Depending on the mutual fund's stated objective, the increase in net asset value is more or less steady. A very regular progression can only be obtained at the cost of profitability.

In order to meet its objectives, each cash mutual fund invests in a selection of Treasury bills, certificates of deposit, commercial paper, repos, variable or fixed rate bonds with short residual maturity. Its investment policy is backed by quite sophisticated interest rate risk management. The management fees of cash mutual funds are paid out of the fund's net asset value (there is no direct entry or exit fee).

Securitisation vehicles are special-purpose vehicles created to take over the claims sold by a credit institution or company engaging in a securitisation transaction (see p. 961). In exchange, these vehicles issue units that the institution sells to investors.

In theory, **bond** investments should yield higher returns than money market or money-market-indexed investments. However, interest rate fluctuations generate capital risks on bond portfolios that must be hedged, unless the treasurer has opted for variable rate bonds. Investing in bonds therefore calls for a certain degree of technical knowhow and constant monitoring of the market. Only a limited number of institutional investors have the resources to invest directly in bonds.

The high yields arising on investing surplus cash in the **equity** market over long periods become far more uncertain on shorter horizons, when the capital risk exposure is very high, well above that of a bond investment. Treasurers must keep a constant eye on the secondary market, and sharp market swings have rendered the few treasurers still invested in the equity market extremely cautious. However, treasurers may be charged with monitoring portfolios of equity interests.

A treasurer's job is to perform the following tasks:

- forecast trends in the credit and debit balances of the company's accounts;

- keep dormant funds to a minimum;

- invest excess cash as efficiently as possible;

- finance borrowing requirements as cheaply as possible.

Cash balances for treasury purposes are not the same as the balances shown in a company's accounts or the accounting balance of its assets held by the bank. In particular, treasurers must take account of value dating. The value date is the date from which a credited amount accrues interest when paid into an interest-bearing account or becomes available when paid into a demand account.

The aim of the cash budget is to determine the amount and duration of cash requirements and surpluses. A cash budget shows all the receipts and all the disbursements that the business expects to collect or make. Day-to-day forecasting, which takes into account value dating, requires paying considerable attention to the payment methods used. Forecasts are more reliable when the treasurer has the initiative both for setting up a payment and for carrying out the fund transfer.

Account balancing is the final stage in the liquidity management process. It eliminates the additional costs deriving from differences between borrowing and investment rates. Lastly, optimised cash management entails the acceleration of the collection process and the extension of suppliers' payment deadlines.

Cash pooling – the centralisation of subsidiaries' account balances within a group – is comparable with the process of balancing all of a subsidiary's accounts. Pooling is generally backed up by an integrated information system and a groupwide agreement concerning banking terms and conditions. At the international level, regulatory difficulties concerning cross-border transfers prevent the direct balancing of subsidiaries' accounts. Instead, the initial pooling process is carried out by a local bank in each country, and then the resulting balances are pooled by an international banking group.

The corporate treasurer's first concern in investing cash is liquidity. The treasurer's second concern – security – is thus closely linked to the first. Security is measured in terms of the risk to the interest and principal. The products he can use can be split between products with a secondary market (Treasury bills, money market funds, ...) or without (time deposit, repos, ...).

SUMMARY

download

BIBLIOGRAPHY

Website of the Association of Corporate Treasurers:

www.treasurers.org

General:

J. Graham, C. Harvey, The theory and practice of corporate finance: Evidence from the field, *Journal of Financial Economics*, **60**(2–3), 179–185, June 2001.
M. Dolfe, *European Cash Management: A Guide to Best Practice*, John Wiley & Sons, 1999.
R. Cooper, *Corporate Treasury and Cash Management*, Palgrave Macmillan, 2003.
T. Opler, L. Pinkowitz, R. Stulz, R. Williamson, The determinants and implications of corporate cash holdings, *Journal of Financial Economics*, **52**, 3–46, 1999.

Chapter 47
ASSET-BASED FINANCING

There is something rotten in this kingdom of accounting

Since the beginning of time, companies have tried to remove assets and liabilities from their balance sheets. The aim is to reduce the company's apparent debt burden or to base financing on specific assets, thereby reducing, theoretically, the cost. The discounting of bills of exchange, an early example, has been part of the banker's bread and butter for centuries. As you will soon discover, many more complicated techniques have since been developed!

After enjoying great popularity in the 1990s, most asset-based financing techniques will now be included in the balance sheet according to IASB[1] rules. In particular, Enron's spectacular bankruptcy towards the end of 2001 is causing the accounting profession to tighten up treatment of some financing products.

1 *International Accounting Standards Board.*

Section 47.1
REASONS FOR USING ASSET-BASED FINANCING

Five nonmutually exclusive objectives might prompt a company to use asset-based financing:

➤ **Find a new source of financing** that is less expensive than the company's overall cost of financing. A Special Purpose Vehicle (SPV) is created to own certain assets. The SPV then obtains a higher rating than the company. By segmenting risks, the company is better able to attract investors looking to specialise in a particular type of risk (property risks, default risk, etc.). They are ready to pay a higher price to gain access to exactly the risk/return profiles they seek. The catch is this: for the transaction to be value-creating, the increase in the perceived risk of the rest of the group must be smaller than the savings derived from the cheaper financing the SPV obtained on the assets transferred. Unfortunately, the theory of perfect capital markets does not leave much room for manoeuvre!

➤ **Transfer risk.** The company may decide that assuming the risk of fluctuations in the property market, in the value of used cars, etc., is not its core business. Selling an asset, then leasing it back may enable the company to get rid of the risk associated with the asset, while still reaping the benefits of its use.

Similarly, deadbeat customers can take a heavy toll on a company, whereas using a factor reduces this risk thanks to the law of large numbers. Factors are skilled in measuring payment risks that the company is ill-equipped to evaluate. They make that expertise available to the company and help it make better client selections in the future. Only in this last way can factoring create value for the company. Transfer of risk alone is simply a risk/return tradeoff and does not create value.

➤ **Re-engineer the company operationally**: outsourcing certain functions so as to increase flexibility constitutes the most advanced form of off-balance-sheet technique (it is then more than just financing). When a company rents its offices, for example, it is less hesitant to move to a location that better accommodates its needs. This flexibility can be limited, however, if the contract signed when the structure is first put in place is a long-term one, especially in case of a very specific asset.

➤ **Reduce taxes**: always a worthy cause!

➤ **Reduce gearing** on the balance sheet and improve financial ratios. As clear as these motives are, achieving them often requires committing to future operating results or assuming higher overall financing costs. Indeed, the choice is often between optimising financing costs and dressing up the balance sheet. In either case, no value is created.

Of the five reasons we have identified, the only questionable one is "Reduce gearing". A company that raises off-balance-sheet financing with this objective in mind is trying to give itself a better image than it really deserves. Nevertheless, we must admit that it has become very commonplace, even for the most respected groups.

Let's think back to Coca-Cola. Coca-Cola's after-tax Return on Capital Employed (ROCE) appears to be excellent (23% in 2004, excluding equity and other investments) and its debt moderate (0.06 times EBITDA[2]). But the bottling assets, worth $35bn or four times the assets shown on the consolidated balance sheet ($6.3bn), are conveniently lodged in 40%-owned affiliates. These affiliates are financed with the $16bn debt (c. 2.4 times EBITDA). Naturally, the affiliates are accounted for using the equity method as Coca-Cola follows US GAAP.[3] Hence, neither the debt nor the assets appear on the balance sheet of Coca-Cola.

The ROCE of these off-balance-sheet assets is 6%. We cannot even imagine Coca-Cola letting these affiliates go bankrupt. They carry its name and constitute an integral part of its business. If we were to reintegrate them into the consolidated balance sheet, Coca-Cola's restated, after-tax ROCE would be 12%, not 23%, and its debt would be c. 1.2 times EBITDA, not 0.06 times. Companies often provide this information, as Coca-Cola does, in the notes to the financial statements, which deserve very attentive analysis!

2 *Earnings Before Interest, Taxes, Depreciation and Amortisation.*

3 *Generally Accepted Accounting Principles.*

1/OVERVIEW

Graphically, the evolution of techniques to remove assets and liabilities from the balance sheet can be represented as follows:

Some forms of outsourcing are in fact nothing more than off-balance-sheet financing carried to the extreme. The company sells industrial assets to a service provider who manufactures for the account of the company. The company then focuses its efforts on research and development, marketing and distribution,[4] considered to be its core competencies.

4 *See p. 127.*

2/DISCOUNTING

Discounting is a financing transaction wherein a company remits an unexpired commercial bill of exchange to the bank in return for an advance of the amount of the bill, less interest and fees.

The discounting bank becomes the owner of the bill and, ordinarily, is repaid when it presents the bill to its customer's customer for payment. If, at maturity, the bill remains unpaid, the bank turns to the company, which assumes the bankruptcy risk of its customer (such discounting is called "discounting with recourse").

In principle, a company uses discounting to obtain financing based on the credit it extends to its own customers, which may be better known to the banking system than the company is. In this way, the company may be able to obtain better financing rates.

In discounting, the bank does not finance the company itself, but only certain receivables in its portfolio – i.e., the bills of exchange. These bills offer the bank a better guarantee of repayment, given the credit quality of the buyers of the company's products.

For the bank, the risk is bounded by a double guarantee: the credit quality of its customer, backed by that of the issuer of the bill of exchange.

In consolidated accounting, discounted bills are reintegrated into accounts receivable and bank advances reported as debt.

For this reason, banks now also offer **nonrecourse discounting**, which is a straight sale of customer receivables, wherein the bank has no recourse to its customer if the bill remains unpaid at maturity. This technique may allow the company to remove the receivables from its balance and from its off-balance-sheet commitments and contingencies.

3/FACTORING

Factoring actually consists of four different services, sold together or separately:

1   Financing at a competitive cost.
2   Outsourcing of the recovery function.
3   Bad debt insurance.
4   Remove assets from the balance sheet.

Factoring is discounting packaged with services.

Depending on the type of service rendered, the receivable may or may not remain on the balance sheet of the company.

4/LEASES

Although banks rarely offer long-term loans (more than 7 years) based solely on the creditworthiness of the borrower, loans backed by specific corporate assets accompanied by an appropriate legal structure are another story. The presence of these assets considerably reduces the credit risk the bank faces and enables the bank to grant the loan for the long term. Financial leases are such arrangements. They take maximum advantage of the collateral offered by the borrower, and the financing arrangements are structured around the collateral.

In a lease contract, the firm (lessee) commits itself to making fixed payments, usually monthly or semi-annually, to the owner of the asset (lessor) for the right to use the asset. These payments are either fully or partially tax-deductible, depending on how the lease is categorised for accounting purposes. The lessor is either the asset's manufacturer or an independent leasing company.

Failure by the firm to make fixed payments usually results in the loss of the asset, and even in bankruptcy, although the claim of the lessor is normally subordinated to those of other lenders.

The lease contract may take a number of different forms, but normally it is categorised as either an operating or a financial lease.

For **operating leases**, the term of the lease contract is *shorter* than the economic life of the asset. Consequently, the present value of lease payments is normally lower than the market value of the asset. At the end of the contract the asset reverts back to the lessor, who can either offer to sell it to the lessee or lease it again to somebody else. In an operating lease, the lessee generally has the right to cancel the lease and return the asset to the lessor. Thus, the lessee bears little or no risk if the asset becomes obsolete.

A **financial (or capital) lease** normally lasts for the entire economic life of the asset. The present value of fixed payments tends to cover the market value of the asset. At the end of the contract, the lease can be renewed at a reduced rate or the lessee can buy the asset at a favourable price. This contract cannot be cancelled by the lessee.[5]

5 *There are two other typologies of financial leases. The **sale and leaseback**, see p. 963. **Leveraged leases** are a three-sided arrangement among the lessor, the lessee and the lenders. The principal difference with other leases is that the lender supplies a percentage of the financing to the lessor – who will use this amount to co-finance the acquisition of the asset – and receive interest payments from the lessor.*

Financial leases are attractive to "lenders" because they allow them to grant loans collateralised by assets that are legally separate from the company's other assets. In fact, leases are often among the lender's best collateralised loans. Leasing can also be used in complex arrangements to reduce taxes.

Through financial leasing, a company can fully use its operating assets (land, buildings or other fixed assets) while renting them, with an option to purchase them at the expiry of the lease at a price specified in the contract.

According to IASB principles, financial leases are integrated into the balance sheet to reflect economic reality. The asset is recorded as a fixed asset and corresponding future payments as financial debt.

Some arrangements aim to remove from the balance sheet some particularly large investments that cannot be financed by debt and would seriously degrade the balance sheet if left in. For example, aeroplanes purchased by airlines or lorries by road hauliers are usually financed by finance leases, the archetypical structured transaction for improving the look of a balance sheet. A separate entity, usually a subsidiary of a financial institution, buys the assets and makes them available to the lessee in return for the stream of lease payments. The lessee therefore can use an asset that doesn't appear on the balance sheet. The lessee can purchase the asset at the expiry of the contract, at a low price that takes into account the wear and tear on the asset. The leasing company meets its commitments through the lease payments it receives and, potentially, the ultimate sale of the asset.

As with investment analysis, the analysis of whether a firm should buy or lease follows the same principles already illustrated. There are basically three alternatives for valuing the relative convenience of leases:

1   The decision can be based according to the present value of incremental after-tax cash flows of the two alternatives. In computing the present value of the cash flows for a lease, we should use the after-tax cost of borrowing since we are comparing two borrowing alternatives. A lease payment is like the debt service on a secured bond issued by the lessee, and the discount rate should be approximately the same as the interest rate on such debt.

2   Alternatively, we can compare the IRR[6] of the two alternatives and choose the one with the lower rate.

3   Or, finally, we could compute the difference between the two cash flows (buying and leasing) and compute the IRR on these differential cash flows. This rate should then be compared with the after-tax cost of debt to determine which alternative is more attractive.

6 Internal Rate of Return.

5/DEFEASANCE

In defeasance, the borrower simultaneously sells debt and a portfolio of assets to a Special Purpose Vehicle (SPV). The portfolio of assets is designed to meet the interest payments and repay the principal of the debt.

Technically, the SPV is independent of the company. Hence, the company is not required to consolidate it. In most cases, the SPV is a subsidiary of a financial institution. The SPV is created especially for the transaction, and the transaction is its only *raison d'être*. The assets of the SPV are risk-free or low risk. They can be government bonds or other, short-term government obligations, or a portfolio of receivables, properties or investments. The sale of assets and liabilities is irrevocable. The approval of the company's creditors is not necessarily required. For that matter, the probability of debt repayment is bigger, because the risk is no longer that of the company, but the government, the portfolio of assets or the securities. For this reason, the transferred debt appreciates in value upon the announcement of a defeasance operation. The value of the company's other debt declines as the overall assets held by the company have become more risky!

Accounting-wise, the transaction removes the assets and the debt from the balance sheet at a value above or below book value. The difference between the two values passes through the income statement. As a result, the company bears the cost of the transaction as a one-off charge. For example, suppose the company issued a bond of 100, at 10%, with a bullet repayment in 3 years. If the yield on government bonds is 3%, the company will have to transfer government bonds of 120 to the SPV to enable it to meet its interest and principal repayment obligations. Such transfer gives rise to a charge of 20, which corresponds to the difference between the net present value of the company's debts and the market value of the government bonds. In this example, 20 is the price the company must pay to "clean up" its balance sheet. The technique enables the company to make a clean sweep of the past. It brings forward the cost of the debt.

Don't forget the fundamental principle: assuming no tax savings, defeasance does not create value. It enables the company to separate the wheat from the chaff, allowing the rest of the company's assets to flourish, "unfettered" by the legacy of a heavy debt burden.

US and international standards do not allow the assets and the debt to be treated as off-balance-sheet items. They allow debt to be removed from the balance sheet only through repayment, expiration or cancellation by the lender.

6/ SECURITISATION

Securitisation was initially used by credit institutions looking to refinance part of their assets – in other words, to convert customer loans into negotiable securities.

Securitisation works as follows: a bank first selects mortgages or consumer loans, as well as unsecured loans such as credit card receivables, based on the quality of the collateral they offer or their level of risk. To reduce risk, the loans are then grouped into an SPV so as to pool risks and take advantage once again of the law of large numbers. The SPV buys the loans and finances itself by issuing securities to outside investors. The new entity – a **debt securitisation fund**, for example – receives the flow of interest and principal payments emanating from the loans it bought from the banks (or nonbank companies). The fund uses the proceeds to cover its obligations on the securities it has issued.

To boost the rating of the securities, the SPV buys more loans than the volume of securities to be issued, the excess serving as **enhancement**. Alternatively, the SPV can take out an insurance policy with an insurance company. The SPV might also obtain a short-term line of credit to ensure the payment of interest in the event of a temporary interruption in the flow of interest and principal payments.

Certain assets of Philippe Co. are sold to an SPV, which finances itself by issuing debt structured so as to respond to investors' various risk/return profiles.

SECURITISATION

Most of the time, the securitisation vehicle subcontracts administration of the fund and recovery to one service provider and cash management to another. More complicated structures, often based on swaps (see p. 979), can also be used when the SPV does not need to reproduce the exact cash flows of the original loans. Instead, cash flows can be reorganised to satisfy the requirements of the various investors involved: no income stream, steady income stream, increasing income stream, etc.

With the help of securitisation specialists, some industrial companies regularly securitise accounts receivable, inventories, buildings or other assets. In short, the whole balance sheet is made liquid. Certain assets, once isolated, are of higher quality than the balance sheet as a whole, thus allowing the company to finance them at preferential rates. This said, the cost of these arrangements is higher than that of straight debt, especially for a high-quality borrower with an attractive cost of debt.

For example, the European group Arcelor is securitising its accounts receivable, Avis its rental fleet, while the Swiss group Glencore is doing the same thing with its lead, nickel, zinc, copper and aluminium inventories.

EUROPEAN SECURITISATION ISSUANCE

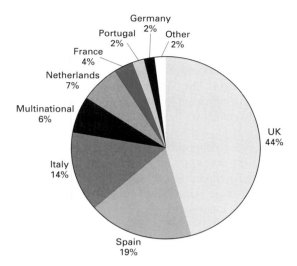

7/SALE–LEASEBACK TRANSACTIONS

In a **sale–leaseback** transaction, a company that owns equipment or other industrial or commercial assets sells the asset to a leasing company, which then immediately makes it available to the company through a leasing transaction. Such transactions are not generally intended to increase the company's liquidity. They usually serve as a source of long-term capital to finance new investments or to consolidate short-term bridge loans and strengthen the balance sheet. Remember, however, that in consolidated accounting, the façade falls away. The leased assets are reintegrated into the balance sheet, while the corresponding financing appears on the liabilities side.

The sale–leaseback technique is often used in property transactions. A partnership is created between the financial institution and the property user. The financial institution manages the partnership and holds most of the capital, thereby financing most of the investment. The partnership, after buying the land and the buildings, leases the properties to the user. At the expiry of the contract, the user may exercise its purchase option by buying up the shares of the partnership.

Alternatively, the user may be the owner of the land on which the buildings are to be built. Instead of setting up a sale–leaseback structure, the user grants a long-term lease on the land, analogous to a transfer of title, to the leasing company. In practice, however, this technique is rarely used.

8/OUTSOURCING

Outsourcing is the ultimate technique to remove assets from the balance sheet. The company voluntarily reduces itself to a service provider that designs products and finds customers, while assigning production to third parties.

A company in the agri-food sector or the textile industry, for example, sets up an SPV owned by a bank and/or financial investors. The SPV buys raw materials.

7 *That is, the goods are first proposed to the company. If the company refuses to buy the finished goods, the SPV will sell them to a third party.*

Under contract with the SPV, the company then processes the raw material into finished products, which belong to the SPV. The company has the right of first refusal[7] on the inventories held by the SPV and has a say in how they are managed. At the same time the inventories do not belong to the company, and therefore do not appear on its balance sheet. The company then buys finished product inventory from the SPV as needed to fill orders from customers.

The company may even sell its factories and equipment, then lease them back from their new owners.

The SPV may choose to finance the inventories by securitising them if the company has made a firm commitment to repurchase them or if the company's customers are contractually forced to buy the finished goods over a certain period of time. The investors in these securities would then be assuming the risk of the company or the company's customers.

Section 47.3
ACCOUNTING TREATMENT

In an effort to stop the most egregious practices, accounting rules now require the restatement of the transactions executed for pure window-dressing purposes. Assets and liabilities must be reintegrated into the balance sheet. Accordingly, discounted bills and leasing transactions have been included in consolidated accounts for a long time. But the cat-and-mouse game is never-ending, and the accounting profession is constantly trying to keep pace. Each time a new off-balance-sheet financing technique is developed, accounting standards are revised in an attempt to separate legitimate use from potentially fraudulent practices. Currently, the principles are as follows:[8]

8 *Payment of all cash flows generated by the asset in exchange for payments based on a reference rate such as EURIBOR.*

1/Unconsolidated financial assets (investments in subsidiaries, receivables, etc.)

US standards here are based on an analysis of legal status, whereas international standards are based much more on economic analysis.

9 *Right to resell the asset to the original seller.*

Under international standards, an asset can be removed from the consolidated balance sheet only if the seller does not have the right to repurchase the asset at a price other than its fair value at the time of repurchase. Therefore, there must be a real secondary market for the asset; in other words, the asset must not be too specific. Similarly, there cannot be a resale agreement allowing the buyer to earn a return similar to what it could have earned by granting a loan to the seller with the asset as collateral. The risks and rewards associated with the asset must not remain with the seller (via a **total return swap**[9] or a put[9] on the seller).

Under US standards, an asset can be removed from the balance sheet only if the seller cedes control over it and if payment made is of something other than the right to all or part of the cash flows to be generated by the asset. To be removed from the balance sheet, the asset must be out of reach of the company and of its creditors in the event the company goes bankrupt. The new owner must be able to sell it at will and there must not be a potentially advantageous repurchase option.

2/ Off-balance-sheet SPVs

Whether an SPV that has purchased assets from a company has to be consolidated or not depends (surprise, surprise!) on the accounting standards used:

➤ Under IASB standards, any controlled entity, even if the selling company does not own a penny capital of the special-purpose vehicle, must be consolidated. Specifically, the selling company is deemed to control the SPV if (i) it has decision-making power or management control over it, through voting rights or a shareholder pact; (ii) it benefits from the results of the SPV, through rights to cash flows or to the residual net assets of the SPV; or (iii) it bears risks related to the SPV (general warranties, etc.).

➤ Under US standards, a distinction is made between financial and nonfinancial assets, as follows:

○ Financial assets. Assets transferred to the SPV have no control features, such as bonds, nonvoting shares or derivatives other than options (swaps, forwards, etc.). If the SPV is a "qualifying" SPV, it must not appear on the balance sheet. To be deemed "qualifying", an SPV must be independent from the seller. The seller cannot have unilateral power to dissolve the SPV and at least 10% of the SPV's beneficial interests must be held by third parties. The SPV's activities must be limited and spelled out in the by-laws.

○ Nonfinancial – i.e., all other assets. In the case of an operating lease with a noncontrolled SPV as lessor, the SPV must be consolidated if:
  – its purpose is essentially to lease assets to a single lessee;
  – the residual risks and rewards related to the leased asset or to the SPV remain primarily with the lessee; and
  – the controlling entity has not invested more than 3% of the value of the SPV's assets, which remain at risk throughout the duration of the lease.

Thus, a noncontrolled and nonqualifying SPV must be nonconsolidated if the ordinary shares held by third parties represent more than 3% of the value of the assets.

IASB standards are strict in this area and emphasise a principle rather than a set of rules. They allow very little accounting leeway. In contrast, US standards are much more flexible regarding removing assets from the balance sheet, because the existence in US GAAP of very precise rules allows transaction designers to create features that comply only with the "letter of the law".

3/LEASES

Leases fall into two categories:

- Financial. Under this type of arrangement, called a finance lease (IASB) or a capital lease (US), the lease payments are intended to finance the asset. The lessee can subsequently become the owner of the asset under certain circumstances.
- Operating. There is no effect on the balance sheet, because there are no provisions enabling the lessee to become the owner of the asset.

Under a finance lease, the leased asset appears on the assets side of the lessee's balance sheet and the future lease payments appear as debt. The amount of debt equals the lesser of the present value of future lease payments and the fair value of the leased asset. Lease payments are apportioned between interest expense and amortisation of debt.

Under an operating lease, there is no balance sheet entry and lease payments are spread evenly over the life of the lease.

IASB rule SIC-15 clarifies the recognition of incentives related to operating leases by both the lessee and lessor. SIC-17 "Dealing with leases", became effective for annual financial statements covering periods beginning on or after January 1999. According to these principles:

- finance leases are those that transfer substantially all risks and rewards to the lessee;
- lessees should capitalise a finance lease at whichever is lower between the fair value and the present value of the minimum lease payments;
- rental payments should be split into (i) a reduction of liability, and (ii) a finance charge designed to reduce in line with the liability;
- lessees should calculate depreciation on leased assets using its useful life, unless there is no reasonable certainty of eventual ownership. In the latter case, the shorter of useful life and lease term should be used; and
- lessees should expense operating lease payments.

US accounting standards use the decision tree displayed at the top of the next page to determine whether a lease is a finance lease or an operating lease:

CLASSIFYING A LEASE UNDER US GAAP

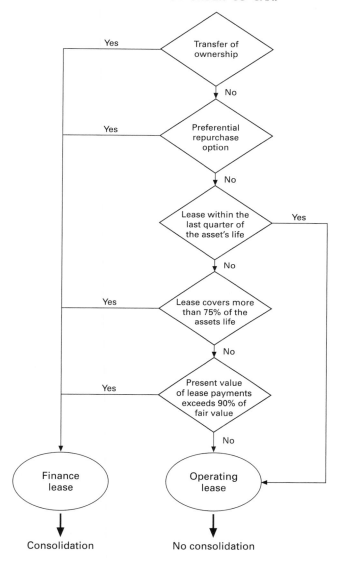

Let us take the example of Company Van Breda NV, which owns an office building with an economic life of 99 years. Van Breda leases the building to an SPV – for example, a trust – and immediately receives the present value of future lease payments. The proceeds equal, given the lifetime of the lease and the economic life of the building (99 years), the fair value of the building. The trust turns around and subleases the building to Van Breda for 30 years. The present value of the 30 years of lease payments equals 85% of the present value of the building. The trust finances 85% of the purchase with a loan and the remainder with capital from an outside investor.

AN ASSET WITH A 99-YEAR LIFETIME

Capital investment: 15% of the fair value of the asset

The headlease is a finance lease. Its duration is more than 75% of the economic life of the asset, and the present value of the lease payment exceeds 90% of fair value. From an accounting point of view, the trust becomes the "owner" of the building.

The sublease is an operating lease. Its duration is less than 75% of the economic life of the building (30 out of 99 years), and the present value of the lease payment (85%) is less than 90% of fair value. Ownership is therefore not transferred from the trust to Van Breda.

Consequently, the asset leaves Van Breda's balance sheet and does not return, under both US and IASB accounting standards.

Economically, we note that the trust has a downside risk of only 15% of the value of the building. If its value declines by more than 15%, given the trust's financial structure, it becomes insolvent. On the other hand, the trust retains all of the upside potential.

Starting with the above scenario, let us now suppose that Van Breda has an option to repurchase the headlease at the end of the sublease and that the trust has an option to sell the headlease to Van Breda at the end of the sublease, guaranteeing it a minimum return. Van Breda still carries the downside risk in the value of the building, because it has given the trust a put option, while its call option allows it to benefit from the upside potential.

Section 47.4
CONSEQUENCES FOR FINANCIAL ANALYSIS

If auditors agree to treat these transactions as off-balance-sheet, the impact on financial reporting will often be complex, but the overall effects are as follows:

- decrease in total assets;
- decrease in net debt;

- generally, a decrease in EBITDA and EBIT, as lease payments reflect both depreciation/amortisation and the cost of financing. Some structures (synthetic leases) reduce this negative impact significantly by limiting the amount of the lease payments to little more than the financing costs. In such structures, the asset must be repurchased at the end of the lease period at a price close to the initial price of the asset when the structure is put together. Conceptually, this is tantamount to a nominee agreement;
- higher cash flow breakeven point, because these transactions substitute a cash expense (lease payments) for a noncash expense (depreciation/amortisation);
- the impact on net profit or loss and on shareholders' equity depends to a great extent on how the transaction is structured. Companies seeking to finance assets off-balance-sheet must weigh the current sale price of the assets against the amount (present value) of future lease payments. The higher the first is, the higher the second will be.

In other words, a company that wants to realise a large capital gain and increase liquidity today will have to commit to a long stream of lease payments that are significantly above the market average for a normal rent.

In certain sectors, such as transport or cinemas, extensive use of these techniques have prompted analysts to reason in terms of "EBITDA before rents" or "**EBITDAR**". Using EBITDAR makes sense only when you compare companies with different rental policies and provided you remember that EBITDAR is not cash flow but a figure further upstream in the income statement. Likewise, when it comes to valuing the company using a multiple of EBITDAR, you must not lose sight of the fact that the lease commitments represent financial – often long-term – debt.

Financial analysts are increasingly familiar with these transactions. They rarely restate them, but they take them into account when formulating their overall opinion of the risks a company runs. The rating agencies systematically reintegrate securitised assets and sale–leaseback transactions into a company's balance sheet. In this regard, if a significant portion of a group's financing (20%) derives from securitisation, sale–leasebacks or other arrangements involving structural subordination, the company may be put on credit watch with negative implications, reflecting possible deterioration in the group's financial condition, as they did when US airlines securitised their spare parts inventories.

In conclusion, you should not hesitate to read the notes to the financial statements in detail. Although they don't explain everything about these techniques, they will often allow you to pick up their scent.

Companies have always tried to remove assets and/or liabilities from their balance sheets in order to reduce the apparent debt burden or base financing on specific assets, thereby reducing, theoretically, the overall cost of debt.

Five objectives may prompt a company to use asset-based financing:

- find a new or less expensive source of financing, backed by assets that present the precise risk profile sought by certain investors;

SUMMARY

download

- transfer a risk that the company is no longer willing to run;
- re-engineer the company so as to increase flexibility;
- reduce taxes;
- reduce the real or apparent debt burden and gearing ratios.

The principal techniques are as follows:

- discounting of bills of exchange, no-recourse discounting, factoring;
- leasing and sale–leaseback;
- defeasance;
- securitisation;
- outsourcing.

The accounting treatment in this instance is fundamental, because it determines whether or not the company must consolidate an asset (or a liability). IASB standards are more strict than US standards as IASB standards emphasise principles whereas US GAAP puts forward strict ratios. In contrast, the "letter-of-the-law" approach of US standards make it possible to structure a transaction so as to circumvent the principles. In any event, the spectacular bankruptcy of Enron, which used off-balance-sheet financing to report fictitious profits and hide debt, will cause both sets of standards to be tightened up significantly. Every cloud has a silver lining!

Off-balance-sheet financing often leads to lower debt, but at the cost of lower or more volatile future profits because of the significantly increasing cash breakeven point.

QUESTIONS

quiz

1/ Does off-balance-sheet financing create value?

2/ Is off-balance-sheet financing a fraudulent practice?

3/ Balzac was already using off-balance-sheet financing by discounting bills. However, consolidated balance sheets only came into being in the early 20th century. State your views.

4/ What advantages are there, on a macroeconomic level, to off-balance-sheet financing?

5/ What is the difference between discounting and factoring?

6/ What services can be offered as part of factoring?

7/ What is the main difference between property leasing and equipment leasing?

8/ In a securitisation transaction, is a company that transfers assets to an SPV at risk if these assets do not cover the debts of the SPV?

9/ In the area of off-balance-sheet financing, is the predominance of form over substance a feature of IASB or US GAAP?

10/ What is a long-term debt? What is a long-term operating lease? Explain why accounting regulators are seeking to harmonise the treatment of long-term operating leases.

11/ What do you think of the following statement: "off-balance-sheet financing only fools those who want to be fooled"?

1/ *As a general rule, no, since the counterpart of, for example, a lower financing cost on certain assets, is a higher financing cost on others.*

2/ *No, as it is permitted by law. What is fraudulent is using off-balance-sheet financing to create fictitious profits, hide sales, and conceal debts which are not asset-backed.*

3/ *The issue here is semantic: off-balance-sheet financing is not the right term. Rather, we should speak of removal from the balance sheet!*

4/ *It gives investors the exact risk and flows profile they're looking for.*

5/ *In factoring, the company can effectively transfer the risk of nonpayment to the factor, while in discounting, the company will always bear the risk.*

6/ *Financing, recovery, bad debt insurance, removing assets from the balance sheet.*

7/ *The type of the asset leased and the term of the lease, which is obviously much longer for property leasing.*

8/ *Normally no. The SPV bears the risk and insures itself against, by oversizing the assets transferred.*

9/ *US GAAP.*

10/ *It is an undertaking to pay flows in the future. Also an undertaking to pay flows in the future. Both are undertakings to pay. Why should one be treated as a debt and the other not?*

11/ *This is just common sense. Auditors' footnotes are there to be read, not for decorative purposes!*

BIBLIOGRAPHY

IASB: *www.iasb.org.uk*, IAS-17, -35, SIC-12 and -27
US GAAP: *www.fasb.org*, FAS-13, -66 and -140.
EITF 90-15: *www.europeansecuritisation.com*, European securitisation site.

Chapter 48
MANAGING FINANCIAL RISKS

Forbidden, but useful tools ...

In the last 30 years, fluctuations have become so severe in interest and exchange rates, raw material prices, and so forth, that companies are now faced with a new set of risks, risks that could threaten their very survival unless properly managed.

As companies have become aware of these risks, they have been increasingly using hedging instruments that allow to diminish or totally eliminate the risks.

The trend of recent years is to break risks down and to offer more sophisticated and more flexible hedging tools where there had been few or no such tools before. The instruments concerned are most often listed and not correlated with traditional assets such as stocks and bonds. These instruments help investors diversify their portfolios just as globalisation is increasing the degree of correlation between traditional products (see p. 398) and thus reduce the impact of diversification.

Section 48.1
THE VARIOUS SOURCES OF FINANCIAL RISK

Companies face four types of financial risk:

➤ **Market risk** is exposure to unfavourable trends in product prices, interest rates, exchange rates, raw material prices or stock prices.

Market risk occurs at various levels:
- a position (a debt, for example, or an expected income in foreign currencies, etc.);
- a business activity (purchases paid in a currency other than that in which the products are sold, etc.); or
- a portfolio (short- and long-term financial holdings).

➤ **Liquidity risk** is the impossibility at a given moment of meeting a debt payment, because:

- the company no longer has assets than can rapidly be turned into cash;
- a financial crisis (a market crash, for example) has made it very difficult to liquidate assets, except at a very great loss in value; or
- it is impossible to find investors willing to offer new funding.

> **Counterparty or credit risk.** This is the risk of loss on an outstanding receivable or, more generally, on a debt that is not paid on time. It naturally depends on three parameters: the amount of the debt, the likelihood of default and the portion of the debt that will be collected in the event of a default.

> **Political risk** results from events, decisions and actions of a political or administrative nature, on a national or international scale, that could lead to losses for importing and exporting companies, and companies that work or invest outside their home country.

Section 48.2
MEASURING FINANCIAL RISKS

Different financial risks are measured in very different ways. Measurement is:

- quite sophisticated for market risks, for example, with the notion of position and Value at Risk (VaR), and for liquidity risks;
- less sophisticated for counterparty risks;
- quite unsatisfactory for political risks.

Most risk measurement tools were initially developed by banks – whose activities make them highly exposed to financial risks – before being gradually adopted by other companies.

1/POSITION AND MEASURE OF MARKET RISKS

Market risk is exposure to fluctuations in value of an asset called the "underlying asset". An operator's **position** is the residual market exposure on his balance sheet at any given moment.

When an operator has bought more in an underlying asset than he has sold, he is **long** (for interest or exchange rates a long position is when the underlying asset is worth more than the corresponding liability). It is possible, for example, to be long in euros, long in bonds or long 3 months out (i.e., having lent more than borrowed 3 months out). The market risk on a long position is the risk of a fall in market value of the underlying asset (or an increase in interest rates).

On the other hand, when an operator has sold more in the underlying asset than he has bought, he is said to be **short**. The market risk on a short position is the risk of an increase in market value of the underlying asset (or a fall in interest rates).

The notion of position is very important for banks operating on the fixed income and currency markets. Generally speaking, traders are allowed to keep a given amount in an open position, depending on their anticipations. However, clients buy and sell products constantly, each time modifying traders' position. At a given moment, a trader could even have a position that runs counter to his anticipations. Whenever this is the case, he can close out his position (by realising a transaction that cancels out his position) in the interbank market.

2/ COMPANIES' MARKET POSITIONS

Like banks, at any given moment, an industrial company can have positions *vis-à-vis* the various categories of risk (the most common being currency and interest rate risk). Such positions do not generally arise from the company's choice or a purchase of derivatives, but are rather a natural consequence of its business activities, financing and the geographical location of its subsidiaries. A company's aggregate position results from the following three items:

* its commercial position;
* its financial position;
* its accounting position.

Let us first consider currency risk. Exposure to currency risk arises first of all from the purchases and sales of currencies that a company makes in the course of carrying out its business activities. Let us say, for example, that a Eurozone company is due to receive $10m in 6 months, and has no dollar payables at the same date. That company is said to be long in 6-month dollars. Depending on the company's business cycle, the actual timeframe can range from a few days to several years (if the order backlog is equivalent to several years of revenues). The company must therefore quantify its total currency risk exposure, by setting receipts against expenditure, currency by currency, at the level of existing billings and forecast billings. By doing so, it obtains its **commercial currency position**.

There is also a risk in holding financial assets and liabilities denominated in foreign currencies. If our Eurozone company has raised funds in dollars, it is now short in dollars, as some of its liabilities are denominated in dollars with nothing to offset them on the asset side. The main sources of this risk are: (1) loans, borrowings and current accounts denominated in foreign currencies, with their related interest charges; and (2) investments in foreign currencies. Taken as a whole, these risks express companies' **financial currency positions**.

The third component of currency risk is **accounting currency risk**, which arises from the consolidation of foreign subsidiaries, including equity denominated in foreign currencies, dividend flows, financial investments denominated in foreign currencies and exchange rate discrepancies (i.e., the use of an average exchange rate for the P&L and the closing rate for the balance sheet). Note, however, that this is reflected in the currency translation differential in the consolidated accounts and therefore has no impact.

The same thing can apply to the interest rate risk. **Commercial interest rate risk** depends on the level of inflation of the currencies in which the goods are bought and sold, while the **financial interest rate** is obviously tied directly to the terms a company has obtained for its borrowings and investments. Floating rate borrowings, for example, expose companies to an increase in the benchmark rate, while fixed rate borrowings expose them to opportunity cost if they cannot take advantage of a possible cut in rates.

In addition to currencies and interest rates, other market-related risks require companies to take positions. In many sectors, for example, raw material prices are a key factor. A company can have a strategically important position on oil, coffee, semiconductors or electricity markets, for example.

3/VALUE AT RISK (VaR)

VaR (**Value at Risk**) is a finer measure of market risk. It represents an investor's maximum potential loss on the value of an asset or a portfolio of financial assets and liabilities, based on the investment timeframe and a confidence interval. This potential loss is calculated on the basis of historical data or deduced from normal statistical laws.

Hence, a portfolio worth €100m, with a VaR of −€2.5m at 95% (calculated on a monthly basis) has just a 5% chance of shrinking more than €2.5m in 1month.

VaR is often used by financial establishments as a tool in managing risk and is closely tied to duration.[1]

VaR is beginning to be used by major industrial groups. TeleDanmark, for example, includes it in its annual reports. However, VaR has two drawbacks:

1 *See p. 500.*

- it assumes that the markets follow normal distribution laws, an assumption that underestimates the frequency of extreme values;
- it tells us absolutely nothing about the potential loss that could occur when stepping outside the confidence interval. Based on the above example, how much can be lost in those 5% of cases: €2.6m, €10m or €100m? VaR tells us nothing on this point, stress scenario can then be implemented.

4/MEASURING OTHER FINANCIAL RISKS

Liquidity risk is measured by comparing contractual debt maturities with estimated future cash flow, via either a cash flow statement or curves such as those presented on p. 224. Contracts carrying clauses on the company's financial ratios or ratings must not be included under debt maturing in more than 1 year because a worsening in the company's ratios or a downgrade could trigger early repayment of outstanding loans.

In addition to conventional financial analysis techniques and credit scoring, credit and counterparty risk is measured mainly via tests for breaking down risks. Such tests include the proportion of the company's top 10 clients in total receivables, number of clients with credit lines above a certain level, etc.

The measure of political risk is still in its infancy.

Section 48.3
PRINCIPLES OF FINANCIAL RISK MANAGEMENT

Financial risk management comes in four forms:

- self-hedging, a seemingly passive stance that is taken only by a few very large companies and only on some of their risks;
- locking in prices or interest rates for a future transaction, which has the drawback of preventing the company from benefiting from a favourable shift in prices or rates should shift favourably;

- insurance, which consists in paying a premium in some form to a third party, which will then assume the risk, if it materialises; this approach allows the company to benefit from a favourable shift in prices or rates;
- immediate disposal of a risky asset or liability.

1/SELF-HEDGING

Self-hedging consists, in fact, in not hedging a risk. This is a reasonable strategy only for very large groups. Such groups assume that the law of averages applies to them and that they are therefore certain to experience some negative events on a regular basis, such as devaluations, customer bankruptcy, etc. Risk thus becomes a certainty and, hence, a cost. Self-hedging is based on the principle that a company has no interest in passing on the risk (and the profit) to a third party. Rather than paying what amounts to an insurance premium, the company provisions a sum each year to meet claims that will inevitably occur, thus becoming its own insurer.

The risk can be diminished, but not eliminated, by natural hedges. A European company, for example, that sells in the US will also produce there, so that its costs can be in dollars rather than euros. It will take on debt in the US rather than in Europe, to set dollar-denominated liabilities against dollar-denominated assets.

Self-hedging is a strategy adopted by either irresponsible companies or a limited number of very large companies who serve as their own insurance company!

One sophisticated procedure consists in setting up a **captive insurance company**, which will invest the premiums thus saved to build up reserves in order to meet future claims. In the meantime, some of the risk can be sold on the reinsurance market.

2/LOCKING IN FUTURE PRICES OR RATES THROUGH FORWARD TRANSACTIONS

Forward transactions can fully eliminate risk by locking in now the price or rate at which a transaction will be done in the future. This costs the company nothing but does prevent it from benefiting from a favourable shift in price or rates.

Forward transactions sometimes defy conventional logic, as they allow one to "sell" what one does not yet possess or to "buy" a product before it is available. However, they are not abstractions divorced from economic reality. As we will show, forward transactions can be broken down into the simple, familiar operations of: spot purchasing or selling, borrowing and lending.

(a) Forward currency transactions

Let us take the example of a US company that is to receive €100m in 3 months. Let's say the euro is currently trading at $1.0510. Unless he is speculating on a rise in the euro, the company treasurer wants to lock in today the exchange rate at which he will be able to sell these euros. So he offers to sell euros now that he will not receive for another 3 months. This is the essence of the forward transaction. Although forward transactions are now a common practice, it is worth looking at how they are calculated.

The transaction is tantamount to borrowing today the present value in euros of the sum that will be received in 3 months, exchanging it at the current rate and investing the corresponding amount in dollars for the same maturity.

Assume A is the amount in euros received by the company; N, the number of days between today and the date of reception; $R_{€}$, the euro borrowing rate; and $R_{\$}$, the dollar interest rate.

The amount borrowed today in euros is simply the value A discounted at rate $R_{€}$:

$$PV = A/(1 + (R_{€} \times N/360))$$

This amount is then exchanged at the R_S spot rate and invested in dollars at rate $R_{\$}$. Present value is thus expressed as:

$$PV = R_S \times PV \times (1 + (R_{\$} \times N/360))$$

Thus:

$$PV = A \times R_S \times \frac{1 + R_{\$} \times \dfrac{N}{360}}{1 + R_{€} \times \dfrac{N}{360}}$$

The forward rate (F_R) is that which equalises the future value in euros and the amount A.

Thus:

$$F_R = R_S \times \frac{1 + R_{\$} \times \dfrac{N}{360}}{1 + R_{€} \times \dfrac{N}{360}}$$

If $R_S = 1.1257$ dollar, $N = 90$ days, $R_{\$} = 1.12\%$ and $R_{€} = 2.15\%$, we obtain a forward selling price of $1.1228.

This is like a forward purchase of euros, in which the operator pledges to receive euros in the future at a rate based on current rates. This is tantamount to the operator buying the euros today while borrowing their corresponding value in dollars for the same period. The euros that have been bought are also invested during this time at the euro interest rate.

The forward exchange rate of a currency is based on the spot price and the interest rate differential between the foreign currency and the benchmark currency during the period covered by the transaction.

In our example, as interest rates are higher in euros than in dollars, the forward euro-into-dollar exchange rate is lower than the spot rate. The difference is called **swap points**. In our example, swap points come to 29.[2] Swap points can be seen as compensation demanded by the counterparty in the forward transaction for providing exposure to a high-yielding currency (the euro in our example), rather than a low-yielding currency (the dollar in our example) up to the moment when

2 $26 = 1,257 - 1,228$.

the transaction is unwound. More generally, currency A is said to be at premium *vis-à-vis* currency B if interest rates on A are below interests rates on B during the period concerned.

Similarly, if the benchmark currency offers a lower interest rate than the foreign currency, the forward rate will be below the spot rate. Currency A is said to be at discount *vis-à-vis* currency B if A offers higher interest rates than B during the period concerned.

As in any forward transaction, the operator knows at what price he will be able to buy or sell his currencies, but will be unable to take advantage of any later opportunities. For example, if he sold his €100m forward at $1.1228, and the euro is trading at $1.1300 at maturity, he will have to keep his word (unless he wants to break the futures contract, in which case he will have to pay a penalty) and bear an opportunity cost equal to $0.0072 per euro sold.

(b) Forward–forward rate and Forward Rate Agreements (FRAs)

Let us say our company treasurer learns that his company plans to install a new IT system, which will require a considerable outlay in equipment and software in 3 months. His cash flow projections show that, in 3 months, he will have to borrow €20m for 6 months.

On the euro money market, spot interest rates are as follows:

3 months	2 1/4% − 2 5/16%
6 months	2 1/4% − 2 5/16%
9 months	2 5/16% − 2 3/8%

How can the treasurer hedge against a rise in short-term rates over the next 3 months? Armed with his knowledge of the yield curve, he can use the procedures discussed below to lock in the 6-month rate as it will be in 3 months.

He decides to borrow €20m today for 9 months and to reinvest it for the first 3 months. Assuming that he works directly at money market conditions, in 9 months he will have to pay back:

$$20 \times (1 + 2\,3/8\% \times 9/12) = €\,20.356\,25m$$

But his 3-month investment turns €20m into:

$$20 \times (1 + 2\,1/4\% \times 3/12) = 20.112\,50$$

The implied rate obtained is called the forward–forward rate and is expressed as follows:

$$T(3.6) = ((20.356\,25 - 20.112\,50)/20.112\,50) \times (12/6) = 2.424\%$$

Our treasurer was thus able to hedge his interest rate risk but has borrowed €20m from his bank, €20m that he will not be using for 3 months. Hence, he must bear the corresponding intermediation costs. **His company's balance sheet and income statement will be affected by this transaction.**

Now, let's imagine that the bank finds out about our treasurer's concerns and offers him the following product:

- In 3 months' time, if the 6-month (floating benchmark) rate is above 2.424% (the guaranteed rate), the bank pledges to pay him the difference between the market rate and 2.424% on a predetermined principal.
- In 3 months' time, if the 6-month (floating benchmark) rate is below 2.424% (the guaranteed rate), the company will have to pay the bank the difference between the market rate and 2.424% on the same predetermined principal.

This is called a *Forward Rate Agreement*, or **FRA**. An FRA allows the treasurer to hedge against fluctuations in rates, without the amount of the transaction being actually borrowed or lent.

If, in 3 months' time the 6-month rate is 2.5%, our treasurer will borrow €20m at this high rate, but will receive, on the same amount, the pro rata difference between 2.5% and 2.424%. The actual cost of his loan will therefore be 2.424%. Similarly, if the 6-month rate is 1.5%, the treasurer will have borrowed on favourable terms, but will have to pay the pro rata difference between 2.424% and 1.5%.

The same reasoning applies if the treasurer wishes to invest his surplus funds. Such a transaction would involve FRA lending, as opposed to the FRA borrowing described above.

Forward rate agreements are used to lock in an interest rate for a future transaction.

It can be seen that, if the FRA does not correspond to a real future cash flow (as in a hedging transaction), it is a speculative product. In this case, accounting rules require companies to show the market value of the FRA – i.e., the profit and losses on this product – at the valuation date and to incur a profit or a loss on the P&L.

The **notional amount** is the theoretical amount to which the difference between the guaranteed rate and the floating rate is applied. The notional amount is never exchanged between the buyer and seller of an FRA. The interest rate differential is not paid at the maturity of the underlying loan but is discounted and paid at the maturity of the FRA.

One last comment: an FRA is free of charge, but, of course, the "purchase" of an FRA and the "sale' of an FRA are not done at the same interest rate. As in all financial products, a margin separates the rate charged on a 6-month loan in 3 months' time, and the rate at which that money can be invested over the same period of time.

You have probably noticed that an FRA is a bet on interest rate trends. Operators have understood this, using the FRA for both hedging purposes as well as to speculate on interest rates. If an operator expects interest rates to go up, he buys an FRA borrower, in order to earn the difference in interest at the maturity of the FRA, and vice versa.

Banks are key operators on the FRA market and offer companies the opportunity to buy or sell FRAs, with maturities generally shorter than 1 year.

(c) Swaps

To swap something means to exchange or trade it for something else. In its broadest sense, a swap is an exchange of financial assets or flows between two entities during a certain period of time. Both operators must, of course, believe the transaction to be to their advantage.

The difficulties that some emerging countries have had in paying off their debt have led to a boom in asset (and debt) swaps. These are meant to prevent too many risks from being heaped on the shoulders of a single debtor. The swaps work by allowing creditors to exchange one debt for another of the same type. Each country is rated in terms of the percentage of the nominal of the debt. Ratings can range from almost 0 (default) to 100% for the safest borrowers.

"Swap" in everyday parlance means an exchange of financial flows (calculated on the basis of a theoretical benchmark called a "notional") between two entities during a given period of time. Such financial flows can be:

- **currency swap without principal**;
- **Interest Rate Swaps**, IRSs;
- **currency swaps** (with principal).

Unlike financial assets, financial flows are traded Over The Counter (OTC), with no impact on the balance sheet and allow the parties to modify the exchange or interest rate terms (or both simultaneously) on current or future assets or liabilities.

Interest rate swaps are a long-term portfolio of FRAs (from 1 to 15 years).

As with FRAs, the principle is to compare a floating rate and a guaranteed rate and to make up the difference without an exchange of principal. Interest rate swaps are especially suited for managing a company's long-term currency exposure.

For a company with long-term debt at 7% (at fixed rates) and wishing to benefit from the fall in interest rates that the company expects, the simplest solution is to receive the fixed rate (7%) on a notional amount and to pay the floating rate on the same amount.

That is:

$$-\text{Fixed rate} + \text{Fixed rate} - \text{Floating rate} = -\text{Floating rate}$$

tantamount to our company's borrowing the notional at a floating rate for the duration of the swap without its creditors seeing any change in their debts. After the 1st year, if the variable benchmark rate (LIBOR,[3] EURIBOR,[4] etc.) is 6%, the company will have paid its creditors an interest rate of 7%, but will receive 1% of the swap's notional amount. Its effective rate will be 6%.

The transaction described is a swap of fixed for floating rates, and all sorts of combinations are possible:

- swapping a fixed rate for fixed rate (in the same currency);
- swapping floating rate 1 for floating rate 2 (called benchmark switching);

3 *London Inter Bank Offer Rate.*

4 *European Inter Bank Offer Rate.*

- swapping a fixed rate in currency 1 for a fixed rate in currency 2;
- swapping a fixed rate in currency 1 for a floating rate in currency 2;
- swapping a floating rate in currency 1 for a floating rate in currency 2.

These last three swaps come with an exchange of principal, as the two parties use different currencies. This exchange is generally done at the beginning and at the maturity of the swap at the same exchange rate. More sophisticated swaps make it possible to separate the benchmark rates from the currencies concerned.

The swaps market has experienced a considerable boom, and banks are key players. Company treasurers appreciate the flexibility of swaps, which allow them to choose the duration, the floating benchmark rate and the notional amount. Note finally that a swap between a bank and a company can be liquidated at any moment by calculating the present value of future cash flows at the market rate and comparing it wirh the initial notional amount. Swaps are also frequently used to manage interest rate risk on floating or fixed rate assets.

3/INSURANCE

Insurance allows companies to pay a premium to a third party, which assumes the risk if that risk materialises. If it doesn't, companies can benefit from a favourable trend in the parameter covered (exchange rate, interest rates, solvency of a debtor, etc.).

Conceptually, insurance is based on the technique of options; the insurance premium paid corresponds to the value of the option purchased.

As we saw in Chapter 29, an option gives its holder the right to buy or sell an underlying at a specified price on a specified date, or to forego this right if the market offers better opportunities. See Chapter 29 for background, valuation and conditions in which options are used.

Options are an ideal management tool for company treasurers, as they help guarantee a price while still leaving some leeway. But, as our reader has learned, there are no miracles in finance and the **option premium is the price of this freedom**. Its cost can be prohibitive, particularly in the case of companies with businesses having low sales margins.

Options have experienced a real boom. Major international banks have become market makers on all sorts of markets. Below we present the most commonly used options:

(a) Currency options

Currency options allow their holders to lock in an exchange rate in a particular currency, while retaining the choice of realising a transaction at the spot market rate if it is more favourable. Of course, the strike price has to be compared with the forward rate and not the spot rate. While banks can theoretically list all types of options, European-style options are the main ones traded.

While standardised contracts are listed, company treasurers generally prefer the over-the-counter variety, as they are more flexible for choosing an amount (which can correspond exactly to the amount of the flow for companies), dates and strike prices. Options can be used in many ways. Some companies buy only options that are far out-of-the-money and thus carry low premiums; in doing so, they seek to hedge against extreme events such as devaluations. Other companies set the strike price in line with their commercial needs or perhaps their anticipations.

Given the often high cost of the premium, several imaginative (and risky) products have been developed, including lookback options, options on options and barrier options.

Lookback options can be used to buy or sell currencies on the basis of the average exchange rate during the life of the option. The premium is thus lower, as less risk is taken by the seller and the volatility of the underlying is below its average.

Options on options are quite useful for companies bidding on a foreign project. The bid is made on the basis of a certain exchange rate, but let us say the rate has moved the wrong way by the time the company wins the contract. Options on options allow the company to hedge its currency exposure as soon as it submits its bid, by giving the right to buy a currency option with a strike price close to the benchmark rate. If the company is not chosen for the bid, it simply gives up its option on option. As the value of an option is below the value of the underlying asset, the value of an option on an option will be low.

Barrier options are surely the most frequently traded exotic products on the market. A barrier is a limit price which, when exceeded, knocks in or knocks out the option (i.e., creates or cancels the option). This reduces the risk to the seller and thus the premium to the buyer. For example, if the euro is trading at $1.2, a US company treasurer who knows he will have to buy euros in the future can guarantee himself a certain exchange rate by buying a euro call at $1.4, for example, and then, to reduce the premium, he would place the knockout barrier at $1. If the euro falls below $1 at any time during the life of the option, the treasurer will find himself without a hedge (but the market will have moved in his direction and, at that moment, the futures price will be far below the level at which he bought his option).

It's easy to imagine various combinations of barrier options (e.g., knockout barrier above the current price or the knockin barrier below, options at various strike prices – one activated at the level where the other is deactivated, etc.). When a bank offers a new currency product with a strange earnings profile (a staircase profile, for example), it is generally the combination of one (or several) barrier option(s) with other standard market products.

Barrier options are attractive but require careful management as the treasurer must constantly keep up with exchange rates in order to maintain his hedging situation (and to rehedge, if the option is knocked out). Moreover, his own risk management tools would not necessarily tell him the exact consequences of these products or their implied specifications.

(b) Interest rate options

The rules that apply to options in general obviously apply to interest rate options. For the financial market, the exact nature of the underlying asset is irrelevant to either the design or valuation of the option. As a result, many products are built around identical concepts and their degree of popularity is often a simple matter of fashion.

A **cap** allows a borrower to set a ceiling interest rate above which he no longer wants to borrow and he will receive the difference between the market rate and cap rate.

A **floor** allows a lender to set a minimum interest rate below which he does not wish to lend and he will receive the difference between the floor rate and the market rate.

A **collar or rate tunnel** involves both the purchase of a cap and the sale of a floor, thus setting a zone of fluctuation in interest rates, below which the operator must pay the difference in rates between the market rate and the floor rate and above which his counterparty pays the differential. This combination reduces the cost of hedging, as the premium of the cap is paid partly or totally by the sale of the floor.

Do not be intimidated by these products, as the cap is none other than a call option on an FRA borrower. Similarly, the floor is just a call option on an FRA lender. In a sense, these products are long options on interest rates that give the implicit right to buy or sell bonds at a certain price. As we have seen, these products allow setting up a borrowing or lending rate *vis-à-vis* the counterparty. These options are frequently used by operators to take positions on the long part of the yield curve.

Swaptions are options on swaps, and can be used to buy or sell the right to conclude a swap over a certain duration. The underlying swap is stated at the outset and is defined by its notional amount, maturity and the fixed and floating rate that are used as benchmarks.

Some banks have combined swaps with *swaptions* to produce what they call "swaps that can be cancelled at no cost". Do not be too impressed by the lack of cost. This product is none other than a swap combined with an option to sell a swap. The premium of the option is not paid in cash but factored into the calculation of the swap rate.

Barrier interest rate options are similar to barrier currency options:

* either the option exists only if the benchmark rate reaches the barrier rate;
* or the option is knocked in only if the benchmark rate exceeds a set limit.

The presence of barriers reduces the option's premium. Company treasurers can combine these options with other products into a custom-made hedge. Like barrier currency options, barrier interest rate options often require careful management.

(c) Confirmed credit lines

In exchange for a commitment fee, a company can obtain short- and medium-term confirmed credit lines from banks, on which companies can draw at any time for their cash needs. A confirmed credit line is like an option to take out a loan.

(d) Credit insurance

Insurance companies specialising in appraising default risk (Euler-Sfac, Altradius, Coface, etc.) guarantee companies payment of a debt in exchange for a premium equivalent to about 0.3% of the nominal.

(e) Credit derivatives

Credit derivatives emerged in 1995 and have taken off since then. They are used to unlink the management of a credit risk on an asset or liability from the ownership of that asset or liability.

Developed and used first of all by financial institutions, credit derivatives are beginning to be used by major industrial and commercial groups. The purpose of these products is mainly to reduce the credit risk on some clients, which may account for an excessive portion of the credit portfolio. They can also be used to protect against a negative trend in margins (see p. 490) on a future loan.

Credit derivatives work very much like interest rate or currency options. Only the nature of the risk covered is different – the risk of default or rating downgrade instead of interest rate or currency risk.

The most conventional form of credit derivative is the credit default swap. In these agreements one side buys protection against the default of its counterparty by paying a third part regularly and receiving from it the predetermined amount in the event of default. The credit risk is thus transferred from the buyer of protection (a company, an investor, a bank) to a third party (an investor, an insurance company …) in exchange for some compensation.

Credit derivatives are traded over the counter and play the same economic role as an insurance contract.

Meanwhile, a second category of derivatives has developed, which is not an "insurance"-type product but a "forward"-type product, via which companies can, from the start, set the spread of a bond to be issued in the future. The spread of an issue is thus bought and sold at a preset level. And, of course, wherever forward purchasing or selling exists, financial intermediaries will come up with the corresponding options. We thus end up with an insurance product called an "option on future spreads!"

Exponential development … Credit derivatives cover an existing risk … or can be used to speculate more efficiently …

@

download

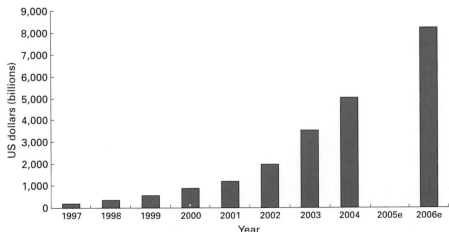

GLOBAL CREDIT DERIVATIVES MARKET EXCLUDING ASSET SWAP ($bn)

Source: British Bankers Association.

(f) Political risk insurance

Political risk insurance is offered by specialised companies, such as Coface, Hermès, AIG and Unistrat, which can cover 90 to 95% of the value of an investment for as long as 15 years in most of the world's countries. Risks normally covered include expropriation, nationalisation, confiscation and changes in legislation covering foreign investments. Initially the domain of public or quasi-public organisations, political risk insurance is increasingly being offered by the private sector.

4/OUTRIGHT DISPOSAL OF THE RISKY ASSET OR LIABILITY

Outright disposal is a last gasp measure that obviously does not unlink the ownership of the asset (or liability) from the management of its risk. Measures include securitisation (see p. 961), defeasance (see p. 960) and nonrecourse factoring (see p. 959).

Section 48.4
ORGANISED MARKETS–OTC MARKETS

1/STANDARDISATION OF CONTRACTS

In the forward transactions we looked at in Section 48.3, two operators concluded a contract, with each exposing himself to a counterparty risk if the other was in default at the delivery of the currency, for example, or before the maturity of the swap. Moreover, other operators were ignorant of the terms of these over-the-counter transactions, and the products' liquidity was unreliable. Liquidity is closely tied to the product's specificity, and usually dependent on the willingness of the counterpart to unwind the transaction.

It is because of these drawbacks that investors turn to standardised products that can be bought and sold on an organised market, such as a stock on the stock exchange. The futures and options markets have responded to this demand by offering:

- fully liquid, listed products;
- with a clearinghouse; and
- specialised traders who act as intermediaries and ensure that the market functions properly.

Moreover, these markets offer the option of taking large positions with a small cash outlay, and on standardised maturities.

A future is a **firm** commitment to buy or sell an agreed-upon quantity of an asset at an agreed-upon price on an agreed-upon date. All futures have the following specifications:

➤ The underlying asset is a benchmark for market operators: Euronext-Liffe, for example, offers:

5 *Morgan Stanley
Composite Index.*

- ○ a notional contract on £100,000 in UK government bonds at 6% maturing in 10 years;
- ○ a notional contract on €1,000,000 3-month EURIBOR;
- ○ a contract on MSCI[5] Euro Index; or
- ○ a contract on cacao, robusta coffee or wheat.

➢ The amount of each contract is standardised.

➢ Quotations are standardised.

➢ Few maturities, generally at the end of March, June, September and December.

Let us take the example of a 3-month EURIBOR traded on Euronext-Liffe, which has a €1m notional value. The contract matures on the 20th of March, June, September and December. It is listed in the form of 100 minus 3-month EURIBOR and can thus be compared immediately with bond prices. The initial deposit is €500 per contract and the minimum fluctuation is 0.20 basis points (or €20).

The high degree of standardisation in futures ensures fungibility of contracts and market liquidity.

Liquidity is often greater on futures than on the underlying asset, as, unlike the underlying assets, futures volumes are not limited by the amount actually in issue.

The Eurex in Germany/Switzerland, the Euronext-Liffe (UK, France, Benelux and Portugal), the Chicago Board of Trade and Chicago Mercantile Exchange offer contracts for managing interest rate risk, including the notional contract, the 3-month EURIBOR, etc.

As listed contracts have become more liquid, standardised options have emerged on these contracts (option on notional, option on 3-month EURIBOR, etc.), which allow financial institutions and companies to take positions on the volatility of contract prices. Organised currency risk management markets are still in their infancy, as the dominance of banks in forward currency transactions constitutes an obstacle to the development of contracts of this type.

2/ UNWINDING OF CONTRACTS

In theory, when a contract matures, the buyer buys the agreed quantity of underlying assets and pays the agreed price. Meanwhile, the seller of the contract receives the agreed price and delivers the agreed quantity of underlying assets. This is the mechanism of delivery. For futures markets to be viable and to function properly there must be at least the theoretical possibility of delivery. The possibility of physical delivery prevents contract prices from being fully disconnected from price trends in the underlying asset. In other words, the value of the contract at maturity is equal to the value of the underlying asset at that time.

Let us take the example of an investor who on 21 March buys cacao contracts maturing in July. Assume that the contract price is $810/tonne, vs. a spot market price of $830. Assume that, at the end of July, cacao is quoted at $900. By using futures contracts, our investor has bought a tonne of cacao in July at $810, whereas it is trading at $900 on the market. Arbitrage trading makes the futures and spot prices converge at maturity. Let us assume that futures contracts were priced below the spot price. Investors would then snatch up these contracts at less than $900 to instantly obtain (as the contract has now matured) cacao that they can resell immediately for $900. On the other hand, if the futures contracts were priced above $900, no investor in his right mind would buy any (after all, who would buy cacao for more than $900 via futures contracts, when they can buy at $900 on the spot market?).

The value of a future at maturity is equal to the value of the underlying asset. The theoretical possibility of delivery prevents the contract price from coming unlinked from the price of the underlying asset at maturity.

However, prior to maturity, the difference between the spot price and future price, called the "base", varies and is only rarely reduced to zero.

So much for the theory. In reality, in more than 95% of cases, no underlying asset is delivered, as this would be costly and administratively complicated. Let us look again at the example of the investor who bought contracts on cacao at $810 on 21 March and sells them at the end of July instead of taking delivery on the cacao, since for him the result is the same. Indeed, what price would these futures be priced at except the cacao spot price of $900, which is also the futures price, since we are at maturity? Once the transaction is unwound, he will buy the cacao on the spot market at $900. This will cost him a total of $810 (purchase of the contracts) + $900 (reselling of the contracts) − $900 (purchase of the cacao) − i.e., $810 per tonne.

The mechanism of delivery exists only to allow arbitrage trading, if, by chance, the price of contracts at maturity moves away from the price of the underlying asset. This is rather rare, as the markets regulate themselves. At maturity, buyers of contracts sell them to the sellers at a price that is equivalent to the price of the underlying asset at the moment.

The purchase of a futures contract is normally unwound by selling it. The sale of a futures contract is normally unwound by buying it back.

3/ELIMINATING COUNTERPARTY RISKS

Derivatives markets offer considerable possibilities to investors, as long as everyone meets their commitments. The possibility of them not doing so is called "counterparty risk". And such a risk, while small, does exist. For example, a contract could be so unfavourable for an operator that he might decide not to deliver the securities or funds promised, preferring to expose himself to a long legal process rather than suffer immediate losses. And even when everyone is operating in good faith, could not the bankruptcy of one operator create a domino effect, jeopardising several other commitments and considerable sums?

Unless specific measures are in place, counterparty risk should certainly be considered the main market risk. But, in fact, markets are organised to address this concern.

Derivatives market authorities may at any time demand that all buyers and sellers prove that they are financially able to assume the risks they have taken on (i.e., they can bear the losses already incurred and even those that are possible the next day). They do so through the mechanism of **clearing**, **deposits** and **margin calls**. The clearinghouse is, in fact, the sole counterparty of all market operators.

The buyer is not buying from the seller, but from the clearinghouse. The seller is not selling to the buyer, but to the clearinghouse. All operators are dealing with an organisation whose financial weight, reputation and functioning rules guarantee that all contracts will be honoured.

Clearing authorities watch over positions and demand a deposit on the day that a contract is concluded. This deposit normally covers 2 days of maximum loss.

Daily price movements create potential losses and gains, relative to the transaction price. Each day, the clearinghouse credits or debits the account of each operator for this potential gain or loss. When it is a loss, the clearinghouse makes a **margin call** – i.e., it demands an additional payment from the operator. Hence, the operator's account is always in the black at least by the amount of the initial deposit. If the operator does not meet a margin call, the clearinghouse closes out his position and uses the deposit to cover the loss. For potential gains, the clearinghouse pays out a margin. When the contract has exceeded the clearinghouse's maximum regulatory amount, price quotation is stopped and the clearinghouse makes further margin calls before quotation resumes.

Margin calls are an integral component of derivatives markets. By limiting the amount of the initial deposit, margins provide considerable leverage to investors. Let's take the example of the cacao contract above and try to work out the transaction's profitability. Our investor used futures contracts to buy July cacao for $810/tonne. At maturity it quotes at $900 on the spot market, hence a $90 gain for a very limited outlay (just the deposit of $25). His gain is considerable: $90/25 = 360\%$), whereas cacao has gone up just $(900 - 830)/830 = 8.4\%$. **Here is an example of the steep leverage of futures, but leverage can also work in reverse.**

Such steep leverage explains why counterparty risk is never totally eliminated, despite precautions that are normally quite effective. Margin calls limit the extent of potential defaults to the losses that are incurred in 1 day, while the initial deposit is meant to cover unexpected events. However, the amounts at stake can, in a few hours, reach sums so high that all operators are shaken. Even if this happens only once in a while, no clearinghouse has ever gone bust.

Futures are a zero-sum game, as what one operator earns, another loses. The aggregate of market operators gets neither richer nor poorer (when excluding intermediation fees).

Let us take the above example of a tonne of cacao quoted at $900 at end-July. We saw that the investor who bought contracts on 21 March has earned $90 per tonne. On the other side, the operator who sold those contracts on 21 March must deliver cacao at the end of July for $810, even though it is priced at $900. He will thus lose $90, the exact amount that his counterparty has earned.

A zero-sum game, not a senseless game.

This is not only a zero-sum game but also a worthwhile game. Derivatives markets are there not to create wealth, but to spread risk and to improve the liquidity of financial markets. On the whole, there is no wealth creation.

All derivatives only allow the transfer of risks, they do not eliminate risk.

Due to the growing volatility of foreign exchange rates, interest rates, share prices or the prices of raw materials, risks to which companies are exposed have significantly increased in the past 30 years. Credit and counterparty risk, along with political risk are also on the rise.

We can identify four major risks:

- market risk – i.e., exposure of the company to unfavourable changes in interest and exchange rates or prices of raw materials or shares;

- liquidity risk – i.e., the inability of a company to make its payments by their due date;

- counterparty risk – i.e., the loss of repayments of a debt in the event of default of the creditor;

- political risk which impacts on importers, exporters and companies that invest abroad.

Market risks are accurately measured with the notion of position and Value at Risk (VaR). Liquidity is measured by comparing debt repayment and expected cash receipts. Techniques for measuring other risks are still in their infancy.

When confronted with risk, a company can:

- decide to do nothing and take its own hedging measures. This will only apply to some of the risks of very large corporates;

- lock in prices or interest rates for a future transaction by means of forwardation;

- insure against the risk by paying a premium to a third party which will then assume the risk if it materialises. This is the same idea that underlies options;

- immediately dispose of the risky asset or liability (securitisation, defeasance, factoring, etc.).

The same types of product (forward buying, put options, swaps, etc.) have been developed to cover the four different risks and are traded either on the OTC markets or on stock exchanges. On the OTC market the company can find products that are perfectly suited to its needs, but there is the counterparty risk of the third party that provides the hedging. This problem is eliminated on the futures and options markets, although the price paid is reduced flexibility in tailoring products to companies' needs.

1/ What are the four financial risks that companies are exposed to?

2/ Describe four ways for a company to deal with risk.

3/ Use arbitrage to calculate forward selling of yens against euros at 3 months. What information do you need to do the calculation?

4/ What is an FRA?

5/ A Portuguese company imports maize from Mexico, which it in turn exports to Canada. The company pays and is paid at 3 months (the maize is in fact shipped direct from Mexico to Canada). Should it buy or sell a peso call option (or put option) against the Canadian dollar?

6/ What is a future?

7/ What are the differences between OTC forward transactions and futures?

8/ What role does a clearinghouse play?

9/ Can credit derivatives be based on options?

10/ Does a derivative product have to be sufficiently liquid to be attractive?

11/ Can you provide examples or hedging products used by ordinary people?

12/ What category of derivative products would personal injury insurance fit into?

13/ Should corporate treasurers take advantage of any arbitrages that they may detect on the markets?

14/ Should traders take advantage of any arbitrages that they may detect on the markets?

15/ Excluding any costs, can a company hedge against all of its risks, taking the risk of opportunity into account? And the trader?

EXERCISES

1/ Calculate the future buy and sell price, at 3 months (dollar against euro) using the following information:

- o   The 3-month euro rate is equal to 4 6/8–4 7/8%.
- o   The 3-month dollar rate is equal to 3 7/8–4%.
- o   The euro is currently trading at $1.0210/20.

2/ Calculate the 6-month interest rate of the dollar on the basis of the following information:

- o   The 6-month euro rate is equal to 4 4/8–4 5/8%.
- o   The euro is currently trading at $1.0210/20.
- o   The euro is trading at 6 months at $1.0150/60.

3/ A market trader is offering a $500m loan agreement in 3 months, for a period of 3 months on the following terms: 3 6/8%–3 7/8%. Using the information provided in Questions 1 and 2, can you identify an arbitrage opportunity? What is the potential gain for the arbitrageur?

4/ Is an arbitrage of this sort really without risk?

5/ If a corporate treasurer finds himself in the situation described above, should he execute the arbitrage?

ANSWERS

Questions

1/ *Market, liquidity, political and counterparty risk.*
2/ *Self-hedging, locking in prices or interest rates now, taking out insurance, disposing of the risky asset or liability.*
3/ *See chapter. 3-month yen borrowing rate. 3-month euro investment rate. Yen/euro spot price.*
4/ *See chapter.*
5/ *Purchase of a call option.*
6/ *A forward buy or sell contract.*
7/ *Futures market = organised market.*

8/ *Eliminate counterparty risk.*
9/ *Yes.*
10/ *No – it is an OTC product.*
11/ *All insurance policies.*
12/ *A floor.*
13/ *No, there is no such thing as a perfect arbitrage, and there is always an element of speculation. Accordingly, it does not fall within the remit of a corporate treasurer.*
14/ *Yes of course – that's what traders do.*
15/ *No, because it cannot wind up its business. Yes, because he can wind up his commitments.*

Exercise

1/ *3-month forward euro exchange rate: 1.0185/$1.201.*
2/ *6-month dollar interest rate 3.299%–3.423.*
3/ *You should borrow $495m at 6 months, invest it at 3 7/8 in dollars for 3 months (you will then have 500m in 3 months) and buy the traders' contract. The value of the arbitrage gain is $1,056 to be cashed in with no risk at maturity of the contract.*
4/ *No, there is always the counterparty risk of the trader offering the contract.*
5/ *No, because there is no way of measuring counterparty risk or any of the other market inefficiencies. For the corporate treasurer, this transaction would amount to financial speculation, and accordingly would not form part of the ordinary course of the company's business.*

On the theory behind the purpose and practice of hedging: **BIBLIOGRAPHY**

G. Brown, Managing foreign exchange risk with derivatives, *Journal of Financial Economics*, 401–448, May/June 2001.
J. Graham, C. Harvey, The theory and practice of corporate finance: Evidence form the field, *Journal of Financial Economics*, 187–243, May 2001.

And for more about credit derivatives:

Euromoney, *Maturity of Hot New Market Faces its Sternest Test*, pp. 34–42, December 2001.
http://www.bba.org.uk

On the transfer of alternative risks:

K. Froot, The market for catastrophe risk: A clinical examination, *Journal of Financial Economics*, 529–571, May/June 2001.

On Value at Risk:

Ph. Jorion, *Value at Risk*, 2nd edn, McGraw-Hill, 2000.
www.gloriamundi.org

Glossary

Agency theory   Agency theory says that a company is not a single, unified entity. It calls into question the claim that all of the stakeholders in the company (shareholders, managers and creditors) have a single goal – value creation. Agency theory shows how, on the contrary, their interests may differ and some decisions (related to borrowing, for example) or how products (stock options) come out of attempts to achieve convergence between the interests of managers and shareholders to protect creditors. It analyses the consequences of certain financial decisions in terms of risk, profitability and, more generally, the interests of the various parties. Agency theory is the intellectual basis of corporate governance.

Balance sheet   The balance sheet represents a snapshot of the cumulative inflows and outflows previously generated by the business. It lists all the assets of a business and all of its financial resources at a given moment in time. The balance sheet is always at equilibrium, guaranteed by the double-entry accounting practice adopted by all businesses.

Beta   Beta is the measure of the contribution of a single asset to the risk of portfolio. It is the covariance of this asset's returns with the returns of the portfolio. Beta measures the volatility of a security.

Bond   A bond is a negotiable debt security that is issued by corporations, municipalities and governments. It pays a coupon and is redeemed in accordance with the prospectus of its issue. Bonds can carry other obligations on the part of the issuer. Bonds are the main medium-term market financing vehicles used by corporations, particularly in the 5–10-year segment. There are various types of bonds, such as convertible bonds, mandatory convertibles, exchangeable bonds, etc.

Capital Asset Pricing Model   The CAPM is based on the assumption that investors act rationally and have at their disposal all relevant information on financial securities. It is the universally used tool for valuing financial securities. CAPM states that all investors should hold the market portfolio, and the risk premium they will demand is proportional to the market beta. According to CAPM, the expected return of an asset will then be a linear function of beta: Expected return of a financial security = Risk-free rate + Beta × (Expected return of the market – Risk-free rate).

Capital employed   Capital employed is the sum of a company's fixed assets and its working capital (i.e., operating working capital and nonoperating working capital). It is therefore equal to the sum of the net amounts devoted by a business to the operating cycle and investment cycle. Also known as operating assets. Capital employed is financed by two main types of funds, shareholders' equity and net debt, sometimes regrouped under the heading of invested capital.

Capital expenditures   Capital expenditures are acquisitions of tangible fixed assets and intangible fixed assets. They are commonly called "capex". *See also* Investment.

Capital increase   From a financial point of view, a capital increase is the sale of shares. Proceeds of this sale go to the company. A capital increase will lead to a change in different indicators: right to dividends, to profits, to liquidation sale proceeds, to equity, to voting rights amongst different funds providers. Capital increases can be made in cash or by asset contribution, following the exercise of warrants or a debt conversion, be reserved or not, and with or without preferential subscription rights.

Capital structure   *See* Financial structure.

CAPM   *See* Capital Asset Pricing Model.

Cash flow   Cash flow is financing that is internally generated by the company. It is equal to EBITDA less net financial expense less corporate income tax. Cash flow can also be calculated by adding to net income depreciation, amortisation and impairment losses, the net result of asset disposals, and the net result of extraordinary events.

Cash flow statement   A cash flow statement is a document containing the information about past trends in the cash flow of the company. Cash flows are usually classified by different categories. One of the possible classifications deals with the business cycle and the investment cycle, which form the industrial and commercial life of the company, and with the debt cycle and the equity cycle, which form the financing life of the company. The cash flow statement is also called the "statement of changes in financial position".

Comparables model   The comparables model is a valuation model that compares all the observable values of assets that can be rationally compared – i.e., which have the same level of risk and growth. More often referred to as the multiples method.

Consolidation   Consolidation is the process of creating the consolidated accounts whose purpose is to present the financial situation of a group of companies as if they formed one single entity. There are three consolidation methods, which are used depending on the strength of the parent company's control or influence: full consolidation, proportionate consolidation and the equity method. The basic principle consists in replacing the historical cost of the parent's investment in the company being consolidated with its assets, liabilities and equity. Consolidation sometimes stands for full consolidation.

Current assets   Current assets consist of inventories, receivables (creditors in the UK), marketable securities and cash. This term reflects the fact that these assets tend to "turn over" during the operating cycle, as opposed to fixed assets, which are not destroyed by the operating cycle.

Debt   Debt is the financing mode, which has the contractually fixed remuneration (*see* Interest rate) and repayment date. It is paid before equity, if and when the company is liquidated.

Dilution   Dilution is the decrease in EPS. It is also the decline in the percentage of a current shareholder interest in the company – i.e., a decrease in his/her current voting rights. It occurs when a capital increase is cash-neutral for a shareholder. Also called dilution of control or real dilution. Where a parent company does not subscribe, either at all or only partially, to a capital increase by one of its subsidiaries that takes place above the subsidiary's book value, the parent company records a dilution profit. This is a noncash profit.

Discount rate   Discount rate is the rate of return required for a project to compensate for its risk. Also called rate of discount.

Dividend   Dividend is a part of net income distributed in cash to shareholders of the company.

Dividend yield   Dividend yield per share is the ratio of the last dividend paid out to the current share price. It can be either gross (including the dividend tax credit if any) or net (without the dividend tax credit). Dividend yield is based on market value, never on book value.

Earning per share   Earnings per share (EPS) represent one of the most widely used indicators measuring the performance of a company. It is calculated by dividing net income by the book value of shareholders' equity.

EBIT   *See* Earnings before interest and tax.

EBITDA   *See* Earnings before interest, tax, depreciation and amortisation.

Earnings before interest and tax   EBIT represents the earnings generated by the investment cycle and business cycle for a given period. The term "business" contrasts with the term "financial", reflecting the distinction between the real world and the realms of finance. EBIT is the product of the company's industrial and commercial activities before its financing operations are taken into account. Also called operating income, trading profit, operating profit or operating result.

Earnings before interest, tax, depreciation and amortisation   EBITDA is the result of the operating cycle, which is equal to the balance of operating revenues and cash operating charges incurred to obtain these revenues. It is also called gross operating profit.

EBIT multiple   The EBIT multiple is one of the enterprise value multiples. It is the ratio of the value of capital employed (enterprise value) to EBIT.

Efficient markets   An efficient market is one in which the prices of financial securities at any time rapidly reflect all available relevant information. In such a market, future returns are unpredictable and prices of securities are always at their "right" value. An efficient market can be weak, semi-strong or strong. Also called perfect market or market in equilibrium.

Financial security   Financial security is a contract whereby the issuer of the security commits to pay to the investor that lends the money today a stream of cash flows in accordance with a given timetable. Also called security.

Financial structure   Financial structure is the proportion of net debt to equity in the company's financing. Capital structure is also called financial structure.

Fixed assets   Fixed assets include everything required for the operating cycle that is not destroyed as part of it, as opposed to the current assets. The decrease in the value of fixed assets is accounted for through depreciation, amortisation and impairment losses. A distinction is drawn between tangible fixed assets (land, buildings, machinery, etc. – known as property, plant and equipment in the US), intangible fixed assets (brands, patents, goodwill, etc.) and investments. When a business holds shares in another company (in the long term), they are accounted for under investments. Accounting policy for fixed assets can significantly affect the accounting and financial criteria of the financial health of a company (profits, solvency, etc.). The state of a company's fixed assets is measured by the ratio net fixed assets/gross fixed assets.

Gearing   Gearing is the ratio of net debt to equity. Also called leverage or financial leverage.

Goodwill   Goodwill is the positive difference between the purchase cost and the fair market value of the assets and liabilities acquired with a company. It may exist due to one of the following: the assets recorded on the acquired company's balance sheet are worth more than their historical cost; some assets such as patents, licenses and market share that the company has accumulated over the years without wishing to or even being able to account for them, may not appear on the balance sheet; the merger between the two companies may create synergies, either in the form of cost reductions and/or revenue enhancement.

Holding company   A holding company owns minority or majority investments in listed or unlisted companies either for purely financial reasons or for control purposes. It is a structure which enables the majority shareholder to maintain control of a company, because minority shareholders are dispersed.

Income statement   The income statement is a document showing all wealth-creating revenues and wealth-destroying charges. There are two major income statement formats: the by-nature income statement format and the by-function income statement format. Also called profit and loss account (or P&L).

Interest rate   The interest rate is interest expressed as an annual percentage rate. It is the cost of borrowing money; the price that a lender charges a borrower for the use of the lender's money.

Internal financing   A company is financed internally when it ensures its development without using external financial resources. Even if internal financing is perceived favourably by the partners of the company, and protects the latter from risks related to an excessive debt burden, internal financing can become harmful when it is used abusively. Its explicit cost being zero, internal financing can encourage not very profitable investment projects and thus cause the impoverishment of shareholders. Only the reinvestment of profits at a rate of return at least equal to cost of equity makes it possible to preserve the value of the reinvested profits.

Investment   Investment is an outlay expected to increase operating cash flows in the future. Investments are carried out from a long-term perspective and have a longer life than that of the operating cycle. Unlike charges, investments are not destroyed in the operating cycle. Investment represents abstinence with a view of increasing future receipts. The increase must be sufficient to ensure the forecast return on investment. Investment is a fundamental process in the life of a company, engaging it for a long period.

LBO   *See* Leveraged buyout.

Leveraged buyout   A leveraged buyout is the acquisition of all a company's shares financed largely by borrowed funds. There are different types of LBOs: management buyout; BIMBO; leveraged buildup.

Leverage effect   The leverage effect explains a company's return on equity in terms of its return on capital employed and cost of debt. It is the difference between return on equity and return on capital employed. It explains how it is possible for a company to deliver a return on equity exceeding the rate of return on all the capital invested in the business – i.e., its return on capital employed. When a company raises debt and invests the funds it has borrowed in its industrial and commercial activities, it generates operating profit that normally exceeds the interest expense due on its borrowings. The company generates a surplus consisting of the difference between the return on capital employed and the cost of debt related to the borrowing. This surplus is attributable to shareholders and is added to shareholders' equity. The leverage effect of debt thus increases the return on equity. If the return on capital employed falls below the cost of debt, then the leverage effect of debt shifts into reverse and reduces the return on equity, which in turn falls below the return on capital employed. The leverage effect is expressed in the following formula:

$$ROE = ROCE + (ROCE - i) \times D/E$$

where ROE is the return on equity, $ROCE$ is the after-tax return on capital employed, i is the after-tax cost of debt, D is net debt, E is equity. The leverage effect itself is $(ROCE - i) \times D/E$.

Leverage   *See* Gearing.

Market capitalisation   Market capitalisation is the market value of a company's equity. It is obtained by multiplying the total number of shares outstanding by the share price.

Merger   A merger consists in combining two or more companies, generally by offering the shareholders of one company securities of the other company in exchange for the surrender of their shares. Often called mergers, these business combinations are, however, almost always acquisitions. They can take the form of a legal merger, asset contribution or contribution of shares.

Modigliani–Miller theorem   The Modigliani–Miller theorem, put forward in 1958, showed that in perfect markets and in the absence of taxation there is no such thing as an optimal capital structure; the overall cost of capital remains the same regardless of the firm's debt policy. Thus, the value of the levered company is equal to the value of the unlevered company. This is the first proposition of the Modigliani–Miller theorem. The second proposition of the Modigliani–Miller theorem states that the cost of equity in a world without taxes rises with the increase in leverage. It can be computed as follows:

$$K_E = K_0 + (K_0 - K_D) \times V_D/V_E$$

where K_E is the cost of equity, K_0 is the cost of equity of an all-equity-financed company, K_D is the cost of debt, V_D is the value of debt and V_E is the value of equity.

Net debt   *See* Net financial debt.

Net financial debt   Net financial debt is the total financial debt net of short-term financial investments. Net financial debt and shareholders' equity together represent the capital invested in the company. Also called net debt.

Net income   Net income is profit after nonrecurrent items and tax. It is one of the most widely used accounting indicators of value creation. Net income is also called profit or earnings or net profit.

Net present value   Net present value, or NPV, of a financial security is the difference between the present value of this security and its market value; NPV changes in the direction opposite to the change of the discounting rate. In an efficient market, NPVs are zero.

Operating assets   Operating assets are all assets used in the company's business activities. *See also* Capital employed.

Operating cash flow   Operating cash flow is the balance of operating outflows and operating inflows generated by the business cycle of the business. It reflects the cash flows generated by operations during a given period. It represents the cash flow generated by the company's day-to-day operations. Operating cash flow differs from EBITDA by the amount of change in the working capital. It is also equal to cash flow less the change in the operating working capital. Operating cash flow is a concept that depends on how expenditure is classified between operating outlays and investment outlays. Since this distinction is not always clearcut, operating cash flow is not widely used in practice, with free cash flow being far more popular. Also called cash flow from operating activities or cash flow from operations.

Operating income   *See* EBIT.

Option   An option is a contract between two parties, under which one party gives the other party the right (but not the obligation) to buy from it (a call option) or to sell to it (a put option) an underlying asset at a predetermined price (see strike price), in exchange for the payment of a premium. Options can be in-the-money, at-the-money and out-of-the-money.

P/E Ratio, PER, price-to-earnings ratio   The P/E ratio, one of the tools most commonly used for valuing a share, is the ratio of the share price to EPS. It can also be obtained by dividing market capitalisation by net income.

Price to Book Ratio (PBR)   The price-to-book ratio is the ratio linking the price of the share with equity per share. It is the ratio of market value to book value.

Profit and loss account   *See* Income statement.

Provisions   The term "provision" covers a wide range of different items: impairment losses; provisions that reflect an increase in the company's liabilities in the shorter or longer term relating to a charge that has not yet been incurred by the financial year-end, but is likely to arise and is connected with operations carried out during the year; tax-regulated provisions (strictly speaking they are not provisions). Aside from tax-regulated provisions, provisions are set aside in anticipation of a charge.

Rate of return   The rate of return is the annual return expressed as a percentage of the total amount invested.

Return   *See* Return on investment.

Return on investment Return on investment is the expected increase in the cash flows generated by the operating cycle as a result of investment outlays. It is compensation for forsaking instant consumption. Return on investment can simply be called return.

Return on capital employed – ROCE Return on capital employed measures the profitability of capital. It is calculated by dividing operating profit (NOPAT, if ROCE is to be measured on an after-tax basis) by capital employed. Return on capital employed can also be considered as the return on equity if net debt is zero. The capital employed can be taken for the beginning of the period in question, for the end of the period or the average over the year; ROCE can be calculated on a before- or after-tax basis. Return on capital employed can be calculated by combining operating margin and asset turnover as follows:

$$\frac{\text{Operating profit}}{\text{Capital employed}} = \frac{\text{Operating profit}}{\text{Sales}} \times \frac{\text{Sales}}{\text{Capital employed}}$$

The first ratio – i.e., operating profit after tax/sales – corresponds to the operating margin generated by the company, while the second – sales/capital employed – reflects asset turnover, which indicates the amount of capital (capital employed) required to generate a given level of sales. Return on capital employed is the most important accounting indicator of value creation.

Return on equity – ROE Return on equity measures the profitability of equity invested in the business. Return on equity is calculated by dividing net income by equity. It is equal to return on capital employed plus the leverage effect. Return on equity is one of the accounting indicators of value creation.

Risk Risk is the uncertainty over future asset values and future returns. It is always present in any investment project. All risks lead to fluctuations in the value of a financial security. In a market economy, risk is measured by the volatility of the price and/or rate of return of a security. The degree of risk depends on the investment timeframe and tends to diminish over the long term.

Risk-free assets By definition, risk-free assets are those that offer a certain return – i.e., the risk-free rate (r_F). These assets are free of the default risk of the issuer and of the coupon reinvestment risk. This is the case with a government bond, assuming of course that the government does not go bankrupt. The standard deviation and variance of its return are thus zero.

Risk premium Risk premium is the difference between the expected return on a financial security and the return on a risk-free asset.

Share A share is a unit of equity ownership in a company. Shares thus constitute a source of financing for the company, just as debt instruments (or debts) do, even though there is clear and well-defined difference between the two. Shares have unlimited maturity (exit is only by transfer/sale of the share, there is no contractually fixed repayment date or value), and shareholders incur the same risks as the company. (They receive no income if the company is in poor health and, in the event of liquidation, shareholders are paid out after creditors when the proceeds of asset sales are distributed. In other words, most of the time, shareholders recover nothing after liquidation proceedings.) In exchange for this risk, a share entitles shareholders to a share in the company's profits and gives them a say in managing the company via voting rights. *See also* Shareholders' equity. Also called stock.

Share buyback   A share buyback is the repurchase of the company's shares by the company itself on the open market. If shares are then cancelled, the share buyback amounts to capital decrease. Share buybacks are also used to control the shareholder structure by buying out "undesirable" shareholders.

Shareholders   Shareholders are individuals or entities that provide a company with capital by buying shares (*see* this term) in the company. Inside shareholders and outside shareholders are two major categories of shareholder.

Shareholders' equity   Shareholders' equity is the capital that incurs the risk of the business. This type of financial resource forms the cornerstone of the entire financial system. Its importance is such that shareholders providing it are granted decision-making powers and control over the business in various different ways. Dividends are a way of apportioning earnings voted on the ordinary general meeting of shareholders once the company's accounts have been approved. Shareholders' equity is not contractually remunerated, does not have a repayment date and, in case of liquidation of the company, is paid off only after debts are paid off. Shareholders' equity is equal to the sum of capital increases by shareholders and annual net income for past years not distributed in the form of dividends plus the original share capital.

Signal theory   A signal is a real financial decision, taken deliberately (e.g., dividend payout), and which may have negative financial consequences for the decision-maker if the decision turns out to be wrong.

Solvency   Solvency reflects the ability of a company to honour its commitments in the event of liquidation – i.e., if its operations are wound up and assets are put up for sale. A company may be regarded as insolvent once its shareholders' equity turns negative. This means that it owes more than it owns.

Takeover bid   A takeover bid is the attempt of one company to buy another company, either in a hostile or friendly manner. The potential acquirer usually offers to buy the target's shares at a higher price than the market price during a limited period.

Value   The present value, or value of a financial security, is the present value of the expected future flows discounted (see discounting) at the rate of return required by investors. Value creation is the objective of any manager. This objective is reached when the investments of the company yield more than the return required by providers of funds.

Volatility   Volatility of the value (or the rate of return) of a financial security characterises the amplitude of the fluctuations of this value (or return). Mathematically, volatility is the variance or the standard deviation. In a market economy, volatility measures the risk: the riskier a financial security, the higher its volatility, and vice versa.

Weighted Average Cost of Capital – WACC   The weighted average cost of capital is the rate of return required by the providers of funds (shareholders and creditors) to finance the company's investment projects. It is the overall cost of financing of a company. According to the theory of markets in equilibrium, and provided there are no tax distortions, this cost is independent of the capital structure of the company; hence, an optimal capital structure does not exist. The weighted average cost of capital can be also called cost of capital.

Working capital   The net balance of operating uses and sources of funds is called the working capital. If uses of funds exceed sources of funds, the balance is positive and working capital needs to be financed. This is the most frequent case. If negative, it represents a source of funds generated by the business cycle. It is described as "working capital" because the figure reflects the cash required to cover financing shortfalls arising from day-to-day operations. Working capital is totally independent of the methods used to value fixed assets, depreciation, amortisation and impairment losses on fixed assets. However, it is influenced by: inventory valuation methods; deferred income and expense (over one or more years); the company's provisioning policy for current assets and operating liabilities and expenses. Working capital can be also called working capital needs, working capital requirements and requirements for working capital.

The Vernimmen's website at *www.vernimmen.com*

The website provides free access to:

- Tools: formulas, tables, statistics, lexicons, glossaries, financial figures for more than 10,000 European and North American listed companies.
- Resources that supplement the book: an Excel file providing detailed solutions to all of the problems set in the book; summaries of recent and interesting research papers, articles, prospectuses of financial transactions, thesis topics, thematic links; and a list of must-have books for your bookshelf.
- Problems, case studies, quizzes (with more than 250 questions and answers) for testing and improving your knowledge.
- A letterbox for your questions to the authors: we aim to reply within 72 hours, unless of course you manage to stump us!
- Archives to the *Vernimmen.com Newsletter* (see below).
- A special section for teachers with original case studies, an instructor's manual and slides.
- Questions and answers, polls, and much more.

New services are put onto the site, which has its own internal search engine, on a regular basis.

The *Vernimmen.com Newsletter*

The *Vernimmen.com Newsletter*, which is sent out via the Web every month, provides, in the spirit of our book *Corporate Finance, Theory and Practice*:

- A conceptual approach to a current corporate finance topic: *European directives on takeovers; is there a limit to the growth of hedge funds?*
- Statistics and/or tables that update the data in the book, and which you may find useful in your daily practice of corporate finance: *corporate income tax rates worldwide; asset betas in Europe.*
- A review of an article on financial research, with a concrete dimension: *Reaction to goodwill writeoffs; private equity performance.*
- Questions asked on the website and the answer: *How to account for stock options? What are PIPEs?*

This letter is sent out free of charge via the Internet to those who have subscribed on *www.vernimmen.com*.

Standard plan for a financial analysis

Two preliminary tasks:

- **get to know the business well**: market(s), products, production model, distribution network, human resources;
- **and understand the accounting policies**: accounting principles, auditors' reports.

A four-stage plan

- **wealth creation**: margin analysis, scissors effect, operating leverage;
- **requires capital employed**: working capital and capital expenditures;
- **that must be financed**: through debt or equity;
- **and provide a sufficient return**: return on capital employed and return on equity.

Conclusion

Comparison of return on capital employed to cost of capital ⇒ value creation ⇒ solvency.

1/PE ratio

The reverse of the PE ratio is nothing but the short-term accounting return for a shareholder who bought the share at a prive of V and who is richer a year later by an amount equal to the EPS.

If the reverse of the PE ratio is very small, this indicates that shareholders expect a strong increase in EPS. The reverse of the PE ratio is then lower than the rate of return required by shareholders.

If the reverse of the PE ratio is large, this indicates that shareholders expect a decrease in EPS, the reverse of the PE ratio is then higher than the rate of return required by shareholders.

Rules for dilution and accretion in earnings per share (EPS)

In case of capital increase

- when the 1/PE ratio > after-tax return of funds raised ⇒ EPS dilution;
- when the 1/PE ratio < after-tax return of funds raised ⇒ EPS accretion.

In case of share buyback

- when the 1/PE ratio > after-tax cost of debt ⇒ EPS accretion;
- when the 1/PE ratio < after-tax cost of debt ⇒ EPS dilution.

In case of an acquisition paid in cash

- when the target's PE ratio > after-tax cost of debt ⇒ accretion of the buyer's EPS;
- when the target's PE ratio < after-tax cost of debt ⇒ dilution of the buyer's EPS.

In case of an acquisition paid in shares (share offer, merger)

- when the target's PE ratio > the buyer's PE ratio ⇒ dilution of the buyer's EPS;
- when the target's PE ratio < the buyer's PE ratio ⇒ accretion of the buyer's EPS.

Multiples

Multiple of turnover, EBITDA or EBIT:
$$\frac{\text{Value of Equity} + \text{Value of net debt}}{\text{Turnover or EBITDA or EBIT}}$$

Multiple of net income (PE ratio), cash flow or equity:
$$\frac{\text{Value of equity}}{\text{Net income or cash flow or equity}}$$

Formulas

Value of an asset
$$V = \sum_{i=0}^{\infty} \frac{F_i}{(1+k)^i}$$
If the asset is capital-employed:
F_i = Free cash flow to firm

Value of an asset with a constant cash flow to infinity:
$$V = \frac{F}{k}$$
If the asset is a share:
F = DPS and $k = k_E$ = Cost of equity

Value of an asset whose cash flow increases at $g\%$ per year:
$$V = \frac{F_1}{k - g}$$
If the asset is a share:
$F_1 = DPS_1$ and $k = k_E$ = Cost of equity

Required rate of return on a share:
$$k_E = r_f + \beta \times (r_m - r_f)$$

Weighted average cost of capital (WACC):
$$k = k_E \times \frac{V_E}{V_D + V_E} + k_D \times (1 - T_c) \times \frac{V_D}{V_D + V_E}$$

$$k = r_f + \beta_E \times (r_m - r_f)$$

Value of an option (Black–Scholes formula):
$$N(d_1) \times V - N(d_2) \times K \times e^{-T \times r_F}$$

$$\text{with } d_1 = \frac{\ln\left(\dfrac{V}{K}\right) + \left(r_F + \dfrac{\sigma^2}{2}\right) \times T}{\sigma \times \sqrt{t}} \text{ and } d_2 = d_1 - \sigma \times \sqrt{T}$$